THE COOK'S BOOK

ABOUT THE AUTHOR

Howard Hillman loves to cook, eat and write about foods. His many books include THE BOOK OF WORLD CUISINES, THE DINER'S GUIDE TO WINES, and a series of epicurean guidebooks to major cities. His writings appear in such publications as *The New York Times, The Wall Street Journal* and *Food & Wine* magazine. Hillman has traveled to all 50 states and to over 100 countries in quest of first-hand culinary knowledge.

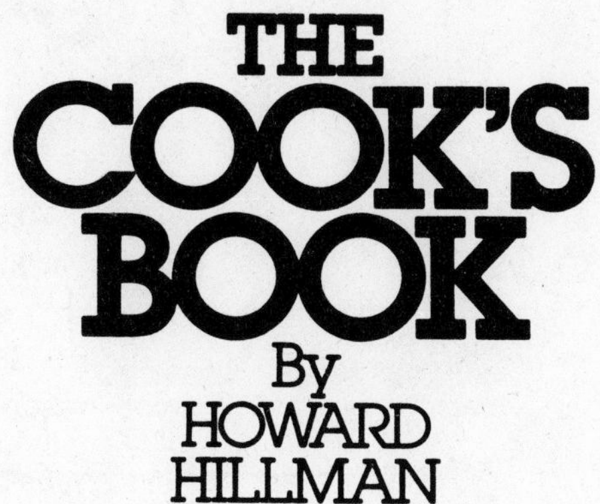

co-authors:
SHANNON OCORK
DANA SHILLING

special research:
CHERRY DUMAUAL

illustrated by:
ANISTATIA GALLEGOS

AVON
PUBLISHERS OF BARD, CAMELOT AND DISCUS BOOKS

THE COOK'S BOOK is an original publication of Avon Books. This work has never before appeared in book form.

AVON BOOKS
A division of
The Hearst Corporation
959 Eighth Avenue
New York, New York 10019

Cover design by Carol Inouye
Published by arrangement with the author
Library of Congress Catalog Card Number: 80-69606
ISBN: 0-380-76794-5

First Avon Printing, April, 1981

Printed in the U.S.A.

DEDICATION

To an endangered species:
the home (and restaurant) cook
who loves and knows how to
identify and prepare quality cooking ingredients.
Without a resurgence in the number
of these caring, knowledgeable people,
the quality of food products and cookery
will continue to decline.

CONTENTS

PREFACE

Long ago it was said, "God created the cooking ingredients and the devil the recipes."

Satan has been getting the upper hand in recent times. For every heavenly cooking ingredient that graces America's larder, there are now hundreds—nay, thousands—of diabolical recipes.

One of the manifold paths to culinary salvation is to know more about your cooking ingredients, the building blocks of any dish. By having that knowledge at your fingertips, you will not be bewitched by blasphemous recipes. You will be able to recognize quickly these demonic recipes that would profane your divine cooking ingredients. Once you spot them, you will be able to cast them into the inferno or convert them into recipes worthy of both your ingredients and discriminating palate.

A knowledge of cooking ingredients will benefit you in another way. You will be a more creative cook because you will be able to select and prepare whatever is best in the marketplace on any given day. As good cooks around the world know, this approach gives you more flexibility and tastier dishes than if you walk into a store with a recipe in hand.

Your ability to improvise creatively will save you money. You will, for example, be able to take advantage of unadvertised daily specials.

The Cook's Book condenses for you in one quick-reference volume essential tips and insights on over a thousand distinct cooking ingredients. It is a labor of love that has taken me, with the generous help of my staff, over ten years to plan and nearly two years to research and write. The background work entailed conducting countless experiments in the kitchen, consulting my multi-thousand-volume food library, interviewing experts in all culinary disciplines, and shopping, cooking, and eating my way a number of times around the world to explore marketplaces and cooking methods in fifty states and over one hundred countries.

Now that *The Cook's Book* is in your hands, I hope it will make your cooking more enjoyable and rewarding. That is its purpose.

Howard Hillman

HOW TO USE THIS BOOK

The alphabetical *Entries-at-a-Glance* section is the heart of *The Cook's Book*. I have organized the individual entries, when appropriate, in this format: *Background*, *Availability*, *Preparation*, and *Classic Uses and Affinities*. The first section, *Background*, provides general information and interesting facts about the food item. *Availability* gives you helpful buying tips. *Preparation* tells you how to store and cook the food once you bring it home. Finally, *Classic Uses and Affinities* presents some of the names of the recipes and pot-mates that—according to generations of cooks—best enhance the ingredient.

As you read through the entries, you will see the names of some ingredients printed in SMALL CAPS. This typographic cross-referencing signifies that related information can be found in another entry.

Following *Entries-at-a-Glance* is the *Glossary*, which defines basic cooking terms. Next come two components to help you adapt recipes: *Equivalents-at-a-Glance* and *Metric Conversion*. The next sections of the book, the *Nutrition Primer* and *Nutrition Chart*, answer some of your health-oriented questions. Following these you'll find a *bibliography* which serves as a starting point for insatiably curious food-buffs who want to learn more about the culinary world, a subject that has no bounds.

At the very end of the book is an *index*. If you'd like to look up a particular term, or if you cannot find an ingredient in its alphabetical place in *Entries-at-a-Glance*, consult this quick-reference aid for the correct page number.

THE COOK'S BOOK

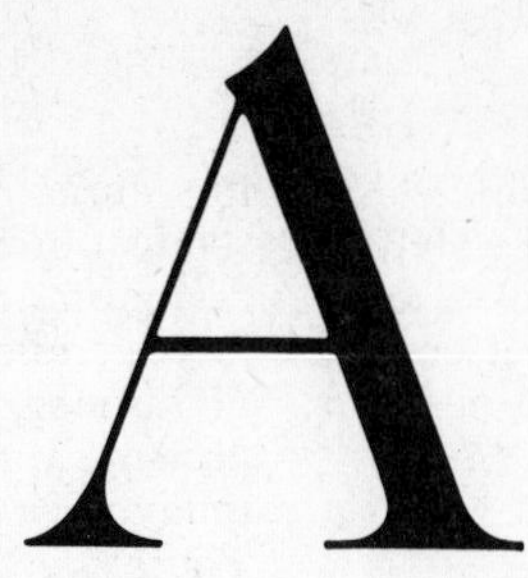

ABALONE

BACKGROUND

Abalone is a univalve mollusk found mainly in the Pacific Ocean. Its single, ear-shaped shell (averaging about 6 inches long in most species) protects its footlike, rock-clinging muscle—the edible portion, which can be eaten raw or cooked. The flavor is clamlike, though slightly more assertive; its texture is chewy and, if improperly prepared, rubbery.

AVAILABILITY

California is this country's abalone capital, but unfortunately for non-Californians, it is illegal to ship fresh abalone beyond the state's borders. The rest of the country, with the exception of Hawaii, must eat the frozen, canned, or dried products, which come in whole, chunk, or steak form, usually from Japan or Mexico.

PREPARATION

The younger the abalone, the more tender it will be. Therefore, select the smallest size for its species. Abalone is very perishable, whether fresh, thawed, or processed (once the can has been opened). Use it sooner rather than later. Abalone is best prepared by slicing the muscle across the grain into thin steaks, then pounding them with a mallet to tenderize them. Note, though, that excessive or prolonged pounding toughens more than it softens and may even mangle the flesh. Dredge the pounded slices with seasoned flour, then briefly sauté (about 1 minute) in a mixture of butter and oil. (Further cooking will turn the abalone pieces into leather fit for soling shoes.) Sauce and serve. Some cooks like a robust tomato-based sauce, others—including us—prefer a simpler sauce that does not mask the abalone's subtle flavor. If you have a less-than-youthful abalone, consider mincing it in your food processor or electric blender, then adding the flesh to fritter batter or to slow-cooked dishes such as stews. Chowder is another use. Tender fresh abalone can be diced, marinated, and added raw to salads.

ACKEE

BACKGROUND

This red-skinned native West African fruit, *Blighia sapida*, is now naturalized in Florida and Jamaica. Each fruit contains three edible, inch-long, creamy white sections, each sheltering a glossy black seed. Immature or overripe ackees can be poisonous. The canned variety is safe but lacks desired texture and flavor.

PREPARATION

Fresh ackee is prepared by removing the

red outer skin, seeds, and pink veins, then boiling the flesh in salted water for about 20 minutes. Canned ackee only needs reheating. Some say that cooked ackee resembles scrambled eggs in appearance and texture.

CLASSIC USES AND AFFINITIES

Salt fish and ackee is one of the national dishes of Jamaica.

ALLIGATOR

BACKGROUND

This large reptile, a native of Florida and Gulf Coast states, was hunted almost to extinction, primarily for its hide, but also for its meat. Florida banned alligator hunting in 1962 and the federal government placed it on the endangered-species list in 1967. It is still on the list, but it has made such a phenomenal comeback that Florida now licenses the killing of numerous alligators a year. Dozens of restaurants have applied for permits to serve 'gator meat, a culinary tourist attraction in Florida. The feet and tails are considered the desirable parts. You are not likely to find alligator meat at your local butcher shop as long as the beast is still on the endangered-species list, but that could change. As one game warden put it, "You can't convince people who see them in their yards that 'gators are endangered. They think it's the people who are endangered."

ALLSPICE

BACKGROUND

Allspice, a 1/4-inch-thick berry, comes from the evergreen pimento tree. It is picked almost ripe, then sun-dried. Drying turns the berry from green to reddish-brown. Its name comes from the resemblance of its slightly pungent flavor and sweetish aroma to a mixture of nutmeg, cinnamon, and cloves. The pimento tree is native to the Caribbean; today, most allspice comes from Jamaica. Therefore, *Jamaica pepper* is another name for allspice; *pimento* (not to be confused with the sweet pimento pepper) is still another name for this spice, whose botanical name is *Pimenta dioica*. (See HERBS AND SPICES for information on buying, storing, cooking, etc.)

AVAILABILITY

Allspice is sold in two forms: whole (the better) and ground. You can grind the former at home in an ordinary peppermill. Alternatively, you can place the whole berries in a cloth and smash them with a hammerhead or with the bottom of a heavy pan.

CLASSIC USES AND AFFINITIES

Allspice is one of the classic pickling spices, and sometimes forms part of the French QUATRE ÉPICES. It goes well in marinades, with pot roasts (including sauerbraten), mincemeat, spiced cake and cookies, fruit compotes, and curry blends. It is also frequently used in soups, sauces (especially tomato-based sauces), preserves, relishes, ground beef, poached fish and meats, steamed puddings, and cranberry dishes. It is a popular baking spice, particularly in Scandinavia. Allspice, which is native to the Western Hemisphere, has an affinity for Western Hemisphere foods such as chocolate, pumpkin, sweet potatoes, and yams.

ANGELICA

BACKGROUND

Medieval herbalists ascribed numerous

medicinal properties to angelica. It was nicknamed the "Holy Ghost plant" and bears the heavenly botanical name of *Angelica archangelica*, but it has many uses. (See HERBS AND SPICES for information on buying, storing, cooking, etc.)

CLASSIC USES AND AFFINITIES

The home or professional baker uses the hollow stems in bright green candied form to give color accents to fruitcakes and puddings. Young shoots can be eaten in salads, while the stalk and leaves of this tall herb can be cooked as a vegetable, as is done in Scandinavia. Tea drinkers know the root can be brewed for tea, which can be further flavored by the addition of the somewhat similar-tasting juniper berry. Marmalade makers sometimes combine angelica stalks with rhubarb or bitter oranges, while spirit producers use the herb to flavor concoctions such as gin, Benedictine, and Chartreuse.

ANISE

BACKGROUND

The anise seed or *aniseed*, the tiny, hairy licorice-flavored part of this plant, is really a kind of fruit. The leaves of *Pimpinella anisum* are also eaten, as is the bulb. The plant is a native of the Mediterranean area, and is popular today in Mexico and India. It should not be confused with STAR ANISE , which has a closely similar flavor. Although anise is not related to licorice, many foods described as "licorice-flavored" are really prepared with anise. Anise oil is used in color photography and is also used as a carminative, expectorant, and antiseptic in medicine. Anisette, pastis, ouzo, and raki are some of the many spirits flavored with anise. (See HERBS AND SPICES for information on buying, storing, cooking, etc.)

PREPARATION

Steam or simmer the anise bulb 10 to 15 minutes, according to thickness and age. As with its look- and taste-alike cousin, the FENNEL, the flesh of the anise bulb may be eaten raw as a *crudité* or in salads.

CLASSIC USES AND AFFINITIES

Many colas, cookies, and candies use anise seed. This flavor is characteristic of Scandinavian baking. The Dutch enjoy hot, sweetened anise-flavored milk. Nonsweet dishes such as sausages, beef stew, fish, and shellfish can benefit from this herb. The French sometimes use anise leaves to season carrots. An average recipe for four servings uses about 1/4 teaspoon of anise seed.

APPLE

BACKGROUND

Can you imagine Adam not eating the forbidden apple; Ichabod Crane without a bobbing Adam's apple; a roast suckling pig without an apple ensconced in its mouth; a county fair lacking candied apples; a Halloween party without a tub of floating dunking apples; Issac Newton sitting safely under an apple tree; New York City without its "Big Apple" nickname; an overworked doctor in a small town where everyone eats an apple a day; Johnny Appleseed staying home; Snow White resisting the poison apple?

When mankind started cultivating the apple several thousand years ago, it was a small, astringent fruit that was a far cry from its succulent twentieth-century progeny. The apple has today become the world's leading temperate-climate fruit. This is particularly true in America, where Washington, Michigan, upstate New York, and New England have helped make the United States the leading producer of the *Pyrus malus*, a member of the rose family. Good old American pomologists have developed a myriad of hybrids—so many that the legendary Johnny Appleseed would be astonished.

Varieties

The Hybrid Conspiracy: Since apple trees cross-pollinate, trees grown from seed will not always replicate the fruit of the parent type. And even though grafts can produce clones, grafts can also yield crosses. Because of the relative ease of developing new varieties, agronomists have plunged headlong into the task of developing the perfect apple. The big question is, perfect for whom—the customer or the food industry? The answer is the food industry, as taste is a low priority for the experimenters who seek a hybrid fruit that is relatively difficult to bruise (making it a good shipper), has long shelf-life (produce managers love this characteristic), and is attractive (most customers buy beauty, not flavor). The woefully bland Red Delicious and Golden Delicious are the two prime examples of this phenomenon. Even some of the quality of the McIntosh apple has been diminished over the last decade through hybridization. If you want to enjoy the great apple of yesteryear, you may have to find and visit orchards tended by conscientious growers—but do not dally; they are disappearing.

Overview: Thousands of distinct apple varieties exist, too many to cover in our book. We have therefore limited our discussion to some twenty common varieties. They fall into three convenient categories: eating, cooking, and all-purpose.

Eating apples are those that are primarily consumed raw, either out of hand or cut up into preparations such as salads. Leading examples include:

Golden Delicious
Red Delicious

Cooking apples are those that are chiefly used for heat-applied preparations such as pies, tarts, cobblers, strudels, fritters, applesauce, applebutter, baked whole apples, and stuffings. For this duty, cooking apples are superior to eating apples because they have a tarter flavor (which counterbalances the natural sweetness of an apple) and a firmer texture (which pleases both the tooth and eye). The best-selling examples include:

Crab
Rhode Island Greening
Rome Beauty
York Imperial

All-purpose apples include those fruits that can be eaten either raw or cooked. Some, of course, lean more in one direction than the other:

Baldwin
Cortland
Granny Smith
Gravenstein
Grimes Golden
Jonathan
Lady
Macoun
McIntosh
Newtown Pippin
Northern Spy
Stayman
Wealthy
Winesap
Yellow Transparent

All the apples mentioned above will now be discussed alphabetically.

Descriptions

Baldwin: With a balanced sweet-tart flavor, the red-skinned Baldwin has become a popular all-purpose apple. Salad makers particularly like it. You will generally find it in the marketplace from mid-fall through mid-spring.

Cortland: As a salad ingredient, this red apple has an advantage over the McIntosh in that the Cortland's cotton-white flesh is less prone to the darkening caused by exposure to air. Uncut, it also has better storage properties than the McIntosh. The Cortland is justifiably called an all-purpose apple, as it can be used to make pies and applesauce. You can also bake it, but do not cook it too long. However, for some palates, the flavor is a little tame, lacking tempting tang. Peak season is early fall through mid-winter.

Crab: Miniature in size, bitterly tart in flavor, and red to purple in skin hue, the crab apple is principally used for cooking such creations as preserves, pickles, and spiced condiments. At other times this fall fruit finds itself decking a platter on the dining table. Though crabs are commercially grown, the sharp-eyed hiker can still find them growing wild.

Golden Delicious: Both the Red and Golden Delicious are for eating rather than cooking, are comparatively large, have elongated shapes, and are the best sellers in their respective color categories. The Golden Delicious has gained its marketplace supremacy because of several factors: its flesh resists darkening more than other apples when exposed to air; it is a good keeper in the warehouse, in the produce bin, and in your home; it bruises less readily than most other apples; it has a relatively long peak season (early fall through late spring); it can be and is grown coast to coast, thereby cutting down on transportation costs. But all those pluses do not change the salient negative of the Golden Delicious: it tastes bland, with barely a hint of tartness. It could be juicier, too. In short, the Golden Delicious is best suited to the artist's still-life bowl, not his palate.

Granny Smith: This new girl in town is too special to ignore. Not only is this green-skinned fruit the only imported apple to have developed an American following, the tart, juicy, crisp, and firm-fleshed Granny Smith is a superior all-purpose apple: excellent for eating raw or cooked, whether in pies, applesauce, or baked apples. Moreover, because she comes mainly from New Zealand and Australia where seasons are opposite to our own, the Granny Smith reaches our shores in summer when the fresh American-grown varieties are out of season. She will soon be available in the cooler months too, because Granny Smith orchards are beginning to take root in the U.S. Because the Granny Smith is a good keeper, it could therefore become the first apple to be available the year round.

Gravenstein: You are more likely to find the Gravenstein on the West Coast (particularly in California) than in the East. Its skin coloration is distinctive: greenish-yellow with red streaking. The Gravenstein is an all-purpose apple but its tart flesh is best when eaten raw. As a cooker, it is better suited for pies and applesauce than for baking whole. Peak season is mid-summer to early fall.

Grimes Golden: If you like to leave your apple cubes unpeeled in your salads, the Grimes Golden lends a decorative touch because of its distinct speckled brownish-yellow skin contrasting its yellow-white flesh. This all-purpose apple is juicy and sweet, but some palates find that it lacks desirable tartness for certain cooked dishes. Season: mid-fall to mid-winter.

Jonathan: Midwesterners particularly enjoy this red-skinned apple with a slightly spicy scent. It is classified as an all-purpose apple—good for eating out of hand, good for pies and applesauce—but it does get a demerit as a baking apple. Peak season is early fall through mid-winter.

Lady: Many shoppers buy this petite apple in the winter season to use principally for decoration or cooking. It can also be enjoyed as an eating fruit.

Macoun: Its name rhymes with "raccoon." This variety is a popular eating apple on the East Coast. Like one of its parents, the McIntosh, the Macoun is a poor keeper. It also looks like a Mac, but the Macoun is considered the better of the two in flavor and texture. Its season is short: late fall through early winter.

McIntosh: Color-conscious salad makers adore the cotton-white flesh of the McIntosh, with or without its red (sometimes green-tinged), relatively tough, peel. Salad eaters also savor the slightly tart and mildly sweet flesh. Most authorities classify the Mac as all-purpose, but in cooking, it is not on a par with its eating quality. This is particularly true when it comes to baking: the McIntosh tends to collapse unless minimally cooked. Compared to most apple varieties, it is a poor keeper—use it soon. Peak season is mid-fall through early spring.

Newtown Pippin (Albemarle): Each successive year one sees less and less of this greenish-yellow (or yellow) apple in the marketplace. Pity, because the Newtown (sometimes spelled Newton) Pippin's tart, juicy flesh is pleasant whether you are eating it out of hand or in a pie or applesauce. Peak season is mid-winter through late spring.

Northern Spy: America's best apple? Some apple connoisseurs would quickly give their vote to the red-skinned Northern Spy. Consensus classifies this good-sized apple as all-purpose, but it comes off better at the cooking end of the spectrum. It has an enviable sweet-and-sour balance that few other varieties can match. When baked, the firm flesh holds its shape. Commercial growers are not replanting some of the trees because the yield is sometimes too unreliable for today's "assured-delivery" market. Peak season is mid-fall through early spring.

Red Delicious: As previously mentioned, the Red Delicious is America's best-selling apple and, at the same time, one of America's worst apples. Red Delicious apples are in season from early fall to early spring. They have a distinctive elongated shape and five bumps at the blossom end. The flesh is crisp, but when bitten into, it does not give the pleasing snap that comes from most other apples. The flavor is sweet but rather bland, principally because the fruit lacks desirable tartness. In short, the Red Delicious may be red, but it is not delicious.

Rhode Island Greening: Domestic bakers consider this green-skinned apple the finest for making all-American apple pie. Its firm yellowish-white flesh holds up to prolonged cooking and the tart flavor gives the pie the needed tang. Moreover, this apple's inherent flavor develops as it cooks (which makes it also ideal for applesauce). Some people love eating this variety raw, but most Rhode Island Greening fans consider it a cooker. It can be kept longer than most apples. Peak season is mid-fall through late winter.

Rome Beauty: Of the various cooking apples, the Rome Beauty is considered the best baker, as it holds its shape well. As a result, this fruit fares well in long-cooking desserts, the baked apple in particular. It has a red skin lightly accented with yellow. The flesh is firm with a mildly tart flavor. Season: mid-fall through mid-spring.

Stayman: Apple lovers use this red variety for eating and, to a certain extent, for cooking. Peak season: mid-fall through mid-spring.

Wealthy: An all-purpose apple, though better for eating than cooking. It especially falls short as a baker. The Wealthy has a bright red, vaguely striped skin. Its season is late summer through early winter.

Winesap: A dark-red all-purpose apple with white, faintly yellow, flesh, the Winesap has a distinct tart flavor. Its texture is crisp, firm, and juicy. It keeps longer than average. The Winesap's season is mid-winter through mid-spring, but it is getting harder to find in supermarkets.

Yellow Transparent: With a peak mid-summer harvest, the Yellow Transparent is one of the first fresh-from-the-tree fruits to mark the beginning of the "apple season." It is a medium-sized, all-purpose apple with a greenish-whitish-yellow skin, and a juicy white pulp.

York Imperial: People who love baked apples love the York Imperial—it keeps its shape and tastes good, as an apple should. The skin of this medium to large fruit is red with a hint of a yellow background. The flesh is firm and tart enough to counterbalance its sweetness.

AVAILABILITY

Seasons

Apples are primarily a cool-season fruit. The exceptions are those grown and imported from Southern Hemisphere lands (like the Granny Smith) and those that have been released from controlled-atmosphere storage. Apples picked at the end of their seasons tend to decrease in acidity.

Buying Tips

Select the best apple available for its intended use. For instance, if you plan to bake the apple whole, buy a variety that holds its shape in the oven. See the individual descriptions above for specific guidelines. Look for apples with skins that are brightly colored (for their variety), clean, and smooth. Avoid apples with bruises, soft (rotten) spots, shriveled skins, and damage caused by worms, insects, birds, machinery, and careless hands. If you have a choice, do not buy apples that have skins with wax coatings (the substance is edible but undesirable) or tan splotches (this *scald* or *russeting* is virtually always harmless, but why take a chance?). The flesh of uncooked apples should be firm, crisp, and at least reasonably juicy; it should not be mealy. Unless you have the facilities to store apples properly, it is best to buy for short-term consumption. Many apples are graded by either federal or subnational inspectors, but unless you buy your apples in a packinghouse container, you are unlikely to know the specific grade. The best grades, in order of rank, are generally U.S. Extra Fine, U.S. Fancy, and U.S. No. 1. Criteria relate to such factors as maturity, general condition, and appearance of the fruit.

PREPARATION

Storage

Apples keep better than most fruits, but they do have their storage limits. If an apple was picked prematurely, it will not mature off the tree in your home. If an apple was picked at the peak of its maturity and is not quite ripe, it will ripen in your home. Should you desire fast ripening, do it at room temperature in a pierced brown bag—this should take one to several days depending on the initial state of ripeness. If you want slow ripening and do not have an ideal environment such as a cellar, place the apples in a plastic bag in your refrigerator crisper. An apple kept at room temperature will ripen many times faster than one stored in a cool (35°–40°F), dry, dark, and airy environment such as a cellar. Apples, because of their moisture content, freeze poorly. As everyone knows, "one bad apple spoils the barrel," because decay spreads quickly from one fruit to another. To minimize bacterial development, wash the apples only just prior to using. Ripe apples give off ethylene gas, which hastens the ripening of both themselves and most other fruits; therefore, do not store apples near other fruit unless you plan to make use of this chemical reaction.

Preliminaries

Wash apples well to rid them of possible insecticide residue and wax coating. The latter is harmless, but distracting to the educated palate. A stainless-steel knife is better than a carbon-steel knife, as the latter tends to give the cut surfaces a light brownish tinge. Various gadgets exist to core and cut apples, but a paring knife in the hands of an experienced cook works better. Those coring devices sometimes remove too little, sometimes too much of the apple's center. When you do core a whole apple, do it before removing the skin. An apple can be eaten with or without its peel. If you pare an apple, take off as little as you can in order to minimize vitamin and mineral loss. All brown spots should be removed from the flesh, not ignored, as they may prove unhealthful and will definitely undermine flavor. Uncooked apple flesh begins to brown when exposed to the air. To retard this oxidation, use lemon or other citrus juices to coat or submerge the surface of the flesh. Mixing the apple pieces with cut-up citrus fruit also works. Ripe apples taste best at room temperature. In baking, whole apples are less likely to burst or become mushy if you let the steam escape by piercing the top of the apple before placing it in the oven. When making pies, cut thicker slices if the apple flesh is soft.

Cooking

Apples are versatile cookers—they can be baked, poached, stewed, steamed, baked, broiled, deep-fried, or sauteed either alone or with other ingredients. Consult the individual descriptions above to see if a particular apple type is suitable for pies, applesauce, baking whole, etc. Bake whole pies in a preheated 350°F oven for 40 to 60 minutes, depending mainly on size. While a propensity to mush is anathema for pies and baked whole apples, some cooks find it a plus when making applesauce. Apples are very high in the thickening agent called pectin, so they make excellent preserves and jellies alone or with other fruits. The ideal cooking apple is neither immature and unripe nor too mature and ripe.

Equivalents

Apples are almost always sold by weight, not by unit. Generally 3 medium-sized apples equal a pound. For a 9-inch pie, figure on 2 to 3 pounds of apples, depending on how thick you want your pie.

CLASSIC USES AND AFFINITIES

Apples are star ingredients in pies, tarts, turnovers, strudels, pandowdies, brown Bettys, fritters, dumplings, salads (including Waldorf), jams, jellies, preserves, pickles, and baby foods. And let us not forget applesauces and apple butters. Dried apples are often used to stuff meats. In the liquid form, we have apple juice and soft cider; for those wishing more wallop, apples yield hard cider as well as brandies such as apple jack and Calvados. Among the better culinary marriages for an aeele are cinnamon, raisins, nuts, brown sugar, lemon juice, and prunes.

APRICOT

BACKGROUND

Although its Latin name, *Prunus armeniaca*, means the "Armenian plum," the apricot is probably a native of China. Virtually all the U.S. apricot crop comes from California. The small, smooth-skinned, golden-yellow fruit with its delectable blush of pink is too delicate to ship easily, so a good portion of the not-so-large harvest is dried or canned, making the fruit available year round. Happily, some flavor survives these processing methods. Indeed, some folks prefer the intensified flavor of the dried product; for us, however, the ideal apricot—albeit ephemeral in season, scarce in quantity, and brief in perfect ripeness—is the fresh fruit.

AVAILABILITY

Season

Fresh apricots are available only from May to August, and then mostly in the Western states. As a rule, the Midwest and the East Coast get fresh apricots only in June and July, but those are the apricot's best months.

Buying Tips

Apricots will ripen away from the tree,

so fresh crops are usually shipped to us before they are fully ripe. They can be ripened at home: place them where they won't get bumped—they bruise easily—at room temperature, in a perforated paper bag so the air can circulate around them, away from drafts and sun. Whether green or ripe, choose apricots that are plump, firm, and unblemished; unripe apricots will be harder, of course, than ripe ones. The ripe fruit will have a glorious golden color and a characteristic fragrant odor.

PREPARATION

Storage

Because of the delicacy of this fruit, we recommend eating apricots as soon as they are ripe. If you can't, store them in the vegetable crisper. Do not wash them until you are ready to eat them, as moisture will hasten bacterial spoilage.

Cooking

Poach apricots in a simple syrup for 15 to 20 minutes. Soak dried apricots in cold water to revive them, then simmer in water or syrup. Bake halved fresh apricots in a pastry shell, with or without a foundation of pastry cream. Or make yourself some apricot butter, to be eaten now or to be preserved for wintertime enjoyment.

Equivalents

On the average, there are 8 large or 14 small apricots in a pound—enough for 3 cups of cut-up fruit, or 6 half-cup servings.

CLASSIC USES AND AFFINITIES

Apricots blend with and enhance other fruits. French chefs have long used an apricot glaze on many of their fruit tarts. In the Middle East, cooks make extensive use of fresh and dried apricots in lamb or chicken dishes. Since apricots are very sweet, lemon juice adds nip and sparkle. Nuts, especially almonds, provide contrast of flavor and texture to apricots, either fresh or dried.

ARTICHOKE

BACKGROUND

The elegant *Cynara scolymus* is a thistlelike plant indigenous to the Mediterranean. Our fresh domestic supply comes from the coastal area of central California in and around Castroville. The part of the artichoke plant eaten is the pineconelike bud that grows on top of a long stem; left to its own devices, the green artichoke bud blossoms into a large violet flower. (The *globe* or *true artichoke* is not to be confused with the vegetable tuber, the JERUSALEM ARTICHOKE.)

Thanks to erroneous information given in some cookbooks, many Americans literally do not know an artichoke's heart from its bottom. Many people even think they are one and the same. An *artichoke bottom* is the tender, thick-dish-shaped flesh lying just above the stem. An *artichoke heart* is what remains of a whole artichoke after you remove the stem and the outer *scales* (*petals* or *leaves*). It comprises the small pale inner scales, the artichoke bottom (as described above), and the fuzzy choke that lies buried under the inner scales and on top of the artichoke bottom. Artichoke hearts can be eaten only when the bud is very young; as the bud develops, the choke grows and becomes inedible. In this country, one seldom finds fresh artichokes young enough to have edible hearts, so one must be satisfied with the frozen or canned hearts.

AVAILABILITY

Season

Artichokes are available all year, with a peak season in April and May. Canned, jarred, and frozen artichoke hearts are readily available at any time.

Buying Tips

The overlapping scales of the artichoke must closely hug each other, with no discernible space between the layers. Once the scales start to open ever so slightly, the artichoke is past its prime. Look for scales that are plump, firm, fresh-looking, and bright green. A few brown surface spots are acceptable in the winter because they are caused by the frost. Nonwinter specimens should not have brown spotting. Artichokes from any season should be free of mold, decay spots, insect damage, bruises, or other injuries. The whole artichoke should be firm (but not rock hard) and be heavy for its size. The smaller the artichoke is for its particular variety, the more tender it will be. However, sometimes a small specimen is too tiny to hold an adequate stuffing, so you must make a compromise. If you are cooking more than one artichoke, choose equal-sized buds for even cooking.

PREPARATION

Storage

Artichokes deteriorate quickly. Seal in a plastic bag and refrigerate for no more than a day or two. Artichokes freeze poorly.

Preliminaries

Holding the artichoke by its stem, swish the bud head up and down in cold water until the dirt between the scales has been dislodged. Make ready a bowl of acidulated water—about 2 tablespoons of lemon juice or vinegar per quart of water. You will submerge the trimmed whole artichoke or bottom in the water to retard the discoloration of the cut flesh caused by exposure to the air. With a knife, cut off the stem flush with the bud. This allows the artichoke to sit flat when served.

Trimming Whole Artichoke: There are many ways to prepare a whole artichoke for cooking. We give you one of the better methods: with a knife, cut off the top quarter of the bud head. Do not feel bad; there's not much to eat there. Some cooks snip off the pointed tip of each scale with scissors. This gives a neat, flat top to the artichoke. Leave the choke in place, or remove it at this point: extra work for you, less work for your guests. To de-choke, stretch apart the middle scales, reach into the center of the artichoke, and scoop out the fuzzy choke with a spoon. Immerse the artichoke, as it is prepared, into the acidulated water.

Trimming Artichoke Bottoms: Cut off the top two-thirds of the artichoke. (Discard or use the severed upper part as you wish.) Trim the lower third of all outer and inner scales as well as the choke, and trim the remaining portion (the bottom) to give it a smooth surface. The artichoke bottom will resemble a thick, miniature saucer. Protect the bottom from oxidation by promptly submerging it into the acid bath.

Cooking

Whole Artichokes: Artichokes are usually simmered or steamed. Do not use iron or aluminum pans or the artichoke may turn battleship gray. Pans of stainless steel, glass, or enamel, and those lined with tin, silver, or Teflon, Silverstone and the like, will not cause as much discoloration. As added insurance against undue discoloration, tie a thick slice of fresh lemon to the bottom of each artichoke with string. The same effect can be attained by cooking artichokes *à blanc*: a few tablespoons of flour in the cooking water. Or add lemon juice (or vinegar) to the cooking water. Some cooks like to add olive oil to the cooking water for richness and to increase the water temperature. Whether simmering or steaming, place the artichokes face down in the pot. To simmer, put the artichokes into boiling salted water to cover. Partially cover with lid, and gently simmer them for 20 to 40 minutes, depending on size. If de-choked, figure on 13 to 25 minutes. To steam, put the artichoke in a pot (preferably with a rack) containing 1 inch boiling salted water. Steam it for the same approximate period of time suggested for simmering. Artichokes must be drained after cooking to get the water out—but be careful; the water is scalding hot. Well-oiled artichokes can also be baked (stuffed or not) in a preheated 350°F oven for 30 to 60 minutes, depending on size. The artichoke is cooked when its bottom can be easily pierced by a fork or sharp-pointed knife, or when one of the middle-sized scales can be easily pulled loose.

Bottoms: Simmer or steam as you would a whole artichoke, except the time period will be 10 to 20 minutes, depending on thickness. If you halve or quarter the bottom, cut down the cooking time. Adding lemon to the pot is especially important when cooking the easily oxidized bottoms.

Eating an Artichoke

Confronted with a whole artichoke, pull off the scales one by one, dip them into the sauce, and scrape off the flesh with your teeth. Put the scraped scales on the side of your plate or in a receptacle provided. If you are aesthetically inclined, artfully arrange the discarded scales, one overlapping the other in a long, curving line around the rim of your plate. When only a few pale inner scales remain, use a knife and fork to remove (and discard) the remaining scales, the choke underneath them, and any other material clinging to the ultimate prize: the bottom. Eat it with a knife and fork.

CLASSIC USES AND AFFINITIES

Hot or cold artichokes take very well to rich sauces: hollandaise, maltaise (hollandaise made with orange juice rather than lemon), *aioli* (a garlic mayonnaise), vinaigrette, and melted butter enriched with lemon juice. Artichoke hearts and bottoms marinate nicely. The chemical composition of the artichoke sensitizes the tastebuds, and makes other foods taste sweet. Therefore, it is often better to serve artichokes as a first course and enjoy the wine with the following course.

ARUGULA

BACKGROUND

Also known as *rocket*, *arugula* (*Eruca sativa*) is a salad green more esteemed in Italy than in America. While northern Italians relish eating a pure arugula salad, Americans generally prefer to lessen the bitter, pungent aftertaste of arugula by mixing it with blander lettuce leaves such as Bibb.

PREPARATION

Select young, bright-colored leaves. Store, wrapped, in the refrigerator and use within a couple of days. Wash arugula gently in cold tap water. When preparing the salad dressing, use a high-quality olive oil.

ASAFETIDA

BACKGROUND

Ferula assafoetida, a dried resin

extracted from a root, is used in India as a seasoning and as a medicine. It is sold in Indian-American markets in powdered form or as a compressed cake, which can be broken or shaved off as needed. At first sniff, some Westerners understand why asafetida got its nickname "devil's dung." It is an acquired taste and is used sparingly even by those addicted to it. (See HERBS AND SPICES for information on buying, storing, cooking, etc.)

ASPARAGUS

BACKGROUND

One sign of spring is a dish of asparagus on the table: the green, white, or violet-tinged *Asparagus officinalis* in cream soup, baked with cheese, or delectably steamed *al dente* and lightly buttered. There are several enthusiastic references to asparagus in classical Greek and Latin literature. The first asparagus each year touches off mass madness in Europe. High prices have—until recent times—limited the popularity of asparagus in the U.S. Today, aided by large, excellent California crops, asparagus is becoming a staple in American kitchens.

Varieties

Most American asparagus is green, grown for long, slender spears. The German, Dutch, Belgian, and other European asparagus addicts prefer fat, soft, white spears grown under earth to prevent the development of chlorophyll. The French *Argenteuil* asparagus is medium-thick and streaked with purple. Since such varieties of asparagus are rarely imported fresh, we will limit our discussion here to green American asparagus.

AVAILABILITY

Season

Asparagus is at its best and its price is lowest from late February through June. April and May are the peak months. Off-season asparagus, when you can find it, tends to be expensive and inferior. Few vegetables suffer as much as asparagus in terms of texture, flavor, and color when frozen or canned.

Buying Tips

One of the most important criteria for selecting good fresh asparagus is the condition of the tip. The bud cluster should be tightly closed. A noncompact bud head is an asparagus past its prime. The bud head should not be wilted, moldy, decayed, sandy, or going to seed. The background color of the stalk should be a rich green from the tip to as close to the root end as possible. (However, the scales can be tinged with purple.) The stalk should have no vertical ridges. The stalk should be ramrod straight—avoid those that are curved or crooked. The stalk should be firm (not limp) and capable of being snapped. The root end should not be coarse and woody. Diameter can vary from pencil-thin to garden-hose-stout, depending on age and variety. The best tend to be the small to medium specimens (about 1/2 to 3/4 inch thick) which offer you some of the full flavor of the larger spears combined with the tenderness of the smaller ones. Choose asparagus of equal thickness for even cooking. The length of the edible portions should be equal too, for the sake of visual appeal when the asparagus lies on the serving platter. If you have a choice, select individual specimens out of an open bin rather than buying a package with unequal qualities and thicknesses.

PREPARATION

Preliminaries

Wash the spears in cold water, scrub-rubbing them with your fingers, being careful not to damage the bud heads. To dislodge the trapped grit in a bud head, run cold tap water over the tip. Young, perfect specimens need no trimming except to slice off the dried cut surface of the end by 1/4 inch. Some asparagus, however, has tough or woody growth at the root end that must be removed. Some people snap off the root ends with their fingers, but this approach has drawbacks: you will end up with uneven lengths, and you may snap off too much and therefore waste good asparagus. Also, snapping often leaves a ragged edge that must be cut with a knife to be neat. A better method is to cut the spears to equal lengths using a knife—if you purchased your asparagus wisely, the differences in the amount to be trimmed will be negligible. Your next step is to use a vegetable parer or knife to scrape off the soft triangular scales on the sides of the stalk below the bud head. Some people go even further by peeling the outer skin of the stalk. If you have young, tender stalks, scaling and peeling may not be necessary or even desirable because you will be discarding flavor, texture, and nutrients. If you have a tough, old stalk, scrape and/or peel away as high up the stalk as may be necessary. Most recipes call for whole stalks. If you plan to stir-fry the asparagus, cut the stalks into 1-to-2-inch-long diagonal segments. If there is a great disparity in diameter between the base and the tip, you may have to cut off the base and give it a head start in the pot or reserve it for soup and the like.

Cooking

Most experienced cooks prefer to steam asparagus. If you have an asparagus steamer (typically, a tall cylindrical covered pot), use it. Otherwise, you can steam asparagus horizontally (it, not you) in a widemouthed nonspecialized steamer—or vertically in two pots, one inverted over the other. In the latter case, tie the spears together into a bundle with kitchen twine, then place the root ends in 1 inch of boiling salted water, then cover the asparagus with the second pot. Pyrex pots are best because you can observe the changes in color, a clue to doneness. As a rule of thumb, asparagus steams in 6 to 14 minutes, depending on age and thickness. Asparagus is also often simmered for the same length of time as steaming. For maximum color retention, simmer uncovered. For optimum vitamin retention, simmer covered. For a compromise, partially cover the pot. One old-time kitchen trick is to steam or simmer twice the amount you need for the meal, and marinate and refrigerate the second half for use as a cold entree for tomorrow's lunch. Remove loose spears from the pot with tongs, being careful not to break off the delicate bud heads. Drain before serving or final preparation. A very popular way to give cooked asparagus panache is to lay the spears in an ovenproof serving dish, top them with bread crumbs, grated Parmesan cheese or mornay sauce, then run the creation under the broiler until slightly browned on top. Alternatively, do the browning in a preheated 400°F oven.

Tests for Doneness

The asparagus is done when it reaches its apogee of vivid greenness. Once it starts overcooking, the hue dulls. Pierce the thick end with a fork—if it enters easily, the asparagus is cooked. If still in doubt, sample a spear. It should be *al dente*; that is, be slightly resistant when bitten into. A limp, mushy asparagus is overcooked.

Eating

The best and most sensual way to eat

whole asparagus is with your fingers. Should you feel leery of doing that at a formal dinner, you could use a knife and fork—or use tongs if available.

CLASSIC USES AND AFFINITIES

Asparagus takes well to rich sauces: hollandaise, mousseline, bechamel. Lemon, melted butter, and Parmesan cheese, separately or together, enhance asparagus. Crumbled egg yolk or nuts such as almonds add flavor and color contrast. Nutmeg is a compatible spice. Asparagus sweetens the flavor of wine, so be forewarned. The bud heads of young, tender asparagus can be eaten raw as a *crudité*. And any dish labeled *Argenteuil* on a menu is prepared with asparagus tips.

AVOCADO

BACKGROUND

The *alligator pear* or *love fruit* is native to Mexico and Guatemala. It was naturalized in South America, and became a significant part of the diet, before Columbus arrived to observe it. Our word *avocado* derives from the Aztec word *ahuacatl*, which literally translates as "the tree's testicles." Some writers say it was so named because of the fruit's alleged aphrodisiac qualities, but more likely, the appellation is based on anatomical resemblance. In Mexico and Guatemala it is often cooked, serving as a meat course. But cooking can turn the avocado bitter and can destroy what you are after when you eat ripe fruit in season.

Varieties

Over a hundred varieties exist in the world, each with distinguishing features. An avocado can be green, maroon, purple, or black; can be sphere-, pear-, or egg-shaped; can have a smooth or goose-flesh skin; and can weigh from several ounces to over 2 pounds. Its meat can be greenish-yellow or whitish-beige-green. In its center lies a single relatively large blackish-brown seed. (In the movie "Oh God!" the deity confessed that He goofed when creating the world: He made the avocado seed too big.)

AVAILABILITY

Season

While avocados are now generally available from greengrocers the year round, their peak season (and the best time to enjoy them) is in late winter and early spring, February through April.

Buying Tips

Avoid rock-hard avocados; they have been picked too early, and will rot before they ripen. Do not buy green-skin varieties if the surface is glistening or dark-skin types if the color lacks depth. Pear-shaped avocados should have fat, symmetrical necks. All avocados should be heavy for their size.

If you plan to eat the avocado the day you buy it, use this test: cradle the fruit in both hands and, with your fingers, squeeze it gently, and then release the pressure. A good avocado will feel soft but the indentations left by your fingers should disappear. A supporting test is to smell the avocado: it should have a slight but identifiable fragrance. Avocados with dents or soft spots, or broken or blemished skins should be left in the bin, as they are either past prime or have been ill-treated during storage.

Chances are you will not find ready-to-eat avocados the day you want them. One reason ripe avocados are in short supply is that the fruit can ripen off its tree (if it has not been picked too early) and, taking advantage of this fact, producers prefer to ship them "very green" into the marketplace. So to be sure, plan to buy your supply 2 or 3 days ahead of time.

PREPARATION

Ripening

If you are in a hurry for your avocado to ripen (let's say you bought it a day later than you should have), place the avocado into a paper bag that you have generously perforated with small holes. Fruit, as it ripens, releases carbon dioxide. Too much CO_2 can retard and even arrest the ripening process; the holes in the bag let the gas dissipate. To increase air circulation, hang the bag. For even speedier ripening, add an apple to the bag. Ripe apples emit an abundance of ethylene gas, which is nature's catalyst in ripening.

To ripen without hastening nature, leave the avocado in an open bowl for 2 to 3 days at room temperature. When it is soft to your touch and you can smell its fragrance easily, your avocado is ready to eat.

Preliminaries

The avocado is an elegant and easy fruit to prepare. First cut lengthwise around the fruit, making a deep incision to (but not into) the large pit inside. Twist the halves free. The seed will adhere to one of the halves. Simply pry it out with a knife. Do not use a carbon steel knife to cut the avocado—it will discolor the pulp. Use stainless steel or silver.

The biggest problem in cutting an avocado is a cosmetic one. Its flesh discolors because of oxidation—and rather quickly, too. While usually this in no way affects taste or nutrition, it is unsightly. To prevent this discoloration, immediately rub or brush the cut surfaces with citrus juice or other mild acid. Lime is the classic choice, but lemon juice will do as well.

Storage

If you wish to store half of your avocado for later use, leave the stone in that half, brush the cut surface well with lime or lemon juice, wrap the half immediately in self-sealing plastic, and refrigerate it. Science does not yet know why, but the avocado seed can slow down the oxidation that browns the pulp. If you have mashed the avocado, bury the seed in the puree, cover the pulp thoroughly with a coating of citrus juice, and refrigerate in a closed container.

CLASSIC USES AND AFFINITIES

The most famous American preparation is guacamole, a Mexican-Guatemalan peasant creation made of avocado, onions, lime or lemon juice, red pepper, and whatever else may be available. The avocado is also classically served "on the half shell," that is, cut in half, stoned, and then stuffed. First slice off a bottom piece of the avocado half for balance. Partially fill the seed-well with a seasoned mayonnaise sauce such as Russian dressing, and drape shrimp attractively around the edges. The avocado, when sliced or cubed, is also a popular salad ingredient.

Grow Your Own Avocado Tree

Wash the seed, let it dry overnight, and peel off the outer membrane. Scar the surface with a few shallow slashes to stimulate. With the point of the seed up, insert three or four toothpicks like the spokes of a horizontal wheel around the seed. Rest the toothpicks on the lip of a glass filled with water, so 1/2 to 1 inch of the larger end of the seed is in the water. Put into a dark corner until the seed sprouts, then transfer to a spot with indirect sunlight. Change the root water once a week. When the roots are several inches long (it may take several weeks), plant indoors with potting soil. With tender loving care and a reasonable amount of sunlight, it will grow leafy and tall. But don't expect blossoms unless it is planted outdoors in a semitropical climate.

AZUKI BEAN

BACKGROUND

The *azuki* (or *adzuki*) bean (*Phaseolus angularis*) is a BB-sized round legume indigenous to and popular in China and Japan. The tiny azuki can be speckled, brownish-crimson, creamy-white, or black.

AVAILABILITY

American health-food shops and Oriental spice and specialty stores often stock dried azuki beans. They are also sometimes available in cans or prepared as a bean paste.

Storage

As with most dried legumes, the azuki stores best in a tightly closed container in a cool, dry environment. Properly stored, your azuki beans should keep up to 1 year.

PREPARATION

(For soaking, cooking, etc., see BEANS.)

CLASSIC USES AND AFFINITIES

The azuki bean goes particularly well with rice and is an excellent protein complement to rice dishes. The dried bean can be ground into a soft flour and used in making delicate pastries.

B

BACON

BACKGROUND

Standard bacon as we know it in America is the cured (and often smoked) belly of the hog. It consists of alternating layers of lean and fat, and may also have an attached rind. Bacon has many culinary uses, but in this country most of it is consumed with breakfast eggs. Due partly to spinach salads and the BLT sandwich, the bacon-eating season peaks during the warm months from June through September.

Much has been written about the possible carcinogenic effect of the nitrates and nitrites in bacon, but the jury is still out. Today, most authorities believe that several slices a week should not cause alarm.

Varieties

You can buy bacon in a number of forms, including sliced, slab, Irish, Canadian, jowl, country-style, canned, ends and pieces, bits, and analog.

Sliced Bacon: Most shoppers bring home the bacon in this form. It is typically sold in either 1/2- or 1-pound windowed packages containing overlapping, rindless, 9-inch-long strips, sometimes called *rashers.* There are three unofficial thicknesses: regular, thin, and thick. *Regular* slices are almost 1/8 to 1/12-inch-thick (roughly 16 to 24 slices per pound). *Thin-sliced* bacon is typically 1/16 to 1/20 inch thick (or 32 to 40 slices per pound). *Thick-sliced* (also called *country-sliced*) bacon is usually 1/4 to 1/6 inch thick (8 to 12 slices per pound).

Slab Bacon: Less often found in the market is the unsliced slab of bacon, usually sold with rind attached. Many gourmets state categorically that it is always better than sliced bacon, but that depends on such factors as the original quality and present freshness. On the average, however, slab bacon is of better quality and is more flavorful than presliced bacon. It is also less expensive and has a much longer storage life. Some people ask the butcher to slice the slab bacon but, unless you plan to cook the bacon within the day, you are better off slicing it just before cooking.

Irish Bacon: Imported from Ireland, this bacon cut includes two distinct portions of the hog's anatomy—the belly (source of the standard American bacon) and the loin—linked together. It is well cured and smoked.

Canadian Bacon: This is not a true bacon. (See under PORK, CURED.)

Smoked Jowl Bacon: This is also not a true bacon, but can be suitably substituted for the real McCoy. (See under PORK, CURED.)

Country-Style Bacon: Generally, this refers to a well-cured and smoked bacon that has been sliced thick.

Canned Bacon: This undistinguished product is not worth buying, except perhaps by people such as campers who lack the means of refrigeration. It is almost always precooked, and needs just a quick heating in a skillet over a campfire.

Ends and Pieces: After the meat packer has trimmed the bacon into the traditional rectangular shape, he sells the ends and pieces (usually to other food processors) for a relatively low cost. Should you come across this type of bacon, use it for dishes that call for cut-up bacon, such as salads and casseroles.

Bacon Bits: Two basic types of bacon bits are marketed: real and fake. The real bacon bits are so full of preservatives that their natural flavor is overwhelmed. The taste of pseudobacon (often made with textured vegetable protein) is even worse. Neither type needs refrigeration.

Analog Bacon: Anyone who loves the taste of true bacon would find it difficult to believe that these ersatz products deserve to be thought of even as a substitute for bacon. Their chief ingredient is soybean protein (which is okay) but their texture and flavor displeases discerning palates. Another type is being made from beef, but this too is not worth the prices even if you maintain a kosher kitchen. Bacon has no adequate substitute.

AVAILABILITY

Bacon can be found throughout the year.

Buying Tips

Different bacon processors use different curing and smoking processes, so some bacon is mild-cured and barely (if at all) smoked, while other bacon is just the opposite. Moreover, a bacon may or may not be highly sugar-cured, and if it is smoked, it may have a distinctive smoked-wood flavor such as hickory. Even the same firm can have several quality levels, each merchandised under a different brand name. Since most imported bacon is not made from corn-fed hogs (as is the case in America) the foreign bacon will taste different from most of our domestic bacon. It therefore pays to try a variety of brands and then stick with those that suit your taste. Select bacon that feels firm, not flabby. The bacon should be free of any off-odor. Examine the bacon through the package window—the slices should look fresh, not dull or slimy, without mold or abnormal discoloration. The texture should be reasonably fine, not coarse. The slices should be uniform in length, width, and thickness. The ratio of fat to lean should be about 3 to 2, one reason being that it is the fat that contributes the sought-after bacon flavor. If you are just interested in the lean, you will be better off buying another type of cured pork (such as ham or Canadian bacon) that gives you more lean per dollar. Buy only for short-term consumption (see STORAGE section below).

Buying for Crispness: If you enjoy crisp bacon, you should buy bacon that has the previously mentioned fat-to-lean ratio of 3:2, not leaner. And you are better off buying slices that show a few broad streaks rather than a lot of narrow streaks of lean. The thinner the slices, the crisper your bacon will be. (Also see COOKING FOR CRISPNESS below.)

PREPARATION

Storage

Sliced Bacon: If you buy a good specimen, unopened vacuum-wrapped bacon should keep at least several weeks in the refrigerator. Once opened, it is very perishable and starts to lose flavor and freshness noticeably within 4 to 7 days, even when tightly sealed in plastic wrap and refrigerated (which should be done). Bacon freezes badly because its high salt content hinders freezing and the high fat content accelerates rancidity. Moreover, the lingering ice crystals (or their melted residue) will increase the tendency of bacon to splatter when fried.

Slab Bacon: If in good condition when purchased, your slab of bacon should keep at least a couple of weeks in your refrigerator if you tightly seal it in plastic wrap and slice off and use the perishable end pieces at least every 4 to 7 days.

Preliminaries

Most people prefer to remove the rind (if any) before cooking the bacon. Others cook and eat that delicacy along with the bacon proper. If the bacon is too salty for your taste, parboil it in simmering water to cover for a few minutes to take out some of the salt, then drain and pat dry with a paper towel to reduce splattering when you cook it. To determine saltiness, cook a sample portion—never sample uncooked bacon, as there is a remote but real chance of consuming the dreadful trichinosis parasites. Sometimes it is hard to separate the slices of cold bacon without tearing and stretching them. To make it easier, let the bacon rest at room temperature for about 30 minutes before cooking. Alternatively, peel off several slices of the refrigerator-cold bacon en masse and cook them for a minute or so—then separate the slices (it should be easy) and continue cooking until the bacon is done as you like it. Stores sell square frying pans just the right size and shape for cooking the standard 9-inch-long bacon strips. If your round pan is not broad enough to accommodate your bacon, you can cut the pieces in half or, better, you can crowd the slices into the pan and then separate them as they shrink. You can also cook the bacon in batches; place the cooked pieces between sheets of paper toweling in a 200°F oven to keep warm. We do not recommend the coffeeshop style of partially cooking the bacon ahead of time. It may make practical sense for a busy coffeeshop with a small kitchen cooking breakfasts for dozens of hurried customers, but much flavor and texture are lost in the process.

Cooking

One of the essential rules of cooking bacon is to use a low-to-moderate temperature (unless you want very crisp bacon; see next section). Too high a temperature causes bacon to shrink drastically and—even more important—to curl and crinkle excessively, which results in uneven cooking. Prolonged high-heat cooking causes bacon to burn and blacken, giving it a disagreeable bitter flavor. And, according to some food scientists, this burnt part may be highly carcinogenic. If you see smoke, you are cooking your bacon with too high a temperature. The bacon strips should be placed on a cold pan, griddle, or rack, never on a preheated one. An oven or broiler, on the other hand, should be preheated. To judge doneness, remember that as the bacon cooks, the opaque fat becomes translucent, then becomes opaque again, while the lean steadily darkens and the bacon shrinks.

Cooking for Crispness: While it is a matter of personal preference whether bacon should be cooked medium-crisp or very crisp, it is a gastronomic faux pas to go to the extremes: soggy-limp or hard-crisp. If you want very crisp bacon, first start with the right type of bacon (see BUYING FOR CRISPNESS above). Second, master a few cooking tips: Cook your bacon at a slightly (but not too much) higher heat than the low-to-moderate heat that we recommend for medium-crisp bacon. Spoon or pour off the fat as it renders. Quickly, and as completely as possible drain and pat dry the cooked slices. Wait a few minutes before eating the bacon.

Pan Broiling: Regular-sliced, refrigerator-cold bacon strips will cook in 4 to 6 minutes. If the bacon strips are thin- or thick-sliced, or if they are at room temperature, make adjustments accordingly. Using tongs (preferably wooden), turn the strips over at least once and press them down whenever they start to curl—for even cooking, you should try to keep as much of the bottom surface as possible in contact with the sizzling fat. Unless you want very crisp bacon, do not spoon or pour off the rendered fat, as it provides a deeper medium in which to fry the bacon, thereby helping the bacon to cook more quickly and evenly. Contrary to popular belief, this extra fat will not increase splatter (unless the heat is too high). Neither will the extra fat give you greasier bacon, if you take the normal step of using absorbent paper to drain and pat dry the bacon immediately after it is cooked. Some cooks save the expense and waste of paper toweling by using paper grocery bags.

Baking and Broiling: The chief drawback of using an oven or broiler is that you will face a clean-up chore if the bacon splatters (with pan broiling you can constantly see the bacon as it cooks, lowering the temperature if necessary). Baking does offer an advantage: if you are cooking a large quantity (say for a bevy of houseguests), you can put the bacon in the oven and give it minimum attention (it needs no turning) until it is done. Place the strips on a rack in a shallow pan and bake in a preheated 375°F oven for 12 to 16 minutes or until the bacon is crisp enough. To broil bacon, place the strips on a rack in a shallow pan and cook 2 to 3 minutes per side, 4 inches from the flame in the preheated broiler set at 375°F. The cooking times given above are for refrigerator-temperature, regular-sliced bacon. Make adjustments for thinner, thicker, or warmer bacon. Lining the bottom of the rack pan with aluminum foil reduces clean-up time.

Bacon Drippings: Some economical cooks save the rendered bacon fat for future frying needs and for seasoning foods such as vegetables. Here is how to do it. Pour off the hot fat into a clean tin can; store it in the refrigerator. When the can becomes nearly full (it may take several weeks), scrape the grease out into a saucepan, discarding as much of the sediment as you can. Add to the saucepan an equal amount of cold tap water and sprinkle the surface with several tablespoons of flour, which will help collect and settle the sediment. Without stirring, bring to a boil and let cool. Pour the solution through several layers of cheesecloth into a clean glass jar or other container. Cover, and refrigerate. The fat will solidify on top of the water. Use as needed.

Barding with Bacon: Many cookbooks recommend using bacon strips to bard food such as fowl. In our opinion, such a practice gives subtly flavored food too much of a bacon taste—why mask the flavor of what you are cooking? A better barding medium is uncured and unsmoked fatback, which can be purchased or cajoled from most butchers. If you wish to bard with bacon, at least parboil it for about 10 minutes to reduce its salty, smoky flavor and fragrance. When you wrap food with bacon (for instance, tenderloin steaks—or oysters for angels-on-horseback), do not use thin-sliced bacon; it is too flimsy for the job.

Serving

Cooked bacon may be eaten hot or cold, the latter temperature for preparations such as salads and sandwiches. The average breakfast serving is 2 to 3 strips of regular-sliced bacon.

BAKING POWDER

BACKGROUND

Baking powder was invented in Boston in 1853. Earlier cooks had leavened quick breads with common BAKING SODA, which must be used with buttermilk, sour milk, molasses, or another acid-bearing ingredient.

How Baking Powder Works

Perhaps you recall from your high-school chemistry experiments that carbon dioxide bubbles are generated whenever a wet acid and alkali are combined, or when water is poured over a dry acid-and-alkali mixture. That is exactly what happens when you use baking powder, because this ingredient is essentially a mixture of an acid (cream of tartar, to name one) and an alkali (sodium bicarbonate, popularly known as baking soda). Add a liquid to this mixture and a chemical reaction results, producing carbon dioxide. This gas creates tiny air pockets within the dough or batter. When placed in a hot oven (or on a hot griddle), the dough or batter rises, for two reasons. First, the heat helps release additional carbon dioxide gas from the baking powder. Second, the heat expands the trapped carbon dioxide gas and air and vaporizes the water thus swelling the countless air pockets and expanding the item being baked. The cooking process firms the expanded dough or batter, which prevents the mass from collapsing back to its original size after the gas cools and escapes into the air.

Varieties

There are three major types of commercial baking powders, described below. Most of us only have to concern ourselves with the *double-acting* variety; it is the type almost exclusively stocked on supermarket shelves. While all three classes use baking soda as the alkaline ingredient, the different acid ingredients give the different types their technical name. These names or their popular equivalents are usually prominently displayed on the container's label. You'll also notice in the printed list of ingredients the name of a starch, frequently cornstarch. This substance serves several functions: to help stabilize and slow down the chemical reaction; to keep the mixture from caking; to absorb, during the storage period, any damaging airborne moisture.

Double-Acting: This variety is also referred to on labels and in recipes as SAS, SAS-phosphate, DA, and combination baking powder. It's the type sold under the Davis label, the brand dominating the American market. Two acids are used: calcium acid phosphate and sodium aluminum sulfate. The former starts chemically reacting with the baking soda as soon as you add the liquid to your mixture, while the latter does not fully react until you place the dough or batter in the oven. Thus the name "double-acting." The chief advantage of this type is that delayed-until-heated chemical reaction minimizes the amount of carbon dioxide gas escaping into the air while you stir the batter or knead the dough. Because of this feature some cookbooks say that batter prepared with double-acting baking powder can be set aside for an hour or so before baking. We suggest you follow this advice only if necessary, because 10 to 20 percent of the carbon dioxide potential of the batter will dissipate into the air. If you must store the prepared batter for more than 30 minutes, cover and refrigerate it, then allow 15 to 30 minutes to bring it to room temperature before baking. You have somewhat greater flexibility in storing dough, because it is less moist than batter; an hour's delay should cause no more than a 5 to 10 percent loss in leavening potency.

Tartrate: This type is sometimes called single-acting baking powder. Its acid ingredient is cream of tartar (a winemaking by-product) and/or tartaric acid. Both these acids start reacting with the baking soda the instant you add the liquid—and, be forewarned, nearly two-thirds of the mixture's carbon-dioxide potential will be generated within the first 2 minutes. Here lies this baking powder's major drawback.

Phosphate: Think of this type as being somewhere between the double-acting and the tartrate baking powders. Most of the chemical reaction between its acid ingredient (calcium acid phosphate or sodium acid phosphate) and the baking soda occurs while you prepare the dough or batter. Still, a reasonable amount of the reaction doesn't take place until the dough or batter is heated.

Buying Tips

Most modern recipes suggest or imply the use of double-acting baking powder, so buy it unless you need or strongly prefer another type. If a recipe merely says "baking powder," assume it means the double-acting type. Buy the smallest container available (usually 8 ounces), as baking powder starts losing its potency the second you open it.

PREPARATION

Storage

Moisture and age are baking powder's two greatest enemies. Dip into your tin only with a dry spoon—and away from steaming pots and other moist air. Keep the powder constantly dry by making sure that the lid is sealed tightly. Any moisture contacting the powder will set off part of the chemical reaction, lessening the potency. Once a tin is opened, the powder should remain usable for 6 months.

Potency Test

If ever you are unsure about baking powder's potency, here is a quick, simple, and reliable test: stir 1 teaspoon of the powder into 1/3 cup of hot tap water. If the powder doesn't fizzle audibly, or at least convincingly, replace it with a fresh supply. After all, the cost of a new can is low when compared to the cost of your other cooking ingredients not to mention your time and disappointment should your culinary triumph prove to be a culinary flop.

Making Baking Powder

If you run out of commercial baking powder you can easily make it yourself, providing you have fresh baking soda and cream of tartar. For each teaspoon of commercial double-acting baking powder called for in a recipe, substitute a scant teaspoon of cream of tartar and a rounded 1/2-teaspoon of baking soda. This mixture will probably lose its leavening power within a day or two, but if you add a teaspoon of cornstarch and store the mixture in an airtight container, your supply should remain adequately potent for several weeks.

Working with Baking Powder

When preparing a baking-powder batter, get into the habit of adding the liquid ingredient only at the last possible moment, stirring the batter as quickly and gently as possible, swiftly spreading the batter into your greased pans, and promptly popping these pans into a preheated oven. Also, do not attempt to stir out all the small flour lumps; this would let too much of the carbon dioxide gas escape into the air, nullifying the desired leavening power. All the above pointers are critical when using a tartrate baking powder, semicritical when using a phosphate baking powder, and reasonably important when using a double-acting baking powder. In the case of a dough (as for baking-powder biscuits), some kneading is necessary to develop the gluten structure in the flour mixture. Thirty seconds is normally ideal. A significantly shorter or longer kneading period usually produces leaden results.

High-Altitude Baking

Recipes require less baking powder at higher altitudes because the lower atmospheric pressure allows gases to expand more readily. This natural phenomenon requires the reduction of the normally prescribed amount of baking powder by about 10 percent at 2,500 feet and about 20 percent at 5,000 feet. For thorough comprehension of high-altitude baking, consult a high-altitude cookbook, since many other adjustments are also necessary.

Equivalents

The three major baking-powder types vary in strength. For each cup of flour, use 1 1/3 teaspoons of double-acting, 1 2/3 teaspoons of phosphate, and 2 teaspoons of tartrate baking powder. Sift these amounts with the flour for even distribution. When substituting tartrate for double-acting baking powder, use slightly more than 1 1/2 teaspoons of tartrate for each teaspoon of double-acting. When substituting phosphate, use 1 1/4 teaspoons for each teaspoon of double-acting baking powder.

What happens if you use too much or too little baking powder? Too much will impart a bitter taste to your baked item. Too little will produce hard objects reminiscent of the proverbial newlywed's biscuits.

Use with Acid Foods

Whenever you alter a recipe by creatively adding buttermilk, yogurt, sour milk, sour cream, molasses, chocolate, honey, vinegar, citrus fruit, tart apples, or any other food containing a relatively large amount of acid, you must reduce, or sometimes eliminate the amount of baking powder called for in the recipe, using baking soda instead. The reason is that the acid in these foods makes the acid in the baking powder partially or totally superfluous. This acid excess will be noticeable in the dish's flavor and will somewhat interfere with the successful execution of the chemical reaction needed to leaven the dough or batter.

When substituting an acid for a nonacid ingredient, the baker must take into consideration the new ingredient's degree of acidity. Let's assume, for instance, the baker is substituting buttermilk for fresh sweet milk. For each cup of buttermilk used, the baker could replace 1 teaspoon double acting baking powder called for in the recipe with approximately 1/2 teaspoon of baking soda. Yogurt, for the record, has roughly the same amount of acid as buttermilk while molasses has a little less. Chocolate and honey have appreciably less acid than buttermilk.

BAKING SODA

BACKGROUND

Other names for the white, crystalline alkali called *baking soda* include *bicarbonate of soda* and, in a chemist's language, *sodium bicarbonate.* When you combine baking soda with an acid such as cream of tartar, you create your own BAKING POWDER which, in the presence of water, chemically alters itself into carbon dioxide which helps raise bread doughs and batters.

CLASSIC USES AND AFFINITIES

Baking soda has many other uses. It is the naming ingredient in soda pop. Some shortsighted cooks add baking soda to the cooking liquid for green vegetables such as green beans in order to make the vegetable pigment more vivid; the strategem works, but it is a Pyrrhic victory, because vitamin C content is nearly obliterated and the vegetables become mushy. A teaspoon of baking soda makes an effective tooth cleanser in an emergency. Some people use an open box of baking powder in the refrigerator as a deodorant (changing the box regularly) because baking soda absorbs food odors. And baking soda can be taken in place of commercial fizzy antacids to alleviate gastric indigestion.

BAMBOO SHOOTS

BACKGROUND

Bambusa gramineae is a giant grass related to wheat, barley, and oats. Most bamboos originate in the Asian subtropics, where they are essential to the economy and ecology of the region. The woody stem furnishes material for everything from furniture to flutes; the young shoots provide food. Ornamental bamboos are now grown in temperate climates around the world.

AVAILABILITY

Fresh bamboo shoots are hard to find in the West. The winter shoots are smaller and softer than the less delicate spring shoots. Canned bamboo shoots are usually imported from Japan or Hong Kong.

PREPARATION

Fresh bamboo shoots must be parboiled 10 to 15 minutes (depending on thickness) before you eat them or add them to a recipe. Once the can is opened, surplus shoots must be refrigerated, with the water covering the shoots freshened every day. But the texture and flavor of the shoots, already impaired by the canning process, deteriorate even further once the can is opened.

BANANA

BACKGROUND

Once exotic and very rare in the United States, the banana (botanically a large berry) has become one of the commonest and least expensive fruits. *Musa sapientum* ("fruit of the wise men") is thought to be indigenous to tropical Asia and is today a major staple in many tropical lands around the world. It requires a consistently warm, wet climate, so Central America and Ecuador are major producers. Each banana tree (really a bush) grows relatively quickly in a year or less. It produces one 50-pound cluster of bananas.

The banana is easy to digest. For this reason, doctors advise it as a solid food for babies, for convalescents, for the elderly and for those with delicate stomachs. The banana has an unusual amount of digestible sugars when fully ripe. These assimilable sugars, plus a high concentration of the mineral salt potassium, have helped establish the banana as a health-food favorite. It is high in carbohydrates, low in protein and fats. Most Americans believe the banana is high on the list of fattening foods, but an average Cavendish banana has only 80 to 90 calories.

Varieties

There are many banana species, but few reach our shores. The yellow Cavendish is the banana the average American knows and loves. Some ethnic Americans—such as those with Caribbean ancestry—also relish the PLANTAIN, as well as the squatter *red banana* and the deliciously sweet *dwarf* or *finger banana*, to name a few.

AVAILABILITY

Available year round.

Buying Tips

The banana is always harvested green, even for local consumption, because it is one fruit which, if left to ripen on its bush, never develops its best flavor. It is still green when importers ship it in temperature-controlled holds of cargo ships—full ripening occurs either in the market or at home. If the banana is still greenish along the ridges or at the tips, it needs ripening at home—this is the kind to buy if you are buying for future consumption or for cooking. Select bananas with a reasonable amount of stem still attached to the fruit as its absence hastens deterioration. This is the prime reason why you usually should not purchase individual—as opposed to bunched—bananas. Choose plump bananas—thin ones will probably never properly ripen. The ideal ripening temperature is about 70°F. If too cold or too warm, the banana will not ripen to its full sweet potential. A fully ripe, ready-to-eat Cavendish banana is yellow, with brown surface specks. These specks (a good sign) are not to be confused with soft, rotten spots or bruise blemishes (a bad sign).

PREPARATION

Ripening

A banana is ripe when an optimum amount of the starch in the flesh has chemically converted into sugar. The disappearance of the green and the development of the brown specks will tell you when that stage has been reached. For normal ripening, store in an uncovered container in a dry, 70°F, draft-free spot. For faster ripening, store in a perforated paper bag.

Storage

Once it has ripened, plan to eat the banana within a day. If not, store in the refrigerator for up to several days (the peel will darken, but the flesh will still be edible). Whole bananas should not be frozen, but should you have a banana surplus, banana paste spiked with an acid such as lemon juice can be frozen if necessary. Once exposed to the air, the banana flesh starts to darken. To prevent this from happening, sprinkle with lemon or other citrus juice. Also, slice with a stainless-steel knife.

Cooking

Cavendish bananas that are slightly unripe are best for cooking because they hold their shape better. (An exception: use ripe ones for banana bread.) A standard way to bake a peeled banana is to dot the flesh with butter and sprinkle the top with brown sugar and place in a preheated 350°F oven for 12 to 18 minutes, depending on whether you left the fruit whole or sliced it.

CLASSIC USES AND AFFINITIES

The banana split, baked banana, and banana cream pie are among the perennial American favorites. The banana has long been pureed, added to flour, and baked into banana bread and cakes, and used in fritters, flapjacks, and crêpes. It is essential to Chicken à la Maryland, not to mention banana ice cream and the banana daiquiri. Popular flavoring agents include brown sugar, certain spices such as cinnamon, and spirits such as rum and orange-based liqueurs such as Cointreau.

BASIL

BACKGROUND

Several dozen green-leaved basil species exist, but it is the *sweet basil*, *Ocimum basilicum*, that dominates the market. The taste of raw basil is minty with a soft pungent background. A member of the mint family, basil probably originated in the Indian, Asian, or African subtropics. Today, it is widely grown and quite popular in the Mediterranean areas: Italy, southern France, and Greece have a high basil metabolism. The English name is derived from the Greek word for "king"; the Greeks called basil "the royal herb." (See HERBS AND SPICES for information on buying, storing, cooking, etc.)

AVAILABILITY

Fresh basil can be found during the summer, dried basil all year. Dried basil is more pungent, less sweet and delicate than the vastly superior fresh leaf. An essential oil of basil is manufactured, but most of this product goes to perfume manufacturers.

CLASSIC USES AND AFFINITIES

The combination of tomatoes and basil is legendary. This herb also goes with a wide range of ingredients including seafood, fowl, pork, lamb, veal, eggs, cucumbers, eggplant, carrots, squash, and green beans. Basil is essential to the celebrated Genoan *pesto* sauce made with garlic, olive oil, Parmesan and/or sardo cheese, and pine nuts. Basil is frequently added to pizza, casseroles, soup, sausages, and salad dressing. Chartreuse and several other liqueurs are flavored with this herb.

BAY LEAF

BACKGROUND

Native to the Mediterranean and to Asia Minor, this leaf of the evergreen sweet *bay* tree, which belongs to the laurel family, is one of the oldest flavoring agents used by mankind. Ancient Greeks and Romans wore it to ward off lightning and made laurel wreaths to crown poets, scholars, and victorious athletes (the origin of the modern terms "winning your laurels," "poet laureate," and "baccalaureate"). (See HERBS AND SPICES for information on buying, storing, and cooking, etc.)

Varieties and Buying Tips

There are several varieties of bay leaf. The Turkish variety, *Laurus nobilis*, has squat oval leaves about 1 to 2 inches long. Its superior flavor is subtler and more delicate than that of the California bay leaf, *Umbellularia californica*, which has narrow-oval leaves about 2 to 3 inches long. Before buying fresh bay leaves, subject them to the squat-versus-narrow oval test. Another good criterion is pliability. When picked from the tree, the bay leaf is reasonably pliable and is at its aromatic peak. As the leaf dries, it starts to lose its aromatic spunk and becomes less flexible. If the leaf is brittle, it is well over the hill and should be replaced. The best bay leaves have a glossy, fresh gray-green color and a sweet pungent scent. Reject broken leaves as whole leaves are easier to keep track of in the pot. Avoid brown-specked leaves or those with insect holes.

PREPARATION

One or one and a half average-sized bay leaves will season 2 to 4 quarts of liquid if other herbs are used. In long-cooked dishes, be prepared to remove the bay leaf early or add it late; otherwise, its flavor will overpower the dish. An infusion of 20 to 40 minutes, depending on the amount of bay leaf used, is about right. If this herb is added at the end of cooking, be sure and remove it before serving; a taste for whole bay leaf is very rare.

CLASSIC USES AND AFFINITIES

Besides being one of the basic herbs in BOUQUET GARNI and in PICKLING SPICE, bay leaves are frequently used to flavor soups, stews, and other casserole dishes. They are also used frequently in marinades, tomato sauces, court bouillon, vinaigrette, and custard creams. Bay leaves are often used in pot roasts, fricassees, and other braised dishes. The classic French cuisine prescribes bay leaves in pâté; many dishes from the south of France employ this herb.

BEAN CURD

BACKGROUND

Tofu (the Japanese name for *bean curd*) is an inexpensive, nonanimal, principal source of protein in many Oriental regional cuisines. It is essentially white soybeans that have been cooked, mashed, drained, and pressed into cakes with a firm, custardlike consistency. Because the flavor is mild, and the tofu readily absorbs other flavors, it is an ideal ingredient when, for instance, stir-fried with more flavorful foods. Bean curd is also excellent when simmered in soups and stews, when deep-fried, and even when served cold and dipped into a soy-based sauce.

Varieties

Bean curd comes in several forms: fresh, canned, dried, and fermented.

Fresh Bean Curd: It comes in three basic styles: Japanese, Chinese, and toasted. The *Japanese*-style tofu has the silkiest, least firm texture, which is the ideal choice for soups and for eating cold with a dip. The firmer *Chinese*-style product is the preferred choice for stir-fried dishes because the curd does not as readily break apart during the cooking process. *Toasted* fresh bean curd is Chinese-style curd that has been given a light brown, soft crust. Bean curd is bland, but it has its own subtle taste, which can vary by the quality of the producer's ingredients and processing methods. When buying fresh bean curd in a store, be sure that the merchant has a high turnover and that the bean curd is properly submerged in water, is not breaking apart, and does not have a sour odor. If you plan to eat the tofu without cooking, buy only from a store where the bean curd is removed from the container with hygienic equipment. Too many stores freely allow customers to reach into the water with unwashed hands. Fresh bean curd is very perishable and should be kept submerged in water in your refrigerator. Thus stored, it will stay reasonably fresh for several days if the water is changed daily.

Canned bean curd: An unworthy commercial product with an inferior, rubbery texture.

Dried Bean curd: The unsolidified bean curd mixture is dried and sold in brittle, brownish-cream colored, flat sheets or long strips (or sticks). It has an interesting, silky, slippery texture and adds excitement when added to meat or vegetable dishes. The sheets can be used as edible wrappings. To reconstitute dried bean curd, soak it in lukewarm water to cover for 30 to 60 minutes.

Fermented Bean curd: Regular bean curd is cut into cubes, then fermented in a rice wine mixture. Unlike other bean-curd products, this variety has its own strong flavor. It is used as a co-ingredient or as the major flavoring agent in meat, fish, or vegetable dishes.

PREPARATION

Cooking

The product was already cooked at the factory before it was pressed into cakes. Therefore, it only needs to be heated through or to have sufficient time to absorb the other flavoring agents. If you suspect that your bean curd was handled with less-than-sanitary hands before you brought it home, you will have to cook it long enough to sterilize it.

BEAN PASTE

BACKGROUND

Yellow bean paste is made from salted, fermented yellow soybeans and is used as a flavoring agent in Oriental cuisine. It and *miso* (its Japanese cousin) are best stored refrigerated in a tightly closed glass jar, though you could store it for a month or two in a dry, dark spot if it is under 60°F. *Red bean paste*, which may or may not be made with soybeans, is often sweetened and used as a filler for Oriental pastries.

BEANS

BACKGROUND

Legumes, especially the *pulses* (beans and certain kinds of peas) are among the oldest known foods of humanity. When dried, they can be stored for a long time. Dried or not, they are inexpensive, filling, and high in certain proteins. However, to get the full value of the protein, you should eat beans in combination with protein-complementing foods such as the cereal grains. Beans do have drawbacks: most legumes taste somewhat bland and starchy unless the cook makes a special effort to season them; beans can cause flatulence.

Varieties

For background information on specific beans, see the following entries:

Azuki bean
Bean sprouts
Black bean
Black-eyed pea
Broad bean
Chick-pea
Cranberry bean
Great Northern bean
Green and Wax beans
Kidney bean
Lentil
Lima bean
Marrow bean
Navy bean
Pea bean
Peas
Pigeon pea
Pinto and Pink bean
Scarlet runner bean
Soybean

AVAILABILITY

Types

Beans are available in several forms: fresh, dried, canned, and frozen.

Fresh: Only a few varieties of beans are commercially available to us fresh: GREEN BEANS, LIMA BEANS, and sometimes *fava* or BROAD BEANS. Fresh beans are almost always sold in their pods.

Dried: A wide variety of dried legumes are available to us year round, usually packaged in airtight plastic bags or windowed boxes, although they can be purchased loose in some specialty food stores. Now and then you can find presoaked, redried beans sold with descriptive phrases such as "quick-cooking beans." Such beans require virtually no soaking—but while you gain convenience, you inevitably lose texture and flavor, and pay a premium price, to boot. For specific information on each type of dried bean, see the individual entries.

Canned: Already fully cooked, these beans need only to be heated at home. Texture is not a strong point—they are invariably mushy. They are sold in cans or jars, either by themselves or mixed with other ingredients such as pork. Marinated "three-bean salad" is also available.

Frozen: The most popular frozen shelled bean is the lima, which is sold in two sizes, baby and regular (Fordhooks). As with canned beans, though not to the same negative degree, the frozen type falls short in the quality of texture, since freezing breaks down the cell walls. On the positive side, frozen beans are convenient and easy to prepare, available year round, and retain much of their original nutritional value. Cooking instructions are found on the package.

Buying Tips

Fresh Beans: They should be plump in their pods, unshriveled, crisp, fresh-looking, and brightly colored for their variety. Avoid fresh beans beyond their initial stage of maturity, as such beans tend to be tough. For even cooking, the beans should be uniform in size. For specific tips, see individual entries.

Dried beans: Dried beans can keep for years, but for best taste and nutrition, buy your dried legumes as newly packaged as possible. Buy your dried beans from stores that have a fairly rapid stock turnover; experiment with different outlets and brands. Once satisfied, stay with the ones you like. This will help you to control the variables of beans, such as knowing roughly how long they have been dried and where they were grown—factors that can affect cooking times. Look for clean, even-sized beans with uncracked hulls and no visible dirt, debris, or small stones. The bags should be strong, unpunctured and well sealed—few things are worse than spilling the beans on your kitchen floor, and exposure to the air is exposure to moisture and bacteria. Beans are priced reasonably enough so that one need not seek out reduced-price beans. Too often such bargains are from broken bags and repackaged. Or they are old, powdery, broken, or dirty. They might also have little tooth-breaking pebbles interspersed among them that must be tediously removed. If buying your dried beans loose from a bin, sift through and choose clean beans with a fresh appearance. Tiny pinholes in the hull usually indicate bug infestation.

PREPARATION

Storage

Dried Beans: For quick identification, store dried beans in their plastic packages or in clear glass jars with tight-fitting lids. Once the plastic bag has been opened, transfer the remaining beans to a newly washed and thoroughly dry glass jar and store in a dry spot. Good-quality dried beans can be kept for up to a year without harm if stored carefully. Do not mix bean varieties or beans purchased at different times. Harder types and older beans have different soaking and cooking requirements than do softer or fresher beans.

Fresh Beans: In general, seal in a plastic bag and refrigerate. Plan to use within a day or two; definitely within the week. For specific bean idiosyncracy, see the individual bean entry.

Preliminaries, Dried Beans

Cleaning: Pour your beans into a colander, sifting through them with your fingers as you do so, looking for shriveled or discolored beans or any objectionable foreign material. (If beans are of good quality and were packaged by a reputable company, chances are you will find few, if any, impurities.) If bought loose, give them an extra-thorough examination and wash. Under strong-running cold tap water give the beans a good rinse and a shake, stirring them around to make sure all the beans get the benefit of the bath.

Soaking: Beans require various soaking times according to their initial hardness, how long they have been in the dried state, the hardness and temperature of the soaking water, and the atmospheric pressure where they are soaked. Getting to know which beans take how long in your kitchen is something learned best by experience. However, here are some workable guidelines:

The *hardest* bean is the soybean. *Hard*

beans are the pea bean, and the navy, Great Northern, marrow, black, pinto, and Roman beans. The *softest* beans are lentils, black- or yellow-eyed beans, and the green and yellow split peas. Consider other common beans to be *medium-hard*. Some cookbooks will tell you that the softest of the dried beans do not need soaking, but all dried legumes are tastier and less flatulence-inducing if they are soaked before they are cooked.

Use about 4 cups of fresh, unsalted water for each cup of beans. Dried beans generally double in volume when thoroughly soaked. Dried mature lima beans only gain about 25 percent increase in size.

There are three methods for soaking.

The Traditional Soak: This is the best method for optimum flavor and texture. Place the beans in fresh cold water, cover with a kitchen cloth, and let stand 8 to 12 hours or overnight. If your kitchen is very warm, let the beans soak in the refrigerator as a precaution against fermentation.

The Simmer-and-Soak: Use this method when you do not have the time for the traditional soak. Bring beans in water to a boil. Reduce to a gentle simmer and cook 2 to 5 minutes. Remove the pot from the heat and let the beans soak for 2 hours, then test. To test if they're sufficiently soaked, see below. If more soaking is needed, keep beans submerged and check every 15 minutes or so thereafter.

The Freezer Soak: Soak beans in water, covered, for 1 to 2 hours at room temperature, then freeze overnight in the freezer. The beans can then be cooked, unthawed. Or, for better results, thaw and cook in fresh tap water. We do not recommend the freezer soak method, as not much time or effort is saved and much texture is lost.

Testing for Moisture Content after Soaking: First throw out any beans that are floating. To check whether the beans have thoroughly soaked, cut through one bean lengthwise with a paring knife. The interior flesh should be all the same color and consistency—if the bean has not completely regained its maximum moisture content, the inner area of the flesh will be whiter, harder, and more raw-looking than the outer parts. If the skin shrivels excessively or loosens and slips off, or if the beans have begun to send up more than a few tiny bubbles in the water, they may have become waterlogged. If so, drain them in a colander and let them dry in the open air for about half an hour before cooking.

Cooking Dried Beans

There are more ways to cook beans than the number of beans in your pot. In this section we will give one simple but effective method. Of the various cooking techniques, the best is pot-cooking on top of the stove or in the oven. Pot-cooked beans need long gentle simmering and occasional attention—beans are more delicate than many people realize. Briefly sauté chopped onions, carrots, and celery in one or more tablespoons of butter, vegetable oil, or rendered pork fat. We advise using fresh water for cooking. While it is true some vitamins and minerals are leached out, the beans are primarily taking water in rather than chemically breaking down during the soak. What is lost to the soaking water is some of the oligosaccharides, carbohydrate substances that cause gas to form in the intestines during the digestive process. To reduce the tendency to flatulence, then, use fresh water for the cooking step. Add to the pot the beans and enough water to cover them, bring to a boil, reduce heat to a gentle simmer; cook with lid. Add flavoring such as herbs and spices (but not salt) at the beginning of the cooking period. Save the salt to the last 20 to 30 minutes of cooking time. Salt (like hard water) tends to toughen beans, and tender but still whole, firm-textured beans are what you are after. For top-of-the-stove cooking, it is especially essential to use a large, heavy pot, a Dutch oven if you have it. If your pot is not heavy enough, use an asbestos pad or a metal Flame-Tamer under the pot to reduce the heat; you may even need it with your Dutch-oven. Use the lowest heat possible to maintain a gentle simmer—never a boil. A wooden spoon or spatula is best for stirring, but stir gently and seldom. Stirring disturbs the beans, breaks them, and causes the skins to fall away. If the beans appear to be absorbing too much of their cooking water before being fully cooked, add a little water as needed. Cooking times (like soaking) must be imprecise because individual variables affect the time—hardness of water, maturity of bean when dried, where grown, and how long dried, among others. As a rough guide, figure about 30 minutes for the softest legumes (lentils, black-, yellow-eyed, green and yellow split peas); 45 minutes for limas; 45 to 90 minutes for the medium-hard type (chick-peas, cannellini, flageolets, broad beans, pink, and kidney beans), 2 to 2½ hours for hard beans (azuki, pea, navy, white, pinto, black) and up to 3 hours for soybeans. Do not worry if your beans cook 20 to 30 percent longer than necessary, because it is difficult to overcook beans—as long as you simmer rather than boil them. Oven cooking has an advantage over stove-top cooking because the bean pot requires less watching. In a 300°F oven, increase stove-top cooking times by approximately 25 percent. Some recipes call for a combination of stove-top (first) and oven cooking. Do as you wish.

Pressure-Cooking: This method takes much less time. Of course you must follow the manufacturer's directions carefully. We do not recommend this method, because bean skins can dangerously clog the escape valve and because we find that beans taste best slow-cooked. The preferred type of pressure cooker cooks at 15 pounds pressure and holds 6 quarts. We suggest following a cookbook specificially designed for the pressure cooker.

Test for Doneness: With a tasting spoon, remove a few beans from the pot. Sample them. Or blow on the beans: if the skins break, the beans are done.

Cooking Fresh Beans

Fresh beans cook more quickly than dried beans. The best method for retaining nutrients of fresh beans is to steam them. One simple steaming method is to add them to a saucepot containing about ¼ inch of boiling water. Add seasonings (but no salt) and butter for flavoring. Immediately cover, reduce heat to a minimum and cook until done, then salt to taste. Simmering takes about the same length of time as does steaming. To simmer, bring beans in a covered heavy pot with water to a slight boil, reduce heat, and gently cook until just tender. Green beans usually take about 10 to 15 minutes; limas maybe 20 minutes; and broad beans may take as long as half an hour.

Equivalents

One cup of dried beans expands to 2 to 2-½ cups of cooked beans. Normally, ½ to ¾ cup of cooked beans per person should be sufficient for a side portion; double the amount if the beans are the main dish of the meal.

CLASSIC USES AND AFFINITIES

In America, there is succotash (lima beans and corn, invented by the Indians); in Boston, baked beans; down South there is Hopping John (black-eyed peas and rice); out West there is chile con carne (although purists will not use the beans); and at Campbell's it is pork and beans in a can. Mexicans like *frijoles refritos* (refried beans). In Brazil, the national dish is feijoada, a bean, rice, and meat medley. Some Spanish-speaking countries humorously call their popular black-bean-and-rice dish "*Moros y Cristianos*" (Moors and Christians). *Hummus* is a Middle-Eastern chick-pea appetizer or side dish and *felaffel* is deep-fried chick-pea balls. Egypt's national dish is the bean-ful *ful medames*. The Japanese have popularized miso, a soybean paste, and tofu, a bean-curd cake. Cold bean salads are favorites everywhere. Almost all herbs and spices—and especially savory, thyme, and bay leaves—go well with beans. Both fresh and smoked pork are classic affinities.

BEAN SPROUTS

BACKGROUND

You can grow your own vegetables without a garden, even without soil, by sprouting beans and seeds. *Mung beans* are the ones most people eat, though SOYBEANS, CHICK-PEAS, *alfalfa* seeds, LENTILS, *millet*, *wheat*, *rye*, and SUNFLOWER SEEDS can also be sprouted. The Chinese call sprouts "the tooth vegetable" because of their crunchy texture.

AVAILABILITY

The dried beans and other seeds are available year around, or you can buy them already sprouted.

Buying Tips

If buying your sprouted beans, choose fresh-looking sprouts with the bean buds still attached. Avoid darkened ones, slimy sprouts, or any that smell musty or even slightly fermented.

PREPARATION

To sprout your own, soak the beans or seeds in four times as much water as beans and leave them in a warm, dark place for 8 hours or overnight. Drain them and put them into a glass or plastic container covered with a loosely woven cloth and return them to their warm, dark spot. Every 8 hours or so, rinse the seeds in fresh cool water, drain, and return to the dark. The sprouts will be ready to eat when they reach about ½ inch in length, though they are still edible when several times that size, with greenish-ivory tips. This should take 3 to 6 days. If you wait until the sprouts develop tiny roots, they are past their prime and should be discarded. For best taste and nutrition, they must be eaten as they sprout. Rinse them in fresh cool water, drain, and if you are an exacting cook, pick off the papery seed coats. They should be eaten raw or just barely cooked to keep their snap and vitamin content.

CLASSIC USES AND AFFINITIES

Sprouts add a bit of exotica at small cost to meals in winter, when few fresh vegetables are available. Add them to salads, marinate them in spice vinegars and mix with nuts, use them as substitutes for lettuce in sandwiches, or serve them as an accompaniment to cooked dishes.

BEEF

BACKGROUND

Beef is a subject worth learning more about—after all, it is the star and most costly food on most American dinner tables. Many factors govern the flavor and tenderness of the meat you eat—the age of the animal it comes from, the quality of the animal, the anatomical location of the cut of meat, and, of course, the preparation. Each of these factors will be discussed below, along with each of the primal cuts of beef. For further information on various cuts, see these other articles:

Beef, Ground
Beef Hanging Tenderloin
Beef Jerky
Beef London Broil
Beef Short Ribs

Also consult these entries:

Blood
Bones
Brains
Head
Heart
Intestines
Kidneys
Liver
Lungs
Marrow
Oxtail
Spleen
Sweetbreads
Testicles
Tongue
Tripe

Age Of The Animal

Bovine meat can be divided into five somewhat arbitrary categories, depending upon its age:

Bob veal
Veal
Baby beef
Beef
Well-matured beef

Bob veal and *veal* are the meat of a young bovine. There is much debate as to when the meat ceases to be veal and starts to become *baby beef*. We think—for reasons of taste and texture—that the cutoff point should be when the animal is about 3 months old, though some stores call the meat veal even when the animal was 6 months old. To us, that meat is baby beef, an inferior substitute for veal. You can tell the difference: veal under 3 months is generally of a pinkish-white color, while older "veal" takes on a cherry-red color. For more on veal and baby beef, see VEAL entry.

Meat is *beef* when the animal is somewhere between 1 to 2½ years old. From a point of taste and texture, the ideal beef is about 18 to 24 months old, though in the rush to get the meat to the market, most of the beef that arrives in our supermarket cases is from animals that were roughly 1 year old. Such meat—and some of it is baby beef—is inferior to what real beef should be in terms of flavor and texture.

Over 2½ years, the meat begins to toughen and darken from a rosy-red to a purplish-red color. At this stage, it becomes *well-matured beef*, and can offer you a rewarding flavor. It will probably be too tough, though, if you cook it with a dry heat. Instead, use a slow, moist-heat cooking method such as braising or stewing. However, if the animal was well fed and little exercised, it is possible to classify and treat a 2½ to 3½-year-old bovine as beef rather than well-matured beef, though such animals are rare.

Quality of the Animal

All animals do not provide equally tender meat—the chuck of one carcass may be as tender (or even more tender) than, say, the porterhouse of another.

USDA Grades: For those meatpackers that request and pay for the service, the U.S. Department of Agriculture grades beef into eight categories. These are:

Prime
Choice
Good
Standard
Commercial
Utility
Cutter
Canner

The specific grade is imprinted all along the outside of the carcass with a special roll-stamp instrument, producing a series of purple shields. The ink is made with a harmless vegetable dye, so it need not be trimmed off before cooking. You seldom see it on small cuts in the meat case, though, because the meat was trimmed or the piece of meat was too small to leave the imprint of a whole shield intact.

USDA Prime grade seldom finds its way into most meat markets or restaurants—it is purchased (at a premium) by quality steakhouses and butcher shops. Most of the meat we find in retail stores is *USDA Choice* grade. Because of this fact and since the category covers a broad spectrum (too broad, to our minds), the usefulness of knowing that your beef has been graded Choice is sometimes nil. *USDA Good* is hard to find in most meat cases. When it is available, it is often sold on a special sale. The lowest five grades, *USDA Standard* to *USDA Canner*, find their way into our homes in the form of processed foods such as canned stew or soup.

Criteria for Grading: The USDA officials grade beef on the net result of several criteria, including:

Marbling: The more marbling (small specks of fat embedded within the lean flesh), the more flavorful, tender, and juicy the meat will be when cooked. The marbling is quite noticeable in better grades and gradually disappears as you move down the quality scale. (It all but disappears by the time you reach the grade of USDA Good.)

Color of Fat: Cattle that feed on grain such as corn produce better meat than do those that eat the less costly grass. The fat of grain-fed animals is bright white; the fat of their grass-fed counterparts has a yellowish tinge. The color of the exterior fat coupled with the amount of marbling is an excellent clue to the quality of the meat in the butcher's display case.

Color of Meat: The brighter, fresher the color, generally the better the meat.

Firmness: The firmer the lean flesh, generally the better the meat.

Texture: The finer the texture of the flesh, generally the better the meat.

Yield: In addition to judging beef quality, the USDA grades the carcass according to the ratio of desirable meat to undesirable meat, bones, and fat. This is done on a scale of 1 to 5, with 1 being the highest accolade. Most of the meat we buy at the market is already trimmed into retail cuts, so this *yield grade* is not practical information for us unless we are purchasing a side or quarter of beef.

Inspection: We have yet another USDA symbol to understand: the circle-shaped federal inspection stamp. Do not confuse this stamp with the USDA grading systems for either quality or yield—both are voluntary except in a few subnational government jurisdictions. The USDA inspection, though, is mandatory for all beef crossing state or national borders. It helps assure us that the animal was healthy, that the packinghouse was sanitary, and that the meat was wholesome when it was shipped. The stamp goes on the carcass or, if the meat is packaged, onto the container.

Anatomical Location

The slaughterhouse worker splits the carcass lengthwise into two halves or *sides*, as they are called by the trade. Each side is then cut crosswise in half, forming quarters. Thus, each carcass contains two forequarters and two hindquarters.

Primal Cuts: The next step, which can be performed at the packinghouse or at the wholesale or retail meat market, is to divide each quarter into *primal* (or *wholesale*) *cuts* as illustrated on page 35. These nine primal cuts are discussed individually in alphabetical order in the sections that follow the PREPARATION section below.

Tenderness: The meat from certain parts of the animal is more tender than that from other areas because some muscles are used more than others. The tenderest muscle is the aptly named tenderloin, which does little work. Next in tenderness ranking is the loin muscle. At the other extreme are the various muscles in the leg (especially the lower leg) and neck, which are well exercised.

PRIMAL CUTS OF BEEF

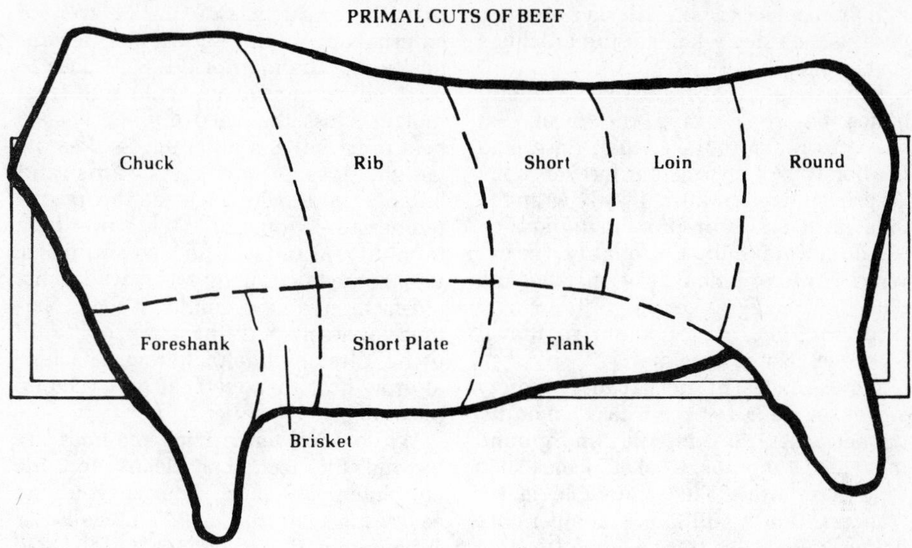

Each individual muscle is not uniformly tender. The closer the location of the portion of the muscle is to the middle of the back (the short loin area), the more tender it will likely be. The converse is also true. Thus, the eye round muscle becomes tougher as it approaches the end of the leg.

PREPARATION

The way meat is stored and prepared of course affects the end result: poor preparation can ruin an excellent cut, and skillful preparation can make the most of an inferior piece of beef. General pointers on storage, tenderizing, and cooking are given in this section; more details are given, where appropriate, for each of the primal cuts in the next sections.

Storage

Refrigeration: If the meat is fresh and is to be cooked within a few hours after purchase, you can leave it in its semiairtight, plastic-wrapped package. But if you will not be cooking the meat for 6 hours or more, than rewrap it loosely with something like wax or butcher paper. This allows the air to circulate, which keeps the surface of the meat somewhat dry and thereby slows down bacterial growth. Cooked meat, on the other hand, should be wrapped tightly. Both fresh and cooked meat are quite perishable and should be used within a day or two, if not sooner. Ground meat is the most perishable. For best results when cooking meat, first bring it to or near room temperature (generally 30 to 90 minutes, depending on the thickness of the pieces.)

Freezing: Freezing meat diminishes its quality in terms of texture, juiciness, and flavor. Nonetheless, there are times when some of us—for instance, those who live a good distance from a suitable meat market—find it advisable, if not absolutely necessary, to preserve meat by freezing. If saving money is your goal, though, freezing is not advised. We believe that in 90 percent of the cases this approach doesn't really save much money at all, after you subtract the cost of the freezer and the electricity, and after you add in the risk factor of unexpected thawing due to a malfunction. In most cases you will save more by buying each day whatever the butcher's special may be.

If possible, trim off the excess fat and bones before freezing the meat. Fat becomes rancid quicker than flesh, and the bones take up precious freezer room. To prevent freezer burn, tightly wrap the meat with a moistureproof material such as aluminum foil or a quality freezer wrap. For later indentification, label and date the packages. Lay them in a single layer for the first 24 hours so they'll freeze as fast as possible.

Large pieces of meat can be safely stored in your freezer 6 to 12 months, cubed meat 3 to 6 months, and ground meat 2 to 3 months. Cooked dishes keep 1 to 3 months. This timetable is for freezers that maintain a temperature below 0°F, not for the ice-cube freezing space found in many home refrigerators. These freezing units seldom get colder than 10° or 20°F. Meat should be stored in such freezers for no longer than 3 to 4 weeks, if that long.

If meat thaws, you can refreeze it without health worries providing the thawed meat is still wholesome (use your eyes and nose to help you judge the meat's condition.) You will lose more flavor, juice, and texture with the second freezing, however, so try to avoid it.

Tenderizing

All meat you buy is tenderized to some degree: within a day or two after the animal is slaughtered, the muscle-toughening effects of rigor mortis subside and various enzymes start to decompose the tough, fibrous connective tissue in the meat.

When the food world talks about "tenderized" meat, however, it is referring to the man-instituted processes which are, to some degree, effective. The process employed by fine steakhouses and butcher shops is called "aging." The meat is hung in a refrigerator at slightly above the freezing point for several weeks or more. This requires that the meat has a thick layer of external fat to slow down the decomposition of the interior flesh. Because 10 to 15 percent shrinkage will result from moisture loss, the piece of properly aged beef must sell at a premium to offset its weight loss. Some restaurants and butchers store the meat at the proper temperature (roughly 35°F), but at high humidity, in order to reduce shrinkage; this method does not work as well as the old-fashioned low-humidity way. Neither do the methods that age beef at 70°F using ultraviolet lights to retard bacterial growth or that age beef in a vacuum plastic bag.

While such tenderizing methods are beyond the technical means and the equipment of most homes, you can easily marinate the beef. This calls for submerging the meat in a mildly acid liquid such as wine, vinegar, or lemon juice for up to a week. If the marinating time is to be more than an hour, refrigerate your marinating meat. Using pectin-laden fruits such as papaya also works. We do not recommend commercial tenderizing agents sold in supermarkets or the chemical solutions used by budget steakhouses. Pounding, scoring and mechanically piercing the meat are other alternatives; they weaken or shorten some of the fibers mechanically. Slicing the meat across the grain helps tenderize the meat because you shorten all the connective tissues. Grinding or chopping does the same thing more thoroughly, of course. (see BEEF, GROUND.) But the most important tenderizer is cooking; the proper method must be used.

Cooking

For best results, the cooking method must be appropriate to the meat. Broadly, the methods can be divided into those that use dry heat and those that use moist heat. Tender cuts of meat are best cooked with dry heat—roasting, broiling, barbecuing, or pan-broiling. These cuts include meat from the short loin, sirloin, and rib primal cuts of, at least, USDA Choice grade. If the meat is minimally upper-level USDA Choice (and certainly if it is USDA Prime grade), you can also cook with dry heat the more tender portions of the chuck and round primal cuts. If you plan to slice the meat thin across the grain, as for London broil, you can use USDA Choice flank steak, for instance. Whatever meat you use for dry-heat cooking, do not cook it beyond a rare or medium-rare stage or the meat will begin to toughen. For best results, the other cuts of meat that we did not mention above should be cooked with slow, moist heat such as braising, stewing, or simmering.

1. Primal Brisket

Located in the forequarter just under the first five ribs of the chuck section, the brisket is the anatomical equivalent of breast of veal or lamb. Besides flavor and texture, the three major differences are: the beef version is bigger, is generally marketed boned, and is sometimes sold cured rather than fresh. Being a well-exercised muscle, the meat is tough while the flavor is full, rich, and tasty, making brisket suitable for slow, moist cooking methods such as braising (pot roasting, for example) or simmering in a liquid (including stewing.) Allow 2½ to 4 hours' cooking time, depending on size and grade. Curing the meat—for instance, in a brine solution, making CORNED BEEF—also helps break down the fibers.

A full boned and trimmed brisket weighs approximately 4 to 6 pounds and is wedge-shaped, ranging in thickness from about 2 inches at the broad flat end and up to 5 inches at the pointed end, the part that lies closest to the head of the animal. More often than not, the butcher cuts the brisket into two pieces: the *flat half* and the *point half*. The flat-half cut (also called *thin cut*, *flat cut*, *first cut*, and *square cut*) costs—or should cost—more than the point-half cut because the first is almost all lean while the point contains a lot of fat. In most instances you gain a better value by paying the higher price, but that of course depends on the comparative prices and on how much fat the butcher trimmed off the point-half cut (also called *front cut*, *point cut* and *thick cut*.)

If you buy your brisket unboned, do not discard the flavorful and nutritious bones and the meat that clings to them; use them for making soups and stock. Figure on ⅓ pound of boned brisket per person. The classic condiments for brisket are sauces based on mustard or horseradish. Most green herbs (especially bay leaf) and certain spices such as peppercorns, clove, nutmeg, cayenne, and allspice marry well with brisket.

2. Primal Chuck

The roughly square chuck section comprises the shoulder and part of the neck. It is worth mastering because it can be a source of bargains for the educated shopper.

Most of the muscles are of the well-exercised variety and, hence, the meat is tough with lots of connective tissue, but with a delicious, well-developed flavor. This is the sort of meat that is usually best moist-cooked or ground for hamburger, though you can use dry heat to cook the tenderest portion (the blade or cross-rib section that lies nearest the primal rib) if from a high-grade animal.

Retail Cuts

Of the nine primal cuts, the chuck is the most perplexing to the shopper because it consists of a complicated array of distinct muscles moving in various directions and a number of bones (blade, arm, back, rib, and neck). Butchers add to our confusion because, in different regions, they use different procedures for dividing the primal cut. For instance, in California and other parts of the West

Coast, certain muscles of the chuck are removed and sold according to the muscle, producing entirely different retail cuts than found in the rest of the United States. The names of the retail cuts vary from region to region, sometimes even from store to store in the same neighborhood. Fortunately, in most parts of the country, the chuck section is cut into three major subdivisions, each named after the distinguishing bone structure: cross rib, arm, and blade. Each will be discussed separately.

Cross-Rib Roast: Most butchers divide the primal chuck into retail cuts by first removing a square subsection of the inner corner, producing the cross rib roast. This cross rib is divided into smaller, more marketable roasts typically weighing 3 to 6 pounds. The meat contains alternating layers of lean and fat and—if not boned—cross sections of the third, fourth, and fifth ribs. The roast is usually tied to cook, and pot-roasted or braised for 1½ to 2½ hours, depending on size and toughness. You can cook it with dry heat such as roasting if the meat is high-grade and comes from the tender end of the cross-rib roast—you can identify this end, which lies next to the rib primal cut, by its truncated-cone shape. Some butchers market the crosscut roast under names such as *English cut, Boston cut, bread-and-butter cut,* and *thick cut.* When the roast is boned, sometimes the leftover bones are sold as beef short ribs, but these are not as juicy and tender as the short ribs that are cut from the upper portion of the plate primal cut. Some butchers cut the cross-rib roast into slices, producing cross-rib steaks, with or without bones.

Arm Pot Roast: After removing the cross-rib subsection, the butcher removes the lower portion of the chuck primal cut. This piece is called the *arm pot roast,* though it goes by other names such as *shoulder roast, round bone roast,* and *arm chuck roast.* Anatomically speaking, the arm pot roast is the shoulder area lying just above the foreshank primal cut. If not boned, its chief identifying feature is the cross section of the humerus (arm) bone, though some arm pot roasts can also contain cross sections of rib bones. Overall, the cut has relatively little bone weight, a reasonable amount of trimmable fat, and quite a lot of lean comprising a cluster of various well-used muscles. Consequently, this meat has toughness, much connective tissue, and well-developed flavor, making it best suited for moist cooking such as stewing or braising (about 1½ to 2½ hours, depending on grade and thickness) or for ground beef. Sometimes the roast is sliced into steaks—if boned and sliced thinly, the meat may be marketed as *Swiss steaks.*

Blade Cut: After the butcher removes the cross-rib and arm-pot-roast subsections, as well as part of the neck and various odd trimmings, he is left with the subsection containing and named after the shoulder blade bone. It is typically cut for roast and steaks perpendicular to the blade bone, producing cross sections of the blade, back, and rib bones (it can also contain part of the neck bone). This perpendicular cutting also produces cross sections of various muscles, some of which are more tender than others (these individual muscles will be discussed a little later).

We cannot emphasize too strongly the importance of memorizing how the cross section of the blade bone changes as it proceeds from the rib section (the most tender part) to the neck (the least tender part). As you can see in the accompanying illustration, the ridge on top of the blade bone increases in height as it moves toward the neck.

If you plan to cook the meat with dry heat such as roasting or pan-broiling, your best bet is to look for the identifying flat bone shape of the first cut—the flatter the better. If of high grade, this meat will be relatively tender—after all, the difference between the first cut of the chuck section and the matching cut from the more expensive rib section is the distance of a knife blade. Moreover, it is a good buy because it sells for the same (or nearly the same) price as the

CROSS-SECTIONS OF THE BLADE BONE

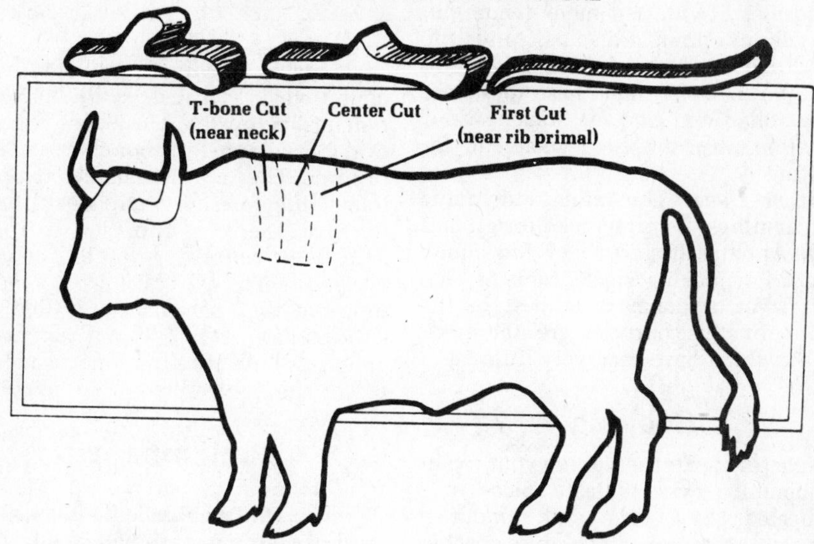

blade center cut.The first cut has a large portion of the eye muscle (a continuation of the rib eye), a fair portion of the blade steak, and not much of the less-than-tender middle muscle.

On the other hand, the 7-bone cut (so named because it vaguely resembles the number 7) is superior if you plan to cook by slow, moist heat. Reason: as you precede from the rib to the neck, the cut has less waste in terms of bone and fat and has a corresponding increase in lean meat, which—because it has been well exercised—is at its flavorful best. For the same reason, this meat is also ideal for cubing for stews.

Interestingly, the center cut is a bad compromise: if you want it for roasting, it is not as tender as the first cut; if you want it for moist cooking, it doesn't offer you as much lean per pound as does the 7-bone cut.

Sometimes the blade cut is boned and divided up into smaller units. The three most important ones are:

Chuck eye: An extension of the rib eye, this meat is relatively tender and is most ample in the first cut section. If of high grade and if it comes from next to the rib primal cut, you can cook it with dry heat; otherwise, use slow, moist heat. Chuck eye goes under other names, including *market* and *Spencer* roasts and steaks.

Chuck steak: This is the small oval muscle to the left of the ridge on top of the blade bone. It is at its largest size in the first cut (where it is the most tender) and the center cut. We recommend cutting out the gristle that runs through its center and, in most cases, cooking it with moist heat. Other merchandising names (there are many) include *flat iron* and *petite steak.*

Mock tenderloin: This is the triangular muscle that runs to the right of the ridge on top of the blade bone. It gets larger as it approaches the neck. Mock tenderloin gets its name because it physically resembles the true tenderloin and, as chuck meat goes, is not all that tough, though it is still best braised. Other names for this muscle include *Scotch tender, Jewish fillet,* and—even though it is not—*chuck eye.*

Another method of dividing the blade

cut is to split it into two parts, the top blade roast (with the mock-tenderloin and chuck-steak muscles) and the underblade roast (with the middle and eye muscles). If boned, these roasts are often rolled and tied for braising or, if cut from near the rib primal cut, for roasting.

Other Uses: The chuck—including its trimmings—is often used for ground beef. Another basic use of the chuck sections is making stock from the rich and flavorful bones. The best of the bones for this purpose are the neck bones, which have relatively little fat.

Cooking

Roasting: After seasoning your room-temperature roast to taste, place in a preheated 325°F oven and remove it when the internal temperature reaches 125°F for rare or 135°F for medium-rare (if you cook it further, the meat will become unnecessarily tough). This roasting process should take 20 minutes per pound, more or less—more if you have a small roast and/or your meat is boned; less if your roast is large and/or contains a substantial amount of bones.

Broiling, Grilling, and Barbecuing: Season your steak to taste and—for a medium-rare steak—cook 4 inches from a high-heat source for a total of 10 minutes for each inch of a steak less than 2 inches thick. If the steak is 2 inches thick or more, cook it 5 inches from your heat source and allow a total cooking time of 12 minutes for each inch of thickness—this will produce a medium-rare steak.

Braising and Stewing: Figure on 1½ to 2½ hours. The larger and/or less tender the piece of meat, the longer it should be cooked.

Slicing and Serving

When slicing any part of the chuck, it is best to cut it across the grain in thin slices. Plan on about ¾ pound per serving. If the meat is boned, reduce the quantity to ½ pound.

3. Primal Flank

Each mature bovine has two 1½-to 2-pound steaks, located in the belly section, just below the loin. These flat, long oval muscles are lean, boneless, and full-flavored. They are also characteristically tough (they are not really steaks in the textural sense) and, accordingly, generally require a moist cooking method such as braising. If cooked properly, they can also be grilled (see BEEF LONDON BROIL). If cut across the grain into thin slices and marinated, the pieces can be stir-fried, Chinese-style.

Preliminaries

If you buy the wholesale flank-steak cut, most of your purchase will be fat. Much of this fat can be sliced thin and reserved for larding beef and veal roasts. The odds and ends of pieces of meat can be cut into chunks for stews or ground into hamburger.

Cooking

The most popular way to prepare a flank steak for braising is to stuff and roll it. To prepare the meat for stuffing, you can either cut a pocket into it or butterfly it. The latter approach is preferred because you can roll the meat crosswise; you end up with shorter muscle fibers when the meat is sliced. The rolled meat can be secured with skewers or string. Bring the meat to room temperature, brown it in fat, then braise it for 1½ to 2 hours.

Figure ⅓ to ½ pound of flank steak per person. Allow slightly less per person if it has been stuffed.

4. Primal Plate

The primal cut called *beef plate* comes from the animal's chest, just below the rib section and in front of the flank steak. It is flavorful but contains a lot of waste—bones and especially fat. If you buy the entire primal cut, cut off the front top portion (the lower part of the animal's rib section) for short ribs. The remaining portion—which is fattier and chewier—generally requires slow, moist cooking such as braising or simmering. When boned, this section of the plate can be cut up in cubes for stews or ground for hamburgers. Pastrami is frequently prepared from the front end of the lower section of the beef plate (this area is sometimes called the *plate flank* as opposed to the *long-bone flanken*, which is located just in front of the flank steak). Another part of the beef primal plate cut is the *skirt steak*, an inner diaphragm muscle that is loosely attached to the main portion of the beef plate; this piece is often rolled and braised, or ground for hamburger, though top-grade skirt steak can be grilled as BEEF LONDON BROIL.

5. Primal Rib

The finest wholesale cut of the forequarter is the *primal rib*, the portion of the animal lying between the primal chuck and short loin. It contains seven ribs, the seventh through twelfth (the first six ribs are located in the primal chuck; the remaining rib, the thirteenth, is found in the primal short-loin section of the hindquarter). Thanks partially to the well-marbled flesh, most of the meat is tasty and tender and, consequently, sells for a tidy sum.

"Prime Rib" vs. Prime Rib

The term *prime rib* has three meanings in the marketplace. Only one is correct: prime rib is USDA Prime-grade meat from the primal rib section. Of the two incorrect definitions, one is a flagrant misnomer: it calls any meat from the prime rib section, regardless of USDA grade, "prime rib." Some butchers and even more restaurant menu writers use that misleading terminology for obvious reasons. The other incorrect definition is a less serious sin: it says *prime rib* signifies any of the "first three ribs." Nevertheless, that definition causes and is the result of much confusion, because the first three ribs of the animal are in fact in the less tender chuck section. What the speaker here means by "the first three ribs" are the tenth, eleventh, and twelfth ribs. Unfortunately, many butchers go along with calling them the "first three ribs." What should be made clear between consumer and butcher is either "the first three ribs cut off the small end of the prime-rib section" or, to prevent any possible confusion, "the tenth through twelfth ribs."

Small vs. Large End

As the prime rib section progresses toward the head of the animal, it becomes larger and, from the buyer's point of view, less desirable. The *small end* (also called *first cut* or *tenth through twelfth ribs*) refers to the portion of the primal rib lying next to the short loin. The *large end*, the portion adjacent to the chuck section, usually includes the sixth through ninth ribs. Sometimes the butcher sells two or three of the middle ribs (eighth through tenth) as *center cut*. This cut can be easily distinguished from the better first cut because it has more fat surrounding the central eye muscle.

Retail Cuts

Butchers can sell you the whole seven-rib section or break it into family-sized two-, three-, or four-rib roasts. They can also cut it into steaks one rib thick or less. They can partly bone your rib roast into what is commonly called a *standing rib roast* (see below), making it easier for you to carve. They can also completely bone it, remove most of the exterior fat, and label the resulting roast (or steak) *Delmonico*, *Spencer*, *boneless rib eye*, or *beauty*, to mention only four of the frequently encountered names. When the rib eye is boned, the leftover portions include short ribs, bones for the stockpot, and a variety of less tender muscles that can be cut up for stewing, left whole for braising, or ground for hamburger.

Standing Rib Roast: In America, this is the classic beef roast, while in England and parts of the Continent the reigning roast is the sirloin, the primal cut that Americans customarily consume in the form of steaks. A standing rib roast is particularly well suited if you are entertaining six to fourteen guests, because not only does it add a touch of class to your dining occasion, it requires relatively little preparation time and effort. (The same is true of a rolled rib roast; tips for cooking are given below.)

Buying Tips

The culinary gold of the primal rib is the large center rib eye muscle. This is part of the long muscle that runs along the animal's back from the hip to the shoulder (in the sirloin section it is called top or eye sirloin; in the short loin section, top or eye loin; in the chuck section, chuck eye).

Standing Rib Roast: Buy at least two, preferably three, ribs. Otherwise, the meat will be top-heavy and will topple over in the oven. If you are buying a boneless rib roast, it too must be long enough to balance. When buying by the pound, make sure the price reflects whether the rib roast has been reasonably trimmed of excess fat. Also be sure that the rib tips have been cut off, leaving a rib length of no more than 6 or 7 inches. If the rib length is 10 inches, the rib tips have not been removed; in this case, instruct the butcher to cut them off in a straight line, from one end of the roast to the other, approximately 2 inches from the eye muscle. Such a line will assure you that the roast will sit evenly in the roasting pan. Save the tips for use as beef spareribs (they will, of course, be uneven because they are cut off relative to the distance from the rib eye muscle). Most butchers will automatically remove or loosen the chine and feather bones from the rib bones before or during your visit to the store. This makes your carving task much easier, so make sure the butcher has done it. Be sure, though, he does it in the traditional way by sawing the bones in the direction of the meat grain. Some modern supermarket butchers (if you can call them that) merely saw through the chine bone perpendicular to the meat grain with a band or a buzz saw; this timesaving ploy not only cuts into the flesh (thereby increasing eventual juice loss), it forces you to serve slices according to the thickness dictated by the butcher. Normally, one buys one rib for every two diners, though a hearty meateater sometimes demands a full rib for himself. If purchasing a rolled rib roast, figure on 1/3 pound per person.

Rib Steak: For average appetites, buy ½ pound per person if the bone is in, 1/3 pound if the steak is boneless.

Cooking

Standing Rib Roast: Seemingly by Divine Providence, a standing rib roast comes with a built-in oven rack (its rib bones) that permits the roast to stand above the pan drippings, keeping the bottom surface of the meat from stewing. These arched ribs also allow hot air to circulate under the roast, producing a better-tasting and a more uniformly cooked mass of meat. What's more, the rib roast is self-basting, thanks to the layer of fat lying on top of the roast as it sits in the pan. Place the roast in a shallow roasting pan in a preheated 425°F oven and immediately lower the temperature to 350°F. For a rare roast (our recommendation), remove it from the oven as soon as your meat thermometer registers 130°F—this should take roughly 18 to 22 minutes per pound, depending principally on the minimum thickness (but not the length) of your rib roast. If you want a medium-rare roast, remove it from the oven when the internal temperature reaches 140°F. The roast will continue to cook after you have removed it from the oven; you can usually count on the temperature rising another 5°F outside the oven. If you want your roast cooked to a greater degree of doneness, go ahead, but you will be transforming your expensive, naturally tender roast into one that is dry and tough. A decorative serving touch is to "French" your roast. Before cooking, cut away the fat surrounding the last 1½ inch of the rib tips that remain on your roast. Wrap the exposed bones with aluminum foil to keep them from charring during the roasting. Just before you bring your cooked roast to the table, replace the foil with clean white paper frills, the type that look like miniature chef's hats. Frenching a roast also has a practical function: removing the fat creates extra space, allowing for even more hot air to circulate under the roast as it is cooked.

Boneless and Rolled Rib Roast: If you want to cook your rib roast boneless, roll and tie the roast with kitchen twine. We also like to tie the removed chine, feather, and rib bones to the boneless rib eye roast because that bone structure makes a perfect oven rack and, as a bonus imparts extra flavor to the meat. When the roast is cooked, simply discard the bones or save them for gnawing by you or your pet dog. If you do not use the bone rack, you will need a metal roasting rack. For a rare roast, cook to an internal temperature of 130°F. For medium-rare, cook to 140°F. Cooking a roast above that internal temperature is not recommended for the sake of the tenderness of the meat.

Rib Steak: Any rib cut less than two ribs thick should be grilled, barbecued, or broiled. If less than 2 inches thick, it should be pan broiled. In both cases, you can roughly figure on cooking the room-temperature meat for a total time of 10 minutes for each inch of thickness.

Seasoning

Salt and pepper are the basic seasonings for primal rib meat, but it is a matter of controversy among experts whether you should do it before or after the meat has been roasted. The "after" party believes that salt draws out the juices, toughening the meat. The "before" party argues that the juice loss is negligible and that preseasoning allows flavoring agents to penetrate the flesh. Flip a coin.

Serving

Loosely cover your roast with a piece of aluminum foil as soon as you take it from the oven and let it rest for 15 to 20 minutes to allow the internal juices to settle and redistribute. When ready to carve, lay the roast on its large, flat end. Carve thin slices across the grain—that is, parallel to the tabletop. Thickness is a matter of choice; we prefer thin slices, other people enjoy thick ones. Free the slice by cutting vertically along the rib bones. Put each slice on a warm plate. Naturally, the slices cut from either end of the rib roast will be less rare than those from the center, so serve the pieces according to the individual preferences of your tablemates. Do not throw away the rib bones—these are excellent to gnaw on, caveman-style.

6. Primal Round

Of the nine primal cuts, the round is the largest and one of the best in terms of offering a high ratio of lean meat to fat and bone waste. It is not, however, as tender as the short loin and sirloin primals because it comes from a well-exercised part of the steer—the muscles work hard to move the weight of the animal from eating bin to water trough and points in between. Think of the primal round as the hind leg of the animal, running from the end of the primal sirloin, down the femur (thigh) and tibia (shin) bones, to the hock (ankle). The other major bone within the primal round is the aitch (rump), which is part of the pelvic structure.

Subprimal Cuts

The primal round is usually divided into six major sections:

Top Round
Bottom Round
Eye of the Round
Sirloin Tip
Rump
Heel of the Round

The first four of these subprimal cuts contain only—and are named after—one of the four major muscles in the round: top, bottom, eye, and tip, the latter being a continuation of a major muscle found in primal sirloin.

Tenderness: Some parts of the primal round are more tender than others. Besides the USDA quality grade and the cooking method employed, the two primary determining factors are the specific muscle and the anatomical location.

The specific muscle: In descending order of overall tenderness, the four major muscles of the primal round are the top, tip, bottom, and eye. The rump and the heel of the round are not in this list because they are made up of combinations of muscles (in the main, the ends of the other muscles), as opposed to a single muscle. When you eat either the rump or heel of the round, its top round portion will be more tender than its bottom or eye portions.

Anatomical location: Each of the muscles—and especially the top, bottom, and eye ones— becomes tougher as it approaches the hoof of the animal and tenderer toward the steer's midsection. Therefore, the first cut of, say, the top round will be more tender than a center cut and even more tender than the final cut. It is also important to note that while, overall, the bottom and especially the eye-of-the-round muscles are tougher than the top round muscle, the first cut of the bottom or eye subprimals will be at least as tender as one of the final cuts of the top round, and probably more so. Because the top round muscle contained within the rump cut is closer to the midsection than that muscle contained in the first cut of the top round, that muscle will be more tender in the rump cut. However, since the rump also contains portions of the bottom and eye muscles, the first cut of the top round is more tender overall.

Rump: When the butcher attacks the whole primal round, his traditional first step is to remove from its upper part the *rump,* a triangular cut that is usually sold as a roast. It is rich in flavor but it possesses lots of connective tissue and bones, including the aitch and tail. The rump is marketed in two forms: *bone-in* (*standing rump roast*)or *boneless.* The standing rump roast is the less desirable of the two because the complicated bone structure makes it extremely difficult to carve. Moreover, the price per pound does not always reflect the heavy internal bone weight. Your best bet is the boned, rolled, and tied rump roast—one that has had some of the connective tissue removed, if the butcher has done his chore. Both roasts, bone-in or boneless, are almost always divided into smaller family-sized roasts and call for the same general cooking instructions (see page 45).

Full-Cut Round Steak: After cutting off the rump, the butcher has two basic options on how to divide the upper two-thirds of the remaining primal round. He can remove the remaining muscles individually and sell them as roasts, steaks, kabobs, stew meat, or ground beef. Alternatively, he can cut the meat crosswise, producing steaks. If left whole, the *full cut steaks* will be oval and will contain a cross section of one bone (thigh), at least three muscles (*top, bottom,* and *eye*), and possibly a fourth (*tip*), as depicted in the illustration on page 45. Or, the steaks can be boned and subdivided into individual top, bottom, eye, and tip steaks.

FULL-CUT ROUND STEAK

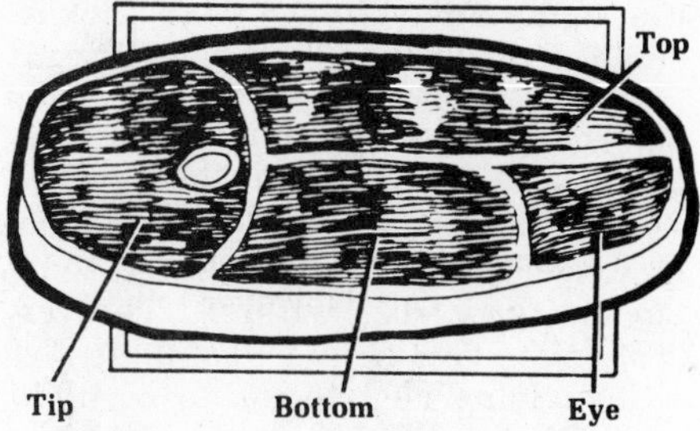

If the steak is a full cut, we have at our disposal at least a couple of visual clues as to where on the leg the meat originally came from and, as a result, its relative toughness. First, we can use the indicator suggested for the top round steak (see above). Second, we can look at the fat slab that lies in the middle of the full-cut steak between the bottom and top muscles; it becomes thicker as the meat approaches the hoof. Sometimes, however, this last clue is not available, because some butchers remove the fat slab before placing the steak in the meat case. If there is a hole where the fat originally was, you can almost be sure that the fat slab was substantial.

If the full cut is available and (as it often is) on sale, here is a tip for the economy-minded: buy and cut it up yourself, using each piece for its most suitable use, be it pan-broiling, braising, stewing, or grinding.

Top Round: This muscle runs down the inside of the leg, does the least work of the rear leg muscles and, consequently is the tenderest muscle in the entire primal round. The top round muscle is also the largest muscle in the primal round, and has no bones, little fat waste except for a moderate layer of external fat, and a large percentage of lean meat with a minimum of marbling.

The first cut is the most tender (for reasons cited above) and is usually sliced about 1 to 2 inches thick, typically reserved for sale at a premium price, often as BEEF LONDON BROIL. The other, less tender end of the top round muscle is frequently used for such purposes as stewing meat, kabobs, and ground round.

There exists an excellent indicator as to where along the leg bone top round originated. The first and most tender cut contains only the "primary" top round muscle. As the meat moves toward the hoof area, a "secondary" top round muscle begins to emerge—it lies between the exterior fat layer and the primary muscle. The two muscles are separated by a thin membrane. The secondary muscle grows larger while the primary one gradually shrinks as we proceed down the inside of the leg. Therefore, the smaller the secondary muscle, the better off you are. If it is nonexistent, all the better.

From the top round, the butcher sells both steaks (when sliced) and roasts. Top round roasts are usually divided into 3-to-6-pound units. One of the few times we encounter a whole top round roast is at those restaurants and sandwich shops that thin-slice the meat for a perennial American favorite, the roast beef sandwich.

Bottom Round: This, the outside muscle of the leg, works harder than the top round muscle and, therefore, can be expected to be less tender. While the bottom round has no bones, good shape, hearty flavor, a relatively small amount of exterior fat, and a high proportion of lean meat, the flesh lacks adequate marbling and contains a noticeable amount of connective tissue. These last two qualities suggest slow, moist cooking as opposed to dry-heat cooking, though the very first cut can be roasted if it comes from an "upper" USDA Choice or USDA Prime steer. One way to help tenderize the lower-grade bottom roasts is by means of marination, as with the Rhenish specialty sauerbraten. Generally, bottom round roasts are sold in 3-to-6-pound units. Bottom round is also sliced for use as steaks, especially for those that must go through some type of tenderizing process—Swiss and cubed steaks are two popular examples. Some butchers sell the bottom and eye of the round attached but use only the bottom round name to identify the retail cut in the meat case.

Eye of the Round: Elongated and oval, the 6-to-8-pound, 3-to-4-inch-thick eye of the round is the smallest, and more importantly, the least tender of the major primal round muscles. Yet, it frequently sells for as much or even more per pound than the more desirable top round. Consumer insanity? Well, not exactly, but we do have a clear case of consumer ignorance. The principal reason for this marketplace quirk is that many people reason that if the eye-of-the-round muscle looks like the true tenderloin muscle (which it somewhat does) then it must be similarly tender (not so; not even remotely so). With so many shoppers asking for the eye, the price naturally goes up—it's the old law of supply and demand. We do not mean to suggest that the eye of the round is undesirable (it has good flavor, much lean meat, no bones, and little waste), just that it's a poor value for your money. If you can find one on sale, go ahead and enjoy it—but plan to cook it with moist heat unless you have the first cut off a USDA prime animal, in which case you can oven-roast the meat. Usually, the whole muscle is subdivided into marketable 2-to-4-pound roasts or sliced into steaks, of which the least tender sometimes are put into a mechanical cubing machine. Whether you have a roast or a steak, remove as much of the outer membrane as possible before cooking.

Sirloin Tip: The division between primal cuts is at times arbitrary, as the *sirloin tip* (also called *top sirloin*) more than verifies. In a sense, it is half round, half sirloin—and in which primal section it ends up is largely determined by the meat cutter. Some butchers leave most of the sirloin tip muscle in the primal sirloin—this is often called *Chicago-style* . Some leave a big share of the muscle in the round—producing what is often referred to as a *diamond cut.* Another meat-cutting procedure more or less equally divides the muscle between the two primal sections. Whatever the cutting philosophy, the sirloin tip should not be thought of as the equivalent of the true sirloin, because the latter is characteristically juicier and more tender. On the other hand, the sirloin tip is boneless and has significantly less waste than the true sirloin. The lean of the sirloin tip has a reasonable amount of flavor and some, but not too much, marbling. The very best of the sirloin tip is, naturally, that portion lying next to the true sirloin. Overall, the sirloin tip is almost as tender as the better cuts of the top round, and, if of USDA Choice or Prime grade, can be oven-roasted—otherwise moist-heat cooking or grinding is necessary. The butcher usually divides the whole sirloin tip (averaging 14 pounds) into 3-to-5-pound retail units, either sold as is or rolled and tied. Or he can slice the roast into steaks (including the "London broil" variety) or cut it into small chunks for kabobs. Part of the tip is also sometimes divided into special cuts such as the *ball tip* or *silver tip* roasts or steaks.

Of all meat sold, the sirloin tip is one of the leaders in terms of being known by a wide variety of names. Besides *top sirloin* (which rivals *sirloin tip* in label popularity), you may come across these among other names: *side of round, knuckle, veiny, crescent, face round, triangle, loin tip,* and just plain *tip* .

Heel of the Round: Each of the three long muscles of the primal round (the top, bottom, and eye) are tightly clustered together in the *heel of the round,* cut just behind the shinbone. Since these are the lower ends of the three muscles, the heel of the round is predictably the least tender major retail cut of the entire primal round. Though this boneless, wedge-shaped cut is quite lean, the cook has to contend with a lot of strong connective tissue. Consequently, the meat demands moist cooking or, as is more often done, grinding for use as ground round. *Pike's Peak* and *Denver pot roast* are the two most popular alternative names for this section of the round.

Shin: After the heel of the round is removed from the hindquarter shin section, the butcher is left with a lot of tough meat. Usually he turns it into ground beef. A careful butcher removes a good share of the chewy tendons prior to grinding the flesh and fat. As for the flavor-filled bones, they make ideal stockpot additions.

Cooking

Roasting: Generally, you should only cook a round roast with dry heat if it is of USDA Prime grade and, in the case of top, bottom, and eye roasts, if it is cut from the upper (and therefore more tender) portions of those muscles. There are two major exceptions to that guideline. First, if the meat is top round or sirloin tip, you can also use high-level USDA Choice grade. Second, if the roast is the heel of the round, do not roast it—period. Because round meat has little if any marbling, it is necessary to bard, lard, and frequently baste it and to roast it at a moderate oven temperature (325°F). To prevent the round meat from becoming unnecessarily dry and tough, it should be cooked no more than rare or medium-rare. For rare meat, cook the room-temperature meat in a preheated oven until the meat thermometer registers 120°F; for medium-rare, the reading will be 130°F. This will take 18 to 24 minutes per pound, depending on thickness, the original tenderness of the roast, and degree of doneness.

Broiling, Barbecuing, and Pan-Broiling: Round steaks to be broiled or barbecued should be between 1¼ to 2½ inches thick. (A 2-inch-thick steak is ideal.) If thinner, the steak should be pan-broiled. If thicker, you should probably roast the so-called steak. For broiling and barbecuing, season the room-temperature meat to taste and cook it 4 inches from the high-heat flame for 5 minutes per side for a rare degree of doneness (for medium-rare, broil 6 minutes per side). For pan broiling, follow the same instructions, but first just briefly sear the steak on both sides over high heat, then reduce the temperature to a medium setting. Cooking round steaks beyond medium-rare produces dry, tough meat and therefore should be avoided.

Moist Cooking: Braising (pot-roasting) and stewing requires 1½ to 2½ hours, primarily depending on two variables: thicker cuts need more, while higher USDA grade cuts require less cooking time than their lower-grade counterparts. When the meat can be pierced with a fork, stop cooking it—it is done. Further cooking will sap flavor and produce stringy meat. Cooking at too high a temperature guarantees tough meat (the liquid cooking medium should be kept comfortably below its boiling point).

Serving

For optimum tenderness, the meat should be sliced thin, across the grain if possible. One pound of bone-in round will generally serve two people. If boned, estimate three servings per pound. Increase the amount of meat needed for hearty eaters.

7. Primal Shank

Most of the meat that you will buy in recognizable form from this primal will be *beef shank cross cuts* (also called *crosscut shanks, center beef shanks, foreshank for soup meat,* and *bone-in*).

Your butcher obtains these crosscuts from the shin section of the front leg of the animal. They are sliced perpendicular to the bone, producing a disk of meat about 3 inches in diameter and 1 to 2½ inches thick, with the cross section of a round marrow-filled bone in the center. Each piece contains a relatively small amount of fat and a high proportion of bone and lean. Because this meat contains much connective tissue, it requires long, slow moist cooking such as braising or simmering in a liquid for 1½ to 3 hours. Alternatively, the meat can be ground (very often the boned shank meat disappears into supermarket hamburger) or chopped, as for chili con carne. Because of the hearty beef flavor and the bones, beef shanks make superb soup and stockpot additions.

8. Primal Short Loin

Of the entire beef carcass, the short loin is unquestionably the tenderest and most expensive primal cut. This hindquarter gem is the section of the back lying between the pinbone area of the primal sirloin and the small end of the primal rib—altogether, it comprises but 10 percent of the total animal's weight.

Retail Cuts

In America the short loin is seldom sold or cooked whole. It is usually divided perpendicular to the backbone into three distinct subsections that ultimately become steaks:

Porterhouse
T-Bone
Club

The second most popular American way of breaking the short loin is according to the muscle, producing two distinct retail cuts in the form of either roasts or steaks:

Tenderloin
Top Loin

Each of these five popular retail cuts will be discussed individually.

Porterhouse Steaks: According to some food historians, this steak received its name because the method of cutting it originated in an old English tavern where porter (a beerlike beverage) was the mainstay. Whether that story is true or not, we may be certain that the porterhouse is regarded by most modern-day Americans as the he-man's special-

PORTERHOUSE STEAK

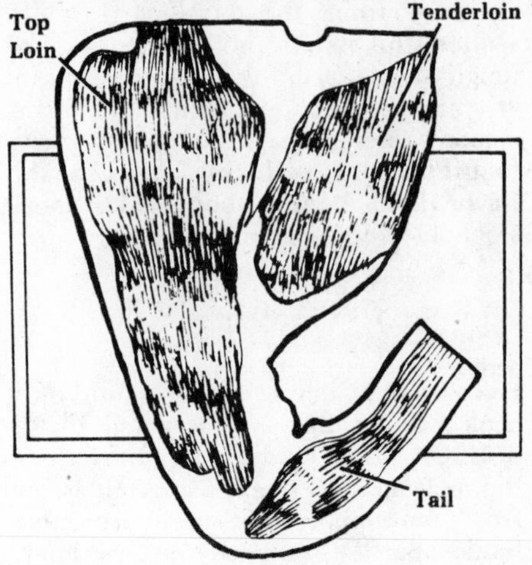

occasion steak. Besides having a bone (shaped like the letter T), the porterhouse steak has cross sections of three fair-sized muscles: the tenderloin, top loin, and tail as shown in the accompanying illustration.

The tenderloin is the tenderest, the top loin is nearly as tender but noticeably more flavorful, while the tail is relatively tough (it is really part of the flank) but quite flavorful. Because of its high price per pound, it pays to make sure that you are buying a relatively large tenderloin muscle (look at both sides of the steak, if possible), a minimum of fat and bone, and a relatively small portion of the tail (remember, you are paying porterhouse prices for flank steak). If the tail, bone, and fat are insufficiently trimmed or the tenderloin muscle is comparatively small, be certain that the price-per-pound reflects those factors. The very best of the porterhouse steaks are well-marbled and, because they come from grain-fed cattle, have a whitish fat layer. A yellowish-white fat layer indicates that the animal was fed a less costly food such as grass. Plan on two servings per pound for a porterhouse steak. You can also use this rough rule of thumb to determine the amount of porterhouse you will require: A porterhouse steak 1½ inches in thickness is generally sufficient for two people, 2¼ inches for three people and 3 inches for four people—but adjust your estimates if the width of steak is narrower or wider than average.

T-Bone Steak: Anatomically speaking, the T-bone steak lies directly in front of the porterhouse. In some ways it is similar to the porterhouse. However, the tenderloin and flank muscles in the T-bone steak become smaller or, as you approach the club steak, nonexistent. The top loin muscle, however, remains approximately the same size for both steaks. The T-bone is a cross-sectional bone created by the intersection of the chine, feather, and finger bones. The first two form the top of the T; the finger bone forms the stem. The characteristic T-bone is not exclusive to the T-bone steak; it also can be found in the adjacent porterhouse and nearby pinbone sirloin cuts. The dividing line between porterhouse and T-bone steak is more arbitrary than physiological. Consequently, because T-bone generally cost 10 to 15 percent less than porterhouse steaks, you usually gain a bargain when you buy the T-bone steak containing the largest possible cross section of the tenderloin—that is, theT-bone steak that lies next to the porterhouse. Half a pound per serving is usually adequate, though slightly more will be required if the T-bone is being served on a special occasion—which tends to be whenever your family or guests spy this beautiful piece of meat.

Club Steak: The only muscle in a club steak is the top loin—unlike the porterhouse and (usually) the T-bone steaks, it has no tenderloin or flank (the "tail") muscle. When well trimmed, the club steak has little waste except for the bone (which is sometimes removed, yielding a *boneless club steak*). Sometimes *strip steaks* are sold as club steaks—and vice versa—but there is a technical difference between the two. A strip steak is a T-bone or porterhouse steak in which the tenderloin (and usually the tail) has been "stripped" away, while the club steak never had that muscle in the first place. You can usually figure on two servings per pound (if boned, calculate about two and a half servings per pound), but you will need more if the meal is a special occasion like an outdoor barbecue or dinner party. A small club steak is an ideal choice whenever you want to serve one steak per diner.

Tenderloin Roast and Steak: Of all the muscles, this is the least exercised and thus the tenderest—and, in turn, the costliest—of beef cuts. Though usually "butter tender," it is noticeably less flavorful than the top loin muscle. Each animal has two tenderloins—one in each hindquarter, running parallel along the back, just below the vertebrae and loin muscle. Each muscle starts in the primal sirloin, passes through the entire subprimal porterhouse, and terminates in the subprimal T-bone. It has an elongated oval shape (somewhat like a loaf of French bread) tapering at the end nearest the animal's head. The flesh is virtually free of fat and marbling and is totally boneless. The only waste comes from the surface fat, which is usually trimmed prior to sale by the butcher. If not, be sure the price per pound reflects its presence, because the exterior fat can equal roughly half the total weight of the cut. That is the reason why some butchers can advertise tenderloins at incredibly low prices—they are selling you a lot of fat along with the flesh. We can buy tenderloin in two basic ways: incorporated within the porterhouse and (sometimes) T-bone steaks, or as tenderloin by itself, either in the form of a steak or roast. The latter can be purchased whole (usually 4 to 6 pounds) or in smaller units such as halves. The tenderloin and its parts are sold by butchers and restauranteurs under a variety of names that are sometimes used interchangeably, much to the ultimate confusion of the consumer. These appellations include *filet mignon*, *chateaubriand* (technically, a specific recipe calling for the thick porterhouse or pinbone sections of the tenderloin muscle and not the cut per se) and

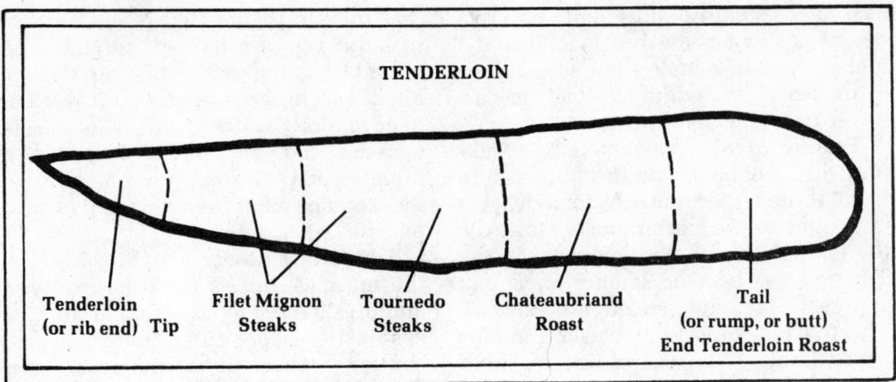

tournedos. Though there is no official or universally accepted definition for the parts of a whole tenderloin, the one presented in the accompanying illustration is favored by a consensus of American food authorities.

On the average, you need 1/4 to 1/3 pound of trimmed tenderloin per serving. Some butchers flatten the tenderloin steak with a heavy mallet, to widen the steaks and, therefore, to make them appear bigger than they actually are. This ploy diminishes the ultimate quality of the steak, so when in doubt, ask the butcher for an unflattened steak.

Strip Steak and Roast: When you "strip" away the tenderloin muscle from the porterhouse and T-bone section of the short loin, you end up with a strip steak (or strip roast, if the meat is cut at least several inches thick). A strip steak basically consists of the top loin muscle plus bones and exterior fat and, if untrimmed, a portion of the flank called the tail. *Top loin* or *strip steaks* (and roasts) are also known by a number of other names. Oddly, in New York they are frequently called Kansas City steaks, while in Kansas City and many other parts of the country, they are often sold as New York strip steaks. *Shell* is another popular name. They go also under the titles of *Delmonico* (also used for eye round, a continuation of the top loin that exists in the primal rib) and *club*, though the latter term rightfully should refer to part of the short loin that never had the tenderloin muscle in the first place. In France, the strip or top loin is called the *faux filet* (false fillet) to contrast it with the tenderloin (*filet*). The strip steak (and roast) can be bone-in or boneless and with or without the tail. The price per pound should reflect these factors, as the weight of fat, tail, and bone in an untrimmed strip steak can be about half the total weight. Plan on an average of three servings per pound for well-trimmed boneless strip steaks and roasts. If semi-trimmed, calculate approximately two servings per pound. For some steak lovers with gargantuan appetites, you may need to buy a whole pound per serving.

Cooking

If you plan to broil, grill, or barbecue your porterhouse, it should be somewhere between 1½ and 3 inches thick, with 2½ inches the ideal. If a porterhouse is over 3 inches thick, it should probably be roasted. If it is less than 1½ inches thick, pan-broil it. The reason is that a too-thick steak will overcook on the surface by the time the interior is properly cooked, while a too-thin steak will be overcooked in its interior by the time the surface develops the desirable crusty texture and flavor.

Porterhouse, T-Bone, Club, and Strip Steaks: Any of the bone-in short loin steaks can be cooked as if it were the star of the lot, the porterhouse. A porterhouse steak should be broiled, grilled, or barbecued until it is rare or medium-rare, never furher, as the meat will start to toughen and lose its prized flavor. For a medium-rare steak, place your seasoned room-temperature steak 4 inches from a high-heat source and, for each inch of thickness, cook for approximately 5 minutes per side. For rare meat, figure 4 instead of 5 minutes; the first side of steak is ready when you first see blood juices rising to the surface. For medium or well-done meat, if you prefer it that way, substitute 6½ and 8 minutes respectively for the 5-minute figure. Do not worry about the difference in cooking time between the meat on the tail end and that on the main section—they will cook at approximately the same rate if you place the tail snugly next to the main section and secure it there with a small implement such as a greased wooden or metal skewer. To prevent the meat from curling as the exterior layer of fat shrinks, cut through that fat every ¾ inch with a sharp knife, being careful to cut as close as possible to the flesh without actually touching it.

***Tenderloin Steak** (Filet Mignon):* When a tenderloin is sliced across the grain into steaks, it is usually labeled *filet mignon* by American butchers. If you plan to broil, barbecue, or grill it, the steak should be ideally 2 inches thick and must be frequently basted. Before cooking, bring the steak to room temperature and season to taste. For a rare steak cook it 4 inches from the heat source for 5 minutes per side per inch of thickness. For medium-rare, add 1 minute per side per inch of thickness. Your tenderloin steak should not be cooked medium or well-done, or it will no longer be tender (and after all, tenderness is what you're paying for). If it is less than 1¼ inches thick, it is best sauteed quickly over high heat with enough butter to keep it from drying out (use the same cooking times as for broiling).

Tenderloin Roast: At no time should your roast be shorter than it is thick. If longer, all the better. Your first steps are to bring your roast to or near room temperature, season it to taste, and remove any excess surface fat and connective tissue. Because the roast lacks sufficient interior marbling, it should be barded. Use thin strips of beef suet—never bacon, as its smoky flavor and chemical additives will overpower the comparatively mild flavor of the tenderloin. If you are roasting a whole tenderloin, fold part of the small end (the "flap") underneath the main body before tying the barding to the roast with an oiled string. This will help keep the small end from overcooking before the thick end is ready. Your roast may also require frequent basting—ideally with unsalted butter. Place your roast in a preheated 425°F oven and immediately lower the temperature to 350°F. If you want a rare tenderloin roast (our recommendation), remove it from the oven as soon as your meat thermometer registers 130°F—this will take 30 to 50 minutes, depending primarily on the thickness (not the length) of your roast. For a medium-rare roast, remove it when the internal temperature reaches 140°F. (The roast will continue to cook after you've removed it from the oven, likely adding another 5°F to the internal temperature.) Cooking your roast more will make your expensive, naturally tender meat unnecessarily tough and dry. Loosely cover your roast with a piece of aluminum foil as soon as you take it from the oven and let it rest for 12 to 15 minutes before serving, to let the internal juices settle.

Strip Roast: For strip roasts (which can weigh up to about 12 pounds), use the cooking guidelines given for standing rib roasts in section 5, Primal Rib, above.

Serving

To carve a large porterhouse steak (or other bone-in steak), first remove the T-bone with a carving or boning knife, then separate the three muscles, trimming away any excess fat. When carving and doling out a three portion cut of porterhouse, do not make the common mistake of dividing the meat into its three basic sections (tenderloin, top loin, and tail), giving each diner one of the three pieces. Whenever that happens, two diners (those who got the tenderloin and top-loin portions) rave about the tenderness of the meat while the hapless third chews silently and grimly away. The best and fairest method, however many are sharing the steak, is to give each person a suitable share of each of the three muscles; that way each one can enjoy the satisfaction of tasting and comparing the three different flavors and textures. A tenderloin steak, of course, is from a single muscle, so can be shared simply. For a tenderloin roast, simply slice the meat across the grain—thin or thick, as you prefer.

Sauce Affinities

Short loin steaks and roasts marry well with melted unsalted butter, with butter-based sauces such as bearnaise, with wine-based sauces, with mushroom-based sauces, and with their own pan juices (preferably not overly thickened with flour into gummy gravy).

9. Primal Sirloin

Of all the nine primal cuts, the sirloin is the most Janus-faced of the group—its front and rear sections vary widely in tenderness. On the side facing the short loin it is tender, while the other end that lies next to the primal round and rump is not as tender as one would expect. Yet most Americans have learned to think that any steak labeled "sirloin" is exceptional and worth the premium price. It pays to know more about this primal.

Retail Cuts

The best way to begin to understand the primal sirloin is to be aware of the three basic options facing butchers when they prepare the wholesale cut for their retail customers. Butchers can:

1. Cut the meat across the grain into steak.
2. Cut the meat with the grain, marketing the muscles individually.
3. Leave the meat whole for a king-sized roast.

When they cut the meat across the grain (perpendicular to the backbone), they gain four distinct types of sirloin steaks, listed here in descending order of tenderness:

Pinbone
Flat bone
Round bone
Wedge bone

These across the grain steaks derive their names from the shape of the hipbone they contain. Since the hipbone passes through every sirloin steak, and since this bone differs in size and shape along its journey, it helps us determine the anatomical origin of the steak, giving us an indication of its potential tenderness. Study the accompanying illustration.

A further aid for identifying the anatomical location of the steaks is the size, shape, and variety of the muscles—but more about that later.

The second of the butcher's options, cutting the primal sirloin with the grain, produces three boneless roasts or, if sliced, steaks:

Tenderloin
Top sirloin
Bottom sirloin

The third option leaves the meat whole (or cut in half, perhaps) for the classic sirloin roast that is more popular in England than in America, where diners prefer their sirloin as steaks.

CROSS-SECTIONS OF THE SIRLOIN BONES

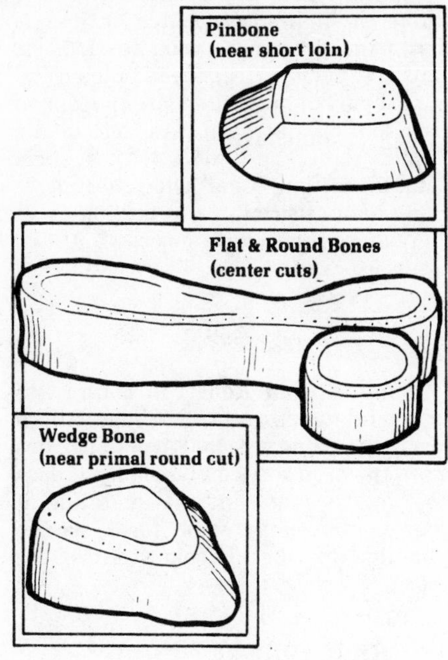

These roasts are marketed bone-in, semi-boneless, or boneless (and usually rolled).

Each of the major types of retail cuts of the primal sirloin will now be discussed individually:

Across-the-Grain Cuts

Pinbone Sirloin Steak: This is also called the *first cut* because it is the first sirloin steak removed by the butcher. In appearance it somewhat resembles the adjacent porterhouse: it has a T-bone; a fair-sized cross section of the tenderloin muscle; a portion of the primal flank referred to as the tail; and a large cross section of the loin muscle (called top sirloin here, top loin in the primal short loin, eye loin or rib eye in the primal rib, and chuck eye in the primal chuck—it is all the same muscle that travels most of the length of the animal's back). The pinbone sirloin differs from the porterhouse in that it contains the pinbone portion of the hipbone; it has more bone waste (usually nearly twice as much) but, at the same time, often has less fat waste; and it is typically about 10 percent less expensive. Compared to other sirloin steaks, the pinbone sirloin has the most bone and fat waste but is by far the tenderest. If you are a neophyte sirloin-hipbone detective, you probably will have a hard time differentiating the pinbone from the round or wedge bone. Identifying the flat bone is easy, so you won't have any trouble in that department. When in doubt, look at the shape of the steak—if it looks like a porterhouse, it is the pinbone sirloin; if not, it is the round-bone or wedge-bone sirloin.

Flat-Bone Sirloin Steaks: As with the pinbone, the center cut contains a cross section of the tenderloin and top sirloin muscles (though of less tender quality), a cross section of the backbone and tail (unless they are removed by the butcher), and a cross section of the hipbone—in this instance, a long, flat bone, hence the name. When the backbone is left in by the butcher, the steak sometimes goes under another name: *double bone*, referring to the existence of two separate bones, the hip and back bones. In terms of tenderness, this steak loses out to the pinbone, but it scores an easy victory over its round and wedge-bone competitors. In terms of the ratio of usable lean meat to bone waste, the reverse is true. Therefore, the flat-bone has become the compromise sirloin steak for many Americans who are willing to sacrifice some—but not too much—tenderness in return for having a little more lean meat for their dollar. (For those to whom tenderness is the compelling criterion, the answer is the pinbone; for those to whom maximum lean per pound is the overriding consideration, either the round-bone or the wedge-bone sirloin is the best choice.)

Round-Bone Sirloin Steak: Relative to anatomy and tenderness, this steak is halfway between the flat-bone and wedge-bone sirloins. It has some of the tenderloin and loin muscles, but not a whole lot in terms of either quantity or quality. It has less gristle than the wedge-bone sirloin, but its percentage of lean meat is almost as high as the wedge-bone sirloin and, consequently, if the price of the two steaks is the same, it is obviously a better buy.

Wedge-Bone Sirloin Steak: The last steak to be cut off the primal sirloin is the one with the wedge-shaped triangular bone. While it is the largest of the sirloin steaks, it is the least tender (it is located near the leg, a well-exercised part of the body), it has the most gristle, and, unless it is of USDA Prime grade, it should probably be cooked with slow, moist heat such as braising. Since the meat is flavorful and since there is relatively little waste in the wedge-bone sirloin, it is a cut of meat worth looking for whenever it is on sale and when the braising mood is upon you.

With-the-Grain Cuts

Cut-with-the-Grain Tenderloin: The butt of the tenderloin is found in the primal sirloin. It is sometimes sold in a 2-pound piece as a roast (for Chateaubriand, etc.) or is sliced into individual steaks called *filet mignons*, among other merchandising terms. At other times, it is left intact as part of the animal's whole tenderloin muscle.

Cut-with-the-Grain Top Sirloin: When the top sirloin muscle (a continuation of the top loin muscle in the primal short loin) is removed from the primal sirloin, it is either sold whole (or in halves, perhaps) as a top sirloin roast or is sliced into top sirloin steaks. Naturally, the parts of the top sirloin that come from closer to the rear of the animal are tougher (and larger in cross section) than the rest. If the steak or roast is cut from the least desirable end and if the USDA grade is less than Prime, you should think of cooking the meat with slow, moist heat.

Cut-with-the-Grain Bottom Sirloin: This is a collection of less than tender but flavorful muscles that should be cooked with slow, moist heat or chopped for ground beef. If the meat is USDA Prime or high-grade-Choice or if it is marinated, it can be used for kabobs. This is especially true if the butcher did not get part of his bottom sirloin from an area that should have been left in the primal round and marketed as such. Sometimes you come across a superb-grade bottom sirloin (or a portion of it) that you can roast with success, but such cases are rare.

Uncut

Whole Sirloin Roast: In contrast to the standing rib roast, the huge sirloin roast, weighing 12 to 20 pounds, has more flavor in the lean but, since it does not have as much internal marbling, it does not have the same flavor as the standing rib when it comes out of the oven.

Servings Per Pound

Normally, plan on two servings per pound for bone-in sirloin, three servings per pound for boneless sirloin—but take into consideration individual appetites and the mood of the dining occasion. The large size of a typical sirloin steak makes it an ideal one-steak-per-small-family purchase, but when you divide it up, try to give each person a fair portion of each of the more desirable tenderloin and top-sirloin muscles.

Cooking

Most sirloin cuts can be cooked the same way as the comparable cuts described in section 8, Primal Short Loin. The across-the-grain steaks and the top sirloin steak use the same guidelines as the porterhouse steak, and the tenderloin is cooked as if it were from the short loin. For either a whole sirloin roast or a top sirloin roast, however, follow the instructions given for standing rib roast in section 5, Primal Rib. For a boneless top sirloin roast, though, let the temperature on the meat thermometer rise 2 or 3 degrees higher than is recommended for the rib roast before you pull it from the oven.

BEEF, GROUND

BACKGROUND

The origin of the common hamburger is obscure. Some food authorities claim it was invented in 1904 at the St. Louis World's Fair. Others vociferously argue that it was born in Hamburg, Germany. Still others pinpoint the birthplace in numerous other parts of the world. More than likely this chopped-meat creation dates back well into history. We do know for certain, for example, that the Tartars who roamed the steppes of Russia were chopping their meat and eating it raw (the predecessor to *steak tartare*).

Whatever the origin, ground meat (whether beef, lamb, horse, pork, veal, or whatever) is universally popular wherever meat is a staple. It goes into making such favorites as hamburgers, meat loaf, meatballs, and steak tartare, each of which is discussed in detail below. It is also the major ingredient in hundreds of other famous prepared foods around the world, such as lion's head and dumplings in China, moussaka and dolma in the Middle East, tacos and tamales in Mexico, empanadas in South America, and sausages in Europe. In this entry, we'll restrict the discussion mainly to ground beef.

Ground vs. Chopped Meat

There is an important difference. Ground meat is meat reduced to a semi-pasty mass principally by means of a pressing action, using a mechanical grinding machine. Chopped meat is cut principally by sharp-blade action, be it the edge of a chef's knife or the rotary steel blade in a food processor. Chopped meat has a lighter, less pasty texture than ground meat and is therefore superior. If you want the best results, chop chunks of meat with a food processor—or, if you have lots of patience, do it by hand with a sharp, heavy knife—and it will be infinitely better than the preground supermarket product.

Varieties

The USDA and most of the meat-industry leaders make the following distinction between the various types of ground beef (the various cuts of meat mentioned below are described in the BEEF entry).

Ground Beef: This meat can come from almost any edible part of the beef carcass except for certain "undesirable" areas such as the ears, snout and innards. Ground beef should be at least 70 percent lean (over 30 percent fat is verboten).

Ground Sirloin: It differs from ground beef in that it is derived solely from the primal sirloin section. Generally, it is the leanest and most expensive of the major types of ground beef. However, it is not always the best choice, as it lacks the flavor of the chuck, round, etc. The fact that unground sirloin is more tender than the chuck and round is irrelevant in the case of ground beef because the grinding (or chopping) process automatically tenderizes the meat by cutting the connective tissue.

Ground Round: This comes exclusively from the primal round section. In most cases it is leaner and more expensive than ground beef or chuck but fattier and less expensive than ground sirloin.

Ground Chuck: This meat is derived totally from the primal chuck and is almost always fattier and less expensive than the ground round and sirloin, but more expensive than ground beef.

Hamburger Meat: This expression

has dozens of conflicting definitions and therefore should not be used to describe a type of ground meat. Rather, *hamburger* should refer only to the American-style meat patty, served with or without a bun.

Leanness

The USDA says that ground beef, round, etc., must contain at least 70 percent lean—in other words, not more than 30 percent fat. Some butchers use distinctions such as *lean*, *extra lean*, and *super lean*, but since there is no national standard, one butcher's lean may be another's extra lean. You can train your eye to detect the approximate amount of fat in the ground meat by the amount of fat specks and by the relative price. When in doubt, ask your butcher to show you the meat before it is ground.

Buying Tips

Try to buy only the amount of ground meat that you plan to use that day—it is more perishable than unground meat because more of its mass it exposed to the air. Fresh hamburger has an appealing rosy-red color. As it sits in your refrigerator, it gradually turns tannish-brown. Therefore, the color of the meat is a good (but not infallible) indicator of freshness. Many markets have dating codes—some are clear, some esoteric. The esoteric can usually be deciphered by comparing the codes of other meat packages—with most coding systems, the higher in sequence the number or letter, the fresher the meat likely is. Never buy ground meat from any retail source that you cannot fully trust to keep its grinding machines sanitary. Also, beware of the butcher who grinds pork in the machine and then grinds beef without first thoroughly cleaning the apparatus. Trichinosis is rare but there's no sense in taking chances (see under PORK, FRESH). Some butchers will grind the beef for you, but remember that unless he cleans out the machine beforehand, you may get an ounce or two of whatever was ground previously. Likewise, a few ounces of beef you bought will be left in the machine.

PREPARATION

Storage

Refrigerating: For optimum storage, remove your store-bought ground meat from its cellophane package (if it came in such a container) and loosely wrap it in butcher or similar paper. Some air circulation is necessary to let the meat breathe. By all means try to use the meat as soon as possible—storing it in the refrigerator for more than a day is generally not recommended.

Freezing: Hamburger meat loses much by freezing but if it must be stored in that manner, do not keep it longer than a week or two in the refrigerator's freezer compartment or longer than a month or so in a subzero freezer. It is best stored in ready-to-cook form (patties, meat loaf, etc.) and must be kept in a suitable airtight wrapping. You can thaw frozen patties in approximately 4 to 8 hours (depending on their thickness) in the warmest part of your refrigerator. A standard-size meat loaf needs roughly 12 to 18 hours to thaw.

Mixing

Perhaps the biggest sin committed against ground beef is excessively kneading it—the more you handle the ground meat, the more compact and heavy and therefore undesirable your final product will be, whether you are preparing hamburger patties, meat loaf, or meat balls. What you should not do is to mix one ingredient at a time such as the salt and then the pepper, and so on. Instead, assemble all the flavoring agents first. Then, gently and quickly mix them into the meat. When you are using ground as opposed to chopped meat, you already have one strike against you: as we said before, the grinding machine by its very nature crushes the meat into a pasty mass. Therefore, you have to be exceptionally light-handed when mixing your seasonings into ground meat. The best method of incorporating the flavoring agents into the meat is, of course, the food processor. Simply put the meat chunks along with all the flavoring agents into the machine's bowl, then chop the meat mixture; be sure to stop before the meat becomes pasty. This process minimizes the handling of the meat and therefore it will be light and airy, not leaden.

Cooking

Hamburgers: Contrary to widespread belief, the best hamburger meat is not the most expensive. The less costly ground chuck is more flavorful than ground sirloin or tenderloin; other flavorful alternatives include round and flank. Moreover, because of its typically higher fat content, chuck meat makes juicier hamburgers. This type of meat must have some fat in it if it is not to dry out during cooking—and do not worry about the extra fat, as most of it is rendered, being left behind in the pan.

When grinding or chopping lean meat at home, you may have to add a little extra fat to it in order to raise the fat content up to 15 percent, the minimum required for a juicy burger. This is especially important when you are using the lean of such meats as round and tenderloin—their flesh contains little fat.

We do not recommend adding thickening or stretching ingredients such as egg yolks and bread crumbs. They are fine for meat loaf, but not for burgers. We are also against the use of commercial hamburger extenders or stretchers. Not only do they disguise the flavor and texture of the meat, they are costly for what you get.

How much meat do you need per serving? The answers vary widely—some fast-food outlets sell 2-ounce burgers while others boast 8-ounce giants. We suggest a 5-ounce 1¾-inch-thick patty for broiling, grilling, or barbecuing and a 4-ounce, 1¼-inch-thick one for pan broiling. Thinner than this, the meat's interior will be overcooked or the exterior will lack sufficient crustiness.

For a rare burger, broil, grill, or barbecue your hamburger 4 inches from a high heat source for about 4 minutes per side per inch of thickness. For medium-rare, substitute 5 minutes for the 4-minute figure. For medium, substitute 6 minutes; for well-done, substitute 8 minutes. Use the same time for pan broiling, but quickly brown both sides over high heat, then reduce heat to a medium setting.

For cheeseburgers, top the meat with the cheese 2 to 4 minutes before the end of the cooking time—the exact timing will vary according to the thickness and type of cheese. Mozzarella and processed American cheese, for instance, melt quickly; natural cheeses such as cheddar and Swiss take a little longer. Other popular cheeses include Monterey Jack and the blues, such as Roquefort.

The best selling hamburger bun is one of the worst: that bland-tasting, airy bread that goes under the name of "hamburger bun" in supermarkets and burger outlets. Hamburgers taste better if the bread has sufficient texture and flavor—American-style English muffins and genuine French bread, for instance. Whatever bread you use, improve the texture and flavor by lightly toasting it.

Popular garnishes and sauces other than cheese include bacon, tomatoes, lettuce, onions, relish, pickles, ketchup, mustard, chili sauce, chutney, Tabasco sauce, A 1 sauce, Worcestershire sauce, mayonnaise—the list is practically infinite, as the hamburger marries well with many food ingredients.

Meat Loaf: While hamburgers require a certain amount of fat, you want to use a leaner meat for meat loaf. Ideally, the fat content should be somewhere between 5 and 10 percent and the meat should be flavorful. Meat from the primal round is a good choice. Alternatively, use a combination of ground beef, veal, and pork—this makes a delicious meat loaf. There are thousands of basic recipes for meat loaf—consult a reliable cookbook for the additions of eggs, bread crumbs, tomatoes, onions, mushrooms, seasonings, and the like. We recommend cooking a standard-sized, room-temperature meat loaf roughly 45 minutes in a preheated 325°F oven, adding 5 minutes to the cooking time if the mixture contains pork. Meat loaf can be served hot or cold. In most cases, you can figure on about three servings per pound.

Meatballs: As with meat loaf, the meat should be relatively lean, and meatballs are especially tasty if concocted from a mixture of ground beef, veal, and pork. Again, consult a reliable cookbook for one of the thousands of meatball recipes from around the world, the Swedish variety being perhaps the most famous.

Steak Tartare: There are several all-important basic rules for steak tartare, the famous raw ground-beef dish: Use only the freshest meat from the most reliable of butchers—otherwise, you are courting a health risk. Chop or grind the meat yourself—do not buy it pre-ground at the store. If possible, *chop* (with a food processor) rather than grind the beef—the result is a lighter, less pasty texture. The meat must be as lean as possible, as eating raw, room temperature fat is unappetizing. The leanest flesh comes from the tenderloin and round—use the first if you want delicately flavored meat, the latter if you prefer more flavor. Though there are countless recipes for steak tartare, the meat is usually mixed with onions, anchovies, capers, parsley, and salt. The typical toppings are a raw egg yolk and a liberal grinding from the peppermill. Side condiments, to be added to the steak tartare at the diner's discretion, include extra chopped onion and parsley sprigs. The meat is spread on small slices of rye or pumpernickel.

BEEF, HANGING TENDERLOIN

BACKGROUND

Despite its name, this muscle—which hangs near the kidney in the hindquarter—is not a tenderloin. It earned the nickname *butcher's tenderloin* because the butcher couldn't effectively market the piece of meat (it is tough and there is too little of it—just 2 or 3 pounds per animal—to make it worthwhile to educate the public on how to cook it), so he simply brought it home for his family to enjoy. Whenever they got tired of it, he mixed it into the hamburger meat that he sold his customers. Ask your butcher to reserve one for you, then maximize its strength (superb flavor) and minimize its weakness (toughness) by grinding it for hamburger, by braising it, or by barbecuing it as London broil. It is highly nutritious and not expensive.

BEEF JERKY

BACKGROUND

Dried beef is called by various names, including beef jerky. When making your own beef jerky, it is essential to buy very lean meat such as eye of the round; otherwise, the fat may become rancid before the drying period has been completed.

BEEF, LONDON BROIL

BACKGROUND

Butchers market various cuts as "London broil," especially *top round steaks* (the most prevalent) and *flank steaks.* The latter is the original and best cut for grilling as London broil, because the muscle fibers of the flank steak run lengthwise.

When you cut the flank steak across the grain into slices (see Sketch A), the muscle fibers are cut into short segments, thereby making the meat less fibrous. On the other hand, the muscle fibers of the top round steak run vertically and, as a result, when you cut it into slices, you are cutting with the grain, ending up with longer muscle fibers and, therefore, chewier meat (B). If you insist on cooking top round as London broil, at least cut the slices at a 45-degree angle (C); this will shorten the muscle fibers.

PREPARATION

Tenderizing

The London broil steak, whether it be a flank steak or top round, can be further tenderized by marinating it in a mixture containing an acid substance such as wine, vinegar, or lemon juice. For added flavor, oil, salt, pepper, herbs, onions, and the like are usually added, but do not make the marinade too assertive and do not marinate the steak for more than 12 hours, lest your overpower the natural flavor of the meat.

Scoring can also help tenderize a flank steak for London broil. Crosshatch both sides of the uncooked meat ¼-inch deep at about ½-to 1-inch intervals, producing a diamond pattern. This process cuts some of the long muscle fibers.

Cooking

For indoor broiling, place your steak 3 inches from the heat source and cook it 2½ minutes per side if it's ¾ inch thick and 3½ minutes per side if 1-inch thick. This timing yields a rare steak—any further cooking will toughen the top round or flank steak. (If you like the meat medium or well-done, you should cook these meats slowly with moist heat, such as braising; see section 3, Primal Flank, in BEEF entry.)

For an outdoor barbecue, set the grate several inches over hot, nonflaming embers. In most cases, the meat will be rare if cooked several minutes per side, but since too many variables (wind, etc.) affect the temperature of a barbecue, you may want to use this test for doneness: turn the steak as soon as dots

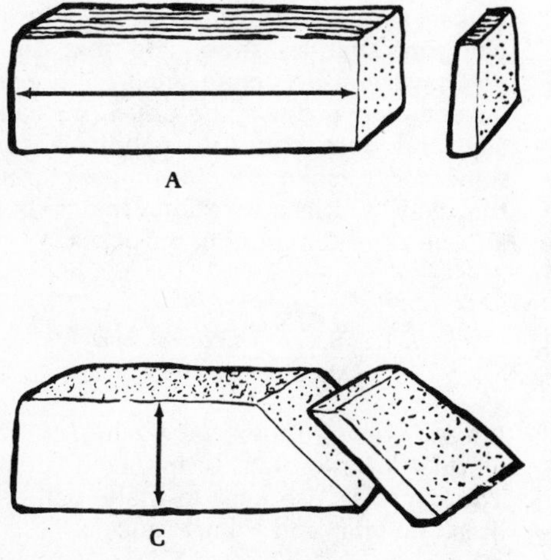

A

C

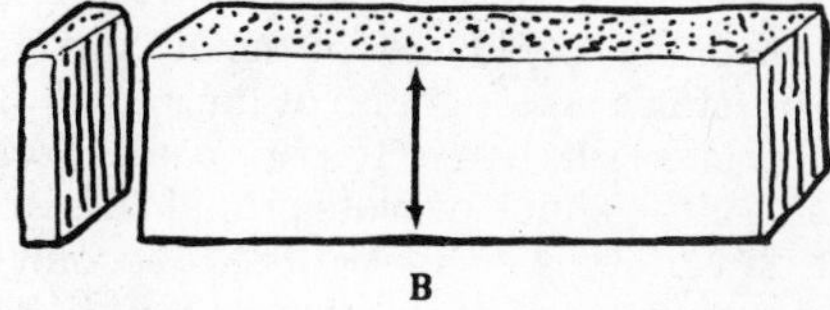

B

of blood begin to appear on the top, uncooked surface of an unsalted steak. Barbecue the other side approximately half as long as you did the first side.

Since London broil steaks are very lean, it is usually a sound idea to baste the meat every minute or so. Baste it with your marinade if it contains at least one-third oil and very little salt. (Salt draws out the juices, and pepper becomes bitter when heated at broiling or barbecuing temperatures, so it's wise to season your London broil after it's cooked.)

Serving

A sharp knife is essential for carving a London broil steak. Cut the steak at a 45-degree angle (starting at the smaller end) into uniform slices 1/8 inch thick. The 45-degree angle makes the muscle fibers in the flank steak slightly longer, but you get broader and therefore more visually appealing slices.

Allow 1/3 to 1/2 pound of London broil per person, depending on individual appetites.

BEEF, SHORT RIBS

BACKGROUND

A typical short rib is a 2-inch cube (sometimes elongated into a rectangle) consisting of layers of meat and fat encasing a cross section of the end of the animal's rib bone. It can come from either the chuck or plate primal cuts; the first variety is leaner while the second is more tender and, in our opinion, better flavored.

PREPARATION

Short ribs are tough and therefore usually require braising or simmering in a liquid, usually for just under 2 hours. Because of the fat content, the calories are plentiful (403 calories per 100 grams, 1,828 calories per pound), but some of this fat can be trimmed by the cook or diner. Allow 1/2 to 3/4 pound of short ribs per person, depending on individual appetites.

BEER AND ALE

BACKGROUND

The brewing of beers has probably been going on since the cultivation of grain. Pottery seals in Mesopotamia and hieroglyphics in Egypt depict the making of beer. The ancient Greeks and Romans enjoyed the beverage. The Romans thought enough of it to name it *Cerevesia* after the goddess of agriculture, Ceres. You can order a beer by the name of Cerveza in a Spanish-speaking country today.

PREPARATION

In the United States, beer and ale are quaffed in volume but are often overlooked as a cooking ingredient in preparations such as stews. The next time you have a leftover opened bottle of beer, do not pour it down the drain. Instead, cap and refrigerate it, saving it for tomorrow's cooking. A fresh beer stored that way will lose its effervescence but still be good for cooking purposes.

CLASSIC USES AND AFFINITIES

Boeuf carbonnades is perhaps the world's best-known beer-spiked dish. You can also use beer to make batters, bread doughs, and robust sauces.

BEET

BACKGROUND

The French and Russians do not agree on much, but they agree that the root vegetable *Beta vulgaris*, proletarian as it is, is very good to eat. Beets are easy to grow, their red roots add color to a monotonous peasant diet heavy on bread or potatoes, and their tops can be cooked as greens. (The sugar beet, which supplies a large share of the world's sugar, is a different beet.)

AVAILABILITY

Year-round, with a peak from June to October.

Buying Tips

Small, firm, well-rounded beets with rich-hued, unblemished, smooth skins and thin taproots are the least likely to have woody cores. A clue to toughness is an elongated shape with a scaly top. If the beets are sold with their greens attached, they are an index to the state of the beets. Fresh beet greens are crisp and bright green (some may be red-streaked).

PREPARATION

Storage

As soon as you get home, cut off the greens; they drain moisture and nutrients from the roots. Leave about 1 inch of stem attached to the roots to prevent bleeding during cooking. The greens should be refrigerated in a plastic bag; the roots can be bagged or loose, in or out of the refrigerator. Cook the greens within a day or two. Cook refrigerated roots within a week.

Preliminaries

The bulb should be washed gently as the thin skin may rupture, allowing color and nutrients to bleed out during cooking. For the same reasons, if you peel your beets, do so only after cooking. Wood and plastic may acquire almost indelible stains when used to prepare beets; use other materials or watch out for staining. Beet greens need to be washed lightly and detached from any remaining stems.

Cooking

Steam or boil whole, stemmed, unpeeled beets 20 to 45 minutes, depending on size and age. Bake butter-coated whole beets in a preheated 350° F oven for 40 to 70 minutes, again determined by size and age. Beet greens should be steamed or boiled for 10 to 15 minutes—but without their stems, or the stems will bleed into the cooking water, dyeing the greens and perhaps the cooking pot.

Equivalents

One pound of beets with detached stems will serve three or four people. Allow about 1/4 to 1/3 pound of beet greens to a person.

CLASSIC USES AND AFFINITIES

Borscht, red flannel hash, Harvard beets, pickled beets.

BIRD'S NEST

BACKGROUND

A classic Chinese banquet will often feature bird's-nest soup, a very expensive delicacy. The bird in question is the swallowlike swift that feeds on fish and seaweed of the South China Sea. The bird transforms this food into a gelatinous saliva to help glue the twigs together to form a nest. This bland, protein-rich binding agent is extracted from the nest and sold in Chinese markets. You need to soak the product for 8 to 12 hours, remove any overlooked waste material such as feathers, then simmer the gelatinous substance for 15 to 20 minutes in your soup.

BITTER MELON

BACKGROUND

If in an Oriental market you see something that looks like a big, wart-ridged cucumber 2 to 3 inches thick, you have probably confronted a bitter melon. The vine (*Momordica charantia*), cultivated in tropical lands around the world, produces green-hued fruits that are 5 to 10 inches long. The cool, stinging, menthollike taste of the melon's flesh comes from quinine.

AVAILABILITY

Bitter melons can be bought at Chinese-American ethnic markets throughout the year, but are at their best during the warm months.

PREPARATION

Once you have it home, a bitter melon can be kept in the refrigerator for up to several days if sealed in a plastic bag.

Cooking

Bitter melons should be cooked. Young melons can be simmered whole; older ones should be trimmed at the stem end, cut open, seeded, and parboiled for several minutes before proceeding with the recipe. The flesh, now with its excessive bitterness removed, can be combined with other ingredients and steamed, boiled, or stir-fried. The seeds of the mature melon should not be eaten. They have a powerful purgative effect.

BITTERS

BACKGROUND

Bitters were first created for their real or imagined medicinal properties, primarily as an aid to digestion. Currently they are most commonly used to flavor cocktails and sometimes foods, when the chef wants to impart a light touch of bitterness to the dish. Bitter herbs, leaves, roots, bark (such as angostura bark), orange rind, quinine, myrrh, rhubarb, Juniper berries, peppermint, cloves, camomile, and others are employed in a variety of combinations with other substances to make aromatic infusions, which sometimes have a high alcoholic content. The precise recipes of brand-name bitters are a closely guarded secret. Angostura, Fernet-Branca, and Campari are a few of the more popular brands.

BLACKBERRY

BACKGROUND

The blackberry (*Rubus fruticosus*), is also called the *bramble* because it grows on thorny bushes or brambles. According to herbal medicine, blackberries are beneficial in curing diseases of the mouth and throat.

AVAILABILITY

The peak season is June, July, and August, with regional variations.

Buying Tips

In choosing blackberries, look for bright, plump, uniformly deep-colored ones that are clean, hulled, and free of surface moisture. If unhulled (with their caps on), the berries are immature, and probably picked too early. Blackberries with dull skins are overripe. Buy a pint of blackberries for two to four servings, depending on appetites.

PREPARATION

Once home, look over the blackberries and discard any that show mold or are leaking. If you store the blackberries in the refrigerator, cover them and use within a day or two. If you do not mind some loss of texture and flavor, you can store your surplus blackberries in the freezing compartment for a couple of weeks, or for a few months in a 0° F freezer.

BLACK BEAN

BACKGROUND

This variety of *Phaseolus vulgaris* is a medium-sized, black-skinned, white-fleshed bean with a full—bodied, distinctive flavor that deepens during cooking. It is also known as the *turtle bean.* For soaking, cooking, and other particulars, see the BEANS entry.

CLASSIC USES AND AFFINITIES

The black bean's flavor makes it particularly good in a hearty winter soup, perhaps flavored with thyme, savory, onions, peppers, and bits of ham. Dry sherry adds piquancy. A white crown of sour cream or yogurt provides a splendid color-contrasting garnish and helps build complete protein. A staple of South America and Mexico, this is the bean of Brazil's famous dish *feijoada* .

BLACK-EYED PEA

BACKGROUND

The black-eyed pea, *Vigna sinensis,* is not a pea but the famous bean of ethnic Southern soul food. A native of Asia, it was originally cultivated in the United States for animal fodder. A black-eyed pea is a smallish chalky-colored bean with a bright black circular outline around the inner curve of the bean coat seam. There is also a yellow-eyed variety which is not so widely distributed. Baby black-eyes are often called cowpeas, reflecting their original purpose. (For soaking, cooking, and other particulars, see the BEANS entry.)

CLASSIC USES AND AFFINITIES

Hoppin' John (black-eyed peas with rice simmered with salt pork and seasonings) is as southern as the drawl. Black-eyed peas are also good in casseroles.

BLOOD

BACKGROUND

The red, life-supporting fluid running through the veins of animals is a staple food among some of the world's people. The Masai tribes in Kenya and Tanzania, for instance, tap the blood from their cattle and either drink it on the spot or use it in cooking. Some nomadic tribes in the Middle East do the same with their camels. Centuries ago, Mongolian warriors drank the blood of their horses. Even highly civilized nations put blood to a culinary advantage. France has its *sanguette* as well as its sausagelike blood pudding called *boudin*. Similar to the latter are the Irish *drisheen* and the British blood pudding. The Philippines enjoys *dinuguan*, made of pork tripe cooked in pig's blood. Blood not only adds flavor and color to sauces and stews, it is also a natural thickener. This is why there are a number of blood-infused stews, such as those made with rabbits and hares. When cooking with blood, do not let it boil or it will curdle—just as mystery writers have long told us.

BLUEBERRY

BACKGROUND

The native North American *blueberry* shrub (*Vaccinium nitidium*) is not demanding: even on "bad" land it produces large crops of round, bluish berries. In the western and southern United States the *huckleberry* is erroneously called the blueberry. Though closely related, the true huckleberry has several distinguishing features: its seeds are fewer and larger, its flavor is generally more astringent and less sweet (this is a positive to huckleberry fanciers), its color is usually darker, its skin is thicker, and it is almost always harvested in the wild state (blueberries are cultivated).

AVAILABILITY

Available fresh from the end of May to the beginning of October, but peaking in June and July, depending on region. Canned and frozen blueberries are available year round.

Buying Tips

Buy blueberries that are uniform in both size and color; deep and rich in color with a silvery but not dull bloom; plump and firm; unblemished, with no mold or surface moisture; and free of dirt, trash, and excess stems.

PREPARATION

Storage

Blueberries are very perishable. As soon as you get them home, pick over the berries, discarding the unripe, overripe, moldy, or crushed ones. Do not wash them until ready to use, as moisture hastens bacterial decay. If not using them immediately, store in a dry, covered container or moistureproof bag in the refrigerator for up to a couple of days, in the freezing compartment for up to a couple of weeks, or in a 0°F freezer for up to a couple of months.

Cooking

One way to store surplus blueberries is to turn them into jam: cook them gently for 10 minutes in a heavy saucepan, using 3 parts blueberries to 1 part (or more, to taste) of sugar.

CLASSIC USES AND AFFINITIES

A summer favorite is blueberries topped with cream and, if one insists, sugar. Blueberries can also be the star ingredient in pies, muffins, pancakes, ice cream, and jams.

BOK CHOY

BACKGROUND

The leafy *bok choy* or *pakchoi* (*Brassica*

chinensis) is a popular and versatile Chinese vegetable, now also cultivated in America.

AVAILABILITY

All Chinese-American ethnic markets sell bok choy. Some supermarkets carry it. It is available the year round, though the winter crop is superior.

Buying Tips

The pale or greenish, smooth, crisp, moist, 12- to 16-inch stalks should have a pearly translucence. If the stalks are wilted or blemished, reject the vegetable. The large, crimped leaves should be dark green, the more vivid the hue, the better.

PREPARATION

Storage

To keep bok choy, seal it in a plastic bag and refrigerate for up to two or three days.

Cooking

Bok choy can be stir-fried, steamed, or added to soups. It cooks quickly. Several minutes in a hot wok is ample for the cut-up stalks. The leaves take even less time.

BONES

BACKGROUND

Bones—be they beef, veal, pork, lamb, or poultry—are rich in flavor and nutrients. And bones from the lower limbs of the animals are high in collagen, a natural THICKENER that gives many soups, stocks, stews, and sauces a desirable gelatinous quality. Some of those bones offer another bonus: marrow. Yet most Americans casually toss bones into the garbage can.

PREPARATION

The age-old method of extracting the sought-after qualities of the bone is to simmer them for hours; producing a stock or soup base for which there are countless recipes. When making a soup or stock, you should start off with uncooked bones, as those removed from cooked meat have already lost much of their flavoring qualities to the meat. One exception to this rule is in the use of the smoked ham bone for soups such as green pea. For maximum extraction, you or your butcher should crack the bones before starting to make the soup or stock.

Cooking

A simple recipe for stock goes like this: put bones in large kettle. Add cold tap water to cover by 2 inches. Bring to boil, lower heat, and simmer for 15 minutes. Remove surface scum (it is edible and nutritious, but not attractive). Add 1/2 to 1 teaspoon of salt per quart of water and—to individual taste—add carrots, clove-studded onion, celery, peppercorns, thyme, bay leaf, and fresh parsley. Partially cover the kettle and gently simmer the developing stock for at least 2 hours, longer if possible. Let stock partially cool and strain it. Place in refrigerator for several hours, until the fat rises to the surface and congeals. When ready to use your stock, peel off the hardened fat and either discard it or reserve it for use as a frying medium.

CLASSIC USES AND AFFINITIES

Beef

Beef bones give stock and sauces a rich flavor and color. To heighten the desired caramel hue, roast the bones in a 400° F oven for a relatively short period, say 20 to 25 minutes, before adding them to the stockpot. Adding caramel or beef extract to the stock also darkens the liquid, but these two culinary shortcuts also add flavors of their own that partially mask the true flavor of homemade stock.

Veal

Veal bones yield a delicate flavor and nearly colorless hue that makes them perfect for stock foundations that will eventually be turned into white sauces.

Pork and Lamb

Unless a preparation contains pork or lamb meat, a chef generally does not use pork or lamb bones for making soups, stocks, sauces, and stews. The reason is that the hearty flavors of the bones may distort the flavor of meats such as veal and/or chicken.

Poultry

Poultry bones are excellent stockpot ingredients. A good chicken soup requires them, as does the famous pressed duck of France, *caneton à la presse.*

BORAGE

BACKGROUND

Borage (*Borago officinalis*) was used in the Middle Ages to cure melancholy, and bathing in water in which borage was steeped was believed to soften the skin. Today, infusions of borage leaves are used as an eyewash. This common south European wild plant can also be cultivated for its edible leaves and flowers. (See HERBS AND SPICES for information on buying, storing, cooking, etc.)

PREPARATION

The gray-green leaves of borage are used for their cucumber flavor. They must be chopped very fine, or their hairy texture can be annoying. They can be cut up raw for salads or cooked like spinach. The leaves can be used in cold drinks, especially in a wine punch. The blue, star-shaped flowers are candied for decorations.

BOUILLON

BACKGROUND

When you simmer meat (or fish) or the meaty scraps and bones in water enriched with vegetables and seasonings, you will produce a stock. Strain that stock and you will have a bouillon, which is often used as a soup. Bouillon is best made from scratch at home, though you can purchase bouillon in concentrated form at the supermarket. One major shortcoming of these commercial products is that they tend to give your preparation a chemical taste that is disconcerting to a discerning palate. Beef and chicken are the two most popular flavors, though some stores also sell cubes made from fish or vegetables. The beef-based commercial bouillon is also available in liquid form. When buying bouillon cubes or liquid, remember that some brands are immensely better than others. Even the same brand may differ depending on its factory of origin. Price generally reflects quality. Bouillon cubes and liquid can be stored at room temperature, but these extracts should not linger for more than a couple of months or so on a shelf.

A variation of bouillon is *consommé*, a clear soup. It is bouillon that has been clarified (for instance, by using egg whites and shells) to rid it of the minute particles that hang in suspension in the bouillon liquid. *Consommé double* is consomme that has been reduced to half its original volume by simmering or boiling for the sake of increasing its strength and consistency. As with bouillon, consomme or its reduced offspring is best made at home, though you can buy it canned and, sometimes, frozen.

BOUQUET GARNI

BACKGROUND

Long-cooked dishes with liquid, such as soups, stews, and braised dishes, are often seasoned with a *bouquet garni*, a bunch of herbs tied together or placed in a small muslin bag. This method of flavoring is fundamental to classic French and Provençal cooking. The custom of using a bouquet garni has been adopted by many American and English cooks. (See HERBS AND SPICES for information on buying, storing, cooking, etc.)

PREPARATION

A basic bouquet garni includes a few springs of parsley, a bay leaf, and a few sprigs of thyme. Other herbs and spices such as peppercorns, dried orange peel, celery leaves, basil, burnet, chervil, rosemary, and tarragon can be added. Make up a fresh bouquet for each dish; tie the herbs with string or thread, or place them in a bag of cheesecloth or muslin.

Cooking

The reason for tying the herbs together is to make it easy to remove the bouquet garni before the dish is served. Just as a chain is only as strong as its weakest link, a combination of herbs and spices should be cooked with other foods only as long as the most fragile ingredient can tolerate their flavor. A bouquet garni should not simmer for more than the 20 to 40 minutes required for optimum bay-leaf flavor, since you don't wish bay to dominate the dish.

BOYSENBERRY

BACKGROUND

This berry is a raspberry-loganberry-blackberry hybrid created by a twentieth-century horticulturist, Rudolph Boysen. It is shaped like the raspberry, but has fewer and larger seeds. Its skin is smooth with a deep blend of purple, red, and black, and it has a full, rich, sweet but tart flavor. For general advice on preparation and storage, see RASPBERRY.

BRAINS

BACKGROUND

Of all the variety meats, brains are the most delicate in terms of texture and flavor. Though the organ is a popular edible in Europe, most Americans have never ventured a single bite as the idea makes them squeamish. Braver souls have sampled brains, but have come away with a negative opinion about them, probably because the dish was improperly prepared. Fortunately, a small but growing number of Americans are learning to prepare brains and, in the process, are putting them on their favorite-food list.

Mankind can and does eat the brains of almost any vertebrate mammal. In the Amazon, for instance, some of the tribes love raw monkey brain, a treat we have ourselves shared with those people. In the Middle East, lambs' brains are the favorite variety. In America and most of Europe, calves' brains reign number one. As the lambs and calves mature, their brains become stronger-flavored and coarser, so beef and mutton brains are less favored. Pigs' brains can be good, but again, for the choicest morsels, select those from young animals.

AVAILABILITY

Buying Tips

It is essential to buy brains that are perfectly fresh. Look for plump, unshriveled brains with a bright, pinkish-white color and a clean-smelling odor. Buy them from a reliable butcher no more than 24 hours before mealtime, as they are extremely perishable, being composed of soft tissue that rapidly decomposes. Some markets sell frozen brains; freezing does greatly reduce the perishability problem, but if you use frozen brains, your finished dish will have noticeably less flavor and desired texture than if you had used fresh brains.

PREPARATION

By all means, handle brains gently. They are fragile and soft and easily tear and break apart.

Preliminaries

Soaking: Whether you plan to cook the brains within one or a dozen hours, it is a practical idea to soak them as soon as you bring them home from the market. This process helps remove traces of blood that would turn brown if cooked, and it makes it easier for you to remove the outer membrane which, if left intact, could possibly shrink during cooking, curling the meat. To soak, immerse the brains in cold, salted, acidulated water (1 tablespoon of vinegar or 2 tablespoons of lemon juice and ½ teaspoon of salt per quart of liquid. Do not use an aluminum or iron bowl). Place in the refrigerator for an hour or so; if you are rushed and have only 30 minutes to soak the brains, do it at room temperature. Drain and gently rinse under cold, running water. Carefully remove the membrane with a small, sharp-pointed knife. This task can be difficult because the membrane clings in the crevices and is somewhat transparent, but if the brains are perfectly fresh, the job is easier.

Blanching: Blanching or parboiling helps whiten the brains and, more important, helps firm their spongy texture, making them easier to handle, cut, and cook. Therefore, unless you plan to braise the brains, blanching should not be omitted. To blanch, place brains in a saucepan (again, not an aluminum or an iron one) of fresh, cold, salted, acidulated water (see Step 1 for formula). Bring the water to a gentle boil, then simmer (boiling would toughen and shrink the meat) for 8 to 20 minutes, depending on the thickness of the pieces and the age of the animal (a more mature brain requires longer blanching). For added flavor, incorporate the ingredients of a *court bouillon* into the acidulated water—parsley, bay leaf, celery, carrots, peppercorns, and onions—but do not make it too flavorful lest it overpower the delicate taste of the brains. When fully blanched, plunge the brains into cold water to stop the cooking process. If you choose to allow the brains to cool in the blanching liquid, be sure to reduce the blanching time by 25 percent. Pat dry with paper toweling and examine the brains to see if you can remove any membrane still clinging in the crevices. Then either proceed to the final cooking step or store in a covered glass or porcelain bowl in the refrigerator until ready to use.

Storage

Blanched brains should be used within 24 hours, the sooner the better. They may be frozen, but this may impair flavor and texture. Blanched brains will keep a couple of weeks in the standard refrigerator freezing compartment or a couple of months in an under-0°F freezer.

Cooking

Brains can be sautéed (the most popular method), broiled, simmered in a liquid, braised, or baked. Whatever the cooking method, be sure to start with brains at room temperature. Sauté ½-inch-thick pieces in butter for approximately 3 minutes per side over medium heat. To broil, use the same (or slightly shorter) timing, and place the brains 4 inches below the heat source; baste often with butter. When simmering in a liquid, increase the blanching time by two thirds and the brains should be properly cooked. When braising unblanched brains, figure on 15 to 30 minutes, depending on thickness and animal maturity. To bake, place in preheated 375°F oven for 15 to 20 minutes, again depending on size and maturity.

Serving

Because there is little waste and because most people prefer to eat small portions of brains, you can generally plan on buying ¼ to ⅓ pound per serving. If your guests are brains devotees, purchase ⅓ pound per serving. Lambs' brains weigh about ¼ pound each, calves' brains about ½ pound, and pork brains somewhere in between. Beef brains weight ¾ pound or more.

CLASSIC USES AND AFFINITIES

The most famous brain dish is the French *cervelles au beurre noir*, which is sauteed and served with a black butter sauce. Other recipes for brains call for them being served on toast, inserted into small pastry shells, incorporated in soufflés and salads, cooked with scrambled eggs, pickled, or simply simmered. The last preparation is often served with a tart dressing such as a vinaigrette sauce in order to add piquancy to the relatively bland-tasting brains. Brains can also be breaded, then pan-fried or deep-fried. They can also be cooked and served whole, split in two, sliced, cubed, diced, or minced. Classic garnishes include chopped bright green herbs (such as fresh parsley or chives) and lemon wedges. Since brains somewhat resemble sweetbreads in terms of texture, taste, and color, the two are interchangeable in some recipes. They also combine well.

BREAD

BACKGROUND

The Biblical "staff of life," bread is often classified in terms of leavening—or its absence, as with unleavened bread. There are three basic leavening agents: *yeast, baking powder* (which produces quick breads), and *hot air* (as with popovers). Bread is also classified by whether the moistened flour mixture was a liquid *batter* or a semi-solid *dough* before being cooked. (For more information, see the following entries: BAKING POWDER, BAKING SODA, BREADCRUMBS, CEREAL GRAINS, CREAM OF TARTAR, CROUTONS, LEAVENING AGENTS, PASTRY, PHYLLO LEAVES, WHEAT, and YEAST.)

Bread made with a fat or oil stays fresh longer than a bread made with just a flour-and-water dough. This is why genuine French bread is a poor keeper. Quick breads, unlike yeast breads, should always be made for short-term consumption. The best place to store bread is a cool, dark, dry place—breadboxes are ideal. Bread should be carefully wrapped to keep out fresh air. If you want longer storage than a breadbox offers, freeze the bread rather than refrigerate it. Wrap it tightly in aluminum foil or freezer paper so that it does not pick up foreign odors.

Varieties

Thousands of distinct bread varieties exist throughout the world. Some of the better-known types include:

Bagel: A chewy, doughnut-shaped yeast bread that is a staple in Jewish-American cuisine. It is poached in water, then baked. To serve, it is split and customarily smeared with butter or cream cheese and perhaps topped with lox.

Bialy: Somewhat resembles the bagel, but it contains onions and has no hole.

Biscuit: In America, the term defines a small, circular, fat-enriched quick bread that is more popular in the South than in the North.

Boston brown bread: A molasses-flavored, steamed quick bread that can be made with a blend of cornmeal, rye, and whole-wheat flour. Popular in New England.

Bread sticks: Long, thin, tube-shaped, brittle bread, often coated with sesame seeds. The original north Italian version is called *grissini.*

Corn bread: A quick bread made with cornmeal. There are many variations.

Cracker: A thin, dry, flat bread that comes in various styles including *soda crackers, hardtack, oyster crackers, pilot crackers,* and *water biscuits.* (The British call crackers "biscuits.")

Flatbreads: A category of very thin, very crisp breads that are especially popular with the Scandinavians. Our best-sellers include *rye crisps.*

French bread: The genuine article is made with white flour, water, yeast, and perhaps a touch of salt—nothing else. It is long and cylindrical. *Baguette* is the thinner version prized for its higher proportion of crust. *Italian bread* is similar to French bread, but can contain other ingredients including a sesame seed coating and is customarily a bit plumper and shorter.

Graham crackers: A flat, rectangular cracker made with graham flour (that is, whole-wheat flour) with one special feature: the outer bran of the kernel is coarsely ground.

Matzo bread: A thin, brittle, unleavened cracker made with wheat flour and water, without salt or any other ingredient. A Passover specialty that helps commemorate the Exodus; the *unleavened bread* of the Bible.

Muffins: In America, muffins are small, round, quick breads usually made of corn or wheat flour. Flat English muffins (which are called crumpets in England) are cooked on a griddle rather than, as with most dome-topped muffins, baked in cupcake-shaped tins. Muffins can be sweetened or not, and may contain nuts, fruits, and the like.

Pancake: A flat, round, griddle-cooked batter bread that is typically leavened with a baking powder, though some—such as *blinis*—use yeast. Other names include *hot cakes, flapjacks,* and—if a thin batter is used—*crêpes.* Pancakes are usually a breakfast food; crêpes, when sweetened with a sauce, can be served as a dessert such as *crêpes Suzettes.*

Pita: A classic Middle Eastern and Greek yeast bread that is flat and round. As the bread bakes, a natural pocket forms in its center, which makes it ideal for holding foods.

Pizza: A flat yeast dough that is smeared and baked with a flavorful topping consisting of tomato and grated cheese, perhaps with sliced pepperoni, mushrooms, and green peppers. Neapolitan pizza is round, and Sicilian is rectangular.

Popover: When a thin batter made of flour, eggs, butter, and water is poured into hot molds and baked at a high heat, a puffy, hollow bread pops up and over the muffin tin. (Expanding hot air is the leavening agent.) They should be eaten while hot. Yorkshire pudding is a popover sibling.

Pretzel: A twisted strand of yeast bread that is poached, coated with coarse salt, then baked.

Rye bread: Since rye flour has very little gluten, it is customarily mixed with wheat flour when used for a yeast bread. Compared to rye bread, pumpernickel is chewier, coarser, and has a higher proportion of rye flour; many bakers darken it by adding molasses or caramel.

Soda bread: Leavened by a baking soda and an acid such as cream of tartar or sour milk. Irish soda bread is the most famous version.

Sourdough bread: A special yeast strain gives this bread its characteristic tang. It was popular with gold prospectors, fur trappers, and cowboys of the Old West and is in vogue with San Franciscans of the New West. Sourdoughs are not exclusive to America, however, as bakers from other lands including France have long known the secret of keeping a small part (called the starter) of each day's batch of dough to incorporate into the next day's batch.

Tortilla: A flat, unleavened pancake-like bread made with a special type of ground corn called MASA HARINA.

Waffle: A crisp-surfaced batter bread cooked between a hinged pair of pattern-indented griddles. Most waffles are leavened with baking powder, though some are yeast-raised. Waffles are a breakfast item, though they can also be transformed into a dessert.

Zwieback: The name means "twice-baked" in German; Zwieback is first baked, then sliced and slowly toasted until it has achieved a dry, crisp texture and a yellowish-brown color. Zwieback can be sweetened or not.

BREADCRUMBS

BACKGROUND

A frugal yet wonderful way to use up leftover bread is to make breadcrumbs, which can be used to make stuffings and *au gratin* preparations and to coat meat, as for Southern fried chicken. Homemade breadcrumbs are much better than the preservative-laden store-bought varieties.

PREPARATION

Preliminaries

To make breadcrumbs, you need slightly dried (stale—but not too stale) crustless bread several days old. If the bread isn't dry enough, place it in a 200°F oven for 10 to 15 minutes. Then grind it in your blender or food processor. Some recipes call for soft breadcrumbs. To make these, use fresher, moister bread than you would for dry breadcrumbs. Fine crumbs adhere to meat better than do coarse ones—but don't make the crumbs too small, or you will have flour. Breadcrumbs are, strictly speaking, made with ordinary bread, but you can use ingredients such as cornflakes or graham crackers if you take their flavor into consideration.

Storage

Store breadcrumbs in a tightly closed glass jar in the refrigerator or, better yet, in the freezer.

Cooking

Breadcrumbs can be used in recipes as they are, or can first be browned in a little butter for better flavor and texture. If you are cooking food with successive coatings of seasoned flour, lightly beaten egg, and breadcrumbs, be sure to allow the coated foods to rest at room temperature for 30 minutes before placing them in the hot oil. This nap allows the crumbs to become more firmly attached to the drying egg; as a result, fewer of the crumbs will drop off, scorch, and turn bitter in the cooking oil.

BREADFRUIT

BACKGROUND

The name *breadfruit* was earned by the

bland taste, starchy texture and white flesh of the young *Articarpus communis*, a tropical staple that looks like a green, bumpy-skinned bowling ball. Breadfruit may be a native of Malaysia; it was popular in Polynesia and Micronesia in 1792, when Captain Bligh took it to Jamaica.

AVAILABILITY

Breadfruit is in peak season in July and August. Choose a firm, well-rounded breadfruit, one that is clean and not too hard.

PREPARATION

To ripen breadfruit at home, remove the stalk, fill the stalk cavity with coarse salt, and leave the breadfruit at room temperature for several days. Breadfruit is not edible raw. It is usually baked—an hour in a 350°F oven is about right. One-quarter to one-half a breadfruit, depending on the size of the breadfruit and the dinner guest, is an average serving.

BREAKFAST CEREALS

BACKGROUND

One of America's best-selling categories of convenience food is breakfast cereals. Their popularity is evidenced by the astonishing amount of space allotted to them in grocery stores. Few foods have prompted as much criticism from consumer groups, which believe too many of these products are too high in price and sugar and too low in nutrients. (Also see CEREAL GRAINS.)

Varieties

Breakfast cereals may be classified into two groups: cold and hot.

Cold (*dry* or *ready-to-eat*) breakfast cereals are easily prepared—they need only some cold milk or cream and perhaps a light sprinkling of sugar and a garnishing of fresh fruit. They come in all manner of shapes, flavors, textures, and colors, and their ingredients, degrees of sweetness and nutritional value vary markedly. Some have had their vitamins and minerals restored, which means that the nutrients in question that were removed in the manufacturing process have been replaced up to the original level. Other cereals have been enriched—that is, the processor added more vitamins and minerals than were in the grains provided by Mother Nature. When eaten with the customary accompaniments such as milk, a few of the enriched cereal brands offer you 100 percent of the U.S. government's adult RDA (recommended daily allowance) of certain key vitamins and minerals—but since we eat other foods during the day, what is the purpose of "100 percent" other than as a sales gimmick? Many of the cereals use terms such as "natural" on their packages—but since sugar is natural, a breakfast cereal could have a 50 percent content of those empty calories and still call itself "natural." We have no ax to grind against breakfast cereals in general—they are a great convenience when the various family members are rushing off into the world in the morning. What we do suggest is to buy whole-grain cereals (containing the bran, germ, and endosperm) that have no sugar, or very little. Read the labels carefully and remember that the ingredients are listed in descending order of quantity.

Hot cereals come in three types: regular, quick-cooking, and instant. When preparing hot cereals such as oatmeal and farina, do not overcook them, or you will end up with an unappetizing substance that will stick to more than your ribs. The chief advantage of hot cereals over cold ones is that their intrinsic warmth adds to your feeling of well-being, especially on a cold morning. Their major drawback is the pot, lid, and stirring spoon that must be washed. We are opposed to quick-cooking cereals—not only are they inferior in taste and texture, they save you only 10 or so minutes of waiting (not clean-up) time. Instant cereals, which are precooked and only need the addition of boiling water, taste even worse than the quick-cooking cereals.

Buying Tips

When buying breakfast cereals, be sure the store has a high merchandise turnover. Examine the packages carefully for any damage. Even though most cereals are loaded with preservatives such as antioxidants, we suggest you sacrifice the luxury of having a variety of different cereals on your shelf for the sake of freshness unless your household happens to eat a lot of breakfast cereals.

Storage

Once a package has been opened, carefully seal its inner lining (if there is one) and lid, and store it on a dry, dark shelf for up to a couple of weeks. For longer shelf life, seal the package inside a plastic storage bag or, even better, put the cereal into a glass jar or metal canister with a tight-fitting lid. If you have a whole-grain cereal that will not be eaten within a week, you are best off refrigerating it, as its germ (embryo) can become rancid quickly.

BROAD BEAN

BACKGROUND

This is the biggest and maybe the oldest bean, and it travels under many names. *Vicia faba* is known in America as the *broad*, or *English broad bean*, in France as *fava* or *faba*, and in England as the *horse* or *Windsor bean*. The pod of the broad bean is very large. The bean itself looks like an outsized cream-colored lima. It has a strong distinctive flavor. As a broad bean matures, it develops a furry growth on the inside lining of the pod which, for some sensitive persons, can cause *favism* , an allergic reaction which can be debilitating or even deadly. Because it is difficult for a host to know which table guests are susceptible to favism, we do not recommend cooking and eating broad beans in their pods even if the legumes happen to be young and tender. Far better to eat just the shelled bean. (For soaking, cooking, etc., see BEANS.)

AVAILABILITY

Rarely available to us fresh, broad beans are usually bought dried or already cooked in cans.

PREPARATION

The mature bean, fresh or dried, ought to be blanched and have its tough skin removed before cooking.

CLASSIC USES AND AFFINITIES

Besides being a good soup bean, this legume makes a nice side dish flavored with cured pork and savory and moistened with butter.

BROCCOLI

BACKGROUND

Broccoli (*Brassica oleracea* var. *botrytis*) is a very close relative of cabbage, cauliflower, Brussels sprouts, and kale—and, like them, it develops an unpleasant odor if overcooked. The harvested 6-to-9-inch-long broccoli plant comprises an umbrella of tightly clustered dark-green (sometimes purple-tinged) edible bud clusters emerging from firm, stout, dark-green, edible stems.

AVAILABILITY

Season

Year round, but mainly a winter and spring vegetable; peaks from October through early May; at its worst in mid-summer.

Buying Tips

Look for fresh-looking broccoli with (depending on variety) vibrant, deep-green or purplish-green buds that are close-packed. Once those buds begin to open and expose their yellow flowers, the broccoli has developed beyond its tender eating stage. Wilted, yellowish, or soggy buds or leaves are also negative signs, as are overly thick or woody stalks.

PREPARATION

Storage

Store broccoli, unwashed and wrapped in plastic, in your refrigerator for no more than 2 or 3 days.

Preliminaries

Wash the broccoli carefully, directing water among the flower buds to flush out lurking dirt or insects. Peel off the skin of the stems, if tough. The problem in cooking broccoli is producing both bud clusters and stems that are done to a turn at the same time. The simplest solution is to trim off the stems and either cook them separately or give them a head start in the pot. Or cut the broccoli stems fine so that they may be cooked simultneously with larger chunks of florets.

Cooking

Broccoli is often cooked in a steamer, an operation that takes 7 to 10 minutes if the bud clusters are broken into small units. It will take about 12 to 15 minutes if the whole broccoli bunch is placed upright (standing on their stems) in a large pot of boiling water, about an inch deep; cover and reduce heat to a gentle boil. Broccoli is also frequently sautéed, stir-fried, or simmered. When parboiled, broccoli is served as a *crudité*.

Equivalents

Broccoli is usually sold by the bunch weighting 1½ to 2 pounds. An average serving is ⅓ pound of broccoli.

CLASSIC USES AND AFFINITIES

Butter, cream sauce, cheese sauce, and hollandaise sauce add richness; lemon juice adds tang; nutmeg adds aroma; oregano adds an herby background. Breadcrumbs and grated cheese add a finishing *au gratin* touch.

BRUSSELS SPROUTS

BACKGROUND

Brussels sprouts, like cauliflower, kale, and broccoli, belong to the same species as the cabbage. In *Brassica oleracea* var. *gemmifera*, the family resemblance is obvious: Brussels sprouts look like miniature cabbage heads. The small, firm, spherical green buds, about an inch in diameter, grow on a thick stem. Brussels sprouts have been cultivated since the Middle Ages and, when over-boiled, have done much to befoul kitchens then and now.

AVAILABILITY

Season

Generally available from September to February, peaking from October through mid-December.

Buying Tips

The green color should be vivid. Wilted, yellow-tinged, or loose-leaved heads are negative indicators. Choose tight, firm, compact buds. Small holes in the surface or ragged leaves may be the result of worm infestation or insect damage. All other variables being equal, the smallest specimens are best; choose even-sized heads for even cooking. If sold in a pint cardboard tub, do not hesitate to remove the cellophane covering to examine the bottom sprouts.

PREPARATION

Preliminaries

Trim the stem ends and the loose or damaged outer leaves of the sprouts. Cut an X in the stem end of each sprout so heat can penetrate into the interior, thereby promoting quick and even cooking.

Cooking

Unless you have an unaccountable nostalgia for an English boardinghouse, do not overcook your Brussels sprouts; there should be some crispness at the heart. Steam or simmer the sprouts for 7 to 14 minutes, depending on size and age. Test them by piercing the heart of one with a fork: when most (but not all) of the resistance is gone, your sprouts are ready.

Equivalents

A pint-sized tub will usually serve three people.

CLASSIC USES AND AFFINITIES

Butter as well as cream, cheese, and hollandaise sauces complement Brussels sprouts, which go well with strong-flavored roast meats such as beef. Chestnuts mixed with sprouts add flavor, texture, and visual contrast.

BURDOCK ROOT

BACKGROUND

A member of the daisy family, the *burdock* (*Arctium lappa*), is a common weed in the United States. Its long, fibrous root, called *gobo* in Japanese and *ngau-pong* in Chinese, is an Oriental delicacy. The roots are very coarse, with white flesh and edible brown skin. Burdock root is often soaked, cooked, soaked again, then flavored. Thin strips of burdock root are eaten as a condiment.

BUTTER

BACKGROUND

To be the real thing, butter must be made from milk, cream, or a combination of milk and cream. By law, butter must be at least 80% fat. The rest consists of water, usually annatto (a natural yellow coloring), sometimes salt, and milk curds left from the separating process. A creamy complement to many foods, butter is a basic household staple—although it has declined in popularity due to its high price and the cholesterol scare. Unique and excellent in flavor and texture, butter's quality depends on the cream it was made from—and the quality of the cream depends on factors such as the season, the geographic area, and the feed of the cows that produced the cream.

Grade

Grading is optional, so a good deal of butter is sold ungraded. When graded, the best butter is Grade AA, also called 93 score; it is made from fresh cream. Grade B butter is made from lesser quality cream, perhaps slightly soured.

Varieties

Sweet butter is made from sweet cream, with no salt added, and its taste is preferred by many cooks and connoisseurs.

Salted butter may be made from either sweet or soured cream; its added salt acts as a preservative, so that salted butter may keep longer than sweet. The salt may also disguise "off" odors or mishandling. Salted butter contains more moisture than sweet butter.

Whipped butter, diluted with air, spreads more evenly as a result. If you cook using whipped butter, you'll have to use more (by volume) than you would if using solid butter.

Clarified butter is what you have when you remove the casein (protein) and certain other nonfat ingredients from butter. On the positive side, your clarified or *drawn* butter will cook at higher temperature without burning and will not become rancid as quickly because you have eliminated the culprit, that is, the casein. On the negative side, your clarified butter loses much of the delicious buttery flavor. *Ghee*, the Indian version, is so clarified that it can be stored for several months or longer at room temperature; regular clarified butter should be refrigerated.

Seasoned butter is made at home by creaming into the butter any of hundreds of possible flavoring agents including herbs, lemon, and garlic—the last being the classic flavor for snails.

AVAILABILITY

Fresh butter is available year round.

Buying Tips

Choose Grade AA butter if available. Butter should be cool and firm, with a fresh smell. The wrappers should be clean and dry, not greasy, and never broken.

PREPARATION

Storage

Keep butter covered to prevent the absorption of other food flavors. More than almost any other food, butter picks up flavors and aroma—not only of food, but of tobacco smoke, paint, and strong-smelling household cleansers. Refrigerate butter, and use it within 2 weeks. Butter should be kept at a constant, cold temperature. If keeping butter longer than 2 weeks, freeze it. It won't be as good as before, but you won't waste it. It will keep frozen for about 2 months. Thaw it for about 3 hours in the refrigerator when ready to use.

Preliminaries

To cut butter into well-shaped pats, wrap the knife in plastic film; the butter sticks to the plastic, not the knife, and can be peeled off easily. Before adding butter to a puff pastry, wash and squeeze the butter under cold water to remove excess water and milk solids. For creaming butter, the best temperature is about 70°F; the butter will be warm enough to mix, yet cool enough to permit air to be incorporated into the batter.

Making Modern Homemade Butter: If you run out of butter but have cream, you can make your own. Crush four or five ice cubes per cup of cream in your blender or food processor. Add the cream and whirl the blades until the butter emerges.

Making Clarified Butter: While there are many ways to clarify butter, our favorite method is not only effective, it is easy: it requires a minimum number of utensils and it demands little close attention on your part. The next time you are using your oven, cut up sticks of sweet butter into cubes and place them in a small- to medium-size glass, porcelain or stainless steel bowl. Place this bowl with its lid or with plastic wrap in the refrigerator. Within a few hours, the butterfat (your clarified butter) will be solidified and separated from the protein and most of the other nonfat ingredients. Remove the solidified butterfat from the bowl and scrape the thin foamy layer off the top and the whitish, casein-infused liquid off the bottom. Wrap the solidified clarified butter in aluminum foil—it will last a month or two in the refrigerator. Break or cut off chunks as you need them.

Cooking

Butter used for deep-frying will burn; butter's smoke point is lower than the temperature needed for frying. When sautéing, add foods to the melted butter after the foam on the butter has subsided but before the butter has browned.

Equivalents

There are four sticks of butter in a pound; each stick is 8 tablespoons of solid butter, or 1/2 cup of melted butter. To cut one tablespoonful from an unmarked stick, mark the halfway point on the stick, then half of that, then half of that again. When substituting other oils or fats: 1 cup butter equals 1 cup margarine, or 7/8 cup vegetable oil.

CABBAGE

BACKGROUND

Cheap, easy to grow, sturdy, and long-keeping, cabbage is more likely to be found on rough earthenware than fine china. A cabbage is any variety of *Brassica oleracea* that forms a large head; kale, cauliflower, and broccoli are members of the same species that take different shapes.

Varieties

The world has many types of cabbages. In America, the best-seller has smooth, compact, greenish-white leaves. Also quite popular is the *red cabbage* with its tight head of deep crimson-maroon leaves that add color interest to salads. Less frequently encountered but culinarily superior is the *Savoy cabbage*, with its head of loose, wrinkled, luxuriously ruffled leaves. Also, see the CHINESE CABBAGE entry.

AVAILABILITY

Available year round, depending on region and variety.

Buying Tips

The outer leaves should have a fresh, vivid appearance. Reject those that are wilted, yellowed, insect-nibbled, or otherwise damaged. If the outer leaves are separating from the tight head, the cabbage is probably overmature and, consequently, of inferior flavor and texture. Choose a head that is firm and heavy for its size. If you have the choice, buy the more nutritious and better-flavored "new" cabbage rather than the "old" cabbage that has been kept in prolonged cold storage. "New" cabbage has a fresh scent. Prepackaged cole slaw is seldom a good buy. The price is too high, and the shreds tend to be in substandard condition.

PREPARATION

Storage

The whole head will keep for 7 to 10 days in the refrigerator, longer in a cool cellar. If you use only part of a head, wrap the remainder well and refrigerate. Plan to use it within a day or two; discoloration and wilting are very rapid.

Preliminaries

To shred cabbage, cut the cabbage head in quarters, remove the core, and make close lengthwise cuts. Or rub the cabbage quarters over a shredder. Or use the shredding blade of a food processor. For diced cabbage, shred the cabbage, then make close crosswise cuts across the shreds. To stuff a whole cabbage, cut out the core from the blossom end (opposite the stem) with a sharp knife, gently separate the leaves, and insert the stuffing mixture between them, preserving the shape of the cabbage. To stuff individual cabbage leaves, break them off one by one, parboil or steam them, and roll them around the filling, tucking in the sides. Then placing each package seam side down in a baking dish, ready for baking. Cabbage can be freshened by a short soak in ice water, but do not leave the cabbage long enough for the vitamin C to soak away.

Cooking

The stench and sog associated with cabbage are really the results of overcooking. Quick-cooked cabbage will be tasty, with a toothsome crunch and high vitamin value; the kitchen will not reek. Shredded cabbage can be steamed or simmered in 4 to 6 minutes, stir-fried in half that time, braised in about 10 to 12 minutes. Cabbage wedges will take 6 to 10 minutes to steam or simmer, depending on thickness and age. Red cabbage turns a less-than-desirable purple in cooking unless an acid ingredient (apple slices, vinegar, or lemon juice, for example) is added. Red cabbage may also discolor if it is cooked in mixed dishes; cook it separately, and add it just before serving.

CLASSIC USES AND AFFINITIES

Cabbage is the basis of raw *cole slaw* and pickled *sauerkraut*. The latter is in turn the basis (along with sausages and smoked meats) of the Polish *bigos*, the Alsatian *choucroute garni* and sometimes the Swiss *Berneplatte*. The Russian *shchi* soup is another well-known cabbage-based specialty. Cabbage leaves are often used by Middle European cooks as the envelope to hold a wide variety of stuffings.

CALVES' FEET

BACKGROUND

Though most cooks use calves' feet mainly for their content of gelatin-producing collagen, they can be substituted for PIGS' FEET in most recipes.

CANDIED FRUIT AND FLOWERS

BACKGROUND

One of the prettiest and sweetest conceits in the culinary repertoire is candied fruits and, especially, flowers. Candied fruits include citrus rinds, pineapple slices, and cherries. They are sometimes incorporated into fruitcakes and breads such as the Italian *panettoni* and Scandinavian *Julekage*. The violet is the most commonly candied flower. Other foods such as ginger and angelica are also candied and used by both home bakers and confectioners extraordinaire.

CANDY

BACKGROUND

One of the world's most popular snacks is candy, which is, most often, a sweet, rich confection made with sugar, SUGAR SYRUP, corn syrup, or honey and combined with other ingredients such as chocolate, nuts, maraschino cherries, and shredded coconut. Candy comes in all shapes, colors, flavors, and degrees of sweetness. It can be hard, chewy, or soft and can be factory- or home-made. Thousands of candy categories exist, including bonbons, caramels, chocolate-covered creams, fudge, gum drops, halvah, hard balls, jawbreakers, kisses, lemon drops, lollipops, marzipan, mints, nougats, pralines, sugarplums, taffy, and toffee. Nutritionally speaking, candy is high in empty calories and, if consumed in excess, is the bane of good health.

Storage

Most candies are best stored in an airtight, dry, cool (about 65° to 70°F) place.

CANTALOUPE

BACKGROUND

We cannot buy a true *cantaloupe* in the United States; this melon, named after a papal villa, grows in Europe and is not imported here. The melon called cantaloupe in the United States is the *netted muskmelon* (*Cucumis melo reticulatus*). Because it is usually picked when still immature, the fruit seldom has a chance to become as sweet, luscious, and juicy as nature had planned. The best American cantaloupes come from small, quality farms.

AVAILABILITY

Season

May through September, peaking in mid-summer. Some markets carry cantaloupes the year round, but these cantaloupes are quite expensive and frequently lackluster.

Buying Tips

A good cantaloupe must be both mature and ripe. To be mature, the melon must not be picked too soon—it does not mature off the vine. The stem neatly separates from a mature cantaloupe, leaving a smooth dry, slightly sunken "moon crater." If bits of the stem remain on or around the lip of the depression, the melon was picked prematurely. Another sign of a mature fruit is the existence of a thick, coarse netting that stands out in clear relief from the smooth skin. And that skin should be well on its way in its natural shift from a green to a creamy-yellow or buff hue. A melon will ripen off the vine providing it was reasonably mature when destemmed. First, look at the smooth undersurface—it should have arrived at its full creamy-yellow or buff color. Next, smell the fruit—the scent should be faintly sweet and fragrant. Finally, gently push in the blossom end (opposite the stem end) with your thumb—it should yield to the pressure. Please note that the last criterion is sometimes unreliable, as the soft blossom end may have been caused by decay or by several days of pressing by other shoppers' fingers. Select cantaloupes that are heavy for their size, for they will be juicier than their slightly dehydrated bin pals. Do not buy cantaloupes that have moldy or injured surfaces, soft spots (these suggest subsurface decay), asymmetrical shapes, or shriveled rinds. Overripeness is also detected by an aroma that is too fragrant or by a skin that has become too yellow or that yields too readily to light squeezing.

PREPARATION

Storage

Cantaloupes ripen best and quickest when stored at room temperature in a closed pierced paper bag. This will take 2 to 4 days for most store-bought cantaloupes. Once ripened, eat your melon as soon as possible because the cantaloupe is very perishable. If you are not going to eat the fruit within the day, refrigerate it. You will have to wrap the melon in plastic wrap, because the cantaloupe will absorb refrigerator odor, and its own odor permeates other foods. This is especially true of cut melons. Do not remove the seeds from a cut melon until ready to eat, because the seeds help keep the flesh moist.

Preliminaries

Cut your melon in half with a sharp knife and (if you are going to eat it soon) seed it with a spoon.

Serving

The melon can be served halved, turned into melon balls with a kitchen utensil especially designed for the purpose, or cut into individual-sized wedges. The cosmopolitan way to serve a melon wedge is to first separate the flesh from the rind with a knife, being careful not to cut into the bitter peel. Leaving the separated flesh on top of the rind, make vertical slices that create bite-sized pieces and which may then be eaten with a fork or with a toothpick. Some people prefer to eat room-temperature cantaloupes; others prefer them slightly chilled. Though it is a matter of personal taste, you will find that the majority of cantaloupe connoisseurs belong to the no-chill club. Even if you enjoy refrigerated melon, it should not be chilled to the point where the fruit cannot release its sweet, musky fragrance and flavor.

EQUIVALENTS

Most cantaloupes weigh between 1½ and 2½ pounds. An average cantaloupe typically serves two people, though some families slice it into three or four servings.

CLASSIC USES AND AFFINITIES

The cantaloupe is a popular appetizer, served with a fig, with a wedge of lemon or lime, or wrapped in prosciutto. The cavity left by the seeds is a natural for filling with cottage cheese, yogurt, ice cream, or fruit salad. Cut or scooped with a melon cutter, bits of cantaloupe are added to fruit compotes.

CAPERS

BACKGROUND

The unopened flower buds of *Capparis rupestris*, a small bush that grows wild in Mediterranean countries, are dried and pickled in vinegar to make *capers*. The flavor develops after pickling because an organic acid called capric acid is produced. The best capers are tiny *nonpareilles* from the south of France.

CLASSIC USES AND AFFINITIES

Whole or minced capers are often used in sauces: milk-based caper sauce (classically served with mutton) and *tartare*, *rémoulade*, *gribiche*, and *ravigote* sauces. The tartness of capers makes them a good complement to fatty fish and meat dishes. Eggplant, tomatoes, olives, and capers combine well.

Storage

Never permit the capers to dry out; store them in the bottle covered in the vinegar they were packed in. Since capers are a preserved product, the opened bottle can be stored a month or two in the refrigerator—after that they start getting mushy.

CARAMBOLA

BACKGROUND

When cut crosswise, the carambola (*Averrhoa carambola*) displays a five-pointed star profile, hence its popularity as a garnish and its other name, star fruit. If you plan to eat this slightly acid tropical fruit raw out-of-hand pear-style, look for a variety with a vibrant yellow color, a clue to ripeness. For cooking, the greenish-yellow skinned specimens are best. Either way, first slice off the darkened, somewhat fibrous edges that run along the peaks of the five lengthwise ridges of the fruit. The remaining thin, waxy peel and the watery pulp—but not the core, seeds and stem end—are edible. Use the carambola for fruit salads and drinks, jams and jellies, pickle mixtures, relishes, stews and soups. Possibilities are endless.

CARAWAY

BACKGROUND

The plant *Carum carvi* is native to Southeastern Europe and Western Asia. It is now grown extensively in the Netherlands. Although the root and leaves can be eaten, the dark, crescent-shaped seeds are the major reason for cultivating this plant. Caraway seeds can be chewed to freshen the breath; they also have a minor effect in promoting digestion. (See HERBS AND SPICES for information on buying, storing, cooking, etc.)

CLASSIC USES AND AFFINITIES

Storage

Raw, dried caraway seeds are very hard; they soften in cooking. Time on the shelf affects the texture of the finished product. Caraway seeds can be stored for about 12 months from time of packing.

CARDAMOM

BACKGROUND

Cardamom, sometimes spelled *cardamon*, is one of the most expensive spices in the world because each small, nutlike pod (each containing 12 to 20 small dark seeds) must be snipped off the plant by hand. *Elletaria cardamomum*, part of the ginger family, is native to India. Today a great deal of cardamom comes from Sri Lanka (Ceylon) and Guatemala. This spice has some flatulent effect and is a strong deodorant; chewed after meals it can neutralize the smell of garlic.

AVAILABILITY

Whole cardamom is sold green or white, the latter having a sun-blanched pod. Connoisseurs prefer green cardamom.

PREPARATION

The pod of whole cardamom is never eaten. If you buy the spice in pod form (which is more aromatic and stays fresh much longer than the ground spice), break the pod apart, then remove and separate the seeds, discarding the whitish connective membranes. Some cooks add the whole, unopened pod to the cooking pot and then discard it before serving the preparation. Use only a small quantity at a time, because the flavor is very strong. One pod can flavor a large pot of coffee, though Levantine cardamom fanciers use one pod per cup.

CLASSIC USES AND AFFINITIES

Cardamom is one of the spices often used in the *masalas* for Indian "curry" dishes. It is a favorite spice of Scandinavians, used in pastry, cakes, and ground-meat dishes. Middle Eastern coffee very often is imbued with it. Cardamom goes well with apples, fruit salads, and hot spiced wine.

CARDOON

BACKGROUND

What looks like mammoth celery, tastes like a mixture of celery and artichoke, and is popular with Italian-Americans? The *cardoon* (*cynara cardunculus*).

PREPARATION

The outer ribs are often wilted or overly stringy and must be discarded or stripped of their fibrous surfaces prior to cooking. The choicer, more tender inner ribs are customarily washed, then simmered for approximately 30 to 60 minutes, according to rib thickness. If you have cut raw cardoons and do not plan to cook them immediately, soak them in acidulated water, as they discolor quickly from oxidation.

CLASSIC USES AND AFFINITIES

Cooked cardoons can be served as a vegetable side dish and topped with a seasoned white sauce. Or, when cooked, they can be part of a salad. The crisp, delicate-flavored stalks can also be braised, added to soups and stews, or breaded and deep-fried.

CAROB

BACKGROUND

The *carob* (*Ceratonia siliqua*), is a tropical evergreen leguminous tree that produces large seed pods up to 10 inches long. Carob is also known by other names, including *St. John's bread* and *locust bean*.

CLASSIC USES AND AFFINITIES

Except for a few hard seeds, the entire carob pod can be eaten fresh or can be dried or ground into a flour and made into candies, cakes, and syrups. Because carob is sweet and tastes somewhat like chocolate, it has become a popular confection in health-food stores.

CARROT

BACKGROUND

Queen Anne's lace, a common weed, has a skinny root that looks something like a *carrot*; fennel, parsnips, and carrots have similar lacy foliage. They all belong to the family of *Umbelliferae*; the carrot is *Daucus carota*. It is a native of the warmer areas of Europe and Western Asia, but it takes very well to American conditions and is very easy for the home gardener to grow. Peter Rabbit's passion is a crunchy favorite of dieters and rich in fiber and carotene (provitamin A). Cooked carrots have more of the vitamin in usable form than raw carrots do.

Varieties

Botanists have developed many kinds of carrots for their qualities of nutrition, taste, keeping, and processing, but the only selection in most supermarkets will be between larger mature carrots and tiny baby carrots, which can be immature carrots or a mature miniature variety such as the Belgian type.

AVAILABILITY

Season

Fresh carrots are available the year round.

Buying Tips

If the carrots are sold in a bunch complete with tops, check the condition of the green lace. If it is bright, fresh, and moist, the carrots are probably fresh and have been well treated on the way to the market. Baby carrots (also called *carettes*) are usually sold in see-through plastic bags and should be whole, reasonably uniform in size, unsprouted, and have bright, unabraded skins. Older carrots should be thin, long, and bright-skinned. Avoid split, cracked carrots and those with green areas on top caused by excessive exposure to sunlight. The "sunburned" areas will have to be discarded, so these carrots are wasteful. Very large, crooked carrots will be hard to peel, and probably are old, dry, and woody at the core. Sprouted carrots have been kept too moist, and have lost nutrients to the sprouts. If the carrots show a small green stub of stalk on top, they were shipped fresh and will be finer-textured and sweeter than storage carrots, identifiable by the total lack of stalk.

PREPARATION

Storage

Immediately after purchase, detach the carrot greens, if any; they cannibalize the roots for moisture and nutrients. Keep packaged carrots in the vegetable crisper. They should stay in good condition for 7 to 10 days. Do not store carrots near apples. The ethylene given off by apples as they ripen, makes carrots bitter.

Preliminaries

Tiny baby carrots just need rinsing. A moderately young carrot can be cooked unpeeled—which saves the vitamins just below the skin—but should be scrubbed with a vegetable brush. Coarser, older carrots should be peeled with a vegetable peeler (a paring knife can cut away too many of the nutrients). A vegetable peeler can also be used to make thick slivers of carrots for salads or garnishes, though a grater and, especially a food processor, works more effectively. Behemoth, coarse carrots can be crisped briefly in ice water before peeling or cutting. You can quarter these antiquities lengthwise and remove their centers, so that you serve tender carrot flesh, not woody cores.

Cooking

Carrots are healthier for you and better tasting if cooked uncut. Cooked carrots should have a bright color and a hint of crispness, not softness, in the final product. Carrots take very well to steaming. Waterless cooking works for very thin carrot slices over very low heat; they steam in their own juices. To boil or steam mature whole carrots, allow 20 to 30 minutes depending on age and thickness. Cook baby, young, halved, or quartered carrots 10 to 20 minutes, depending on age and thickness. Add carrots to a stew or pot roast 30 to 45 minutes—again depending on age and thickness—before the meat is scheduled to be done.

Equivalents

A pound of carrots makes three to four average servings.

CLASSIC USES AND AFFINITIES

Carrots combine delectably with cream sauce. They are often teamed with peas, though this may be more a visual than a taste affinity. Nutmeg accents the sweetness of carrots. Parsley adds flavor and color contrast; raisins do likewise in shredded carrot salads enriched with mayonnaise.

CASABA

BACKGROUND

The first *casaba melons* were imported into the United States about 1870 from Kasaba, a town near Izmir, in Turkey. Like the CANTALOUPE and PERSIAN MELON, the casaba is a member of the species *Cucumis melo*. A farmer friend describes the casaba as resembling a giant fig with poorly plowed furrows running lengthwise. Under its thick rind is one of the juiciest melon fleshes.

AVAILABILITY

Casabas are now grown in the United States, mostly in California, and are available in some markets from July through November, but they are at their best in September and October.

Buying Tips

The casaba is odorless when ripe, so we cannot use the sniff test. Neither can we check maturity by looking for a stem-free "moon crater" at the stem end, as the casaba must be cut from the vine in the field. Fortunately, there are two criteria we can use: The blossom end, opposite the stem end, yields when gently pushed with the thumb. Also, as the casaba ripens, the skin color changes from green to a golden yellow. But do not be deceived by a dyed rind, which is recognizable by a vibrant, artificial-looking yellow color. Stay away from casabas with soft spots (a sign of sub-surface decay), bruises, injuries, and mold. A good casaba should be heavy for its size (indicating maximum moisture content) and not soft to the touch.

PREPARATION

Storage

As melons go, casabas have good storage properties. Ripen yours at room temperature in a closed, pierced paper bag. When ripe, eat it within the day or store the whole casaba tightly sealed in plastic wrap in the refrigerator—it will stay fresh for 4 to 7 days and possibly longer, depending on original conditon. A cut casaba can also be stored in plastic wrap in the refrigerator, but plan to use it within a day or two.

Serving

Serve a casaba as you would a CANTALOUPE or a HONEYDEW.

CASSAVA

BACKGROUND

The botanical name for *cassava* is *Manihot utilissima*. Other names are *Brazilian arrowroot*, *mandioca*, *manioc*, and in Spanish, *yuca* to list a few. The multiplicity of native names shows that this plant is part of the diet of many cultures. Originally a native of South America, this brown-skinned, white-fleshed tuber, 6 to 10 inches long and 2 inches thick, is now also grown in Asiatic and African tropics. Its usefulness depends on cooking; uncooked cassava is poisonous. Both bitter and sweet cassava contain prussic acid, which is driven out by heat.

PREPARATION

Storage

Keep cassava in the refrigerator and use within a few days.

Cooking

Cassava is often prepared by stripping off the peel, slicing the hard flesh into 1-

to 1½-inch pieces, and boiling them in salted water. Use 1 teaspoon of salt per quart of water and boil for 1 to 1½ hours.

CLASSIC USES AND AFFINITIES

Latin American cuisines use cassava as a starch staple. *Cassava meal* (*farinha* or *farofa*) is popular in Brazil and Central America. *Cassava juice* (*cassareep*) flavors a pepperpot soup or stew of the same name. Cassava is also the source for tapioca.

CAULIFLOWER

BACKGROUND

Cauliflower is a mass of tiny flowers set on clustering stems. Usually the flowers are creamy white, though some cauliflower varieties are green or purple-tinged. The green leaves around the curd (flower mass) look a little like cabbage leaves; and cauliflower, being a *Brassica oleracea* var. *botrytis*, belongs to the CABBAGE species.

AVAILABILITY

Season

Some fresh cauliflower is usually available, at a price; but this is basically a fall and early-winter vegetable, peaking from September to early January. Frozen cauliflower is always in the marketplace.

Buying Tips

The curds of the fresh vegetable should be firm and compact, not spreading apart. Whatever the color of your cauliflower, look for even color without discoloration, dark spots, or bruise marks. Head size is not a reliable age criterion. The leaves should be a vivid green, untinged by yellow. Tiny green leaves peeking through the curd are acceptable. Frozen cauliflower lacks pleasing crispness.

PREPARATION

Storage

Cauliflower is very fragile, so keep it well wrapped and do not attempt to store it, even refrigerated, for more than 2 days.

Preliminaries

If cooking the cauliflower whole, trim off the excess outer leaves and rinse the crevices well with cold tap water, as the space between the leaves and the white curds tends to harbor dirt. Also gently wash the curd surfaces. If preparing the vegetables into florets, break the cauliflower into pieces of desired size, then rinse them individually. Hollowed-out raw cauliflower heads can be used to serve sauces or salad dressings at a buffet. If you have reason to suspect that insects are hiding in the head, sacrifice some tenderness and flavor and soak the cauliflower in cold salted water for half an hour to drive out the vermin.

Cooking

Cauliflower can be eaten raw as a *crudité*, so prolonged cooking is obviously not necessary for health, flavor, or tenderness. Brief cooking is all it needs: steam or simmer the florets for 5 to 10 minutes, depending on thickness. Whole heads will take 12 to 20 minutes, according to size. Overcooking leads to mushy texture, loss of nutrients, and a rank odor drifting through the house. Do not salt the cooking water, as it may toughen the curd. Adding a tablespoon of milk or a teaspoon of lemon juice to the cooking water helps keep the curd white. If you cook with hard water, though, your white cauliflower will probably pick up a yellow tinge whatever you do. There are advantages and disadvantages to cooking a whole head of cauliflower with the foliage attached. The leaves help keep the cauliflower firm and stately, but they are less delicate in taste and take longer to cook than the curd does. If you decide not to cook the leaves, save them for your stockpot or steam them with a mixture of greens. A whole head of cauliflower cooks faster if you hollow out the stem with a paring knife. A good-tasting, good-textured cauliflower puree can be made by gently sautéing raw florets in butter for about 8 to 10 minutes (adding a few drops of boiling water when it threatens to stick), combining with milk, butter, or other vegetables, then pureeing. Leftover cooked cauliflower marinated in vinaigrette makes a delicious cold salad or hors d'oeuvre. You can marinate raw florets with success, too.

Equivalents

A pound of cauliflower makes about four servings.

CLASSIC USES AND AFFINITIES

Delicate cauliflower pairs up beautifully with rich sauces such as Mornay sprinkled with chopped parsley or chives. Cauliflower with cheese or bread crumbs browned under the broiler is also appetizing in both sight and taste. The subtle sweetness of mace and the pleasing tartness of lemon juice make them good partners.

CAVIAR

Virtually all the *caviar* comes from the Caspian Sea, an 800-mile-long landlocked body of water shared by the Soviet Union and Iran. In the late 1800s, Americans were catching sturgeon in the Hudson River within or near New York City and commercially selling the caviar to Russia. Pollution and overfishing soon put that bonanza to an end. The sturgeon of the Caspian Sea are nowadays facing the same two problems as well as having to contend with declining water levels. Some experts foresee doom for the caviar industry, others are a little more optimistic.

Varieties

Beluga, Osetrova, Sevruga, and Sterlet: The three principal types of sturgeon are beluga, osetrova, and sevruga, in descending order of size. The *beluga* ("white" in Russian) sturgeon, which can grow 15 feet long and weigh a ton, produces the softest and largest eggs, somewhere between a BB and a pea in diameter. Americans consider beluga the *ne plus ultra* of caviar, but beluga has no corner on quality. The color of the caviar can range from steel-gray to nearly black; the color is a function of development (the eggs are palest just before spawning). To our tastes, the steel-gray eggs are better than the darker ones, but not by as much as some gourmets insist or as the price differential suggests. *Osetrova* caviar varies from greenish-gold to brown and is smaller, firmer, and less expensive than beluga caviar. Few American stores carry it. *Sevruga* caviar, which is also firmer than beluga, ranks second in popularity in this country and usually is the least expensive, though still dear by all but a Greek shipping tycoon's standard. Some epicures consider the grayish-black sevruga the best caviar of them all. Most well-traveled connoisseurs, however, opt for the golden caviar of the rare *sterlet* sturgeon that was once reserved for the Shah of Iran or the Czar of Russia.

Pressed Caviar: Eggs that are too immature, too fragile, or damaged by mishandling are sold as *payasnaya*, pressed caviar. This product, which may contain a blend of the eggs of more than one type of Caspian Sea sturgeon, is often an excellent value compared to the whole-egg beluga, osetrova, or sevruga caviars. It will definitely not look as pretty, and it will probably not taste nearly as good, but for the price it is nothing to complain about.

Malossol caviar: *Malossol* means "light salt" in Russian and is applied to the eggs of any type of Caspian sea sturgeon (beluga, osetrova, sevruga, etc.) that are in such excellent condition that only the minimum quantity of salt need be added to help preserve the caviar for shipment. Malossol caviar is never pasteurized.

Pasteurized caviar: Only the best egg specimens are sold fresh. The rest are pasteurized and are typically packaged in vacuum-sealed tins or jars. Pasteurization partially cooks the eggs, giving them a noticeably chewy skin.

Artificial "sturgeon caviar": With less and less genuine caviar available, the Soviet Union has created an artificial caviar made with milk albumen and casein thickened with gelatin and given a caviarlike taste by the addition of sturgeon sperm, then dyed black, gray, or red. We have sampled this product in Moscow and have found it to be a dreadful substitute for the true caviar.

Buying Tips

The quality of caviar you eat depends upon a number of variables beyond whether the egg-bearing fish was a beluga or whatever. Other influences include the condition of the individual fish, how well the processor, shippers, and merchant performed their jobs, and the freshness of the caviar. Except in the case of pressed caviar, the individual eggs should be separate, not mashed together. The skins should have a lustrous glow and should not be shriveled. Avoid caviar that has an oily or milky surface. If the merchant allows, sniff the contents. There should be little odor and that should be reminiscent of the first springtime whiff of the sea. Fishiness or other "off" odors are negative signs. Merchant allowing, sample-taste the contents. The flavor should not be salty, bitter, sour, or hint of additives. The texture should be smooth, not chewy. When buying in ounce portions out of a large tin, find out when the tin was opened. One hopes that the caviar was first exposed to the air just before you walked in the door, but certainly not more than a week or two before, even if it was properly stored. Price and quality of caviar often do not go hand in hand. Like Chablis and Burgundy wines, more beluga caviar is sold than is produced—there is too much profitable temptation for a tradesman to mislead the customers. Check the label or, if the caviar has been removed from its original container, ask to see the label. Because of trade tradition, one pound of caviar weighs 14, not 16, ounces, so if a merchant sells 1 ounce of caviar for $10 and 1 pound for $140, he is not giving you a quantity discount.

PREPARATION

Storage

Unopened tins and jars of pasteurized caviar can be kept in a cool, dark spot for 2 to 4 months (the higher its quality, the less time it should be stored, because better caviars have more subtleties to lose). Once opened, keep the container tightly closed in the refrigerator for up to 1 to 2 weeks. Fresh caviar is very perishable and should be kept, ideally, at about 32°F. It freezes at about 28°F, a temperature to which it should never be subjected. Above 40°F, the eggs rapidly spoil; even an hour at 40°F or higher can cause irreparable damage. A tin or jar of fresh caviar can be kept at 32°F to 35°F for 1 to 4 weeks, depending on its original condition and on how often and how long you have exposed its contents to room-temperature air.

Serving

Caviar is traditionally served in a crystal

bowl (though glass will do), which is set inside another bowl filled with shaved ice. Purists simply set the original caviar container in the ice-filled bowl; they rightly argue that transferring the caviar from container to bowl would unnecessarily bruise the fragile eggs. Ice is absolutely necessary to keep the caviar cold and hinder its deterioration. A silver spoon is the classic serving implement, but some metallurgically-minded gourmets prefer wooden or glass spoons because silver can tarnish in contact with caviar. Most Americans serve caviar accompanied by lemon wedges, butter, chopped raw onions or scallions, chopped cooked egg yolk and whites, cream cheese, sour cream, and black pepper. These are abominations if you have good caviar, because they do nothing but mask the subtle flavor. Some food writers assert that these accompaniments are permissable to mask the taste of less-than-good caviar; we say do not eat such caviar in the first place. What should be served with caviar is crustless, toasted, high-quality white bread. Rye bread is sometimes too strongly flavored; buckwheat blinis always are. Ice-cold vodka is the classic accompanying drink, though *brut* champagne of good pedigree is worthy, too.

"CAVIAR" AND OTHER ROES

BACKGROUND

The eggs of fish are *roe*. Caviar is a term that should be reserved strictly for the roe of the sturgeon. Only female fish, of course, give roe, though the males do have edible sperm which is called *milt*, but it is not as widely prized.

AVAILABILITY

Some processors foist onto the unwary American public psuedocaviar made by dyeing black the light-hued roe of, for instance, the inferior lump-fish. Such products are detestable—look at the label carefully for the name of the species of the fish. The unadulterated roe of certain other fishes such as salmon and shad, however, can be good in their own right if properly purchased and prepared.

The red salmon roe is best when the fish was caught just as it was starting its upstream migration to its spawning grounds. The roe that comes from fish caught while still living in the sea is not as pale in color nor as delicate in flavor.

PREPARATION

The Japanese enjoy salmon roe raw. (In fact, nearly all roe can be eaten raw if it is fresh and in good condition.) *Shad roe*, an Eastern American speciality, can be broiled or baked, but it is at its best when it is parboiled, then sauteed whole in butter. The minuscule eggs come, and are cooked and served, in a brownish-red membrane pouch that is, on the average, about 5 inches long, 2 inches wide and 1/2 inch thick.

The eggs of almost any other fish are edible, too, including those of the *alewife, bluefish, carp, catfish, haddock, herring, mackerel, mullet, red snapper, striped bass, weakfish, whitefish* and *whiting*. If the fish is medium-sized or larger, the roe is usually removed and cooked separately. With small fish, the eggs are often left in it and cooked with the whole fish.

CELERIAC

BACKGROUND

Celery knob and *celery root* are other names for this 3-inch-thick oval, root vegetable with a rough, fibrous, knobby brown peel bearded with rootlets. It is not the root of ordinary celery, but the root of a celery relative widely grown in France for its firm flesh and unique celerylike flavor. The green leaves are not eaten.

AVAILABILITY

Celeriac is available from October through April.

Buying Tips

Small celeriacs are best; the larger ones may have too high a ratio of woody core to chewy flesh. Press the bulb, especially the top. If there is a yielding soft spot, the bulb has internal decay. To minimize waste in preparation, pick relatively smooth bulbs with few rootlets. Since celeriacs are gnarled and loaded with rootlets, these are relative terms.

PREPARATION

Storage

Without cutting into the flesh, trim the rootlets and leaves (if any) soon after purchase. Celeriac can be refrigerated for several days in the vegetable compartment.

Preliminaries

Wash, slice off top and bottom, and pare. The skin is tough enough to defeat some vegetable peelers; a paring knife may be a better choice. Keep prepared celeriac in acidulated water until you cook it; that will prevent oxidation and discoloration.

Cooking

Celeriac can be eaten raw or cooked. Allow 20 to 30 minutes for steaming or boiling whole vegetables, 5 to 15 minutes for portions, depending on thickness. Celeriac may also be sautéed, mashed, or added to soups and stews.

Equivalents

Small to medium celeriac knobs weigh about 1/3 to 1/2 pound each; the first would provide one average serving.

CLASSIC USES AND AFFINITIES

The deep, almost musky flavor of celeriac is complemented by basil, parsley, tarragon, or oregano, and is enlivened by lemon juice and mustard. Celeriac puree is very good with richly flavored roast meat such as beef. *Céleri rémoulade* (raw or lightly blanched celeriac with mustard mayonnaise) is a classic hors d'oeuvre in fancy French restaurants.

CELERY

BACKGROUND

Apium graveolens (var. *dulce*) is one of the workhorses of the western world cuisine. In our country it is virtually mandatory for the weight reducer and practically indispensable when preparing *crudités* as well as egg, chicken, or tuna salad (but do not overuse it as a stretcher). Because you can use the whole celery (stalk, leaves, seeds and all) and can store it for a reasonable length of time, celery returns a lot on a moderate investment.

Varieties

Most celery sold in the United States today is *Pascal celery*, an unbleached green variety which forms large bunches. Some "*golden*" *celery* is sold; it has been blanched (grown beneath soil to prevent the development of chlorophyll) and offers less nutrition. *Celery hearts* are the tender and desirable centers of the celery stalk that have had the larger top leaves and coarser outer ribs removed. Technically speaking, a bunch of celery is called a stalk; each branch is called a rib.

AVAILABILITY

Celery is abundant the year around.

Buying Tips

A good stalk of celery is medium-sized, unblemished, and crisp; the ribs are rigid, not flexible. Soft or darkened spots, and chips missing from the ribs are bad signs. So are seedstems: round, almost solid stems in the center in place of normal heart formation. Such celery is seriously overmature.

PREPARATION

Storage

Celery will stay fresh from five to seven days if refrigerated in a plastic bag. Remove the ribs from the stalk as you need them.

Preliminaries

Scrub the celery—especially the inner surface of the base of the celery ribs; these are gathering places for dirt. Trim celery ribs of thickened bases and leaves, then use the rest of the rib whole, cut it lengthwise into sticks, dice it, or cut it into diagonal "U" shapes. If eating celery raw as a *crudité*, crisp the ribs for an hour or two in refrigerated ice water. If you do not serve the leaves, save them along with the trimmings for your stockpot.

Cooking

Celery is usually eaten raw; it can also be added, with advantage, to soups and stews. Chinese-American restaurants wishing to stretch a dish will load their woks with celery in lieu of more expensive Chinese vegetables. Celery hearts are often braised for about ten to fifteen minutes, sometimes with a rich cream or cheese sauce.

CLASSIC USES AND AFFINITIES

Cheese and peanut butter are among the many foods that contrast agreeably in taste, texture and color with raw celery. A celery rib makes a flavorful, color-contrasting swizzle stick in a Bloody Mary.

CELERY SEED

BACKGROUND

Celery seed is the fruit of a plant which is related to, but not identical with, head celery and celeriac. Celery seed is native to Central Asia and the Mediterranean; the major commercial sources are India and France. *Celery salt* is a mixture of ground celery seed and plain salt. The taste of celery seed is slightly bitter; the seeds themselves are crunchy. (See HERBS AND SPICES for information on buying, storing, cooking, etc.)

CLASSIC USES AND AFFINITIES

Celery seed can be used to accent dishes where head celery would be appropriate. The seed goes very well with tomato juice and tomato aspic. Clams and oysters have an affinity with celery seed; so do egg dishes, bland vegetables, baked fish, and mayonnaise salads such as potato salad and cole slaw.

CEREAL GRAINS

BACKGROUND

The world's most popular cereal grains are *barley, corn, millet, oats, rice, rye, sorghum, triticale, wheat,* and *wild rice.* (*Buckwheat* is not really a grain, but we have included it here because cooks generally treat it as such. For CORN, RICE, and WHEAT, see those entries.)

Cereal grains are the seeds of grasses. Each grain contains a *germ* (embryo) from which a new plant can grow; an *endosperm* (the starchy interior) to help feed the potential new plant; the *bran* (one or more ultra-thin surface layers); and perhaps an outer protective *husk* or *hull.* All components except the husk are edible.

PREPARATION

Most grains such as wheat or rice need to be threshed to remove the inedible husks and other debris. These grains can then be cooked and eaten whole; or they can be further processed: cracked, rolled into flakes, or ground to a coarse meal or a fine flour. Often the bran and the germ are removed from rice and wheat to prolong their storage life and to satisfy consumer preference for a white product. Much of the texture, flavor, and nutrition are also removed in the process.

Grains are starchy and therefore filling. The traditional peasant meal in much of the world is a hunk of bread or a plate of cracked grain with a small amount of vegetable or meat mixture. Often the sauce is heavily flavored to enliven the bland-tasting grain. From the nutritionist's point of view, even whole grains provide incomplete protein—their protein is low in isoleucine and lysine—and therefore should be supplemented with foods such as meat, fish, beans, brewer's yeast, or milk products. In short, the peasants were right after all.

Storage

Cereal grains and flours should be stored in an airtight container and placed in a dry, cool, dark spot. If you store them in their original bags or boxes, be very careful about insect infestation and moisture absorption. Once the original bag or box is opened, we recommend transferring the contents to a glass jar or metal canister with a tight-fitting lid. Unless you plan to use whole grains, and especially whole-grain flour, within a week or two, we suggest you refrigerate them as the high oil content of the germ within each grain promotes rancidity. Whole-grain (brown) rice will have longer non-refrigerated shelf life than most other whole grains, but it, too, must not be left at room temperature for more than a month.

Varieties

Barley: Most of the *barley* (*Hordeum vulgare*) grown in the Western world winds up as animal fodder—or in liquid form for human consumption. The process that turns beans into beansprouts turns barley into malted barley, an eminently useful product that is used in making beer and whiskey. The Scots, having all that barley around anyway, evolved dishes such as *Scotch broth* that combine barley with mutton and other local staples. Barley is esteemed in Japan and China. *Tsampa,* or barley meal, is basic to the Tibetan diet. Eastern European cooks mix barley with fresh or dried mushrooms as a side dish or in thick soups. Both *whole-grain* and *pearl* barley are available. Pearl barley, which has had the bran removed, comes in coarse, medium, and fine grinds. Barley is also sometimes ground into *flour.* If you want to cook some barley *porridge* at home the simple way, add pearl barley to a pot of lightly salted boiling water (1 cup barley per 3 cups water), cover and simmer until tender and the water has been absorbed, which will take 40 minutes, more or less. *Barley water,* an old-fashioned nourishment for invalids, is made by boiling barley and lemon peels in a large quantity of water, then straining.

Buckwheat: As we mentioned earlier, *buckwheat* (*Fagopyrum esculentum*) does not come from a grass, so it is not a true grain. Its relatives are rhubarb, sorrel, and dock. The commercial forms of buckwheat are *groats* (hulled kernels) and *flour*. Buckwheat groats, which come in coarse, medium, and fine grinds, are sometimes called *kasha*, but kasha really is an Eastern European generic name for various grains or grain pilafs. Buckwheat flour, which comes in light or dark hues and is often mixed with wheat flour to mitigate its assertive flavor, makes good if leaden pancakes and blinis. *Soba* (a buckwheat noodle) is a popular fast food in Japan. One traditional way to cook buckwheat groats is to pour them into a pot of lightly salted boiling water (1 cup buckwheat to 2 cups water), then cover the pot and gently simmer the groats for 15 to 20 minutes; they will double in volume. Or mix 1 cup of groats with a beaten egg; then toast them, en masse, in an ungreased frying pan until the concoction separates (proof that the egg is cooked); finally add 2 cups of boiling water or broth, cover, and steam for 15 to 20 minutes. *Kasha varenishkas*, Eastern European Jewish soul food, combines groats cooked this way with lots of fat, onions, mushrooms, and bowtie-shaped pasta—delicious, but loaded with calories. You can get a distinctive buckwheat flavor in bread even if the buckwheat flour comprises only 10 percent of the total. To develop maximum gluten, add the buckwheat flour after the lighter flours have been incorporated—and near the end of the kneading period.

Corn: See CORN entry.

Millet: The tiny, pale yellow spheres of *millet* (*Panicum miliaceum*) are full of high-quality protein. In the Western world they are unjustly neglected and are usually used as animal fodder or relegated to birdseed, though some American cooks convert whole millet into porridge and millet flour into breads. Millet is the leading staple in some of the economically disadvantaged regions of Africa and Asia. Millet grain has no pronounced taste of its own, but that only makes it a better background for complex, highly-spiced main dishes. A basic recipe calls for adding one cup of millet to a pot of two cups of rapidly boiling, lightly salted water. Then cover and gently simmer the millet for about 25 to 30 minutes. The millet will double in volume. Sauce and season to taste.

Oats: Long associated with nosebags and breakfast cereal, *oats* (*Avena sativa*) win the nutritional first prize in competition with the other cereal grains. The whole oat, husk and all, is fed to animals. Human stomachs prefer the oat *groat* (the hulled berry), which is almost as nutritious. *Oatmeal* is commercially marketed in this country in three basic forms: regular, quick-cooking, and less often, Scotch. *Regular oatmeal*, the type most often found on grocery shelves, is rolled oats, made by crushing the groat between steel rollers. Because this oatmeal comes in various thicknesses, it is essential to check the processor's label for specific cooking times. Whatever you do, never overcook oatmeal or it will congeal into a sticky, gummy mass. Since standard-cooking oatmeal is so quick and easy to cook, we see no reason to use the *quick-cooking* variety, which is vastly inferior in terms of flavor and texture. It only saves you a few minutes of waiting (not working) time, and you still must wash the pot. Genuine *Scotch* or *Irish oatmeal*, which can be found in some health-food stores, requires longer cooking than the regular-cooking type, partially because the groats are cut into coarse pieces. Oat groats further pulverized make *oat flour*. It is not rich in gluten, so it is not good as the sole flour in bread. However, the oat flour has antioxidant properties, so bread containing oat flour stays fresh longer.

Rice: See RICE entry.

Rye: *Secale cereale* is a hearty grain that flourishes in damp, cold climates and is an Eastern European staple. *Rye* *flour* has no appreciable gluten, so bread made from pure rye flour will be heavy-textured and a low riser. A standard-sized slice of rye bread (customarily made with a combination of rye and wheat flour) is more filling than a slice of whole-wheat or white bread because it is much denser. *Light rye* bread or flour contains a large quantity of wheat flour which most likely has been sifted to remove some of the bran. *Dark rye* (or true *pumpernickel*) contains little or no wheat flour and usually has most of its original bran. Many modern bakers add molasses to achieve the sought after dark hue. Whether light or dark, rye flour must be refrigerated. One hazard of rye culture is the grain's susceptibility to the fungus *ergot*, a natural psychedelic with extremely unpleasant effects known collectively as "St. Anthony's fire," responsible for several outbreaks of mass psychosis. Fortunately, modern agricultural methods in this country have virtually eliminated ergotism, and you can enjoy rye bread or rye whiskey with impunity. *Whole rye berries*, found in some specialty shops and health-food stores, make a change-of-pace starch side dish: Add the berries to thrice their volume of boiling, lightly salted water, cover and gently simmer for 40 to 60 minutes (depending on berry dryness). Remove the covered pot from the heat, briefly and gently stir the rye, and let it rest for five minutes. Drain off excess water (if any), then season, sauce (with butter, for instance), and serve.

Sorghum: As a food for humans, the cereal grain called *sorghum* (*Sorghum vulgare*) is more popular in the poor, semi-arid tropical areas of Africa and Asia than in America. It was first introduced to our country as a low-cost food for slaves, who often transformed it into a porridge. Today, much of the sorghum crop ends up as fodder; sweet sorghum is used as a substitute for sugar cane to make molasses.

Triticale: Wheat belongs to the genus *Triticum*, rye to the genus *Secale*. A hybrid of hard, red, winter wheat, durum wheat and rye has been produced called *triticale* (four syllables, long *a*). Triticale is a hardy, high-protein grain with a very palatable sweet flavor. It is low in gluten and therefore not a baker's dream.

Wheat: See WHEAT entry.

Wild Rice: The thin, dark grains of *Zizania aquatica* do not look much like rice grains, and the two are not related botanically. Both, however, grow in shallow water and their flavors are compatible, so they are often mixed together as an economy measure to offset wild rice's very high price. Wild rice is scarce because it cannot be successfully commercially cultivated. It grows where it pleases, in modest quantities. To keep this rare plant from being harvested to oblivion, it has been made illegal in parts of the country to use any harvesting method except the traditional, deliberately inefficient, Indian way. Moreover, the harvester must be an Indian. You paddle your canoe up to a stand of wild rice and whack the plants with a flail. Some of the grains fall into your harvesting box, some fall into the water to propagate new plants. When buying wild rice, remember the best (and most expensive) are the whole, unbroken grains. A basic way to cook 1 cup of wild rice is to wash the grains thoroughly in several changes of water, then pour them (gradually, over 10 seconds) into 1 quart of boiling, lightly salted water. Cover tightly, and simmer until the water is absorbed—about 30 to 40 minutes, depending on the storage age of the grains. Season to taste, sauce with butter, and serve. Wild rice is especially delicious with roasted hearty meat or game, either as a vegetable side dish or as a stuffing.

CHAMOMILE

BACKGROUND

The name *Chamomile* (also spelled as pronounced—*camomile*) is applied to two medicinal herbs, *Anthemis nobilis* and *Matricaria chamomilla*. Tea brewed from 1 teaspoon of dried white flowers per cup of hot water has a host of traditionally ascribed virtues. It is supposed to cure indigestion and other stomach ailments, headaches, and general malaise. Italian wives use it as a sort of indirect birth-control method; they fondly believe that a cup of chamomile tea after dinner will send a husband straight to bed—and put him to sleep instantly. An after-shampoo rinse with chamomile tea brings out the highlights in blond hair. The *Matricaria* chamomile can be one of the herbs in vermouth; cigarettes of dried *Anthemis* chamomile are said to help asthma sufferers breathe freely. Chamomile is usable as long as it retains its sweet, applelike scent. (See HERBS AND SPICES for information on buying, storing, cooking, etc.)

CHARD

BACKGROUND

Chard (*Beta vulgaris*, often called *Swiss chard*) is easy to grow. People have been cultivating it for over 2,000 years. It was first introduced into the United States in 1806. A small patch produces a superfluity of foot-long edible stalks and leaves, the latter reminiscent of spinach leaves. Some varieties are reddish, but most are either dark green (with a fuller flavor) or light green (milder).

AVAILABILITY

If you relish chard, you may have to plant your own; it is rarely available commercially, as it does not ship or store well. The peak season is mid-summer through early fall.

Buying Tips

Yellow leaves are overmature and will give an off-taste. Stalks and leaves should be crisp.

PREPARATION

Storage

Wrapped chard can be stored in the refrigerator for 2 or 3 days.

Cooking

Wash the chard well in cold tap water. Separate the leaves from the stalks. Cut the stalks into 2- to 3-inch lengths. Steam or simmer them for about 12 minutes, or until tender yet firm. Cook the leaves separately in a covered pot for about 4 minutes, using only the water clinging to them after washing.

CHAYOTE

BACKGROUND

Chayote (*Sechium edule*) is also called the *vegetable pear, mirliton, mango squash*, and *christophine*. This climbing-vine squash grows all year round in warm regions like Mexico, Central America, Florida, and other states bordering the Gulf of Mexico. Chayote is typically ribbed, cool green, and pear-shaped. It ranges from 3 to 10 inches. Some varieties have fine spines.

AVAILABILITY

Chayote is available throughout the year but makes the best eating mid-fall through mid-spring.

Buying Tips

The chayote should be firm, not soft or wrinkled.

PREPARATION

Storage

Raw chayotes will keep up to one week in the refrigerator.

Cooking

Young chayotes do not have to be peeled before cooking. The vegetable can be substituted in any recipe for summer squash. The taste of the flesh is mild with a hint of quinine bitterness.

Equivalents

As a rough estimate, the average chayote will weigh 1½ to 2 pounds and provide three to five servings.

CHEESE, NATURAL

BACKGROUND

Cheese, one of the most nutritious of foods, has been made by man since animals were first domesticated some 10,000 years ago. Legend has it that an Arab traveling through the desert with a supply of milk stored in a sheep's stomach found that the milk had curdled at the end of the day—into cheese. People have been enjoying cheese throughout the ages in all parts of the world for its keeping qualities, its wide variety of flavors, aromas, and textures, and its high level of protein. Cheese can be made from any mammal's milk, including that of cows, horses, sheep, and goats—familiar to most people; but it can also be made from the milk of horses, yaks, whales, reindeer—and yes, even humans.

Cheesemaking

The basic cheesemaking process is simple: all milk will eventually sour and separate into soft, white curds and whey, the remaining thin liquid. Yet a host of factors affect the eventual product, and no two cheeses will be alike if made in different places. Climate, soil, vegetation, altitude, economic development, taste, kind of milk-producing animals, temperature and handling in curing, how and where cured, additives—all will affect the eventual product. The type and quality of milk used—and whether the curds, whey or both are used—are of paramount importance. A cow eating bitter food will give bitter milk—and a bitter cheese. In most cases, the milk is first separated by the addition of rennet, a curdling agent taken from the stomachs of young calves. It is the curing process that brings out the various flavors and aromas in cured (or aged) cheeses made from rennet curds. Small variations in time, temperature, and humidity of curing determine the character of the cheese.

Varieties

The most popular way of classifying cheeses is according to hardness. The hard cheeses keep longest, and hold their shape well when cut. Semisoft cheeses can be resilient or crumbly to the touch, but do not become runny. Soft cheeses keep for the shortest length of time, contain the most moisture, and are the most spreadable.

Perhaps a more useful way to divide cheese from a cook's and diner's standpoint is as follows:

- Blue
- Firm to Semifirm
- Surface-Ripened
- French Double- and Triple-Cremes
- Fresh
- Grating
- French Goat
- Miscellaneous

Blue Cheeses

These are characterized by blue or blue-green veins, which are widespread and evenly distributed throughout the white interior of the cheese. Although virtually all are made from cow's milk, the most famous, Roquefort, is made from sheep's milk. In texture, blues are semisoft and sometimes slightly crumbly. They are sharp and piquant with a creamy texture, which should look moist, not granular. When too old, they will look dry and cakey. Because they easily dry out, they are best stored wrapped in a damp cloth or covered with a cheese dome, and refrigerated.

Roquefort, if authentic, will carry a sheep symbol on its foil wrapping. In terms of quality, this is an erratic cheese: some is superb, most is good, and some is inferior. Therefore, if possible, sample it first when choosing; don't buy it if it is too salty, dried-out, overly crumbly, or lacking in creaminess—or if its interior is grayish-white or has too few delicate blue-green veins. This king of the blues has a strong, sharp taste.

Stilton is considered the finest of the English cheeses by many turophiles. It has a strong, ripe, intense flavor, but is less strong than its French rival, Roquefort. It should be moist and slightly flaky. The paste is off-white, with blue-green veins which tend to concentrate towards the center of the paste. The tradition of scooping out the cheese and pouring port into it will only distort the flavor and dry the cheese out.

Gorgonzola is the famous Italian blue. It has a wrinkled, red crust, blue-green or pale-green veins, and a creamy white paste. Usually packed in aluminum foil, it spreads well and is excellent as a dessert cheese.

Bleu de Bresse is a popular French blue: rich, creamy and moist, with blue streaks in the body and a thin, pebbly, pinkish crust.

Pipo Crem, from France, is similar to Bleu de Bresse, but yellower in the paste; moist and creamy, it is very delicate in taste, milder than most other blues.

Danablu (or *Danish Blue*) is a rich, very salty but sweet cream-white blue cheese from Denmark.

American Blue is generally a blander, less distinguished cheese than its European counterparts.

Firm to Semifirm Cheeses

This group includes a variety of cheese families, each of which share certain characteristics of taste and texture. In terms of condition, these are perhaps the easiest cheeses to choose: if they look good, they probably are. There should be no surface cracks or flecks of white mold in the body of these cheeses, and those with rinds should not look too dark near the rind. These cheeses are best stored in the refrigerator, tightly wrapped in plastic wrap or aluminum foil.

Cheddar family: Cheddar is the most popular cheese in the United States, both as a natural cheese and as the basis for processed cheese. Cheddar ranges in color from white to pale yellow to pumpkin orange, the color produced by adding annatto-seed dye. Its flavor comes with aging; a young cheddar will taste mild and a mature cheddar will be very sharp. In no case should a cheddar taste bitter, or leave a bitter aftertaste; "sharp" does not mean bitter. Cheddar may be stored for a long time without losing its excellent quality.

Cheddar was born in England. The classic English cheddar is hard, with a natural rind, and a light yellow-white interior. It should not be crumbly.

Cheshire, the oldest of English cheeses, is mellow, rich, and medium-strong; it is firm in texture but not as compact as an English cheddar.

Gloucester is a firm, satiny-smooth, buttery cheese, usually slightly pungent; the cheese body should not look greasy or grainy.

Leicester is moister than English cheddar, with a thin, smooth rind; the interior should be a uniform orange or pale red. Mild when young, it becomes medium-sharp when aged, with a hint of lemon, and is a good melting cheese.

Dunlop, a mild Scottish cheese, resembles a young English cheddar, but is moister and creamier, with a smooth, white interior.

American cheddars usually come in rindless blocks, or are paraffin-dipped. Most American types are orange in color and are labeled "mild," "medium," "sharp," and "very sharp," according to the age of the cheese—but be forewarned that the sharpness of the mass-marketed brands is overstated; for instance, "very sharp" is merely sharp. The New World cheddars should be firm to the touch, not crumbly. Those with mottled spots may be either bitter or damaged.

Herkimer County, produced in New York State, is sharp, fairly dry, and a light ivory in color; and of high quality.

Longhorn is a good, mild cheddar traditionally produced in Wisconsin in the shape of a horn.

Tillamook is an excellent medium-sharp cheddar from Oregon.

Colby, also called *Colby Cheddar* or *Crowley,* is usually orange. Made in Vermont and Wisconsin, it has a softer, moister texture than standard cheddar, and a mellow flavor.

Coon is a dark, crumbly, very sharp cheddar; it is considered one of the best of the fully cured, tangy American cheddars.

Cheddars are also produced in many other countries, including New Zealand. In Canada, *Cherry Hill* and *Black Diamond* cheddar-types are exceptionally fine.

Swiss family: The genuine Swiss cheese in the traditional sense is *Emmentaler,* produced only in Switzerland. It is a firm, smooth, elastic cheese of a light yellow color with large holes in the interior, carrying the words "Switzerland Swiss" or "Switzerland" stamped on the rind in red and radiating from the center of the cheese like spokes of a wheel. The characteristic holes, or eyes, in the cheese, develop in the curd as the cheese ripens. Flavor ranges from mild to piquant, with a nutty, fruity, zesty quality.

Another famous cheese from Switzerland is *Gruyère,* similar to Emmentaler, but moister and creamier, with a sharper, more robust flavor. It melts easily and is one of the classic cheeses for fondue. France produces a good copy of Gruyère, though the Gallic version is less tangy than the original. Two other well-known Swiss family cheeses from Switzerland are *Raclette* (famed for its melt-by-the-fireside use), and *Appenzeller,* soaked in cider or wine and spices during the ripening process.

Denmark makes several types of Swiss-style cheeses: *Samsø,* which becomes pungent with age, is the classic Danish Swiss; *Danbø,* quite similar to Samso, but less distinguished in flavor; and *Tybo,* resembling Samsø, though some Tybos have caraway seeds.

Norway produces a good Swiss-style cheese called *Jarlsberg.*

The American Swiss-style cheese is much blander than the European versions.

Trappist: This is a term used for monastery-type cheeses, which were produced at one time by Trappist monks. *Port-Salut* (sometimes called *Port-du-Salut*) is the prototypical Trappist cheese, soft yet firm, mild in flavor, with a creamy yellow interior. There are a great number of brands like Port-Salut. *Saint-Paulin,* slightly firmer than Port-Salut, has more "bite" and a lingering taste. It should not be bitter or gummy.

Gouda and Edam: Produced in Holland, either Gouda or Edam is one of the safest cheeses to buy; if it looks good, it probably is. *Gouda* is a whole milk cheese with a creamy, nutlike buttery-mild flavor. When aged, it acquires a tangy, more pronounced nutty flavor. It is sold in the U.S. in a wax-coated flattened sphere. A *Baby Gouda* is the same cheese in a smaller package. Like Gouda, *Edam* has a mellow, nutty flavor, but is partly made with skim milk and has a lower fat content.

Others:

Bel Paese is a soft, mild, sweet, creamy-yellow cheese. It is produced both in Italy and the New World. The Italian version is superior and can be easily identified by the map of Italy on the wrapper. The one produced in America, on the other hand, displays a map of the Americas.

Tilsit or *Tilsiter*, originally a German cheese, has a creamy texture with small eyes in the cheese body and a mild to slightly tangy flavor. With age it acquires a sharp, full flavor. *Havarti* is the Danish equivalent of Tilsit.

Provolone, a mellow-to-sharp, salty Italian cheese, which becomes much stronger with age, is smooth and firm, and a creamy yellow-white in color. The American type is blander and tastes quite different.

Monterey Jack (or *Jack* or *Monterey*) is a mild U.S. product with a pale yellow interior. When old, it makes a good grating cheese.

Fontina is an Italian mountain cheese with a semifirm texture and usually a few small eyes. Its flavor is slightly nutty to almost smoky. It is both a table and a cooking cheese. You can easily distinguish between the authentic Italian version from Val d'Aosta and the Danish imitation: the first has a light tan rind while the latter has a bright red rind.

Surface-Ripened Cheeses

As the name implies, these cheeses begin ripening on the surface. The beneficial surface mold imparts some of the characteristic flavor, body, and texture to the interior of the cheese. Most surface-ripened cheeses have downy-soft, thin rinds that vary in color from white to rose to mottled brown and white. Others have thin rinds with a slightly varnished appearance. All are creamy-smooth when ripe—but be forewarned that many surface-ripened cheeses are sold underripe or overripe. If possible, press the cheese gently from the edges to the center; if ripe, the center should be as resilient as the edges, and, once opened, there should be no hard chalky line running through the center. The interior should look creamy, slightly runny, and glossy throughout. Don't buy a surface-ripened cheese that has an acrid, ammoniac, or barnyardy scent, even if your cheesemonger insists that "that's the way French gourmets love them." They don't. Surface-ripened cheeses are generally not in the best of condition during the middle and late summer months.

Brie: Called the queen of cheeses, this famous French flat, disc-shaped product is characterized by a soft white edible crust and (when ripe) a satiny, pale-yellow body. It has a savory lingering flavor, sometimes a touch earthy, always harmonious. It is best to buy fresh-cut rather than precut wedges. Once a whole brie wheel is cut open, it will no longer ripen—it will just start to decline in flavor and taste. It is extremely perishable and should be bought bulging with ripeness and slightly runny, and eaten within 24 hours, if not sooner. A cut piece of brie is best not refrigerated if you plan to eat it within the next 12 hours; tightly wrap it in plastic and store it in a cool spot.

Camembert: Another famous French cheese, Camembert is a complex, delicate, yet piquant cheese when good, with a supple, yellow, smooth, very soft creamy texture at its peak. When overripe, it is almost fluid and must be eaten immediately, if at all. Prewrapped wedges sold in U.S. in supermarkets bear little resemblance to the French product. And buying the Gallic version is no guarantee of satisfaction, as quality varies markedly.

There are a number of other well-known surface-ripened cheeses: *Carré de l'Est*, a French cheese similar to Camembert but blander and less complex in flavor. It has a downy white rind and a soft ivory paste and is marketed in a box. It keeps well for a number of days if properly stored: it and all other boxed and wrapped cheeses are best kept in the warmest spot of your refrigerator. Once opened, they should be eaten as soon as possible. *Coulommiers* is less subtle than a Brie in flavor, but with a nutty, sweet-almond flavor. It has a downy, white rind and a soft and creamy interior, and is marketed in a slightly larger box than a Camembert in the U.S. *Pont l'Evêque*, one of France's best-liked cheeses, is rich and pronounced in flavor, with a lingering taste. Small, flat, and square, it has a soft, pale-yellow body with tiny irregular holes and, when ripe, a golden-brown skin. *Reblochon* is a mild, creamy rich, rather nutty cheese with an ivory-hued, thick, supple body. This French Alpine cheese takes on bitterness when too old. *Beaumont* is a creamy, mild, yet earthy cheese. *Tomme* (or *Tome*) *de Savoie* is an ivory-colored cheese with a natural red-orange rind; it tastes mild and nutty when young, and becomes stronger with age. *Taleggio* hails from northern Italy. This is a square, flat, pale-yellow or ivory cheese, smooth and creamy with a slightly tart edge in flavor. *Munster* is a pungent cheese with a flavor a bit earthy or mushroomy. It sometimes has a rough reddish rind and a yellowish, semisoft interior with many small eyes. This Alsatian or German-produced cheese should be moist. (Note: American muenster has nothing in common with European munster other than its name. It is a mild, unassertive simple cheese, and is not surface-ripened.)

Strong-smelling: Members of this category of cheeses do not generally taste as pungent as their aromas may suggest—but they are quite strong. Although they can smell overwhelming or almost rank, they should not smell of ammonia. It is advisable to keep them stored in airtight containers in the refrigerator to keep their smell from affecting other foods. Some of the best-known: *Limburger* is a redolent, semisoft cheese with a thin rind and a plump, resilient white body. It was originally produced at Limburg, Belgium, though there is a copy now made in America. *Liederkranz* is a U.S.-invented relative of Limburger; as American cheeses go, it is not a bad one. Milder in flavor and aroma than Limburger, this pale yellow, spreadable cheese should smell pungent and full, but not acrid, and is pungent to the taste. *Handkäse* ("hand cheese") is made today both in Germany and the U.S. from sour milk or skimmed and sour buttermilk. It has a white-yellow, thick, gelatinous interior and a very strong smell; it can be as strong as or stronger than Limburger. It ranges in taste from mild to pungent and, like all strong-smelling cheeses, is considered to be an acquired taste.

French Double- and Triple-Crème Cheeses

Extremely rich, soft and creamy, mild and milk-sweet in flavor, the crème cheeses are distinguished by their high butterfat content, due to the cream added during the cheesemaking process. By French law, double-crèmes must contain at least 60 percent butterfat, and triple-crèmes 75 percent. Their rich taste makes them suitable as a dessert cheese. When ripe, they are almost runny, and should be eaten at room temperature for maximum enjoyment. *Boursault* is a rich triple-crème with a soft downy rind, rich, delicate, and slightly tangy. *Caprice des Dieux* is a double-crème, buttery-rich with a white crust and ivory interior. It comes prewrapped, shaped in an oval loaf. *L'Explorateur* is a triple-crème with a very rich, salty, buttery, tangy flavor. *Crema Dania* (or *Danica*), a rich, delicate, pale-white rectangle, comes from Denmark. With 72 percent fat, it is almost a triple-crème.

Fresh Cheeses

In essence, these are uncured cheeses. They have mild, milk-sweet flavors and aromas, and most are relatively low in fat. They can be stored for only short periods—several days to a week, depending on type, original condition, and facilities.

Cottage, Pot, and *Farmer's cheese* are the three most popular fresh cheeses in America. While the definitions for each vary and overlap in different regions, generally it can be said that pot cheese tends to be drier than cottage cheese, and that farmer's cheese is even firmer (it can be sliced) and is typically molded into loaf shapes. Cottage cheese is marketed in both small and large curd sizes and may be enriched with added cream (labeled "creamed"). Cottage cheese may be made of whole milk or of partly skimmed milk. It usually is sold plain, but some types have additions of fruit, pineapple being the most popular. Cottage cheese is highly nutritious but contains more calories than most weight-watchers realize—86 calories per 100 grams, 390 calories per pound, for the plain, whole-milk variety. The cream variety has 106 calories per 100 grams, 481 per pound. Diet cottage cheese has fewer calories, but really does not taste very much like cottage cheese.

Mozzarella is a molded, moist, pliable, delicate fresh cheese still made from buffalo's milk in southern Italy but from whole or part-skim cow's milk in America and elsewhere. It has a short life and is used mostly in cooking (it is the classic cheese for pizza because of its melting properties). There is also a partially cured mozzarella sold in some stores; it is inferior to the fresh variety in terms of both flavor and melting qualities, but it has a longer shelf life.

Ricotta is best known as a fresh, whey cheese that is low in fat (4 to 15 percent). Pure white, smooth and moist, and slightly nutty in flavor, ricotta is often made from sheep's-milk whey in Italy, but in the U.S. it is derived from cow's milk, or cow's milk and whey.

Queso blanco is the principal Latin American fresh cheese, usually farm-made from skim or whole cow's milk. It is bland, white, soft, and springy, and it varies in quality and taste from region to region.

American cream cheese also fits into the fresh-cheese category. It is slightly tangy, very soft, smooth, and made of cream or cream and milk (35 to 40 percent fat). It can also be lightly cured, is marketed both plain and with additions such as pimientos and olives. It is popular as a sandwich spread.

American Neufchatel is similar to American cream cheese but is lower in fat, has more protein, and spreads easier.

Grating Cheeses

These extremely hard varieties cure slowly (times measured in years) because of very low moisture and high salt content. They are very sharp in flavor, used as flavoring in a wide variety of dishes.

Parmesan, when it is the genuine Italian product, carries the words "Parmigiano-Reggiano" stenciled on its tough, thick brown rind. It is pale yellow, very hard and dry in texture, yet soft and moist in the mouth. It has a complex taste, full yet not strong. It should not be too salty nor bitter. It will keep for a very long time if properly stored. The U.S.-made copy which must be aged 14 months, is a poor relative.

Pecorino Romano, (in Italy, *pecorino* refers to cheeses made from sheep's milk) is a part-skim sheep's-milk cheese which is very white in color, mildly tangy when young and noticeably sharp when aged. Its flavor is not as subtle as the Parmigiano-Reggiano, but, unlike the American version, it is interchangeable as far as recipes go.

Sapsago, a truncated-cone-shaped cow's-milk cheese from Switzerland, is very hard. Its light creamy-green color and its pungent, unique clover scent keep it from being universally popular.

French Goat Cheeses

Called *Chèvres* in France, these are tangy yet mild when young, but can become powerful when aged. *Montrachet* is pure-white, very soft and creamy, mildly rich, slightly sour to the taste, and log-shaped. *Sainte-Maure* is tangy, creamy, and log-shaped. *Valençay* or *Pyramide* is creamy-thick, sometimes strong-tasting, and shaped as the second name suggests. Still other best-selling chèvres include *Banun*, disc-shaped and wrapped in chestnut leaves; *Capricorne*, cartwheel-shaped with a hole in its center; *Crottin* (literally "dung," because its shape and size—but not its flavor or smell—resemble its namesake); and the various products sold under the *Lezay* proprietary label.

Miscellaneous Cheeses

Feta, extremely popular in Greece, can be made from the milk of the goat or sheep, or a mixture of goat's and cow's milk. It is a soft, crumbly, rindless cheese which ripens in brine, is tangy and very salty. It should not taste bitter.

Brinza is a rustic sheep or goat's milk cheese made in Hungary, the Balkan countries, and the U.S. Somewhat off-white in color, creamy but granular, salty, biting and oily, it resembles feta.

Kasseri is made mainly in Greece, but there is an American version. This hard cheese can be made from sheep or goat's milk, is cream-colored, looks moist, tastes oily and pungent. It can be overly salty.

Gjetost is a hard Norwegian whey cheese. Genuine gjetost is made from goat's whey; other varieties abound, such as the softer *Primost* or *Flotost*, which contains 10 percent buttermilk or cream; and *Mysost*, made from cow's-milk whey. This cheese looks like a small, hard, light-brown bar of soap, tastes sweetish and caramely, and has a buttery consistency. Its unique flavor makes it an acquired taste.

Buying Tips

Judging a Cheese Store: A reliable store should be clean and smell fresh; have room between stored cheeses for air circulation; keep cheeses under refrigeration or at very cool temperatures; keep strong-smelling cheeses away from delicate ones; keep cheeses well-wrapped; stress quality rather than quantity. You should be able to sample most cheeses, examine the rind or label, and return a spoiled, damaged, or otherwise unsatisfactory cheese.

Judging a Cheese: Appearance is one of your best guides; look at the cheese, if you can. However, many cheeses come wrapped and boxed, and the packaging prevents us from seeing the cheese. Open the box and gently touch the inner wrapping. A cheese such as a Camembert should feel plump and a little springy. And if the wrapping is not fresh and clean, is broken, gummy, or smells, don't buy the cheese. Boxed soft cheeses should always look pleasingly plump, the center of the cheese not sunken and the outside rim not standing in a ridge.

When selecting cheese, keep in mind that flavor becomes more pronounced with age in all cheeses—and that a mature, or aged, cheese, is more expensive than a young one because of storage and inventory costs. After a cheese reaches its peak, it continues to age, and flavor will deteriorate from then on. Surface-ripened cheeses will become excessively runny and may develop a hint of ammonia—avoid cheese in that condition. And in purchasing, remember that most cheeses can be eaten at any time of the year, but certain imported cheeses—such as Bel Paese, Camembert, Munster, Pont L'Evêque, Gorgonzola, and Stilton—are not at their best during the warm months. For specific tips about judging cheese, see specific sections above.

PREPARATION

Storage

Ideally, cheese should be stored in a cool cellar, but if you don't have one, a refrigerator will have to suffice. To minimize moisture and flavor loss caused by the cool refrigerator environment, store cheeses in the vegetable crisper or the inside door of the refrigerator, where the temperature is warmest. Always wrap the cheese tightly in plastic wrap or aluminum foil. Hard cheeses may be wrapped in a damp cloth to keep them moist. Draw the flat of a knife over the cut surface of hard cheeses to seal in moisture. Keep a wheel or large cheese in the refrigerator and cut or slice from it what you will use; while the large wheel set out for display may dazzle your guests, fluctuations in its temperature caused by frequently removing a large cheese from the refrigerator will cause texture, flavor, and aroma to deteriorate. Cheese picks up odors, so store it away from foods with strong odors, and don't wrap different kinds of cheese together. Wipe, scrape, or cut off mold spots which develop on a cheese. If the mold has penetrated the cheese, cut away a layer. The remainder of the cheese is fine. With a dry cloth, wipe off the fat drops that form on hard cheeses stored too long at room temperature.

We don't recommend freezing cheese, because freezing often brings about loss in flavor, aroma, and texture. But if you do freeze, wrap the cheese as airtight as possible. Hard cheeses freeze more satisfactorily than soft cheeses. Cheddar types may be frozen about six weeks, after which flavor will fade. When thawing, put the cheese in the refrigerator section before removing to room temperature, to allow it to thaw gradually and minimize loss of flavor and texture. A thawed cheese that has become mealey or crumbly may be used in cooking.

Keep in mind that once a cheese is ripe, refrigeration will not halt its deterioration. In general, the more moisture a cheese has, the shorter its life, so buy and store accordingly. For specific tips about storing, see specific sections above.

Cutting

There are traditional ways to cut certain cheeses. You generally cut wheel-shaped cheeses such as Brie into wedges as you would a pie; brick or log-shaped cheese such as Montrachet into slices as you would a loaf of bread; ball-shaped cheeses such as Edam first into wedges as you would an apple, then into bite-sized hunks; pyramidal cheeses such as Velançay into four vertical wedges.

Serving

To fully enjoy the taste and aroma of cheese, allow it to reach room temperature before serving. Remove it from the refrigerator at least an hour before serving. The harder and larger the cheese, the longer it will take to lose its chill.

Cheesetasting: For the sake of eye appeal, cheese should be served on a wooden board or marble slab. Offer at least four varieties to allow for different tastes; for example: surface-ripened, Swiss-style, blue, and double-crème. Supply individual knives or cheese slicers and servers, especially for soft or strong-flavored cheeses. Preslicing or cutting will rapidly dry the cheese out. But do cut one portion if the cheese is in a whole uncut state (such as a ball of Edam); this makes for an inviting display. Arrange the cheeses roomily so they can be easily cut. Don't remove the rind from soft, ripened cheeses. Do remove at least part of the rind from hard- or waxed-rind cheese.

Cheese can be enjoyed by itself, or with a wide range of accompaniments. Serve two or three fresh breads, a white and one or two darker, such as pumpernickel or rye. A crusty French bread is best. Other popular accompaniments include unsalted crackers and dry biscuits; unsalted pecans; pickles, scallions, chives, shallots, and parsley with cream and cottage cheeses; sweet (unsalted) butter, especially with blue cheese; juicy, crisp fruits. With delicate cheeses, avoid robust breads and beverages, which tend to overpower them.

Wine is the natural beverage choice with cheese. Serve the cheese to complement the wine—generally, a strong cheese accompanies a strong wine. A good wine choice for a wide range of cheeses is a Beaujolais. Strong, tangy cheeses such as cheddars go well with ale or beer.

At meals: A versatile food, cheese can be offered at many points of a meal. Serve small amounts of cheese as an appetizer—it can be filling; with the salad or right after; with the last of the dinner wine between the main dish and dessert; with fruit for dessert after a heavy meal; after the dessert, as the English do. Before serving, always taste the cheese. Appearance does not always reveal a defect in flavor.

The rinds of hard cheeses (which may contain wax, plastic, charcoal, or dyes) should not be eaten, but it is a matter of taste whether the rind of surface-ripened cheese is eaten.

Cooking with Cheese

Cheese is the main ingredient of many dishes and a flavoring in numerous others. Melting quality, flavor, and texture of a cheese are the main qualities to look for in selecting a cheese to cook with. Some dishes, such as fondue and pizza, will call for a cheese that is stringy when melted—here, a Gruyère or Mozzarella is suitable. A hot cheese canapé, on the other hand, will want a creamy melted cheese. For soups and salads, use a piquant grating cheese, and in soufflés, a well-aged cheese to keep the soufflé light.

To avoid stringiness and lumpiness in melting cheese, shred, grate, use a blender, or break the cheese into small pieces before melting; use a double boiler or a thick-bottomed pan for melting; and keep the heat low to moderate.

In gauging the amount of cheese to use in cooking, remember that the stronger the cheese, the less will be needed in seasoning; that approximately four ounces of cheese equal one cup of grated; one ounce of cream cheese is approximately two tablespoons; one pound of cottage cheese contains two cups.

Leftovers

Cheese that is too dry, crumbly, or grainy has a variety of uses as flavoring. Grind or grate it and store in airtight glass containers in the refrigerator. Use it in casseroles, soups, pizzas, salad dressings, and omelets. Or make a cheese spread. Dried blue cheese, for example, can be mixed with the same amount of butter, moistened with brandy, and worked into a spread; stored in a small crock, capped and refrigerated, it will keep for at least a month.

CLASSIC USES AND AFFINITIES

The list of dishes that include cheese as an important ingredient is virtually endless. It includes cheese omelets, sandwiches (ham and cheese, etc.), quiche, Welsh rarebit, lasagne, cheese puffs, cheese soufflé, Mornay sauce, raclette, pizza, fondue, fonduta, cheese blintzes, enchiladas, and cheesecake.

CHEESE, PROCESSED

BACKGROUND

Since most of the cheese sold in supermarkets is processed cheese of various types, it is helpful to know about them. Unlike naturally aged cheese, processed cheese undergoes a manufacturing process. A blend of bits of fresh and cured natural cheese is mixed and heated quickly at very high temperatures—pasteurization. Then this blend is sometimes studded with additions of fruits, pimientos, vegetables, or meats. The heat applied to the cheese halts ripening, enabling the cheese to be transported, stocked, and finally stored in the consumer's refrigerator with less care and attention than is required for natural cheeses.

Varieties

Domestic Processed Cheeses: The label that assures you that you are getting the highest proportion of cheese says *Pasteurized Processed Cheese*—one of the three basic varieties of processed cheese. The flavor of a pasteurized processed cheese depends largely on the cheese or cheeses used in its manufacture—for instance, pasteurized processed Swiss cheese. Any additions, such as smoke flavor, pimentos, fruits, vegetables, or meats, must be listed on the label.

The second type is *processed cheese food*, prepared in much the same way, but containing less cheese, more moisture, and less fat than processed cheese. It spreads more easily, melts faster, and has a milder flavor. It too may have added ingredients.

The third type, *processed cheese spread*, has more moisture than the cheese food, and less butterfat. It is the most spreadable, and is used mostly for snacks. It is usually sold in glass jars or in loaves and is frequently flavored with added ingredients.

Pros and Cons: All of the processed cheese and cheese products will keep longer than natural cheese, and are easier to spread and melt. These advantages are offset by the bland to almost nonexistent flavors and aromas of processed cheese, when compared to natural cheese.

Coldpack Cheese: *Coldpack* or *club cheese* differs from pasteurized processed cheese. Though it is a blend of one or more fresh and aged natural cheeses, it is mixed without heating. Most coldpack cheeses have a sharp flavor and keep longer than natural cheese. There is also a *coldpack cheese food*; it contains more noncheese ingredients.

European Processed Cheese: France offers its own processed cheese, among which are *Rambol*, a processed cream cheese with 60 percent fat, often flavored or covered with nuts; and *Fromage Fondu*, a very bland processed cheese of gummy texture, often covered with nuts or herbs.

Analogs: Relatively new to the market, *artificial cheeses* are made in all styles which are roughly analogous in look and smell to real cheeses, and sold under real cheese names, such as Colby, Cheddar, and Gouda. These analogs are made from a range of chemical and organic materials including vegetable oils. They contain less fat than cheese, but a similar amount of calories, protein, vitamins, minerals, and moisture content. They can be stored much longer than natural cheese—for example, an imitation mozzarella will keep for a year compared to up to three months for a natural mozzarella—and are cheaper to produce and buy. They have a rubbery, wet-paper texture and are lacking in flavor.

CHERIMOYA

BACKGROUND

Like coffee beans, the best *cherimoyas* grow in high altitudes and rarified air. *Annona cherimola*, a variety of custard apple, is native to the mountains of Ecuador and Peru and now grows successfully in Southern California. The cherimoya is usually irregularly shaped or oval and large—some specimens reach 15 pounds. It sports a thick, tough, green jacket of "imitation alligator skin"—the rind is indented with thumbprint-like impressions. Inside, there are black seeds to set off the pulp, which is creamy-white, custardlike, fine-grained, and highly esteemed for the delicacy of its taste.

AVAILABILITY

In California, cherimoyas can be bought fresh from November through May. They ship fairly well, so look for them in big city markets throughout the rest of the nation during the winter months, where availability will depend upon the extent of California's crop.

Buying Tips

Buy big ones that are firm-just-going-soft, with no cracks. Avoid those with brown skins—an indication of overripeness. Cherimoyas do not keep. Eat as soon as possible.

CHERRIES

BACKGROUND

Cherries, the petite members of the *Prunus* family—the stone fruits that include plums and peaches—are grown in temperate lands around the world, much to the delight of their most ardent fans: birds. Botanists believe they were first cultivated in Western Asia, but because their seeds are easily carried long distances in the intestines of birds, no one knows for certain the home of the first wild cherry trees. These wild trees still flourish today from California to the Middle East to China.

Varieties

While hundreds of cherry varieties exist (with skin color varying from a pale yellowish-pink to a deep reddish-black), they fall into three basic culinary classifications:

Sweet cherries (*Prunus avium*)
Sour cherries (*Prunus cerasus*)
Sweet-Sour cherries (*P. avium* x *cerasus* hybrids)

Sweet Cherries: These are sweet enough to be eaten fresh, but they can also be cooked. Best-selling varieties include the deep reddish-black *Bing*, *Lambert*, and *Tartarian* cherries, as well as the pale yellowish-pink *Royal Ann*. The latter is sometimes converted into MARASCHINO CHERRIES. Other popular sweet cherries include the *Chapman* and *Windsor*.

Sour Cherries: Usually a sour cherry can be distinguished from a sweet one by its configuration: the fruit is more globular, less heart-shaped than the latter. A few sour cherries can be eaten raw, but most are too astringent and end up in pies and preserves or are canned. The three most popular sour cherries—in order of their seasonal availability—are the *Early Richmond*, *Montmorency*, and *English Morello*.

Sweet-Sour Cherries: Many of these hybrid varieties are marketed as *Dukes*.

AVAILABILITY

Season

Fresh sweet cherries are generally available from May through August, with mid-June through July being the peak season. Sour cherries reach the market several weeks later than sweet cherries. Processed cherries can be found in the markets canned and, less often, frozen. Neither type comes even close to the desirable flavor, fragrance, and texture of fresh in-season cherries.

Buying Tips

For optimum succulence, cherries should be picked in a state of full ripeness, as they do not ripen appreciably off the tree. Unfortunately, for the sake of ensuring safe shipping and prolonging shelf life, most cherries are picked prematurely. For ripe cherries, look for a surface color that is deep and full for its variety—for instance, the darker the look of Bing or Lambert cherries, the riper they will probably be. Therefore, if cherries are sold in open lugs (the flat wooden boxes), do not hesitate to select the darker ones, leaving the lighter ones behind. Cherries should be firm, but not hard. Sour cherries will, however, be naturally a bit softer than sweet cherries. Choose plump, glossy-skinned cherries: Avoid cherries with dull, shriveled, bruised, cracked, scaly, moldy, leaky or sticky skins. The cherries should not smell fermented. Cherries with stems attached will keep longer but obviously have less usable flesh per pound, so the price should be lower. The stems should be fresh and supple, not dried-out or brittle. If in doubt, eat a sample cherry before you buy, if your greengrocer permits it. Be sure to wipe it with a tissue to remove possible pesticide residues and germs.

PREPARATION

Storage

Cherries in good condition will stay fresh for two or more days in the refrigerator in a sealed plastic bag. Do not wash them until just before serving, as moisture hastens bacterial growth. Treat the cherries gently as they are readily bruised. Cherries do not freeze well.

Preliminaries

Some cooks submerge cherries in water, discarding any that float, an indication that the fruit has spoiled from an affliction such as worm-infestation. If you use this test, soak the cherries only briefly lest they become waterlogged. If you cook cherries often, it may be worthwhile to invest in a mechanical cherry-pitter. Several are on the market. Otherwise, use a hairpin or paperclip and push the wire loop into the stem end of the destemmed cherry; then scoop out the pit. If the cherries are very ripe, you may be able to cut a small slit in the stem end with the point of a sharp knife or a vegetable peeler, and then squeeze out the pit, but be prepared for a squashed, messy cherry. For cooking cherries with fatty meats such as goose, sour cherries like the Montmorency are *de rigueur*, because the tartness helps cut through the fatty taste.

CLASSIC USES AND AFFINITIES

Schwarzwalder kirschtorte (Black forest cherry cake), cherries jubilee (ice cream topped with a flaming hot cherry sauce), *clafouti limousin cerise* (cherries topped and baked with a sweetened batter), cherry-topped cheesecake, *canard montmorency* (duckling with cherry sauce) and, of course, the all-American cherry pie and cobbler.

CHERVIL

BACKGROUND

Chervil is a component of the classical FINES HERBES. Its leaves have a delicate taste somewhat reminiscent of parsley, with faint anise undertones. Southern Russia and Western Asia are the homelands of this herb, but the major producer in modern times is France. True chervil is *Anthriscus cerefolium*: medieval recipes calling for chervil are often designed to use *sweet cicely* (*Myrrhis odorata*), an unrelated plant with a somewhat similar flavor. (See HERBS AND SPICES for information on buying, storing, cooking, etc.)

PREPARATION

The essential oils of chervil are very volatile, so the herb must never be boiled. Raw leaves used for salad should be cut at the last minute before serving. The taste of chervil is very delicate, so a healthy sprinkle of the herb can be used at a time.

CLASSIC USES AND AFFINITIES

Chervil combines very well with other herbs. Ravigote sauce often combines chervil, tarragon, and chives. Fine-cut chervil leaves enhance simply prepared lean fish and delicate meats such as veal, rabbit, and baby lamb. Tender poultry can be complemented by this herb. Omelets and cream soups often contain chervil; the leaves can be eaten raw in salad, or steeped in white-wine vinegar to embellish the salad dressing.

CHICKEN

BACKGROUND

The chicken has come a long way since it first began scratching the floors of the primordial Asian tropical rain forests. Once domesticated, the chicken spread from village to village, eventually reaching a global population approximately equal to that of mankind's four billion.

Henry IV of France reputedly guaranteed his sixteenth-century subjects "a chicken in every pot every Sunday," a political promise that was repeated centuries later by President Herbert Hoover in the early 1930s in the midst of the Great Depression. Until after World War II, the cost of chicken in America was relatively high, sometimes matching the cost of beef, so a whole chicken was indeed a special treat for the average household. Not so today. The American chicken industry has developed sophisticated mass-production methods that speed the chicken from incubation to 3-pound slaughter weight in about 2 rather than 4 months, dramatically lowering the husbanding cost in the process. Regretably, there is a trade-off: while the 2-month-old chicken is as big as its 4-month-old ancestor of previous decades, its flavor remains that of a 2-month-old chicken: semi-insipid. You cannot rush Mother Nature without a penalty, at least in this instance. Our modern TV-advertised chicken is literally a jailbird, typically being raised in close quarters in multistoried indoor factory farms, untouched by sunlight. The diet is scientifically designed and controlled, laced with hormones, chemicals, antibiotics, and coloring agents—almost anything that will increase growth and lower costs.

Now that we have painted a grayish picture of the American chicken industry, let us examine the other side. The monetary savings resulting from lower production costs have largely been passed on to the consumer, giving us an economical, nutritious, high-quality protein alternative to the decidedly more expensive beef. Furthermore, chicken is preferable to beef in at least three important ways: it has fewer calories, it has less cholesterol-producing fat and—thanks to its shorter muscle fibers—it is easier to digest. Chicken is also quick and easy to prepare and, because it marries well with most flavoring ingredients, its taste can be readily changed from semi-insipid to savory, and you can cook a different chicken every night for a year without coming close to recipe repetition.

Varieties

Cooking Classification and Age: Most chickens are merchandized with names that suggest the preferred cooking method. Today, three major classifications exist:

Broiler-fryer: Chickens of this class generally weigh 2 to 3½ pounds dressed. Age is usually 2 to 2½ months, give or take a week or two. Sex is male or female. Broiler-fryers are best broiled or fried, as the appellation indicates, but the heavier specimens can also be roasted, and thus are sometimes called *all-purpose chicken.*

Roasters: These birds typically weigh 3½ to 5 pounds dressed and have an age range of 4 to 7 months. Compared to broiler-fryers, roasting chickens have a higher ratio of meat to bone, are more flavorful, and have more fat, making them ideal for oven roasting and rotisserie cooking. Larger roasters can be cooked with moist heat, but their meat will not have as much desirable deep flavor as a stewing chicken.

Stewing Chickens: You may see these birds being sold under other names, such as *fowl, hen, elderly hen, stewing hen,* and *stewer*. Their full, rich flavor makes a stewing chicken a perfect choice for stews (including the fricassees), as well as for cold salads, sandwiches, soups, and stocks.

Chicken Parts: Not too many years ago most chicken was sold whole, usually with the giblets (liver, gizzard, and heart) tucked inside the stomach cavity. Because of public demand, most fresh chicken today is sold halved (usually split lengthwise) or quartered (divided into two breasts-cum-wings and two legs), or further divided into serving-size pieces: drumsticks, thighs, breasts (whole or halves, bone-in or boned) and wings. Giblets and especially liver are also separately packaged. Parts of little culinary interest to most Americans include the feet, cockscomb, and the undeveloped eggs. The individual parts of a chicken virtually always collectively sell for much more than the whole chicken, a fact that reflects the extra labor and packaging costs.

Other Classifications: These descriptions do not directly suggest the cooking method, but each is best cooked certain ways.

Rock Cornish Game Birds: Old cookbooks do not have recipes for this 1- to 2-pound mini-chicken because it did not exist until several decades ago, when the Plymouth Rock hen was first crossbred with a Cornish game cock. The *Cornish Game Hen*, as the original and subsequent crossbreeds are known, is not as flavorful and as meaty as its producers would have us believe. And, judged by edible meat per pound, it is quite expensive. Its saving grace is that it makes an attractive presentation when served whole, one to each diner. The bird is widely available frozen; in some areas it is also available fresh-killed—immeasurably better than the frozen product. Rock Cornish game birds are best roasted or broiled.

Capon: Plump-breasted and oversized, the capon gets those physical properties as a direct result of being castrated at a very young age. Its plentiful white breast meat is succulent and tender, making the desexed male chicken a natural for roasting (there is no finer chicken for that purpose). Most capons are slaughtered at about 6 months old, and weigh 6 to 8 pounds dressed. Because capons fetch hefty prices, some markets delude the public by selling plump roasters as capons. These pseudocapons are sometimes hormone-fattened but always lack the true capon's high proportion of juicy breast meat. If the breast is not noticeably expansive, it probably is not a capon.

Squab chicken: This bird should not be confused with the SQUAB which is an immature pigeon. Neither is a squab chicken a Rock Cornish Game bird. Squab chickens are typically 1- to 1½-month-old chickens weighing approximately ¾ to 1½ pounds. Squab chickens are best broiled, though the larger ones can be also fried with success.

Cock or Rooster: Generally this refers to a male chicken too old and tough to be of much use besides enriching the stock pot.

USDA GRADES: The federal government (or sometimes a state government with USDA approval) quality-grades five types of poultry—chicken, turkey, duck, goose, and guinea hen—if requested and paid for by the commercial processor. It is important to note that these grades do not reflect tenderness per se—the age of the bird is the primary determinant in that department. USDA Grade A is the highest quality designation. A bird of that grade will be meatier and plumper and have a better overall appearance than one judged USDA Grade B—which in turn will be better than a USDA Grade C specimen. If you do see an official USDA grademark, it will be almost certainly the Grade A shield, because Grade B and C birds are seldom marketed as such, since no one is required by law to do so. Should you not see a grade shield, you will have to let your eyes do their own quality-grading. All birds that cross state borders (and some that do not) are governmentally inspected for wholeness. This inspection includes examining the carcass and processing plant for possible diseases and unsanitary conditions. The official seal of wholesomeness is indicated by a round stamp, the code number specifying the processing plant. Sometimes the wholesomeness mark is printed on a label or tag on the whole chicken, seldom on chicken parts. More and more stores display whole chickens with a wing tag that shows the quality grade mark, the seal of wholesomeness, and the cooking class.

AVAILABILITY

Fresh or Preserved

You can purchase chicken fresh, frozen, canned and freeze-dried throughout the year.

Fresh (or Fresh-killed): This term encompasses more than one definition, and it is important for us as consumers to know the difference between them. The first definition refers to a chicken that has been stored and shipped under standard (about 35°F) refrigeration. This is the best type and the one most people think (often erroneously) they are buying when they see a sign saying "fresh" or "fresh-killed." Chickens that fall under the second definition are less desirable, as they have been stored and shipped in *ice pack*—buried in shaved ice to prolong their storage life. The least desirable of the fresh chickens are those that fall within the third definition: *deep-chilled*. These *chilled chickens*, as they are known by some tradesmen, are quick-cooled at the processing plant to an internal temperature of about 30°F, then shipped to market at that temperature. Technically, the bird does not freeze (unlike water, which freezes at 32°F, chicken freezes at about 28°F), but it comes very close to it, enough to do some cellular damage.

Frozen: Chickens of this ilk have been frozen solid at the processing plant and are shipped and sold that way. A frozen bird will never be as succulent, flavorful, well-textured, tender, and nutritious as its unfrozen counterpart. Reason: the freezing process bursts some of the flesh cells which, when thawed, lose some of their internal juices and develop a mushy texture. If you do have a frozen bird, see the thawing instructions later in this entry. A different type of frozen chicken is the prepackaged ready-to-cook or heat-and-serve variety (such as TV dinner or breaded chicken parts) that come under the general umbrella of convenience foods. Seldom are these products of serious culinary interest.

Canned and Freeze-dried: Chicken of these sorts should be left to army mess-hall chefs or to campers far from refrigerators. Canned chicken meat needs only to be heated through, though most can also be eaten cold without risking one's health. Freeze-dried chicken needs to be reconstituted with water (read package directions).

Buying Tips

The bird and especially the breast should be plump and semifirm, with excellent conformation. The legs should be squat and well-fleshed. Between the flesh and skin should be a fair layer of fat. Look for skin that is soft, smooth, slightly moist, and not too thick. Lingering pin feathers and unnecessarily punctured or ripped skin are signs of sloppy processing, as are bruises and blood stains. The color of the skin should have a healthy glow, but whether it is off-white or yellow depends on breed, feed, and regional preferences. In sections of the country where customers are convinced that yellow is always better than white, the chicken rearers feed their charges a coloring agent such as marigold petals. What you do not want is a chicken that is too white for its breed, and since some breeds are regionally entrenched, no national standard can be given. Always smell the chicken, even if you have to do it through the cellophane wrapping. It must have a fresh, not a foul (pun intended) odor. Off-odors are a sign of decay. Buy chickens to match the cooking method by noting the cooking class on the label or sign: broiler-fryer, roaster, stewing chicken, and so on. Look for the official USDA grademark—if none is there, it does no harm to ask your meatman. Many markets put a date on the label which may indicate when the meat was packaged or the last day it can be sold. Sometimes the date is coded. If so, ask the meat person to teach you how to decipher the code. The age of a chicken is related to cooking method, not quality: a young bird (broiler-fryer) would be too bland for a fricassee, while a stewing chicken would be too tough for broiling. Age can be approximately judged by bending the breastbone: the forward tip is pliable on a young bird, inflexible on an older one. Other age indicators include relative size and the feet: those of a young bird are sharper and softer and smoother than those of a mature bird. On a pound-for-pound basis, the female will have more breast meat than the male. The exception is the desexed male, the capon. A dry-plucked bird is superior to one plucked after being dipped in hot water (the *scalding* method). Whenever you have the choice, buy a fresh-killed rather than a frozen bird, for the reasons we discussed earlier. If you must buy a frozen chicken, examine the package for visible frozen liquid, a telltale sign that the bird was thawed and refrozen, thus likely in poor condition. Do not buy a "fresh-killed" bird that has liquid in the bottom of the package—it was probably frozen or near-frozen, then thawed. Many markets frequently put on special sale certain chicken parts, or perhaps whole birds of a particular cooking class. You will save money by buying these specials rather than going to the market with an unshakable intention such as "I will buy chicken breasts today." Almost any chicken part is delicious and easy to prepare. Another way to save money is to buy a whole chicken and cook it whole. Or cut it up yourself—it is not that difficult, it just takes a little practice, a good boning knife, and perhaps a pair of poultry shears. Chickens sold with head and feet attached are easier to judge for quality and freshness. When examining such a bird, look for eyes that are bright and not dull or sunken, a cockscomb (if it's a male) that is a fresh red, and a thick neck. When examining a live chicken, look for an energetic, healthy countenance plus the other relevant factors discussed here.

PREPARATION

Storage

Chicken is often sold in tight-fitting cellophane-wrapped packages. Unless you plan to cook the chicken within a few hours, remove the wrapping, place the bird on a clean platter and loosely rewrap the chicken in wax or butcher paper so that air can circulate around the exposed skin and flesh. This free flow of air helps keep the surface of the chicken dry, thus hindering the buildup of spoilage-causing bacteria. If the giblets are in the body cavity, remove and store them separately. Always remove the stuffing of a cooked chicken prior to refrigerating or freezing it lest the bacterial count of the stuffing rise to an unhealthy level before the stuffing has had a chance to become sufficiently cold. Use fresh chicken parts and giblets within a day, a fresh whole chicken within a day or two. If you must freeze chicken, the limit is about 7 to 10 days in the frozen-food compartment, and several months in a 0°F freezer. Because of the risk of food poisoning, never partially cook chicken before storage. Either refrigerate or freeze it raw, or cook it completely before storing it.

Thawing Frozen Birds

The best way to minimize the loss of flavor and nutritious internal juices that leach out of the flesh when a bird thaws is to thaw it slowly in the refrigerator.

This will take 2 to 6 hours for chicken parts, depending on thickness. A whole chicken will thaw in 8 hours (for small Rock Cornish Game birds) to 36 hours (for large capons). Once thawed, remove the original wrapper and loosely rewrap in butcher paper. The less desirable "rapid method" involves submerging the whole bird in its watertight wrapping in cold tap water for 1½ to 6 hours depending on size. Change the water every hour or two. If the original wrapping is not watertight, seal it in a watertight plastic bag. Squeeze excess air out of the bag to keep the bird from floating. If it insists on floating, weigh it down. At no time should you try to thaw a bird by letting it stand at room temperature because the thawed portions will be warm enough for pathogenic bacteria to multiply before the bird is completely thawed. Despite what some recipes tell you, do not put a frozen bird in the oven unless absolutely necessary—the culinary results are abominable at best. Rather, let the bird properly thaw in the refrigerator.

Preliminaries

Since over 99.9 percent of the chickens marketed today in America are sold dressed and drawn, very few of us have to learn how to kill, eviscerate, and pluck a chicken. For those of us city folk who want to master this complicated and messy art, the best teacher is an experienced country cousin, not a book. If you purchase a dressed and drawn bird from a local poultry farm, it is a good idea to store it overnight in the refrigerator if it was killed on the day of purchase. This gives the carcass a chance to rid itself of any toughening effects of rigor mortis. If your bird has some remaining pinfeathers (small, underdeveloped feathers that have just broken through the skin surface), you will have to singe them with a flame such as a candle or gas burner. When singeing, be careful not to scorch and therefore partially cook the bird's surface. If only a few pinfeathers exist, pull each one out individually with a pair of tweezers. The bird should be at or near room temperature before cooking. Since the bird has a large, exposed stomach cavity, it will warm up faster than a beef roast of the same weight. Depending on size, allow roughly 20 to 45 minutes for a bird brought directly out of a 40°F refrigerator. A longer warmup increases the risk of a high bacterial count. The typical store-bought bird need not (and should not) be washed in water. Wiping the inside cavity and outside surface with a wet paper towel should suffice. Pull or cut off any excess fat found near the cavity opening.

Disjointing: There is no single correct way to disjoint a whole chicken. The approach you take will largely depend on family custom, the recipe, and your tools and experience. All together, there are at least a dozen basic ways to do it. Here is perhaps the simplest and easiest method. First, place the bird breast-side down on your working surface. Remove the backbone (save it for the stockpot) by making two parallel cuts along both sides, working from the back to the front of the carcass. Poultry shears work best, though you can use a knife, if need be, for this operation.

Turn the chicken over and cut down the middle through the entire length of the breast, from front to rear. You now have two chicken halves ready for broiling, roasting or barbecuing. To divide the halves into quarters, cut through the skin to the natural seam line between the leg and the breast muscles. With the aid of the blade of your knife, gently pull and cut apart these two sets of muscles. The leg can be further divided into thigh and drumstick pieces. Sever the two parts by cutting through the cartilage at the joint in the middle of the leg. The wing can be separated by cutting through the joint that links the wing to the body. The disjointed wing will fry or broil more evenly if you make an incision through the V-shaped skin to the joint connecting the two larger bones of the wing, then snapping the joint with your hands to make it lie flat. Cutting off the easily scorched wing tip also promotes even cooking (save the tip for your stockpot).

Seasoning a Whole Chicken: Here is but one of countless ways to accomplish this step: First brush the stomach cavity with a mixture of 3 parts melted butter to 1 part lemon juice, plus salt, pepper, and herbs to taste. Place into the cavity half a medium-sized onion, half a medium-sized carrot, a few leaf sprigs of celery, and a few sprigs of fresh parsley. These will flavor the bird and will be discarded after the cooking. Close the cavity by trussing it (see below). Brush the outer surface of the bird with the same mixture used for the cavity. The bird is now ready to be roasted whole in the oven.

Stuffing: *Dressing* is another word for stuffing in some parts of the country. If you elect to stuff a bird, do so only just before cooking. To do otherwise creates a risk of food poisoning as the bacteria count of the stuffing can reach a dangerous level before the oven heat reaches the stuffing and halts the growth. And to minimize the time needed to heat the stuffing properly as it sits inside the bird's cavity, bring the stuffing to room temperature before spooning it inside the bird. For each pound of dressed bird, you will need about 3/4 cup of stuffing. Any surplus stuffing can be cooked by wrapping it in aluminum foil and placing it in the oven about 30 to 40 minutes before the bird will be finished cooking. Stuffing expands as it cooks, so do not pack it tightly inside the cavity—otherwise, you will end up with a gummy stuffing and, just as likely, one that will ooze out of the bird, creating a mess. Gently spoon in the stuffing until the cavity is about 80 percent filled, then get out your trussing needle. With large birds, you may wish to stuff the neck cavity as well.

The basic stuffing can be defined as a seasoned mixture on a moist starchy base. The starch substance is usually bread cubes or crumbs, though cooked ingredients such as rice, wild rice, mashed potatoes, mashed sweet potatoes, cornbread, and cracked wheat also work well. Many recipes call for stale bread, but this is poor advice because most cooks interpret "stale" as meaning "very stale." What you want is fresh bread that has lost most of its moisture so that the stuffing does not become unappetizingly soggy. If you do not have fresh semidry bread, partially dry some fresh bread by placing it in a 200°F oven for about 15 to 30 minutes, depending on the bread's thickness and moisture content. Before using the bread, trim off the crusts, saving them for other culinary uses. If you want to use breadcrumbs, do not use finely textured ones or you will be eating a mush rather than a light and airy stuffing. The starch base can be enriched with precooked giblets or sausages, or raw oysters, fruits, nuts, and mushrooms. Basic moistening agents include melted butter, chicken broth, wine, cognac, lemon juice, eggs, yogurt and milk. Other ingredients can be added just for flavoring—herbs and spices (see Classic Uses and Affinities section), as well as minced onions, carrots, and celery leaves. You can buy the packaged bread stuffing in supermarkets, but the variety made from scratch is vastly superior. To get you started, here is a basic mildly seasoned recipe for one cup of stuffing (for larger amounts, proportionately increase the ingredients). Gently saute over moderate heat 1 tablespoon of chopped onions in 2 tablespoons of butter; when the onions become translucent, turn off the heat and add 1/2 teaspoon of poultry seasonings (herbs and spices of your choice), a scant 1/4 teaspoon of salt, a scant 1/8 teaspoon of ground peppercorns and 1 cup of bread cubes; gently mix all the ingredients together; allow the mixture to cool. Once having mastered this basic recipe, you can begin to explore the variations limited only by your desire to experiment.

Trussing: The purpose of trussing is threefold: to keep the stuffing from falling out of the cavity; to help promote even cooking (by preventing the oven heat from freely flowing into the stomach cavity and by helping to keep the drumsticks and wings from cooking quicker than the thigh meat); and to help preserve the shape of the bird as it cooks. As with making stuffing, there are a number of effective ways to truss a chicken. We shall briefly outline one of the more common methods, which calls for the use of a trussing needle and kitchen twine. First, soak the string briefly in cooking oil (to help prevent the string from scorching). Then thread the needle. Sew the stomach cavity closed. Next, tie the ends of the two drumsticks together just below the exposed bone tips. Twist the wings flat against the back of the bird, securing them with the string (or skewer). If the neck cavity has a skin flap, pull it over the cavity and secure the skin with the string (or a skewer). Some people prefer to cut off the "pope's nose" (the tail extremity) in the belief that it disflavors the rest of the meat as it cooks. If the bird is young and healthy, it will not give the rest of the meat an "off" flavor. And cutting off the tail may make it difficult to close the stomach cavity when trussing. If you do not like the flavor of the tail (some people do), we suggest you snip it off after the bird has been cooked.

Cooking

While a mature chicken has to be cooked until well-done because it requires long, slow cooking to make it tender, a broiler-fryer or a small roaster needs to be cooked only until medium-well-done. Too many home chefs overcook these younger chickens because they assume that the presence of red juices in the flesh surrounding the thigh bone is a direct violation of the venerable rule to cook until the juices run clear. The reddish-brown juices that suffuse the meat lying next to the thigh bone are not flesh blood per se, but rather blood that has leached out from inside the bone marrow, a natural occurrence when a young chicken is cooked. Not only is the resulting blood-infused flesh fully cooked and safe to eat, these particular red juices will not show, and therefore will not give you a false reading when you make the standard "clear juice" test for doneness. In short, a slight trace of marrow blood in the thigh flesh of a young chicken is perfectly okay. Dark meat takes longer to cook than white meat, primarily because the thigh flesh is thicker. When cooking chicken pieces, give the thicker pieces a head start. Boned breasts make excellent fare and some dishes such as chicken *cordon bleu* absolutely call for them. However, if you have a choice, cook bone-in breasts: the bones add flavor, nutrients, and sauce-thickening substances and they reduce shrinkage. The lower the cooking temperature, or the shorter the cooking time, the less the shrinkage. As a rough rule of thumb, the older (and sometimes the larger) the bird, the longer the cooking period and the lower the temperature should be (see Roasting Times below).

Cooking a Whole Chicken

Roasting: Always lightly grease the rack and the bottom of the roasting pan; this will make washing the pan easier. It will also help keep the first pan drippings from scorching and hence from becoming bitter. Place the seasoned, trussed, room-temperature bird breast-side up on a rack in a shallow roasting pan. (The vertical roasting stands that perch the bird rump-side down, neck-side up are counterproductive as they allow too much of the internal juices to fall from the flesh.) Some cooks turn the bird upside down or on its side for set periods during the cooking process in order to give it an evenly browned skin. In most cases, the slight cosmetic advantage gained does not offset the damage done to the bird (as it cooks, it becomes increasingly fragile).

Do not cover the bird with a lid or aluminum foil—that may reduce splatter but will give you a mushy, steam-roasted bird rather than a firm-fleshed but succulently roasted one. For the same reason, do no add a liquid to the pan. Also, do not rest the bird on the bottom of the pan—a rack not only keeps a bird from steaming in its own juices, it permits proper circulation of the oven heat. If you are cooking more than one bird at a time, leave at least two inches of space between the birds, and between them and the oven walls, again for the sake of proper heat convection. If you wish to minimize splatter on your oven walls, the best way to do it without covering the bird is by decreasing the cooking temperature while increasing the cooking time.

Should you salt the skin of the bird before it is cooked? If you want the brownest possible skin, do not use salt (even in the basting mixture) until after or just before the bird comes out of the oven. Otherwise, feel free to salt first; the skin becomes only slightly less brown—an inconsequential loss considering the gain of giving the salt a chance to permeate into the flesh of the whole bird. One of the biggest challenges you will have is keeping the breast from overcooking and drying out while you are waiting for the slower-cooking thigh muscles to roast. The best technique is to cover the breast with a double layer of cheesecloth that has been soaked in melted butter, cooking oil, or the basting liquid. Remove that cloth 30 minutes before the bird is cooked to allow the breast to brown. Or bard the chicken breast rather than using the cheesecloth. Plan to baste the bird every 20 minutes, giving extra attention to the breast. Work quickly (but safely) to minimize loss of oven heat. You can baste with substances such as melted butter (herb-seasoned or not), cooking oil, or pan drippings.

Roasting Times: And now for the roasting times. We have experimented with dozens of well-publicized methods—"steady high heat," "constant low heat," "high then low heat," "low then high heat," and "turn off a 500°F oven"—all of them contributing to the bewilderment of the home cook. Which is best? The answer is none; all have their strengths and weaknesses, including the one we are about to give you. We have elected this method because it is the simplest to follow, the easiest to remember, and takes into consideration the size and type of bird.

Roast *Rock Cornish game birds* in a preheated 400°F oven for 20 minutes plus 15 to 20 minutes per pound.

Roast *broiler-fryers* in a preheated 375°F oven for 20 minutes plus 15 to 20 minutes per pound.

Roast *roasters* in a preheated 350°F oven for 20 minutes plus 15 to 20 minutes per pound.

Roast *capons* in a preheated 325°F oven for 20 minutes plus 15 to 20 minutes per pound.

As you can see, there are two variables. One is the oven temperature (the larger the bird, the lower the setting) and the second is the cooking minutes per pound, which will depend on how well done you want your bird. The shorter time, 15 minutes per pound, will give you the most succulent chicken. As you increase the time, the bird will become drier. Use our figures as guidelines, not as laws (see Test for Doneness). If your bird is stuffed, add about five minutes per pound to the above suggested cooking times. If you have not brought your refrigerator-cold bird to room temperature, add 15 to 30 minutes (depending on size) to the total cooking time. If your bird is frozen and is oven ready (no giblets in the cavity), doubling the suggested times will work, but do not expect satisfactory results. (See Thawing Frozen Birds).

When the bird has finished cooking, remove it from the oven, place it on a warm platter, and lightly cover it with aluminum foil (if the covering is too tight, the flesh will steam and become mushy). Before carving, allow the bird to rest 10 to 20 minutes, depending on size, in order to let the internal juices settle and redistribute. This will make carving easier and will minimize the quantity of juices that will seep out of the flesh as it is carved.

Spit-Roasting: (Note: Also follow relevant advice given in the previous sections.) Starting at the tail, push the rotisserie skewer through the bird's stomach cavity, having the rod come out in the middle of the "V" of the wishbone. Truss tightly. A small-to-medium-sized roaster chicken (your best bet) will take approximately 20 minutes plus 15 to 20 minutes per pound, depending on your electric rotisserie. Test for doneness as below.

Test for Doneness: Some cooks use the pinch test, some the thermometer test, some the clear-juice test, some the fork-tender test, some the drumstick test, some the scent-and-sight test—while others use none at all, relying on fate and the presumed accuracy of the typical cooking-time table.

Pinch Test: Of the various tests, this is generally the most reliable. With protected fingers (use a cloth or paper towel, for instance), squeeze the thickest section of the thigh. When the texture has become tender, the bird is done. Determining what "tender texture" means can only be gained through trial-and-error experience, temporarily using the thermometer or juice tests to corroborate your educated guesses.

Thermometer Test: You have two options. If your bird is large enough, you can insert a standard meat thermometer into the thickest part of the inner thigh muscle before you start the roasting process. You can briefly insert into the same anatomical location one of the small instant thermometers near and at the end of the cooking period. We prefer the instant thermometer method regardless of bird size because the wider diameter of the permanently inserted larger thermometer creates an easy escape route for the bird's internal juices. Whatever method you employ, you must be careful not to touch the bone which would give you an erroneously high reading. The bird will be medium-well-done when the thermometer registers 165°F, well-done at 180°F. Forget about those miniature pop-up thermometers that are inserted into the breast—they are too unreliable.

Clear-Juice Test: Pierce the thickest part of the outer thigh muscle, reaching between 1/4 and 1/2 inch below the skin, depending on the size of the bird. If the oozing juices are red-tinged, continue cooking. The bird will be properly done the moment the juices begin to run clear, with just a yellowish tinge. If you do use this test, do it as seldom as possible and do not use a thick, multitined fork to do the pricking, or your bird will lose an excessive quantity of juices, reducing the succulence and flavor of the thigh flesh.

Fork-Tender Test: This test is a cross between the pinch and prick tests. To determine if the chicken's flesh has become tender, and thereby cooked, the chef inserts the fork (or tip of a knife) into the thickest part of the bird's leg muscle. As with the pinch test, only experience can tell you what "fork-tender" is. And, again, test rarely to preserve juices.

Drumstick Test: Many cookbooks say that if you can easily wiggle the drumstick in its hip joint, the bird is done. As a matter of fact, by the time the drumstick can be readily jiggled in its socket, the bird is overdone. Another factor that makes this fatuous is that it is difficult to move the drumstick if the bird's legs are trussed together.

Scent-and-Sight Test: Professional cooks with years of experience can often tell when a bird is done solely with the nose and eyes. When in doubt, they confirm their assessment with the pinch or fork-tender test.

No Test: Cooks who blindly rely upon cooking-time tables for roasting birds will have inconsistent results even if the tables are reliable (few are), because there are too many variables. For instance, the size, age, quality, and type of bird; the temperature of the bird when it went into the oven; the unique characteristics of the oven. For best results, use the suggested cooking times (such as those we recommend) only as a rough guideline, making your final determination based on empirical evidence such as the pinch test.

Pan Gravy: A simple but tasty way to make pan gravy is to remove the roasted chicken and the rack from the roasting pan, then pour off all but about two or three tablespoons of the pan drippings. Place the pan on top of the stove over a moderate flame. With a wooden spoon, scrape off any solidified pan drippings that cling to the bottom of the pan until they will dissolve. Immediately remove the pan from the heat, and mix into the remaining liquified pan drippings 1 to 2 tablespoons of standard (noninstant) flour—the more flour you add, the thicker your gravy will be. (Making a gravy with instant flour is easier and quicker, but produces less desirable results.) Place the pan over a low to moderate flame, and stir the paste (called a *roux*) for several minutes. Stir into the *roux* one cup of broth (perhaps enriched with cream, wine, cooked and minced giblets, or some of the juices that you previously poured out of the pan); add the broth slowly (a few tablespoons at a time), or the developing gravy will become lumpy. Cook while stirring for several minutes or so, until the gravy thickens. Season to taste and serve.

The Oysters: A chicken has two so-called *oysters* or *nubbins*, each imbedded in a cavity on either side of the rear half of the backbone. An average-sized oyster is about an inch long, oval, and dark-fleshed. Many gourmets—with good reason—consider these delicately flavored twin morsels to be the best part of the chicken. Yet only a minority of cooks and diners are aware of their existence. If you remove the backbone of an uncooked chicken, pull these mini-muscles out of their recessed pockets and either briefly saute them in butter or simmer them for about five minutes (perhaps in the saucepan containing the giblets), then season and serve them as an appetizer on a small square of buttered toast. If you are carving a cooked chicken, search the backbone for the two precious culinary jewels; too often they are thrown away in the garbage pail with the backbone.

Cooking Chicken Parts

Broiling: (Note: Also follow relevant advice given in previous ROASTING A WHOLE CHICKEN section.) The ideal chicken for broiling is a broiler-fryer. Brush the room-temperature pieces with a combination of butter and cooking oil. Place the pieces skin-side down in a single, nontouching layer on a lightly greased broiler rack set into a lightly greased broiler pan. Season before or after cooking, as you wish, but go easy on the spices such as black pepper and well-spiced flavorings such as barbecue sauce until the chicken is almost cooked, because the spices may burn and become bitter. Also go easy with the salt at first lest it draws meat juices to the surface and, thus, keeps the pale chicken skin from acquiring the desirable rich, deep brown complexion normally associated with broiled meats. One of the secrets of successfully broiling chicken halves or quarters in a typical home broiler compartment is to cook the flesh farther away from the heat source and at a lower temperature than most cooks are in the habit of doing. For chicken with a succulent interior surrounded by a crisp exterior, try broiling the pieces approximately 5 inches away from a preheated 400° F gas burner or electric coil for a total of 30 to 45 minutes, depending on thickness. If the pieces vary in thickness, start cooking the thicker ones first. Every ten minutes, turn the pieces, brushing them each time with the butter-and-cooking oil basting mixture. Test for doneness by making a cut in the thickest part of the meat near but not next to the bone.

Barbecuing: (Note: Also follow relevant advice in the previous sections on roasting and broiling.) The ideal chicken for barbecuing is a broiler-fryer. Whole birds should not be barbecued unless you have a domed barbecue oven, in which case you should consult each manufacturer's instructions. Timing for barbecuing halves, quarters, or smaller pieces of chicken, however, is universal for all barbecue units, if they are left uncovered. Brush the pieces with a protective coat of oil. Place the room-temperature pieces skin-side up 4 to 6 inches (the thicker the piece, the farther the distance) above nonflaming, moderately hot briquettes. Cook approximately 40 to 70 minutes, depending on thickness of the pieces, their distance from the heat source, and variables such as wind velocity. Test for doneness near the end of your estimated cooking period. If pieces are of differing thicknesses, give the thicker pieces a head start. Turn the pieces every 10 minutes, basting them each time. Do not baste with a standard barbecue sauce until the final 15 minutes of cooking, because the sugar and spices may burn, giving your chicken a bitter flavor and scorched facade. If you marinated the chicken in a barbecue sauce, brush most of it off and brush on an unspiced oil mixture before you start barbecuing them.

Frying: For best results, select broiler-fryers. Always let the pieces come to or near room temperature before cooking them, or the interiors may not fully cook. For best browning, pat the pieces dry with paper toweling before proceeding with the recipe. And, if you are going to fry the pieces without a coating, do not salt or pepper them until after they have been browned, as the salt will draw out moisture (hindering browning) and the pepper may burn (producing bitterness).

Of the many ways to coat chicken pieces, the simplest and most popular is to dredge them with seasoned flour. Some cooks dip the pieces in beaten egg before dusting them with the flour. The next most popular coating method is to bread the pieces by giving them successive coatings of seasoned flour, beaten egg, and breadcrumbs. Once breaded, allow the pieces to rest at room temperature for 20 to 30 minutes to allow the coating to dry a bit. This step will help minimize the number of breadcrumbs that fall off and burn in the oil. It also helps reduce the amount of oil that reaches the chicken flesh. For deep-fried chicken, a batter coating is also popular. Place the pieces in a thick-bottomed skillet or sauté pan skin-side down (when deep-frying, submerge them into the oil edgewise). Leave at least ½ inch of space between the pieces and the pan walls. If you overcrowd a skillet or sauté pan, steam will be trapped beneath the cooking pieces, making them soggy. If you overcrowd a deep frying pan, you may drastically lower the temperature. For even cooking, add the thickest pieces first.

To sauté: Use 2 to 4 tablespoons (depending on pan diameter) of a 2-to-1 mixture of butter and cooking oil. When the fat is moderately hot, add the pieces and brown them on both sides, then reduce the cooking temperature and cook uncovered for about 7 to 15 minutes per side, depending on thickness. Test for doneness with a fork. An alternative to the basic sautéing method is to cover the pan after the pieces have been browned, then reduce the heat to moderately low and cook for a total of 20 to 35 minutes. Or place the covered pan of browned pieces in a preheated 350° F oven for about 30 to 50 minutes. Both these methods should be thought of as braising rather than frying techniques, and while both give satisfactory results, the pieces will have soft, not crisp, crusts. Crisp crusts are one of the advantages of frying.

To pan-fry: Heat ½ inch of fresh cooking oil to 365° to 375°F. Add the pieces and cook them for a total time of 10 to 25 minutes, depending on thickness. Turn once or several times, as you prefer. Test for fork-tender doneness.

To deep-fry: Make sure the cooking oil is fresh and preheated to 365° to 375° F. Too high a temperature will overcook the surface of the chicken before the interior is properly cooked. Too low a temperature will permit the chicken to absorb too much of the cooking oil, making the chicken oily. Estimate 6 to 12 minutes per piece, depending on thickness. Longer periods will toughen and dry out the flesh.

When cooked, regardlesss of frying method, drain the pieces on paper toweling. Serve the cooked pieces immediately. If that is not possible, keep them warm in a preheated 275°F oven, but not for more than 15 minutes, as fried chicken becomes soggy as it waits for the diner.

Simmering: *Simmering*, or *poaching*, is the preferred method for cooking a mature bird whose flesh will end up in a preparation such as a cold chicken sandwich or salad—or as the star ingredient in chicken soup made with the nourishing broth. Put a whole or disjointed chicken in a large pot and cover it with several inches of water to spare. Bring the water to a boil, then reduce to a simmer and wait about ten minutes. Skim the surface scum, then add to the water various flavoring agents, such as salt (about 1/2 to 1 teaspoon per quart of liquid), peppercorns, thyme, bay leaf, parsley, carrots, celery, onions, white wine, and lemon juice. Continue to simmer a whole bird 1 to 2 hours, chicken parts for 30 to 60 minutes, depending on age and size. One clue to doneness is when the meat shrinks noticeably away from the exposed bone tips. If you are serving the chicken cold, allow the meat to cool in the broth for added flavor.

Stewing: Follow the relevant advice given in the previous section on simmering, but this time use a smaller, heavy pot, and put in just enough liquid to cover, no more. Be more eclectic in your selection of seasonings: for instance, use ingredients such as tomatoes, fruit juice, and garlic, depending on your goal. After the liquid has been skimmed and seasoned, cover the pot tightly, and reduce the heat to produce no more than a gentle simmer. Continue cooking on top of the stove (or in a 325° F oven) for 1 to 2 hours, depending on chicken age and thickness.

Braising: Follow the relevant advice given in the previous sections on simmering and stewing, but this time first brown the whole or disjointed chicken in hot fat or oil, then add almost 1/2 inch of preheated seasoned liquid to the pot. Ingredients like sauteed onions and peeled tomatoes help give character to braised chicken. Cover and cook on top of the stove or in the oven, as suggested for stewing. You may have to add liquid near the end of the cooking time, if the liquid in the pot gets too low.

Equivalents

One pound of bone-in chicken furnishes about two servings, while boneless chicken offers about three and possibly four servings, depending on individual appetites. The older the bird, the more meat you will likely get from each pound of dressed weight.

CLASSIC USES AND AFFINITIES

Some of the better known chicken preparations include: chicken Kiev, coq au vin, Southern (and Maryland) fried chicken and its Austrian progenitor *backhendl*, chicken fricassee, paella, *arroz con pollo*, chicken with dumplings, country captain, chicken cacciatore, barbecued chicken, suprêmes de volaille, chicken Marengo, chicken pot pie, chicken a la king, chicken paprika, chicken salad, chicken tandoor, and the all-time Jewish "penicillin," chicken soup. Chinese cuisine abounds with chicken dishes: moo goo gai pan, chicken with walnuts, and lemon chicken, to name a few. Among the classic herbs and spices for chicken are tarragon, thyme, bayleaf, parsley, basil, dill, rosemary, sage, savory, mustard, paprika, nutmeg, curry—and poultry seasoning, which can be almost any combination. Other popular affinities include white or red wine, vinegar, lemon juice, and members of the onion family.

CHICKEN FAT

BACKGROUND

Mild-flavored chicken fat—and particularly the type found near the entrance to the stomach cavity—makes a fine cooking medium. Some cuisines, such as Jewish, make *schmaltz*. They pan-fry the chicken fat with onions and perhaps apples, drain and store it for use as a butter substitute. The hardened skin segments, a byproduct of rendering, are enjoyed as *grebenes*, or Jewish cracklings.

CHICKEN GIBLETS AND VARIETY MEATS

BACKGROUND

Chicken *liver* is the most popular poultry *variety meat*, followed by the *heart* and cleaned *gizzard*. All three of these edible organs are collectively known as the *giblets*. Other variety meats are noted at the end of this entry.

PREPARATION

Preliminaries

If you buy a whole chicken, the giblets and the neck will probably be tucked inside the stomach cavity. (For the record, the giblets put inside the cavity of the bird you buy in a supermarket were probably not from the same bird, but—thank goodness—most of the time do come from similar-sized birds.) Remove them as soon as you get home, and refrigerate them separately. (If you have a frozen bird, the giblets cannot be removed until the bird is nearly thawed.) Before storing or cooking giblets, give the sniff-and-look test: if they have an off-odor or off-color, discard them. Unless it is absolutely necessary, do not freeze giblets because they (especially the liver) do not freeze well. Fresh giblets (especially the liver) are very perishable and should be used within the day of purchase. Wash them in cold water, being particularly careful not to damage the delicate liver. When examining the liver, pay close attention to its color. If it is yellow-tinged, it may be from a mature bird, and therefore will not be as delicate in flavor as you would want. If the liver is green-tinged, throw it away—more than likely one of the workers at the processing plant allowed the gall bladder to leak its bitter bile into the liver. When buying a batch of chicken livers in the supermarket, check carefully for such discoloration, as the terrible bile flavor may permeate the other livers.

Cooking

Giblets: Place the heart, gizzard, and neck (and other scraps such as wing tips, or backbone, should you have them) into a saucepan. Cover with water and add about 1/2 teaspoon of salt per quart of liquid. Bring to a boil, reduce heat, cover, and simmer for 1/2 to 1 1/2 hours, depending on the age and size of the bird. If you wish to add the liver, add it the last 10 to 15 minutes (depending on the size and age of the bird) of the cooking. Drain the liquid, reserving it for making a sauce. Discard the backbone, neck, and wing tips. Save the giblets for use in preparations such as a sauce, stuffing or rice casserole. Giblets may also be sauteed or braised.

Liver: One of the easiest ways to cook chicken livers is to sauté them in butter over moderate heat, turning them gently to promote even browning. When the centers have lost all but a slight pinkish cast, the livers are ready. If no pink remains, they are overcooked and have likely toughened. When cooked, season to taste. Besides being for simply sautéed dishes and giblet-based creations, chicken livers are excellent for making pâtés, sandwich spreads, salads, and brochettes, perhaps wrapped in bacon.

Gizzard: The biological function of the gizzard is to grind the seeds and grains the chicken eats. The part that does the chore is in the center of the organ and must be cut out; this is virtually always done before a gizzard reaches the meat display case. The outer, fleshy part is the edible portion. It is tough-textured and needs to be cooked with slow moist heat—simmer or braise it, but never let it boil or be cooked with dry heat unless it has been finely chopped.

Heart: Little preparation is required for the heart, except perhaps to trim any protruding blood vessels. Being not quite as tough as the gizzard, the heart can be sautéed, if from a young bird. Cook it just to the point where some internal pink remains.

Other Variety Meats: Other chicken variety meats are the *feet* (braised and eaten, or used to flavor and thicken soups by many ethnic groups including the Chinese), *cockscomb* (used as a colorful, edible garnish by the French) and the developing *eggs* (can be used as regular eggs in most culinary functions, including as a sauce thickener and enricher).

CHICK-PEA

BACKGROUND

Think of the *chick-pea* (*Cecer arietinum*) as the poor man's filbert. Chick-peas taste vaguely like a nut and, if fresh, can be eaten raw in small quantities or roasted like true nuts. The chick-pea is a hard, round, knobby legume the size of a giant pea that is commonly buff or white, but sometimes red or black. An old food and one of the most nutritious legumes, the chick-pea is called *garbanzo* in Spanish and *ceci* in Italian. (See BEANS for information on soaking, cooking, etc.)

AVAILABILITY

Chick-peas are available dried, canned, and, in some regions, fresh.

CLASSIC USES AND AFFINITIES

The chick-pea is especially popular in cold marinated salads. Tomato, thyme, onions, parsley, sesame seeds, nuts, black pepper, vinegar, and garlic all go well with the chick-pea, as do other beans in combination. *Hummus* is the traditional Middle-Eastern bean paste made from chick-peas and flavored with sesame seeds.

CHICORY

BACKGROUND

Chichorium intybus grows wild in Europe, Asia and North America. During July and August the bright blue flowers of the wild chicory plant decorate many of America's rural roadsides. The plant is a botanical cousin of both Belgian and curly ENDIVE—and to add to the confusion, the latter is often called chicory.

CLASSIC USES AND AFFINITIES

Chicory is grown commercially for its root, which is often used as a flavorful coffee extender or substitute. The root can also be braised or simmered like a turnip. However it is used, chicory adds a bitter flavor to the recipe.

CHILI POWDER

BACKGROUND

A spice blend, not a single spice or herb, chili powder is a mixture of ground hot peppers and other spices such as cumin, garlic, oregano, cloves, and allspice. It was invented in the American southwest in the late nineteenth or early twentieth century. There is no one official recipe. Since most supermarket varieties are overly mild, many chili-powder lovers usually blend their own (it is the best bet), or spike the commercial mixture with added chili pepper such as cayenne.

(See HERBS AND SPICES for information on buying, storing, cooking, etc.)

CLASSIC USES AND AFFINITIES

Tex-Mex style foods such as chili con carne, tacos, enchiladas, and refried beans need chili powder. The spice blend can also be used in cocktail or barbecue sauces and in corn and egg dishes. Add untested chili powder initially in cautious increments because it may be hot. Avoid contact with skin and eyes to prevent irritation.

CHINESE CABBAGE

BACKGROUND

The *Tientsin*, *Chinese cabbage*, or *celery cabbage* is called *Brassica pe-tsai* by the botanists and delicious by everyone else: by the Chinese who have grown it for centuries, by the French, who have grown it for over a century and a half, and by Americans, who have grown it since the turn of the century. The vertical, yellow-green-white leaves grow in a tight 8- to 16-inch-long cylinder. Each leaf has a broad celery-like rib at its center, tapering to the top.

AVAILABILITY

Chinese cabbage is available the year round in Chinese groceries. Sometimes you can find it in supermarkets.

Buying Tips

Select pale specimens for the best, most delicate flavor.

PREPARATION

Tightly wrapped Chinese cabbage will keep about 3 to 6 days in the vegetable compartment of your refrigerator. It can be cut fine and used as a raw salad green. It can also be cooked in Chinese and Oriental-style dishes, or, with a slightly shortened cooking time, used in recipes for head cabbage.

CHIVES

BACKGROUND

Chives, a member of the onion family, have been used by cooks from the East and West since prehistoric times. Though some pickle the bulbils, most of us just use the thin, hollow, 6- to 9-inch leaves as a seasoning. While over 99 percent of the chives consumed in America are *Allium schoenoprasum*, several other edible varieties exist, including the Chinese chives, a more pungent species available in Oriental markets.

AVAILABILITY

Fresh chives are commercially available year round, with a peak in spring and early summer. Most food markets also sell minced chives, either freeze-dried or frozen. Both are inferior to fresh chives in terms of flavor, fragrance, color and texture, but at least the frozen type bears some resemblance. Moreover, the frozen version can be used directly on a dry food, while the freeze-dried variety must first be reconstituted in a little water for several minutes. (This step is unnecessary if the freeze-dried chives are going directly into a hot or cold liquid dish, so long as you wait several minutes before eating it.)

Buying Tips

When buying fresh chives, select unblemished and unsoggy leaves with vivid green color and unwilted tips. When purchasing potted chives, check for pests, as they can infest your other houseplants.

PREPARATION

Grow Your Own

Chives are hardy perennials that are relatively easy to grow from seed or bulbil in gardens or on windowsills so long as your plant has good soil, a minimum temperature of 50°F, sufficient humidity (most apartments fail this requirement), adequate watering, and plenty of sunshine. When you buy potted chives from a store, replant them outdoors or in a larger container, giving them more space—one reason store-bought potted chives deteriorate so quickly indoors is that there are too many plants for the soil in the pot.

Cutting Your Chives

Use scissors to remove the amount of chives you need. Do not cut off the top like a crew-cut; this will cause unsightly brown tips as well as extra work when you have to trim those blemishes. Rather, snip off several whole blades at a time, cutting approximately half an inch above the soil surface. If the plant is properly looked after, the leaves will regrow and can be harvested several times in one season. But cutting the same leaf more than four times a season is not recommended if you want the plant to rejuvenate next spring.

Storage

Fresh, trimmed whole chives should be washed in cold running water, patted dry, wrapped in paper toweling, sealed in a plastic bag, and stored in the refrigerator vegetable crisper. Alternatively, place the chives, bottom end down, into a glass jar partially filled with water and cover with a plastic bag secured by a rubber band, then place in the refrigerator. Both these storage methods are effective for 1 to 3 days, depending on the original condition of the chives. Frozen minced chives that come in plastic tubs should always be kept in the frozen food compartment. To reduce frost buildup inside the tub (it is a major problem), minimize the time the chives are exposed to fresh air out of the freezing compartment—and be sure to seal the lid tightly. A well-stored, infrequently opened tub of chives should last a month or two. If the frost builds up excessively—or if you inadvertently stored the chives tub above 32°F—then rinse the chives, pat dry, and plan to use them within hours in a suitable dish or sauce. You have numerous options. If you have a surplus of freshly trimmed chives that you cannot use within a few days, freeze them whole, mincing them later, when needed. If you try to freeze your own minced chives, you will end up with a less-than-desirable, unmanageable frozen patty. Freeze-dried chives will last several months if kept in a tightly closed container, away from direct sunlight and high heat.

Mincing

The chive leaf is almost always minced. This is easy to do: hold a bunch of chives in one hand and use a scissor to snip them into ⅛-inch segments. Or hold the bunch of chives on a cutting board and slice into ⅛-inch segments with a knife. Other choices include using an electric blender, food processor, or mincing jar, though these tools do not produce uniform pieces essential for a visually appealing garnish. Once cut, chives begin to lose their refreshing volatile oils and start developing a slightly bitter, acrid, "off" taste. So observe these pointers: Always mince fresh chives just before use. Sprinkle them on top of cooked foods rather than adding them to a cooking dish. Do not mix chives with other uncooked ingredients such as cream cheese if they are to be stored for more than an hour or two.

CLASSIC USES AND AFFINITIES

Chives are used by chefs when a delicate onion flavor or a bright green garnish is desired. A sprinkling of chives is basic on soups (especially creamy ones like vichyssoise), golden omelets and scrambled eggs, baked or boiled potatoes, sliced tomatoes, and fish. Chives are popularly mixed into cottage cheese, sour cream, yogurt, cream cheese, creamed butter, spreads, and sauces as *vinaigrette* and mayonnaise.

CHOCOLATE AND COCOA

BACKGROUND

Chocolate and *cocoa* are products of the hulled bean of the *Theobroma cacao*, a tropical tree native to the New World, though now also commercially cultivated in Africa (especially in Ghana) and Southeast Asia. Montezuma (and his high-ranked Aztec followers, who were allowed the privilege) relished a cocoalike drink made from the *cacoa bean*, believing it to be an aphrodisiac as well as delicious; he was right on at least one score. The words *chocolate* and *cocoa* come from the Aztec word *cacahuatl*, meaning "bitter juice."

To produce chocolate, processors first extract from the hulled cacao bean a substance known in the trade as *cocoa liquor*.

Varieties

Chocolate:

Unsweetened (baking or *bitter) chocolate* is the pure form of the cocoa liquor. It is sold in packages containing one-ounce squares and is the form of chocolate most often preferred by serious cooks and bakers.

Semisweet or *bittersweet chocolate* is cocoa liquor enriched with sugar and, typically, with some extra cocoa butter (the fat in the cacao bean). Many recipes for icings, coating sauces, and pie or cake fillings call for semisweet chocolate.

Sweet or *sweet cooking chocolate* has an even higher sugar content than semisweet chocolate and can be eaten as a snack, or—in some circumstances—in cooking. What is sold in this country as *German chocolate* is a type of sweet chocolate. Like unsweetened and semisweet chocolate, this chocolate is sold in measured squares in bar form. Like semisweet chocolate, it should not be substituted for unsweetened chocolate unless you know its exact sugar and cocoa-butter content and can make the proper allowances for those contents in the recipe.

Milk chocolate is the star ingredient of most American candy bars. It is chocolate liquor infused and made milder with extra cocoa butter, dry milk, and a sweetener such as sugar. Do not substitute milk chocolate for nonmilk chocolate in a recipe.

Chocolate chips are usually made of

semisweet chocolate and, if so, can be used instead of semisweet in most recipes. The exception is when, as with some *chocolate-flavored chocolate chips*, the manufacturer has substituted hydrogenated vegetable oil for the cocoa butter in such a way as to seriously alter the taste or fat content of the chocolate. The *raison d'être* of chocolate (and chocolate-flavored) chips is twofold: they melt quicker than chocolate squares, and the chips can be employed effectively in some preparations as an eye-appealing topping. Chocolate chips are also made, though less prevalently, with sweet chocolate.

Chocolate syrup is a mediocre instant sauce people buy for such purposes as mixing into milk or pouring over ice cream. It is well-sweetened with sugar or corn syrup and flavored with various ingredients according to the producer's proprietary recipe.

Liquid chocolate is a convenience food in that it eliminates the need for a cook to melt chocolate squares. However, since the chocolate liquor has been enriched with vegetable oil rather than cocoa butter, liquid chocolate will not yield the same satisfactory results in terms of flavor, aroma, and texture.

Artificial chocolates are increasing their supermarket shelf space, which means that people are buying more of them. When you see the words *artificial chocolate* or *chocolate-flavored* or do not see the word *chocolate* on the label, move down the aisle to the real chocolate products.

White chocolate is not true chocolate but a vegetable-oil mixture, typically flavored with vanilla or, more likely, an artificial flavor such as vanillin. Sometimes cocoa butter is added, but that ingredient does not make the product chocolate.

Cocoa:

Cocoa is the result when approximately half the cocoa butter (the fat or oil in the bean) is removed from the cocoa liquor. The result is the powdered ingredient we buy to make a hot cup of cocoa. The cocoa powder is sold plain or is blended with other granular ingredients such as sugar and dry milk (and, perhaps, further processed) to make instant cocoa mixes. Because these convenience foods usually have a very high sugar content, it is best to buy the plain product and add sugar in keeping with sensible good-health practices. You will also be saving money. Plain cocoa is sometimes sold in three forms: *breakfast cocoa*, *cocoa* and *low-fat cocoa*, in descending order of cocoa-butter content. *Dutch cocoa* has been refined with an alkali which, because it partially neutralizes the natural acid of cocoa, helps give the product a richer, distinct character.

Buying Tips

When chocolate is stored improperly or too long, cocoa butter rises to the chocolate's surface, giving it a grayish-white "bloom." Many cookbooks say this does not affect quality; our tests show that it does affect the flavor and texture to a slight, but noticeable, degree. A piece of prime chocolate has a uniform color with a soft glossy glow. Nowadays, much of the chocolate in candy bars is specially treated to raise its melting point to counteract the effects of warm weather. This is done for the producer's and store's benefit, not your palate's. A telltale sign of this tempered chocolate is that it will not readily melt in your mouth. It will also tend to have a grainy rather than a satiny texture and may smack of chemicals.

PREPARATION

Storage

Keep your chocolate tightly wrapped and dry at about 60° to 72°F.

Melting Chocolate

Since chocolate scorches easily and

therefore may become bitter, it should be slowly melted (for about 8 to 12 minutes) over very low heat in a double boiler or in a bowl placed in a pan of gently simmering water. Be careful not to splash water into the melting chocolate, as this may give your preparation a firm or crusty texture.

Substituting Cocoa for Chocolate

If you run out of unsweetened chocolate, you can use cocoa. Since cocoa has had some of its cocoa butter removed, you must add some form of fat to the cocoa powder. For each ounce or square of unsweetened chocolate that the recipe calls for, substitute three tablespoons of regular standard cocoa power plus one tablespoon of unsalted butter.

CIDER

BACKGROUND

The juice of the apple, if unchecked, will ferment into an alcoholic beverage. It was quite popular with our early American forefathers. *Sweet* (or *soft*) *cider* differs from *hard cider* in that the former has not reached a potent fermentation stage. You have sweet cider if you drink it early in the fermentation stage or if you stop the fermentation by any of several means, including pasteurization and by the addition of benzoate of soda. Hard cider can attain an alcoholic content of 14 percent (sometimes slightly higher), but most of the hard cider we drink is under 10 percent. When cider is distilled, it becomes *apple brandy*. The popular variety in America is *applejack*, in France it is *Calvados*. Both can be used in cooking with great success.

CINNAMON AND CASSIA

BACKGROUND

True *cinnamon, Cinnamomum zeylanicum*, is imported from the Spice Islands (Molucca Islands) and Sri Lanka (Ceylon), but most cinnamon sold in the West is really *cassia, Cinnamomum cassia*, a spice that is tangier and more bitter than the darker true cinnamon. There is nothing wrong with the lighter-hued cassia per se; it is just that the genuine cinnamon is so vastly superior in flavor and fragrance that cinnamon is the only one you should purchase, even though you will have to pay a premium price. (See HERBS AND SPICES for information on buying, storing, cooking, etc.)

Both cinnamon and cassia come from the dried inner bark of evergreen trees. Curled bits of bark are sold as *cinnamon sticks* or *quills*. The bark is very hard and almost impossible for most cooks to grind at home, so ground cinnamon is also sold. The cooking of the Indian subcontinent as well as the Middle East use a good deal of cinnamon and cassia, in part because these spices contain antiseptic phenols that impede food spoilage.

Storage

Stick cinnamon kept dry and out of direct sunlight has a long shelf life. Ground cinnamon should be examined frequently for negative scent and taste qualities.

CLASSIC USES AND AFFINITIES

Cinnamon is one of the most important spices for the home baker. Apples and cinnamon taste wonderful together. Other fruit pies, salads, preserves, and cakes also take well to cinnamon. Sweet potatoes, squash and rice pudding are all traditionally sprinkled with cinnamon. Cinnamon toast is a teatime and nursery classic. Ground cinnamon is a major flavoring in many Greek lamb and beef dishes. The combination of chocolate and cinnamon is popular in Mexican cooking. Cinnamon sticks are used in pickling, in meat dishes, and as stirrers for hot drinks such as cider, mulled wine, chocolate, and coffee. Stick cinnamon is used in pickles, clear jellies, or any dish where the appearance of ground spice is undesirable. Stick cinnamon is also preferable in dishes where only a hint of cinnamon flavor is desired. The stick can be removed partway through the cooking period.

CIPOLLINI

BACKGROUND

Cipollini is the tender young bulb of the *grape hyacinth (Hyacinthus orientalis)*, popular in Italian and Greek communities.

AVAILABILITY

A few Italian-American markets carry the bitter, onionlike cipollini during the fall, its peak season.

PREPARATION

To lessen bitterness, some chefs peel and simmer the small brown-skinned bulbs for about 10 to 20 minutes in acidulated water (one tablespoon of vinegar per quart of liquid). The cipollini are then seasoned, coated with olive oil, and served hot or cold as an appetizer. Pickling the bulb is another culinary avenue open to the cook.

CITRON

BACKGROUND

Think of an oversized (up to 1-pound) lemon with a very thick, bumpy, greenish-yellow skin and you'll have a mental approximation of what a *citron* (*Citrus medica*) looks like.

Buying Tips

If you should come across a fresh citron, look for one with a firm, unshriveled skin. If it has been cut into sections, be sure the rind is fragrant and moist, not dried out.

CLASSIC USES AND AFFINITIES

Unlike its cousin, the lemon, the citron is grown primarily for its thick rind, which is often candied and used by bakers to add color and flavor to cakes, pastries, and breads. Can you imagine a fruitcake without candied citron peel?

CLAM

BACKGROUND

Clam-eating in America tends to be a coastal affair. Easterners favor their local *hardshell* and *softshell clams*, while Westerners believe their local clams, such as *pismo* and *geoduck* are best. Both shores come out winners. The Gulf Coast, however, does not have clams worthy of regional chauvinism.

Varieties

Atlantic Clams: The most popular

East Coast clam is the *hardshell*, sometimes called by its Indian name *quahog*. The hardshell clam is often sold under three distinct names depending on size. *Littleneck clams* are the smallest (customarily less than 2 inches in shell diameter) and are the preferred type to eat raw on the half shell because they are the sweetest and most tender. Next in size comes the *cherrystone*, 2 to 3 inches across. A cherrystone is sometimes called the "all-purpose" clam, because it is suitable for eating raw or for cooking. The largest of the three is the *chowder*—it is seldom eaten raw because of its toughness and its intimidating size as it sits on its shell. While this big boy gets its name from the fact that it is often relegated to clam chowder, it can also end up in other preparations, such as clam fritters. The only difference among littleneck, cherrystone, and chowder clams is their age.

Second in culinary popularity to the hardshell clam is the *softshell clam*, which is especially favored in New England. It physically differs from its hardshell cousin in that it is more oval and has a projecting rubber-hose-like neck (the *siphon*). The hardshell clam is typically thought of as the one to eat raw on the half shell, while the softshell (nicknamed *steamer* if small) conjures up the image of being steamed or dipped in batter and fried. Both types are popular chowder and fritter ingredients.

Pacific Clams: The best-tasting West Coast clam is the *pismo*; regrettably, it is becoming scarce. Winner of the funny-looks award is the *geoduck* (pronounced goo-ey-duck) which is about a half foot long with a necklike siphon projecting 2 feet or more. Its trimmed siphon flesh can be cooked like ABALONE. Other leading Pacific clams include the *razor* (shaped like your great-grandfather's straight razor), *softshell* (the Atlantic variety transplanted), *littleneck* (differs from the Atlantic variety in species) and *butter* clams. *Cockle* clams also exist, but are not as tasty as their distant European relatives.

AVAILABILITY

Fresh clams are in peak season from September through early May, though some can always be found in the marketplace the rest of the year. They are sold in the shell, or, sometimes, shucked. Frozen, canned, and dried clams are sold the year round. Commercially processed clam juice, a watered-down clam liquor, is sold in bottles. It is a poor imitation of the fresh clam liquor.

Digging Your Own

A well-entrenched American sport is *clamming* or clam-digging. Hardshell clams can be harvested by walking in shallow water at low tide while using your toes to detect the mollusk's presence—once found, you bend down and dig it out of the water-covered sand with your fingers. Softshell and razor clams can be dug up on the wet sand at low tide—the spouting siphon of the softshell clam gives away its location. When clamming, be sure the water is not contaminated and that the sport is legal and has no restrictions such as the need for a license—check with the local authorities.

Buying Tips

Buy your clams only from a reliable merchant with a high stock turnover. If the clam is the type that can tightly close its shell, give the shell a light rap; if the clam has a siphon, lightly tap its neck. If the shell does not close or its neck does not contract, the mollusk is dead or well on its way, and therefore should not be bought. Nor should you buy a clam that has a broken shell or feels light or heavy for its size. If the fishmonger's supply has too many of these rejects in the bin, do not buy even his good specimens. If possible, select even-sized clams; they look better when served together and, if you cook them, they will cook uniformly. As a general rule, the smaller the clam for its species, the tenderer it will be. When buying shucked clams, look for plumpness, clear liquid, and no smell except a hint of the sea.

PREPARATION

Storage

You can keep clams in good condition for one to three days in a bucket of ice in a cool, dark place such as a celler—or in a container at 40°F in a refrigerator. Clams with siphons have the shortest storage lives.

Preliminaries

Your first step is to give the clams the same relevant test suggested under Buying Tips above. Before opening a clam, the shell should be well scrubbed—and, if possible, the live clams should be soaked overnight in a bucket of water to allow them to rid themselves of some of their digested food and sand inside their shells. This purging is sometimes facilitated when you sprinkle fine-grained cornmeal on top of the water—as it sinks, the clams may eat it, thereby helping them to eliminate some of their previously digested food. When the clams have been sufficiently soaked, discard any that float or, after you have drained the pot, any whose shell does not close (or whose neck does not contract slightly) when tapped—such clams are dead or dying and should not be eaten. Some softshell clams need to have their beardlike growth removed and discarded.

Opening Clams: If you are experienced, a clam knife will open most live hardshell clams. First, firmly hold the clam in the palm of your hand, with the hinged end of the clam pointed to the palm. Using pressure, insert the sharp edge of the clam knife into the seam and pry apart the two shell halves, being careful not to lose the delicious clam liquor inside the shell. Sever the flesh from both shell halves and, if you are going to serve the clams on the half shell, keep the flesh inside the larger half. If you are concerned about cutting yourself, use (and reserve for future clam opening) a pair of heavy-duty cotton work gloves. If you are inexperienced, use a guillotinelike clam apparatus. Clams are easier to open if they are put in the freezer for 5 to 15 minutes beforehand. Freezing them completely does an even better job, but the flavor and texture of the flesh will suffer. When steaming clams, simply put the unopened shells in the pot—they will automatically open when cooked. If any do not open, the obstinate clams are suspect and should not be eaten.

Cooking

Clams (especially the young ones) need not be cooked to make them tender. One cooks clams to develop their flavor. If clams are cooked too long, they become tough. Add shucked clams to soups, stews, and sauces during the last 3 to 6 minutes (depending on their size) of the cooking period—and simmer, never boil them. Clams will bake in a preheated 350°F oven in 10 to 20 minutes, depending on their size and whether they are being cooked in a sauce. Clams can also be sautéed, deep-fried, and steamed.

Equivalents

Six to twelve clams on the half shell make one serving, depending on the size of the clam and the diner's eyes.

CLASSIC USES AND AFFINITIES

Purists say the only thing that should go with fresh raw clams is a hearty appetite. Other diners enjoy sprinkling clams with lemon juice, and/or with horseradish, cocktail sauce, melted butter, or a simple grind of peppercorns. World-famous clam-based dishes include clams casino (baked clams cooked and garnished with bacon, parsley and breadcrumbs), clams *oreganate*, red or white clam sauce for spaghetti, and clam fritters. Clam chowder has created a culinary controversy: the Manhattan version uses tomato; the New England recipe—the original—calls for cream or milk. A clambake is a New England tradition originated by the Indians.

CLOUDBERRY

BACKGROUND

Cloudberry (*Rubus chamaemorus*) is a species of raspberry native to the northern parts of New England. It bears a soft amber fruit that resembles a raspberry. Cloudberries are too tart to eat raw. They are usually transformed into a jam that sells for a king's ransom.

CLOVES

BACKGROUND

A *clove* is an unopened flower with part of its stem that has been dried until it has acquired its characteristic reddish-brown hue and pebblelike texture. Each *Eugenia caryophyllata* is surprisingly lightweight—it takes over 1,000 whole cloves to make 1 pound. The tree is a native of the Indonesian Spice Islands; today, most cloves exported to the West come from Pemba, an African island north of Zanzibar. About half of the world's clove production is not used for cooking. *Kretek* cigarettes, 1 part ground cloves to 2 parts tobacco, are extremely popular in Indonesia and absorb much of the spice produced. Another portion of these nail-shaped buds is turned into *oil of cloves*, which is used as an antiseptic and a dental anesthetic. Finally, a few cloves are chewed whole as breath fresheners. (See HERBS AND SPICES for information on buying, storing, cooking, etc.)

PREPARATION

Cooking

To test freshness, crush the head of a whole clove. Fresh cloves exude pungent oil. Brittle, stale cloves do not. Clove is very powerful; it must be used with discretion. One clove in a meat stew gives subtle flavor, five or six can be used in a spicy meat marinade, six to eight in the syrup for several quarts of fruit compote. Only 1/8 teaspoon ground cloves flavors 2 cups of vegetables, 1/4 teaspoon spices an average-sized meatloaf. Many baked-ham recipes call for studding the ham with a small army of cloves. While we totally agree that an artistic arrangement of cloves garnishing the ham surface is an attractive sight, we are—with one exception—opposed to this technique, because the clove flavor will overpower the taste of the ham, the star of the preparation. If you wish to clove-stud your ham, add the cloves after the ham has been cooked to minimize flavor transference. Also remember to remove the cloves before serving the ham on a plate, because cloves are proven tooth crackers.

CLASSIC USES AND AFFINITIES

The shape of a clove makes it ideal for studding orange skins for pomander balls and onions for use in stocks. Whole cloves are often used in pickling. Ground cloves are used in baking, fruit compotes, soups, stews, and with sweet vegetables such as yams and winter squash.

COCONUT

BACKGROUND

The *coconut* palm has contributed to the image of the tropics as paradise, but it also produces many useful products: wood, fiber, *coconut water*, *coconut milk*, *toddy* (a potent drink), *oil*, *copra* (dried coconut meat), and hard shells that can be used as food or drink containers. A typical *cocos nucifera* tree yields thousands of coconuts over its lifespan of several decades. The coconut (technically a drupe, not a nut) consists of four basic parts: the outer fibrous husk (which is usually removed before transocean shipment); the hard monkey-faced inner shell; the white flesh and the coconut water. Virtually all the coconuts shipped to the American mainland are mature, and therefore the white interior flesh has a firm texture. Most inhabitants of the coconut-producing tropics prefer the slightly green or immature coconut, whose flesh still has a jellylike texture (it can be eaten with the fingers or a spoon) and whose coconut water is deliciously sweet.

Cholesterol-watchers beware—the coconut is high in saturated oils. Most often, however, you need not worry because coconut is usually consumed in small amounts.

AVAILABILITY

Whole coconuts are available year round, with a peak in November and December. Coconut can also be purchased pre-shredded—the canned variety is significantly fresher tasting than the cellophane-packaged type. Coconut milk and cream (see below) are available in cans.

Buying Tips

Here is the most important guideline: If you cannot hear and feel the internal coconut water sloshing when you shake a coconut, do not buy it, as it will probably be too old or well on the path toward spoilage. The more the liquid sloshes, the fresher and therefore the better the coconut is likely to be. The best coconut is heavy for its size. Avoid any coconut with wet or moldy eyes (those three nature-plugged holes that help give the coconut its monkey-face appearance). A cracked coconut may be bacterially infested.

PREPARATION

Storage

Depending on degree of freshness, whole undrained coconuts can be safely stored in a dry, room-temperature environment for up to a couple of months; store shredded coconut tightly covered in the refrigerator for up to several days if fresh, or up to a couple of weeks if dried. Shredded coconut can be frozen, but be prepared for some flavor and texture loss. Coconut cream, milk, and water should be refrigerated and used within a day or two.

Opening

There are many ways to open a coconut, but one of the easiest for the neophyte is this: Pierce two of the eyes with a screwdriver, skewer, or icepick. Pour out the coconut water, reserving it for other use (such as flavoring a sauce). Place the drained coconut in a preheated 325°F oven for 20 minutes. Sometimes this cracks the hard coconut shell. If not, allow the coconut to cool slightly. Split the shell by rapping it with a heavy object such as a hammer. Tap it all over the surface until you find the natural fault-line, then keep hitting the coconut to lengthen that line until the coconut breaks apart. Wrapping the coconut in a towel prevents the small pieces from scattering. Pry out the white flesh with a knife or screwdriver. Using a paring knife or vegetable peeler, scrap off the brown membrane (it is edible, but the white coconut flesh looks more appetizing without it).

Shredding

For long shreds, use a metal grater. For quick shredding, use a blender or food processor. You can get 2 to 4 cups of loosely-packed shredded coconut from an average-size coconut, depending upon the shred size and your shredding efficiency.

To Make Coconut Milk

Contrary to many cookbook authors, the liquid that sloshes inside the coconut is *coconut water*, not *coconut milk*. The latter is extracted from the white flesh. To make it yourself, soak equal parts hot water and shredded coconut flesh for several minutes, then strain through a fine-meshed or cheesecloth-lined sieve, pressing as much liquid as possible out of the pulp, then discard the latter. It is best not to use prolonged high temperatures when cooking with coconut milk or cream.

To Make Coconut Cream

Follow the same procedure as for coconut milk, but use only one part of hot water to 4 or more parts of coconut.

Toasting

Spread out shredded coconut in a flat pan and bake in a preheated 325°F oven for approximately 12 to 15 minutes, turning the coconut several times until it is brown-tinged. Or, pan-toast it in a sauté pan over moderate heat for 3 to 5 minutes, shaking the shreds until all are brown-tinged.

CLASSIC USES AND AFFINITIES

Shredded coconut can be used as a topping for custards, puddings, and ambrosia. The flavor of coconut enhances tropical rum drinks, ice cream, curries, and candy bars. Chocolate and coconut go well together. Both are sweet, creamy and rich, but they have pleasantly contrasting textures.

COFFEE

BACKGROUND

America's favorite beverage is believed to be native to northeast Africa, perhaps the mountains of Ethiopia. Once man discovered how to roast and brew the beans of the coffee tree, the custom of drinking coffee spread throughout the Middle East and then, from Turkey, into Europe via Vienna. Of the several existing coffee species, *Coffea arabica* and *Coffea canephora* dominate the plantations around the world. *Aribica* is the finest. *Robusta*, as the second species is popularly known, is inferior, but since it produces a larger yield, is hardier and can be grown in more climates, it is by far the world's most-planted coffee species. High-quality coffees use 100 percent *Arabica* beans. Most of the coffee widely sold in vacuum-packed cans or in jars is made from *robusta* beans.

Coffee contains *caffeine*, a nerve stimulant, and therefore should not be drunk in excess. If you are a coffee hound (as many of us are), consider buying quality decaffeinated coffee beans, and alternating the regular beans with the decaffeinated ones. If the decaffeinated beans are of good quality, freshly ground, and well-brewed, few people notice the difference in terms of flavor and aroma. What give decaffeinated coffee a bad image in the eyes of gourmets are the factory-processed, preground or powdered varieties.

Classifications

Like wine, coffee can be classified in a number of ways.

Place of Origin: Whole-bean coffees are often labeled by place of origin. While it would be tempting to give you the precise gustatory characteristics (acid, mellow, etc.: see below) for each type of coffee, we have kept these descriptions to a minimum, because too often the coffees from a given country or region can vary markedly in attributes, depending on weather, the particular plantation, and so forth.

Arabian: This term refers to a collection of various coffees including those from *Yemen. Mocha* used to be shipped from a port of the same name in this area, but now the word describes a genre of coffee from different parts of the world that are high in acidity, low in mellowness. True mocha was traditionally blended with coffee from Java which had the opposite characteristics: superb mellowness, insufficient acid. The resulting blend was pleasant and was called Mocha-Java. Today, Mocha-Java is seldom made with beans from Mocha and Java. What goes into the blend depends on the blender's formula and the available supply.

Brazilian: The world's largest coffee producer is *Brazil*, and most of its output is mediocre. *Bourbon Santos*, however, makes a fair-to-good cup of coffee when blended with good-quality, high acid beans.

Caribbean: The best coffee beans in the Caribbean come from *Jamaica*, the nation that produces *Blue Mountain*, one of the world's greatest coffees. It is easily the world's most expensive coffee. The best Jamaican coffees are winy and full-bodied, with a heavenly aroma. *Haiti* occasionally produces a fair-to-good coffee bean. *Cuba* and the *Dominican Republic* are also active in the industry.

Central American: These coffee beans can be very good. They are usually rich and have sound body and sufficient acid content. They are usually sold under their individual country names: *Costa Rica, Guatemala, Honduras, El Salvador*, or *Nicaragua*.

Colombian: The beans exported from *Colombia* have a good quality level and some are outstanding, with a full-bodied mellowness and a proper acid foundation. *Colombian Supremo* is a top grade. *Colombian Excelso* is a notch or two down on the quality scale.

Hawaiian: In good years, *Kona* can be one of the world's best coffees and worth its high price. In off-years, the coffee is acceptable, but overpriced.

Indian: Southern *India* produces many coffees, especially those of the Malabar area.

Indonesian: The island of *Java* gave us a nickname for coffee. From the *Sulawesa* (formerly Celebes) *Islands* grow the superb *Kalossi* coffee beans. Bali also cultivates excellent coffee. The flaw of Indonesian coffee is its low acid content (see Arabian, above).

Other major coffee-growing areas include *Ethiopia, Kenya, Malagasy Republic, Mexico* (its best bean is the *Altura Coatepec), Tanzania, Uganda, Venezuela, Zaire*, and *West Africa* in general.

Gustatory Characteristics: Coffee connoisseurs use a common language to describe and differentiate various coffees. The most important terms are:

Acidity: A sharp, piquant flavor. Good coffee will have some acidity, but not an excess, and it requires some mellowness to soften that acid.

Aroma: The scent of brewed coffee.

Bitter: The objectionable taste of coffee that has been over-extracted, over-brewed, scorched, or kept too long on the warmer.

Body: The feeling of substance that your mouth perceives when you sip the coffee.

Green: The raw flavor of underroasted beans.

Mellow: A pleasant, soft taste. Good coffee has some acidity to balance the mellowness.

Stale: Flavor of an over-the-hill coffee. Opposite of fresh.

Thin: Watery, lacking body.

Winy: A rich mellowness combined with obvious body.

Altitude: As a rule, the best coffees are grown at high altitudes—in the hills or mountains or on the slopes of volcanos at about 3,000 to 5,000 feet above sea level. Low-altitude coffees are often grown on rolling hills or on plains.

Whole vs. Ground: Most coffee is sold preground, which is a shame because ground coffee exposed to air loses much of its freshness within hours, or at least within a day. (If you enjoy coffee, a good home coffee grinder is a wise investment.) Whether you buy a coffee preground or you do the chore yourself, the coffee grounds should be the right size for your method of making coffee (see the GRINDING COFFEE AT HOME section below).

Degree of Aging: Once picked, few coffee beans are aged, except in the normal course of storing and shipping. Some coffee beans, however, are aged in storehouses for up to ten years; this gives them a fuller body and flavor, but deprives the beans of desirable acidity. People buy these aged coffee beans because they reason that if wine improves with age, so will coffee. Balderdash.

Method of Processing: The dried, hulled coffee beans can be simply roasted and sold as a normal coffee. Or, by means of special processing techniques, they can be *decaffeinated.* The coffee manufacturer can also produce *freeze-dried* and *instant* coffees by dehydrating brewed coffee.

Type of Roast: The green (unroasted) coffee bean can be roasted to several stages of doneness. The more the beans are roasted, the darker their color and the stronger their flavor will be. Though the terms sometimes overlap or contradict each other in different regions, the four basic stages of roasting are American, Viennese, French and Italian, in ascending order of intensity of roasting. *American* is the roast you use for the typical American cup of coffee. *Viennese* is the choice of an after-dinner cup of coffee. *French roast* makes a good strong brew for *cafe au lait. Italian,* the strongest of the four, is used for espresso.

Straight vs. Blend: Virtually all coffees sold in cans or jars are blends, some with a score or more different coffees, in order to help assure the manufacturers (and customers) a consistency of flavor and aroma from year to year. Even many of the whole-bean coffees sold out of the barrel are blends—Mocha-Java for instance.

Added Ingredients: Coffee can be plain or flavored with ingredients such as cinnamon or chocolate or chicory. The last ingredient is also used sometimes to stretch the coffee and sometimes to satisfy regional taste preferences—for instance, chicory goes into most coffee sold in New Orleans.

AVAILABILITY

Coffee, in one form or another, is available in every season in virtually every part of the world.

Buying Tips

Beans: The best coffee merchant is one who roasts his own beans at least every several days. If there is no such retailer in your neighborhood, buy from a store with a high merchandise turnover, as roasted coffee beans that sit in barrels or burlap sacks go stale within several weeks after they are roasted. For the same reason, buy beans for short-term consumption. A line of glass jars filled with coffee beans may appeal to the eyes of your friends, but not to their taste buds. Do not buy loose coffee beans in a store such as a cheese shop, as the beans can readily pick up foreign odors. Too many importers, wholesalers, and stores mislabel their products, selling, for instance, a common Haitian product for Jamaican Blue Mountain—and to add insult to injury, at the latter's price. Your best safeguard against such ploys is to give your trade to a reliable merchant.

Often the best buy of a conscientious merchant is his house blend, as pride often enters into his choice of beans. If you have your own blend formula, remember that its flavor and aroma will almost certainly change at times, since the flavor and aroma of the individual varieties of beans change due to factors such as weather at the plantation.

Ground Coffee: Even ground coffee packaged in unopened vacuum-packed tins is perishable—after a couple of months or so, staleness starts to become apparent to a discerning palate. Therefore, buy from a store with a fast turnover. Freeze-dried and instant coffees are almost as perishable.

PREPARATION

Storage

Green coffee will last a year or more if stored in a cool, dry, dark, airtight container. Whole beans will last several weeks beyond their date of roasting if stored in an airtight container out of direct sunlight. If you must keep coffee beans longer than that, store them in the freezer (for up to several months at 0°F). Ground coffee at room temperature starts to go stale and lose its aroma and flavor within a day or two and, if the coffee has delicate qualities, within an hour or less after it has been ground. For storage up to two weeks, ground coffee should be kept in an airtight container in the refrigerator.

Grinding Coffee at Home

For best flavor and aroma, grind only as much coffee as you plan to use immediately. Use a dry brush to keep the grinding area of the machine clean; leftover particles can turn stale, contaminating your next batch. High-quality grinders are worth the extra money, because they do a better job of making uniform grinds, which in turn helps ensure even extraction when the coffee is brewed. Percolators require a coarse grind. Make a medium grind for drip coffee, a fine grind for espresso and an even finer grind for Turkish coffee. Follow the manufacturer's directions, but remember that some beans are softer or harder than the norm and will therefore require a shorter or longer grinding time.

Brewing

One of the worst ways to make coffee is to percolate it. The coffee may fill the room with an evocative aroma, but since you are boiling the coffee (which should never be boiled), the essential oils will turn bitter. The best method for making an American-style cup of coffee is the drip method. Both the automatic drip-style coffee makers and the less costly plastic funnel apparatus will give you equal results. It is essential to keep the equipment clean; the stains that build up on its interior walls can taint subsequent batches of coffee. If the coffee is kept too warm too long or is allowed to come even close to a boil, the coffee will turn bitter.

CLASSIC USES

Classics include *café au lait* (strong French roast with hot milk), Turkish coffee (strong black roast, served with grounds in), espresso (black roast, made under pressure of steaming-hot water), cappuccino (espresso with frothy steamed milk) and Irish coffee (American roast coffee flavored with Irish whiskey and sugar, topped with whipped cream). Affinities include cardamom, cinnamon, lemon rind, sugar, cream or milk, and liqueurs such as anisette. Tia Maria and Kahlua are coffee-based liqueurs. Coffee is one of the popular ice cream flavors. When blended with chocolate, the flavor is called mocha (not to be confused with the chocolateless mocha or mocha-type coffee beans).

COLA NUT

BACKGROUND

In the United States *cola* means one of a number of popular soft drinks, which may or may not use extracts from the cola nut for its flavor. In tropical Africa, *cola* means a reddish nut possessed of almost magical properties. This nut of the cola tree, *Cola acuminata*, is chewed to sustain human vigor under sweltering conditions. It quenches thirst, diminishes fatigue, lessens sleepiness, and is considered by some an aphrodisiac. The cola nut's stimulating properties are due to its high caffeine content. It is held in such high regard in many parts of Africa that it is used as money.

COLLARD GREENS

BACKGROUND

Soul food developed out of the need to make good meals out of the foods slaves could produce or gather. Collard greens, a variety of nonheading cabbage, was a soul food star in several ways. The greens added deep color and strong flavor to a monotonous, pale, starchy diet, and they contributed plenty of vitamins A and C, calcium, and iron. Even today, with more varied diets available, collard greens are still popular dietary mainstays in the South.

AVAILABILITY

Season

A winter and early-spring crop that is available year round in some markets.

Buying Tips

The leaves should be a deep green with a hint of brightness, with no tinge of yellow, and should be smooth, thick, unbroken, and free of insect nibblings. Seedstems indicate excessive age.

PREPARATION

Storage

Collard greens should be used quickly. Store them in the refrigerator in a plastic bag for no more than a few days.

Preliminaries

Cut off the tough, fibrous stems. If the midribs of the leaves are very coarse, cut them out. Discard or trim damaged leaves. Wash collard greens in several changes of water if necessary; they can be gritty.

Cooking

Unlike most greens, which can steam tender in a tiny amount of water, collards are tough enough to require simmering. Chop the greens and boil them until just tender, about 12 to 15 minutes. Overcooking produces a needlessly strong odor and reduces nutrition. A little salt pork or bacon fat in the cooking water adds richness. Be sure and drink the pot liquor or use it in soup. It has plenty of nutrition and taste to offer. Serve boiled collards with butter or bacon fat, or top them with butter and grated cheese and broil them until the cheese melts.

CLASSIC USES AND AFFINITIES

Do not serve collard greens with subtly flavored foods.Team them instead with smothered pork chops, cornbread, fried chicken or catfish, and cold beer.

CONCH

BACKGROUND

The footlike muscle of this univalve mollusk can be tenderized, eaten raw, or cooked like its cousin, the ABALONE. *Conch* (pronounced "konk") is an especially popular food with Floridians and Caribbean-Americans. Italian-Americans, who call it *scungilli,* often serve it with a spicy tomato sauce. Fresh conch is most available in the summer; frozen conch has no season.

CORIANDER

BACKGROUND

Both the seeds and the leaves of the native Mediterranean *Coriandrum sativum* are used in cooking. The spherical seeds are yellowish or brown, about 1/8 inch in diameter, and marked with ridges. The green, lacy leaves—also known as *Chinese parsley* or *cilantro*—have a pungent and distinctive odor that some American and European palates consider an acquired taste. Other cultures, from Mexico to India to the Orient, love coriander unabashedly. (See HERBS AND SPICES for information on buying, storing, cooking, etc.)

CLASSIC USES AND AFFINITIES

The whole seed is used in pickles, cold drinks,and hot drinks such as coffee and mulled wine. Crushed coriander seed flavors many American frankfurters and Scandinavian baked goods, roast pork, puddings, cookies, gingerbread, and other cakes. Coriander forms part of the Indian *garam masala* and commercial curry powders. The seed has an affinity with apples, pears, and peaches.

CORN

BACKGROUND

Corn, also known as *maize* (whence the botanical name, *Zea mays*), is one of the most American of foods. Pre-Columbian Indian agriculture centered on the triad of corn, beans, and squash. When the English arrived, they saw the grain the Indians ate and called it *Indian corn* or just *corn,* which was a generic English name for grain or anything else very small. When the first English settlers arrived in North America, their wheat crop failed, and the corn the Indians taught them to plant helped sustain them. Today, it is one of America's most beloved foods.

Varieties

An ear of corn consists of the edible kernels arranged in snug parallel rows along the cylindrical cob; overlapping green husks protect the contents. But fitting that description are hundreds of corn varieties. Some varieties are grown and used for special purposes: for POPCORN, CORNMEAL, harvest-time decoration, and animal fodder, for example. The type we buy fresh in the produce department is called *sweet corn.* The most popular sweet corn has yellowish kernels, though some Americans prefer the white kernels. There is also a corn with two-colored kernels, though it is not available in all regions.

AVAILABILITY

Season

Fresh Corn: The height of the corn season runs from June (for corn grown in the warm states) through September (for corn harvested further north). Sometimes you can find excellent fresh corn in May and October, but the specimens that reach the produce bins in mid-winter are seldom worth the price.

Processed Corn: Corn is available the year around in cans, jars, and frozen-food packets in various forms: whole kernel, creamed, or in combination with other vegetables. There is even a baby-sized corn on the cob, about 2 inches long, that is popular with Chinese and Thai cooks. Whatever the type of these processed corn products, they lack the desirable texture and flavor of fresh corn. Processed corn can be worthy, however, when it is converted into other products such as CORNMEAL, cornstarch (see under THICKENERS), HOMINY, grits, CORN SYRUP, corn oil (see under OILS AND FATS), and whiskey. Corn flakes, corn chips, and even corncob pipes are also marketed. Corn is versatile.

Buying Tips

The best corn is fresh off the stalk. As each hour goes by, the sugar content converts to starch and the sweetness diminishes. Even corn harvested yesterday has lost much of its goodness. For maximum goodness, you must buy locally grown corn in the height of the local season. Corn may be in season in June in Florida, but by the time it is trucked to Minnesota, the sugar-to-starch conversion is well under way. Do not buy unhusked ears that feel warm as the heat is a byproduct of the sugar-to-starch transformation. If you see corn being sold at a roadside produce stand, do not automatically assume that it is local corn.

Never, unless absolutely necessary, buy corn that has been husked, even partially, to show the kernels—naked corn deteriorates rapidly. Look for ears of corn with bright green, soft, fresh husks that tightly and completely surround the kernels. Reject corn with dry, wet, yellowed, wilted, or otherwise damaged husks. Smell the husk—freshness should be apparent. Examine the exposed silks at the blossom end of an ear of corn. It should literally be silky and be free of decay, worm infestation, and other injury. Check the stem end—it should give readily to finger pressure and must not be woody, oxidized, or dry. Overall, the ears should look well formed. There is nothing wrong with a slender ear of corn if the other selective criteria are met. For even cooking, buy equal-sized ears of corn.

Some greengrocers allow you to pull back the husks to examine the kernels—provided, of course, that you pull the husks carefully and rearrange them to their original position. If the grocer minds, consider shopping elsewhere, because such investigation is crucial to determining the eating quality of an ear of corn. First scrutinize the top 2 inches of the ear—there should be no wormholes, rotting areas, or other deformity, and the kernels must not be underdeveloped. Next, examine all the kernels on the cob—they should be in straight rows and neither be jammed close together (indicating overmaturity) or have barren space between the rows (indicating immaturity). The individual kernels should be plump (but not bloated) and should not be dented or flattened. Press a few kernels—they should feel slightly resistant and soft (but not mushy) to the touch, as opposed to being tough and coarse. The kernels should be filled with milky juice—immature specimens have watery juice, overmature ones have thickened juices. Also examine the color—yellow varieties should be a vivid (but not dark) yellow. Either the yellow or white variety should have a glossy, uniform color.

PREPARATION

Storage

Every minute a harvested ear of corn waits to be cooked, it decreases in flavor, texture, and nutrients. The ultimate of purists do not pick the corn from the stalk until the cooking water is boiling, and they run from garden to stove.

While few of us have such fortunate circumstances, we can at least maximize the eating qualities of corn by buying good specimens the day we plan to enjoy them. If you must store ears of corn, keep them in their unwashed husks until ready to cook them. Also seal them in a plastic bag and refrigerate them, as they need a cold and moist environment. If you are thinking of freezing fresh corn, forget it.

Preliminaries

Strip off the husks, remove the silk and any underdeveloped or damaged part of the ear. Some people like to trim off both the stem and blossom ends to improve the appearance. For informal dining, this step is not necessary. Since the kernels have been protected by the husks, a husked and desilked ear of corn needs just a quick rinse in cold water. Some cooks eliminate this step. of you have refrigerated an ear of corn, bring it to room temperature (allow about 30 minutes) before cooking it. If you are cooking the kernels separately, you can remove them with a special gadget called a corn stripper—or you can cut them off the cob with a knife, attacking several rows at a time. For a creamed-corn preparation, use a knife to slice open the eernels along each row. Then, with the flat side of the knife, scrape the pulp and milky juice into your work bowl and proceed with your recipe. This is particularly a good idea if the corn has become too tough to eat on the cob—or if one of your diners cannot eat corn on the cob or whole kernels. It is a chore, though.

Cooking

Each kernel of corn is filled with a milky substance. In perfectly cooked corn, this substance is just set by heat, not coagulated (coagulation results in poor texture and flavor). The most common and perhaps the best way to cook corn is to boil it. Immerse the ears of corn in a large pot of fiercely boiling water. Do not salt the water, as this promotes toughness (let each riner sprinkle salt to taste at the table.) The volume of water should be at least six times the volume of the ears—if not, you may have to add a minute or two to the boiling time. If an ear is too large for the pot, snap it in half. The pot must be covered so that the top of a floating cob will cook in steam. Boiling time is 3 minutes for fresh-from-the-stalk corn, about 5 to 6 minutes for very fresh store-bought corn, and up to 10 minutes for older corn. Do not overcook corn—that makes it tough. As soon as the ears are cooked, remove them with large tongs (or a slotted spoon), drain, and serve promptly.

Corn can also be barbecued. To prepare, carefully and completely pull back the husks, remove the silk, rub the kernels with butter, push back the husks to their original position, and secure them at the end with a small piece of kitchen twine. Next, soak the ears of corn in water for 10 to 20 minutes, then drain and place 4 inches above hot coals and cook for 10 to 15 minutes, turning frequently. Or bury the ears of corn in hot coals and cook for 8 to 12 minutes. Alternatively, husk completely, rub the kernels, with butter and wrap the ear snugly in aluminum foil and cook as instructed above.

Fresh kernels cut from the cob cook in a simmering liquid in 6 to 12 minutes, depending on thickness and age.

Serving

Corn on the cob can only be eaten with the fingers. Mini-skewer holders do exist and they have the redeeming (but not sensual) value of keeping your fingers clean. To eat corn on the cob, brush with butter and sprinkle with salt. Or roll the ear in a plate specially designed to hold melted butter under the rotating cob.

CORNED BEEF

BACKGROUND

The word *Corned* applied to meat means "cured in brine." The term originated because the size of the salt grain used to cure meat in Merry Olde England was approximately the size of corn—meaning cereal grains and other small particles. Beef brisket (see Primal Brisket, under BEEF) is the classic cut for making corned beef, although rump, eye round, bottom round, tongue, and other cuts are sometimes used, too. Pork, veal, and lamb are also sometimes corned.

AVAILABILITY

You can make your own corned beef at home or buy it ready cured. While the ready-cured variety offers you convenience (just remove it from its plastic wrap, place it into a pot of water, then simmer), it will probably be bland and contain all too much sodium nitrate or potassium nitrate, popularly called saltpeter. A few old-fashioned butchers still cure their own briskets, sometimes offering it for sale directly out of their huge curing tubs; it can be superb.

PREPARATION

Cure Your Own

It really is not that difficult to make your own corned beef from scratch at home. The first step is to prepare your corning solution. The ratio of water to salt should be about 10 to 1. If higher, the meat may spoil (but if you cure your meat in the refrigerator, you can use a ratio of about 15 to 1). For each 2½ quarts of water, add 1 cup of salt, 2 to 3 tablespoons of PICKLING SPICE, and a discretionary amount of whatever other flavoring agents appeal to your fancy. If you wish your corned beef to be purplish-red rather than greyish-red, add ½ to 1 teaspoon of saltpeter (available at some drugstores), but its use is a matter of individual and regional preference. (We do not believe that the more attractive appearance of the meat is worth putting sodium nitrates and the like into the body system.) Bring the brine solution to a boil in a large kettle, then cool it to room temperature. Place the meat in a suitable curing container—it can be a glass or enamel bowl or a glazed crock, but never use metal, as the salt will chemically react with it. To accommodate ample brine, the container's volume should be twice that of the meat's. Cover meat with the brine and, if you wish, add onion slices and garlic cloves to taste. You must have enough of the brine to completely submerge the meat. Keep the meat below the liquid surface by means of a sterilized nonmetal weight such as glass bowl filled with some of the brine. Cover the curing vessel and keep in a cool spot for 1 to 2 weeks (the thicker or the lower the grade of the meat, the longer it will take to tenderize the meat). The mold that forms on the liquid is harmless if the meat is rinsed before cooking. If your coolest storeroom is warmer than 60°F, we suggest that you cure the meat in the warmest spot in your refrigerator, but allow a little more curing time in deference to cooler temperatures.

Cooking

If the meat is well-cured and therefore likely excessively salty, you may have to presoak it for several hours overnight in several changes of cool water. Place the cured meat in a large kettle with enough water to cover the meat liberally. Bring the water to a boil. Then simmer (do not boil or the meat will toughen) for 2 to 4 hours, depending on the thickness of the meat. If you like, add sliced onions, diced carrots, herbs, spices and other stock-flavoring agents to the cooking liquid.

Serving

Allow about 1/3 pound per person, depending on appetites. Corned beef should be sliced as you would a BEEF LONDON BROIL: thin, across the grain, at an angle. Corned beef may be eaten hot or cold. The classic condiments are mustard, mustard sauce, and horseradish sauce.

Leftovers

Don't worry about preparing too much corned beef—in fact, plan on leftovers. On day two have sliced corned-beef sandwiches. On day three have corned-beef hash. On day four....

CLASSIC USES AND AFFINITIES

Corned beef is the star ingredient of both corned beef and cabbage and the New England boiled dinner. The latter is accompanied by whole vegetables such as potatoes, carrots, and turnips plus wedges of cabbage. There is a heated debate whether the vegetables should be cooked with the corned beef or separately. We prefer the latter because it helps preserve the individual flavors. If you do add the vegetables to the kettle, add the whole ones about 30 minutes before and the cabbage wedges about 15 minutes before the end of the cooking period. Adding them earlier will yield mushy vegetables and an unpleasant cabbage odor.

CORNMEAL

BACKGROUND

By definition, *cornmeal* is ground dried corn kernels. It can be *yellow* or *white* (depending on the corn variety), is usually marketed in three grinds (fine, medium, and coarse) and can be *water-ground* (or *stone-ground*) or *steel-roller ground*.

The only two significant culinary differences between yellow and white cornmeal are their colors and the fact that the white variety has only a trace of vitamin A.

Water-ground cornmeal is better flavored and textured and more nutritious than the mass-produced steel-rollered embryo-less cornmeal, the type usually sold in grocery stores. Water-ground cornmeal is also more expensive and, because it retains the embryo, has a shorter shelf life. Look for it in specialty and health-food stores.

PREPARATION

Storage

Cornmeal is best stored in an airtight jar or canister on a cool, dry, dark shelf. If the cornmeal is water-ground, it needs to be refrigerated unless it is fresh and you plan to use it within a week or two.

Basic Cooking

For a basic cornmeal mush, slowly add cornmeal to 3 to 5 times its volume of lightly salted, boiling water. The more water or the coarser the cornmeal grind you use, the thinner the consistency. Cook uncovered and stir frequently about 20 minutes (for fine grind) to 30 minutes (for coarse grind).

CLASSIC USES AND AFFINITIES

Cornmeal is basic to many American culinary classics, including cornbread, corn muffins, spoonbreads, cornpone, hoecakes, corn sticks, hush puppies and corn fritters, Indian pudding, and hasty pudding. Cornmeal also helps make famous foreign bread-mushes, including Rumania's *mameliga* and northern Italy's *polenta*.

CORN SALAD

BACKGROUND

Corn salad—also called *lamb's lettuce*, *field salad*, or *mâché*—has small, firm, round or oval leaves with a delicate lettucelike taste. Though it is a common cornfield weed, it tends to be scarce and expensive in American markets. *Valerianella olitoria* emerges in the fall and grows until spring, when it is gathered. The leaves can be eaten raw as a salad green, or steamed like spinach.

CORN SYRUP

BACKGROUND

Manufactured principally from the glucose found in cornstarch, the sticky liquid is marketed in this country in two shades: light and dark. *Light corn syrup* has been clarified and is milder in flavor than *dark corn syrup*; the latter is a blend of pure corn syrup and refiner's sugar (the liquid that remains after extracting granulated sugar from sugar cane or beets).

Storage

Store corn syrup, capped, on a cool, dry, dark shelf.

CLASSIC USES AND AFFINITIES

Corn syrup is poured by some diners over waffles and pancakes and is used in cooking as a sweetener in the making of candy, jams, frostings, cookies and desserts in general. It has two culinary advantages over other syrups, such as maple: it costs less and it does not crystallize—a helpful quality for concocting smooth sweets such as caramel.

COSTMARY

BACKGROUND

The herb *costmary* (*Chrysanthemum balsamita*) has a number of religious links: it is associated with the Virgin Mary and with St. Mary Magdalene, and its long, serrated leaves make such good placemarkers that the plant is called *Bible leaf*. Another name for the plant is *alecost*, because the leaves have been used in beer brewing. The lemon-mint taste of the leaves is also welcome in salads, cold drinks, sausages, soups, and stuffings for white meats. (See HERBS AND SPICES for information on buying, storing, cooking, etc.)

CRAB

BACKGROUND

One of America's greatest natural treasures is its wealth of crabs, including the blue crabs of the Atlantic and Gulf coasts, the stone crabs of Florida, the Dungeness crabs of the West Coast, and the king crab of Alaska.

Crabs are aquatic arthropods with five pairs of legs. The front legs are pincers or claws, the rear legs can be paddle-shaped if the crab belongs to a swimming family (*blue crab* is the best-known example). Other major crab families include the *rock crab* (such as the *Dungeness*), *mud crab* (*stone crab*, for instance), and *land crabs* (very popular in the Caribbean).

Varieties

Blue Crab: This delicious crab is sold in two forms: hardshell and softshell. These terms describe not crab species (as many people erroneously think) but rather refers to growth states of the crab. A crab is normally *hardshell*—its protective shell is hard enough to thwart most predators. As the crab grows, it outgrows its shell and molts—that is, it sheds its shell. Gradually (over several days) its soft skin hardens into a new, larger shell; during that time, it is a *softshell* crab. The blue crab typically undergoes this transformation several times a year. Other species of crabs also molt, but it is the softshell blue crab that is perfect for the table.

Dungeness: With good reason, the Dungeness crab is the pride of Pacific Coast gourmets, who cannot find too much praise for its delectable flesh. Most marketed Dungeness crab weighs 2 to 3 pounds.

Alaskan King Crab: Also called the Japanese king crab, this monster crab can measure nearly 10 feet between leg tips. The commercially profitable parts of the anatomy are the legs (of small to medium crabs) which are typically cooked, frozen, and shipped throughout the U.S. Gastronomically, Alaskan king crab legs are minor league compared to the blue and Dungeness crabs.

Stone Crab: Only the claws of the stone crab are eaten, so Florida fishermen snap one or both claws off and throw the crab back into the sea to regenerate new weapons (in a year or two). Stone crab claws are expensive, but well worth their price.

Other Species: The meat of *snow crabs* comes from various oversized spiderlike crab species that live in the ocean depths. On the opposite end of the scale are the under-one-inch-wide, permanently softshelled female *oyster crabs* that live inside their hosts, the oysters: delicious sautéed in butter when you can find them. Still other edible species include the *calico*, *green*, *Jonah*, and *red crabs*.

AVAILABILITY

Once out of water, crabs are very perishable. This is why live crabs are seldom marketed far from where they are taken. Cooked whole crabs have a broader marketing area, while cooked, shelled crab meat is shipped even farther. Frozen and canned crabmeat have no geographical limitation.

Grades of Shelled Crabmeat

Lump crabmeat is the best and most expensive form. It consists of large chunks taken from the body of the crab. *Backfin* crabmeat comes from the body proper, too, but the pieces are smaller. *Claw* crabmeat comes from the pincers. With some crabs (such as the stone crab) this claw meat is the choice part, while with others (such as the blue crab) the claw meat has a brownish tint and is less desirable than the body meat. *Flake* crabmeat is the least expensive grade, made up of small pieces taken from the claws or body.

Crab Roe

The orange eggs of the female crab are a culinary prize (though catching roe-bearing females is banned at times in some areas). The most famous use of crab roe is in she-crab soup, a South Carolina specialty. Telling the difference between the crab sexes is easy with most species, since the *apron* (the shieldlike plate at the rear of the crab's lower shell) is broader on females than on males. Also, in blue crabs, the female's claw is red-tipped even before it is cooked.

Buying Tips

Meat from the fresh live crabs that you cook is significantly better in flavor and texture than the meat from precooked whole crabs and especially to the precooked, shelled crabmeat that is sold in fish stores. Even the last type is better than the mushy frozen or canned crabmeat.

Live Crabs: When buying a live crab, always make sure it is alive and kicking.

If it doesn't move its legs when picked up or poked, don't buy it. But remember that a crab stored on ice will be more sluggish than one in the water. The smaller a crab is for its species, the younger and therefore the more tender the meat will be. Make sure that the crab has all its God-given claws and feet. Buy for use on day of purchase—and do business with a reliable fishmonger with a quick stock turnover. Crabs are edible the year round, but are least expensive and most abundant during the warm months. The softshell crab season runs from late spring through August, but the early-season and smaller crabs tend to be best.

Crabmeat: If you have to buy a precooked crab, be sure to sniff it closely for signs of off-odors—there should be none. When buying shelled crabmeat, buy the more expensive lump meat when appearance is important (such as for making salads) and the lower-priced flake meat when making preparations such as crabcakes. Sniff the meat closely for off-odors. Also examine the color—it becomes yellower and/or darker as time passes.

PREPARATION

Storage

Live or unfrozen crab is very perishable and should be used on the day of purchase. Then keep them in the refrigerator until the moment you need them. Crabmeat can be frozen, though we do not recommend it.

Cooking

The simplest way to cook live hardshell crabs is to simmer them in plain or (preferably) seasoned water. With tongs or protected hands, plunge the live crabs head first into plenty of rapidly boiling water. (If you soak them for several minutes beforehand in a sink or deep container of hot tap water, they normally react less ferociously and spastically when they first come in contact with the boiling water.) Reduce to a simmer and cook 5 to 20 minutes, depending on crab size. The shells become bright red when cooked. Do not overcook or the meat will become tough. With tongs, remove the crabs and allow them to cool until you can comfortably handle them. To eat a hardshell crab snap off the two claws, then crack the shells so you can get out the meat with a tool such as a pick. Snap off the walking legs and, if you truly love crab, suck out the legmeat and juices. Open the shell and enjoy the white flesh.

Softshell crabs are cooked and eaten whole after you have done a few preparatory chores: kill the crab by using a scissors to cut off the front of its head (the eyes and mouth); turn the crab upside down and, with a knife, cut off the apron; lift up the flaps on both sides of the shell and remove the grayish, spongy lungs; pull out the digestive tract located behind the head. It is now ready to cook. Wash it and pat dry, dredge it in seasoned flour, then sauté it in a sizzling mixture of butter and oil for 2 to 4 minutes, depending on thickness. Enjoy.

CRANBERRY

BACKGROUND

Bogs in New England produce crops of *cranberry* (*Vaccinium macrocarpon*), a hard shiny berry with a very tart, somewhat bitter flavor. Another name is *bounceberry*: when dropped, a cranberry has enough resilience to spring up unharmed.

AVAILABILITY

Fresh cranberries are found on the market between October and December, just at the right time for the holiday dinner tables.

PREPARATION

Storage

Cranberries can be frozen (at some loss in texture and flavor) in their original package with no processing, for later use.

Equivalents

Each pound (or quart) of cranberries will make 3 to 3 1/2 cups of cooked sauce.

CLASSIC USES AND AFFINITIES

There are the traditional cranberry sauces, and cranberries are often used in puddings and batter breads. The juice of this acid berry, rich in Vitamin C, is also used as an appetizer or breakfast drink and is sometimes blended with apple juice.

CRANBERRY BEAN

BACKGROUND

Other names for the native New World *cranberry bean* are *shell bean* and *shellout*—it is always shelled, even when young, because of the toughness of its pods. Cranberry beans are characterized by red splotches on the tough outer pod and cream-colored red-streaked bean seeds within. (For soaking, cooking, and other particulars, see BEANS.)

AVAILABILITY

They ripen in the summer and are used fresh and can be dried for winter use.

PREPARATION

Fresh or dried, the beanskin is thick and tough, too. A slit cut in the skin seam along the inner curve of the bean before cooking will help the bean reach tenderness more quickly.

CRAYFISH

BACKGROUND

Strictly defined, a *crayfish* or *crawfish* is one of several hundred species of freshwater aquatic arthropods that usually resemble midget lobsters, complete with claws. Some books extend the definition to marine crustaceans such as the spiny lobster, but from a zoologist's viewpoint, that is incorrect. French gourmets have long had a gastronomic love affair with crayfish or, as they call them, *écrevisses*. Crayfish also excite other palates around the world, from Scandinavia to New Zealand to New Orleans.

PREPARATION

You can simmer live crayfish as you would LOBSTERS if you adjust the cooking time downward. From the time you plunge the crayfish into boiling seasoned water, figure on 8 to 12 minutes, depending on size. Like lobsters, crayfish turn bright red when cooked. Unlike lobsters, they will probably need to be washed and soaked in water before you cook them, to rid them of the slime and grit they pick up from living on the bottoms of rivers, ponds, or canals.

CREAM

BACKGROUND

Unhomogenized milk separates naturally on standing into skim milk and a top layer of rich, butterfat-heavy cream. There are a number of varieties of cream available to the consumer. (See also SOUR CREAM.)

Varieties

Heavy (or whipping) cream is 40 percent butterfat; cream to be whipped should be at least that rich, because it is the butterfat content that determines how well the cream will whip up. When whipping, use very cold bowls and beaters—the cold keeps the fat firm, not oily or buttery. A high, narrow bowl, with the cream not quite covering the blades of the beaters, will aid in increasing the volume of the whipped cream. And day-old cream will be more viscous than fresh. Sweetened whipped cream has a softer texture than unsweetened.

Double cream, with a 50 to 60 percent butterfat content, called for in many European recipes, is not available commercially in America.

Light cream is 32 percent fat; it is pasteurized (heated to 161° to 170°F for 15 to 18 seconds) and has a shelf life of a few days.

Coffee cream is 18 to 20 percent fat.

Ultrapasteurized cream, heated to 275° to 300°F for a few seconds, has a long shelf life (up to a month if not opened), because the high heat kills the microorganisms that cause spoilage; but it is difficult to whip and has a cooked taste that many cream-lovers find unsatisfactory.

Clotted cream, made by skimming the clots of cream from heated fresh milk or equal amounts of heavy cream and milk, is delicious with tea scones and strawberry jam, for one, and will keep refrigerated for 2 to 3 days.

Crème fraîche is a 30 percent butterfat cream, fermented by bacteria in the air to a rich, thickened, sweet taste—sometimes slightly sour—and a velvety texture. It is a lavish complement to fresh fruit. Used as a substitute for heavy sweet cream or sour cream in desserts, in cream soups, or as filling for tortes, this lavish French invention is superb. An ultrapasteurized product that approximates *crème fraîche* is sold in America; it is expensive.

Nondairy creamers, made from coconut or palm oil, do not taste like real cream, are high in saturated fats, and contribute to high cholesterol levels in the blood.

Readymade whipped cream: Some members of this category contain real cream, but have additives to extend their shelflife and promote stability. Their flavor and texture are not on target with freshly whipped cream. Another type of aerosol-whipped "cream" is neither whipped nor even cream—it is completely artificial, made with hydrogenated vegetable oils and artificial flavorings. This type is referred to as a *dessert topping.*

CREAM OF TARTAR

BACKGROUND

Tartar is the acid sediment deposited on the sides of casks during wine-making. Refined, it becomes the white, fine-grained crystalline *cream of tartar,* which was once the main acid used to make commercial baking powders. (You can combine it with baking soda to make your own; see BAKING POWDER.) Recipes call for cream of tartar to improve the creamy texture of candies and cake frostings as well as to help stabilize the volume of beaten egg whites.

CRENSHAW

BACKGROUND

The *crenshaw* or *cranshaw* is a member of the same species as the cantaloupe, called *Cucumis melo*. This 6- to 9-pound melon is considered one of the very best in terms of sweetness, lusciousness, and juiciness by discriminating melon-lovers. Some people confuse the crenshaw with the good, but not-as-good, casaba. The crenshaw, however, has less pronounced furrows running from its slightly pointed stem end to the round blossom end, a smoother skin, and a detectable fragrance when ripe. Under its thick rind is the flesh with a pastel salmon-orange hue.

AVAILABILITY

The season for crenshaw lasts from July to October, but you will usually find the best specimens from August through mid-September.

Buying Tips

As the crenshaw ripens, its skin changes from green to a deep golden-yellow; this is the best ripeness indicator. The one exception is the crenshaw that arrives in September, which is more green than yellow. It also is more deeply furrowed and has a more pointed stem end, making its shape a little more like the casaba's. Another buying guide is to smell the fruit—a pleasing scent should be noticeable. Also, gently push the blossom end (opposite the stem end) with your thumb—the rind should yield to the pressure. For optimum moisture content, the crenshaw should be heavy for its size. Avoid those that have soft spots (a sign of subsurface decay) and those with moldy, bruised, injured, or shriveled skins.

PREPARATION

Storage

A whole crenshaw keeps better than a cantaloupe. Once ripened, tightly seal it in plastic wrap (to keep its odor in and foreign odors out) and refrigerate for up to 4 to 7 days and possibly longer, depending on original condition.

CLASSIC USES AND AFFINITIES

A crenshaw may be prepared and used as you would a CANTALOUPE or a HONEYDEW (see those entries).

CROUTON

PREPARATION

Slice slightly dried, crustless bread into small cubes, sauté them in butter to a golden brown, and you have croutons that will taste immensely better than the preservative-laden store-bought ones. For flavor, add ingredients such as fresh herbs, garlic, or sautéed onions. Use cubed croutons to garnish soups and salads and as the bulk item in a stuffing. You can also cut croutons into flat rectangles, squares, or discs and you can sauté them in other fats beside butter or toast them with fat or oil in the oven.

CUCUMBER

BACKGROUND

Cucumis sativus is no Johnny-come-lately. The Chinese have been growing cucumbers for about 3,000 years, the Romans relished them, and they are mentioned in the Bible. Nor are cucumbers limited to one class. They range from England's aristocratic tea sandwiches to the working-class crunch of a sour pickle.

Varieties

The cucumber usually available in American markets is smooth, green, and approximately 6 inches long. These cucumbers are likely to have been waxed by the processor. Smaller, lighter green cucumbers, sometimes streaked with yellow or white, with bumpy rinds, are sold for pickling. A virtually seedless variety is now on the market: it is about 1 to 2 feet long, about 1½ to 2 inches thick, and relatively expensive but worth its premium price. Countless other cucumber varieties exist ranging in size from an inch to over 2 feet and come in a wide choice of surface hues.

AVAILABILITY

Year round, with a summertime peak.

BUYING TIPS

The best cucumbers are firm, well-proportioned, and have a rich green skin color, though minute traces of white are not necessarily a negative sign. Avoid those with skins that are shriveled or soft-spotted; particularly examine the two ends for these flaws. The smaller the cucumber for its variety, the better it is. As a cucumber grows, its seeds develop, producing a wasteful core and a bitter flavor that permeates the flesh. All else being equal, select nonwaxed cucumbers.

PREPARATION

Storage

Tightly seal whole cucumbers in plastic wrap to retain their moisture. They can be refrigerated in the vegetable compartment for three to five days. If you must store cut cucumbers, keep them well covered; they give off an odor that can permeate other foods; they also can absorb scents. Use cut cucumbers within a day or two.

Preliminaries

Scrub cucumbers well. If the skin is very waxy, peel it off. If not, scoring the skin of a whole cucumber, lengthwise, with the tines of a fork adds a decorative touch when it is sliced. Cucumbers to be used in salad will be firmer, tastier, and less watery if the pulpy seeds, if any, are removed. One quick and easy seeding method is to halve the cucumber lengthwise and then—dugout canoe style—scoop out the seeds. Seeding will also make cucumbers less upsetting to sensitive digestive tracts.

Cooking

Slices or small chunks of young cucumbers can be sautéed for a few minutes in butter, or can be steamed or poached for about five minutes using a broth as the liquid base. Braised cucumbers are also tasty. Cooked or raw cucumber can be marinated, chilled, and served.

CLASSIC USES AND AFFINITIES

Dill weed and seeds are traditional flavoring agents for cucumbers. So are yogurt and sour cream. Sliced cucumbers go perfectly with poached fish as well as into sandwiches. Cucumbers marinated in seasoned vinegar make a splendid salad. Another summertime favorite is cold cucumber soup.

CUMIN

BACKGROUND

The fruit of *Cuminum cyminum* (called a seed because it is only about ¼ inch long) looks, but does not taste, like caraway seed. Cumin is native to the Nile and Eastern Mediterranean; Iran, Morocco and India are major commercial producers in the twentieth century.

Ground cumin becomes rancid quickly. Smell it before using. Cumin seeds can keep for a year if properly stored. (See HERBS AND SPICES for information on buying, storing, cooking, etc.)

CLASSIC USES AND AFFINITIES

Commercial chili and curry powders almost always contain cumin. Chili con carne, huevos rancheros, and other Mexican dishes use cumin; so do Indian dishes. Swiss, Dutch, and Scandinavian cumin-flavored cheeses are manufactured, and this spice can be used in homemade cheese spreads. The Germans use cumin with sauerkraut and roast pork. This spice is also popular in Greece and North Africa.

CURRANT

BACKGROUND

The *dried currant* used in fruitcakes is really a small dried seedless grape, the Zante, and is therefore treated like a RAISIN. In the Middle Ages, it was imported from Greece; it was called *rayson of Coruante* (Corinth), which became the name *currant*. The same name was later applied to a Northern fruit that was in some ways similar—the tart red or white berry of *Ribes rubrum* or the sweet black *R. nigrum*, related to the gooseberry. This currant, native to the cool, moist regions of North America and Northern Europe, is the one considered here.

AVAILABILITY

Fresh currants are available in June, July, and August.

Buying Tips

Choose plump currants free of hulls and other debris.

PREPARATION

Storage

Currants can be stored in a refrigerator for 1 to 2 days. If you are willing to sacrifice some texture, you can freeze currants for up to a couple of weeks in the freezing compartment, or for several months in a 0°F freezer.

Preliminaries

Wash currants just before use as moisture hastens decay.

Equivalents

Each quart (about 4 cups) provides six to eight servings, depending on appetites.

CLASSIC USES AND AFFINITIES

Cassis is French for black currant, and for the syrup or liqueur with that flavor. *Bar-le-duc* is traditionally made with currants. Now this famous tart jelly, usually eaten with game or cream cheese, is sometimes made with other berries.

CURRY

BACKGROUND

The *curry* that Westerners use (a fairly specific yellowish blend of spices) is unknown in traditional India. The word *kari* in Tamil means "sauce," and the cooks of India have different names for different types of spice blends and sauces. Thus, a Westerner who orders "chicken curry" in India is being as vague as an Indian who orders "chicken with sauce" in America—one must be more precise and name the particular sauce.

Traditional Indian cooks grind fresh whole spices at home or buy preground spices in market stalls or from itinerant peddlers, provided that the merchant has ground his spices on the spot or at least sometime that day. Even the growing number of convenience-seekers in India who buy packaged ground spices off the shelf seldom buy an all-purpose curry powder—they take home the individual ground spices or base mixtures such as GARAM MASALA and blend them according to the nature of the particular dish they are preparing. Western cooks are advised to do the same, despite the temptation to buy an all-purpose curry powder.

Commercial curry powder made for Western world markets is a ready-to-use mixture of numerous spices such as turmeric, coriander, black pepper, cayenne pepper, cumin, cardamom, cinnamon, ginger, mace, fenugreek, bay leaves, saffron, and mustard seed. Understandably, the more expensive spices in most commercial blends appear in proportions determined by economics, not gastronomy—consequently, one is apt to find a disagreeable overabundance of turmeric in all but the top-quality curry powders. Turmeric is also used to give the curry powder its characteristic yellow hue; superb blends let the costly saffron perform part of that mission. (See the various spice entries, and HERBS AND SPICES for general information.)

Buying Tips

If you must purchase an all-purpose curry powder, remember that hotness varies from brand to brand, and that "Madras-style" is hotter than the standard mixture. Buy in small quantities, because freshness disappears in a matter of a month or two. Once opened, oil-based curry pastes are best refrigerated.

Cooking

Never subject a curry blend to hot heat such as sautéing over a high flame, or some of the component spices such as turmeric may become bitter.

CLASSIC USES AND AFFINITIES

In our country, curry blends are most often used in Indian-style dishes. Curry blends can also be used in egg dishes, soups, cheese dishes, cheese spreads, and fruit salads.

CUSTARD APPLE

BACKGROUND

The *custard apple*, (*Annona reticulata*), a close relative of the soursop and the sweetsop, and sometimes confused with the latter, is a native of tropical America. In our country it is grown to a limited extent in the orchards of California and Florida. It is a roundish fruit, usually the size of a large orange. It has a dimpled, tough, green, greenish-brown, or reddish-brown rind. The flesh is sweet, soft, and white, with a delicate flavor and a custardlike texture. Black seeds within the flesh can be removed with your teeth or with a pointed knife as you come upon them.

CUTTLEFISH

Many shoppers use the word *cuttlefish* interchangeably with *squid*, though biologically the cuttlefish is a distinct type of cephalopod. Culinarily, it can be treated as a SQUID.

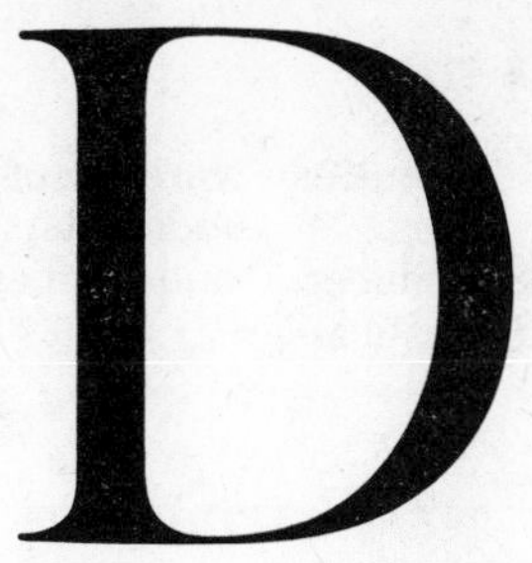

DANDELION GREENS

BACKGROUND

Do not curse if your lawn has been overrun by *Taraxacum officinale*; get a bucket and pull up the young plants by the roots. If you have waited long enough for the yellow flowers to appear, gather them for homemade wine; but the best dandelion eating is in the bitter tenderness of the baby springtime leaves. The jagged-edged leaves reminded Medieval people of lion's teeth; their Latin *dens leonis* became the Anglo-French *dent de lion* and our *dandelion*.

PREPARATION

Pick fresh, bright-looking, unblemished leaves just prior to use. Wash them well and use them for salads (alone, or as a background companion to supermarket greens). Or simmer or braise them in butter for several minutes.

DANGLEBERRY

BACKGROUND

The *dangleberry* (*Gaylussacia frondosa*) or *tangleberry* is a close relative of the HUCKLEBERRY and the BLUEBERRY , and is in desperate need of a good public-relations firm. Many people think it is poisonous. Even the derisive term "dingleberry" may have derived from the poor culinary reputation of the dangleberry. Wild-food gourmets, however, know that the dangleberry can be delicious as a game sauce.

DATE

BACKGROUND

Americans generally regard the *date* as sort of a desert dessert, but the *Phoenix dactylifera* is an essential of life in many arid regions of the Middle East and North Africa. In those lands, the desert dwellers revere the date palm for its ability to thrive with minimum water; for its source of concentrated food energy that can be eaten fresh, dried for future use, or refined for sugar; for its nonedible fiber, which is converted into ropes, mats, and baskets; and for its very presence, which furnishes a noonday respite at isolated oases where the only other cooling shade may be under the belly of a camel.

Dates grow in clusters, hanging high above the ground. As each single-seeded fruit matures and ripens, its skin color changes from green to golden or mahogany (depending on the variety), and the pulp sweetens. Most date varieties are oval, though some are practically globular; most are 1 to 2 inches long, though some varieties measure as much as several inches.

Iraq is the world's top date producer; California and Arizona lead domestically.

Varieties

There are many ways to classify the enormous number of date varieties. Marketers often categorize them by their texture: *soft* or *hard*, with gradations between. *Khadrawy* is a soft date, *Thoory* is a dry (or bread) date, and *Deglet Noor* and *Hallowi* fall between.

AVAILABILITY

Some markets carry fresh dates from late summer through mid-fall. Most markets carry dried dates the year round.

Buying Tips

Both fresh and dried dates should be plump, soft to the touch (relative to the variety) and have a fresh luster. Do not purchase any with sticky, overly shriveled, moldy, or sugar-crystal-encrusted skins nor any that have a fermented sour scent. If sold loose, ask the seller if you can sample (or at least buy, then sample) one date before you commit yourself to a bagful. Some dates are pitted, others are not—be sure the price reflects that situation. For your teeth's sake, eat pitted dates cautiously, as seed fragments may remain. Check the box labels (if any) for the possible existence of excessive additives.

PREPARATION

Storage

Dried dates naturally keep much longer than fresh dates. Also, the hard dates store longer than the soft ones. All dates keep well in a well-closed container at room temperature or, for prolonged storage, in the refrigerator. Storage life varies from several weeks to a year or more, depending on condition, variety, and temperature.

Uses

Dates may be eaten raw or, if used with discretion, to flavor such preparations as rice pilaf, nut breads, and fruitcakes. To stuff a date, make a lengthwise slit on top, remove the seed, and, for example, insert an almond or a dollop of almond paste. Do not try to chop dates too fine; you will end up with a gluey date pâté instead.

DEWBERRY

The *dewberry* (*Rubus flagellaris*) is a smaller variety of the blackberry. For general preparation and storage advice, see BLACKBERRY.

DILL

BACKGROUND

Both the feathery green leaves and the tan, flat oval seeds of *Anethum graveolens* are eaten. There is a hint of similarity between the taste of *dill leaves* (also called *dill weed*) and FENNEL. The seeds taste and look somewhat like CARAWAY seeds. Dill weed is available dried or fresh, the latter being superior in flavor and fragrance. (See HERBS AND SPICES for information on buying, storing, cooking, etc.)

PREPARATION

Fresh dill weed must be cleaned carefully—an amazing amount of dirt adheres to the tiny fronds.

CLASSIC USES AND AFFINITIES

Dill is essential to Scandinavian cooking, and very often it is used by central European, Russian, and Jewish cooks. Dill weed has an affinity for mild, creamy foods such as sour cream, cottage cheese, white sauce, and yogurt. It is a classic herb for fish, lobster, shrimp, and crayfish. Potatoes, carrots, cucumbers, and cauliflower are dill-loving vegetables, and the delicate fresh leaves make a pretty garnish. Dill seeds are fundamental to dill pickles and excellent in cheese spreads, potato salad, cole slaw, sauerkraut and tomato juice.

DITTANY

BACKGROUND

This gray-green bush, a member of the mint family, is native to Crete. Its leaves are eaten, finely chopped, in salads. *Origanum dictamnus* is related to oregano, marjoram, and thyme, and its leaves can be used to impart a somewhat similar flavor wherever one of these herbs would be used. (See HERBS AND SPICES for information on buying, storing, cooking, etc.)

DUCK

BACKGROUND

Two of the world's finest-tasting domesticated ducks are the varieties from Rouen, France, and from Peking, China. Fortunately for Americans, the famous white-feathered, dark-fleshed Long Island duck is none other than a direct descendent of the Peking duck, having been transported halfway around the world to New York aboard a Clipper ship in 1873. Most ducks sold in this country are from that strain.

This entry covers the domesticated duck. For wild duck, see under GAME BIRDS. Ducks and chickens share many culinary traits, so much of the advice given in the CHICKEN entry on the following subjects is relevant:

- Background:
  - USDA Grades
- Availability:
  - Fresh or Preserved
  - Buying Tips
- Preparation:
  - Storage
  - Thawing Frozen Birds
  - Preliminaries
  - Cooking

Also see the separate entry, CHICKEN GIBLETS AND VARIETY MEATS. However, keep in mind the following information that applies more specifically to ducks.

AVAILABILITY

Fresh ducks are available seasonally, from late spring through late fall, because most of the major duck farms are located in chilly climates. Frozen ducks, which comprise 90 percent of the duck sales in America, are available the year round. Typically, they weigh between 3 and 5½ pounds. Since they are usually 7 to 12 weeks old, they are technically ducklings, not ducks, and are correctly sold as such.

Buying Tips

Look for a plump, well-formed bird with a broad, meaty breast. The smaller the duck for its variety, the younger and therefore more tender it will be. If you are buying a frozen duck, be sure the bird is solidly frozen and the wrapping is intact. Frozen ducks are usually sold under brand names, most of which can be trusted to give you a consistently good product. Experiment and stick with the brands in your region that you deem best.

Amounts

Because a duck has a lower ratio of edible meat to fat and bone waste than a chicken, you will need to buy a greater quantity of duck for each person. Figure on about 1½ pounds per person. On special dining occasions, half a bird is the norm; with day-to-day meals, a whole 4½ pound bird will serve three diners, or two diners with some left-overs. If you have four at the table, buy two 3-pound ducks rather than one 6-pounder.

PREPARATION

Storage

A frozen duck can be kept in its original wrapper for up to two weeks in the frozen food compartment and for several months in a 0°F freezer.

Thawing

Depending on size, allow 24 to 36 hours to thaw in the refrigerator for a 3 to 5½ pound frozen duck. It will take 2 to 3 hours with the cold-water method, which we do not recommend unless absolutely necessary.

Preliminaries

With some ducks, you will have to remove some of the fat near the opening of the stomach cavity. Render and then clarify that fat for other uses such as frying or pastry-making, if the flavor suits your palate. While it is beneficial to rub the skin and stomach cavity of a chicken with an acid liquid such as lemon juice, it is almost essential to do it to a duck to help counteract its fatty flavor.

Stuffing

Do not expect a stuffing cooked inside a duck's stomach cavity to gain rave reviews, because a duck is too fatty. We recommend that you partially fill the cavity with ingredients such as quartered onions, carrot chunks, orange segments, various herbs (especially fresh parsley springs) and spices, and the like—and then discard those flavoring agents once the bird is cooked. If you insist on baking an edible stuffing inside rather than outside the stomach cavity, at least cut down on the fat or oil called for in the stuffing recipe. Perhaps the best-known duck stuffing is made with apples, prunes, and/or apricots.

Cooking

Ducks are fatty and, partially for that reason, are best roasted, even if sold under the name of "young duckling," "broiler-fryer duckling," "roaster duckling," or just plain "duckling." Mature ducks (few are to be found in the market) are best cooked with slow moist heat such as braising or stewing. Using a sharp-pointed knife or fork, prick the skin all over the bird and particularly in the thick fat areas before you put the duck into the oven and, if necessary, during cooking. This step allows a lot of the melting fat to drain out of the bird, thus giving you a less fatty duck with a crisper skin. When pricking the skin, do not make the punctures too deep, nor make too many. Because a duck is fatty and may cause excessive oven splatter, roast your room temperature duck at 325°F for 20 minutes plus 18 to 22 minutes per pound. The shorter time will give you the most succulent flesh, the longer time a drier flesh that is closer to the preference of the average American diner. If stuffed, add 3 to 5 minutes per pound. If you want a crisper, browner skin and do not mind the messy splatter, turn the temperature up to 400°F for the last 30 minutes, reducing the total cooking time by 5 minutes. Always test for doneness. Basting a duck is not necessary because, unlike a chicken, its thick layers of fat serve as natural barding. Nevertheless, brushing the bird once or twice with the fat drippings will not do any harm. Because the bird is so fatty, you will probaby have to pour off the fat that accumulates in the roasting pan once or twice during the cooking period. Too much fat in the pan may produce annoying smoke and even a safety hazard.

CLASSIC USES AND AFFINITIES

Famous French duck dishes include *canard bigarade* (duckling in a sour orange sauce) and pressed duck. From northern China comes the celebrated Peking duck (this name refers to a preparation as well as to a variety of duck), from southern China the honey-glazed roast duck. Cookbooks and restaurants usually perpetuate the presumed affinity of sweet sauces with duck. While the duck is full enough in flavor to stand up to some sweetness, a cloying taste overshadows the subtle flavor tones of the duck meat. What duck needs is a sauce with an acid base such as citrus juice (orange or lemon), wine or vinegar, which helps the diner's taste buds to reduce their perception of the fattiness of the duck. Wild rice is the classic American accompaniment to roast duck, at least in restaurants.

DURIAN

BACKGROUND

Durian is the fruit of a Malaysian tree, *Durio zibethinus*. The typical durian is a little larger than a football, weighs 5 to 10 pounds, and is covered with stout "cleats" rising from a semihard brown (sometimes tinged with green) outer husk. The durian is a paradox. It is malodorous to the nose, marvelous on the tongue. The durian pulp is creamy in color, thick and custardy in consistency, not juicy or cloyingly sweet, but deliciously rich. For the people of Southeast Asia it is a popular food. When just underripe, it can be eaten raw or cooked as a vegetable. Its seeds, when roasted, are also good to eat. In Malaysia, they make it into ice cream.

EEL

BACKGROUND

An *eel*, to be sure, is a fish, but its snakelike appearance has done much to intimidate most Americans even though the Eastern coastal rivers offer a sizable potential eel harvest. This gustatory reluctance seems strange to Europeans and Orientals, who willingly pay high prices for eels. Hollanders eat *aal*, as they call them, with gusto, either in stews or soups, or sautéed, broiled, baked, smoked, or jellied. *Anguilles au vert*, eels in green sauce, is a classic Benelux specialty. Raw eel is cherished by the Japanese. Spaniards fry *elvers* (baby eels) with garlic in oil. Americans usually relegate the white, firm, fatty, rich yet deliciously delicate flesh as fishing bait.

AVAILABILITY

Fresh eels are most likely to be found in Eastern fish markets during the late summer and early fall. Ask the fishmonger to skin and dress the eels for you. Smoked fresh eel is sometimes sold in gourmet deli shops. Eel is also sold canned and frozen across the country. Canned eel if well prepared is fine as an appetizer or as an ingredient for open-faced sandwiches; frozen eel is too mushy to create much culinary excitement.

PREPARATION

If you catch or are given fresh eels, clean them as soon as possible, as the fish is perishable. The old-fashioned yet still effective method is to rub off the surface skin with dry sand, then to impale the head of an eel on a post or wall with a nail. Make a circular skin-deep cut around the neck and then, using pliers, pull off the skin stocking-style with a strong downward movement. Gut the eel and cut off its head and tail tip. Wash the skinned flesh, then slice it across the grain into 1- to 3-inch segments.

Cooking

The younger the eel, the more tender the flesh. Eel segments will simmer in 20 to 40 minutes, depending on their thickness and the maturity of the flesh.

EGGPLANT

BACKGROUND

Eggplant is a member of the nightshade family, thus related to the tomato and potato. It is referred to in some chic American circles by its French name, *aubergine*. Scientifically it is known as *solanum melongena*. Though only mildly popular in America, eggplant is consumed in abundance in the Mediterranean, Middle Eastern, and Balkan regions as well as in China and India. It probably is native to northern India. Up until the nineteenth century, most Westerners considered it poisonous—and some Europeans, believing it caused insanity, nicknamed this fruit the *mad apple*.

Varieties

Just about the only eggplant that can be found in American grocery store produce bins is the purple-black, 5- to 10-inch, egg-shaped variety. But many other varieties exist: eggplants are also white, yellow, red, or striped; are also pear-, cucumber- or ball-shaped; and vary in length from 2 to 12 inches. The small varieties are almost always culinarily superior, and can usually be found in Italian and Oriental ethnic food stores. The discussion that follows, though, deals primarily with the common American grocery-store variety, the one we are most likely to encounter.

AVAILABILITY

Available year round. Peak: late July through September.

Buying Tips

A good eggplant is always firm to the touch, not soft or flabby, which indicates overripeness. It should still be a long, long way from reaching its maximum growth size. The flesh of a young eggplant tastes better and its seeds and skin are far less bitter than those from a fully mature one. If you have no choice but to buy the "giant" breed, at least pick out the smallest fruits. It should be heavy for its size, indicating optimum moisture content. The skin should be smooth and shiny, free from scars, cuts, and brownish blemishes. The latter is a sign of decay, which can spread quickly within the eggplant. Don't take a shriveled eggplant; a wrinkled skin is usually the result of excessive moisture loss caused by prolonged or improper storage.

PREPARATION

Storage

Use your eggplant as soon as possible, as bitterness increases with storage time. If storage is necessary, put it in a cool dry place—it will keep up to a day or two if the fruit is in perfect condition. If a slightly longer storage time is required, or if the fruit is nearly overripe, place it in your refrigerator crisper compartment and bring to room temperature an hour before use.

Preliminaries

The flesh and skin of the eggplant are edible, the stem and green-leafed cap are not. The latter is simply removed by slicing it off, along with the tip of the fruit. Some flesh will be wasted, but the stem end is the least palatable area, so little of value will be lost. Peel off the skin of an overly mature eggplant before cooking or it will make the rest of the ingredients bitter. Skins of young eggplants are delicious. To peel skin, use a vegetable peeler or paring knife on the whole fruit—or cut it into slices, then trim the skin. Cut open your uncooked eggplant just prior to use, as the flesh discolors quickly. If you're not using the exposed raw flesh immediately, either rub lemon juice on its surface or drop the pieces into cold salted water. Contrary to widespread notion, soaking the flesh of an eggplant for 30 to 60 minutes in salted water before cooking usually is not necessary. If the fruit is too ripe and its flesh overly bitter, do soak it, but only for about 15 minutes. Or, even better, cover the exposed flesh with salt (coarse salt, if you have it) and press it down with a 5-pound weight for 20 minutes, then rinse. Both these ancient methods draw out water and, in the process, some of the bitter flavor.

Cooking

Think of an eggplant as a sponge or blotter. It can soak up a lot of butter or oil. (This is best illustrated by the classic Turkish story about *imam bayildi*—in English, "the fainting Muslim priest"—who passed out when he learned that his bride used up her entire dowry of several barrels of olive oil preparing a few eggplant dishes.) If you're calorie conscious, your best bet is to bake, broil, or stew the eggplant, rather than fry it. The favored methods are deep-frying (always coat the chunks of flesh with batter or an adhesive bread-crumb mixture to retard oil absorption), pay-frying (always flour it for the same reason), broiling, roasting, baking (best when halved and stuffed), and stewing. Avoid simmering and steaming, as the flesh becomes uninvitingly water-logged. Cooking times will vary according to the eggplant's variety, age, condition, and size—and to your recipe and personal preferences. The following are averages for the fruit found in most grocery stores, and are designed to serve only as rough guidelines if you are not using a set recipe. To bake whole eggplants, lightly grease and pierce them (to allow the steam to escape, thus preventing bursting), bake in a preheated 375° oven for 50 minutes, then remove and let them cool slightly before serving. If you like, scoop out the flesh and mash it, then season. To bake eggplant halves, baste them with butter or oil, place in preheated 350° oven for 30 minutes, adding 5 minutes if stuffed. To broil ½ slices, liberally brush them with oil or melted butter, then cook 4 inches from heat source for 5 minutes per side. To pan-fry ½-inch slices, sauté in butter or oil over medium heat for 5 minutes per side. To deep-fry ¾-inch cubes, coat with batter or crumbs, cook in 375°F oil for 5 minutes or until golden brown, then thoroughly drain on paper towels.

Equivalents

The average grocery-store eggplant weighs slightly more than 1¼ pounds. It will yield approximately a dozen ½-inch slices, or 3 cups of ¾-inch cubes. Used as a side dish. One fruit is enough for three or four servings. As a main dish, figure one eggplant for two people.

CLASSIC USES AND AFFINITIES

Eggplant's blandness makes it a welcome complement to most foods. Tomato is its chief cooking companion, especially in the Mediterranean world. Other popular potmates include zucchini, the onion family, sweet peppers, lamb and cooking cheeses like Mozzarella. Herb and spice match-ups include basil, tarragon, parsley, oregano, thyme, savory, sage, cinnamon, and nutmeg. Eggplant parmigiana, moussaka, ratatouille, baba ghanouj, and imam bayildi are a few famous eggplant dishes.

EGGROLL SKINS

BACKGROUND

These flat sheets are made with an egg-enriched dough. When the skins are wrapped around a mixture of savory chopped meat or seafood and vegetables, then deep-fried, you have the famous Chinese egg roll, a perfect dish for making the most out of leftovers. If well wrapped, eggroll skins can be refrigerated for up to several days or stored in the deep freezer for a month or two. In the latter circumstance, you must thaw the skins before proceeding to your recipe.

EGGS, CHICKEN

BACKGROUND

"You can't," as Lenin said, "make an

omelet without breaking eggs." But you can make hard- or soft-boiled eggs, and serve the egg in its natural package. Eggs can be white, brown, or even freckled. Inside, an egg is an egg; the color of the shell simply indicates the breed of hen that produced it (though the brown variety tend to have thicker shells and therefore to be slightly superior when it comes to making boiled eggs). Most commercial eggs are unfertilized; some health-food stores sell fertilized eggs, if you want them. Eggs are valuable in cooking for their excellent taste, and for their chemical and physical properties. Eggs cause foods to cohere; egg yolks emulsify sauces; beaten egg whites trap air and raise soufflés and angel-food cakes.

Grades

Quality: Eggs are letter-graded AA, A, B, or C, based not on size or freshness, but on the physical condition of the egg—how stiff or viscous the eggs are and therefore, how they are best used. The stiffer and more compact the yolk and white, the higher the grade. *Grade AA* (or *Fancy*) eggs are the stiffest, with a firm, high-standing yolk and a firm white that stays compact when the egg is broken. They are good poached or fried. *Grade A* is a little runnier than AA, but is also a stiff egg. The lower grades have progressively flatter and wetter yolks and whites, less separation between the two: *Grade B* eggs perform well in cakes, mixtures, and as scrambled eggs; *Grade C* eggs usually go to commercial food processors and don't appear at the stores.

Size: This U.S. government-sanctioned system refers to the minimum weight per dozen, not to quality. The minimum weights in ounces for a dozen eggs are: *Peewee*, 15; *Small*, 18; *Medium*, 21; *Large*, 24; *Extra-Large*, 27; *Jumbo*, 30.

AVAILABILITY

Available year round.

Buying Tips

Most recipes are calibrated on medium or large eggs; using other egg sizes may throw the recipe out of kilter. When in doubt, use large eggs. Open the carton and examine each egg closely to see that it is uncracked and clean. Cracked or soiled eggs may contain harmful bacteria. Fresh eggs are slightly dull-looking; only stale eggs are shiny. A fresh egg makes no noise if you hold it up to your ear and shake it; overage eggs slosh. The freshest eggs will lie flat at the bottom of a bowl of water; an egg that floats is bad news.

PREPARATION

Storage

Eggs lose quality fast when stored at room temperature. Keep eggs refrigerated until they are to be used. The rack in the refrigerator door is not the best place to store eggs; concussion from opening and closing the door can crack the eggs. If you experience this problem, keep the eggs in their original carton, on the coldest shelf of the refrigerator. Store eggs with the large end up. If you crack an egg accidentally, use it right away or freeze it—but never in its shell. Fresh egg yolks will keep about three days in the refrigerator. Put them in cold water and in a covered container. Fresh egg whites, covered and refrigerated, may be kept a little longer. Keep eggs away from strong-smelling foods in the refrigerator; eggshells are porous and absorb food odors. Yolks and whites may be frozen, if separated and stored in different containers. Add water to cover the yolks. An egg white fits into an individual ice-cube container; cover with aluminum foil. Thaw at room temperature, drain water from yolks, and use immediately.

Preliminaries

Bringing to Room Temperature: In most cases, you should bring eggs to or near room temperature (allow about an hour or so) before cooking them. This rule covers a wide assortment of preparations: fried eggs, scrambled eggs, omelets, sauces, to name a few. Exceptions to the rule include soft- and hard-boiled eggs made by the "pierced egg shell" method (described later). Cold eggs straight from the refrigerator separate better than warm eggs.

Separating Eggs: Eggs to be separated should be fresh enough to have a distinct, firm yolk. If you need training separating eggs, practice on eggs you'll use whole for scrambling, omelets, or cakes; then you'll be adept when you really need to separate eggs. If you find a bloodspot in an egg, pick it out and use the egg. The bloodspot is harmless.

Beating Egg Whites: The whites will not beat to optimum volume if any water, oil, or fat (including egg yolk) adheres to the whites, the pan, or the whisk. Use a copper, glass or stainless steel bowl instead of a plastic one because oil can linger on the latter material, even after repeated washings. An untinned copper bowl reacts chemically with egg whites to give them greater volume. If you don't have a copper bowl, add a pinch of cream of tartar—it produces the same type of chemical reaction. Start beating slowly, then gradually increase the pace. When making meringue, add the sugar only after the egg whites have begun to stiffen, or you'll end up with a stiff arm and a gooey mess. Use beaten egg whites right away—the foam will soon liquefy, and the whites can't be beaten again. Fold, never stir, egg whites into another mixture.

Cooking

Treat eggs gently in cooking. Eggs, except in the fast-cooked omelet, should not be cooked at too high a heat—they become rubbery, lose flavor, and are difficult to digest.

Thickening with Eggs: Both the yolk and the white can be used to thicken preparations such as sauces, custards, puddings, and pâtés. But since the yolk is immensely more efficient at this task and produces a smoother sauce, the yolk is usually separated from the white and used alone. The yolk also serves to color and flavor the preparation. As a general rule of thumb, it takes one raw large-sized yolk to firm 2/3 of a cup of liquid of a dish such as custard (thus, three such eggs will thicken one pint). One raw medium sized yolk performs the same culinary magic on slightly less than 5/8 of a cup of liquid. When making a preparation such as a sauce, remember that the yolk will curdle if the mixture boils or if the yolk is heated too quickly. Therefore, when adding yolks to a hot liquid, follow this procedure: lightly beat yolks in a small bowl, then blend into them several tablespoons of the hot liquid, a little at a time. Then stir the heated yolks into the hot liquid. Egg yolks, of course, are essential for the emulsified, butter-rich, hollandaise sauce.

Whole-Egg Dishes:

Boiled eggs should be simmered, or even steeped in just-boiled water. They should never be—as their name suggests—boiled. Use a wide, deep saucepan, one that does not have an iron or aluminum inner surface.

Boiled eggs can be prepared in many ways. Of all the techniques, the "pierced egg shell" one is the quickest and produces the surest and most consistent results. (Other methods such as the "bring-to-room-temperature-and-start-in-cold-water" one involve variables that cannot be accurately estimated.) Bring the water to a boil. Remove the eggs from the refrigerator. Using a sharp-pointed instrument such as a push-pin, pierce a narrow, ¼-inch hole into each egg's larger end. That portion of the egg contains the air cell, the culprit that can cause eggs to crack as they simmer. The hole allows the gas in the air cell to escape as the heat expands it. Because pressure won't build up in the air cell, you can use cold eggs and thus, need not have to remember to remove the eggs from the refrigerator beforehand. With a slotted spoon, gently place the eggs in the boiling water. Immediately, reduce the heat to a simmer level. Cook 5 to 7 minutes for soft-boiled and 12 to 15 minutes for hard-boiled eggs. (Through experimentation, you'll be able to determine the precise cooking time relative to your taste, to the type and water level of your pan, to the egg size of your choice, to the storage temperature of your refrigerator, and to your culinary plans. For instance, you would probably want to cook the eggs for 12 minutes if they are to be eaten out-of-hand and for 15 minutes if they are to be sliced.) When the eggs are cooked, promptly cool them in a container of cold running water for about 10 seconds for soft-boiled, and about a minute for hard-boiled eggs. This step helps stop the cooking process and makes the eggs easier to handle. In the case of hard-boiled eggs, it also prevents a layer or greenish ferrous sulphide from forming on the yolk. The green "ring" will form in any case if the eggs are overcooked. When you need perfectly smooth, peeled, hard-boiled eggs for a garnish, use this method: after cooking and cooling the eggs as described above, return them to the simmering pan for about 10 seconds. The shell will contract with the cold, then expand with the heat, making it easy to peel. The fresher the egg, the more difficult it is to peel, so use your older eggs.

Poached eggs are generally those cooked in simmering water or other liquid—best made from very fresh, cold eggs, which hold their shape best. To prevent sticking and make cleaning easier, lightly grease the bottom of your pan. Add about 2 inches of water and a teaspoon of vinegar (it helps set the egg white). Break the eggs to be poached into individual saucers. Slide each egg gently from saucer to the boiling water. Lower the heat to a simmer; watch the egg until it is done, about 3 to 5 minutes, depending on whether you want soft or firm eggs. Remove each egg with a slotted spoon, and hold over a paper towel to drain. For extra flavor, poach the eggs in a liquid other than water—try broth, wine, or tomato sauce. If you are making a lot of poached eggs or a dish such as eggs Benedict, keep the poached egg warm by slipping it into a pan of ½ inch of warm water.

Coddled eggs are often described as whole eggs cooked in hot water off the heat; other writers use this term for poached eggs which are covered, taken off the fire, and steeped for 8 to 12 minutes.

Scrambled eggs: Beat the eggs until well blended, but not foamy, with a fork, wire whisk, or the beater of a mixer (not too much: you don't want to incorporate air). You can add a teaspoon of cream, milk, or water to your scrambled egg or omelet mixture; the added liquid helps give the finished product a fluffy texture. Pour them into sizzling melted fat in a skillet, stir them lightly with a fork over low, gentle heat. Stir constantly as the mixture slowly cooks; when it is thick throughout but not moist or yet fully set, remove from the heat and serve promptly. You will have perfect scrambled eggs—well, good ones anyway. For tender, soft scrambled eggs that will wait without separating or toughening, use a double boiler. Melt the fat over hot water, add the eggs, and stir occasionally. Some cooks add bits of butter to the cooked eggs just before serving—but do add salt and pepper *after* the eggs are cooked; salt can toughen the cooking eggs, and pepper, when fried at high heat can become bitter.

Omelet: If you cook the scrambled eggs into a flat sheet, not a mass of curds, you will have an omelet. Speed (and therefore practice) is the key to success: a golden, light-textured omelet with a creamy center. Have all the equipment and ingredients ready when you begin cooking. Have the filling, if you want one, ready and warm before you start. A sacred omelet pan, untouched by soap and used for nothing else, is not essential—but if you use the traditional cast-iron pan, it really helps to set aside a special one so that it will stay seasoned and won't pick up the flavors of other foods. The pan should be free of scratches or surface marrings. A small, heavy pan (7 to 8 inches for a 2- or 3-egg omelet) with rounded, sloping sides and a longish handle is best and handiest for omelets. Too large a pan will be clumsy and the eggs may cook too quickly and become dry. Too small a pan may toughen the bottom of the omelet. Clean the pan with a little salt and wipe with a paper towel. Because you want the egg to spread out in a thin layer, don't try to cook a vast omelet capable of serving a football team; make individual omelets. If you're using butter, it should be hot, foaming, and sizzling—but don't let it brown. Pour the eggs (beaten as for scrambled eggs) into the heated pan—to avoid sticking, pour the eggs in a swift, circular motion, distributing the liquid uniformly. There are many ways to form an omelet. Here is the most popular of the sensible methods: Pour the eggs into the pan, wait a few seconds, then stir the omelet with a fork while simultaneously shaking the pan back and forth, until the bottom is set and the top warmed. This operation takes only seconds. As you shake the pan, lift the edges with a fork, to let the unset egg run underneath the set egg to the hot pan. Keep this up until most of the egg has solidified. When the omelet is set, add the filling (if any), then roll or fold the omelet onto the serving platter. To roll, lift the pan handle vertically and roll the omelet away from the handle toward the opposite edge of the pan. Serve the omelet immediately, preferably on a warm plate. The fillings added to an omelet are almost infinitely varied—grated cheese, sautéed mushrooms, chicken livers, crumbled bacon, ham, cooked vegetables, seafood, herbs, fruit, preserves. Many people enjoy a fluffier omelet, made by beating the yolks and egg whites separately, then folding them together and cooking.

Steam-fried eggs are started in a little hot fat, then drizzled with a teaspoon to a tablespoon of water per egg and covered about 3 to 5 minutes until done.

Oeufs sur le plat, or *mirrored eggs*, are broken onto a buttered heatproof dish, cooked on top of the stove or under the broiler, to a shiny finish.

Shirred eggs are baked in buttered ramekins, casseroles, or other shallow dishes, often with a bed of some savory food. The oven temperature should be about 325°F; an individual shirred egg will take 8 to 10 minutes, a casserole 12 to 15 minutes.

Raw eggs: Most of us have consumed raw eggs without realizing it—if you have had an egg nog, you have done it. A small number of people eat raw eggs in the unsubstantiated belief that doing so cures hangovers, gives added strength—or impresses their friends.

The Other Half of the Egg: Some recipes leave you with extra egg whites or yolks. What to do? Remember that egg whites are basic to many dessert preparations, including mousse, meringue, angel cake, frostings (as a glaze). They can be added to soufflés, or used in place of whole eggs with bread crumbs for a coating for meat or vegetables. Use extra *egg yolks* in mayonnaise, egg custard, omelets, scrambled eggs, chocolate mousse, or added to pastry cream, butter frosting, chocolate icing, blancmange, or biscuit mix.

Either whites or yolks can be added to a scrambled egg or omelet mixture. In the former case, the finished product will be firmer, while in the second, it will be of a lighter texture.

The Cleaning Chore: Soak egg utensils in warm water; hot water sets the egg, and makes matters worse.

Equivalents

A cup of egg equals approximately seven small, six medium, five large, a little more than four extra-large, or roughly four jumbo eggs. For a cup of egg whites, you need eleven whites from small eggs, ten from medium, eight from large, six from extra-large; for a cup of yolks, increase the number by about two-thirds in each case.

Egg Substitutes

The popular substitutes sold in supermarkets are made from egg whites with corn oil to replace the fat of the egg yolks, leaving the egg substitute free of cholesterol. It is nutritionally comparable to whole eggs, though it contains a little more fat—and about 20 more calories per serving. It can be used in anything, as eggs are used—but it does not have a true egg flavor, and costs almost twice as much as a fresh egg.

CLASSIC USES AND AFFINITIES

Emulsified sauces (e.g. mayonnaise, hollandaise), egg-raised cakes (angel, chiffon), meringues, meringue cakes and pies (baked Alaska, vacherin, Pavlova, *Spanische windtorte*), custard, quiche (shell of pastry or bread dough filled with a savory ingredient or mixture and custard), egg and potato salad, Egg Foo Yung, Spanish tortilla, and so on and so on....

EGGS, NONCHICKEN

BACKGROUND

Mankind's favorite egg is that of the chicken, but other eggs are also exciting to palates, at least in some cuisines.

Varieties

The *duck egg* is popular in the Orient. Filipinos make *balut*, a hard-boiled duck egg containing the partially developed embryo embedded in the yolk.

Goose eggs do not necessarily have to be zeros or golden. Properly cooked, they are delicious.

Quail eggs, which have a delicate flavor, are more cherished in the Orient and in Europe than in America.

Ostrich eggs are popular in parts of Africa. The bird (over 8 feet tall and several hundred pounds heavy) lays a clutch of about a dozen eggs, each a half foot long and a few pounds in weight. One egg can make an omelet for a dozen diners, but if you want a successful omelet, you must dilute the fat-rich egg with a volume of about 10 to 20 percent water. The flavor is a little more robust than that of chicken eggs, partially because of the ostrich's free-foraging diet.

For a discussion of *roe*, the eggs of fish, see CAVIAR and "CAVIAR" AND OTHER ROES.

EGGS, THOUSAND-YEAR-OLD

BACKGROUND

Thousand-year-old eggs is one name for this Chinese specialty; others are *ancient*, *century*, and *hundred-day-old eggs*. The last is most accurate. These eggs develop a brown or black shell, a blackish-amber egg white, and a greenish egg yolk as a result of being buried in the ground surrounded by wood ashes, salt, and lime for about 100 days. The earth's natural moisture chemically makes the lime hot which in turn slow-cooks the eggs. To serve this pungent-scented appetizer, peel and slice it lengthwise—it does not need to be cooked. You can store the eggs at room temperature for a week or two.

ELDERBERRY

BACKGROUND

The *elder* tree (*Sambucus canadensis*) is a member of the honeysuckle family and is a hardy native of the Northern Hemisphere. Both blossoms and berries are produced by the elder and both are edible.

PREPARATION

Elderflowers may be dipped in batter and fried like fritters. Elderberries are too tart and bitter for eating raw, but they are outstanding when cooked into preserves or fermented into elderberry wine or vinegar.

ENDIVE, BELGIAN

BACKGROUND

The *Belgian* or *French endive*, (*Cichorium endivia*), also called *witloof chicory*, is a close relative of the CURLY ENDIVE and ESCAROLE but does not resemble those salad greens. Belgian endive has many crisp leaves that dovetail tightly together into a shape resembling an oversized bullet, about 6 inches long and 1½ inches thick. The vegetable is purposely grown underground to deprive it of chlorophyl-producing sunlight in order to preserve its creamy whiteness. This labor-intensive cultivation process helps make the Belgian endive one of our more expensive vegetables.

AVAILABILITY

September through May.

Buying Tips

Select Belgian endive that are as white as possible, tinged with yellow only at the tips. The vegetable should be firm, with crisp, snug-fitting leaves. Avoid blemished, limp, and gargantuan specimens.

PREPARATION

Storage

Belgian endives become bitter when soaked in water or exposed to light for more than a brief spell. Therefore, store them in a tight, opaque covering such as a dry towel inside a plastic bag or a close wrapping of dark paper, wax paper, or foil. Use endives as soon as possible, preferably the day of purchase, certainly within a couple of days.

Preliminaries

Wash whole endives or their separate leaves in cold tap water with a very gentle and brief swishing motion. Drain and gently pat dry. Meticulous cooks simply wash the endives by dabbing them with a moist paper towel. Be sure to remove the hard, bitter stem core from the bottom of the endive. To crisp the leaves for a raw salad, place them briefly in refrigerated ice water.

Cooking

Belgian endives are popularly used as a raw salad ingredient or, when braised, as a side vegetable dish. Braise whole in butter infused with white wine for roughly 8 to 10 minutes, then gratinée by covering them with a white cream sauce, grated cheese, and bread crumbs, and place the dish into the broiler long enough to brown the topping.

Equivalents

A pound of Belgian endive should serve three to four persons.

ENDIVE, CURLY

BACKGROUND

Cichorium endivia is the botanical name for both Belgian and *curly endive*. To confuse the issue further, curly endive is often simply called chicory in the

United States. Curly endive produces slim, crumpled, edge-indented leaves that form an attractive green-rimmed, white centered floret, which has a bitter but pleasant flavor.

PREPARATION

The leaves are quite perishable. Refrigerate the greens and count on using them within a day or two of purchase. They can be used in a mixed green salad or they can be cooked briefly as a vegetable.

ESCAROLE

BACKGROUND

Escarole, the third type of *Cichorium endivia*, can be distinguished from Belgian endive and curly endive by its wider, flatter green leaves and its loose head. The flavor has a bitter edge.

AVAILABILITY

Escarole is available from late summer through the winter, but is at its best during the cool months.

Buying Tips

Select escarole with bright, fresh color and crisp leaves that snap when broken. Avoid wilted, limp specimens.

PREPARATION

Escarole can be stored in a plastic bag in the refrigerator for several days. True grit is a characteristic of escarole. Before using, wash it in several changes of cold water to clean. Escarole is used raw as a salad green, but it is also a good soup green. Boiled or braised with butter for a few minutes, it is a side dish.

EXTRACTS

BACKGROUND

Flavoring extracts are concentrated essences of ingredients such as almond, anise, banana, bergamot, brandy, cherry, cinnamon, clove, coconut, coffee, ginger, lemon, maple, mint, mocha, orange, peach, pineapple, pistachio, raspberry, rosewater, rum, sherry, strawberry, vanilla, and walnut. They are usually manufactured by distilling the substance's oil and preserving it in ethyl alcohol. Some so-called extracts are artificially made from molecularly identical chemicals in a laboratory, but such creations are not, as yet, the quality equals of their natural brothers. If the label displays such words as "imitation," "style," and "flavored," the product is not a pure extract. Natural products often emphasize the word "pure" on their labels.

PREPARATION

Extracts, real or artificial, are mainly used by shortcut cooks. In some instances, extracts are used by gourmet chefs in desserts or sweet purees where the "flavor" is wanted but not the texture or appearance of the ingredient in question. Our question: why do those chefs use vanilla extract when a steeped vanilla bean would perform the same, yet better, culinary role? To put our position straight, we are not against extracts if, and only if, the cook has no alternative. Usually, he does.

Storage

Buy small amounts at a time and keep the bottles tightly capped, as the alcohol in which they are preserved does evaporate. Extracts are best stored in a dark, cool, dry place. For month-long storage, your refrigerator is the preferred spot.

Cooking

Extracts are volatile, so add them near the end of the cooking, lest flavor disappear. Or, if the food (say a custard) must be subjected to prolonged heat, add more extract than usual.

FATBACK

BACKGROUND

Fatback is the first layer of fat that runs along the pig's back. It is sometimes confused with SALT PORK, which comes from the animal's belly. Fatback can be purchased fresh or sometimes cured with salt. It can also be transformed into lard.

PREPARATION

Storage

Fresh fatback can be stored for 4 to 6 days and cured fatback for 4 to 6 weeks in the refrigerator. Neither freezes well, especially the cured version.

Preliminaries

If the fatback is cured, you may have to blanch it, to rid it of excess salt, before adding it to the dish you are preparing.

CLASSIC USES AND AFFINITIES

Fatback is used to bard or lard meat dishes and to season soups, stews, and many bean and vegetable dishes.

FENNEL

BACKGROUND

The leaves, dried fruit (called seeds) and fleshy stalks of *fennel* (*Foenicum vulgare*) are used. Fennel is a favorite food in Italy and southern France. Medieval medicine ascribed wide curative powers to this licorice-flavored plant, especially for eye diseases. The sympathetic magic of fennel's slim leaves and the hunger-assuaging properties of its seeds endeared the plant to early weight-watchers.

PREPARATION

The seeds will keep their potency for a year after packing if they are kept free of moisture. Use just a few seeds in salads or bean dishes, perhaps 1/8 teaspoon of the seeds in a sauce for four portions of fish. (Also see HERBS AND SPICES for relevant information.) The fennel bulb can be eaten raw or cooked. For the latter, steam or simmer it for 5 to 10 minutes if sliced or chunked, for 10 to 15 minutes if whole, depending on thickness. It can also be braised or added to soups and stews.

CLASSIC USES AND AFFINITIES

The bulbs of Florentine fennel (the bulbous type) can be used as you would use ANISE—and some grocers interchange the two licorice-flavored bulbs without changing the sign, whichever name it has. Fennel has an affinity to fish; the seeds can be used in *court bouillon* to poach fish, in stuffings, and in sauces such as mayonnaise served with fish. Italian sausages often contain fennel seed. Other pork products and wild boar take well to this herb. Dry beans and mayonnaise salads such as cole slaw and potato salad can benefit by the addition of fennel seed.

FENUGREEK

BACKGROUND

The *Fenugreek* plant (*Trigonella foenum-graecum*) can be grown for animal fodder; its young leaves can be eaten by humans in salad. But most of the interest, culinary and otherwise, comes from its very small reddish seeds. The slightly bitter seeds can be brewed into tea which, in quantity, is laxative. They can be ground into Indian dishes or Western curry powders. They contain *coumarin*, a substance used in making artificial maple flavoring. Last but not least, fenugreek seeds also contain *diosgenin*, a steroid that can be used as one of the raw materials in making birth-control pills. Fenugreek is sold in two forms: whole and ground, the latter having a short shelf life. (See HERBS AND SPICES for information on buying, storing, cooking, etc.)

FERMENTED BLACK BEANS

BACKGROUND

A staple in Chinese (especially Cantonese) cuisine, *fermented black beans* are black soybeans that have been preserved by being salted and partially dried. Though it is not absolutely necessary, some cooks first soak the fragrant, moist beans for about 30 minutes in water to rid them of excess salt. These beans are used in small amounts as a flavoring agent in savory dishes in general and seafood in particular. As an added advantage, fermented black beans supply color contrast to light-hued foods and sauces. They are best stored in a tightly closed glass jar at room temperature or, for year-long keeping, in the refrigerator.

FIDDLEHEAD

BACKGROUND

The *ostrich fern* (*Matteucia struthiopteris*) is unlike the ostrich; in New England during May it sticks its head out of the sand, producing a gracefully curled edible sprout resembling the spiral tip of a violin. To be at their best, *fiddleheads* must be sproutings, no longer than 2 inches.

PREPARATION

They are prepared by washing, then steaming, simmering, or sautéing for several minutes at most. Canned fiddleheads are poor substitutes for the marvelous flavor of the fresh-picked variety.

FIG

BACKGROUND

The *fig* (*Ficus carica*) has been eaten fresh or dried for thousands of years and has contributed a great deal to obscene images and innuendo throughout the ages. Figs are believed to be indigenous to Asia and are today devoutly adored by people from the Mediterranean to the Indian subcontinent. Consumption in America, by contrast, is low.

Varieties

Hundreds of distinct varieties are cultivated; they range in skin color from pale whitish-green to purplish-black, in size from one to several inches in diameter, in shape from onion to teardrop, and in flesh tones from pinkish-white to striated violet-cerise. Whatever the variety, the flesh of a good specimen is scrumptiously sweet, but not cloying. The leading varieties include:

Smyrna (or *Calimyrna* when grown in California): This world-acclaimed fig was originally and still is today grown in and around the Turkish city of Smyrna (now called Izmir). The relatively large, yellow-green-skinned Smyrna is sold fresh or dried and traditionally pressed into a squat, squarish shape.

Mission: California's best known fig is the Mission, so named because the trees were first planted in that state by the early Spanish Franciscan missionaries. The fruit—which is marketed fresh or dried—has a deep purple skin, small seeds, and a grainy texture.

Kadota: Home and commercial canners love this yellow-green-skinned minimally seeded, thick-skinned fig. It is also sold fresh or dried for eating out of hand.

Other major fig varieties include the ***Celeste*** and the ***Magnolia,*** both of which are particularly popular in the Southern states.

AVAILABILITY

Season

Fresh figs can be found in most markets from early July through late October. Dried figs are available the year round.

Buying Tips

Fresh Figs: A sourish fragrance indicates that the fig has started to ferment, a result of prolonged or improper storage. Do not count on a fig ripening much more once it has been picked. A ripe fig will feel soft (but not mushy) when gently squeezed. Color is not necessarily a good clue to ripeness, but in general we may say that the background skin color of the standard supermarket variety of fig should have transformed from green into a deep, purplish-black glow. A good fig is plump, not collapsing inwardly. Avoid figs with skins that are cracked, leaky, sticky, scaly, bruised, or decay-spotted.

Dried Figs: A dried fig should not be dried out. It should yield to pressure when squeezed. Avoid dried figs with "off" odors, such as the sour smell of fermentation. They should smell of figs, nothing else.

PREPARATION

Storage

Ripe figs are very perishable. If you must store them, seal them in a plastic bag in the refrigerator and plan to use within 36 hours, if not sooner. Dried figs can be kept for months in a closed jar. Store the jar in a dark, not-too warm, cabinet.

Use

After washing a fig to rid it of germs and pesticides, you can eat it raw, skin and all. If you prefer, you can eat the pulp and not the skin by separating the pulp with an implement or with your teeth, if you're eating it out of hand. Serve your figs at or just below room temperature. Stew fresh figs in syrup. Soak dried figs; then spice, for example with ginger, and simmer them into a compote. If a package of dried figs has coalesced into a solid mass, a few minutes in a 300°F oven should allow you to separate the figs.

CLASSIC USES AND AFFINITIES

Figs have an excellent affinity with prosciutto, a popular hor d'oeuvre combination. Cream is another good matchup.

FILÉ POWDER

BACKGROUND

Filé powder, a Choctaw Indian invention, is made from the dried leaves of the tree called SASSAFRAS. (See HERBS AND SPICES for information on buying, storing, cooking, etc.)

In the Creole cooking of New Orleans and environs, filé is used to flavor and especially to thicken gumbos: soup-stews that can be made of seafood, meat, or vegetables. Viscous okra pods are also used to thicken gumbos, but no purist would use okras and filé in the same recipe.

PREPARATION

Filé becomes stringy when subjected to prolonged or high heat. You must stir it into your preparation only after it has been cooked and the pot is off the flame.

FINES HERBES

BACKGROUND

A mixture of delicate-tasting herbs, chopped small, is called *fines herbes*. Parsley, chervil, tarragon, and chives are the traditional quartet, though you can also compose beautiful music by substituting or adding herbs such as burnet, savory, marjoram, and basil. The stong tastes of tarragon and basil can dominate other herbs, so these should be soft-pedaled. (See HERBS AND SPICES for information on buying, storing, cooking, etc., as well as the individual herb entries.)

Fines herbes cannot be cooked for long without loss of flavor. This mixture can be used with fish, cheese, veal, poultry, eggs, and other foods that can use a taste lift, but would be overwhelmed by strong herbs and spices. The *omelette aux fines herbes* is a French classic that has entered the English and American cooking repertoire.

FISH

BACKGROUND

Over two-thirds of the earth's surface is ocean, lakes, and rivers teeming with over 25,000 fish species, yet less than 200 of them find their way into American kitchens. Most of our fellow countrymen have sampled only a dozen or so species. Americans as a whole are not great fish eaters; we eat only about 13 pounds a year compared to roughly 50 pounds of chicken and 150 pounds of red meat. Japanese and Scandinavians consume at least six times as much fish as we do.

While it is untrue that we become smarter by eating fish, we can call ourselves smart if we do eat fish. Not only does the flesh have all the essential amino acids, but one of them—lycine—is so prevalent that fish acts as a protein extender when eaten with rice, a food low in lycine. Orientals have long made use of this healthful combination. Fish flesh—including that of the fatty fishes—has many fewer calories per pound than beef. Also, nearly all the fat of fish is polyunsaturated, which is good news for cholesterol watchers. Finally, fish is easier to digest than animal meat because it has scant connective tissue.

Fish Types

Fishes vary in size from the less-than-1-inch-long gobi of the Philippines to the over-60-foot-long whale shark. (The largest sea creature of them all is the 100-foot-long blue whale—which is, of course, a mammal and not a fish.)

For the plural of the word *fish*, there is a distinction between the use of the words *fish* and *fishes*. The first is the usual plural; the latter is used when discussing different varieties.

Freshwater vs. Saltwater: A major difference between the freshwater and ocean fishes involves bone structure. The first type cannot afford the luxury of having the thicker bones that ocean fishes possess because freshwater provides less buoyancy than does saltwater. Nature (that is, evolutionary selection) designed freshwater fishes with a multitude of thin bones, much to the displeasure of diners everywhere.

Cold-Water vs. Warm-Water Fishes: Marine fishes can vary in flavor according to the temperature of their water habitat. In most cases, and up to a point, the colder the water, the tastier the fish. To illustrate, nearly all tropical fishes tend to be unappetizingly bland when compared to temperate-water fishes such as the cod.

Active vs. Inactive Fishes: The freshwater fishes that have to do a lot of arduous swimming usually are more flavorful than their slow-moving, lake-bottom counterparts. A fish caught in a cold, fast-running stream, for instance, usually tastes infinitely better than one hooked from a pond.

Lean vs. Fat Fishes: The fat content of fishes varies markedly, from under 1 percent (flounder and cod) to over 15 percent (for mackerel and salmon, for instance). The figures used here are averages; the exact fat content changes by season, environment, and the fish's luck in catching other fish. In most instances, the higher the fat content of a fish, the fuller-flavored, darker-hued, more caloric and more nutritious the fish will be. Here is a breakdown of some of the more popular fishes:

LEAN
Less than 2½ percent fat

Black sea bass
Cod
Croaker, Atlantic
Haddock
Hake
Halibut, U.S.
Lake herring
Pollack
Ocean perch, Atlantic
Red snapper
Rockfish
Sea bass
Smelts, Atlantic
Sturgeon
Tilefish
Trout, brook

MODERATE FAT
2½ to 5 percent fat

Alewife
Barracuda, Pacific
Bluefish
Butterfish, Gulf waters
Herring, Pacific
Striped bass
Swordfish
Tunafish
Whiting

FAT (OR OILY)
More than 5 percent fat

Butterfish, Northern waters
Eel
Herring, Atlantic
Lake trout
Mackerel
Mullet
Salmon
Shad
Sheepshead, Atlantic
Smelts, eulachon
Trout, rainbow
Weakfish
Yellowtail

Varieties

The following is a brief guide to some of the fishes we eat.

Anchovies: This pungent flavoring

agent and garnish for sauces and antipasto plates is made from a 3-to-5-inch-long silver-skinned fish that may or may not be fermented. It is marketed as fillets (packed flat or wrapped around capers in tins) or as a paste in tubes which can give gusto to egg-, cheese- and tomato-based preparations. Fat content is 10.3 percent.

Barracuda: Atlantic, Pacific, and Caribbean species exist; the last may be toxic. The Pacific variety, with a long, slender body and sharp, dangerous teeth, is the one that is most often eaten. Its flesh is full-flavored and firm-textured. Most marketed barracudas weigh between 4 and 15 pounds and are sold whole or cut into steaks, chunks, or fillets. Fat content is 2.6 percent.

Bass: True bass and often unrelated fish species are sold under the name of *bass*. One of the best-sellers is the *black sea bass*, a staple in Chinese restaurants in America. The other widely sold ocean bass is the *striped bass*. If you know an angler, you may also be able to sample a variety of freshwater bass including the *smallmouth* and *largemouth bass*. Raw striped-bass flesh has a fat content of 2.7 percent.

Blowfish: Also known as *sea squab*, *globefish*, and *puffer*, the *blowfish* has an interesting defense against larger fish intent on swallowing it whole: it rapidly expands its size by bloating itself with water, making itself look like an underwater basketball with attached head, fins and tail. Only the meat along the rear portion of the body is eaten; because the retail cut vaguely resembles a chicken leg, the blowfish gets its "sea squab" nickname. In some species such as the *fugu* of Japanese fame, the flesh can be deadly poisonous if the liver and the ovaries are allowed to contaminate the edible flesh.

Bluefish: Considered one of the fiercest and best-tasting Atlantic fishes, the *bluefish* has a rich, delicate flavor, especially when the cook removes the dark, oily strip of meat from the lighter-colored flesh. Most marketed blues weigh 3 to 8 pounds, and are often baked whole or broiled as fillets. Fat content is 3.3 percent.

Carp: A number of *carp* species are found in freshwater lakes and rivers around the world. The *Eastern European carp* is a key ingredient along with pike and whitefish in the making of the Jewish staple *gefiltefish*. Carp is at its best in winter. Because it spends much time in the muddy bottoms of its environment, many cooks insist that carp first be allowed to swim in a freshwater tank for a couple of days to rid itself of its muddy flavor. You can usually buy live carp (3 to 10 pounds) in tanks in seafood markets in major Chinatowns. Carp can be cooked whole or divided into steaks or fillets; sometimes it is pickled or smoked. Fat content is 4.2 percent.

Catfish: The barbeled freshwater *catfish* is revered in the South where it is often deepfried. Folksy Southern politicians love giving fish fries, hoping to bribe votes with free catfish and beer. Many catfish species exist, ranging in weight measured in ounces to over a hundred pounds, but it is the 1-to-3-pound, mild-flavored *channel catfish* that most people eat. Fat content is 3.1 percent.

Chub: See *whitefish*.

Cisco: See *whitefish*.

Cod: Of the various fishes in the *cod* family, the *Atlantic cod* is commercially the most important, much more so than the *Pacific cod*. The cold-water, winter-season cod is sold both fresh (as steaks, fillets and, if under 4 or so pounds, whole) or dried as salt cod, a staple in Iberia that is produced mainly in cold-climated Scandinavia. Salt cod is also popular in tropical lands principally because it stores well and because the fish caught in the local waters tend to be bland. Another cod product, cod-liver oil, was one of Grandma's favorite medicines, much to the displeasure of tots. Other leading members of the cod family include the *ling*, *pollack*, *haddock* of finnan haddie fame, and the stronger-flavored *hake*. *Burbot* is the freshwater cod. The young of the cod family, generally not more than 2½ pounds, is often sold as *scrod*. Fat content is minimal: 0.3 percent.

Eel: Discussed in its own entry.

Flatfish: Three basic fish groups fall under the *flatfish* umbrella: *sole, flounder,* and *halibut*. All three have lean, firm-textured, white flesh, a characteristically flattened body that rests on the ocean floor, and have both eyes topside. The sole and flounder differ physically: the first is thicker vertically, the latter has a rounder, less ovoid outline. Geographically, the sole mainly thrives in European water, the flounder in New World seas. Culinarily, the sole is significantly superior in flavor and texture to the flounder—this is why much of the flounder sold in America is deceptively called "sole" by fishmongers and restaurateurs. To illustrate, *gray sole* (the best of the flounders), *lemon sole, rex sole* and the *pseudo-Dover sole* of the Pacific Coast are all flounders. Often they are the *white flounders* or *summer flounders*, sometimes called the *fluke*. Genuine soles are the *true Dover sole, English sole,* and *turbot*; when these fish are available in the United States, they are usually shipped frozen (or buried in shaved ice) from Europe. *Halibuts* are the largest members in the flatfish troika, and sometimes weigh in at over 500 pounds. The flesh of the halibut is coarser and the flavor is stronger and less refined than the flounder's and, especially, the sole's. Small flatfish are often cooked whole; dressed, medium-sized specimens are typically sold filleted; halibuts are often sold in the form of steaks. On the average, raw flatfish flesh such as that from flounders has 79 calories per 100 grams, 358 per pound while raw halibut flesh has 100 calories per 100 grams, 454 per pound. Fat content of flounder is 0.8 percent and of halibut, 1.2 percent.

Flounder: See *flatfish*.

Fugu: See *blowfish*.

Game fishes: Most fishes that are commercially caught are hooked by sports fishermen as well. Certain fishes, such as the *blue marlin*, the *sailfish*, and the *tarpon*, however, are particularly associated with anglers.

Goldfish: Though most people think of goldfish as a pet destined to peer out at the world through a tabletop glass bowl, some seafood markets sell a large version of this fish, a member of the carp family. Fortunately for the goldfish, its flesh is too bland to cause a widespread culinary rage beyond household cats and dotty old gents reliving their goldfish-swallowing college days.

Globefish: See *blowfish*.

Gray Snapper: See *red snapper*.

Haddock: See *cod*.

Hake: See *cod*.

Halibut: See *flatfish*.

Herring: Three basic *herring* groupings exist as far as American cooks are concerned: the small to medium, silvery-skinned *Atlantic, Pacific* and the anadromous (that is, living in saltwater, spawning in freshwater) species such as the *alewife* and *blueback*. Herring is eaten raw (especially in Holland and surrounding lands), cooked, pickled, salted or smoked. Fresh herring average 1 pound in weight and are usually cooked whole or filleted. Well-known herring products include the English specialties *kippers* (split, salted, dried, and smoked) and *bloaters* (larger herrings that are not as highly salted or smoked and thus are more perishable). Both kippers and bloaters are often grilled and served at breakfast, perhaps with scrambled eggs. There is also the German specialty called *rollmops*, consisting of vinegar-cured, unskinned herring fillets wrapped around an ingredient such as a pickle. Scandinavians produce canned herring fillets in various sauces such as mustard or dill. Americans eat a lot of pickled herring sold and served in a sour-cream-type sauce. Some canned sardines are made from herring. Fat content is 11.3 percent for the Atlantic herring and 2.6 percent for the Pacific; the alewife's fat content is in between.

Lake Herring: See *whitefish*.

Mackerel: Tuna is a *mackerel*, but when people buy and eat mackerel they think of species such as the *Spanish mackerel* or the *king mackerel*, also called *kingfish*. Whatever the mackerel, the flesh is oily and firm-textured, and the rate of spoilage is rapid. The flesh is often sold in steak form, though small mackerels can be purchased whole. Fat content averages 9.8 percent.

Mullet: Many fish are sold as *mullets*, but few really are. Among the fish inaccurately sold as mullets in the marketplace are the *Canadian sucker* and, from the Mediterranean, the *red mullet*; the first is mediocre, the second is superb. The best-selling true mullets are mild-flavored Southerners: the *silver* and *striped mullets*, the latter being fattier. The striped mullet's fat content is 6.9 percent.

Muskellunge: See *pike*.

Perch: There are *freshwater* and *ocean perches*. The latter (not a true perch) is often a convenient catchall marketing term for frozen fish fillets of various fish including the *redfish*. Invariably, these products are too mild in flavor and coarse in texture to excite most sophisticated palates. The best of the freshwater perches is probably the *yellow perch*, a delicate-flavored fish which is best sautéed whole when in the 3/4-to-1-pound range. Its fat content is 0.9 percent.

Pickerel: See *pike*.

Pike: Members of the long, slender freshwater *pike* tribe include the *common pike* as well as the *pickerel*, *northern pike*, and the comparatively large *muskellunge* or *muskie*. The meat tends to be very lean and therefore needs basting if it is sautéed, broiled, or baked. The mild-flavored pike is used in the making of the Jewish *gefiltefish* as well as the French *quenelles de brochet*. Fat content is approximately 1.1 percent.

Pompano: One of the culinary prides of the Gulf Coast is the *pompano*, a silvery, flat-sided fish with a rich, delectable taste. Average market weight for a whole pompano is 2 to 3 pounds; fillets are also sold. The fish can be broiled, sautéed, or baked. A renowned New Orleans specialty is pompano *en papillote*, which is baked in an oiled paper bag. Pompano's fat content is 9.5 percent.

Porgy: When small, a *porgy* or *scup* can be annoyingly bony. It is a relatively inexpensive fish that is usually sold whole, weighing 1/2 pound to 2 1/2 pounds. None of the many porgy species, technically, should be called *sea bream*, a superb fish found in Oriental waters. Fat content is 3.4 percent.

Red Snapper: The *snapper* crowd includes the abundant *gray snapper*, but it is the *red snapper* from the semitropical Southern Atlantic and the Gulf Coast waters that is the piscatory delight. The snapper name can be confusing: *yellowtail snapper* is a true snapper, but the so-called *yellow snapper* is a tilefish. And the *rouget* of Louisiana Creole fame is not the *red mullet* (*rouget*) of the Mediterranean, but rather the local *red snapper*. The smaller red snappers (1/2 pound to 4 pounds) are usually sold whole, the larger specimens cut up into steaks and fillets. Fat content is 0.9 percent.

Salmon: A good *salmon* will make an epicure ecstatic and the one most likely to do so is the super-sized *Chinook* (or *king*) *salmon*, identified by its deep coral flesh. Other *Pacific salmons*, in descending order of preference, are the *coho* (*silver*), *sockeye*, and *chum*, the last having the coarsest texture, palest flesh hue, and least succulent flesh. The *Atlantic salmon* is as—or nearly as—good as the chinook. Salmon is sold fresh (typically in steaks) or smoked, in the form of nova, lox, kippered salmon, etc. Salmon is the star ingredient in Scandinavian *gravlax* and, usually, in Russian *coulibiac*, two jewels in the international culinary crown. Canned salmon is widely available but is a poor substitute for fresh. Salmon roe is also sold processed (See "CAVIAR" AND OTHER ROES). Pacific salmon is in season from spring through fall, Atlantic salmon from summer through early winter. Raw chinook's fat content is 15.6 percent.

Sardine: The word *sardine* is both the name for a specific Mediteranean fish and a generic term for small, soft-boned fish canned in oil. The latter type can be *brislings* (usually your best bet), *her-*

rings, *pilchards* or one of several other fishes. Canned sardines are packed whole or, for the nonpurist, dressed without their heads and tails and, sometimes, without their skin and bones. Quality varies noticeably among brands and generally corresponds with price. Drained canned Atlantic sardines have a fat content of 11.1 percent.

Scrod: See *cod*.

Sea Bream: See *porgy*.

Sea Squab: See *blowfish*.

Shad: Though noted for its roe (See "CAVIAR" AND OTHER ROES), the *shad*'s flesh is a treat unto itself. Since shad—which lives in the sea but spawns in rivers—is a very bony fish, it is more often sold filleted than whole. When whole, the market weight is about 1½ to 5 pounds. *Cut shad* (female with its roe removed) is preferable to *buck* (or male) shad flesh because it is more succulent. Shad is most abundant from mid- to late spring on the East Coast and slightly later on the Pacific Coast. Fat content is 10.0 percent.

Shark: The flesh of some *shark* species such as the *mako* is delicious and, unlike the ferocious personality of a shark, is relatively mild in flavor. Sometimes shark is substituted by greedy fishmongers and restaurateurs for swordfish steaks.

Silver Hake: See *whiting*.

Smelts: Eat these fishes whole—head, tail, bones, entrails, and all. If the guts make you squeamish, draw the fish, but leave in the succulent head and soft bones where God intended. Popular serving-size is 4 to 7 inches long—these smelts can be dredged in seasoned flour, then fried and served, perhaps with a tartar sauce. Smelts are at their best and most abundant in the nonsummer months. Fat content can vary from 2.1 percent to 6.2 percent, depending on species.

Sole: See *flatfish*.

Striped Bass: See *bass*.

Sturgeon: The flesh of the *sturgeon* is characteristically dry and fine-grained and is usually sold in this country smoked rather than fresh. The sturgeon, of course, is the source of CAVIAR. Fat content is 1.9 percent.

Swordfish: Since the mercury scare of a decade ago, the rich, firm-textured flesh of the *swordfish* has rebounded in popularity as well as in price, which has prompted some fishmongers to sell *mako shark* as swordfish. Even though whole mako shark is almost as good as swordfish, it should sell for a fraction of the price of genuine swordfish because of the law of supply and demand. An alert shopper can distinguish between whole swordfish and mako shark steaks with the following indicators: The skin color of both swordfish and mako shark is whitish on the belly underside, but swordfish is brownish-gray and mako is bluish on the top. The overall flesh hue of the raw swordfish steak is paler than that of the mako shark. Another clue is that a whole swordfish steak has two kite-shaped dark oil-rich spots. The flesh texture of the swordfish is firmer. The shape of the whole swordfish steak is a smooth, oval curve, while the shark steak has a more irregular circumference. Swordfish fat content is 4.0 percent.

Tilefish: The yellow-spotted *tilefish* can be called the gourmet of the deep because it feasts on lobster and crabs, a superb diet that gives its flaky flesh a delicate flavor. *Yellow snapper* and *yellow pike* are marketing (and inaccurate) names for the tilefish, which is caught by commercial fishermen miles beyond the Atlantic coastline. Fish of 7 to 40 pounds are usually cut into steaks; smaller specimens are frequently sold whole. Fat content is just 0.5 percent.

Trout: All sorts of *trouts* exist, including the brook, rainbow, cutthroat, brown, steelhead and the large-sized lake trout. The gourmet's favorite is the brook trout though commercial fish farms inundate American restaurants with frozen rainbow trout. Brook trout are at their best when small (six to eight inches long) and when panfried within the hour of the catch from a running mountain brook teeming with trout food and when minimal extraneous flavorings are used by the cook. It need not be scaled but should be skinned, before or after cooking. Famous trout preparations include *truite au bleu* (poached in a vinegar-spiked liquid) and *truite meunière* (dredged in seasoned flour and sautéed in butter). The raw flesh calorie count is 101 per 100 grams, 458 per pound, for brook trout; 195 per 100 grams, 885 per pound, for rainbow trout. Fat content is, respectively, 2.1 percent and 11.4 percent.

Tuna: A member of the mackerel clan, *tuna* can vary in weight from several pounds up to over a half ton. The flesh is fatty and firm-textured and can come from several species: *albacore* (has the whitest meat and the highest price tag), *bluefin*, *yellowfin* and *bonito* (the strongest-flavored of the four). Canned tuna is discussed in the Buying Hints: Canned Fish section. Raw bluefin tuna has a fat content of 4.1 percent.

Turbot: See *flatfish*.

Weakfish: This high-quality fish of the Atlantic seaboard received its name because when a fisherman catches it, the fishhook can easily rip away from the tender cheek flesh—*weakfish*, is not easy game. It is sometimes called *sea trout*—erroneously, though its cousin from the Southeastern American coastline is correctly called *spotted seatrout* (spelled as one word). The weakfish is typically sold whole in the 3- to 6-pound range. Its fat content is 5.6 percent.

Whitebait: The fish called *whitebait* are fairly immature fishes of several saltwater species that are usually flour-dredged or batter-coated, then briefly fried. Whitebait are so small that it can take several hundred to satisfy a hungry epicure.

Whitefish: Mild-flavored, freshwater fishes that fall within this collective marketing name *whitefish* include the *cisco* (or so-called *lake herring*), the *chub* and the *lake whitefish*. This last is the best. It is often sold whole in the 2- to 4-pound range and—because it has much more fat than the cisco (8.2 vs. 2.3 percent)—it can be more effectively cooked with dry heat such as baking, though poaching is usually the best cooking method for whitefish in general.

Whiting: This relative of the cod has a delicate flavor, yet is usually underpriced, perhaps because its flesh tends to fall apart if not properly handled and cooked. It is also called the *silver hake* because of its belly hue. Fat content is 3 percent.

Yellow Snapper: See *tilefish*.

Whales, Porpoises, and Other Mammals

The fact that these creatures should not be eaten because they are now endangered or semi-endangered species should not bother the seafood epicure, because their flesh falls leagues behind fish flesh in terms of tenderness and subtle flavor. Not to be confused with the mammal dolphin is the fish dolphin, a tasty game fish that deserves the attention of seafood cooks.

AVAILABILITY

Live fish are seldom available except to anglers, although certain seafood markets—notably in Chinatowns—sell fish live from tanks.

Fresh fish is the phrase used for fish that is no longer alive but still in a fresh state. It is sold in five basic forms: whole, drawn, dressed, steaks and fillets. *Whole* (or *round*) is the entire fish just as it comes from the water, with head, scales, intestinal tract, and all. *Drawn* is a whole fish minus its entrails and, sometimes, its gills. *Dressed* (or pan-dressed) is a drawn fish minus its scales and, perhaps, the head, tail and fins as well, depending on the policy of the fishmonger or the wishes of the customer. If the head and tail are left intact, the phrase *whole dressed* may be used. *Fillets* are the plank-shaped, usually boneless pieces of flesh cut lengthwise off each side of the fish along the back bone. They may be skinned or not, or partially skinned. When the fillets from each side of the fish are left attached, it is called a butterfly fillet. *Steaks* are pieces of large, dressed fish cut crosswise into thicknesses of ½ inch to 1½ inches. Still other market forms include fish *sticks* and *chunks*.

Frozen fish is a poor substitute for fresh, because the freezing process diminishes flavor, texture, and nutrients. Frozen fish is widely available as fillets, steaks, balls, cakes, or sticks and may be plain or breaded, raw or precooked.

Canned fish includes tuna, salmon, sardines, and anchovies, to name the most popular. Other types of processed fish include *salted*, *dried*, *smoked*, and *pickled*.

Buying Tips

Live Fish: Do not hesitate to insist that the merchant pick out the particular fish you want, not the easiest fish from the tank to net. The fish should be prime in appearance, without body mutilations caused by fishing or handling implements, other fish, or disease. Look for an alert swimmer—if the fish is listless or listing to one side, reject it. If the tank water is dirty or has too many floating (that is, dead) fish in it, you are probably better off not purchasing even the energetic specimens. Some shoppers prefer to let the fish die in the bag as it is transported home. More consciously humane consumers ask the fishmonger to give the fish its *coup de grâce* promptly after it is removed from the tank. The latter method also makes weighing it a lot easier. If the fish is killed at the shop, ask the fishmonger to eviscerate and de-gill it then, too, in order to slow down bacterial decay.

Fresh Fish: Fish-buying savvy is important, especially if you live away from the source of the fish.

Buy from a merchant who has a fast stock turnover and a clean shop that is not fishy smelling. Sunday is usually the worst day to buy fresh fish. This is particularly true in restaurants, because fish suppliers seldom work past Saturday dawn. Most fish have seasons of availability. A fish in season will be less expensive and, likely, better tasting than during its off-season. Often the fish that sits in your local fish store was caught days ago and hundreds of miles away. Get to know the fish of your area.

Some fishmongers prolong the storage life of their fish by burying them in ice. This is unwise: such treatment can give the fish freezer burns and can partially ruin its flavor and texture. The best way for a merchant to display fish is to keep it on a cloth resting on top of a tray of crushed ice. Sometimes merchants thaw frozen fish and sell the product as fresh. This is unethical. Clues to this ploy include an opaque rather than translucent flesh, mushy rather than firm texture, and liquid that has leached out of the flesh, which you can see only if the fish is stored in an iceless pan.

If it's a whole fish, look it right in the eye. It should appear to be alive, with a bright, clear, glistening gaze. Cloudiness, milkiness, and dullness indicate a fish that has been dead too long. The eyes should bulge, as opposed to being sunken. Bloody eyes suggest mishandling or prolonged storage (bear in mind, however, that a few species such as the red snapper have naturally reddish eyes).

Sniff the fish—it should smell fresh like a sea breeze, not fishy or sourish. The more fishy or sour it smells, the longer or more improperly it has been stored. The best anatomical area to sniff-test a whole fish is its gills, which are reached by lifting off the earlike gill flaps located behind the eyes. Some shoppers are squeamish about sniffing gills, but it is much better to risk sniffing a foul odor at the store than to taste or have to discard a bad fish later at home. When you are sniffing the gills, be sure to examine their color (if the merchant has not already removed them). The gills should be bright red. As the fish decomposes, the gills turn pink, then brownish- or greenish-gray.

If the scales are still there, they should be shiny, not slimy—and they should be firmly attached to the skin. If scaled, the skin should be iridescent, not dull.

Fresh flesh should be firm rather than flabby to the touch—and it should be resilient enough to regain its form after being poked by your fingertip. A whole fish should feel somewhat stiff, never limp, when you hold it horizontally by the head and tail. If a piece is sold bone-in, the flesh should cling tightly to the bones.

A center-cut steak will be more tender than a tail-cut steak. The first can be identified by its horseshoe shape; the space is part of the abdominal cavity. The exposed flesh of both steaks and fillets should have a slightly moist, not dried, surface. The edges of the fillets must not have a brownish-yellow tint. For uniform cooking, buy equal-sized fish or fish portions.

When you ask the fishmonger to cut off the head and tail of the fish, ask him to pack them for you in a separate bag. They are excellent for making *court bouillon*, sauces, and soups. You might also ask him if he has any heads that another customer left behind—chances are he will give them to you free or very cheaply.

We do not recommend buying prewrapped fresh fish. If you do, be sure the package is tightly wrapped in moisture-proof material and that the fish is given minimum opportunity to mingle its scent with the other foods in your shopping bag.

More and more fish such as trout and catfish are being grown in commercial fish farms. Because these fish are less active in their restricted, controlled environments, their meat tends to be less flavorful and more flabby than their "born-free" counterparts in rivers, lakes and oceans. If in doubt as to the fish's upbringing, ask the merchant—some will level with you.

Frozen Fish: The first rule about buying frozen fish is "do not." If you insist, here are a few guidelines: The fish must be purchased solidly frozen. The package should be stored at the market at a subzero temperature. If the package is misshapen or otherwise out-of-balance—say with one of the sides noticeably lumpier or heavier than the other—the product was likely thawed, then refrozen, which makes frozen fish even worse than it was in the first place. The protective wrapper should cling to the fish with minimum airspaces and should not be ripped or otherwise damaged. If you can see the fish through the wrapper, the flesh or skin should have no discoloration—a sign of bacterial decay, freezer burns, etc. Sniff the package—there should be no odor. When judging the price and value of breaded fish, take into consideration that the product likely contains no more than 50 percent fish. Return the fish to the store for a refund or exchange if, when you've thawed it at home, it smells fishy or has otherwise deteriorated.

Canned Fish: Canned fish such as tuna, sardines, and anchovies will stay in good conditon for a year, but only if stored in an under-65°F environment. Since the temperatures in some warehouses, trucks, and stores can be much higher, it is a prudent idea to buy cans from a store with a frequent merchandise turnover. Do not buy or use the contents of tins that are puffed, dented, or rusty. Canned tuna ia available packed in water or vegetable oil. Buy water-packed tuna, because the oil is typically of inferior or mediocre grade. If you want oil-coated tuna, add good oil at home. If you are a weight-watcher, you have saved a number of calories and the bother of trying to squeeze out as much oil from your tuna as possible. The meat in canned tuna can come from several fish species, including bluefin and albacore. Only the latter is permitted by law to be called *albacore* or *white-meat* rather than *light-meat* tuna. The three basic tuna meat size-designation grades, in descending order of price are *solid* or *fancy* (up to several large pieces), *chunk* (smaller pieces), and *flaked* or *grated*. For salads, the first is best because of its more attractive appearance. For sandwiches and other preparations where large pieces are not essential, flaked tuna can be a wise choice. Some canned tuna carries a federal inspection approval. While its existence is a positive sign, its absence is not necessarily a negative sign because the program is voluntary on the part of the canner.

As a general rule, the deeper and richer the red hue of canned salmon, the better its quality.

Sardines are packed whole or, for the nonpurist, dressed without their heads and tails and, sometimes, without their skin and bones.

Smoked Salmon: The very best smoked salmon comes from Ireland (peat-smoked) and Scotland, followed by that from Nova Scotia or Eastern Canada. Too many delicatessens sell the broader-beamed, deeper-hued Pacific salmon as "nova" or "Nova Scotia." There is nothing intrinsically wrong with smoked Pacific salmon, it is just that it is simply not as good as the richer, subtler-flavored, and finer-grained genuine Nova Scotia product. Wherever the salmon's home, the best smoked salmon is cured by the dry-salt method, rather than with the less costly brine method. The latter produces a noticeably saltier flesh that is often merchandised as *lox*, the star ingredient with the Jewish bagel and cream cheese. When buying smoked salmon, try to ascertain whether the fish has been frozen—if so, chances are it will have a mushy texture. Once sliced, smoked salmon rapidly deteriorates, so avoid the presliced variety. Ask for the center cut, as the tail-cut meat tends to be drier and, often, saltier. Before the deli person starts slicing, examine the slab of smoked salmon—it should not be discolored around the edges. Ask him to slice your selection as thin as he can. If he slices with too heavy a hand, shop elsewhere. The salmon that is sold presliced in vacuum-sealed packages is unworthy.

PREPARATION

Storage

Never store an ungutted fish, as the contents of the abdominal cavity spoils quicker than the flesh of the fish. The same is true for the gills. Fish should be rushed from market or boat to your refrigerator. If you plan to cook the fish within the hour, store it in its original wrapping in the coldest part of your refrigerator. If longer storage is necessary, pat it dry and store it in a fresh moisture proof wrapping and use it within the day. If you must store it overnight, place the airtight package on a tray of ice in the refrigerator. Except for the successful sport fisherman who has no other choice but to preserve his bumper catch, we do not recommend freezing fish. If you must buy frozen fish, store it in its original wrapping. If you have purchased unfrozen fish, tightly wrap it in suitable freezer paper and store it no longer than four days in the frozen food compartment, or one (if a fatty fish) or two months in the deep freezer. Before storing the fish, remove blood spots and, preferably, the skin. If a fatty fish has a red strip of flesh running along the lighter-hued flesh, remove that oily section before freezing the fish.

Cleaning Fish

Most shoppers buy their fish fully dressed or ask their fishmonger to do the chore for them. If you are a sports fisherman—or if you know a generous, lucky one—you will probably have to clean and dress the fish yourself. While each fisherman has his own preparation technique, this section summarizes one of the sound approaches.

The Anatomical Names: Besides knowing the obvious terms such as *head* and *tail*, it is useful to learn these names as well. The *gills* allow the fish to extract vital oxygen from the water. The *lateral line* comprises a series of sensi-

THE ANATOMICAL FISH

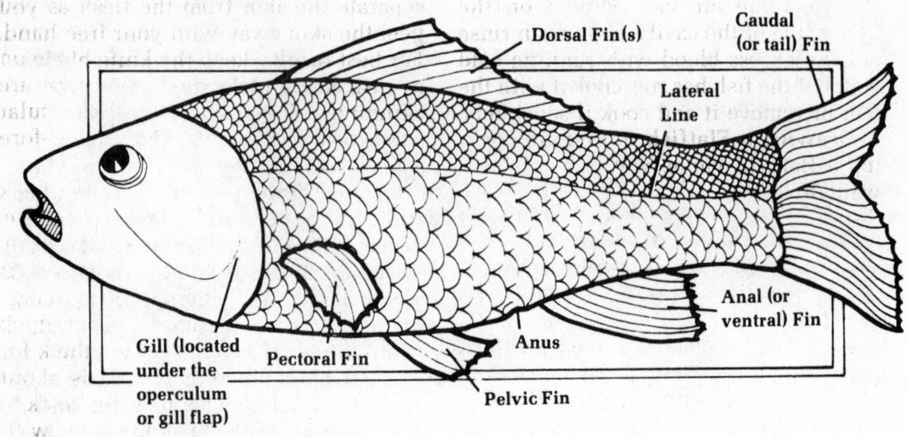

tive nerves that detect low-frequency vibrations, warning the fish of an approaching predator. The line is not readily visible on all fish.

Tools of the Trade: You will need a small-to-medium sharp-pointed *knife* (ideally a boning knife) as well as a *scaler* which can be a commercially produced implement specifically designed for the task or simply a bottle cap nailed to a stick. In a pinch, a paring knife works, too.

Type of Cut: Large fish are usually cut into steaks, medium ones into steaks or fillets, or are cooked whole. Small specimens are often cooked whole or as fillets.

Edible Parts: Very small fishes, such as whitebait, are eaten in their entirety, intestines and all. Most fish, however, need to be scaled, eviscerated, and degilled; and some fish—such as the catfish—should be skinned. Most Americans never eat the fish head, although the lips, tongue, eyes, and cheeks are delicious to some epicures. While eating the first three named parts may make a conservative diner squeamish, the cheek (a delicious morsel of muscle flesh located just below and behind the eye) is similar to the regular flesh of the fish, only better. The liver and gonads of most fish are edible, as is the delicious roe (See "CAVIAR" AND OTHER ROES).

Scaling: Most fish need to be scaled, but fish such as trout don't. Scaling is easier if the fish is wet, so first briefly rinse the fish under cold running water. This will also remove dirt and slime. Place the fish in a sink or on top of week-old black-and-white newspapers (the ink of comic pages or today's paper may contain toxins). Firmly grasp the fish tail (or head, if you wish) with one hand (left, if you are right-handed). With the other hand, scrape off the scales with a scaler, working against the grain from tail to head. Short, quick, rhythmical strokes will help keep the scales from flying beyond your contained work area. If you plan to cook the fish whole-dressed, be sure to remove all the scales, including those on often-overlooked areas such as around the head.

Drawing Nonflat Fish: With a sharp-pointed knife, slit the belly open lengthwise, from the anus to the throat. Remove and discard the viscera with your hands and with the help of a knife. Once the viscera are removed, be sure to slit open the air sack located on the upper side of the cavity so you can rinse out the excess blood with running cold water. If the fish has roe, cook it with the fish or remove it and cook it separately.

Drawing a Flatfish: If you are cooking a flatfish whole, you probably will want to decapitate it—this step makes the cleaning of the abdominal cavity easier.

De-Gilling: Remove and discard the gills if you plan to cook the fish whole or if you plan to store it. The gills can be cut out with a knife or kitchen shears, or pulled out with pliers or (if the fish is young) perhaps with your fingers.

De-Finning: If you plan to serve the fish whole, you need to remove the fins. Two fins, the dorsal and anal ones, should never be snipped with shears as the root bones will remain embedded in the body. Instead, use a sharp-pointed knife to make two lengthwise parallel slices as close as you can to the fin you are removing, then grasp the fin (being careful not to prick yourself) and jerk it quickly toward the head—it should pull free easily, root bones and all. The pectoral and pelvic fins can be cut off (at the skin level) with shears or a knife, if you like. Some cooks remove the fins after the fish is cooked, but sometimes this technique can disfigure the flesh.

Removing the Head and Tail: A sharp knife, perhaps with the aid of a rubber mallet, will sever the head (start the cut from the underside at the throat) and tail of most fish. If decapitation proves difficult, place the fish on a work surface. Turn it on its back, hang its head over the edge, and sharply yank the head downward—the obstinate bone should snap. Trim any scrap pieces from the body. Save the head and tail for the stockpot.

Skinning: Some fishes, such as catfish, require skinning; with most others it's often best to leave the skin on. It infuses flavor into the flesh, and it helps keep the flesh from losing its shape and some of its juices. For most fish, the skin is removed by starting at the tail end. Use the cutting edge of a knife to separate the skin from the flesh as you peel the skin away with your free hand. For best results, keep the knife blade on a near-horizontal plane. If you are skinning a whole fish, make a circular flesh-deep incision near the tail before you start the skinning process.

Cutting Steaks: Starting at the neck and ending near the tail of a whole, dressed (and usually unskinned) fish, use a sharp knife to make a series of equally thick (for uniform cooking) cross-section steaks. Under ½ inch thick is too thin, over 2 inches is too thick for most cooking situations. Ideal is about 1¼ inches. If the backbone is too thick to cut with a knife, tap the knife blade with a rubber mallet, use a cleaver, or saw the bone with a kitchen saw.

Filleting a Nonflat Fish: The best of the easy methods for a neophyte is to lay an eviscerated fish on its side. With a sharp knife, make a downward incision near the tail to the backbone (Line A in sketch). Next, slide the knife on a horizontal plane close to and over the backbone and ribs toward the head up to just behind the gills. Remove the knife and make a downward incision at the neck to the backbone (Line B), then peel off the fillet from the rest of the carcass. Remove any bones with the tip of your knife. Turn the fish over and repeat the process for the second fillet. If you plan to skin the fillet, that is easier to do before you remove the fillets from the carcass.

FILLETING A NONFLAT FISH

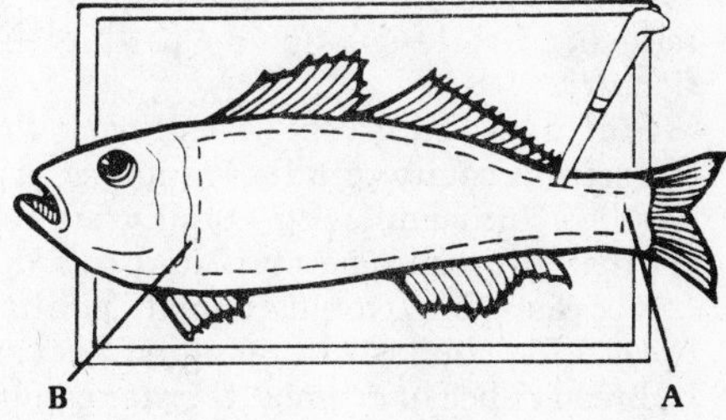

FILLETING A FLATFISH

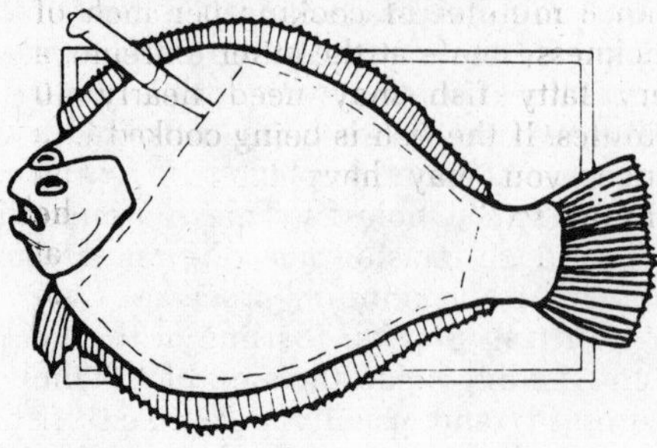

Filleting a Flatfish: The technique is similar to filleting other fish except that the shape of the fillet will be different, and the severing cut will be made somewhat obliquely rather than straight across the fish.

Other Preliminaries

Thawing Frozen Fish: In most instances, you should not thaw commercial fish products (especially the breaded variety) before cooking. When in doubt, follow label instructions. Fish you have frozen should be slowly thawed in the refrigerator and, once thawed, should be cooked promptly. Thawing in the refrigerator will take anywhere from several hours to a day, depending on size and whether the fish was in the frozen food compartment or a deep freezer. Thawing at room temperature, or in warm water, or in a plastic bag under running cold water will cause the fish flesh to become even mushier. Once thawed, do not refreeze. When frying thawed fish, be sure to reduce possible splatter by patting the fish dry.

Stuffing: You can stuff and truss the abdominal cavity of a fish much as you would a bird and with equally superb results. You can also stuff and roll the fillets as you would boned poultry breasts. The bulk stuffing ingredient can be bread cubes or crumbs, the star can be oysters, clams, or crabmeat flavored with herbs, spices, and wine. The opportunities to experiment are endless. Stuffing does expand as it cooks, so do not overstuff a cavity. And, when gutting the fish, cut the slit a little shorter than usual.

Marinating and Pickling: Whatever recipe you are following, use only the freshest of fish for marinating. Your container must be made of a noncorroding material such as glass, porcelain, or stainless steel—never of aluminum or iron. Avoid glazed pottery unless you're sure the glaze is lead-free, as the acidulous liquid in the marinade or pickling solution might leach out the toxic lead.

Cooking

The first rule of fish cookery is that unlike beef, the flesh of fish does not need to be cooked to tenderize it. If you overcook fish, it will become mushy and will tend to break apart into an unappetizing mess. Fish as it comes from the water is tender enough to eat raw, as the Japanese well know. The three prime reasons for cooking fish are to destroy harmful bacteria (if they exist), to develop flavor, and to firm the texture by coagulating the protein. The last, incidentally, can be done without heat. Peruvians, for instance, do it by marinating raw fish in lemon or lime juice, calling their delightful specialty *ceviche.*

When broiling, sautéing, or baking, fish should be cooked with a moderate to high temperature. Heat that is too low will extend the needed cooking period, making the flesh dry and tough and drawing out the juices, flavor, and nutrients in the process. Very high heat over a short period will also produce practically the same negative results. When poaching, the ideal is a simmer; no fish should ever be boiled. Fatty fishes are better suited for dry-heat methods such as broiling; lean fish fare better with moist-heat methods such as poaching. Of course, you can broil a lean fish if you frequently baste it. You can poach a fatty fish, too, but likely with less success than if you baked it.

Fish is fragile and tends to break apart unless gently and carefully handled. While this is especially true with cooked fish, sometimes the reason a cooked fish falls apart is that the fish was handled too often or carelessly before it went into the pan. A lot of people—including fishmongers—forget this fact.

Virtually all the fish sold in fish markets or caught by sports fishermen has a delicate flavor—and each fish species has its own distinct flavor. You will mask those flavors if you cook or serve the fish with assertive flavoring agents, so—except for the sake of variety—use strong cooking mediums and sauces sparingly.

In most cases, you can substitute one fish for another in a recipe if you take into account the variables such as fat content, texture, and thickness.

Cooking Times: Not too many years ago, the Canadian Department of Fisheries said that the time it would take you to poach (once the liquid returns to a simmer), to broil or sauté (with moderate to high heat), or to bake (at 450° F) a room-temperature steak or fillet or whole fish would be a total time of 10 minutes per inch of maximum thickness. Thus, you would cook a 1-inch-thick steak, fillet, or whole fish for 10 minutes. While we compliment its creators for conceiving a method that is so easy to remember, we believe the fixed factor of 10 in the time equation leads to overcooked fish. Our kitchen experiments have shown that a factor of 9 rather than 10 is the ideal number in most instances. Thus, with our Modified Canadian Timing Method, a 1-inch-thick steak, fillet, or whole fish would poach, broil, sauté, or bake in 9 rather than 10 minutes. When cooking fish, even a minute's difference is crucial to perfect results.

Our magic number works for the average fish, but since not all fish are average, you must take into consideration a small handful of variables. A very lean fish may require only slightly more than 8 minutes of cooking per inch of thickness, while at the other extreme, a very fatty fish may need nearly 10 minutes. If the fish is being cooked in a sauce, you may have to add a few minutes to the total cooking time. If the fish is refrigerator cold rather than at room temperature, add slightly less than 2 minutes per inch of thickness. If the fish is being cooked frozen, double the amount of time it would require if cooked thawed at room temperature.

Poaching: You can poach thick fish steaks, fillets, and chunks though whole fish seems best suited for this method. Leave the head and tail attached to the body during the poaching; they add flavor and help seal in the body juices.

The liquid can be water with a scant teaspoon of salt per quart of liquid. Or you can use a seasoned liquid, simply or complexly concocted. Just add some milk or, perhaps, add all or some of these *court bouillon* ingredients: *mirepoix* (carrots, onions, and celery), *bouquet garni* (parsley, thyme, and bay leaf), an acidulous liquid (lemon juice, vinegar, or wine), and peppercorns. Experiment by varying the ingredients.

You will need a pan large enough for your fish. If you are cooking a whole nonflat fish, the elongated, oval metal fish poacher that fits over two stove burners is usually ideal. If your whole fish is too long for the pan, you may have to cut off the head and tail. Some cooks cut the whole fish in halves instead, poach them separately in two pans, then reassemble the two parts on a serving platter, hiding the division line with a thick, opaque sauce. Unless you have a specialized fish poacher with a removable tray, wrap the fish in cheesecloth, leaving enough material at each end to serve as handles for submerging and removing the fish. Use a rack when poaching, to lift the fish away from the hot metal pan bottom.

Put enough liquid in the pan to cover the fish by about an inch. Depending on the pan and fish shape, you will likely need about 1½ to 2½ quarts of liquid for each pound of fish. Bring the liquid to a boil—and if you have seasoned it with herbs, spices, etc., let it boil for about five minutes before you proceed to the next step.

Add the fish. The liquid will cease boiling; when the first bubbles emerge again, reduce the heat to a soft, "shimmering" simmer. You must not let the liquid boil. From this moment, poach the fish for approximately 9 minutes per inch of thickness, taking into account the variables discussed under Cooking Times above.

When cooked, remove the fish. Be gentle with it, as cooked fish is fragile and may break apart. Do not let the fish sit in the cooking liquid or it will overcook. Poached fish that is to be served cold, however, can benefit from this additional steeping, but you must shorten the cooking time in that case.

Poached fish is usually enhanced with a sauce, perhaps based on the reduced and strained cooking liquid. Or, use stock that you kept and froze from last week's fish preparation. When preparing the sauce, keep the fish warm in a preheated 200°F oven or on a warmed platter.

Steaming: This technique involves cooking the fish above the liquid rather than in it, as is the case with poaching. Most of the guidelines discussed in the previous poaching section are relevant to the steaming method. Start the timing the moment the steam starts to escape between the lid and pot, and make sure no part of the fish touches the simmering liquid.

Stews, Soups, and Chowders: Follow the relevant guidelines in the Poaching section. The commonest error is adding the fish to the preparation too soon. Firm-textured fish that are low or medium in fat content are generally best for these dishes.

Baking: You can bake almost any dressed freshwater or saltwater fish if your pan and oven are big enough. You can also bake steaks and fillets. Fish with high fat content are the best bakers. Leave the head and tail attached to the body; cutting them off would let juices flow out and cause the exposed flesh to toughen and dry. A whole fish also is more handsome on a serving platter. Do not slash the sides as some recipes dictate, or valuable juices will seep out of the flesh. Place the fish in a greased, shallow roasting pan in a preheated 450° F oven and bake approximately 9 minutes per inch of thickness. The leaner the fish, the more often you will have to baste it. For baking in a paper bag (*en papillote*), add approximately 3 to 5 minutes to the total cooking time because heat will take longer to penetrate the greased paper wrapping.

Broiling: Fatty fish broil better than their leaner counterparts. If you do broil a lean fish, baste it well and often. Besides steaks and fillets, you can broil whole small fish (or medium-sized whole ones if they are first split). Wrap the heads and tails well with aluminum foil to keep these parts from burning. Before broiling the fish, dredge it with flour, then brush or dollop it with butter or other fat. Salt, pepper, and other seasoning should be added after the fish is cooked. The ideal broiling thickness is about 1¼ inches. Fish that is less than ½ inch thick or over 2 inches thick generally should not be broiled; the first will dry out and the second will overcook on the surface before the interior is done. If the fillet is unskinned, broil it skin-side down. Place the fish on greased aluminum foil in a broiling pan. The foil reduces clean-up time and, as a bonus, allows you to remove the foil and fish, once cooked, from the pan that would otherwise keep cooking the fish. The foil is hot enough to keep the cooked fish warm, but not hot enough to continue cooking it. Place the broiling pan in a preheated 450°F broiler 4 inches from the heat source and broil for 9 minutes per inch of maximum thickness. If the fish is over 2 inches thick, broil 5 inches from the heat source and ever so slightly extend the cooking time. Fillets need not be turned, but all but very thin steaks and whole fish do. Brush them well with melted butter or fat as soon as you turn them.

Charcoal Broiling: Follow the relevant guidelines given under Broiling. Always oil the grill to prevent the fish from sticking. Hinged grills are very useful for steaks, fillets, and small whole fish.

Sautéing: Fish steaks and fillets and small whole fish can be sumptuously sautéed or pan-fried. Prepare them by dredging them in flour or cornmeal, or by giving them a breadcrumb coating. If you sauté them plain (or if you soak them in milk or beaten egg) be sure to let them dry or pat them dry to prevent splattering. Use a heavy-bottomed sauté pan or skillet over a moderate to high heat. Cook them in clarified butter or in a mixture of clarified butter and vegetable oil that is hot (but not smoking) for a total time of 9 minutes per inch of maximum thickness, or until golden brown. Do not overcook.

Deep-Frying: Fish steaks, fillets, or sticks, as well as very small fish, can be deep-fried. The usual custom is to bread or batter-coat the pieces. Our modified Canadian timing is not applicable to deep-frying: cook the fish in fresh 375°F vegetable oil for 2 to 4 minutes (depending on thickness), or until golden brown. Do not overcook. Do not crowd the pan with too many pieces or the oil temperature will drop, causing the fish to become soggy and greasy.

Cold Fish Dishes: Poach the fish ahead of time, at least six hours before serving. If you plan to coat the fish with an aspic or a *chaud-froid* sauce, you will have to allow even more lead time. Keep the fish covered in the refrigerator. To develop flavor, marinate the fish before cooking or—if you reduce the poaching time—allow it to cool in the seasoned cooking liquid.

Fish Stock: Put uncooked fish heads, tails, and bones in a pot. Cover them with water, and add salt, peppercorns, *mirepoix*, *bouquet garni*, and a little lemon juice, wine, or vinegar. Lightly boil for 20 to 30 minutes, then strain. Use the stock for soups, stews, etc. For aspics or clear soups, clarify the stock.

Raw Fish: Many famous fish specialties are uncooked: *sushi*, *sashimi*, *ceviche*, and *gravlax*, for example. While we do not recommend that you give up these delicacies, we do urge discretion, because raw fish may contain parasitic worms or noxious bacteria and may inflict you with a disease such as hepatitis. Always start with a fish that was swimming in uncontaminated waters no more than 24 hours ago, and purchase from a reliable dealer.

Test for Doneness

The traditional test involves gingerly probing the thickest part of the flesh with the tines of a fork. If the flesh separates into flakes, the fish is done. If underdone, the flesh will rip or resist separating, rather than flake. If overdone, the flesh will be mushy. The fork test by itself is not conclusive. Therefore, also examine the interior of the flesh—it should be opaque all the way through. A thin translucent line means the fish needs more cooking. Some cookbooks suggest that the fish is done when the raw, translucent surface turns opaque. This is an unreliable test as the surface turns opaque before the rest is cooked. Another test is to cut into the thickest part of the flesh, looking for the telltale line of translucence that shows it isn't done. That method works, but—unless deftly performed—will damage the fish's appearance. Experienced fish cooks also can test by gently poking the flesh with a blunt tool like a wooden spoon. The fish is ready when the flesh becomes slightly resistant to the touch—how resistant can be learned only through trial and error, not words. If you plan to serve the fish in the cooking pan, take it off the heat when it is slightly undercooked, because the hot pan will continue to cook the fish for a few minutes.

Serving: Always serve fish on a heated platter and, ideally, on heated plates, as cooked fish cools quickly.

Customary garnish comprises parsley or dill leaves and lemon wedges or slices. Of the many good boning techniques for a standard fish, here is one of the simplest and easiest for a neophyte to follow. After laying the fish on a platter, use a knife to make a backbone-deep incision behind the gill flap and in front of the tail.

Next, make a lengthwise incision along the back of the fish from the head to tail, just deep enough to reach the backbone. Working from the belly, finish separating the top fillet from the backbone and ribs. Carefully lift the fillet away from the backbone and remaining carcass; if the fish is large, you'll have to remove the fillet in segments. Sever the backbone from the head and tail sections with your knife, then lift up and discard the backbone, freeing it from the remaining bottom side fillet. Both fillets are now ready to serve.

Leftovers: One excellent way to use leftover cooked fish is to marinate the flesh in a *vinaigrette* sauce overnight in the refrigerator, then serve it as a cold salad the following day. This technique is especially good when you have leftover poached fish.

Equivalents

For the average serving, you will need 1 pound of whole-dressed fish, or slightly more than 1/2 pound of dressed fish without head and tail, or 1/3 pound of steak, or slightly less for fillets.

CLASSIC USES AND AFFINITIES

Because fish is relatively neutral in flavor, it marries well with a host of flavors. Herbs often used in fish cookery include dill, parsley, thyme, bay leaf, oregano, tarragon, coriander, sage, basil, rosemary, and summer savory. On the spice list are peppercorns, paprika and cayenne, capers, mustard seeds, nutmeg, cinnamon, cardomon, coriander seeds, fennel seeds, cumin, and some curry blends. Other flavoring agents include butter, members of the onion family, fresh ginger, fermented black beans, lemon, vinegar, wine, cream, sour cream, yogurt, cucumber, mushrooms, tomatoes, and nuts, especially almonds. Sauces for fish abound; for openers, there are various butter sauces (clarified butter, *beurre noir*, lobster, shrimp, anchovy, etc.) and white sauces including *béchamel*, *velouté*, and *mornay*. Other traditional sauces for fish include tartar, mustard, *vinaigrette*, hollandaise, *béarnaise*, mayonnaise, and *sauce verte*.

FIVE-SPICE POWDER

BACKGROUND

A blend of five ground spices is favored in China (especially in Szechuan) and in Southeast Asia. The most usual combination is one of star anise, cinnamon, Szechuan peppercorns, fennel seeds, and cloves. (See the HERBS AND SPICES for information on buying, storing, cooking, etc., as well as the individual spice entries.)

PREPARATION

Half a teaspoon, in conjunction with other spices, will usually suffice for a pound and a half of spareribs, six pork chops, or four whole chicken breasts. Use a teaspoon for a whole chicken. A tightly closed jar of five-spice powder should keep for about a year.

CLASSIC USES AND AFFINITIES

This powder, with a pungent taste of licorice, has an affinity for chicken, pork, and duck.

FLAGEOLET

BACKGROUND

Long favored by the French, the *flageolet* (*Phaseolus chevrier*), is just now beginning to make the American culinary scene. It somewhat resembles the baby lima in color and size. (For soaking, cooking, and other particulars, see BEANS.)

AVAILABILITY

More often than not it is available dried, though you can find frozen flageolets and, even less often, fresh ones.

PREPARATION

One excellent way to cook flageolets is to steam them in a tightly covered pot, using butter and minced onions as the base medium. So cooked, the flageolets become a classic accompaniment to preparations such as roast leg of lamb.

FOOD COLORINGS

BACKGROUND

These liquid dyes are U.S. Certified food colors held in a glycerine solution. They are usually sold in small individual bottles or in small boxes containing four tiny plastic bottles of red, yellow, blue, and green. Instructions on the back of the box tell how to blend the various colors into different hues such as violet or turquoise. Use with a light hand, as each drop is very concentrated. Most frequently, food colorings are used to give special tints to icings, fillings and pastry confections. At Eastertime, the colorings dye the shells of hard-boiled eggs. If you think your family will be sport for it, you may get a laugh by serving green mashed potatoes on St. Patrick's Day or chartreuse rice on Halloween. What a cook should not do is overuse food colorings, as there is no substitute for natural coloring agents such as saffron to give, for example, *paella* an appetizing yellow hue.

FROGS' LEGS

BACKGROUND

While many Americans have dissected frogs in high school biology labs, few have experimented with them culinarily. Of the frog's body, only its hind legs are edible. Some food writers say frogs' legs resemble young chicken or rabbit in flavor and texture, but, in truth, they have a lower-keyed, subtler flavor that makes these amphibian morsels an epicure's delicacy.

AVAILABILITY

Frogs' legs are available the year round in many fine fish stores—though sadly, they are almost always frozen, which means you will be eating mushy flesh. Moreover, freezing does much to obliterate what delicate flavor the legs have, thus making the legs even blander than they were when fresh. For best taste and succulence, you need fresh frogs' legs. They are normally available in some fish markets from late spring through late summer. Or you can go frogging (a Southern sport) yourself. Most frogs (including bullfrogs) do provide gourmet fare. Toads do not. Be sure the water they live in is not polluted. The American frog industry is concentrated in the states along the Gulf Coast from Florida to Louisiana. Frozen frogs' legs are imported from lands such as Japan, China, Indonesia, India and Italy.

Buying Tips

Frogs' legs are traditionally sold in attached pairs. Their size varies from about 1/8 to 1/2 pound each. Buy the smallest ones for the species (they will be the most tender) and even-sized specimens (for uniform cooking). Look for plump, well-formed legs with a pinkish-white flesh that springs back into shape when pressed with your fingers. Avoid soggy, wet-surfaced, off-odor specimens. If you must buy them frozen, be sure the package is solidly frozen and is not sticky, a sign that the product was partially thawed, then refrozen. Figure on two to five pairs of legs per person, depending on the size of the legs and the diner's appetite.

PREPARATION

Preliminaries

Fresh or frozen, frogs' legs are customarily sold skinned and ready to cook. If you have captured a live frog, first decapitate it. Sever both rear legs as close to the trunk as you can. Leave the pair hinged, or separate the legs, as you wish. Cut off and discard the feet. Wash and dry the legs and, for easier skinning, refrigerate them for an hour. Starting at the thigh end, turn the edge of the skin inside-out, pull it off, and discard it. Use the legs immediately or, if necessary, lightly cover and refrigerate them for up to one day. Thaw frozen legs in the refrigerator—this may take a full day if the legs are solidly frozen in a package. Some recipes specify cooking the legs either in tandem or singly. The first makes a more striking presentation, the latter are easier to cook. Many recipes suggest soaking the legs in milk for an hour or two before cooking. If the legs are young, tender, and fresh, this step is not necessary.

Cooking

Frogs' legs are similar to fish in that the flesh is naturally tender and therefore needs to be cooked only to enhance the taste. If overcooked, the flesh becomes tough. Most frogs' legs are sautéed, typically in olive oil, clarified butter, or both. The simplest and best method is to pat the legs dry, dredge them in seasoned flour, and sauté them over moderate to high heat for 3 to 5 minutes (depending on thickness), until lightly golden brown. Turn them with a spatula for even browning—but be careful, as they tend to stick to the pan and break apart if mishandled. Serve with the pan juices and garnish with parsley and a lemon wedge. The most famous recipe is *cuisse de grenouille provençale*, the garlic-infused French Mediterranean recipe. Do not overdo the garlic, as most French-American cooks do, or you will mask the subtle flavor of the meat. Likewise, go easy on the use of spicy tomato or tartar sauces. Frogs' legs are delicious breaded and deep-fried in a 375°F oil for 2 to 3 minutes, depending on their thickness. Frogs' legs can also be broiled or braised.

FUZZY MELON

BACKGROUND

Available in Chinese markets, the relatively bland *fuzzy* (or *hairy*) *melon* is prized as a soup ingredient because of its ability to pick up the flavors of the other ingredients. The whitish flesh can also be stir-fried, braised or stewed. The light-to-dark green skin, which must be peeled off, has a fine fuzzy covering. A fuzzy melon is cylindrical, typically between 6 and 10 inches long and 2 to 3 inches thick. Store in a sealed plastic bag in the refrigerator for up to about five days.

GAME ANIMALS

BACKGROUND

By definition, game meat comes from an undomesticated animal (and also from undomesticated GAME BIRDS and from FISH, which are discussed in separate entries). When we talk about these game creatures, we must differentiate between the ones reared in the wild and those raised on game farms. Both types are (or should be) identical species; the major difference is that the game-farm creatures were born and raised in a less active, diet-controlled, man-supervised environment. Both types are distinct from and should not be confused with the domesticated varieties—the domesticated sheep, for instance, is a descendant of the wild sheep, but has a different shape, flavor, and texture because, over the centuries, it has been developed via selective breeding into a somewhat different creature.

Varieties

Common Large Game:

Venison: In the limited sense, venison refers to the meat of the American *deer*, our country's most popular large game meat. By broader definition, the term also incorporates the flesh from other related antlered species such as the moose, elk, reindeer, caribou, and antelope. All are cud-chewing vegetarians. Our informal poll of game gourmets indicates that New World *elk* wins the blue ribbon for the best venison. *Moose*, the giant of the deer family, comes in a close second, followed by the American *deer*. *Reindeer* and its cousin the *caribou* are delicious, but not as delicate as the first three. Of all the members of the deer family, only the reindeer has been successfully domesticated, furnishing fresh milk and sled-pulling power to people such as the Lapps of Northern Scandinavia. The midgets of the deer family are the *antelopes*—most species have a more assertive flavor than the typical American deer.

Wild boar: "Several hundred pounds of danger" aptly describes the *wild boar*, indigenous to the Old World. Our native New World version, the *peccary*, is much smaller but can compete in matters of succulent taste. A boar's diet comprises wild vegetation perhaps enhanced by the meat of small creatures such as field mice or lizards, which help give its flesh a slightly stronger flavor than its evolutionary progeny, the pig. In cooking wild boar, you can follow the general guidelines suggested for the domesticated pig (see PORK), but take into consideration such differences as the boar's lower fat content and more exercised muscles. You will also have to remove the musk gland located on the boar's back. The most renowned specialty is the Christmastime appetizer, wild boar's head, which is boned, stuffed, slowly simmered and brought to the table in Merry Olde England on a decorative platter with much pomp and circumstance. A whole roast suckling wild boar can also be ceremoniously carried into the dining room on a parsley-ringed silver platter.

Bear flesh tastes like pork, but much stronger. The best bear meat comes from the *black bear*, and particularly if the animal was young and had been recently feeding on ambrosia, such as ripe berries, wild nuts, and honey. Bears often augment their diets with non-vegetarian foods such as salmon freshly plucked from the cold mountain stream or, perhaps, small land animals. Those flesh foods are good for the bear, but not for their prey or for the flavor of the bear meat. The extreme negative example is the *polar bear*, whose diet of arctic seals and seafood gives the meat a very fishy flavor. Most cooks trim bear meat of all excess fat because they do not like its cooked flavor. On the other hand, rendered fat, called *bear grease*, makes a good lard, as many backwoodsmen avow. *Bear paw* is one of the ancient eight delicacies of the classic Chinese banquet; it is usually skinned, simmered or roasted, and served in thick slices. A limited amount of bear meat is commercially available from game farms or from hunters who have legally shot bears in order to keep the bear population in balance with the ecology.

Buffalo, bison, and beefalo: The American *buffalo* is not a true buffalo—it's a *bison*. (The two major types of true buffalo are the *Asian water buffalo*, which has been domesticated for dairy and draft use, and the wild *African water buffalo*, which defies domestication.) American buffalo meat is legally available from game farms and from the wild animals killed to reduce oversized herds. The meat somewhat resembles beef (but is leaner and stronger-flavored) and—with adjustments such as barding—can be cooked as beef. Choice cuts include the hump and tongue as well as the loin, rib, and sirloin sections. *Beefalo* is a recent cross between the American buffalo and bovine, with the cattle strain predominating. Though beefalo ranchers claim that the meat is superior to both beef and American buffalo, our palates are yet to be convinced.

Other Large Game: Some of the animals discussed below are endangered species. Our discussion refers to the meat from animals that were legally slaughtered (for instance, for the purpose of reducing an oversized herd or killing a rogue elephant).

Camel meat is proscribed to Orthodox Jews by Talmudic law, but is relished by Arab nomads. The prized cut is the hump—and unfortunately for the Arabs the camel of their part of the world is the single-humped dromedary while the camel from Central Asia is the twin-humped bactrian. Besides being a source of flesh, the domesticated camel (wild ones do exist) provides transportation as well as a fat-rich milk which is often converted into various cheese products.

Elephant meat from the fatty loin area is tasty and, for such a huge animal, is surprisingly light—that is, in flavor. However, it is the well-exercised trunk muscle and the feet that are considered choice selections by globe-trotting epicures. One of the ways the huge foot is cooked in the savannahs of Africa is by roasting it for half a day in an earth oven dug into the ground. When cooked, the skin peels off with ease. The elephantlike *mastodon* has been extinct for thousands of years, but its flesh has been eaten recently by a few scientists who discovered frozen specimens embedded in glaciers. The meat tastes like modern-day elephant flesh, they report.

Wild sheep and *mountain goat* meats are rarely available to city folk because the animals live in remote mountains that make them difficult to hunt and to lug back to civilization. The flesh of the wild sheep is more delicate and desirable than that of a mountain goat; if it comes from a young animal,it can be cooked as you would a mature lamb or yearling mutton.

Kangaroo tail is a well-known ingredient for a soup. Regrettably, the other delectably flavored cuts such as the loin or leg are often left uneaten by the hunters of this Australian marsupial.

Lion, tiger and other members of the ferocious feline clan such as the *leopard, jaguar,* and *mountain lion* have meats that are as delicately flavored as that of a mild-mannered lamb. Young feline meat is ideally suited for roasting, while the flesh from the stronger—hence tougher—older animals is best stewed or ground for preparations such as tiger-burgers, if you add a little fat to the lean.

Zebra meat tastes similar to HORSEMEAT and can be cooked as if it were.

Small Game: As with the large game animals, we are talking in this section about legally killed game (for instance, to trim the herd) in the case of an endangered species.

Armadillo: Its white tender flesh, which in taste vaguely resembles a cross between pork and chicken, is protected by an armored shell. This defense does not daunt its prime enemy, the two-legged hunter, who simply turns the animal over and scoops out the flesh through the armadillo's soft underside—an Achilles belly, so to speak. Millions of easy-to-capture wild "dillos" roam countrysides from Florida to Texas, providing a delicious, inexpensive meal to the savvy Southerners who roast, broil, saute, or bake the meat, using their favorite pork recipes.

Beaver: The delicately flavored tail of this vegetarian rodent is a favorite with some hunters, who cook it buried in campfire coals, then peel off the skin and enjoy the flesh. At home the beaver tail is usually skinned and simmered. Once trimmed of fat, the red lean from the body can be successfully cooked using various pork recipes. Young animals, weighing 20 to 30 pounds, are tenderest.

Hare: See RABBIT AND HARE entry.

Muskrat: Also known as the *marsh* or *swamp rabbit*, the herbivorous muskrat is appreciated by furriers for its warm pelt and by cooks for its deep red flesh. The excess fat and scent glands should be removed prior to cooking.

Opossum: Southerners love roasting the pale flesh of young (under 10 pounds) 'possums and serving it with sweet potatoes or persimmons. The taste of the meat of this marsupial is reminiscent of pork and may be cooked using most pork recipes.

Porcupine: This vegetarian rodent has been called the "starving woodsmen's salvation" because it is easy to find, kill (with a heavy instrument such as a rock), and cook in the wilds. One just has to avoid being pricked by the thousands of quills sticking out of the animal's body. The easy way to cook the porcupine is to eviscerate it, then bury the unskinned whole carcass in campfire coals. In an hour or two, the porcupine is ready to eat once you peel off the skin. Porcupines under 15 pounds will yield the tenderest flesh.

Raccoon: Here we have the "masked robber" of nature—an apt sobriquet considering that this bear-related farmyard chicken-thief wears what looks like a black Lone Ranger mask. His pelt is prized by furriers, and, with the black-ringed tail attached, it is the basis of the Davy Crockett coonskin hats. For best eating, cook an under-10-pound raccoon whose scent glands and excess fat have been removed. The mildness of the dark flesh is on a par with that of pork.

Squirrel: A number of young two-legged predators shoot this furry mammal for the sport of the kill, never realizing that the tender dark meat they leave in the woodlands as carrion for other animals has culinary value. Use rubber gloves when eviscerating and skinning the squirrel because it might (though unlikely) carry the dangerous *tularemia* disease. Most rabbit recipes work. Like rabbit meat, squirrel flesh needs barding or basting if dry-cooked. The most famous squirrel dish is Brunswick stew, a good dish if you have a young squirrel.

Woodchuck: Once trimmed of excess fat and the scent glands, the mild-flavored *groundhog* (as it is also called) can be cooked using recipes for rabbits.

The woodchuck's relative, the *prairie dog*, can be cooked the same way.

Factors in Flavor and Tenderness

The flavor and tenderness of game animals depend on a number of factors. Those that have to do with the animal as you find it are discussed here; those you can control are discussed under Preparation below.

Type of Animal: It has been often said that flavor of game meat such as venison is beeflike, that of bear is porklike, and that of snake is chickenlike. There is nothing wrong with such comparisons as long as you use them only as a very rough rule of thumb. No one animal tastes exactly like another.

Age: The older the animal, the less naturally tender and less delicately flavored its meat. In almost all game, the best-quality meat comes from animals that are past their infancy but have not yet reached the first stages of maturity. Reasonably reliable age indicators include relative *size*; color and texture of *bone* cross-sections (they change in time from soft and reddish to brittle and white), color of *fat* (white indicates youth, creamy white, maturity), *flesh texture* (fine grain suggests youth, coarse grain, age); and *flesh color* (the paler it is the younger the animal).

Sex: In most cases the male has a slightly better flavor while the female has a slightly more tender flesh. Take your pick.

Feed: A change in diet from, say, bark to berries can produce pronounced flavor changes in an animal's flesh. Some woodsmen can even taste the differences between two beavers that have been eating the bark of different tree species.

Exercise: The more an animal exercises, the less naturally tender and the leaner the meat will be.

Season: Most game animals are at their culinary best in the fall after feasting on the riches of spring and summer. The worst time is usually from mid-winter through early spring.

How Killed: There is some truth in the old hunter's wisdom that the flesh of an animal that was shot unawares and instantly is more tender than one killed in a startled state and especially one that was killed after a slow death or a lengthy chase. A good hunter, therefore, stealthily approaches his prey, completing his mission with one well-targeted bullet.

Anatomical Location: As with the domesticated meat animals, the tenderness of a cut is conditional on its anatomical location—and the anatomy of most game animals resembles that of the steer, hog and sheep sufficiently to ease your learning task (see BEEF, PORK, and LAMB for details). The most tender section is the immobile *loin* (or the *saddle*, if both loins remain united), followed closely by the *rib* and *sirloin* sections. The least tender meat comes from the active muscles in the *neck* and *shanks*. Other cuts such as the *shoulder* and *hind leg* fall somewhere in between the extremes; with such cuts, the age of the animal is usually the primary determinant in whether to cook the meat with dry or moist heat.

PREPARATION

Dressing and Transporting

Millions of pounds of otherwise perfect game meat is wasted or diminished in quality each year by the hunters' post-kill actions. To minimize spoilage and maximize tenderness, flavor and nutritive value, the animal should be bled and eviscerated within an hour of the kill, with the stomach cavity propped open by a stick to hasten the cooling of the carcass. How the carcass is transported from the woods to the home also affects quality. We have observed too many sportsmen driving hundreds of miles through heat and road dirt with deer strapped to the fenders. We certainly would not want to sample the pride and joy of such a hunter, even if it were given to us free on a silver platter. If you are not going to hang the carcass, then, as soon as you get home, skin and cut the animal into cooking-sized pieces. Then refrigerate them, or, if you must, freeze them. If you do not know how to cut up the carcass, some butchers will do it for you for a fee or a share of the meat. Negotiate.

Hanging

Almost all game animals except the very young benefit to some degree from proper *hanging*, which gives the meat a sought-after "high" flavor and does some tenderizing in the process. But contrary to what some hunters believe, hanging is not an absolute necessity—it merely improves the already pleasant flavor and texture of the flesh. And a too "high" flavor is an acquired and perhaps not a sophisticated taste. As for the woodsmen's wisdom that hanging counteracts the flesh-stiffening caused by rigor mortis, that can be accomplished equally well by butchering the animal and storing the pieces overnight in the refrigerator. When hanging an animal, be sure you have an insect-free, cool (about 35°F is ideal) environment with ample air circulation. Remove the excess fat (it becomes rancid easily) but not the skin. For a small animal such as a hare, 2 days is usually ample. For a large mammal such as a deer, up to a week or more may be satisfactory. The older the animal, the longer you will probably have to hang it. For detailed advice on hanging, consult a reliable hunter's manual or a knowledgeable sportsman.

Storage

Game meat stored too long or improperly will obviously deteriorate or be ruined. Unless you have a bevy of hungry friends, freezing the game meat is often a necessity, but realize that the act of freezing negatively affects texture, flavor, and nutrients. So if you do not absolutely need to freeze your game meat, do not. If you have to freeze it, remove as much of the rancid-prone fat as possible and store the well-wrapped meat in a subzero deep-freeze. When defrosting the meat, do it slowly in the refrigerator; rapid defrosting draws out too much of the internal juices. Unfortunately, most of the game meat sold in butcher shops has been frozen. If the meat man wants to hoodwink you, he surreptiously thaws the meat in his walk-in refrigerator before displaying it for sale as "freshly killed" in the meat case. The times of the year when meat markets will most likely have freshly killed game meat are during the local hunting seasons, especially in the fall when the butcher's sportsmen friends may have a surplus kill.

Flavoring, Marinating, Etc.

The traditionally assertive game marinades, flavoring agents, sauces, and garnishes were originally developed out of necessity: to disguise near-spoiled or ill-treated meats. Many modern cookbook writers, loyally following the advice of their predecessors, continue to promote the use of such overpowering flavorings for game meats across the board, even though major improvements in areas such as refrigeration often make strong-flavored marination unnecessary. If you need to marinate the meat, contemplate how much loss of natural game flavor you are willing to sacrifice for the sake of tenderness. For minimum loss of natural flavor, keep the marinating period to several hours and do not overload the liquid with assertive seasoning agents. Some tough game meat from older animals, however, may benefit from longer marination, perhaps 2 days or more. Popular game marinating ingredients include red wine, wine vinegar, and/or lemon juice infused with peppercorns, onions, garlic, thyme, bay leaf, and sage. Parboiling your game meat 10 to 15 minutes helps rid it of unwanted gamy flavor; subtract that amount from your regular cooking time. You would seldom want to use this technique if the meat is to be cooked with dry heat such as roasting.

Cooking

Much game meat has entered the kitchen in excellent state only to exit in deplorable condition. This should not imply, however, that game cookery is difficult, requiring arcane knowledge. If that were the case, how did our cave-dwelling ancestors survive without the aid of electric-powered rotisseries and a full shelf of spices and game cookbooks? The false notion that game cuisine is markedly different from beef cookery emanated from the bygone days when a cook had to be a wizard to cope with a spoiled, too "high," or otherwise ruined game carcass that was stored too long in the larder or that was just plopped on the kitchen table by a hunter at the end of a day-long outing. For the record, you can cook game flesh as you would other meat, allowing for a few adjustments. One major difference is wild animals are well-exercised and, consequently, their meat tends to be less tender and less fatty than their domesticated counterparts. This means that if we are cooking with dry heat—say roasting—we must take special care to lard, bard, or baste the meat, and we must not cook the meat beyond medium-rare lest it becomes dry and tough. The surface fat of most game animals does not cook as pleasantly and flavorfully as the fat of domesticated animals, so many cooks remove most of it, replacing it with a thin layer of beef suet or pork fatback. However, using bacon is not a good idea; its flavor may make the meat taste of bacon, not game. And salt pork may impart too much salt.

Another key difference between the game meat and, say, beef is that the game is typically stronger-flavored. But this does not mean we have to adulterate venison to make it taste like beef any more than we have to make beef taste like veal. We should appreciate each meat for its own virtues. As noted before, some game meat may benefit slightly from hanging. This step is not necessary for domesticated animals. As a very rough rule of thumb, you can treat most large game meat such as venison as you would beef or lamb, other large game such as bear and wild boar as pork, and most small game as chicken or pork, depending on flavor intensity.

As with domesticated animals, you can roast the animals whole (if small) or can cut the carcass into roasts, steaks, and stew meat, or you can grind the meat for elkburgers, mooseburgers, whatever. When preparing ground game meat, you will probably have to add 10 to 25 percent fat from a domesticated animal, as game meat is usually too lean to begin with and what fat exists may not cook to a desirable flavor. Save the bones for the stockpot.

Trichinosis can be a problem with certain game meat, especially with that of bear and wild boar. It is therefore prudent to treat all game meat as pork in terms of not tasting it until the flesh has reached an internal temperature of at least 137°F, the heat needed to assure the demise of the deadly trichinosis parasites (see discussion under PORK). At the same time, don't let caution drive you to the other extreme of overcooking the meat.

The exact cooking time for game is hard to peg; there are too many variables, such as age. For venison and most other land game, we suggest taking the roasting meat out of the oven when the meat thermometer registers 135°F (no need to fret about trichinosis, because the internal temperature will continue to rise 5° or more after the roast leaves the oven). This will leave your roast rare to medium-rare. For bear and wild pork, the take-out figure should be about 140°F. In both cases, the meat will take roughly 15 to 20 minutes per pound in a preheated 350°F oven for most cuts, but take into consideration all the key variables such as thickness. Very small game such as rabbit or squirrel can be and perhaps should be roasted at a high oven temperature (400° to 425°F), for a shorter period of time, if barded, basted, or both. A steak or chop in a broiler will take a total cooking time of about 10 minutes per inch of thickness when set 4 inches from a 450° F heat source (turn the meat once). Allow 1 to 2 1/2 hours for stewing or braising, depending on variables such as age, cut, and thickness.

Serving and the Diner's Prejudices

If someone has a built-in prejudice against eating, say, opposum meat, that viand will not taste good no matter how juicy and tender the chef may cook it. Splendid, well-prepared game meat deserves an educated, or at least an appreciative, palate.

CLASSIC USES AND AFFINITIES

In our strong opinion, popular game sauces such as Cumberland sauce and currant jelly are too sweet for game dishes. A better choice includes some other equally popular sauces: bread sauce, *sauce poivrade*, Madeira sauce, *chausseur* sauce. Excellent garnishes include mushrooms, broiled tomatoes, onions, sweet potatoes, lima beans, and peas.

GAME BIRDS

BACKGROUND

In this day and age you practically have to be well-heeled, know a hunter, or be a crack shot to enjoy game birds. Gift birds are few and those that can be purchased are expensive because the true wild variety is scarce and protected with short hunting seasons, and the game-farm variety is expensive to rear.

Varieties

Wild Turkey: The wild turkey, usually weighing between 8 and 20 pounds, is the largest of the popular game birds. The most noticeable physical difference between the whole carcasses of wild and domestic turkeys is the projecting breast bone of the wild turkey. This bird also has leaner flesh (though it is much juicier than that of most other game birds). Spring is the standard hunting season for wild turkey, so if you expect to have a legally hunted bird for Thanksgiving dinner, it is going to have to be frozen. (A game-farm wild turkey, on the other hand, can be bought fresh the year round, though some game-farm birds are frozen too, so ask.) Although the male (or tom) turkey has finer, firmer texture and is tastier than the hen the female is in greater demand because of her abundance of white breast meat. You can tell the intact male from the female—the male has a long beard, a spur near each foot, fleshy lobes (wattles) hanging from the chin, and a wart on the forehead, whereas the female does not. For each diner, allow 1 pound of a whole, dressed turkey.

Wild Goose: Another large game bird is the wild goose, whose dark flesh teems with rich flavor and texture. Almost all of the many varieties of wild goose are very tasty, although beware of a goose that has recently eaten strong-smelling vegetation such as cabbage. The wild goose most likely to end up on the dinner table is the 6- to 12-pound *Canada goose*, though some connoisseurs prefer the *white-fronted goose*, which feeds on heath berries and is found in the Western United States. Another popular wild goose is the *blue goose*, sometimes referred to as the *emperor goose*, which is a strict vegetarian. Still some other delicious varieties you will enjoy are the *brants*, *snow geese*, and *specklebellies*. Cholesterol-watchers please note that the wild goose has significantly less fat than the domestic goose. For each diner, plan on buying (or shooting) 1 pound of wild goose.

Wild Duck: The wild duck, a medium-sized game bird, may be separated into three categories: early season, diving, and sea ducks. The *early season ducks* are *mallards*, *godwalls*, *ruddy ducks*, *black ducks*, *pintails*, *widgeons*, *green-winged teals*, *blue-winged teals*, *cinnamons*, and *wood ducks*. The mallard is not considered the best-tasting of the early-season ducks because it often feeds on almost anything—yet the mallard is frequently eaten, principally because it is the most abundant wild duck in the United States and Canada. Early-season ducks that are tastier include the *widgeon* and *teal* that feed on grass-seed and grain. Members of our next category, the *diving ducks*, are generally not as pleasing to the tastebuds as the early-season duck. The *canvasback* and *redhead*, though scarce and protected, are exceptions because, like the early-season ducks, they feed on grass, seeds, and grains. Other diving ducks are the *wing duck*, *golden eye*, *scaup*, *shovelers*, and *old-squaw* . They are not as highly regarded, for if there is no other source of food, they will eat fish. The third category is the *sea duck*; they are the least desirable of all the varieties of the wild duck, for they feed on fish. However, the breasts of fish-eating ducks can be made pleasurable to some tastes if they are marinated, thereby removing some of their fishy flavor. Any duck that has a serrated bill should be avoided. Do not even try to cook it, unless it is a matter of economics or survival. One duck will more than likely serve two people; of course, this depends on the size of the appetites and of the duck.

Pheasant: One of the tastiest of medium-sized game birds is the pheasant which originally came from the Eastern shores of the Black Sea. The best-known variety is the *ringneck*, although also quite popular is the *English pheasant*. The ringneck is an upland bird, found in flocks from the Atlantic to the Pacific in the central and northern parts of the United States. The bird from the wild is becoming scarce and its hunting season is short, so feasting on it is indeed a rare treat. Fortunately, there are a number of game farms that rear pheasants—ask your butcher if he can order one for you. While the female of the species is smaller than the male, her flesh is more flavorful and juicier. This last point is particularly salient because the pheasant tends to have dry flesh, even when compared to other game birds. Pheasant-under-glass may be one of the glamour dishes of the epicurean world, but cooking your bird under a glass bell is not roasting but steam-roasting, a process that gives the flesh a slightly mushy texture.

Grouse, Partridge, and Quail: These three birds cause a lot of culinary confusion because they are referred to interchangeably and inconsistently in various parts of the United States. And to make matters worse, the grouse, partridge and quail that are imported from the Old World are not even close relatives to the ones that fly wild in the New World. Birds that are called grouse, therefore, vary too much in qualities such as size and taste for us to give you specific culinary instructions without knowing exactly which of several dozen species you have. The same is true for partridges and quails. For instance, most of the birds named quail in America are medium-sized, while the Old World species (the true quail according to ornithologists) are small-sized.

Small-Game Birds: Several species are categorized as small-game birds. One of the most popular among American sportsmen is the *woodcock*, which is found mainly in the United States, though it has been known to breed in Canada. The best season for hunting woodcock is fall, when these migratory birds fly south in giant flocks. The woodcock feeds on earthworms. When serving woodcock allow one or two birds per person. Other small-game birds are the full-breasted *hazel hen* (which is imported from Siberia) and the *plover*. The plover, though found rarely in the United States, is illegal to hunt, but may be enjoyed without guilt as it is imported from Europe and raised on game farms. The hazel hen and plover, like the woodcock, feed on earthworms and one bird will feed one person, depending on size. Other small-game birds include the *dove*, which may be cooked the same way as woodcock, the *thrush*, *lark*, *ortolan*, and *snipe*. There is usually no need to hang most small and young wild game birds, as they are very tender. The same is true for eviscerating them as their entrails meld into the body—but if you feel squeamish if you omit this step then go right ahead and gut your birds. Small-game birds are best when cooked as fresh as possible. They can be roasted but are often best prepared with the "five-B" method: bard, broil, and baste your bird on a piece of bread.

Buying Tips

When purchasing a game bird at a market, you are usually assured that the meat has been properly aged and dealt with. However, to make certain of the quality of your bird, check to see that it has a fresh odor, and a skin that is neither dried out nor dull in color. The younger the bird, the more tender and desirable the flesh. There are a number of ways to tell the age of the bird; the most popular is to check breastbone tip: it is soft and pliable when the bird is young, but grows hard and inflexible as the bird reaches maturity. The same is usually true with the feet and legs. Check the shape of the outer flight feathers: most young birds have pointed feather tips; on older birds they are rounded. (This test does not work when the feathers are wet, as round ones may appear pointed.) Another way to judge age is to examine the bursa. This is a small opening on the upper side of the vent on a young game bird. When the bird reaches sexual maturity this opening will become smaller or close completely. To perform the test, insert a small stick, such as a wooden match, into the bursa.

PREPARATION

Dressing Game Birds

There are many factors that contribute to the ultimate flavor of your wild game bird. Proper attention once the bird has been shot is of the utmost importance. If the hunter does not handle the freshly killed bird properly, it will probably spoil long before it reaches the oven. The steps in handling a game bird are: bleeding the bird, evisceration, hanging, plucking, skinning, singeing, removing tendons, washing.

Bleeding: This chore should be done as soon as possible after the bird is shot. To bleed the bird, split the jugular vein in the neck and hang the bird head downward, draining the blood. (If possible, preserve the blood—there is little pan juice in game cookery, and the blood is an ideal sauce ingredient, thickening as well as flavoring it.) After draining the blood from your bird, remove any food you find in the throat.

Evisceration: The next step is to remove the bird's entrails. For health reasons, this step is especially important in warm weather. However, if the weather is cool and the hanging period short (or, in the case of a small-game bird which will be cooked with entrails intact within 24 hours), it is not absolutely necessary. To eviscerate the bird, cut off its head, then carefully pull the skin from the neck down the shoulders. Cut the neck off very close to the body. Using your hands, remove from just under the breast skin the attached tubes and the crop, a small fleshy sac at the bottom of the neck. Just below the breastbone, make an incision large enough to insert your hand and carefully remove the solid gizzard; in the process, the heart, intestines, and liver should also pull out. If not, remove them as well. Next remove the lungs, kidneys, and any fat deposits and blood clots in the cavity of the bird. Keep the liver, heart, and cleaned gizzard (if fresh, they may be used in cooking), but discard the other organs. With a sharp knife, cut off the oil sac, which is located on the back near the tail. Finally, wipe your game bird inside and out with a damp cloth. Be sure to pat completely dry, for water aids bacterial growth and spoilage.

Hanging: To achieve the most tender and flavorful wild game bird, it may be necessary to hang it. During the hanging period, the bird should be protected from insects and other predators with either screening or cheesecloth. If you are hanging more than one bird, separate them to allow the air to circulate around them. The environment should be cool, dry and away from direct sunlight. Authorities differ widely on how long a bird should be hung; recommendations vary from 24 hours to 2 weeks or more. In most instances, several days to a week should suffice. However, you must take into consideration the variables: the age of the bird (older birds need more hanging time); the weather (in warmer weather a bird is hung for a shorter period); the size of the bird (a large game bird is hung longer than a small one); and your taste preference (for "high" flavor, the longer the hanging period). One way of determining if your game bird has been hung long enough is to look below the breast bone. If it is turning blue or green (depending on the type of game bird) your bird has been hung long enough. Another criterion is smell: it should not, all that much (this is particularly true with young birds). Still another sign is that the tail feather can be easily plucked. Keep a close watch on your bird during hanging. There should be no discoloration around the vent; if there is, your bird has been hung too long.

Plucking: The longer you wait to pluck the feathers, the more difficult your task. However, do not pluck any wild game birds until you are ready to cook, refrigerate, or freeze them, or the carcass is likely to spoil (due to its exposure to the air) before the bird has become tender. In removing the feathers, pull small amounts at a time, downward toward the tail. If you have waited to pluck the bird and the feathers have become stiff, you can avoid breaking the skin while removing them if you dip the bird repeatedly in scalding water until the feathers are soaked. But it is best to dry-pluck any game birds that are going to be frozen or held for even a short period, since soaking the bird will break down the fatty tissue of the skin. All game birds should be dry-plucked, though very small ones should be singed rather than plucked. Do not wash wild game birds between plucking and cooking. Exceptions are fish-feeding ducks, of which only the breast meat will be eaten, and a bird whose cavity is filled with blood clots and viscera. Pluck all other ducks dry, as their feathers are very oily. To remove the remaining down, dip the duck in a pot filled with 2 gallons of boiling water with 1/2 pound of paraffin melted in it. It will take a few dips into the pot before the duck has a thick coat of wax on. Once the paraffin has cooled and hardened, you scrape it, and the down, off your duck with a dull knife; only a few pin feathers will remain. These may be singed away.

Skinning Very small game birds must be skinned. Do not skin larger birds, for they will dry out during cooking. Of course, if the bird has been badly shot up, it may have to have some skin taken off, but remove as little as possible. To skin a small game bird, slit the neck lengthwise, then gently pull the skin off the carcass. It is a skill gained with practice.

Singeing: All game birds should be singed before cooking in order to remove the remaining feathers and hair. Use an unscented candle or long wooden matches to avoid scorching its skin.

Removing Tendons: In large game birds, as well as large domestic fowl, the tendons in the legs are often tough and should be removed. To do this, make a cut in the skin approximately 1½ inches above the joint in the knee. Take care not to cut the tendons. Place the bird on a table with the cut at the edge of the table. Snap the bone by sharply pressing the foot and ankle downward at the knee joint. Then on the bird's foot; the tendons should pull away along with the lower leg bone and foot. If they don't, you will have to remove them one at a time, using an implement such as a skewer and forcing it under each tendon individually.

Washing: Many cooks feel a wild game bird should not be washed out before it is cooked. However, if the cavity is not clear of blood clots or if bits of entrails remain, it is best to wash the bird out with cold water and lightly pat dry. Another but less effective way of freshening the bird is to rub with lemon inside and out. This will also enhance the flavor, but do not overdo the lemon.

Freezing: Freezing wild game birds may be considered if you have more game than you can use. However, if you do freeze your bird, keep in mind that as with other meats, this process tends to make the flesh mushy. Do not keep wild game birds frozen (at 0°F) for more than six months, as their fat tends to become rancid.

Preliminaries

Barding: Because game birds are well exercised, they are very lean, generally lacking the fat of their domestic cousins. Thus, before you roast or broil your game bird, you should *bard* it—add fat to the outside of the bird, usually tying on a thin slab of beef or pork fat. (Frequent basting while cooking also helps.) Many cooks use bacon fat for barding, but we prefer not to for it gives the bird a smoky taste.

Flavoring: Wild game birds generally do not require as much flavoring with herbs and spices as domestic birds do, for their flavors are distinct and delicious. Some cooks, however, like to use a marinade before cooking game birds. This serves two purposes—it helps tenderize the flesh; and it adds flavor, which may be desired to mask the gamy taste. To lessen the gamy taste, place either an onion or a potato in the cavity of the bird before roasting; discard it before serving. This also reduces the fishy flavor in a wild duck.

Stuffing: Allow ¾ to one cup of stuffing for each pound of bird. Do not force-pack the stuffing, as it expands during cooking.

Trussing: It may not be as easy to truss a game bird as it is a domestic one because a game bird which has been shot may have missing joints. In such cases you will have to become a creative surgeon, using the trussing needle and string in odd ways to tie the bird into a compact mass, thus minimizing uneven cooking. Problem-free trussing is outlined in the CHICKEN entry.

Cooking

Age is a key determining factor on which cooking method should be used. If a game bird is young, roasting is strongly suggested. An older bird is more suitably cooked with slow, moist heat; braising is good. Older birds are also fine for stock, soup, sauces, hash, or forcemeat. If the legs of your game bird are tough or full of tendons, they may be simmered along with wings, necks, and giblets to make a game stock, for game cooking produces relatively little pan drippings for making sauce.

There are many schools of thought on how long a wild bird should be cooked. On one extreme, there are those who say the bird should be merely set for a moment in a warm oven; other extremists argue that it should be roasted until well done. The truth (at least our definition of the truth) lies somewhere between these two poles, but slightly favoring the rare-meat adherents—in other words, medium-rare is ideal. Here are our suggestion for the proper cooking times and temperatures for a room-temperature bird:

Roasting: Place large game birds (over 4 pounds) on a rack in a shallow roasting pan in a preheated 450°F oven, then reduce heat setting to 325°F and roast 14 to 18 minutes per pound. Do the same for medium-sized game birds (1 to 4 pounds), but estimate 18 to 22 minutes per pound. (The larger the bird, the fewer minutes per pound.) Small game birds (under 1 pound) should be roasted at a constant 425°F oven temperature for a total time of 8 to 25 minutes, depending on size. If you stuff the bird, increase the cooking period by 10 to 15 percent. Adjust the suggested time downward if you want rare meat, upward for medium or well-done. The most popular way to test for doneness is to prick the thickest part of the thigh. If the juice that comes out is bloody, the meat is still rare, if it is pinkish clear, it is medium-rare and if it is clear, it is cooked to at least a medium level.

Broiling: Small birds or thick bird parts should be broiled 5 inches from the heat source about 18 to 22 minutes, thinner parts 3 inches from the heat for 8 to 12 minutes. These times are for medium-rare meat; adjust according to taste preference.

Braising: Time varies from 1½ to 2½ hours—the thicker, older and tougher the piece, the longer the period required.

We have suggested roasting for a young bird and braising or a moist-heat recipe for an older bird; however, game birds may be prepared in a variety of other ways. For instance, use your wild turkey to make soup or chowder, turkey salad, turkey à la king, turkey burgers, even sweet-and-sour turkey. Another example is making wild duck into a pâté.

GARAM MASALA

BACKGROUND

Indian households often prepare a mixture of hot spices such as fresh-ground cardamon seeds, cinnamon sticks, coriander seeds, black peppercorns, and cloves, producing *garam masala*. Indian medicine ascribes the power of heating the body to these spices. *Garam masala* can be mixed with other spices to make what we Westerners may call a curry blend. Only small quantities of *garam masala* should be prepared at one time; long storage would result in stale spices. Commercial *garam masala* blends can be found in Indian-American markets but are inferior to the fresh home-mixed variety. (See HERBS AND SPICES for information on buying, storing, cooking, etc.).

GARLIC

BACKGROUND:

Allium sativum, an onion cousin, has been used as a seasoning since time immemorial. Today, *garlic* is widely cultivated around the world, especially in the warm climates of the Mediterranean, Chinese, Indian, and Hispanic lands. It was used as food for the ancient Egyptian pyramid-builders, a courage-builder for Roman soldiers, and an antiseptic for common folk in the Middle Ages. Raw garlic eaten in quantity will certainly decrease the chance that anyone will come close enough to transmit an infection.

The entire garlic bulb is called a *head*, each section of the bulb a *clove* . These cloves are individually encased in a papery membrane and range in length from about ½ to 1½ inches, depending on maturity and species. The white-skinned variety is the smaller of the two more popular types, the purplish-red one is the larger. Neither is appreciably stronger than the other, but garlic, regardless of pedigree, tends to increase in assertiveness as the growing climates and seasons get colder.

AVAILABILITY

Fresh Garlic

The fresh garlic we buy in stores—available year round—is not, strictly speaking, *fresh* but *dry;* the outer skins (not, however, the moist interiors) have been dehydrated, either by sunlight or by hot mechanical blowers. This step is necessary if the garlic is to be stored without refrigeration for more than a week. (Dry garlic should not be confused with *dried garlic,* which is peeled, chopped, and completely dehydrated. Because of the possible confusion, it's best to continue to call it fresh.)

Processed Garlic

There are many kinds. *Garlic powder* is made from ground, dehydrated garlic. *Garlic flakes* or *chips* are dehydrated garlic cut into slices or chips; unless added to a liquid preparation, they must be reconstituted by soaking them in a small amount of tepid water for about 5 minutes. *Garlic salt* is a blend of salt, garlic powder, and an anticaking agent. Another type of processed garlic is *garlic extract.* Whatever the processed garlic product, it is a poor and not recommended substitute for the better-tasting, less expensive unprocessed garlic. Since unprocessed garlic is so readily available and easy to store, few of us have rational excuses for using processed garlic.

Buying Tips

Fresh garlic is usually sold loose in the bin or packaged in small, windowed boxes. The first arrangement is better because it readily allows you to examine the bulbs for positive factors (plumpness, firmness, reasonable dryness) and for negative signs (broken skins, brown or soft spots, shriveled appearance, wetness). If only the boxed garlic is available, open and examine the contents, if possible. Avoid separated cloves sold in cellophane packets, as the individual cloves are likely to be dry, rancid, or both. If you plan to be using a lot of garlic at a time, buy the larger garlic bulbs because this reduces peeling time.

PREPARATION

Storage

Place unwashed garlic in a topless glass jar or small plastic basket in a cool, dark, dry, well-ventilated spot. An unopened head should last 1 to 10 weeks, depending on its condition when purchased as well as the qualities of your storage environment. An individual unpeeled clove will be over the hill after 2 to 10 days. Storing garlic in the refrigerator is not recommended as it encourages sprouting, and the garlic will both assimilate and emit perceptible odors. Once peeled, garlic should be used promptly—it does not store well.

Preliminaries

Removing the Peel: Break off the clove from the garlic head. Unless the clove is dirty, you need not wash it. Next, cut off any coarse material from both the root and neck end of the clove. Remove the skin with your fingers—or, if you don't want the odor on them, do it with a sharp paring knife. If the skin clings tight to the garlic flesh, hit the clove lightly but firmly with the flat of a broad knife; the skin should come off easily. Or drop the end-trimmed cloves into boiling water for 5 to 10 seconds, then into cold water, then drain; the peel should slide off with ease.

Mincing: The common method is the best: mince the peeled clove with a French chef knife or small Chinese cleaver. Cutting novices can add a bit of salt to the garlic; this makes mincing easier, but adjust the salt in the recipe accordingly. Garlic can be minced in an electric blender or processor, but this method seldom yields the even-sized pieces that are essential in precision cooking.

Garlic Press: This kitchen gadget, a twentieth-century invention, is not a must for the kitchen. Not only is it a chore to clean, but the press imparts a metallic taste. Better ways to release the garlic flavor and fragrance are described in the next section.

Cooking

The intensity of garlic fragrance diminishes with cooking time. One long-simmered French regional specialty that calls for forty cloves of garlic is tamer than you may imagine. When sautéing garlic and onions together, add the garlic just before the onions are done, and be sure the heat is low to moderate; high heat will scorch garlic, making it unpleasantly bitter. There are many ways to add a light garlic touch to food without using the garlic flesh. You can add a slightly crushed whole clove (peeled, for the sake of flavor) to a cooking or marinating preparation, discarding the clove when it has done its job. Salad bowls can be rubbed with a cut garlic clove before the greens are added. For even subtler garlic flavor (normally a contradiction in terms), a piece of dried bread can be rubbed with raw garlic, tossed in the salad bowl with greens and dressing, then removed before the salad is served.

Garlic Odors

Raw garlic, to be sure, is assertive, but the relative degree it attacks your senses is largely a function of your eating biases and habits. As with hot chilis, the more regularly you eat garlic, the less its sensory impact (on you, not necessarily on the people around you). When garlic offends someone, it is primarily due to its fragrance, not its taste. One good way to lessen garlic breath (which lasts for hours, sometimes days) is to remember this aphorism: "The man who eats parsley/Need not eat garlic sparsely."

Equivalents

When a recipe calls for a clove of garlic, it usually means one average-sized clove, roughly 3/4 to 1 inch in length. We do not recommend any processed garlic product. However, if you must use garlic powder or flakes, substitute 1/8 or 1/4 teaspoon respectively for each clove. For garlic salt, substitute 1/2 teaspoon per clove, but be sure to subtract nearly 1/2 teaspoon of salt from your recipe.

CLASSIC USES AND AFFINITIES

Garlic accents many popular salads, stews, pot roasts, sauces, salad dressings, marinades, sausages, and pickles and it gives a resounding punch to *pesto* sauce, *aioli* sauce, garlic bread, and garlic butter. Some chefs insert slivers of garlic into slits cut into a leg of lamb that is to be roasted. For a subtler flavor, rub lamb or any meat with a slightly mashed garlic clove.

GELATIN

BACKGROUND

Gelatin—a protein—is extracted from bones, connective tissue, and certain other parts of animals and fish. It is used to firm preparations such as aspics and the sweet, fruit-flavored gelatins such as Jell-O. Gelatin is also used to coat meats and fish that are to be served at a buffet, to make *chaud-froid* dishes, to thicken cold soups such as *consomme madrilene*, to mold salads, to make marshmallows, and—when diced—to serve as a garnish.

AVAILABILITY

You can buy granulated gelatin in small airtight envelopes, either unflavored or flavored. The unflavored type is virtually tasteless, odorless, and colorless. The flavored variety is typically a dessert mixture of gelatin, sugar, and genuine or artificial flavorings. Besides granulated gelatin, there is also the leaf variety. Some food specialty shops stock it. All these types gel when mixed with hot water and then cooled in the refrigerator. Reheated, the mixture becomes liquid; if chilled again, it gels.

PREPARATION

Variables

A cooled gelatin mixture can be anything from a liquid to a jelly bean. The degree of firmness depends on three variables: the ratio of gelatin to liquid; the temperature of the mixture; and any ingredients added to the mixture.

The customary *ratio* of unflavored granulated gelatin to liquid is one packet (about 1 tablespoon) of dried gelatin to 2 cups of water. Four gelatin leaves accomplish the same deed. Too little gelatin and the consistency of your product will be undesirably limp; too much gelatin and it will be rubbery. The ideal is when the chilled gelatin mixture can stand (when unmolded) on its own, yet still quiver "nervously" when shaken. For flavored gelatin, consult the directions on the package.

The higher the *temperature*, the less firm the solution will be. Even the effects of a 10°F change in temperature are noticeable.

Certain *ingredients* retard gelatinization. Sugar, if used in excess, is one. Fresh or frozen pineapple is another, though canned pineapple (or any pineapple that has been cooked) may be used with impunity.

Mixing

Most recipes specify water as the liquid base for the dried gelatin (though some recipes substitute fruit juice, vegetable juice or stock for part of the water). If you add the granulated gelatin directly to hot water, some of the gelatin granules will lump together or cake to the side of the vessel. You can eliminate this problem in several ways. The most reliable method is to sprinkle the granules on the surface of 1/4 cup of cold water, then wait several minutes without stirring the mixture. Then—after briefly stirring the mixture—add 1 3/4 cups of boiling water, together into a solution. Flavored gelatins are easier to dissolve and sometimes will dissolve in merely warm water, mainly because the sugar in them helps the gelatin enter into a solution. To dissolve leaf gelatin, read the package directions.

Adding Ingredients: Once the gelatin has been dissolved, you can add other ingredients. You can add as much as a cup of solid ingredients to each cup of gelatin solution, sometimes a bit more. When adding solid ingredients, be sure they are chilled and well-drained. Some ingredients (such as fresh apples, bananas, nuts, peaches, pears, and strawberries) tend to float to the top. Others (grapes and most citrus and canned fruit) tend to drift to the bottom, giving you a not-quite-right-to-the-eye product when the solution gels. For even distribution, chill the gelatin solution until it reaches a thick syrupy consistency before adding your solid ingredients. If the additions settle before the gelatin has set, stir them up again, but gently.

Using a Mold: The mold you use can be an ordinary bowl or a specially shaped mold. Lightly rinse it with cold water just before you add the mixture. Do not, as some recipes advise, coat it with oil, as that technique gives your finished preparation a filmy surface and probably a touch of the oil's flavor. Pour in the gelatin mixture, cover it, and place it in the refrigerator. A typical solution without added ingredients will take 1½ to 3 hours to gel, depending on the ratio of gelatin to liquid, the temperature of your refrigerator, and the depth of the mold. If you have added ingredients, you may have to double the gelling time.

Shortcuts: If you want your solution to gel more quickly, do not put it into the freezer, as the texture will suffer greatly. Instead, stir the unset mixture in a bowl set inside another bowl containing cracked ice. Or you can use ice cubes instead of part of the water in the mixture. Add them after the gelatin is dissolved; stir occasionally until the cubes melt and their water is mixed into the solution.

Serving

When unmolding, keep the gelatin in the refrigerator until the last possible moment. There are several reliable ways to loosen and unmold the gelatin. One is to place a serving platter (slightly wet on its surface so you can later center the unmolded gel) upside-down over the mold. Then turn them both over with a quick, sure movement. If the gelatin does not separate from the mold place a warm towel over it. Unless you are a professional at it, do not try dipping the mold in hot water, as sometimes the mixture gets too warm and becomes flabby, losing its intended shape. If you are serving your gelatin buffet-style, place the serving platter on top of crushed ice—it will stay firm longer.

Make Your Own

You can easily make your own aspic at home by boiling bones (especially those from the feet) for an hour or two, then straining, clarifying, and reducing the stock. The liquid will firm when chilled.

GINGER

BACKGROUND

Ginger is a sharply pungent spice that comes from the gnarled, multilobed root (really a rhizome, or underground stem) of *Zingiber officinale*, a plant native to Asia. Ginger was believed to cure the Black Death. Ginger does promote sweating, so it can cool the body in hot climates. Gingerbread was a favorite food in ancient Greece and in sixteenth-century England. Many contemporary European and American bakers still use lots of ground ginger for specialties such as ginger snaps.

AVAILABILITY

Fresh ginger is sold in two forms: young and mature. *Young ginger*, which has been recently harvested, has a soft, thin, pink-tinged tan skin and a green-tinged ivory flesh. It is more aromatic than *mature ginger*, whose semihardened tan peel protects the moist ivory-hued interior and prolongs its storage life. The longer-keeping mature ginger is the type usually sold; young ginger can be found in Oriental markets during the springtime. Fresh ginger is strikingly better than *dried ginger*, the variety found, chopped or powdered, in bottles or tins on the spice shelves of your supermarket. Ginger is also sold *crystallized*, *pickled*, and *preserved* in syrup.

Buying Tips

When buying fresh ginger, look for negative tell-tale signs such as hard, dried-out surfaces where the flesh has been exposed. Other bad indicators are a shriveled, moldy, bruised, cracked, or otherwise damaged skin. Good ginger should smell freshly piquant, not musty;

sniff it before you purchase it. If the ginger has been broken into smaller segments, look for the thicker specimens, as the slenderer ones have more waste and take longer to peel for any given amount of usable volume. For the same reason, look for specimens with a minimum of small protruding lobes.

PREPARATION

Storage

The best way to store fresh ginger is to peel it completely, place in a glass jar with dry sherry or madeira to cover, close the lid, and refrigerate. The ginger will stay fresh for at least a couple of weeks, and the fortified wine can be reused for the same purpose a number of times. As an added advantage, you don't have to peel the ginger every time you need a small piece. You can also store the unpeeled ginger in the refrigerator vegetable crisper in a sealed plastic bag or aluminum foil. For month-long storage, peel, wrap, and freeze the ginger; when you need a bit, take out the ginger but don't thaw it, slice off what you need, and place the rest back into the freezing compartment. If you have a large supply of unpeeled ginger, store the surplus buried in your backyard—it will not only stay fresh in this manner, it may also start growing, giving you a bonus.

CLASSIC USES AND AFFINITIES

Beverage manufacturers concoct ginger ale and ginger beer. Sauerbraten and other pot roasts can have a ginger accent. Indian chutneys and curry dishes very often include ginger. The cuisines of China and Japan use ginger frequently in main dishes, especially with fish and seafood, partially because ginger helps neutralize fishy scent.

GINSENG

BACKGROUND

Ginseng powder is the dried, ground, red or white root of *Panex ginseng*, a plant believed indigenous to China. *Man-root*, as it is also called, has long been world-famous for its supposed aphrodisiac powers for the male and for its beneficial restorative properties for the bodies of either sex. Its sometimes humanlike shape is the primary basis for such folklore. And, the closer its shape resembles man's, the more expensive it is (some obvious specimens have sold for thousands of dollars). In America, ginseng is most often steeped as a tea or taken by tablet for its alleged salutary effects. Although some ginseng is grown commercially in the U. S., the preferred and higher-priced varieties are imported from Korea and Manchuria.

GOOSE

BACKGROUND

Despite the free plug that Charles Dickens gave to the goose in *A Christmas Carol*, most Americans have never tasted this succulent bird. One is more likely to see it gracing the tables of Europe, where it is frequently roasted whole. Goose (meaning both goose and gander in the cook's language) is also often butchered into pieces and prepared in unlimited ways. The French in the region between the cities of Toulouse and Carcassonne, for instance, preserve the flesh embedded in goosefat and eventually eat this "buried treasure" as part of the celebrated bean-based *cassoulet*, one of the greatest of all peasant dishes.

This entry covers the domesticated goose. For wild goose, see under GAME BIRDS. Geese and chickens share many culinary traits, so the advice given in the CHICKEN entry on the following subjects is relevant.

- Background:
  - USDA Grades
- Availability:
  - Fresh or Preserved
  - Buying Tips
- Preparation:
  - Storage
  - Thawing Frozen Birds
  - Preliminaries
    - Disjointing
    - Seasoning a whole chicken
    - Stuffing
    - Trussing
  - Cooking
    - Roasting
    - Spit-Roasting
    - Test for Doneness
    - Pan Gravy
    - The Oysters
    - Broiling

Also see the separate entry, CHICKEN GIBLETS AND VARIETY MEATS. Besides making obvious adjustments for the difference in size between chicken and goose, take into consideration the following tips and insights that relate more to goose than to chicken.

AVAILABILITY

Frozen goose is available the year round, fresh goose from late spring through Christmas, the day when roast goose is a tradition. Most geese sold in America are frozen, and typically weigh 5 to 9 pounds, though some weigh as little as 4 or as much as 18 pounds. Those under 9 pounds can rightly be called goslings.

Buying Tips

It is especially critical to buy a small goose (a gosling) if you want tender meat. The tenderest will be the smallest one you can find—providing, of course, that the bird is plump and well-formed.

Amounts

You will need to buy at least 1 pound of goose for each diner, as the bird has much less edible meat relative to bone and fat than a chicken does. If you're planning to serve a party of six or more, consider buying two small geese rather than one outsize creature.

Storage and Thawing

Frozen goose will keep up to 2 weeks in the frozen-food compartment, several months in the 0°F freezer. Depending on size, estimate 30 to 48 hours in the refrigerator to thaw a 5- to 9-pound frozen goose. The less preferable cold-water method will require 3 to 4 hours.

PRELIMINARIES

Trim off excess fat around the entrance of the stomach cavity. Render and clarify that fat for other cooking uses, such as frying, or making pastry or *confits* (potted goose). *Pâté de fois gras* is made from the liver of specially fattened geese—you will not be able to produce the same results with the liver of the goose you buy from your local butcher. Do not throw your goose liver away, though, because you can still create creditable delicacies with it. Rubbing the skin and stomach cavity with lemon juice does help cut down your palate's perception of the fatty taste of a cooked goose.

STUFFING

A goose is so fatty that trying to cook a palatable stuffing inside is often a waste of time. If you want a stuffing, bake it separately in aluminum foil. The bird should, however, be stuffed with flavoring agents (which will be thrown away after the goose is cooked) such as quartered onions, carrot chunks, and herbs and spices such as fresh parsley sprigs. Orange sections also work well. If you insist on cooking an edible stuffing in the bird, one based on apples and prunes is often used. Some cooks even stuff the bird with sauerkraut, serving it as a side dish.

Cooking

Because of its high fat content, a gosling is best roasted, though it can also be broiled, barbecued, or spit-roasted. A mature goose is even fattier, but is not naturally tender enough for cooking with dry heat. It is best cooked with slow, moist heat as in stewing or braising. The best roasting temperature for a goose is 325°F—allow 20 plus 18 to 22 minutes per pound. The shorter time will give you succulent flesh, the longer time, drier flesh that comes closer to the preferences of most Americans. If the goose is stuffed, add 3 to 5 minutes per pound. Though the times suggested above will give a brown, crisp skin, some cooks like this characteristic exaggerated. If you do, raise the temperature to 400°F for the last 30 minutes and reduce the total cooking time by 5 minutes. Always test for doneness. You need not baste a goose; its thick fat layer is natural barding. Nonetheless, brushing now and then with the fat drippings will not do any harm. Prick the skin with a sharp-pointed knife or fork before and perhaps one or two times after the bird goes into the oven. This helps release the melted fat through the skin, and it also promotes a crisper skin. Do not make your punctures too deep or too great in number. There will be a lot of fat in the roasting pan. Pour it off once or twice during the cooking period and, if you like, save it for other uses such as frying potatoes with onions, a celebrated European peasant side dish.

Carving

Be aware that you will have much more difficulty carving a goose than a chicken.

Sauce

A sauce for your goose does need some acidulous liquid such as lemon or orange juice in order to counteract the fatty taste of the goose. What the sauce does *not* need is the excessive sweetness called for in most recipes; a little sweetening is okay, but too much will mask the subtleties of the goose meat.

GOOSEBERRY

BACKGROUND

Shaped like a small, striped grape, the *gooseberry* (*Ribes grossularia*) can be green, yellow, white, or red. Some varieties have fuzzy skins. This very tart berry is rare in the United States because its bush carries white-pine blight, so several states have outlawed gooseberry growing.

PREPARATION

If you do find some on the market, wash them (just before use) and remove tops and tails; it's easiest to do this with a scissor. Gooseberries are too tart to eat neat, so make a preparation such as gooseberry pie or jelly. The French approach is to make a sour *gooseberry sauce* for oily-fleshed mackerel or rich meats, particularly game. The English approach is to make *gooseberry fool* (from the French *fouler*, to crush), a puree of gooseberries mixed with cream, whipped cream, or custard.

GRAPE

BACKGROUND

Leif Ericson was so impressed with the abundance of grapes growing wild along the Northeast coast of North America that he named his discovery "Vinland." The grapes were probably a hardy ancestor of the Concords, one of a number of New World species grouped under *Vitis labrusca*. The Old World species, *Vitis vinifera*, did not prosper in America until monks at the Mission San Diego introduced *vinifera* grapes to California in 1769. Since then the European varieties have prospered along the milder Pacific Coast.

The *vinifera* is considered the superior grape. The *labrusca* has a characteristic foxy taste, somewhat like the flavor of mass-produced grape juice, that is not relished by most grape aficionados. Besides the difference in taste, the two prime species differ in that *Vitis vinifera* is harder to peel and that the seeds of *Vitis labrusca* tend to cling annoyingly to the pulp.

Classifications

Grapes are divided into two general classes, *white* and *black*. The white types are usually a pale greenish-yellow, while the black types usually have a reddish-purple or bluish color.

Grapes may also be classified as to use. There are *table* (eating) *grapes*, *wine-making grapes*, *raisin-making grapes*, *jam-and-jelly-making grapes*, and *juice-making grapes*. Table grapes do not produce good wine because of their low acidity, and wine-making grapes are usually too acid for eating out of hand.

Varieties

Here is a brief rundown of the varieties you are most likely to see displayed in your supermarket produce department.

Catawba: A deep maroon, medium-to-large, slightly oval *Vitis labrusca* with a sweet, foxy flavor. Like most of the *labruscae*, the Catawba is grown in New York State and ends up principally as a jam, jelly, or wine.

Concord: A *Vitis labrusca* of medium size and deep bluish-black skin, with a sweet, foxy taste, this is the popular jam, jelly, and wine grape. Not all produce markets carry fresh Concord grapes because they are poor shippers and have a short shelf life. But where they are sold, they are plentiful.

Delaware: *Vitis labrusca* is definitely one part of the ancestry of this hybrid, but no one knows for sure yet whether the other part of the union includes *Vitis vinifera* or another species. Whatever the case, this sweet, small-to-medium, red-skinned grape is better regarded than the Catawba, Concord, and Niagara grapes because of its comparatively less foxy taste. Much of the crop ends up in wine bottles.

Emperor: One frequently sees this thin-skinned, red *Vitis vinifera* in produce bins because it has a relatively long season. The flavor is not foxy.

Malaga: There are two types of the round, tough-skinned, mild *Vitis vinifera* Malagas, the red and the white. Reds are in season before whites.

Niagara: A greenish-white round-to-oval *Vitis labrusca* grape with a sweet, somewhat foxy taste.

Ribier: The mild flavor and the long season of this round, relatively large, tough-skinned, deep bluish-black *Vitis vinifera* have helped make it one of America's best selling grapes.

Thompson seedless: Of all the fresh grapes sold in America, this elongated, greenish-white *Vitis vinifera* hybrid leads in sales, and by a wide margin. It is medium-sized, thin-skinned, firm-fleshed (making it ideal for salads), and virtually seedless. Its drawback is its lackluster, mild flavor.

Tokay: The red, somewhat oval, thick-skinned, sparsely seeded, mild Tokay is a *Vitis vinifera*.

Other commercially sold table grapes include the *Almeria*, *Cardinal*, and *Olivette Blanche* (all three are *Vitis vinifera*), as well as the greenish-white *Scuppernong*—a native American, but a southern *muscadine* as opposed to a *labrusca*.

AVAILABILITY

While grapes are nowadays available the year round (due mainly to modern cold-storage techniques), grapes are at their best and cheapest from late summer through late fall. Many grape-lovers pinpoint mid-September through mid-October as the high season.

Buying Tips

Grapes should be firmly attached to their stems; it is a bad sign to see unattached grapes in the display box. The stems should be green and supple, not dried and brittle. The skin color of a red or black grape should be deep and full for its variety. Almost all green or white grapes should not be a pure green, but instead be greenish with some yellow pigmentation, a sign that the fruit was not picked too early. Bypass grapes with whitish discolorations beneath the skin. The grape should be well-shaped and plump, not soft, cracked, or shriveled. A good test (your greengrocer permitting) is to sample a grape from the cluster you intend to purchase. Wipe the sample grape on a tissue first; most grapes found in the market are covered with insecticides and germs. Avoid prepackaged grapes. Before weighing, do not hesitate to remove all obviously bad grapes from your cluster.

PREPARATION

Storage

If fresh and in good condition, a cluster of unwashed grapes will keep for several days in the refrigerator if kept in a plastic bag along with a paper towel to absorb moisture.

Preliminaries

Wash grapes only just before serving, as moisture hastens spoilage. Shake and pat dry. Or serve grapes unwashed and give each guest a small bowl of water for rinsing the berries. For the best flavor, serve grapes at just below room temperature, about 60°F. For salads, grapes like the Thompson seedless may be served whole, but most other varieties need pitting. Slice the grape in half and remove seeds with the tip of a knife. To peel a grape, start from the stem end. Hard-to-peel grapes are easier to skin if you submerge them in boiling water for 10 seconds, then immediately plunge them into ice water. For best results, grapes being used for jams and jellies should be slightly underripe.

GRAPEFRUIT

BACKGROUND

In the seventeenth century, a British sea captain named Shaddock brought a rather sour *pomelo*, a type of citrus fruit, from Oceania to the Americas. Soon this fruit was renamed Shaddock, and eventually it was bred into a sweeter, juicier, more delicate food. Because the yellow globes often grow in clusters, *Citrus paradisi* became known as the *grapefruit*. Today, this fruit is extensively grown in Texas, California, Florida, and Arizona, so the price in America is low compared to the price charged in most of Europe.

Varieties

Many grapefruit varieties exist: some are oval or slightly teardrop-shaped rather than round; some are sweeter than others; some have had most of their seeds eliminated by means of selective breeding. The main distinction, however, involves flesh color: one has yellowish-white pulp, the other pink pulp. The difference is not solely cosmetic, as the pink-fleshed grapefruit is richer in Vitamin A.

Grading

The USDA grades grapefruit. The best specimens are U.S. Fancy, second best are U.S. No. 1, and so on. But since this program is not mandatory, most grapefruits are sold ungraded.

AVAILABILITY

Fresh grapefruit are available all year, but they are at their best in winter and early spring.

Grapefruit juice is sold canned, bottled, and as a frozen concentrate. Grapefruit segments are sold canned, frozen, and in bottles; all lack the fresh flavor and texture of the freshly prepared fruit.

Buying Tips

Select a grapefruit that is heavy for its size, therefore juicy; firm yet springy when pressed with the palms of the hands; and symmetrical, not deformed. The skin should be thin, not thick and spongy; it should be smooth, not shriveled, which suggests tough internal flesh. The fruit should be free of bruises, cuts, decay, mold, and most discoloration. Two discolorations that should not overly alarm you are russeting and regreening. Russeting is frequently caused by the russet mite, and affects the outer surface of the rind, not the flesh. Regreening is an idiosyncracy of some citrus fruits; after fully ripening, part of the peel sometimes becomes green again.

PREPARATION

Storage

For maximum storage life and minimum loss of Vitamin C, place the whole grapefruit in a plastic storage bag in the refrigerator vegetable crisper. It should keep for 1 to 2 weeks. You can keep a grapefruit half for a day or two if you tightly seal the exposed flesh with a plastic wrap and refrigerate it.

Preliminaries

Always wash the fruit before using. The traditional way to enjoy a grapefruit is to cut it in half and eat the flesh with a spoon. To minimize squirting (which can be slapstick-funny or annoying, depending on which end of the squirt you are on), it helps to loosen the flesh from the rind with a specially designed grapefruit knife, the one with a curved, serrated blade. Next, remove excess membrane and seeds and—using a knife—separate the segments into bite-size portions. Many diners have learned from their parents the habit of sprinkling sugar on grapefruit, but nowadays, most grapefruit is naturally sweet enough, and such adulteration is not required.

Equivalents

A typical grapefruit weighs about a pound, and makes two first-course servings.

CLASSIC USES AND AFFINITIES

Fresh grapefruit—either as a garnish or as part of the sauce—marries well with poached fish. Grapefruit juice blends pleasingly with orange and pineapple juice. Grapefruit rinds make a good marmalade. Grapefruit segments make a tart addition to most fruit salads. A topping of brown sugar followed by a quick run under the broiler gives grapefruit an interestingly different flavor and texture.

GRAPE LEAF

BACKGROUND

Greek and Middle Eastern cooks use the leaves of grape vines—thus known either as *grape leaves* or *vine leaves*—to hold stuffings or in salads.

PREPARATION

For fresh grape leaves, select tender, small ones; parboil them in simmering water for 8 to 10 minutes or they will be too crisp to stuff. Canned vine leaves in brine are the most accessible to Americans. They are somewhat softer than fresh vine leaves, which is an advantage. The brine makes them salty, so briefly rinse and soak the leaves and decrease the amount of salt in your recipe. A teaspoonful or so of the selected filling, often rice-based, is placed in the center of the leaf; the sides are folded up around the filling, envelope-style, and the leaf is rolled into a neat cylindrical package. Pack the stuffed leaves in fairly tight layers in a flat-bottomed pot and simmer according to the recipe.

GREAT NORTHERN BEAN

BACKGROUND

The mellow but distinctive flavor of the Great Northern bean makes it one of the popular baking beans across the U.S. The Great Northern (so-called because of its Michigan home address) is a big bean, just under the marrow bean in size. It is round and flattish, somewhat like the lima bean in appearance, though not so curvaceous. The Great Northern bean is usually available in only one form: shelled and dried. For soaking, cooking, etc., see BEANS.

GREEN AND WAX BEANS

BACKGROUND

Tutankhamen ate *string beans*—at least Pliny says Egyptians of that period did. He may even have called them the Egyptian equivalent of "string bean" too, but today that designation is an anachronism. Modern botany has researched away the fibrous strings that used to run down the seam-side of the pod and beyond to trouble the slave-chefs of King Tut. Better to refer to this variety of *Phaseolus vulgaris* as *green bean* if it has an elongated green-colored pod, or *wax bean* if it has a yellowish or wax-colored one. If the pods are more slender, curved, and wrinkly than our sturdy-straight American type, call them *Italian*. If over a foot in length, they are probably of *Oriental* persuasion. *Haricots verts* are the classic French variety. "French" (or "Frenched") green beans in this country refer to the method of slicing the bean pod on the diagonal. There is also the SCARLET RUNNER BEAN. (For general information, see BEANS.)

AVAILABILITY

Fresh green beans are now available year round.

Buying Tips

When buying fresh green or wax beans, buy the youngest and smallest for their variety. Select bright-colored, unblemished pods. Crack one across—it should snap and spit juice. The pods should be flexible but feel crisp. If they're too stiff, the beans are too mature for best flavor and texture. Hand-pick your own if you can, and—for the sake of uniform cooking—try to choose beans of the same size.

Amounts

One pound of green beans should give you three average-sized portions.

PREPARATION

Storage

Green or wax beans can be stored in the refrigerator, well sealed in plastic wrap, for 3 to 5 days without injury, but after that time, expect deterioration.

Cooking

Cook gently, as with most fresh vegetables. Beans can be steamed or simmered for 15 to 20 minutes. If you simmer the beans without a lid, your cooked vegetables will have a more vivid green hue. On the other hand, if you use a lid, you preserve more of the vitamins. If in doubt as to your priorities, then compromise: partially cover the pot. Season them with onions, mushrooms, pork fat, savory, and dill, and with salt and pepper to taste.

CLASSIC USES AND AFFINITIES

Garnish with sliced almonds or chopped walnuts. Serve with dark-red roast meat or with pale-sauced dishes of poultry or fish. More simply, cut them into bite-size pieces, marinate in vinegar and oil, and eat them raw as an appetizer or side salad.

GRENADINE

BACKGROUND

A sweet red syrup that is used to flavor cocktails and desserts. Once grenadine was made exclusively from pomegranate juice (grown and processed on the Caribbean island of Grenada), but nowadays other fruits may also be employed.

GUAVA

BACKGROUND

A South American native, the *guava* is grown in our country in Florida, California, and Hawaii. Like so many of the lush warm-climate fruits, *Psidium* comes in different colors, shapes, and sizes in its different varieties. The typical guava is an oval about 2 inches in diameter, although it may be round or pear-shaped with twice the waist span. The thin skin can be yellow to red to purple, one Caribbean variety is black. The pulp is aromatic, sweet and somewhat acid; its hue ranges from creamy-white to yellow to yellowish-red to coral to red.

AVAILABILITY

In guava-growing country, the fruit is available year round. Elsewhere, shoppers must resort to the canned variety or to a good preserve to get to know the distinctive guava flavor.

PREPARATION

While good to eat raw, the guava is generally preferred cooked into a paste, jam, jelly, condiment, sauce, or syrup.

GUINEA FOWL

BACKGROUND

Though food scholars cannot be certain

that this delicious bird is indigenous to Guinea, it is named after that West African land. Allowing for a few exceptions, you can prepare Guinea fowl like CHICKEN. See that entry for relevant information. Please take note, however, of the following special tips and insights that pertain more to Guinea fowl than to chickens:

AVAILABILITY

The Guinea fowl reared and sold in America is from the domestic bird and will probably be frozen. Fresh-killed domestic Guinea fowl is superior—some butchers can special-order it for you.

Buying Tips

The meat of the Guinea fowl is drier than chicken and especially needs to be barded or frequently basted if cooked with dry heat. For the same reason, buy a Guinea hen rather than a male, because the former is fattier and therefore will cook more tenderly. The hen is also more naturally tender. Guinea hens range in size from 1 pound (the so-called Guinea squab) to 4 pounds. The younger the bird, the more tender it will be. Guinea hens over 2½ pounds should be cooked with slow, moist heat, such as stewing or braising.

Amounts

Figure on 1 pound to 1¼ pounds of whole Guinea hen per person. Serve a whole Guinea squab to each diner.

PREPARATION

Preliminaries

If you plan to roast or broil your Guinea fowl, bard it well to compensate for the dry flesh.

Cooking

Roast a room-temperature 1-pound Guinea squab in a preheated 400°F oven for 30 to 40 minutes (add 5 minutes if the bird is stuffed). The shorter period will give you a succulent bird, the longer time a drier one that is more in keeping with the American norm. Roast a 2 pound bird in a 350°F oven for 45 to 60 minutes (add 10 minutes if the bird is stuffed). Small Guinea hens can also be broiled, spit-roasted, barbecued, or sautéed.

H

HAM

BACKGROUND

The hind leg of the hog from the middle of the shank bone to the aitch (hip) bone is *ham*. Notwithstanding what some food writers would have us believe, ham does not necessarily mean the cured (and possibly smoked) meat, because the rear leg of a swine can be sold fresh and be rightfully called ham. (Often, for clarity, it's called *fresh*.) In this entry, however, we will restrict our discussion to the rear leg that is cured and possibly smoked; for details on fresh ham, see the PORK, FRESH entry. Picnic ham (not really a ham) is discussed under PORK, CURED.

Almost all ham—including country ham—processors use the preservative saltpeter to cure their hams. Potassium nitrate and sodium nitrate additives are being investigated by Federal agencies as possible carcinogens—but the consensus of authorities presently sees no danger if intake is held to a reasonable amount.

Ham Classifications

Hog's Biography: How the ham was cured, smoked, aged, stored, and cooked certainly helps determine how the meat will ultimately taste. Often overlooked, however, is the effect of the preslaughter variables such as *breed*, quality of *husbandry*, animal *age*, and type of *feed*. Corn and not hogwash is the principal feed for most of the common ham porkers. If the destiny of the hog's hind leg lies in the direction of a prized ham, the animal may be fed a diet that includes peanuts, acorns, chestnuts, hickory nuts, beechnuts, peaches, sugar beets, or even whey. Those special diets give the ham subtle but distinctive flavor undertones.

Length of Cut: Hams such as the Smithfield variety are long-cut—that is, they contain most of the hind leg from the shank through and including the pelvic bone. Noncountry hams are virtually always butchered into short-cuts which produce a squat ham, the type usually seen at the butcher's.

Bone Content: A full ham contains several bones: the *hip* (or *aitch*) bone, the *thigh* (femur) bone, and the *shank* (tibia and fibula) bones. To make carving easier, sometimes the aitch and shank bones are removed to produce what is called a *partially-boned* or *semi-boned* ham. Shankless hams have had only the shank bone removed. A ham labeled "boneless" is exactly that. Remember, bones give flavor when cooked and, therefore, you do sacrifice taste for ease of carving.

Country or "Urban": While virtually all ham connoisseurs would agree that *country hams* are clearly superior to *"urban"* (or *noncountry*) hams, the latter type outsells the first by a wide margin. The reason for the market success of *urban hams* are several: they cost less, are more accessible, are easier to prepare, and have a blander flavor that appeals to most Americans. In fact, most of these urban hams are so insipid that untrained palates would not be able to tell one from another if it were not for the brand name on the label. Few of the urban hams receive more than a brief stay (if any at all) in the smokehouse and are rarely (if ever) aged.

Country hams are extensively produced in Virginia, Georgia, Tennessee, Kentucky, and—to a lesser extent—in other states such as Missouri, Maryland, North Carolina, Pennsylvania, and New York, each region giving us a ham with distinctive characteristics. Yet, they generally share certain traits. First, they usually come from porkers that are fed special costlier-than-corn diets, possibly peanuts, hickory nuts, acorns, or a combination. These hams are typically dry-cured, slowly smoked and aged somewhere between 1/2 to 1 year, sometimes for 2 years. These prolonged smoking and aging processes shrink the meat (often up to 25 percent), which partly explains why country hams cost so much more than their urban cousins. Their flavor is rather salty (unlike urban hams, country hams need to be soaked before cooking), strong, and smoky. The texture is much dryer, firmer, and leaner than their urban counterparts. Flesh color ranges from reddish-brown to mahogany, while the meat's surface is often characteristically moldy. Most of the better country hams are sold uncooked, though a recent market trend is increasing the percentage of precooked hams.

The Smithfield Ham: By epicurean consensus, the Smithfield is the Tiffany of country hams. All Smithfields are processed in the Virginia town of that name, though the hogs can be raised in surrounding lands that extend beyond the Virginia border. After the razorback hogs are reared on a diet of nuts (acorn, hickory, etc.), they are generally allowed to free-forage for overlooked legumes on harvested peanut farms. Following slaughter of the pigs, a typical ham is dry-cured and stored at about 35° F for 4 to 6 weeks. The surface of the ham is then cleaned and rubbed with black pepper, then the ham is hickory-smoked for about a month. Aging averages 1 year, though some are aged 2 years (there is a point of diminishing returns: if aged too long, you may end up with an inedible petrified leg of pork). Ham is big business in Smithfield—on an average workday, several thousand hams come off the production lines. You can purchase Smithfield hams from gourmet butchers and food stores, or they can be ordered by mail.

Domestic or Imported: With the exception of premium country hams such as Smithfield, imported hams are generally more savory and superior in quality to our domestic product. Perhaps the most famous foreign ham is the *prosciutto* of Parma, which is dry-cured and air-dried but not smoked or cooked. It is cut into tissue-thin slices and eaten raw (no need to fret, Europe does not have the trichinosis problem). Other well-known to-be-eaten-raw Continental hams include Germany's *Westphalian* and France's *Bayonne*. Except for certain dishes like *saltimbocca*, these three hams are seldom used in cooking because heat tends to toughen their flesh. They are best served by themselves or with a compatible food such as a melon or a fig. Other major ham-producing countries include England (famed for its *York* ham), Poland, and Denmark. The last three countries export a great amount of canned ham to America, but it should be pointed out that, out of deference to the Yankee taste, those shipped hams tend to be much blander than the ham consumed in the Old World. (Note: As of this writing, the importation of raw hams from Italy is illegal. Many an epicure, as well as the Italian government, is trying to persuade the U.S. government to rescind this recently instituted embargo.)

Curing Process: Three basic curing methods exist: dry cure, sweet pickle cure, and injection cure.

Dry curing involves rubbing the surface of the meat with salt (normally seasoned), then usually storing the ham in a dry, cool (about 35° F) place until the natural juices within the flesh absorb the salt up to the point where the entire ham has become permeated with salt. Alternatively, the meat may be packed in salt in a barrel, a method that accounts for the meat processor being called a *packer*.

Sweet-pickle curing calls for the fresh ham to be completely immersed in a sweet (usually sugared) seasoned brine until the proper salinity is reached.

Injection cure is the modern and prevailing method. Essentially it is the old-fashioned sweet-pickle cure with an added twist: to speed up the pickling time, the brine is injected into the hams's interior with a series of hyperdermic needles. A variation is to pump the brine through the meat's blood vessels.

All three curing methods have the same purpose: to hinder bacterial decay. Before refrigeration became widespread, curing was a practical necessity. Today, curing is done mainly for reasons of flavor. Less salt is required, since the ham can be refrigerated after curing. Though the general curing processes are not a secret, the way the salt or brine is seasoned is—some manufacturers live in fear of industrial espionage and give their formulas top-secret security treatment. Popular ingredients include peppercorns and garlic as well as sugar and saltpeter. (This last substance is a nitrate chemical which helps preserve the flesh and gives the ham its characteristic rosy-pink color. It also raises the hackles of many consumerists and food scientists who believe saltpeter to be carcinogenic.)

Degree of Cure: Most hams sold in this country are *mild-cured*, out of deference to mass American taste. In contrast, country hams are geared for a smaller but more sophisticated market which appreciates a saltier and stronger-seasoned flavor.

Sweetness of Cure: *Sugar-cured* means that sugar was added to the curing mixture or solution. Even the best of processors add sugar, because it helps counteract the toughening effect of salt upon the flesh, but too much sugar can throw the flavor of a ham off-balance. Though the term "sugar-cured" can mean anything from a grain to a handful of sugar, you can usually assume you have a sweet-tasting ham when the processor puts the phrase on his label.

Smoking Process: After the ham is cured, it is ready for smoking. The primary purposes of smoking are to add desirable flavor and color. To some degree, smoking also helps preserve the meat, but not as significantly as salt curing. Not all hams are smoked, and of those that are, the intensity runs the gamut from barely noticeable (typical of mass-marketed canned hams) to strong and assertive (typical of hams like the famous Smithfield). Hot smoke can partially or totally cook the meat; for canned hams, the smoking technique must heat the interior flesh to at least 140° F, a temperature that assures that any disease-causing trichinae parasites are killed. The length of the smoking period varies from a matter of hours (for common hams) to a month or more for premium country hams. Type of wood is also important. It should be nonresinous wood such as hickory or maple; pine, for instance, would not be suitable. Logs or chips are preferred, though some cost-cutting firms use sawdust. Even worse, some processors use the liquid smoke-flavoring agent, but that method must be so stated (though in fine print) on the label whenever it is employed.

Length of Aging: Once cured and smoked, some hams are aged to further develop flavor. The aging period ranges from a few days to a year or more—the premium country hams get the longer treatment. The vast majority of canned hams are never aged—those 90-hour wonders go from the carcass to the brining step to the cans in that time or less. Labels seldom tell you if or for how long a ham has been aged—you must rely upon your knowledge of a particular brand and on your senses: the longer a ham is aged, the stronger flavored, saltier, and firmer-textured it will be. Long-aged hams can also be identified by their moldy exteriors.

Degree of Cooking: Hams can be fully cooked, partially cooked, or uncooked. Most canned hams are of the *precooked* variety and, technically, can be eaten cold straight out of the can, though you will improve their flavor by heating them to an internal temperature of about 130°F. Such hams carry descriptive wording such as "fully cooked," "ready-to-eat," "heat-and-serve," and "heat-and-eat." To be so classified, the ham must be heated by the processor to an internal temperature of at least 148°F. Since some processors heat their hams to 160°F or higher without specifying the fact on the label, there is no way for the consumer to know how well-done an untried brand may be—this does pose a problem to those of us who do not relish overcooked hams. The only solution is to learn the various brands by trial and error.

Partially cooked canned hams carry descriptive phrases such as "cook before eating." They have been heated to an internal temperature of at least 140°F, three degrees above the temperature needed to assure the killing of any trichinae parasites. For optimum flavor and texture, cook these hams to an internal temperature of 155°F to 160°F, never higher.

Uncooked hams have not necessarily been heated to at least 140°F, though many have been during the smoking process. It is best to be cautious and assume that live trichinae may exist; therefore you should not sample the ham until you have properly cooked it.

Noncanned hams generally but not always tell you on the label whether the ham is precooked, partially cooked, or uncooked. If it doesn't, ask the butcher. When in doubt, consider the ham uncooked and treat accordingly.

Water Content: Sometimes the processed ham weighs more than it did in its fresh state. The extra weight is due to water that the ham absorbed and retained from the brine. Those waterlogged hams must clearly state on the label words such as "water added" or "natural juices added." If the increase is more than 10 percent of the original weight, the ham must be labeled "imitation ham."

Storage Requirements: Almost all hams have to be refrigerated. Exceptions are certain whole uncooked country hams, such as the Smithfield. Other exceptions are the small sterilized canned hams which do not need refrigeration because the meat is already overcooked in the can. (It is best never to buy such a ham unless you happen not to have access to refrigeration.) Hams that require refrigeration virtually always say so on their label. If the label does not indicate whether or not the ham needs refrigeration, it is prudent to assume that it does.

Packaging: Most hams are canned. They are not, incidentally, cut to shape the can; that would be too wasteful. Instead, the hams are pressure-molded into the necessary shape.

Other hams are packaged in a vacuum-packed or ordinary plastic wrapping; still others come to the store in the netting in which they were smoked and aged. Certain uncooked country hams such as the Smithfield are shipped and sold in a close-fitting cloth bag. Butchers sometimes cut hams into more marketable sizes and repackage them in cellophane.

Canned Whole or Bits: Some canned hams are one single piece of meat. Others—especially the less expensive types and the smaller sizes—are made up of separate chunks and bits of meat that have been pressed together and solidified by means of gelatin. These chunks are usually scraps of better portions and, to make matters worse, some of them break off when sliced. A fine-print phrase such as "sectioned and formed" on the can helps prewarn the customer. Those mediocre hams that are molded in loaves and cylinders (the type of ham customarily sliced into squares or rounds and used in sandwiches) are virtually always of the "sectioned and formed" variety, but the customer is seldom so apprised.

Whole or Partial Cut: Hams are sold whole, in halves, and by the slice. Butchers almost always cut the slices from the center portion of the ham, producing the customary oval slab of meat containing a single section of the round leg bone. These *center-cut slices* or *steaks* range in thickness from 1/4 to 2 inches, though 1/2 to 1 inch is the norm. When the meat cutter divides the whole ham in two parts, he ends up with the *butt* (or upper) half and the *shank* (or lower) half. Should the butcher remove center-cut slices from a ham half, the label on the half should inform you of that action, and the price per pound should be less, because the partial half has a lower meat-to-bone ratio than does the whole (or full) half.

Weight: Canned hams are usually marketed in sizes of 1, 1½, 3, 5, and 8 pounds. The larger the can, generally the better the ham, because the large hams retain the cooking juices better. Also, the processor generally assigns the better cuts for the larger cans. And, as noted elsewhere, the smaller the can, the greater the chance that it contains "sectioned and formed" meat. Moreover, the larger canned hams cost less per pound. Of course, a super-sized ham is not a value for everyday needs if you are a single person or have a small family because, as everyone knows, such a ham may take all too many meals to finish.

Whole country hams vary in weight from 10 to 25 pounds. The heavier specimens come from older animals which yield less tender meat. The preferred weight for a ham like the Smithfield is about 10 to 13 pounds.

Quality: Some hams are merchandised as "premium." That term has no official meaning, and a processor could call any of his hams "premium." The more reputable firms, however, use the word only for hams of above-average quality.

Name Brands: Some companies process hams of different quality grades and—in order not to confuse the public—market them in the same stores under different brand names. Some producers also sell the same-quality hams under different names—their own, and supermarket private-label brand.

AVAILABILITY

All hams are available throughout the year.

Buying Tips

Most of the buying tips have been discussed in the various Classifications sections. Here are a few other guidelines worth knowing: If you are purchasing a noncanned ham, whether urban or country, select one that is plump and firm to the touch. Hams with stubby- as opposed to long-shank ends will offer you a higher proportion of meat to bone. Buying a whole ham is not unlike buying the proverbial pig in the poke—you are seldom given a chance to see what is inside the bag, wrapping, or can. If you have that chance—as is usually the case when you are buying a portion of a whole ham—you should look for a fine-grained flesh that has a fresh rosy-pink glow. Do not be alarmed by the rainbow-hued sheen on the exposed sliced meat, as this iridescent phenomenon is seldom caused by chemical additives. Rather, it is almost always the result of natural light refraction of the fat molecules interspersed within the flesh. Well-aged premium country hams usually have rather moldy surfaces. Once you scrub it off, no harm will befall you. Each year there must be hundreds of people who receive a mail-order gift of a Smithfield-type ham only to throw it away because they think it is spoiled—and then, out of fear of hurting the giver's feelings, dash off a thank-you note extolling the ham's virtues. Moldy is okay, but that does not mean that excessively moldy is, so do not be taken in by an avaricious butcher who—out of desire to sell his slow-moving stock—tries to convince you that a ham whose mold has badly permeated the cloth sack is still good. Chances are it is not.

Amounts

For most adult appetites, you can estimate 1/4 to 1/3 pound of boneless ham or 1/2 pound of bone-in ham per person. Most whole bone-in hams weigh 10 to 18 pounds, while full halves, either butt or shank, weigh 5 to 9 pounds each. A boneless whole averages 8 to 14 pounds, its halves 4 to 7 pounds. Most canned hams weigh from 1 to 8 pounds.

PREPARATION

Storage

A recently canned, unopened, sterilized ham has a nonrefrigerated lifespan of approximately one year. A "keep refrigerated" canned ham should be consumed within several months. If in doubt whether the ham is sterilized, play safe and assume that it needs refrigeration. An uncooked country ham will keep indefinitely in a dry, cool place—but if you keep it too long, it will shrink via evaporation into a mummified hind leg of pork, ill-suited but for the toughest of jaws. Once the uncooked country ham has been cut into, store it as leftover ham. Ham halves and slices brought home from the store have exposed flesh, so they should be wrapped in plastic wrap, refrigerated, and used within approximately a week. Leftover ham should be used within several days or at least completely reheated every two days or so. Because of its relatively high salt content, ham fares poorly in the freezer.

Preliminaries

Country Hams: First, use hot running water and a stiff brush to scrub off as much of the surface mold and black pepper as possible. Then submerge the ham in cold water to cover and soak for 12 to 24 hours, using the longest time for hams aged for over a year (some hams are dated). Also use the longest time if you want to minimize the salt flavor. Changing the water once or twice also helps reduce salinity. If you want to serve your hanging ham to unexpected weekend guests, you can shorten the soaking period by parboiling the ham in simmering water for 1 hour, but this shortcut will produce inferior results. After soaking (or parboiling), rinse the ham well in hot running water, scrubbing away any lingering mold or black pepper. If your cooking pot is too small for your leg of ham, you will have to saw off a portion of the shank, cooking that piece separately or perhaps reserving it to flavor stews and soups.

Urban Hams: Urban hams seldom need more advance preparation than removing them from their can or plastic wrap.

Cooking

Country Hams: After the ham is soaked, scrubbed, and (if necessary) truncated, immerse it in cold water to cover and bring to a simmer and skim as necessary. If the meat is placed on a trivet, all the better because this implement keeps the ham from touching the pot's hot bottom. If no cooking instructions are given on the package, simmer the whole ham skin-side down for 20 minutes plus 15 to 20 minutes per pound or until the bones protrude from the flesh about 1½ to 2 inches. Check at regular intervals to make sure the water continues to completely cover the ham. If the ham is boned (not often done with country hams) you will have to allow an additional 2 or 3 minutes per pound to the time. Turn off the heat, and when the ham is cool enough to handle, remove it from the water. Now is the time to remove the skin. With the aid of your fingers and a paring knife, the skin should easily peel away from the fat and flesh. Trim the excess fat to a thickness of about 1/2 inch. At this point, your ham is ready for one of several options. For example, you can let it cool for an hour or two in its cooking liquid, then serve it at room temperature; or you can brown or glaze it in the oven (described below).

Urban Hams: Follow package instructions. If there are none, place the room-temperature ham on a rack in a shallow roasting pan in a preheated 325°F oven. The ham should be fatty-side up if whole, cut-side down if a half. It will be properly baked when the meat thermometer registers 155°F, which should take about 15 minutes (for large sizes) to 30 minutes (for small sizes) per pound. Subtract 2 or 3 minutes per pound for bone-in hams. If the fat covering is thin or nonexistent, baste the meat every 20 minutes. See instructions below if you wish to brown and glaze the ham. If not, remove it from the oven and, for serving at room temperature, let it cool. If you wish to serve the ham warm, let it rest with a loose covering of foil for 15 to 20 minutes. This allows its internal juices to redistribute and resettle, and makes carving easier.

Some urban hams are completely precooked. Even if you plan to eat these hams cold, their flavor and attractiveness are markedly improved if you place the room-temperature meat on a rack in a shallow roasting pan in a 325°F oven until the meat thermometer reaches 130°F, which should take approximately 1/2 to 11/2 hours, depending on the size. If whole, place fatty-side up; if half of a ham, place it cut-side down. Bone-in hams will heat slightly faster.

Ham Slices: Trim the surrounding fat to a thickness of 1/4 inch, then slash the fat at 1-inch intervals to prevent curling. Bring the meat to or near room temperature before cooking. Season to taste before or, preferably, after cooking.

Ham slices and steaks less than 3/4 inch thick are best pan-broiled. Using moderate heat, and turning the meat only once, it will take a total cooking time of about 5 minutes for a 1/4-inch slice, 8 minutes for a 1/2-inch slice, and 10 minutes for a 3/4-inch slice of cook-before-eating ham. Reduce the time by about half for fully cooked urban ham and precooked country ham.

Ham slices and steaks between 3/4 and 11/2 inches thick are best broiled. Adjust the broiler tray to a distance of 4 inches under a moderate flame. Allow a total broiling time of 8 minutes for a 3/4-inch- and 16 minutes for a 11/2-inch-thick slice of cook-before-eating ham. Fully cooked urban hams and precooked country hams take half that time. Turn the meat once.

Ham slices and steaks over 11/2 inches thick are best baked in a preheated 325° F oven. If your ham is one of the cook-before-eating variety, figure on about 1 hour for a 11/2-inch-thick slice, a little longer for a 2-inch-thick piece. Reduce the time roughly one-third for the fully cooked or precooked ham. Unless you have glazed the top surface, baste it once or twice, or cook the slice in a shallow layer of liquid such as diluted white wine or orange juice.

Browning and Glazing

These techniques are primarily cosmetic in purpose: they make a succulent ham all the more tempting as it sits on the table. Whatever the type of ham, you should skin it if it has a rind. This chore is easiest when the ham has just come from the oven or pot. If your unskinned ham is cooked but at room temperature, you may wish to pop it into a 300°F oven for about 15 minutes to make it easier to peel.

To *brown* the ham, simply place it on a rack in a shallow roasting pan in a preheated 400°F oven for 15 to 20 minutes. If the ham is already in the oven, increase the temperature to 400°F for about 15 to 20 minutes before it would normally be finished. Of course, you would not brown the ham if you plan to glaze it.

Scoring is often done before a glaze is applied. The most popular design is diamond-shaped. Use a sharp knife to make crossing lines 1 inch apart in the top fatty surface of the ham, making incisions through the fat and just into the flesh. It has become almost a cliché to stud the center of each diamond area with a clove. If you choose to do so, wait until after the ham is out of the oven, otherwise the aromatic power of cloves is likely to dominate the flavor of the ham. And, before serving each slice, remove the cloves out of deference to your favorite aunt's remaining teeth. An alternative to scoring and clove-studding the ham is to cover the top surface with thin slices of orange or pineapple.

Glazing involves spreading paste on top of the ham, then placing the meat on a rack in a shallow roasting pan in a preheated 400°F oven for about 15 to 20 minutes. A standard glaze is made of about 3/4 cup of brown sugar blended with 1 teaspoon of dry mustard and moistened into a paste with a fruit juice (orange, pineapple, apple, etc.) or an alcoholic beverage (Madeira, hard cider, rum, etc). Molasses or honey can be substituted for the sugar, but in this case, a substance such as breadcrumbs, ground nuts, an apricot puree, or a fruit preserve such as marmalade or jam should be added to thicken the paste. Spices such as cinnamon and fresh ginger can give the paste extra character. The glaze will adhere better and glisten if it is applied to the fatty side of the ham.

If you want to score or glaze a ham that is baking in your oven, remove it 20 minutes before it would normally be done and turn up the oven heat to 400°F. After the ham is cool enough to handle, skin it (if necessary), score it, and apply the glaze, then put it back into the oven for 15 minutes.

Serving

Premium country ham as well as the imported Parma-type hams should be sliced as thin as possible. Purists insist such hams are best enjoyed at room temperature. Knowledgeable nonpurists add "warm" to the okay temperature list, but definitely rule out chilled or piping hot. Conventional urban hams should be sliced reasonably thin—the exception, of course, being ham steak.

Leftovers

Few foods lend themselves as well to leftover cookery as does a whole ham. Not only is it large enough to usually require a series of meals, it can be used in a wide variety of food prepartions including soups (split pea, lentil, etc.), stews, casseroles (including the famed *cassoulet*), bean pots, sandwiches, appetizers, egg concoctions (omelets, eggs Benedict, etc.), croquettes, salads—let your imagination run wild. Serve it with pasta as in *ham Tetrazzini*, mix it with potatoes to make ham hash, cream it, pot it; the list is endless.

HEAD

BACKGROUND

From a culinary standpoint, the younger the animal, the better the head, be it that of a calf, sheep, or pig. The closest most Americans come to eating an animal's head is head cheese. Even then, most Americans do not know the source of that "cheese." In the Middle East and southern Italy, the sheep's head is held in high regard and is often roasted, sometimes simmered. England has its wild boar's head specialty at Christmas. A number of edibles come from the head: cheeks (they can be delicious), tongues, brains, and ears. Some people even love the eyeballs and snouts.

PREPARATION

The simplest way to cook an animal's head is to leave it on and barbecue or roast the entire animal. It is necessary to wrap the ears in aluminum foil to keep them from charring. Also, remove the eyes as they cook too quickly, and stuff the mouth with an aluminum foil ball to keep it from sealing shut, thus hindering the flow of heat from reaching the inside of the head. If the head is separated from the body, you can simmer the cleaned and parboiled head for 1½ to 2 hours, depending on size.

HEART

BACKGROUND

The leader of ancient hunting parties often demanded and ate the prey's heart, believing it to be a source of strength and courage. Today, the animal's heart as meat is not held in much esteem by most contemporary Americans. Pity; the heart is rich in flavor, texture, and nutrients such as protein, iron, riboflavin, and niacin. As a bonus, the heart—because of its widespread unpopularity—sells for a bargain.

AVAILABILITY

You can enjoy the heart of any type of animal, though it is beef and veal (technically "calf's") hearts that are commonly available. Between the two, the calf's is more tender and desirable and therefore carries a higher per pound price tag. You may be able to find delicacies such as the heart of the very young sheep (baby lamb), pig (piglet), and goat (kid) in an ethnic neighborhood market. For a discussion of poultry hearts, see CHICKEN GIBLETS AND VARIETY MEATS.

Buying Tips

Heart must be purchased as fresh as possible. Look for those that are plump and bright red. Avoid any that have taken on a brownish or grayish hue and that lack a clean, fresh scent. The younger the animal, the tenderer the meat will be.

PREPARATION

Storage

You can refrigerate a fresh heart, if necessary, for a day or possibly two in the refrigerator if you wrap it loosely (this allows for air circulation, which helps keep the heart surface dry, thereby slowing down bacterial growth). Surplus hearts may be stored (with some loss in flavor and texture) for a couple of weeks in the frozen food compartment or for several months in a 0°F freezer—but when freezing, wrap the meat tightly with suitable moisture-proof paper.

Preliminaries

Gently wash each heart under cold running tap water. Pat dry. With a small, sharp knife, trim the exterior and cavity of as much of the vessels, tubes, connective tissue, membrane, and fat as is possible. Beef heart will have the highest ratio of waste to lean meat. At this stage, some cooks marinate the heart, but this step is not necessary if you cook the heart properly. Leave the heart in one piece if you plan to stuff it. Otherwise, slice it lengthwise into strips ⅓ to ½ inch thick. For diced or small-cubed meat, cut those strips crosswise across the grain.

Cooking

As one would expect from a well-worked muscle that contracts and expands in split-seconds, the heart is not naturally tender, despite what romantic poets would have us believe. Semi-tender, however, are the hearts of the extremely young animals such as milk-fed calves, lambs, piglets, and kids. These may be cooked with dry heat such as sautéing, broiling, or roasting provided that they are well basted or barded and are not cooked beyond medium rare (some internal pinkness must remain). All other hearts must be cooked with slow, moist heat, as in braising or simmering. For an average-sized (4½ pound) beef heart, cook it for 3 to 4 hours if whole or 1½ hours if diced. For a whole, average-sized (½ to 1 pound) veal heart, estimate 1½ to 2½ hours, depending on size. The roasting times for the heart of a young animal are 30 to 60 minutes (depending on size) in a preheated 325° F oven.

Equivalents

Figure on ¼ to ⅓ pound per person, depending on appetites. Ideal for individual portions are the hearts of the young lamb (about ¼ pound) and of the young pig (about ⅓ pound).

CLASSIC USES AND AFFINITIES

Many cooks around the world love to stuff hearts for good reason: the stuffing keeps the heart plump, adds an exciting contrast in flavor and texture, and—for the budget-minded—stretches the already inexpensive meat even further. If the heart is stuffed, add 10 percent to the cooking times suggested in the cooking section. Heart is also frequently diced and added to stews and casseroles, either by itself or in combination with other meats. Try adding heart to your next ground-meat preparation—you will discover a new, pleasing flavor. Small hearts are sometimes pickled.

HERBS AND SPICES

BACKGROUND

Herbs and spices are both seasonings, but they do differ in definition. An *herb* is usually a leaf of a plant, and sometimes the stem of a nonwoody plant. A *spice* is usually the seeds, bark, roots, or other parts of a plant. Herbs generally come from temperate climates, spices from tropical ones.

Even before the time of Christ, spices were transported halfway around the world from the tropical rain forests of Southeast Asia to the snow-covered European plains. Traders were willing to risk purse and life carrying the spices over ancient caravan routes because Europeans were willing to pay exorbitant prices. The need existed because the spices slowed down and masked food spoilage in the era when there was no refrigeration. Another reason for the insatiable desire for spices was that Europeans depended on local supplies of food, and few could be stored during the long winters; this meant the cook had a limited variety of food staples. Flavored with spices, those staples became less repetitious and more exciting.

In an attempt to break the Eastern spice-trading monopoly, European explorers set out to find a direct sea route to the Spice Islands of Indonesia. One of these explorers—Christopher Columbus—decided to reach the faraway goal by sailing westward because he believed that the world was round. Columbus did not find the fabled Spice Islands, but he inadvertently did find something of greater long-term commercial importance: the New World. If spices were not so prized, the post-Viking discovery of the Americas might have been delayed for nearly a half century, perhaps longer.

People living in the tropics require more spice in their diets than Medieval Europeans did. Their spice need stems from at least four basic factors: Without refrigeration, preservatives are even more important in a hot climate. Except for the fruits, the staple foods (including fish) of tropical areas tend to be blander than those harvested in cooler climates—and, thus, spices are especially necessary to perk up the dishes. Hot, sultry weather is an appetite depressant. Spices pique the tastebuds and encourage eating. When consumed, some spices—such as Indian ginger or American chili peppers—make the body sweat. When the perspiration evaporates, it cools the body. Fortunately, being close to the sources, the tropical inhabitants could get their spices with little effort or money.

Europeans had access to inexpensive herbs even when spices were rare and costly. Herbs were used, sometimes effectively, for healing. In an age when few vegetables were available, herbs were eaten by the bunch, providing significant amounts of vitamins. (Half a teaspoon of an herb in a twentieth-century dish for four is not a meaningful source of nutrition.) The practice of strewing sweet-smelling herbs on floors made life much more pleasant when toilets were exceedingly scarce and washing of clothes and bodies infrequent.

Today spices and herbs are less vital in our Western diet, but more often used. In these sanitary days, food is preserved in cans and refrigerators; the variety of available food has increased; diseases are treated with drugs, not herb teas. But sophistication about food has increased. People know more about other cuisines. Imported ingredients are available quickly via airplane rather than after a months-long voyage in a sailing ship. Scientific farming has made food more plentiful, but less flavorful. A bland frozen chicken takes on some life when judicious amounts of seasonings are added. Twentieth-century cooks can do without spices, but they would hate to have to do so; so much can be gained by using herbs and spices wisely.

Varieties

For discussion on individual spices, see these entries.

Allspice
Angelica
Anise
Asafetida
Basil
Bay Leaf
Borage
Bouquet Garni
Capers
Caraway
Cardamom
Celery Seed
Chamomile
Chervil
Chili Powder
Chives
Cinnamon and Cassia
Cloves
Coriander
Costmary
Cumin
Curry
Dill
Dittany
Fennel
Fenugreek
Filé Powder
Fines Herbes
Five-Spice Powder
Garam Masala
Ginger
Horseradish
Hyssop
Juniper Berries
Lavender
Leek
Lemon Balm
Lemon Grass
Lemon Verbena
Lovage
Mace
Marjoram
Mint
Mustard
Nutmeg
Oregano
Parsley
Pepper, Chili
Pepper, Sweet
Peppercorns
Pickling Spice
Poppy Seeds
Poultry Seasoning
Quatre Épices
Rose Hips

Rosemary
Rose Petals and Water
Rue
Saffron
Sage
Salt
Sassafras
Savory
Sesame Seed
Shallots
Sorrel
Star Anise
Tamarind
Tansy
Thyme
Turmeric
Vanilla
Watercress
Woodruff

AVAILABILITY

Parsley is nearly always available fresh. Sometimes you can also find other fresh herbs, such as dill, mint, basil, coriander (also called Chinese parsley or cilantro), thyme, and tarragon. Dried herbs and spices are available year round.

Buying Tips

Fresh Herbs: Look for vivid green specimens. Bypass herbs if their leaves or stalks are beginning to wilt or brown. Another negative sign is a sour scent—always give fresh herbs the sniff test before opening your wallet.

Dried Herbs and Spices: High quality and freshness are the keys to herb and spice selection. You want the best, freshest spices, not fancy containers or gourmet hoopla at inflated prices. Supermarket tins or bottles of spices and herbs are seldom either very good or very bad; they probably will not be adulterated or very low in quality, but they will not be the finest either. The tins are not best for preserving freshness. But tins and particularly bottles are superior to cellophane packages, because the latter type allows too much air to reach the ingredients.

Some dealers sell their goods out of large glass jars. Be sure the contents are fresh. Just as important, remember that the less desirable pieces and stems gradually sift through the lighter whole leaves to the bottom. Therefore, each time the merchant removes some of the contents, what is left in the jar tends to be slightly lower in overall quality. A good spice dealer with a quick turnover is the best source for herbs and spices. Rapid turnover is necessary to insure freshness; you do not want to be on the receiving end of a bargain the dealer got several years ago. Mail-order operations provide more variety than most people can find near home. On the other hand, you can't inspect the product before buying.

Whole spices and herb leaves stay fresher much longer than their crushed, ground, or powdered counterparts. However, some hard spices, such as cinnamon, require more trouble and time to grind than most home cooks are willing to expend. Buy small quantities. The bulk price may be much lower, but it is no saving to buy 4 ounces and throw out 3½ of them.

PREPARATION

Storage

Storage—Fresh Herbs: If you expect to use all your fresh herb supply in a day or two, simply seal it in a plastic bag and refrigerate. If, however, you use herbs at a slower speed, use a canning jar. It allows you to keep most herbs up to 7 days and parsley up to 14 days. You will need a large glass canning jar, the one that comes with a metal clamp and a rubber ring. The 1.5 liter size is ideal. First, put 1 inch of fresh cold tap water in the jar. Place the washed bouquet of herbs stem-side down into water as you would flowers, but with the entire bouquet inside the jar. If it is too tall, trim the stems. Close the jar (it will have an airtight seal) and place it upright in the refrigerator. You will need to change the water every two or three days. A variation of the above method is to place the bouquet in a regular glass jar with an inch of water, then cover the bouquet with a plastic storage bag, sealing it to the jar with a rubber band. This method is less effective than the other, since it's less airtight; also the contraption is more likely to tip over in your refrigerator.

Dried Herbs and Spices: Heat, moisture, air, foreign odors, and light are enemies of dried herbs and spices. Store your seasonings away from the stove, radiator, or other heat source. Keep the seasonings in airtight containers; the zipper-lock plastic bags and most cork-topped jars are not sufficiently hermetic. Be sure the jar is completely dry before adding the seasonings. Try to minimize *ullage*, the air space between the contents and the lid. Before adding an herb or spice to a new container, sniff the container for residual odors as they can alter the fragrance of the seasoning. Glass is an excellent material for minimum odor retention. Keep herbs and spices out of direct sunlight. Storing them in clear glass bottles in normal room light will not drastically affect the quality over a short period of time, and the advantage of being able to see the contents usually makes this type of storage a positive trade-off. However, if you plan to store a particular herb or spice for a lengthy period, you are advised to store the clear glass bottle in a closed cabinet or to transfer the contents to an opaque container.

Basic Cooking

Whole spices can be ground in an electric blender or a grinder, but lingering odor from the machine may transfer itself to the seasonings, and vice versa. The most efficient way to grind a small amount of whole spices is to use a mortar and pestle (marble and porcelain ones are less likely to retain odor than wooden ones). If a coarsely cracked texture is desired, the spices can be wrapped in cloth and whacked with a hammer or the flat side of a cleaver. Fresh herbs are usually chopped on a cutting board with a knife point held steady, the blade going up and down, and the herbs being pushed under the blade from one side. You can also cut the fresh herbs with kitchen scissors. Or, use your blender or food processor if the more difficult clean-up and the less uniform pieces do not bother you.

Tying whole spices or herbs into a bit of cheesecloth or muslin allows the cook to remove the spices when maximum flavor is obtained, and before a diner breaks a tooth on a clove. Or, if you are making a liquid preparation such as a sauce, you can remove the hard whole spices by using a sieve.

Most dried herbs (if still at their peak) are twice or three times as strong as an equal volume of minced fresh herbs, so a teaspoon of dried herb replaces up to a tablespoon of fresh herb. Bay leaf is an exception: fresh bay leaf is twice as strong as dried. The flavor of herbs comes from volatile aromatic oils; to liberate these oils, crush the dried leaves in your palm with your free thumb—or crush them between finger and thumb just before adding the dried herbs to food. Dried herbs can be added directly to moist dishes such as soups or stews; before adding them to low-moisture dishes, steep them in a little hot water for a minute or so. Once again, the purpose is to impart the essential oil to the dish.

If you're unfamiliar with a new spice or herb, begin adding a conservative amount. Wait a few minutes, then test. You can always add more; you cannot subtract. Most spices become very bitter if subjected to very hot temperatures for more than a brief period. Remember this rule when using cooking methods such as sautéing or stir-frying.

HOMINY

BACKGROUND

An American Indian creation, *hominy* is hulled, embryoless, dried corn kernels. Whole hominy arrives in the marketplace either in the dried form (which needs to be reconstituted overnight with water, then cooked in a liquid such as water or milk for hours) or in cans (which needs only to be heated through, as it has already been reconstituted and cooked). If the dry hominy kernels are broken into large pieces, you have *samp*. If the kernels are further ground into a coarse, medium, or fine grind, you have *hominy grits* (or *grits*, for short). Grits are a star starch staple at breakfast (and, sometimes, lunch and dinner) tables in the American South.

PREPARATION

One simple way to cook hominy grits is to slowly pour them into lightly salted, boiling water (three to four times the volume of the grits), then cover and simmer for 45 to 60 minutes, depending on the coarseness of the grind. Stir occasionally. When they're cooked and the water is absorbed, serve the grits topped with butter or gravy.

HONEY

BACKGROUND

Honey was the world's leading sweetener until a little over two centuries ago, when it became technologically possible to produce crystallized sugar from sugar cane and sugar beets on a mass-production level. Even though honey is much more costly than sugar today, it is still popular because of its distinct and agreeable taste. Honey has many culinary uses, including serving as bread spread, as a sweetening and browning agent for baked goods, as the base of the alcoholic beverage mead, and as a food preservative. Honey is a preservative because it contains a special enzyme that helps counteract mold—which is why honey, if properly stored, does not require refrigeration.

Honey has two chief nutritional talents: it provides quick energy to the body and it is very easy to digest. However, despite claims by some food faddists, honey should not be considered a health food because the amount of vitamins and minerals it offers is scant compared to the plethora of empty sugar calories it contains.

Varieties

What determines the color, flavor and scent of a particular honey is not the bees that made it but rather the source of the nectar, the flower. That is why certain honeys, such as that produced by killer bees, are gimmicks. Clover is the most prevalent flower from which honey is made, though scores of other types of honey are commercially sold, including sage, buckwheat, tupelo, orange blossom, thyme, alfalfa, and heather. Some honey companies blend the various types to produce a consistent proprietary characteristic or to save money. Some companies also stretch their blends with nonhoney sweeteners, then pasteurize the product to extend its shelf life.

Classifications

Honey is also classified by its physical form. *Comb honey* is honey as the bees made it. It contains the honey and the chewy honeycomb framework—both parts are edible, and many purists insist on enjoying their honey in this form.

Comb honey is sold whole or broken into smaller-sized sections. *Liquid honey* is extracted from the honeycombs. This is the type we see in glass jars dominating supermarket shelves. From a grocery store's point of view, liquid honey is preferable because it has a much longer storage life than does comb honey. *Chunk honey*, sold in jars, contains honeycomb pieces suspended in liquid honey. It is sort of a compromise between comb honey and liquid honey. New-fangled honeys crop up in the marketplace regularly: *honey spreads*, *honey toppings*, *honey butters*, to name three.

PREPARATION

Storage

Honey is best stored in a tightly closed jar in a cool, dry, dark spot. Unless the jar is tightly closed, the honey may ferment or develop a moldy crust. When honey is refrigerated, it crystallizes and thickens into a difficult-to-spread mass. If your cupboards are too warm and long-term storage is required, do refrigerate your honey. Each time you are ready to use it, place it in a pan of hot tap water and the honey will thin in a short time.

Cooking

Honey blends with other cooking ingredients more easily if it is first warmed. Place the jar in a pot of warm water for about 10 to 15 minutes. When substituting honey for sugar in a recipe, take into account that honey is usually slightly sweeter than sugar on a volume basis, so reduce the measurement called for by about 10 percent. Also take into consideration the honey's moisture content. Reduce the amount of liquid called for in the recipe by one-fourth the volume of the honey you use. Honey contains acid. If the recipe calls for a specific amount of baking powder and you are extemporaneously adding honey, slightly reduce the quantity of baking powder and replace that amount with baking soda. In most cases, honey should not be cooked at a very high heat, as it tends to caramelize and, as a consequence, will give your preparation a darker hue and a different flavor than you intended.

HONEYDEW

BACKGROUND

The whitish mint-colored flesh of the oval-shaped, 4- to 9-pound *honeydew* (*Cucumis melo*) is visually most inviting. So is its sweet scent and flavor. The same may be said for the honeydew's smaller brother, the round *honeyball*. The honeydew is the same family as the cantaloupe.

AVAILABILITY

Honeydews can be purchased in some big-city markets the year round, but the best are sold from July through October. August and September are the best two months of all.

Buying Tips

Look for rinds with creamy or yellowish-white pigment, a sign that the honeydew has ripened. A chalky or greenish-white honeydew should be left at the market—it will probably never ripen into a luscious fruit. Caress the melon slowly with your hand. If the honeydew is mature, you should be able to feel a minutely wrinkled texture. A smooth texture suggests that the melon was picked prematurely. Unlike cantaloupe, a mature honeydew must be cut from the stem, so do not look for a smooth crater at the stem end. Not only should all honeydews be heavy for the size (an indication of maximum juiciness), they should be heavy, period.

Taste tests have shown that large honeydews are usually better than the 4- or 5-pound "midgets." Sniff the fruit. It should have a faint, agreeable fragrance. Gently push the blossom end (opposite the stem end) with your thumb—the rind should yield. Avoid honeydews with asymmetrical shapes and those with mold, blemishes, soft spots (a sign of internal decay), or shriveled skins.

PREPARATION

Storage

A honeydew has much better storage capabilities than its market rival the cantaloupe, but is still perishable. Store it in a closed, pierced paper bag until the previously mentioned indicators tell you that the fruit is ripe. Once it's ripe, eat it within the day if you can. If you must wait, a whole fruit can be stored in the refrigerator for 4 to 6 days. Tightly cover a refrigerated honeydew with plastic wrap as it will absorb and create refrigerator odors. This is especially true with cut melons. Do not de-seed a cut portion of a melon until you are ready to eat it, as the seeds help the flesh retain its moisture. If you prefer your honeydew chilled, do not serve it so cold that its beautiful fragrance and flavor are not released.

Preliminaries

With a sharp knife, slice the honeydew lengthwise and scoop out the seeds with a spoon. You can cut the halves into lengthwise wedges. Then, cut the flesh from the rind by making a curved cut parallel to the rind, being careful not to cut into the bitter peel. Next, make vertical cuts to produce bite-size pieces that can be eaten with a fork or toothpick. Alternatively, you can use a melon-cutter to scoop melon balls out of the halved melon for a compote. Mixing honeydew and cantaloupe melon balls makes an attractive color contrast.

HORSEMEAT

BACKGROUND

While most Americans cringe at the thought of eating *horsemeat*, the French have numerous *boucheries hippophagiques*, butcher shops specializing in the flesh of the equine animal. Their customers swear that horse meat is superior in flavor and succulence to beef. We do not go that far but would agree that it is the equal of beef.

AVAILABILITY

You can purchase horsemeat in some areas of the United States, but it must by law be clearly merchandised as horsemeat.

PREPARATION

Cook the horsemeat like BEEF, taking into consideration such factors as cut and age. Because horsemeat is leaner than beef, it will require extra larding, barding, or basting.

HORSERADISH

BACKGROUND

Eastern Europe is the original home of *Armoracia rusticana*, but horseradish is now very popular in Germany as well as in France, England and the United States.

AVAILABILITY

Fresh horseradish is most likely to be found in supermarket produce departments just before Passover, the Jewish festival commemorating the Exodus. Bottled horseradish sauce, whether natural white or dyed purple with beet juice, is marketed year around, but it is a second-rate substitute for a freshly made sauce. Dried horseradish is a third-rate supernumerary for the freshly-grated type.

PREPARATION

The young leaves can be chopped up for salads, but it is the grated root of horseradish that is the star attraction. Grated horseradish root should not be cooked as its pungency disappears with heat. Any sauce that features the grated root will be noticeably less tangy and tasty if allowed to stand. Your only defense is to grate fresh horseradish just before serving.

CLASSIC USES AND AFFINITIES

Grated horseradish root is eaten by itself as a condiment or combined with other ingredients in numerous sauces. Horseradish added to tomato sauce makes a cocktail sauce for seafood. Whipped cream, *béchamel* sauce or cream is mixed with horseradish to make sauces for boiled tongue, roast beef or lamb.

HYSSOP

BACKGROUND

The shrub *Hyssopus officinalis* is *not* the hyssop mentioned in the Bible. With that out of the way, it remains to say that *hyssop* leaves are bitter, with a taste reminiscent of mint and camphor. According to ancient medical lore, they are beneficial to the complexion and help cure chest ailments. They can be cooked with fatty fish or meats; they combine well with cranberries; and they can be used in stuffings, marinades for meat, potato salad, and lentil dishes. The leaves can be used raw in green or fruit salads or cooked into fruit pies. (See HERBS AND SPICES for information on buying, storing, cooking, etc.)

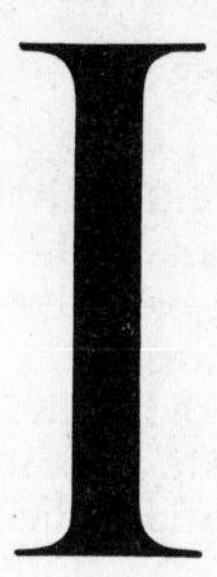

ICE

BACKGROUND

The basic forms of ice are block, cube, shaved, and crushed. The new food processors are particularly adept in crushing ice. The term "ice" also refers to various types of sweetened products, icings, etc.

AVAILABILITY

The cold water tap, ice tray, and refrigerator have pretty much put the ice man out of business. Ice cubes are sold in plastic bags in grocery stores—usually for a profiteer's price. But if you are having a large last-minute cocktail party, what alternative do you have?

PREPARATION

An educated palate does not necessarily perceive ice as tasteless and odorless frozen water. First, ice has the flavor of the water used to make it. If your local water supply is mineral-laden, you might put bottled spring water in your ice tray, but do not use the sparkling varieties, because the bubbles will quickly disappear, and those varieties tend to have a higher mineral (especially sodium) content than the still mineral waters. Second, the surface of ice readily picks up refrigerator odors. Before using ice cubes, sniff them. If you detect an off-smell, briefly run water over the loose cubes and most of the odors will be washed down the drain. When preparing an ice bucket to chill wine, do not make the common mistake of adding the ice, then the water to the container or you will end up with clusters of cubes frozen together. To keep the ice cubes separate add the water, then the cubes. And, remember that a 50-50 mixture of water and ice cubes will cool a wine much quicker than will pure ice.

ICE CREAM AND ITS RELATIVES

Frozen desserts originated in mountainous regions, most likely of ancient China, when someone thought of adding a flavoring to a handful of snow. That discovery was further developed upon so that today we have ice cream, pseudo ice cream, and sherbets. Each of these variations on a theme will be discussed individually.

ICE CREAM

Thomas Jefferson brought a primitive ice-cream recipe to the United States from Europe. He and his fellow Americans fell in love with the preparation and further improved on the formula and techniques so much that rich ice cream may be almost thought of as an American creation. America is now a nation of ice-cream eaters—only the Russians and certain other Eastern

Europeans rival our avidity for and consumption of the product. Ice cream, of course, is enjoyed by itself or can be concocted into well known specialities such as sundaes, banana splits, baked Alaskas, cakes, sandwiches, chocolate-covered sticks, floats, sodas, shakes, and malts.

Manufacture

Ice cream is made from fresh, condensed, or dried milk products, blended with various flavorings and sweetening agents and sometimes with colorings and other agents as well. The milk products can be cream or milk and the flavorings run the gamut from almond to whortleberry, though vanilla, chocolate and strawberry are the most popular, in that order. Sweeteners can be sugar, corn syrup, honey, or—for dietetic ice cream—sugar substitutes. Except in certain brands, coloring agents are widely used. Stabilizers help keep the ice cream from melting or crystallizing prematurely in temperatures normally found in store and home freezers. Other additives thicken the ice cream or help retard bacterial proliferation.

In recent years a host of home ice-cream-making machines have come onto the market. The better ones can make better ice cream than the typical mediocre store-bought variety. Homemade ice cream cannot, however, compete in excellence with high-quality commercial ice cream, because sophisticated plant equipment can, for instance, obtain the precise temperature needed for each production stage.

Overrun: When buying ice cream, consider the overrun. Ice cream needs to be somewhat fluffed with air; the measurement of this aeration is called overrun. If no air has been whipped into the ice cream, there is a 0 percent overrun. If the ice cream is all air (which, of course, is theoretical), the overrun would be 200 percent. If half the volume of the ice cream is whipped-in air, the overrun is 100 percent, which is the maximum legal limit. Some aeration—about 20 to 50 percent—is desirable. Since ice cream is sold by volume and not weight, many ice cream manufacturers increase their overrun to the 100 percent legal limit, which gives the product an inferior texture. An ice cream with a 25 percent overrun will be 12½ percent air, while one with a 100 percent overrun will be 50 percent air. Therefore, do not think you are being overcharged if the 25 percent type sells for 75 percent more than the 100 percent overrun brand—that would amount to the same price on a weight basis. The surest way for a shopper to compare overrun percentages (they are not listed on the label) is to weigh and compare brands. Ice cream with a 100 percent overrun will weight about 9 ounces per pint (be sure to subtract for the weight of the package—about 1 ounce for the rectangular paper package, and nearly 2 ounces for the typical cardboard tub).

Label Terms: If ice cream is made with natural flavors, it can be called, for instance, "strawberry ice cream." If artificial flavorings are used, but the natural flavors predominate, the label will read "strawberry-flavored." If the artificial flavoring is over 50 percent, the label will read "artificial strawberry." "French ice cream" must be made with egg yolks. "Vanillin" is not vanilla. It is an artificial substitute.

Buying Tips

Ice cream has a short storage life, even when kept in a deep freezer. Buy from a store with a high merchandise turnover, and one that has ice cream stored in an efficient freezer with a door that is tightly closed. The package should feel stiff and solid. Reject containers that are sticky—a sign that the ice cream may have partially thawed before being refrozen, and thus developed a crystal-flecked texture. Pick up your ice cream last on your shopping trip, and have it put into an insulated bag. Go quickly home and immediately put it in your freezer—subzero if possible. Keep it in a plastic bag to prolong its storage life. The colder your storage environment, the longer your ice cream can be stored. Figure on 1 or 2 days in the frozen food compartment, 5 days or so in the deep freezer. Beyond those times, the ice cream has a tendency to crystallize and to pick up foreign odors. To judge a new brand, try vanilla ice cream first, as it will give you a good base comparison against other brands. Besides judging for flavor, give the ice cream the melt test. High-quality ice cream generally melts at room temperature slower than products with high overruns. The exception are those high-overrun, low-quality ice creams that are loaded with thickening agents. Ice cream of that sort has a telltale dryish, chalky look rather than a creamy, glossy appearance, and tends to have minute, frothy bubbles rising to its surface as it melts.

Ice Milk And Other Pseudo-Ice Creams

Ice milk contains less butterfat than ice cream. *Frozen custard*, the type that is customarily extruded from a nozzle into cones, may or may not contain cream. *Frozen yogurt*, a new-style product, is not as grand a nutritional star as some advocates would have you believe, as it tends to be sugar-infused.

Ice And Sherbet

The terms *ice* and *sherbet* are sometimes used interchangeably in America, but traditionally, an ice (or *granité*) is a frozen mixture of water, sugar, and fruit flavoring. A sherbet (or *sorbet*) on the other hand, has a less granular texture, the result of adding ingredients such as eggwhites, milk, or gelatin. A *snowball* or *snow cone*, an altogether different product, is a mound of fine-shaved ice that has been drenched with a colorful liquid flavoring. A *Popsicle* is a frozen ice on a stick.

IGUANA AND OTHER LIZARDS

BACKGROUND

The flesh of the large New World lizard is a highly acclaimed delicacy in the tropical Americas where it lives. The flavor is delicate, almost rabbitlike, and is best served with a not-too-assertive sauce, though some cooks spike the sauce with hot chili peppers. There is no reason why you could not cook most small lizards, but they have too little edible flesh to make their preparation worthwhile for all but penniless cooks.

INTESTINES

BACKGROUND

The best and most popular variety of intestines come from young pigs. In the South where they have become one of the stars of the soul-food table, they are called *chitlins*, which is the popular—and proper—way of pronouncing the word spelled *chitterlings*. Pork intestines are also used as both a sausage casing and, in French *andouilles*, a sausage stuffing.

PREPARATION

You can purchase pork intestines from the butcher already cleaned and partially cooked.

Preliminaries

If you have fresh-from-the-carcass pork intestines, your first step is to clean them. Cut them into 1- to 3-foot lengths (depending on how you wish to use them) and wash out their insides with cold running water. Turn the intestines inside out. Scrape away mucus and most but not all of the fat; the latter substance adds flavor. Some earthy cooks prefer not to wash out the intestines thoroughly, in the belief that the undigested food clinging to the internal walls adds even more flavor, but that is a matter of personal preference.

If you are not making sausages and therefore do not need to preserve the natural tubular shape, you can make your task easier by splitting the intestines lengthwise before starting to clean them.

Your next step is to cover the cleaned intestines with salted water (1 teaspoon per quart of liquid) for 12 to 24 hours in the refrigerator. Drain and discard the water. Rinse the intestines well in several changes of water.

Basic Cooking

Add fresh water to cover the intestines, again with 1 teaspoon of salt per quart of liquid. For improved flavor, add *court-bouillon* ingredients such as onions, carrots, celery, bay leaf, parsley, and peppercorns. Bring to a gentle boil, then cover with a lid, reduce heat, and slowly simmer for about 1½ to 2 hours, depending mainly on the age of the animal and on how you plan to use the intestines. (For sausage casings, cook for a shorter period.) Once they've been simmered, you can serve them with a sauce, add them to a soup or stew, dredge them with flour and sauté them for a couple of minutes, or coat them with breadcrumbs or batter and deep-fry them. Or, instead of simmering them at all, you can, after soaking them, braise them or add them directly to slow-cooking soups or stews.

JACKFRUIT

BACKGROUND

The Asiatic tropics (especially Sri Lanka and Indonesia) and Brazil are the homes of the *jackfruit*, a huge relative of the breadfruit and fig. *Artocarpus integra* and *A. heterophyllus* produce spiny oval or oblong fruits that usually weigh about 10 pounds but can grow up to 100 pounds. Green jackfruit is used in curries, or parboiled and baked as a side dish. Ripe jackfruit flesh is sweetened and used in desserts. Unripe jackfruit has fibrous flesh that exudes a sticky latex.

JELLY AND ITS RELATIVES

BACKGROUND

Distinct differences exist among jellies, jams, preserves, conserves, marmalades, and other spreads.

Varieties

Jelly is the strained juice of cooked fruits that solidifies into a quivering mass due to the release by heat of the fruits' natural pectin. Sometimes the fruits' natural pectin is so weak that you need to add a THICKENER such as processed pectin or gelatin. Sugar is added primarily to satisfy the sweet tooth.

Jam differs from a jelly in that the cooked pulp of the fruit is not strained. The product can be seedless or not.

Preserves differ from jam in that the fruit—whole or in large pieces—is cooked just enough to release the gelatinizing pectin but not enough to reduce the fruit to pulp. The sugar helps the fruit to hold its shape.

Conserve is a jam that contains more than one type of fruit.

Marmalade is a preserve that contains pieces of the fruit rind. Typically, the fruit is a citrus—most often, that of the bigarade, sour, Seville, or bitter orange.

Fruit butter is a thick, sweet, spicy, slow-cooked, smooth puree. You can make it with orchard fruits such as quinces, apricots, and plums, but the most common type is apple butter.

Applesauce, a different product, is coarse-textured and not cooked as long as apple butter, is rarely spiced, and is used as a side dish or garnish rather than a spread.

Storage

Once opened, jelly and its relatives must be refrigerated.

JERUSALEM ARTICHOKES

BACKGROUND

Jerusalem artichokes are neither native to Jerusalem nor artichokes. Botanically they are the edible tuber from the *girasole* (*Helianthus tuberosus*), a variety of sunflower. (*Girasole*—meaning "sun-turner"—the Italian name for sunflower, became *Jerusalem* by folk etymology.) The small, lumpy, sometimes branched tubers resemble ginger roots, but Jerusalem artichokes have a thin, reddish-brown skin and white flesh. Early American Indians loved the sweet, nutty-tasting tubers. Europeans, introduced to the Jerusalem artichoke in the seventeenth century, took to its crunchy texture. But most twentieth-century Americans have never tasted a Jerusalem artichoke. Commercial growers, who are starting to call them *sunchokes*, are trying to remedy the situation. Dieters and diabetics can make use of sunchokes, as they contain inulin, a carbohydrate that is not metabolized as starch.

AVAILABILITY

Mid-fall to early spring.

Buying Tips

If sold in sealed plastic bags, scrutinize the contents. Choose small ones (about 2 inches long), and avoid those with moldy soft spots, blemished skins, or a musty odor.

PREPARATION

Storage

Keep Jerusalem artichokes in a bag, in a cool place or in the refrigerator. They should last a week. Diced raw Jerusalem artichokes immersed in acidulated water and refrigerated should hold for a day or two. Cooked Jerusalem artichokes will keep about 2 days under refrigeration.

Preliminaries

Jerusalem artichokes' irregular shape makes them a happy home for dirt, so scrub all the crevices well with a vegetable brush. Use a vegetable peeler or paring knife to remove the skin: a tedious and somewhat wasteful job, again because of the uneven shape. But why not leave the skin on? It is edible and nutritious. Slice or dice them, or cook them whole.

Cooking

Use Jerusalem artichokes raw as an appetizer or marinated in a salad. Or boil or steam them until they are tender, but still give some resistance to the teeth. This should take 10 to 15 minutes, depending on size.

Equivalents

A pound yields about 2½ cups of prepared, sliced chokes, enough for three or four servings.

JÍCAMA

BACKGROUND

Pronounced HEE-kah-mah, this root vegetable comes from a Mexican variety of morning-glory vine (*Exogonium bracteatum*). Jícama looks and cooks like our Southern type of sweet potato. The jícama is often eaten raw in its native environments, but its flesh is less sweet and more stringy than our lush sweet potato, and Americans usually prefer to cook it. The jícama is available in some

Latin-American ethnic markets fresh (in season, from November to June). Fresh jícama will keep for a couple of days in a cool place or in the refrigerator. A pound of jícama should provide four servings.

JUJUBE

BACKGROUND

The jujube (*Zizyphus jujuba*, sometimes called the *Chinese date*), is an oval fruit about the size of an olive, covered with a tough, leathery skin most commonly red, but sometimes also white (on the *honey jujube*) and sometimes black. Beneath the skin is a hard, pointed stone covered with dry yellow flesh that is esteemed for its sweet taste. Chinese cooks use fresh or, more often, dried jujubes in soups, as sweetmeats, and in pastry fillings. Dried jujubes must be soaked for an hour before being used.

JUNIPER BERRIES

BACKGROUND

The dark-blue berries of the small tree, *Juniperus communis*, have a strong, bitter taste. A few crushed dried berries can be used with cabbage dishes (especially sauerkraut), in marinades, and with small game birds, venison, and fat meats such as pork. The dominant flavoring agent in gin is juniper berries. You can make vodka taste like gin by steeping a few berries in the bottle overnight. Your "instant gin" will not look like gin, however, because the berries will have given the liquid a slight purplish tinge. Distillers make sure the berry dye does not color commercial gin. (See HERBS AND SPICES for information on buying, storing, cooking, etc.)

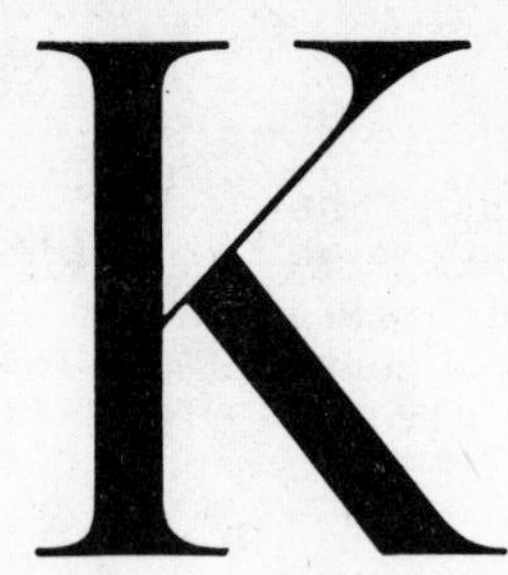

KALE

BACKGROUND

A variety of leafy, nonheading cabbage, *kale* (*Brassica oleracea acephala*) is a coarse, strong-flavored green that has provided vitamins and iron in the limited winter diets of European peasants for centuries. Some kale mavens believe it should not be picked until after the first frost, so that the leaves will become more tender and the intense flavor modified somewhat.

Varieties

Many varieties exist, with different colors and leaf shapes. The ones sold in America usually have curly, ragged-edged leaves that grow in a bouquet cluster, colored dark green with a tinge of gray, purple, or blue.

AVAILABILITY

Season

Winter through mid-spring.

Buying Tips

Choose untorn, crisp leaves firmly attached to the stalk. Leaves should have a rich, deep hue, whatever the color. Avoid leaves that are wilted or darkened at the edges. Stems and midribs should be crisp, not limp. Larger leaves tend to be less tender and more assertively flavored than smaller ones.

PREPARATION

Storage

Kale is more fragile than it looks. Refrigerate it, and plan on using it within 2 or 3 days of purchase.

Preliminaries

The stalks of kale are stringy and too tough to eat, so cut or tear them off the leaves and discard. Or save the stalks for the stockpot—but use them in very small quantities as the flavor may overpower the broth. Remove the midribs if tough, and break the leaves into small pieces. Kale may be dirty. Wash it well with cold water.

Cooking

Steam or simmer kale for about 10 to 15 minutes. Do not cook kale in untreated aluminum or iron pots as they may discolor the vegetable.

Equivalents

A pound of kale makes three to four servings.

CLASSIC USES AND AFFINITIES

Potatoes complement the texture, taste and color of kale. Fat back, salt pork, and bacon add richness. So does butter. The strong green enlivens bean soups, and teams up with coarse garlic sausage.

KID

BACKGROUND

By definition, a kid is an immature goat, usually less than a year old. Few mature goats are eaten in this country, as their meat is strong-flavored and on the tough side. Kids consumed in America are almost always under 6 months because the younger the animal, the more tender and delicately flavored the meat will be. Kid is popular in many nations in Africa, the northern Indian subcontinent, southern Europe, and Latin America, and you can sometimes find kid being sold in the appropriate American ethnic markets. Kid can be cooked following the same general guidelines given for LAMB.

KIDNEY BEAN

BACKGROUND

This popular American variety of *Phaseolus vulgaris* is a medium-sized, medium-hard, dark-red-skinned, white-fleshed, kidney-shaped (naturally), full-flavored legume and that family's leading inducer of flatulence. A smaller white variety of kidney, the Italian *cannellini*, lacks that exuberance of character and the robustness of flavor of our red one, and is preferred by some cooks for these reasons. Red kidney beans are widely used in chili con carne; both white and red are good in cold bean salads, in meat stews, and in casseroles with rice and cheeses.

AVAILABILITY

Seldom available fresh, red kidney beans are sold year round, either dry or already cooked in cans, alone or in soups and chili. The white *cannellini* is available to us only dried or canned. (For soaking, cooking, and other particulars, see BEANS.)

KIDNEYS

BACKGROUND

Each quadruped has a pair of kidneys that can be exhilaratingly delicious if properly cooked—and if they come from a young animal. The flavor and aroma is more assertive and the texture is tougher in kidneys from mature animals; their sole advantage is their much lower price. All kidneys are nutritiously rich in protein, iron, riboflavin and niacin.

AVAILABILITY

Most butchers will have kidneys available; just ask.

Buying Tips

All kidneys should be semi-firm to the touch without any soft spots, should have a glowing appearance, and should smell clean and fresh. Avoid any kidneys that have a dull surface or show signs of drying out. Most American markets sell only beef and veal kidneys. The easiest way to distinguish the two, if in doubt, is by the color: the paler the color, the younger the animal. (A kidney starts off with a whitish-reddish-brown hue and, as the bovine matures, becomes a deep reddish-brown.) To tell the bovine (beef and veal) kidney from that of the pig and sheep, examine the shape: the first is multi-lobed; the others are single-lobed. To tell a lamb kidney from a pork kidney, remember that the first is smaller and more the shape of the kidney bean (which was named because of that striking resemblance).

PREPARATION

Storage

Fresh kidneys are highy perishable and, therefore, should be used on the day of purchase, if possible. To refrigerate, place in a loose wrapping—this insures a circulation of air which helps keep the meat surface dry, thereby minimizing bacterial growth. If you must buy frozen kidneys, tightly wrap and store them in the frozen-food compartment for up to a couple of weeks or in the 0°F freezer for up to several months—but you will lose some flavor, texture, and nutrients.

Preliminaries

Trimming: If the butcher has not already done so, peel off the thin outer membrane with a small, sharp-pointed knife. Next, split the kidney in half lengthwise (or, if using lamb kidney, split nearly in half, leaving the halves connected to each other). With the same knife or a small, curved pair of scissors, remove the whitish core in the center and any excess tubes, fat, gristle, etc. If the kidneys are from milk-fed animals, you don't need to remove the core, as it does not become hard until after the baby has been weaned. When cutting out the core, be careful not to convert a small kidney into a mutilated mass. If the kidney comes encased in fat, keep that top-quality suet for such duties as barding, pastry-making, and adding to beanpots, casseroles and meat pies.

Washing: Do not wash the kidneys of young animals, as they readily absorb water, thereby hindering proper dry-heat cooking; the added moisture will create steam, which lowers the cooking temperature, which weakens the delicate flavor. Kidneys from mature animals can be washed, though, since they must be cooked with moist heat. Wash them under cold, running water, then pat dry.

Soaking: One way to help rid mature kidneys of their strong odor is to soak them in an acidulated liquid (1 tablespoon of vinegar or 2 tablespoons of lemon juice to 1 quart of water) for 1 to 2 hours, depending on size. The delicate kidneys of young animals should not be soaked for the reason given above.

Parboiling: Another way to reduce the odor of mature kidneys is to parboil them for 2 to 4 minutes, depending on size. Some cooks briefly parboil the kidney of young animals if they are making a white sauce (parboiling helps remove some of the blood, which can discolor the sauce-producing pan juices) but they pay dearly in terms of the moisture the kidneys will absorb. It is a classic trade-off: texture for color.

Cooking

Dry Heat: Only the kidneys from young animals can be cooked with dry heat such as sautéing or broiling. In all cases they should be cooked quickly over medium-high heat to no more than a medium-rare state (some internal pinkness should remain). They also need to be cooked with ample butter or oil. Otherwise, the meat will unnecessarily toughen. Depending on size, this will take roughly 3 to 6 minutes per side if whole or merely a few minutes total if diced. Lamb kidneys are often broiled on a skewer: slice them lengthwise nearly in half, open them flat, and skewer them in such a way to prevent them from curling when heated; baste often and cook 2 to 3 minutes per side, 4 inches away from the heat source.

Moist Heat: Unless ground, all kidneys from mature animals must be cooked with slow, moist heat, such as braising or simmering. Whole beef kidneys take 1 1/4 to 2 hours. Whole veal and young pig kidneys require about 30 minutes less; whole lamb kidneys require but 40 minutes. Diced beef kidneys take about 1 hour. Whatever the case, do not let the liquid boil or the kidney meat will toughen.

Equivalents

Purchase 1/4 to 1/3 pound per person, depending on appetites. An average-sized beef kidney weighs about 1 pound, a veal kidney between 5 and 10 ounces, a pork kidney 3 to 4 ounces, and a lamb kidney 2 to 3 ounces.

CLASSIC USES AND AFFINITIES

The kidney chop (or, as it is sometimes called, an English chop) is one of the most elegant ways to serve the kidney. Basically, it is a loin steak that still has part of the suet-encased kidney attached to it. The suet-encased kidney is also cooked by itself in places like Ireland. Skewered-broiled kidneys are popular around the world. The traditional English mixed grill calls for lamb's kidney. Another English favorite is steak-and-kidney pie. The French love their *ragnons* sautéed with a sauce such as bordelaise. In France and beyond, kidney stews and casseroles are legion. Some cooks enjoy adding kidney to their ground-meat preparations such as hamburger or meat loaf. Traditional culinary partners for the kidney include mushrooms, shallots, lemon juice, fortified wines, butter, fragrant green herbs, and—for a bed—a small slice of toast.

KIWI FRUIT

BACKGROUND

New Zealand named the *Chinese gooseberry* (*Actinidia chinensis*) the *kiwi fruit* after its native hairy brown bird that can't fly. A kiwi fruit does resemble one's fanciful idea of a kiwi's egg—it is the size and shape of an egg and covered with a dull reddish-brown fuzz over a thin tan skin. Inside, the flesh is lime green, juicy, and pleasantly sweet-tart, with a smattering of tiny black seeds strewn about its central creamy-white core. The delicately crunchy seeds are edible—and removing them would be a nuisance. A fresh kiwi is rich in Vitamin C. Native to eastern Asia, the fruit is now cultivated largely in New Zealand and California.

AVAILABILITY

Kiwi fruit ripens as the cold weather comes in. Since New Zealand's winter reverses ours, kiwis are available fresh, although in limited quantities nearly year round—from June through March.

PREPARATION

Storage

Unripe kiwi fruit stores well. If bought slightly firm, ripen to softness at room temperature in a pierced paper bag and then refrigerate for up to 2 or 3 weeks.

Serving

If the fuzz is rubbed off, kiwis can be eaten whole, but usually they are peeled. You can slice them into lengthwise segments, but the fruit best displays its beauty when it is sliced crosswise. Alternatively, slice an unpeeled kiwi in half lengthwise and eat with a spoon, melon style.

CLASSIC USES AND AFFINITIES

Kiwi juice tenderizes meat; just rub a slice of the fruit over the flesh. The fruit makes an exotic addition to fruit macédoines. A sprinkling of lime juice is a splendid affinity. Kiwi fruits are commonly made into preserves in New Zealand.

KOHLRABI

BACKGROUND

Kohl means "cabbage," *rab* means "turnip"; the *kohlrabi* (*Brassica caulorapa*) is also called *cabbage turnip*. It has two edible portions, the leaves, which can be cooked like *turnip greens*, and the thick, turnip-shaped, purple-tinged white stem.

AVAILABILITY

Kohlrabi is available fresh from late spring through early fall, with a peak in mid-summer.

Buying Tips

For greatest tenderness and sweetness of flavor, choose small bulbs, under 2½ inches in diameter. Large kohlrabis tend to be woody, fibrous, and bitter. Look for fresh green leaves, if they are still attached. A tender skin covering a firm body is a positive sign. Do not buy bulbs with blemishes, withering, a yellow tinge, numerous scars, or soft spots.

PREPARATION

Storage

Kohlrabis will stay fresh for several days in a refrigerator; much longer in a cool, well-ventilated cellar.

Preliminaries

Wash before cooking. Tender young kohlrabi are most nutritious cooked and served with skins attached. Tough kohlrabis generally require peeling—for best nutrition, do that chore after cooking.

Cooking

Whole small-to-medium kohlrabis take 15 to 25 minutes to steam or boil; cubes and slices take 5 to 10 minutes, depending on thickness. Continental chefs julienne fresh kohlrabi, briefly steam or boil the strips for about 5 minutes, then steep them while still hot in a seasoned oil-and-vinegar dressing, refrigerate them, then serve the dish as an appetizer or a side vegetable. Kohlrabi can also be sautéed, added to stews, or mashed. They are delicious raw, too.

Equivalents

One medium-sized kohlrabi gives one average serving.

CLASSIC USES AND AFFINITIES

Sour cream with dill and caraway seeds makes a pleasing complement to kohlrabi. A nutmeg-laced cream sauce also does justice.

KUMQUAT

BACKGROUND

At first glance, the oval or round *kumquat* looks like a miniature orange. Though they are distantly related and share certain resemblances (for instance, color and surface texture), the orange and the kumquat have distinct flavors. The kumquat, in fact, has two flavors—sweet (from the rind) and tart (from the pulp). Since you eat the kumquat skin and all, these two flavors intermingle, producing a delightful taste sensation. A branch of kumquats, complete with green leaves, is a favorite Chinese New Year present; it symbolizes good luck throughout the year.

Buying Tips

Select firm, plump kumquats that are blemish-free, heavy for their size, and—if you are going to eat them raw—ripe. Choose nearly ripe specimens if you are going to cook them—they go well with fatty meat such as duck, either as an edible whole or sliced garnish or as a sauce ingredient.

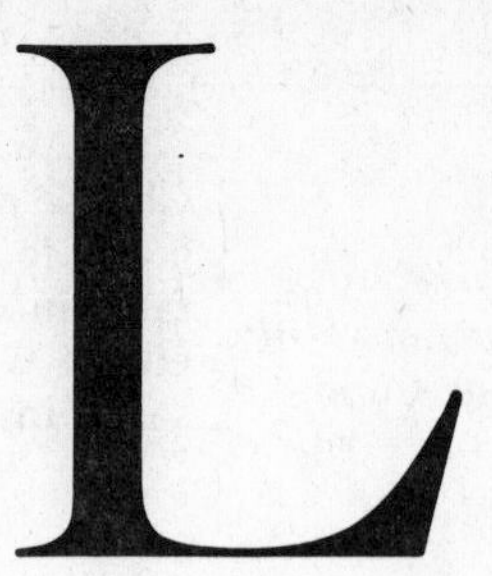

LAMB AND MUTTON

BACKGROUND

Lamb is a major and adored food in many parts of Europe, throughout the Middle East, and in the northern regions of the Indian subcontinent and China. It is also popular with the American ethnic groups with roots in those lands, but not with Americans in general, despite the fact that lamb is well entrenched in our country in terms of Biblical history and symbolism. Statistics tell us that the consumption of lamb meat in the United States is rather low: less than several pounds per capita per year compared to nearly 100 pounds of beef. Why? One reason is that most American cookbooks encourage their readers to cook lamb well-done—that is to an internal temperature of 170°F or more. This advice virtually guarantees that the meat will be dry and tough and unappetizingly grayish-brown. If these cookbooks would recommend cooking the lamb rare or medium-rare (130° to 140°F), their readers would be able to enjoy lamb with a tender and juicy texture, a delicate flavor, and an appealing pinkish interior. Another reason lamb is not a staple in most American homes is the common misconception that the meat has a strong muttony flavor. Since the average age of the lambs slaughtered for meat in this country is only about six months, the animals' flesh, fat, and bones have not yet developed the characteristic mutton flavor found in the mature sheep. Simply defined, *lamb* is the meat of a lamb, an immature sheep, while *mutton* is the meat of one that has reached maturity. The widely accepted point of demarcation between the two is the animal's first birthday. Another criterion is the "break point" test used by a slaughterhouse personnel: if a leg on the carcass easily snaps in two just above the ankle, the animal is considered a lamb.

Butchers use the following seven, sometimes overlapping, designations, largely governed by age:

- Unborn lamb
- Baby lamb
- Milk-fed lamb
- Hothouse lamb
- Genuine spring lamb
- Spring lamb
- Lamb
- Mutton

Unborn Lamb: Few meats are so identified with Greek shipping tycoons' dining tables as the extremely expensive *unborn lamb*. It was a particular favorite, for instance, of Aristotle and Jacqueline Onassis. To our tastes, the meat is too delicate, too tender, too flavorless to be anything but a culinary conceit.

Baby Lamb: An ovine is unofficially classified as *baby lamb* from the age of 1 day to 2 or 3 months. On a price-per-pound basis, it is very expensive. If the baby lamb is very young, its carcass usually reaches the retail marketplace whole, with the head and tail attached. In most cases the meat of a 2-month baby lamb is more desirable in terms of developed flavor and texture than one with an age of only a month or less.

Milk-Fed Lamb: This designation defines a baby lamb that has never tasted grain or grass, only mother's milk or a commercial milk formula.

Hothouse Lamb: This defines a baby lamb that has been raised indoors during the cold season. The lamb is usually slaughtered when 1 to 10 weeks old.

Genuine Spring Lamb: When you see the *genuine spring lamb* stamp on the carcass, you are generally assured that the animal was slaughtered at an age of less than 6 months, and somewhere between March and the beginning of October. The best of the genuine spring lambs are those slaughtered between the ages of 2 and 4 months and have an average dress-weight of approximately 20 to 35 pounds. These prized lambs usually reach the retail market fully dressed, but with head and skin attached.

Spring Lamb: Nowadays, a lamb can be called *spring* regardless of its birth-month just as long as it is less than 6 months old. However, the seller cannot use the term *genuine spring lamb* if the animal was slaughtered between the beginning of November and the end of February. Few diners other than lamb connoisseurs can detect any appreciable difference between spring lamb and the more expensive genuine spring lamb.

Lamb: An ovine too old to be called spring lamb and too young to be labeled mutton is known simply as *lamb*. However, some of the meat sold as lamb in your supermarket may be entitled to the phrase "spring lamb" but, for various reasons, the butcher decides not to print the word "spring" on his label or display sign. The typical dressed market weight of a whole nonspring lamb is about 48 to 60 pounds.

Mutton: Between 1 and 2 years of age, the sheep is called *yearling mutton*, and has an average weight in the neighborhood of 100 pounds. After its second birthday, its meat is called *mature mutton* or just plain *mutton*. As with other animals, as the sheep matures its muscles become more exercised and its metabolism changes, which results in tougher, stronger-flavored, darker-red flesh. Simultaneously, the fat becomes more yellow and brittle, the bones increase in size and hardness, and the price per pound drops. It is important to realize that there is nothing wrong with mutton—it is delicious but it is an acquired taste. Some preparations such as Scotch broth even benefit from the strong mutton flavor.

Quality and Breed

USDA Quality Grades: The federal government classifies lamb by quality, but only if this service is requested and paid for by the slaughterhouse. The grades take into account factors such as the finish and conformation of the carcass. The better the grade, the more tender and delicately flavored the meat will be for its breed and age. In order of descending quality level, lamb is awarded one of these five grades:

Prime
Choice
Good
Utility
Cull

The appropriate purple-ink, shield-shaped grademark is roller-stamped along the length and across the shoulders of the carcass. It is clearly visible on an untrimmed wholesale cut, but you may see only a portion of a shield—or none at all—on a retail cut. The vast majority of the graded lamb that reaches the display case is USDA Choice grade. Gourmet butcher shops often carry the USDA Prime grade as well. Budget meat outlets sometimes sell USDA Good lamb. USDA Utility and USDA Cull grades virtually never reach the consumer directly, as such meat usually goes to canners and other processed food manufacturers.

Other USDA Inspection Systems: The USDA (or a similar state government bureau) examines all lamb carcasses and processing plants for wholesomeness and sanitary conditions. Approved meat gets stamped with a round purple ink inspection mark with the abbreviated phrase "US Ins'd & P's'd" along with the code number of the processing plant. Unapproved meat cannot be sold. The USDA classifies lamb carcasses by yield (the ratio of flesh to fat and bone waste) on a scale of 1 to 5, with 5 indicating the highest yield. The shield-shaped yieldmarks serve a wholesale, not a retail, function.

Varieties: Sheep are classified by breed (and there are many of them) but few, if any, breed names ever reach the consumer's ear. Most breeds fall conveniently into either the "meat" or "wool" category—if a sheep is perfect for one role, it will not be ideally suited for the other. Some sheep are classified by their rearing environment. *Agneau pré-salé*, for instance, is the celebrated lamb that grazes on the salt marshes along the Brittany and Normandy coasts of France.

Anatomical Location

Primal Cuts: Other than size, the lamb's anatomy differs only slightly from that of the steer—a lamb loin chop, to illustrate, bears a striking resemblance to a beef porterhouse steak. However, lamb comes from a far younger animal than beef, and therefore most cuts from areas such as the shoulder or leg can be perfectly cooked with dry heat if the lamb is at least USDA Choice grade. Lamb also differs from beef in the form the dressed carcass reaches the butcher shop. Beef arrives divided into quarters while lamb is shipped whole, or if it is a large lamb, cut into the foresaddle and hindsaddle. The butcher then usually divides the lamb into the following six major primal cuts (the first two from the hindsaddle, the remaining four from the foresaddle):

Primal Leg
Primal Loin
Primal Rib (or Rack)
Primal Shoulder
Primal Breast
Primal Shank

See the illustration on page 247 for their anatomical locations.

The butcher now has the option of selling these primal cuts as they are or further dividing them into more marketable smaller pieces such as chops.

Primal Leg: For most Americans, this is the most desirable cut of lamb, and it connotes "special occasion" when it is brought to the table. A *whole leg of lamb* includes the *hind shank, round, rump*, and *sirloin* parts along with the leg, aitch (hip) and chine (back) bones. The last two bones make carving difficult, so consider removing them (or having your meat cutter do it), or buying a *short leg*, as described below.

Beside being sold whole, the leg is sold in smaller units:

American Leg
French Leg
Short Leg
Sirloin Roast or Chops
Sirloin and Shank Halves
Leg Steaks
Butterflied Leg
Kabobs
Hind Shank

American Leg: If you or the butcher remove the shank bone at the stifle joint and fold back the hanging, boneless shank meat into a pocket in the leg and secure it with skewers, you will have an American leg. It is shorter than a whole leg and will fit into smaller pans and ovens.

French Leg: Generally, this phrase refers to a leg whose shank bone has been stripped of an inch or two of flesh so it can be decorated with a paper frill before serving. (If you do French the leg, cover the exposed bone with aluminum foil to keep it from scorching during cooking.) The term may also refer to a leg of lamb we just described, but with one difference: the sirloin section has been removed.

Short (or Three-quarter) Leg: To create this cut, you or your butcher must

PRIMAL CUTS OF LAMB

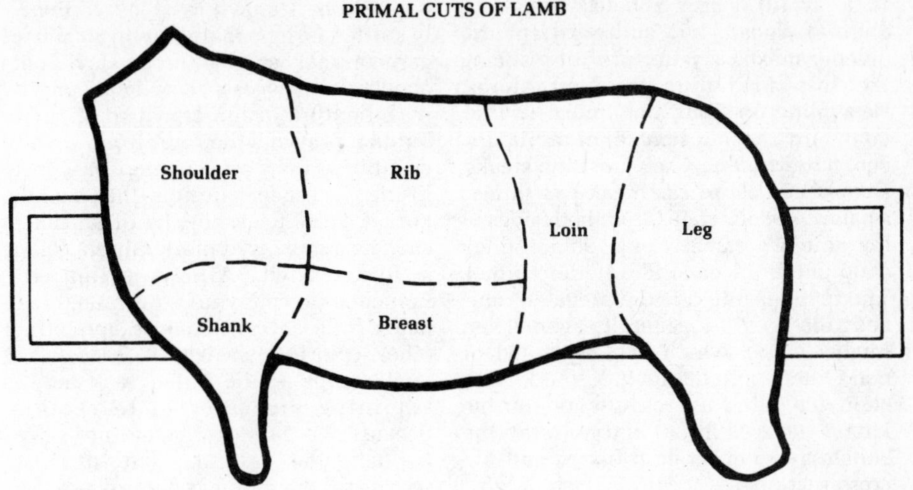

remove the sirloin section from the whole leg. It is easier to carve and fits into smaller ovens.

Sirloin Roast and Chops: The portion cut off the whole leg to make the short leg of lamb is the sirloin section (the larger end of the whole leg). It is then sold either as a 2- to 3-pound bone-in roast or, more likely, as a boned roast or as three or four individual chops. As with their anatomical equivalents, beef sirloin steaks, the tenderest of these sirloin chops are the ones that were cut closest to the loin section.

Sirloin and Shank Halves: For some families, a whole leg is too large. This is why butchers often saw the leg in two, creating a sirloin half and a shank half, each weighing about 2½ to 5 pounds. The *sirloin* (or *upper* or *rump* or *butt*) *half* has the most tender meat and the least connective tissue. But on the negative side, it has a lower ratio of lean to bone and fat waste, and—unless boned—it is much harder to carve. The *shank* (or *lower*) *half*, because of its higher proportion of lean, generally sells for 15 to 30 percent more than does the sirloin half. If both halves sell for the same price, as is sometimes the case, take the shank half unless tenderness is your sole goal. When buying either half, make sure—unless the price per pound has been correspondingly lowered—that the butcher has not removed some slices to be sold separately as leg steaks. If he has, the meat should not be labeled "half" or "full-half."

Leg Steaks: These are the steaks (or chops) cut from the center of the leg and have a very high proportion of lean. Depending on how they have been cut, these steaks are the anatomical equivalent of the ham steak or the beef round steak.

Butterflied Leg: Perfect for barbecues, this retail cut is a boned leg of lamb that is split almost in half, then spread open for easy grilling.

Kabobs: First divide the leg muscles along their natural seams (so the meat will not break apart during cooking), then cut the lamb into cubes about 1½ inches on a side.

Hind Shank: This cut, the lower part of the whole leg, is best braised, butchered for use in soups or stews, or ground into lamb patties and loaves.

Primal Loin: As with its equivalent the beef short loin, the lamb loin is the tenderest and most expensive primal cut. Sometimes this 2-or-so pound loin is sold as a bone-in roast (or as a saddle of lamb when both loins of the animal are sold unsplit) or as a boneless (single or double) roast, but more often the butcher makes a better profit by slicing the loin into four to eight chops. Depending on their anatomical source, lamb loin chops resemble, in miniature, beef porterhouse, T-bone, or club steaks. Double loin chops can mean two things: a pair of unsplit chops from both sides of the animal's carcass, or a double-thick chop cut from one side of the animal. The first definition is the prevalent one, and the cut is generally called an English chop, which can be boned or not. Other loin cuts include the kidney chop (contains a cross-section of the kidney encased in fat) and *noisette* (the boneless eye of the loin that is cut into cross-sectional slices). When judging the value of a lamb loin roast or chop, take into account the size of the so-called tail (consisting of fibrous flank steak and fat; see BEEF, Primal Loins, for details).

Primal Rib (or Rack): As with beef, the *primal rib* cut of the lamb lies along the animal's back, between the loin and shoulder. A single *rack* contains the eye muscle and various smaller, less tender muscles, plus fat, the chine (back) bone and, customarily, rib bones. If the butcher "borrowed" one or two ribs from the primal shoulder, the *"Eve" rack* will have eight or nine ribs. A single rack roast usually weighs between 2½ and 3 pounds, but since it only provides you with about 1 pound of lean (the rest is bone or fat waste), it will serve only two or three people. A *double rack*, consisting of the unsplit rib sections from both sides of the carcass, will feed twice as many diners. A single or double rack may be boned-and-rolled or not—if unboned, ask your meat cutter to crack the chine bone to facilitate carving. If you bend two or more single racks into a circle and secure them together with twine, and French the rib ends, you have a *crown roast* (which can also be made of veal or pork rather than lamb sections). A typical crown roast has fourteen to eighteen ribs, which will feed seven to nine people, allowing two ribs per person. A crown roast is traditionally stuffed (after cooking) with a colorful garnish such as peas or parsley. Some cookbooks suggest cooking a ground pork mixture in the crown roast cavity but that prevents the roast from cooking evenly. To help prevent the roast from losing its shape during the cooking period, stuff the cavity with an object such as a large wad of aluminum foil or a Pyrex bowl. After roasting, the Frenched rib ends can be decorated with paper frills, cherry tomatoes, apricots, or other colorful garnish. A *bracelet* of lamb comprises the double rack and the adjoining breast or plate section. Because the curving ribs are not sawed in half, the resulting cut—a cross-section of the animal's carcass—resembles a giant bracelet, hence its name.

Rib chops are usually cut ¾ to 1 inch thick, each one containing a rib bone. Those chops cut nearest to the loin will give you the highest ratio of lean to fat and will be the most tender; those cut nearest the shoulder will be larger in cross section. If both sell for about the same price per pound, or if tenderness is your principal goal, always buy the chops from the small (loin) cut of the primal rib. A *double rib* chop can be one that includes matching, unsplit chops from both sides of the carcass or one that is a double thickness, that is, about 1½ to 2 inches thick. The thicker the chop, the juicier and more tender it will cook. Some retailers sell chops only ½ inch thick—leave these in the display case. All rib roasts and chops containing one or more rib bones can be Frenched: trim off 1 to 1½ inches of the meat and fat from the tip of the rib bone and, after cooking, add decorative paper frills. In the case of a rack or crown roast, the exposed bone tips should be wrapped with aluminum foil to prevent them from scorching in the oven.

Primal Shoulder: Anatomically, this cut somewhat corresponds to the beef chuck and therefore comprises a number of different muscles moving in various directions and a complicated structure of bones that include the chine, blade, rib, and arm bones. If of USDA Choice grade or higher, the shoulder cut can be cooked with dry as well as with moist heat. The basic shoulder cut is called the *square-cut shoulder*. This 5- to 8-pound roast can be cooked as is (a devil to carve), or can be presliced and tied back together before cooking (okay for people who like dry, tough meat). Wiser alternatives include boning the shoulder and transforming it into a *rolled roast* or—if you want to stuff the meat with a savory filling—into a square *cushion roast*. Another way to deal with the difficult-to-carve whole shoulder cut is to slice several steaks off both the blade bone and arm bone ends. The *arm-bone steak* contains cross-sections of the round arm bone and, usually, the first rib bones. The *blade-bone steak* has a cross-section of the blade bone and, perhaps, part of a rib or the chine bone. The blade- and arm-bone steaks often sell at the same price, but the blade-bone steak will be more tender and delicately flavored. The best blade-bone steaks are those cut closest to the rib section (such steaks will have a blade-bone cross section without the protruding bump or knob). A *Saratoga chop* is a slice from a boned-and-rolled roast made of the inside shoulder muscle. A *wing* is a single cut of lamb comprising the animal's entire shoulder (both halves), its two foreshanks, its breast, and its neck. The whole shoulder can be *cubed* for stew meat or kabobs, or *ground* for meat patties and loaves. Meat from the neck area is usually stewed. Scraps and trimmings are best ground.

Primal Breast: Flat and oval, weighing 1½ to 2 pounds, a lamb *breast* consists of the breast muscle interspersed with layers of fat as well as breast and rib bones. When compared to veal or pork breast, lamb breast has too much fat and too little lean, but the price per pound sometimes reflects that situation. Lamb breast is best braised or, if marinated and basted, barbecued, either whole or cut between the ribs into 1- by 4-inch *riblets* (*lamb spare ribs*). Or the breast can be boned and rolled jelly-roll style, stuffed or not. The meat and part of the fat can be ground for meat patties and loaves.

Primal Shank: Lamb *shank* should designate only the 1 to 1½-pound foreshank of the animal, though some butchers use the phrase interchangeably with *hindshank*. With so much connective tissue and gristle, it needs to be cooked slowly with moist heat, such as braising and stewing. With so much bone and a fair amount of fat, you should plan to buy one shank per hungry diner. If you do not plan to serve the shank whole, ask your butcher to crosscut it in halves or into 2-inch-thick slices.

Flank Steak: The customer seldom sees this cut in whole form, as it is too thin to be treated as a London broil. Usually the butcher converts it into ground lamb.

Variety Meats: See the following entries: BRAINS, HEAD, HEART, KIDNEYS, LIVER, SWEETBREADS, TAIL, TESTICLES, and TONGUE. Also see BLOOD and BONES.

Buying Tips

The younger the animal, the more tender and delicate its flesh. (But remember, extremely young lamb lacks desirable texture and flavor.) You can easily identify relative age of lamb of the same breed by comparing the sizes of two pieces of meat cut from identical carcass areas. If, for example, you see a 6-pound and a 9-pound whole leg of lamb, the 6-pounder will be from the younger animal. Likewise, a loin chop that is 2 rather than 3 inches wide will be from the younger sheep. The diameter of like bones also reveals relative age. Still another visual clue to relative age between animals of the same breed and feed is flesh color. The younger the animal, the paler the flesh will be. Milk-fed baby lambs have a white-pinkish hue. As the animal matures, the color gradually changes into a pinkish-red, then starts developing a brownish-red tinge.

The flesh should be firm, neither soft nor tough, and fine- rather than coarse-grained. Marbling (flecks of fat imbedded within the lean) contributes to tenderness and flavor. However, because the degree of marbling increases with age, do not reject young lamb if it has but scant marbling.

The younger the animal, the whiter the fat will be for its breed and feed. As the animal ages, the fat takes on a creamy yellowish tinge. Too much exterior fat is a sign of lesser quality and value. Overly brittle fat suggests an older animal, or lamb that has been frozen too long. The ideal fat is firm-textured with a slightly waxy consistency.

The cross sections of bones of very young sheep are infused with blood, giving the bones a pinkish hue. As the lamb matures, the bones change from being soft, moist, and porous to hard and dry. If the lamb is young, the previously mentioned *break joint*, which lies just above the lamb's hoof, will have four spongy, easily seen ridges. If the break joint is hard and jagged, you know you have an older lamb. If there is no break joint, you probably have yearling mutton (or mutton), because the leg of an older animal cannot be readily snapped in two at the break joint because natural ossification has been completed.

Regardless of its size, any cut should be well-proportioned. The configuration of a leg or shank should be plump. If prepackaged lamb swims in its own juices, the meat was probably frozen then thawed and, consequently, may cook dry and tough.

PREPARATION

Storage

If you plan to refrigerate unground lamb, loosely rewrap it in butcher paper—this allows for enough air to circulate to reduce surface moisture, and thereby hinder bacterial growth. Plan to use refrigerated lamb chops, steaks, and chunks within a day or two. A roast will stay fresh for 2 to 3 days. Cooked lamb will stay good for 2 or 3 days, longer if reheated every 2 days. Refrigerate ground lamb in its original wrapping and use within a day. We do not recommend freezing lamb unless it is absolutely necessary, because that process significantly diminishes flavor, texture, and nutrients. If you must, seal it tightly in freezer paper. Store small cuts such as chops for no more than 10 days in the frozen-food compartment and for a maximum of 2 months in a 0°F freezer. (Holding a roast in the frozen food compartment has too many drawbacks to be recommended.) The fattier the cut, the shorter the freezing period should be, because fat does not freeze as well as lean. Do not freeze lamb for more than a short duration if it has been cooked with salt, as the salt keeps the meat from freezing as solid as it would if it were unsalted.

Preliminaries

The Fell: Covering the exterior fat of the sheep is the fell, a thin, tissuelike membrane. It is left on the whole carcass when it is shipped, because it helps to prolong storage life. The butcher usually removes the fell from all cuts save the leg. Too many cookbooks erroneously say the fell gives lamb a strong, objectionable flavor. Not so, at least not for lamb that is typically sold in this country, as our kitchen experiments have shown. Our best advice is to remove the fell from cuts such as chops, as it has a slight tendency to curl them. Remove it or not, as you wish, from other cuts except for the leg. Do not remove the fell on the leg of lamb, because it helps retain the leg's juices and shape. The exception is when you plan to marinate the leg, because the fell hinders infusion by the marinade. What about the fell of mutton? Granted, mutton fell is strongly flavored, but so is mutton flesh. Therefore, follow the same guidelines.

General: As with all meats, bring

lamb to or near room temperature prior to cooking. Defrost frozen lamb slowly in the refrigerator—this minimizes loss of internal juices. All four legs of the sheep (as with many other quadripeds) have what are commonly called musk glands, so named because of the incorrect belief that the glands give lamb an unpleasant musklike odor. Butchers usually remove the protruding, yellowish gland from each leg at the shop. If not, we suggest you cut it out yourself (it is easy to do with a sharp knife or poultry shears), because it may detract from the appearance of your leg roast.

Cooking

Broiling and Sautéing: Do not salt lamb that is to be broiled or sautéed until after it has been browned, because salt draws moisture to the surface, hindering the browning. Likewise, do not pepper those cuts until near the end of the cooking, as the heat may burn the pepper, producing a bitter taste. A thick lamb chop (or steak) will cook more tenderly and be more juicy than a thin one; 2 inches thick is best. Though some markets sell 1/2-inch-thick chops, the thinnest you should buy is 3/4 inches, and even then you will not be savoring the meat's full potential. Chops between 1 1/2 and 2 inches thick are best broiled; thinner ones usually taste best sautéed (pan-broiled); pieces thicker than 2 inches should be cooked like a roast. For medium-rare meat, saute a 3/4-inch chop for about 4 minutes per side, and a 1-inch chop for 5 minutes per side. Broil 1 1/2-inch-thick chops 3 inches from the 450°F heat source for 7 minutes per side; if 2 inches thick, add 3 minutes per side. Shorten the time for rare chops, increase it for medium to well-done chops. For most lamb shoulder chops, you should slightly reduce the temperature while slightly increasing the cooking time. Baste as needed. Test for doneness by slicing into the thickest part of the meat, preferably near but not to the bone. Rare meat is reddish-pink, medium-rare is pink, medium is brown with a barely perceptible pink tinge, and well-done is grayish-brown.

For a change of pace, bread your chops. Kabobs 1 1/2 inches thick will take a total broiling or charcoal-broiling time (3 inches from either heat source) of about 12 minutes for medium-rare meat. Shish kabob tastes best if the lamb has been marinated. Baste often. Broil the standard accompaniments—mushrooms, onion wedges, cherry tomatoes, green-pepper squares—on separate skewers for less time, otherwise they may be scorched by the time the lamb cubes are properly cooked. Patties 1 inch thick require 5 to 8 minutes per side, depending on doneness.

Roasting: We have tested a number of common roasting methods for lamb and have proven to ourselves that the two most popular ones produce good results. One calls for first searing the meat at 425°F for 15 minutes, then reducing the temperature to 300°F for the rest of the cooking. The other method is the simplest: roast the meat at a constant 325°F temperature. The searing method gives you an attractive brown-crusted roast while the constant-temperature technique assures you a juicier and less-shrunk roast. Both methods require just about the same length of cooking time. Take your pick.

Lamb tastes best when rare or medium-rare. The meat is rare when the meat thermometer registers 125°F (the internal temperature will increase another 5 to 7 degrees within 15 minutes after you remove the roast from the oven). The pull-out-of-the-oven temperature for medium-rare is 135°F, for medium is 145°F and for well-done is 155°F or higher. For a medium-rare roast (our recommendation), estimate 17 to 22 minutes per pound for a whole leg or 22 to 27 minutes per pound for a leg half or for a square-cut shoulder roast. Estimate 40 to 50 minutes' total time for a tailless single loin roast. For a single rib roast, we suggest a constant temperature of 375°F for a total time of 35 to 45 minutes (or 40 to 60 minutes for an unstuffed crown roast), because without the high heat level, the outside surface would not be adequately browned by the time the inside is properly cooked. For much the same reason, we suggest cooking milk-fed baby lamb in a constant 400°F oven.

Your roast will taste better and shrink less if it is cooked bone-in. However, some roasts, such as the square-cut shoulder, are so difficult to carve that boning is usually advisable. If you cook a boned-and-rolled roast, increase the bone-in times by about 10 percent. Roast the meat fat-side up on a rack in a shallow roasting pan in a preheated oven. You will not need the metal rack for the rib, tailless loin, or crown roast as they have their own built-in racks. Do not cover a roast as it cooks—otherwise, you will be partially steaming the meat, giving it a mushy texture. Baste well with drippings, butter, or other oil every 20 minutes or so. Insert the meat thermometer in the center of the thickest part of the flesh, being careful not to touch a bone (it is hotter than the surrounding lean) or the fat (fat will register a lower reading than the lean). Many recipes call for inserting a small army of garlic slivers into leg of lamb. While there is nothing wrong with enjoying the assertive garlic taste and smell now and then, if you do it too often, you will seldom have a chance to enjoy the true, natural, delicate flavor and fragrance of the lamb, a treat indeed. (This principle holds, too, for using too much of other strong seasonings.) A better alternative is to rub the meat's surface with a cut clove of garlic.

Braising: Lamb shanks, breasts, and riblets are usually braised. Allow 1¼ to 1½ hours for the riblets, 1½ to 2 hours for the whole breast, shanks, and other large cuts.

Stewing: The neck meat is often stewed. Do not remove the bone, as it not only adds flavor and thickening power, it is difficult to remove without much effort and waste. Neck meat cut into 1-to-2-inch chunks will cook in 1½ to 2 hours.

Mutton: Only the tenderest sections of yearling mutton or mutton should be cooked with dry heat such as broiling or sautéing; it should be done at temperatures slightly lower and for cooking periods slightly longer than those we suggested for lamb. Tender primal sections of mutton include the rib, loin and sirloin. You will also need more time for braising and stewing—the methods necessary for most mutton.

Serving

In America and England the cliché accompaniment to lamb is green mint jelly. Few choices could be worse as far as taste is concerned, as the jelly's cloying sweetness and excessively minty flavor overpower the subtle taste of the lamb. The best sauce for lamb besides a hearty appetite is just the natural juices without any flour thickener. While cooked beef can be served cold to good advantage, the same is seldom true with lamb. If you are slicing lamb, try to make the slices as thin as possible for the sake of tenderness. A sharp carving knife certainly helps.

Equivalents

Estimate ¼ to ⅓ pound of boneless lamb and ½ to 1 pound of bone-in lamb per serving. For ribs, figure on 1 to 1½ pounds, as they contain much bone and fat waste. A whole shank should satisfy one hungry person.

Carving a Leg of Lamb

There are two basic ways to carve a leg of lamb: Continental and American style. The first entails carving the meat parallel to the leg bone, but we believe that the American method is superior. In this method, the meat is carved perpendicular to the bone, which means you are cutting the flesh across (rather than with) the grain, thereby making each slice more tender in the process.

Here are simplified directions on one way to carve a leg of lamb American-style. Place leg on a carving platter with the shank bone pointing to the right (or to the left, if you are a southpaw). Carve a couple of slices off the base of the leg near the knee joint.

Balance the leg on the cut surface. Starting a couple of inches from the exposed shankbone, make perpendicular (downward) slices of desired thickness, working your way toward the end opposite the shank bone. Make as many slices as you require.

Next, free the slices by making one long horizontal cut parallel to and touching the leg bone.

Place the slices on a warm serving platter. If you later need more meat, continue to carve as before, then repeat the process on the other side of the leg (the slices will be much smaller). Finally, remove the remaining meat from the bones; sorry, you will just have to follow your best instincts, letting experience teach you the ins and outs of carving the remaining meat from a very complicated bone structure.

CLASSIC USES AND AFFINITIES

As we have already mentioned, mint jelly is a famous but horrible accompaniment to lamb. So are other sweet sauces and jellies, including currant. A mild, not-too sweet chutney does work, however. Classic and worthy seasonings are rosemary, garlic, and lemon juice, if not overused. Also high on the favored list are basil, bay leaf, curry, dill, ginger, marjoram, mint, mustard, olive oil, onion, oregano, parsley, sage, savory, thyme, vinegar, and wine. Popular garnishes and side dishes are baby carrots, broiled tomato halves, eggplant, *flageolets*, green beans, lima beans, mushrooms, pan-browned or baked stuffed potatoes, parsley sprigs, pearl onions, peas, and watercress. Some of the well-known preparations that always or often include lamb are: cassoulet, chelo kebab, couscous, crown roast, dolma, English mixed grill, Irish stew, kibbeh, korma, Lancashire hot pot, moussaka, navarin, pilaf, Scotch broth, shepherd's pie, shish kebab, and souvlaki.

LARD

BACKGROUND

Lard is rendered pork fat. *Leaf lard* is made from the more delicate belly fat with leaflike veins. Unprocessed lard has a greasy, soft texture and a pronounced flavor. Frequently lard is hydrogenated, giving it a firmer texture, longer shelf life, and a milder flavor. This commercially processed lard can be stored at room temperature. (For more information, see OILS AND FATS.)

PREPARATION

Basic Cooking

Lard's crystalline texture is excellent for making fluffy biscuits or piecrust, but not very good for cake. When substituting lard for butter or margarine in a recipe, use 20 to 25 percent less. The smoke point of lard varies from 350° to 375°F, but it will not burn below 482°F. A careful cook can use lard to fry savory doughnuts or fritters that can be a cardiologist's nightmare.

LAVENDER

BACKGROUND

English cooks made a good deal of use of the leaves of *lavender* (*Lavandula officinalis*), a relative of mint, during the

Elizabethan age. Today, in the West, it is used more often in perfumes and sachets than in kitchens. However, it is an important spice in Moroccan cooking; sometimes Spanish *chorizo* sausages use it. Lavender can be used with small game birds, in marinades (especially with venison), in fruit jellies, in salads, and with sauerkraut. The leaves can also be brewed for tea. (See HERBS AND SPICES for information on buying, storing, cooking, etc.)

LEAVENING AGENTS

BACKGROUND

BAKING POWDER is now the leavening agent most often used in making cakes, pancakes, muffins, biscuits, and other quick breads. However, other leavenings are frequently employed too. For instance, YEAST is the leavening for most breads, while steam is the leavening agent for air-risen baked goods such as popovers and cream puffs. Likewise, beaten egg whites leaven angel cake and soufflés. Without any of these various leavening agents, the vast majority of bakery items would be hard and compact rather than soft and fluffy.

LEEKS

BACKGROUND

The *leek* is rich in history and lore. Nero supposedly ate leeks to improve his voice, and it is said that a victorious sixth-century Welsh army wore them on their helmets to distinguish themselves from the enemy. (In honor of that episode, the leek was made the national emblem of Wales.) The ancient Egyptians and Greeks loved leeks; so do modern northern Italians and Frenchmen. The latter call them "the asparagus of the poor," a label that seems strange in America, where leeks command a fairly high price.

Allium porrum tastes somewhat like its relative the onion, but is definitely milder and more subtle. With its green top, white stalk, and bearded roots, the leek looks like a giant scallion. The leek has long, medium-green, flat, wraparound leaves that are ridged like corduroy. Its white stem is generally between 3/4 and 1 1/2 inches in diameter and several inches long, the base is slightly bulbous. The extensive whiteness is caused by piling dirt around the stalk (this process, called *blanching*, is why so much grit and dirt is imbedded between the leaves).

AVAILABILITY

Traditionally, leeks are a cold-weather vegetable, although they are available in some markets all year.

Buying Tips

For best flavor and tenderness, choose young, small leeks. Whatever you buy, stay clear of the fibrous second-year crop. These leeks are quickly identified by their oversized bulbs. The green tops should be vivid green, crisp, and unwilted; the white portion should be relatively long and free of soft spots and blemishes. If you plan to prepare them whole, halved, or in chunks, choose leeks of roughly the same size, so they will cook at the same rate.

PREPARATION

Storage

Keep fresh, untrimmed leeks in a plastic bag in the vegetable crisper of the refrigerator for 1 to 4 days, depending on original condition. Do not wash until ready to use.

Preliminaries

Trimming: Remove the tough outer leaves, cut off the roots and all but 1 to 5 inches of the green tops, depending on the condition of the leaves and your taste preference, then peel the tissuelike skin from the white portion. If they're in good condition, save the leaf trimmings for flavoring and soups and stocks.

Washing: It is essential that you wash away the grit and dirt lodged between the leaves. If the leek is to be sliced or diced, simply wash the pieces after cutting. If the vegetable has been cut in half lengthwise, soak the two sections for 15 minutes, then run a fast stream of cold tap water between the leaves, spreading them a litle with your fingers, taking care not to ruin the half-cylinder shape. If the leek is to be used whole, first soak the trimmed cylinder for 20 minutes, then run the tap water down through the leaves and the grit should flush out on the other side. This last method may be insufficient for very gritty leeks. In that case, make one or two lengthwise slits completely through the soaked leek, but only to within 3/4 of an inch of each end. Run water through the openings, spreading the leaves gingerly with your fingers.

Cooking

Whole leeks can be simmered in salted water for 12 to 25 minutes, depending on thickness. Or they can be braised: parboil them for 4 to 8 minutes, then braise them for 12 to 25 minutes, depending on thickness. Halved leeks are difficult to simmer or parboil as they easily fall apart, so braise them for 10 to 15 without the preliminary parboiling step. A good way to cook sliced leeks is to parboil them for several minutes, then braise them for 8 to 12 minutes.

Equivalents

Six small or three large leeks weigh approximately a pound. Used as a side vegetable, this amount will usually serve two to three people.

CLASSIC USES AND AFFINITIES

Leeks are often used in soups, stews and—if young and tender—raw in salads. They can be used as a seasoning as well as a vegetable. They take well to braising, simmering, steaming, and deep-frying and can be eaten hot or cold, especially *à la vinaigrette.* Marjoram and lovage are agreeable herbs for leek cooking. Compatible sauces include those based on cream, cheese, and egg yolk. Famous preparations include vichyssoise, cockaleekie soup, leek pie, and leek quiche.

LEMON

BACKGROUND

The common *lemon* is a versatile and valuable fruit, one of the culinary workhorses. *Citrus limonium* is believed to be indigenous to Southeast Asia. It is now widely cultivated around the world and has become one of the cornerstones of many a cuisine. California almost monopolizes production in America. Our other leading citrus state, Florida, prefers to concentrate on growing juice oranges.

AVAILABILITY

Fresh lemons are available all year, but best in June, July, and August.

Processed Lemon Products

Lemon juice can be purchased in the supermarket in two basic forms: unrefrigerated in a glass bottle and frozen in a plastic bottle. The first—the reconstituted, additive-laden variety—is not recommended, as its flavor is poor. The frozen variety, however, is at least a fair (but not perfect) substitute for freshly squeezed lemon juice. The frozen lemon-juice concentrates that come in cans are infused with sugar and often other ingredients—read the label carefully. Candied lemon peels designed for cocktails are found in most supermarkets.

Buying Tips

The best lemons are heavy for their size, firm, plump, with a well-developed bulge on the blossom end. The skin should be smooth and a deep, bright, healthy yellow without green tinge, brown or soft spots, blemishes, injuries, or dullness. The fruit should smell fresh and fragrant, not odorless nor pungent.

PREPARATION

Storage

Unless you plan to use your lemons within a couple of days, they should be stored in the refrigerator vegetable crisper. Placing them in an airtight plastic storage bag helps keep moisture and fragrance in and helps prevent the lemon and other foods from exchanging odors. That way, a lemon should stay in good condition for about a week. You can store lemon halves for a day or two if you wrap them tightly in cellophane, then refrigerate them. Freshly squeezed lemon juice should be used promptly, but if you must store it, keep it in a tightly closed, nonmetal container in the refrigerator for up to a couple of days, in the frozen food compartment for up to a couple of weeks, or in a 0°F freezer for up to a few months. Lemon peel, either grated or cut into strips, quickly loses its essential oils, thereby its fragrance. Therefore, peel is not suited for proper storage.

Preliminaries

Always wash a lemon before using. To increase juice production, soak the whole lemons in hot water for several minutes (or at least have them at room temperature). Then roll each lemon on a flat surface. This breaks up the pulp, forcing out more juice. When you need only a few drops of juice, pierce the lemon with a toothpick, squeeze out the necessary juice, then refrigerate the lemon with the toothpick installed as a plug. When cutting lemon peel, remove only the yellow, aromatic, surface skin (called the *zest*), not the white membrane which is bitter.

Equivalents

An average lemon will give you 1½ to 2 ounces (or 3 to 4 tablespoons) of juice, and 1 to 2 teaspoons of grated peel.

CLASSIC USES AND AFFINITIES

It is hard to imagine a lemonless world of cooking. To illustate, the lemon is used for: giving a tart flavor to fish, vegetables, etc.; preserving foods; marinating foods; keeping food like the apple from turning brown from oxydation; dressing salads; giving the twist to a martini; garnishing (with its cliché partner, a sprig of parsley); adding life to iced tea; quenching our thirst in lemonade; and flavoring desserts, such as lemon meringue pie and sherbet. The lemon is indeed a flexible tool for the imaginative chef.

LEMON BALM

BACKGROUND

This herb, also called *vervain*, flourishes in Europe. Its pleasant smell is attractive to bees, which explains its botanical name, *Melissa officinalis: melissa* is the Greek word for bee.

CLASSIC USES AND AFFINITIES

The leaves of this plant can be brewed for tea, a potion said to promote longevity. Balm leaves are also used to impart a slightly tart, fresh flavor to cold drinks such as white wine punch; and in cream soups, stuffings for poultry and pork, salads, and roast lamb. The Dutch call balm the *eel herb* because it cuts the fatty taste of eels. Germans enjoy balm with poultry, mushrooms, and soup. (See HERBS AND SPICES for information on buying, storing, cooking, etc.)

LEMON GRASS

BACKGROUND

Southeast Asian cooks often use the herb called *lemon grass* (*Cymbopogon citratus* and *C. flexuosus*). The long green stalks have a scallionlike swollen base and a lemon-sour aroma and taste. This flavor comes from *citral*, an essential oil also present in lemon peel. (See HERBS AND SPICES for information on buying, storing, cooking, etc.)

AVAILABILITY

Lemon grass is available fresh, or more often dried, in Oriental markets—especially Vietnamese or Thai.

CLASSIC USES AND AFFINITIES

Lemon grass is one of the star ingredients in the famous Thai soup *tom yam koong*. It can also be brewed into a tea rich in Vitamin A.

LEMON VERBENA

BACKGROUND

The long, slender leaves of *lemon verbena* (*Lippia citriodora*) have been used as an herb at least since early Grecian times. Recently, the herb has gained popularity among some of the French chefs who espouse the so-called *nouvelle cuisine*. Lemon verbena's virtues are its lemonlike flavor and fragrance, which perk up such foods as plainly poached fish. Its major drawback is that it can be overpowering unless used in minute portions. *Citronalis*, as it is also called, is used in making sachets as well as herb teas. Some lovers say the tea can be aphrodisiac. (See HERBS AND SPICES for information on buying, storing, cooking, etc.)

LENTIL

BACKGROUND

This legume is never eaten fresh. Two chief varieties of *lentil* (*Lens esculenta*) exist: the French and Egyptian lentils. Both are tiny, round, long-valued substitutes for meat and are available dried year round. The *French* or *European lentil* is brownish-gray-skinned, yellow-fleshed, and the more common in this country. The *Egyptian* or *Middle Eastern lentil* is reddish-yellow-orange, sold without its seedcoat, and preferred by the particular cook for its more delicate flavor and for its ability to commingle with other foods to good effect. Nutritionally high even for a legume, the lentil is a food staple in the Middle East as well as in India where it is called *dhal*. (For soaking, cooking, etc., see BEANS.)

CLASSIC USES AND AFFINITIES

Best known in America as a soup, the lentil is also very good added to stews, in casseroles with cream sauces, and in curries with rice. A bit of mint makes an unusually nice flavoring agent.

LETTUCE

BACKGROUND

Californians eat their salad at the beginning of dinner; the French eat theirs after the meat and before the cheese; dieters crunch with determination through platter after cellulose-filled platter. Lettuce salads are a mainstay of the Western diet.

Varieties

Of the countless lettuce varieties grown in the world, these are the ones you are most likely to find at your greengrocer's:

Iceberg: America's least flavorful lettuce is its best seller. The only saving graces of the fairly firm, round-headed, pale-leaved iceberg are its long storage life and its crisp texture when shredded for foods such as tacos. For salads, you are better off using other greens.

Romaine: Also called *cos*, the romaine is a 6-to-12-inch-long loose cylinder of feather-shaped green leaves, each with a thick midrib, a crisp texture, and a pleasant hint of bitterness. The best leaves found near the center, are a must for the perfect Caesar's salad.

Boston and Bibb: Both are also called *butterheads*, and have soft, loosely clustered, crinkled, whitish-green leaves that form a rosette. Both are prized by connoisseurs for their subtle flavor, but it is the bibb—because of its smaller size—that is the four-star choice. Greengrocers despise both for their fragility and perishability.

Leaf lettuce: This name is collectively given to a class of loose-headed lettuces that are merchandised under many names. Their colors shade from light to dark green, and some have red-tipped leaves. Salad buffs love their crisp but succulent texture and delicate flavor. Unfortunately, they store poorly, bruise easily, and are rarely found in stores (look for them in farmers' markets and a quality greengrocers').

Other salad greens: While some people think lettuces are the only salad greens, you can also make raw salads out of other leafy vegetables, including ARUGULA, CHINESE CABBAGE, CORN SALAD, DANDELION GREENS, ENDIVE, FIDDLEHEADS, PURSLANE, SPINACH and WATERCRESS.

AVAILABILITY

Iceberg is abundantly available all year; other varieties tend to become a little more scarce and expensive during the cool weather months.

Buying Tips

The head should be well-proportioned. Surface lumps are symptomatic of a head that has gone to seed. The color should be bright and fresh-looking for its type. Uncharacteristic paleness is a sign of overmaturity. Wilted, brown-tipped lettuce is deteriorating (some greengrocers hide the fact by peeling off the outer leaves, and selling the soon-to-rot center). Certain lettuce types have specific characteristics. Iceberg, for instance, should have a firm but resilient head and snugly-folded (but not welded-together) leaves. Iceberg and romaine lettuce leaves should be crisp, but butterhead has a soft texture. Butterhead lettuce has naturally oily leaves, so a slightly slick feel is to be expected.

PREPARATION

Storage

Lettuces must be refrigerated, covered tightly in plastic or paper bags. Use leaf or butterhead lettuces within a day or two, romaine within several days, and iceberg within the week.

Preliminaries

Washing: Lettuce tends to be gritty and must be rinsed thoroughly but gently in cold water. Exceptions are the internal leaves of the iceberg lettuce—

they may be eaten unwashed, but for safety's sake, we advise a quick rinsing. The whole heads of Boston and bibb lettuces may be washed by holding them by their stems and then swishing their faces up and down in a container of fresh water.

Cutting: Some cooks say you will bruise lettuce less if you rip the leaves by hand rather than cut them into smaller pieces. Our kitchen experiments show that a sharp knife works just as well if not better. It is the dull blade that has given the knife a bad reputation in this task.

Drying: Moisture on a salad leaf keeps it from absorbing your dressing, so drying is highly desirable. There is an army of gadgets for shaking or spinning lettuce dry. We find that tabletop spin-dry models do the job effectively. The only more thorough method is tedious: Patting each leaf with a paper- or lint-free-cloth towel.

Crisping: Washed and dried lettuce leaves benefit from crisping. Cool them, loosely packed in a plastic bag, in the refrigerator for an hour or two before adding the dressing.

Dressing and Tossing

Too many American homes and especially restaurants use an oil-to-vinegar ratio of 3 to 1 or less. The best dressing has a ratio of at least 4 to 1. If your oil is good and your leaves are dry, you can use a 6-to-1 ratio, the ideal. The best oils include high-quality walnut and olive oils. The worst are blends of inexpensive vegetable oils and those that have become old and rancid. The best vinegars include wine, sherry, and rice vinegars from dependable producers. The common supermarket variety will seldom inspire a lettuce leaf. Do not buy an herb-flavored vinegar; adding the herb yourself produces a fresher bouquet and a more creative dressing. Freshly squeezed lemon can be effectively substituted on a 2 to 1 basis for all or part of the vinegar allowance. You can successfully use almost any herb or spice, but they must be fresh and used with a light touch. Flavorings such as minced onions, garlic, and ginger root as well as whole green peppercorns and capers can add excitement if used judiciously. The first choice for pepper is freshly ground peppercorns and for salt is sea salt. For best flavor, do not mix the dressing until just before use. While the leaves benefit from a short nap in the refrigerator, the dressing will fall soundly asleep. If you must store dressing in the refrigerator for more than a couple of hours, do not add onions or garlic as they may give the dressing a bitter off-flavor. Purists mix the dressing directly into the salad. They add the oil first, so it will have a chance to reach the leaves before they are coated by the vinegar. Use a bowl large enough for free tossing action. Some people toss with a salad fork and spoon; others use their fingers, insisting that it is more effective.

Cooking

Sometimes lettuce is braised as a side dish, or cooked with young peas to provide moisture. This is a splendid way to use surplus lettuce that would otherwise wilt in your refrigerator. Cooking time is very short: a few minutes.

LICORICE

BACKGROUND

Licorice is a plant grown for the characteristic flavor obtained from juice pressed from its roots. It is used in medicines and confections. Food manufacturers often substitute the similar-tasting ANISE and FENNEL plants, but retain the descriptive "licorice" term on the label of their products.

LIMA BEAN

BACKGROUND

Phaseolus lunatus macrocarpus is a New World legume and one of the most beautiful. Whether palest green or creamy white, the *lima bean* is sensuously curved, round, and full-bodied under a fine-veined, translucent skin. Aesthetically, limas enhance any plate. There are two basic varieties—the *baby lima* and the *Fordhook*. The baby lima is not an immature Fordhook, but a mature, small-seeded type; some prefer its milder flavor. Others accuse the baby of being a bit to bland and prefer the larger Fordhook, which is also mild, but fuller in flavor and crunchier in texture. In the South, dried, bleached-white Fordhooks are known as *butter beans*, and there is a purple-streaked type, also available in the South, called a *calico bean*. (For cooking, soaking, etc. see BEANS.)

AVAILABILITY

Fresh limas can be bought from June to September. Dried limas—boxed by slice, baby or Fordhook—and frozen limas are available year round.

Buying Tips

Buy crisp, firm, well-filled, dark green, unspotted pods. Limas can, slightly immature, be cooked in their pods, but most often fresh limas are shelled before cooking.

CLASSIC USES AND AFFINITIES

Lima beans are good simply seasoned with parsley or tarragon and butter, and—for piquancy—a touch of mustard. They are a tradition combined with corn in *succotash*, a dish given to us by the American Indians. Limas are also very nice as a soup; with meat, as a side accompaniment or in delicate stews; and they become distinctive when dewdropped with lime.

LIME

BACKGROUND

The common *lime* (*Citrus aurantifolia*), native to Southern Asia, is today grown in abundance in the Caribbean and Mexico and to a lesser extent in Florida and California. The mildly pejorative word *limey* (denoting a British sailor) derives from the fact that the Royal Navy was put on a ration of this long-keeping citrus fruit in 1795, not long after it was first discovered that the lime prevented scurvy, the scourge of the days of sail. Not until this century was the antiscorbutic agent isolated and named Vitamin C.

Varieties

The green *Persian* is the most popular lime in America. The highly esteemed yellow *Key lime* is seldom found outside its Florida home except in a few big-city gourmet markets.

AVAILABILITY

Persian limes are sold year round, but they are at their best and most plentiful from late May through the end of August.

Buying Tips

Select limes with—depending on the variety—a bright green or yellow color. Some brownish mottling or scald is not necessarily an indication of inferior quality, but a dried, shriveled skin certainly is. Look for smooth skins. Also avoid limes with soft spots, bruises, and those with moldy or punctured skins. All limes should have a fresh characteristic lime scent, and be heavy for their size, a sign of maximum juice content.

PREPARATION

Storage

Whole limes retain their freshness and Vitamin C longest stored in a sealed plastic bag in the refrigerator. That way, prime-condition limes should keep fresh for up to 7 to 10 days. A sliced lime will keep for a couple of days in the refrigerator if the cut surface is tightly covered with plastic wrap. Freshly squeezed lime juice keeps a day in the refrigerator, for several weeks in the frozen food compartment, and for several months in a deep freezer.

Preliminaries

Always wash before using. For tips on juicing a lime, see LEMON.

Equivalents

You can usually get 1 to 2 ounces of juice from an average-sized lime, or about 3 tablespoons.

CLASSIC USES AND AFFINITIES

Bartenders put the deep, tart taste of lime juice to work in well-known drinks such as gin-and-tonic, daiquiri, and margarita. Mexicans love a quick suck of lime to chase a sip of the potent tequila. Limeade and lime rickeys are popular with all ages. Lime in fresh food dishes include the avocado-based *guacamole*, the marinated Peruvian raw-fish concoction *ceviche*, various chutneys made in India, and, in the case of the Key lime, Florida Key lime pie. Because lime may be substituted for lemon in most preparations, this citrus fruit can give you a refreshing variation on the lemon theme.

LIQUORS AND LIQUEURS

BACKGROUND

Liquors, liqueurs, brandies, and other spirits have their own distinctive tastes and aromas in terms of strength, sweetness, and flavoring agents. Those variables must be taken into consideration before using them in cooking. Do not be worried that a child will consume alcohol if you cook with an alcoholic beverage, as long as the beverage has been flambéed, briskly reduced in a sauté pan, or slow-cooked in a pot, because the alcohol boils and, in the process, evaporates at about 175°F (compared to 212°F for water). However, many dessert recipes calling for rum, brandy, or other spirits get little or no cooking after the alcohol is added. If these desserts are eaten reasonably soon after preparation, the alcohol's intoxicating powers will still be evident, but to such a small degree that it shouldn't cause concern to most parents.

Flambéing

This technique is used more for theatrical than culinary purposes and, as such, should be done on rare occasions. Your spirit may not ignite when touched with a lit match, unless you preheat it to about 110° to 130° F. The best and safest way to do that is to pour the spirit you need into a warm Pyrex measuring cup, then place it in a pot or bowl containing an inch or two of just-boiled water. Within several minutes the alcohol should be warm enough to flame readily. Do not flambée a food with too much alcohol, as the spirit's flavor may dominate the dish. Do not blow out the flames until they have subsided of their own accord, because you want the alcohol to burn off.

LITCHI

BACKGROUND

Thousands of years ago, *Litchi chinesis*, a fruit native to Southeast Asia, was adopted by China and became its most cherished fruit. The *litchi* (or *leechee*—it is spelled many ways) grows on trees in small bunches like cherries. Fresh, it looks like a large scaly strawberry, about an inch or so in diameter. It is familiarly called a nut—probably because dried, its red shell darkens to walnut color and its juicy, creamy-white, soft flesh browns and hardens. They are grown domestically in California, Hawaii, and Florida.

AVAILABILITY

On the West Coast and around the Gulf you might find fresh litchis through June and July, but in the rest of the country expect them only from about late June into early July. They will keep a week or so if refrigerated and not shelled. Chinese and specialty shops carry the litchi canned and dried all year round.

CLASSIC USES AND AFFINITIES

Use as a dessert alone or with other fruits, or cook in Cantonese-style duck dishes.

LIVER

BACKGROUND

America's favorite organ meat is liver, rich in body-building nutrients, particularly protein, iron, and Vitamin A. Mankind eats the liver of a wide variety of beasts, fowl, and sea creatures, but the all-American best-seller is liver from cattle. It is called *calves'* (or *veal*) *liver*, *baby beef liver*, or *beef liver*, depending on the age of the animal. Culinarily speaking, calves' liver is decidedly superior to beef liver and the significant price difference reflects that fact. Moreover, beef liver may provide you with a possible excess of unwanted additives because liver has a propensity for storing the medicines, growth-stimulants, and other chemicals given to cattle—and the older the animal, the greater the residual buildup.

Varieties

Beef vs. Calf: Some butchers try to hoodwink the unwary shopper by switching beef (or at least baby beef) liver for calves' liver, and by selling it at a calf's ransom. There are several ways to differentiate between the two. (Baby beef liver—from an animal between 6 and 12 months old—falls between calf and beef livers in the qualities discussed.) Beef liver has a darker reddish-brown color than calves' liver, which should have a pinkish-brown tone. A whole liver usually weighs about 10 or more pounds. Calves' livers usually weigh in at about 1½ to 3 pounds. Beef liver is firmer than calves' liver. A good on-the-spot test is to press the flesh with the tips of your fingers. Beef liver has a stronger aroma than calves' liver, whose odor is sometimes barely detectable. Beef liver has a more pronounced taste than the more subtly flavored calves' liver. The color is usually the quickest quality test, and size less so—the butcher can always sever the 2-to-3-pound small lobe of the whole beef liver, palming it off as calves' liver.

Lamb vs. Calf: Tricky butchers also sometimes switch lamb liver for calves' liver. This would not be all that bad if the liver came from a young lamb, because such liver is similar to—even, to most palates, indistinguishable from—calves' liver. In that case, the sin would be charging you high calves'-liver prices for the lamb liver, which should cost less because of the smaller demand. When the switch is indeed nefarious is when the liver of older sheep is substituted. While their weight may be equal, the difference in their flavor and texture is quite noticeable to any discerning diner. Fresh, unprocessed lamb liver is seldom seen in meat markets outside of certain ethnic neighborhoods.

Pork vs. Calf: Pork liver is easy to distinguish from calves' liver: the first is three-lobed, the latter two-lobed. If it comes from a piglet, the liver of pork can be good, but if it comes from a mature porker, it is coarse and strong-flavored. Except for the small quantity that finds its way into ethnic markets, most pork liver is ground up by commercial processors for products such as sausages, pâtés, and spreads.

Poultry: Poultry liver is discussed under CHICKEN GIBLETS AND VARIETY MEATS.

Buying Tips

Top quality liver—whether calves', beef, lamb, or pork—should be fresh in smell and look, and not faded or too brownish. The surface should appear bright and moist, not slimy. Many markets sell frozen liver. It is inferior to fresh liver in both flavor and texture.

PREPARATION

Storage

Like all fresh organ meats, liver is highly perishable. If you cannot use it the day you buy it, store it loosely wrapped in the refrigerator for no more than a day. If you must freeze liver, store it, tightly wrapped, for no more than a couple of weeks in the refrigerator freezing compartment, and a couple of months in an 0°F freezer. Try not to have leftover cooked liver, as reheating it will make it tough.

Preliminaries

Do not soak or marinate liver if you plan to sauté or broil it, as the meat will absorb too much moisture. The only time marinating may be necessary is if you have the liver of an older animal; in this case, braise the marinated liver. Before cooking, clean the surface of the liver with a damp paper towel. Liver has an outer membrane that will curl the meat as it cooks. If the butcher did not remove it, carefully peel it off with a sharp knife. Liver has a number of vessels running through it. These (especially from an older animal) become tough when cooked, so it is a good idea to pull or cut out the large tubes before cooking, if at all possible.

Cooking

Liver is at its best when cooked rare and should never be sautéed or broiled beyond medium-rare (the moment it starts to lose its internal pink color) unless one prefers shoe leather. The reason you need to cook liver only briefly is that it is already tender. Your goal is ever so slightly to firm the interior flesh while giving the exterior surfaces an appetizing brown color. Slice the liver as thin as possible (1/4 inch or less) to insure uniform pieces and even cooking. Sauté over medium-high heat (high heat will toughen the meat) in preheated butter, fat, or oil for 2 to 3 minutes at most. Braise whole or large pieces 1½ to 2 hours, and slices 20 to 40 minutes, depending on thickness. Braising should be used only for mature livers. The texture of liver makes it difficult to grind; some cooks partially firm the liver that is to be ground by slicing then sautéing it for a few seconds.

Sauce

Before deglazing the pan drippings for making sauce, taste them to make sure they are not bitter or otherwise objectionable. Bitterness can be a result of overcooking, cooking over too high heat, or using the liver of a too-mature animal.

Equivalents

Buy 1/4 to 1/3 pound per person.

CLASSIC USES AND AFFINITIES

The classic combination is (calves') liver and onions, with Italy's *fegatto alla veneziana*, one of many fine European examples. Calves' liver is also popularly broiled on a skewer with a wrapping of bacon, producing a clichéd hors d'oeuvre. Liver is the star (or co-star) in many other recipes: liver dumplings, English mixed grill, various pâtés, to name a few. The adaptable liver cooks well with butter, fats, and oils and blends well with fresh green herbs, mild spices, lemon juice, wine and mushrooms.

LOBSTER

BACKGROUND

From a culinary point of view, there are three basic categories of crustaceans that fall within the broad *lobster* grouping: the standard *Homarus* lobster, the *spiny lobster*, and the lobsterlike *prawn*. The latter two of these marine creatures will be discussed at the end of this entry.

Homarus Lobster

The *Homarus* lobster is the familiar type with the large, threatening pincer claws that scare fish and men alike. The darker and thicker-shelled *Homarus vulgaris* lives in European waters, while the *Homarus americanus* lives along the Atlantic coastline of Canada and the northern United States. Most restaurants and seafood stores call the latter type the "Maine" lobster, even though most *Homarus americanus* lobsters are collected in Canadian waters.

Comparisons

Left- vs. Right-Clawed Lobsters: Lobsters are not symmetrical; their two claws are different in size, shape, and function. The large claw is the crusher or "molar-tooth" claw, while the smaller, defter claw has finer teeth for ripping and tearing the food into bite-sized pieces. A lobster is categorized as left- or right-clawed depending on which side has the large claw. If you examine 100 lobsters, about 50 will be southpaws. While a right-clawed lobster tastes the same as a left-clawed lobster, the two claws are far from the same: the larger has more meat while the smaller tastes sweeter.

Female vs. Male Lobsters: The female lobster is the prized sex because it contains the delectable sweet coral-hued roe. The *coral*, as the eggs are called, can be cooked with the whole lobster or can be removed and used as a sauce ingredient. There are two ways to determine sex: The female is slightly broader-beamed in the forward part of the tail section. Examine the lobster's underside just behind the last pair of walking legs. You will see a pair of minute leglike appendages. The male's pair will be longer, thicker, and firmer than the female's, which will be feathery and pliable.

AVAILABILITY

Whole lobsters are sold live or precooked. Lobster meat is sold freshly cooked, frozen or canned. Fresh live lobsters, by far the best alternative, are available the year around (thanks to lobster farms consisting of artificially enclosed bays) but they are priced the lowest during the warm months when the lobstermen can more easily do their chores.

Buying Tips

Live Lobsters: An uncooked lobster must be alive when you buy it, because its carcass quickly develops bacteria. There is no sure way to tell how long a lobster has been dead. To be sure a lobster is alive, use this test: its tail will curl underneath its body when you lift the lobster up. The more its feet struggle, the healthier the lobster is (but if it was sitting on ice, it will be slow though healthy). The longer a lobster is stored, the more its flesh shrivels and toughens. Always buy lobsters from a merchant with a high stock turnover.

For your hands' sake, be sure the lobster's claws are closed with bands or wooden pegs. If you are buying more than one lobster, ask the merchant to bag them separately. Lobsters are cannibals, and one may do serious damage to the other if a band or peg comes loose. And buy equal-sized specimens for uniform cooking.

The lobsters from Canada and northern Maine are better tasting than those collected from warmer waters to the south. The latter can usually be detected by their lighter-hued shells. If you wish the coral, buy the female (see Comparisons above). *Culls*, lobsters with one claw missing, are less expensive than whole lobsters but their meat is not as tender, perhaps because of the added tension the one-clawed lobster undergoes. If you do buy a cull and want to get the most meal for your dollar, be sure its remaining claw is the larger one. When buying a live lobster cooked to order in a restaurant, select the lobster out of the tank yourself to ascertain its condition and, if you like coral, its sex. Unethical restaurants may try to hoodwink you—for example, by giving you a cull lobster with an extra, detached claw. Lobsters are sometimes classified by weight. Most tradesmen use the following definitions: *Jumbo* (over 2½ pounds), *large* (between 1½ to 2½ pounds), *quarter-pounders* (from 1¼ to 1½ pounds), *eighth-pounders* (from 1 to 1¼ pounds) and *chicken* (less than 1 pound but above the lobster's minimum legal weight limit, which varies regionally). Are small lobsters more tender? Some say that a 1½ pound lobster, for example, is better tasting and more tender than a 3-pound lobster. The other side argues there is absolutely no difference. Our controlled taste tests indicate that the smaller lobster is indeed sweeter and more tender, but the difference is so small that it is virtually irrelevant for most palates.

Unless you happen to have your own home lobster tank, buy live lobsters on the day you intend to cook them. If you do not plan to cook the lobster within the hour, store it in your vegetable crisper or in a burlap sack on top of ice.

Precooked Lobster: Some seafood stores sell whole lobsters that are precooked (identifiable by their red shells and higher price tags). Unless you know that the fishmonger has the highest of standards, we do not recommend buying precooked lobsters, because too often they were the dying or dead lobsters in the merchant's supply. If you must buy such a lobster, examine the tail: if it is not curled, the lobster was dead when cooked. Also smell the lobster for off-odors.

PREPARATION

Preliminaries

Killing the Lobster: A common way of giving a live lobster the *coup de grace* is to plunge it head-first into boiling water. Some cooks think this is unnecessarily painful to the lobster. An alternative—severing the spinal cord—is less painful to the lobster. Plunge the point of a chef's knife into the crack on top of the back between the body and tail sections. This will sever the spinal cord. The lobster may undergo a few quick spasms, but these are natural involuntary reflexes of the autonomous nervous system. When the deed is done, proceed with your recipe. A third method is to place the lobster in a container of hot tap water for ten minutes, then drop the lobster into the pot of boiling water. The theory behind this technique is the hot water puts the lobster "to sleep," perhaps killing it in the process. Of the three methods, we think severing the spinal cord causes the least pain to the lobster.

Cleaning the Lobster: Inedible parts of the lobster are few and include (besides the shell, of course) the intestinal tract, the spongy gills, and the stomach sac, located just behind the lobster's head. Remove the internal parts after the lobster has been cooked or, if you are splitting the lobster before you cook it, remove those items then. Unless you plan to use them in a sauce, do not remove the *coral* (eggs) or the greenish *tomalley* (liver), as they are delicacies.

Cooking

A whole lobster can be simmered or steamed; if split or shelled, broiled or sautéed. To enjoy lobster at its best, simmer or steam the lobster whole and serve it with clarified butter and lemon wedges.

Simmering: For every pound of lobster, bring to a rapid boil 1 gallon of water or, preferably, *court bouillon*. Use one tablespoon of salt per gallon (unless you are using sea water). Plunge the live (or just-killed) lobster head-first into the boiling water. Cover the pot. As soon as the water returns to a boil, reduce the heat to a simmer and continue to cook the lobster for an additional 5 minutes plus 3 minutes per each pound of weight. (If you are cooking two lobsters, use the weight on one lobster for the calculation.) When cooked, immediately remove the lobster from the water, as overcooking toughens and dries out the flesh, and shrinks it in the process.

Steaming: With this method, you must kill the lobster before you start to cook it (see under Preliminaries). Put the lobster in the steam pot containing rapidly boiling water and cover with the lid. When the water returns to a boil, steam will start escaping from around the lid. From that moment on, steam the lobster for 5 minutes, plus 3 minutes per pound. Do not overcook.

Broiling: Kill the lobster, split it in half, and remove the inedible internal organs such as the stomach sac. Brush the lobster with melted clarified butter and cook, flesh-side up, under a preheated broiler (medium-to-high setting) for 6 to 12 minutes, depending on thickness of the lobster and distance from the heat source. To prevent the flesh from drying, baste frequently.

Serving

If the diner is to cut open his whole lobster at the table, he will need a metal lobster cracker (or nut cracker), a lobster fork (or cocktail fork), a bowl for discarded shells, a bowl of melted clarified butter for dipping, lemon wedges, napkins, and lots of elbow room. Lobster bibs are for babies. The way to attack a whole cooked lobster Maine-style is to first snap off the two claws, then snap the tail section off the body. Crack the claws with the nutcracker and remove the meat with the fork. To remove the large chunk of tail meat in one piece, snap off the rear tail fins, then, using a fork or your thumb, push the piece of meat out of the tail-section shell, pushing from the narrow end. Alternatively, cut the underside membrane lengthwise and remove the tail meat. The main body section has a little meat, too, plus the tomalley and, in a female, the coral. Remove the body core from the shell by stripping the latter away. Before eating the body meat, discard the intestinal tract, gills and stomach sac (or you can simply eat around them). The meaty juice of the legs is obtained by snapping off each leg, one at a time, and sucking out the contents. As you retrieve the meat from the various parts of the lobster, dip it into the butter, then pop it into your mouth. Some cooks and most restaurants save the diner the chore of cracking and opening his own lobster by doing it in the kitchen. Any purist will tell you that such kindness takes all the fun out of eating a lobster.

CLASSIC USES AND AFFINITIES

Lobster is featured in lobster *à l'Americaine*, lobster cardinal, lobster *fra diavolo*, lobster Newburg, lobster Savannah, and lobster thermidor, to name a few classic dishes.

Spiny Lobsters

The *spiny* (or *rock*) *lobster* (or crayfish, as it is sometimes erroneously called) can be physically distinguished from the *Homarus* by its lack of claws; all ten of its legs are about the same. The spiny lobster's distinguishing feature is a pair of long, relatively thick antennae that flop backwards over its body. It is the tail muscle that provides virtually all the edible meat. Perhaps because the spiny lobster lives in warmer water than the *Homarus* lobster, its meat is comparatively coarser, firmer, less sweet and flavorful, and therefore less desirable. Moreover, most of the rock lobsters sold in this country are frozen, which further widens the quality gap. Rock lobster tails are nevertheless delicious, however, if fresh and not frozen; regrettably, such specimens are seldom found outside the Gulf states and California. Most of the frozen lobster tails are marketed as "South African lobster tails" though they may be imported from such Southern Hemisphere countries as Australia, New Zealand, or Chile. These lobsters are biologically different from our domestic spiny lobsters, but are, except for being frozen, on par when it comes to flavor and texture.

When you see "lobster tails" on a menu, chances are overwhelming that they will be from spiny rather than *Homarus* lobsters. If you see "langouste" on a French menu, it is (or should be) a spiny lobster; *homard* is the French word for the *Homarus* type. If you insist on buying frozen lobster tails, be sure to thaw them completely in the refrigerator, then bring them to room temperature before cooking them. Add them to boiling water and, when the liquid returns to a boil, simmer them for approximately 1 minute per ounce of weight. Consult the "*Homarus* Lobster" section above for relevant buying, etc. tips.

Prawns

Prawns are petite lobsterlike crustaceans. Members of the clan include the famous Italian *scampo* (*scampi* is the plural), Dublin Bay prawn, and France's *langoustine*. Prawns have claws like the *Homarus* lobsters, but because their claws are so thin, only an epicure would find it worthwhile to extract the scant flesh they contain. Like the spiny lobster, therefore, it is only the tail meat that is normally eaten. When you see "scampi" or "prawns" on a stateside menu, the odds are at least 1,000 to 1 that you are being served oversized shrimp. These pseudo-prawns typically are from the Gulf of Mexico and, in most cases, are shipped frozen.

LONGAN

BACKGROUND

Oriental markets in the United States stock canned *longans*; sometimes this fruit, also called *Dragon's Eye*, is available fresh. *Nephilium longana*, related to the litchi, bears a fruit the size of a large grape, perhaps an inch in diameter. Inside the spice-brown shell is a juicy, soft white fruit used as a between-meal treat or pastry filling in Chinese cuisine.

LOQUAT

BACKGROUND

Although it is called the *Japanese medlar*, the *loquat* (*Eribotrya japonica*) probably originated in China. Because it ripens in early March, it is one of the first signs of spring. The grape-shaped fruit is about 1½ inches long and has a yellow-orange skin and a pale yellow flesh that has a moderate sweet-and-sour flavor. Ripe, it is very juicy and makes a good thirst-quencher.

AVAILABILITY

The loquat is normally available fresh only in California, Florida, and other Southern states where it is cultivated because it does not ship well. It is often found, though, in the Chinatown markets in big northern American cities. It can be found canned in specialty stores throughout the country.

LOTUS ROOT

BACKGROUND

Several foods are derived from the *lotus* (*Nelumbo nucifera*), an Oriental plant. The leaves are boiled as a potherb. The stamens of the flowers are brewed for tea in Southeast Asia. The seeds are canned as a dessert fruit, or are dried, roasted, and ground into meal, or sweetened as lotus jam. But it is the crisp underwater root, which can reach a length of 4 feet and a diameter of 4 inches, that is the part most commonly eaten. The root's natural shape is that of a string of sausages, with red-brown skin and creamy white flesh.

AVAILABILITY

Fresh lotus root is available in Chinese markets from mid-summer through mid-winter, with a fall peak. Canned, pickled, or dried lotus root is available the year around.

PREPARATION

After removing the inedible peel, soak the flesh in acidulated water to help prevent oxidation. Cut the root into thin discs. Each crosswise slice of lotus root has a ring of ten large and small perforations. These lacy discs float on Oriental soups and are used in stir-fries and casserole dishes.

LOVAGE

BACKGROUND

Lovage (*Levisticum officinale*) was a very popular herb in Medieval times. Many virtues were ascribed to this plant—curing coughs and stomach trouble, aiding the lovelorn, and removing offensive odors and freckles. Today, lovage is grown for its flavor, which is somewhat like that of celery but stronger. (See HERBS AND SPICES for information on buying, storing, cooking, etc.)

PREPARATION

Lovage leaves can be chopped in salad

(use only a few leaves; the flavor is powerful) or cooked in soups or in mixed vegetable dishes. The stems can be lightly cooked and eaten as a vegetable; the seeds can be used like celery seeds. Lovage stems can also be candied as a sweet or garnish. The root can be brewed for tea.

LUNGS

BACKGROUND

In 1971 the USDA prohibited the public sale of *lungs* because it was too difficult for their inspectors to ascertain the wholesomeness of this variety meat. *Lights*, as they are also called, are still popular in Central Europe. Typically, the lungs are ground and used as a stuffing or sausage ingredient, or are added to soups and stews.

M

MACE

BACKGROUND

The nutmeg tree, *Myristica fragrans*, bears fruits that look like peaches. The kernel of this fruit is the spice NUTMEG. The aril, or fiber around the kernel, is the spice *mace*. The aril is bright red. When it is removed from the nutmeg, pressed or dried, it becomes an orangish "blade" of mace. Mace tastes rather like nutmeg, but more delicate. This spice, a native of the Moluccas, also grows in other parts of Southeast Asia, particularly Malaysia. (See HERBS AND SPICES for information on buying, storing, cooking, etc.)

AVAILABILITY

Mace is available in two forms, *blade* and *ground*. The latter can become rancid in a matter of a month or two.

CLASSIC USES AND AFFINITIES

Mace has an affinity for cherries and for chocolate. It flavors doughnuts and poundcakes. It can be used in white sauces, cream soups, and with bland vegetables such as cauliflower and potatoes. A blade of mace can be used to flavor sauces, aspics, and clear soups where flecks of ground spice would be a visual distraction, the blade is removed before serving.

MALT

BACKGROUND

Sprouted, fermented grain (usually barley) is called *malt*. The malt is then kiln-dried and powdered. In this form it can be mixed with hot water to produce the mash that is basic to beer and malt whiskey. Or it can be prepared as nutritious and easily digestible extract to combine with other foods. *Malted milk* is a blend of powdered malt and powdered milk, often with a chocolate flavor. Soda jerks need it to make genuine malted-milk drinks.

MANGO

BACKGROUND

Known as "the fruit of India" and the magic in Major Grey's famous chutney, the *mango* (*Mangifera indica*) is today grown in California and Florida as well as everywhere else in the world where the climate is warm enough to permit it. Mangoes grow in many shapes and sizes, but the ones available to us (whether imported or domestic) are typically 3 to 5 inches long, and either kidney-shaped, oval or round.

The mango has a thin but relatively tough peel which is initially green and becomes yellow or orangey-red as it ripens. When fully ripe, a mango may have a mottled surface of pinks, reds, and yellow, perhaps over some lingering green. The flesh of a ripe mango is yellow-orange, aromatic and juicy, with its own very distinctive sweet-and-tart taste. In the middle of the mango is a single, long, large, flattish seed with clinging fibers. In the best mangos those fibers are almost unnoticeable; in the worst, the seed fibers invade and ruin the texture of the flesh.

AVAILABILITY

The mango is sporadically available fresh year round as imported specimens arrive. The American season spans May through August with the peak time for most mangoes being the month of June.

Buying Tips

You can buy a greenish mango and ripen it at home, but do not buy one that is hard and fully green. Rather choose a somewhat firm-feeling, plump mango with an unblemished, unbroken skin with some color change to yellow, orange or red already evident. To buy almost ripe, select one that yields to gentle pressure without being too soft and shows more red and yellow than green. Since much of the mango is seed, a larger (but not outsize) mango is usually a better buy and tends to have less fiber-invaded pulp. Avoid the mango dotted with black spots and the mango with a fermented aroma.

PREPARATION

Ripening

Mangoes must be ripe to be delicious. Unripe, they have a sour, turpentiny aftertaste. Ripen your mango in a pierced paper bag at room temperature until it has almost completely lost its greenness, has a fresh aroma and, though still firm, yields to your touch. Once ripe, it is best to enjoy the fruit immediately because the mango goes past its prime very quickly, shown by a diminution of its aroma and coloration. If it must be held, seal it in a plastic bag, keep in the refrigerator, and use as soon as possible.

Serving

The most striking way to serve a mango was created a thousand years ago. First, slice the mango into three sections by making two slices through it parallel to the flat sides of the fruit. These slices should be as close to the flat, oval seed as possible.

With a sharp knife, score the pulp of both the top and bottom slice in a cross-hatched pattern. The grooves should be about ½ inch apart and reach but not cut through the peel.

Push the pulp upwards by pushing with your thumbs from the skin-side, bending the slice into an arch as you push. In other words, reverse the shape of the slice from concave to convex. The diamonds of flesh will stand out in bold relief from the surface. Serve on a dish with a spoon—or eat out of hand using your teeth to cut the flesh away from the peel. Do not throw away the middle slice, the one with the seed. Trim off the peel and eat the remaining flesh out-of-hand, sucking the succulent pulp from the seed—it *is* messy, but if the mango is ripe, it is more than worth the effort of cleaning up afterwards. The mango can also be served whole. Cut the skin in strips and partially folded back (rather like a banana). Hold the fruit in your hand or impaled on a fork; eat the flesh down to the seed, pulling the skin away as needed. Note: Some people get an allergic reaction to the oil in mango skin. Avoid the possibility of a rash by peeling the mango before serving it to guests.

CLASSIC USES AND AFFINITIES

Mangos are served as a dessert fruit alone and in fruit salads. They are used to make pickles, sauces, and especially chutneys. They can be pureed and stewed, used in baking, ice creams, and sherbets and preserved as jams and jellies. Slightly green mango flesh cooked with duck produces a memorable dish. Mango and lime juice are a classic pair.

MANGOSTEEN

BACKGROUND

No relation to the mango and unknown to most Americans, the tropical *mangosteen* (*Garcinia mangostana*) is a popular and highly-prized fruit in tropical Asia, where it is widely cultivated. Typically the size and shape of a large tangerine, the mangosteen has a hard purplish-reddish-brown skin which must be cut away with a knife; usually the top third of the rind is removed to shape a natural cup. The flesh is thick, creamy-white, rich, and juicy and is divided into five to eight vertical convex segments; it rises out of the shell like a natural scoop of ice cream with an alluring aroma. The taste is extraordinary, refreshingly sweet and tart. Because the rind contains a pigment that stains, the mangosteen is usually served with a napkin and eaten with a spoon. In the Northern Hemisphere its peak season is from September into November.

MAPLE SYRUP

BACKGROUND

A favorite with the American Indian long before Columbus reached the New World, *maple syrup* is simply the sap of maple trees that has been boiled down to, ideally, one-fortieth of its original volume. With most of the water evaporated, the maker ends up with a sweet, thick, dark-brown liquid. It is the classic American sauce for waffles and pancakes, though it does have other culinary uses, as a topping for ice cream and as a candy ingredient. If more of the water is boiled away *maple sugar* is the result.

The finest maple syrup is made in Vermont, New York, and Canada. Each area has its own grading system—in Vermont, for instance, Grade AA is tops. Not everyone prefers the top grades. Some connoisseurs consider the lower grades (just as long as they are pure maple syrup) to have a more robust and therefore desirable flavor. Because of its high cost, pure maple syrup is often stretched with less expensive syrups (usually corn) and called *maple-flavored syrup*, a product that is inferior to pure maple syrup but usually superior to *pancake syrup*, which contains no genuine maple syrup or just a nip of it.

Storage

Once opened, maple syrup and its substitutes should be stored in the refrigerator. Bring to room temperature, or warm them before serving.

MARASCHINO CHERRY

BACKGROUND

A *maraschino cherry* is any cherry (often a Royal Ann) that is pitted, preserved in a syrup infused (traditionally) with maraschino liqueur, and then dyed red or green. Until recently, potentially harmful chemical coloring agents were used, but these have now been banned by the federal government. Maraschino cherries are used to garnish cocktails and desserts. Once the jar is opened, refrigerate the contents.

MARGARINE

BACKGROUND

No matter what the commercials say, *margarine* cannot be confused with butter: you can't make butter without cream, an expensive product with other uses. Gourmets prefer butter. But good margarine is acceptable for most palates, and will flavor cakes, vegetables, or breakfast toast satisfactorily. Also known as *oleomargarine* or *oleo*, margarine was developed in the late nineteenth century, in part as a butter substitute. Better technology and demand from knowledgeable consumers led to improved varieties. Today's product is usually 100 percent vegetable oil and comes in 1-pound cartons of four 1/4-pound sticks. Aside from its use as a table spread, cooks use it in baking, for frying, and for broiling. (Also see OILS AND FATS.)

Varieties

Regular margarine contains a minimum of 80 percent fat by law; the remaining ingredients include moisture (usually 16½ percent), salt, low-fat milk solids, color, flavoring, and antioxidants.

Premium margarine is generally made of more expensive, polyunsaturated corn or safflower oils—good for cholesterol counters.

Soft margarine always made entirely of vegetable oil, remains soft and spreadable.

Whipped margarine has as much as 50 percent of its volume as air added, so it is fluffier, spreads easily, yields more servings per pound, and melts faster than regular margarine. It is somewhat lower in calories than hard margarine, but you need to use more in cooking because a good deal of it is air.

Diet (or *imitation*) *margarine* has half the calories of regular margarine because it contains only 40 percent fat—the rest is largely air and water. It is not recommended for baking because of the lower fat content but it is fine as a spread, or in toppings.

Liquid margarine available in squeeze bottles, remains liquid even when refrigerated. It is used in basting, in sauces, or on pancakes and the like.

Other margarines include *unsalted*, *vegetarian*, and *kosher*.

Buying Tips

Check the label when choosing; the best margarines list polyunsaturated safflower or corn oil as their first ingredient. Stick margarine is a good selection for sautéing or for making cake. Soft, whipped, or diet margarine is appropriate for spreading on bread or topping vegetables. The soft margarine burns very quickly and has the wrong texture for cake, but is economical for spreading and melting. All margarine should be refrigerated. The less expensive margarines contain hydrogenated and/or saturated oil, the anethema of the anticholesterol league.

MARJORAM

BACKGROUND

Sweet marjoram (*Origanum majorana* or *Marjorana hortensis*) is similar to oregano in flavor and fragrance, but lighter. Its perfume made sweet marjoram popular in the Middle Ages for scenting baths and for strewing rush-covered floors; colonial Americans used it in furniture polish. *Pot marjoram* (*Origanum onites*), another native of the Mediterranean, is a sturdier plant and has a more pungent, bitter flavor. (See HERBS AND SPICES for information on buying, storing, cooking, etc.)

AVAILABILITY

Sweet marjoram is sold fresh or, more often, dried.

CLASSIC USES AND AFFINITIES

Cooks use sweet marjoram in herb blends, such as poultry seasoning. It complements most meats, with a special affinity for liver and veal. Many green vegetables and dried legumes taste better when marjoram is added. The fresh leaves can be chopped raw and used in salads.

MARROW

BACKGROUND

The rich, soft, easy-to-digest, fatlike substance that fills the middle of certain bones such as the leg (the choicest) and the spine is called *marrow*. It has many culinary applications. The Milanese savor it when they eat their famous braised veal-shank dish called *osso buco*. The French make marrow dumplings and marrow-filled pastries. American Indians used it as one of the prime ingredients for pemmican. American prospectors and cowboys called it prairie butter because they spread it on their campfire-baked biscuits. Beef roasters produce an exciting flavor when they bard their meat with it. Sauciers add it to classics such as *bordelaise* and *marchand de vin*. Soups and stews do well by it, too.

PREPARATION

Perhaps the simplest of the excellent ways to enjoy marrow is to put beef leg bones (crosscut into 2-inch lengths) in a 325°F oven for 25 minutes; do not cook them too long, as the marrow easily renders. Then remove the marrow, season with salt and pepper to taste, and smear on some crusty French bread. Another version is to put the marrow on a small piece of toast, run the open-face sandwich under a broiler until the marrow starts to run, sprinkle it with salt and pepper, and serve it hot as a first course.

MARROW BEANS

BACKGROUND

Biggest and roundest of the white beans, the *marrow bean* is widely used in our country like pasta: simply buttered, or cooked and served in a tomato-onion or cream and garlic sauce. They are not available fresh unless locally grown, but can be found dried year-round in packages and boxes. Sometimes—to the horror of purists—marrow beans are substituted for their diminutive cousin, the pea bean, in Boston baked beans, where they perform reasonably well. (For soaking, cooking, etc., see BEANS.)

MARSHMALLOW

BACKGROUND

Originally, *marshmallow* was made from the root of a plant called the marsh mallow. Today, the confection is made with sugar or corn syrup, gelatin, beaten egg whites, and various stabilizers. Its popular uses include being roasted on a stick over a fire, and garnishing desserts, hot cocoa, and baked sweet potato—the flavor is neutral enough to adapt to many foods so long as the marshmallow is not too sweet.

AVAILABILITY

Marshmallows are usually sold in 2-inch-thick cylinders in plastic bags or as 1/4-inch *miniatures*. Marshmallow *cream* and a *spread* are also available.

MARZIPAN

BACKGROUND

Made of almond paste, sugar, and egg whites, *marzipan* is used in confections, including small candies shaped like fruits. Marzipan is more popular in Europe than in America.

MASA HARINA

BACKGROUND

Used to make Mexican tortillas and tamales, *masa harina* is finely ground parched corn treated with lime. It is available in Mexican-American ethnic markets and, sometimes, in general supermarkets.

MEAT TENDERIZERS

BACKGROUND

Long ago, cooks in tropical papaya-growing lands discovered that if you rubbed meat with the fruit pulp or leaves of the papaya tree, the meat would become more tender. Resourceful food processors now isolate the enzyme *papain* from the papaya fruit, dry it into crystals, and sell it in grocery stores as a modern miracle. The use of a little of these chemical meat tenderizers is probably okay, but overdoses tend to make the meat mushy. And before you use these tenderizers in the first place, remember you have other options: marinating, pounding, scoring, cubing, or grinding the meat or cooking it with slow moist heat.

MILK

BACKGROUND

Milk from cows has been a part of human history for as long as man has domesticated animals. A 20,000-year-old cave drawing in the Pyrenees depicts a cow being milked. The 5,000-year-old Vedic hymns of India sing the praises of the cow and the milk she gives. Over the years and in different parts of the world, people have drunk the milk of many animals—goats, asses, horses, and camels, to name a few—but in this entry we will be concerned only with cow's milk.

Milk, designed by nature, is the nearly complete food for young growing bodies. As some people grow older, they become increasingly unable to digest milk. Milk gives them digestive upsets or other problems (such as intense itching). This tendency, called *lactose intolerance*, can be alleviated by choosing fermented and cultured milk products where the lactose, or milk sugar, has already been digested by bacteria—buttermilk, YOGURT, and CHEESE are traditional, well-known choices; acidophilus milk (see below) is a newer alternative.

Besides being high in protein, milk contains sugar, calcium, phosphorus, riboflavin and fat-soluble Vitamins A and D. The natural sodium content of milk is very high; those on low-sodium diets must control their milk consumption. Unless skimmed it also has a high amount of highly saturated butterfat, an important consideration for cholesterol counters.

Varieties

Pasteurized Milk: In 1860 Louis Pasteur discovered that if you heat milk to a high but not boiling temperature, you kill microorganisms that cause many diseases, including undulant fever, salmonella, infectious hepatitis, and even tuberculosis. As a bonus, pasteurization increases the storage life of the milk without changing its flavor a great deal. Modern milk-producing companies use essentially the same method devised by Pasteur.

Homogenized milk has undergone a process that prevents the cream from separating from the milk. Unless a milk is homogenized, the cream will slowly rise to the top, creating a less-than-whole milk on the bottom.

Raw milk has not been pasteurized. Partisans of raw milk say that pasteurization destroys vitamins, destroys certain beneficial enzymes, and damages the taste of milk. A few dairies are permitted to sell raw milk. Because these dairies are held to rigid standards of cleanliness and their herds are inspected often for disease, the milk is called *certified*. Uncertified raw milk, if unhygienic, can be a source of many diseases, including the ones mentioned in our discussion about pasteurized milk. But certified raw milk can be bought at health-food stores or directly from the dairy. Its higher price and potential danger in relation to pasteurized milk must be balanced against the taste and possible nutritional advantages of raw milk.

Whole milk contains all the butterfat of raw milk and is almost always sold with Vitamins A and D added, usually pasteurized and homogenized. No cream has been added to or taken from the milk: it is just as it came from the cow, with roughly 3.7 percent fat.

Skim milk has had all or most of the butterfat removed. It usually has 1 percent fat (sometimes labeled as 99 percent fat-free). Some middleground milks, often called *lowfat*, have about a 2 percent fat content. Most skim and lowfat milks are fortified with Vitamins A and D. When you see the phrase "protein fortified" on a container, it means that the skim or lowfat milk has been fortified with nonfat milk solids. The addition of those nonfat milk solids does more than provide extra nutrients. It also helps give skim and lowfat milks desirable body and richness.

Buttermilk is a type of skim milk. It is a naturally occurring product; after butter-making, a sour liquid with bits of butterfat remains in the churn. But buttermilk sold in supermarkets is cultured: a lactic-acid bacterial culture is added to skimmed or partly skimmed milk. Frequently salt is added to extend the shelf life of the product and to mask possible off-flavors; be sure to investigate your brand if you must reduce your intake of sodium. Buttermilk, which seems to get colder than whole milk, is a refreshing summer drink. Or it can be blended with fruit or fruit juice to make "milkshakes," or used as a sauce for vegetables and grains. Dieters often enjoy buttermilk, which is comparable to skim milk in calorie and protein content.

Evaporated milk: Remove about half the water content of whole milk and you have evaporated milk. This concentrated product is cooked, canned, and heat-sterilized, so the small, compact cans can keep at room temperature for 6 months or longer. Because evaporated milk is more concentrated than whole fluid milk, it tastes richer; and it is thick enough to whip. Adding an equal volume of water to evaporated milk produces reconstituted whole milk, with approximately the nutritional makeup of the original whole milk, but with a caramel taste as a result of heat. Once the can is opened, it should be refrigerated, and the contents used within about 5 days.

Condensed milk: To make condensed milk, the manufacturer removes much of the water, and also adds up to 40 percent sugar, for a sweet, thick, rich fluid. Each fifteen-ounce can has the same amount of protein, calcium, thiamine, and riboflavin as in a quart of milk, but the added sugar means it has twice as many calories. The unopened can will stay good about 6 months on a pantry shelf. Once the can is opened, it must be refrigerated and should be used within 5 days. There is some evidence that some cans used for condensed milk present a lead hazard. Condensed milk can be baked in a pie plate in a 425°F oven for an hour, to produce a kind of caramel pudding. Or, you can make frozen desserts and pie fillings.

Nonfat dry milk: All the protein and calcium of milk, with none of the fat or water, wrapped up in a less-expensive, convenient-ready-to-mix food: nonfat dry milk sounds ideal. However, there are a few catches. It does not have the taste of whole milk, and it tends to reconstitute to a grayish color and be lumpy. But the *instant nonfat dry milk* dissolves easily in hot or cold liquids (noninstant dry milk tastes better and makes better yogurt, but is more expensive). Nonfat dry milk comes packaged in bulk or in packets that make 1 quart of skim milk each. Brands with the "U.S. Extra Grade" shield have been subjected to stricter quality control and sanitary inspection than the others; they are likelier to taste fresher. Unopened, dry milk powder can be kept in a cool, dry place up to 6 months. Opened packages should be refrigerated to help keep freshness and flavor. The powder keeps well in sealed glass jars. For slightly more than a quart of skim milk, mix 1⅓ cups instant dry milk (1¼ cup noninstant) with one quart water. Reconstituted milk should be refrigerated and used within 5 days or so—as if it were fresh skim milk. Reconstituted milk has a "cooked" flavor; overnight storage in the refrigerator may reduce this taste. No more than ¼ cup of dry milk per cup of flour is recommended in baking—more and your bread or cake may have a too-heavy texture. Dry milk can be used in cooking soups, gravies, custards, and sauces.

Acidophilus milk: Some lactose-intolerant individuals can drink acidophilus (or *LBA culture*) milk without discomfort. Some nutritionists believe that it promotes the growth of healthful bacterial flora in the digestive tract, and relieves digestive disturbances. Acidophilus milk (whole, skim, or lowfat) has had acidophilus bacteria added; it is thus *cultured*, in the sense that yogurt is cultured. It has the same nutritional value as milk, and is homogenized and fortified with Vitamins A and D. The older, traditional method produced a very sour or acid milk with a characteristic odor. A newer, or sweet, method grows the acidophilus bacteria outside the milk, then adds them to whole milk, which remains sweet. This newer, sweeter, less startling product has gained in popularity and is available in some supermarkets and in health-food stores.

Ultrapasteurized milk may be stored on a shelf until opened. It is milk which is flash-heated to about 300°F and vacuum-packed in sterilized containers: the high heat kills microorganisms that may cause spoilage and, on the negative side, gives the milk a "cooked" flavor. Once opened, it should be refrigerated like ordinary milk. It is more popular in Europe and Canada than in the United States.

Buying Tips

If you can get your milk in recyclable glass bottles, the milk will stay colder and won't pick up refrigerator odors. Keep milk bottles out of direct sunlight, which destroys riboflavin. Plasticized cardboard milk cartons do have the advantage of being light and easy to carry. Buy milk with the last available date—and be sure to learn what that date signifies in your locale. It may tell you the date the milk was packaged, or it may indicate the last date on which it may be sold.

PREPARATION

Storage

Refrigerate fresh milk, cream, and milk products right after purchase. Use milk and cream within 3 to 5 days for best flavor. Don't store milk near strong-smelling foods. The best way to judge whether milk or cream is still good or has turned sour is to trust your nose.

Basic Cooking

Don't boil milk, or it will burn, taste bad, and form a skin or curds, depending on the degree of overcooking and the freshness of the milk. To scald milk, heat it gently just until bubbles appear at the edge of the pan. A heavy saucepan or double boiler is helpful in cooking with milk.

MINT

BACKGROUND

The green leaf herb, *mint*, which has been known for thousands of years, has many species and subspecies. *Spearmint* (*Mentha spicata*) is one of the most common; *peppermint* (*Mentha piperita*) is a hybrid of spearmint and another species, *water mint*. Mint is usually used in drinks and desserts in Western cooking; it is a common herb in savory dishes in India and the Middle East. *Peppermint oil* contains *menthol*, which anaesthetizes the mouth slightly, so that a tingling sensation of cold is experienced. Therefore, peppermint oil is used in toothpaste and mouthwashes to produce a sensation of freshness and to impart its pleasant scent to the mouth. (See HERBS AND SPICES for information on buying, storing, cooking, etc.)

CLASSIC USES AND AFFINITIES

Fresh or dried mint leaves are used in salads, with new potatoes, peas, carrots, zucchini, and eggplant. Mint sauce and mint jelly are traditional with roast lamb. Peppermint and chocolate go well together; so do peppermint or spearmint with fruit salads and juices. The mint julep of Kentucky Derby fame is a drink of sweetened bourbon and crushed mint leaves. Fresh or dried mint leaves can be brewed, alone or with tea leaves, into tea. Commercially, mint is used to flavor candy, gum, and cordials such as *crème de menthe*.

MOLASSES

BACKGROUND

Nearly all *molasses* is a viscous, brown-to-black liquid byproduct of sugar. When sugar is extracted from sugar cane or beets, the residual boiled liquid is molasses. If it comes from the first boiling, it is *light molasses*; from the second boiling, it is *dark molasses*; from the third boiling, it is *blackstrap molasses*. Blackstrap is the thickest and darkest of the three and is greatly overrated as a source of nutrition. Though it does offer some vitamins and minerals, it also contains a lot of empty sugar calories as well as some indigestible residue, not to mention its bitter flavor. Molasses can also be made from other ingredients, especially sorghum (see under CEREAL GRAINS.)

Storage

Once opened, molasses should be refrigerated. If it will be used within a week or two, it may be stored in a cool, dark, dry spot.

CLASSIC USES AND AFFINITIES

Molasses (especially the light variety) is poured over waffles and pancakes. Cooks use it as a sweetening agent, though less than in past centuries. Some American classics require it, including Boston baked beans, Indian pudding and, from the Pennsylvania Dutch, the shoofly pie.

MONOSODIUM GLUTAMATE

BACKGROUND

Monosodium glutamate, or *MSG*, as it is popularly known, is the powdery white sodium salt of glutamic acid, an amino acid. It has always been naturally present in many organic foods, but was first isolated by two Japanese scientists in the 1920s. Since then, commercially extracted MSG has spread around the world for use as a "flavor enhancer," but the interpretation of that phrase is controversial. MSG does, among other things, intensify the flavor of the salt content of foods. If a vegetable is past its prime or otherwise inferior, MSG does make it more flavorful, but... A far better course of action is to buy and cook fresh, high-quality ingredients—not only do they not need MSG, it will interfere with the natural flavor.

MSG and Health

There is some evidence that too much MSG can be harmful to the brains of infants. Some adults who absorb more than a scant amount of MSG develop the so-called "Chinese restaurant syndrome," a feeling of tightness in the temples and neck, flushing, and allied discomforts. With most adults, these symptoms are obviously psychosomatic, otherwise they would suffer similar symptoms when they dine in coffee shops, private homes, and non-Chinese restaurants that use MSG with equal or greater abandon. For the record, Chinese restaurants do not have a monopoly on the overuse of MSG—and a good Chinese chef will either forego the MSG or use it with restraint.

AVAILABILITY

Monosodium glutamate is widely sold under its generic full name or initials or—for a higher price—under proprietary names such as Ac'cent. MSG is also a component of seasoned salts such as Lawry's. It also enters our homes as an ingredient in most of the processed foods we buy, be they seasoned frozen vegetables, canned stews or cold cuts.

Test for MSG

To train one's taste buds to recognize the presence of MSG is not difficult, because a metallic flavor is produced when MSG reacts chemically with salt. To help yourself acquire this MSG-detecting expertise, conduct this simple experiment. Half-fill three glasses with tap water. Using separate spoons, stir 1/8 teaspoon of MSG into Glass A, 1/4 teaspoon of salt into Glass B, and 1/8 teaspoon of MSG plus 1/4 teaspoon of salt into Glass C. Take a sip from Glass A and notice the surprising mildness of the MSG when it is sampled by itself. Next, take a sip from Glass B, making a mental note of the natural taste of this briny liquid. Finally, take a sip from Glass C. Notice how the natural salt flavor has been amplified, a direct result of the reaction of the MSG with salt. More important, notice the distinctly metallic taste of the combination. It is this unique flavor that tells you when a dish has been prepared with the virtually tasteless MSG.

MUSHROOM

BACKGROUND

A *mushroom* is a fungus, not a plant. It has no roots and no chlorophyll, and cannot make its own food by photosynthesis. Mushrooms get their food from a natural host, or from a growing medium supplied by a mushroom farmer. There are hundreds of types of mushrooms and related fungi; many are poisonous (infamous ones include the *destroying angel* and the *fly agaric*), and some are harmless but inedible. The importance of avoiding all fungi except those known to be edible cannot be overstressed.

Varieties

Popular culinary mushrooms include:

American Cultivated Mushroom: Its skin is white, its diameter is 1 to 3 inches, and its flavor, sadly, is bland and ordinary. This is the mushroom sold fresh at your greengrocer's.

Morel: A gourmet favorite that is imported canned into this country. A morel is about 1½ to 2½ inches high with a whitish stem supporting a golden-brown top that resembles a pockmarked dunce cap.

Chanterelle: Another epicurean delight that is imported canned. The yellowish cap is multileaved with a spongy texture.

Cèpe: A large European mushroom (imported into the USA canned as well as dried) that somewhat resembles our cultivated mushroom in shape, but certainly not in quality, texture, and aroma. The cèpe has character.

Enok: The *enoki-dake* mushroom has long, thin stems topped by a minute button cap. Indigenous to Japan, but now grown and sold fresh in America.

Other Types: Chinese food stores sell a variety of dried fungi, including the *cloud* (or *tree*) *ear* or *mo-er*, a sort of bracket fungus. The Japanese are considered to be the world's finest producers of dried mushrooms.

Button: This term refers to a youthful umbrella-type mushroom, not to a variety.

AVAILABILITY

Buying Tips

For the best flavor and longest storage, the caps of the standard supermarket variety of mushroom should be completely closed over the stem, with no gills showing. An "open umbrella" mushroom is past its peak. The skin should be white or creamy-white, particularly if you plan to use the cap as garnish. A slightly brown-flecked surface, however, is not necessarily a negative sign and indeed, in some parts of the country, that quality is considered desirable. Reject mushrooms that are soft, misshapen and dirty, or dark-tinged, broken, bruised, or otherwise injured. Since the cap is tenderer than the stem, look for short-stemmed specimens. Equal-sized mushrooms cook evenly. Though loose mushrooms generally sell for more than the packaged variety, you will likely save money because you can pick the best specimens and need not buy more than you need. Some fresh mushrooms (especially packaged ones) are coated with a preservative chemical such as sodium bisulphite which imparts an off-taste unless thoroughly washed. Read the small print on the label. Canned and frozen mushrooms have lost much of their intrinsic texture and flavor. When buying canned mushrooms, beware of the dented or puffy can—it may be harboring lethal botulism.

PREPARATION

Storage

Mushrooms need air, coolness, and humidity. Store them in an open container (perhaps draped with a damp paper towel) in the refrigerator. Do not seal them in a bag. Mushrooms are very perishable—use them within a day or two. If they become too dark to be decorative, chop them and use for flavoring.

Preliminaries

Mushrooms darken quickly when cut or exposed to room temperature, so prepare them at the final moment. If they must wait, gently rub them with an acid liquid, such as lemon juice. Mushrooms can absorb water if washed in water. For better results, wipe them with a damp cloth. If your mushrooms were coated with a preservative chemical, you should wash them thoroughly under hot running water—they will absorb a lot of water but at least you've sent most of the additives down the kitchen drain rather than down your gullet. Only the mature varieties of some wild mushrooms need peeling. Cultivated mushrooms do not, unless seriously blemished. Trim off the base of the stem if it is coarse or unattractive. If you remove the stem from the cap, save it and any trimmings to use in sauces. To make neat lengthwise slices, use a very sharp knife or a hard-boiled-egg slicer. To flute a mushroom, cut a tiny incision into the skin with a paring knife; make a parallel cut nearby, and lift out the strip of skin. Rotate the mushroom slightly, repeating the process around the mushroom cap. To reconstitute dried mushrooms, soak them in tepid water for 20 to 60 minutes, depending on their thickness, age, and variety. If you are not sure if they are hygienic, use boiling water, and reduce the soaking time slightly. When reconstituted, drain and squeeze them partially dry, saving the liquid (once you've strained it to get rid of possible sand particles and the like) to flavor a sauce or stock.

Cooking

Though mushrooms are excellent eaten raw as a *crudité* or salad ingredient, or when marinated for use as an appetizer, their flavor deliciously develops when cooked. Mushrooms are often sautéed in butter for 3 to 5 minutes, depending on size. Overcooking produces tough and rubbery results. Do not crowd the pan, as their flavor and texture fare better when they are truly sautéed, not steamed. If caps and stems are separated, give the slower-cooking stems a slight headstart in the pan. The French call mushrooms "*les assassins du beurre*," the butter-killers, and mushrooms do absorb a lot of butter, so be warned. Fortunately, they also absorb the flavors of their other pan mates. Be sure to use the sinister-looking but delicious pan liquid if any remains. Be prepared for some shrinkage, as mushrooms are mainly water. Mushrooms are also often stuffed and baked (brush with butter and cook in a 375°F oven for about 20 minutes), steamed (5 to 8 minutes), or added to simmering soups, stews, and sauces.

CLASSIC USES AND AFFINITIES

Mushrooms are compatible with many foods, including butter, cream, and sour cream. Their subtle yet earthy flavor is accented by a wide choice of herbs, a squeeze of lemon, a discreet rubbing of garlic, a grinding of black pepper, or a touch of paprika. Mushrooms go into soups (mushroom-barley and cream of mushroom), casserole dishes, omelets, sauces and purees (*duxelle*), salads, and stuffings. They are toppings for pizza, steaks, and burgers. They garnish dishes of all sorts, are mixed with brightly-colored vegetables such as peas, and are a popular member of the shish-kebab team. They are frequently marinated (*champignons à la grecque*). Perhaps mushrooms are at their best when stuffed and baked with delicacies such as snails, oysters, or crabmeat.

MUSSEL

BACKGROUND

Mussels have a long culinary history. Archaeologists have found piles of mussel shells dating back to 20,000 B.C. in European caves. These tasty creatures were also consumed on a regular basis by many pre-Columbian Indian tribes.

While modern Americans have a culinary love affair with the clam and oyster, they tend to spurn the equally delicious and nutritious mussel. As a result, vast quantities of these oblong bivalve mollusks lie unharvested along our Atlantic and Pacific shorelines. Yet in France and Italy the mussel is such a sought-after delicacy that the natural supply must be augmented with high-priced mussels cultivated on commercial sea farms.

Mussels live in all oceans, though they are more prolific and succulent along the seashores in the temperate climates. Of the dozens of species so far identified, the *blue mussel* (sometimes called the *common mussel*) is the most abundant. This species—with its creamy-tan, delicately flavored lean meat—is considered the choicest.

When young, a mussel moves about freely until the adolescent day it decides to attach itself permanently to a rock, jetty, pier, or fellow mussel via its *byssus*, a grasslike beard growth. There it lives for the rest of its days, usually in a tight clustered colony. A few burrow into the sand or mud. Full-grown mussels range in size from 1 to 6 inches, depending on their species and environmental conditions. The blue muscle (its shell is really bluish-black in color) reaches 2 to 3 inches in length.

AVAILABILITY

Mussels are available year round, but they cost the most during winter when the chilly waters make harvesting more difficult, and they lose flavor with most epicures from late spring through summer, because that is when the mussel is spawning.

Buying Tips

Buy mussels only from a reliable fishmonger with a high turnover. Do not buy any mussel with a broken shell—or any that refuses to close when tapped (it is dead or well on its way). Avoid any that feel noticeably light for their size (dead, more than likely). Also avoid any that feel noticeably heavy for their size or that make a sound when rattled (probably is filled with sand—and it takes only one sand-filled mussel to ruin an entire sauce). If the merchant's supply has too many defective mussels, do not buy even his good ones. If possible, select equal-sized mussels—they will cook uniformly and will look more attractive on the table. In most cases, the smaller the mussel for its species, the more tender its flesh will be.

Gathering Your Own

Many people gather their own mussels as a sport or as an economic necessity. To gather your own, wait till low tide when the rock-clinging mussels are exposed, then detach them with a knife or small crowbar. Give them a quick-on-the-spot scrubbing to remove excess slime. In their natural state, they are not as clean as you might expect; the mussels in a store have already been partially scrubbed. Keep your nature-given bounty in cold water or moist seaweed until you get home.

When gathering mussels, be aware of two critical factors. The first is the condition of the water. Healthy, delicately flavored mussels come from the unpolluted shallow seawater—hopefully away from the pounding surf, which can make their bodies leathery. Harbor-water mussels run the risk of being contaminated and, in all probability, will smack of sewage. Fresh-water mussels, a separate species, are to be avoided in this day of desecrated rivers. When in doubt about water purity, check first with local authorities. (They will also tell you if mussel-gathering is legal and if it requires a license.) The second factor is the time of year. On the West Coast, mussels can be noxious between May and October. East Coast mussels are safe to eat the year round.

PREPARATION

Storage

Keep mussels in a cool, dark place (such as a cellar) on ice. Or keep them in a container in the refrigerator until you are ready to prepare them. If they're reasonably fresh when purchased, you can keep mussels this way for a day or two, though the sooner you use them, the better.

Preliminaries

Examine your mussels again, giving them the tests suggested under Buying Hints. Discard any defective specimens. Scrub each acceptable mussel under cold running water to remove every bit of slime, mud, sand, and any other foreign matter on the shell's outer surface. Scrape barnacles off with a dull knife. Pull out or cut off the beardlike byssus (it is indigestible). Soak the mussels in cold water for at least a couple of hours. This gives the mussels a chance to suck the water in and out and, in the process, expel some of their internal sand and intestinal waste. Discard any that float (they are dead or dying). An old restaurant ploy is to stir a handful of fine cornmeal or wheat flour into the water in the hope that the mussels will eat it and thus become plumper. It also helps the mussels to rid themselves of previously digested food. Finally, drain and rinse the mussels, discard any that refuse to close when tapped, and cook them immediately.

Cooking

Though occurrences are rare, mussels can spread typhoid fever. This is one of the main reasons why mussels, unlike clams and oysters, are seldom eaten raw. If the mussels carry typhoid bacteria, the cooking should destroy them. One of the simplest and most delicious ways to cook mussels is to sauté, in a large heavy-bottomed sauce pan, some chopped onions briefly in butter. Then add cleaned, live mussels in, their shells along with salt, pepper, herbs (such as parsley, thyme, and bay leaf), and some dry white wine. Bring the liquid to a boil, cover, reduce heat to a gentle simmer and—without once lifting the lid—cook for about 5 minutes. Serve the cooked and opened mussels along with the pan liquid (your sauce) in a bowl. As a rule, you can cook mussels just as you would oysters or clams. For example, you can bake, skewer-barbecue, grill, deep-fry, stuff, wrap, or poach them. You can also buy them at your local food specialty shop canned, pickled, or smoked, ready to eat. Mussels will become tough and chewy if they are overcooked or steamed over too high of a flame. They will also lose their inherent tenderness if they are kept in a warming device for more than 10 minutes before serving them—so rush them to the table the moment the dish is cooked.

Equivalents

Allow eight to twelve mussels per person if served as an appetizer, sixteen to twenty-four if as a main course.

CLASSIC USES AND AFFINITIES

Besides *moules marinière*, other famous mussel dishes include *cozze alla marinara* (the Italian version of *moules marinière*), *moules Normande* (*moules marinière* enriched with cream and, sometimes, egg yolk), *moules ravigote* (steamed mussels served cold in a *vinaigrette* sauce laden with onions, capers, and herbs), and *billi-bi* (a hot or cold soup made with a *moules-marinière*-type sauce lavishly infused with cream). Mussels can also play a supporting role in many dishes such as the Spanish *paella* and the Provencal *bouillabaisse*.

MUSTARD

BACKGROUND

Mustard has been used in cooking for several thousand years by the Chinese and nearly that long by the Europeans for both its piquant flavor and its oil. The English word *mustard* derives from the old French word *moutarde* which comes from *moust*, or *must* (unfermented grape juice), which was mixed with mustard seed to make prepared mustard.

Botanically, two major mustard seed species exist: *Brassica hirta*, known as *yellow* (or *white*) *mustard*, and *Brassica juncea*, called *brown* (or *black*) *mustard*. The yellow seeds have over twice the diameter of the brown seeds and are less sharply pungent. Yellow seeds are used for jobs such as pickling, seasoning cooked vegetable dishes, and for making American-style mustard. Black seeds are used for Chinese and French mustards. English mustard usually is a blend of the two seed types. Mustard is sold as whole seeds, ground into powder, or commercially processed into a paste, the type we buy in jars.

PREPARED MUSTARD

Prepared mustard runs the spectrum of flavor from mild to hot, of texture from smooth to grainy, and of color from creamy yellow to brown-specked caramel. Prepared mustard is made with the ground mustard seeds combined with a liquid such as wine vinegar, must, water, champagne, or beer—and perhaps a small amount of sugar, herbs, spices, and chemical additives. The precise recipes are closely guarded secrets. Some manufacturers flavor their mustard with a pronounced amount of an ingredient such as green peppers or tarragon. We advise you not to purchase these flavored mustards, because you can easily season a plain mustard at home to suit each specific dish and your creative urge at the moment.

Mustard products tend to have regional characteristics. The most famous mustard manufacturing center is Dijon, France, which has scores of firms with respected brand names such as Maille, Bornibus, and Pikarome. Traditionally, Dijon mustard is pastel yellow with concentrated piquancy, though nowadays numerous types—some flavored—are shipped from Dijon. One type that French producers have rejuvenated is *moutarde à l'ancienne* ("old-style mustard") which is milder and grainier than the usual contemporary style. English and Chinese mustards are customarily even more pungent than most French products. Typical German mustard is milder, sweeter and darker than the English, Chinese and French counterparts. Germany has its mustard capital, too: Dusseldorf. Italy is noted for its *mostarda*, a medley of fruits preserved in mustard. American "ballpark" style mustard is generally high in tumeric and vinegar and mediocre in quality.

PREPARATION

Storage

Mustard seeds can be stored at room temperature in a dry, sunless place for a year or more. Figure 6 months as maximum for mustard powder. Prepared mustard must be refrigerated once the container has been opened.

There is no danger in storing prepared mustard in a glazed crock that came with the mustard produced by a quality firm. Do not, however, transfer an acid-base mustard for storage into another crock unless you know for certain that its interior has been properly glazed. Otherwise, you are courting lead poisoning. Another tip is not to buy those oversized crocks unless you have a large family of mustard mavens. We bet more mustard from those crocks gets old and thrown away than is consumed.

Making Your Own

An alternative to using commercially prepared mustards is blending your own at home. Several guidelines are in order. If you have seeds rather than powder, grind them. For each tablespoon of powder, mix in approximately two teaspoons of liquid, which can be vinegar, wine, milk, cream, beer, what have you.

Add other flavoring agents such as herbs, spices, and sugar to suit your taste. If you want a lighter consistency, add a little extra water. Allow the mixture to rest for at least ten minutes before serving it in order to mellow the mustard's natural bitterness. However, do not wait too long, because homemade mustard starts to lose its freshness within 30 minutes if made with water or within an hour or two if made with an acidulous liquid such as vinegar.

CLASSIC USES AND AFFINITIES

Prepared mustard is usually served raw, as a condiment for hearty meats such as pastrami or garlicky hot dogs—or for bland meats, fowls, and fish. It can also be blended into cold sauces such as mayonnaise or *vinaigrette*. You can also add prepared mustard in discreet amounts to hot sauces such as *béchamel*, soups, egg dishes, and cheese dishes such as Welsh rarebit; the key is to add the mustard after the food has (or almost has) been cooked, so that the mustard paste does not separate. At one time people used mustard to smear on the chest whenever afflicted with a deep cold—today, thank heavens, we take aspirin and other drugs.

MUSTARD GREENS

BACKGROUND

Mustard greens (*Brassica sinapis*) rank second to the related collard greens as the staple leaf vegetable in soul food cookery. Americans grow several varieties of mustard greens, all with dark-green leaves that give the palate a pungent mustardy aftertaste.

AVAILABILITY

Mustard greens are a winter vegetable, though a few markets offer it year round.

Buying Tips

Young plants cook more tender and have a milder bite. The leaves should have a rich, deep-green hue and be free of wilting, yellowing, insect holes, and fibrous or flabby stems. Seedheads indicate a mature and therefore less desirable plant.

PREPARATION

Storage

You can keep mustard greens in a bag in the refrigerator for a few days.

Preliminaries

Remove roots, stems and, if tough, the midrib. Discard or trim damaged leaves. Wash well in cold tap water. Mustards are often gritty.

Cooking

Steam or simmer for 12 or 15 minutes. A ham bone or diced fatback, salt pork, or bacon adds richness and flavor. Drain before serving, but save the pot liquor.

CLASSIC USES AND AFFINITIES

Butter, onions, garlic, lemon juice, and cured pork all go well with mustard greens.

MUSTARD GREENS, CHINESE

BACKGROUND

The leafy, 8-to-12-inch-long *Chinese mustard greens* (*Brassica erispifolia*), a cabbage relative, has dark green leaves with a texture like coarse cabbage and tangy, mustardy, slightly bitter taste. The leaves and (if tender) the thick, curving greenish stalks are used in Chinese soups and stir-fries; cook them as you would BOK CHOY. The seeds are pressed to make cooking oil. The leafy vegetable can be purchased in Chinese markets and can be refrigerated for several days if sealed in a plastic bag.

NAVY BEAN

BACKGROUND

The legume used in the ubiquitous canned pork and beans is the white *navy bean*, also known as the *Yankee bean*. Though small, this bean is hard and tough, requiring long cooking. It can be transformed into a wonderful soup as anyone who has eaten in the U.S. Senate dining room has likely discovered. It is also good baked slowly, heartily flavored with a generous amount of pork fat and a reasonable amount of brown sugar or molasses. Popular seasonings include onions, garlic, and lemon juice. (For soaking, cooking, etc., see BEANS.)

NECTARINE

BACKGROUND

The *nectarine* (*Prunus persica nectarina*) is a mystery fruit. Is it, as some foodbooks claim, a cross between a plum and a peach, or is it, as others say, a mutated peach? More likely, the peach and the nectarine did not spring one from the other but are both descendants of a common, now extinct, ancestor. Our research of centuries-old written descriptions of peaches and nectarines indicates that both were more distinctive than they are today. Over the years, the peach and nectarine have gradually become more like one another due partly to natural cross-pollination and partly to the work of horticulturists. (It is possible for the same tree to produce both fruits.) In another generation or two we may not be able to tell the difference between the two fruits, for they will perhaps have assimilated each other's characteristics to the point where markets will be selling a new variety, the "peacherine." Let us hope not.

Compared to a peach, a nectarine (as it exists today) has a smooth rather than a fuzzy skin, and is generally firmer-fleshed, less succulent, and higher in calories by as much as two-thirds. It used to be much smaller than a peach, but today it is almost as large. A prime virtue of the nectarine is that it gives us a gustatory alternative to the peach.

Like the peach, the nectarine is a drupe (stone fruit, and thus related to cherries, plums, and almonds). Also like the peach, the nectarine can be either *freestone* or *clingstone*; there are numerous varieties within each of the two groupings. Nectarine skin color ranges from pale white to yellow to golden red; the commercial trend is gravitating toward the last hue.

AVAILABILITY

Nectarines are readily available from mid-June through late-September and are at their peak from mid-July through mid-August.

Buying Tips

A green-tinged nectarine is one that has been harvested prematurely; it will not appreciably ripen nor, consequently, will it develop sweetness and aroma. Since most market-sold nectarines are picked at a deplorably unripe stage, it is essential to be on the lookout for telltale green surface tint. Another excellent test for ripeness is smell: the scent should be wonderfully fragrant. The skin color differs among varieties, so a red blush is not necessarily a sign of ripeness. A fresh, bright color is. When you press the pulp, it should feel firm but not hard (immature) nor overly soft (over-the-hill). Do not buy nectarines whose skin is bruised, blemished with decay, cracked, leaky, or sticky. Small pin-sized holes sometimes indicate internal worm infestation.

PREPARATION

Storage

Ripe nectarines are highly perishable, but if necessary, they can be kept for a day or two in the refrigerator sealed in a plastic bag. For the best flavor, bring the fruit almost to room temperature before eating. Treat nectarines gently, as they are easily bruised. A hard nectarine can be softened by being stored at room temperature in a pierced paper bag for 2 days or more, but do not expect much flavor development.

Preliminaries

Always wash nectarines to rid them of likely pesticide residue and germs. However, do not wash them until ready to use them, as moisture hastens surface bacterial growth. Unless you plan to serve nectarine slices immediately, coat the exposed pulp with citrus juice to help retard the natural browning caused by oxidation. To remove the skin of a nectarine, immerse it in boiling water for 10 to 15 seconds, then plunge it in ice water. You will then be able to slip the skin from the flesh by peeling small strips away with a sharp paring knife. Nectarines can be substituted for peaches in almost all recipes including pies and other desserts. Nectarines, like peaches, have a heaven-made affinity for cream.

NUTMEG

BACKGROUND

A whole *nutmeg* is hard and ovoid, about 3/4 to 1 inch long. It is the seed of the tree *Myristica fragrans*; MACE is this seed's lacy covering. Chief growing regions are the Spice Islands and other parts of Southeast Asia such as Malaysia. (See HERBS AND SPICES for information on buying, storing, cooking, etc.)

Freshly ground nutmeg was so popular a spice in Western kitchens in the seventeenth and eighteenth centuries that a nutmeg grater was a common accessory of everyday female dress. When nutmegs were scarce, canny Yankee peddlers allegedly substituted hand-carved wooden nutmegs, carved by sailors on the high seas to help them alleviate their boredom. Later, when this legendary bit of Americana became known, canny Yankee antique dealers sometimes substituted real nutmegs for the wooden ones when they became scarce.

AVAILABILITY

Whole nutmegs are sold plain or dusted with a white powder—connoisseurs prefer the undusted type. Ground nutmeg is, of course, available. An inexpensive metal nutmeg grater is a good investment, because freshly grated nutmeg has a much better flavor than ground nutmeg.

CLASSIC USES AND AFFINITIES

Nutmeg is versatile and has a special affinity for spinach. It is used in commercial sausages and cold cuts. Eggnog and other milk- or cream-based drinks and dishes are often sprinkled with a smattering of nutmeg. It can also be used in cheese or meat, especially beef, dishes.

NUTS

BACKGROUND

From a cook's or diner's point of view, a number of foods are *nuts*, including acorns, almonds, beechnuts, black walnuts, Brazil nuts, butternuts, cashews, chestnuts, English walnuts, filberts (hazelnuts), ginkgo nuts, hickory nuts, macadamia nuts, peanuts, pecans, pine nuts, and pistachios. Botanists, however, disagree with this broad definition, because while some are genuine nuts (such as acorns), others are seeds (Brazil nuts) or legumes (peanuts). In this book, we will take the perspective of the kitchen rather than the laboratory. The "nuts" on our list do share many culinary characteristics. What we do not consider in the same genre are foods such as COCONUTS, LITCHIS, and WATER CHESTNUTS, which are discussed in their individual entries.

Varieties

Acorns: Most people leave the tiny acorns alone to become giant oak trees because not all American acorn types are edible without tedious preparation. In Europe and the Middle East, and sometimes in America, the acorns are roasted like chestnuts, or ground into a flour for making breads or used as a coffee substitute.

Almonds: Botanically, an almond is much closer to a peach than it is to true nuts such as the acorn. Cooks and snackers buy the *sweet almond*, not the *bitter almond*, which is used for flavor extracts. Sweet almonds are probably indigenous to the Mediterranean; most of our domestic crop comes from California. *Nonpareil* is the best-selling almond variety. Runner-ups include the *Mission* and the connoisseur's delight, the *Jordanola*, which has little to do with the sugar-coated candy called Jordan almonds. Almonds are essential to *amandine* dishes, whether the chief ingredient is sole, trout, or green beans. Almonds are ground to make *almond paste* which in turn can be transformed into *marzipan*, Danish pastry filling, and, with coconuts, macaroons.

Beechnuts: This small nut, which is seldom sold commercially, can be substituted for hazelnuts or chestnuts in recipes.

Brazil nuts: Native to tropical South America, the Brazil nut is a white-fleshed seed covered with a brown, rock-hard three-sided shell that is very difficult to crack. Its relatively large size makes it an ideal contrast in a bowl of mixed nuts, but since the Brazil nut is particularly oily, it is generally the first nut of the mixture to go rancid.

Butternut: Also known as the *white walnut*, the butternut is noted for its richness, which makes it perfect for candies, cookies, and cakes. The native American nut is a relative of the English (Persian) walnut, but is of less commercial importance because it is harder to shell and its high oil content hastens rancidity.

Cashews: Though native to the tropical Americas, the cashews we buy are mainly grown in India and Mozambique. The pudgy comma-shaped cashew is the shell-less seed of the *cashew pear*. While the fruit can be eaten raw, the seed must be processed to help rid it of its prussic acid. Cashews are usually sold roasted and salted. They are very good in quickly cooked dishes such as the Chinese stir-fry preparations, but as bakers, they score low because prolonged heat robs them of their crisp texture.

Chestnuts: Winter is the season for fresh chestnuts, roasted in fireplaces or on the portable braziers of street vendors. The chestnut, without its lustrous brown, thin shell, has many other culinary uses—as a stuffing for game birds, as a flour for thickening sauces or making puddings and cakes. Canned chestnuts are imported whole or pureed, usually sweetened (for desserts such as *Mont Blanc aux marrons*). Unsweetened, chestnuts may be used as a vegetable side dish. This latter use is possible because the chestnut is higher in carbohydrates and lower in fat than other nuts; it also has less calories. Dried chestnuts are also imported and must be reconstituted in water for several hours or overnight.

Filberts (Hazelnuts): Technically, the brown-hulled, white-fleshed marble-sized *filbert* is the cultivated Old World variety while *hazelnuts* are the smaller, less prized, wild New World type. Today, both terms are synonomous in the cook's vocabulary. The filbert has less oil than almonds, pecans, and walnuts, and is acclaimed as a superb baker, though it is certainly as versatile as any other nut.

Ginkgo nut: In China, the tree is noted for its sweet, white, crisp nut that is used in soups and in fowl and seafood dishes. In America, the large, spreading tree is prized for its shade. Unfortunately for lovers of fresh ginkgo nuts, the trees planted in parks and along residential streets are seldom the nut-producing female ginkgos.

Hickory Nut: The granite-hard shells help keep this delicious nut from being commercially significant. Hickory-nut meats can be substituted for pecans, and resemble them with their brainlike twin-lobed configuration.

Macadamia Nuts: The marble-sized macadamia nut, with its crisp texture and faintly sweet flavor, is considered the world's finest nut by gourmets. It is also the world's most expensive nut. They are usually sold shelled, roasted, and salted; the surface of the white twin-kerneled nut then has a honey-brown color. Sometimes, especially in California, you can find the nuts sold raw and unhulled. Macadamia nuts are not nuts in the scientific sense, but seeds native to Australia, now grown commercially in Hawaii and California.

Peanut: The two major varieties of this native New World legume are the smaller, round *Spanish peanut* and the larger, oilier, and stronger-flavored oval *Virginia peanut*. The seeds are also called *goobers* (from *nguba*, a West African word) and *groundnuts* (because the pods mature in the ground). Most of our domestic crop ends up as peanut butter; other major products include peanut oil and peanut flour. The peanut is also widely used in making cookies, candies (such as peanut brittle), cakes, soups, and even ice cream. The peanut plays a major role in the cuisines of West Africa and Indonesia.

Commercial *peanut butter*, by law, must contain at least 90 percent shelled, roasted peanuts. The remaining 10 percent can be salt, a scant quantity of natural sweeteners (such as sugar, honey, or dextrose), and stabilizers (often hydrogenated vegetable oils) to keep the natural oil from separating and rising to the top. (Because natural peanut butter contains no stabilizers, the user must periodically stir the separated oil back into the paste.) Artificial food coloring, flavors, and sweeteners are prohibited, as are chemical additives—though some of these ingredients may be used in products labeled *peanut spreads* as long as the ersatz paste is at least the nutritional equal of peanut butter. The two major styles of peanut butter are *creamy* (smooth-textured) and *chunky*.

The best peanut butter is the fresh homemade variety. For best results, you need a mixture of Spanish and Virginia peanuts. Put 1 cup of shelled and skinned roasted peanuts in your food processor or blender and briefly whirl the blades. Then add 1½ to 2 tablespoons of a bland oil, such as peanut or safflower oil. If the peanuts are unsalted, also add salt to taste, about ½ teaspoon. Blend to desired consistency, chunky or smooth. Whenever the peanut chunks rise to the top of the developing paste, turn off the machine, push them back into the mixture, and continue to process.

Pecans: Oklahoma and Texas are the pecan-growing capitals of this native American nut, though this usually oval nut with the polished brown shell is a well-entrenched tradition in most of the Deep South. The pecan's twin-lobed, brain-shaped kernels are good bakers (pecan pie, pecan coffee cake, etc.) and they are a favorite confection in the form of pralines. The pecan has a high fat content and therefore becomes rancid easily.

Pine Nuts: *Pignoli* or *Indian nuts,* as they are also called, vary in length from ⅓ to 2 inches. The high cost of these usually cylindrical nuts is largely a result of the labor required to extract them from the cones of certain pines. Though not the best bakers, they are marvelous in classic preparations such as Genoa's famed *pesto* sauce and the Middle-Eastern-style stuffed mussels and grape leaves. Pine nuts become rancid easily.

Pistachio Nuts: Native to the Middle East, pistachio nuts are widely cultivated from Afghanistan to Turkey, and are grown in California as well, but the finest and most expensive specimens are the darker-green pistachios from Italy, Sicily, to be specific. The hard outer shell reaches the market partially open, clam-style. If the shells are reddish, they have been vegetable-dyed; white shells have been blanched, and brownish-ivory shells are *au naturel.* The ½- to-1-inch-long kernels are usually pale green, can be salted or not, and provide an intense color contrast to preparations such as pâtés and sausages, confections, and savory dishes. Pistachio nuts provide interesting flavor and texture contrast as well. A warm-weather favorite is pistachio ice cream.

Walnut: The two major types of walnuts are the *black* and *English* (or *Persian*) varieties. (A third type, the white walnut, is the butternut discussed previously.) The native American black walnut has a stronger, more bitter flavor than the English walnut. Other reasons for its lack of popularity are the hardness of its dark-brown shell and the speed with which it turns rancid. Black walnut cake is its best-known use. The tan-shelled, golf-ball-sized English or Persian walnut is native to the Old World, but now California is the planet's principal producer. When properly shelled, the double-lobed, brain-shaped nutmeats make attractive fare for eating out of hand or for garnishing. Products include walnut oil, pickled walnuts, candied walnuts, and even walnut catsup.

AVAILABILITY

Most nuts are sold in the shell or shelled. Shelled nuts can be blanched or not, can be whole or halved or cut into slices or slivers, can be chopped or grated, or can be ground into a dry flour or a moist paste or butter. The nuts can be sold fresh from the bin or packed in airtight jars and tins. Some bags are hermetically sealed, others are not. Nuts are sold raw, dry-roasted, or roasted in oil, and can be smoked (often with artificial smoke), salted, sugared, or candied, as in Jordan almonds. Take your pick.

Buying Tips

Unshelled Nuts: Remember the "shake, rattle, and roll" rule: if a nut you shake rattles, roll it back into the produce bin, as it is probably stale. The exception is the peanut. Look for nuts with uniform sizes and colors and those that are heavy for their size. Select nuts with clean, polished shells. Avoid those with holes (a clue to worm infestation), mold, cracks, or other surface injury. Always buy from a store with a high merchandise turnover, whether you are buying shelled or unshelled nuts.

Shelled Nuts: Nuts with skins have longer shelf lives than skinned ones but entail a chore if you want to blanch them. Look for plumpness, uniform size and color, and a bare minimum of broken pieces or powder at the bottom of the glass jar or see-through bag. Shelled nuts sold in jars and cans will almost always be much fresher than those sold in bags. The remaining tips in this section concern those sold in see-through bags. Sniff-test the bag for rancid or other off odors. The nutmeat texture should be crisp—with the grocer's permission, break one of the nut kernels or pieces in half without piercing the bag. If the nutmeat snaps, the contents will likely be at least reasonably fresh. If there is no crisp snap, the nutmeats are probably well on the path to staleness and rancidity.

PREPARATION

Storage

Nuts in their shells store longer than shelled nuts. Unshelled oily nuts (such as Brazil nuts and butternuts) store longer than their less oily counterparts. Unskinned nutmeats store longer than skinned. And the thicker the piece of broken or chopped nutmeat, the longer the storage life, so do not grind nuts until just before using them. The storage enemies of nuts are time, heat, moisture, light, and vermin and worms. Unshelled nuts can usually be stored in a cool, dry, sunless, pest-free spot for a month or more. If you have no cool room, seal the unshelled nuts in a plastic bag and refrigerate. The same advice is valid for nuts in airtight, unopened containers, though you will not need the plastic bag, of course. All other nuts should be refrigerated in tightly closed containers such as jars; a 2-to-3-week storage life is the norm. You can freeze the nuts, too, but they will lose much of their flavor and their crisp texture.

Preparation

Shelling: Practically everyone can use his fingers to shell peanuts, and some can do the same with almonds. A few people can pressure-crack a pair of walnuts between the palms of their hands (or in one hand!). We do not recommend this show-off technique because the sharp-edged shells make it a hazardous exercise for neophytes, and the nutmeats usually break into pieces. Except for peanuts, and chestnuts, and—if you are able—almonds, your best shelling aid is a good nutcracker or a hammer. When cracking the shell, use only a moderate force, and crack the shell in several places so as to not break the kernals. With exceptionally hard nuts like Brazil nuts, you can make them more crackable by placing them in a bowl of boiling water for 3 to 10 minutes, depending on their thickness and obstinacy. Chestnuts are best peeled by first making a crisscross cut into the shell on, preferably, the curved side. If the chestnuts resist peeling, parboil or partially roast them first.

Cutting: A nutmeat—especially a raw one—is easier to chop, slice, and so forth if you first place it in a 350° F oven for about 5 minutes. The best all-around tool for *cutting* nuts is a sharp French knife or Chinese cleaver. For *grating*, special nut graters exist. Electric food processors produce mediocre results when *chopping* because you end up with irregularly shaped pieces. Processors do, however, save time and bother when *grinding* nuts into a powder or paste. Electric blenders are useful but not as effective for this last function. When using an electric blender, it is best to grind only about a quarter of a cup of nuts at a time—and be careful not to make a moist paste if you want a semi-dry powder. Special nut grinders can be purchased, but unless you are a nut freak your investment will sit idle much of the time.

Blanching: To blanch a nut means to remove the tissue-thin brown skin that clings to the nutmeat. Unless it is desirable to blanch, do not do so because the skin is nutritious and, in most cases, flavorful. There are two situations when blanching is desirable. First, when the skinless white flesh of the kernel will add visual beauty to a dish (for example, when serving spinach with almonds). Second, when the skin may become bitter when subjected to high heat—it is a good rule to always blanch a nut when you plan to employ a cooking method such as sautéing, stir-frying, or deep-frying. One easy way to blanch nuts is to place them in a bowl, cover them with boiling water, let them rest for 3 to 5 minutes, drain off the liquid and, using your fingers, strip off the skins. Some nuts, such as cashews or pine nuts, of course, do not need to be blanched. Other nuts, like walnuts and pecans, will be difficult to blanch perfectly because some of the skin will tenaciously cling to the kernel's folds and recesses. Nuts such as almonds pose no problem.

Cooking

Roasting: Roast raw shelled nuts in a single layer in an ungreased shallow pan in a 350°F oven for 13 to 25 minutes, depending on thickness. If unshelled, allow 20 to 40 minutes, depending on both body and shell thickness. Whether shelled or not, stir occasionally to ensure even roasting. Shelled nuts can also be slowly toasted in a skillet or sauté pan on top of the stove.

Recipe Substitutions: Most nuts can be substituted for other nuts in a recipe providing that you take into consideration the differences in their individual tastes, aromas, and textures; sometimes these differences are subtle, other times quite noticeable. Generally, milder-flavored nuts include almonds, pine nuts, chestnuts, cashews, and macademias. Stronger-flavored nuts are peanuts (the Virginia type), pecans, and walnuts. Also consider any processing the nuts have undergone. The most overlooked factor is freshness—it is always better to use, say, walnuts in your grandmother's cherished pecan pie recipe if the walnuts are fresh and pecans are stale.

CLASSIC USES AND AFFINITIES

Nuts are particularly cherished for their flavor and texture as well as the color accent they give to other foods. Nuts can be added to preparations in the role of a garnish (as in a chopped hazelnut topping for cakes), a co-star (chicken with walnuts, for instance) or the sole star (chestnut puree). Nuts are versatile. Processed nut products include nut pastes (especially almonds), nut purees (particularly chestnut), nut butters (peanut is the most popular, though cashew and almond butters are also sold), nut flour (chestnut is a classic here), and nut oils (see OILS & FATS).

OCTOPUS

BACKGROUND

The name *octopus* derives from the two Greek words *octo* ("eight") and *pod* ("foot") because the octopus—a cephalopod mollusk—has eight tentacles, each covered with suction cups. Both its body sac and the attached tentacles are edible; the eyes, operculum (mouth), and visceral sack are discarded. (As in the case of the SQUID, the contents of its ink sac can be used to color and flavor the preparations.) Species size varies from less than a foot up to almost Hollywood monster-of-the-deep size, the latter being rare. Most octopi are in the 1-to-2-foot range. The smaller the octopus is for its species, the younger and therefore the more tender its flesh will be.

PREPARATION

Your octopus should be sautéed or deep-fried for a minute or two. Or try it as the Japanese enjoy it—eaten raw, with the tentacles sliced across the grain. Mature octopus is best cooked by simmering it in liquid for 30 minutes to 2 hours, depending on its age, thickness, and tenderness. The last quality can be increased by marinating or, as some Mediterranean natives do, by flinging the octopus against a rock or by pounding it with a flat board.

OILS AND FATS

BACKGROUND

Oils and fats have the same general chemical structure; the difference between them is that, at room temperature (about 70° F), an *oil* is liquid, while a *fat*, such as butter, margarine, or solid vegetable shortening—is more or less solid. For a cook, the important difference between various oils and fats lies in their heating properties, flavor, and the like; for a person conscious of health and diet, the nutritional factors are most important.

Diet and Health

Nutrition and Calories: A certain amount of oil or fat (about 2 teaspoons a day; most of us far surpass that minimum) is necessary to a balanced diet. Fats help form membranes in the body and aid in the absorption of fat-soluble vitamins (A, D, E, and K). Fatty acids are required for brain and nerve function and for the synthesis of hormones. And fats are a concentrated source of energy (calories): Pure fat has 902 calories per 100 grams, 4,091 per pound.

However, many American diets have half the daily calories supplied by fat—too much of a good thing. The AMA recommends that no more than one-third of the day's calories come from fats and oils. Not more than one-third of those calories should come from saturated fats, and at least one-third should come from polyunsaturated oils. The balance should come from monosaturated oil.

Chemical Structure and Saturation: In structure, every fat or oil is made up of a molecule of *glycerol* (an organic acid, commonly known as *glycerin*) joined to three molecules of any of several *fatty acids*. It's the differences among the fatty acids that account for individual characteristics of fats and oils. Each fatty acid is made up of an *acid group* (of hydrogen, oxygen, and carbon), a long chain of *carbon* atoms (commonly 15 or 17), and a number of *hydrogen* atoms attached to the carbon atoms.

The crucial differences are in the molecule's long chain. Each carbon atom can make four *bonds*; two of these potential bonds are made with the next carbon atoms on each side, forming the chain. The other bonds are with the hydrogen atoms. If each of the carbons has two hydrogens attached, so that all the bonds are occupied, the fatty acid is said to be *saturated*—it has all the hydrogen it can hold. If it has less than the maximum potential amount of hydrogen, it is *unsaturated*. In that case, two adjacent carbon atoms have only one hydrogen apiece; they make the fourth bond with each other, making it a *double bond*. If there's one such double bond, the fatty acid is called *monounsaturated*; if there are two or more double bonds (and thus the potential for four or more additional hydrogen atoms), it is *polyunsaturated*. Most natural fats and oils are mixes of the various types of fatty acids; the most saturates there are in the mixture, the solider the fat will be. A *highly polyunsaturated oil* is made up mostly of polyunsaturates, and with few monounsaturates and saturates.

Cholesterol: Most life scientists believe that saturated fats are implicated in excessive serum cholesterol and atherosclerosis. Some of these scientists believe that eating polyunsaturated oils can reduce serum cholesterol; others believe that polyunsaturates and monounsaturates are neutral. In general, the more saturated a fat is (and thus, more likely to be a solid), the more likely it will increase the blood's cholesterol, whereas polyunsaturates reduce that level. A course that almost all doctors would applaud would be to reduce the intake of fats in general in the diet, especially saturated fats—and to use polyunsaturated oils rather than the other types of fat whenever it doesn't make that much of a culinary or gustatory difference.

Generally speaking, vegetable oils are predominantly polyunsaturated, while animal fats are saturated. While the proportion of polyunsaturates in oils varies from brand to brand, here is a rough ranking of the most popular oils:

Safflower oil most polyunsaturated
Soybean oil
Corn oil
Sesame oil
Peanut oil
Olive oil
Vegetable shortening most saturated

Please note that the last two, olive oil and vegetable shortening, have so little polyunsaturated in proportion to saturated fats that their possible effect in lowering the blood's cholesterol level is minimal. Also, if any oil—including safflower oil—has been *hydrogenated* to prolong shelf life or has been overused for frying, its ability to lower the blood's cholesterol level will have been significantly lowered, or sometimes even reversed. The reason for this is that hydrogenation supplied the "missing" hydrogen atoms, making the fat more saturated.

Oil Extraction Methods

Solvent-extraction uses chemicals to remove oil from the seeds.

Cold-pressed oils are extracted by

pressure only—the name is not very accurate, because the press can reach temperatures up to 160°F. Even though cold-pressed oils are more nutritious than the solvent-extracted oils, the advantage is minimal, because one doesn't (or shouldn't) consume that much oil.

Crude or virgin oils, with pronounced color and flavor, are not processed after pressing. Their shelf life is actually longer than that of "refined" oils, because the natural Vitamin E in them acts as an antioxidant. "Virgin" may also mean that it is from the first pressing.

Refined oils are treated to prevent clouding, remove residues, and maintain standard light color and delicate flavor. They are good for frying because they can be heated hotter than crude oils without smoking or burning. But they are often treated with antioxidants, preservatives, and stabilizers—a plus if you prefer a neutral, standard product, a minus if you want to avoid additives in your food.

Smoke Point

The smoke point of an oil is the temperature at which wisps of smoke appear and also the point where the oil begins to decompose and generate off-odors and off-flavors. All other factors being equal, a high smoke point is desirable in an oil, especially if you want to reuse the oil, as each use lowers the smoke point. Smoke points vary from brand to brand for specific oils, but here are some rough averages:

Safflower oil	510°F
Soybean oil	495°F
Corn oil	475°F
Peanut oil	440°F
Sesame oil	420°F
Olive oil	375°F

Varieties

Oils:

Coconut oil is unusual among vegetable oils: it is highly saturated. It is used in many imitation dairy products, most processed foods, and cheaper margarines.

Corn oil is a good general-purpose oil; it is high in polyunsaturates, inexpensive, mild-tasting, and suitable for deep-frying. The smoke point of corn oil is high, well above the normal frying temperature. American-style corn oil contributes very little flavor to food, which is either an advantage or a limitation, depending on your point of view.

Cottonseed oil is one of America's most often used cooking oils, but few people have heard about it because it is often used in combination with other oils in vegetable-oil products. Cottonseed oil is not a high-quality oil.

Olive oil has a pronounced, distinctive flavor, enjoyed by many people in salads and in Mediterranean and Middle Eastern dishes. For a full discussion, see OLIVE OIL.

Palm-nut oil, rich in Vitamin A, gives characteristic flavor and reddish-orange color to much of West African and Brazilian cooking. It is highly saturated.

Peanut oil, American-style, is bland, suitable for use in salads; some cooks prefer the Chinese-style peanut oil, which has a definite peanut flavor. As its smoke point is high, it is a good frying oil, often used in France and China for that purpose. Its disadvantage as a cooking oil is that it does not last as long as most other varieties. Peanut oil is polyunsaturated to a modest degree.

Safflower oil is very highly polyunsaturated, so it is a good choice for those who are worried about cholesterol. It also has a high smoke point, but it should never be the only source of oil in a diet, because it lacks Vitamin E. Safflower oil first came into vogue when it was believed that it had a magical power to melt away fat.

Sesame oil, nutty in flavor, is a component with other vegetable oils of traditional Indian cooking, and is also used, in tiny quantities, to flavor

Chinese dishes. It is good for sautéing vegetables and in salads.

Soybean oil is traditional in Chinese cooking, but is becoming increasingly popular in America. It ranks high both in terms of smoke point and polyunsaturates.

Walnut oil is an excellent ingredient for salad dressings, preferred in much of France for this purpose. The French import has a distinct walnut aroma and flavor, while the health-food-store variety tends to be bland.

Other sources of oil include *avocado*, (the oil is used in both cooking and cosmetics), *apricots, sunflowerseeds, mustardseeds, grapeseeds, almonds, hickorynuts*, and *beechnuts*. The best all-around source for these oils is usually health-food stores.

Fats:

Butter is made by churning the cream taken from milk—usually cow's milk. For a full discussion, see BUTTER.

Lard: Rendered pork fat. For details, see LARD.

Margarine: A blend of vegetable (and sometimes animal) fats to form a solid mass. See MARGARINE.

Vegetable shortening is sold in cans under various brand names. All of them are bland and highly saturated, though to different degrees. They are inexpensive, have a long shelf life, and need not be refrigerated. Some brands are colored a deep yellow; this is accomplished by the addition of carotene (Provitamin A), a harmless—and, in fact, beneficial—substance. Piecrust made with shortening is not quite as good as that made with lard. The versatile shortening can also be used for deep-frying and in cakes. Because solid vegetable shortening is 100 percent fat, and butter or margarine is typically 15 to 20 percent water, you must use 15 to 20 percent less shortening than butter or margarine when substituting. Even so, the texture of cake made with solid vegetable shortening will be slightly different.

Other animal fats used in cooking include *schmaltz* (rendered chicken fat) and the *suet* of certain animals such as beef and sheep. If properly rendered, these fats can be stored at room temperature.

Buying Tips

Buy precisely labeled products if you are worried about cholesterol. Products that do not provide precise information about their contents may contain saturated or hydrogenated oil, which can increase the body's cholesterol level. An unspecified vegetable oil or shortening will probably contain inexpensive oils such as cottonseed or soybean in whole or in part. Baking mixes, such as cake mixes, pancake mixes, and the like, frequently contain oil high in cholesterol. Clear plastic oil bottles are frequently made of PVC, a suspected carcinogen. If possible, buy no more than 1 or 2 months' supply at a time (see below).

PREPARATION

Storage

Unopened oils and cans of solid vegetable shortening do not require refrigeration. Butter and margarine should be refrigerated. Rendered fats such as lard need not be refrigerated, if fresh and properly rendered. Don't leave oils standing out—they should not be exposed to sunlight or air, and may become rancid. Olive oil is especially suspectible to light, so a solid can is a better container than a clear bottle. Refrigerated oils tend to cloud; this is a natural response to cold, not a sign of deterioration. The clouding usually clears up when the oil is brought to room temperature. If you have a large container of oil, pour it into smaller, preferably opaque, containers. Fill them to the brim to exclude air, and seal them. Mixtures of olive oil and other oils become rancid more quickly than pure olive oil; prepared salad dressings deteriorate even faster.

Cooking

Measuring: The most accurate way to measure fat for a recipe is by displacement. To measure a precise half cup of shortening, for example, first half fill a large transparent measuring cup with cold water. Then add shortening until the water level has risen half a cup.

Salad Dressings: The choice of strong-flavored or bland oil in salad dressing is purely subjective. In either case, the oil—if you want it to adhere to the leaves—should not be applied to salad greens that are wet or that have been doused with vinegar.

Add the oil with the vinegar—or even better, before you add the vinegar. To avoid soggy leaves, a salad should be dressed just before eating. Salad dressings taste fresher and better if they are made less than an hour before serving.

Substituting: "Butter" cakes made with margarine will have a similar texture, but a different flavor. If you go to the trouble of making puff pastry, it pays to use butter for flavor and texture. Using oil instead of butter in a cake recipe will tend to impart an overly-grainy texture to the baked goods. It is generally better to use oil only in frying, although some cakes (such as chiffon cakes and dense, rich tea breads) are designed to be baked with oil, not butter. These foods have less saturated fats, but usually more sugar, than butter cakes. Lard or vegetable shortenings give flaky piecrust; nuggets of solid fat surrounded by flour explode in oven heat, and give the desired texture.

Tenderizing: Oil can be used to tenderize tough meat: cover with oil and marinate 3 to 4 hours at room temperature. For even better results, add some acidulous liquid such as lemon juice or vinegar to your marinade.

Frying: Sautéing, or cooking in shallow fat, can be done in any fat or oil if the temperature is low enough for the fat not to burn. If your temperature is too high for butter but you want the butter flavor, then raise the smoke point by using a mixture of butter and oil.

Any food that is to be deep-fried must be at or near room temperature, and should be immersed in hot oil or melted fat that has a volume of at least six times that of the food that is being cooked. In choosing the oil or fat you will use for deep-frying, keep in mind the smoke point of the fat *medium* (see above). The traditional deep-frying temperature is about 375°F; if you use too high a temperature, the food will be overcooked on the outside and undercooked on the inside, whereas too low a temperature produces greasy food. At 375°F, olive oil can't be used, but safflower, soybean, corn, sesame, and peanut oils, or vegetable shortening, can be, because their smoke points are comfortably above 375°F. A frying thermometer is very helpful, but an alternative is to throw a 1-inch cube of bread into the hot fat and watch it brown. It will be done to a uniform brown in 20 seconds at 385°F, 40 seconds at 375°F, and 1 minute at 350°F. Reduce the frying temperature by 5° to 10°F if you cook 1,000 to 5,000 feet above sea level and 10° to 15°F at altitudes over 5,000 feet.

For grease-free fried foods, use uniform pieces of food with minimal surface area. Add a few pieces of food at a time, so the fat stays hot enough to form a crust on the food. After frying, drain the food on crumpled paper towels or napkins (crumpling increases the fat-absorbing surface area); keep the food warm in the oven if necessary. Serve the fried food on heated plates—as these foods cool, they look and taste greasy.

Reusing: Fat or oil used for frying can be safely used and is digestible, up to a point. Here is an effective way to strain oil: line a funnel with cheesecloth or paper toweling, insert it in your storage bottle, then pour the oil. If any particles seep through your filter, they will sink to the bottom as sediment within 24 hours; the next time you use the oil, slowly pour out the oil (leaving at least 10 percent), being careful not to disturb the sediment. Frying the used oil with a few raw potato slices helps clarify and neutralize fat—especially if it was used to fry strongly-flavored foods such as fish. (Interestingly, if an oil smells no more than lightly of fish, it will not pass that odor onto another type of food). If a reused oil becomes dark and thick-looking as it is used, is smelly, or smokes at the normal frying temperature, discard it.

CLASSIC USES AND AFFINITIES

Various regions of French cuisine characteristically use butter, lard, or olive oil; olive oil flavors southern Italian, Iberian, and Middle Eastern dishes. Onions well-fried in lard typefy Hungarian cuisine, whereas onions in chicken fat are the foundation of European Jewish cuisine and sesame oil floats on Chinese stir-fry dishes. Olive oil makes an excellent salad dressing; the rarer and more expensive walnut oil is especially compatible with bitter greens.

OKRA

BACKGROUND

Slaves from West Africa brought the word *gumbo* and likewise the vegetable called *okra* to the American South. The ridged, tapered, green-hued *Hibiscus esculentus* pods, when cut, exude a mucilaginous substance useful for thickening soups and stews.

AVAILABILITY

Fresh okra is available from late spring through early fall, with a peak from July to September.

Buying Tips

Young pods, under 4 inches long, are the tenderest. Their tips should easily bend when pressed with your fingers. Mature pods are often fibrous and woody. Look for bright green color and a moderately firm texture. Limp, shriveled, pale, blemished pods are best left for the greengrocer's garbage pail.

PREPARATION

Storage

Keep in a plastic bag in the refrigerator for 1 or 2 days.

Preliminaries

Remove the stems and wash the pods in cold water. Cut the okra into round slices anywhere from 1/4 to 1 inch long, according to your recipe.

Cooking

Steam or simmer whole okra pods for 7 to 10 minutes, depending on diameter. Sliced okra will take four to seven minutes, according to the thickness. Overcooked okra becomes slimy; if you're adding to a stew or soup, remember that fact. Okra can also be sautéed or deep-fried with a batter coating. Okra will thicken the liquid it is cooked in; the thickness mainly depends on the okra-to-liquid ratio. To reduce the thickening effect, cook the okra whole.

Equivalents

You will get three to four side-dish servings in a pound of okra.

CLASSIC USES AND AFFINITIES

Tomatoes, ham, onions, green peppers, and lemon juice are good companions with okra. Okra soup-stews are often served over rice, the dark stew contrasting with the bright white rice that soaks up the juices. If you are making a gumbo dish, purists insist that you either thicken the liquid with the okra or FILÉ POWDER (ground sassafras leaves), but never both simultaneously.

OLIVE

BACKGROUND

The *olive* tree (*Olea europaea*) is a Middle Eastern native. Today, the tree is widely cultivated for its fruit throughout most of the Mediterranean. In the U.S., it is cultivated in California, Arizona, and New Mexico. The olive tree can survive very harsh conditions and lives to a lusty old age. Its wood is strong and hard, its branch is a symbol of peace, and its fleshy fruit can be eaten or pressed for oil. Uncured olives are bitter and indigestible, though, so to make the olive palatable, it is cured in brine, or sometimes with dry salt.

Varieties

American producers often label their olives with the following designations, in descending order of size: *special-supercolossal, supercolossal, colossal, jumbo, giant, mammoth, extra-large, large, medium,* and *small* (or *select* or *standard*). Since these terms are meant more to impress than to inform, and since the exact size can be determined by looking at the picture on the label or at the olives in a glass jar, these size designations are next to useless. What counts most in terms of quality is the variety, the processor's skill and the storage. An example of a superior variety is the wrinkled, oily-purple-skinned *Kalamata* from Greece and the firm, green, noticeable acid Queen olive from Spain. These olive types are available in cans or jars, as well as out of the barrel; as with all olives, the barrel variety is the best. Of low interest to olive connoisseurs is the bland black *Mission* olive which, regrettably, is the best-seller in America. Olives are sold in cans or jars, whole, sliced, or chopped, and pitted or not, and stuffed or not. Green olives are the ones usually sold in glass jars, because the black ones tend to cloud their liquid, creating a cosmetic problem. Green olives are also the ones selected for stuffing, usually with almonds, pimentos, or anchovies.

PREPARATION

Storage

Unopened cans and jars will last for a year or longer, depending on the storage environment. Once opened, olives will keep their desirable firmness, flavor, and freshness for almost a week, if kept submerged in the original packing liquid.

CLASSIC USES AND AFFINITIES

Olives are excellent when eaten as hors d'ouevres or martini companions, or when mixed into cream cheese, cold cuts, sauces, and stuffings. They make an attractive edible garnish and are used in place of sliced truffles by deceptive chefs.

OLIVE OIL

BACKGROUND

The fresh fruit of the olive tree (*Olea europaea*) is crushed in a press for the strongly flavored oil that emerges. The oil is a characteristic food of Mediterranean Europe, the Middle East, and North Africa, and is also used in dishes from other cultures. Olive oil is monounsaturated, so it will affect your palate but not your arteries. (For general information, see OILS AND FATS.)

Varieties

Virgin olive oil is cold-pressed, without additives, and should be thick, green-gold, and richly flavored. The top grade, labeled *Extra*, has only 1 percent acid. The second grade, *Fine*, has 1.5 percent acid. The intermediate grade is not labeled; the bottom grade, called *Lampante*, has more than 3.3 percent acid and is marred with off-flavors. *Pure* olive oil is solvent-extracted from olive pulp, skins, and pits, then refined. It is lighter in color and blander than virgin olive oil. *Blended* oils are usually 10 percent olive oil, 90 percent other oils.

Buying Tips

Olive oil is an expensive commodity, subject to cheating and adulteration, so buy only from reliable shippers and merchants. Opaque containers are better than transparent ones—light is bad for olive oil.

PREPARATION

Storage

Opinions differ as to whether olive oil should be refrigerated. It does turn cloudy when cold, and it doesn't taste its best, but refrigeration forestalls rancidity. Fine olive oil has a long shelf life even without refrigeration—up to one year. Keep olive oil in several small, full containers, instead of one large, half-full one; the less air that touches the oil, the less likely it is to become rancid.

Cooking

The classic proportion for a salad dressing are 3 parts olive oil to 1 part good vinegar, but many salad lovers prefer an even higher proportion of olive oil (if it is of high quality) in the mixture. Even if you could afford to deepfry in olive oil, the low smoke point would make it inadvisable.

CLASSIC USES AND AFFINITIES

Hot-weather foods—tomatoes, eggplant, zucchini, Mediterranean fish—take well to olive oil.

ONION

BACKGROUND

No other major food is as essential to as many cuisines around the world as is the *onion*, a subterranean bulb native to Southwest Asia, *Allium cepa*, a relative of the lily. Because onions are so common, so adaptable, and relatively inexpensive, shoppers take them for granted. If onions were scarce, most good cooks from Paris to Peking to Phoenix would pay $10 a pound for them rather than let their culinary creations suffer from the absence of onions. (This entry deals only with the onion. For its relatives, see the entries on CHIVES, CIPOLLINI, GARLIC, LEEK, RAMP, SCALLION, and SHALLOT.)

Dry Onions

Sometimes a shopper hearing the expression "dry onions" understandably assumes that it refers to chopped or powdered onions that have been dehydrated, an entirely different item. In the produce trade, "dry" refers to the onions that can be stored without refrigeration (because their dry skins protect their juicy interiors). Others, such as scallions and chives, are "green" and are quite perishable.

Varieties

One of the areas of greatest perplexity

for the shopper is in the onion section of the produce department. The roots of the confusion are deep and tangled. First, there are numerous hybrids, with new ones cropping up each year. Second, the terms used in one region or supermarket often overlap or contradict those used in others. Finally, most food writers disagree with each other's definitions. The only solution is to think of onions in terms of their culinary functions. Using this approach, you can group them in four major classifications:

Miniature Onions: These marble-sized white onions are often pickled to use as appetizers or garnishes or in Gibson cocktails. Unpickled, the *pearl* onions can be cooked and creamed and served as a vegetable dish, sometimes mixed with green peas.

Pungent Cooking Onions: These are the best onions for cooking because they do not become overly sweet when cooked and their strong flavor and firm shape will stand up well under prolonged heat. Onions in the cooking class are called *globe* or *boiling* onions, and come in various colored skins (yellow, white, and even red), shapes (round or oval) and sizes (usually 1 to 3 inches in diameter). Generally, the yellow-skinned varieties are 2 to 3 inches wide and have a slightly less sharp taste than do the white (also called *silverskin*) varieties which normally are 1 to 2 inches thick. When the whites are very small, they are sometimes sold as *pearl* onions, and are ideal for stews such as the French peasant masterpiece, *blanquette de veau.*

All-Purpose: You can cook these onions or eat them raw. While it is convenient to have an all-purpose everything, remember that jacks of all trades are often masters of none, and so it is with the all-purpose onion. Unless the all-purpose is cooked only briefly, you are better off using the pungent cooking onion. And unless you are going to add just a touch of chopped onions to, say, a salad, your palate will be happier with the mild onions described in the next paragraph. Generally, all-purpose onions vary in diameter from 2 to 4 inches (the bigger they are, the milder they tend to be). Skin hue is typically yellow, sometimes white. All-purpose onions are also known as *granex-granos* (a specific type) and *new* onions (because they first reach the marketplace from warm-climate farms in the springtime).

Mild Onions: Also called *sweet*, this onion group includes the *Bermuda*, *Spanish*, and *Italian* onions, names that are sure to bewilder us since many greengrocers consider these (usually) 2-to-4-inch-thick onions identical. A Bermuda onion typically is flattened on one or both ends, and can be yellow, white or red. A Spanish onion, the largest of the three, is almost always spherical and can be yellow or white. An Italian onion, the smallest, is often ovoid and can be yellow, white, or red. Mild onions are ideal for eating raw in salads, as a sandwich garnish, and so on. The red ones are especially attractive when sliced. Mild onions are not good cookers except in the instance of french-fried onion rings where their juiciness and the thickness of their layers are ideal characteristics. Another advantage is that mild onions will make you cry less when you peel or chop them.

AVAILABILITY

Fresh Onions

Fresh onions (meaning the "green" or "dry," but not the dehydrated types) are available the year around, though there are peak periods for each variety. The pungent cooking onion is most common from late summer through late winter. The all-purpose onion, with a spring and summer prime, follows the pungent cooking onion. The mild onions start peaking in the spring if Bermuda, the fall if Spanish.

Processed Onions

Dried or freeze-dried onion products include *onion powder, onion flakes, onion salt*, *onion soup* and *onion gravy* mixes. Canned onion preparations include *soup* and boiled whole *pearl onions*. Frozen onion products include whole *pearl onions*, possibly swimming in a "cream" sauce, and *chopped onions* alone or mixed with other vegetables. Jarred and bottled onions include *onion juice* and the tiny pickled whole *cocktail onions*. Except for the latter type, the difference in the culinary quality between a fresh and a processed onion is astronomical.

Buying Tips

Buy the type, size, and amount of onion you need for your culinary purposes. Remember, color does not indicate strength or flavor. And neither color nor size indicates quality. If possible, select your onions from an open bin rather than buying a prepackaged bag. You may have to pay more per pound, but you almost always come out on top when you consider quality and spoilage. Buy onions that are firm (new onions will be slightly less firm than the long-stored type), well-shaped, and heavy for their size. The protective papery skins should be dry, clean, glistening. The skin should not be soft, dark-spotted, or stained, or have green "sunburn" blotches, cuts, bruises, or other injuries. The onions should have small, tight necks; a sprouting or thick, woody, opened neck are signs of overmaturity or improper storage. A soft neck indicates immaturity or decay. Misshapen onions such as those with double bulbs are, when cut, wasteful. If you have an informed greengrocer, ask him where his onions grew, as the answer will help you determine the strength of flavor. Onions grown in warm climates are typically milder (and larger) than their cool-weather counterparts.

PREPARATION

Storage

Onions are best stored in a cool, dry, dark place. Ideally, they should be stored in a single layer or in a hanging net bag to allow air circulation. Under these conditions, onions can last two or three months. If you do not have the perfect storage conditions, store onions in the coolest, darkest spot in your kitchen, and plan to use them within a week. Dry onions should not be refrigerated, because dampness hastens decay. Pungent cooking onions tend to keep longer than all-purpose onions, which in turn are usually better keepers than mild onions. If an onion does begin to sprout, you can use the green sprout as you would a green onion. Whether the bulb can still be used will depend on its condition—chances are you will have to discard it.

Once cut, a dry onion is very perishable. Tightly seal a cut onion in plastic wrap, refrigerate it, and plan to use it within a day or two. Refrigerate chopped onions in a tightly closed glass jar—use within a day. Do not use a plastic container, as onion odor lingers.

Preliminaries

Peeling: Some whole onions (especially the small white ones) are difficult to peel. One effective way to peel a whole onion is to submerge it in boiling water for a minute or two, then plunge it into cold water. The skin should slip free easily. It is not necessary to peel a whole onion if you are going to halve or quarter it. Once an onion has been cut into parts, the skin is easily stripped away.

Dicing and Mincing: First halve the onion lengthwise, neck to root end. Cut off any coarse portions of the neck end of each half and slip off the peel. Leave the root end on. Rest one half cut-side down on your cutting board. Make parallel vertical cuts completely through the onion half from the neck end to within 1/2 inch of the root end—that is, the end you are holding (see dark lines, sketch A). The spacing of the cuts depends on whether you want the onion minced (make all cuts 1/8 inch apart) or diced (1/4 inch apart). The closer the cuts,

DICING OR MINCING AN ONION

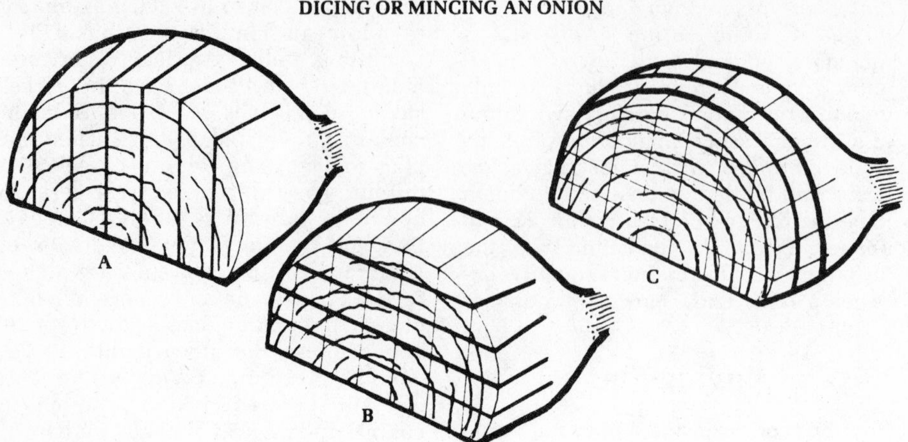

the more difficult the task; practice and master dicing before you attempt mincing. Your second series of cuts will be horizontal (see dark lines, sketch B), again to about ½ inch of the root end. Finally, cut down to the cutting board (see dark lines, sketch C), across the grain of the onion. As you make each of these cuts, tiny cubes of onion will fall to the board; push them to the side as you make each cut. Discard the root-end stub, and proceed with the second half.

Another method is to halve, trim, and peel the onion as outlined above, then to cut it into uniform thin slices, then to mince these slices with a French-style knife. While this method will not produce uniform pieces (essential for precision cooking), it is acceptable for most cooking needs. And it's a snap for cooks without enough savvy in the use of knives—which requires practice, not talent. We do not recommend the glass jars with a chopping blade attached to the lid. They are hard to clean, they tend to mash the onion, and the pieces they make are far from uniform. Food processors have the same drawbacks but to a lesser degree.

Minimizing Tears: We have tested many techniques intended to come to the rescue of crying onion cutters. Some of the tricks, such as clenching a piece of bread in your mouth or cutting the onions under water are more bother than they are worth. One key to success is to use a very sharp knife with slow, deliberate strokes; this diffuses a minimum of tear-producing volatile oils into the air. If you are especially susceptible to "onion tears" (some people are more so than others), the best method is to wear a pair of airtight safety goggles (ski goggles are not as effective because their ventilation holes will allow the onion vapors to reach your eyes).

Onion Juice: For a hint of fresh onion flavor, you can use a few drops of onion juice. Half an onion can be squeezed on a juice reamer; a quartered onion can go into a lemon squeezer. Either of these methods leaves you with the problem of getting the smell of onions out of your juicer. A better method is to scrape the side of a cut onion with a spoon or paring knife to produce onion juice.

Removing Odors: Rubbing your hands, pots, and utensils with lemon juice or vinegar helps eliminate lingering onion odor. If your equipment is made of rustable iron or aluminum, use salt instead.

Miscellaneous Tips: If you use a carbon knife to cut onions, be sure to wash and dry it immediately afterwards, as the acid in the onions can discolor the blade. Scoring a cross into the root end of onions to be cooked whole helps keep them intact. Another technique is to pierce the onion to its core once or twice with a small skewer, this will allow the trapped steam to escape from between the layers as the onion cooks. Before adding raw onion rings to salads, crisp them in ice water for an hour or two.

Cooking

Onions can be eaten raw or can be cooked to various stages of doneness, from lightly cooked to dark and caramelized. But it is essential to know the cooking limitations as onions can easily give your home an offensive lingering odor or can become bitter if cooked with too high of a heat. Onions will taste better and less harsh if they are gently sautéed for a few minutes before being added to preparations such as stews or omelets.

Sautéing: The secret of sautéing is to cook the onions over low to moderate heat; a higher heat scorches them and makes them bitter. For even cooking, the onion pieces should be cut uniformly thick. To lightly sauté onions, cook them in a small amount of fat or oil for 3 to 5 minutes (depending on thickness), until they start to become soft and translucent. For a darker color and a mellower but richer and sweeter flavor, sauté the onions for 8 to 12 minutes, using a lower temperature and less butter than you would for lightly sautéed onions.

Simmering and Steaming: Onions should be simmered, not boiled. To simmer whole onions, drop them into salted water (1 teaspoon salt per quart of liquid) and simmer for 15 to 25 minutes, depending on size, until fork-tender. Drain, season and coat with butter or sauce, and serve. Onion slices or wedges will cook in 5 to 8 minutes. You can also steam onions using the same guidelines. With either method, it is best to remove the outermost skin layers before cooking the onions. This is particularly essential if you are cooking a yellow-skinned onion, as the skin may discolor your pot or a light-hued stock.

Other Methods: Bake butter-rubbed whole onions in a rack over a pan containing 1/2 inch water in a preheated 350°F oven for 1 to 1 1/2 hours, depending on thickness. Remove the skin and slice off tops and bottoms, then season, sauce, and serve. Onions can also be stuffed and baked, much like squash. Batter-coated onion rings should be deep-fried in a 375°F cooking oil about 1 minute per side or until golden-brown. Drain on paper toweling and serve immediately, lest they become soggy. Onions can also be braised or barbecued (either on a skewer or wrapped in foil).

CLASSIC USES AND AFFINITIES

Most cooking ingredients benefit from an affair with onions—and that includes meats from beef to poultry. Hamburger, meat loaf, sautéed liver, and pot roasts would be lonely without them. Tomatoes and onions, raw or cooked, pair up well, too. And without onions, you would not be able to make *mirepoix* (a mix of onion, carrot, and celery) one of the foundations of French cooking.

ORANGE

BACKGROUND

In the nineteenth century, Americans consumed an average of only one *orange* per person per year. It wasn't a matter of taste; oranges were rare and quite expensive, especially in cities far from the groves. Today, thanks to vast plantings in California and Florida (which produce supply) and modern technology, fresh or frozen orange juice provides flavor and Vitamin C in millions of breakfasts each morning. And the flesh of oranges is eaten in abundance either plain or in fruit salads. Most food historians believe the orange is native to southeast Asia. Over 100 varieties now exist, the result of natural mutations and the work of hybridizers. Most oranges are descended from the *sweet Chinese orange, Citrus sinensis.*

Basic Types

From a consumer's point of view, there are three basic types of oranges: eating, juice, and bitter.

Eating Oranges: California produces most of our eating oranges which are characterized by their well-balanced sweet-tart taste and their easy-to-remove peel. Members of this group include the *navel, temple, tangelo, tangerine, mandarin,* and *clementine.*

Juice Oranges: Florida grows most of the juice oranges which are lower in acid and harder to peel than eating oranges and generally have many more seeds. The *Valencia* and *Parson Brown* are the two leading varieties.

Bitter Oranges: Our third type, the bitter orange, is too tart for orange juice or for eating out of hand, but is ideal for marmalades and certain sauces. The *Seville* or *bigarade* (as the French call it) is the classic example.

Names such as Sunkist (from California) and Indian River (from Florida) are proprietary names, not botanical varieties.

Varieties

Blood Orange: This one is characterized by a reddish pulp. The tarter varieties such as the *maltese* are used to flavor sauces such as the French *Maltaise.*

Clementine: A cross between a standard orange and a tangerine, which it somewhat resembles. Most of our supply is grown in Morocco.

Hamlin: A thin-skinned juice orange.

Jaffa: A juicy, navel-type Israeli eating orange with a deservedly high reputation.

King: A very good Florida eating orange. This hybrid with loose, rough skin and a flattened spheroid shape looks somewhat like a tangerine.

Mandarin: A number of common orange varieties including the *clementine, king, murcot, satsuma, tangelo, tangerine,* and *temple* are descendants of this relatively small, loose-skinned, easily segmented fruit. Its flavor is deliciously sweet but could use more acid.

Navel: California's pride and joy is an outstanding eating orange, particularly during the peak season: late fall through mid-spring. While no one specific navel exists, those called "navel" share certain characteristics: larger than average size; thick peel; navellike blossom, and seedless (or virtually seedless) flesh.

Parson Brown: A popular early-season Florida juice orange.

Pineapple: A good mid-winter juice orange.

Seville: This, the most celebrated of the bitter oranges, has a rough, thick skin and a pulp too tart for eating. That flesh, however, is perfect for marmalades. It is also *de rigueur* for *canard bigarade* (roast duck with Seville orange sauce), because sweeter oranges have too little acid to cut across through the fat. The Sevilles are also used in making orange-flavored liqueurs such as Cointreau, Curacao, Grand Marnier, and Triple Sec.

Sour Orange: This lime-and-orange hybrid is a favorite in Caribbean cuisines.

Temple: Loose- and thick-skinned, this easy-to-peel eating orange with a somewhat flattened globular shape is a cross between the standard orange and a member of the mandarin family. The temple's shortcoming is that it has too little acid to balance its sweetness.

Tangelo: This hybrid derives its name from its two ancestors: the *tangerine* and the *pomelo* (a relative of the grapefruit). Nowadays, the tangelo has been hybridized from different types of grapefruits and loose-skinned oranges and thus we find in the marketplace tangelos differing in size, shape, skin texture, and flavor. More often than not, this eating orange is a little short on desirable acid.

Tangerine: Of the various members of the mandarin orange family, the tangerine (named after the city of Tangiers) is the most common in America. Its skin is rough, thick, loose, and easily peeled. The pulp is readily segmented. It could be a better eating orange if it were slightly more acidic.

Valencia: Of all the major varieties of oranges, the Valencia comes closest to being considered both an eating and juice fruit, though it is best for juice. Valencias are grown in Florida, California and other states; those from California tend to have a higher acid content and are thus usually the finest eating Valencias. It differs from its main marketplace rival, the navel, in that the Valencia has a thinner, paler skin and is more difficult to peel and segment.

AVAILABILITY

Fresh oranges are not the strictly seasonal commodity they were a few decades ago. Among the many horticultural advances was creating subtle changes in existing varieties to extend their overall harvesting periods. It was also learned that the fruit of some of the Valencia orange trees could stay fresh on the tree for months after ripening.

Seasons

Nevertheless, some varieties normally have peak seasons as follows:

Blood—early to mid-spring
Clementine—mid-winter
Hamlin—late fall to early winter
Jaffa—early to mid-spring
Mandarin—early to mid-winter
Navel—late fall to early spring
Parson Brown—mid-fall to early winter
Seville—late winter
Tangelo—early to late winter
Temple—early to late winter
Valencia—early spring to early fall

As you can see, winter and early spring offer the broadest selection of oranges.

Buying Tips

Fresh Oranges: Virtually all oranges are picked when mature, so a green surface coloration is seldom a sign of unripeness. Strangely, certain varieties such as the Valencia can become partially green around the seam once the fruit has ripened; this is called *regreening* and should not appreciably affect quality. Choose oranges that are heavy for their size; lightness indicates dryness. Select oranges that are firm for their variety—even tangerines should not be spongy. Soft spots suggest internal decay. The skin should be bright, not dull. Avoid oranges that have wrinkled, moldy, blemished, or punctured rinds. However, some varieties have russeting, which should not affect the quality of the orange. If possible, do not buy oranges packaged in any type of container, including net bags. Just one bad orange can usually change a bargain into a poor value. If you have a choice, do not buy artificially colored oranges. Authorities tell us that dyes like Citrus Red. No. 2 are, in all likelihood, harmless, but no one knows for sure. While the shipping boxes of artificially colored oranges must, by law, carry the phrase "color added," we seldom see the box and the greengrocer rarely gives public notice at the display case. The peel of such oranges usually has a phosphorescent glow reminiscent of orangeade. When in doubt, ask to see the crate.

Processed Oranges: Never buy *frozen orange juice* with sticky containers—the juice may have partially thawed during storage. Not all frozen orange juice is alike. The weather and the selection standards and style preferences of the processors combine to produce a wide variety of flavors for different tastes. The orange juice sold in jars or cartons is often shipped in from Florida in concentrated form, then reconstituted at a regional plant. Its flavor ranks below that of freshly squeezed and home-reconstituted frozen juice, but ahead of canned and doctored orange juices. *Canned orange juice* tastes like orange juice only to those who are used to drinking it. Except in certain circumstances, such as a camping trip, there seems little reason to buy it when frozen juice is competitively priced and is so easy to reconstitute at home. The same is true for "super" orange juice that has been doctored with ingredients not grown on the evergreen orange tree. Supermarkets carry a wide variety of *orange-flavored drinks*, but this book refuses to take these man-made products seriously. Almost invariably they are low in nutrition and value and high in sugars. Not to be condemned are the *orange extracts* and *orange-blossom waters* that are used by some cooks to impart a subtle flavor to various dishes and drinks.

Grading

The USDA grades oranges only for those producers who want and pay for the service. U.S. Fancy is best; next is U.S. No. 1. Most oranges, however, are ungraded.

PREPARATION

Storage

Fresh whole oranges can be kept in a cool, dry place for several days. But for minimum Vitamin C loss and prolonged storage life (1 to 2 weeks), place them in the refrigerator vegetable crisper. Ideally, oranges and orange juice should be at 35° to 40°F. Putting the oranges in a plastic storage bag helps keep moisture in and refrigerator odors out.

Preliminaries

Always wash oranges before using. The neatest way to peel a tight-skinned orange is to slice off the top and bottom peel, making a firm base for the orange. Then shave off the peel in vertical strips with a paring knife. If your objective is orange peel for use in drinks or desserts, however, scrape off the peel with a citrus zester or vegetable parer; that way you will not taste the bitter white membrane. For well-shaped sections for salads, cover the tight-skinned orange with boiling water for five minutes before peeling. The water helps loosen the peel and membrane, but you will lose some Vitamin C content in the process. The least messy way to eat a tight-skinned orange out of hand is to quarter it lengthwise, and eat each section of pulp from the peel.

Juicing

Use juice oranges which are sweeter and less acid than eating oranges. To increase the amount of juice that you can squeeze out of an orange, roll it on a flat surface, using the palm of your hand. But do not push too hard or for too long lest you release too much of the bitter flavor of the membrane. If you select prime-conditioned juice oranges, then freshly squeezed orange juice is the best tasting and the most nutritious. If, on the other hand, your oranges are less than prime—perhaps having been stored too long or improperly—you are much better off preparing frozen orange juice. In today's supermarket, frozen orange juice is one of the best values, and it reduces the take-home weight of your shopping bag.

Equivalents

A medium-sized orange will provide you with roughly 3 ounces of juice and 2 tablespoons of grated peel.

CLASSIC USES AND AFFINITIES

The orange is one of the most versatile of foods. Besides being widely enjoyed as orange juice or as a whole fruit, it goes into fruit salads such as ambrosia; is standard for most marmalades; is a superb flavoring agent in the hands of skilled cooks, sauciers, and bakers, whether in the form of juice or zest; is a mild preservative and tenderizer when used with other fruits and meats. Further afield, it is the core of the clove-studded pomander ball, makes a colorfully attractive plate garnish when sliced or fluted, and is essential for screwdrivers, Harvey wallbangers, and a number of liqueurs. Last but not least, the orange is the primary source of the average American's daily requirement of Vitamin C.

OREGANO

BACKGROUND

A number of *oregano* varieties exist around the world. The Mediterranean type, *Origanum vulgare*, is used in Italy, Provencal, and Greek cooking. It is related to marjoram, but is stronger in flavor and fragrance. Except for Americans of Mediterranean extraction, oregano was little known in the United States until after the Second World War. GIs stationed in Italy developed a taste for oregano-spiked dishes such as pizza, and brought their new taste home with them. (See HERBS AND SPICES for information on buying, storing, cooking, etc.)

AVAILABILITY

Fresh oregano is hard to find in this country—you will probably have to grow it as a pot herb. Dried branches of oregano can usually be found in Mediterranean-American ethnic neighborhoods. Prepackaged dried oregano is widely available.

CLASSIC USES AND AFFINITIES

Oregano is excellent in Mediterranean-style tomato sauces. Zucchini, eggplant, olives and other hot weather vegetables take to this herb; so do roast and grilled meats. Basil, another strong herb, combines well with oregano. Forget oregano for delicate or refined dishes unless used in scant quantities.

OXTAIL

BACKGROUND

In the days of our ancestors, the oxtail used by cooks was just that: an oxtail. Now butchers merely cut up the tail of the steer, which is younger and is raised for food rather than for work; understandably, its tail is tenderer. That is why old-fashioned recipes that have been reprinted in contemporary cookbooks that call for several hours of cooking are outdated and erroneous. Nonetheless, even our modern 1-to-2-pound oxtail still needs slow, moist cooking, because the tail of any bovine—with flies to swat—has well-exercised muscles. It also has a rich, well-developed flavor that enriches soups and stews. Oxtail is especially popular in Central Europe and in parts of the old Spanish Empire such as the Philippines, where the braised oxtail dish named *kari kari* is a classic.

Buying Tips

Select fresh oxtails with bright red flesh and a pleasant smell. Avoid those that have become brown-tinged. Equal-sized oxtail cross sections cook uniformly. Oxtails are mainly bone—you will need to buy nearly a pound of oxtail per person.

PREPARATION

Storage

Fresh oxtail should be used within a day or two of purchase. Store loosely wrapped in the refrigerator. Tightly wrapped in freezer paper, oxtail may be stored for up to a couple of weeks in the frozen food compartment and up to a couple of months in the deep freezer, but be prepared for some loss of flavor and texture.

Preliminaries

If your butcher has not already done it, skin the tail and remove the excess surface fat and connective tissue. Disjoint through the cartilage, not through the vertebrae.

Cooking

Depending on size and animal age, oxtail segments should be simmered or braised 1¼ to 1¾ hours. Overcooking or cooking with too high heat (including a rapid boil) will toughen the flesh.

OYSTER

BACKGROUND

Oysters may not be the best-looking of bivalve mollusks, but to most epicures their succulent creamy-gray meat wins the culinary blue ribbon. Oysters proliferate best in tidal waters, bays, and river mouths where the ocean's normal salinity is diluted with fresh water.

There are hundreds of distinct oyster species with shells ranging from less than an inch to over a foot long. The tiny ones are tasty but require more shucking work than they are worth. The larger varieties, such as the *Japanese oyster*, are used in preparations such as stews and fritters but are too immense to be eaten on the half shell. The perfect size range is between 1½ and 5 inches long. The taste, texture, and size of oysters within a given species can vary markedly also due to differences in diet and in such factors as mineral content and temperature of the water where they grew.

Do not look for pearls in your oysters, as those precious gems come from large species found in tropical waters. Also do not give too much credence to the belief that raw oysters are aphrodisiacal. Of course, if you think they are, they are.

Varieties

The leading Atlantic oysters include the *blue point* (Long Island, New York), *Chincoteague* (Virginia and Maryland), *coluit* (Massachusetts), *malpeque* (Canadian Maritime provinces), and *Wellfleet* (Cape Cod, Massachusetts). From Florida comes the *Apalachicola*, from Louisiana the *Mobile Bay* and *New Orleans*. The two leading Pacific Coast oysters are the small, subtly flavored *Olympio* oyster from Puget Sound, Washington, and the foot-long *Japanese* (or *Pacific*) oyster. Europeans have their delicious French *bélon* and Irish *Galway* oysters, which are vastly superior to the more abundant *Portuguese* oysters.

AVAILABILITY

Season

"Eat oysters only during months spelled with an R": That rule is now out of date. It originated before the days of widespread refrigeration, when harvested oysters quickly spoiled during the warm summer months. There is now nothing noxious about eating oysters during May, June, July, and August, and they can be a treat. However, keep in mind that oysters during this period are spawning and tend to be more watery and less plump than they are during the cooler months. Live oysters in the shell, because of their weight, are seldom shipped far beyond their regional environs. The blue point oyster is the prime exception because the well-publicized name allows the fish store or restaurant to charge a hefty price to offset the shipping cost. Shucked oysters are sold fresh, frozen, dried, or canned (usually smoked) the year around. Oysters are also sold in commercially prepared products such as soups.

Buying Tips

Live Oysters: The less time a harvested oyster is stored, the better it will taste. In ideal circumstances, the period between oyster bed and oyster platter is less than an hour. But since in our real world the fishmonger's oysters will probably be at least a day to possibly a week, out of the sea, we must make do with less than perfection. What we can do is buy oysters from a reliable seafood store with a fast stock turnover. Do not buy oysters that have broken shells, that do not close when rapped (they are dead or dying), or that feel light or heavy for their size. If the merchant's supply has too high of a proportion of those rejects, do not even buy the apparently good specimens. Size of the oyster shell is not conclusive evidence of the size of its meat. When buying oysters in bulk, always open one to check the meat size as well as its general condition. The smaller an oyster is for its species, the younger it will likely be and therefore the sweeter and more tender it will be. One way to estimate age is to examine the concentric shell rings which were formed because an oyster grows more rapidly in the warm summer than in the cold winter months. This principle is the same as with tree rings; each ridge represents one year of age. Select even-sized oysters for uniform cooking and a more attractive platter presentation.

Shucked Oysters: The first rule for buying pre-shucked oysters is: Do not, if you can buy live oysters. (The fishmonger will usually shuck them for you on the spot and, on request, give you the delicious liquor.) If you must, look for plumpness, uniform size, a pleasant sea-breeze scent, and a clear rather than a cloudy or milky liquor. Be sure the fishmonger gives you the liquor along with the oysters in a leakproof container.

PREPARATION

Storage

Keep live oysters on ice in a cool, dark place such as a cellar—or in a container at 40°F in a refrigerator. Store the oysters sitting on their deeper shell half. If in good condition when purchased, oysters in the shell will stay fresh for at least several days, but the sooner you use them, the better they will taste.

Shucking

Scrub the oyster shells at least 30 minutes before you plan to shuck them. Then handle the oysters gently for the last 30 minutes, because an alarmed oyster, understandably, will contract, obstinately fighting for its life—and making your job harder. Properly removing live oysters from their shells is easy for an experienced shucker (who can do a dozen or more a minute) or impossible for the neophyte (whose rate may be zero per hour). The best teacher is experience, under the tutelage of a skilled friend. You need a more angular-pointed oyster knife rather than the rounder-pointed clam knife. Hold the oyster firmly in your hand with the hinge against your palm. To keep the juice from spilling out, the thicker half of the shell should be on the bottom. Insert the tip of the knife between the shell halves, opposite the hinged side. Sever the adductor muscle from the upper shell. Lift and snap off the top shell. Finally, separate the meat from the lower shell half. If you are worried about cutting yourself, use a heavy-duty pair of cotton work gloves reserved for this task. Place a bowl under the oysters as you open them if you think you may spill their juices. If you cannot open your oysters the proper way, pay the fishmonger to do it. This is better than suggestions such as hammering off a corner of the shell (bits of shell may become imbedded in the meat). And if you are going to eat the oysters on the half shell, do not place them—as some cookbooks suggest—on a hot burner or in a hot oven until they open. What is acceptable, however, is placing them in the freezer for 5 to 15 minutes (depending on size) in order to help relax the adductor muscle. Do not wash the oyster. If there are shell bits, remove them with your fingers or tweezers.

CLASSIC USES AND AFFINITIES

Oysters on the half shell are these creatures' greatest moment, at least from the diner's point of view. Purists place the opened oysters on a platter of crushed ice, then lift out the meat from one oyster at a time, eat the meat neat, then sip the liquor from the shell. Less demanding palates sprinkle the oysters with lemon juice, horseradish sauce, Tabasco sauce, shallots, cocktail sauce, vinegar, or anything else that will mask the subtle oyster flavor. Well-known cooked oyster specialties include oysters Rockefeller, oyster stew, angels on horseback, fried oysters, and oysters *Bien-ville.* The mollusk is also used as a stuffing ingredient for poultry.

PALM HEART

BACKGROUND

The *cabbage palm* (*Sabal palmetto*), a native of Florida, produces an edible shoot called a *palm heart* or *swamp cabbage*. The shoot weighs about 2 pounds. Palm hearts are quite bland, but extravagant; they are sometimes made into "millionaire's salad," so called not only because of the price but also because the fledgling tree has to be chopped down to get at its heart. Canned palm hearts are available but fall short of the fresh variety in flavor and texture.

PREPARATION

To cook a *palm heart*, the outer covering and fibrous top must be removed. Then the heart is sliced thin and soaked in water for an hour. Next, it is blanched, drained, and simmered for about 30 to 45 minutes. An alternative preparation is to roast the whole palm heart for an hour in a preheated 325°F oven, then peel it.

PAPAYA

BACKGROUND

The *papaya* (*Carica papaya*) is one of the world's fastest-growing trees—it can sprout from seed to a 20-foot-tall fruit-bearing tree in less than a year. In some markets the papaya is sold as *tree melon* and in others as *papaw* or *pawpaw*. (The last two names create some confusion, because another, unrelated, fruit goes under the same two names. And a word of warning: if you happen to be in Cuba, ask for a *fruta bomba*; *papaya* is a very uncouth word.)

Key domestic production areas for this native tropical American fruit are Hawaii, Puerto Rico and Florida. A papaya's size can range from less than 1 pound up to 20; most markets stock the 2-to-4-pound specimens, the ones that are deemed the best tasting. The shape varies from round to (more typically) one resembling a football with tips like a lemon's. The skin is thick and smooth (though sometimes slightly pocked); it is colored green when unripe and, depending on variety, anywhere from green to a deep golden yellow when ripe. The latter color is typical of most papayas that reach our stores. The ripe pulp is usually salmon to pastel orange, with a juicy, melonlike texture, only softer. It has a mild, sweet-tart flavor with strong, musky overtones (if too pungent, the papaya is likely overripe). The inside cavity swarms with tiny dark seeds that can be easily scooped out with a spoon.

The leaves and fruit of the papaya contain an enzyme, *papain*, that will tenderize tough meat. (Papain, incidentally, is the key ingredient in the commercial meat tenderizers.) Papain is at its most potent in the underripe fruit. This substance makes the papaya a mild digestive—but do not fret, as it cannot digest your stomach. There is even some evidence that our stomach acids diffuse the enzyme before it has a chance to do its digestive chores.

Some people develop an allergic reaction when their skin comes into contact with raw papaya pulp or juice. If you belong to that club, wear gloves or wash your hands thoroughly after handling the cut-up fruit.

AVAILABILITY

In some markets, papayas are available the year round, but they are generally at their finest several weeks before and after Memorial Day. Food manufacturers process papaya into a number of products including sherbet, ice cream, and canned juice.

Buying Tips

A ready-to-eat papaya will yield slightly to palm pressure and will (except for a few varieties) develop a rich golden-yellow hue and a pleasing aroma. Bad signs include excessive softness, "off odor" such as one of rot or fermentation, and a skin that is blemished, bruised, decay-spotted, cracked, or otherwise damaged.

PREPARATION

Ripening

You can ripen most papaya varieties at home with some success so long as the fruit is not too green. Store the papaya in a pierced paper bag at room temperature for one to several days, depending on the original degree of ripeness. Once ripe, a papaya decays swiftly, so plan to enjoy your fruit within the day or, if that is not possible, refrigerate it in a sealed plastic bag for no more than a day or two. Always handle a papaya gently as it bruises easily.

Cooking

Papayas may be cooked like a squash or made into pies, preserves, and chutneys. For such purposes, select a papaya just slightly underripe.

Serving

For the best flavor, serve your papaya at or slightly below room temperature. The most common way of eating a papaya is to slice it into halves or wedges, seed it, and sprinkle the flesh with lime juice. Then spoon out bite-sized portions of the flesh. For added pleasure, fill the cavity with shrimp, cottage cheese, or ice cream. The seeds are edible and can be reserved for use as a garnish or as an addition to salad dressings, to mention two of many possibilities.

PARSLEY

BACKGROUND

One of our most popular herbs, *parsley* is often used as a garnish but is well worth eating for itself. It has a light, fresh flavor, very few calories, and a great deal of calcium and Vitamins A and C—but its vitamin content is academic since few of us consume handsful of parsley. A necklace of parsley was a usual ornament at a Roman banquet, because it was believed that parsley staved off drunkenness. British children are found in a parsley bed, not brought by the stork. Parsley is rich in chlorophyll and acts as a breath freshener.

The two major varieties of *Petroselinum crispum* are the ornamental *curly-leaved parsley* and the *Italian* or *flat-leaved parsley*. The first makes a more striking garnish, the second is more flavorful. *Hamburg parsley* is a variety grown for its edible root. *Chinese parsley* is not parsley at all, but fresh CORIANDER (also see HERBS AND SPICES for information on buying, storing, cooking, etc.).

AVAILABILITY

Parsley is available dried and freeze-dried, but since the fresh product is so widely available the year around, so easily stored, and relatively inexpensive, we do not see the value of processed parsley except, say, to campers or to people living in remote areas. If you buy dehydrated parsley, use it before it loses color and flavor.

CLASSIC USES AND AFFINITIES

Vivid-green fresh parsley used as a garnish enlivens pallid dishes such as mashed or boiled potatoes, noodles, cauliflower, and cottage or cream cheese. Deep-fried parsley is a tasty garnish for meat. Most sauces look attractive given a sprinkle of chopped parsley. Chopped parsley is used in many herb blends such as FINES HERBES and BOUQUET GARNI, and in classic French sauces such as *tartare, vinaigrette, ravigote,* and *beurre à la maître d'hotel.*

PARSNIP

BACKGROUND

The *parsnip,* a creamy-yellow edible root with white-flesh, resembles its cousin, the carrot, but is usually somewhat thinner. *Pastinaca sativa* is loved by some people and loathed by a great many others. Perhaps if its Medieval reputation as an aphrodisiac were better known, it would be more popular. It is myth that parsnips must freeze before they are eaten; a temperature somewhat above the freezing point is sufficient to trigger the enzymatic change from starch to sugar.

AVAILABILITY

Parsnips are spottily available all the year round, but their peak seasons are winter and early spring.

Buying Tips

Choose unwilted, unwrinkled parsnips without visible blemishes. Small to medium roots are the least fibrous and most tender. For stews or sautéing, choose long, slim parsnips; for pureeing, choose parsnips with thick meaty tops for greater yield. In either case, avoid the over-sized parsnip, as it may prove woody and dry.

PREPARATION

Storage

If the parsnips are sold with green tops, remove them as soon as possible, as the green growth will drain moisture and nourishment from the root. If there are blemishes and bruises, trim them off lest they spoil the rest of the parsnip. Use those parsnips as soon as possible. You can keep parsnips refrigerated for 7 to 10 days sealed in a plastic bag.

Preliminaries

Trim both ends, and scrub well. For a sweeter taste and maximum nutrition, and to prevent oxidation, cook parsnips with the skin on. Peel them afterward if you wish. Parsnips can be left whole for braising or the stock pot. For stews and vegetable dishes, cut them into chunks or thick slices.

Cooking

You can treat the parsnip almost as you

would a carrot. Steam or boil whole parsnips 20 to 35 minutes, depending on size; if cut into chunks, 10 to 15 minutes should be adequate. Bake unpeeled buttered parsnips in a 350°F oven for 30 to 45 minutes, depending on size. You can also sauté or puree parsnips, or use them in soups, stocks, and stews.

CLASSIC USES AND AFFINITIES

Parsnips are a good side dish for dark-fleshed meats. Ginger, mace, dill, and chervil emphasize the sweet flavor of parsnips. Butter and cream add richness.

PASSION FRUIT

BACKGROUND

The tropical fruit *Passiflora edulis* is noted for two things: its name and unique flavor. It is called *passion fruit* not because it has any aphrodisiac qualities, but because the flowers of this vine vaguely resemble and symbolize Christ's crown of thorns and the wounds of the Crucifixion. The egg-shaped passion fruit (also called *purple granadilla*) is about 3 inches long with a thick outer hull that changes as it ripens from a smooth, tight-fitting green to a well-wrinkled purple. When ripe, the juicy yellowish pulp is sweet in smell and taste, and has many tightly clinging dark edible seeds, which are virtually impossible to remove from the flesh. Its juice has a special, permeating quality that mixes well. It is usually sparingly blended with other juices to make festive punches—even Hawaiian Punch contains some. Indigenous to Brazil, the passion fruit is now cultivated as a major crop in Australia; in the United States it is grown in limited acreage in both California and Florida.

AVAILABILITY

The passion fruit matures in the fall. In most parts of our country it is difficult to find fresh—usually part of a small shipment to a specialty shop or ethnic market.

Buying Tips

If you do find fresh passion fruit, buy one with as deep a purple color as possible. The fruit should give a little when pressed but be firm overall.

PREPARATION

Once ripened, the passion fruit is perishable and will not keep. To serve it as a dessert fruit, cut through the hard rind with a sharp knife, dribble fresh lime juice over the halves, add a dusting of ground coriander, if you have it, and eat with a spoon, flesh and seeds together.

PASTA

BACKGROUND

If you grind the hard kernels of *durum wheat*, you get *semolina*—a hard, fine-grained substance. If you mix semolina with water and shape it, you get *pasta*, a collective name for an array of starchy foods such as spaghetti and macaroni.

Pasta is closely associated with Italy, but noodles of wheat, rice, and buckwheat are extremely significant in Oriental cuisines. For the record, Marco Polo did not bring pasta to Italy from China (or vice versa) as legend has it. Historical documents prove that noodles existed in both lands before Marco Polo was born.

Pasta can be fresh or dried. Fresh pasta is superb. Dry pasta is practical; it keeps much longer than bread. Either type can be combined with almost anything to make a satisfying meal. Armed only with a rolling pin and knife, you can make squares of pasta or long noodle strips. Special pasta machines extend the home cook's options even further. The dies and machinery of a pasta factory turn out hundreds of different shapes.

Varieties

Italian pasta lovers classify pasta dishes as *pasta in brodo*, "in broth," or *pasta asciutta*, "dry"—pasta that is in anything else, typically in sauce. They also distinguish between *pasta fresca*, fresh dough made at home or bought fresh for immediate consumption, and *pasta secca*, long-keeping dried factory pasta. Beyond those broad classifications, things become confusing. There are at least 500 varieties of pasta and, to make matters worse, some of these varieties are called by different names in different regions. Any shape can be manufactured in various sizes and can be cut smooth or grooved (*rigati*), its edges can be straight or ruffled (*riccie*), it can be uncolored or colored with spinach juice (*verde*) or beet juice. Some pastas are enriched with eggs.

Spaghetti ("strings") is pasta in long threads. *Linguine* ("little tongues") is spaghetti with a flattened, rather than a round, cross section. *Fusille* is spaghetti fashioned into an elongated spiral. *Vermicelli* and *capellini* ("little worms" and "fine hair" respectively) are ultra-thin spaghetti. *Tagliatelle* and *fettuccine* ("small ribbons") are long, thin flat noodles. *Mafalda* are broad flat noodles with rippled edges.

Shaped hollow types of pasta are called *macaroni*, and the farther south you travel in Italy the more popular they tend to be. *Bucatini* and *perciatelli* ("tiny pierced") are almost as thin as spaghetti. *Maruzze* look like shells. *Ditali* ("thimbles") and *elbows* are curved tubes. *Penne* and *mostaccioli* ("tiny mustaches") are straight tubes cut on the diagonal. *Ziti* ("bridegrooms") are medium-sized tubes. *Occhi di lupo* ("wolf eyes") are large-sized tubes.

Pasta to be stuffed includes *cannelloni* and *manicotti*, which are flat squares or tubes to be filled with meat or cheese, sauced, and baked. *Lasagne* are flat sheets baked in layers interspersed with meat, sauce and cheese. Pasta available prestuffed includes the square *ravioli*, the half-moon *agnolotti*, and the "little hats," *cappelletti*.

Special-shaped pasta includes the bowtie-shaped *farfalle* ("butterflies"), the corkscrew-shaped (sometimes wheel-shaped) *rotelle*, the twisted helix-shaped *gemelli* ("twins"), the shell-shaped *conchiglie* ("conch shells"), and the thin dumpling-shaped *cavatelli*.

Ideal for soups are *acini*, *anelli* ("rings"), *capelli d'angelo* ("angel's hair"), *funghini* ("little mushrooms"), *orzo* ("barley"), *stelle* ("stars"), and *tubetti* ("tiny tubes").

These are only the elementary varieties. For a graduate course, visit an Italian grocery store.

AVAILABILITY

Dried pasta is universally available. Fresh pasta must be bought at a specialty store.

Buying Tips

Dried Pasta: Dried pasta imported from Italy is almost always superior to the domestic product. The pasta should be in a reasonably airtight carton or bag—examine the package for rips or other openings that will let in air and perhaps bugs and hasten the pasta's downfall. If you buy green or red pasta, check the label to see that the color comes from natural spinach or beet juice and not from food coloring. Dried pasta is fragile and easily damaged if dropped. Look through the see-through package or window to make sure the pasta is intact. At the same time, check for a lack of freshness, excessive powderiness, and the like. A grocery shelf is not the ideal storage environment. Buy from markets with high merchandise turnover. With so many pasta types available, experiment and add variety to your menus.

Fresh Pasta: "Fresh" is relative. Some stores sell pasta as "fresh" that was made 6 to 12 hours earlier. Purists, rightfully, consider such food as partially dried pasta. For the best results, no more than an hour after the pasta is made should it be plunged into the boiling water. The longer the time delay, the more the fresh pasta deteriorates in quality. If you must temporarily store fresh pasta, place it in a sealed plastic bag and refrigerate.

Frozen Pasta: Some stores sell pasta that is frozen immediately after it is made. It has a limited freezer life, usually a week or two. When stored too long, this frozen pasta dries out and becomes brittle; look for telltale signs such as small broken fragments in the package.

PREPARATION

Storage

Keep pasta cool and dry. Tall glass jars with well-closed lids are perfect, and a variety of pastas makes a pretty display so long as you do not store the contents beyond your short-term needs. If you plan to store your pasta for more than a couple of weeks, however, it should not see the light of day.

Cooking

A basic secret for cooking *bellissima* pasta is to have enough boiling water in the pot to hold its temperature when you add the room-temperature pasta. For each half pound of pasta, we recommend at least 3 quarts of salted, oiled water (1 teaspoon each of salt and olive oil for each quart of liquid). The salt adds flavor and slightly raises the boiling point of the water—and the hotter the water, the better the pasta. The olive oil does likewise and also helps keep the pasta from sticking together. Add the pasta when the water is at its maximum, most tumultuous boil. And put the pasta into the water a little at a time (but do not take too long) so as to minimize the drop in water temperature. You will need a fairly large pot for boiling long-stem pasta. If the pasta is too long, it is better to "melt" it into the boiling water so that full-length strands can be served. Breaking the strands in half takes away some of the joy of eating pasta. As the pasta boils, occasionally stir it. Dried pasta usually doubles in volume as it cooks and absorbs water; fresh pasta does not appreciably change in size. The thinner and fresher the pasta, the quicker it will cook. Slender, board-fresh pasta cooks in a minute or two. Thick, dried, shelf-aged pasta can require 20 to 30 minutes' cooking time. Typical store-bought spaghetti needs about 7 to 10 minutes.

Test for Doneness

Pasta is at its best when cooked to the point the Italians call *al dente*—literally, "to the tooth." Most American home cooks overcook pasta and end up with a limp, soggy food lacking texture. The traditional Italian peasant test for doneness of noodle or spaghetti-type pasta is to throw a strand against the wall. It should stick for a count of two or three. If the test specimen falls down sooner, it is undercooked; if it becomes a fixture, it is overcooked. Less dashing, but easier, is to test the pasta as it cooks. It should be firm, offering a little resistance to the teeth. A surer way for neophytes is to cut through a pasta sample at its thickest point. The pasta is ready the second you can no longer see starchiness in the core. Because the pasta will continue to cook a bit after it leaves the pot, it should be removed from the heat source when there are still a few starchy specks or a starchy hairline in the middle of the pasta.

Serving

Once cooked, drain the pasta immediately. Unless you want the pasta to cool for use in another preparation, never follow the advice of cookbooks that tell you to rinse the hot pasta with cold water to stop the cooking process. After quickly draining the pasta, put it in a heated bowl, or directly on hot plates. Serve it promptly—time, tide, and pasta wait for no man. In most instances, you should not mix the pasta and sauce together (American-style) before serving it but rather serve the pasta and let each diner sauce his own. Not only does this method make a more attractive presentation, it gives the diner the chance to choose the amount of sauce he (or she) prefers. When serving (or cooking) with grated parmesan cheese, be aware that there is a world of difference between the freshly grated cheese and the pre-grated store-bought variety.

CLASSIC USES AND AFFINITIES

Tomato-based sauces, red and white clam sauces, herb, wine, and garlic-spiked sauces, sausage-starring sauces—these are some of the tried and tested ways to flavor the relatively bland taste of pasta. So are additions of butter, cheese, raw eggs, cream, mushrooms, olive oil, and a final sprinkling of freshly chopped parsley. World-renowned pasta dishes include *fettuccine Alfredo* and *lasagne al forno*, as well as pasta *alla bolognese*, *alla carbonara*, *alla pesto*, *alla matriciana*, *alla marinara*, *alla* . . . An American but not Italian tradition is baked macaroni and cheese. The same is true of spaghetti and meat balls. But *pasta vinaigrette*, cold pasta dressed with a sauce of seasoned oil and lemon juice, is becoming an international favorite for mid-summer *al fresco* meals.

PASTRAMI

BACKGROUND

That favorite Jewish-American delicatessen specialty, hot *pastrami* sandwich, has thrust this cured slab of beef into deserved fame. The name derives from *pastra*, meaning "to preserve" in Romanian.

PREPARATION

The classic way of making pastrami calls for a boneless slab of trimmed beef, preferably from the plate section of the animal. Other cuts can be used, including brisket, but they will not match the plate in succulence. Its entire surface is rubbed with salt and a paste of various spices such as peppercorns, garlic, cayenne, allspice, cloves, cinnamon, cumin, coriander seeds, sugar, and ginger—pastrami should be highly seasoned. Traditionally, saltpeter is also used, but we don't recommend it because it is potentially hazardous to health. The seasoned beef is dry-cured for about a week, then rinsed and patted dry. A fresh batch of the paste seasoning, this time with an abundance of crushed peppercorns, is applied to the meat. Finally, the meat is smoke-cooked for several or more hours until tender.

Serving

Serve pastrami cold or hot. If you reheat it, steam it to keep the meat juicy. To make pastrami as tender as possible, slice the meat thin across the grain as you would BEEF, LONDON BROIL. Serve pastrami with its two classic accompaniments: rye bread and mustard.

PASTRY

BACKGROUND

Pastry has been enjoyed ever since some ancient Greek thought it might be a good idea to add some honey to his bread, producing the first honey cake. In Medieval times sweet pastries were so highly valued by the nobility that the indispensable pastry chef became a person with political power. One of the earliest trade unions was the association of pastry chefs that was founded in Paris in 1270. By the mid-sixteenth century, French pastry chefs were granted titles and special privileges by royal decree. Those days are gone, and pastry is now for the common man. In fine restaurants throughout the Western world, however, the pastry chef still demands a certain degree of special attention.

Varieties

The types of baked goods that are classified as pastries are too numerous to cite in detail. Among the best known are *cakes*, *pies* and *cookies*, as well as *brioches*, *croissants*, *Danish pastries*, *doughnuts*, *éclairs*, *napoleans*, *petit fours*, *profiteroles* and *strudels*. Everyone has his or her favorites.

AVAILABILITY

The best pastries come fresh from a baker's oven—or your own.

Buying Tips

One of the biggest telltale differences between high-quality and mediocre pastries is the amount of butter used. To cut costs, many bakeries cut down on the butter and use vegetable oil substitutes.

Storage

Unlike BREADS, most pastry requires and often desperately needs refrigeration, especially if it contains eggs. Bring it to room temperature or heat it before serving.

PEA BEAN

BACKGROUND

The smallest of the four major types of white beans is the *pea bean* (the other three, in ascending order of size, are the navy, Great Northern, and marrow beans). Perhaps the pea bean reaches its culinary apogee in the humble but excellent Boston baked beans. Sometimes commercial packagers of dried beans do not differentiate between the pea and navy beans, so you may find them mixed in packages and boxes simply merchandised as "white beans"; but for the record, traditional New Englanders only use the pea bean for Boston baked beans, then only with blackstrap molasses. (For soaking, cooking, etc., see BEANS.)

PEACH

BACKGROUND

The botanical Latin name *Prunus persica* means "Persian plum," but most food scholars trace the *peach*'s earliest roots to China. As a stone fruit (or *drupe*), it is a member of the genus that includes cherries, nectarines, plums, almonds, and apricots. America's two leading peach-producing states are California and, of course, Georgia, whose name is practically synonomous with the word "peach."

Varieties

Innumerable peach varieties exist, ranging in skin color from red-tinted creamy white to yellow, and in pulp color from pale whitish-yellow to deep gold, often with reddish streaks near the pit. Virtually all peach varieties fall into one of two basic culinary classifications: freestone and cling. Freestone peaches are distinguished by their easily removed pit. In contrast, the pit of the cling peach does exactly that: it obstinately adheres to the pulp. Freestone peaches prevail in retail markets, while cling peaches are the runaway favorites of commercial canneries, partly because of their firmer and smoother texture and more uniform general appearance. Peach fuzz is seen less and less; much of it is removed by mechanical brushes or is being bred out in an attempt to please a mass market swayed more by sight than taste.

AVAILABILITY

Peaches are abundant from mid-May through mid-October and at their very best in July and August. Cling peaches generally arrive and depart earlier than freestones. Peaches are also widely marketed canned or frozen, packed in either water or syrup. Besides scoring reduced marks in terms of nutrition and natural peach flavor and fragrance, those preserved fruits are deplorably mushy. Yet they sometimes fare better than the evil on the other end of the spectrum: the hard, insipid, immature peaches found in most produce bins.

Buying Tips

A ripe peach is succulent, flavorful and fragrant; an unripe peach is not. Unfortunately, the overwhelming majority of commercially grown peaches are picked prematurely so as to stretch their shipping and storage life. Since these non-tree-ripened fruits will not appreciably ripen once picked, they are best left in the bin. The surest ripeness test is to smell the peach—it should be fabulously fragrant. A second major clue is skin color. However, contrary to popular notion, a reddish tint is not necessarily an accurate indicator; what is is the absence of a green tint on the creamy yellow background. And that background color should have a fresh, perky glow. The peach should feel firm, but yield slightly when squeezed. If the fruit is too hard, it was picked prematurely. If too soft, the peach is overripe or decaying. The skin should not be bruised, blemished, cracked, shriveled, leaky or sticky. Subsurface worm infestation can often be detected by examining the peel for telltale entry holes. Plump, spherical peaches are better than those with semi-flattened shapes. Within the same variety, medium-sized peaches are better than large or small ones.

PREPARATION

Storage

Buy only for short-term consumption, as ripe peaches are highly perishable. Handle ripe peaches gingerly; they are easily bruised. Store ripe peaches in a sealed plastic bag in the refrigerator and use within a day or two. For best flavor, bring the peach to just below room temperature before eating. If a peach is hard and therefore immature, you can soften the flesh by storing the fruit at room temperature for 2 or more days. But do not count on miracles—it will not develop a celestial flavor and fragrance.

Preliminaries

To remove the skin from a ripe peach, immerse in boiling water for 10 to 15 seconds, then immediately submerge it in ice water, then strip the skin from the peach in small segments using a paring knife. Exceptionally soft peaches can sometimes be peeled just by rubbing the dull edge of a butter knife thoroughly over the skin to loosen it; the skin can be crumpled off in your hand. Stone cling peaches by slipping a knife tip into the blossom end until it reaches the pit, then cutting around the peach lengthwise. Twist, and the two peach halves should separate. Pry out the seed with a spoon. When preparing large quantities of peach slices (for a pie or salad, for example) use lemon juice or a sprinkling of brown sugar to prevent browning. The citric acid acts as an antioxidant; the sugar forms a syrup coating which helps exclude the air. To poach peaches in a syrup, simmer about 7 minutes for slices, 10 to 12 minutes for halves. Before eating a peach raw, wash it to rid the skin of possible pesticides and germs.

Equivalents

Some peaches are much larger than others; about 4 to 5 ounces is average. A pound of peaches will yield approximately 2 cups of sliced, 1 cup of pureed fruit.

CLASSIC USES AND AFFINITIES

The peach's most celebrated dish is the dessert created by Escoffier, *Peach Melba*: vanilla ice cream topped with a poached fresh peach half and a raspberry-based sauce. Peaches are often used in ice cream, liqueurs, jams, pies, cobblers, fruit cocktails, and cottage-cheese salads. Classic affinities include brandy, Sauternes wines, sugar, raspberries, cinnamon, and especially, cream.

PEAR

BACKGROUND

The triumphant refrain of "The Twelve Days of Christmas" is "a partridge in a pear tree." In these days of inflation, few of us can afford partridge, but most can manage a *pear* or two. *Pyrrus communis*, the common pear, is indigenous to the Old World but is now cultivated in temperate climates everywhere. France is especially noted for her pear harvest, though the quality has been slipping over the last decade or two, as the growers are opting for the higher-yielding American hybrids. Most of America's commercial orchards are found in the three Pacific states of California, Oregon, and Washington.

A pear is not necessarily "pear-shaped"; some varieties are spherical, while others have such elongated necks that they would better be described as gourd-shaped. A pear at its best is juicy, not coarse and grainy. Surface color ranges from a milky green to yellow to russet, sometimes with a rose-red blush. Some new hybrids are almost red. Pulp can be creamy greenish-white or virtually snow white. Flavor runs the gamut from luscious sweetness to a hint of spiciness.

Varieties

Many varieties exist and new hybrids crop up periodically, but most American fruit markets limit their offerings to the big five:

Anjou: Named for its original home, an area of France, the *poire d'Anjou* is an all-purpose (cooking, canning, eating) pear that is distinguished by its winy taste, squat neck, and yellow-green, sometimes russeted skin. When ripe, this fruit can be superb.

Bartlett: America's best-selling pear goes under the name of *poire Williams* in France. A good specimen is juicy, fragrant and moderately acid. The medium-large fruit is bell-shaped with a greenish-yellow, sometimes red-blushed peel (the skin of one new hybrid is predominantly red). The more yellow and less green the skin hue, the more mature and ripe the pear is likely to be. The Bartlett is all-purpose; use it for eating raw, cooking or canning.

Bosc: If you see a medium-to-large pear with an exaggerated, slender, elongated neck, it is probably an all-purpose Bosc. Its yellow skin is russeted, its flavor has an agreeable tartness.

Comice: The all-purpose Comice is medium to large in size, has a squat neck and a red-blushed yellow skin. Its flesh is sweet and juicy when ripe.

Seckel: Compared to other leading pear varieties, the russeted, yellow-skinned Seckel (a *Pyrrus serotina*) is a runt in size but not in quality. Its piquant but sweet taste is a welcome characteristic, especially for cooks and canners, though it can be eaten raw.

Other pear varieties include the *Cayuga, Chinese sand pear, Clapp Favorite, Kieffer, Ovid, Sheldon, Snow pear, Tyson,* and *Winter Nelis.*

AVAILABILITY

Season

Pears are available at an opportune time: fall and winter, when the selection of fresh fruits is limited. Of the five leading pear varieties, the Bartlett is the early arrival, and with a late-July through mid-October season. Next comes the Seckel with its late-August through early-November season. October marks the market entry of the Comice, the Bosc, and Anjou, all three being generally available through mid-winter. Modern cold storage extends the normal seasonal lifetimes of the pears, but the end product is too often insipid and mealy. Canned pears are available the year around for those who enjoy minimum flavor coupled with maximum mushiness.

Buying Tips

Avoid a pear whose skin is cracked, bruised, blemished, decay-spotted, scaly, leaky, or sticky. An odd-shaped pear should be left behind in the bin. If you plan to cook or can pears, use slightly unripe specimens. Unlike most fruits, a pear that undergoes its final ripening process off the tree tends to have a less coarse texture than one that is left on the tree to ripen. Also the shopper usually has to ripen pears at home, because they almost unavoidably reach the market unripe. Accepting that as a fact of life, it is more prudent for us to supervise the ripening at home than to buy a pear that has "ripened" in the unsalubrious produce bin where thousands of testing fingers have squeezed the poor little fruit. (Pears do bruise easily.)

PREPARATION

Ripening

It is wiser to bring a virtually unpinched pear home, store it in a pierced paper bag at room temperature and then patiently wait one to several days until the fruit ripens. A pear is ripe and ready to eat when the flesh (especially that at the stem end) yields to gentle pressure. If it yields too much, it may be overripe. (Please note: a pear tends to ripen from the inside out, so if the outside is perfect, the core area is probably overripe, or worse.) If the pear is rock-hard, all the proper home-ripening will prove futile. As a pear ripens, its fragrance develops. Skin color is not the best measure of ripening as the surface hue differs among varieties. Generally, however, yellowing of the greenish skin is a good sign. The same may be said about a red blush, but do not blindly rely upon that clue. Once ripe, serve the juicy pear at or just below room temperature. If you cannot eat it immediately, seal the pear in a plastic bag in the refrigerator for no more than a day or two.

Preliminaries

Do not wash your pear until ready to eat it, as moisture hastens bacterial growth. But be sure to rinse it carefully at the appropriate time to rid it of germs and pesticides. Pears have a relatively low acid content, and therefore are not as good for cooking as apples. To offset this limitation, you may wish to add lemon juice, wine, or another acid to your pears when cooking them. Unless you are going to eat your pear sections immediately, coat the exposed flesh with citrus juice to retard the natural darkening caused by oxidation. Or, for a short time only, submerge the pieces in cold water. Peel the pear or not, as you please.

CLASSIC USES AND AFFINITIES

The classic French dessert *poire Hélène* consists of vanilla ice cream topped by poached vanilla-infused pears and a hot chocolate sauce. Pears are often pickled with spices, go into fresh fruit or cottage-cheese salads, become an ingredient in stewed compotes, and accompany ripe cheeses such as Brie or Camembert as a climactic ending to a meal.

PEAS

BACKGROUND

Think of peas and you probably see the *English* or *garden pea*, our most popular variety of *Pisum sativum*, a plump, little ball with bright green skin and pale green flesh that mixes happily with almost anything else you are serving. This legume, when young, is the *petit pois* of France. However, there are also the Chinese snow pea (or sugar pea) and the new kid on the block, the sugar snap pea. The latter, a cross between the English and snow peas, holds much promise because of its sweet taste.

In addition, there is the smaller, harder *field pea* that becomes the green or yellow split *dried pea* that is often used for purees and soups, as well as in meat loaves and vegetable casseroles. In this entry, we will not discuss the field pea; for soaking, cooking, and other advice relevant to the dried pea, see the BEANS entry.

English Pea

AVAILABILITY

Peas are spring vegetables that are at their peak generally from late March until the end of May. Frozen peas are available year around, but are inferior to fresh peas in taste and texture. Nonetheless, the damage caused to peas by freezing and thawing is less severe than is the case with most other vegetables. Moreover, frozen peas are certainly superior both gastronomically and nutritionally to either canned peas or those so-called fresh peas that have taken a slow journey from field to plate.

Buying Tips

When buying fresh English peas, buy them as young as you can, looking for clean, leprechaun-green, unblemished pods swelling with plump peas. Split a pod lengthwise (your fingernail will do it) and examine the peas inside. They should shine, be well separated, all look alike, and smell fresh as new grass. If you sample one, it should be crunchy with a juicy snap. Rub two pods against each other—young and fresh, they will squeak. Yellowness on the pods indicates age, and spots indicate possible fungus or insect infestation.

PREPARATION

Storage

Fresh peas will not hold their flavor beyond 2 or 3 days. Refrigerate, and use as soon as possible.

Cooking

English peas can be cooked in their pods if very young, but usually they are shelled, and steamed or simmered in very little liquid for about 10 minutes until just tender. Often they are seasoned with basil and cut or whole baby onions, pimento, or mushrooms or engulfed in a well-peppered cream sauce.

Equivalents

One pound fresh peas in the pod will give you 1 cup cooked shelled peas or 2 typical servings.

Snow Pea

The *snow pea* (*Pisum sativum macrocarpon*) is the Chinese variety of the edible-pod pea.

AVAILABILITY

It is available fresh except in deep winter months in Chinatowns and in a growing number of greengroceries. Frozen snow peas are available year round, but are not crisp—and crispness is what the snow pea is about.

PREPARATION

Snow peas are best stir-fried or steamed and are correctly served and eaten in their broad, flattish, vibrantly green pods, though the string that runs along one side of the pod should be removed prior to cooking. If not overcooked, snow peas are a delicate, crisp, beautiful, and distinctive-tasting legume offering a contrast in texture between the pod and the pea within. Their color makes them an attractive complement to pale foods, such as breast of chicken, fillets of fish, and veal.

Sugar Snap Pea

AVAILABILITY

The height of the sugar snap pea season is from late spring to early summer.

Buying Tips

For optimum sweetness, select sugar snap peas that have just reached maturity. Those peas will be vivid green and plump. Since sugar snap peas are generally more expensive than snow peas, some unscrupulous retailers market fully mature snow peas as sugar snap peas to unwary customers. The bogus specimens will not have the sugar snap pea's characteristically plump pod.

PREPARATION

Storage

Refrigerate and use sugar snap peas as soon as possible because their sought-after sweetness starts to diminish once the peas are harvested.

Cooking

Once you have washed the sugar snap peas and removed their lateral strings, you are ready to cook (or eat raw) the pod and all. Steam sugar snap peas for about 5 minutes. Or, stir-fry them for about 2 minutes. Overcooking will ruin their desirable snappy texture.

PECTIN

BACKGROUND

Occurring naturally in most fruits and some vegetables, *pectin*—virtually tasteless, odorless, and colorless—is used by home cooks to thicken their jams and jellies. While gelatin is a protein, pectin is a carbohydrate. Pectin is superior to gelatin in at least two regards: it creates a finer-textured gel and will not liquefy as easily at room temperature.

For pectin to do its thickening work, there must be enough of it relative to the other ingredients, and particularly the liquid. And there must be enough sugar and acid in the mixture.

High- and Low-Pectin Fruits

Some fruits are high in pectin—apples, crab apples, cranberries, currants, grapefruit, lemons, and sour oranges, among others. Quinces rate high in pectin, too, but fall short in acid. Low-pectin fruits include apricots, cherries, grapes, peaches, pears, pineapples, raspberries, and strawberries. Even naturally high-pectin fruits will have insufficient pectin if they are too unripe or too mature. Most fruits are richest in pectin just before they are fully ripe.

Increasing Pectin

Pectin in, say, a jelly can be increased by blending a high-pectin fruit with a low-pectin one. Or you can supplement pectin available naturally with a commercial concentrate of it (powered or syrup), which is sold in many supermarkets. As the thickening power of these concentrates varies from brand to brand, follow the manufacturer's instructions. If you use too little pectin, your preparation will not gel properly; too much will give you an unpalatable, overly firm mass. Do not cook pectin too long or at too high a heat or its thickening ability will deteriorate.

PEPPER, CHILI

BACKGROUND

Chili peppers, indigenous to the New World, got the first half of their name from the Nahautl Indian word *chilli* and the second half from Christopher Columbus, who mistook them for native Asian PEPPERCORNS. In fact, the chili pepper genus, *Capsicum*, is more closely related to tomatoes, potatoes, and eggplant—they all belong to the same botanical Nightshade family. (See HERBS AND SPICES for information on buying, storing, cooking, etc.)

Virtually all *Capsicums* conveniently fall into two groupings: chili peppers (the sole subject of this entry) and sweet peppers (see PEPPER, SWEET). About 90 percent of the capsicums are chili peppers and are, to varying degrees, hot. Sweet peppers are not. Once the explorers brought the chili pepper back to Europe, it quickly spread to North and West Africa, Ethiopia, Hungary, India, Thailand, Indonesia and even to the Szechuan province of China. Today, the chili pepper plays a major role in those cuisines.

Varieties

Over 200 varieties of chili peppers are commercially grown in the world, with new hybrids being developed annually. They vary in hotness from mildly pungent to outright devilish, in length from 1/2 inch to over 1/2 foot, in shape from a thin taper to spheroid, and in color from green to yellow to orange to flaming red.

Nomenclature in the chili-pepper world can be confusing. *Cayenne pepper*, for instance, can be made with various *Capsicum frutescens*—and even that generic name "cayenne" is being phased out by the American spice industry for the equally generic *red pepper*.

Paprika generally refers to peppers of the *Capsicum annuum* species and is particularly popular in Hungary, where it is generally sold in three strengths: mildly pungent, moderately hot, and fiercely hot. The imported product is almost always better than the domestic, and the Hungarian far better than the harsher Spanish paprika.

Ranking the individual chili peppers by degree of hotness is difficult, as different climates, weather, soil, and farmers will create varying results. If we take rough averages, some of the better known chili peppers may be ranked in ascending order of hotness as follows: the large, mildly hot *ancho*, the green, mildly hot *poblano* (which becomes an *ancho* when dried), the typical supermarket varieties (*Anaheim, New Mexico No. 6*, etc.), the small-to-medium *serrano*, the green, medium-small, hot *jalapeño*, the tiny, red-hot *pequin*, and the tiny, red-hot *tabasco* (not to be confused with the proprietary condiment). Even more incendiary than all of the above are chili peppers such as the Japanese *santaka*.

AVAILABILITY

Fresh chili peppers are usually available from mid-summer through the fall. Dried chili peppers are sold year round.

Buying Tips

Fresh Chili Peppers: As most chili peppers mature, the skin changes color from green to yellow, orange, or red. Green is perfectly okay if the chili is sufficiently mature, which is indicated by a thick skin and a vivid color for its variety. Paleness is a sign of immaturity. Overmaturity or prolonged or improper storage is evidenced by soft spots, shriveling, surface blemishes, and general injury. Well-formed specimens will be easier to cut and will have less waste than their deformed mates.

Dried Chili Peppers: Though dried, the chili pepper must be as fresh as possible so that it will cook with robust aroma and flavor and, if being used as a ground garnish, will have a vivid hue. Ground paprika is better for garnishing than ground red pepper or cayenne, because of its bright red hue. Of the paprikas, the mildly pungent type works best as a garnish for most American preparations.

Chili Pepper Products: Well-known liquid table condiments made with chili peppers include Tabasco Sauce, (see SAUCES AND CONDIMENTS, COMMERCIAL), Red Hot Sauce, and Pickapper. Both Hungarian-style paprika and the North African *harissa* paste are available in tubes. Chili oil is sold in ethnic Oriental and India stores; supermarkets carry chili sauce and, sometimes, whole or chopped chilies as well as chili pastes in tins and jars, and ground red pepper or cayenne in the spice section. Red pepper is also marketed in the crushed, flaked form, the type we find in glass containers with perforated tops in pizza parlors and Neapolitan-American eateries. The best all-around stateside source for chili-pepper products is Mexican-American grocery stores.

PREPARATION

Storage

Fresh chili peppers should be stored in a pierced paper bag in the vegetable crisper of the refrigerator. Dried whole or ground chili pepper can be stored in an airtight container at room temperature, but its fresh aroma will last longer if stored in such a container and refrigerated.

Preliminaries

We do feel obligated to warn neophytes that chili peppers can painfully irritate eyes and skin if improperly handled. Wash your hands, utensils, and work area thoroughly after cutting open a chili pepper; the hotter the variety of chili pepper, the more important this precaution is. Be especially careful not to rub your eyes while working with the chili pepper. Should the irritant accidentally reach your eyes, quickly and gently flush out your eyes with water.

De-Flaming Chili Peppers

Should the chili pepper you are using be too hot for you or your diners, there are ways to cut down its hotness. Since the culprit *capasaicin* is concentrated around the seeds and in the internal membrane, remove and discard those elements and use only the chili flesh. That part of the chili offers more than hotness—it also has a fresh, pleasing flavor. To further reduce hotness, soak the trimmed peppers in water for an hour or parboil them for a few minutes. Of course, the simplest way to cut down on hotness is to use less.

Cooking

A touch of cayenne pepper enlivens white sauce, cheese dishes, stews and roasts, and deviled eggs. Use with discretion, cayenne pepper can improve almost any savory dish. Whole or ground chili peppers become bitter when cooked with too high a heat. When using cooking methods such as sautéing or pan-frying, it is generally best to add the chili pepper near the end of the cooking process.

Chili Tolerance

One's physical reaction to chili peppers is individual. Some people have high, some have low natural tolerance levels to capsaicin, the substance in the chili pepper that causes palates to burn. Moreover, the more often you consume capsaicin, the more you become immune to its effects. When we returned from the island of Bali, our palates had become so immune from eating the local meals that American-grown peppers did not seem very hot. But a few weeks later, they did. If your mouth blazes with pain because of eating too much chili, do not follow instinct and guzzle water or beer, as those liquids may spread some of the capsaicin from your now semidesensitized tastebuds to the not-yet-desensitized buds in the other parts of your mouth. A wiser countermeasure is to take a big bite of an absorbent food such as bread or rice.

PEPPER, SWEET

BACKGROUND

The sweet pepper, like the potato and tomato, belongs to the Nightshade family of the New World—and, like the hot pepper, is a *Capsicum*. (It is not related to the PEPPERCORNS that make common black and white peppers.) The sweet pepper's capacious middle is perfect for stuffing. It is crisp and colorful when raw and tender when cooked, and has been naturalized in a wide variety of cuisines on all continents.

Varieties

The glossy green *bell pepper* is the most common: a red color simply indicates full maturity. *Italian*, or *frying*, *peppers* are longer, narrower, paler green, or red or yellow, and are slightly more assertive in flavor. Gourmet cooks prefer them.

Availability

Sweet peppers are available the year round, with a peak time from late spring into the early fall.

Buying Tips

Look for a full glossy color, a firm, unshriveled thick flesh with no cracks, soft spots, bruises, or other injuries. The pepper should be heavy for its size and be well-proportioned—a deformed specimen is wasteful. If buying more than one to stuff, choose equal-sized peppers.

PREPARATIONS

Storage

Keep sweet peppers sealed in a plastic bag in the vegetable crisper for up to several days—they are more perishable and more likely to lose moisture than most people believe. Once cut, seal tightly wrapped in plastic and use within 24 hours.

Preliminaries

Wash just before using. Slice off the top and cut out the unpalatable ribs and seeds. Depending on your recipe, leave whole, slice into rings, segments, squares, or julienne strips. Some cooks believe that sweet-pepper dishes are more elegant and cook faster if the skins are removed first. To do it, impale the whole pepper on a long fork, then turn it over a moderate gas flame until the skin is uniformly blackened, charred, and blistered. Let the pepper cool slightly and pull off the skin. Or place the peppers 1½ to 2 inches beneath a preheated broiler until the skins are equally distressing-looking—then seal them in a brown paper bag, wait 15 minutes, and then skin them. Use the roasted peppers right away, or cover with olive oil and refrigerate in a covered jar. Parboiling reduces the strength of the flavor, if you feel it to be too assertive.

Cooking

Do not overcook sweet peppers or they will become bitter. Sweet pepper pieces can be sautéed in olive oil in 4 to 7 minutes, depending on thickness. Segments can be steamed in 5 to 8 minutes. Before baking stuffed peppers, be sure the shell has been parboiled (about 5 minutes), drained, and rubbed with oil. Bake the stuffed peppers in a preheated 350°F oven for 15 to 25 minutes if stuffed with cooked food. Bake 30 to 50 minutes if stuffed with an uncooked mixture.

CLASSIC USES AND AFFINITIES

Italian cooks use sweet peppers to top pizza, and as an antipasto ingredient. Chinese-American chefs use sweet peppers freely in preparations such as sweet and sour pork and pepper steak. The most popular European stuffing for peppers is a mixture of rice and chopped meat. Mexicans use a cheese stuffing. True and proven cooking mates include beef, veal, tomatoes, onions, mushrooms, and garlic.

PEPPERCORN

BACKGROUND

The *peppercorn*, the dried berry of the climbing vine *Piper nigrum*, is the world's most widely used spice. The vine is believed to be indigenous to India; today the commercial peppercorn powers of the world are India, Indonesia, and Malaysia.

Before European sailing ships began transporting the berries in quantity back to their home ports in the sixteenth century and thus displaced most of the ancient caravan trade, peppercorns were quite expensive—sometimes worth their weight in silver. Despite the exorbitant prices, cooks bought the dried berries. Not only did peppercorns add flavor to bland staples, they could mask the taste of rancid meats, stale breads, and sour vegetables—common phenomena in the days before refrigeration and sophisticated regional food transportation systems.

Modern cooks can buy peppercorns at non-budget-straining prices and use them to give their fresh foods a hot savor with an undertone of sweetness. Most Western cuisines put at least a touch of black pepper into their dishes. Even sweet foods such as spice cakes benefit from a grind of black pepper. Diverse flavors are harmonized by pepper and bland dishes are enlivened by it. Coarsely-crushed whole black peppercorns are used as a decorative and flavoring element in steak *au poivre*, pastrami, and other smoked meats. Whole peppercorns are used in pickling, in pot-roasted meats, in crab boils, and in sausages such as Italian salamis. (See HERBS AND SPICES for information on buying, storing, and cooking.)

From a doctor's point of view, peppercorns contain *piperine*, an alkaloid that aids digestion by stimulating your gastric juices. Also, since pepper is free of sodium, many persons on low-salt diets can use it to perk up their foods.

Peppercorns and Chili Peppers

Peppercorns and chili peppers (PEPPER, CHILI) are entirely different—the first is native to Asia and a member of the *Piper* botanical genus, the second is native to the New World and is a *Capsicum* genus. Columbus called the *Capsicums* peppers because, after tasting them, he erroneously concluded they were *Pipers*, the expensive spice he was trying to find. He also misnamed the natives "Indians," thinking he was in or near India. We are now stuck with both of his misnomers.

Varieties

Black vs. White Peppercorns: The black and white peppercorns are botanically identical. The black type are harvested unripe, then dried (usually under the sun) until their outer skins become wrinkled and black. White peppercorns, which are also dried, are picked ripe (or nearly so) and have their outer shell removed. White peppercorns are milder than black peppercorns and are ideal for preparations such as white sauces or light-hued flesh where tiny black specks would be objectionable. Culinary critics of the use of white peppercorns argue that the cosmetic advantage is slight compared to the loss of the beautiful perfume that only the skin-intact black peppercorn possesses. Whether black or white, not all peppercorns are of equal quality. By gourmet consensus, the world's finest black peppercorn is the *Tellicherry*, grown on the north Malabar Coast of India. The other areas of the Malabar Coast also produce worthy black peppercorns as does the *Lampong* area in Sumatra, Indonesia. Some connoisseurs are of the opinion that the best white peppercorns come from *Muntok* on the island of Bangka in the East Indies.

Green Peppercorns: These soft-textured, immature berries have been preserved in brine or vinegar. Green peppercorns are noticeably less pungent than their black and white brothers. Green peppercorns are a favorite of French chefs and, for good reason, are rapidly growing in popularity in American kitchens as a garnish and flavoring agent for fish, fowl, and meat dishes, especially *bifteck au poivre vert*. Green peppercorns also do wonders in sauces such as *vinaigrette* salad dressings.

Pink Peppercorns: New to the culinary scene and dear to the nouvelle cuisine chefs are the freeze-dried, slightly sweet, rose-hued berries which have the shape of the true *Piper Nigrum*.

Szechuan Peppercorns: Though not *Piper nigrum*, the reddish-brown Szechuan peppercorns can be used interchangeably with black peppercorns. Each pepper, however, has its own distinctive flavor and fragrance. Szechuan peppercorns are native to the Szechuan province of China and are basic to its cuisine, which has become popular in the United States. Contrary to popular belief, Szechuan peppercorns do not impart the characteristic palate-scorching hotness to Szechuan-style foods—it is the chili pepper that is principally responsible for that quality.

AVAILABILITY

Black and white peppers, both whole and ground, are universally available. Green peppercorns, pink peppercorns, and Szechuan peppercorns are found in specialty stores.

Buying Tips

The difference between freshly ground peppercorns and the pregound variety is vast, as any test will prove. Once ground, the taste and fragrance of peppercorns begin to dissipate into the air. Within hours, if not within minutes, loss is already apparent, so you can imagine the condition of the ground pepper in those boxes lining supermarket shelves or in the shakers sitting on restaurant and home dining tables. If you do not have a peppermill, buy yourself one of good quality (the inexpensive ones tend to be short-lived and do not grind uniformly). Better yet, buy two—one for the kitchen and one for the dining table. If you use white pepper, too, you could use a third mill. Giant peppermills are strictly showpieces for flashy restaurant *maîtres d'* and captains; medium-sized mills are best for home use; small ones need to be re-filled too often.

PREPARATION

Storage

Whole dried peppercorns have 1-year shelf lives. Once ground, peppercorns quickly lose their sought-after flavor and fragrance and, in time, begin to turn bitter. Green peppercorns are sold in small jars and cans. Once opened, refrigerate them in their original liquid. Thus stored, they will stay in good condition for a week, in fair condition for several weeks, then will start to deteriorate noticeably and become mushy.

Cooking

When using high heat, as in sautéing or pan-frying, it is a good idea to add the ground pepper near the end, because ground pepper becomes bitter when scorched. Whole dried peppercorns can be used in long-cooked dishes. If you want to remove them before serving, enclose them in a spice bag. If you are making a stock or sauce, strain them out with a sieve. Whole dried peppercorns can also be immersed in marinades and pickling solutions. Green peppercorns need not be cooked to be edible if consumed in small quantities.

PERIWINKLE

BACKGROUND

Sometimes called the "sea snail," a periwinkle is a tiny, spiral-shelled univalve mollusk. It is typically cooked in its shell—the diner has the chore of pulling out the cooked muscle. Periwinkles as a food are popular in Europe and seldom encountered in America.

PERSIAN MELON

BACKGROUND

Though it somewhat resembles the cantaloupe, the *Persian melon* is generally larger (approximately 5 pounds), has a finer surface netting and a more orange flesh, and—at its best—is definitely better scented and flavored. You can use most of the general guidelines given under CANTALOUPE for buying, storage, preparation, and classic affinities. However, a Persian melon is seldom found in domestic markets outside the hot, late summer months. One Persian melon can usually satisfy three or possibly four persons.

PERSIMMON

BACKGROUND

Two basic *persimmon* species exist: the *Asiatic* or *Japanese* (*Diospyros kaki*) and the *North American* (*Diospyros virginiana*). Both species are somewhat tomatolike in appearance, and can vary in shape from spherical to oblong, with the blossom end curvaceously tapering off to a point. The surface color of both species varies from green (when immature) to yellow or reddish-orange, depending on the variety. When ripe, both species have a distinctive sweet flavor balanced by a pleasing tangy background; when unripe, both offer you an awful, astringent, mouth-puckering experience. Both species can be seedless or not. The *kaki* persimmon is generally bigger and is almost always superior in succulence, sweetness and overall flavor than the domestic variety. Most of the persimmons sold in the U.S. are of the *kaki* species and are grown principally in California and, to a lesser extent, in Florida.

AVAILABILITY

Season

Persimmons are at their peak in November and are in season from October through the first of the year. Persimmons are best when picked slightly unripe and left to ripen quietly off the tree. Unfortunately, for the sake of shipping and storage, the overwhelming majority of persimmons are picked very unripe, giving us a fruit that will never live up to its succulent sweet promise. It is therefore essential to know how to buy and store persimmons.

Buying Tips

Your persimmon should be plump and, when gently squeezed, should feel somewhat soft but not mushy. The skin should be smooth and glossy like a tomato and be free of cracks, punctures, blemishes, scales, and decay-spots. Some skin wrinkling is a favorable sign for some varieties. The green stem and cap should be still attached and not be excessively dry and shriveled. The color of the peel should be deep, perky, and full for its variety. However, skin hue is no guarantee of ripeness, as some fruits are artificially ripened—for instance, with an overdose of ethylene gas. The skin color produced by that process is proper, but the pulp remains distastefully puckerish. A too-soft persimmon is overripe, and is very likely well along the road to internal decay.

PREPARATION

Ripening

If you have bought a persimmon that is nearly but not fully ripe, store it in a dry, somewhat cool place in a pierced paper bag for one to several days. To hasten the ripening, store it with a ripe apple, as the latter gives off some ethylene gas (but not too much), which produces a bonus enzymatic action that reduces the persimmon's tannin content. Once it's ripe plan to eat your persimmon as soon as possible as it is highly perishable at this stage.

Storage

If you must delay eating it, seal the ripe persimmon in a plastic bag and refrigerate for no more than a day or two. A persimmon is best enjoyed at about 60°F, slightly below room temperature. Handle your persimmon with care as it is easily bruised, and bruises precipitate decay.

Preliminaries

A persimmon must be washed to rid it of possible germs and pesticides. However, to minimize bacterial surface decay, never wash it until just before you plan to use it. The skin is edible, but if you wish to remove it and it doesn't readily peel off, submerge the fruit in boiling water for 10 to 15 seconds, then plunge it into ice water, then peel. One popular way of eating the persimmon flesh is to cut the fruit in half vertically and eat the flesh with a spoon, melon-style. Another method is to slit the skin at the blossom end, peel it back, hold the stem and eat the persimmon banana-style.

Cooking

Because persimmon pulp has a tendency to become bitter when cooked too long, plan to add the pulp to whatever you are preparing near the end of the cooking.

CLASSIC USES AND AFFINITIES

The persimmon has found its way into many recipes for jams, jellies, and desserts such as pies, cakes, and sherbets. Citric juices such as lemon and lime have a special affinity with the persimmon.

PHYLLO PASTRY

BACKGROUND

Of Middle Eastern origin, *phyllo pastry* is a tissue-thin (*phyllo* is Greek for "leaf") flour-and-water dough used to make creations such as the honey-rich *baklava* dessert and the spinach-and-cheese-filled *spanakopita*. It is virtually the same as strudel dough. Some stores now sell a frozen, factory-made phyllo that is unfortunately much thicker than the hand-rolled leaves, but since making good phyllo leaves is a task that requires consummate skill, this thicker "convenience phyllo" is a blessing for most home cooks. Instructions come with the package.

PICKLES

BACKGROUND

The art of *pickling* developed out of the age-old need for preserving food for consumption during the cold winter seasons. Pickling, basically, is preserving a food in a brine flavored with, for instance, vinegar, lemon juice, peppercorns, dill seeds, coriander seeds, allspice, mustard seeds, chilies, cloves, cardamom, fresh ginger, bay leaf, tumeric, and perhaps garlic and onions. Pickles need not be made of cucumbers, though most are. Other popular pickle bases include watermelon rind, cabbage, cauliflower, hot or sweet peppers, green or red tomatoes, and even fruit such as lemons and pears. And do not forget pigs' feet, herring, and other meats and seafood as well. Only the pickler's imagination sets the limit.

Varieties

Countless varieties of pickled cucumbers exist, often with overlapping names and pickling methods. The many types of *dill pickles* have in common the use of dill seed. A *kosher* pickle need not be religiously kosher; the pickle term refers to the process as well as to the use of garlic in the flavoring. *Sour pickles* are typically fermented in brine. *Sweet pickles* have been sugared to produce a sweet-and-sour taste. *Gherkins* are miniature cucumber pickles. *Cornichons* are the French counterpart of gherkins, but are not as sweet. Pickles are sometimes mixed with a well-seasoned sauce as is the case with *piccalilli* and *chowchow*, the latter being a mustard-spiked Pennsylvania Dutch favorite.

AVAILABILITY

Buying Tips

Pickled cucumbers should be firm, well-formed and void of skin blemishes, soft spots, and excess wrinkling. The smaller a pickled cucumber is for its variety, the better it will tend to be, as large ones tend to have seedy, soggy interiors and a bitter aftertaste. The skin hue should be a vivid, not a pallid or brownish, green. When bitten into, a pickle should snap. Fresh-from-the-barrel pickles are superior in flavor and texture to the type preserved in sealed glass jars.

PREPARATION

Pickling Your Own

One of the numerous ways to pickle cucumbers is to submerge well-scrubbed whole specimens (buy Kerbys or another type of pickling cucumber) in boiled-and-cooled salted water (6 to 7 tablespoons per quart of liquid) for 3 to 7 days, depending on desired pickle strength. Many picklers prefer Kosher salt because, unlike most table salts, it won't cloud the brine. If you add vinegar, you can cut down the salt a bit. As for pickling spices, figure on about a couple of tablespoons or so per quart of liquid.

PICKLING SPICE

BACKGROUND

Various manufacturers produce proprietary blends of pickling spices, but you can easily make your own. Whole peppercorns, cloves, mustard seeds, bay leaves, and chilies are common constituents of these mixtures. So are cardamom, coriander, cinnamon, mace, ginger, and allspice. (See HERBS AND SPICES for information on buying, storing, cooking, etc.)

PREPARATION

A tablespoon or so of pickling spice can be used in the brine for a pint of pickled cucumbers, beets, or other vegetables and relishes. Pickling spice can also be used in water for simmering shrimp or other seafood; 1 tablespoon per quart of water is a reasonable ratio. A *sauerbraten* or other pot roast can use a teaspoon or so of pickling spice per pound of meat. Because ground spices can cloud your pickling liquid, use whole spices. They will be much easier to remove if you enclose them in a cheesecloth or muslin bag.

PIGEON PEA

BACKGROUND

Why *Cajanus indicus* is called the *pigeon pea* we do not know. It is also variously called the *Congo pea*, *Goongoo pea*, and the *no-eyed pea*. It grows in the tropics in a long, lumpy, fuzzy sectioned pod; its seeds, the size of the standard English pea, are dark-gray or yellowish-gray. (Since it is a legume, it can be treated like a dry bean; for soaking, cooking, etc. see BEANS.)

AVAILABILITY

In the U.S., the pigeon pea is grown mainly in the South, but it is available across the country dried and usually split, year round. Sometimes it can be found frozen whole, and, of course, already cooked in cans.

PREPARATION

The pigeon pea can be used in any pea recipe. It is a favorite in the Bahamas with rice in their own variation of our Hoppin' John.

PIGS' EARS

BACKGROUND

While you cannot make a silk purse out of a sow's ear, you can make delicious dishes. Singe the ears to remove any hairs, then scrub well under tepid running water. Parboil for 15 minutes, discarding the liquid. Cover with fresh boiling water and simmer (do not boil) for 3/4 to 1 1/2 hours, depending on size. Save the cooking liquid. Proceed with final cooking step. For instance, bread, deep-fry, and serve with a sauce based on the cooking broth. Alternatively, pickle the ears—this will take several days in your refrigerator—and add to cold salads.

PIGS' FEET

BACKGROUND

Trotters, as *pigs' feet* are sometimes called, are rich in collagen, the protein that produces gelatin when long boiled. The gelatin-containing liquid is fluid when warm, solid (in a loose sense) when cold.

AVAILABILITY

You can purchase trotters as well as pigs' knuckles pickled, smoked (a good soup ingredient), or fresh.

PREPARATION

If your butcher hasn't already done so, split the fresh feet lengthwise (unless your recipe suggests otherwise). Do not remove the skin. Wash well under cold running water, using a scrub brush if needed. Parboil the trotters for 15 minutes. Discard the first water and cover the trotters with fresh boiling water. Add 1 teaspoon of salt per quart of liquid. Partially cover and simmer for 1 1/2 to 2 hours, depending on size. Proceed with final cooking step. For instance, bread the trotters and bake in a preheated 325°F oven for 30 minutes and serve with a sauce using the broth as a base. Or coat them with a batter and deep-fry them. You have many options.

CLASSIC USES AND AFFINITIES

Famous dishes based on pig's feet include souse, France's *pieds de porc Sainte-Menehould*, and plain old pickled pig's feet. Both the flesh and bones often enrich soups, stews, and sauces.

PINEAPPLE

BACKGROUND

Since it is neither pine nor apple, *pineapple* is a misnomer. It derived its curious appellation when seventeenth-century Spanish and British adventurers visited the pineapple's native land (tropical northern South America) and came to the understandable conclusion that the fruit looked like a pinecone. Pinecones were then called "pineapples" because "apple" was used to describe any fruit. The Guarani Indians called the same thing *anana* ("excellent" or "fragrant fruit"); this name passed into most of the European languages, and into botanical nomenclature as *Ananas comosus*.

Hawaii is the world's leading pineapple producer; most of its crop ends up canned. Americans also eat a lot of pineapple from Puerto Rico, but also imports the fruit in quantities from Central America, Mexico, and certain Caribbean island nations.

Varieties

Depending on variety, pineapples vary in pulp pigmentation from creamy white to golden yellow; in skin color (when ripe) from brownish-gold to a reddish-brown, in size from 1 to 20 pounds (most pineapples sold in our markets range from 1 1/2 to 4 pounds), and in shape from squat bulging oval to elongated bulging cylinder. All varieties have the characteristic diamond-shaped knobbed skins (creating a distinctive oblique cross-hatched pattern), a greenleaf crown, and a pulp whose grain radiates from the axis of the vertical core.

Of the many varieties, the *Smooth Cayenne* and the *Red Spanish* are the two major commercial pineapples. The Smooth Cayenne is the typical fruit of Hawaii and, when ripe, has a golden-yellow skin. Most impartial pineapple connoisseurs consider it to be slightly superior in flavor to the Red Spanish, a reddish-orange-brown-skinned fruit that is abundantly cultivated in Puerto Rico, America's second pineapple capital. There are other ways to distinguish the two types: the Smooth Cayenne is usually taller and has a single-tuft greenleaf crown, while the Red Spanish often has a multiple-tufted one.

A third variety is the subtly flavored Sugar Loaf, which is judged by some experts to be one of the best pineapples in the world. Unfortunately, it is seldom domestically cultivated or imported, partly because of its poor shipping and storage properties, and mainly because it is green when ripe. That color leads most American shoppers to the erroneous conclusion that the fruit is extremely unripe and, as a consequence, few of us are willing to take a Sugar Loaf home. An identifying feature is a crown of leaves that are relatively broad and long for the size of the fruit.

AVAILABILITY

Fresh Pineapple

But no matter what variety, when ripe, a pineapple is succulent and has a sweetness balanced with a light, pleasant tartness. Most of us, however, have never tasted such a fruit. Why? Because once picked, pineapples cannot appreciably ripen. If we let the pineapple fully ripen on the plant, it is quite perishable—once picked, it must be eaten or processed within a day or two. Pineapple canners have no problem in this regard. They simply process the properly ripe pineapple within 12 to 24 hours after the pineapples are brought in from the fields. Shippers of fresh pineapples, on the other hand, have no other option but to have the pineapples picked before they come ripe. Shippers who must send their merchandise by slow boats over long distances must have it picked even more unripe. The pineapples shipped by air will taste better (and be significantly more expensive) than those of the first kind. In terms of value, you are almost always better off paying the premium price.

Processed Pineapple

Pineapple is sold frozen, canned, and preserved, but the texture and flavor of those products is a far cry from those of the fresh fruit. Pineapple juice is available canned and, to a lesser extent, frozen. Crystallized pineapple is sold in some fancy candy or gourmet shops. Pineapple-flavored cream cheese is carried by many supermarkets but, we are sad to report, it has little, if any, of the genuine fruit.

Buying Tips

The silliest of tests is pulling out one of the spikes from the central crown leaves. All too many food writers tell you that if a spike comes out readily, the pineapple is ripe. The simple truth is that all center leaves separate from all but the most unripe pineapples, and if the fruit is that unripe, you will know it at a glance from the otherside of the supermarket aisle. What is a reliable quality indicator is the color and size of the crown leaves. Their color should be fresh, deep, and vividly green, not brown or wilted. Their size, relative to the fruit and variety, should be as small as possible. Skin color is not an assurance of quality. Color differs from variety to variety. As a general rule, look for golden-yellow in a Smooth Cayenne and reddish-orange-brown in a Red Spanish. The color of both should be as deep and perky as possible and show few, if any, lingering green traces.

The best buying guide is your nose—the pineapple will nearly always taste as sweet or acid or rotten as it smells. When measuring the aroma's intensity, take into account the temperature of the pineapple. The cooler it is, the less it will yield its fragrance, whether positive or negative.

The skin should be free of blemishes, decay spots, bruises, mold, cracks, or other surface damage. Decay makes a speedy journey through the pulp. Examine the base. Any telltale external rot or mold has probably already contaminated the center. The pips (or eyes) of a ripe pineapple are plump and stand out in striking relief from the background cross-hatched grooves. The pips should not be hard or sunken. The fruit as a whole should be plump and well-shaped. The pineapple should be heavy for its size. Up to a point, the larger the pineapple is, the greater the proportion of edible pulp. Squeezed with your fingertips, the ripe pineapple will yield slightly. The extremes—too hard or too soft—are undesirable.

PREPARATION

Ripening

A pineapple will not noticeably sweeten once harvested. Nevertheless, you can make a slightly unripe pineapple less acid by storing it at room temperature in a pierced paper bag for one to several days, depending on its initial degree of ripeness. There is a point of diminishing return, for if you store your fruit too long, it will become rotten before it loses its excess acid.

Storage

As soon as it is as ripe as it will become, either eat your pineapple promptly, or refrigerate in a sealed plastic bag and plan to enjoy it within a day or two. Pineapple slices should be wrapped tightly in plastic wrap and refrigerated.

Cutting and Serving

There are as many ways to cut a pineapple as there are pips in a pineapple. Here are three of the popular methods: Slice the fruit into 3/4-inch-thick discs, then pare and core into rings, which may be left whole or cut into bite-sized chunks. Cut the pineapple in quarters lengthwise, through both the tuft and pulp. Then loosen the meat from the shell and slice it, put back, and present the slices in the "boat." Cut the pulp and leaves of the pineapple in half the long way. Cut and scoop out the woody core and the flesh, retaining a shellcase about 1/8-inch-thick. Dice the flesh, and serve in the shell, either alone or in combination with other fresh fruits. For the best flavor, serve pineapple slightly below room temperature.

Pineapple Peculiarities

The core of a fully ripe pineapple is delicious; for less than fully ripe pineapples, the core is usually discarded as it tends to be woody. Because of an enzymatic action, fresh or frozen (but not canned, which is cooked) pineapple will keep aspics and gelatin concoctions (including Jell-O) from setting. Those enzymes are destroyed by boiling the pineapple pieces for a few minutes. Fresh or frozen pineapple has the capacity of curdling milk and cream.

CLASSIC USES AND AFFINITIES

Pineapple is the star ingredient in pineapple upside-down cake and a co-star in Chinese sweet-and-sour pork. Chefs use pineapple rings to garnish roast meat specialities, including baked ham. Fresh pineapple can be readily converted at home into juice and preserves and can be mixed with most other fruits in salads. Pineapple combined with cottage cheese is a light, nourishing lunch entry. Other pineapple affinities include mint, ice cream and rice. The empty shell of a pineapple makes an eye-catching container for Polynesian-style drinks.

PINTO BEAN AND PINK BEAN

BACKGROUND

Skin coloration differs between these two varieties of *Phaseolus vulgaris*—the *pinto* (Spanish for "painted") *bean* is the more showy. It has a pale pink background overlaced with intricate streaks of reddish-brown. Its outer surface is rough. The *pink bean* (also called the *Red Mexican*) is smooth-coated, with an all-over reddish-brown more than pink color. Other than that, consider these beans interchangeable. They cook and taste alike—and during cooking their color changes to an identical reddish-brown, so that if cooked together they are indistinguishable in the finished dish. (For soaking, cooking, etc., see BEANS.)

CLASSIC USES AND AFFINITIES

Very popular out West, these medium-hard legumes are the beans in *frijoles refritos*, the once only Mexican but now Americanized dish, refried beans. Chili, onions, tomatoes, and garlic are classic flavorings. A favorite way to enjoy them is made into a patty and blanketed in a tortilla or simply served as a side dish.

AVAILABILITY

They are available year round in the dried form.

PLANTAIN

BACKGROUND

Compared to the ordinary yellow BANANA the light green to green-yellow *Musa paradisiaca* is larger, thicker skinned, coarser in texture, and contains more starch and less sugar. Most important of all, the *plantain* must be cooked. This fruit is used as the primary starch vegetable by many people in tropical Latin America.

AVAILABILITY

Available year round.

Buying Tips

Select firm, plump plantains and avoid those that have blemishes or soft areas. Plantains are most readily found in Mexican and Caribbean ethnic markets.

PREPARATION

Ripening

The plantain can be cooked green (as long as it is mature) or fully ripe (indicated when most of the skin area becomes brownish-black). To ripen, store in a dry, 70°F draft-free environment. Once ripened, either use within a day, or refrigerate for up to several days.

Cooking

Plantains are often fried, broiled, stewed, or baked. To bake, make a lengthwise incision down one side (to prevent steaming or bursting), then place the unpeeled plantain in a preheated 350°F oven for 30 to 45 minutes, depending on size.

CLASSIC USES AND AFFINITIES

Being relatively bland in flavor, the plantain marries well with many vegetables including onions, tomatoes, and peppers. It also goes well with meat.

PLUM

BACKGROUND

Members of the species *Prunus domestica* crossbreed readily. This biological trait has resulted in a broad spectrum of new but not necessarily better plums. These drupes (stone fruits) differ widely in terms of quality, flavor, shape (oval or round), size (from ½ to 3 inches in diameter), and color (yellow, red, purple, bluish-black). The plum tree grows wild and is cultivated extensively around the world from Asia to Europe to North America, where California is that continent's prime commercial producer. Most plums can be eaten either fresh, dried as the PRUNE, or cooked and sugared as a jam or jelly. Spirits such as the plum brandies of Eastern Europe and the Balkans are distilled in great quantities.

Varieties

Beach plum: A small purplish-blue-skinned plum that grows wild along the sandy beaches of the Northeastern seaboard. Its high acidity makes it ideal for jams and jellies, but not for eating fresh.

Damson: A small, indigo-skinned, oval plum. Its firm, greenish-yellow flesh is very tart, which makes it suitable for preserves, tarts and spirits. Its etymological root: the Syrian city of Damascus.

El Dorado: A medium-sized, slightly oval, reddish-blue-skinned plum with greenish-yellow flesh.

Greengage: You can use this medium-sized, greenish-yellow-fleshed plum to make jam, jelly, and spirits. It is also a good plum to eat raw if it is fully ripe—indicated when the green skin develops a yellow tinge.

Italian Prune: This small, oval plum does not come from Italy and is seldom dried for prunes—more often than not, it is eaten out of hand or converted into preserves. Underneath its dark purplish-blue skin is a sweet, greenish-yellow pulp.

Santa Rosa: A best-seller across the nation. The skin is a deep red with a characteristic bloom, the shape is roundish, the pulp is greenish-yellow, and the flavor is slightly tart but ordinary at best.

Other leading members of the plum family include the *cherry plum*, the magenta-hued *Laroda*, the dark-blue *DeSoto*, and the big, purplish-black *President*. The small black *sloe* is used in Europe to flavor spirits and to make preserves.

AVAILABILITY

Fresh plums are available throughout the summer, with a mid-July through mid-August peak. During the winter months some plums are imported from Southern Hemisphere lands, but those fruits are normally high in price and mediocre in quality. Bear in mind that there are many subvarieties: a plum marked as a Santa Rosa in one section of the country may be different from a Santa Rosa sold in another.

Buying Tips

For the sake of improved shipping and storage qualities, over 90 percent of American-grown plums are picked before they have sufficiently ripened. This gives the buying public a sourish, nonsucculent plum that will never fully ripen. A ripe plum is firm but should give to gentle pressure (if the flesh feels hard in your hand, you have an unripe, sour fruit). A good plum is plump, with a smooth, uniformly colored skin. Avoid those that are misshapen or those with soft spots or skins that are cracked, bruised, shriveled, or sticky. A brownish surface suggests damage caused by excess sun exposure. If an opened plum has a split pit, it is probably a victim of prolonged or improper storage.

Storage

Keep ripe plums in a sealed plastic bag in your refrigerator for up to several days. For the best flavor, bring to just under room temperature (about 60°F) before eating.

POMEGRANATE

BACKGROUND

The *pomegranate*, archetypal "apple of many seeds," originated somewhere in western Asia and is mentioned in the Bible, sung of by Homer, and used in pagan fertility rites. To the modern eye, it looks like a small grapefruit trying to become an apple; to any taste, it has an ambrosial juice.

The pomegranate is round with a leathery rind. The skin color can vary from light yellow to dark reddish-purple, with tinges of yellow. The pulp is a striking bright red bulging with plump gelatinous seeds that are full of pectin and have a nutty taste. The small membranes which divide the pulp into segments are bitter and not edible. The pomegranate is grown widely today in Asia, around the Mediterranean, and, to a much smaller extent, in California.

AVAILABILITY

The pomegranate matures in the fall and can be found fresh in specialty shops most often in October and November.

Buying Tips

Buy pomegranates that look fresh (not tired and dull), have good color, and are heavy for their size. The larger they are, the juicier they will usually be. Check for an unbroken rind and no surface signs of decay.

PREPARATION

Storage

Pomegranates will keep several days in a cool, dim, dry spot, but if you intend to use only the juice and seeds it is best to ream the pomegranate as you would an orange, strain, and refrigerate the juice immediately. The seeds, removed from the pulp and free of moisture, can be stored in an airtight container in the frozen food compartment of your refrigerator for a month or so to be used as desired as an addition to your salads, poultry stuffings, sauces, soups, and desserts.

Serving

To eat fresh, halve it or cut into wedges, and serve with a grapefruit spoon to wedge out the pulp and seeds from the membraneous lining. Caution your guests to remove the seeds with a delicate touch—the juice spurts and it stains.

POPCORN

BACKGROUND

Many movie theaters would go broke if their popcorn equipment permanently broke down—the fluffy white morsels help pay the rent. Popcorn is a particular variety of corn that explodes when the countless water molecules trapped within the heated kernel turn to steam. When the kernel can no longer contain the expanding steam, it pops, turning inside out and greatly swelling in the process.

Buying Tips

The longer dry kernels are stored, the more they lose their internal moisture, so for superb popcorn, it is essential to use freshly purchased popcorn from a store with a high stock turnover. It is also essential to buy good popcorn; not all brands are equal. Premium brands cost more but give you more and better-tasting popcorn. If you must store popcorn, keep it in an airtight jar or canister away from heat.

PREPARATION

Most of the automatic, home popcorn machines now on the market work well, but unless the members of your family are popcorn freaks, you can save dollars and storage space by using one of your large, heavy-bottomed skillets or sauté pans with a tight-fitting lid. First, heat a thin layer of oil in the pan, then add a single layer of popcorn. Cover and gently shake the pan back and forth over the heat until you hear a decrease in the intensity of the popping. Turn off the heat, wait a minute or two, then uncover and discard the unpopped kernels. Flavor with melted butter, salt to taste, and serve.

POPPY SEEDS

BACKGROUND

The tiny, lustrous *poppy seeds* (it takes nearly a million to make a pound) come from the opium poppy, *Papaver somniferum*. But you can eat poppy-seed cakes and pastries forever without experiencing any narcotic effects, because the plant cannot form seeds until all the narcotic alkaloids have disappeared from the plant. The best poppy seeds are imported from Holland. They are bluish-black and shiny. A dullish sheen often indicates rancidity. (See HERBS AND SPICES for information on buying, storing, cooking, etc.)

PREPARATION

The poppy seeds you buy are raw—you must toast them for full flavor. This process will take care of itself when you sprinkle the seeds on dough to be baked. In other situations, toast the raw seeds for about 5 minutes in a heavy frying pan over a low flame (shake the pan periodically to assure even toasting). Or, place the seeds one layer deep on a rimmed baking sheet or rimmed piece of aluminum foil for 15 minutes in a 350°F oven.

If you wish to grind the seeds, first soak them in a little warm water, then crush them in a mortar with a pestle, or roll them beneath a rolling pin. Or use a blender, food processor, or—if you have a highly specialized *batterie de cuisine*—in your poppy-seed grinder.

CLASSIC USES AND AFFINITIES

Poppy seeds are most often used in Central and Eastern European dishes. Whole poppy seeds can be used to top bread and rolls, or they can be mixed with butter and hot noodles or green beans. Crushed or whole poppy seeds can be sweetened and used to fill strudel, cake, or other pastries.

PORK, CURED

BACKGROUND

Meats can be preserved and flavored by curing, usually with salt and sugar, and by smoking. The processes are described in the entries on HAM and BACON. Pork is the meat most often cured; other major cured and smoked pork products are described here—picnic ham, pork butt, Canadian bacon, loin, jowl, and ham hocks.

Varieties

Smoked Picnic Ham: The retail cut consisting of the lower portion of the ham's shoulder is variously called *callie* (*cally*, *calas*, or *calais*), *pork shoulder*, or *picnic ham*. It is less expensive than the true ham but it has more waste in terms of bone, skin, and especially fat. It also has more connective tissue, which is why you want to cook the picnic ham slightly more thoroughly than you would the true ham (to 165°F vs. 155°F). Another comparative negative is that a whole picnic ham is more difficult to carve, because it has a more complicated bone structure. Finally, a whole picnic ham does not have the cachet and visual appeal of the true ham. Despite those negatives, the picnic ham bears at least some resemblance in flavor to the true ham and—even with its waste—does offer more meat per penny.

Smoked picnic hams usually weigh between 5 and 10 pounds, and are almost always brine cured. However, there are some dry-cured, country-style picnic hams. Fully cooked picnic hams need only about an hour in a 325°F oven. Uncooked brine-cured hams require 25 to 30 minutes in a 325°F oven. Uncooked dry-cured smoked picnic hams should be prepared like the country hams (see under HAM), though you should add about 5 to 7 minutes per pound to the suggested cooking times. Because of the high proportion of waste, you will need to figure on anywhere from 1/2 to 3/4 of a pound per serving.

Smoked Pork Butt: Other market names for this boneless cut include *smoked Boston butt*, *Daisy ham* and *Cottage roll*. It comprises part of the upper shoulder and neck and is fattier and less tender than true ham and Canadian bacon. Most smoked pork butts on the market have an objectionable chemical flavor due to an overabundance of additives. Average weight is 1 to 4 pounds. Select the elongated rather than the squat specimens, as the former usually has a higher ratio of lean to fat waste. Almost all smoked port butts are precooked and just need heating to bring out their flavor: simmer or bake (in a 325°F oven) for 30 to 60 minutes, depending on size. Or, slice and panbroil 1/4-inch-thick slices for several minutes per side. Or broil 1/2-inch slices 4 inches from a moderate flame for about 5 minutes per side, basting several times. Plan for 1/3 pound (or 1/2 pound, if fatty) per serving. Once heated, you can serve it cold, but it will taste better warm or hot.

An Italian version of the smoked pork butt is the cylindrical *coppa*, which is also known as *capocolla*, *capicola*, *capacola*, etc., depending on where you live. It is rubbed with pepper and slowly air-dried. Slice *coppa* thin and serve it raw, as you would prosciutto.

Canadian Bacon: *Back bacon*, as it is generally known to Canadians, is the cylindrical loin or eye muscle running along the animal's back. It is not to be confused with regular BACON, which is cut from the belly. It is leaner than regular bacon and drier than ham. Most Canadian bacon is fully-cooked (check the label to be sure), but needs some additional cooking to bring out its flavor. It is often prepared by slicing it into 1/2-inch slices and baking it at 325°F for 15 to 20 minutes or broiling it 4 inches from a moderate flame for a total cooking time of about 10 minutes, turning it once. In both methods, the slices should be basted. Or you can slice the meat into 1/4-inch slices and panfry for several minutes each side. Canadian bacon is sold unsliced (in pieces from 1 to 9 pounds) or sliced (usually vacuum-packed). Somewhat akin to Canadian bacon is the European *Lachsschinken*. Whatever type you buy, look for uniform thickness and allow 1/4 to 1/3 pound per person for average appetites.

Smoked Loin: While Canadian bacon is boned, smoked loin is not. Smoked loin is popular in German and other ethnic cuisines and generally is sold in weights of 3 to 6 pounds. (Sometimes individual chops are available.) For easier carving, ask your butcher to loosen the chine bone. Heat fully cooked smoked loin in the oven to an internal temperature of 130°F. Cook uncooked smoke loin to an internal temperature of 155°F. Both methods call for basting. Or use smoked pork loin as the classic German dish *Kasseler Rippenspeer.* Allow about 1/3 pound per serving.

Smoked Pork Jowls: The cheek of the pig is never wasted: it is cut into 4- to 8-inch squares, then cured and smoked. Jowls can be substituted for bacon and are sometimes called *bacon squares.* They have more fat and less lean than true bacon, and therefore are less costly.

Smoked Ham Hocks: Culinarily, the *hock* is the lower leg, which is often crosscut into sections about 2 to 3 inches thick. Each hock contains lean muscle, a cross-section of the tibia (shinbone), fat, gristle, and connective tissue, all surrounded by a tapered tube of skin. *Pork* (or *ham*) *hocks* are usually cured, smoked, or both, but they can also be bought fresh. Smoked ham hocks are used for flavoring and thickening slow-cooked bean dishes, stews and soups. Hocks can also be braised. Unless you want the flesh to fall off the bones during cooking, leave the outer skin on.

PORK, FRESH

BACKGROUND

Pork is the name for the flesh of the porcine animal variously called *pig, swine, hog* (when mature), *sow* (female adult), *gilt* (young female), *boar* (uncastrated male), *barrow* (castrated male), *piglet* (young of either sex), *porker* (young and fattened), *shoat* (weaned youngster), and *suckling pig* (unweaned).

Only about one-third of the meat of the pig reaches the American marketplace in the fresh state; the rest comes into our homes cured, smoked, or spiced, in cans, casings, or plastic wrap, as hams, bacon, pâté, and sausages. As the cliché aptly informs us, we can be nourished by practically everything of the pig except its oink, and that means everything between and including the flat snout and the curled tail. This entry describes fresh pork flesh, in terms of quality, health, butchering, preparation, etc. For cured pork and variety meats, see the following related entries in their alphabetical places:

Bacon
Blood
Bone
Brains
Fatback
Ham
Head
Heart
Intestines
Kidneys
Liver
Lungs
Marrow
Pigs' Ears
Pigs' Feet
Pork, Cured
Salt Pork
Sausage
Spleen
Sweetbreads
Tails
Testicles
Tongue
Tripe

Estimates place the pig's domestication some five thousand years ago in China. Over the course of time the craving for the tender, juicy, tasty flesh spread around the world from tropical Tahiti to winter-chilled Helsinki. Prime exceptions include those regions whose principal populace eschew the meat for reasons of religion or philosophy, be it Moslem, Jewish, or vegetarian.

Recently, the pork industry has been developing a leaner pig, out of deference to the trend toward less animal fats in the American diet. As a result, today's pork has a higher proportion of lean to fat. Another marked change is the pig's slaughter age: nowadays it averages 5 to 9 months; formerly, it was roughly 12 months. This means that pork is more tender than before. Because our pork is less fatty and more tender than in grandmother's day, many of her favorite pork recipes will probably need serious revision if we do not want to overcook the meat.

In at least one respect, the pig is like the struggling artist who is destined to gain due acclaim posthumously. No matter how much the gourmet praises the pork on the fork, the stereotype is of an animal stupidly wallowing in a filthy pigsty. The living pig is further maligned by the pejorative connotation of the words *pig*, *hog*, and *swine*. To set the record straight, let us emphasize that the pig is more intelligent, fun-loving (some people have pet piglets), and cleaner than city folks realize. The pigsty is muddy only if the owner throws garbage into it or does not periodically tidy it. A common work horse or even the family's pet poodle would look a mess, too, if it were made to live in such a place. Virtually all contemporary commercial pork producers rear their pigs on acceptably sanitary pig farms, not in stys.

But the image isn't all bad. Popular everyday expressions include "go the whole hog," "living high off the hog," and "bring home the bacon." Words of wisdom include "you can't make a silk purse out of a sow's ear" and "Neither cast ye your pearls before swine." Anthropomorphic fictional characters include the Three Little Pigs and Porky Pig. And where would the stereotypical twentieth-century little girls and the nineteenth-century Chinese coolies be without pigtails? Literature includes Charles Lamb's "A Dissertation on Roast Pig." Commercial products include gloves, handbags, bristle brushes, and in days past, the pigskin football.

Quality of the Animal

USDA Grades: The top U.S. Department of Agriculture grades for pork are USDA No. 1, USDA No. 2, and USDA No. 3, but slaughterhouses almost always forego asking (and paying) the federal authorities to make this voluntary evaluation. The chief reason is that the difference between one pig and another is not nearly as great as is the case with beef cattle, partly because most pigs are butchered at a tender young age. When the pork is graded, the USDA stamps the skin or exterior fat with a shield-shaped mark containing the appropriate grade. Even if the meat is stamped, you probably will not see it on the typical retail cut.

Inspection: All pork shipped between states must be inspected by USDA officials; most of the test is subject to state or local inspection. They examine the carcass for wholesomeness (though the presence of trichinae—see below—usually cannot be detected by the inspectors). They also check the sanitary conditions of the processing plant. The USDA indicates its approval by stamping the skin or exterior fat with a round, blue-ink seal. Unless you buy a wholesale cut, you probably will not see the seal on the meat.

Trichinosis

We run a small risk of being infected with *trichinosis* whenever we eat the uncooked or undercooked meat of a pig that contains the live microscopic organisms called *trichinae*. Unbeknownst to most people, the trichinae can also live in the flesh of other creatures such as dog, cat, rat, and yes, even in deer and bear, so hunters beware. When we eat the contaminated meat, the minute worms attach themselves to our intestinal walls, then breed. Their baby offspring are small enough to travel through our bloodstream to reach our muscles. As they grow, they cause pain, inflammation, muscle deterioration, general debilitation, and even death.

Fortunately, the trichinosis problem is not worldwide; raw pork is eaten in parts of Southeast Asia with impunity, and certain European hams such as the famous prosciutto of Parma are perfectly safe to eat raw. As far as our country is concerned, trichinosis has become a near rarity. Public education about the need to cook pork thoroughly has helped reduce the disease. So have improved feeding procedures, such as killing the parasitic worms by cooking any garbage (a favorite trichinae haunt) destined for the pig's stomach, or feeding only prepared foods.

Not only is it possible for the trichinae to live in the pork cuts found in the butcher's meatcase, they can also exist in bacon and especially uncooked pork sausages. Thanks to governmental standards, there is no trichinosis threat in cured hams (whether ready-to-eat or cook-before-eating) or in precooked sausages produced by reliable meat processors.

If the meat you buy is infected, you can kill the trichinae in one of two ways: cook the meat to an internal temperature of at least 137°F or freeze the meat for several weeks at a temperature below -10°F. The latter method is the less desirable, because freezing ruins the cellular structure of the meat, making it mushy when it's cooked.

Though the odds of getting a trichinae-infected piece of pork are today astronomically low, you should always assume that they are present in American-produced pork, since the possible consequence of their existence is utterly dreadful. You should never sample uncooked pork mixtures and should throughly wash, with hot, soapy water, anything that comes in contact with the raw pork—including your hands, utensils, dishes, and cutting boards. If you use a meat grinder, sterilize it with boiling water to prevent the possibility that the trichinae may contaminate whatever you grind next. Most municipalities require by law that butchers either use two separate meat grinders (one for pork and one for other meats) or that they sterilize the grinder before switching from pork to other meats.

But sensible precaution does not mean being so paranoid that you cook the meat to the 170°F-to-185°F temperatures recommended by most cookbooks. This overcaution leads to overcooking, which is guaranteed to make your pork less tender, less juicy, less tasty, and less nutritious than it would be if you cooked the pork less. Prolonged cooking also causes the meat to shrink, a big drawback to budget-minded families. For optimum culinary rewards, cook your pork to 160°F, a temperature that gives you a comfortable 23°F safety margin.

Anatomical Location

The pig is divided into fewer *primal* or *wholesale cuts* than the steer, and therefore the cuts are anatomically different (compare the illustration on page 346 with the one for beef on page 35). The pork loin, for instance, contains the equivalent of not only the beef primal short loin and primal sirloin, but also the beef primal rib.

Another way pork differs is in the form it reaches the butcher shop. Except for suckling pigs, pork is seldom shipped to the butcher shop as a whole, halved, or quartered carcass, as is usually the case with beef, veal and lamb. The slaughterhouse generally divides the carcass into primal cuts that are sent to wherever the demand is greatest for each particular wholesale cut. Curers of ham, for example, buy almost all the *legs* and a lot of the *picnic shoulders*. Bacon producers nearly monopolize the pork *bellies*, while lard renderers purchase a good deal of the *fatback* and *belly* trimmings. The three primal cuts most often purchased by the retail butcher are the *loin*, *Boston butt*, and *spareribs*, because they are the type of fresh pork favored most by this

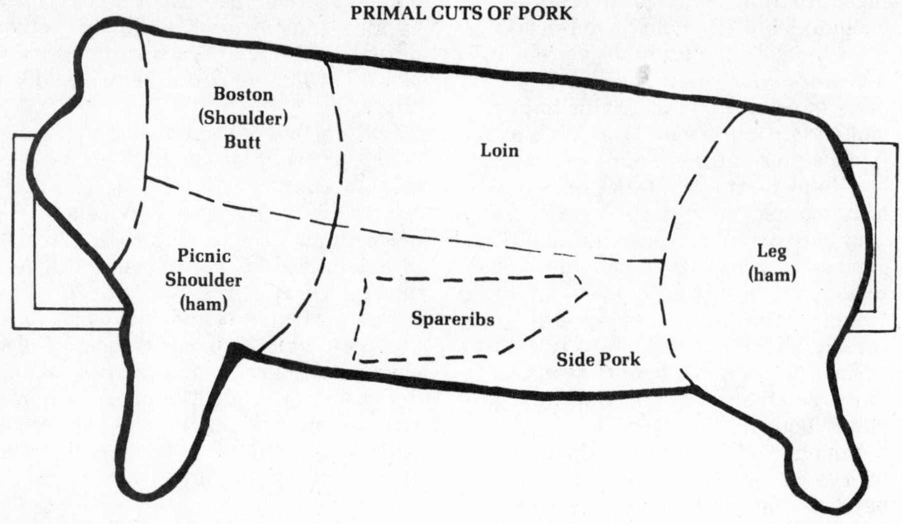

customers. Butchers seldom sell cuts like the fresh leg of ham or pork belly unless they are special-ordered by a shopper.

Primal Loin: The whole loin of a young pig, which weighs about 10 to 14 pounds, runs along the back of the animal from the shoulder area to the ham. It is the tenderest of the wholesale pork cuts and contains many retail cuts, including various *roasts*, the *tenderloin* and several types of *chops*. From this primal section also comes *country-style ribs*, *Canadian bacon*, *butterfly chops* as well as the regal *crown roast*.

The primal loin is seldom sold whole at the retail level, partly because the entire loin cannot fit into most home ovens. Usually, the butcher divides it in one of two basic ways.

The first method is to cut the primal into two halves and, perhaps, then again into quarters, producing the retail cuts shown above. Each full half weighs about 5 to 7 pounds, each center quarter 3 to 4 pounds, and each end quarter 2 to 3 pounds.

The second butchering method is the most common. The primal loin is cut into three sections as shown and discussed below.

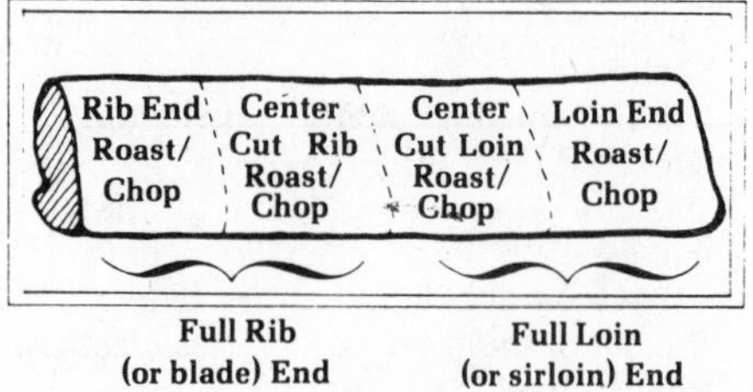

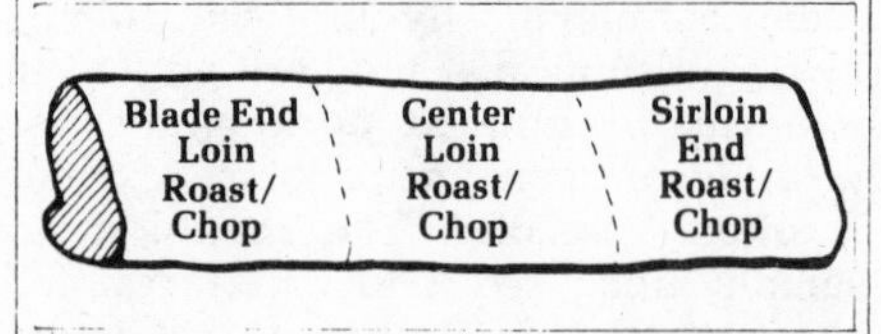

Center Loin—Roast or Chops: Of the three major subdivisions of the primal loin, this is the choicest. Rarely do we find it sold as a roast because butchers know it usually sells for a better profit when sliced into center loin pork chops. The very best of these chops are those that contain the highest proportion of the tenderloin muscle—the more the pork chop resembles the shape of the porterhouse beef steak, the better. Thus, the best chops are cut from the end of the center loin lying near the sirloin end rather than the blade or rib end.

Sirloin (or Loin) End—Roast or Chops: This retail cut is generally sold as a roast rather than divided into sirloin chops (if you buy these chops, remember that the closer they were to the center loin, the better they will be). On the desirability scale, the roast from the sirloin end ranks below the one from the center loin but above the one from the blade end, principally because the latter has more fat waste. The sirloin end roast's chief negative is its bony structure, which not only creates waste, it makes carving bothersome. Some butchers will sell it boned, but—understandably—for a premium. The longer a sirloin roast is for its size, the better value it will be, because the butcher has left on more of the meat that lies next to the center loin area.

Blade (or Rib) End Loin—Roast or Chops: Like the sirloin end roast, the blade end loin roast is usually sold whole rather than divided into chops. The best chops, of course, come from the area nearest the center loin. The best roast will be the longest one, for the reasons given in the previous paragraph. While the blade end loin roast has more fat than the sirloin end roast, it has less bone waste. If you buy the roast with the bone in, have the butcher remove or loosen the backbone from the ribs to facilitate carving. Be forewarned—some meat cutters merely saw the bones perpendicular to the back (chine) bone. This procedure saves the butcher time, but it forces you to serve slices at the thickness dictated by the meat cutter's, rather than your or your dinner guest's, choosing. And, sometimes, the butcher slices beyond the bone and well into the meat. This desecration makes it easy for the meat's interior juice to escape during the cooking process. Result: a tougher, dries, and less flavorful victual.

Tenderloin: Of the entire pig, this muscle is the tenderest and most expensive. A major source of tenderloin muscles are the makers of Canadian bacon, who remove the tenderloin from the top loin muscle, the basis of their product. The tenderloin muscle weighs 3/4 to 1½ pounds and can be roasted if barded, larded, or well basted. It can also be braised or (when sliced) sautéed.

Double Chops: Because of their thickness—2 to 2½ inches—these cuts are sometimes stuffed and almost always braised.

Butterfly Chops: These are boneless double chops that have been opened butterfly-style after first slicing them across the grain almost but not quite in half. Butterfly chops are often stuffed.

Country-Style Ribs: To create this popular-to-barbecue cut, the butcher saws a blade end loin roast lengthwise almost but not quite in half, leaving the two elongated pieces hinged together butterfly-style. Some butchers saw all the way through and sell the two pieces separately.

Crown Roasts: You can make an excellent veal or lamb crown roast, but it is the pork crown roast that is considered the true king by sophisticated palates. Whatever meat you select, your finished dish is almost guaranteed to elicit oohs and ahs from your assembled dinner guests. You will need one to three rib end racks (ask your butcher to crack the chine bone to facilitate carving); somewhere between a rack and a half and two and a half (about 12 to 20 chops) is best, as a single rack makes an object more like a shin bracelet than a crown, and a three-rack crown seems more like a stadium. Strip 1½ inches of flesh from the rib tips. Curve and sew together the individual racks into a circle with the ribs facing outward and the exposed rib ends pointing up. To keep the tips from scorching during the roasting, cover them with aluminum foil. Place the roast in a 325°F oven. It will be cooked when the internal temperature reaches slightly less than 160°F (it will rise after the roast comes out of the oven). This will take about 1½ (if from a young animal) to 2 hours. We do not recommend stuffing the crown roast before it is cooked, as the filling will overcook, and (if it is ground meat) it will hinder the proper cooking of the meat in the roast. Once cooked, you can fill the central cavity, for example, with colorful cooked vegetables. Remove the aluminum foil and garnish the rib tips with paper frills, cherry tomatoes, or pitted small fruits such as kumquats. At the table, slice the crown roast between the ribs into individual chops. Figure on two chops per person.

Canadian Bacon: See under PORK, CURED

Smoked Loin: See under PORK, CURED.

Primal Leg of Pork: Also called *fresh ham*, this primal has the highest proportion of lean to bone and fat of any other pork primal; it is of course the section cured for a HAM. It is the hind leg, the anatomical equivalent of the cattle's sirloin tip, round, and shank cuts. The leg of pork is sold with some exterior fat and skin covering, the latter being easily removed after the cut has been roasted. Fresh ham is an ideal cut for serving a large gathering of a dozen or so friends, but because it is in high demand for cured ham, it is both expensive and scarce—you may have to special-order it from your butcher. Try to find a plump leg with firm white exterior fat and smooth skin, and as short a stump as possible; younger animals have smaller legs and, therefore, small legs are generally the most desirable. The 10- to 15-pound leg can be purchased whole or as two 5- to 8-pound parts: the *butt end* (or upper half) and the *shank end* (or lower half). The butt end is the better choice because it is more tender. On the other hand, it is much more difficult to carve, especially when the butcher has not removed the aitch (hip) bone. Whenever you buy half of a leg, check to see if the label says *full* butt or shank end. Without the word "full," you can almost be assured that the butcher has carved cross-sectional slices off the half in order to sell them as ham steaks. These ham steaks come from the desirable center portion of the leg, so if you are not buying a full half, make sure the price reflects that fact. If you buy the full half, you may wish to cut off your own ¾-to-1-inch slices from your roast and reserve them for the next meal.

Primal Boston (or Shoulder) Butt: The pig's shoulder is cut into two primals: the Boston butt (the upper half) and the picnic ham (the lower half). A large percentage of the Boston butt primal is purchased by commercial curers (See under PORK, CURED). When available fresh, the 4=to 8=pound Boston butt can be braised (your best option) or simmered, either bone-in or—for easier carving—boned and rolled; roasting is generally not recommended for this less than tender meat. The Boston butt can also be sliced into *blade steaks* and other steaks; *cubed* for stews or (if marinated) kebobs; sliced into *strips* for stir-frying; or *ground* for use in patties, meatloaf, pâtés, or sausages. The Boston butt is a tasty cut, but it does have a relatively high fat and gristle content.

Primal Picnic Shoulder: Only a handful of butchers sell this cut fresh, as most of it is bought by commercial houses who cure and smoke it (See under HAM). When it is available fresh, it may be marketed under the name *callie* (or a spelling variant). The picnic shoulder is not the culinary equal of the hind leg, because the foreleg is less tender and has more fat and gristle. It is, however, quite flavorful and is worth buying if the price is right. The 5- to 8-pound picnic shoulder is often boned and rolled for easy carving. Sometimes the *hocks* are removed (to be used for other dishes such as stews or soups) and the remaining meat may be sold as an *arm roast*. This cut, like all other large parts of the picnic shoulder, is best braised, pot-roasted, or simmered, but never roasted. The arm roast can in turn be cut into *arm steaks*. Another well-known cut from the primal picnic shoulder is the several-pound boneless, square "cushion," whose natural pocket makes an ideal package for your favorite stuffing. The picnic shoulder can also be cubed for stews and kabobs, sliced for stir-fried dishes, or ground for concoctions such as meatloaf.

Primal Side Pork (Pork Belly): How many high-rolling investors have not felt the uncontrollable urge to invest in pork-belly futures, a trading commodity that has made and busted millionaires overnight? To most of us, the pork belly's significance is BACON, which is the cured and smoked midsection of the 10- to 15-pound pork belly. What remains after the bacon section is removed mainly ends up as salt pork, sausages, and lard. Fresh pork bellies are rarely sold to the public except in certain ethnic neighborhood stores such as those found in Chinatowns. They are excellent when cut into cubes then braised.

Primal Spareribs: Lying just under the layer of the primal side pork is the primal sparerib section. It comprises the breastbone and lower ends of the rib bones, as well as the lean and fat directly connected to those bones. A whole sparerib section is usually referred to as a *slab* and can weigh anywhere from 2 to 5 pounds. Since young hogs have tenderer meat than older ones, it stands to reason that the whole slabs that weigh less have the tenderer meat, an important factor that is especially critical if you plan to barbeque the spareribs. You can barbeque spareribs 5 inches from the coals in a total cooking time of 40 to 60 minutes, depending on thickness. It is not a good idea to barbecue pork spareribs closer than 5 inches. Neither is it advisable to baste the ribs with the barbecue sauce until the last 20 minutes or so of cooking, as that will allow the sauce and therefore the meat to develop a bitter flavor. Your spareribs can also be baked in a 325°F oven or braised in a suitable pot for 1¼ to 2 hours, again depending on thickness. Braising is recommended for spareribs from slabs weighing over 3½ pounds.

Suckling Pig: Few culinary presentations are as picturesque as a whole roast suckling pig, apple in mouth, crouching on top of a parsley-ringed silver platter. The best weight is usually 10 to 15 pounds, because if it were larger, it might not fit into your oven. Even if you have a huge oven, stay below 25 pounds; this older baby pig would probably no longer be suckling, and quite definitely its flesh would no longer be as tender and succulent. Those pigs of 50 to 100 pounds served at large-scale luaus are sort of teenage pigs whose principal virtue is saving the cooks the expense and bother of preparing a number of smaller (but better-tasting) piglets. You will probably need to buy 1½ pounds (2 pounds, if the occasion is festive) per person, because not only does a whole suckling pig have a high proportion of bone and waste, the typical diner is conservative, preferring not to eat the delicacies found in such places as the head and lower legs—they even bypass the crisp skin. Before placing the piglet into the oven, it is necessary to stuff the abdominal cavity in order to prevent the loin area from being cooked faster than the legs. You also need to wrap the tail and ears with aluminum foil to keep them from scorching. Keep the mouth open with a ball of aluminum foil, while the piglet cooks, or you won't be able to insert the apple before serving. Remove the eyes of the pig before cooking. Insert a cranberry or other suitable garnish into each cavity after the pig is roasted. To get a crisp, deep-brown skin, place the prepared pig in a preheated 400°F oven, then immediately reduce the temperature to 300°F and roast for 30 minutes. Then cook for an additional 15 minutes for each pound of weight, or until the meat thermometer registers 160°F. Baste regularly. When cooked, remove it from the oven and cover it lightly with aluminum foil. Let the pig rest at room temperature for about 20 minutes before carving and serving; this allows the internal juices to redistribute and settle.

Cracklings: Roast or fry some pork skin until it is crisp and you have *cracklings*, as they are called in the South. If your square or rectangular cracklings are to be superb, their dry, crunchy exteriors will be contrasted with slightly moist interiors. Cracklings are usually served as a snack or as an appetizer.

AVAILABILITY

Season

All forms of fresh pork are available the year round. However, because Old Man Winter puts an economic strain on pig farmers, many slaughter an abnormally large share of their spring-born animals during the last few months of the year, making the supply go up and prices go down during that period. And prices of certain cuts can vary with the season: spareribs soar in price during the summer barbecuing months, the time when loin prices fall, because roasting heats up an already hot kitchen. When the cool season arrives, the price trends are reversed.

Buying Tips

The best-tasting pork generally comes from pigs that are young and have been fed the right type of diet (for instance, corn and protein supplements rather than slop made from ordinary throwaways). This high-quality pork can be identified in the meatcase by looking for the following factors: The skin (if still attached) should be pale creamy white and thin, not tough. The bones should be pink-tinged and soft, not fully white and hardened. The smaller the cut is for its type, the younger and more tender the flesh. The fat should be firm and snow-white, not yellowish. The flesh should have a very high lean-to-fat ratio, but some fat is needed to give cooked pork its desirable flavor. The lean should be at least slightly marbled (though this quality will be absent in extremely young pigs). The lean should be as light a shade of pink as is possible for the pig's breed, because the color of the flesh deepens as the animal grows older; the lean should be reasonably fine-grained and firm, not flabby. The meat should have a minimum quantity of bone and gristle for its cut. Please note that the level of quality of one cut of pork compared to another is not always reflected in the price: as mentioned earlier, sparerib prices go sky-high in summer, and fresh legs of ham are usually overpriced.

PREPARATION

Storage

Depending on the condition of the meat when you bring it home, fresh pork can be stored one to several days in the refrigerator if loosely wrapped, allowing for the air circulation that will retard bacterial growth. You can—if you must—freeze fresh pork for up to a couple of weeks in the frozen food compartment or up to several months in a deep freezer. In both instances, the meat should be tightly wrapped and sealed in freezer paper. And, in both instances, the meat will suffer in terms of flavor, texture and nutrients. None of the above times refer to ground pork, which is highly perishable and should be used within a day.

Cooking

Just as it is a culinary *faux pas* to cook pork too much beyond the 160°F level, it is equally a shame to cook it much below the 160°F mark. The reason is not fear of incurring trichinosis—137°F is sufficient to kill any trichinae. Rather, it is a matter of flavor; pork, unlike beef or lamb, tastes better when cooked to 160°F rather than, say, 140°F. Why? Principally because the extra cooking time gives the fat a little more time to melt and infuse its special flavor into the lean. As noted before, the fat of the pig plays a prominent role in making cooked pig taste great.

Roasting: Pork is a superb roasting meat, but it is critical not to roast pork at too high a temperature. The ideal temperature seems to be roughly 325°F. A room-temperature roast on a rack in an uncovered roasting pan will cook to an internal temperature of 160°F in a total cooking time of about 30 minutes plus 15 minutes for each pound of weight. Because heat reaches the center of the meat from the shortest radius, a long, slender roast cooks faster than a squat one. Add a few minutes per pound if the meat has been boned or if it contains a lot of fat, because bones conduct heat faster than lean, and fat slower. If you do not have a meat thermometer, use your eye to estimate the degree of doneness. The juices should be just beginning to run clear, and the center of the flesh should have lost its rosiness. It should still have just a blush of pinkness, though; if it doesn't, it was overcooked. Cookbooks that tell you that absolutely no pink should remain are out of step with modern trichinosis research. After the roast is cooked, remove it from the oven, place it on a warm platter, loosely cover it with aluminum foil, and let it rest for 15 to 20 minutes to let the internal juices redistribute and settle before you start to carve.

Stewing: Simmer or stew pork for 1½ to 2½ hours, depending principally on thickness. Meat cut from the less tender part of the anatomy or from older animals will obviously require the longer cooking times.

Braising: Braising a 1-inch-thick pork chop or steak requires about 15 minutes. A 2-inch-thick piece needs about 25 minutes.

Sautéing or Broiling: Sautéing or broiling a pork chop or steak is generally not recommended because the meat has a tendency to become tough and dry with these cooking methods. If you want to sauté or broil them, then at least use no more than moderate heat, allowing 8 minutes for the first side, 4 minutes for the other for a 1½-inch-thick piece. Test for doneness by making a cut in the thick lean near a bone. If the juices do not run clear or if there is more than a blush of pink in the lean, cook the meat a little longer.

Equivalents

If meat is lean and boneless, allow ¼ to ½ pound per serving. If meat is bone-in, allow at least ½ to 1 pound per serving, with cuts such as spareribs requiring the higher allowance.

CLASSIC USES AND AFFINITIES

Herbs in general go well with pork—thyme, sage, and bayleaf are cookbook favorites. Garlic and mustard are classic affinities, too, as are sauerkraut and fruits, especially apple, prunes, and pineapple. Sweet-and-sour sauces go particularly well with barbecued pork, but too many Americans make those sauces so cloyingly sweet that they overshadow the delectble pork flavor.

POTATO

BACKGROUND

Long ago, before Pizzaro and his Spanish conquistadores invaded and destroyed it, the now legendary Incan civilization of Peru domesticated the *potato*, a wild brown root ball that grew in the Andes Mountains amid purest air and strong sun. From such a genesis came the tuber *Solanum tuberosum*, our everyday spud. Today, America's ubiquitous meat-and-potatoes man almost eats his weight just in potatoes every year. Though too often mundanely served in America, the New World potato has been creatively exploited in many European cuisines. But that took time. When the Spaniards brought the potato into Europe in the sixteenth century, it was at first misunderstood and maligned. Its warty, dumpy appearance went against it. And suspicions of its wholesomeness flew from *femme* to *hausfrau* to *senora*, because the potato is a member of the *Solanaceae* or nightshade family, of which there are poisonous specimens, such as the fatal nerve-relaxing herb belladonna. To make matters even worse, foot-stomping Scottish preachers denounced the potato as unfit for Christian consumption because it is not mentioned in the Bible. Once accepted, the potato's European problems were not over as Ireland's potato blight in the 1840s was a national catastrophe: millions of Irish either starved to death or were forced to emigrate, especially to the United States.

Potatoes have been much maligned as the enemy of weight watchers. In truth, the potato does not have that many calories for the bulk it provides. It is the butter, gravy, sour cream and other high-fat toppings that make potato-eating fattening. This means that the calorie count is about 70 calories for a small potato, 100 calories for a medium potato, and 150 calories for a large russet. Potatoes have generous amounts of phosphorous and potassium and some Vitamin C, but not much protein or B Vitamins. They are, of course, relatively high in carbohydrates, and having very little fiber, they are easily digestible.

Varieties

Types of Potatoes: The many varietal names of the American potato are meaningful only to commercial planters and private gardeners. The type of potato for its intended culinary purpose is what concerns us. There are four basic types: the round-white, the round-red, the russet or Idaho, and the all-purpose long-white.

Round-white (a "boiling" potato): This is the familiar *"Irish"* potato, of medium size and good for many purposes: boiling, pan-frying and pan-roasting. It is most often grown in the Northeast and has firm, waxy, whitish-beige flesh and darker-freckled, brown, relatively thick skin. It is also called the *Katahdin*.

Round-red (a "boiling" potato): Except for its distinctive reddish-brown outer coat, the round-red (or *red Pontiac*) is identical to the round-white in cooking uses, texture, and general appearance. It is, however, predominantly grown in the Northwest. In comparison to the russet and long-white potatoes, both types of round potatoes contain less starch and more moisture, which gives them their waxy look.

Russet or Idaho (the "baking" potato): The russet is large, a long flattened cylinder that rounds out on the ends. Its flesh is buff-white and its skin is brown, rough, thick, and coarse. The *russet Burbank*, named after the famous botanist who refined it to its present perfection, is the baking potato *nonpareil*. But any russset is a fine baker. This type of potato is still grown mainly in the Midwest—in general parlance, the name "Idaho" has become synonymous with the russet potato type, but more and more local governments are insisting that only russet potatoes actually grown in Idaho be commercially so labeled. It is the high starch and low moisture content in the russet that causes the dry, fluffy "mealiness" so desired in the baked potato. This is a key reason why the russet potato is preferred for baking, french fries, and *pommes soufflées*.

Long-white (an "all-purpose" potato): Most farmers call this potato the *white rose* or *California long-white*, though it is also grown in the Northeast, where it may end up in produce bins under the appellation *Maine* or *Eastern*. (In some regions, these last two names also are given to round whites.) The long-white resembles the russet in shape, but features a thin, smooth beige-tan skin and almost no eyes. The long white can be mashed or baked (but not as well as the russet) and can be pan-fried, pan-roasted or boiled (but not as well as the two rounds). If you have the choice, it is always better to buy the preferred potato for your cooking needs, rather than the all-purpose one.

Age:

New Potatoes: All four types of potatoes can be bought *new*. The word applies to a very young potato that has developed to the sugar stage but has still to undergo the final enzymatic change of sugar-into-starch that signals maturity. They also have not fully developed (or *set*) their skins. Consequently some of the skin has often pealed away before you buy them. New potatoes are usually very small and hard; their high moisture content gives them a waxy consistency. New potatoes of whatever type cannot be successfully baked: they are much too waxy. They are best made into hot and cold potato salads, and are very good steamed or boiled in acidulated water and seasoned with salt, pepper, butter and chopped parsley. Boiled new potatoes with dried surfaces can be fried.

Mature Potatoes: Mature potatoes are harvested fully grown. Properly stored after harvest, the potato slowly ages; it becomes drier and drier and gradually increases its concentration of starch. One of the professional secrets of successful *pommes soufflées* is the use of well-aged russet potatoes. By well-aged we do not mean, of course, over-the-hill potatoes that have begun to deteriorate.

Processed Potatoes: Processed food manufacturers offer a range of potato products. The all-American *potato chip* was invented in Saratoga Springs, New York, which explains why its early name was the *Saratoga chip*. Today the old-fashioned chip has developed into a wide variety of sizes, flavors, and shapes, most often skinless, well-seasoned, and full of additives. Some "chips" are even made into a paste, then formed into uniform chips that conveniently fit into a cylindrical container. The best are homemade, the second best are those made of natural slices with no additives—read the labels. Whatever the type, potato chips should be fresh, free of a rancid odor. Store in an airtight container in a cool, dry place. *Instant mashed potatoes* are widely sold, but we cannot recommend any of these highly processed, packaged horrors. *Frozen potatoes* come in many forms: *french fries, hash browns, croquettes, pancakes, skinned boilers, whole stuffed baked potatoes, preassembled potato dishes*—the lists increases yearly. The biggest weakness of frozen potatoes is a very serious one: most of the desirable texture is destroyed in freezing.

AVAILABILITY

New potatoes precede the seasonal full harvest of mature potatoes by several weeks and sometimes months. Traditionally, new potatoes are available in the spring and early summer. Mature potatoes are available year round, but so many are held in controlled storage and then released as wanted that sometimes potatoes sold in early summer can be suspected of being last year's crop—especially when sold in closed bags that offer limited viewing. Processed potatoes are widely available year round.

Buying Tips

Before shopping, decide what you will do with the potatoes, and buy the best type for that purpose. The highest grade is U.S. Extra No. 1, but the second best grade, U.S. No 1, is more commonly available. U.S. No. 1 potatoes will vary in size, but none can be smaller than 1⅞ inches in diameter. Grade labeling is voluntary; if sold in closed bags, federal law requires the specific grade or the word "unclassified" to be printed on the package. The potato should look fresh, be well-formed for its type, and be firm with no soft spots. It should be clean of visible dirt, have no sprouting in the eyes, no blemishes, discoloration, or cracks. Avoid any potato that is spotted or tinged with green. The greening comes from a bitter alkaloid, *solanin*, which a potato will produce when disturbed by light. In some sensitive persons there is an allergic reaction, and for all of us the taste is spoiled. New potatoes are so delicate that some have bald spots where the skin has rubbed off. Mature potatoes should not. The skin should fit the potato snugly. A potato shrunken within its jacket has internal decay. When in doubt, give each potato the sniff test. It should smell fresh, not musty or moldy-sweet. For uniform cooking times, select uniform-sized potatoes.

PREPARATION

Storage

Unless you have an appropriate cool, dark storage area—such as a draft-free 45°F cellar—do not buy mature potatoes for future use beyond a two-week period, and new potatoes for beyond several days. Potatoes are economical enough to buy in frequent small amounts and they are always available. Eventual loss through spoilage or waste only increases cost. If you're fortunate enough to have an ideal hibernating lair for potatoes, remember only that while potatoes are hardy and good keepers, they are easily bruised. One bad potato can spoil any others it touches, spreading decay or infection throughout the lot. Store your unwashed potatoes in a bug-free, clean, dark place. If you don't have that ideal cellar, store potatoes in soft, loosewoven, light-shielding material such as burlap if you have it. If not, use wood or something else that "breathes," not plastic. To hold just a few potatoes, a brown paper sack will do nicely. Tuck them into the coolest corner of a dark shelf or closet. As the stereotyped bachelor never knows, raw potatoes should not be refrigerated: under 40°F, their starch will convert back to sugar and destroy consistency and taste. The USDA advises that if held at room temperature for two weeks, the sugar will convert again to starch, but after such internal shock, your potato will definitely be affected. Above 70°F (most homes average around 75°F), potatoes begin to shrivel and sprout within a week or so. If this happens, the little eye sprouts can be simply plucked out with the tip of a vegetable peeler or rubbed off with your fingers and discarded as you prepare the potato for cooking. If you had to buy potatoes in a sack, open it as soon as possible, sort out any potatoes that are bruised or show any signs of injury, and set them aside to be used at once. Cut away the affected sections, wash the potatoes, and use. Do not store potatoes with onions. Each vegetable gives off a gas detrimental to the other.

Preliminaries

Just before cooking potatoes, wash them in fresh cool water, scrubbing them very well with a vegetable brush, removing any tiny eye sprouts, and cutting away bruised or infected parts. Ideally, you should leave the skin on for cooking. But if you are peeling the potatoes before boiling, use a vegetable peeler. A paring knife, however sharp, tends to cut too deeply into the outermost layer of flesh, where the potato has much of its valuable nutrients. If you peel the potatoes, cover them with acidulated water (1 tablespoon of vinegar or 2 tablespoons of lemon juice per quart) to prevent darkening the flesh by oxidation. Some nutritionists suggest that coating the exposed surfaces with lemon juice rather than soaking the potatoes preserves more vitamins and minerals.

Basic Cooking

There are countless ways to cook a potato, the basic ways being boiling (and steaming), baking, pan-frying, and deep-frying.

Boiling and Steaming: The basic way to boil unpeeled potatoes is to cover them with cold water, adding salt to taste (1 teaspoon salt per quart of water is usual). Bring the liquid just up to a boil, reduce to a simmer, and cover the pot. Cook for 20 to 40 minutes, depending on size. To steam potatoes, put 1/4 to 1/2 inch of water in the pan and salt to taste. Bring it to a boil, add the potatoes and lower the heat for simmering. Cover the pot and let the potatoes steam for 15 to 35 minutes. (You may have to add a little liquid halfway through the cooking process.) Test for doneness after 15 minutes: pierce the thickest potato to its center with the tip of a knife; if it slides in easily, your potatoes are ready. As soon as the potatoes are boiled or steamed, immediately drain off any water that remains in the pot. Firmly hold the pot lid and handle and put the pot back on the heat, shaking it back and forth for about 30 seconds. This will evaporate most of the excess moisture still clinging to the potatoes. Now is the easiest and most nutritious time to peel the potatoes, if you choose to do so. Just let the potatoes cool slightly before handling.

Baking: For best results, use the russet Burbank, but any russet is a better-tasting baker than the other types. Place the potatoes in a preheated 425° to 450°F oven. This high heat shortens cooking time and gives your potatoes a crisper, darker skin, which will set off their fluffy white interior when served. If you prefer a softer, shiny skin, grease the jacket before baking with butter or a light vegetable oil. For a medium-large potato, figure 45 minutes to an hour, depending on size. We do not recommend the baking nail or potato rack. These so-called kitchen aids do shorten the cooking time by about one-third and they do pierce a potato to allow steam to escape, but we think a few discreet fork pricks atop the potato and unhurried cooking times give you the whitest, driest, fluffiest, best-tasting potato. Test for doneness by piercing with a paring knife—the potato is done when the blade slides easily into the center. Or squeeze a potato, using a potholder or towel. If the potato feels soft, it is done. Moisture cannot escape from a foil-wrapped potato. Consequently, it cannot bake; it gets steamed and develops a mushy texture. To insure a free flow of hot oven air when baking several potatoes, space them generously apart. Serve at once or keep warm in the oven. Once a baked potato has grown cold, its desirable mealiness is gone forever.

Pan-Frying: Slice or cube the potatoes. They will be more nutritious if you leave the skins on. In a heavy pan, preheat 1/4-inch of vegetable oil or bacon fat. Add the potatoes, and cook over moderate heat for 15 to 25 minutes (depending on thickness), turning occasionally with a spatula for even browning. If you wish, fry onions along with the potatoes. Season to taste.

Deep-Frying: Cut the peeled potatoes into uniform pieces—the size and shape is up to you. Generally, Americans like long and narrow french fries. Now give the potatoes a 10 to 20 minute rest in cold water. This soaking absorbs some of the surface starch and firms the potatoes. Dry as thoroughly as possible with paper towels. Fill the pot with 4 or more inches of fresh vegetable oil and bring slowly to 375°F (use a frying thermometer). Add the potatoes a few at a time and do not crowd them. They will sputter, but if you dried them well they should not splatter. Fry for 5 to 10 minutes until golden brown. Remove and allow them to dry on paper toweling. Serve immediately or, if you have to, place them in a 250°F oven for no more than 10 minutes.

Mashed Potatoes: This is not really a cooking method, as the potatoes have already been boiled (or baked or steamed). After cooking and peeling the hot potatoes, gradually add warmed cream or milk, butter, salt and pepper to taste, mashing them with a potato masher, fork, or electric mixer until the lumps are gone and the potatoes are light and airy. When using a potato masher, use an up and down rather than a circular motion; you incorporate more air and, thus, your mashed potatoes will have a lighter consistency. Do not cover them, lest they steam and become soggy. Serve at once.

Equivalents

For an average serving, figure one medium potato, or half a large one, or two to four small ones.

CLASSIC USES AND AFFINITIES

Meat goes well with potatoes as do milk, cream, cheese, onions, chives, bacon, caviar, paprika, and fresh parsley, thyme, and dill. Potatoes love butter, gravy, and sour cream; if calories concern you, try topping your potato with yogurt. Or use salt, pepper, and just a light touch of melted butter. The French have a way with potatoes. Here are some of their better-known *pommes* specialties that are often found on restaurant menus: *allumette* (matchstick-sized, deep-fried potatoes); *Anna* (thin-sliced potatoes baked in layers in a casserole dish with clarified butter); *au four* (baked potato); *château* (potatoes cut into ovals, then oven-roasted); *croquette* (egg-enriched mashed potatoes shaped into balls or ovals, then breaded and deep-fried); *dauphine* (*duchesse* potatoes [see below] combined with sugarless puff paste, then shaped into small cylinders, then breaded and deep-fried); *dauphinoise* (thin-sliced potatoes baked with butter and cream or milk and made *au gratin* with grated gruyère cheese); *duchesse* (egg-yolk-enriched mashed potatoes—often used to garnish main dishes, applied with a piping bag and then baked until brown-crusted); *gaufrettes* (waffle-patterned potato chips, cut on a mandoline); *lyonnaise* (sliced potatoes sautéed with onions); *pailles* (strawlike deep-fried potatoes); *Pont Neuf* (rectangular, thumb-sized, deep-fried potatoes); *pommes soufflées* (1/8-inch-thick oval potato slices that puff up after being deep-fried first in 325°F and then in 375°F oil). The word *Parmentier* attached to a dish implies "with potatoes." *Frites* simply means "fried." France has many types of french-fried potatoes, but *pommes frites* usually suggests a deep-fried potato slightly thinner than the usual American french fry.

POULTRY SEASONING

BACKGROUND

Many herbs and spices have an affinity for chicken, turkey, and duck. Commercial poultry seasonings are blends of dried herbs such as sage, thyme, rosemary, savory, marjoram, and parsley, and spices such as ground pepper, nutmeg, allspice, ginger, and cloves. These mixtures, which you can blend yourself, can be used in the stuffing for roast poultry, spread on the poultry before roasting, or used in cooking other bland meats such as veal and mild-tasting fish. (See HERBS AND SPICES for information on buying, storing, cooking, etc.)

PREPARATION

For most tastes, a teaspoon of poultry seasoning will be enough for a 5-pound roasting chicken. Each cup of bread cubes or crumbs for stuffing will take about 1/4 teaspoon of the herb mixture. Using prepared poultry seasoning means that the seasoning you use will be only as fresh as the stalest ingredient in the mixture; it also means that you lose the opportunity to use your own favorite herbs and spices creatively and to suit the spicing of the main dish to that of the other dishes on the menu.

PRICKLY PEAR

BACKGROUND

You can enjoy the juicy fruit of several species of the genus *Opuntia*, cacti that are native to the New World tropics and Southwestern United States. The *prickly* (or *cactus*) *pear* ranges in shape from spherical to flattened-oval, in diameter from 1 to 3 inches, and in pulp color from yellow-green to vibrant burgundy. The exterior skin is spiny (hence the graphic name) but those sharp pins are customarily removed before the fruit reaches the retail market. The flesh and seeds may be cooked or eaten raw, but do not consume the skin.

AVAILABILITY

Peak season is mid-fall to early winter.

Buying Tips

Select prickly pears that are reasonably but not totally hard. As the fruit ripens, the skin changes from green to yellow or reddish, depending on species. Generally, medium-sized fruits are superior to the larger ones. Avoid fruits whose skin is cracked, shriveled, dried, moldy, or otherwise damaged.

PREPARATION

Store prickly pears in a dry, cool place. Raw prickly pears are often peeled and diced or sliced and added to salads or eaten as is, perhaps with a sprinkling of lime juice. They are also converted into jams, jellies, pickles or pastes.

PRUNES

BACKGROUND

A *prune* can be made by dehydrating any plum, but some plums are better suited for the purpose because of their greater fragrance, sweetness, and firmness. The *plum d'Agen* is a case in point. Historically, prunes were dried in the sun, but modern technology uses artificial heat.

AVAILABILITY

Prunes are available the year round, but early fall brings us the year's finest prunes as they are made from the recently harvested plum crop.

Buying Tips

Select prunes that are slightly pliable, as some moisture should remain. The skin should be bright bluish-black and not damaged nor decayed. When buying packaged prunes, be sure that the container is tightly sealed and that the merchant has a reasonably fast stock turnover. Prunes are sold by themselves or in combination with other dried fruits, such as apricots and apples.

PREPARATION

Storage

Do not store your prunes on a shelf near the kitchen stove. If you have no convenient cool, dry storage place, keep your prunes in a covered jar in your refrigerator. There they will keep for up to several months.

Cooking

Uncooked prunes are safe to eat. If you want to add prunes to (for example) a roast pork or goose, do not cook them too long or at too high a heat, lest they become mushy.

PUMPKIN SEEDS

BACKGROUND

A favorite among health food devotees, pumpkin seeds—like nuts—are tasty, nutritious, and rich in vegetable oil. Pumpkin seeds can be eaten shelled or in the shell, fresh or dried, raw or toasted, salted or not, as you prefer. Though they are most often thought of as a snack, pumpkin seeds can be added to many dishes with success. Store the seeds in a tightly closed glass jar in the refrigerator. (For pumpkins, see under SQUASH, WINTER.)

PURSLANE

BACKGROUND

You can grow *Portulaca oleracea*, or gather it—it is a common weed in the United States and Europe. The narrow, triangular leaves are usually reddish-green. They grow on a fleshy forked stalk of green splotched with red or purple. Young leaves are used raw in salad; older leaves are boiled. Their texture is slightly sticky, and their flavor has a hint of acid.

QUATRE ÉPICES

BACKGROUND

In culinary French, *quatre épices* (literally, "four spices") is a mixture of sweet spices. The blend is usually made of white pepper, cloves, nutmeg, and ginger, all ground. It can be bought ready-made in France or prepared at home; it is harder to find in the United States, and is not used often enough to be more convenient than individual spice blends prepared for each dish cooked. The French use *quatre épices* frequently, in dishes such as stews and hearty soups; in preparing sweet vegetables such as carrots, sweet potatoes, and yellow squash; in sweet sauces such as raisin sauce; in wine sauce; and, mixed with salt, over meat to broil. (See HERBS AND SPICES for information on buying, storing, cooking, etc.)

QUINCE

BACKGROUND

Middle Eastern and Mediterranean peoples have been enjoying the *quince* (*Cydonia oblonga* and *C. vulgaris*) for thousands of years. But until recently, Americans have limited their use of the quince largely to filling in six-letter crossword-puzzle spaces. The fruit resembles a deformed, lumpy apple; of the many varieties now grown in America, most are round or pear-shaped and have a smooth or somewhat fuzzy skin.

AVAILABILITY

Buying Tips

Fall is the season. For the quintessential quince, choose those that are relatively large, firm (but not hard), reasonably yellow (as yellow as you can find them), as their yellowness is a sign of ripeness in most varieties. Avoid damaged fruits, as those with surface injury can spoil quickly, but do expect to see some scarring on quinces in the market.

PREPARATION

Ripening

If your quinces are mature but not yet fully ripe, you can hasten ripening by storing them at room temperature in a pierced paper bag. For better but slower results, store them in a cool, dry spot such as a cellar—quinces keep well in such places. Once they're fully ripened, keep them in your refrigerator. At all times, treat your quinces gently, for they bruise readily.

Cooking

The quince must be cooked to make its astringent flesh edible, but most cookbooks demand excessive cooking periods. You can bake a whole quince in 25 to 40 minutes (depending on size) in a preheated 325°F oven, or can poach segments in 15 to 20 minutes. Quince pulp may turn slightly pink when cooked. Many recipes call for the addition of an equal portion of sugar to quince pulp in order to offset the natural tartness of the fruit, but you can use much less or no sugar with equal or better results.

CLASSIC USES AND AFFINITIES

Because of the high pectin content, the quince often ends up as the base for a jam, jelly, or a marmalade. The quince—with or without peel—can be baked whole, or sliced in a pie; it is often combined with other fruits such as apples. Quinces can also be pureed for pastes and sauces. Lemon juice and cinnamon are natural affinities.

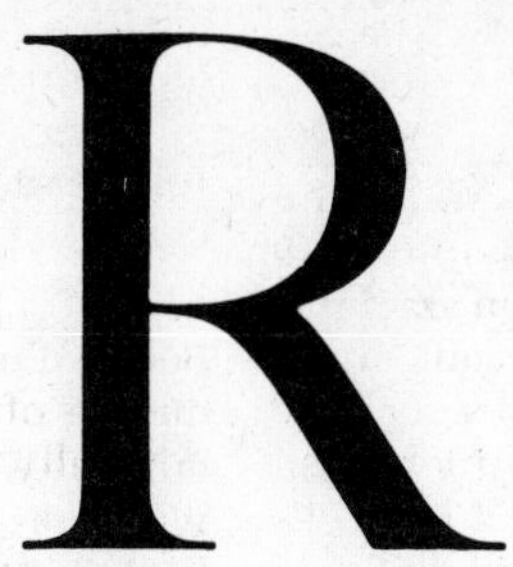

RABBIT AND HARE

BACKGROUND

There are many distinct differences between these two look-alike animals. For instance, a mature *rabbit* weighs about 3 to 5 pounds, versus about 6 to 13 pounds for a *hare*. We also have to distinguish between wild rabbit—such as the *cottontail*—and the *domesticated rabbit* that is reared in cages. The latter type, the "bunny," has a milder flesh and a higher fat content, and is the only type of rabbit we are apt to find in the meat store. The source for the likes of the wild rabbit and the *jackrabbit* (really a hare) are usually young sharpshooters we happen to know.

Buying Tips

The choicest domesticated rabbits are about 2 months old and weigh about 2 to 2½ pounds. A good test for young—and, hence, for the most tender-fleshed—whole animals involves examining the ears; as the animal ages, its ears change from being soft and pliable to semifirm. The flavor of domesticated rabbit meat is as mild as chicken. As with chicken, the strength of flavor will vary with age. Feed also plays a role: a rabbit raiser who places, say, alfalfa pellets in the bins will produce better-tasting meat than a raiser who feeds his animals cabbage.

PREPARATION

There is a scant but real chance that a rabbit or hare (or the vermin that hitchhiked on its fur) may harbor the dangerous *tularemia* disease, so it is wise to wear rubber gloves when eviscerating and skinning the animals. Unless they are young, wild rabbits and hares may benefit slightly from 1 or 2 days of hanging (see GAME ANIMALS entry). Marinating sometimes benefits older rabbits and hares, but overpowers the delicate flavor of the younger animals.

Cooking

A young animal can be roasted whole (usually stuffed) or cut up into pieces for sautéing, frying, or broiling. A 2½ pound rabbit should be roasted in a preheated 425°F oven for roughly 40 minutes, basting every 12 to 15 minutes. Mature domesticated rabbits weigh about 4 to 6 pounds and are best stewed or braised in 1¼ to 2 hours, depending on age and size of pieces. Cook hares as you would rabbits, taking into consideration variables such as age. Hares, like wild rabbits, will be leaner than domesticated rabbits; therefore, measures such as barding or basting become very important to help keep the meat from cooking dry and tough.

RADISH

BACKGROUND

The commonest form of the *radish* on the American table is the small globular or oval red radish, *Raphanus sativus*, about an inch in diameter. It is white-fleshed and juicy, crisp and pungent. There are also the milder *icicle radish*—a longish (3 inches and more) white-skinned, white-fleshed variety—and a less-common black-skinned type.

Americans are also becoming familiar with the *daikon*, a giant Oriental radish—it is 6 to 15 inches long and 2 to 3 inches in diameter. The *daikon*'s skin can be creamy-white or black. The white flesh is crisp, but like the "icicle," mellower than the red radish. Japanese and Chinese cooks serve the *daikon* shredded raw into salads, cooked, or pickled.

AVAILABILITY

Red radishes are available fresh all year round. Early radishes in the spring are smaller and sweeter, and winter radishes, first pulled in early fall, are larger and more pungent.

Buying Tips

Most red radishes are sold pretrimmed, in plastic bags, but some greengrocers offer them in bunches with their top leaves and taproots still attached. Whichever way you buy them, choose unblemished, bright-looking radishes with no cuts, cracks, scars, or soft spots.

PREPARATION

Storage

If you buy radishes with tops on, remove the foliage before using or storing. In the refrigerator, radishes will keep in good condition for several days.

Preliminaries

All radishes are crisp, but some people prefer to make them even crisper by soaking the peeled vegetable in refrigerated ice water for a few hours. This ploy also helps to reduce some of the radish's pungent bite.

Serving

Radishes are usually just washed and trimmed before being eaten raw whole, but they can be sliced into rounds, carved into rosebuds, or peeled, German-style, into one thin continuous, curling strip.

CLASSIC USES AND AFFINITIES

Radishes are a popular addition to salads, as *crudités*, and as garnishes to finished dishes.

RAISIN

BACKGROUND

A *raisin* is no more than a grape dried either by the sun (an age-old practice) or by artificial heat. Though the *Thompson seedless* or *Sultana* grape is often used to make raisins, the seed-laden grape usually offers the most satisfactory flavor; the seeds of the latter are removed by special equipment. Dried currants are made from tiny Zaute grapes, not from the berries called CURRANTS.

PREPARATION

Storage

Prolonged or improper storage makes

raisins tough and chewy; buy your raisins from stores that have a fast stock turnover. Once a package has been opened, seal it in an air-tight plastic bag or transfer the unused raisins to a covered glass jar.

Basic Use

Raisins are often eaten by themselves or as an ingredient in sauces, breads, and desserts such as cakes. To help keep the raisins from slipping to the bottom of a cake batter, dredge them first with flour.

RAMBUTAN

BACKGROUND

This Indonesian fruit, related to the litchi, grows in clusters of small, hard-shelled fruits. The spiny shell of the *rambutan* (*Nephelium lappaceum*), is red or bright orange tinged with green. Inside is a 2-by-½-inch translucent white fruit which is eaten raw. Its taste is reminiscent of grapes.

RAMPS

BACKGROUND

The Appalachian mountain area in West Virginia gives most of the limited production of ramps, a member of the lily family. With its elongated bulb and green leaves, it looks somewhat like its cousin the scallion and can be used interchangeably in most recipes.

RAPE

BACKGROUND

Rape (*Brassica campestris*), is another relative of cabbages and turnips. As *broccoli di rape*, it is very popular with Italian-Americans. The 6- to-9-inch-long stalk-bunches have dark green, chard-like leaves. Though rape has a slightly bitter flavor, it is not as bitter as collard or mustard greens.

Buying Tips

The best rape is harvested in winter, is young, has a rich color and looks fresh. There should be no leaves that have been wilted, yellowed, bruised, or gnawed by bugs.

PREPARATION

A broccolilike flower indicates maturity, but if you buy such rape, sauté those delicious morsels in olive oil with garlic or onions, and season to taste with basil, lemon juice, and perhaps tomato. To prepare the leaves for cooking, remove the roots and any tough stems and midribs, discard or trim damaged leaves, wash well in cold tap water. Steam or simmer the useable stems for about 20 minutes, adding the midribs and leaves during the last 7 to 10 minutes.

RASPBERRIES

BACKGROUND

Delicate and expensive, the *raspberry* comes in two varieties: *red* (*Rubus idaeus*) and *black* (*Rubus occidentalis*). The raspberry is a composite fruit, made up of numerous sweet, tart, juicy cells, each with a distressingly large seed.

(Each cell, in fact, is technically a drupe—a miniature plum or cherry.)

AVAILABILITY

Fresh raspberries are at their best in June and July.

Buying Tips

Choose raspberries that are clean, plump, fragrant (but not fermented), uncrushed, free of mold, and free of stem caps; if the stem caps cling, the berries are immature. All of the raspberry cells should have a red or black (depending on variety) coloration that gleams—when overripe, the surface sheen diminishes. Avoid any that have even one green cell, a sign of unripeness.

PREPARATION

Storage

Use within a day or two, as raspberries are highly perishable. They may be frozen in a freezing compartment for a couple of weeks, or in a 0° F freezer for several months, though they will lose much texture and flavor because they are so delicate. They are so fragile, in fact, that they are best stored in a single layer, never in a berry box as so often happens.

Preliminaries

Chill raspberries before gently rinsing them, so they will be less likely to be bruised and to absorb water. Do not rinse or expose them to moisture until ready to use, because water accelerates decay.

Serving

Serve raspberries with heavy cream or whipped cream. Citrus fruits and juices also harmonize well with raspberries. You can justify the monetary extravagance because raspberries are low in calories, high in Vitamin C, and incredibly delicious. They are also high in natural pectin, so they make excellent jam by themselves or as a conserve—though modern science has not yet devised a way to keep the seeds from getting stuck between your teeth.

RHUBARB

BACKGROUND

The 10-to-20-inch stalks of *Rheum rhaponticum* look like celery dipped in red ink. Two basic types are marketed: the pinkish "hothouse" and the deeper red "field" rhubarbs, the latter having a more pronounced flavor. Rhubarb is also referred to as *pieplant*, because it is most commonly stewed with sugar or honey and baked in pies, producing a sweet-tart flavor. Strawberry-rhubarb pie and jam are homespun classics.

AVAILABILITY

Rhubarb is at its best in late winter through late spring, peaking in May.

Buying Tips

Choose crisp, brightly hued stalks with (if attached) fresh green leaves. Reject outsized, mature, limp, wilted, or bent specimens. The stalks should be medium-thick, not skinny or overly broad. Young stalks are tenderer than mature ones.

PREPARATION

Storage

Store rhubarb in a bag in the refrigerator and use within a day or two.

Preliminaries

Never cook or eat rhubarb leaves; they contain enough oxalic acid to be toxic. Trim the stalks, and, if from a mature plant, peel them. Crosscut the rhubarb into ½-inch to 3-inch sections, depending on your recipe.

Cooking

Rhubarb pieces can be steamed, simmered, or stewed in about 20 to 35 minutes, depending on thickness.

RICE

BACKGROUND

The cereal grain *Oryza sativa* is the basic foodstuff in large parts of China, Japan, India, and Southeast Asia, and extremely significant in the world diet as a whole. We used the qualifying word "parts" because, contrary to widespread American opinion, wheat reigns as king in most of northern China and India. The reason is one of climate rather than any innate food preferences of different groups of people. Rice grows well in tropical and subtropical lands, while wheat grows best in temperate areas. People—wherever they live—adopt the most efficiently grown cereal grain into their culinary framework, passing down the taste preference from generation to generation as a cultural value.

Rice consumption in America is on the increase, mainly because of the growing influence here of Chinese cuisine. More and more Americans are using rice as a once-a-week alternative to the leading starch staples—bread, potatoes, and pasta. Rice also finds its way into the American kitchen in the form of breakfast cereals, rice pudding, rice noodles, chicken-rice soup, rice vinegar, rice wine, *saki*, and if you drink Kirin, as beer.

Varieties

Short-, Medium-, and Long-Grained Rice: Marketers classify rice, whether brown or white, by its grain length. *Long-grain rice* includes the flavorful *patna, bashmati*, and *Carolina* types—they are prized for their dry, fluffy texture and separate grains when cooked. *Short-grain rice* has a squat, oval shape and includes the delightful-tasting *Arborio* of Northern Italian fame and the *glutinous Japanese* variety, which is heralded for its thick, slightly moist, adhesive consistency. *Medium-length rice* can have the qualities of long- or short-grain rice, or be a compromise, depending on the particular variety.

Paddy vs. Hill Rice: Paddy rice is grown in the water. Hill rice is grown on dry land. Paddy rice easily wins the awards for flavor and texture.

Wild Rice: Though a cereal grain, this is not true rice (see WILD RICE entry). If you prepare a mixture of white rice and wild rice, remember that the latter ingredient requires about twice the cooking time. Either give it a head start in the pot or cook the two grains separately, then combine them.

AVAILABILITY

Brown and White Rice: When the inedible husk is removed from the rice kernel, you have *brown rice*, which includes the white starchy interior (the endosperm) as well as the nutritious brownish-yellow outer layer (the bran) and embryo (the germ). If the miller removes all or most of the bran and germ, he has a blander, less nutritious *white rice*. Why then does white rice significantly outsell the chewier, nutty-flavored brown rice? First, most diners prefer white rice because it lends an appealing color contrast to other foods. Second, cooks prefer white rice because it cooks in half the time. And white rice can be stored longer than brown rice, because it is less subject to rancidity. Nowadays, nutrition-conscious cooks can buy *converted white rice* which, while not the nutritional twin of brown rice, comes respectably close to being equal. Moreover, some of the better imported white rices such as *bashmati* have not been polished as much as some of our conventional domestic white rice, so it does retain more of its nutrients. Our recommendation, if rice plays a major role in your diet, is to choose brown rice. If rice is not one of your day-to-day main sources of nutrition, let flavor and your taste be your guide.

Converted Rice: Before polishing the bran off the rice, the miller partially cooks the brown rice in such a way that many of the vitamins and minerals (especially the thiamine, niacin, and iron) that lie in and just under the bran layer are infused deep into the kernel's core, the starchy endosperm. Once that mission is accomplished, the miller removes the bran and germ. Voila! he has converted white rice, which can usually be distinguished from ordinary white rice by its slight brownish tint. It also requires more cooking (about 3 to 5 minutes) than ordinary white rice.

Coated Rice: To improve the visual appeal of uncooked white rice, many millers used to coat the rice with talc and glucose. To rid the rice of this despicable coating, the cook had to rinse the rice and—regretably—wash away some of the rice's nutrients in the process. Today, virtually all rice is sold uncoated; if it is coated, the label must clearly state that fact and list the ingredients used.

Instant Rice: One of the worst of convenience foods is instant rice. Not only does it have a curious flavor and texture, it does not really save you that much work or, for that matter, time in relation to cooking normal rice.

Preseasoned Rice: Another deplorable rice product is preseasoned rice, the type that is sold with the dried flavoring agents incorporated inside the rice package. You can flavor your rice more creatively and with fresher, higher-quality flavorings by using your own; at the same time, you can cut the cost approximately in half and eliminate the additives.

Rice Flour: Rice that is finely ground becomes rice flour, an ingredient that is much used by Orientals to make elegantly textured baked goods including cakes and cookies, to thicken sauces, and to prepare puddings. Westerners who are allergic to wheat and certain other cereal-grain flours also use rice flour to good advantage.

PREPARATION

Storage

White rice is best stored in a tightly sealed canister in a cool, dry place—and, if stored in a clear glass jar, in a dark spot. So stored, it will stay in splendid condition for months, often longer. Because brown rice can easily become rancid or insect-infested, it should be kept refrigerated if you do not expect to use it within a month. If you do not have the refrigerator space to devote to rice storage, buy in quantities for short-term consumption. Also, buy from a clean store that has a high stock turnover.

Washing

Rice sold in packages on grocery shelves is quite clean and, for sake of maximum nutrient retention, should not be washed unless it has been coated (in which case you should not buy it in the first place). If you have bought the rice loose out of a store display sack or barrel, place the rice in a sieve, look for and discard pebbles and other foreign matter, then gently rinse the rice in the sieve with a stream of cold water.

Cooking

The cooking time and (if steam-simmering) the amount of water needed to cook rice depends on several factors: The longer the rice has been stored, the dryer it is and thus the more cooking time and liquid it will require. Generally, the shorter-grain varieties of rice take a little longer to cook. Brands of rice sometimes have individual styles, so follow the label's instructions the first time, then adjust the time or water upward or (usually) downward if needed. Brown rice takes twice as long to cook and 50 percent more water than does converted white rice—which takes a little longer to cook and a little more water than does plain white rice.

Steam-Simmering Plain White Rice: Numerous aunties around the world have the "one and only" perfect way to cook rice. Some of these methods produce good, most produce mediocre, results. We believe that the best method for preparing plain cooked rice is the Chinese steam-simmer technique.

First, it is practically essential to have a suitably large, heavy-bottomed pot or wok with a tight-fitting lid. If your pot has a thin bottom, the bottom layer of rice will likely cook into a scorched, hard-to-clean crust. If the lid does not fit snugly, the needed steam will escape. Unless you have the proper pot or an automatic electric rice cooker, we suggest you use the boiling method that we will describe later.

For each cup of rice, add more or less 1¾ cups water. The ideal water-and-rice level should reach slightly above the pot's one-third mark. This allows proper room for both grain expansion and steam. Some recipes call for adding of about ½ to ¾ teaspoon salt and, perhaps, a pat or two of butter. Oriental cooks and some Western cooks (including ourselves) prefer to steam-simmer the rice without salt or butter. Bring the water to a boil in the uncovered pot. Immediately give the rice a quick stir (excessive stirring may encourage stickiness), cover the pot, and reduce the heat to a very low setting. Let the rice gently steam-simmer for approximately 12 to 15 minutes. At no time during this cooking period should you lift the lid; if you do, the steam will escape, the water temperature will drop, and you are guaranteed less-than-superb rice. The rice should be cooked the moment the water has just been absorbed. This moment will vary, depending on the particular type of rice you are cooking, a variable you will have to learn through trial and error. Turn off the heat, lightly fluff the rice grains with a fork, cover the pot again, and let the rice rest for about 5 minutes before serving.

Boiling Plain White Rice: Slowly pour the rice into a pot of rapidly boiling water—at least six times as much water as rice. The water can be salted and/or buttered or oiled if you prefer that approach. Keep the water boiling in the uncovered pot for 15 to 20 minutes; test for doneness. When cooked, drain in a sieve or colander and serve.

Converted Rice: Follow the guidelines given above for plain rice, but you will probably have to add 3 to 5 minutes to the cooking time and, if steam-simmering, use about 2 cups of water per cup of rice.

Brown Rice: Follow the guidelines above for plain rice, but figure on 35 to 45 minutes' cooking time and, if steam-simmering, use about 3 cups of water per cup of rice.

Pilaf: Brown the white rice in a little oil in a broad, heavy-bottomed pan, then add boiling water or broth (about 1¾ cups of liquid per cup of rice) and other ingredients (such as meat, vegetables, and flavorings), then tightly cover and simmer until the rice has completely absorbed the liquid.

Fried Rice: Steam-simmer or boil the rice (without adding salt or butter) at least several hours ahead of time or, if possible, the previous day. Then refrigerate it until 30 minutes before you are ready to proceed with your recipe. The famous Chinese fried-rice dishes of Yangchow are basically ways to use leftover rice. Chinese-American recipes customarily call for fried rice well-colored with soy sauce. Authentic Chinese recipes usually suggest little or no soy sauce.

Toasting: Some cooks like to give their white rice a nuttier flavor by toasting the grains in a single layer in a shallow ungreased pan in a preheated 350° F oven for about 8 minutes. When it's toasted, proceed with the regular recipe or store the rice for future use.

Test for Doneness

Cool a few grains on a tasting spoon. Bite into the grains. If you can detect hardness in the grain cores, the rice is undercooked; cook it a little longer and test again. When each rice grain feels soft but gives a gentle resistance in its center, your rice is cooked. If the grains are soft throughout and offer no resistance to your bite, the rice is probably overcooked and will soon become a gummy mass.

Leftover Rice

Yesterday's steamed or boiled rice can be reheated directly from the refrigerator by placing it in a steamer for 5 to 10 minutes, depending on the quantity. Or it can be reheated in a pot in a 300° F oven for about 25 to 30 minutes. To keep it from drying out, you may have to sprinkle a little water on the rice before putting it in the oven. Or you can make fried rice. Leftover rice readily combines with other leftover foods such as chopped meat and vegetables. Also consider adding it to soups, omelets, pancake batter, stews, vinaigrette-dressed tomato slices or wedges, stuffings, croquettes and sauces. Or turn the rice into a cold salad—perhaps enriched with parsley, tuna, tomatoes and a vinegar-and-oil dressing—for a main luncheon course on a hot summer day.

Equivalents

About 1/3 to 1/2 cup of cooked rice should be an adequate serving for a typical American meal. For an Oriental-style meal, 1 cup or more may be in order. Depending on its type, 1 cup of raw rice will produce varying quantities of cooked rice. For plain white rice, the yield is about 3 cups. For converted white rice or brown rice, it is 3½ to 4 cups. For instant rice, it is about 2 cups. Of course, the method and length of cooking as well as the storage time of the rice will also influence the cooked yield.

Brown and, to a lesser extent, converted white rice, is a good source of high-quality protein and other nutrients when supplemented with meat, fish, or legumes. A "peasant's" diet heavy in highly polished non-converted white rice, however, can be and has been a cause of beriberi, an extremely severe disease of nutritional deficiency.

CLASSIC USES AND AFFINITIES

Well-known rice preparations include *paella, arroz con pollo, pilaf, risotto alla Milanese, riz à l'impératrice, chelo kebab, moros y cristianos*, dirty rice, jambalaya, Chinese fried rice, Spanish rice, *risi e bisi*, and, of course, rice pudding. The Dutch colonists in Indonesia created an entire grandiose meal around rice: *rijsttafel*, literally "rice table." Ingredients that can be added to white rice before or after it is cooked include color-contrasting foods such as minced or chopped parsley, carrots, celery, tomatoes, mushrooms, nuts, raisins, and freshly blended curry powder. Other flavor enhancers include sautéed minced onions, garlic, and ginger as well as grated parmesan cheese. When steam-simmering rice, you can substitute liquids such as broth or a fruit juice for part of the water. Rice is quite adaptable, so experiment boldly.

ROSE HIPS

BACKGROUND

One species of rose, the *dog rose* (*Rosa canina*), produces a bulbous fruit called a *rose hip*, which is an excellent source of Vitamin C. Rose hips can be dried and ground into a powder; that can be compressed into a tablet and sold as a Vitamin C supplement in health-food stores. Rose hips are also processed into a tonic tea and made into jellies and jams which are more popular in northern Europe than in America. The Scandinavians enjoy a cold soup made from rose hips, honey, and sour cream.

ROSEMARY

BACKGROUND

Rosemary (*Rosemarinis officinalis*) is a native of the Mediterranean area. Its leaves are dark green on top, silver below, and pine-needle-shaped. According to herbal lore, rosemary promotes memory—whether studying for exams or commemorating the dead. This herb also symbolizes fidelity. Herbal medicine claims that rosemary cures trembling, female complaints, and nervous headaches. If the nervous head belongs to a brunette, it is true that rosemary tea or rosemary oil will condition the hair and bring out its highlights. (See HERBS AND SPICES for information on buying, storing, cooking, etc.)

PREPARATION

The leaves of dried rosemary can be sharp and very hard; if so, chop them fine with a knife before using. If a whole sprig of rosemary is used in a long-cooked dish such as a stew or soup, let the rosemary simmer for about 15 minutes to develop its flavor, then remove the sprig before serving.

CLASSIC USES AND AFFINITIES

Rosemary has an affinity with thyme. It is traditional in Italy with lamb, fennel, and suckling pig; many other cultures use rosemary with meats such as lamb, veal, chicken and pork. Whole branches of rosemary can be strewn on coals for barbecuing to perfume the meat. A sprig of rosemary, or chopped or powdered rosemary leaves, can be used in stews, soups, and stock for cooking fish. Fruit salad, oranges, and rhubarb can benefit from a discreet touch of rosemary.

ROSE PETALS AND WATER

BACKGROUND

Various species of roses have highly perfumed petals. Since aroma and flavor are intimately related, it is not surprising that roses have been used for millennia to flavor foods and drinks. Wine with *rose petals* steeped in it was a popular drink in ancient Rome; rose liqueurs are made today in Europe and the Orient. Rose petals crystallized in sugar are used as decorations. Rose-petal jam is a popular sweet in many parts of the world. *Rose water* is a significant flavoring for desserts, pastries, and some main dishes in India and the Middle East. Rose water is made by steeping water with fresh rose petals or by spiking water with essential oil of the rose.

RUE

BACKGROUND

Prescientific medicine attributed almost a hundred healing virtues to *rue* (*Ruta graveolens*) and the flints of early guns were boiled with this herb to make the guns supernaturally accurate. Shakespeare described rue as "the bitter herb of grace"; grace is a matter of opinion, but rue leaves are very bitter and some people are allergic to the herb. Used cautiously, rue leaves stimulate the appetite, flavor cream cheese, go into salads or tea sandwiches, season broiled chicken or lamb, or complement baked potatoes. Grappa, the crude Italian brandy, is sometimes sold with a few rue leaves steeped in it.

RUTABAGA

BACKGROUND

There are few vegetables less glamorous than *rutabaga* (like rape, it is botanically *Brassica campestris*), an edible root which looks like a pale yellow cannonball, 3 to 5 inches in diameter. Sometimes called *swede*, *Swedish turnip*, or *Russian turnip*, the rutabaga is not strictly a turnip, although it closely resembles one and can culinarily be treated as one.

AVAILABILITY

Rutabagas are available fresh all year round, with a long peak season lasting through the fall and winter.

Buying Tips

Buy smooth-skinned, uncracked rutabagas that are heavy for their size. (If the rutabagas look unnaturally bright, they may be waxed—that is sometimes done to prolong their storage life.)

PREPARATION

Storage

If not immediately used, rutabagas should be refrigerated or kept in a cool, semimoist place. They should remain in good condition for a week in the refrigerator, or for a month or so in a cool cellar.

Cooking

Rutabagas are cooked, usually steamed or boiled. First wash them well, and peel if waxed. Boiling and steaming take approximately the same length of time; steaming preserves more nutrients. Allow 30 to 40 minutes for either cooking method, depending on the rutabaga's size. (If quartered, estimate 20 to 25 minutes.)

Serving

After cooking, they can be cut or sliced or served pureed. Rutabagas go well with full-flavored meat, but may eclipse the flavor of mild-mannered flesh such as chicken or pork.

Equivalents

One medium-sized rutabaga should give you four or five servings.

S

SAFFRON

BACKGROUND

The *saffron* crocus, *Crocus sativus*, is a small blue or lavender flower with three stigmas (female organs). Seventy-five thousand crocuses, more or less, must be picked by hand and the stigmas removed by hand to produce one pound of saffron, the world's most expensive spice. (Fortunately, a little saffron goes a long way.) The twentieth-century price is so high that saffron is used mainly for cooking, but saffron was once a popular dye for anything from the hair of classical Roman ladies of easy virtue to the pristine robes of Buddhist monks. Saffron was a very popular spice in England during the Renaissance. Today, it is used mostly in the Mediterranean area and in the Middle East and India. Saffron quality varies regionally. The best saffron comes from trans-India around Kashmir. Saffron from Spain can be good. Mexican saffron is usually not a true saffron and is inferior. (See HERBS AND SPICES for information on buying, storing, cooking, etc.)

PREPARATION

The whole stigmas (avoid ground saffron, which is easier to adulterate and goes stale faster) should be gently crushed in a mortar or between your fingers just before using. Steep the spice in a little bit of hot liquid before adding it to the other ingredients. Saffron becomes bitter if cooked at too high a heat.

Substitutions

Some cookbooks assert turmeric can be substituted successfully for saffron. While turmeric will color food yellow, it will not give your dish the heavenly saffron flavor and fragrance—and, if too much turmeric is used, it may even leave your palate with a hellish, pungent aftertaste.

CLASSIC USES AND AFFINITIES

Authentic Spanish *arroz con pollo* and *paella* require saffron. So does a real *bouillabaisse* (though true *bouillabaisse* also requires *racasse*, a fish so far unavailable at the A&P, so the purist's version of a *bouillabaisse* is unlikely to be confected in the United States). The Italian *risotto milanese* has a delicate tinge of saffron. Sweet breads made with saffron are traditional in Cornwall and in the Scandinavian countries.

SAGE

BACKGROUND

Sage is an herb native to the Mediterranean, where it continues to grow wild in profusion. Dudes who come across the sagebrush of the American West are advised to avoid confusing this plant with cooking sage. Herbal medicine ascribed so many virtues to sage that it was believed to confer immortality. This hypothesis, so easily tested, proved to be false. Nonetheless, the fresh or dried leaves of *Salvia officinalis* are minty and pungent and have many uses in cooking. They must be added at the end of cooking, and must not be subjected to very high temperatures, or a taste of camphor will predominate. (See HERBS AND SPICES for information on buying, storing, cooking, etc.)

CLASSIC USES AND AFFINITIES

Sage combines well with fatty meats such as roast pork and sausage. It is often used in bread stuffings for chicken, turkey, goose, and other birds. The pungent flavor of sage can stand up to the strength of rosemary and thyme; it also combines well with gentle parsley. Homemade and factory cheeses sometimes contain sage. Beans can be enhanced with a little sage. This herb is one of the most popular in the Anglo-American kitchen; it is also used with great enthusiasm in Italy in such dishes as calves' liver with onions and *saltimbocca* (pounded veal scallops with sage leaves, ham, and cheese).

SALSIFY

BACKGROUND

Salsify (*Tragopogon porrifolius*) is a member of the daisy family. This root vegetable looks like a gnarled old carrot with a thick taproot. Salsify can grow up to 10 inches long and 2 inches in diameter. Many people think the cooked flesh has a taste and texture similar to oysters—it is popular in England as *oyster plant*. We don't taste the resemblance, though we do appreciate the subtlety of the salsify's flavor. Usually the skin is grayish-cream, with juicy, white flesh, but there is a black-skinned salsify, and a golden-skinned one, though we rarely see these types in the United States.

Buying Tips

The smaller specimens, unwithered, heavy for their size, unscarred, and firm, will be the best choices to buy. Salsify will keep for a week or so in the refrigerator.

PREPARATION

To cook, first scrub it well. Cook it unpeeled and whole, or peel and cut into cubes or slices, as you prefer. If cut and not cooked immediately, immerse the pieces in acidulated water to retard darkening of the flesh by oxidation. Boil or steam whole small-to-medium-salsify (steaming preserves more nutrients) for 10 to 15 minutes, then peel and serve. Salsify can also be pureed, sautéed, fried, or braised in butter. A good cream sauce complements the delicate flavor.

SALT

BACKGROUND

Common *salt*, or *sodium chloride*, is the most fundamental of seasonings. The human body requires salt to regulate the balance of fluids. In hot weather, enough sweat is produced to endanger this balance; therefore, hot climates often favor salty cuisines, and salt pills are sometimes recommended for those who must work hard in the heat. Salt helps preserve foods. It also seems to blend and point up food flavors; saltless bread tastes flat, most grain foods and vegetables seem to require it to bring out their full flavor. Very salty foods induce thirst—which explains why salty snack foods such as peanuts and pretzels are provided "gratuitously" by your local bartender.

Varieties

Almost all commercially sold salt comes from one of two sources: salt mines and directly from the sea.

Salt mines contain the solid sodium chloride residue of extinct ancient seas. This is the type of salt you are apt to find in the cylindrical cardboard containers that line supermarket shelves.

Sea salt is more costly because it must be extracted by evaporating the water of extant seas. Sea salt is superior to mined salt in terms of flavor, but remember, some sea salts are better than others. For instance, most connoisseurs readily agree that Malden salt from the east coast of England is finer tasting than the common but good French sea salt from the Mediterranean.

Kosher salt is coarsely crushed so that it can aid Orthodox Jews in preparing meat at home according to strict religious laws. It is also used by savvy gentile gourmet cooks who appreciate its jagged edges that enable it to cling better to food.

Rock salt is salt in larger chunks, the type we put into ice-cream makers and use as a platform to cook oysters Rockefeller. Such salt is edible, but it contains more (though safe) impurities than does standard salt.

Seasoned salts are flavored with ingredients such as onion, garlic, and celery, and many are infused with MSG. Most of the commercially produced seasoned salts are mediocre at best.

Salt and Health

Our body needs salt for normal functions including to help it maintain an acid-alkaline balance. Most Americans, however, probably consume too much salt for their bodies own good. Generally speaking, the more vegetables and grains in a person's diet, the more salt is required. Meat-eaters get much of their salt from the flesh they eat. Salt encourages the body to retain fluid, so if you abnormally cut down on your salt intake, you will lose a pound or two of water, but not, weight watchers be advised, fat. A low-sodium diet is desirable, however, for people with high blood pressure.

Salt substitutes have recently become major grocery store items. Either they contain no salt or they contain salt that has been diluted by about 50 percent with ingredients such as potassium chloride and dextrose. Educated palates will easily detect their curious medicinal flavor. A more sensible alternative is to reduce by half (or whatever) one's consumption of standard salt (rather than replacing it with an equal volume of substitute salt), while at the same time getting to know how to use flavorings such as herbs, spices, lemon juice, and vinegar more effectively.

Most commercial salts contain added *iodine* (look for the word on the label). While this element helps prevent goiter, most people (especially those that live in coastal areas and eat seafood) get a sufficient amount of iodine from the other ingredients they consume. For these people, plain salt is fine.

PREPARATION

Storage

Most table salts contain anti-caking additives. If you buy salt without those additives, or if your home is too damp for even "free-running" salt, keep a dozen or so grains of rice in the salt shaker. Your salt will run freely because the rice absorbs atmospheric moisture and, when you shake the container, the rice hits the salt, breaking up any cakes. Salt, of course, should never be stored in the refrigerator, which is too humid. In your cupboard, properly stored salt—sealed in glass or plastic in humid climates—will last almost indefinitely.

Cooking Tips

When following a printed recipe, keep in mind that the quantity of salt recommended is almost always based upon the strength of common supermarket table salt. If you are using coarse sea or Kosher salt, use a greater volume relative to its coarseness. To illustrate, you will need about 2½ teaspoons of the average Kosher salt to substitute for 1 teaspoon of the average table salt.

"Salt to taste" is a favorite cookbook phrase. Though such instructions are frustrating for novice cooks, the authors have reason for their vagueness: different people like different amounts of salt; what is too salty for one will be too bland for another. One's perception of the taste of salt is partly inherited and partly learned. For this reason, it is egotistical and unscientific for a chef to feel insulted if someone salts the food at the table. What is an affront is for a diner to salt the food before sampling it. If you are cooking a dish that will be served cold, remember that the intensity of the salt increases as the dish cools, so make your "salt to taste" test accordingly.

Salt is added to boiling pots of water not only to flavor the cooking foods, but also to increase the liquid's temperature by a degree or two.

When not sure how much salt to add, be conservative in your estimate; you can always add more but cannot easily subtract your miscalculated quantity. One way to rectify a too-salty liquid preparation such as a soup is to add saltless ingredients such as water, pasta, or vegetables. If you do not want to dilute or permanently add more ingredients, place a peeled quartered potato in the pot, simmer for about five minutes, then remove the salt-infused potato pieces and save them for another dish.

Salt changes the chemistry of food, creating an atmosphere unfavorable to the growth of bacteria; so salting and brining are millennia-old methods of preserving food. However, since most table salts cloud the brine, many cooks use kosher salt for preserving.

Placing a salt mill filled with coarse sea salt on the dining table is a nice touch, but realize that the flavor difference between fresh-ground and preground sea salt is much less than the difference between fresh-ground and preground pepper.

SALT PORK

BACKGROUND

White bacon and *side meat*, as *salt pork* is also called, is made from the layer of fat that lies along the belly of the pig. This is the same slab from which the meat packer cuts the fat-and-lean piece for making bacon. It becomes salt pork when it has been cured with salt. Unlike bacon, it is not smoked. Salt pork—because it is cut from the ends rather than from the middle of the pork belly (or side pork) slab—has less streaking (lines of lean meat) than bacon; some has no streaks at all. Salt pork should not be confused with fatback which comes from the top rather than the bottom of the swine's torso and which is not usually salted.

Buying Tips

Some producers use more salt in their salt pork than others. Since the amount of salt used cannot be judged by eye, it is a good idea to know and stick with one firm's product.

Storage

Tightly wrapped salt pork will keep in the refrigerator for about 4 to 6 weeks before it starts to become rancid. It does not freeze well, principally because of its high salt content.

Cooking

Salt pork's culinary missions are many. Its major role is to season slow-cooked stews, soups, and vegetable dishes such as Boston baked beans and pot liquor. Most salt pork is too salty for some dishes, so blanching may be in order.

SANTA CLAUS MELON

BACKGROUND

At first glance, one may think this 6-to-9-pound football-shaped *Santa Claus* (or *Christmas*) *melon* is a small watermelon. Appearances can be misleading—in color and flavor, its flesh is reminiscent of a honeydew.

AVAILABILITY

December is the peak season for the melon, hence its two names. In some areas of the country you can find it several months earlier, but those specimens will not be as juicy, fragrant and sweet.

Buying Tips

As the melon matures and ripens, some of the lengthwise bands of its thick green rind begin to develop a golden hue. Another test for ripeness is the blossom end: it slightly yields to gentle pressure. A good Santa Claus melon will be heavy for its size, an indication of maximum moisture content. Avoid those melons with soft spots (a sign of decay) and those with shriveled, moldy, bruised, or otherwise injured skins.

PREPARATION

You can generally prepare a Santa Claus melon as you would a HONEYDEW (see that entry).

SAPODILLA

BACKGROUND

The *sapodilla* tree grows in the West Indies and Central America and in southern Florida. It produces a resin that is tapped to get chicle which is used to make chewing gum. It also bears a fruit called the sapodilla or *sapodilla plum*, which is rough of rind, brownish of color, and about the size of a pomegranate. The sweet, usually yellowish-beige flesh of the sapodilla can be eaten alone, with other fruits, or blended to make sweet custards and ice creams. The sapodilla is hardy enough to be shipped and therefore can sporadically be found in big-city "gourmet" fruit markets.

SASSAFRAS

BACKGROUND

A tree native to the eastern United States, *Sassafras albidum*, produces several products for use in cooking. The root is used for flavoring root beer, and can be brewed for tea. Young sassafras leaves can be eaten in salad. Older leaves can be brewed for tea; but sassafras tea should be consumed in moderation, because it contains saffrole, a potentially toxic substance. The major culinary use of sassafras is FILÉ POWDER.

SAUCES AND CONDIMENTS, COMMERCIAL

BACKGROUND

Supermarket shelves are lined with numerous cooking and tabletop sauces and condiments that realistically fall under the "convenience food" classification. Some—such as mayonnaise—can be prepared (and made better) by the home cook, while others, such as Angostura Bitters or soy sauce, are clearly beyond the resources of home kitchens.

Varieties

Ketchup and Its Relatives: *Ketchup* (or *catsup*) is our country's second-best-selling sauce and a near-essential for hamburgers and french-fried potatoes in America. It derives its name from Malay *kechap* and Chinese *ke-tsiap*, names for a pickled fish brine. In our country, ketchup is almost always made with tomatoes, though walnut, mushroom, and even banana ketchups are available in specialty stores and ethnic markets. Recipes vary by manufacturer, but the principal secondary ingredients usually are vinegar, sugar, onions, salt, and spices in various proportions.

Chili sauce is a gently spiced-up variation of ketchup. Some of its flavoring ingredients (such as onions, garlic, and peppers) are different, or are used in greater quantity than those found in the mild ketchup.

Barbecue sauces vary widely according to proprietary formulas. A typical bottle probably contains tomatoes, vinegar, sugar, onions, garlic, salt, and a blend of herbs and spices. If you use a sugar laden brand, as most are, do not brush the sauce on your barbecuing meat until the last 20 minutes or so of cooking or the sauce may become bitter.

Steak sauces: *Worcestershire, A.1, Robert's,* and *Albert's* sauces are four of the better-known dark-brown steak sauces, though they can be used to give a piquant lift to homemade sauces, stocks, soups, and stews. The soy-based *Worcestershire sauce* is imbued with vinegar, anchovies, tamarinds, molasses, red onions, shallots, garlic, chili peppers, cloves, and other full flavored ingredients. The basic recipe was conceived in Old India by an Englishman who brought it to Worcestershire, England; the rest is history. *A.1 Sauce* is prepared from tomatoes, vinegar, corn syrup, raisins, oranges, garlic, etc. In *Albert's*, horseradish predominates. *Robert's* sauce should (but does not always) have mustard as its distinguishing ingredient.

Ethnic sauces: Ethnic sauces used widely in America are often of the fruit-based sweet-and-sour persuasion. *Chutney*, the table condiment that is ordinarily *de rigueur* in this country for curry dishes, is usually made from fruits on the order of mangoes, tamarinds, and raisins that have been pepped up with vinegar, sugar, onions, herbs and spices. *Plum* (or *duck*) *sauce* is the condiment you find alongside the mustard in most Chinese-American restaurants; nowadays, the commercial product is often made with ingredients other than plum (apricot, for example) even though the label reads "plum sauce." Another popular Chinese condiment is the thick, soybean-based *hoisin* (or *Peking*) *sauce* enriched with garlic and spices including a bit of chili. *Oyster sauce* is still another.

Soy sauce is the thin, dark brown, salty flavoring agent basic to most Oriental cooking. It is made from lightly fermented soy beans, and varies in its characteristics according to manufacturer or origin. American-made soy sauces tend to be slightly sweet and do not have the full flavor of the Japanese imports. Chinese soy sauces tend to be even stronger than the Japanese, and are therefore usually better suited to the kitchen than the dining room.

Mayonnaise and Its Relatives: *Mayonnaise* is America's best-selling sauce. It is basically an emulsion of egg yolks and vegetable oil that has been given a tart edge by the inclusion of lemon juice or vinegar and pleasantly perked by a light touch of spices. Manufacturers sometimes use sweeteners and emulsifiers, other than egg yolk as well. You can make mayonnaise at home with an electric blender—or a strong arm, a pliable whisk, and a large bowl, preferably copper. Though the homemade variety is vastly superior to the store-bought mayonnaise, most home cooks prefer the latter because it is more convenient and keeps longer in the refrigerator: a month or two vs. a day or two.

Mayonnaise-type sauces are variations on the mayonnaise theme. There is no official recipe for these sauces, but here are brief tips on how you can concoct your mayonnaise into the mayonnaise variations. For *green* (or *verte*) *sauce*, add minced fresh herbs such as parsley or chives. For *Green Goddess* dressing, add tarragon vinegar, fresh herbs, scallions, and anchovies. For *Thousand Island* dressing, add chili sauce (which gives the mixture its characteristic pinkish hue) along with color-contrasting minced ingredients such as olives, capers, pickles, red peppers and chives. Modern *Russian dressing* is the same as Thousand Island, though originally it contained caviar. *Tartar* dressing is somewhat like Thousand Island except it contains no chili sauce and is spiked with more pickled ingredients and might contain chopped egg yolks. *Gribiche* is also similar but must contain chopped egg yolks. Sometimes one particular seasoning is characteristic of a mayonnaise-type sauce; for instance, garlic in *aioli sauce*. You can mix most flavoring agents in your larder to make a special mayonnaise—for example, a mustard mayonnaise. If the ingredients you choose have sufficient texture, you can concoct what is sold as *sandwich spread*. And, with daring, you can evolve your own *specialité de la maison*, unique in all the world—just take stock of your larder and experiment.

The white emulsified product you see on grocers' shelves labeled *Salad Dressing* is another mayonnaise-type sauce, but this version is cooked rather than raw, can freely use emulsifiers other than egg yolks, tends to be sweeter, and is genuinely inferior in taste to genuine mayonnaise.

Oil-and-Vinegar Dressings: Seasoned oil-and-vinegar based dressings for salads abound in American supermarkets under names such as *vinaigrette* or *french dressing* or *italian dressing*. If a major flavoring ingredient is added, they bear labels such as *roquefort* or *blue cheese* dressing. Whatever the type, we do not recommend either the pre-mixed bottle or dehydrated package types, as homemade oil-and-vinegar dressings prepared with fresh ingredients are so easy to concoct when you need them. Moreover, you can use fine oil and vinegar (those used for the pre-mixed bottle brands are mediocre at best); this does make a big difference.

Chili-Pepper Sauces: *Tabasco Sauce*, from New Iberia, Louisiana, and its competitors such as *Red Hot* and the Jamaican *Pickapper* are made from pureed red hot chilies blended with vinegar and "secret" other ingredients. There is nothing wrong with these instant chili sauces, so long as the cook does not automatically reach for the bottle when alternatives such as fresh chili peppers are available.

Spaghetti Sauce: Spaghetti sauces come in cans and jars and are usually tomato-based and made of flavorful and aromatic ingredients such as herbs, spices, onions, garlic, mushrooms, chili peppers, sweet peppers, vinegar or lemon juice, wine and oil. Spaghetti sauces can be *meatless* or not. The *clam sauces* come in two basic forms: *red* (with tomato) and *white* (without). The best spaghetti sauces are homemade. If you have to use one of the commercial sauces, do lift its flavor a little by adding some fresh ingredients, such as herbs in season, lemon juice, wine, and sautéed onions.

Gravy: *Gravy* is commercially available canned or dehydrated. These products offer little incentive to the conscientious home cook. Of better, though still far from perfect, quality are the frozen sauces now being marketed in gourmet food outlets. *Gravy browning agents* are of limited interest. The commercial products are usually used to give gravies, sauces, soups, and stews a deeper brown hue—and, sometimes, a flavor smacking of additives.

Buying Tips

For maximum flavor and fragrance, these sauces must be fresh—too many over-the-hill bottles such as Tabasco Sauce sit on kitchen shelves. When the liquid starts to develop a brown tinge and lose its bright hue, throw out the old bottle and buy a new one. Some products are dated to tell the grocery clerk—and you, if it's not coded—the suggested final date of sale. Look for those dates, as two bottles of the same sauce on the same shelf may have been manufactured weeks or months apart. If you cannot decipher the dating code, ask.

Storage

Once opened, sauces and condiments such as mayonnaise must obviously be stored in the refrigerator. When in doubt, look at the label. Under normal conditions, condiments such as ketchup need not be refrigerated for a short time, but unless you have the turnover of a coffeeshop, your ketchup will stay fresh longer in the refrigerator. If you go through your sauces such as Worcestershire and Tabasco at a snail's pace, refrigerate them, also. Except for the sauces sold frozen commercially, sauces rarely freeze well, because freezing tends to cause them to separate.

SAUSAGES

BACKGROUND

One definition of a sausage goes like this: chopped or ground meat mixed with seasonings and preservatives and typically stuffed into casings. For starters it is adequate, but the world of sausages is more complicated than that. And it is partly that complexity that makes sausage-eating such a rewarding experience.

Sausage-making is an age-old technique that arose from two necessities: to economize and preserve. Putting into practice the "waste not, want not" principle, ancient men discovered that the post-slaughter trimmings of the animal (usually a hog) could be made even more palatable if not outright delectable by converting the trimmings into sausage meat. By adding preservatives such as salt (the words *salt* and *sausage* both derive from *sal*, Latin for "salt") and certain spices. Smoking and air-drying helped, too. Our distant ancestors could safely store the previously perishable meat for future use, a procedure that was of particular importance in the days before refrigeration.

Today nearly every land has its distinct sausage or, sometimes, pantheon of sausages. Taking a globe-trotting culinary tour, we could, for instance, enjoy the famous

chorizo of Mexico and Spain,
drischeen of Ireland,
andouille of France,
bratwurst of Germany,
kielbasa of Poland,
párky of Czechoslovakia,
mortadella of Italy,
biltong of South Africa,
lop chong of China, and
longaniza of the Philippines.

Not only does our own country have its unique sausages, it also consumes a greater array of sausage than any other nation, thanks to the immigrants who brought their recipes and ingrained preferences. Perhaps, therefore, America can justifiably be thought of as the sausage capital of the world. In terms of variety, it is. In terms of overall quality, it is not, as most American-made sausages are on the bland side. A knowledgeable shopper, however, can find and enjoy great sausages.

Sausages are often a subject of heated debate among food nutritionists because of their fat and their additives. The fat is deplored because it makes up a large percentage of the sausage's weight, is high in calories, and is a saturated fat. The additives cause alarm principally because saltpeter (sodium nitrate and nitrite) is thought by many medical researchers to be carcinogenic. However, if sausage is consumed in reasonable quantity, and if you stay away from the sausages that are heavily doused with chemical salts, there seems to be no overpowering reason why properly cooked sausage cannot be part of your diet—unless for health's sake you must carefully watch your intake of saturated fat, sodium, or calories.

Classifications

To be an astute sausage buyer, it helps to know the major ways in which any given sausage may be classified. Regrettably, no simple system exists. We cannot place each sausage into one of several convenient categories (as some books do) because too many sausages could be logically placed in more than one. Here, then, are a dozen-plus workable ways to classify available sausages.

By Primary Ingredient: Most sausages are made with pork alone or combined with beef, veal or both. There are also sausages made with only beef or veal, as well as with lamb, mutton, chicken, turkey, venison, bear, horsemeat, and variety meats in general, to name some possibilities. Currently a new type is appearing in stores across the country—various imitation sausages made with textured vegetable protein rather than meat. They're nutritious, but the flavor and texture leave much to be desired.

By Secondary Ingredient: Some sausages are pure meat save for their seasonings and preservatives. Others have been extended with less costly ingredients (called *fillers*) such as dry milk solids, cereal, soybean flour, and even water (see the Frankfurter description below).

By Flavorings: As a general rule, the more a particular type of sausage is made for the American mass market, the blander it tends to be. Thus, one processor's *kielbasa* (for instance) may vary greatly in flavor strength from a competitor's. Full flavored sausages can be best found in America's many ethnic markets. Labels usually simply list the collective word "spices" for whatever herbs and spices have been used; one reason the processor does not give you a listing is that the formula is usually a jealously guarded secret. For a list of some of the common sausage flavorings, see the Making Sausages at Home section below.

By Additives: Besides flavorings and fillers, processors also use a variety of other additives for specific purposes: these include preservatives (antibacterial agents, mold inhibitors, botulism killers such as sodium nitrate and nitrite, etc.) as well as emulsifiers and thickeners (such as eggs and gelatin) and coloring agents. Some processors use these additives minimally while others overdose their products with them so much that doctors and nutritionists are waving red warning flags, and the sausages unappetizingly smack of chemicals.

By Shape: "Link" is the most common shape—such a sausage can be sold individually, in pairs (a Central European custom), or in lengthy chains. The links are sometimes curved into circular or horseshoe-shaped loops—or, if they are long and soft enough, coiled into flat spirals. A thin, stiff link such as the rectangular *landjager* is often called a *sausage stick*. A thick, cylindrical tubelike link is sometimes referred to as a sausage roll, which is normally sliced into disks, usually 1/16 to 1/2 inch thick. A *loaf-shaped* sausage is exactly that; it may be purchased whole or sliced, the latter being ideally suited to square American bread. Still other sausage meat is sold in *bulk* that the cook typically molds into serving-sized patties or balls.

By Curing: Sausages are cured (usually salt-cured) primarily to extend their storage life. Sausages made for short-term storage such as *bratwurst* are seldom cured, but those made for long-term storage such as salami are often cured. However, there is nothing to keep a processor from not curing his sausage if he does not wish to, as he has other preserving techniques at his disposal. And even when he does cure his sausage, the outcome can vary from mild- to well-cured.

By Smoking: Fresh sausages are seldom smoked (*Mettwurst* is an exception), while cured sausages such as *cervelat* are often smoked. Nowadays, the chief reason for smoking is to add character to the taste and smell of the sausage. Smoking also helps preserve the sausage, though the contribution is minimal. In the old days, smoking also helped keep away insects during the initial time the sausage was being dried. The smoke flavor and fragrance can vary from mild to strong, depending on the processor's wishes. The more the processor smokes his sausage, the darker, firmer, and fuller-flavored it will become. (By smoking we mean natural smoke, not liquid smoke, which is used in some substandard products.)

By Dryness: A number of sausages such as *cervelats* and salamis are dried—in the air, in smoke, or both—to extend their storage life by removing much of their moisture, a medium that fosters bacterial decay. With today's refrigeration, drying is not as necessary as it was a few generations ago. That need used to be vital in warm climates, which largely explains the phenomenon that the farther south you travel in Europe, the drier the sausages tend to be. Contemporary processors continue to make dry sausages in the Mediterranean mainly in response to long-held cultural preferences, not because of an overwhelming shortage of refrigeration. Another name for *dry sausage* is *summer sausage*, because it was almost the only type available during the summer in Rome, Lyon, and other sun-drenched areas. Dry sausages cover a spectrum from semi-dry to hard-dry, the latter being aged from 1 to 6 months, which makes them drier and firmer, and gives them a more concentrated flavor than if they were dried for only a few days or weeks. Dry sausages have usually been cured or smoked, but not always cooked. An uncooked dried sausage should be safe to eat if it is in good condition. By and large, dry sausages have more and stronger seasonings than moist ones.

By Precooking: Sausages can be *uncooked*, *partially cooked* or *fully cooked*. The last type is also known by such names as *ready to eat* and can be eaten without further cooking, but the flavor of some—such as the frankfurter—is markedly improved if heated. Partially cooked sausages generally have been heated enough to kill any trichinae but not enough to give the sausage the developed flavor it deserves. Some uncooked sausages such as salami may be eaten without further cooking because any possible trichinae and harmful bacteria would have been killed during the curing, smoking, and/or drying. Other uncooked sausages such as fresh *bratwurst* must positively be cooked before eating.

By Texture: The phrase *country sausage* usually indicates that the grind of the meat is coarse rather than fine. Texture has also to do with softness versus hardness—*mettwurst* and *landjager* are graphic examples of the respective qualities.

By Manufacturer: The very best sausages are often homemade (or farm-made) variety shaped by adept, experienced hands. The quality of factory-produced sausages can be excellent but it often seems that as processing plants grow larger, quality declines.

By Origin: With exceptions, imported sausages are far superior to our domestic products. Unfortunately, you cannot sample some foreign sausages such as the true frankfurter of Frankfurt, Germany, here in America, because the United States prohibits their importation. If you eat a frank in Germany, you may fall in love with it and vow never to taste the lackluster all-American hot dog again. Moreover, some of the foreign-made sausages that come into our country are not identical to the product consumed abroad because of federal health requirements. Some of these are absurd. For instance, the true *mortadella* of Italy is perfectly safe to import and eat, but it does not satisfy the U.S. law that imported pork must be prepared in a certain way to guarantee the destruction of possible trichinae. For the record, our trichinosis parasite is unknown in Italian pigs. The sad truth is we are burdened with eating the American-made mortadella which is a transmogrification of the authentic Italian product. An interesting sidelight of geographic origins are the many sausages named for their real or imagined birthplaces: the Genoa salami, bologna from Bologna, Italy, the frankfurter, lebanon (Pennsylvania) bologna, and *berliner*, to name a few.

Varieties

The facts given below are for sausages typical within their respective categories. It is always possible, for instance, that a sausage-maker will break custom by not precooking a particular type of sausage that is traditionally marketed cooked. If in doubt, check the label or ask your butcher. If still in doubt, treat the sausage as uncooked.

Andouille: Intestines are seasoned, stuffed into a casing (itself an intestine), then simmered and sold ready to eat as *andouille*. This 2-to-3-inch-thick, highly acclaimed French specialty is sliced and served cold or browned in butter. The petite version called *andouillettes* can also be grilled whole.

Bangers: A general term for a number of different English-made sausages.

Bauernwurst: At first glance, Germany's "farmer sausage" may remind you of the American frankfurter, but it has a slightly coarser texture, is more strongly seasoned and smoked, and is better tasting. Usually they are sold raw; less often, they are precooked.

Blood Sausages: The various *blood sausages* of America, *Blutwursts* of Germany, *boudin noirs* of France, *blood puddings* of England, *drischeens* of Ireland, and *morcillas* of Spain all have at least one ingredient in common: pork blood is used to give the sausage added flavor, nutritional value, visual appeal, and firmness (blood is a natural thickener when cooked). Besides the blood, the sausages contain ground or chopped pork meat, usually diced or cubed pork fat, and in some varieties, such as *Zungenwurst*, pieces of pork tongue. Most blood sausages are ready to eat. The gelatinized varieties are best served sliced and at room temperature; most other types improve by heating (if precooked as most are) or cooking.

Bockwurst: Traditionally sold and eaten during the springtime bock beer festival (hence its name) in Germany. Typically made with finely ground veal and some pork blended with eggs, milk, parsley, and chives, the last two ingredients giving the delicately flavored white flesh its characteristic green specks. Except for a few precooked types, the *Bockwurst* is very perishable and must be thoroughly cooked prior to eating. Serve hot.

Bologna (or *Baloney*): This popular American sandwich sausage was named after the Emilia-Romagna capital, a fact that rankles citizens of that proud sausage-making Italian city. The typical ready-to-eat American bologna is smoked quickly (if at all), and made without distinction from finely ground pork and beef with—save for the possible addition of garlic—mild seasonings.

Most of it is marketed in round or squared links or loaves, sometimes whole, more often presliced. Among the numerous variations of American bologna are *Lebanon bologna* (see below), *chub bologna* (bacon added), *ham bologna* or *Schinkenwurst* (ham chunks embedded in the bologna mixture) and *kosher bologna* (all beef and garlic-laden; see Kosher sub-section below). In addition, you can buy bologna made solely or principally with chicken or turkey. While bologna is usually served at room temperature, it can be successfully heated and served hot. Down South, it is often pan-fried.

Bratwurst: The name of this celebrated German sausage means "frying (or roasting) sausage," though you can also simmer or grill it. This plump, medium-sized link sausage is made with pork (sometimes with veal added), with seasonings such as sage, caraway, and lemon juice. Depending on the maker, the *bratwurst* can be of coarse or fine grain and sold raw or cooked (coarse and raw prevails).

Cervelat: A *cervelat*—which is also called *summer sausage* in various languages—is typically made of cured pork, beef, or both, blended with herbs and spices, then stuffed into a medium or medium-large casing, air-dried, and smoked. Though seldom cooked, it is safe to eat raw—slice thin and serve with firm-textured bread. A tasty but less popular alternative is to heat a whole *cervelat* in an oven or steam-pot. Well-known varieties include the *farmer cervelat* (coarsely chopped pork and beef, 50-50), *Goteborg* (cardamom-infused; Swedish); *Gothaer* (usually pork, finely chopped; German) *Holsteiner* (loop-shaped), *Touristenwurst* (soft-textured; not really made of tourists, as some travelers say), and *Thuringer* (lives up to Germany's Thuringian sausage-making reputation). (See the "Salami vs. Cervelat" section below for a brief rundown on basic differences between these two oft-confused sausages.)

Chorizo: A medium-sized, hot and spicy, smoked, air-dried pork (sometimes with beef) link sausage that is much admired in Spain as well as in Mexico and the bordering U.S. states. It can be cut into 1/8-inch slices, sautéed in olive oil, and used to flavor rice or bean dishes or enjoyed as a hot appetizer. Alternatively, it can be sliced extremely thin and served raw at room temperature.

Country Sausage: This term has a number of meanings. To most people it connotes any coarse-ground sausage, especially one made of pork, with mild or moderate seasonings.

Frankfurters: Whether they are called *frankfurters, hot dogs, weiners*, or whatever, Americans devour a lot of them—billions a year, at home and at the ballpark. But what we eat is a distorted reflection of the succulent sausages produced in the namesake city, Frankfurt, Germany. You will find on the package labels of most American franks one of three terms: "beef," "meat," and just plain "frankfurter," each word governed by law. To qualify for the first, the frank must be made exclusively of beef and must contain no binders such as dry milk solids or textured soybean protein. Seasonings and preservatives are permitted, however. "Meat" franks follow the same rules, except they can be made with a number of other types of meat. A mixture of 60 percent beef, 40 percent pork is typical of many "meat" franks. Except to one following a kosher diet, there is nothing inferior with a frank made partially or wholly of pork; to many tastes, including our own, pork flavor is practically indispensable for a good sausage. "Frankfurter" franks differ from the "meat" kind in that they can (and almost always do) contain up to 3½ percent in binders. All three types of franks may contain up to 30 percent fat and 10 percent added water, and may have natural or synthetic casings or none at all. Their meat is usually fine-ground, cured, and smoked mildly if at all. The sausage is precooked, ready-to-eat, though it needs to be served hot for optimum flavor. Unknown to most people, the sausage meat is mainly scraps, including ears and snouts—all of which are flavorful, nutritious, and inexpensive. Virtually all franks contain chemical salts such as sodium nitrate and nitrite, that are suspected of being carcinogenic, but some manufacturers use mild doses while others use megadoses. Without the saltpeter, the franks would turn a grayish-reddish-brown, a hue that is (to most consumers) uninviting and unappetizing. This is a pity, because there is nothing wrong with the grayish tinge except for running counter to well-entrenched consumer preferences. Franks are made with other meats than beef and pork; veal, chicken, and turkey are examples. Today, the names *frank* and *wiener* are used interchangeably, though some packers still properly differentiate between the two: wieners are traditionally longer and thinner than franks. *Cocktail* or *Vienna* sausages are miniature franks used as hors d'oeuvres. *Kosher franks* (see Kosher Sausage section below) tend to have at least a touch more garlic than do regular beef franks.

Fresh Sausage: A label term that defines uncooked sausages in general and, specifically, those that require refrigeration and cooking.

Frizzes: A dry, garlicky, well-seasoned salami-type sausage with a contorted configuration. Usually cured pork, sometimes beef added.

Haggis: The national dish of Scotland. A sheep's stomach is stuffed with chopped variety meats from the same animal, oatmeal, and various herbs and spices, then slowly simmered for hours.

Head Cheese: Bits of meat (especially from the hog's head and tongue) are attractively bound by the cooked, naturally gelatinous cooking liquid. Slice and eat slightly chilled or at room temperature.

Italian Sausage: In America, the name normally refers to a coarse-ground, well-seasoned, cured pork-based link sausage. There are two types: *hot* (chili-hot) and *sweet* (nonfiery). Seasonings can include fennel, garlic, and wine. Pan-fry, boil, or grill. Serve hot. It is a staple pizza topping.

Kielbasa: Also called *Polish sausage.* In America, *kielbasa* refers to a sausage of pork (often with beef or veal added) accented with varying amounts of garlic and other seasonings. It is formed into long, 1 2-inch-thick links and normally sold smoked and precooked (just requiring heating). In some outlets you can purchase uncooked *kielbasa*, the type made in the Old World.

Knackwurst: It resembles the American frankfurter except that it is thicker and has a pronounced garlic flavor. The true German *Knackwurst* wins hands down over its milder American imitator. Our domestic *knackwursts* are almost always precooked, needing only to be heated through.

Kosher Sausage: A nonpork (usually beef) sausage made under the supervision of a rabbi adhering to strict religious dietary proscriptions. *Kosher salami* and *frankfurters* are widely available wherever there is a large Jewish-American community.

Landjäger (or Land Jaeger): One normally buys these small, rectangular stick-shaped, well-smoked, hard, dry, dark *cervelat*-type, "hunter" sausages in linked pairs. They are best enjoyed served in very thin slices at room temperature, or used to flavor hot casserole dishes.

Lebanon Bologna: A coarse-ground all-beef sausage named after its birthplace, a city in Pennsylvania. Its distinctive sharp flavor is imparted by a lactobacilli culture used in the curing process.

Leberkäse: Germany's "liver cheese" is really a pâté-sausage, if you will permit a neologism. It is usually served hot, though some eaters enjoy it best at room temperature.

Liverwurst: "Liver sausage" is indeed made with livers (pork), but it usually also has the muscle flesh and fat of the hog, and perhaps those of other animals as well. It may or may not be smoked or contain onions. Different makers use different blends of herbs and spices. One of the finest liverwursts is Germany's smoked and egg-and-milk-enriched *Braunschweiger* (the American edition bearing the same name is less glorious but superior to the typical American liverwurst). Liverwurst is ready-to-eat, and is generally served with bread at room temperature, though there is no reason why the firmer specimens cannot be heated and served hot.

Longaniza: A dry Iberian pork sausage that is also avidly enjoyed in many ex-Spanish lands, including the Philippines. It resembles a *chorizo*, but is generally not as heavily seasoned.

Lop Chong: A dry fatty Chinese sausage made of pork and/or pork liver. Some *lop chongs* have a hint of sweetness.

Mettwurst (or *Teewurst*): A cured, smoked, fatty link sausage made of fine-ground beef and (usually) pork. It is so soft and spreadable that some Germans have given it a third name, *Schmierwurst*. Smear this uncooked but ready-to-eat sausage on firm-textured bread or crackers and enjoy the rich flavor that is often counterpointed with the taste of coriander seeds and pepper.

Mortadella: The original version from Bologna, Italy, looks like a watermelon masquerading as a football, but tastes heavenly. The cubed pork fat is imbedded within the fine-ground, seasoned, cured pork-and-beef mixture. After being stuffed in an oversized casing, the sausage is smoked and air-dried. It is now ready to eat—slice thin and serve at room temperature, even though uncooked. The cylindrical American-style *mortadella* is a different creature—basically no more than Yankee-style bologna meat interlarded with unsmoked cubes of pork fat, lacking the flavor and texture of the original. Even the Italian-made *mortadella* that we sometimes find in this country is unlike the product consumed in Bologna, because *mortadella* cannot be imported into America unless it undergoes certain nontraditional cooking steps that invariably modify flavor and texture.

Pâtés and Terrines: Closely related to sausages and perhaps legitimate members of the family, are pâtés and terrines. They may also be accurately thought of as glorified meat loaves (though many of us have probably tasted simple meat loaves that were better than some of the fancy pâtés served in pseudo-gourmet restaurants). A pâté is a baked mixture of ground meat such as livers of pork or fowl, seasoned with herbs, spices, and other flavoring agents such as cognac. Sometimes truffles are added for taste and visual contrast. *Country-style* usually refers to a pâté with a coarse texture. The terms *pâté* and *terrine* are used interchangeably today, but in the past they were differentiated: a pâté was surrounded by a pastry crust, while a terrine was wrapped in a protective layer of fat and usually served out of the terrine dish in which it was baked.

Pepperoni: This air-dried, coarse-ground pork (and often beef) slender sausage of Italian ancestry is most famous in America as a pizza garnish. It is usually well-seasoned with ingredients such as coarse-ground black and red peppers (hence its name). *Pepperoni* is ready to eat; slice it tissue thin if you are serving it at room temperature as an appetizer.

Pork Sausage: A catchall word for (usually) uncooked, coarse-ground sausage made totally or principally of hog meat and fat. In America, pork sausage tends to be mildly seasoned and is sold in link, patty, or bulk form.

Salami: Most salamis are made with a combination of pork and beef. Popular seasonings include wine and garlic, especially in Italy. (Germans generally cut down or entirely eliminate garlic from their salami recipes.) Of Italy's many famous salamis, including the *Sicilian* and *Milanese*, the best by consensus is the *Genoa* salami, with its rich, fatty texture and flavor accented with white peppercorns. Other well know salamis include the *kosher* (see Kosher Sausage above), *Hungarian* (relatively mild), *Lyonnaise* and *Arles* (both French), *cotto* (whole peppercorns; Italian), *alpino* and *alesandri* (both Italian-

American concoctions). A *salamette* is one term for a small salami. Siblings of the salami include the *frizzes* and *pepperoni* (see both above). Salamis are best enjoyed when sliced thin and served at room temperature with firm-textured bread or a hard cheese.

Salami vs. Cervelat: The distinction between the two sausage families is becoming increasingly blurred, as more and more shops use the two words interchangeably. There is a difference. Compared to a cervelat, a salami is usually of coarser texture; more heavily seasoned; less likely to be smoked; drier; and a better keeper without refrigeration. The last two factors make sense in light of the fact that the climate of southern Europe (where most salamis come from) is warmer than central Europe (where most cervelats are produced).

Salsiccia: A squat version of the Italian sausage (see above), often made with fine-ground meat.

Sandwich Cold Cuts and Spreads: America's penchant for producing food on a mass scale gave us a huge cold-cut industry off whose assembly lines come presliced, vacuum-packed luncheon meats flavored with numerous ingredients such as pimentos and olives. Sadly, the lion's share of the production contributes little more to an exciting sandwich than does the cottony white bread most people buy to hold the cold cuts. The same may be said for virtually all the canned sandwich meats and spreads, such as deviled ham, that line supermarket shelves. You would be wiser to pay a slight premium for freshly cut slices of better quality sausages from the delicatessen counter.

Scrapple: A Pennsylvania Dutch and Philadelphia specialty. Ground pork (mainly scraps, as the name suggests) is cooked with cornmeal, onions, herbs, and spices, then molded into a loaf and allowed to cool and firm. Many cooks cut it into ½-inch slices and fry them until brown, serving them hot for breakfast.

Smokies: A term generally used for either heavily smoked frankfurters or a commercial type of small, dry, well-seasoned sausage. Neither variety often rises above mediocrity.

Souse: Similar to head cheese (see above) except that souse (1) is likely to have a higher proportion of other slaughter-time by-products such as the pig's foot and (2) has a more pronounced sweet-and-sour flavor. Souse is a Pennsylvania Dutch specialty that is an adaptation of its close relative, the European *sulze*.

Thuringer: The former German state of Thuringia gave its name to many types of well-known sausages including the Thuringer *Blutwurst* (blood sausage), Thuringer *cervelat*, and the general class of Thuringer fresh sausages.

Weisswurst: The "white sausage" of Munich is similar to the bockwurst (see above).

Zampino (or Zampone): The casing of this visually striking cured and air-dried pork sausage is the boned pig's foot, skin and all. It requires long, gentle simmering before being eaten hot or at room temperature.

AVAILABILITY

Mass-produced packaged sausages are universally available. Finer-quality sausages are available from some butchers and ethnic food stores.

Buying Tips

When buying airtight sausage packages, avoid those that are bloated (likely caused by bacterial decay), moisture-laden, or torn. The sausage surface should not be slimy, wet, or moldy. The skin of a whole sausage should have no surface lesions. The scent should be fresh without any off-odor. If you don't want to eat nitrites and the like, remember that a bright rosy-red hue often indicates an abundance of those chemical salts. Check the label closely for such additives. Scrutinize the label for facts such as weight (two apparently equal packages from different processors could vary by as much as 25 percent in net weight) and for the list of ingredients. The latter are listed in order of quantity—largest amount first, second next, and so on. The chief weakness of the list is that it does not give you exact percentages—for instance, if water is the second largest ingredient, does it amount to 1, 5, or 10 percent of the total weight? When possible buy sausages with natural casings (rather than those with synthetic ones or none at all) because such sausages have a more desirable crisp snap when you bite into them. Rather than buying presliced sausage in packages in the meat case, consider paying a slight premium at the delicatessen counter. You should be able to buy smaller quantities and get a greater variety for the same total weight. You will also be getting fresher sausage meat, as it will be sliced only when you buy it. If you are not going to eat the sausage meat immediately, buy it unsliced (if possible); it will stay fresher longer. Picnic-basket and lunch-pail packers as well as backpackers know that dry sausages such as salami stay fresh longer without refrigeration than moister ones. And a whole dry sausage will stay fresh many times longer than a cut one. When buying sausages for hot-dog buns, be sure that, when cooked, they will be at least as long as the buns. You will find other buying tips scattered about in other sections of this entry.

PREPARATION

Storage

Uncut dry sausages can be safely hung in a cool, dry place practically forever, but after a year or so dehydration reaches the point where the sausage disagreeably mummifies. If you don't have a cool, dry place, you're better off storing your sausages in the refrigerator. There they will keep fresh for a month or two, if you wrap them carefully to keep as much moisture from reaching them as possible. Since they are salty, they will tend to absorb any available moisture. Sometimes a harmless, white mold-looking substance forms on the outer skin. Do not despair. This is probably the salt residue of the brine that has risen to the surface and evaporated; simply cut that portion off before eating. Dry sausage with exposed flesh can be stored in a 35° to 40°F refrigerator for up to a month if well-wrapped. Fresh sausage is very perishable and should be refrigerated (35° to 40°F) for no more than 2 or 3 days. Most other sausages, such as frankfurters and sandwich meat, can be refrigerated for 1 or 2 weeks in the original wrapper or for 3 to 7 days once opened and carefully rewrapped. Sausages are not good freezers, because of their high fat and salt content.

Cooking

To pierce or not to pierce? That is the question asked by many cooks. Some authorities say yes, others say no. Our answer is that it depends on internal moisture and your own personal priorities. Exceptionally moist sausages, such as most blood sausages, should be pierced to prevent them from bursting during cooking. (An alternative is to cook them with very low heat.) The majority of other encased whole sausages should not be pierced unless you are willing to sacrifice juiciness and flavor for increased crispness and reduced fat calories. Never sample-taste fresh uncooked sausage such as bratwurst. To check the seasoning of uncooked bulk sausage, first cook a small amount in a skillet to kill any trichinae or harmful bacteria that may exist. To see if a batch of cooking sausages is done, cut into the center of one of the links or patties. If the core is still pinker or of a noticeably different color than the surrounding meat, then the sausages need further cooking. Sausages and patties usually have a surface layer of liquid fat when they come out of the pan. You have two options: you can pat them dry with paper towels or you can let the sausages reabsorb the fat while resting on a warm rack or platter for a few minutes. There are many ways to cook sausages. The two most popular and generally the two best ways are simmering and pan-frying (sautéing). Practical but less desirable are broiling and baking. Each of these four basic methods will now be discussed.

Simmering: This is a simple method for sausages with casings. Drop the room-temperature sausage into boiling water to cover, reduce the heat and gently simmer. Uncooked ones should simmer for about 10 to 25 minutes and precooked ones for 5 to 8 minutes, depending on thickness. Another basic way to heat precooked sausages in liquid is to immerse them in boiling water, remove the pan from the heat and let it rest covered for 8 (for frankfurters 3/4 inch thick) to 12 minutes. Consider adding wine, stock, herbs, spices and other flavoring agents to your boiling water—your sausages will pick up a delicious new flavor. If the sausages have only slight amounts of chemical additives, save the broth for other cooking uses.

Pan-frying: To pan-fry uncooked links, add approximately one quarter inch of water to a lightly greased skillet or sauté pan and bring to boil. Add the room-temperature sausages, reduce the heat, cover, and gently simmer for 4 to 8 minutes, depending on sausage thickness. Then pour off water and pan-fry the sausages uncovered for 4 to 8 minutes more, turning often with tongs until the links are evenly browned. To pan-fry uncooked patties or slices 1/2 inch thick, place them in a cold skillet. Turn heat to moderate and sauté for roughly 10 to 15 minutes, turning with spatula as necessary until done. To pan-fry precooked links, slices, and patties, start by placing them in a cold, lightly greased pan, turn heat to moderate, and cook for 4 to 8 minutes, turning as necessary. If you slice frankfurters lengthwise almost in half, reduce the cooking time slightly, and be sure to start with the skin side downward to minimize curling.

Baking: The chief advantage of baking sausages is that you can cook a large quantity with minimum attention. Granted, simmering is even easier, but your sausages will not acquire that special appearance and texture that only oven-browning can give. First, place your sausages in a single layer on a lightly greased rack in a shallow pan in a preheated 350°F oven. Bake uncooked links 20 to 40 minutes and precooked ones 10 to 20 minutes, depending on thickness. For even all-over browning, it helps to turn the sausages with tongs one or more times. If splattering becomes a problem, pour off rendered fat as it accumulates.

Broiling: This method is not recommended for moist sausages, as they have a penchant for bursting when broiled. For most other sausages, first brush them with a cooking oil such as butter. Then place the room temperature links or patties in a single, nontouching layer on a lightly greased broiling pan 4 inches under the flame or electric heat coil at a preheated 375°F setting. Broil links or patties for 10 to 20 minutes if uncooked and for 5 to 10 minutes if precooked, depending on thickness. If you are charcoal-broiling your sausages, follow the relevant guidelines above, but keep the sausages 5 inches above medium-hot, nonflaming coals. Many cooks like to butterfly sausages such as frankfurters for broiling. If you do, broil them a couple of minutes cut-side down, then turn them over on their backs and broil till done. Generally, however, we do not recommend broiling split frankfurters, as they tend to curl excessively, thus cooking unevenly.

Serving

To determine how thick or thin you should slice any given sausage, remember this useful rule of thumb: the harder the texture, the thinner the slice. To illustrate, pepperoni should be sliced tissue-thin, while liverwurst can be cut a quarter of an inch thick or more. Some sausages, such as salami, are meant to be served at or slightly below room temperature (but never chilled). Other sausages, such as bratwurst, must always be served piping hot. A third group of sausages—bologna—may be served either way, depending on use. If a sausage slice has a skin, the diner generally removes and discards it if it is synthetic (though some artificial casings are edible) but eats it if it is made of animal entrails and has been prewashed. It is considered—for good reason—a dining *faux pas* to eat the pastry crust or fat that rims a slice of pâté or terrine. That surrounding layer has been placed there by the chef to help protect the meat mixture during and after cooking rather than to titillate the palate of the diner. Moreover, eating that (usually) awful-tasting protective coat will make it difficult for your taste buds to appreciate the subtleties of the meat mixture, the sole star of the preparation. When you are served a slice of pâté or terrine, you should remove a section of crust rim with fork and knife and set it off to the side of your plate. You now have easy access to the pâté proper. When serving a frankfurter in a hot-dog bun, make sure that the bun is no longer than the sausage it envelops and that the bun is either warm or (even better) toasted. Popular frank-and-bun garnishes besides mustard are sauerkraut, pickled relish, ketchup, chili sauce, chopped or fried onions, and any combination of these things. A good baseball or football game is perhaps the best garnish of them all. Potatoes, beans, sauerkraut, apple sauce, onions, full-textured breads, and beer are classic sausage accompaniments. Sausage links and patties are typically served whole, either alone or in pairs, depending on their size and the diner's appetite. It may require several (or more) baby-sized links to satisfy a hearty eater. In terms of weight, figure about 1/4 to 1/3 pound per person (appreciably less if serving sausage as an appetizer). Most menu-planners increase the weight when serving hot dogs, and decrease it when serving thin-sliced dry sausages.

Making Your Own

There are numberless ways you can create sausages, ranging from complex to simple. To illustrate how easy it is for you to do at home, here is perhaps the most basic way.

If you plan to make link sausages rather than patties, first buy animal entrails from your butcher. The intestines will have been hygienically cleaned—all you need to do is rinse and soak them to get rid of the salt used to help preserve them. Rinse the casing quickly in medium-hot tap water; this should eliminate most of the salt. To soften the dried casings, soak them for a couple of hours in tepid acidulated water (1 tablespoon of vinegar per quart), changing the water once. Drain and rinse again, this time allowing the tap water to flow through the inside of the casings. Pat dry. They are now ready to use.

For the stuffing, buy a relatively inexpensive cut of meat (preferably pork) such as one cut from the shoulder of the animal. The ratio of lean to fat should be 2 to 1 (or, at least, no higher than 3 to 1); the fat gives a sausage its juiciness and most of its flavor, so do not skimp in that department. If you're worried about eating too much fat, it's better simply to eat fewer sausages, but good ones, than to make inferior sausage.

Cut your lean and fat into small cubes (if they are refrigerator-cold, they will be easier to cut and later to grind or chop). For every pound of lean-and-fat, mix in about 1 teaspoon salt, 1/2 teaspoon freshly ground black pepper, and 2 teaspoons of crushed or 1 teaspoon of powdered dried sage (of course, fresh sage is best if you have it; in that case, use 2 tablespoons chopped.)

Coarsely grind the mixture with a

meat grinder or coarsely chop it with your food processor. If you have neither instrument, use the French haché method: cut the meat and fat into small pieces with a sharp chef's knife. A food blender is not ideal for this coarse-ground homemade sausage; it tends to turn the mix into too much of a paste.

If you want patties, shape the mixture into discs about 3 inches across and 1/2 inch thick. If links are your goal, and you do not have a mechanical stuffer with a nozzle (many meat grinders have a sausage-stuffing attachment), you can easily stuff the sausage mixture into the casing with the tip of the handle of a long wooden spoon. Once the casing is semifirmly stuffed, tie it into links with kitchen string.

You are now ready to cook and enjoy your homemade sausages.

Once having mastered the basic recipe, you can start experimenting and developing sausages of your own invention; this is where the fun begins. You can use almost any type of herb or spice, by itself or in medley with others. To spur your thinking, we have prepared a list of some of the seasonings most frequently used by sausage-makers: allspice, aniseed, basil, bay leaves, caraway seeds, cayenne, cardamom, cassia, celery seed, chili peppers, chives, cinnamon, cloves, coriander, corn syrup, cumin, dill, fennel, five-spice powder, garlic, ginger, mace, marjoram, mustard, nutmeg, onions, oregano, paprika, parsley, peppercorns, salt, savory, sugar, and thyme.

Making a dry sausage is not a simple task. It requires expertise, the right environment and controlled timing. So do not attempt to dry your own without proper guidance from a knowledgeable source.

SAVORY

BACKGROUND

This herb comes in two varieties: *summer savory* (*Satureia hortensis*), and *winter savory* (*Satureia montana*). The more aromatic and culinarily popular is the summer species. Both are useful in salt-free diets because they add piquancy to food without adding sodium. (See HERBS AND SPICES for information on buying, storing, cooking, etc.)

AVAILABILITY

Savory is seldom sold fresh in America. Dried, it is widely available.

CLASSIC USES AND AFFINITIES

Summer savory enhances the appearance and flavor of pale vegetables like cauliflower. It has an affinity with the cabbage family, including Brussels sprouts, and often goes into poultry seasoning. Veal and sausage are sometimes prepared with summer savory in classic French cuisine. Bean soup and other dishes prepared with dried legumes take well to summer savory. Winter savory, tasting like a delicate blend of marjoram and thyme, is used in egg dishes, long-simmered soups and stews, in cold sauces, and in potato salad.

SCALLIONS

BACKGROUND

Spring onions and *green onions* are other market names for the *scallion*. Adding further confusion is the fact that in some areas such as Louisiana, scallions are known as *shallots*, a name most Americans use to describe an entirely different member of the onion family (see SHALLOTS entry). Even the so-called Welsh onion of Oriental popularity is sometimes sold in this country as a scallion.

Depending on region, store, and season, the two types of scallions we are most apt to see in the greengrocer's bin will be either a specific variety of the onion family called scallion or simply a standard ONION that was harvested long before reaching maturity. The authentic scallions have straight sides; the base of an immature onion will be just beginning to show the characteristic bulbous shape of an onion. The authentic scallion has a finer texture and a slightly less assertive flavor, but otherwise these two types of scallions are culinarily interchangeable.

A scallion has two major parts: the white base and the green leaves. Both parts are edible, though most Americans, not knowing that the leaves have many excellent uses in the kitchen, throw them away.

AVAILABILITY

Scallions are available all year, though they are at their best and are least expensive from spring through summer.

Buying Tips

Select crisp, clean, vivid green leaves free of withering, fibrousness, yellow edges, bruises, and other injuries. The white stem area should be firm, free of soft spots—and as long as possible relative to the scallion's overall length. Usually, middle-sized neck diameters are better than the two extremes.

PREPARATION

Storage

Scallions are very perishable. Seal them (trimmed of any damaged leaves) in a plastic bag, store them in the refrigerator's vegetable crisper, and use within two or three days. Do not wash until just before use.

Preliminaries

Trim off the woody base tip along with the attached roots and discard. Cut off all but about 1 to 3 inches of the green leaves (if they're in good condition, save them to flavor stocks or sauces or to garnish meats and vegetables). Using your fingers, peel off and discard the thin membrane covering the white stem area. You are now ready to slice the resulting scallion cylinder into thin rings or to halve the cylinder lengthwise prior to cutting it into long strips. Or you can leave the cylinder whole for braising. Or you can mince it.

Cooking

Scallions offer their best qualities in flavoring a preparation such as a sauce or meat dish, after they have been lightly sautéed in a little butter or oil over low-to-moderate heat for several minutes. Too high a heat will scorch the scallions, giving them a bitter flavor. You can braise scallion cylinders in butter as you would leeks. Figure on 8 to 10 minutes total braising time, then drain and season and serve as a side vegetable dish.

Raw Uses

Scallions can be eaten raw, perhaps dipped in a bit of salt or melted butter, and eaten as an appetizer. Chopped raw scallions can be used as a topping garnish for preparations such as sandwiches and salads. The Chinese make a "scallion brush," the indispensable edible utensil that brushes the sauce onto the thin flour pancake that will wrap the delicate skin of the celebrated Peking duck. To make your own brushes, use a knife to make a dozen ¾-inch-deep incisions (as you would cut a pizza) into the flat circular surface of one or both ends of a trimmed scallion cylinder. Place the scallions in ice water and refrigerate for an hour or two. The end(s) will flare, brush-style.

SCALLOPS

BACKGROUND

Most bivalve mollusks, such as clams and oysters, are usually sold live in their shells. Not so with *scallops*. The reason is that scallops quickly die outside their saltwater environment—because, as one commercial fisherman told us, "they cannot keep their mouths shut." American scallop dredgers, therefore, remove the cream-colored adductor muscle which closes the shell; the muscle is the only part of this shellfish we eat in America. The marshmallow-shaped muscle is shipped to the market on ice; the radiating-ribbed shell is usually tossed back into the sea. Europeans, in contrast, eat everything inside the shell, including, if it exists, the delicious orange coral (the eggs).

Varieties

There are hundreds of scallop species, but they are usually classed according to their habitat: bay or sea. The better is the *bay scallop* (the edible muscle averages ½ inch in diameter) because its flesh is more tender, sweeter, and juicier. The stronger-flavored *sea scallop* (the edible muscle averages 1½ inches in diameter) is firmer, chewier and should sell for much less per pound than its counterpart. But remember, it is better to have a properly cooked sea scallop than to have a poorly prepared bay scallop.

AVAILABILITY

The scallop season runs from early fall through mid-spring.

Buying Tips

When buying shucked and trimmed scallops, sniff them: they should possess no more than a delicate sea-breeze aroma. When pressed, their flesh should be resilient. The surface should glisten and be fresh-looking. If they are very white, chances are that someone has soaked the scallops in water to increase their weight. A pool of water in the bottom of the tray is another clue to that deceptive practice. Other ploys include stamping "scallops" out of inexpensive fish fillets or cutting up sea scallops into bay-scallop-sized pieces. However, high labor costs have made these last two tricks less common than certain alarmists would have us believe.

PREPARATION

Cooking

Scallops are ideal for the busy cook—they require no preparation and they cook quickly. In fact, if you overcook them, they will toughen. The perfect way to cook scallops is to sauté them. First, you will need to bring them to or near room temperature, pat them dry, and, if you want, dredge them with seasoned flour. Put them into a sauté pan or skillet (containing sizzling butter mixed with a little oil) over moderate to high heat. This heat is necessary to sear the scallop surfaces so as to keep the juices inside. Do not overcrowd the pan, or the scallops will steam rather than fry. Shake the pan frequently to promote even browning. Bay scallops will cook in approximately 2 to 3 minutes, sea scallops about 3 to 6 minutes, depending on thickness.

CLASSIC USES AND AFFINITIES

Scallops can also be broiled or simmered, and can be a soup ingredient. The most famous scallop recipe is *coquille Saint-Jacques*, creamed scallops baked on the half shell.

SCARLET RUNNER BEAN

BACKGROUND

The native South American *scarlet runner bean* (*Phaseolus multiflorus*) is today firmly entrenched in the American West. It has a large, long, slender pod like the green bean's. The medium-to-large seed is whitish-beige with streaks that are sometimes red, sometimes wine, and sometimes roan-colored. Slightly immature and fresh, the scarlet runner can be cooked in its pod like the green bean. Most often, perhaps because it is available nationally only shelled and dried, the scarlet runner is cooked like the pinto or pink bean, and is used in soups, chilis, and meat stews flavored with strong spices, tomato sauces, and onions. (For soaking, cooking, and other particulars, see BEANS.)

SEA CUCUMBER

BACKGROUND

This shell-less mollusk that crawls along the bottom of ocean floors is called a *sea cucumber* because of its shape. It is sometimes called a *sea slug* or *bêche-de-mer*. It varies from 1 to 2 inches thick and from several inches to 2 feet long.

AVAILABILITY

Sea cucumbers are sometimes available fresh, but more likely they will be sold dried. In some Chinese-American markets, dried ones that have been presoaked are sold.

PREPARATION

Storage

Dried sea cucumbers will stay good for up to 6 months if sealed in a bag and stored in a cool, dry, dark environment. Fresh or presoaked sea cucumbers should be kept submerged in fresh water in the refrigerator and used within a day or two.

Preliminaries

You must soak a dried sea cucumber for about 24 hours, changing the water several times. It will double in volume and will acquire a semifirm, gelatinous consistency. Next, if this has not been done, cut out the vital organs and scrub it well.

Cooking

Simmer the sea cucumber in fresh, perhaps seasoned, water for 3 or 4 hours or until tender. Serve it in a soup or in tandem with another main ingredient such as pork, duck, or chicken.

SEA URCHIN

BACKGROUND

Americans seldom eat the *sea urchin*; Japanese and Mediterraneans consider it a delicacy. *Oursins*, as the French call them, are marine animals that cling to (usually) rocks beneath the low tide mark. They have a hard discoid or spheroid shell covered with sharp projecting spines. If a swimmer accidentally steps on one of these "pincushions," excruciating pain will result. The edible portion of the sea urchin is its interior. This pulpy flesh can be briefly cooked, but the sea urchin is at its best when eaten raw out of the shell, with a spoon and, perhaps, a sprinkling of lemon or lime juice. Before reaping your own supply of fresh sea urchins, check with the local authorities to make sure the water is unpolluted and the species is edible.

SESAME SEED

BACKGROUND

The tiny, oval beige seed of *Sesamum indicum* is prized for its mild, rich flavor and its high oil content. The *sesame* plant is a native of Central Asia, and is very common today in the Middle East, Africa, China, and Japan. The seeds are rich in protein; the oil is polyunsaturated. The slaves brought to the United States from Africa called the sesame seed "benne"; this name is still current in the Southern United States. (See HERBS AND SPICES for information on buying, storing, cooking, etc.)

Cooking

Sesame seeds can be toasted in a heavy frying pan over low heat, or baked in a single layer in a rimmed pan in a 350°F oven for 15 minutes.

CLASSIC USES AND AFFINITIES

Raw or toasted sesame seeds are good sprinkled on noodles, casserole dishes, breads and vegetables. A few toasted seeds can enhance a green salad or a *vinaigrette*. The Japanese make a low-sodium condiment called *gomasio*, five parts of toasted sesame seeds to one part of salt. Sesame butter, pureed whole sesame seeds, and *tahini*, made of pureed hulled sesame seeds, are Middle Eastern staples; they substitute for butter and are combined with vegetables such as chick-peas and eggplant.

SHALLOT

BACKGROUND

The *shallot* (*Allium ascalonicum*), is a member of the onion family, and has long been a favorite flavoring agent with French chefs. Today, it is rapidly gaining popularity across the United States and around the world from West Africa to Indonesia. Most of our domestic crop of shallots comes from our Southern states; France supplies the U. S. with imported shallots. The shallot forms several small bulbs like a head of garlic, rather than forming a single multi-layered head like the onion. The thin papery skin around each shallot can be brown, gray, or rosy. Its whitish flesh can be green- or mauve-tinged. Like all members of the onion family, shallots enhance the taste of food by irritating the membranes of the mouth and nose, thus increasing sensitivity to flavor and smell. Some sensitive stomachs and eyes that rebel at onions accept shallots with ease and pleasure.

Varieties

Two basic types of shallots reach the American greengrocers' shelves: the *common* or *"true" shallot* and the *Jersey* or *"false" shallot*. The first is the better in terms of subtle flavor, the second is superior in one regard: since it is much larger, your peeling chore will be appreciably shortened for any given weight of shallots. (In some regions such as Louisiana the SCALLION is called a shallot. Since the vast majority of American regions use the word "shallot" to define the common or the Jersey shallot rather than the scallion, we shall do the same.)

Dry, Dried, and Fresh

Most shallots sold in this country are *dry*, a term that should not be confused with *dried*. Dry shallots have dry skins and moist interiors and are sold whole. Dried shallots are peeled, chopped, and dehydrated. The third category, fresh shallots, are those that have been recently harvested and may still have their green tops attached; if so, remove them (save them for the stockpot) as they drain nutrients and flavor out of the bulbs.

AVAILABILITY

Traditionally, shallots are planted on the shortest day of the year and harvested on the longest. Today, they are available all year, with a peak in the winter.

Buying Tips

Select shallots with firm, full cloves and well-attached bright skins. Avoid shallots that are shriveled or that have soft spots, bruises, or mold. It usually costs more to buy shallots loose out of an open bin rather than in a package, but you save money that way in the long run, since you can select the pick of the crop.

PREPARATION

Storage

Fresh shallots are very perishable and should be washed, wrapped in paper toweling, sealed in a plastic bag, and stored in the refrigerator's vegetable crisper—for only a day or two. Dry shallots—the type you are most likely to buy—should not be stored in the refrigerator, but rather in a dry, cool, dark, well-ventilated spot. Under perfect conditions, dry shallots will last a couple of months; under typical kitchen conditions, they can be stored for 7 to 10 days. When shallots start to sprout or shrivel, you have kept them too long.

Preliminaries

Trim off the root and then insert the point of a knife into the peel; slit, then remove the peel. Shallots can be sliced, minced, or diced. If your recipe calls for one shallot, use one stout, medium-sized clove about an inch long, not a whole multi-cloved bulb. Freeze-dried shallots need to be reconstituted unless you are adding them to a liquid preparation.

Cooking

Shallots need not be cooked (and are excellent raw in salads), but they do develop flavor when subjected to heat. Sauté minced shallots in butter for several minutes. Like onions, shallots must be sauteéd over low to moderate heat or they may scorch and become bitter. Shallots may also be simmered in liquid.

Equivalents

Two or three medium-sized shallot cloves will enliven a four-serving salad or a large chicken prepared as *coq au vin* or four servings of steamed mussels. If you cannot find fresh or dry shallots, substitute scallions. Dried shallots are an inferior substitute for fresh or dry shallots. If you must use dried shallots, use about one-eighth the volume of fresh or dry shallots called for in the recipe.

CLASSIC USES AND AFFINITIES

Shallots are welcome wherever a flavor like that of onions, but sublter and milder, is desired. Haute cuisine often combines shallots with fish, chicken, and seafood. Famous preparations include shallot butter, sauce *béarnaise*, sauce *Bercy* and *moules marinière*.

Vinegar-soaked shallots are popular in Chinese and Vietnamese cooking.

SHARK'S FIN

BACKGROUND

An expensive highlight of a Chinese banquet is shark's fin soup, made with the bland, transparent, gelatinous, stringlike, protein-rich cartilage of the dorsel or tail fin of the shark.

AVAILABILITY

It is sold in two forms: processed and nonprocessed. Nonprocessed shark's fin is sold with the cartilage still imbedded in the fin along with the skin and bones. Removing the cartilage is a long, painstaking operation.

Buying Tips

Most cooks are better off buying the processed fin, which is the extracted cartilage *sans* skin and bones. When buying shark's fin, remember that the longer the cartilage, the higher the quality and price will be. Better specimens are also the most translucent and palest and have the least waste in terms of bone or skin fragments.

PREPARATION

Preliminaries

If wrapped in an airtight bag, shark's fin can be stored in a cool, dry, dark spot for up to several months.

Cooking

To cook it, first soak the dried cartilage for 8 to 12 hours, remove any bits of bone or skin that may have been overlooked by the processor, then simmer the cartilage in your soup stock for about an hour and a half.

SHRIMP

BACKGROUND

Hundreds of edible shrimp species exist, weighing anywhere from less than 1/10 of an ounce (the sub-Arctic variety) to over a pound (developed by aquaculturists). Each American coast—the Atlantic, Gulf and Pacific—has a number of shrimp species, though it is the Gulf Coast that leads the nation in commercial sales. Shrimp species are more or less interchangeable in recipes. What counts more, in most cases, is the size. The cooler a shrimp's water habitat, the smaller, more succulent, and more flavorful it tends to be—but exceptions to the rule exist.

AVAILABILITY

Fresh shrimp is available the year round, though it is most plentiful and least expensive during the warm months.

Varieties

Unless the shrimp boats dock near your home, you will seldom see whole live shrimp being offered for sale. Chances are they will be shipped and sold headless, with or without the shell and the legs. Such shrimp may be *deveined* or not, and may be *fresh* (called *green*) or *frozen*. In the latter case, the shrimp may be *plain* or *breaded* and/or *stuffed*. Shrimp are also available *potted* (packed in solidified clarified butter), *canned*, and, in Oriental foodstores, *dried* or as *shrimp paste*.

Buying Tips

Fresh Shrimp: *Jumbo, large,* and so on are market terms for size that vary in weight from region to region and, sometimes, from store to store. Jumbo shrimp almost always sell for a higher price per pound than their smaller counterparts, yet they offer approximately the same proportion of edible meat to waste as do the smaller species. They are usually less sweet and tender than their smaller cousins. On the other hand, jumbo shrimp are less of a chore to prepare, and, they are the best type if you want to serve stuffed shrimp. When comparing the price per pound of two types of shrimp, take into consideration whether they are being sold whole, headless, or shelled. On the average, a pound of whole shrimp yields about half a pound of edible, deveined flesh, and a pound of headless shrimp in the shell yields slightly more than ¾ pound of edible, deveined flesh. The difference in shell and flesh color of the various species is not an indicator of quality. Some fishmongers and restaurateurs innocently or deceptively sell jumbo shrimp as prawns, an entirely different, though related, decapod crustacean (see under LOBSTER.) Be aware that most of the so-called "fresh" shrimp sold in retail markets has been frozen, then thawed. This ruse gives the flesh a mushy texture and a blander flavor. You can spot frozen-and-thawed shrimp by their limp rather than firm texture, by their opaque white rather than translucent white flesh and, possibly, by the presence of leached-out water in the bottom of their container. The longer a shrimp is stored, the more the flesh shrinks. Therefore, when buying fresh shrimp in the shell, be sure the shell snugly encases the meat. Sniff the shrimp. It should smell sea-fresh, not fishy. Reject any with an off-odor; the smell of ammonia tells you that this stale shrimp is not worthy of your dollar, pot, or stomach. It is natural for shrimp to possess a faint hint of iodine taste; the saltier the water, the more pronounced this undertone. Some shrimpmen illegally add chemicals such as sodium bisulfite or chlorine to prolong the storage life or to mask the spoiled nature of their bounty. Often these chemicals accentuate the flavor of the iodine, so if the shrimp smacks too much of iodine, you should seriously consider switching your source of supply.

Frozen Shrimp: First, let us say we do not recommend purchasing frozen shrimp, as too much texture and flavor is lost. If you insist on frozen shrimp, your best bet is to buy it in a see-through package so that you can scrutinize the shelled meat. Each shrimp should be completely coated with a thick ice glaze which means that each shrimp was individually frozen (as opposed to being lump frozen) and that the shrimp has remained frozen since it left the factory. When buying heavily ice-glazed shrimp, read the label to ascertain whether the frozen water was included as part of the net weight. If it was, the price per pound should reflect that fact.

PREPARATION

Preliminaries

The edible part of the shrimp is the so-called tail, the large muscle below the head and above the tail fin. However, if you buy shrimp with heads still attached, you may not want to decapitate them, as some preparations call for serving the whole shrimp. If you cut off the heads, add them (along with the shells) to a stock to make a sauce. Unless you are positive that no chemical preservatives have been used, it is a good idea to briefly rinse the shrimp under cold running water.

Shelling: The shell and the attached legs can be pulled off with your fingers or with the assistance of a paring knife. Some preparations such as butterfly shrimp require that you leave the tail fins on. That end piece is a natural handle when dunking the shrimp into a dip.

Deveining: If the shrimp is in prime condition, the *intestinal tract* is not noxious, though it can be gritty and can ruin the pristine appearance of the shrimp. Some gourmets eat it, others remove it; take your pick. If you are cooking shrimp in their shells, you will have to remove the vein afterwards. Otherwise, it is easier to extract the black *vein* (as it is sometimes called) before the cooking process. Some neophyte cooks assume that the nerve vein that runs down the belly (or inside curve) of the shrimp is the intestinal track. Not so. The true intestinal tract runs down the back (or outside curve) of this crustacean. How big and large the intestinal tract will appear depends principally on how much, how recently, and what the shrimp ate before it died. To remove the digestive tract, score the shrimp's back lengthwise with a paring knife. The incision should be just enough to allow you to remove the "black vein" using the knife tip, a toothpick, or a long, sharp fingernail. Deveining underneath running cold water makes the task easier.

Butterflying: Decapitate and shell the shrimp, but leave the tail fins attached to the flesh. When you are making the incision to devein a shrimp, cut deeper, almost but not through to the underside. Remove the black vein and flatten the shrimp into the characteristic butterfly shape. Some cookbooks suggest butterflying from the underside, but that approach does not produce as attractive a form.

Cooking

As with most seafood, shrimp does not need to be cooked to tenderize it—as the Japanese well know (they eat it raw or just briefly cooked to develop an appealing red surface color). If you overcook shrimp, as many American chefs do, the meat will toughen. The flesh should be cooked just long enough to develop its flavor and firmness. The simplest cooking method is to bring to a boil approximately one quart of liquid per pound of shrimp—ideally, a seasoned liquid such as *court bouillon*—with 1 teaspoon of salt per quart of liquid. Add the shelled, room-temperature shrimp, reduce the heat, and simmer (never boil) for 2 to 5 minutes, depending on thickness. Add roughly 1 minute to your estimate if the shrimp is unshelled. When cooked, the flesh will have a marblelike pink exterior and a snowy white interior. At that point, immediately remove the shrimp from the water to stop the cooking. Shrimp may also be battered and deep-fried in 375°F oil from 1 to 3 minutes, depending on thickness or until golden brown. Or they can be sautéed—cook them quickly at moderate to high heat. Cooking shrimp in their shells allows the flavor of the shells to permeate the flesh.

SNAIL

BACKGROUND

The best *snail* for eating purposes is the *Helix pomatial*, a gastropod that feeds on grape leaves. Most of the snails we eat in America are imported in cans from France—though, unknown to most American diners, most of these land mollusks have been imported into France from lands such as Turkey, Yugoslavia, and Taiwan. To make matters worse, the latter type of snail is not the true *escargot*, but a swamp-living mollusk that has a pointed, rather than a globular, shell. Because this snail feeds on swamp foods such as insects rather than vine leaves, its taste and texture are inferior. Imported cans that contain such snails should, but do not always, carry the word *azatine* somewhere on the label, if only in small print.

AVAILABILITY

Most snails are sold in cans, with or without the accompanying, reusable, empty shells. The quality and flavoring agents of these snails do vary—generally, you get what you pay for. Snails are also sold frozen in the shells, sauced and ready for the oven. The best snails are fresh. If you can find them fresh in this country, by all means try them and compare their superior texture and taste to the processed variety. The usual serving of snails is a half-dozen or a dozen per person.

PREPARATION

Canned Snails

These are already cooked and need only to be drained and heated through.

Live Snails

First, you must literally starve the snails to allow them to rid themselves of any noxious waste. This will take a minimum of several days, a maximum of a week or two. If the period extends beyond three days, feed the snails a little lettuce. Second, soak them in lukewarm to tepid water for 30 minutes. Discard any that do not slightly crawl out of their shells because, most likely, they are dead and risky to eat. Drop the live snails (still in their shells) into boiling salted water and simmer for about 5 minutes. Drain and cool, then use a small instrument such as a skewer to pull them out from their shells. Trim off head, tail, secretions, and any hard or foreign substances. Simmer the trimmed snails in a stock such as *court bouillion* for ½ hour to 2 hours, depending on their size. When cooked, allow them to develop flavor by letting them cool in the stock. Drain them. They are now ready to use in your recipe as you would canned snails. If you wish to keep the shells, they can be cleaned and disinfected by boiling them in salted water infused with one or two tablespoons of baking soda per quart for approximately an hour. Drain, then dry them in the oven.

Cooking

The classic snail dish is *escargot â la bourguignonne*. Tuck into the shell a little *beurre d'escargot* (butter blended with garlic, shallot, parsley, salt, and pepper), then insert the precooked snails. Seal the opening with some more snail butter. Place the shells in an indented *escargot* pan or on a thick layer of rock salt that keeps the shells open-side up. Put the pan into a preheated 350°F oven for 10 minutes or until you hear the herb butter sizzling. Serve immediately. For the most enjoyment, you should have the special *escargot* equipment: platter, tongs, and fork. If you do not have such equipment, consider baking the snails inside butter-basted mushroom caps—the results are ambrosial.

SNAKE

BACKGROUND

You can eat many snakes such as the python or boa, but it is the meat of the deadly rattlesnake that is the most widely available and highly esteemed in this country. Rattlesnake flesh is mild like chicken or rabbit meat but, despite what some gourmets tell us, it has its own distinct flavor, a rather good one at that, once the diner gets over the hurdle of eating the first bite.

Buying Tips

The best rattlesnake meat comes from a fresh, young reptile (3 to 5 feet in length) caught in the fall when small live creatures such as baby quails and rabbits give it the tasty nourishment that produces a plump torso. Be sure that the rattlesnake you buy (or trap) is not on the endangered species list.

PREPARATION

Sautéing is a succulent way to cook 1-inch-thick cross sections; those cut from the center of the body are the best. Season lightly so as not to mask the delicate flavor, and whatever you do, do not overcook lest the meat become dry and chewy.

SORREL

BACKGROUND

Sourgrass and *dock* are other names for *sorrel*; in some areas, different types have different names. The characteristic flavor of the 2-to-3-inch green African-shield shaped *sorrel* leaves is noticeably acid, the intensity depending on type and age (the older the plant, the more pronounced the tartness).

PREPARATION

Storage

Sorrel is perishable; keep it in a plastic bag in the refrigerator and use within a day or two.

Cooking

The milder varieties, if young, can be mixed in raw salads, but most sorrel varieties need cooking. Discard any roots and damaged leaves, rinse sorrel, drain and steam-cook the leaves (either whole or shredded) with the clinging water for a few minutes until the leaves just begin to wilt. Serve with sage-enriched butter, cream or sour cream.

CLASSIC USES AND AFFINITIES

Cream of sorrel soup and the Eastern European *schav* soup are famous preparations.

SOUR CREAM

BACKGROUND

Hungarian, Polish, and Russian food does not taste right without sour cream. Sour cream is simply heavy cream that has fermented. What you buy in a store as sour cream, however, is cultured sour cream, produced by pasteurizing 18 percent butterfat cream, cooling it to 72°F, and adding a culture of *Streptococcus lactis* bacteria. After 15 hours, a thick, high-fat product with a rich, tart taste and 30 calories a tablespoon is ready. Sour cream can be refrigerated about 10 days, divided between the grocer's refrigerator and yours. The liquid that forms on top is whey; it can be stirred back in or poured off and discarded. Sour cream curdles when it gets too hot, so when you prepare a dish with it, first warm it by mixing in some of the hot sauce; then add the sour cream to the hot food off the heat—don't cook it.

SOURSOP

BACKGROUND

The *soursop* (*Annona muricata*) is a large tropical fruit (it can weigh up to 5 pounds) with a warty skin that ranges from greenish to purplish. The almost-white flesh inside is juicy, heavily seeded, with a taste sometimes compared to black currants. The soursop is eaten raw, or pureed for use in iced drinks and sherbets.

SOYBEAN

BACKGROUND

A staple legume for vegetarians and health-cultists, the *soybean* (*Glycine soja*) is considered the most nutritious bean in the family. It is also the hardest. The soybean is round, the size of a small pea, and comes in assorted colors—green (the young soybean), grayish-green, yellow, black, and brown. For centuries in the Orient, the versatile soybean has been sprouted, pressed into oil, powdered into flour, pounded into paste, sieved and pureed and fermented into curds, squeezed into cakes, strained into sauces, and dried for indefinite, long-term storage. Today, America produces so much of the product for export and domestic fodder that soybean farmers have become powerful lobbyists.

AVAILABILITY

Dried soybeans are available year round in Chinatown shops and most other Oriental shops, as well as in health-food stores. Soybeans are also available in many processed forms including miso (fermented soybean paste), tofu (soybean curd—see BEAN CURD), soy sauce, and soy flour.

PREPARATION

Do not try to pressure-cook the soybean—it is notorious for clogging escape valves. Also note that soybeans have an as yet not fully identified substance called a trypsin-inhibitor which—unless the soybean is thoroughly cooked—hinders your body's ability to assimilate protein. To be sure of getting all the nutritive protein that soybeans are valued for, then, cook soybeans the requisite time (2½ to 3 hours). (For soaking, cooking, and other particulars, see BEANS.)

CLASSIC USES AND AFFINITIES

The soybean is almost the perfect legume, but its flavor goes against it in some cooking situations; its taste is more than slightly assertive and can overwhelm other flavorings and ingredients. Because of this strong flavor, the soybean cooks well with other dominating tastes such as cheeses, tomatoes, corn, anchovies, hot chilis, and as a substitute for meat in burgers, loaves, pâtés, and stews.

SPANISH MELON

BACKGROUND

This hybrid resembles a cross between a CRENSHAW and a CASABA MELON (see those entries). The flavor of the Spanish melon, however, is more like that of the crenshaw. The season runs from late summer to late fall. Store, prepare, and serve the Spanish melon like the crenshaw.

SPINACH

BACKGROUND

Popeye the Sailor loves *Spinacia oleracea*; some children do not. Parents are right in insisting that *spinach* is good for your health, but too much of a good thing can be bad: spinach—and particularly, uncooked spinach—contains oxalic acid, a substance which taken in excess can hinder the body's normal metabolism.

Varieties

Most spinach sold in America is curly-leaved, though some varieties are smooth-leaved. In taste and cooking properties, they are practically indistinguishable. *New Zealand spinach* (*Tetragonia expansa*) is botanically distinct; when young, it looks reasonably like our spinach, but it has a thicker stem, and its flat leaves are spade-shaped and sometimes fuzzy. New Zealand spinach is seldom available beyond the Pacific coast. Cook it as you would true spinach.

AVAILABILITY

Spinach is available year round, though it is at its best from mid-winter through late spring. Frozen spinach is always available. Spinach, incidentally, suffers less from freezing and thawing than do most other vegetables.

Buying Tips

If possible, buy loose rather than packaged spinach. The leaves should be a fresh, dark green and be void of insect holes, grit, blackened decay spots, wilted or yellow edges, rips, and slimy surfaces. Some clinging moisture is okay; a completely dry leaf is not. The stems should be crisp, but pliable, not dry, limp, or fibrous. Don't take any spinach with seedstems. The entire plant should be squat and bushy, not elongated and sparsely leaved. Spinach must have a fresh odor. Sniff packaged spinach; if it has any trace of sour scent, it is over the hill.

PREPARATION

Storage

Use spinach promptly; do not keep it in the refrigerator more than two to three days.

Preliminaries

Separate the leaves and stems from the roots. Pick off any tough stems and discard or trim damaged leaves. If the spinach is to be eaten raw, also remove any tough midribs. Rinse in cold (or tepid, if very gritty) water. Drain well.

Salad

Classic ingredients for the popular spinach salad are chopped eggs, mushrooms, bits of bacon, and dressing. Raw spinach can be also substituted for or mixed with lettuce in most green salads.

Cooking

A standard way to cook spinach is to put a little butter in a heavy pot. When it sizzles, add chopped onions and sauté a few minutes until the onions are translucent. Add the spinach, tightly cover, and steam-cook for about 5 minutes or just until the leaves wilt. "Wilt" is the operative word here; spinach shrinks amazingly. You may have to stir the spinach in the pot at first, to assure that all leaves cook evenly and shrink. Do not add water to the pot; the liquid that clings to the leaves after washing and draining will suffice. Use an enameled, stainless steel, or Teflon- or Silverstone-coated pot; cast iron or untreated aluminum will darken the spinach and give it a metallic flavor. Before serving, lightly press the spinach to release excess juices; they could pose a problem by running off into other food on a diner's plate. Season to taste. Spinach can also be stir-fried or simmered.

Equivalents

One pound of raw spinach should serve two persons when cooked.

CLASSIC USES AND AFFINITIES

Almost any dish described on an American menu as "Florentine" is served on a bed of spinach. A Greek favorite is *spanakopita*, spinach-stuffed flaky pastry. Northern Indians and Pakistanis have many *sag* dishes incorporating their regional variety of spinach. Italians sometimes dye their pasta with spinach juice. Americans are growing increasingly fond of spinach salad. Spinach is used for Oysters Rockefeller. Affinities include cream, butter, nutmeg, mace, basil, garlic, onions, blanched almonds, hard-boiled eggs, and crisp bacon.

SPLEEN

BACKGROUND

This little-known organ usually ends up as pet food. Some cuisines, however—Slavic and Jewish, for instance—do wonders with the spleen by stuffing, then braising it. The spleen can also be used as a soup or stew ingredient. Spleen is sometimes called *melt* and, in Jewish ethnic cooking, *miltz*.

SQUAB

BACKGROUND

A squab is a domesticated month-old pigeon whose flesh is very tender, partially because the bird has never flown. The pigeon that is bred and raised for the dinner table is not to be confused with the common park-bench variety, a less tasty creature.

AVAILABILITY

Squabs are sold frozen the year around. Fresh squabs have better flavor and texture; they are available mainly from late spring through early fall.

Buying Tips

Youth is culinarily very important with a squab, so reject those specimens weighing over a pound. If the bird is not frozen, you can also use these clues: the younger the bird, the more pliable the breastbone and the lighter in shade the dark flesh will be. Select squabs that are very plump (but firm) and well-formed.

PREPARATION

Squabs, with certain exceptions, can be prepared and cooked like chickens and especially like the rock cornish game bird. Rather than repeat lengthy material, we refer you to the CHICKEN entry for information on buying, storing, preparing, and cooking. However, the following tips and insights particularly concern squabs:

Cooking

The best way to cook a squab is roasting, provided that you bard it, baste it every 15 minutes, or both. Roast a room-temperature 1-pound squab in a preheated 400° F oven for 30 to 40 minutes (add 5 minutes if it is stuffed). The shorter period will give you succulent flesh, the longer time a drier flesh more pleasing to most Americans. For each ounce a pigeon weighs under 16 ounces, subtract 2 minutes from the total cooking time. Over 16 ounces, add 2 minutes per ounce. A squab can also be braised whole (about 45 minutes), spit-roasted whole (30 to 45 minutes, depending on distance from and intensity of heat source), broiled split or quartered (15 to 25 minutes, according to thickness as well as the heat source's strength and distance), or sautéed split or quartered (12 to 20 minutes). Sautéed squab is especially good when the pieces have been dredged in seasoned flour. Squab is simmered (45 to 60 minutes) when the cook wishes to remove the flesh for another preparation such as *bastila*, the classic North African pigeon pie.

Serving

You will need one squab per person. If serving squab meat on the bone, politely tell your guests that not only is it permissible etiquette to eat squab with the fingers, it is almost a necessity if they want to enjoy all the delicately flavored meat.

SQUASH

BACKGROUND

Cooks divide squashes into two classifications: *summer* and *winter squashes*. While both types are indigenous to the New World and come in a variety of colors, shapes, and sizes, there are salient differences other than their traditional seasons: Summer squashes are picked and eaten when immature rather than mature. While mature summer and immature winter squashes are edible, they are not usually palatable. Summer squashes have tender, thin skins that are eaten; the hard, thick skins of winter squashes are not. Summer squashes have soft, edible seeds that are eaten with their flesh, rather than removed. Summer squashes have a higher water content and consequently a lower calorie count per unit of weight. They have a more delicate flavor and softer texture. They require less cooking. They can be stored for only a short time, while winter squashes can be stored for long periods.

Summer and winter squashes are discussed individually in the two entries that follow.

SQUASH, SUMMER

BACKGROUND

The varieties of summer squashes that we are most apt to find in a greengrocer's bin are listed below.

Varieties

Zucchini: The commonest summer squash variety in America today is the 4-to-10-inch-long, 1-to-2-inch-thick, cylindrical green zucchini with a pronounced blossom cap. (The best specimens are young, and only 4 to 6 inches long.) A summer squash similar to the zucchini is the *cocozelle*, identified by its white striping on the green background.

Yellow Straightneck: Shaped like a bloated miniature baseball bat, the straightneck has a vivid yellow skin and a pale yellow flesh. As the squash matures, the skin deepens in color and starts to develop a bumpy rind. For optimum flavor and tenderness, choose the juveniles, under 6 inches.

Yellow Crookneck: Similar to the straightneck except for its arching neck.

Pattypan: Also called the *cymling* or *scalloped squash*, the pattypan is a saucer-shaped pale green squash with a scalloped circumference. The best and most tender specimens are under 4 inches in diameter. As a pattypan matures, its skin turns white and its shell hardens.

AVAILABILITY

While some other squashes are now available the year round in some warmer regions, only the zucchini is generally marketed year round throughout the country. The time of the year for greatest freshness and flavor and lowest cost, however, is late spring through the summer.

Buying Tips

The younger the squash, the more tender it will be, so select the tiniest ones you can find—unless you are planning to stuff them. Thinness of skin is another clue to youth. The skin hue should be vivid, not dull, and the skin should be free of cuts, soft spots, and blemishes. The squash should be firm, well-proportioned, and heavy for its size.

PREPARATION

Storage

Keep squashes in a plastic bag in the refrigerator. Plan to use them within 2 or 3 days.

Preliminaries

Gently wash the squash with a soft brush under tap water. Drain well. Unless the squash is on the old side, do not peel it, as the skin is colorful and protects nutrients just below the surface. Trim off both ends and any blemishes and cook whole, or cut into bite-size chunks, or if sautéing, into slices.

Cooking

Summer squashes are culinarily interchangeable. They are all better steamed than simmered. Figure on 8 to 15 minutes, depending on thickness and age. Summer squash also fares well when baked (350° F oven for 25 to 35 minutes), sautéed (about 5 minutes), or deep-fried in a batter coating.

Equivalents

One pound of summer squash will furnish about three side-dish servings.

CLASSIC USES AND AFFINITIES

Summer squashes marry well with tomatoes, onions, garlic, olive oil, basil, oregano, and other Mediterranean flavorings. A grating of cooking cheese or a topping of sour cream also works well.

SQUASH, WINTER

BACKGROUND

Pre-Columbian Indian agriculture centered around corn, beans and squashes. Some of the squashes grown were hard-rinded, long-keeping members of the species *Cucurbita maxima* and *Cucurbita moschata.* The hard rind protects the firm, fibrous flesh inside. Some winter squashes have vibrant colors and markings, and make good decorations and centerpieces. Unlike most decorations, they can be eaten when you get tired of looking at them, if you don't wait too long.

Varieties

Acorn: This acorn-shaped squash weighs 1 to 2 pounds, measures 4 to 7 inches long. It has a smooth, glossy, fluted rind colored dark-green, sometimes streaked with yellow-orange. Inside, the flesh is pastel orange.

Buttercup: Like other turban squashes (see below), the buttercup has a bulbous cap swelling from its blossom end. It is typically 4 to 8 inches in diameter and 2 to 3 inches high with a pale-gray turban perched atop its gray-flecked green rind, which encloses its yellowish-orange flesh.

Butternut: The bright caramel-yellow butternut squash has a distinctive bulbous blossom end and a long neck, making it look like a pear-shaped club. It is 8 to 12 inches long and weighs 2 to 3 pounds.

Calabaza: The word is Spanish for "squash" as well as the specific name of various squashes found in different lands. The calabaza we are most apt to see in America is the West Indian-type with a thick, whitish-green rind, a pumpkinlike shape and size, and a stringy orange-yellow pulp.

Hubbard: The behemoth of the common winter squashes is thick as a basketball with two tapering ends, the stem end protruding the farther. The rind is usually bumpy and slightly ridged, and ranges from dark green to deep orange. The flesh is orange-yellow.

Pumpkin: Most Americans think of pumpkin only as a Halloween jack-o'-lantern, a Thanksgiving pie, or a coach for Cinderella. But pumpkin is a winter squash that can be used in virtually any recipe for winter squash. Pumpkins vary in shape (globular or oval), in weight (several to over 100 pounds) and in color (though typically bright orange). The word "pumpkin" refers to an entirely different group of squashes in some other English-speaking lands.

Spaghetti Squash: When cooked, the flesh of this 4-to-7-pound yellow flattened-oval squash separates into spaghettilike fibers, hence its name. It is cooked differently from the other winter squashes (see below).

Turban Squash: A group of squashes that come in a host of sizes and bright color combinations, sometimes with a swirl of orange, yellow, and cream on a warty green background. Each has the characteristic turban crown on top of a doughnut-shaped base that can measure anywhere from several inches to over a foot in diameter. In most homes, the turban squash is used principally as an autumn decoration, not as food. The flesh is orange-yellow.

AVAILABILITY

Most winter squashes mature at the very end of summer or in early fall, and are on the market in autumn and winter. Storage technology has made it possible for certain types such as the acorn squash to be available the year around, but their springtime and mid-summer quality is not prime.

Buying Tips

To be at its best, a winter squash must be harvested fully mature. Look for a hard, deep-colored rind for its variety. Also select squashes that are heavy for their size—if too light, the squash may be either immature or over the hill. A squash can easily decay once its protective rind has been injured, so reject any with a skin that is cut, scarred, soft-spotted, moldy, discolored, or blemished.

PREPARATION

Storage

Winter squashes do not require refrigeration. If they're in good condition, you can store them at room temperature for up to a week (a little longer if the very thick-rind variety). You can store them for a month or more in a cool, dark place such as a cellar. Refrigerate cut squash, and plan to use it within a day or two, wrapping the piece well in plastic.

Preliminaries

After washing the outer rind, leave the squash whole—or halve, quarter or cube it, removing the seeds and fibers in the cavity. Save the seeds; they're good roasted (see below). Before baking, rub the rind and exposed flesh with softened butter to help prevent the squash from drying out in the oven.

Cooking

Small and medium winter squashes can be baked whole in a preheated 350° F oven for 40 to 80 minutes, depending on thickness. (De-seed and season after cooking.) Squashes of all sizes can be baked halved, quartered, in wedges, or chunks rind-side-down in a preheated 350° F oven for 30 to 60 minutes, according to thickness. The flesh of the hubbards and turbans may require a little longer cooking time. If the squash is stuffed, add about 5 to 10 minutes. Squash chunks can be steamed or simmered in 10 to 20 minutes, depending on thickness. For *Spaghetti squash*, first pierce the skin. Simmer the squash whole for 20 to 30 minutes, or bake it whole in a preheated 350° F oven for 1 to 1½ hours, depending on thickness. Cut open, deseed, and pull out the flesh lengthwise to preserve the long strands and season with butter, salt, and pepper—or top with your favorite spaghetti sauce. To *roast squash seeds*, remove them raw from the squash and let them dry. Oil them lightly, spread them on a shallow pan, and roast them in a preheated 375° F oven for 10 to 20 minutes, until properly brown. To make a squash (including pumpkin) pie, here is a brief recipe outline: first bake the vegetable, scoop out the flesh, puree it, add the liquid, emulsifyers and flavorings of your choice, pour the filling into a pie shell, and bake in a preheated 375° F oven for about 45 minutes or until set. Consult a recipe book for details and variations.

CLASSIC USES AND AFFINITIES

The sweet flavor of winter squash goes well with sweet spices such as cinnamon, nutmeg, and allspice. Brushing the cut edges of the squash with honey adds sweetness and a pretty brown glaze. A wide variety of savory stuffings can be baked within the cavity of halved squash.

SQUASH BLOSSOMS

BACKGROUND

An epicurean delight are the yellow or orange blossoms of various squashes such as the zucchini or pumpkin. They and their tender stems are traditionally sautéed briefly in olive oil or butter, or are dipped in batter and then deep-fried.

SQUID

BACKGROUND

The *squid* is a cephalopod that has a conical body and ten tentacles (as opposed to eight for the octopus) covered with suction discs. Length varies from a half-foot up to the Jules Verne behemoths, 80 feet long, that live in the ocean depths.

Squid is more popular as food in the Mediterranean and the Orient than it is in the U.S. Here, most of the squid that is caught ends up as bait to catch other seafood. As a result, squid is usually a great protein bargain in America. The edible meat has a sweet, subtle flavor and a firm, chewy texture.

AVAILABILITY

Squid is sold in this country fresh, canned, and dried, but is not universally available.

Buying Tips

For squid at its finest, it should be bought fresh and whole. The smaller the squid is for its variety, the younger and therefore more tender it will be. The freshest squid has clear bright eyes and a sweet sea scent. The purplish-mottled outer membrane should not have been excessively rubbed away. Avoid squid that is slimy or limp, or that has been bruised or otherwise mishandled. If possible, buy fresh squid that has not been stored or packed in ice, which partially freezes the meat.

PREPARATION

Preliminaries

It is not that difficult to dress a whole squid. First, separate the section consisting of the tentacles, eyes, head, bony mouth, and visceral sac from the tail section by pulling the first section out of the second. Sever (and reserve) the tentacles from the head just in front of the eyes. If you plan to use it, remove and reserve the ink sac, being careful not to puncture it prematurely. Pull out the cartilage (tail skeleton). Discard everything except the edibles: tentacles, ink sac, and the tail along with its two attached caudal fins. Wash these edible parts in water and, using your fingers, rub off the tail's mottled covering membrane. Leave the tail section whole (if you plan to stuff it) or cut it across the grain into rings.

Cooking

Squid needs to be cooked only to develop its flavor. In fact, the Japanese serve squid raw in their *shushi* preparations. If you cook squid too long with too high a heat, it will become so tough the children will be right when they say it reminds them of fried rubber bands. Only young squid rings should be sautéed or deep-fried. Estimate a minute or two for sautéeing, about the same time for deep-frying in a 375° F oil. Simmer squid in soups or stews for anywhere from 20 minutes to 2 hours, depending on age—but never let the liquid come to a boil. Cooked squid can be marinated and served *vinaigrette*-style. When stuffing a squid, the tentacles can be cooked separately or chopped and added to the stuffing. When cooked, expect squid to shrink by at least a third of its original size. When making dishes such as *calamares in su tinta* ("squid in its ink"), press the ink out of its sac and add it to the cooking liquid. It provides both color and flavor.

STAR ANISE

BACKGROUND

Eight dark-brown seed pods of *Illicium verum* are joined in a star shape; each pod contains a shiny flat seed the size of a small bean. The seeds contain anethole, the same essential oil that characterizes aniseed. Whole star anise is used in Chinese (especially Szechuan) cooking; ground, it is often one of the spices in FIVE-SPICE POWDER. The essential oil extracted from star anise is frequently used in the West in the manufacture of liquors and other anise-flavored products. Whole star anise keeps for 6 to 12 months in a covered glass jar at room temperature. (see HERBS AND SPICES for information on buying, storing, cooking, etc.)

STRAWBERRY

BACKGROUND

From the botanist's point of view, the strawberry (genus *Fragaria*) is neither straw nor a berry, nor even a fruit; it is a swollen stem end dotted with black fruit (the "seeds"). There are many indigenous New and Old World varieties, the best being the wild strawberry (the classic *fraise des bois* of France) which is smaller, sweeter, and more fragrant than the cultivated American-developed variety. Sadly, virtually all the strawberries sold in this country are of the latter type.

AVAILABILITY

Fresh strawberries are available in spring and summer, with a peak in April, May, or June, depending on region. Frozen strawberries, and to a lesser extent, canned ones are available year round.

Buying Tips

Check the bottom and sides of the basket for stains or wetness, which indicate crushed, overripe, or moldy strawberries. Avoid green- or white-tinged strawberries—they are unripe and were picked too soon. Your strawberries should have a uniform, bright reddish color. Select firm-fleshed, plump strawberries. The fragrance should be pleasing and noticeable, without any fermented or moldy scent. All the strawberries must have their green caps still attached. Round strawberries usually have a better flavor than the conical ones. All else being equal, the smaller the strawberry, the better the flavor. The oversized Japanese-developed variety is certainly no bargain. Avoid the temptation of purchasing the first strawberries of the season: they tend to be sour and woody-textured.

PREPARATION

Storage

Sort through the strawberries immediately and discard any that are crushed or moldy. Decay spreads quickly. Until ready to use them, leave the hulls (the green caps) on—otherwise Vitamin C content will decline and decay will accelerate. Spread out the unwashed strawberries in shallow layers and cover. Refrigerate them and use within a day or two. Or wash and freeze them whole, crushed, or sliced, and use within two weeks if stored in your freezing compartment. If in a 0°F freezer, use within several months. Freezing, of course, diminishes texture and flavor.

Washing

Wash strawberries by placing them in a bowl of cool water and agitating the bowl several times. Strawberries are often too delicate to be washed under running water and will definitely absorb water if soaked. To further minimize water absorption, hull them only after washing.

Equivalents

Strawberries are usually sold in pint boxes which serve 3 to 4 people, depending on appetite.

CLASSIC USES AND AFFINITIES

Strawberries taste wonderful by themselves or covered with cream, sugar, chocolate, citrus juice, or even freshly ground black pepper. Strawberries play a leading role in ice cream, fruit sauces (their color adds a nice contrast to oranges and bananas), jams, preserves, and that all-American favorite, strawberry shortcake. To the purist, the latter must always be made with baking-powder biscuits (never spongecake) and real whipped cream.

SUGAR

BACKGROUND

The word sugar refers to any of several sweet, water-soluble crystalline carbohydrates that are extracted from the juices of certain plants, especially sugar cane and sugar beets. Other sugar sources include maple sap, fruits, and sorghum.

Sugar is used by mankind primarily as a sweetener and secondarily as a preservative. Americans use too much of it—about a hundred pounds of cane and beetsugar a year per person. Most people do not realize how much sugar they consume, because after all, how much sugar can be sprinkled on cereals and poured into coffee cups? But most of the sugar that reaches our stomachs comes as an unseen ingredient in commercial beverages, confections, baked goods, jams, sauces, canned and frozen foods, breakfast cereals, and convenience foods in general. Therefore, for us to decrease our sugar intake appreciably, we must not only cut down on the sugar that we use directly, we must also minimize the use of convenience foods and, instead, cook our foods from scratch. Even when baking a cake, a cook has the opportunity to use much less sugar than is contained in a commercial cake mix or in a store-bought ready-to-eat cake.

Varieties

Chemical:

Sucrose is the principal type of sugar obtained from plants such as sugar cane, sugar beets, and maple sap. *Glucose* often comes from fruits such as grapes and vegetables such as corn. *Dextrose*, a particular form of glucose, is the type used in our own bloodstreams. *Fructose* is the primary sugar obtained from fruits in general. *Invert sugar* is created when sucrose is heated, especially so when in the presence of an acid. The sucrose is transformed into glucose and fructose, which are capable of forming smaller crystals. This phenomenon is desirable when making preparations such as candies because of the resulting fine and smoother texture. Other common forms of sugar are *maltose* (malt sugar) and *lactose* (milk sugar).

Commercial:

Brown sugar differs from white sugar in that it is not completely refined and thus retains some molasses, which gives brown sugar its characteristic color, scent, and flavor. Many health-food enthusiasts use brown sugar in the belief that it is more nutritious; it is, but to such a scant degree that brown sugar should never be thought of as healthful. It is empty calories just like white sugar. Nowadays, the product sold in supermarkets as brown sugar is usually made by adding molasses to refined white sugar and, therefore, is not a true brown sugar. Like genuine brown sugar, it comes in two shades: light brown and stronger-flavored dark brown.

Raw sugar: is the crystallized sugar remnants, molasses and impurities found in the bottom of the mill's vat after the desirable sugar and molasses have been taken out. Unless it is purified, it cannot be sold. When purified, you are buying a lot of empty calories.

White sugar: is highly refined sugar. Most is sold in the granulated form. Because standard *granulated* sugar is sometimes difficult to dissolve in cold liquids such as iced tea, granulated sugar is sometimes ground into smaller crystals. It is called by names such as *superfine* or *extra fine*, and costs more, but is the best all-purpose choice for most kitchens. When ground into a powder, the sugar becomes XXX or *powdered sugar* and is used for certain baked goods. It is not ideal for sweetening drinks because it tends to lump. Powdered sugar will also cloud the liquid if the processor added cornstarch as an anti-caking agent (check the label). The most finely ground sugar is XXXX or *confectioners' sugar*, which usually makes icing better than powdered sugar.

Colored sugar: or *confetti sugar*, is used for decorating cakes, cookies, and the like.

Flavored sugars: are permeated with the scent of aromatic foods such as vanilla, citrus rinds, cardomom, or cinnamon.

Rock candy: is prepared by allowing the sugar in a concentrated syrup to crystallize around a string or thin stick.

Spun sugar: is a sugar SYRUP that has been boiled to the thread stage (230°F), then drawn out into threads and allowed to cool. A variation is *cotton candy*, which is colored, then spun using a centrifuge.

Maple sugar: is MAPLE SYRUP that has been boiled down to a more concentrated form, then cooled and allowed to crystallize.

Sugar Substitutes:

These products are marketed as liquids, powders, or tablets. Many sugar substitutes, such as cyclamates (currently outlawed in this country as possible carcinogenics) and saccharin, contain no or virtually no calories. Others, such as Xylitol, more or less match the calorie count of sugar. We suggest these products be used only by people who must use them for dietary reasons, because sugar substitutes give foods an off-flavor. We recommend that you reduce the amount of sugar you use rather than replacing it with substitutes.

Storage

Store white sugar in a dry, tightly closed container and it should last a year. In a sugar bowl or shaker, though, sugar will stay fresh for a much shorter period. Brown sugar tends to cake. Store it in a tightly sealed moisture-proof container on a cool cupboard shelf.

SUNFLOWER SEEDS

BACKGROUND

Unlike pumpkin seeds, *sunflower seeds* are hard-shelled and must be husked. You can eat them out of hand raw or roasted, or cooked in various dishes. You can toast them in a single layer in a 300°F oven until they acquire the color you want. Because sunflower seeds contain a lot of oil, they should be stored in an airtight container in the refrigerator. This oil is polyunsaturated, and thus sunflower seed oil is one of the leading vegetable oils (see under OILS AND FATS).

SWEETBREADS

BACKGROUND

Among variety meats, sweetbreads are the ones most coveted by connoisseurs of fine eating. This demand has escalated the cost of sweetbreads into the "gourmet" price range.

Sweetbreads are the two thymus glands located in the upper chest. While the precise function of these lymphoid organs is still a mystery to physiologists, they seem to help in creating antibodies. Whatever their exact duty may be, it is apparently not necessary for adults.

The two sweetbreads are the elongated lobe located in the throat area and the round lobe nestled near the heart. A tube connects the two. The *heart* (also called the *belly* or *kernel*) *sweetbread* is the larger of the two and is the most preferred from a taster's point of view—it has a more subtle, elegant flavor. Connoisseurs like to buy the intact *pair* (or *cluster* or *set*) of sweetbreads, complete with the connecting tube. A pair of calves' sweetbreads weighs between 1/2 and 1 pound; baby beef sweetbreads weigh approximately 1 1/2 pounds. Broken pairs or pieces of sweetbreads are less in demand, and thus usually sell for lower prices, typically 10 to 33 percent less.

Varieties

Of the four major varieties of sweetbreads—veal, lamb, baby beef, and pork—the first is the most prized in America and most of Europe. *Veal* sweetbreads are at their ephemeral best when they come from milk-fed calves. *Lamb* sweetbreads are also fine, but they are often hard to find in the market, and are quite small, making it a chore to prepare them (though they are perfect to fill pastry shells). *Baby beef* sweetbreads (from animals 6 to 12 months old) are larger, but less delicate in flavor and texture. *Pork* sweetbreads are seldom marketed, because they are small and because, unless you have piglet sweetbreads, their flavor is relatively strong. Often pork and piglet sweetbreads are used by food processors in spreads and pâtés.

AVAILABILITY

Sweetbreads can be found at better butcher shops year round.

Buying Tips

The whiter the sweetbreads, the younger the animal was, and thus, the more desirable the sweetbreads will be. As the baby animal approaches puberty, the sweetbreads become redder (milk-fed calves' sweetbreads have virtually no reddish hue), and develop a tougher membrane and internal texture. This last factor can be detected by pressing a finger against the surface of the meat. Sweetbreads should be plump, and unshriveled, look bright and glossy, and have a clean, fresh odor. If not, they may have been hanging around the market too long. Since sweetbreads are highly perishable, buy only from a reliable butcher, and plan to use them within 24 hours, preferably within hours after your purchase. Some unethical butchers sell the pancreas gland as sweetbreads. The two types of glands do resemble each other to some degree, but the pancreas is coarser in texture and less delicate in flavor; for these reasons, this gland should be labeled as the pancreas it is and sold at a fraction of the price generally asked for sweetbreads.

PREPARATION

Storage

Sweetbreads should be soaked, blanched, and pressed as soon as you get them home from the butcher, then refrigerated for no more than about 20 hours and, if possible, for no more than a few hours. Freezing extends storage life (to a couple of weeks in the standard refrigerator freezer compartment and to a couple of months in a 0°F freezer), but you will be sacrificing desirable texture and flavor.

Preliminaries

Soaking: Sweetbreads should be soaked before cooking, mainly to rid them of as much blood as possible. Blood traces that remain within the sweetbreads will darken upon cooking—considered a blemish. Soaking also helps to whiten and firm the meat and to make it easier for you to remove the outer membrane. Before soaking the sweetbreads, sever the connecting tube. Either discard the tube or use it as a flavoring agent in your stock pot. Place the separated lobes in a nonaluminum bowl and cover with cold acidulated water (1 tablespoon vinegar or 2 tablespoons lemon juice, plus ½ teaspoon salt per quart of water), and store in the refrigerator for 1 to 2 hours. If you only have 30 minutes for the soaking, then do so at room temperature. When soaked, rinse the sweetbreads under cold running water; handle them gently, as they are quite fragile. Next, carefully trim off as much as possible of the outer (but not the inner) membrane, the blood vessels, and connective tissue, using a sharp knife. This task takes a bit of skill and practice, as the membrane is thin and has a nasty habit of sticking in the crevices on the surface of the meat. If you are a novice, it is better to leave some of the membrane attached than to butcher the sweetbreads. But don't leave the trimming task until after blanching, as some cookbooks recommend, or you may end up with brown stains caused by the unremoved blood vessels.

Blanching: Another name for this step is *parboiling*. Blanching has two important functions: it helps develop and preserve the whiteness of the meat and it helps firm the sweetbreads' texture, making it easier for you to handle, cut, cook, and serve this fragile variety meat. Just about the only time you can skip the blanching step is when you will be braising the sweetbreads, but even then, a brief blanching will not do any harm and may do some good, especially if the braising medium is low in acid. To blanch, place the sweetbreads in a nonaluminum, noniron saucepan and cover them with fresh, cold, acidulated water (the same formula as for soaking). Bring the liquid to a gentle boil. Simmer for 5 to 15 minutes (thicker pieces from older animals take the longer period.) At no time let the water actively boil, or your sweetbreads will unnecessarily shrink and toughen.

You can give your sweetbreads more flavor by adding various *court-bouillon* ingredients to your blanching liquid—parsley, bay leaf, celery, carrots, peppercorns, and onions are some examples. But do not overdo it, lest the flavorings subdue the delicate sweetbread taste. As soon as the meat has been sufficiently blanched, drain and plunge it into cold water to stop the cooking. Alternatively, you can let the sweetbreads cool in the blanching water, but reduce the simmering period by a fourth. Pat dry with paper toweling and check to see if you can remove some of the outer membrane that you may have missed earlier.

Pressing: Also called *weighing down*, this step is strongly recommended if you plan to cook the sweetbreads with dry heat, such as sautéing or broiling. Its purpose is to remove some of the moisture from the sweetbreads. This makes the sweetbreads firmer and therefore easier to handle, cook, cut and serve, lessens the drop in pan temperature when you add the sweetbreads; and reduces splattering when the sweetbreads touch the hot fat in the pan. To press the sweetbreads, first place them between layers of paper or cotton towels, then place them on a flat plate. Next, cover them with a heavy object such as a flat-bottomed bowl or pot filled with water, or a flat plate with a heavy weight on top of it. Refrigerate for 1 to 3 hours (if unrefrigerated, press the sweetbreads for 30 to 50 minutes).

Cooking

The most common cooking method for sweetbreads is sautéing in butter (either breaded or with a light coating of seasoned flour) for a total cooking time of about 6 minutes (turning once) over medium heat. Broiled sweetbreads should be cooked 4 inches from the heat source for 5 to 6 minutes total cooking time, turning them once and basting them liberally with butter. Unblanched sweetbreads require 15 to 30 minutes braising time, depending on thickness and animal maturity. To poach, follow the pointers given for blanching, but simmer for a total period of 8 to 20 minutes (the thicker pieces from older animals require the longer period). To bake, cook 15 to 20 minutes (depending on piece size and animal age) in a preheated 375°F oven. With any method, the sweetbreads should be at room temperature before cooking.

Equivalents

In most instances you can figure on 1/4 pound per serving, as there is little waste. If your dining table has a high percentage of sweetbread fanciers, you'd better buy 1/3 pound more per person.

SWEET POTATO

BACKGROUND

Many people erroneously call *sweet potatoes* "yams." This entry exclusively deals with the sweet potato; the true YAM is discussed in its own entry. Two types of the vegetable tuber *Ipomoea batatas* are commercially grown in the United States. Superficially, they look alike, although if you compare them side by side, there are obvious differences. One type—the *"pale" sweet potato*—has a light skin (yellow just shading to orange) and a pale yellow flesh. The other, and more popular, type of sweet potato has a darker orange skin and a vivid, almost coral-orange flesh. This type is also called *yam*. The confusion began with African slaves given the cheap and prevalent Southern sweet potato to eat; being familiar with the true yam of Africa, called the sweet potato *nyam* in their native tongue.

The two types have different cooking properties. The pale is more like the white potato (although it is unrelated)—it cooks dry and mealy, and does not taste sweet unless it has been candied, sugared, pureed or souffléed—which are good, if rich, ways to prepare it. The other type, the pseudo-yam is moist-cooking, higher in natural sugar, hence truly sweeter than the pale variety, and can grow only in our Southern climate. (The pale type is commercially planted as far north as New Jersey.)

AVAILABILITY

Fresh sweet potatoes are generally, if sometimes spottily, available the year round. Peak season for newly harvested sweet potatoes is from mid-fall into the winter. In late spring and summer, the offerings are often last year's crop released from controlled cold storage, and are usually higher-priced.

Canned sweet potatoes are always available. The dark, sweet type are often labeled as *yams* (or *fancy yams* if candied) to differentiate them from their paler, drier cousins and often sell for several pennies more. If you read the label's small print under "contents," however, the yams are further identified as sweet potatoes. Frozen sweet potatoes, usually pureed in some form, are also easily procured at almost any supermarket. Fresh is best.

Buying Tips

As sweet potatoes of either type mature, they grow fibrous external "beards" (long white strings and proof positive of advancing age) and develop tougher and stringier internal fiber. Look for medium-small to medium sweet potatoes, with smooth unbroken skin, of good shape and color for their type. Smaller, younger specimens are less woody inside and thus more tender and better tasting. Sweet potatoes look hardy but they are almost excessively delicate. They bruise and crack very easily, and once bruised, the injury spreads and soon spoils the entire potato. Pick over sweet potatoes carefully, and reject those with any indication of bruising. Sunken off-color areas on the skin indicate dry rot. Buy sweet potatoes of uniform size for uniform cooking, and only enough for your immediate needs.

PREPARATION

Storage

Sweet potatoes are difficult to store properly in home environments. Do not refrigerate; dampness or high humidity encourages rapid spoilage and cold temperatures are harmful to them. Above 65°F, sweet potatoes are also unhappy. Store in the coolest, dark, draft-free spot available and use within the week. Of course, if you have the perfect environment (about 55°F) and the place is dry and dark, your sweet potatoes will hold in good condition for a month or so.

Preliminaries

Scrub the sweet potato well, removing the fibrous strings, if any. Do not peel; cooking them in their coats helps prevent the nutrients and natural sugar from leaching out. Peel after cooking, when it is easier.

Cooking

Sweet potatoes can be used interchangeably in any potato recipe, but most often they are baked (the dry pale type is the better choice) or boiled and then mashed, pureed, candied, or souffleed (the moist Southern pseudo-yam is recommended). Bake sweet potatoes at 400° to 425°F for 40 to 60 minutes, depending on size. To boil, drop the sweet potatoes into boiling, salted water; then cover, reduce to a simmer, and cook for 20 to 35 minutes, depending on size; drain the excess liquid. They can now be peeled or not, and prepared according to your favorite recipe.

Equivalents

There are usually two to three average-sized sweet potatoes to a pound. Baked, one potato to a person is the average serving. If pureed, three-quarters of a potato per person should be adequate.

CLASSIC USES AND AFFINITIES

Candied sweet potatoes and sweet-potato pie are classic American dishes. Sweet potatoes combine well with cured pork (ham and sausage, especially) as well as with brown sugar, maple syrup, marshmallow, cinnamon, ginger, orange juice, raisins, apples, and nuts.

SWEETSOP

BACKGROUND

(*Anona squamosa*) is an ovoid tropical fruit. Its green rind is sometimes tinged with purple; its pulp is segmented, like a citrus fruit. Sweetsop is eaten raw, after simply removing the skin and seeds. The sweetsop is sometimes confused with the related CUSTARD APPLE.

SYRUP

BACKGROUND

By definition, a *syrup* (sometimes spelled *sirup*) is a sweet, thick solution of water, sugar, and perhaps some flavoring agents. It may be directly derived from nature (maple syrup is simply boiled-down maple sap) or made of refined sugar added to water. Other sweeteners (such as honey) and other forms of liquid (such as fruit juice) may be substituted for the sugar and the water. To make a syrup thicker, you can add more sugar or, for best results, evaporate some of the water by boiling the solution. Sugar syrup, the primary subject of this entry, is made at home on the stove. For other types of syrup, see CORN SYRUP, MAPLE SYRUP, and MOLASSES.

A sugar syrup is used in preserving methods such as canning. It can also be used for making stewed fruits, icings, candies, confections, and sweet drinks.

PREPARATION

Simple Syrup

There are two basic types of sugar syrup. A *simple syrup* is easy to prepare. Mix sugar and water in a ratio of 1 to 3 (for thin syrup), 1 to 2 (for medium syrup) and 1 to 1 (for thick syrup). Boil the mixture briefly, stirring until all the sugar is dissolved.

Candy-Syrup Stages

A more involved syrup making process is used for making candies. Using an absolutely clean wooden spoon and a large, heavy-bottomed, very clean pot, stir together about 1 cup of cold tap water for every 2 cups of sugar. Bring to a boil, but long before it reaches that point, be sure all the sugar crystals have been dissolved into liquid.

Once the solution comes to a boil, never stir it again and, immediately, cover the pot for several minutes. This allows the steam to dissolve any sugar crystals that may be clinging to the inside walls of the pot. Uncover and continue to boil, using moderate heat.

The longer you boil the solution, the more the sugar will cook and the more the water will evaporate—and therefore the thicker your syrup will be. The desired degree of thickening will be determined by what you are planning to make. At the minimum extreme, you can bring the solution to the *thread stage*; at the opposite extreme is the *carmelized stage*. In between, as the syrup becomes thicker, are the *soft ball*, *firm ball*, *hard ball*, *soft cract*, and *hard crack* stages.

You have two basic ways to ascertain when the sugar has reached the stage specified in your recipes. One way is to use a candy thermometer—and the following table:

STAGE	BEGINS AT
Thread	230°F
Soft ball	234°F
Firm ball	244°F
Hard ball	250°F
Soft crack	270°F
Hard crack	300°F

At 310°F and above, your sugar will carmelize or brown noticeably. When using the thermometer, make sure it is clean and that its bulb does not touch the bottom of the pot. You must be alert, because the temperature rises slowly to about 220°F and then scurries upward.

If you do not have a candy thermometer, you can see what stage the syrup has reached by spooning a few drops of the boiling syrup into a measuring cup of cold water.

Thread stage is reached when a 2-inch-long soft thread solidifies in the water.

Soft ball stage is reached when a ball develops that flattens when taken out of the water.

Firm ball stage is reached when the removed ball needs finger pressure to flatten it.

Hard ball stage is reached when it requires considerable finger pressure to flatten or break the ball.

Soft crack is reached when bits or strands form that are pliable when removed from the liquid.

Hard crack stage is reached when the removed bits or strands are brittle.

Caramelized sugar is reached when the solution starts to brown noticeably.

When the solution has reached the desired thickness, remove the pan (without shaking it) immediately from the heat so that the syrup will not cook up to the next stage. Allow it to cool in the pan to 105°F to 115°F before proceeding with your recipe.

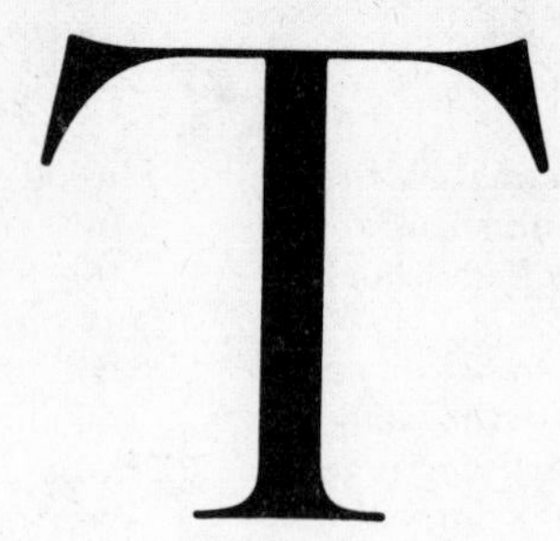

TAIL

BACKGROUND

The flesh-and-bone *tails* of most animals—including cattle (see OXTAIL), pigs, and sheep—are both edible and flavorful. They should be first singed, scrubbed well, and parboiled. Tails—with the exception of those from baby animals—require slow, moist cooking. In Iraq and some neighboring countries the fat-tail sheep is much prized for its extremely large tail, which can comprise 15 percent of the animal's total body weight. The rendered fat of this animal is used as a cooking medium as well as a flavoring agent. Tails of pigs (especially piglets) are a delicacy in many parts of the world, including China.

TAMARIND

BACKGROUND

An Asian tree often grown in India, the *tamarind* (*Tamarindus indica*) produces a 5-inch-long pod with small shiny seeds and a reddish pulp. This pulp, when extracted and dried, is a sour condiment used in Southeast Asian, Indian, and Middle Eastern food. Tamarind pulp is soaked in water to produce a juice that is used in seasoning curries and other long-cooked dishes, and in a syrup used to make soft drinks. Worcestershire sauce also contains tamarind.

AVAILABILITY

Whole tamarind pods as well as canned tamarind paste can be found in Indian-American ethnic markets and sometimes in Oriental ones.

TANSY

BACKGROUND

One of the bitter herbs eaten at the Jewish seder, *tansy* (*Tanacetum vulgare*) was extremely popular in medieval England. This herb, which has an affinity for eggs, was eaten at the end of Lent in omelets and custards called "tansies," which were believed to purify the blood. External applications of tansy were supposed to bleach away freckles. In the twentieth century, tansy is usually grown for its yellow flowers; but a few leaves, mixed with rosemary, can be used in herb breads, mixed herb omelets, and savory custards. (See HERBS AND SPICES for information on buying, storing, cooking, etc.)

TARO

BACKGROUND

No, not the name of Scarlett O'Hara's beloved plantation, but any one of several edible plants including *dasheen*, the genus *Colocasia* grown in the American south. *Taro root* (really a rhizome) is an important starch staple in the diet of many tropical cultures, including West Africa, Caribbean, and its original home, Polynesia. In Hawaii it is converted into the famous *poi*, a cooked and usually fermented paste. Some taro plant varieties have edible leaves. They can be prepared much like MUSTARD GREENS or TURNIP GREENS.

AVAILABILITY

The skin of the taro root is brown and fibrous, its length can vary from several inches to well over a foot, its width from one to several inches. The flesh can range from white to purplish, especially when cooked. Select firm, smooth and well-proportioned specimens.

PREPARATION

Store taro root in the refrigerator and use within a few days. The skin must be scrubbed, but need not be removed before cooking. Steam or boil 1-to-1½-inch chunks for 1 to 1½ hours. Taro roots can also be baked or added to soups and stews.

TEA

BACKGROUND

Several thousand specific varieties of *tea*, the world's most popular beverage, exist, yet all are the harvested young leaves (and center bud) of the tropical evergreen tree *Camellia sinensis*. Tea drinking originated in China at least 4,000 years ago. Britain was largely responsible for bringing the custom to Europe and to the American colonies. Just prior to our revolution, tea was the national beverage. If it were not for the Boston Tea Party and the following boycott, more tea than coffee would probably be consumed in America today. Sri Lanka (Ceylon), India, and China are the world's foremost tea producers, though large-scale plantations can be found in other lands such as Indonesia and parts of Africa.

A given weight of tea leaves has about twice the caffeine content of the same weight of coffee beans, but since you can brew over 160 cups of beverage per pound of tea versus 40 cups per pound of coffee, a cup of tea will have less than half the caffeine of a cup of standard coffee.

Varieties

Fermentation: All teas fall into one of three classifications—*black*, *green*, and *oolong*. The difference among them is not the kind of tea bush, but rather the degree of fermentation that the tea leaves and buds undergo.

Black tea has been fermented (oxidized) during the drying period. Black tea typically produces a reddish-brown tea in the cup and is by far the favorite type in America and England. The best known varieties include *Darjeeling* and *Assam* from India and *Keemum* and the smoke-flavored *Lapsang Souchong* from China. *Earl Grey* is a fragrant blend of Indian and Sri Lankan teas. Other popular black teas are named after personages, including *Prince of Wales* and *Queen Mary*. *Breakfast teas* are blends and tend to be more robust in flavor than standard black teas: *English Breakfast* and the even stronger *Irish Breakfast* teas are prime examples. *Orange Pekoe* refers not to a specific tea but to a leaf size.

Green tea undergoes virtually no fermentation and gives us a greenish-yellow liquid that tends to be less full and assertive in flavor than black tea. Green tea is exceedingly popular in Japan. An interesting Chinese green tea is the pellet-shaped *gunpowder tea.*

Oolong tea is a compromise between black and green teas as it is partially fermented.

Scented Teas: Some teas are infused with other fragrant ingredients, especially flowers: *jasmine* and *chrysanthemum* teas are the most famous examples. *Lemon tea* is also popular.

Herbal Teas: Not to be confused with true teas are herbal teas and tisanes that are made with aromatic ingredients such as chamomile, hyssop, and rose hip.

AVAILABILITY

Tea is sold in this country in various forms. *Tea bags* consist of measured quantities of tea encased in a porous paper envelope. Most of these products are mediocre at best, though tea bags of good imported brands can provide you with a good but not great cup of tea. *Instant teas* are also quite popular in this country and are even worse than ordinary tea bags. They are powdered products that are soluble in hot or cold water. They come plain, though more often have sugar and sometimes lemon flavor. *Pre-mixed teas* are sold in cans like soda pop and are likely to be cloyingly sweet and reek with additives. *Filter blend teas* are new concoctions designed for us in automatic drip-style coffee makers. *Loose teas* provide you with the best opportunity for a glorious cup of tea. They are typically sold in tins, boxes, or out of the barrel. Loose teas range in quality from poor to magnificent. The leaves can be sold *powdered, broken,* or *whole,* with the first state the least desirable, the last one the ideal.

Buying Tips

Even though stored in airtight tin containers, tea will lose much of its aroma and flavor within a year of the harvest. Tea sold in cellophane-wrapped paper boxes will deteriorate three to four times as quickly. It is essential, therefore, to buy tea from a merchant who has a rapid stock turnover and to buy in quantities that you will use within months (if stored in an airtight container) or weeks (if stored in a paper box). Do not buy tea out of a barrel in stores selling other aromatic foodstuffs such as cheese, because tea readily absorbs foreign odors. When buying loose tea out of an open storage bin, use these tests: sniff it for fresh, characteristic odor and crumble a leaf to see if it disintegrates into a powder (if it does, the tea is probably stale). For even extraction, buy uniform-sized tea leaves. As a general rule, high-quality tea is almost always equal-sized, inexpensive tea often is not.

PREPARATION

Storage

For greatest freshness, store all tea, including tea bags, in a tightly closed, moisture-proof container, preferably opaque, as light adversely affects tea. Do not place more than one variety in the same container or their aromas will mix. Keep each container on a dry, cool, dark shelf, never in the refrigerator. Green teas (with the exception of gunpowder tea) have shorter shelf lives than do black teas. Whole leaf tea will keep longer than broken tea—which will, in turn, keep longer than powdered tea.

Brewing

Loose tea: On the average, you will need 1 level teaspoon of tea for each standard cup (about 6 ounces) of tea. Place the tea in a warmed, clean teapot (preferably porcelain). Add freshly boiled water, cover the teapot, and let the tea steep undisturbed for 3 to 5 minutes, depending on how strong you want your tea. Do not steep the leaves for more than 5 minutes or the tea may become bitter. When properly steeped, briefly and gently stir the tea. Serve the tea immediately by straining it into individual cups or into a warmed, clean pitcher.

Iced Tea: You have two options for brewing iced tea. The traditional way is to brew hot tea at twice the normal strength, then add ice cubes or shaved ice equal to the volume of water. The best way is the cold-water method. Put the usual amount of tea (1 level teaspoon of loose tea for each 6 ounces of tea that you want) in a clean glass jar, then add cold water and, to taste, sugar and lemon juice and perhaps mint leaves. Refrigerate for 8 to 12 hours, then stir, strain, and serve. Always remember that your iced tea will only be as good as the tea leaves you are using.

Tea Bags: Depth of color is not necessarily an indication of the strength of flavor. Do not overextract the leaves, or the tea will become bitter and the tea will lose its inherent subtleties. If you prefer a stronger brew, use a stronger type of tea, an extra tea bag, or less water.

Serving

Many Americans and most Britishers are accustomed to adding milk, cream, or sugar to the tea, a custom that masks the delicate flavor of a good tea. Adding a bit of lemon juice is fine for a change of pace, but not if it is done all the time. (Iced tea, however, always seems to benefit from a small amount of lemon or lime juice.) The classic herb for flavoring tea is mint, but again, do not make the addition a regular habit.

TESTICLES

BACKGROUND

Of all the edible variety meats, it is undoubtedly the *testicles* that shock and embarrass most American diners. Yet, they are deservingly popular delicacies in many cuisines, particularly in Mediterranean lands such as Italy and southern France, where they are called *mogliatelle* and *animelles* respectively. In America the testicles of a calf (and sometimes of a lamb) are euphemistically called *mountain* or *prairie oysters*. *Fries* is the stateside appellation for lamb's testicles, which are sold in Italian ethnic neighborhood markets. Piglet testicles are best found in Chinese ethnic markets.

Buying Tips

The younger the animal, the better the testicles will be. It is sometimes necessary to order the meat ahead of time from the butcher. Testicles are very perishable and therefore must be very fresh and used within a day of purchase.

PREPARATION

Preliminaries

Cleaning: Wash testicles under cold running water. If the butcher has not already done so, make a lengthwise cut down the outer sack (scrotum). Gently ease the inner oval meat out of the scrotum. Snip off the connecting tube. Discard the scrotum and the loosely attached membrane that surrounds the oval-shaped meat. Gently wash the meat under cold running water until liquid runs clear.

Parboiling:Cover with cold water, add salt (1 teaspoon per quart) and bring to a gentle boil. Reduce the heat to a simmer and parboil for 5 minutes. Drain, discard the water, and pat the meat dry with paper toweling.

Cooking

Sauté: Dredge with seasoned flour and sauté the room-temperature testicles in butter, oil, or a mixture, until a light golden brown. *Deep-fry:* Bread the testicles and cook in 375°F oil until golden brown. *Braise:* Dredge with seasoned flour, lightly brown in hot butter or oil, cover with lid, reduce heat, and braise for 15 to 20 minutes, depending on size and age of animal. *Poach:* Add parboiled testicles to seasoned simmering water and cook for 25 to 35 minutes. *Marinate:* Poach the parboiled testicles for 10 to 15 minutes. Place drained testicles in a lemon-based marinade and refrigerate for 1 to 2 days. Serve cold.

TEXTURED VEGETABLE PROTEIN

BACKGROUND

Textured vegetable or *plant protein* is concentrated protein derived from protein-rich vegetables such as soy beans. It is often used to stretch commercial meat products such as frozen prepared meat dishes. It is also used to make *meat analogs* (such as ersatz bacon). Budget-minded home cooks mix it with ground meat in preparations such as meat loaf. There is nothing wrong with the nutritious textured vegetable protein so long as you know it is not a substitute for meat in terms of flavor, aroma, texture, and appearance.

THICKENERS

BACKGROUND

Cooks have at their disposal a number of ways to thicken sauces, soups, stews, and puddings. The most common *thickeners* are flour and other starches; others include EGGS, GELATIN, PECTIN, and even BLOOD (see all), plus rennin, seaweed, and others discussed at the end of this entry.

STARCH THICKENERS

Starch is food stored for future use by most plants in their seeds, fruits, roots, or tubers. Each plant stores the food in *starch granules* of a characteristic shape and structure. Starches are complex carbohydrates; each molecule is made up of many simple SUGARS (commonly several hundred) bound together in a characteristic pattern—a kinky chain or a branching structure. When you digest starches, they are broken down into the component sugars, which your body can use for fuel. You can use starchy foods in many ways—whole (as beans or potatoes), ground up into flour (which may be whole or have the bran sifted out), refined into a purer starch (as arrowroot and cornstarch), or converted to malt sugar and fermented (as in beer). In the form of a flour or a refined starch, it can be used as a thickener.

Thickening occurs when the starch and liquid are heated together to a specific range of temperature (which varies with the type of starch, but is typically in the neighborhood of 140°F to 180°F). Below that range, the granules do not absorb much water or swell as much as they can. At the proper temperature, absorption and swelling are at the maximum—and thus so is thickening. But if the mixture is cooked too long, or if it is stirred too much once it has thickened, or if it is heated beyond the proper point, the starch granules will be overly strained and will release some of the trapped water; as a consequence, the liquid will begin to thin again.

Methods

Most flours cannot be added directly to a hot liquid. If you do, the flour will lump, giving your sauce an undersirably lumpy texture. There are several ways to overcome this problem

Paste (or slurry) Method: Slowly mix

cold water into the flour (usually 2 parts water to 1 part flour) to develop what is called a *paste (or slurry)*, although it should be quite thin, like light cream. Slowly blend the watery paste into the hot liquid.

Roux Method: Here is the basic recipe for a *roux* (rhymes with "true"). For each cup of liquid, you will need 2 tablespoons each of butter and white wheat flour to make a medium-thick sauce (use 1 tablespoon of each for a thin sauce or 3 tablespoons of each for a thick one). Melt the butter without browning it in a heavy-bottom saucepan. Remove the pot from the heat and blend the flour into the butter with a whisk or wooden spoon. You now have an uncooked *roux*. Return the pot to the heat and cook the *roux* over low heat for 3 to 10 minutes, stirring frequently. A minimum of 3 minutes is necessary to rid the flour of its uncooked flavor as well as to increase the absorbency of the flour. The longer you cook the *roux* beyond that point, the darker and more flavorful your *roux*, and thus your eventual sauce, will be. As a rule of thumb, white sauces require 3 to 5 minutes, brown sauces 5 to 10. When the *roux* is cooked enough, start slowly blending the liquid into it adding just a tablespoon or two of the liquid at first. When the first bit of liquid is smoothly blended in, add more liquid, increasing the amount you add by about 50 percent. When this is blended into the developing sauce, continue to repeat the last step (each time increasing the quantity of added liquid by 50 percent) until all the liquid has been incorporated into the developing sauce. Then continue cooking over low heat, stirring frequently, for 3 to 7 minutes until the sauce has properly thickened.

Beurre Manié Method: By definition, *beurre manié* ("kneaded butter") is a 1/4-to-1/2-inch ball of butter and flour. To make these balls, rub together flour and softened butter in approximately equal proportions. Add a few of them into your hot liquid, stir until blended, then repeat the process until you have enough thickening power (the surplus *beurre manié* balls can be refrigerated or frozen for future use). This method works because flour granules that have been coated with a fat or oil will not lump together when they enter the hot liquid.

Tips

If your flour obstinately lumps despite your best efforts, the remedy is to strain the liquid through a sieve or layers of cheesecloth. Some cooks use their electric blenders or food processors to break up the lumps.

When thickening with flour, remember that sugar can inhibit the swelling of the flour granules, so if more than a scant amount of sugar is to be added to the liquid, add most or all of it after the liquid has thickened. Acid can create the same problem, too. Acid can also hasten the thinning of a cooked sauce.

Starch is a wonderful adhesive, as glue makers well know. This quality can cause cleanup problems if you let a starch paste dry (or overcook) on your utensils. Get in the habit of immediately rinsing as much of the starchy deposits off your utensils as you can, then soaking them to get off the last bits. Lukewarm or cold water works best; hot water can cook and therefore firm the paste.

Varieties

Wheat Flour: Use *white* rather than *whole wheat flour* for thickening because what you need is the starch (found in the endosperm) rather than the bran or embryo. (You need as much starch as you can get; even white flour is only about 90 percent pure starch.) White flour is the most popular starch thickener in American homes not because it is the best, but because it is the most commonly available and, therefore, is the one most cookbooks specify in their recipes. A good cook experiments with and gets to know other thickeners as well (described below). The chief virtues of white flour, compared to other starch thickeners, are its stability (the sauce will not thin as quickly) and its ability to withstand higher temperatures. A shortcoming is that it makes sauces grainier and more opaque than, say, cornstarch does. *Instant wheat flour* is a specially processed white flour that can be added directly to hot liquids without first making a paste, a *roux*, or a *beurre manié*. The time and work you save are offset by a loss in the thickened sauce's stability.

Cornstarch: America's second most popular starch thickener is *cornstarch* (sometimes called *corn flour*), which produces a smoother, more transparent thickened liquid than does white flour. This quality makes it better suited for making puddings (such as *blancmange*), fruit-pie fillings, and sauces. Most Chinese stir-fry recipes specify it. If a recipe calls for flour as a thickener, you can substitute cornstarch—but cut the amount in half, as cornstarch has twice the thickening power. Bear in mind, though, that a cornstarch sauce is more delicate than a flour sauce; you cannot cook it as hot or as long, or it will break down and thin. The best way to add cornstarch to a hot liquid is by the paste method.

Arrowroot: Even better than cornstarch in terms of producing a satiny, transparent thickened sauce, pie filling, etc., is *arrowroot*, the finely ground root of certain tropical plants. Arrowroot, however, fares worse than cornstarch in terms of sauce-thinning if cooked too hot or too long. Since arrowroot is flavorless, you need not cook it to remove its raw taste. And, since it thickens at a comparatively low temperature, arrowroot is ideal for egg-based dishes such as custards that might curdle if cooked over too high a heat. Arrowroot happens to be a very digestible starch and thus is often used (in place of wheat flour) in foods cooked for invalids and babies. The name *arrowroot* derives from the fact that the root was used in the tropical Americas to treat wounds inflicted by poison arrows. Arrowroot has slightly more than double the thickening power of white flour, so when substituting, use slightly less than half as much arrowroot.

Potato Starch: *Potato starch*, is similar to cornstarch and arrowroot in giving a liquid a silky texture and transparency as well as in its vulnerability to high or prolonged heat. When combined with the gluten-containing white wheat flour, *potato flour* is used to make potato bread. Potato starch is sometimes called potato flour, but in fact it is more refined, with a higher starch content and finer texture.

Tapioca: Made from the root of the tropical CASSAVA plant, *tapioca* is most familiar as the star ingredient in tapioca pudding. The starch comes in several forms, especially as pea-sized spheres (called *pearls*) for making the pudding, or as smaller granules, and as flour for use as thickener.

Other Starch Thickeners include filé powder as well as buckwheat, peanut, rice, rye, sago, soy, and waterchestnut flours.

Other Thickeners

Rennin: Used principally by cheesemakers to coagulate milk, *rennin* is an enzyme from the lining of the fourth stomach of calves and certain other young mammals. Rennin (or *rennet*, the rennin-containing membrane or extract) is also used as the thickening agent for other foods including junket, a sweet, often flavored dessert made with milk and sugar.

Seaweed: Some forms of seaweed are used to thicken liquids. Gaelic cooks use *carrageen*, popularly known as Irish moss. Oriental cooks use *agar-agar*, a flavorless substance that, when dried, resembles dried rice noodles.

Miscellaneous Thickeners: The cook has other options, including the use of *gum arabic* and *gum tragacanth* and the addition of ingredients that absorb moisture and take up space, such as rice, breadcrumbs, or soup-sized pasta. Even cream has thickening properties, as does OKRA. Finally, a sauce can be boiled down to get rid of water by *evaporation* (called *reducing* in culinary parlance).

THYME

BACKGROUND

Thymus vulgaris is ordinary cultivated *thyme*—ordinary because it is so easy to grow and has so many uses. *Mother-of-thyme* is *wild thyme* (*Thymus serpyllum*), a plant that forms a creeping blanket across the garden. *Lemon thyme* is a subvariety of *Thymus serpyllum*; it accentuates the lemon aspect of garden thyme's minty, lemony bouquet. The Hymettus honey of classical Greece came from thyme blossoms. The herbalist Culpepper recommended thyme tea before bedtime to prevent nightmares; the botanist Linnaeus prescribed it as a hangover cure. Experiments in either direction are harmless. (See HERBS AND SPICES for information on buying, storing, cooking, etc.)

AVAILABILITY

Fresh thyme is seldom marketed in America. Sometimes you can come across dried sprigs of thyme; these are superior to dried thyme leaves, which in turn are better than powdered thyme.

CLASSIC USES AND AFFINITIES

Perhaps because it retains much of its flavor when dried, thyme is one of the basic herbs of the French cuisine. It combines well with bay leaf, and is a common ingredient of BOUQUET GARNI. Thyme perks up cream sauces and creamed foods: fish and seafood chowder, for example, or creamed onions. Chicken takes well to thyme; so do bread stuffings and meatloaves. Tomatoes, eggplant, asparagus, and string beans are some of the vegetables with an affinity for this herb.

TIGER-LILY BUD

BACKGROUND

Golden needles is the Chinese name for *tiger-lily buds*, which look like 2-to-3-inch bits of dry, ocher-brown yarn. They are the dried buds of the tiger lily (*Lilium tigrinum*). Their best-known role is as a principal ingredient in the northern Chinese dish *moo shi ro*, though they can be equally effectively used as a flavoring and garnish in stir-fried dishes containing pork, poultry or seafood. In most cases, light color means good quality.

PREPARATION

Before cooking, soak the buds in water 30 to 60 minutes. Dried tiger-lily buds will stay fresh for at least a year if kept in a tightly closed glass jar in a cool, dark place.

TI LEAVES

BACKGROUND

Polynesian cooks use the leaves of the tropical *ti* tree as place mats and as a wrapping for foods as they cook. If you find them being sold in mainland states, the ti leaves will likely be dried rather than fresh, and therefore will have to be soaked in water before using them as a food wrapper.

TOMATO

BACKGROUND

The *tomato* (*Lycopersicon esculentum*)—like the potato a member of the nightshade family—is indigenous to the New World. When the European explorers brought the tomato back with them, the fruit was small and yellow—which gave rise to its modern Italian name, *pomodoro* (from *pomo d'oro* or "apple of gold"). The Italian horticulturists were largely responsible for breeding the small yellow tomato over the centuries into its present common form: large and red.

The tomato was only slowly accepted in Europe; it was thought to be poisonous, like some of its nightshade cousins. Some people, however, ate them with gusto for their alleged aphrodisiac powers; they were called *pommes d'amour* in French—"love apples."

Within the last several decades, American horticulturists have engineered a thick-skinned, inferior fruit to lower the costs of growing, harvesting, transporting, and storing tomatoes. The industry gains, the consumers lose.

Varieties

The most common tomato in America is the round, red type (including the larger, lumpy *beefsteak tomato*). Next in popularity are the 1-inch red *cherry tomatoes*, which are popular as garnishes or salad ingredients. Rapidly gaining acceptance is the excellent, egg-shaped Italian *plum tomato*—usually red, sometimes yellow. It is sometimes available fresh, widely available canned. Mexican-American markets sell fresh or in cans the small, globular *green tomato* which, unlike the other tomatoes, must be cooked.

AVAILABILITY

Alleged tomatoes are available all year, but true tomato season is high summer: July, August, and early September. For the best flavor, fragrance, texture, and appearance, a tomato should be ripened on the vine. Such tomatoes are red when picked and are very perishable. In order to prolong the storage life of a tomato, most commercial growers pick their tomatoes while the tomatoes are still green on the vine. These tomatoes are then ripened by intensely exposing them to ethylene gas. While they reach the market with a red skin, they are not and never will be ripe, and these tomatoes will have a cottony texture and minimal taste, scent, and succulence.

Tomatoes are also available canned. The four main types are *whole tomatoes* (good cooks select the peeled plum variety), *tomato puree* (most brands are unseasoned), *tomato sauce* (puree that is seasoned, usually ineptly), and *tomato paste* (a concentrate of cooked tomatoes that smacks more of the metal container than do the other canned tomato products).

Buying Tips

Unless you have a dire need for tomatoes, buy only vine-ripened ones. If none are available, we suggest you either forego them or, in cooked dishes, use good-quality canned Italian plum tomatoes. A good tomato will be well-shaped and heavy for its size. It should feel slightly soft (neither firm nor mushy) when gently squeezed. The skin color should be as deep red (or, in some varieties, orange-red) as possible. Examine the stem end. Reject tomatoes if you see green or yellow patches ("sunburn"), or deep growth cracks. Also reject tomatoes with bruised, moldy, blemished, or otherwise damaged surfaces. Buying tomatoes in a carton is chancy because you cannot examine the entire tomato. If unsure whether a tomato was vine- or gas-ripened, sniff it; the latter type will have little scent.

PREPARATION

Ripening

Unripe tomatoes should not be refrigerated or they will not ripen and will become mushy and mealy. The best ripening conditions are warmth (65°-70°F) and high humidity. The ideal environment for ripening tomatoes is a pierced paper bag containing a very ripe apple. The nonairtight environment allows carbon dioxide, which would slow down the ripening process, to escape. The apple gives off a small quantity of ethylene gas, which speeds up the ripening. Keep ripe tomatoes in the refrigerator or at cool room temperature, in the dark. Use tomatoes within a day or two of ripening.

Preliminaries

Wash tomatoes to rid their surfaces of chemicals, etc. Many recipes call for skinned tomatoes because the skin, when cooked, becomes shriveled and chewy. To remove the skin, submerge the tomatoes in boiling water for about a half minute, then immediately plunge them into cold water. The skin will be easy to remove. Or rub the dull edge of a knife gently against the tomato until the skin wrinkles and pulls off easily. To seed, scoop out the seeds with a pointed instrument such as a grapefruit spoon. Tomatoes drip and leak less if they are sliced vertically rather than horizontally, though the latter configuration is more attractive. Wedges make neater, dryer salads than slices do.

CLASSIC USES AND AFFINITIES

Tomatoes are delicious eaten raw with a sprinkling of salt and pepper. Basil is the classic tomato herb. Oregano, thyme, parsley, and chives are also excellent. Tomatoes are excellent when marinated in an olive-oil based *vinaigrette* sauce and served at room temperature. A salad of thick-sliced tomatoes and onion rings is a traditional accompaniment to steaks, roasts, and other robust meat dishes. As an attractive and tasty garnish, sprinkle seasoned and oiled tomato halves with breadcrumbs, then run them under the broiler. Tomato sauce is basic to southern (but not to northern) Italian cuisine. Tomatoes, raw or cooked, are good with most kinds of cheese. Tomatoes, of course, are essential for "BLT" sandwiches, ketchup, tomato sauce, tomato soup, tomato juice, *ragu bolognese*, pizza . . . the list could go on for pages.

TONGUE

BACKGROUND

The culinary highlight of some lavish Roman feasts was a dish of the tongues of tiny songbirds; you can imagine how many tongues were necessary for just a single portion. Today, the large beef tongue leads in consumer appeal. Tongue is an economical piece of meat when you consider the cost and waste are relatively low, and the nutrients, including protein, are high. But because it is a well-exercised muscle, it needs slow, moist cooking.

AVAILABILITY

Beef tongue is available fresh, cured (pickled, corned, or smoked), and cooked in cans and jars or sliced-to-order in delicatessens. Pickled lamb tongue is also available in some markets. A whole beef tongue weighs between 2 and 5 pounds. The smaller it is, the better it will probably be. Tongue of veal (1/2 to 2 pounds), lamb (1/4 pound) and pork (1/2 to 1 pound) are also available, but seldom in an unprocessed state. The reason beef tongue is more in demand than veal tongue is that it has more flavor (tongue can be bland after being cooked for hours) and, because of it size, is easier to slice into attractive pieces.

PREPARATION

Storage

Fresh tongue is extremely perishable. It should not be stored for more than 1 day in the refrigerator, for more than a couple of weeks in the refrigerator freezing compartment, or for a couple of months in a 0° F freezer. Cooked tongue will last a little longer in the refrigerator; if you freeze it, put it in its strained cooking stock for added flavor (use the stock for sauce or soup when you thaw the tongue). Cured tongue will last several days in the refrigerator if wrapped; it is generally not frozen, because some of the preservatives such as salt may keep the meat from properly freezing.

PREPARATION

Scrubbing and Soaking

Scrub the uncooked tongue with a stiff brush under tepid running water. If it has been cured, we advise soaking it for 2 to 3 hours in the refrigerator to help leach out some of its excess salt and any other residual preservatives.

Cooking

Parboiling: Blanching or parboiling is recommended primarily to give you a chance to get rid of the scum that will otherwise build up on top of your stock. Of course, you can skip the parboiling and skim the stock as it cooks, but this method is not as thorough. In a pot that is neither aluminum nor iron, cover the tongue with cold water. Bring to a gentle boil and simmer for 10 to 20 minutes, depending on the size of the tongue. Discard the water, rinse the tongue, and replace it in the cleaned pot.

Simmering: Cover the tongue with cold water (add 1 teaspoon salt per quart of water, unless it is a corned tongue). Because plain cooked tongue can be on the bland side, we suggest adding *court-bouillon* ingredients to the water (for instance, parsley, bay leaf, carrots, celery, onions, and peppercorns). Adding a touch of vinegar or lemon juice is also helpful; use a lot of vinegar if you want a pickled flavor. Bring the liquid to a gentle boil, cover with a lid, reduce the heat, and simmer till tender. This will take, depending on size, 2½ to 3½ hours for beef tongue and 1½ to 2½ for veal tongue. Do not let the water boil, or you will be serving a tough piece of meat. Test for doneness by piercing the thickest part of the tongue with a long-tined fork or skewer—if it goes in easily, the meat is done.

Skinning and Trimming

Remove the tongue from the simmering water and immediately plunge it into cold water. This makes the skin easier to peel off. As soon as the tongue is cool enough to handle (5 to 10 seconds), drain and pat it dry. Next, slit the skin lengthwise on the bottom side of the tongue, commencing at the root (thick) end. Peel off the skin from root to tip as you would a delicate glove—that is, with reasonable care. Sometimes the skin will stick here or there, but a sharp knife will help you separate the skin from the flesh when that happens. The only times you will have difficulty peeling off the skin are when the tongue is undercooked or when it was allowed to cool.

After skinning the tongue, trim away any small bones, fat, and gristle in the root end. If you do not plan to serve the tongue at once, put it back in its broth, which should still be hot enough to keep it warm. If you plan to serve your tongue cold, give it added flavor and juiciness by letting it cool in the refrigerator in its broth. If you have cooked a fresh tongue, strain and reserve the stock for making sauce or soup. If your tongue was processed, throw the stock away, as it will probably be filled with salt and other preservatives.

Carving

Tongue should be sliced across the grain, as thin as possible. The colder the tongue, the easier it is to slice: you should be able to cut 1/8-inch slices from cold tongue. With hot tongue, you may have to be satisfied with slices twice that thick. You can start slicing from either the root or tip end. We recommend the tip, since the root end is easier to hold onto. In order to make the slices as equal in size and thus as attractive as possible, start off by cutting the tip end at a diagonal and gradually make your slices vertical as you move toward the root end. Reserve the very tip for another use (such as a puppy scrap), as it will probably be on the tough side. Small tongues, such as those from lambs, can be sliced lengthwise, in order to make larger slices, but you will be cutting with the grain, sacrificing some tenderness, and the two outer slices will be definitely chewy.

Equivalents

Purchase 1/4 to 1/3 pound per person depending on appetites and eating attitudes.

CLASSIC USES AND AFFINITIES

The New York Jewish deli scene has made sliced-tongue sandwiches an American classic. In Brazil, tongue is one of the star ingredients in the national dish, *feijoada*. Europeans enjoy tongue in aspic or *gelée*, best prepared using a special circular tongue press. Tongue is also a popular addition to pâtés, salads, casseroles, and stuffings—and the muscle may also be stuffed itself. Many cooks interchange corned tongue for corned beef in recipes, as in New England Boiled Dinner. Spicy and piquant sauces are popular companions to tongue, mainly because of tongue's relative blandness. A second reason is that an assertive sauce makes tongue-eating more acceptable to the timid diner (with enough sauce, most people cannot tell the difference between corned beef and corned tongue). Among the most common sauces are mustard, horseradish, and sweet-and-sour raisin sauces.

TRIPE

BACKGROUND

Tripe is the lining of the stomach of a bovine. Some people extend the definition to include the stomach linings of all ruminants, such as sheep, goats, and deer. Most neophytes assume that tripe has a strong flavor. Not so. Tripe has a mild delicate flavor and, when properly cooked, a soft but chewy texture that makes even millionaires appreciate this inexpensive meat. Calves' "honeycomb" tripe is the choicest of all, but since little is found in the marketplace, this entry will focus on beef tripe.

Varieties

Unlike ours, a ruminant's stomach is multi-chambered. From the first stomach (the *rumen*) comes the "plain" or "flat" tripe that has a characteristic smooth, slippery surface. From the second stomach (the *reticulum*) comes the tenderest, most delicately flavored, and highest priced tripe, the *honeycomb*. It derives its name from the fact that its inner side has a honeycomblike pattern; the reverse side is relatively smooth. A variant of the honeycomb tripe is the *pocket* tripe, cut from the end of the second stomach. It is pocket-shaped with a honeycombed pattern on its inner surface.

Processing

By law, U. S. meat packers must wash, scrape, lime-soak, and partially cook the tripe before delivering it to wholesalers and retailers. In the old days, one had to perform these chores oneself—the pre-cooking alone took 8 to 12 hours.

AVAILABILITY

Tripe is sold in supermarkets fresh (that is, partially cooked). Canned tripe is also available, though its flavor and texture leave much to be desired. If you live in New England, you can usually find tripe pickled. This is fully cooked, but most cooks wisely parboil it for 15 minutes, or simmer it in water for a couple of hours, to reduce the assertive pickled taste. For the ultimate in pickled tripe, cure it yourself.

Buying Tips

The whiter, thicker (for the size of the animal), and more honeycombed the tripe, the better it will probably be. Avoid any tripe that is noticeably brown-tinged or that has lost its fresh scent.

PREPARATION

Storage

Even though tripe in this country is always sold partially cooked, it is quite perishable whether resting in the butcher's meat case or in your refrigerator. If you plan to refrigerate it, remove it from its original storage container. Then place it in a paper wrapping that is loose enough to allow some air circulation—this helps keep the surface dry, thereby slowing down bacterial growth. We advise cooking the tripe within a day of purchase.

Cooking

Parboiling: Some cooks parboil the tripe, others do not. We recommend doing it, especially if you plan to use the final delicious stock for a soup or sauce. First, thoroughly wash the tripe in cold water. If necessary, cut it into pieces that will fit into your kettle. Then, place the pieces in a large kettle and cover them with cold water, adding 1 teaspoon of salt for each quart of liquid. Bring to a gentle boil, then reduce the heat, cover with a lid, and simmer for 15 minutes. At no time during this or the next cooking step should the water actively boil. (That would produce the tough, rubber texture that has given tripe its undeserved bad reputation.) Drain and discard the water.

Simmering: It seldom makes any difference whether you are going to broil or deep-fry your tripe; you must first slowly simmer it until tender, as the muscle is well-used and therefore naturally tough. If you haven't parboiled the tripe, wash it, put it in a kettle, and cover with cold water. If you have parboiled it place the hot tripe in an empty kettle and cover with boiling water. Add 1 teaspoon of salt per quart of liquid. We recommend also adding *court-bouillon* ingredients, such as onions, carrots, celery, parsley, salt, and peppercorns. Bring to a gentle boil, then cover and simmer until tender. This will take 1½ to 2½ hours, depending on animal age, type of tripe (the honeycomb is tender and requires less time), amount of precooking done by the meat processor (it varies), size and thickness of pieces, and whether or not you parboiled the tripe. Then drain, reserving liquid for other uses.

Final Cooking: Lightly dry the tripe on paper toweling. When cool enough to handle, cut into bite-sized pieces (for instance, ½ -inch strips). It is now ready to eat with a sauce (such as red-hot tomato or seasoned *béchamel*), with a mixture of sautéed onions and green peppers, or in a soup or stew. There are other options: Dredge the squares or strips with flour and sauté them for a couple of minutes. Dip them in seasoned flour, then a beaten egg mixture, and coat them with breadcrumbs, then fry or deep-fry them. Coat them with a batter then deep-fry them. Broil them for 4 minutes per side 5 inches from the heat, basting them well with melted butter. Simply sprinkle them with vinegar or a vinaigrette sauce. You can also stuff the uncut tripe; when using pocket tripe, turn it inside out so that the honeycomb surface is visible.

Equivalents

Estimate 1/4 to 1/3 pound per person, depending on appetites and taste preferences. A whole honeycomb tripe will weigh a couple of pounds or so, but most tripe is sold cut into pieces weighing a pound or less.

CLASSIC USES AND AFFINITIES

The most celebrated tripe dishes include France's *tripes à la mode de Caen*. Philadelphia pepper pot, the Wild West's son-of-a-bitch stew, and *menudo*, a soup-stew found throughout most of the Spanish-speaking world. Though made with a sheep's (or deer's) stomach rather than that of a bovine, we cannot forget *haggis*, the national dish of Scotland. The paunch is stuffed with a mixture of heart and other offal, suet, onions, herbs, and oatmeal, then sealed and slowly simmered. At banquets, the haggis is triumphantly carried into the dining room with great fanfare.

TRUFFLE

BACKGROUND

Champagne and caviar are not the *ne plus ultras* of free-spending gourmets—*truffles* are. One reason they are expensive (several hundred dollars a pound) is because they are rare: truffles are edible fungi that live in symbiosis with tree roots (usually oak) and cannot be coaxed into growing. Sniffing dogs and pigs are used to locate the precious truffles, which grow several inches to a foot underground. The size of these wrinkle-faced fungi ranges from that of a peppercorn to a pomegranate, with walnut-sized being the average. Good truffles have a unique, elusive, permeating, ineffable aroma that can only be described by your nose.

Varieties

It is possible to find truffles around the world, from Asia to Africa to California, but it is in Périgord in France and in the Italian Piedmont that they flourish and are at their very best. Epicurean consensus is that the *black truffle*(or the "black diamond") of Périgord is the finest in the world. Some gourmets disagree: they believe the stronger, more earthy-flavored *white* (really cream-beige) *truffle* of Piedmont wins the contest. What counts most, in our opinion, is how good the individual truffle is, not whether it came from France or Italy, because the strength and quality of aroma and flavor vary greatly from specimen to specimen.

AVAILABILITY

The season for imported fresh truffles varies from year to year; typically it is from October through early December for the white truffle, January through mid-February for black truffles. Canned truffles are available the year round, but they are poor examples of the truffle in its full sensuous glory. A can (or glass jar) of truffles can either contain whole truffles or bits and pieces; the latter is less expensive, though still dear to most budgets.

Buying Tips

When buying a fresh truffle, look for a plump, well-formed, firm (but not hard or soft) fungus. Avoid those with bruises or abnormal color. Smell the truffle—it should effervesce with its characteristic aroma. When buying a truffle-laced pâté, beware of the dastardly doings of some chefs: they substitute chopped black olives or another jet black ingredient for the genuine article.

PREPARATION

Storage

Fresh truffles should be used as soon as possible. If they must be stored for a few days, place them in a glass container, cover them with a dry Sherry or Madeira, tightly close the container, and store in the refrigerator. Once opened, canned truffles can be kept for about a week in a glass container if submerged in their original liquid, tightly capped, and refrigerated.

Cooking

Truffles can be eaten raw or cooked. Either way, gently wash fresh truffles and peel off the skin, if it has not already been done. Save the peelings for flavoring sauces and the like. Truffles are usually sliced thin. Their flavor is easily infused into foods, so a little truffle goes a long way. To preserve the maximum flavor of a truffle, add it to a dish being cooked near the end of the cooking period.

CLASSIC USES AND AFFINITIES

Famous preparations featuring the truffle include *poularde demi-deuil*, *fonduta con tartufi*, and versions of *pâté de fois gras*. Many recipes call for the addition of truffles to various sauces (including *sauce périgueux*), omelets, salads, and pasta creations. The truffle, often cut decoratively, is used as an elegant garnish.

TURKEY

BACKGROUND

The domesticated turkey that graces most of our Thanksgiving Day tables has an interesting historical itinerary: its ancestors began life in the New World, spent a century in Europe, then returned to North America. After Cortez brought them from Mexico to Spain in 1519, the turkey spread into France, then England. The Europeans gradually bred the turkey into a plump, domesticated bird to such an extent that when the pilgrims settled in Massachusetts in 1620 they did not recognize any connection between the Europeanized turkey and its ancestor, the leaner wild turkey (see under GAME BIRDS). Being creatures of gustatory habit, the colonists imported the domesticated turkey to America, bringing it full circle. Modern American breeders have further evolved the turkey with an eye to mass production: the bird has been bred for a high proportion of white meat; within 20 weeks after hatching, it will grow to a hefty 12 to 16 pounds, ready for slaughter.

Turkeys share many culinary characteristics with chickens, so that, allowing for such obvious differences as size, much of the advice given in the CHICKEN entry on the following subjects is relevant:

- Background:
  - USDA Grades
- Availability:
  - Fresh or Preserved
  - Buying Tips
- Preparation:
  - Storage
  - Thawing Frozen Birds

Preliminaries
- Disjointing
- Seasoning a Whole Chicken
- Stuffing
- Trussing

Cooking
- Roasting
- Spit-Roasting
- Test for Doneness
- Pan Gravy
- The Oyster
- Broiling

Also see the separate entry, CHICKEN GIBLETS AND VARIETY MEATS. And keep in mind the following information that applies more specifically to turkeys.

AVAILABILITY

Season

Not too long ago, the turkey was a seasonal bird. Most were consumed at Thanksgiving, some ended up as Christmas fare, and very few were eaten during the rest of the year except in forms such as TV dinners, pot pies, and coffeeshop "chicken" soup or salad (it is no secret that some cooks substitute turkey for the more expensive chicken). The multi-billion-dollar turkey industry is trying to make the turkey a non-seasonal food by selling smaller turkeys that are family- rather than feast-sized, by selling turkey parts such as breasts, legs, and wings separately, by fashioning special pieces such as cutlets and rolled breasts, and by creating ersatz products such as turkey hams, hot dogs, bologna, sausages, and even pastrami. If success is measured in sales, the industry is succeeding.

Sizes and Varieties

Most turkeys raised in America are of the White Holland breed, usually sold as frozen *young hens* weighing 8 to 16 pounds. An increasing number of *fryer-roaster turkeys* are coming to market; they may be of either sex and weigh from 5 to 8 pounds. Mature *tom turkeys* of 20 pounds or more (the record is over 70 pounds) are becoming scarcer as American families and ovens grow smaller. Oversized birds are best simmered for use in salads, soups, and sandwiches; they tend to be too tough for roasting. Of special interest to thick-walleted gourmets is *smoked turkey*—especially smoked turkey breasts. It is usually sold precooked (read label), and needs only to be heated through. It is also wonderful when sliced paper-thin and eaten cold as an appetizer.

Buying Tips

If necessary, measure your oven before buying a whole turkey. If you want a fresh turkey, place your order with your butcher at least a week before Thanksgiving, as the demand sometimes outstrips the supply. We do not recommend the so-called "basted" or "self-basting" turkey. They are pumped with vegetable oil or butter combined with ingredients that give the flesh a curious flavor. Even worse, the injected juices tend to congeal into an unappetizing mass when the cooked turkey cools. And they cost more.

PREPARATION

Thawing

For reasons of hygiene, all frozen turkeys over 10 pounds should be thawed in the refrigerator. To minimize the loss of juices that leach out during thawing, we recommend that smaller turkeys also be refrigerator-thawed. As a rough rule of thumb, allow 1 day for a 6-pounder, 2 days for a 14-pounder, and 3 days for a 22-pounder. Since turkeys tend to be sold older (and bigger) than chickens, disjointing will be more difficult. Also, if you plan to divide the bird into serving-sized pieces, you will have to cut it into more parts than you would a chicken. Some frozen turkeys are sold prestuffed. If you buy such a bird (a choice we do not recommend), put it in the oven while still frozen. Follow the instructions on the label.

Cooking

Since a turkey will be in the oven longer than a chicken, you will have to take decisive measures to keep the breast from drying out. The best and easiest method is to place a piece of butter- or oil-soaked cloth or a double layer of cheesecloth on the breast, removing it 30 to 45 minutes before the end of the cooking period so that the breast will brown. We do not recommend using an aluminum-foil tent or a covered roaster, as the breast may steam and become mushy. Roast a stuffed, room-temperature turkey in a 325°F oven; figure on a time of about 20 minutes plus 14 to 17 minutes per pound. The lower figure gives the most succulent meat, the higher figure a drier bird that comes closer to the average American's preference. Either way, use these figures as guidelines—you must test for doneness. If your turkey is unstuffed, subtract 2 to 3 minutes per pound from the total cooking time. If the turkey is refrigerator-cold when you place it in the oven (a technique we do not recommend), add 20 to 40 minutes (depending on bird size) to the total cooking time. For easier carving and a juicier meat, allow the cooked turkey to rest 20 to 30 minutes under a loose tent of aluminum foil before making the first slice. Though turkeys are best roasted, small turkeys can also be broiled, barbecued, or spit-roasted as you would a chicken—with two major differences: cook the turkey farther from the heat and for a longer time than you would a chicken.

Equivalents

As holiday fare, allow 1½ to 2 pounds of whole turkey per diner—that should be enough for generous second helpings as well as for a midnight raid on the ice box. If you like turkey leftovers, buy 3 pounds per guest. For an everyday meal, figure on ½ to 1 pound per person of a whole turkey or ¼ to ⅓ pound of boneless breast meat, depending on appetities. Remember that there is proportionately more meat on a heavier bird.

TURMERIC

BACKGROUND

A relative of ginger, *turmeric* comes from the rhizome (underground stem) of *Curcuma longa.* Turmeric is an excellent, fairly colorfast, orange-yellow dye. It will dye textiles, tablecloths, the cook's clothes, and even chipped dishes, so be warned. (See HERBS AND SPICES for information on buying, storing, cooking, etc.)

AVAILABILITY

Turmeric is almost always sold as a powder; the rhizomes are difficult to grind at home. Unlike the case with some spices, you need not worry about a manufacturer adulterating your turmeric—it is not expensive enough to tempt him.

CLASSIC USES AND AFFINITIES

Turmeric is often used in curries, chutneys, and other Indian foods and in common American prepared mustard. A pinch of turmeric can also be added to dishes such as cream sauces, deviled eggs, rice, or broiled chicken—not enough to color or flavor the dish strongly, but just enough to add a hint of the turmeric color and fragrance. If you try to use turmeric to color food yellow, your tastebuds will, almost certainly, detect an unpleasant pungent aftertaste.

Some cookbooks say you can use turmeric as a saffron substitute. This is not true—or, at least, not advisable. Saffron is in a supreme class by itself.

TURNIP

BACKGROUND

The *turnip*, *Brassica rapa*, is one of the earliest known food crops, going back at least 4,000 years. It is probably native to the temperate portions of Europe and Asia. It is a root vegetable, easy to grow and long-keeping; it adapts well to the cold when it has to. The turnip provides two edible portions: the white-fleshed, purple-skinned root, and the green leaves, called *turnip greens*; the greens are a soul-food staple.

AVAILABILITY

Turnips and turnip greens are available fresh all year with their peak season in the fall and winter.

Buying Tips

Choose small, young turnips; large, older ones can give a coarse flavor and texture. If the green tops are attached, choose bunches with fresh, crisp, well-colored, unwilted foliage. The same standards apply when buying greens. Avoid cracked, ropy-looking turnips, or turnips with torn or scarred skins.

PREPARATION

Storage

Detach the root from the greens. The leafy parts draw moisture and nutrients from the roots. Use the greens as soon as possible, within a day or two. If sealed in a plastic storage bag, the turnip itself can be kept in the refrigerator for about a week.

Preliminaries

Turnips cooked in the skin are sweeter and more nutritious. If you must peel them, use a vegetable peeler as a paring knife can cut too deeply into the nutritious flesh near the surface. To minimize any bitter flavor, blanch older turnips before cooking them. For the greens, clip and discard the fibrous stems, and rinse the leaves well.

Cooking

Turnips are usually steamed or boiled for 15 to 25 minutes; steaming preserves more nutrients. Turnips may then be mashed or pureed, once peeled. Or try cutting turnips in tiny cubes and sautéing them with small cubes of bacon. A very popular Southern method of using turnips is to boil the turnip greens, turnip pieces, and fat pork together until the pieces of turnip are done. The result is odoriferous and very down-home, but the greens will be soggy and vitaminless. It's better to steam the greens separately in a scant amount of water (the wet leaves will be providing water, too) for 5 to 10 minutes, depending on personal taste. Turnip greens tend to darken and develop a metallic flavor if cooked in iron or aluminum pots, so use a stainless steel, tin-lined, or enamel-coated pot. Flavor with butter, salt and green pepper. Southerners flavor turnip greens with a ham bone or pork fat.

CLASSIC USES AND AFFINITIES

Turnips tend to overpower delicate seafood or chicken dishes. Serve them instead with hearty meat dishes such as pot roast, baked ham, or roast pork. Dill seed is a good seasoning for turnips. Or try a cream and mustard sauce.

TURTLE

BACKGROUND

Most lexicographers use the word *turtle* to include both aquatic and terrestrial varieties of this reptile, while most cooks use the following definitions: *turtles* lives in the sea, *terrapins* swim in salt marshes or fresh water, and *tortoises* are landlubbers. Tortoise meat is not considered as good as sea turtle or terrapin. Most people leave the tortoise to run its race with the hare.

Varieties

Turtle: A number of turtles have been put onto the endangered species list, but thanks to turtle farming in the Caribbean, the quarter-ton, sea-going green turtle is becoming increasingly available to the food industry. The greener its flesh, the better its meat. In all types of turtle, the female tends to have the tenderer flesh and, as a bonus, provides a treasure trove of undeveloped eggs which are delicious when cooked.

Terrapin: The best-tasting terrapin in America is the snapper, which usually weighs in at 6 to 20 pounds, though one of 88 pounds has been reported. This species is the prized ingredient in snapper soup made famous by Old Bookbinder's in Philadelphia. Besides soup, a diner can enjoy terrapin (as well as turtle) steak which is a pounded, thin slice of meat dredged in flour, then quickly sautéed.

Mock Turtle: There is also a mock turtle soup made with, of all things, bovine flesh such as a calf's head.

AVAILABILITY

Chinese-American ethnic markets are often a good source for fresh turtles. On request, they will clean your turtle and make it pot-ready. Ask for a female, and do not let the merchant keep the eggs for his own family. Turtle meat is very perishable and should be refrigerated and used within the day of purchase. Canned or frozen turtle meat, which is stocked in some gourmet stores, lacks the desirable flavor and texture of the fresh ingredient.

UGLI FRUIT

BACKGROUND

The Jamaicans call the *ugli fruit* the "hoogly," and it is. It looks dented and irregular, like a grapefruit that has been used as a punching bag. The thick, loose, spongy, easily peeled rind seems too big for its contents, a ball of juicy citrus sections waiting to be divided and eaten out of hand. While the flavor vaguely resembles that of grapefruit with orange overtones, its parentage is still open to debate. The ugli fruit is most readily available in this country during the winter months.

VANILLA

BACKGROUND

The vine *Vanilla planifolia* produces a yellow orchid and a long skinny seed pod called a *vanilla bean*. Inside each vanilla bean are thousands of minute seeds, the substances that give us the sought-after vanilla flavor and fragrance. So when a recipe calls for one-tenth of a vanilla bean, do not try to split one of those almost microscopic seeds. Though native to the Americas, the vanilla bean is now mainly grown on Madagascar and nearby islands.

AVAILABILITY

Since not enough vanilla is produced to satisfy the world's craving for this tropical seasoning, over 90 percent of "vanilla"-flavored foods (such as most vanilla ice creams) are flavored with *vanillin*, a synthetic chemical substitute, and not with nature's true vanilla. "Vanillin ice cream" would therefore be a more truthful appellation. Some manufacturers of high-quality ice cream make sure aficionados know they are tasting the real thing by leaving the vanilla seeds in the ice cream. Look for those tiny specks the next time you buy a cone—they are a sign of quality, not cockroach droppings, as some kids claim. Under federal law, anything sold as *vanilla extract* must contain only vanilla, alcohol and water. It may not contain artificial flavoring, although *vanilla flavoring* or *artificial vanilla* may.

PREPARATION

The longer a vanilla bean is stored, the harder and less aromatic it becomes. There are various techniques for storing a whole vanilla bean. One way is to simply keep it in an airtight glass jar in the refrigerator. Alternatively, whole or split beans (splitting the bean permits flavor to diffuse more easily) can be buried in a tightly closed container of granulated sugar. Several weeks later, the beans will be intact and the sugar will be impregnated with the aroma and taste of vanilla and will taste sweeter than ordinary sugar. A hot liquid can be vanilla-flavored by removing the preparation from the heat, inserting a piece of vanilla bean, and letting it steep for 10 to 20 minutes. The vanilla bean can then be washed, dried and reused several times. Or vanilla can be added directly to the preparation by scraping the black seeds from inside the split skin of the bean.

CLASSIC USES AND AFFINITIES

Vanilla intensifies the flavors of fruit, chocolate, and coffee. It makes sugar taste sweeter. It is marvelous with cream, custard, and whipped cream and flavors America's favorite ice cream. Almost any kind of dessert benefits from vanilla, either as a primary flavoring or as a flavor-enhancer. A tiny bit of vanilla bean can also be used in brewing coffee.

VEAL

BACKGROUND

Even in Biblical days, *veal* was considered a special edible; when the prodigal son returns, his father says, "Bring the fatted calf and kill it, and let us eat and make merry." Veal—the meat of a bovine calf of either sex—is still highly regarded today, but the enthusiasm for it is not equally shared in all countries. France and Italy have a culinary love affair with veal; in contrast, the average American eats only a couple of pounds of veal a year compared to over a hundred pounds of beef. And a lot of that American "veal" is really baby beef, not true veal.

Veal is easier to find in big cities than rural areas. If there is an Italian-American neighborhood nearby, you stand a good chance of buying fine quality. It will be expensive—but not, finally, as dear as you may think, for two reasons. First, there is little fat waste. Second, a study of eating habits confirms that a given weight of lean veal usually provides more servings than would an equivalent amount of beef, pork, or lamb.

Age of the Animal

The meat of the young bovine falls into three basic age groupings:

Bob veal
Veal
Baby beef

No precise official age standards exist; the USDA classifies veal by factors such as carcass conformation and bone development rather than age per se. But since some age determinant is more useful than none at all, we have informally polled meat experts across the country. Here is the consensus: the meat of a bovine from birth to the age of 1 month is *bob veal*; between 1 and 3 months it is *veal*; between 3 and 12 months it is *baby beef* (or *calves' meat*); over 12 months it is *beef*, though for the best beef you must wait until the animal reaches 18 months. The average carcass weight is about 100 pounds for bob veal, 150 to 200 pounds for veal, 300 to 500 pounds for baby beef, and 1,000 pounds or so for beef. These are very rough estimates, as the weight depends as much on breed and feed as on age.

Bob Veal: Some people jump to the conclusion that since veal is better than baby beef, then bob veal must be superior to veal. Not so. Bob veal lacks desirable firm texture. Just as bad, its flavor is too delicate for the cooking methods that can effectively be used for this lowfat meat. Sound advice is not to be seduced by the cute, miniature veal chops in your butcher's display case even if the flesh is a pale creamy pink.

Veal—Milk-Fed: By strict definition a milk-fed calf is a suckling calf, nourished exclusively on its mother's milk. (Nearly the same, but not quite, is the formula-fed calf described in the next paragraph.) Once the calf starts eating other food such as grass or grain, its pink-tinged, creamy-white flesh begins to darken. First it becomes pinkish-red, then rosy red, and then cherry red. The cause of this change is chiefly the iron in the new food—cow's milk has virtually no iron, so a calf's flesh remains pale until it finds a source of iron. The change involves more than color; texture and flavor are affected, too. Both normal growth and the switch to a nonmilk diet help to diminish the delicate veal flavor and to create a coarser texture. Contrary to popular notion, it is for the flavor and texture, not color, that gourmets prefer the meat of young milk-fed calves. The color is a sign of quality, not quality in itself.

Veal—Formula-Fed: The Netherlands was the principal pioneer in the

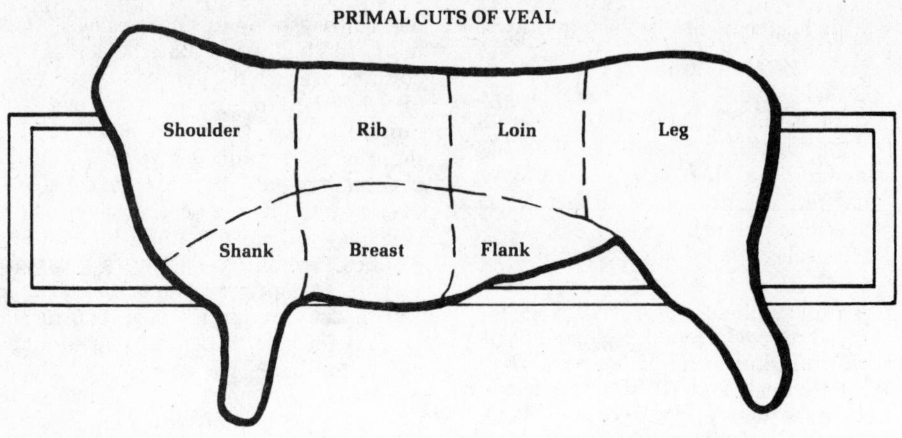

development of the "special-formula" feeding system, and consequently it is sometimes called the Dutch method. Essentially, healthy calves are fed dry milk solids that have been scientifically mixed with fats (to replace the butterfat removed from the milk), water, and selected nutrients. Some nutrients are proscribed: iron in specific and minerals in general, as these darken the flesh and therefore lower the market price of the meat. The feeders go so far as to not put metal pails or other metal objects within reach of a calf's tongue. For the record, these calves become anemic animals by man's, not by nature's, design. There are about a half-dozen major Dutch-method producers in this country.

The Dutch method does produce firm-textured, delicate, pale creamy-pink veal which is markedly better than the so-called veal sold in most American markets; its color comes close to matching that of true milk-fed veal. On the other hand, it is not on par with the superb quality of veal that comes from a calf fed solely on mother's milk, for at least two reasons. First, the special formula is not as rich as cow's milk in substances such as butterfat. Second, Dutch-method veal comes from calves about 15 weeks old and, accordingly, it is less delicate than if the same animal were slaughtered at, say, 10 to 12 weeks—the usual limit for milk-fed calves. Still, in all fairness, the 15-week-old formula-fed calf is not the equivalent of a 15-week-old calf that has been allowed to roam a ranch. The formula-fed calves are almost always kept in small pens where they cannot do much more than eat and gain weight—muscle-toughening exercise is not part of their regimen.

Baby Beef: Once the bovine passes the age of several months, its meat becomes discernably less delicate in flavor, tougher in texture, and redder in color. The flesh remains at this undesirable transitional state until the animal reaches maturity, at which time its meat develops the positive qualities associated with beef. Unfortunately, many butchers sell this baby beef as veal—and, worst of all, charge veal prices for it. Certain restaurateurs expand the culinary crime by chemically tenderizing this baby beef and then advertising on the menu the tender but mushy-textured result as veal.

Anatomical Location

The seven basic primal (or wholesale) cuts are shown in the illustration. The *shoulder, shank, rib*, and *breast* compose the *foresaddle*; the *loin, flank* and *leg* make up the *hindsaddle*. The area we know as the primal sirloin in the beef carcass is not separated in the veal carcass, but is divided between the primal loin and the primal leg in proportions that vary from meatcutter to meatcutter. (For a more detailed discussion of the muscle and bone structure of the bovine carcass, see the BEEF entry, especially each of the Primal Cut sections.)

Primal Leg: This is the source of veal *scallops* (described at the end of the cooking section below) and *cutlet steaks* (slices or cross-slices slightly thicker than scallops) as well as a number of basic *roasts*. The 3-to-6-pound *rump roast* should be boned and rolled, because its aitch bone makes carving difficult. The 3-to-6-pound *round roast* (or *center cut roast*, depending on how it was severed from the carcass) can be roasted as is, can be boned and rolled, or can be divided into smaller roasts such as *top round* and *top sirloin*. The 4-to-8-pound *shank half* cut can be roasted but is best braised because of its inherent toughness and its abundance of connective tissue.

Primal Loin: One seldom encounters a veal *loin roast* because butchers almost always cut the loin into 3/4-inch to 1½-inch *chops*—the anatomical equivalent of the beef club, T-bone, and porterhouse steaks. It is the "porterhouse" veal chop that gives you the best value, as it contains a fair portion of the tenderloin muscle and, usually, has more lean and less waste per pound than do the equal-priced "T-bone" and "club" veal chops. Any of the chops can be stuffed; they are particularly attractive when they are Frenched, with paper frills adorning the trimmed ends of the rib bones. A tasty variation on the theme is the *veal kidney chop*: a cross-section of part of the kidney is left attached with suet to the standard loin chop. You will likely have to special order this cut from a premium butcher. Some butchers slice the loin muscle into so-called *scallops*. If you can find a *loin roast* (3 to 6 pounds), make carving easier for yourself by having the butcher loosen the chine bone or have him bone and roll your loin roast. For a festive treat for a large dinner party, buy a 10-pound *saddle* or *double loin* in which both the right and left loin sections are kept attached.

Primal Rib: This wholesale cut normally contains seven ribs (the sixth through the twelfth), but we rarely see this rack of veal in a meat case; it is usually butchered into more marketable *single* or *double-rib chops*. The first is ideal for Frenching, the latter for stuffing. Both are best braised. Rib chops cut closest to the loin section are better because they are more tender and have a greater proportion of desirable lean to bone and fat waste. The 3-to-5-pound *rib roast*, if you find one, can be roasted standing or can be boned and rolled. The primal rib should sell for less per pound than the primal loin, because it has less tender meat and more waste. A stunning dinner-party dish is the *crown roast*. To prepare it, buy two or more racks of veal (ask your butcher to crack the chine bones to facilitate carving). French them—that is, trim the last 1½ inches of flesh and fat from the ends of the rib bone. Then curve (with the rib bones facing outward) and sew together these racks into a circle. Stand the crown on its backbone with the rib ends pointing skyward; protect them from scorching by wrapping each tip in aluminum foil. When roasted, fill the cavity with a cooked vegetable or meat stuffing (some cookbooks tell you to cook the stuffing along with the roast, but this keeps the roast from cooking evenly). Remove the foil and garnish the exposed rib tips with paper frills, cherry tomatoes, or pitted apricots. Bring the crown roast to the table and slice between the ribs to produce individual rib chops, allowing two chops per person.

Primal Shoulder: Anatomically, and in terms of flavor and value, this cut is the equivalent of the primal beef chuck. It can be boned and rolled whole but more often it is divided into smaller, more marketable units: a *blade roast* (containing the scapula) and an *arm roast* (containing the arm bone and at least three of the first five ribs). Both of these 3-to-5-pound retail cuts can be boned and rolled for easier carving or can be sliced into 3/4-to-1 1/2-inch-thick *blade* and *arm steaks*. Whatever the cut, the meat should be cooked with slow moist heat, such as braising. Cutting scraps can be ground.

Primal Shank: Meat markets sell both veal *foreshank* and *hindshank*, but they seldom differentiate it as far as labeling goes. The best is the foreshank, a crosscut slice of which stars in the classic Milanese *osso buco*. (The name literally means "bone hole," referring to the marrow nestling inside the slice of bone.) The shank needs slow moist cooking to help break down the large amount of connective tissue and to tenderize the relatively tough lower leg muscles. Shank meat and bones are good for soups, sauces, and stews, giving them flavor, nutrients, and collagen, a liquid-thickening substance. French chefs throw these and other veal bones into their stockpots to make their white-sauce foundations.

Primal Breast: Breast of veal comes from the area that, in a mature steer, provides two primal cuts: breast and plate. Veal breast is bony, but the retail price more than reflects that fact. It is also more versatile than most shoppers believe. You can braise it bone-in; bone and roll it, then braise it; stuff it, either bone-in or boned; cut it into *riblets* ("spareribs") for braising or stewing; bone and cut it into lean chunks for stewing; or grind it. A primal veal breast can weigh roughly 8 pounds and be about 2 feet long, but butchers usually sell it in 3-to-4-pound *halves* or in smaller pieces. If you plan to stuff a bone-in veal breast half, be sure to buy the rib-filled rear half, the one that comes from the area near the loin section. It is distinguishable from the front half in that it is squarish rather than having one side curved like the tip of a knife. To make the cavity, use your hands to separate the ribs and their surrounding meat from the lean that lies next to them. Once stuffed, sew the cavity shut with kitchen twine.

Primal Flank: You will seldom see this cut sold as flank because the butcher either tosses it into his meat grinder or cuts it up and labels the resulting chunks as veal *stew meat*. It is too thin to be cooked like a London broil.

AVAILABILITY

Veal is available year round, but it does have its season when supplies peak and prices move downward: spring.

Buying Tips

High-quality veal is expensive but worth its price. Low-quality veal and baby beef are seldom a bargain, because for the same or less money you can usually buy full-fledged beef, a superior food. The color of milk-fed veal is pink-tinged creamy white. Veal that is pinkish-red, rose-red or, worst of all, cherry-red comes from a calf that is too old and should be left in the meat case. Good quality veal has a reasonably firm, velvety, fine-grained texture. Leave any veal that is soft, excessively dry or moist, or brown-tinged. Browning usually indicates prolonged or improper storage. Fine veal has a fresh scent. Avoid veal if you see liquid in the package. The meat was probably frozen, then thawed—the flavor and texture will never be the same again. Good veal has no marbling and only minimal exterior fat, if any. That fat should be firm and creamy-white, not brownish- or whitish-yellow. The highest USDA veal grade is Prime. Next comes Choice (the best seller), followed by Good. Lesser grades are seldom encountered in the retail market.

PREPARATION

Storage

Veal is much more perishable than beef. Veal scallops and ground veal should be used within hours of purchase. Veal cubes, chops, and cutlets can be kept for up to 24 hours in the refrigerator if loosely wrapped so that air circulation will keep the surface reasonably dry, thereby hindering bacterial development. Large veal cuts should be treated in the same manner, though they will probably stay fresh for up to a day longer if the meat was in perfect condition to begin with. No meat freezes well; this is particularly true of veal. You will always lose some flavor, texture, and juiciness. If you must freeze it, tightly seal it in freezer wrap and store it up to a couple of weeks in the frozen food compartment or up to a few months in the 0°F freezer. Up to a point, the larger the piece the longer it can be frozen.

Cooking

Veal is the most difficult of the "big four" animal meats to cook. Unlike beef, pork, and lamb, veal has little natural fat to keep it moist and juicy if it is cooked with dry heat. The relatively high amount of connective tissue and the absence of internal marbling also argue against dry-heat cooking. Consequently, with the exception of sautéing veal scallops and roasting cuts such as the loin, veal almost always needs slow, moist heat such as stewing or braising.

Another idiosyncrasy of veal is that for greatest flavor and tenderness, it must be cooked until it is relatively well done. But don't cook a veal roast to an internal temperature of 170°F or higher, as most cookbooks recommend; 160°F is fine. If veal is cooked too long or at too high a heat, it becomes dry, tough, coarse, and stringy.

The flavor of veal is so delicate that some call it bland; it needs seasoning, a sauce, or a stuffing to enhance its savor. But the veal taste should not be smothered, so keep assertive flavorings out of the pan: subtlety is the objective.

Roasting: Many cooks believe that veal is not suitable for roasting, and to some degree they are right. For those cooks who like roast veal, here are a few tips. The meat must be barded, larded, or basted every 15 minutes. The meat should not be seared in a hot oven. Rub the surface of a room-temperature roast well with butter or oil, then season, then cook it on a rack in an open roasting pan in a preheated 325°F oven for 25 to 35 minutes a pound. The thicker the piece, the fewer minutes per pound; rolled or stuffed roasts require the longer times. Cook until the meat thermometer registers 150° to 155°F; the roast will continue cooking up to 160°F once it is removed from the oven. Test for doneness by pricking the roast: it is ready when the juices start to run clear. Remove the roast from the oven, lightly cover it with aluminum foil, and let it sit for roughly 15 minutes to allow the internal juices to settle. The roast is now ready to carve.

Braising: There is debate over whether the meat should be browned before braising: some say browning ruins the delicate texture; others (ourselves included) say a bit of browning improves the flavor. It is a trade-off. Large cuts of veal take about 1½ to 2½ hours to braise. Meat that is thick or that has been stuffed will obviously require the longer cooking. Veal shanks need about 1½ hours. Veal chops and rib steaks—whether breaded, dredged, or plain—can be braised in about 25 minutes.

Stewing: If you want to eliminate some of the edible but unsightly veal scum that collects in a stewing liquid, then parboil the meat for 5 to 10 minutes and discard the water before stewing the meat. Estimate 1½ to 2 hours' stewing time for 1½-inch-thick chunks. For a fricassee such as *blanquette de veau*, the meat should not be browned. Good veal cuts for stewing are the relatively inexpensive breast and shoulder. When making stews, do not forget to add veal bones to the pot—they contribute flavor and nutrients, and their collagen helps thicken the liquid.

Sautéing Scallops: Americans call them *scallops*, the British *collops*, Italians *scaloppini*, and the French *escalopes*. Whatever their name, scallops are thin, boneless slices that technically should be cut from the upper portion of the leg, though some butchers also cut them from the loin, rib, or shoulder. You can buy scallops ready to cook, or you can slice your own: with a sharp knife cut the meat across the grain into 1/4-inch slices, then pound the slices into a thickness of about 1/8 inch. If your slices are much more than 1/4 inch, your pieces should more appropriately be called *cutlets* than scallops. Each scallop must be a cross-section of one muscle rather than two or more connected by a membrane, because the separate muscles will break apart or curl away from each other when sautéed. Your pounder can be a specially designed scallop mallet, the bottom of a heavy pan, or you name it. Place the to-be-pounded scallops between layers of plastic wrap—this works much better than the usual waxed paper. Whatever the thickness of your pounded slices, they must be uniform for the sake of even cooking. Each flattened piece can measure anywhere from an oval of several inches in length, for *saltimbocca*, up to a size that almost fills the bottom of the sauté pan, for *Wiener Schnitzel*. Pound the pieces from the center outward. Be firm but not brutal, as excessive force will mutilate the scallop. Take out your aggressions elsewhere. Some of the veal sold in markets is cut with rather than across the grain. Should you mistakenly take home such a scallop, you can make the best of a bad situation by scoring one or both sides of the meat with latticework slashes. The flavor of scallops is generally enhanced by being either breaded or flour-dredged. Sauté the scallops quickly lest you overcook them and thereby create tough, dried-out flesh; 2 to 3 minutes (depending on thickness) per side over medium to high heat should be sufficient. Leave space in the sauté pan between the individual scallops. Otherwise, excess moisture will be trapped under the meat; the resulting steaming action will make the flesh mushy. Scallops almost invariably need some type of sauce—for which there are a myriad recipes from Vienna to San Francisco. The sauce can be elaborate or can simply be a squeeze of lemon juice and a sprinkling of chopped fresh parsley.

Ground Veal: Too lean to be cooked by itself, ground veal needs some form of added fat. Without the fat, your veal meat loaf or patties would be unappetizingly dry. For each pound of ground veal, add a couple of ounces of fat. Alternatively, do as the Scandinavians do: mix veal with an equal amount of a not-too-lean combination of pork and beef—or mix equal parts of each of these three meats. Generally, the less expensive veal cuts such as shoulder, breast, and plank are used for ground veal. City chicken and veal Pojarski are two well-known ground-veal specialties.

Equivalents

The average diner will likely be satisfied with 1/4 to 1/3 pound of boneless veal or 1/2 to 3/4 pound of bone-in veal.

CLASSIC USES AND AFFINITIES

Restaurant menus teem with dishes such as:

Vitello scaloppini alla Marsala
Vitello Milanese
Saltimbocca alla Romana
Involtini (veal birds)
Veau cordon bleu
Naturschnitzel
Wiener Schnitzel à la Holstein
Escalopes de veau Prince Orloff
Veal Marengo
Vitello tonnato

Veal, with its unassertive taste, is adaptable to many flavorings, including these well-established affinities: sage, rosemary, thyme, tarragon, lemon juice, dry white wine, subtle ham, mild cooking cheese, and tomatoes. These flavorings, however, must not overpower the principal cooking ingredient.

VINEGAR

BACKGROUND

Vinegar is used as a flavoring, as an ingredient in marinades, and in pickling solutions. The word *vinegar* means "sour wine"—it stems from the French words *vin* (wine) and *aigre* (sour). It is so named because most of the French prepare their homemade vinegar from wine that has gone sour (intentionally or accidentally) after being attacked by a special type of bacteria. Excellent vinegar is also made from other fermented liquids such as apple cider and rice wine. The best wine vinegars generally come from France, especially from Orleans and nearby. Superb vinegar is also made in Spain from sherry, a fortified wine. Japan makes quality rice vinegar. America's mass-produced malt and cider vinegars are generally undistinguished, though some good local producers do exist.

You can make your own vinegar at home, but for a worthy product you need a *mother of vinegar*, the starter. A little can be "borrowed" from a vinegar-making friend or, sometimes, can be bought from a local vinegar producer.

Flavored vinegars—with ingredients such as tarragon—are sold. Our advice is not to buy them but instead to steep your own at home to your taste. You will probably save money, too.

Verjuice is not to be confused with vinegar, though in most instances it can be substituted for it. Verjuice—literally "green juice"—is the sour unfermented juice of green fruit, including grapes and crab apples.

WASABI

BACKGROUND

The pungent *wasabi* is a condiment served with *sashimi*, a raw-fish preparation. Wasabi—the "Japanese horseradish"—is best when freshly grated. It is available in this country in powdered form in small cans; when reconstituted with a touch of water, it becomes a ready-to-serve green paste.

WATER

BACKGROUND

The human body is mostly water—for adults, the figure is about 75 percent. People can live without food for a number of weeks, but can survive only a few days without water. To stay healthy, the average adult needs to imbibe about 2½ quarts per day. However, it doesn't all have to be downed straight. Much of the H_2O consumed is in the solid food people eat and in the wine, beer, coffee, tea, milk, orange juice and other beverages they drink.

Varieties

Tap Water: The water that flows from the kitchen tap varies significantly across the U.S. Its taste—largely determined by the amount of dissolved chemicals and minerals—varies according to its source, storage, treatment and delivery system. At its worst, tap water will be brackish, highly chlorinated, sulphurous, or have an iron taste. At its best, it will taste clean with just a hint of minerals. No tap water is flavorless, though if you drink a particular source for a few months or more, your ability to detect its flavor diminishes.

Although U.S. municipal tap water is adjudged by the consensus of international experts as the best in the world, it has its critics. These antagonists believe that the drinker's health is endangered when a public water system adds chemicals to its water (as most do). Most authorities disagree. They believe that the chemicals do more good than harm. For example, chlorine is a necessary disinfectant and flouride helps prevent tooth decay. (Flourides, it should be noted, are naturally present in about half of our nation's water supplies.) Moreover, some additives—such as copper sulphate, which is used to control algae—are removed before the water reaches your tap.

Not all the foreign matter in your water comes courtesy of your local water system management. Microorganisms, dirt, and other impurities are in the water from the start. (Even rain water isn't pure since it picks up pollutants from the atmosphere.)

For those concerned about chemical additives and impurities in their tap water, there are activated charcoal filters (similar in concept to some cigarette filters). These devices, which attach to the tap, are not as effective in removing foreign matter from water as some manufacturers claim. If you do use a filter system, keep it clean or it will play host to countless germs.

Bottled water: There are many ways to classify bottled waters. The most common way is:

Natural mineral water
Purified water
Distilled water
Soda water

Natural mineral water is also known as "natural mineral table water," "natural spring water," or "natural mineral spring water." It should be just that: natural, containing no additives and flowing naturally to the earth's surface, where it is generally bottled on the spot. There are two types of natural mineral water. *Still* mineral water is uncarbonated and often bland. *Sparkling* mineral water, on the other hand, has natural CO_2 and a tingly taste. Sparkling mineral waters generally have more sodium and still mineral waters have less sodium than tap water. Because of the presence of sodium sulphate, some sparkling mineral waters have a laxative effect.

Purified water is less expensive than natural mineral water. It comes capped by a number of different names such as "spring-type," "spring-pure," "spring-fresh," "filtered," "formulated," "processed," or "treated." Purified bottled water contains only a small amount of natural spring water, if any at all. In many cases, it is merely tap water that has been treated to remove all minerals or trace elements, and then formulated to replace certain minerals. It is increasingly popular in those parts of the country where the local tap water tastes bad or is suspected to be unhealthy.

Distilled water is virtually free of all chemicals, minerals or elements. It is generally used in baby formulas, hospitals, and industries. It tastes flat.

Soda water is water that has acquired its effervescence by artificial means. Bottlers suffuse H_20 with carbonic acid, the basis of the bubbles, and sell their product under such names as "soda water," "club soda," and "seltzer water." Salts give these beverages their characteristic alkaline or "soda" flavor. They are also usually sweetened to various degrees and can be given a distinct personality by the addition of, for example, the bitter alkaloid quinine to make quinine water of gin and tonic fame. Often these effervescent tonic solutions are infused with citrus flavor and/or bitters which partially explain why most palates never detect how much sugar these beverages usually contain. Carbonated water is also used in the preparation of the countless varieties of soft drinks that line supermarket shelves.

Buying Tips

A glass bottle is the best storage container. A plastic container creates odors and affects taste when plastic molecules leach into the water. All bottled water is subject to FDA regulations; states also set their own standards. "Spring water" must declare its source; other types of water are not required to. Imported bottled waters (which make up the majority of natural mineral water consumed in the U.S.) must meet FDA standards for foods and beverages. All bottled water should be purer than tap water. Occasionally, however, there may be a brand which has a higher concentration of contaminants than tap water. To be on the safe side, buy a known and reliable brand. Check the bottle cap to see that the bottle has been well sealed. This assures you that no foreign substance has entered and possibly contaminated the water, and that no one has changed the contents.

PREPARATION

Cooking

Your choice of water for cooking or brewing does make a difference in taste, as brewers have known for a long time. An old maxim says that a beer is only as good as the water used to make it. The same principle applies to a cup of tea. If your tap water has an off-flavor, consider using bottled still water. Because of its clean taste, bottled still water can be made into ice or used in making juices, tea, coffee, or used in cooking in general. Don't use water from the hot tap for cooking—this water has likely picked up a metallic taste from the hot water heater and pipes. Let the cold tap water run for a short period before drawing it—the water standing in the pipes has probably collected an off-flavor. The level of mineral salts in water does affect its cooking performance. Cooking vegetables in hard water has its disadvantages. If you cook one half of a batch of vegetables in soft water and the other half in hard water, the second half will be tougher. If your vegetables are potatoes, rice, or onions, the second half will also develop more of a yellow tinge. Hard water, however, is better for making yeast doughs because soft water can make dough gummy and soggy. Water boils atsealevel at 212°F (100° C). For every 1000 feet above sea level, the boiling point drops by about 2°F (1°C). The boiling point of water is raised with the quantity of particles dissolved in it which includes the salt you add when cooking. If you are unsure of the potability of water, boil it for 20 minutes. This process should kill almost every possible organism. When water that has been boiled tastes flat, pour it from one vessel to another and let the air freshen it. Soft and softened water, incidentally, are better than hard water for cleaning because they produce more suds from soap or detergent. And when the H_2O evaporates, there will be less film residue on your glasses and other objects you have washed.

WATER CHESTNUT

BACKGROUND

In the Orient and Southeast Asia, the aquatic *Eleocharis dulcis* is often intercropped with rice; it grows well in the dampness of the rice paddies. The edible part of the plant is the brown or black tuber, somewhat like a western chestnut in shape and size. The flesh inside is white, with a bland flavor but an agreeable, juicy crunch, which is especially welcome when a meal consists of a few stir-fried vegetables and a comparatively large volume of soft rice. Water chestnuts are also used in soups or as a garnish.

AVAILABILITY

Fresh water chestnuts are available the year round in Chinese markets—look for firm specimens. The vegetable is also sold canned, dried, or ground into a flour which makes an excellent thickener and batter base.

PREPARATION

Refrigerate the unpeeled tubers; use them within five days. To prepare a fresh waterchestnut, wash and then peel it. It can then be eaten raw, or sliced for stir frying. A water chestnut can also be peeled and eaten after it has been boiled for 3 to 5 minutes.

WATERCRESS

BACKGROUND

You may be able to find *watercress* (*Nasturtium officinale*) growing wild along freshwater banks from mid-spring through early summer. If not, do business with your greengrocer. The dark greencround, half-inch-wide leaves and the crisp, juicy stalks render a pleasing, pungent, mildly bitter aftertaste.

AVAILABILITY

Watercress is typically sold bouquet-style. Select a bunch with a bright, deep color and a healthy surface glow. Avoid those that are wilted, yellow-tipped, or sour-scented.

PREPARATION

You can store fresh watercress in a plastic bag (or, stem down, in a half-inch of water in an airtight glass jar) for two or three days in the refrigerator. Wash it gently in cold water just before using. Raw watercress is used as a salad green or as a colorful garnish for roast meat. The leaves and stalks may also be simmered or braised in butter for a few minutes.

WATERMELON

BACKGROUND

Of the half-dozen most popular melons, the *watermelon* is the least sophisticated because of its watery and less-than-rich flavor. One explanation for this difference is that the watermelon is a member of the *Citrullus* genus, while the others belong to the *Cucumis* genus. A watermelon comes into its glory on a hot summer afternoon when cooling refreshment rather than style brings the most pleasure. Little of the watermelon needs to be wasted. Asians and health-food enthusiasts love the roasted seeds, while people on nearly all continents relish the pickled rind.

Varieties

The number of watermelon hybrids is virtually beyond count. America's best-selling type is the elongated oval watermelon whose rind is mottled or striped dark green, or grayish with green stripes, depending on specific variety. The round, blackish-green cannonball variety is also found in many markets. (For the record, the Santa Claus or Christmas watermelon is a *Cucumis* and therefore is not a watermelon in the narrow definition of that word; while it is shaped like a watermelon, its flesh is more reminiscent of the honeydew.)

AVAILABILITY

The watermelon is generally available from May through September, but peak season runs from mid-June to late August.

Buying Tips

Whole Watermelon:Buying a whole watermelon is like buying a pig in a poke. You can judge other melons accurately by inspecting the exterior, but a watermelon gives you only sketchy clues. If your seller won't cut a sample plug or slice so you can examine the flesh, you must make the best of the following guidelines: The deeper the surface color of a watermelon (for its variety), the more mature it is. As the watermelon matures on the vine, the white underbelly (the part that rests on the ground hidden from direct sunlight) develops a creamy-yellow hue. This is perhaps the most reliable indicator. A ripe watermelon has a somewhat dull, but not overly dull, surface. And that surface can usually be shaved with a stroke of your fingernail. (Understandably, greengrocers hate this test.) Give the watermelon a sharp slap with the palm of your hand. If it replies with an echoing, hollow, thumping sound, you have a good sign of ripeness. But if it responds with a flat, dull thud, the melon was picked prematurely. If the sound is too hollow, the watermelon is over the hill. The shape should be symmetrical, never flattened along one side. The two ends should be round and well-developed. Press the two ends with your fingertips. If ripe, the rind will just slightly yield to the pressure. Overall, the rind should be firm and devoid of soft spots (which suggest internal decay) as well as mold, bruises, cracks, and other injuries. Some showcase watermelons reach 50 pounds or more. The best melons usually seem to weigh from 15 to 30 pounds.

Cut Watermelon: The flesh should be a bright rose red. Pastel red or white streaked flesh likely means the melon was picked prematurely. A mature watermelon has hard black or brown seeds. An immature one has a noticeable number of soft white seeds. The flesh should be firm and moist, not fibrous, mushy, grainy, or dry, which suggest that the melon was picked too late or was stored too long or improperly. Finally, sniff the flesh to check for a fresh, sweet fragrance.

PREPARATION

Storage

Watermelons do not ripen much after they're picked, so use it as soon as possible, and don't buy an immature watermelon in the hope that a miracle might occur. A whole watermelon should be stored in the refrigerator, if you have the space. Otherwise, keep it in the coolest part of your home until ready to eat. It should keep in the refrigerator for a week or so, depending on original condition. A cut watermelon should be eaten as soon as possible, as the exposed flesh rapidly deteriorates. If refrigerating is necessary, tightly seal the cut portions in plastic wrap and use within a day or two.

Serving

Watermelons should be served colder than other melons. The simplest way to eat a watermelon is, of course, to slice a wedge and eat it out of hand. This can also be the messiest method, but the sensual satisfaction may be worth the soiled shirt or lap. A more elegant way of serving watermelon is to slice a wedge into bite-sized cubes which are left in place on top of the detached rind. You can also use a melon-cutter to make watermelon balls, but we do not recommend adding them to a mixed fruit compote, as the watermelon may make the sweet combination too watery.

WHEAT

BACKGROUND

A kernel of wheat (*Triticum*) consists of three main parts. Its outer covering, or *bran*, is very fibrous—not very nutritious, but important in the diet nonetheless. The oily *germ* is mainly the *embryo*—the future plant—and contains most of the vitamins and minerals of the kernal and quite a bit of protein. The *endosperm* is the rest of the kernel, roughly 70 percent. It is mostly starch, but has significant amounts of protein, iron, and niacin in its outer layers.

Unlike other CEREAL GRAINS, *wheat* is rich in gluten, the protein necessary for light-textured yeast BREADS. The gluten in the flour forms long strands that—when filled with the gas emitted by growing YEAST cells—stretches into a delicate framework that firms when baked. Wheat flour is also used in quick breads (with BAKING POWDER used for leavening), in hot-air breads such as popovers, in most types of PASTRY, in unleavened foods such as PASTA, and as a THICKENER.

Varieties

There are countless varieties and strains of wheat, developed for different characteristics of yield, disease resistance, nutrition, etc. Following are some of the major types:

Hard red spring wheat produces thick, chunky kernels that make the best flour for breads. It is high in protein and gluten.

Hard red winter wheat with thinner, longer kernels, also makes good bread flour.

Soft red winter wheat has long, chubby kernels. This wheat has more starch than hard wheat, and is used for pastry flour.

Durum wheat, with its pointed amber kernels, very high in gluten, is not good for baking. It is ground coarsely into *semolina*, the foundation for the best pasta.

Commercial Forms

Other than as flours (see next section), wheat is generally available in the following forms:

Whole berry, the whole kernel, is sold for cooking or grinding at home.

Cracked wheat is made by crushing whole berries into several pieces.

Bulgur wheat (also called *wheat pilaf*) is made by cracking kernels of partially cooked whole berries. Typically, bulgur wheat comes in three grinds: fine, medium, coarse. The first two grinds are generally used in making dishes such as *tabbuleh*, a cold salad from the Middle East.

Wheat germ is the high-protein, nutritious, but very perishable embryo of the wheat. Health-food enthusiasts use it as a nutritional supplement.

Bran, the coarse outer covering of the wheat kernel, is used in high-fiber diets.

Flours

Flour is made by grinding the wheat kernels, then perhaps sifting out the bran and germ; the whole process is called milling. The characteristics of a given flour depend on two factors—the variety (or varieties) of wheat used, and the way it is milled and processed.

Varieties: Hard, Soft, and All-Purpose Flours: *Soft flours* are made from high-starch wheat varieties and are best for making cakes and biscuits, which don't depend on gluten. *Hard flours*, made from high-gluten varieties, are best for yeast breads. *All-purpose flours* are a blend of hard and soft, with the blend varying from region to region. The blend marketed in the South, for instance, has more soft than hard wheat, mainly because much of the flour there goes into biscuits; the ration is reversed in Yankee land, principally because home bakers prefer to make yeast breads. Local brands are not the only ones affected; even the major national brands follow suit. Our best advice is to avoid the compromise all-purpose flour and rather to buy soft or hard flour according to your baking plans. If your supermarket does not sell soft and hard flours separately, try a specialty or health-food store.

Milling:

White and Whole-Wheat Flours: By law, *whole-wheat flour* or bread must be made with 100 percent of the husked kernel: bran, germ, and endosperm. *White flour* or bread has had some or all of the bran andxerm sifted out. If you want whole-wheat flour or bread, do not assume you are getting it when you see the phrases *wheat flour* or *wheat bread*; all that tells you is that the flour is made totally of wheat rather than, say, rye or sorghum. Look for the phrase whole wheat or, redundantly, *100 percent whole wheat*. Whole wheat's strong points are fuller flavor, more interesting texture, higher fiber content, and superior nutritional value. The benefits of white flour include its longer shelf life and, from a marketer's point of view, its greater public appeal. Most important, though, is that white flour is better for making high-rising, delicate baked goods; the rough edges of the bran particles in whole-wheat flour cut the gluten strands, resulting in coarser baked goods.

Stone-ground flour, whether whole wheat or not, is ground between stone wheels. Because the millstones do not get as hot as the steel roller mills usually used, the flour is somewhat more nutritious and better tasting than steel-milled flour. It is more expensive.

Graham flour is a whole-wheat flour that has the bran ground coarser than is the case with ordinary whole-wheat flour.

Other Processes:

Bleaching: Flour can be made whiter with chemicals, to prolong their shelf life and to appeal to those who think whiteness is good. Unbleached flours are favored by consumers interested in minimum-processed foods.

Enriching: Milling can remove most of the vitamins and minerals contained in the original kernels; white flour has only about 25 percent of most nutrients left. When the miller replaces the nutrients in at least the original quanities, the label will carry the word *enriched*.

Aging: A "matured" flour bakes better than a freshly ground one. Bleached flours do not need to be aged as long as unbleached flours, because the chemicals used to bleach the flour speed up the normal maturation.

Other Flour Types: *Self-rising flour* has had a form of BAKING POWDER and salt incorporated into it at the mill. The result certainly is one of the silliest convenience foods, because it costs more and you cannot use it for making yeast breads or for thickening sauces. The labor "saved" is minimal, since it is so easy to add your own baking powder when the recipe calls for it, and you know that it is fresh.

Pastry or *cake flour* is very finely ground, soft flour with an exceptionally high starch content. This flour feels silky when rubbed between your fingers.

Instant flour has been processed to dissolve quickly into liquids. While it will blend into a sauce instantly without lumping, it will not form as smooth or long-lasting a sauce as regular flour will.

Gluten flour is made by washing the starch out of the whole-wheat flour and drying the remaining material. It can be used in baking to combine with low-gluten flours such as rye; since it is high in protein it is used as a meat substitute.

Storage

Wheat flour should be transferred to an airtight jar or canister as soon as you bring it home. Otherwise, you risk insect infestation and staleness. Store the flour in a cool, dry place—and, if you're using a glass jar, in the dark. If you plan to keep whole-wheat flour for more than a week or two, it is best refrigerated, as the bran and germ can become rancid easily.

Equivalents

The longer a flour is stored (either at the store or in your home) or the drier the storage environment, the more the flour loses moisture. This is one reason why baking cannot be codified with precise recipes that work consistently. If you have a long-stored flour or a very dry storage environment, make a recipe adjustment by using slightly less flour than is called for in the recipe. However, if the day or climate is especially humid, you may have to add a bit more flour. A pound of all-purpose flour is about 4 cups. A pound of whole-wheat flour is 3¾ cups. A pound of cake flour is 4¾ cups. To substitute all-purpose flour for cake flour, use about 2½ tablespoons less per cup called for in the recipe. Whole-wheat flour and white flour can be exchanged cup for cup, but the texture of the things baked will be different. Use 13 tablespoons (instead of the conventional 16 tablespoons) of gluten flour as a substitute for 1 cup of white flour. Again, the texture will be different. Do not substitute instant flour for any other type of flour. Please remember that these substitutions, though generally applicable, still will be affected by climate, storage conditions, and age of the flour. Only through actual experience with different flours at different times can your mind and eyes "read" your dough.

Never cook with whole-wheat kernels intended for planting. It is likely to be mercury-treated to prevent fungus and therefore poisonous.

WHELK

BACKGROUND

Some customers and fishmongers interchange the terms *whelk* and *conch*, though they are distinct (but related) univalve mollusks. Physically, the whelk has a more pronouncedly spiral shell than does the conch. A whelk can be substituted for ABALONE and CONCH in most recipes. In America it is often used in place of conch in the spicy tomato-dressed Italian dish called *scungilli*.

WINE

BACKGROUND

The miller needs a mill, the blacksmith needs a forge, but the winemaker needs only grapes and containers for the juice. Because the fermentation of grape juice is a completely natural process, wine is one of the few commercial products that can be made without machinery. For this reason, wine is probably the oldest intoxicant known to man. Wine has probably been used in cooking for almost as long as it has been used as a beverage. Many chefs consider it as essential as herbs and spices for the proper preparation of many dishes. Here are a few tips on the use of wine in the kitchen.

Many recipe writers insist that the wine used in the dish be identical to the wine being served at the table. If you do use the same wine, fine; if not, do not be overly concerned—all that significantly matters is that the two wines be reasonably similar. And if you merely use a few drops in your preparation, that gap can even be greater.

Quality of the wine does matter. You need not pour a very expensive wine into your cooking pot—that would be a waste of funds. But you should not use a poor wine. After all, when the alcohol and water in the wine evaporate during the cooking, you will be left with the essence of the wine. If the wine is poor to begin with, you will end up with a disagreeable concentrate.

We strongly—very strongly—recommend that you not use the cooking wines sold in grocery stores. It is better to use no wine at all than contaminate your food with such typically distasteful products.

Some recipes call for champagne. This is fatuous, because the bubbles don't survive the cooking, and flat champagne is not the best-tasting wine. (If you have not already discovered that truth, try sipping yesterday's champagne.)

Many novice cooks erroneously reason that if a little wine works minor magic in a dish, more wine would perform majestic wonders. Wine's mission in the kitchen is to enhance, not to eclipse, the major cooking ingredients.

When should the wine be added? The answer will depend on your goal. If you are *marinating* a dish such as sauerbraten, the wine will be incorporated into the marinade days before the meat is cooked. For most *slow-cooked* preparations such as stews, the wine should be added early in the cooking period (and never less than 30 minutes before the end); the alcohol and water in the wine need time to evaporate, and the remnants of the wine need time to permeate the food and react with the other flavors. For *sautéed* dishes, the wine is usually added after the food has been cooked and transferred to a heated platter. The wine is then reduced with the pan juices over moderate to high heat. When lacing a soup with a fortified wine such as sherry or Madeira, add the wine just a minute or so before serving. The aroma of a fortified wine is quite volatile, capable of escaping into the air before the diner has had a chance to enjoy its fragrance. Do not, as many home cooks and restaurant chefs do, put too much fortified wine in the soup or it will mask the subtle flavors of the soup.

WINTER MELON

BACKGROUND

An Oriental vine, *Benincasa hispida*, produces a 1-to-2-foot-thick squash (it is not a melon) that looks something like an oversized pale green pumpkin. The thick rind has a natural frosty white bloom.

AVAILABILITY

Winter melon is sold fresh in Chinese-American markets. Because a whole winter melon is too large for most family needs and too expensive for all but a few budgets, it is usually sold by the wedge—a pound is a typical portion.

PREPARATION

Storage

When the rind is intact, the springy white, relatively bland flesh can keep for months. Cut winter melon can be plastic-wrapped and refrigerated for 2 to 3 days.

Preliminaries

Seed it as you would a cantaloupe, pare off the rind, and cut the flesh into ½-to-1½-inch cubes.

Cooking

Simmer the cubes in your soup for 10 to 20 minutes, depending on thickness. While they marvelously absorb the flavor of the stock, overcooking can cause the chunks to lose their desirable texture.

CLASSIC USES AND AFFINITIES

A classic Chinese banquet dish is winter-melon soup: the scooped-out shell is filled with a steaming soup made from the cut-up flesh; on very special occasions, an artistic design is etched on the outer shell.

WOODRUFF

BACKGROUND

A common use for *woodruff* (botanically *Asperula odorata*) is in Maibowle, a sort of German sangria: white wine, champagne, woodruff, and strawberries. Five or six bunches of fresh woodruff, or half a cup of dried, per punchbowl is about right. The Germans and Austrians also use woodruff in candy, sausages, and in braised dishes such as pot roast; it is the flavoring of May wine. Dried woodruff is available at herb and spice shops in America. (See HERBS AND SPICES for information on buying, storing, cooking, etc.)

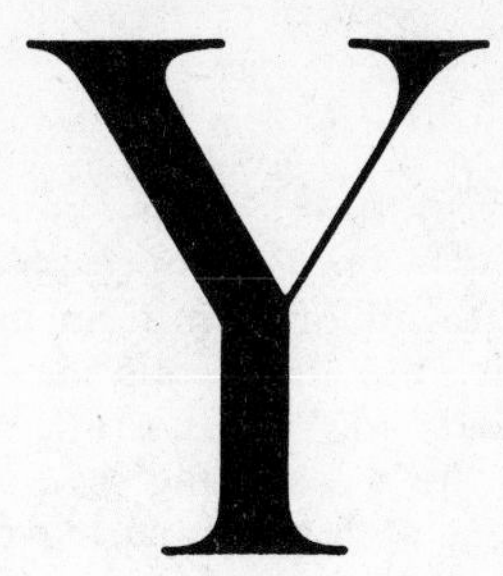

YAM

BACKGROUND

In America, *Dioscorea bulbifera*, the true *yam*, is rarely seen fresh. Like the Southern SWEET POTATO that has appropriated its name, the true yam is a vegetable tuber, but one of a tropical climbing vine. Although the yam is (or can be) similar in shape and external appearance to our sweet potato, the yam has a wider range of skin and flesh colors and can grow to over 7 feet in length and 100 pounds in weight. The yam has more natural sugar than the American sweet potato, and a moister texture. It has virtually no Vitamin A (with which the sweet potato is abundant) and only the average vegetal amount of Vitamin C. Nowadays it is sometimes found in Latin-American ethnic markets, usually cut into chunks and sold by weight. Cook as you would the American sweet potato.

YEAST

BACKGROUND

Yeast—a unicellular fungus—was used by Egyptian bakers to leaven breads over five thousand years ago and by makers of fermented beverages such as wine for millennia before that period in time.

In one pound of yeast there are over 3 trillion microscopic cells that, when fed a diet of sugar in a moist environment at a beneficial temperature, will divide. If there is no sugar, certain yeast enzymes can convert the starch in flour into the needed sugar. As the living organisms feed and divide, they convert most of the sugar into approximately equal parts of alcohol and carbon dioxide. Producers of wine, beer, and spirits welcome the alcohol and (except in making beer and champagne) let the CO_2 escape. Bakers take the opposite tack. They use the carbon dioxide gas to raise the bread dough and do not mind when the alcohol (which evaporates as the bread is baking) escapes into the air.

Yeast cells multiply best between 70° to 85°F, a range that includes the normal temperature of most American homes. If the temperature is too cold, the cells "hibernate" or procreate languidly. If too hot, the yeast cells die; the lethal temperature is about 120° to 140°F, depending on the particular strain of yeast.

Varieties

Bakers' yeast comes in three basic forms: active dry, compressed, and as part of a starter.

Active dry yeast or *dry granular yeast* is the form nowadays most often available. A blend of yeast and starch, it is typically sold in moisture-proof 1/4-ounce packets, though 4-ounce jars are also sometimes available for the busy home baker. To activate the yeast, sprinkle the contents of a packet (a scant tablespoon) into 1/4 cup of 105° to 115°F water, then wait 10 minutes before stirring, then blend the liquid into the other ingredients. Some cooks add a smidgen of sugar to spur the yeast growth. Store unopened packets and jar in a cool, dry, dark spot and use the yeast before the expiration date stamped on the container. Once you open a jar, tightly close it and keep it in an under-60°F storage area—if you have no such spot, store your supply in the refrigerator. If unsure of the potency of the yeast, mix a little with an equal volume of sugar into a little warm water and wait about 5 minutes; if the yeast is healthy, it will become visibly bubbly and will start to expand perceptibly. This test is called "proving" the yeast.

Compressed yeast or *fresh yeast*, is not as widely sold in America as it was a decade or two ago. It comes in moist, small, brick-shaped cakes, typically weighing about 3/5 ounce. This size can be substituted for a standard packet of dry yeast. Unlike dry yeast, compressed yeast is very perishable and must be refrigerated. If fresh when purchased, it should last 7 to 10 days in the refrigerator or for a month or two in the frozen food compartment. To test compressed yeast for freshness, crumble the cake with your fingers; it should easily break into angular-edged chunks. Also, this yeast should not have a sour odor or a brown or blotched crust. You can also use the test suggested for dry yeast. To dissolve compressed yeast, let it soak in lukewarm water for about 5 minutes or until it is soft enough to form a coarse solution with the liquid. Some bakers add a touch of sugar to it to accelerate cellular division.

Starter: When you reserve a portion of today's batch of dough for tomorrow's or next week's, you call it a starter. It comprises flour, water, and living yeast. San Francisco's *sourdough starter* is the most famous. When you are ready to make a new dough, you incorporate the yeast-laden starter which, in time, will permeate the entire dough with growing yeast cells. Another and more common approach is to mix the reserve portion into an unleavened batter, let the yeast cells leaven that batter, then store it in the refrigerator for future use. Depending on its strength, 1 to 2 cups of this now leavened batter can be substituted for one standard packet of dry yeast. The amount of flour and liquid in your starter must, of course, be subtracted from the quantity called for in your recipe.

Brewer's yeast: This product is not a leavening agent. Rather, brewer's yeast is used by many health-food enthusiasts as a food supplement because it is rich in thiamine and other B vitamins. Most people prefer to eat it sprinkled on or mixed into other food ingredients in order to mask the unpleasant flavor.

PREPARATION

Cooking Tips

The reason recipes say "keep the yeast dough away from a draft" or "cover the bowl with a cloth" is that moving air cools the dough, thus slowing the yeast growth.

While some sugar (or flour that can be converted to sugar) is essential to yeast development, too much sugar can noticeably slow it down or even stifle it. This is why you must allow a longer leavening time for rich doughs such as those for coffeecakes.

Another stifler of yeast growth is salt. However, as professional bakers know, a little salt can be desirable (especially on a hot day) to slow down the yeast's growth rate so that the resulting baked bread will be evenly light-textured. Salt, of course, also lends flavor to the bread.

As a very rough rule of thumb, one standard cake or packet of yeast will raise approximately 3 to 4 cups of flour. It is always better to use too little than too much yeast. If you are a little short on yeast, give the dough a little longer time to expand. If you use too much yeast, your final product may end up with a disagreeably yeasty flavor, a malformed shape, or an uneven texture.

YOGURT

BACKGROUND

Although it is not a wonder food as it has been touted—it won't melt off pounds, immunize you against infection, or make you live to 120—yogurt, especially when homemade without additives, is a healthful food. It is about as nutritious as the milk from which it is made, but is slightly more digestible, somewhat more concentrated in protein, and—some, but not all, experts say—can be helpful in maintaining a healthy bacterial population in the digestive tract. Yogurt is milk fermented with the help of friendly bacteria. Originally (starting thousands of years ago) yogurt was a way of preserving milk. Then as now, it could be made from the milk of cows, horses, sheep, goats, camels—even water buffaloes, as it still is in Egypt. Virtually all the yogurt made and consumed in America is produced from cow's milk.

Varieties

Plain whole milk yogurt should be smooth and creamy in consistency and taste somewhat astringent but fresh.

Plain skim milk yogurt is more watery, lower in fat and calories, and has less of the traditional yogurt flavor.

Flavored yogurt has added sugar and calories—as much a a total of 250 per container.

Swiss-style yogurt, the kind that doesn't have to be stirred, also contains gelatin or some other stabilizer to keep the flavoring in suspension.

Frozen yogurt is a commercial, hard-frozen yogurt; most of the beneficial bacteria are probably destroyed. Freezing inhibits the growth of nutrients; but the shelf life is prolonged by pasteurizing and sterilizing. This popular variety, much of which looks like soft ice cream, has the advantage for weight-watchers of being lower in calories than a comparable amount of ice cream—about 145 to 150 per cup. Most of the available brands have stabilizers, emulsifiers, and artificial flavorings and colorings added. They are also sugar-infused.

PREPARATION

Cooking

Plain yogurt can be used instead of sour cream in many recipes; the calorie saving compensates for the thinner texture.

Making Your Own

Like baking your own bread, making yogurt at home is easy, moderately tiresome, and requires a knack. A quart of milk (whole, skim, or reconstituted milk powder, preferably not instant) plus a package of yogurt culture or a tablespoonful of plain yogurt containing active cultures becomes a quart of yogurt. If the milk you use is raw (unpasteurized), scald and cool the milk to 110° before the next step. Add the starter to the milk, and mix thoroughly. Pour the milk into one or more clean, warm containers. Cover the containers and incubate them at 110°F for 8 to 12 hours. You need a source of steady, gentle heat: a heating pad, commercial yogurt maker, or an oven warmed only by its pilot light. Don't disturb the developing yogurt, and keep it out of direct sunlight. Some yogurt-making equipment has a heat source on the bottom: this makes containers of yogurt that are thick at the bottom, thin on top. Most homemade yogurt is thinner than commercial yogurt; add extra dry milk powder if this bothers you.

GLOSSARY

Words set in SMALL CAPS will be found defined in their alphabetical place.

AL DENTE (Italian; "to the tooth"): Describes pasta cooked to just the point where your teeth can still detect some firmness.

AU GRATIN (French): Describes a dish sprinkled with bread crumbs and/or cheese, then browned in an oven or, more authentically, under a flame.

AU JUS (French; "with juice"): Describes meat—especially beef—served with its own natural, unthickened juices.

BAKE: To cook with dry heat, especially in an oven. Baking and roasting are the same technique, although, customarily, you say you bake bread or ham but roast beef, fresh pork, poultry, etc.

BAKE BLIND: To bake pastry such as pie crust before adding the filling.

BALLOTINE (French): Beef, poultry or fish that is boned, rolled like a bundle (*ballot*), and tied with a string, then cooked.

BARBECUE: To cook meat, etc., on a grill or on a spit over hot coals.

BARD: To cover food such as meat with slices of fat such as suet or bacon to keep the flesh moist while cooking with dry heat.

BASTE: To coat the surface of food such as roasting meat with a liquid such as melted fat, to keep it from drying out in the oven.

BATTERIE DE CUISINE (French): Your collection of cooking tools including pots, pans, knives, and gadgets.

BEAT: To stir a mixture vigorously and in such a way as to incorporate air into it, making it lighter and fluffier.

BEURRE MANIÉ (French; "kneaded butter"): Butter and flour kneaded together into small, raw paste balls used to thicken liquids.

BIND: To give ingredients cohesiveness by means of adding eggs, cream, flour, breadcrumbs, etc.

BLANCH: 1. To plunge a food briefly into boiling water to retain or enhance color, to loosen the skin, to reduce objectionable flavors, to leach out salt or other ingredients, or to destroy enzymes prior to freezing. 2. To whiten by preventing sunlight from reaching a growing vegetable—often done with Belgian endive, celery, and asparagus.

BLANQUETTE (French; diminutive of *blanc*, "white"): A rich, creamy stew made with unbrowned meat such as veal, chicken, or rabbit.

BLEND: To stir or mix two or more ingredients together into a homogenous combination.

BOIL: To cook a liquid (or in a liquid) at a temperature high enough so the bubbles actively break the surface. At sea level, water boils at 212°F.

BONE: To remove the bone(s) from flesh.

BRAISE: To cook meat (or vegetables) by first browning in hot fat, then simmering in scant liquid in a heavy, covered pot.

BREAD: To coat a food with breadcrumbs prior to cooking.

BRINE: A saline solution used to preserve or flavor ingredients.

BROIL: To cook with dry heat under a flame or, sometimes, to cook on a grill over a heat source.

CARAMELIZE: 1. To brown and melt sugar with heat. 2. To coat food with such sugar.

CASSEROLE: 1. A heavy, covered pot for cooking in the oven or on top of the stove. 2. A slow-cooked dish prepared in such a vessel.

CHAFING DISH: A tabletop vessel on a stand with a candle or spirit lamp, used to cook or keep dishes warm.

CHAPON (French; "capon"): A crusty piece of garlic-rubbed bread that is tossed with salad, then removed and discarded before serving.

CHILL: To cool food without freezing it.

CHOP: To mince.

CLARIFY: 1. To make a stock clear by removing bits of suspended matter in the liquid. 2. To remove the protein (casein) and any impurities from butter or fat.

CODDLE: To simmer foods such as eggs slowly in water.

COURT BOUILLON (French; "short boiling"): A water seasoned with ingredients such as herbs and wine. Often used to poach fish and vegetables.

CREAM: 1. To mix flavorings such as herbs and garlic into softened butter. 2. To give a dish or ingredient a creamy consistency.

CRIMP: To use fingers or fork to make a decorative edge on a pastry or pie crust.

CRISP: 1. To firm the texture of an ingredient such as a carrot stick by soaking in cold water. 2. To toast bread until brittle.

CROQUETTE (from French for "crunch"): A molded morsel of minced food coated with breadcrumbs or batter, then deep-fried.

CROUSTADE (French): A small, crisp bread or pastry shell filled with a savory stuffing.

CROUTON (from French for "crust"): A small, fried piece of bread used to garnish soups and salads.

CUBE: 1. To cut food into cubes about 1/2 inch thick (larger than diced but smaller than chunked pieces). 2. To tenderize meat by using a patterned mallet or press.

CURE: To preserve food by any of various processes including salting, pickling, or smoking.

CUT IN: To mix a shortening or butter with flour with the use of a pastry blender or two knives. The mixture is coarse, not blended.

DEEP-FRY: To cook foods by submerging them in hot oil or fat.

DEGLAZE: To loosen and dissolve solidified particles (congealed pan drippings) from a pan with the use of heat and a liquid such as wine or water.

DEGREASE: To separate the fat from soup, stock, or other liquids.

DEVIL: To highly season a food with flavorings such as hot red pepper.

DICE: To cut food into cubes about 1/4 inch thick (smaller than cubed but larger than chopped pieces).

DOT: To distribute small pieces of (usually) butter uniformly over the surface of a food before cooking.

DOUGH: A mixture of flour and liquid. A dough is solid, a batter is thin enough to be poured.

DRAW: 1. To EVISCERATE an animal or fish; that is, to remove its innards. 2. To take liquid, as water or beer, from a tap.

DRAWN BUTTER: Clarified butter.

DREDGE: To sprinkle flour—or sometimes sugar, breadcrumbs, or seasoning—over a food. Also called DUSTING.

DRESS: To make an animal or fish ready for cooking by drawing, scaling, plucking, etc.

DRIPPINGS: The rendered fat and natural juices that cooking meat releases into the pan.

DRY-HEAT COOKING: Cooking foods with no added liquid (except perhaps to baste); includes the following methods: roasting, baking, broiling, pan-frying, sautéing, and deep-frying. Moist-heat cooking includes boiling, poaching, simmering, braising, stewing, and steaming.

DUST: See DREDGE.

EVISCERATE: See DRAW.

FILLET: 1. A boneless piece of meat or fish. A poultry fillet (or filet) refers to the breast. A fish fillet is the side. A meat fillet (or filet) is usually cut from the tenderloin muscle. 2. To remove the bones of a chicken breast, etc.

FLAMBÉ (French; "flaming"): To douse food with alcohol and set it aflame, to give the food added flavor, heat, or glamour.

FLOUR: To give a piece of food a light coating of flour, often seasoned.

FLUTE: 1. To CRIMP. 2. To cut decorative grooves into a food such as a mushroom cap.

FOLD: To blend a delicate, unstable mixture such as beaten egg whites into a less fragile mixture such as a sauce or custard. A light lifting-and-turning motion is needed to avoid bursting the air bubbles.

FRENCH: To trim flesh and fat from the end of a rib bone.

FRENCH-FRY: To deep-fry a food such as potatoes.

FRICASEE (from French): Food (especially veal or chicken) browned in fat or butter, then simmered in a liquid.

FRITTER: A food mixed or coated with batter, then deep-fried.

FRIZZLE: To fry foods such as bacon until crisp.

FRY: To cook or brown in hot fat, butter or oil. The method can range from SAUTÉING to DEEP-FRYING.

FUMET (French; "fume" or "smoke"): A concentrated (usually fish) stock or broth.

GALANTINE (from French; related to *gelatin*): A dish of boned meat or fish that is stuffed and rolled, then coated with aspic and served old.

GARNISH: 1. Decorative foods added to a preparation principally for visual appeal. 2. To add a garnish.

GEL or JELL: For a liquid to turn semisolid due to gelatin suspended in it. The gelatin may come from the food cooked in the liquid or may be added as gelatin or pectin.

GLAZE: 1. To give foods a surface shine by means of browning or by coating with beaten egg whites, preserves, etc. 2. The resulting surface or coating.

GRATE: To shred or divide a food such as cheese into small pieces by means of a tool with sharp-edged holes.

GREASE: To rub fat or oil on a pan to help prevent cooking foods from sticking.

GRILL: To cook on a grating, gridiron, rack, or similar instrument over hot coals or fire.

GRIND: To reduce a hard substance to fine pieces or powder.

HULL: 1. The dry hard or leafy outer covering of some fruits, nuts, and seeds. 2. To remove the hull. Certain foods, such as corn, are HUSKED, not *hulled.*

HUSK: See HULL.

INFUSE: 1. To extract the flavor of an ingredient such as tea by steeping it in liquid. 2. To imbue a food with the flavor of another ingredient.

JELL: See GEL.

JULIENNE (from a French name): 1. Describes foods such as potatoes or ham cut into uniform pieces about the size and shape of a kitchen match. 2. To cut food that way.

KNEAD: To mix and work a substance (especially yeast dough) into a smooth, elastic, uniform mass. Kneading may be done by hand or machine.

LARD: 1. Pork fat that has been rendered and clarified. 2. To insert strips of fat called *lardoons* into lean meat to add flavor and to prevent the meat from becoming dry as it roasts.

LEAVEN: To cause a dough or batter to rise by means of a *leavening* such as yeast or baking powder.

LIAISON (French; "bond" or "connection"): A substance or mixture used to thicken sauces, soups, etc.

MACÉDOINE (French; "Macedonia"): A preparation of mixed vegetables or fruits, the latter often macerated (see).

MACERATE: To steep food in a *flavorful* liquid such as liqueur or syrup. One generally uses the term *macerate* for fruits and MARINATE for meats and vegetables.

MANDOLINE (French): A rectangular instrument for cutting vegetables and fruits into slices, julienne strips, cubes, etc.

MARBLING: The small specks or lines of fat interspersed within the flesh of animals and sometimes fish.

MARINATE: To tenderize and flavor a food by steeping it in a seasoned acidic and/or oily solution.

MASK: To coat or cover a food with, for example, a thickened sauce or aspic.

MEAL: Food (especially cereal grains) ground coarser than flour.

MERINGUE (from French, from a place name): Stiffly beaten egg whites with or without sugar.

MINCE: To cut a food into bits about 1/8 inch thick.

MIREPOIX (French; from a name): A mixture of finely diced vegetables (typically carrots, celery, and onions) and, perhaps, ham, used for flavoring.

MOCHA: 1. Originally, a type of coffee. 2. Now, more commonly a mixture of coffee and chocolate, as a drink or a flavor.

MOIST HEAT: See DRY-HEAT COOKING.

MULL: To season and heat a liquid such as wine or cider.

OFFAL: The British term for what are called *variety meats* in the U.S.—edible internal organs, heads, tails etc.

PAN-BROIL: To cook briefly and rapidly in a pan with no or very little fat.

PAN-FRY: Similar to PAN-BROILING, but a little more fat is used. Also called SAUTÉING.

PARBOIL: To partially cook a food by placing it briefly in boiling water. Also called BLANCHING.

PARE: To cut off the skin or peel of a fruit or vegetable.

PICKLE: To preserve and flavor a food by soaking it in a solution, usually of brine or vinegar.

PIPE: To force a soft substance, such as a dough or pureed potatoes, through the tube of a pastry bag, to decorate a dish, make pastries, etc.

PIT: 1. The (often large) seed of any of several fruits. 2. To remove the pit(s) from fruit.

PITH: 1. The pale, soft, shapeless, juiceless substance inside some plant stems and fruits. 2. The white, often bitter, substance between the peel and flesh of citrus fruit.

PLUCK: To remove the feathers from a bird.

POACH: To cook food in a liquid heated to just below the boiling point. See SIMMER.

POT-ROAST: 1. To BRAISE a large, usually tough, piece of meat. 2. A roast so cooked.

PUREE (from French, "mashed"): To turn food into pulp by using a sieve, food mill, electric blender, or food processor.

QUICK BREAD: Bread LEAVENED without yeast.

RANCID: Having the offensive smell and taste characteristic of spoiling fat.

RECONSTITUTE: To restore the original water content of dried foods.

REDUCE: To boil a liquid to evaporate some of its water and thus to concentrate its volume, flavor, and consistency.

REFRESH: To plunge hot, cooked, or blanched food into cold water to stop the cooking process and/or to set the color.

RENDER: To melt and separate the fat away from nonfat substances such as flesh and bone. Also called *try out*. See CLARIFY.

RICE: To press food such as cooked potatoes through a special perforated instrument called a *ricer*.

ROAST: To cook meat with dry, radiant heat in an oven, on a spit, or in the ground as with an earth oven.

ROUX (from French; "russet"): A mixture of flour and fat (usually butter) used to thicken liquids such as sauces. In ascending order of cooking time and depth of color, there are white, blond, and brown roux.

SALAMIS (French): A preparation of (usually) game birds that are partially roasted, then stewed.

SALPICON (French): A mixture of cubes or small pieces of meats and vegetables.

SAUTÉ (French; "tossed"): The French term for PAN-FRIED.

SCALD: 1. To plunge vegetables or fruits into boiling water to facilitate skin removal. 2. To heat milk or cream just below the boiling point.

SCALLOP: 1. A shellfish; see entry in main text. 2. A thin slice of meat; see under VEAL in main text. 3. To bake food such as sliced potatoes in layers in a rich sauce in a casserole dish. Often the dish is topped with bread crumbs.

SCORE: To make shallow incisions (often in a cross-hatched pattern) on the surface of a food such as meat to decorate or tenderize it.

SEAR: To quickly brown the surface of meat with very hot heat in order to seal in its juices.

SEASON: 1. To flavor food with *seasonings* such as salt, herbs, and spices. 2. To give a protective coating to cast-iron cookware.

SHORTENING: Fat or oil used in baked goods.

SHRED: To cut, grate, or shave into small, thin slivers.

SIEVE: 1. To strain particles of food through a wire mesh. 2. The utensil so used.

SIFT: To pass food such as flour through a fine-meshed screen to give lightness and to eliminate lumps and coarse particles.

SIMMER: To cook in a liquid just below the boiling point. At sea level, 180°F is a low simmer, 195°F is a medium simmer, and 210°F is a high simmer.

SKIM: 1. To remove from the surface of a liquid any scum, fat, etc. 2. Specifically, to remove the cream from unhomogenized whole milk.

SPIT-ROAST: To broil or roast food (usually meat) on a fixed or rotating skewer, traditionally over hot coals.

STEAM: To cook food on a rack in a covered pot with steam rising from boiling water.

STEEP: To soak a food in liquid to extract flavor or unwanted properties such as excessive saltiness.

STEW: To slowly cook food in a simmering, well-seasoned liquid in a covered pan.

STIR-FRYING: The American term for SAUTÉING in a Chinese wok.

STOCK: A flavored liquid made by simmering food such as beef bones along with seasonings. The liquid is strained and used as a base for soup, sauces, etc.

SUET: The hard, brittle, choice fat from the loin and kidney areas of animals such as beef cattle and sheep.

TRUSS: To use string or skewers to keep the legs and wings of a bird close to its body as it roasts. This method promotes a well-shaped, evenly cooked, juicy bird.

WHIP: To incorporate air into a substance such as egg whites or cream by rapidly beating it with a whisk, electric mixer, etc.

ZEST: 1. The outermost surface of the peel of a citrus fruit. 2. To remove zest in tiny strips. 3. To flavor a preparation with those strips or their oily essence.

EQUIVALENTS-AT-A-GLANCE

Basic Equivalents

1 drop = about 1/50 fluid ounce
1 dash = about 5 drops or 1/10 ounce
1 pinch = about 1/8 teaspoon
1 jigger = 1½ fluid ounces (or, sometimes, 1)
3 teaspoons = 1 tablespoon
2 tablespoons = 1 fluid ounce
8 fluid ounces = 1 cup
2 cups = 1 pint
2 pints or 4 cups = 1 quart
4 quarts = 1 gallon
2 gallons = 1 peck
4 pecks = 1 bushel
16 ounces avoirdupois = 1 pound

Oven Temperature Equivalents

500°F = broil (average)
450°F = very hot
400°F = hot
375°F = moderately hot
350°F = moderate
325°F = moderately slow (or low)
300°F = slow (or low)
250°F = very slow (or low)

High-Altitude Cooking

The higher you are above sea level, the lower the boiling temperature of water. This means that you must cook foods longer, since the boiling water will not be as hot.

Altitude in Feet	Boiling Point of Water
0	212°F
1,000	210°F
2,000	208°F
3,000	207°F
4,000	205°F
5,000	203°F
7,500	198°F
10,000	194°F

High altitude affects other culinary methods, including baking, candy making, leavening, and whipping egg whites. Consult a cookbook geared for your altitude, and inquire whether your local college home-economics department distributes information.

METRIC CONVERSION

Though America has committed itself to changing over to the metric system, general use of the system in the American kitchen is many years away. While we favor and encourage the change, it seems premature for American cookbooks to start listing the metric equivalents in the recipes—it creates more confusion than it is worth, and the apparent accuracy is often spurious. A published recipe will flatly state, for instance, that the cook should use "1 tablespoon (14.79 milliliters) of lemon juice." In order to measure 14.79 milliliters, a cook would require the type of precision instruments normally used in chemical laboratories, not in home sweet home. Moreover, no recipe really requires an exact tablespoon (or whatever) of lemon juice (or of virtually any other ingredient), so why 14.79 milliliters as opposed to 14 or 15, or—for that matter—20 milliliters?

If you encounter a metric-numbered recipe in the near future (as you probably will, especially if you are interested in foreign cooking), this concise appendix should help you in most of your arithmetic conversions. Just keep in mind that you seldom need to use scientifically precise measurements in cooking.

Temperature Equivalents

Fahrenheit is the traditional temperature scale in the U.S.; Celsius is its metric counterpart. To convert Fahrenheit (F) to Celsius (C), subtract 32 from the Fahrenheit number, then multiply by 5 and divide by 9.

$$(F - 32) \times \frac{5}{9} = C$$

If you have a calculator, it may be as easy to multiply by 0.56:

$$(F - 32) \times 0.56 = C$$

To convert Celsius (C) to Fahrenheit (F), multiply the Celsius number by 9, then divide by 5 and add 32.

$$(\frac{9}{5} \times C) + 32 = F$$

Alternatively:

$$(1.8 \times C) + 32$$

Sample temperature equivalents:

Fahrenheit	Celsius	
600°	316°	
500°	260°	
400°	204°	
300°	149°	
212°	100°	water boils (at sea level)
200°	93°	
150°	66°	
100°	38°	
68°	20°	normal room temperature water freezes
50°	10°	
32°	0°	
0°	−17°	
−10°	−23°	
−40°	−40°	
−459°	−273°	absolute zero

Volume Equivalents

1 kiloliter = 1000 liters
1 liter = 1000 milliliters
1 milliliter = 1 cubic centimeter

1 teaspoon = 4.93 milliliters
1 tablespoon = 14.79 milliliters
1 fluid ounce = 29.57 milliliters
1 cup = 237 milliliters
1 pint = 473 milliliters
1 quart = 946 milliliters
1 gallon = 3.78 liters

1 milliliter = 0.03 fluid ounce
100 milliliters = 3.38 fluid ounces
250 milliliters = 8.45 fluid ounces or 1.06 cups
500 milliliters = 16.91 fluid ounces or 1.06 pints
1 liter = 33.81 fluid ounces or 1.06 quarts
10 liters = 2.64 gallons

Linear Equivalents

1 kilometer = 1000 meters
1 meter = 100 centimeters or 1000 millimeters
1 centimeter = 10 millimeters

1 inch = 2.54 centimeters
1 foot = 30 centimeters
1 yard = 91 centimeters
1 mile = 1.61 kilometers

1 millimeter = 0.04 inch
1 centimeter = 0.39 inch
1 meter = 39.37 inches or 3.28 feet or 1.09 yards
1 kilometer = 3281 feet or 1094 yards or 0.62 miles

Weight Equivalents

1 kilogram = 1000 grams

1 ounce = 28.35 grams
1 pound = 453.59 grams

1 gram = 0.03 ounces
100 grams = 2.84 ounces
1 kilogram = 28.35 ounces or 2.20 pounds

NUTRITION PRIMER

This is a brief, quick-reference primer that is intended to give an overview rather than be comprehensive.

CALORIE: Energy values of food are measured by the calorie, a standardized heat unit. For every 3,500 calories we consume in excess of our bodily needs, we gain a pound. Conversely, we will lose a pound when our calorie intake is 3,500 calories less than required by our metabolism. Calories come from *proteins, carbohydrates*, and *fats*.

PROTEIN: Our bodies need protein as a source of energy as well as to help create, repair, and sustain tissues, enzymes, body fluids, and hormones. Complete protein sources (containing all essential *amino acids*) include the flesh of animals, poultry, and seafood plus eggs and dairy products. Vegetarians must obtain complete protein by consuming at the same meal the right combinations of cereal grains and legumes.

CARBOHYDRATES: When our bodies use this source of energy, we free the protein to do its body-building and maintenance work. Carbohydrates also help our body effectively use fat. Carbohydrate sources include *starches* which are found in abundance in *cereal grains, potatoes*, etc..

FATS: Besides serving as a reserve source of energy, fats help the body to metabolize other nutrients. Fat sources include *butter, animal fats* and *vegetable oils*.

VITAMINS: These nutrients help other nutrients perform their functions. If we eat a balanced diet, vitamin supplements are seldom necessary. Our body can store fat-soluble vitamins, but not the B-complex and C vitamins which are water-soluble. For optimum health, we should replenish our bodies' supply of water-soluble vitamins daily.

Vitamin A promotes growth and helps keep eyes, skin and internal membranes healthy; night blindness results from a deficiency. *Dark green, yellow,* and *orange vegetables*, such as *broccoli, squash* and *carrots*, are good sources of Vitamin A.

Thiamine (Vitamin B1): Benefits include healthy nerves and good digestion. Deficiency creates appetite loss. Thiamine sources include *organ meats, pork, legumes*, and *cereal grains*.

Riboflavin (Vitamin B2): Our bodies use riboflavin to help metabolize our carbohydrates and to keep our eyes and lip skin healthy. Riboflavin sources include *liver, lean meats, dairy products, eggs*, and *green leafy vegetables*.

Niacin helps keep skin healthy and helps the body use oxygen efficiently in creating energy. Good sources include *liver, cereal grains*, and the *lean flesh* of animals, poultry, and fish.

Vitamin B12: Anemia results from a lack of Vitamin B12, which is found in *organ meats, dairy products, leafy vegetables*, and *seafood*.

Vitamin C (ascorbic acid) helps to build and maintain bones, teeth, and gums, helps wounds heal quickly and hygienically, promotes strong cells and blood vessels. Its possible ability to cure the common cold is debatable. Sources are *citrus fruits* and many *green vegetables.*

Vitamin D deficiency can lead to rickets (bone malformation). Growing children as well as pregnant and nursing women especially need Vitamin D. If the body gets enough sunshine, it can manufacture its own Vitamin D. Other sources include *fish liver oils* and *Vitamin-D-fortified milk.*

Vitamin E: Though popularly—and unprovably—supposed to encourage sexual prowess and to delay aging, Vitamin E does have some proven benefits, including helping muscles do their job. Sources include most *vegetable oils, eggs,* and *legumes.*

Vitamin K is necessary for blood clotting; it can be found in many foods including *cabbage* and *spinach.*

Minerals: Our bodies require certain minerals, including *calcium* (for healthy teeth and bones), *iron* (for healthy red blood cells), and *iodine* (for a healthy thyroid gland). Other essential minerals include *cobalt, copper, fluorine, magnesium, manganese, molybdenum, phosphorus, potassium, sodium, sulphur,* and *zinc.*

NUTRITION CHART

A growing number of cooks and diners are becoming increasingly interested in nutritional specifics of food, such as the exact Vitamin C content. For that reason, we have included in our book the official U.S. Government analysis of the composition of foods in edible portions of 100 grams, which is approximately 3½ ounces. Multiply the numbers given for 100 gram portions by 4.54 if you wish to convert them to pounds, or by 0.28 to convert to ounces. Please note that the phrase "food energy" means food calories, the same units of measurement that particularly concern weight watchers.

TABLE 1.—COMPOSITION OF FOODS, 100 GRAMS, EDIBLE PORTION

[Numbers in parentheses denote values imputed—usually from another form of the food or from a similar food. Zero in parentheses indicates that the amount of a constituent probably is none or is too small to measure. Dashes denote lack of reliable data for a constituent believed to be present in measurable amount. Calculated values, as those based on a recipe, are not in parentheses]

Item No.	Food and description	Water	Food energy	Protein	Fat	Carbohydrate		Ash	Calcium	Phosphorus	Iron	Sodium	Potassium	Vitamin A value	Thiamine	Riboflavin	Niacin	Ascorbic acid
						Total	Fiber											
(A)	(B)	(C)	(D)	(E)	(F)	(G)	(H)	(I)	(J)	(K)	(L)	(M)	(N)	(O)	(P)	(Q)	(R)	(S)
		Percent	*Calories*	*Grams*	*Grams*	*Grams*	*Grams*	*Grams*	*Milligrams*	*Milligrams*	*Milligrams*	*Milligrams*	*Milligrams*	*International units*	*Milligrams*	*Milligrams*	*Milligrams*	*Milligrams*
	Abalone:																	
1	Raw	75.8	98	18.7	0.5	3.4	0	1.6	37	191	2.4	—	—	—	0.18	0.14	—	—
2	Canned	80.2	80	16.0	.3	2.3	0	1.2	14	128	—	—	—	—	.12	—	—	—
3	**Acerola** (Barbados-cherry or West Indian cherry), raw, pulp and skin.	92.3	28	.4	.3	6.8	.4	.2	12	11	.2	8	83	—	.02	.06	0.4	[1] 1,300
4	**Acerola juice**, raw	94.3	23	.4	.3	4.8	.3	.2	10	9	.5	3	—	—	.02	.06	.4	[2] 1,600
5	**Albacore**, raw [3]	66.2	177	25.3	7.6	0	0	1.3	26	—	—	40	293	—	—	—	—	5
	Ale. See Beverages: Beer, item 394.																	
	Alewife:																	
6	Raw	74.4	127	19.4	4.9	0	0	1.5	—	218	—	—	—	—	—	—	—	—
7	Canned, solids and liquid	73.0	141	16.2	8.0	0	0	3.4	—	—	—	—	—	—	—	—	—	—
	Algae. See Seaweeds, items 2027–2031.																	
	Alimentary pastes. See Macaroni, Noodles, Pastinas, Spaghetti.																	
	Almonds:																	
8	Dried	4.7	598	18.6	54.2	19.5	2.6	3.0	234	504	4.7	4	773	0	.24	.92	3.5	Trace
9	Roasted and salted	.7	627	18.6	57.7	19.5	2.6	3.5	235	504	4.7	198	773	0	.05	.92	3.5	0
	Sugar-coated. See Candy, item 613.																	
10	**Almond meal**, partially defatted	7.2	408	39.5	18.3	28.9	2.3	6.1	424	914	8.5	7	1,400	0	.32	1.68	6.3	Trace
11	**Amaranth**, raw	86.9	36	3.5	.5	6.5	1.3	2.6	267	67	3.9	—	411	6,100	.08	.16	1.4	80
12	**Anchovy**, pickled, with and without added oil, not heavily salted.	58.6	176	19.2	10.3	.3	0	11.6	168	210	—	—	—	—	—	—	—	—
	Apples:																	
	Raw, commercial varieties: [4]																	
	Freshly harvested and stored:																	
13	Not pared	84.4	58	.2	.6	14.5	1.0	.3	7	10	.3	1	110	90	.03	.02	.1	4
14	Pared	85.1	54	.2	.3	14.1	.6	.3	6	10	.3	1	110	40	.03	.02	.1	2
	Freshly harvested:																	
15	Not pared	84.8	56	.2	.6	14.1	1.0	.3	7	10	.3	1	110	90	.03	.02	.1	7
16	Pared	85.3	53	.2	.3	13.9	.6	.3	6	10	.3	1	110	40	.03	.02	.1	4
	Stored:																	
17	Not pared	83.9	60	.2	.7	14.8	1.0	.4	7	10	.3	1	110	90	.03	.02	.1	3
18	Pared	84.8	55	.2	.3	14.4	.6	.3	6	10	.3	1	110	40	.03	.02	.1	2
	Canned. See Applesauce, items 28–29.																	
	Dehydrated, sulfured:																	
19	Uncooked	2.5	353	1.4	2.0	92.1	3.8	2.0	40	66	2.0	7	730	—	Trace	.06	.6	10
20	Cooked, with added sugar	79.6	76	.2	.3	19.6	.5	.3	6	10	.3	1	106	—	Trace	.01	.1	1
	Dried, sulfured:																	
21	Uncooked	24.0	275	1.0	1.6	71.8	3.1	1.6	31	52	1.6	5	569	—	.06	.12	.5	10
	Cooked:																	
22	Without added sugar	78.4	78	.3	.5	20.3	.9	.5	9	15	.5	1	162	—	.01	.03	.1	Trace
23	With added sugar	69.7	112	.3	.4	29.2	.8	.4	8	13	.4	1	144	—	.01	.03	.1	Trace
24	Frozen, sliced, sweetened, not thawed	75.1	93	.2	.1	24.3	.7	.3	5	6	.5	[5] 14	68	20	.01	.03	.2	7
25	**Apple brown betty**	64.5	151	1.6	3.5	29.7	.5	.7	18	22	.6	153	100	100	.06	.04	.4	1
26	**Apple butter**	51.6	186	.4	.8	46.8	1.1	.4	14	36	.7	2	252	0	.01	.02	.2	2
27	**Apple juice**, canned or bottled	87.8	47	.1	Trace	11.9	.1	.2	6	9	.6	1	101	—	.01	.02	.1	1
	Applesauce, canned:																	
28	Unsweetened or artificially sweetened	88.5	41	.2	.2	10.8	.6	.3	4	5	.5	2	78	40	.02	.01	Trace	1
29	Sweetened	75.7	91	.2	.1	23.8	.5	.2	4	5	.5	2	65	40	.02	.01	Trace	1
	Apricots:																	
30	Raw	85.3	51	1.0	.2	12.8	.6	.7	17	23	.5	1	281	2,700	.03	.04	.6	10
31	Candied	12.0	338	.6	.2	86.5	.6	.7	—	—	—	—	—	—	—	—	—	—
	Canned, solids and liquid:																	
32	Water pack, with or without artificial sweetener	89.1	38	.7	.1	9.6	.4	.5	12	16	.3	1	246	1,830	.02	.02	.4	4
33	Juice pack	84.5	54	1.0	.2	13.6	.4	.7	17	23	.5	1	362	2,700	.03	.03	.5	6
	Sirup pack:																	
34	Light	81.9	66	.7	.1	16.8	.4	.5	11	15	.3	1	239	1,780	.02	.02	.4	4
35	Heavy	76.9	86	.6	.1	22.0	.4	.4	11	15	.3	1	234	1,740	.02	.02	.4	4
36	Extra heavy	72.9	101	.6	.1	26.0	.4	.4	11	15	.3	1	230	1,720	.02	.02	.3	4
	Dehydrated, sulfured, nugget-type and pieces:																	
37	Uncooked	3.5	332	5.6	1.0	84.6	3.8	5.3	86	139	5.3	33	1,260	14,100	Trace	.08	3.6	15
38	Cooked, fruit and liquid, sugar added	66.7	119	1.3	.2	30.5	.9	1.3	20	33	1.3	8	299	2,800	Trace	.02	.8	2
	Dried, sulfured:																	
39	Uncooked	25.0	260	5.0	.5	66.5	3.0	3.0	67	108	5.5	26	979	10,900	.01	.16	3.3	12

	Cooked, fruit and liquid:																	
40	Without added sugar	75.6	85	1.6	.2	21.6	1.0	1.0	22	35	1.8	8	318	3,000	Trace	.05	1.0	3
41	With added sugar	66.2	122	1.4	.1	31.4	.9	.9	19	31	1.6	7	278	2,600	Trace	.04	.9	2
42	Frozen, sweetened, not thawed	73.3	98	.7	.1	25.1	.6	.8	10	19	.9	4	229	1,680	.02	.04	.8	28
43	**Apricot nectar,** canned (approx. 40% fruit) [4]	84.6	57	.3	.1	14.6	.2	.4	9	12	.2	Trace	151	950	.01	.01	.2	3
	Artichokes, globe or French:																	
44	Raw	85.5	(7)	2.9	.2	[8] 10.6	2.4	.8	51	88	1.3	43	430	160	.08	.05	1.0	12
45	Cooked, boiled, drained	86.5	(7)	2.8	.2	[8] 9.9	2.4	.6	51	69	1.1	30	301	150	.07	.04	.7	8
	Artichokes, Jerusalem. See Jerusalem-artichokes, item 1150.																	
	Asparagus:																	
46	Raw spears	91.7	26	2.5	.2	5.0	.7	.6	22	62	1.0	2	278	900	.18	.20	1.5	33
47	Cooked spears, boiled, drained	93.6	20	2.2	.2	3.6	.7	.4	21	50	.6	1	183	900	.16	.18	1.4	26
	Canned spears:																	
	Green:																	
	Regular pack:																	
48	Solids and liquid	93.6	18	1.9	.3	2.9	.5	1.3	18	43	1.7	[9] 236	166	510	.06	.09	.8	15
49	Drained solids	92.5	21	2.4	.4	3.4	.8	1.3	19	53	1.9	[9] 236	166	800	.06	.10	.8	15
50	Drained liquid	95.6	11	.8	Trace	2.4	Trace	1.2	15	24	1.4	[9] 236	166	Trace	.06	.07	.8	15
	Special dietary pack (low-sodium):																	
51	Solids and liquid	94.7	16	2.0	.2	2.7	.5	.4	18	43	1.7	3	166	510	.06	.09	.8	15
52	Drained solids	93.6	20	2.6	.3	3.1	.7	.4	19	53	1.9	3	166	800	.06	.10	.8	15
53	Drained liquid	96.8	9	.8	Trace	2.0	Trace	.4	15	24	1.4	3	166	Trace	.06	.07	.8	15
	White (bleached):																	
	Regular pack:																	
54	Solids and liquid	93.3	18	1.6	.3	3.3	.5	1.5	15	33	.9	[9] 236	140	50	.05	.06	.7	15
55	Drained solids	92.3	22	2.1	.5	3.6	.8	1.5	16	41	1.0	[9] 236	140	80	.05	.06	.7	15
56	Drained liquid	95.4	11	.7	Trace	2.5	Trace	1.4	13	18	.7	[9] 236	140	Trace	.05	.04	.7	15
	Special dietary pack (low-sodium):																	
57	Solids and liquid	95.0	16	1.4	.2	3.0	.5	.4	15	33	.9	4	140	50	.05	.06	.7	15
58	Drained solids	94.0	19	1.9	.2	3.5	.7	.4	16	41	1.0	4	140	80	.05	.06	.7	15
59	Drained liquid	97.2	8	.6	Trace	1.8	Trace	.4	13	18	.7	4	140	Trace	.05	.04	.7	15
	Frozen:																	
	Cuts and tips:																	
60	Not thawed	92.3	23	3.3	.2	3.6	.8	.6	23	66	1.3	2	239	850	.16	.14	1.2	25
61	Cooked, boiled, drained	92.5	22	3.2	.2	3.5	.8	.6	22	64	1.2	1	220	850	.14	.13	1.0	23
	Spears:																	
62	Not thawed	92.0	24	3.3	.2	3.9	.8	.6	23	69	1.2	2	259	780	.18	.15	1.3	29
63	Cooked, boiled, drained	92.2	23	3.2	.2	3.8	.8	.6	22	67	1.1	1	238	780	.16	.14	1.1	26
	Avocados, raw:																	
64	All commercial varieties [10]	74.0	167	2.1	16.4	6.3	1.6	1.2	10	42	.6	4	604	290	.11	.20	1.6	14
65	California, mainly Fuerte	73.6	171	2.2	17.0	6.0	1.5	1.2	10	42	.6	4	604	290	.11	.20	1.6	14
66	Florida	78.0	128	1.3	11.0	8.8	(1.5)	.9	10	42	.6	4	604	290	.11	.20	1.6	14
	Baby foods: [11]																	
	Cereals, precooked, dry, and other cereal products:																	
67	Barley, added nutrients	6.6	348	13.4	1.2	73.6	1.2	5.2	736	821	53.2	452	413	(0)	3.71	1.20	32.2	(0)
68	High protein, added nutrients	5.9	357	35.2	3.7	48.1	2.2	7.1	815	904	63.1	653	1,078	—	3.67	1.15	24.0	(0)
69	Mixed, added nutrients	6.5	368	15.2	2.9	70.6	1.1	4.8	820	741	56.4	470	345	—	3.15	1.35	22.3	(0)
70	Oatmeal, added nutrients	7.0	375	16.5	5.5	66.0	1.5	5.0	757	734	48.2	437	374	(0)	2.58	1.05	21.3	(0)
71	Rice, added nutrients	7.2	371	6.6	1.6	80.0	.5	4.6	858	646	50.2	530	208	(0)	2.56	1.24	19.7	(0)
72	Teething biscuit	5.6	378	11.1	2.3	78.0	.7	3.0	322	347	4.6	421	250	—	.47	.57	3.0	(0)
	Wheat. See Farina, instant-cooking: items 995–996.																	
	Desserts, canned:																	
73	Custard pudding, all flavors	76.5	100	2.3	1.8	18.6	.2	.8	64	62	.3	150	94	100	.02	.12	.1	1
74	Fruit pudding with starch base, milk and/or egg (banana, orange, or pineapple).	75.7	96	1.2	.9	21.6	.3	.6	27	34	.3	128	75	100	.03	.05	.1	3
	Dinners, canned:																	
	Cereal, vegetable, meat mixtures (approx. 2%–4% protein):																	
75	Beef noodle dinner	88.2	48	2.8	1.1	6.8	.3	1.1	12	29	.5	269	159	620	.02	.05	.5	2
76	Cereal, egg yolk, and bacon	84.7	82	2.9	4.9	6.6	.1	.9	29	60	.8	301	36	520	.05	.06	.4	—
77	Chicken noodle dinner	88.5	49	2.1	1.3	7.2	.1	.9	27	30	.3	297	42	800	.03	.06	.4	1
78	Macaroni, tomatoes, meat, and cereal	84.5	67	2.6	2.0	9.6	.3	1.3	21	35	.5	381	77	500	.14	.12	1.0	1
79	Split peas, vegetables, and ham or bacon	81.5	80	4.0	2.1	11.2	.2	1.2	29	79	.7	295	112	600	.08	.05	.5	1
80	Vegetables and bacon, with cereal	85.7	68	1.7	2.9	8.7	.4	1.0	17	28	.6	282	130	2,200	.07	.05	.6	1
81	Vegetables and beef, with cereal	87.0	56	2.7	1.6	7.6	.4	1.1	17	39	.8	307	143	2,800	.03	.04	.9	1
82	Vegetables and chicken, with cereal	87.8	52	2.1	1.4	7.7	.2	1.0	33	33	.4	307	55	1,000	.03	.04	.5	Trace
83	Vegetables and ham, with cereal	85.6	64	2.8	2.2	8.3	.3	1.1	25	42	.3	360	90	1,000	.08	.05	.5	3

[1] Average for fully ripened fruit grown in Florida, Puerto Rico, Hawaii; range is from 1,000 to 2,000 mg. per 100 grams. At firm-ripe stage, average is 1,900 mg.; range, 1,200 to 2,700 mg. At partially ripe stage, average is 2,500 mg.; range, 1,200 to 4,500 mg.

[2] Average for juice from ripe fruit; range is from 1,000 to 2,200 mg. per 100 grams.

[3] Almost all of catch is canned as tuna.

[5] Average weighted in accordance with commercial freezing practices.

[6] Average weighted in accordance with commercial freezing practices. For products without added ascorbic acid, average is about 9 mg. per 100 grams; for those with added ascorbic acid, about 65 mg.

[7] Values may range from 9 Calories per 100 grams for freshly harvested raw artichokes to as many as 47 for stored product; the corresponding range for boiled artichokes is 8 to 44 Calories.

[8] A large proportion of the carbohydrate in the unstored product may be inulin, which is of doubtful availability. During storage, inulin is converted to sugars.

[9] Estimated average based on addition of salt in the amount of 0.6 percent of the finished product.

[10] Values weighted according to production, estimated as 90 percent from California, 10 percent from Florida.

[11] Values for items in this group apply to both strained and chopped (or junior) foods, unless otherwise specified.

TABLE 1.—COMPOSITION OF FOODS, 100 GRAMS, EDIBLE PORTION—Continued

[Numbers in parentheses denote values imputed—usually from another form of the food or from a similar food. Zero in parentheses indicates that the amount of a constituent probably is none or is too small to measure. Dashes denote lack of reliable data for a constituent believed to be present in measurable amount. Calculated values, as those based on a recipe, are not in parentheses]

Item No.	Food and description	Water	Food energy	Protein	Fat	Carbohydrate		Ash	Calcium	Phosphorus	Iron	Sodium	Potassium	Vitamin A value	Thiamine	Riboflavin	Niacin	Ascorbic acid
						Total	Fiber											
(A)	(B)	(C)	(D)	(E)	(F)	(G)	(H)	(I)	(J)	(K)	(L)	(M)	(N)	(O)	(P)	(Q)	(R)	(S)
		Percent	Calories	Grams	Grams	Grams	Grams	Grams	Milligrams	Milligrams	Milligrams	Milligrams	Milligrams	International units	Milligrams	Milligrams	Milligrams	Milligrams
	Baby foods [11]—Continued																	
	Dinners, canned—Continued																	
	Cereal, vegetable, meat mixtures (approx. 2%-4% protein)—Continued																	
84	Vegetables and lamb, with cereal	87.0	58	2.2	2.0	7.7	0.3	1.1	23	37	0.7	269	148	2,200	0.03	0.05	0.7	1
85	Vegetables and liver, with cereal	87.8	47	3.1	.4	7.8	.3	.9	17	57	2.7	236	162	4,700	.04	.37	1.6	3
86	Vegetables and liver, with bacon and cereal	87.2	57	2.4	1.9	7.5	.3	1.0	11	42	2.6	284	131	4,600	.03	.33	1.3	2
87	Vegetables and turkey, with cereal	88.9	44	2.1	.8	7.2	.2	1.0	22	26	.3	307	46	400	.01	.03	.4	1
	Meat or poultry (approx. 6%-8% protein):																	
88	Beef with vegetables	81.6	87	7.4	3.7	6.0	.2	1.3	13	84	1.2	304	113	1,100	.07	.17	1.6	2
89	Chicken with vegetables	79.6	100	7.4	4.6	7.2	.2	1.2	22	85	.9	265	71	1,000	.09	.15	1.6	2
90	Turkey with vegetables	81.3	86	6.7	3.2	7.6	.5	1.2	38	63	.6	348	122	1,000	.13	.13	1.8	2
91	Veal with vegetables	85.0	63	7.1	1.6	5.1	.2	1.2	11	71	.8	323	95	800	.08	.15	2.0	2
	Fruits and fruit products, with or without thickening, canned:																	
92	Applesauce	80.8	72	.2	.2	18.6	.5	.2	4	7	.4	6	64	40	.01	.02	.1	Trace
93	Applesauce and apricots	76.7	86	.3	.1	22.6	.5	.3	4	14	.3	(4)	105	600	.01	.02	.1	2
94	Bananas (with tapioca or cornstarch, added ascorbic acid), strained.	77.5	84	.4	.2	21.6	.1	.3	13	10	.2	29	118	70	.02	.02	.2	35
95	Bananas and pineapple (with tapioca or cornstarch).	78.5	80	.4	.1	20.7	.1	.3	20	12	.2	59	72	30	.01	.01	.1	2
96	Fruit dessert with tapioca (apricot, pineapple, and/or orange).	77.6	84	.3	.3	21.5	.2	.3	15	9	.4	53	73	450	.02	.01	.2	4
97	Peaches	78.1	81	.6	.2	20.7	.5	.4	6	14	.3	(4)	80	500	.01	.02	.7	3
98	Pears	82.2	66	.3	.1	17.1	1.0	.3	7	8	.2	4	62	30	.02	.02	.2	2
99	Pears and pineapple	81.5	69	.4	.2	17.6	.9	.3	7	12	.2	(4)	72	20	.03	.02	.2	2
100	Plums with tapioca, strained	74.8	94	.4	.2	24.3	.3	.3	5	12	.4	38	44	250	.01	.02	.2	2
101	Prunes with tapioca	76.7	86	.3	.2	22.4	.3	.4	7	21	.9	33	120	400	.02	.06	.4	4
	Meats, poultry, and eggs; canned:																	
	Beef:																	
102	Strained	80.3	99	14.7	4.0	(0)	(0)	1.0	8	127	2.0	228	183	—	.01	.16	3.5	0
103	Junior	75.6	118	19.3	3.9	(0)	(0)	1.4	8	163	2.5	283	242	—	.02	.20	4.3	0
104	Beef heart	81.1	93	13.5	3.8	.4	(0)	1.2	5	155	3.7	208	—	—	.06	.62	3.6	0
105	Chicken	77.2	127	13.7	7.6	(0)	(0)	1.5	—	129	1.9	263	96	—	.02	.16	3.5	0
106	Egg yolks, strained	70.0	210	10.0	18.4	.2	(0)	1.4	81	256	3.0	273	59	1,900	.12	.22	Trace	Trace
107	Egg yolks with ham or bacon	70.3	208	10.0	18.1	.3	(0)	1.3	71	185	2.8	313	82	1,900	.10	.23	5	—
	Lamb:																	
108	Strained	79.3	107	14.6	4.9	(0)	(0)	1.2	9	124	2.1	241	181	—	.02	.17	3.3	—
109	Junior	76.0	121	17.5	5.1	(0)	(0)	1.4	13	156	2.7	294	228	—	.02	.21	4.1	—
110	Liver, strained	79.7	97	14.1	3.4	1.5	(0)	1.3	6	182	5.6	253	202	24,000	.05	2.00	7.6	10
111	Liver and bacon, strained	77.0	123	13.7	6.6	1.3	(0)	1.4	6	157	4.2	302	192	22,000	.05	1.99	7.8	7
	Pork:																	
112	Strained	77.7	118	15.4	5.8	(0)	(0)	1.1	8	130	1.5	223	178	—	.19	.20	2.7	—
113	Junior	74.3	134	18.6	6.0	(0)	(0)	1.3	8	144	1.2	237	210	—	.23	.23	2.8	—
	Veal:																	
114	Strained	80.7	91	15.5	2.7	(0)	(0)	1.1	10	145	1.7	226	214	—	.03	.20	4.3	—
115	Junior	76.9	107	18.8	3.0	(0)	(0)	1.4	8	157	1.6	276	206	—	.03	.22	6.0	—
	Vegetables, canned:																	
116	Beans, green	92.5	22	1.4	.1	5.1	.8	.9	33	25	1.1	213	93	400	.02	.06	.3	3
117	Beets, strained	89.2	37	1.4	.1	8.3	.6	1.0	18	27	.7	212	228	20	.02	.03	.1	3
118	Carrots	91.5	29	.7	.1	6.8	.6	.9	23	21	.5	169	181	13,000	.02	.03	.4	3
119	Mixed vegetables, including vegetable soup	88.5	37	1.6	.3	8.5	.5	1.1	22	36	.9	272	170	4,700	.05	.04	.6	2
120	Peas, strained	85.5	54	4.2	.2	9.3	.8	.8	11	63	1.2	194	100	500	.08	.09	1.2	10
121	Spinach, creamed	88.1	43	2.3	.7	7.5	.4	1.4	64	63	.6	272	142	5,000	.02	.13	.3	6
122	Squash	92.1	25	.7	.1	6.2	.8	.9	24	17	.4	292	138	2,400	.02	.04	.3	8
123	Sweetpotatoes	82.3	67	1.0	.2	15.5	.5	1.0	16	34	.4	187	180	4,900	.04	.03	.4	8
124	Tomato soup, strained	83.4	54	1.9	.1	13.5	.2	1.1	24	52	.4	294	300	1,000	.05	.12	.7	3
	Bacon, cured:																	
125	Raw, slab or sliced	19.3	665	8.4	69.3	1.0	0	2.0	13	108	1.2	680	130	(0)	.36	.11	1.8	—
126	Cooked, broiled or fried, drained	8.1	611	30.4	52.0	3.2	0	6.3	14	224	3.3	1,021	236	(0)	.51	.34	5.2	—
127	Canned	16.7	685	8.5	71.5	1.0	0	2.3	15	92	1.4	—	—	(0)	.23	.10	1.5	—
	Bacon, Canadian:																	
128	Unheated	61.7	216	20.0	14.4	.3	0	3.6	12	180	3.0	1,891	392	(0)	.83	.22	4.7	—
129	Cooked, broiled or fried, drained	49.9	277	27.6	17.5	.3	0	4.7	19	218	4.1	2,555	432	(0)	.92	.17	5.0	—

No.	Food																	
	Baking powders: [12]																	
	Home use: [13]																	
	Sodium aluminum sulfate:																	
130	With monocalcium phosphate monohydrate	1.6	129	.1	Trace	31.2	Trace	—	1,932	2,904	—	10,953	150	(0)	(0)	(0)	(0)	(0)
131	With monocalcium phosphate monohydrate and calcium carbonate.	1.0	78	.1	Trace	18.9	Trace	—	5,778	1,452	—	11,618	—	(0)	(0)	(0)	(0)	(0)
132	With monocalcium phosphate monohydrate and calcium sulfate.	1.3	104	.1	Trace	25.1	Trace	—	6,320	1,560	—	10,000	—	(0)	(0)	(0)	(0)	(0)
133	Straight phosphate	1.6	121	.1	Trace	29.3	Trace	—	6,279	9,438	—	8,220	170	(0)	(0)	(0)	(0)	(0)
	Tartrate:																	
134	Cream of tartar, with tartaric acid	1.0	78	.1	Trace	18.9	Trace	—	0	0	0	7,300	3,800	(0)	(0)	(0)	(0)	(0)
	Special low-sodium preparations:																	
135	Commercial powder	2.2	172	.1	Trace	41.6	Trace	—	4,816	7,308	—	[14] 6	10,948	(0)	(0)	(0)	(0)	(0)
136	Noncommercial formula [15]	1.1	83	.1	Trace	20.1	Trace	—	—	—	—	—	20,729	(0)	(0)	(0)	(0)	(0)
	Commercial use:																	
	Pyrophosphate:																	
137	No additional leavening acid	1.4	109	.1	Trace	26.5	Trace	—	0	11,954	—	16,804	—	(0)	(0)	(0)	(0)	(0)
138	With monocalcium phosphate monohydrate	1.4	105	.1	Trace	25.5	Trace	—	900	12,245	—	16,210	—	(0)	(0)	(0)	(0)	(0)
139	With monocalcium phosphate monohydrate and calcium lactate.	1.3	103	.1	Trace	25.0	Trace	—	[16] 993	11,580	—	15,947	—	(0)	(0)	(0)	(0)	(0)
140	**Bamboo shoots,** raw	91.0	27	2.6	.3	5.2	.7	.9	13	59	.5	—	533	20	.15	.07	.6	4
	Bananas:																	
	Raw:																	
141	Common	75.7	85	1.1	.2	22.2	.5	.8	8	26	.7	1	370	190	.05	.06	.7	10
142	Red	74.4	90	1.2	.2	23.4	.4	.8	10	18	.8	1	370	400	.05	.04	.6	(10)
143	Dehydrated, or banana powder	3.	340	4.4	.8	88.6	2.0	3.2	32	104	2.8	4	1,477	760	.18	.24	2.8	7
	Bananas, baking type. See Plantain, item 1634.																	
	Barbados-cherry. See Acerola, item 3.																	
144	**Barbecue sauce**	80.9	91	1.5	6.9	8.0	.6	2.7	21	20	.8	815	174	360	.01	.01	.3	5
	Barley, pearled:																	
145	Light	11.1	349	8.2	1.0	78.8	.5	.9	16	189	2.0	3	160	(0)	.12	.05	3.1	(0)
146	Pot or Scotch	10.8	348	9.6	1.1	77.2	.9	1.3	34	290	2.7	—	296	(0)	.21	.07	3.7	(0)
147	**Barracuda, Pacific,** raw	75.4	113	21.0	2.6	0	0	1.3	—	—	—	—	—	—	—	—	—	—
	Basella. See Vinespinach, item 2408.																	
	Bass, black sea:																	
148	Raw	79.3	93	19.2	1.2	0	0	1.2	—	—	—	68	256	—	—	—	—	—
149	Cooked, baked, stuffed [17]	52.9	259	16.2	15.8	11.4	—	3.7	—	—	—	—	—	—	—	—	—	—
150	**Bass, smallmouth and largemouth,** raw	77.3	104	18.9	2.6	0	0	1.2	—	192	—	—	—	—	.10	.03	2.1	—
	Bass, striped:																	
151	Raw	77.7	105	18.9	2.7	0	0	1.2	—	212	—	—	—	—	—	—	—	—
152	Cooked, oven-fried [18]	60.8	196	21.5	8.5	6.7	—	2.5	—	—	—	—	—	—	—	—	—	—
153	**Bass, white,** raw	78.8	98	18.0	2.3	0	0	1.0	—	—	—	—	—	—	—	—	—	—
	Beans, broad. See Broadbeans, items 481–482.																	
	Beans, common, mature seeds, dry:																	
	White:																	
154	Raw	10.9	340	22.3	1.6	61.3	4.3	3.9	144	425	7.8	19	1,196	0	.65	.22	2.4	—
155	Cooked	69.0	118	7.8	.6	21.2	1.5	1.4	50	148	2.7	[9] 7	416	0	.14	.07	.7	0
	Canned, solids and liquid:																	
156	With pork and tomato sauce	70.7	122	6.1	2.6	19.0	1.4	1.6	54	92	1.8	463	210	130	.08	.03	.6	2
157	With pork and sweet sauce	66.4	150	6.2	4.7	21.1	1.7	1.6	63	114	2.3	380	—	—	.06	.04	.5	—
158	Without pork	68.5	120	6.3	.5	23.0	1.4	1.7	68	121	2.0	338	268	60	.07	.04	.6	2
	Red:																	
159	Raw	10.4	343	22.5	1.5	61.9	4.2	3.7	110	406	6.9	10	984	20	.51	.20	2.3	—
160	Cooked	69.0	118	7.8	.5	21.4	1.5	1.3	38	140	2.4	[9] 3	340	Trace	.11	.06	.7	—
161	Canned, solids and liquid	76.0	90	5.7	.4	16.4	.9	1.5	29	109	1.8	3	264	Trace	.05	.04	.6	—
162	Pinto, calico, and red Mexican, raw	8.3	349	22.9	1.2	63.7	4.3	3.9	135	457	6.4	10	984	—	.84	.21	2.2	—
163	Other, including black, brown, and Bayo, raw	11.2	339	22.3	1.5	61.2	4.4	3.8	135	420	7.9	25	1,038	30	.55	.20	2.2	—
	Beans, hyacinth. See Hyacinth-beans, items 1137–1138.																	
	Beans, lima:																	
	Immature seeds:																	
164	Raw	67.5	123	8.4	.5	22.1	1.8	1.5	52	142	2.8	2	650	290	.24	.12	1.4	29
165	Cooked, boiled, drained	71.1	111	7.6	.5	19.8	1.8	1.0	47	121	2.5	1	422	280	.18	.10	1.3	17
	Canned:																	
	Regular pack:																	
166	Solids and liquid	80.8	71	4.1	.3	13.4	1.3	1.4	26	67	2.4	[9] 236	222	130	.04	.04	.5	7
167	Drained solids	74.7	96	5.4	.3	18.3	1.8	1.3	28	70	2.4	[9] 236	222	190	.03	.05	.5	6
168	Drained liquid	93.3	20	1.3	Trace	3.9	Trace	1.5	22	60	2.3	[9] 236	222	Trace	.04	.03	.6	10
	Special dietary pack (low-sodium):																	
169	Solids and liquid	81.7	70	4.4	.3	12.9	1.2	.7	26	67	2.4	4	222	130	.04	.04	.5	7
170	Drained solids	75.6	95	5.8	.3	17.7	1.8	.6	28	70	2.4	4	222	190	.03	.05	.5	6
171	Drained liquid	94.4	19	1.4	Trace	3.5	Trace	.7	22	60	2.3	4	222	Trace	.04	.03	.6	10

[9] Estimated average based on addition of salt in the amount of 0.6 percent of the finished product.

[12] Values for energy and proximate constituents are based on starch content.

[13] List of ingredients on label indicates type of baking powder.

[14] Value based on single brand.

[15] Values are based on formula in "Planning Low-Sodium Meals," Newton Health Dept., Newton, Mass., 1951, as cited in National Academy of Sciences–National Research Council Publication No. 325 "Sodium-Restricted Diets," p. 20, 1954, Washington, D.C.

[16] Calcium content depends largely on amount of monocalcium phosphate in the product. Values range from 200 to 1,600 mg. per 100 grams.

[17] Prepared with bacon, butter, onion, celery, and bread cubes.

[18] Prepared with milk, bread crumbs, butter, and salt.

TABLE 1.—COMPOSITION OF FOODS, 100 GRAMS, EDIBLE PORTION—Continued

[Numbers in parentheses denote values imputed—usually from another form of the food or from a similar food. Zero in parentheses indicates that the amount of a constituent probably is none or is too small to measure. Dashes denote lack of reliable data for a constituent believed to be present in measurable amount. Calculated values, as those based on a recipe, are not in parentheses]

Item No.	Food and description	Water	Food energy	Protein	Fat	Carbohydrate		Ash	Calcium	Phosphorus	Iron	Sodium	Potassium	Vitamin A value	Thiamine	Riboflavin	Niacin	Ascorbic acid
						Total	Fiber											
(A)	(B)	(C)	(D)	(E)	(F)	(G)	(H)	(I)	(J)	(K)	(L)	(M)	(N)	(O)	(P)	(Q)	(R)	(S)
	Beans, lima—Continued	Percent	Calories	Grams	Grams	Grams	Grams	Grams	Milligrams	Milligrams	Milligrams	Milligrams	Milligrams	International units	Milligrams	Milligrams	Milligrams	Milligrams
	Immature seeds—Continued																	
	Frozen:																	
	Thick-seeded types, commonly called Fordhooks:																	
172	Not thawed	72.7	102	6.2	0.1	19.5	1.7	1.5	23	96	1.9	[19] 129	490	230	0.10	0.06	1.2	22
173	Cooked, boiled, drained	73.5	99	6.0	.1	19.1	1.6	1.3	20	90	1.7	101	426	230	.07	.05	1.0	17
	Thin-seeded types, commonly called baby limas:																	
174	Not thawed	67.8	122	7.6	.2	23.0	1.9	1.4	38	131	2.8	[19] 147	438	220	.10	.06	1.2	19
175	Cooked, boiled, drained	68.8	118	7.4	.2	22.3	1.9	1.3	35	126	2.6	129	394	220	.09	.05	1.2	12
	Mature seeds, dry:																	
176	Raw	10.3	345	20.4	1.6	64.0	4.3	3.7	72	385	7.8	4	1,529	Trace	.48	.17	1.9	—
177	Cooked	64.1	138	8.2	.6	25.6	1.7	1.5	29	154	3.1	[4] 2	612	—	.13	.06	.7	—
178	**Bean flour, lima**	10.5	343	21.5	1.4	63.0	2.	3.6	—	—	—	—	—	(0)	—	—	—	(0)
	Beans, mung:																	
179	Mature seeds, dry, raw	10.7	340	24.2	1.3	60.3	4.4	3.5	118	340	7.7	6	1,028	80	.38	.21	2.6	—
	Sprouted seeds:																	
180	Uncooked	88.8	35	3.8	.2	6.6	.7	.6	19	64	1.3	5	223	20	.13	.13	.8	19
181	Cooked, boiled, drained	91.0	28	3.2	.2	5.2	.7	.4	17	48	.9	4	156	20	.09	.10	.7	6
	Beans, snap:																	
	Green:																	
182	Raw	90.1	32	1.9	.2	7.1	1.0	.7	56	44	.8	7	243	600	.08	.11	.5	19
	Cooked, boiled, drained, cooked in—																	
183	Small amount of water, short time	92.4	25	1.6	.2	5.4	1.0	.4	50	37	.6	4	151	540	.07	.09	.5	12
184	Large amount of water, long time	92.4	25	1.6	.2	5.4	1.0	.4	50	37	.6	4	151	540	.06	.08	.3	10
	Canned:																	
	Regular pack:																	
185	Solids and liquid	93.5	18	1.0	.1	4.2	.6	1.2	34	21	1.2	[9] 236	95	290	.03	.04	.3	4
186	Drained solids	91.9	24	1.4	.2	5.2	1.0	1.3	45	25	1.5	[9] 236	95	470	.03	.05	.3	4
187	Drained liquid	95.9	10	.4	.1	2.4	Trace	1.2	15	14	.9	[9] 236	95	Trace	.03	.03	.3	4
	Special dietary pack (low-sodium):																	
188	Solids and liquid	94.8	16	1.1	.1	3.6	.6	.4	34	21	1.2	2	95	290	.03	.04	.3	4
189	Drained solids	93.2	22	1.5	.1	4.8	.9	.4	45	25	1.5	2	95	470	.03	.05	.3	4
190	Drained liquid	97.3	8	.4	.1	1.8	Trace	.4	15	14	.9	2	95	Trace	.03	.03	.3	4
	Frozen:																	
	Cut:																	
191	Not thawed	91.7	26	1.7	.1	6.0	1.0	.5	42	33	.8	1	167	580	.07	.10	.4	9
192	Cooked, boiled, drained	92.1	25	1.6	.1	5.7	1.0	.5	40	32	.7	1	152	580	.07	.09	.4	5
	French style:																	
193	Not thawed	91.6	27	1.7	.1	6.1	1.1	.5	40	32	.9	2	153	530	.07	.09	.4	10
194	Cooked, boiled, drained	91.9	26	1.6	.1	6.0	1.1	.4	38	30	.9	2	136	530	.06	.08	.3	7
	Yellow or wax:																	
195	Raw	91.4	27	1.7	.2	6.0	1.0	.7	56	43	.8	7	243	250	.08	.11	.5	20
196	Cooked, boiled, drained	93.4	22	1.4	.2	4.6	1.0	.4	50	37	.6	3	151	230	.07	.09	.5	13
	Canned:																	
	Regular pack:																	
197	Solids and liquid	93.7	19	1.0	.2	4.2	.6	.9	34	21	1.2	[9] 236	95	60	.03	.04	.3	5
198	Drained solids	92.2	24	1.4	.3	5.2	.9	.9	45	25	1.5	[9] 236	95	100	.03	.05	.3	5
199	Drained liquid	96.1	11	.4	.1	2.5	Trace	.9	15	14	.9	[9] 236	95	Trace	.03	.03	.3	5
	Special dietary pack (low-sodium):																	
200	Solids and liquid	95.2	15	.9	.1	3.4	.6	.4	(34)	(21)	(1.2)	2	95	(60)	(.03)	(.04)	(.3)	(5)
201	Drained solids	93.6	21	1.2	.1	4.7	.9	.4	(45)	(25)	(1.5)	2	95	(100)	(.03)	(.05)	(.3)	(5)
202	Drained liquid	97.7	7	.4	.1	1.4	Trace	.4	(15)	(14)	(.9)	2	95	Trace	(.03)	(.03)	(.3)	(5)
	Frozen, cut:																	
203	Not thawed	91.1	28	1.8	.1	6.5	1.1	.5	36	32	.8	1	180	100	.08	.09	.5	12
204	Cooked, boiled, drained	91.5	27	1.7	.1	6.2	1.1	.5	35	31	.7	1	164	100	.07	.08	.4	6
	Bean sprouts. See Beans, mung: items 180–181; and Soybeans: items 2143–2144.																	
205	**Beans and frankfurters,** canned	70.7	144	7.6	7.1	12.6	1.0	2.0	37	119	1.9	539	262	130	.07	.06	1.3	Trace
206	**Beaver,** cooked, roasted	56.2	248	29.2	13.7	0	0	.9	—	—	—	—	—	—	.08	.38	—	—
207	**Beechnuts**	6.6	568	19.4	50.0	20.3	3.7	3.7	—	—	—	—	—	—	—	—	—	—

	Beef: [4]																	
	Carcass:																	
	Total edible, including kidney and kidney fat, raw:																	
208	Prime grade (54% lean, 46% fat)	44.8	428	13.6	41.	0	0	.6	8	124	2.0			80	.06	.12	3.3	—
209	Choice grade (60% lean, 40% fat)	49.4	379	14.9	35.	0	0	.7	9	136	2.2			70	.06	.13	3.6	—
210	Good grade (66% lean, 34% fat)	54.7	323	16.5	28.	0	0	.8	10	152	2.5			60	.07	.15	4.0	—
211	Standard grade (73% lean, 27% fat)	60.1	266	18.0	21.	0	0	.9	10	166	2.7			40	.08	.16	4.3	—
212	Commercial grade (64% lean, 36% fat)	52.4	347	15.8	31.	0	0	.8	9	145	2.4			60	.07	.14	3.8	—
213	Utility grade (76% lean, 24% fat)	62.5	242	18.6	18.	0	0	.9	11	172	2.8			40	.08	.17	4.5	—
	Total edible, trimmed to retail level, raw:																	
214	Choice grade (75% lean, 25% fat)	56.7	301	17.4	25.1	0	0	.8	10	161	2.6			50	.07	.15	4.2	—
215	Good grade (78% lean, 22% fat)	60.3	263	18.5	20.4	0	0	.8	11	171	2.8			40	.08	.16	4.4	—
216	Standard grade (82% lean, 18% fat)	63.9	225	19.4	15.8	0	0	.9	11	180	2.9			30	.08	.17	4.7	—
	Separable fat:																	
	Raw. See individual cuts.																	
217	Cooked	15.7	729	5.7	78.1	0	0	.5	—	—	—			—	—	—	—	—
	Retail cuts, trimmed to retail level:																	
	Chuck cuts:																	
	Entire chuck, 1st–5th ribs, arm, and neck:																	
	Choice grade:																	
	Total edible:																	
218	Raw (82% lean, 18% fat)	60.8	257	18.7	19.6	0	0	.9	11	188	2.8			40	.08	.17	4.5	—
219	Cooked, braised or pot-roasted (81% lean, 19% fat).	49.4	327	26.0	23.9	0	0	.7	11	140	3.3			40	.05	.20	4.0	—
	Separable lean:																	
220	Raw	70.3	158	21.3	7.4	0	0	1.0	12	214	3.2			10	.09	.19	5.1	—
221	Cooked, braised or pot-roasted	59.7	214	30.0	9.5	0	0	.8	13	160	3.8			20	.05	.23	4.6	—
	Separable fat:																	
222	Raw	16.9	716	6.6	76.3	0	0	.2	4	72	1.0			150	.03	.06	1.6	—
	Chuck rib, 5th:																	
	Choice grade:																	
	Total edible:																	
223	Raw (70% lean, 30% fat)	51.7	352	16.2	31.4	0	0	.7	9	148	2.4			60	.07	.14	3.9	—
224	Cooked, braised (69% lean, 31% fat)	40.3	427	22.4	36.7	0	0	.6	10	110	2.9			70	.04	.17	3.5	—
	Separable lean:																	
225	Raw	67.4	188	20.7	11.0	0	0	.9	12	192	3.1	[20]	[21]	20	.09	.18	5.0	—
226	Cooked, braised	56.5	249	28.9	13.9	0	0	.7	13	143	3.7			20	.05	.22	4.5	—
	Separable fat:																	
227	Raw	14.3	745	5.5	80.0	0	0	.2	3	45	.8			160	.02	.05	1.3	—
	Good grade:																	
	Total edible:																	
228	Raw (74% lean, 26% fat)	56.3	303	17.5	25.3	0	0	.8	10	162	2.6			50	.08	.16	4.2	—
229	Cooked, braised (73% lean, 27% fat)	44.8	377	24.2	30.3	0	0	.7	10	121	3.1			60	.04	.19	3.8	—
	Separable lean:																	
230	Raw	69.8	163	21.2	8.0	0	0	1.0	12	197	3.2			20	.09	.19	5.1	—
231	Cooked, braised	59.2	219	29.8	10.2	0	0	.8	13	147	3.8			20	.05	.23	4.6	—
	Separable fat:																	
232	Raw	17.8	705	7.0	74.9	0	0	.3	4	60	1.0			150	.03	.06	1.7	—
	Arm:																	
	Choice grade:																	
	Total edible:																	
233	Raw (86% lean, 14% fat)	64.2	223	19.4	15.5	0	0	.9	12	180	2.9			30	.08	.17	4.7	—
234	Cooked, braised or pot-roasted (85% lean, 15% fat).	53.0	289	27.1	19.2	0	0	.7	12	134	3.4			30	.05	.21	4.2	—
	Separable lean:																	
235	Raw	72.0	141	21.6	5.4	0	0	1.0	13	201	3.2			10	.09	.19	5.2	—
236	Cooked, braised or pot-roasted	61.7	193	30.5	7.0	0	0	.8	14	150	3.8			10	.06	.23	4.6	—
	Separable fat:																	
237	Raw	15.2	736	5.8	78.8	0	0	.2	3	48	.9			160	.02	.05	1.4	—
	Good grade:																	
	Total edible:																	
238	Raw (89% lean, 11% fat)	67.3	191	20.3	11.6	0	0	.9	12	188	3.1			20	.09	.18	4.8	—
239	Cooked, braised or pot-roasted (88% lean, 12% fat).	56.3	253	28.4	14.6	0	0	.7	13	140	3.7			30	.05	.21	4.3	—
	Separable lean:																	
240	Raw	73.2	129	21.8	4.0	0	0	1.0	13	203	3.3			10	.09	.19	5.2	—
241	Cooked, braised or pot-roasted	63.1	179	30.9	5.2	0	0	.8	14	151	3.9			10	.06	.23	4.7	—
	Separable fat:																	
242	Raw	17.9	704	7.1	74.7	0	0	.3	4	61	1.1			150	.03	.06	1.7	—

[4] Estimated average based on addition of salt in the amount of 0.6 percent of the finished product.

[19] Average weighted in accordance with commercial practices in freezing vegetables.

[20] Average value for 100 grams, all cuts, is 65 mg. for raw beef and 60 mg. for cooked beef.

[21] Average value per 100 grams of beef of all cuts is 355 mg. for raw meat and 370 mg. for cooked meat.

TABLE 1.—COMPOSITION OF FOODS, 100 GRAMS, EDIBLE PORTION—Continued

[Numbers in parentheses denote values imputed—usually from another form of the food or from a similar food. Zero in parentheses indicates that the amount of a constituent probably is none or is too small to measure. Dashes denote lack of reliable data for a constituent believed to be present in measurable amount. Calculated values, as those based on a recipe, are not in parentheses]

Item No.	Food and description	Water	Food energy	Protein	Fat	Carbohydrate		Ash	Calcium	Phos-phorus	Iron	Sodium	Potas-sium	Vitamin A value	Thiamine	Ribo-flavin	Niacin	Ascorbic acid
						Total	Fiber											
(A)	(B)	(C)	(D)	(E)	(F)	(G)	(H)	(I)	(J)	(K)	(L)	(M)	(N)	(O)	(P)	(Q)	(R)	(S)
	Beef[4]—Continued	Percent	Calories	Grams	Grams	Grams	Grams	Grams	Milligrams	Milligrams	Milligrams	Milligrams	Milligrams	International units	Milligrams	Milligrams	Milligrams	Milligrams
	Retail cuts, trimmed to retail level—Continued																	
	Flank steak:																	
	Choice grade:																	
	Total edible:																	
243	Raw (100% lean)	71.7	144	21.6	5.7	0	0	1.0	13	201	3.2			10	0.09	0.19	5.2	—
244	Cooked, braised (100% lean)	61.4	196	30.5	7.3	0	0	.8	14	150	3.8			10	.06	.23	4.6	—
	Good grade:																	
	Total edible:																	
245	Raw (100% lean)	72.1	139	21.8	5.1	0	0	1.0	13	203	3.3			10	.09	.19	5.2	—
246	Cooked, braised (100% lean)	61.8	191	30.8	6.6	0	0	.8	14	151	3.9			10	.06	.23	4.7	—
	Hindshank:																	
	Choice grade:																	
	Total edible:																	
247	Raw (67% lean, 33% fat)	57.6	289	18.2	23.4	0	0	.8	11	168	2.8			50	.08	.16	4.4	—
248	Cooked, simmered (66% lean, 34% fat)	46.1	361	25.1	28.1	0	0	.7	11	125	3.3			50	.05	.19	3.9	—
	Separable lean:																	
249	Raw	72.7	134	21.7	4.6	0	0	1.0	13	202	3.3			10	.09	.19	5.2	—
250	Cooked, simmered	62.5	184	30.7	5.9	0	0	.8	14	151	3.9			10	.06	.23	4.7	—
	Separable fat:																	
251	Raw	27.0	602	11.1	61.5	0	0	.4	6	100	1.7			120	.05	.10	2.7	—
	Good grade:																	
	Total edible:																	
252	Raw (71% lean, 29% fat)	62.3	239	19.7	17.2	0	0	.8	12	182	3.0			30	.08	.17	4.7	—
253	Cooked, simmered (70% lean, 30% fat)	51.0	307	27.2	21.1	0	0	.7	12	136	3.6			40	.05	.21	4.2	—
	Separable lean:																	
254	Raw	73.5	126	21.8	3.7	0	0	1.0	13	203	3.3			10	.09	.19	5.2	—
255	Cooked, simmered	63.4	176	31.0	4.8	0	0	.8	14	151	3.9			10	.06	.23	4.7	—
	Separable fat:																	
256	Raw	34.6	517	14.5	50.4	0	0	.5	8	132	2.2			100	.06	.13	3.5	—
	Loin or short loin:																	
	Porterhouse steak:																	
	Choice grade:											(20)	(21)					
	Total edible:																	
257	Raw (63% lean, 37% fat)	48.3	390	14.8	36.2	0	0	.7	8	136	2.2			70	.06	.13	3.6	—
258	Cooked, broiled (57% lean, 43% fat)	37.2	465	19.7	42.2	0	0	.9	9	168	2.6			70	.06	.16	4.2	—
	Separable lean:																	
259	Raw	69.7	164	21.1	8.2	0	0	1.0	12	196	3.2			20	.09	.19	5.1	—
260	Cooked, broiled	57.9	224	30.2	10.5	0	0	1.4	12	242	3.7			20	.08	.23	5.9	—
	Separable fat:																	
261	Raw	11.5	777	4.2	84.1	0	0	.2	2	33	.6			170	.02	.04	1.0	—
	Good grade:																	
	Total edible:																	
262	Raw (64% lean, 36% fat)	50.2	370	15.3	33.8	0	0	.7	8	140	2.3			70	.06	.14	3.7	—
263	Cooked, broiled (58% lean, 42% fat)	38.9	446	20.5	39.7	0	0	1.0	9	173	2.6			70	.06	.17	4.3	—
	Separable lean:																	
264	Raw	72.0	141	21.5	5.5	0	0	1.0	12	200	3.2			10	.09	.19	5.2	—
265	Cooked, broiled	60.3	197	31.1	7.1	0	0	1.4	12	247	3.7			10	.08	.24	6.0	—
	Separable fat:																	
266	Raw	11.6	775	4.3	83.9	0	0	.2	2	34	.6			170	.02	.04	1.0	—
	T-bone steak:																	
	Choice grade:																	
	Total edible:																	
267	Raw (62% lean, 38% fat)	47.5	397	14.7	37.1	0	0	.7	8	135	2.2			70	.06	.13	3.5	—
268	Cooked, broiled (56% lean, 44% fat)	36.4	473	19.5	43.2	0	0	.9	8	166	2.6			80	.06	.16	4.1	—
	Separable lean:																	
269	Raw	69.7	164	21.2	8.1	0	0	1.0	12	197	3.2			20	.09	.19	5.1	—
270	Cooked, broiled	57.9	223	30.4	10.3	0	0	1.4	12	243	3.7			20	.08	.23	5.9	—
	Separable fat:																	
271	Raw	11.7	774	4.3	83.8	0	0	.2	2	34	.6			170	.02	.04	1.0	—
	Good grade:																	
	Total edible:																	
272	Raw (64% lean, 36% fat)	50.6	366	15.4	33.3	0	0	.7	9	142	2.3			70	.07	.14	3.7	—
273	Cooked, broiled (58% lean, 42% fat)	39.2	442	20.6	39.2	0	0	1.0	9	175	2.7			70	.06	.17	4.3	—

	Separable lean:																	
274	Raw	71.9	142	21.5	5.6	0	0	1.0	12	200	3.2			10	.09	.19	5.2	—
275	Cooked, broiled	60.2	199	31.1	7.3	0	0	1.4	12	247	3.7			10	.08	.24	6.0	—
	Separable fat:																	
276	Raw	12.9	761	4.8	82.1	0	0	.2	3	39	.7			160	.02	.04	1.2	—
	Club steak:																	
	Choice grade:																	
	Total edible:																	
277	Raw (64% lean, 36% fat)	49.1	380	15.5	34.8	0	0	.7	9	142	2.3			70	.07	.14	3.7	—
278	Cooked, broiled (58% lean, 42% fat)	37.9	454	20.6	40.6	0	0	.9	9	175	2.7			70	.06	.17	4.3	—
	Separable lean:																	
279	Raw	67.9	182	20.8	10.3	0	0	1.0	12	193	3.1			20	.09	.19	5.0	—
280	Cooked, broiled	56.0	244	29.6	13.0	0	0	1.4	12	238	3.6			20	.08	.23	5.8	—
	Separable fat:																	
281	Raw	15.6	731	6.0	78.2	0	0	.2	3	50	.9			160	.03	.05	1.4	—
	Good grade:																	
	Total edible:																	
282	Raw (70% lean, 30% fat)	54.5	324	16.9	27.9	0	0	.8	10	156	2.6			60	.07	.15	4.0	—
283	Cooked, broiled (64% lean, 36% fat)	42.8	398	22.9	33.3	0	0	1.0	10	192	3.0			60	.06	.18	4.7	—
	Separable lean:																	
284	Raw	70.3	158	21.2	7.5	0	0	1.0	12	197	3.2			20	.09	.19	5.1	—
285	Cooked, broiled	58.5	217	30.5	9.6	0	0	1.4	12	243	3.7			20	.08	.23	5.9	—
	Separable fat:																	
286	Raw	17.0	716	6.6	76.2	0	0	.2	4	56	1.0			150	.03	.06	1.6	—
	Loin end or sirloin:																	
	Wedge and round-bone sirloin steak:																	
	Choice grade:																	
	Total edible:																	
287	Raw (73% lean, 27% fat)	55.7	313	16.9	26.7	0	0	.8	10	155	2.5			50	.07	.15	4.1	—
288	Cooked, broiled (66% lean, 34% fat)	43.9	387	23.0	32.0	0	0	1.1	10	191	2.9			50	.06	.18	4.7	—
	Separable lean:																	
289	Raw	71.8	143	21.5	5.7	0	0	1.0	12	200	3.2			10	.09	.19	5.2	—
290	Cooked, broiled	58.7	207	32.2	7.7	0	0	1.5	13	261	3.9			10	.09	.25	6.4	—
	Separable fat:																	
291	Raw	11.8	773	4.4	83.6	0	0	.2	3	35	.7			170	.02	.04	1.1	—
	Good grade:																	
	Total edible:																	
292	Raw (75% lean, 25% fat)	58.7	281	17.8	22.7	0	0	.8	10	164	2.7			50	.08	.16	4.3	—
293	Cooked, broiled (68% lean, 32% fat)	46.9	353	24.5	27.5	0	0	1.1	11	202	3.1	(30)	(31)	50	.07	.19	5.0	—
	Separable lean:																	
294	Raw	73.2	129	21.8	4.0	0	0	1.0	13	203	3.3			10	.09	.19	5.2	—
295	Cooked, broiled	61.6	183	31.7	5.3	0	0	1.4	13	250	3.8			10	.08	.24	6.1	—
	Separable fat:																	
296	Raw	14.4	744	5.5	79.9	0	0	.2	3	45	.8			160	.02	.05	1.3	—
	Double-bone sirloin steak:																	
	Choice grade:																	
	Total edible:																	
297	Raw (72% lean, 28% fat)	53.7	333	16.4	29.1	0	0	.8	9	151	2.5			60	.07	.15	3.9	—
298	Cooked, broiled (66% lean, 34% fat)	42.1	408	22.2	34.7	0	0	1.0	10	186	2.9			60	.06	.18	4.6	—
	Separable lean:																	
299	Raw	70.3	158	21.3	7.4	0	0	1.0	12	198	3.2			20	.09	.19	5.1	—
300	Cooked, broiled	58.5	216	30.6	9.5	0	0	1.4	12	244	3.7			20	.08	.23	6.0	—
	Separable fat:																	
301	Raw	10.1	793	3.6	86.2	0	0	.1	2	27	.5			170	.02	.03	.9	—
	Good grade:																	
	Total edible:																	
302	Raw (75% lean, 25% fat)	57.6	293	17.6	24.1	0	0	.8	10	161	2.7			50	.08	.16	4.2	—
303	Cooked, broiled (67% lean, 33% fat)	45.7	365	24.1	29.1	0	0	1.1	11	198	3.1			50	.07	.19	4.9	—
	Separable lean:																	
304	Raw	72.6	135	21.7	4.7	0	0	1.0	13	202	3.3			10	.09	.19	5.2	—
305	Cooked, broiled	61.0	190	31.5	6.1	0	0	1.4	13	249	3.8			10	.08	.24	6.1	—
	Separable fat:																	
306	Raw	13.8	751	5.3	80.7	0	0	.2	3	43	.8			160	.02	.05	1.3	—
	Hipbone sirloin steak:																	
	Choice grade:																	
	Total edible:																	
307	Raw (61% lean, 39% fat)	46.0	412	14.5	38.8	0	0	.7	8	132	2.2			80	.06	.13	3.5	—
308	Cooked, broiled (55% lean, 45% fat)	35.1	487	19.1	44.9	0	0	.9	9	163	2.5			80	.06	.16	4.0	—
	Separable lean:																	
309	Raw	68.2	179	20.9	9.9	0	0	1.0	12	194	3.1			20	.09	.19	5.0	—
310	Cooked, broiled	56.3	240	29.8	12.5	0	0	1.4	12	239	3.6			20	.08	.23	5.8	—
	Separable fat:																	
311	Raw	12.0	771	4.5	83.3	0	0	.2	3	36	.7			170	.02	.04	1.1	—
	Good grade:																	
	Total edible:																	
312	Raw (64% lean, 36% fat)	50.4	367	15.7	33.2	0	0	.7	9	143	2.3			70	.07	.14	3.8	—
313	Cooked, broiled (58% lean, 42% fat)	39.0	441	21.0	39.0	0	0	1.0	9	176	2.7			70	.06	.17	4.4	—

[30] Average value for 100 grams, all cuts, is 65 mg. for raw beef and 60 mg. for cooked beef.

[31] Average value per 100 grams of beef of all cuts is 355 mg. for raw meat and 370 mg. for cooked meat.

TABLE 1.—COMPOSITION OF FOODS, 100 GRAMS, EDIBLE PORTION—Continued

[Numbers in parentheses denote values imputed—usually from another form of the food or from a similar food. Zero in parentheses indicates that the amount of a constituent probably is none or is too small to measure. Dashes denote lack of reliable data for a constituent believed to be present in measurable amount. Calculated values, as those based on a recipe, are not in parentheses]

Item No.	Food and description	Water	Food energy	Protein	Fat	Carbohydrate		Ash	Calcium	Phosphorus	Iron	Sodium	Potassium	Vitamin A value	Thiamine	Riboflavin	Niacin	Ascorbic acid
						Total	Fiber											
(A)	(B)	(C)	(D)	(E)	(F)	(G)	(H)	(I)	(J)	(K)	(L)	(M)	(N)	(O)	(P)	(Q)	(R)	(S)
		Percent	Calories	Grams	Grams	Grams	Grams	Grams	Milligrams	Milligrams	Milligrams	Milligrams	Milligrams	International units	Milligrams	Milligrams	Milligrams	Milligrams
	Beef[1]—Continued																	
	Retail cuts, trimmed to retail level—Continued																	
	Loin end or sirloin—Continued																	
	Hipbone sirloin steak—Continued																	
	Good grade—Continued																	
	Separable lean:																	
314	Raw	70.9	152	21.4	6.7	0	0	1.0	12	199	3.2			10	0.09	0.19	5.1	—
315	Cooked, broiled	59.2	209	30.8	8.6	0	0	1.4	12	245	3.7			10	.08	.23	6.0	—
	Separable fat:																	
316	Raw	14.4	744	5.5	79.9	0	0	.2	3	45	.8			160	.03	.05	1.3	—
	Short plate:																	
	Choice grade:																	
	Total edible:																	
317	Raw (59% lean, 41% fat)	47.2	400	14.8	37.3	0	0	.7	8	135	2.2			70	.06	.13	3.6	—
318	Cooked, simmered (58% lean, 42% fat)	36.0	474	20.6	42.8	0	0	.6	9	101	2.7			80	.04	.16	3.2	—
	Separable lean:																	
319	Raw	69.7	164	21.1	8.2	0	0	1.0	12	196	3.2			20	.09	.19	5.1	—
320	Cooked, simmered	59.1	222	29.7	10.5	0	0	.8	13	146	3.8			20	.05	.22	4.5	—
	Separable fat:																	
321	Raw	15.3	734	5.9	78.6	0	0	.2	3	49	.9			160	.03	.05	1.4	—
	Good grade:																	
	Total edible:																	
322	Raw (62% lean, 38% fat)	51.3	356	16.1	31.9	0	0	.7	9	147	2.4			60	.07	.14	3.8	—
323	Cooked, simmered (61% lean, 39% fat)	39.9	432	22.3	37.3	0	0	.6	9	110	2.9			70	.04	.17	3.4	—
	Separable lean:																	
324	Raw	71.5	146	21.5	6.0	0	0	1.0	12	200	3.2			10	.09	.19	5.2	—
325	Cooked, simmered	61.1	199	30.3	7.7	0	0	.8	13	149	3.8			10	.05	.23	4.6	—
	Separable fat:																	
326	Raw	18.2	701	7.2	74.3	0	0	.3	4	62	1.1			150	.03	.06	1.7	—
	Rib:																	
	Entire rib, (6th–12th ribs):																	
	Choice grade:																	
	Total edible:																	
327	Raw (64% lean, 36% fat)	47.2	401	14.8	37.4	0	0	.6	9	151	2.2			70	.06	.13	3.6	—
328	Cooked, roasted (64% lean, 36% fat)	40.0	440	19.9	39.4	0	0	.7	9	186	2.6	(20)	(21)	80	.05	.15	3.6	—
	Separable lean:																	
329	Raw	66.8	193	20.7	11.6	0	0	.9	12	208	3.1			20	.09	.18	5.0	—
330	Cooked, roasted	57.2	241	28.2	13.4	0	0	1.1	12	256	3.6			20	.07	.21	5.1	—
	Separable fat:																	
331	Raw	12.8	762	4.8	82.2	0	0	.2	3	54	.7			160	.02	.04	1.2	—
	Ribs, 11th–12th:																	
	Choice grade:																	
	Total edible:																	
332	Raw (55% lean, 45% fat)	43.0	444	13.7	42.7	0	0	.6	8	124	2.1			90	.06	.12	3.3	—
333	Cooked, roasted (55% lean, 45% fat)	36.3	481	18.3	44.7	0	0	.7	8	153	2.4			90	.05	.14	3.4	—
	Separable lean:																	
334	Raw	66.9	192	20.7	11.5	0	0	.9	12	192	3.1			20	.09	.18	5.0	—
335	Cooked, roasted	57.3	240	28.2	13.3	0	0	1.1	12	237	3.6			20	.07	.21	5.1	—
	Separable fat:																	
336	Raw	13.3	756	5.0	81.5	0	0	.2	3	41	.8			160	.02	.04	1.2	—
	Good grade:																	
	Total edible:																	
337	Raw (63% lean, 37% fat)	[illegible].5	376	15.5	34.3	0	0	.7	9	142	2.3			70	.07	.14	3.7	—
338	Cooked, roasted (63% lean, 37% fat)	41.9	417	20.9	36.3	0	0	.9	9	175	2.7			70	.06	.16	3.8	—
	Separable lean:																	
339	Raw	69.5	166	21.1	8.4	0	0	1.0	12	196	3.2			20	.09	.19	5.1	—
340	Cooked, roasted	59.7	215	28.9	10.2	0	0	1.3	12	242	3.7			20	.07	.22	5.2	—
	Separable fat:																	
341	Raw	16.0	726	6.2	77.6	0	0	.2	4	52	.9			160	.03	.06	1.5	—
	Rib, 6th or blade:																	
	Choice grade:																	
	Total edible:																	
342	Raw (71% lean, 29% fat)	50.7	363	16.0	32.7	0	0	.7	9	146	2.4			70	.07	.14	3.8	—
343	Cooked, braised (70% lean, 30% fat)	39.3	437	22.1	38.0	0	0	.6	10	109	2.9			70	.04	.17	3.4	—

	Separable lean:																	
344	Raw	66.1	200	20.5	12.5	0	0	.9	12	190	3.1			20	.09	.18	4.9	—
345	Cooked, braised	55.1	263	28.5	15.7	0	0	.7	13	142	3.7			30	.05	.22	4.4	—
	Separable fat:																	
346	Raw	12.6	764	4.7	82.5	0	0	.2	3	38	.7			160	.02	.04	1.1	—
	Good grade:																	
	Total edible:																	
347	Raw (77% lean, 23% fat)	56.6	300	17.5	25.0	0	0	.8	10	162	2.6			50	.08	.16	4.2	—
348	Cooked, braised (76% lean, 24% fat)	45.1	373	24.3	29.9	0	0	.7	10	121	3.2			60	.05	.19	3.8	—
	Separable lean:																	
349	Raw	69.3	168	21.1	8.6	0	0	1.0	12	196	3.2			20	.09	.19	5.1	—
350	Cooked, braised	58.6	225	29.6	10.9	0	0	.8	13	146	3.8			20	.05	.22	4.5	—
	Separable fat:																	
351	Raw	14.7	741	5.6	79.5	0	0	.2	3	46	.8			160	.02	.05	1.3	—
	Round, entire (round and heel of round):																	
	Choice grade:																	
	Total edible:																	
352	Raw (89% lean, 11% fat)	66.6	197	20.2	12.3	0	0	.9	12	203	3.0			20	.09	.18	4.8	—
353	Cooked, broiled (81% lean, 19% fat)	54.7	261	28.6	15.4	0	0	1.3	12	250	3.5			30	.08	.22	5.6	—
	Separable lean:																	
354	Raw	72.7	135	21.6	4.7	0	0	1.0	13	217	3.2			10	.09	.19	5.2	—
355	Cooked, broiled	61.2	189	31.3	6.1	0	0	1.4	13	268	3.7	(30)	(31)	10	.08	.24	6.0	—
	Separable fat:																	
356	Raw	18.7	696	7.5	73.6	0	0	.2	4	80	1.1			150	.03	.07	1.8	—
	Rump:																	
	Choice grade:																	
	Total edible:																	
357	Raw (75% lean, 25% fat)	56.5	303	17.4	25.3	0	0	.8	10	160	2.6			50	.08	.16	4.2	—
358	Cooked, roasted (75% lean, 25% fat)	48.1	347	23.6	27.3	0	0	1.0	10	197	3.1			50	.06	.18	4.3	—
	Separable lean:																	
359	Raw	70.3	158	21.2	7.5	0	0	1.0	12	197	3.2			20	.09	.19	5.1	—
360	Cooked, roasted	60.4	208	29.1	9.3	0	0	1.3	12	243	3.7			20	.07	.22	5.2	—
	Separable fat:																	
361	Raw	16.0	726	6.2	77.6	0	0	.2	4	52	.9			160	.03	.06	1.5	—
	Good grade:																	
	Total edible:																	
362	Raw (76% lean, 24% fat)	59.4	271	18.3	21.4	0	0	.8	11	168	2.7			40	.08	.16	4.4	—
363	Cooked, roasted (76% lean, 24% fat)	50.7	317	24.9	23.4	0	0	1.0	11	207	3.1			40	.06	.19	4.5	—
	Separable lean:																	
364	Raw	72.0	141	21.6	5.4	0	0	1.0	13	201	3.2			10	.09	.19	5.2	—
365	Cooked, roasted	62.0	190	29.6	7.1	0	0	1.3	13	248	3.7			10	.08	.22	5.3	—
	Separable fat:																	
366	Raw	19.0	692	7.5	73.2	0	0	.3	4	65	1.1			150	.03	.07	1.8	—
	Hamburger (ground beef):																	
	Lean:																	
367	Raw	68.3	179	20.7	10.0	0	0	1.0	12	192	3.1	—	—	20	.09	.18	5.0	—
368	Cooked	60.0	219	27.4	11.3	0	0	1.3	12	230	3.5	48	558	20	.09	.23	6.0	—
	Regular ground:																	
369	Raw	60.2	268	17.9	21.2	0	0	.7	10	156	2.7	—	236	40	.08	.16	4.3	—
370	Cooked	54.2	286	24.2	20.3	0	0	1.3	11	194	3.2	47	450	40	.09	.21	5.4	—
	Beef and vegetable stew:																	
371	Cooked (home recipe, with lean beef chuck)	82.4	89	6.4	4.3	6.2	.4	.7	12	75	1.2	37	250	980	.06	.07	1.9	7
372	Canned	82.5	79	5.8	3.1	7.1	.3	1.5	12	45	.9	411	174	970	.03	.05	1.0	3
373	**Beef, canned, roast beef**	60.	224	25.	13.	0	0	2.	16	116	2.4	—	259	—	.02	.23	4.2	0
	Beef, corned, boneless:																	
374	Uncooked, medium-fat	54.2	293	15.8	25.	0	0	5.0	9	125	2.4	1,300	60	—	.03	.15	1.7	0
375	Cooked, medium-fat	43.9	372	22.9	30.4	0	0	2.9	9	93	2.9	1,740	150	—	.02	.18	1.5	0
	Canned:																	
376	Fat	55.3	263	23.5	18.	0	0	3.2	19	98	4.0	—	—	—	.01	.22	3.2	0
377	Medium-fat	59.3	216	25.3	12.	0	0	3.4	20	106	4.3	—	—	—	.02	.24	3.4	0
378	Lean	62.0	185	26.4	8	0	0	3.6	21	110	4.5	—	—	—	.02	.25	3.5	0
379	Canned corned-beef hash (with potato)	67.4	181	8.8	11.3	10.7	.5	1.8	13	67	2.0	540	200	—	.01	.09	2.1	—
	Beef, dried, chipped:																	
380	Uncooked	47.7	203	34.3	6.3	0	0	11.6	20	404	5.1	4,300	200	—	(.07)	(.32)	(3.8)	0
381	Cooked, creamed	72.0	154	8.2	10.3	7.1	Trace	2.4	105	140	.8	716	153	360	.06	.19	.6	Trace
	Beef, potted. See Sausage, cold cuts, and luncheon meats: item 2008.																	
	Beef potpie:																	
382	Home-prepared, baked	55.1	246	10.1	14.5	18.8	.4	1.5	14	71	1.8	284	159	820	.11	.12	2.0	3
383	Commercial, frozen, unheated	63.3	192	7.3	9.9	18.0	.1	1.5	10	48	1.0	366	93	410	.03	.06	1.2	Trace
	Beer. See Beverages, item 394.																	
	Beets, common, red:																	
384	Raw	87.3	43	1.6	.1	9.9	.8	1.1	16	33	.7	60	335	20	.03	.05	.4	10
385	Cooked, boiled, drained	90.9	32	1.1	.1	7.2	.8	.7	14	23	.5	43	208	20	.03	.04	.3	6

[30] Average value for 100 grams, all cuts, is 65 mg. for raw beef and 60 mg. for cooked beef.

[31] Average value per 100 grams of beef of all cuts is 355 mg. for raw meat and 370 mg. for cooked meat.

TABLE 1.—COMPOSITION OF FOODS, 100 GRAMS, EDIBLE PORTION—Continued

[Numbers in parentheses denote values imputed—usually from another form of the food or from a similar food. Zero in parentheses indicates that the amount of a constituent probably is none or is too small to measure. Dashes denote lack of reliable data for a constituent believed to be present in measurable amount. Calculated values, as those based on a recipe, are not in parentheses]

Item No.	Food and description	Water	Food energy	Protein	Fat	Carbohydrate		Ash	Calcium	Phosphorus	Iron	Sodium	Potassium	Vitamin A value	Thiamine	Riboflavin	Niacin	Ascorbic acid
						Total	Fiber											
(A)	(B)	(C)	(D)	(E)	(F)	(G)	(H)	(I)	(J)	(K)	(L)	(M)	(N)	(O)	(P)	(Q)	(R)	(S)
		Percent	Calories	Grams	Grams	Grams	Grams	Grams	Milligrams	Milligrams	Milligrams	Milligrams	Milligrams	International units	Milligrams	Milligrams	Milligrams	Milligrams
	Beets, common, red—Continued																	
	Canned:																	
	Regular pack:																	
386	Solids and liquid	90.3	34	0.9	0.1	7.9	0.5	0.8	14	17	0.6	[9] 236	167	10	0.01	0.02	0.1	3
387	Drained solids	89.3	37	1.0	.1	8.8	.8	.8	19	18	.7	[9] 236	167	20	.01	.03	.1	3
388	Drained liquid	92.2	26	.8	Trace	6.2	Trace	.8	5	15	.4	[9] 236	167	Trace	.01	.02	.1	3
	Special dietary pack (low-sodium):																	
389	Solids and liquid	90.8	32	.9	Trace	7.8	.5	.5	14	17	.6	46	167	10	.01	.02	.1	3
390	Drained solids	89.8	37	.9	.1	8.7	.8	.5	19	18	.7	46	167	20	.01	.03	.1	3
391	Drained liquid	92.8	25	.8	Trace	5.9	Trace	.5	5	15	.4	46	167	Trace	.01	.02	.1	3
	Beet greens, common:																	
392	Raw	90.9	24	2.2	.3	4.6	1.3	2.0	119	40	3.3	130	570	6,100	.10	.22	.4	30
393	Cooked, boiled, drained	93.6	18	1.7	.2	3.3	1.1	1.2	99	25	1.9	76	332	5,100	.07	.15	.3	15
	Beverages, alcoholic and carbonated nonalcoholic:																	
	Alcoholic:																	
394	Beer, alcohol 4.5% by volume (3.6% by weight)	92.1	[22] 42	.3	0	3.8	—	.2	5	30	Trace	7	25	—	Trace	.03	.6	—
	Gin, rum, vodka, whisky:																	
395	80-proof (33.4% alcohol by weight)	66.6	[22] 231	—	—	Trace	—	—	—	—	—	1	2	—	—	—	—	—
396	86-proof (36.0% alcohol by weight)	64.0	[22] 249	—	—	Trace	—	—	—	—	—	1	2	—	—	—	—	—
397	90-proof (37.9% alcohol by weight)	62.1	[22] 263	—	—	Trace	—	—	—	—	—	1	2	—	—	—	—	—
398	94-proof (39.7% alcohol by weight)	60.3	[22] 275	—	—	Trace	—	—	—	—	—	1	2	—	—	—	—	—
399	100-proof (42.5% alcohol by weight)	57.5	[22] 295	—	—	Trace	—	—	—	—	—	1	2	—	—	—	—	—
	Wines:																	
400	Dessert, alcohol 18.8% by volume (15.3% by weight).	76.7	[22] 137	.1	0	7.7	—	.2	8	—	—	4	75	—	.01	.02	.2	—
401	Table, alcohol 12.2% by volume (9.9% by weight).	85.6	[22] 85	.1	0	4.2	—	.2	9	10	.4	5	92	—	Trace	.01	.1	—
	Carbonated, nonalcoholic:																	
	Carbonated waters:																	
402	Sweetened (quinine sodas)	92.	31	(0)	(0)	8.	(0)	—	—	—	—	—	—	(0)	(0)	(0)	(0)	(0)
403	Unsweetened (club sodas)	100.	0	(0)	(0)	0.	(0)	—	—	—	—	—	—	(0)	(0)	(0)	(0)	(0)
404	Cola type	90.	39	(0)	(0)	10.	(0)	—	—	—	—	—	—	(0)	(0)	(0)	(0)	(0)
405	Cream sodas	89.	43	(0)	(0)	11.	(0)	—	—	—	—	—	—	(0)	(0)	(0)	(0)	(0)
406	Fruit-flavored sodas (citrus, cherry, grape, strawberry, Tom Collins mixer, other) (10%–13% sugar).	88.	46	(0)	(0)	12.	(0)	—	—	—	—	—	—	(0)	(0)	(0)	(0)	(0)
407	Ginger ale, pale dry and golden	92.	31	(0)	(0)	8.	(0)	—	—	—	—	—	—	(0)	(0)	(0)	(0)	(0)
408	Root beer	89.5	41	(0)	(0)	10.5	(0)	—	—	—	—	—	—	(0)	(0)	(0)	(0)	(0)
409	Special dietary drinks with artificial sweetener (less than 1 Calorie per ounce).	100.	—	(0)	(0)	—	(0)	—	—	—	—	—	—	(0)	(0)	(0)	(0)	(0)
	Biscuits, baking powder, baked from home recipe, made with—																	
410	Enriched flour	27.4	369	7.4	17.0	45.8	.2	2.4	121	175	1.6	626	117	Trace	.21	.21	1.8	Trace
411	Unenriched flour [23]	27.4	369	7.4	17.0	45.8	.2	2.4	121	175	.5	626	117	Trace	.04	.10	.5	Trace
412	Self-rising flour, enriched	26.8	372	7.1	17.4	46.0	.2	2.7	[24] 209	[24] 317	1.7	[24] 660	64	Trace	.22	.22	2.1	Trace
	Biscuit dough, commercial, with enriched flour:																	
413	Chilled in cans	37.5	277	7.3	6.4	46.4	.2	2.4	53	497	1.7	868	65	Trace	.26	.17	2.1	0
414	Frozen	30.9	327	5.7	11.9	48.9	.1	2.6	71	400	1.4	910	86	Trace	.22	.17	1.7	Trace
	Biscuit mix, with enriched flour, and biscuits baked from mix:																	
415	Mix, dry form	7.5	424	7.7	12.6	68.7	.3	3.5	27	265	[25] 3.1	1,300	80	Trace	[25] .44	[25] .26	[25] 3.0	Trace
416	Biscuits, made with milk	28.5	325	7.1	9.3	52.3	.2	2.8	68	232	[26] 2.3	973	116	Trace	[26] .27	[26] .25	[26] 2.0	Trace
417	**Blackberries,** including dewberries, boysenberries and youngberries, raw.	84.5	58	1.2	.9	12.9	4.1	.5	32	19	.9	1	170	200	.03	.04	.4	21
	Blackberries, canned, solids and liquid:																	
418	Water pack, with or without artificial sweetener	89.3	40	.8	.6	9.0	2.8	.3	22	13	.6	1	115	140	.02	.02	.2	7
419	Juice pack	85.8	54	.8	.8	12.1	2.7	.5	25	17	.9	1	170	150	.02	.03	.3	10
	Sirup pack:																	
420	Light	81.0	72	.8	.6	17.3	2.7	.3	21	12	.6	1	111	130	.01	.02	.2	7
421	Heavy	76.1	91	.8	.6	22.2	2.6	.3	21	12	.6	1	109	130	.01	.02	.2	7
422	Extra heavy	71.2	110	.8	.6	27.1	2.6	.3	20	12	.6	1	107	130	.01	.02	.2	7
	Blackberries, frozen. See Boysenberries, items 436–437.																	
423	**Blackberry juice,** canned, unsweetened	90.9	37	.3	.6	7.8	Trace	.4	12	12	(.9)	(1)	(170)	—	(.02)	(.03)	(.3)	(10)
	Blackeye peas. See Cowpeas, items 896–904.																	

No.	Food																	
	Blackfish. See Tautog, item 2275.																	
	Blanc mange. See Puddings, item 1824.																	
	Blueberries:																	
424	Raw	83.2	62	.7	.5	15.3	1.5	.3	15	13	1.0	1	81	100	(.03)	(.06)	(.5)	14
	Canned, solids and liquid:																	
425	Water pack, with or without artificial sweetener	89.3	39	.5	.2	9.8	1.0	.2	10	9	.7	1	60	40	.01	.01	.2	7
426	Sirup pack, extra heavy	73.2	101	.4	.2	26.0	.9	.2	9	8	.6	1	55	40	.01	.01	.2	6
	Frozen, not thawed:																	
427	Unsweetened	85.0	55	.7	.5	13.6	1.5	.2	10	13	.8	1	81	70	.03	.06	.5	7
428	Sweetened	72.3	105	.6	.3	26.5	.9	.3	6	11	.4	1	66	30	.04	.05	.4	8
	Bluefish:																	
429	Raw	75.4	117	20.5	3.3	0	0	1.2	23	243	.6	74	—	—	.12	.09	1.9	—
	Cooked:																	
430	Baked or broiled [27]	68.0	159	26.2	5.2	0	0	1.4	29	287	.7	104	—	50	.11	.10	1.9	—
431	Fried [28]	60.8	205	22.7	9.8	4.7	—	2.0	35	257	.9	146	—	—	.11	.11	1.8	—
	Bockwurst. See Sausage, cold cuts, and luncheon meats: item 1981.																	
	Bologna. See Sausage, cold cuts, and luncheon meats: items 1982–1985.																	
432	**Bonito,** including Atlantic, Pacific, and striped; raw	67.6	168	24.0	7.3	0	0	1.4	—	—	—	—	—	—	—	—	—	—
433	**Boston brown bread**	45.0	211	5.5	1.3	45.6	.7	2.6	90	160	1.9	251	292	[29]0	.11	.06	1.2	0
434	**Bouillon** cubes or powder	4.	120	20.	3.	5.	—	68.	—	—	—	24,000	100	—	—	—	—	—
	Boysenberries:																	
435	Canned, water pack, solids and liquid, with or without artificial sweetener.	89.8	36	.7	.1	9.1	1.9	.3	(19)	(19)	(1.2)	1	85	130	(.01)	(.10)	(.7)	7
	Frozen, not thawed:																	
436	Unsweetened	86.8	48	1.2	.3	11.4	2.7	.3	25	24	1.6	1	153	(170)	.02	.13	1.0	13
437	Sweetened	74.3	96	.8	.3	24.4	1.8	.2	17	17	.6	1	105	(140)	.02	.10	.6	8
438	**Brains,** all kinds (beef, calf, hog, sheep), raw	78.9	125	10.4	8.6	.8	0	1.4	10	312	2.4	125	219	0	.23	.26	4.4	18
	Bran:																	
439	Added sugar and malt extract	3.6	240	12.6	3.0	74.3	7.8	6.5	70	1,176	([30])	1,060	1,070	(0)	[31].10	.29	17.8	Trace
440	Added sugar and defatted wheat germ	3.0	238	10.8	1.8	78.8	6.5	5.6	73	977	8.8	490	—	(0)	.28	.21	14.0	(0)
441	**Bran flakes** (40% bran), added thiamine	3.0	303	10.2	1.8	80.6	3.6	4.4	71	495	4.4	925	—	(0)	.40	.17	6.2	(0)
442	**Bran flakes with raisins,** added thiamine	7.3	287	8.3	1.4	79.3	3.0	3.7	56	396	4.0	800	—	Trace	.32	.13	5.3	(0)
	Braunschweiger. See Sausage, cold cuts, and luncheon meats: item 1986.																	
443	**Brazilnuts**	4.6	654	14.3	66.9	10.9	3.1	3.3	186	693	3.4	1	715	Trace	.96	.12	1.6	—
	Breads:																	
444	Cracked-wheat	34.9	263	8.7	2.2	52.1	.5	2.1	88	128	1.1	529	134	Trace	.12	.09	1.3	Trace
445	Toasted	22.5	313	10.4	2.6	62.0	.6	2.5	105	152	1.3	630	160	Trace	.11	.11	1.5	Trace
	French or																	
446	Enriched	30.6	290	9.1	3.0	55.4	.2	1.9	43	85	2.2	580	90	Trace	.28	.22	2.5	Trace
447	Toasted	19.3	338	10.6	3.5	64.4	.2	2.2	50	99	2.6	674	105	Trace	.26	.25	2.9	Trace
448	Unenriched	30.6	290	9.1	3.0	55.4	.2	1.9	43	85	.7	580	90	Trace	.08	.08	.8	Trace
449	Toasted	19.3	338	10.6	3.5	64.4	.2	2.2	50	99	.8	674	105	Trace	.08	.10	.9	Trace
	Italian:																	
450	Enriched	31.8	276	9.1	.8	56.4	.2	1.9	17	77	2.2	585	74	(0)	.29	.20	2.6	(0)
451	Unenriched	31.8	276	9.1	.8	56.4	.2	1.9	17	77	.7	585	74	(0)	.09	.06	.8	(0)
452	Raisin	35.3	262	6.6	2.8	53.6	.9	1.7	71	87	1.3	365	233	Trace	.05	.09	.7	Trace
453	Toasted	22.0	316	8.0	3.4	64.6	1.1	2.0	86	105	1.6	440	281	Trace	.05	.11	.8	Trace
	Rye:																	
454	American (⅓ rye, ⅔ clear flour)	35.5	243	9.1	1.1	52.1	.4	2.2	75	147	1.6	557	145	(0)	.18	.07	1.4	(0)
455	Toasted	25.0	282	10.6	1.3	60.5	.5	2.6	87	171	1.9	648	169	(0)	.17	.08	1.6	(0)
456	Pumpernickel	34.0	246	9.1	1.2	53.1	1.1	2.6	84	229	2.4	569	454	(0)	.23	.14	1.2	(0)
457	Salt-rising	36.5	267	7.9	2.4	52.2	.2	1.0	23	69	.6	265	67	10	.04	.05	.6	Trace
458	Toasted	29.4	297	8.8	2.7	58.0	.2	1.1	26	77	.7	294	74	10	.04	.05	.6	Trace
	White:																	
	Enriched, made with—																	
459	1%–2% nonfat dry milk	35.8	269	8.7	3.2	50.4	.2	1.9	70	87	2.4	507	85	Trace	.25	.17	2.3	Trace
460	Toasted	25.3	314	10.1	3.7	58.7	.2	2.2	81	101	2.8	590	99	Trace	.23	.20	2.7	Trace
461	3%–4% nonfat dry milk [33]	35.6	270	8.7	3.2	50.5	.2	2.0	84	97	2.5	507	105	Trace	.25	.21	2.4	Trace
462	Toasted	25.1	314	10.1	3.7	58.8	.2	2.3	98	113	2.9	590	122	Trace	.23	.24	2.8	Trace
463	5%–6% nonfat dry milk	35.0	275	9.0	3.8	50.2	.2	2.0	96	102	2.5	495	121	Trace	.27	.20	2.4	Trace
464	Toasted	24.4	320	10.5	4.4	58.4	.2	2.3	112	119	2.9	576	141	Trace	.25	.23	2.8	Trace

[9] Estimated average based on addition of salt in the amount of 0.6 percent of the finished product.

[23] Values are based on biscuits made with baking powder, item 130, and cooking fats, item 999.

[24] Based on use of self-rising flour, item 2445, containing anhydrous monocalcium phosphate. With flour containing leavening ingredients noted in footnote 169, approximate values per 100 grams are: Calcium, 124 mg.; phosphorus, 363 mg.; sodium, 826 mg.

[25] With unenriched flour, approximate values per 100 grams are: Iron, 0.6 mg.; thiamine, 0.05 mg.; riboflavin, 0.05 mg.; niacin, 0.7 mg.

[26] With unenriched flour, approximate values per 100 grams are: Iron, 0.5 mg.; thiamine, 0.04 mg.; riboflavin, 0.10 mg.; niacin, 0.5 mg.

[27] Prepared with butter or margarine.

[28] Prepared with egg, milk or water, and bread crumbs.

[29] Applies to product made with white cornmeal. With yellow degermed cornmeal, value is 70 I.U. per 100 grams.

[30] Values range from 4 to 12 mg. per 100 grams.

[31] For product containing added thiamine, value is 0.4 mg. per 100 grams.

[33] When amount of nonfat dry milk in commercial bread is unknown, values for bread with 3 to 4 percent nonfat dry milk, item 461 or item 467, are suggested.

TABLE 1.—COMPOSITION OF FOODS, 100 GRAMS, EDIBLE PORTION—Continued

[Numbers in parentheses denote values imputed—usually from another form of the food or from a similar food. Zero in parentheses indicates that the amount of a constituent probably is none or is too small to measure. Dashes denote lack of reliable data for a constituent believed to be present in measurable amount. Calculated values, as those based on a recipe, are not in parentheses]

Item No.	Food and description	Water	Food energy	Protein	Fat	Carbohydrate		Ash	Calcium	Phosphorus	Iron	Sodium	Potassium	Vitamin A value	Thiamine	Riboflavin	Niacin	Ascorbic acid
						Total	Fiber											
(A)	(B)	(C)	(D)	(E)	(F)	(G)	(H)	(I)	(J)	(K)	(L)	(M)	(N)	(O)	(P)	(Q)	(R)	(S)
		Percent	Calories	Grams	Grams	Grams	Grams	Grams	Milligrams	Milligrams	Milligrams	Milligrams	Milligrams	International units	Milligrams	Milligrams	Milligrams	Milligrams
	Breads [32]—Continued																	
	White—Continued																	
	Unenriched, made with—																	
465	1%–2% nonfat dry milk	35.8	269	8.7	3.2	50.4	0.2	1.9	70	87	0.7	507	85	Trace	0.09	0.08	1.2	Trace
466	Toasted	25.3	314	10.1	3.7	58.7	.2	2.2	81	101	.8	590	99	Trace	.08	.09	1.4	Trace
467	3%–4% nonfat dry milk [33]	35.6	270	8.7	3.2	50.5	.2	2.0	84	97	.7	507	105	Trace	.07	.09	1.1	Trace
468	Toasted	25.1	314	10.1	3.7	58.8	.2	2.3	98	113	.8	590	122	Trace	.06	.10	1.3	Trace
469	5%–6% nonfat dry milk	35.0	275	9.0	3.8	50.2	.2	2.0	96	102	.7	495	121	Trace	.07	.13	.9	Trace
470	Toasted	24.4	320	10.5	4.4	58.4	.2	2.3	112	119	.8	576	141	Trace	.07	.15	1.0	Trace
	Whole-wheat, made with—																	
471	2% nonfat dry milk	36.4	243	10.5	3.0	47.7	1.6	2.4	99	228	2.3	527	273	Trace	.26	.12	2.8	Trace
472	Toasted	24.3	289	12.5	3.6	56.7	1.9	2.9	118	271	2.7	627	325	Trace	.25	.15	3.4	Trace
473	Water	36.4	241	9.1	2.6	49.3	1.5	2.6	84	254	2.3	530	256	Trace	.30	.10	2.8	Trace
474	Toasted	24.3	287	10.8	3.1	58.7	1.8	3.1	100	302	2.7	631	305	Trace	.29	.12	3.3	Trace
	See also Biscuits; Boston brown bread; Cornbread; Muffins; Rolls; Salt sticks.																	
475	**Breadcrumbs**, dry, grated	6.5	392	12.6	4.6	73.4	.3	2.9	122	141	3.6	736	152	Trace	.22	.30	3.5	Trace
476	**Bread pudding** with raisins	58.6	187	5.6	6.1	28.4	.1	1.3	109	114	1.1	201	215	300	.06	.19	.1	1
	Bread sticks (vienna). See Salt sticks, item 1966.																	
	Bread stuffing mix and stuffings prepared from mix:																	
477	Mix, dry form	6.3	371	12.9	3.8	72.4	.8	4.6	124	189	3.2	1,331	172	Trace	.22	.26	3.2	Trace
	Stuffing:																	
478	Dry, crumbly: prepared with water, table fat	33.2	358	6.5	21.8	35.6	.4	2.9	66	97	1.6	896	90	650	.09	.12	1.5	Trace
479	Moist: prepared with water, egg, table fat	61.4	208	4.4	12.8	19.7	.2	1.7	40	66	1.0	504	58	420	.05	.09	.8	Trace
480	**Breadfruit**, raw	70.8	103	1.7	.3	26.2	1.2	1.0	33	32	1.2	15	439	40	.11	.03	.9	29
	Breakfast cereals. See Corn, Oats, Rice, Wheat, also Bran, Farina.																	
	Broadbeans, raw:																	
481	Immature seeds	72.3	105	8.4	.4	17.8	2.2	1.1	27	157	2.2	4	471	220	.28	.17	1.6	30
482	Mature seeds, dry	11.9	338	25.1	1.7	58.2	6.7	3.1	102	391	7.1	—	—	70	.50	.30	2.5	—
	Broccoli:																	
483	Raw spears	89.1	32	3.6	.3	5.9	1.5	1.1	103	78	1.1	15	382	[34]2,500	.10	.23	.9	113
484	Cooked spears, boiled, drained	91.3	26	3.1	.3	4.5	1.5	.8	88	62	.8	10	267	2,500	.09	.20	.8	90
	Frozen:																	
	Chopped:																	
485	Not thawed	90.6	29	3.2	.3	5.2	1.1	.7	58	59	.7	17	241	2,600	.07	.13	.6	70
486	Cooked, boiled, drained	91.6	26	2.9	.3	4.6	1.1	.6	54	56	.7	15	212	2,600	.06	.12	.5	57
	Spears:																	
487	Not thawed	90.7	28	3.3	.2	5.1	1.1	.7	43	60	.7	13	244	1,900	.07	.13	.6	78
488	Cooked, boiled, drained	91.4	26	3.1	.2	4.7	1.1	.6	41	58	.7	12	220	1,900	.06	.11	.5	73
	Brown betty. See Apple brown betty, item 25.																	
	Brownies. See Cookies, items 813–814.																	
	Brussels sprouts:																	
489	Raw	85.2	45	4.9	.4	8.3	1.6	1.2	36	80	1.5	14	390	550	.10	.16	.9	102
490	Cooked, boiled, drained	88.2	36	4.2	.4	6.4	1.6	.8	32	72	1.1	10	273	520	.08	.14	.8	87
	Frozen:																	
491	Not thawed	88.4	36	3.3	.2	7.3	1.2	.8	22	62	.9	16	328	570	.10	.11	.6	87
492	Cooked, boiled, drained	89.3	33	3.2	.2	6.5	1.2	.8	21	61	.8	14	295	570	.08	.10	.6	81
	Buckwheat:																	
493	Whole-grain	11.0	335	11.7	2.4	72.9	9.9	2.0	114	282	3.1	—	448	(0)	.60	—	4.4	(0)
	Flour:																	
494	Dark	12.	333	11.7	2.5	72.0	1.6	1.8	33	347	2.8	—	—	(0)	.58	.15	2.9	(0)
495	Light	12.	347	6.4	1.2	79.5	.5	.9	11	88	1.0	—	320	(0)	.08	(.04)	(.4)	(0)
	Buckwheat pancake mix. See Pancake mix, item 1461.																	
496	**Buffalofish**, raw	77.4	113	17.5	4.2	0	0	1.1	—	—	—	52	293	—	—	—	—	—
	Bulgur (parboiled wheat):																	
	Dry, commercial, made from—																	
497	Club wheat	9.	359	8.7	1.4	79.5	1.7	1.4	30	319	4.7	—	262	(0)	.30	.10	4.2	(0)
498	Hard red winter wheat	10.	354	11.2	1.5	75.7	1.7	1.6	29	338	3.7	—	229	(0)	.28	.14	4.5	(0)
499	White wheat	(9.)	357	10.3	1.2	78.1	1.3	1.4	36	300	(4.7)	—	310	(0)	(.30)	(.10)	(4.2)	(0)
	Canned, made from hard red winter wheat:																	
500	Unseasoned [35]	56.0	168	6.2	.7	35.0	.8	2.1	20	200	1.3	599	87	(0)	.05	.03	2.4	(0)
501	Seasoned [36]	56.0	182	6.2	3.3	32.8	.8	1.7	20	195	1.4	460	112	(0)	.06	.04	3.0	(0)
502	**Bullhead, black, raw**	81.3	84	16.3	1.6	0	0	1.0	—	—	—	—	—	—	—	—	—	—

No.	Food																	
	Bullocksheart. See Custardapple, item 949.																	
	Burbot:																	
503	Raw	81.1	82	17.4	.9	0	0	1.0	—	190	—	—	—	—	.39	.14	1.5	—
504	Cooked, fried	60.5	—	37.0	—	0	0	—	—	—	—	—	—	—	.54	.23	3.7	—
	Burghul. See Bulgur, items 497–501.																	
505	**Butter** [37]	15.5	716	.6	81.	.4	0	2.5	20	16	0	987	23	3,300	—	—	—	0
506	**Butter oil** or dehydrated butter	.2	876	.3	99.5	0	0	0	—	—	—	—	—	4,080	—	—	—	0
	Butterfish, raw:																	
507	From northern waters	71.4	169	18.1	10.2	0	0	1.4	—	—	—	—	—	—	—	—	—	—
508	From gulf waters	78.2	95	16.2	2.9	0	0	2.9	—	—	—	—	—	—	—	—	—	—
	Buttermilk:																	
509	Fluid, cultured (made from skim milk)	90.5	36	3.6	.1	5.1	0	.7	121	95	Trace	130	140	Trace	.04	.18	.1	1
510	Dried	2.8	387	34.3	5.3	50.0	0	7.6	1,248	970	.6	507	1,606	220	.26	1.72	.9	—
511	**Butternuts**	3.8	629	23.7	61.2	8.4	—	2.9	—	—	6.8	—	—	—	—	—	—	—
	Cabbage:																	
	Common varieties (Danish, domestic, and pointed types):																	
512	Raw	92.4	24	1.3	.2	5.4	.8	.7	49	29	.4	20	233	130	.05	.05	.3	[38] 47
	Cooked, boiled until tender, drained:																	
513	Shredded, cooked in small amount of water	93.9	20	1.1	.2	4.3	.8	.5	44	20	.3	14	163	130	.04	.04	.3	33
514	Wedges, cooked in large amount of water	94.3	18	1.0	.2	4.0	.8	.5	42	17	.3	13	151	120	.02	.02	.1	24
515	Dehydrated	4.	308	12.4	1.7	73.7	10.3	8.2	405	287	3.9	190	2,207	1,300	[39] .45	.40	3.0	[39] 211
516	Red, raw	90.2	31	2.0	.2	6.9	1.0	.7	42	35	.8	26	268	40	.09	.06	.4	61
517	Savoy, raw	92.0	24	2.4	.2	4.6	.8	.8	67	54	.9	22	269	200	.05	.08	.3	55
518	**Cabbage, Chinese** (also called celery cabbage or pe-tsai), compact heading type, raw.	95.0	14	1.2	.1	3.0	.6	.7	43	40	.6	23	253	150	.05	.04	.6	25
	Cabbage, spoon (also called white mustard cabbage or pakchoy), nonheading green leaf type:																	
519	Raw	94.3	16	1.6	.2	2.9	.6	1.0	165	44	.8	26	306	3,100	.05	.10	.8	25
520	Cooked, boiled, drained	95.2	14	1.4	.2	2.4	.6	.8	148	33	.6	18	214	3,100	.04	.08	.7	15
	Cabbage salad. See Coleslaw, items 801–804.																	
	Cakes:																	
	Baked from home recipes: [40]																	
521	Angelfood	31.5	269	7.1	.2	60.2	0	1.0	9	22	.2	283	88	0	.01	.14	.2	0
522	Boston cream pie	34.5	302	5.0	9.4	49.9	0	1.2	67	101	.5	186	89	210	.03	.11	.2	Trace
	Caramel:																	
523	Without icing	23.0	385	4.5	17.3	53.7	.1	1.5	78	106	1.3	305	68	180	.02	.08	.2	Trace
524	With caramel icing	20.9	379	3.7	14.8	59.1	0	1.5	84	95	1.5	252	64	200	.02	.07	.1	Trace
	Chocolate (devil's food):																	
525	Without icing	24.6	366	4.8	17.2	52.0	.3	1.4	74	137	.9	294	140	150	.02	.10	.2	Trace
526	With chocolate icing	22.0	369	4.5	16.4	55.8	.3	1.3	70	131	1.0	235	154	160	.02	.10	.2	Trace
527	With uncooked white icing	21.3	369	3.8	14.6	59.2	.2	1.1	59	106	.7	234	110	180	.02	.08	.2	Trace
	Cottage pudding, made with enriched flour:																	
528	Without sauce	26.6	344	6.4	11.3	54.3	.1	1.4	90	115	1.4	299	88	140	.15	.17	1.2	Trace
529	With chocolate sauce	27.9	318	5.3	8.8	56.7	.3	1.3	71	109	1.4	233	140	100	.12	.14	1.0	Trace
530	With fruit sauce (strawberry)	36.6	292	5.1	8.8	48.4	.3	1.1	73	93	1.2	233	93	120	.12	.15	1.1	12
	Fruitcake, made with enriched flour:																	
531	Dark	18.1	379	4.8	15.3	59.7	.6	2.1	72	113	2.6	158	496	120	.13	.14	.8	Trace
532	Light	18.7	389	6.0	16.5	57.4	.7	1.4	68	115	1.6	193	233	70	.10	.11	.7	Trace
533	Gingerbread, made with enriched flour	30.8	317	3.8	10.7	52.0	.1	2.7	68	65	2.3	237	454	90	.12	.11	.9	0
	Plain cake or cupcake:																	
534	Without icing	24.5	364	4.5	13.9	55.9	.1	1.2	64	102	.4	300	79	170	.02	.09	.2	Trace
535	With chocolate icing	21.4	368	4.2	13.9	59.4	.2	1.1	63	104	.6	229	114	180	.02	.09	.2	Trace
536	With boiled white icing	22.9	352	3.8	10.5	61.8	Trace	1.0	49	77	.3	262	64	130	.02	.07	.2	Trace
537	With uncooked white icing	20.6	367	3.4	11.8	63.3	Trace	.9	50	75	.3	227	61	200	.02	.07	.1	Trace
	Pound:																	
538	Old-fashioned (equal weights flour, sugar, table fat, eggs).	17.2	473	5.7	29.5	47.0	.1	.6	21	79	.8	110	60	280	.03	.09	.2	0
539	Modified	19.4	411	6.4	18.7	54.7	.1	.9	40	104	.8	178	78	290	.04	.11	.2	Trace
540	Sponge	31.8	297	7.6	5.7	54.1	0	.8	30	112	1.2	167	87	450	.05	.14	.2	Trace
	White:																	
541	Without icing	24.2	375	4.6	16.0	54.0	.1	1.2	63	91	.2	323	76	30	.01	.08	.2	Trace
542	With coconut icing	21.3	371	3.7	13.3	60.7	.3	1.0	45	72	.3	257	106	20	.01	.07	.2	Trace
543	With uncooked white icing	20.0	375	3.3	12.9	62.9	0	.9	48	65	.1	234	58	110	.01	.06	.1	Trace
	Yellow:																	
544	Without icing	23.5	363	4.5	12.7	58.2	.1	1.1	71	112	.4	258	78	150	.02	.08	.2	Trace
545	With caramel icing	21.8	362	4.0	11.7	61.3	.1	1.2	77	103	.7	226	73	170	.02	.08	.2	Trace
546	With chocolate icing	21.2	365	4.2	13.0	60.4	.2	1.1	68	112	.6	208	108	160	.02	.08	.2	Trace
	Frozen, commercial, devil's food:																	
547	With chocolate icing	21.0	380	4.3	17.6	55.6	.3	1.5	54	92	.8	420	119	430	.02	.08	.2	Trace
548	With whipped-cream filling, chocolate icing	29.7	371	3.5	21.9	43.8	.2	1.1	80	122	.6	190	113	270	.02	.08	.2	Trace

[33] When amount of nonfat dry milk in commercial bread is unknown, values for bread with 3 to 4 percent nonfat dry milk, item 461 or item 467, are suggested.

[34] Value for leaves is 16,000 I.U. per 100 grams; flower clusters, 3,000 I.U.; stalks, 400 I.U.

[35] Processed, partially debranned, whole-kernel wheat with salt added.

[36] Processed, partially debranned, whole-kernel wheat with chicken fat, chicken stock base, dehydrated onion flakes, salt, monosodium glutamate, and herbs.

[37] Values apply to salted butter. Unsalted butter contains less than 10 mg. of either sodium or potassium per 100 grams. Value for vitamin A is the year-round average.

[38] For freshly harvested cabbage, average value is 51 mg. per 100 grams; for stored cabbage, 42 mg. per 100 grams.

[39] Applies to unsulfited product. For sulfited product, values per 100 grams are: Thiamine, 0.10 mg.; ascorbic acid, 300 mg.

[40] Unenriched cake flour used unless otherwise specified. Values for cakes that contain baking powder and/or fat are based on use of baking powder, item 130, and cooking fats, item 999.

TABLE 1.—COMPOSITION OF FOODS, 100 GRAMS, EDIBLE PORTION—Continued

[Numbers in parentheses denote values imputed—usually from another form of the food or from a similar food. Zero in parentheses indicates that the amount of a constituent probably is none or is too small to measure. Dashes denote lack of reliable data for a constituent believed to be present in measurable amount. Calculated values, as those based on a recipe, are not in parentheses]

Item No.	Food and description	Water	Food energy	Protein	Fat	Carbohydrate: Total	Carbohydrate: Fiber	Ash	Calcium	Phosphorus	Iron	Sodium	Potassium	Vitamin A value	Thiamine	Riboflavin	Niacin	Ascorbic acid
(A)	(B)	(C)	(D)	(E)	(F)	(G)	(H)	(I)	(J)	(K)	(L)	(M)	(N)	(O)	(P)	(Q)	(R)	(S)
		Percent	Calories	Grams	Grams	Grams	Grams	Grams	Milligrams	Milligrams	Milligrams	Milligrams	Milligrams	International units	Milligrams	Milligrams	Milligrams	Milligrams
	Cake mixes and cakes baked from mixes:																	
	Angelfood:																	
549	Mix, dry form	1.8	385	8.4	0.2	88.5	Trace	1.1	108	125	0.4	190	112	0	0.01	0.17	0.2	0
550	Cake, made with water, flavorings	34.0	259	5.7	.2	59.4	Trace	.7	95	119	.3	146	60	0	Trace	.11	.1	0
	Chocolate malt:																	
551	Mix, dry form	3.8	412	4.0	10.7	79.0	0.2	2.5	100	270	1.0	551	119	70	.04	.08	.4	0
552	Cake, made with eggs, water, uncooked white icing.	19.8	346	3.4	8.7	66.6	.1	1.5	63	166	.7	318	80	190	.03	.07	.2	Trace
	Coffeecake, with enriched flour:																	
553	Mix, dry form	3.8	431	5.9	11.0	77.2	.2	2.1	36	191	[41] 2.0	613	87	Trace	[41] .30	[41] .14	[41] 2.4	Trace
554	Cake, made with egg, milk	30.0	322	6.3	9.6	52.4	.1	1.7	61	174	[42] 1.6	431	109	160	[42] .18	[42] .16	[42] 1.4	Trace
	Cupcake:																	
555	Mix, dry form	4.9	438	3.7	13.6	75.8	.3	2.0	173	263	.4	596	46	0	.05	.06	.3	0
556	Cake, made with eggs, milk, without icing	25.6	350	4.9	12.0	55.8	.2	1.7	161	235	.5	453	84	150	.04	.11	.2	Trace
557	Cake, made with eggs, milk, chocolate icing	22.2	358	4.5	12.6	59.2	.3	1.5	130	197	.8	335	117	170	.04	.11	.2	Trace
	Devil's food:																	
558	Mix, dry form	3.9	406	4.8	11.7	77.0	.3	2.6	80	120	1.2	457	121	Trace	.03	.08	.5	Trace
559	Cake, made with eggs, water, chocolate icing	23.6	339	4.4	12.3	58.3	.3	1.4	59	105	.8	262	130	150	.03	.08	.3	Trace
	Gingerbread:																	
560	Mix, dry form	3.0	425	5.4	10.4	78.2	.1	3.0	180	200	1.4	463	418	Trace	.04	.14	.4	Trace
561	Cake, made with water	37.0	276	3.1	6.8	51.1	Trace	2.0	90	100	1.6	304	274	Trace	.03	.09	.8	Trace
	Honey spice:																	
562	Mix, dry form	3.5	443	4.3	14.0	76.3	.4	1.9	74	274	.2	373	99	Trace	.02	.08	.3	Trace
563	Cake, made with eggs, water, caramel icing	22.7	352	4.1	10.8	60.9	.2	1.5	71	193	.8	245	82	160	.02	.09	.2	Trace
	Marble:																	
564	Mix, dry form	4.0	425	4.9	13.5	75.6	.1	2.0	130	270	1.0	381	188	Trace	.03	.09	.4	Trace
565	Cake, made with eggs, water, boiled white icing	23.6	331	4.4	8.7	62.0	.1	1.3	78	171	.8	259	122	90	.02	.08	.2	Trace
	White:																	
566	Mix, dry form	3.4	434	4.1	11.9	78.4	.2	2.2	150	270	.2	373	88	Trace	.02	.07	.3	Trace
567	Cake, made with egg whites, water, chocolate icing.	21.1	351	3.9	10.7	62.8	.2	1.5	99	179	.5	227	116	60	.02	.08	.2	Trace
	Yellow:																	
568	Mix, dry form	3.3	438	4.0	12.9	77.6	.1	2.2	140	270	.2	407	86	Trace	.02	.07	.3	Trace
569	Cake, made with eggs, water, chocolate icing	25.6	337	4.1	11.3	57.6	.2	1.4	91	182	.6	227	109	140	.02	.08	.2	Trace
	Cake icings:																	
570	Caramel	14.1	360	1.3	6.7	76.5	0	1.4	102	63	2.0	83	52	280	.01	.06	Trace	Trace
571	Chocolate	14.3	376	3.2	13.9	67.4	.4	.9	60	111	1.2	61	195	210	.02	.10	.2	Trace
572	Coconut	15.0	364	1.9	7.7	74.9	.8	.5	6	30	.5	118	167	0	.01	.04	.2	0
	White:																	
573	Uncooked	11.1	376	.5	6.6	81.6	0	.2	15	12	Trace	49	18	270	Trace	.02	Trace	Trace
574	Boiled	17.9	316	1.4	0	80.3	0	.4	2	2	Trace	143	18	0	Trace	.03	Trace	0
	Cake icing mixes and icings made from mixes:																	
	Chocolate fudge:																	
575	Mix, dry form	.8	409	2.5	9.8	86.4	.6	.5	18	82	1.3	95	78	Trace	.01	.06	.3	0
576	Icing, made with water, table fat	15.3	378	2.2	14.4	67.0	.5	1.1	16	66	1.0	156	63	270	.01	.04	.2	0
	Creamy fudge (contains nonfat dry milk):																	
577	Mix, dry form	3.1	386	3.2	7.4	85.1	.6	1.2	45	102	1.3	265	111	Trace	.02	.09	.3	Trace
	Icing:																	
578	Made with water	15.1	339	2.8	6.5	74.6	.5	1.0	39	89	1.1	232	97	Trace	.02	.08	.3	Trace
579	Made with water, table fat	15.1	383	2.6	15.2	65.9	.5	1.2	37	81	1.0	321	89	390	.02	.07	.3	Trace
	Candied fruits. See Apricots, Cherries, Citron, Figs, Ginger root, Grapefruit peel, Lemon peel, Orange peel, Pear, Pineapple.																	
	Candy:																	
580	Butterscotch	1.5	397	Trace	3.4	94.8	0	.3	17	6	1.4	66	2	140	0	Trace	Trace	0
	Candy corn. See Fondant, item 602.																	
	Caramels:																	
581	Plain or chocolate	7.6	399	4.0	10.2	76.6	.2	1.5	148	122	1.4	226	192	10	.03	.17	.2	Trace
582	Plain or chocolate, with nuts	7.1	428	4.5	16.3	70.5	.4	1.6	140	139	1.5	203	233	20	.11	.17	.2	Trace
583	Chocolate-flavored roll	5.6	396	2.2	8.2	82.7	.2	1.2	68	119	1.8	197	123	Trace	.02	.07	.1	Trace
	Chocolate:																	
584	Bittersweet	1.8	477	7.9	39.7	46.8	1.8	2.3	58	284	5.0	3	615	40	.03	.17	1.0	0
585	Semisweet	1.1	507	4.2	35.7	57.0	1.0	1.2	30	150	2.6	2	325	20	.01	.08	.5	0
586	Sweet	.9	528	4.4	35.1	57.9	.5	1.2	94	142	1.4	33	269	19	.02	.14	.3	Trace

	Chocolate, milk:																	
587	Plain	.9	520	7.7	32.3	56.9	.4	1.9	228	231	1.1	94	384	270	.06	.34	.3	Trace
588	With almonds	1.5	532	9.3	35.6	51.3	.7	2.0	229	272	1.6	80	442	230	.08	.41	.8	Trace
589	With peanuts	1.0	543	14.1	38.1	44.6	.9	2.0	174	294	1.4	66	487	180	.25	.26	5.0	Trace
	Chocolate-coated:																	
590	Almonds	2.0	569	12.3	43.7	39.6	1.5	2.3	203	343	2.8	59	546	Trace	.12	.53	1.7	Trace
591	Chocolate fudge	6.2	430	3.8	16.0	73.1	.2	.9	101	110	1.3	228	193	Trace	.04	.13	.2	0
592	Chocolate fudge, with nuts	6.0	452	4.9	20.8	67.3	.4	1.0	101	137	1.5	205	219	Trace	.06	.13	.2	Trace
593	Coconut center	6.6	438	2.8	17.6	72.0	.6	1.0	48	77	1.1	197	165	0	.02	.07	.2	0
594	Fondant	5.8	410	1.7	10.5	81.0	.1	.9	57	54	1.1	185	91	Trace	.03	.06	.1	Trace
595	Fudge, caramel, and peanuts	8.3	433	7.7	18.1	64.1	.4	1.7	179	186	1.4	204	301	Trace	.16	.22	1.9	Trace
596	Fudge, peanuts, and caramel	7.0	459	9.4	23.1	58.7	.7	1.7	127	192	1.1	128	222	Trace	.26	.15	3.7	Trace
597	Honeycombed hard candy, with peanut butter	1.7	463	6.6	19.5	70.6	.4	1.5	80	135	1.8	163	225	Trace	.05	.09	2.9	Trace
598	Nougat and caramel	7.7	416	4.0	13.9	72.8	.2	1.4	127	123	1.6	173	211	40	.06	.17	.2	Trace
599	Peanuts	1.0	561	16.4	41.3	39.1	1.2	2.0	116	298	1.5	60	504	Trace	.37	.18	7.4	Trace
600	Raisins	4.8	425	5.4	17.1	70.5	.6	2.1	152	174	2.5	64	603	150	.08	.21	.4	Trace
601	Vanilla creams	7.5	435	3.8	17.1	70.3	.1	1.2	128	110	.6	182	178	Trace	.05	.07	.1	Trace
602	Fondant	7.6	364	.1	2.0	89.6	Trace	.7	14	6	1.1	212	5	0	Trace	Trace	Trace	0
	Fudge:																	
603	Chocolate	8.2	400	2.7	12.2	75.0	.2	1.8	77	84	1.0	190	147	Trace	.02	.09	.2	Trace
604	Chocolate, with nuts	7.8	426	3.9	17.4	69.0	.4	1.8	79	114	1.2	171	177	Trace	.04	.09	.3	Trace
605	Vanilla	10.0	398	3.0	11.1	74.8	0	1.1	112	83	.5	208	127	Trace	.02	.13	.1	Trace
606	Vanilla, with nuts	9.4	424	4.2	16.4	68.8	.2	1.2	111	113	.8	187	114	Trace	.05	.13	.1	Trace
607	Gum drops, starch jelly pieces	11.7	347	.1	.7	87.4	0	.1	6	Trace	.5	35	5	0	0	Trace	Trace	0
608	Hard	1.4	386	0	1.1	97.2	0	.3	21	7	1.9	32	4	0	0	0	0	0
609	Jelly beans	6.3	367	Trace	.5	93.1	Trace	.1	12	4	1.1	12	1	0	0	Trace	Trace	0
610	Marshmallows	17.3	319	2.0	Trace	80.4	0	.3	18	6	1.6	39	6	0	0	Trace	Trace	0
	Mints, uncoated. See Fondant, item 602.																	
611	Peanut bars	1.5	515	17.5	32.2	47.2	1.2	1.6	44	273	1.8	10	448	0	.43	.08	9.4	0
612	Peanut brittle (no added salt or soda)	2.0	421	5.7	10.4	81.0	.5	.9	35	95	2.3	31	151	0	.16	.03	3.4	0
	Sugar-coated:																	
613	Almonds	2.3	456	7.8	18.6	70.2	.9	1.1	100	166	1.9	20	255	0	.05	.27	1.0	0
614	Chocolate discs	1.2	466	5.2	19.7	72.7	.3	1.2	135	140	1.3	72	250	100	.06	.20	.3	Trace
	Cantaloups. See Muskmelons, item 1358.																	
	Cape-gooseberries. See Groundcherries, item 1092.																	
	Capicola. See Sausage, cold cuts, and luncheon meats: item 1989.																	
615	**Carambola,** raw	90.4	35	.7	.5	8.0	.9	.4	4	17	1.5	2	192	1,200	.04	.02	.3	35
	Caribou. See Reindeer, items 1855–1858.																	
616	**Carissa** (natalplum) raw	80.8	70	.5	1.3	16.0	.9	.4	—	—	—	—	—	40	.04	.06	.2	38
617	**Carob flour** (St. Johnsbread)	11.2	180	4.5	1.4	80.7	7.7	2.2	352	81	—	—	—	—	—	—	—	—
618	**Carp,** raw	77.8	115	18.0	4.2	0	0	1.1	50	253	.9	50	286	170	.01	.04	1.5	1
	Carrots:																	
619	Raw	88.2	42	1.1	.2	9.7	1.0	.8	37	36	.7	47	341	[43] 11,000	.06	.05	.6	8
620	Cooked, boiled, drained	91.2	31	.9	.2	7.1	1.0	.6	33	31	.6	33	222	10,500	.05	.05	.5	6
	Canned:																	
	Regular pack:																	
621	Solids and liquid	91.8	28	.6	.2	6.5	.6	.9	25	20	.7	[9] 236	120	10,000	.02	.02	.4	2
622	Drained solids	91.2	30	.8	.3	6.7	.8	1.0	30	22	.7	[9] 236	120	15,000	.02	.03	.4	2
623	Drained liquid	93.3	22	.4	0	5.5	Trace	.8	14	15	.8	[9] 236	120	Trace	.02	.02	.4	2
	Special dietary pack (low-sodium):																	
624	Solids and liquid	93.7	22	.7	.1	5.0	.6	.5	25	20	.7	39	120	10,000	.02	.02	.4	2
625	Drained solids	93.0	25	.8	.1	5.6	.8	.5	30	22	.7	39	120	15,000	.02	.03	.4	2
626	Drained liquid	95.2	16	.4	0	4.0	Trace	.4	14	15	.8	39	120	Trace	.02	.02	.4	2
627	Dehydrated	4.	341	6.6	1.3	81.1	9.3	7.0	256	234	6.0	268	1,944	100,000	.31	.30	3.0	15
	Casaba melon. See Muskmelons, item 1359.																	
628	**Cashew nuts**	5.2	561	17.2	45.7	29.3	1.4	2.6	38	373	3.8	[44] 15	464	100	.43	.25	1.8	—
629	**Catfish,** freshwater, raw	78.0	103	17.6	3.1	0	0	1.3	—	—	.4	60	330	—	.04	.03	1.7	—
	Catsup. See Tomato catsup, item 2286.																	
	Cauliflower:																	
630	Raw	91.0	27	2.7	.2	5.2	1.0	.9	25	56	1.1	13	295	60	.11	.10	.7	78
631	Cooked, boiled, drained	92.8	22	2.3	.2	4.1	1.0	.6	21	42	.7	9	206	60	.09	.08	.6	55
	Frozen:																	
632	Not thawed	92.9	22	2.0	.2	4.3	.8	.6	19	42	.6	11	225	30	.06	.06	.5	56
633	Cooked, boiled, drained	94.0	18	1.9	.2	3.3	.8	.6	17	38	.5	10	207	30	.04	.05	.4	41
	Caviar, sturgeon:																	
634	Granular	46.0	262	26.9	15.0	3.3	—	8.8	276	355	11.8	2,200	180	—	—	—	—	—
635	Pressed	36.0	316	34.4	16.7	4.9	—	8.0	—	—	—	—	—	—	—	—	—	—
636	**Celeriac,** root, raw	88.4	40	1.8	.3	8.5	1.3	1.0	43	115	.6	100	300	—	.05	.06	.7	8
	Celery, all, including green and yellow varieties:																	
637	Raw	94.1	17	.9	.1	3.9	.6	1.0	39	28	.3	126	341	[45] 240	.03	.03	.3	9
638	Cooked, boiled, drained	95.3	14	.8	.1	3.1	.6	.7	31	22	.2	88	239	230	.02	.03	.3	6
	Cereals, breakfast. See Corn, Oats, Rice, Wheat, also Bran, Farina.																	

[9] Estimated average based on addition of salt in the amount of 0.6 percent of the finished product.

[41] With unenriched flour, approximate values per 100 grams are: Iron, 0.5 mg.; thiamine, 0.07 mg.; riboflavin, 0.06 mg.; niacin, 1.0 mg.

[42] With unenriched flour, approximate values per 100 grams are: Iron, 0.6 mg.; thiamine, 0.05 mg.; riboflavin, 0.11 mg.; niacin, 0.6 mg.

[43] Average for carrots marketed as fresh vegetable.

[44] Applies to unsalted nuts. For salted nuts, value is approximately 200 mg. per 100 grams.

[45] Average for all varieties. For green varieties, value is 270 I.U. per 100 grams; for yellow varieties, 140 I.U.

TABLE 1.—COMPOSITION OF FOODS, 100 GRAMS, EDIBLE PORTION—Continued

[Numbers in parentheses denote values imputed—usually from another form of the food or from a similar food. Zero in parentheses indicates that the amount of a constituent probably is none or is too small to measure. Dashes denote lack of reliable data for a constituent believed to be present in measurable amount. Calculated values, as those based on a recipe, are not in parentheses]

Item No.	Food and description	Water	Food energy	Protein	Fat	Carbohydrate		Ash	Calcium	Phosphorus	Iron	Sodium	Potassium	Vitamin A value	Thiamine	Riboflavin	Niacin	Ascorbic acid
						Total	Fiber											
(A)	(B)	(C)	(D)	(E)	(F)	(G)	(H)	(I)	(J)	(K)	(L)	(M)	(N)	(O)	(P)	(Q)	(R)	(S)
	Cervelat. See Sausage, cold cuts, and luncheon meats: items 1990–1991.	*Percent*	*Calories*	*Grams*	*Grams*	*Grams*	*Grams*	*Grams*	*Milligrams*	*Milligrams*	*Milligrams*	*Milligrams*	*Milligrams*	*International units*	*Milligrams*	*Milligrams*	*Milligrams*	*Milligrams*
	Chard, Swiss:																	
639	Raw	91. 1	25	2. 4	0. 3	4. 6	0. 8	1. 6	88	39	3. 2	147	550	6, 500	0. 06	0. 17	0. 5	32
640	Cooked, boiled, drained	93. 7	18	1. 8	. 2	3. 3	. 7	1. 0	73	24	1. 8	86	321	5, 400	. 04	. 11	. 4	16
641	**Charlotte russe,** with ladyfingers, whipped-cream filling.	45. 5	286	5. 9	14. 6	33. 5	Trace	. 5	46	91	. 7	43	64	740	. 03	. 10	. 1	Trace
642	**Chayote,** raw	91. 8	28	. 6	. 1	7. 1	. 7	. 4	13	26	. 5	5	102	20	. 03	. 03	. 4	19
	Cheeses, natural and processed; cheese foods; cheese spreads:																	
	Natural cheeses:																	
643	Blue or Roquefort type	40.	368	21. 5	30. 5	2. 0	0	6. 0	315	339	(. 5)	—	—	(1, 240)	. 03	. 61	1. 2	(0)
644	Brick	41. 0	370	22. 2	30. 5	1. 9	0	4. 4	730	455	(. 9)	—	—	(1, 240)	—	. 45	. 1	(0)
645	Camembert (domestic)	52. 2	299	17. 5	24. 7	1. 8	0	3. 8	105	184	. 5	—	111	(1, 010)	. 04	. 75	. 8	(0)
646	Cheddar (domestic type, commonly called American).	37.	398	25. 0	32. 2	2. 1	0	3. 7	750	478	1. 0	700	82	(1, 310)	. 03	. 46	. 1	(0)
	Cottage (large or small curd):																	
647	Creamed	78. 3	106	13. 6	4. 2	2. 9	0	1. 0	94	152	. 3	229	85	(170)	. 03	. 25	. 1	(0)
648	Uncreamed	79. 0	86	17. 0	. 3	2. 7	0	1. 0	90	175	. 4	290	72	(10)	. 03	. 28	(. 1)	(0)
649	Cream	51.	374	8. 0	37. 7	2. 1	0	1. 2	62	95	. 2	250	74	(1, 540)	(. 02)	. 24	. 1	(0)
650	Limburger	45.	345	21. 2	28. 0	2. 2	0	3. 6	590	393	. 6	—	—	(1, 140)	. 08	. 50	. 2	(0)
651	Parmesan	30.	393	36. 0	26. 0	2. 9	0	5. 1	1, 140	781	. 4	734	149	(1, 060)	. 02	. 73	. 2	(0)
652	Swiss (domestic)	39.	370	27. 5	28. 0	1. 7	0	3. 8	925	563	. 9	710	104	(1, 140)	. 01	(. 40)	(. 1)	(0)
	Pasteurized process cheese:																	
653	American	40.	370	23. 2	30. 0	1. 9	0	4. 9	697	[46] 771	. 9	[46] 1, 136	80	(1, 220)	. 02	. 41	Trace	(0)
654	Pimiento (American)	40.	371	23. 0	30. 2	1. 8	Trace	5. 0	—	—	—	—	—	—	—	—	—	—
655	Swiss	40.	355	26. 4	26. 9	1. 6	0	5. 1	887	[46] 867	(. 9)	[46] 1, 167	100	(1, 100)	(. 01)	. 40	. 1	(0)
656	Pasteurized process cheese food, American	43. 2	323	19. 8	24. 0	7. 1	0	5. 9	570	[46] 754	(. 8)	—	—	(980)	(. 02)	. 58	. 2	(0)
657	Pasteurized process cheese spread, American	48. 6	288	16. 0	21. 4	8. 2	0	5. 8	565	[46] 875	(. 6)	[46] 1, 625	240	(870)	. 01	. 54	. 1	(0)
658	**Cheese fondue,** from home recipe	54. 2	265	14. 8	18. 3	10. 0	Trace	2. 7	317	294	1. 2	542	165	880	. 06	. 34	. 2	Trace
659	**Cheese souffle,** from home recipe	65. 0	218	9. 9	17. 1	6. 2	Trace	1. 8	201	195	1. 0	364	121	800	. 05	. 24	. 2	Trace
660	**Cheese straws**	21. 7	453	11. 2	29. 9	34. 5	. 1	2. 7	259	206	. 6	721	63	390	. 02	. 16	. 3	0
661	**Cherimoya,** raw	73. 5	94	1. 3	. 4	24. 0	2. 2	. 8	23	40	. 5	—	—	10	. 10	. 11	1. 3	9
	Cherries:																	
	Raw:																	
662	Sour, red	83. 7	58	1. 2	. 3	14. 3	. 2	. 5	22	19	. 4	2	191	1, 000	. 05	. 06	. 4	10
663	Sweet	80. 4	70	1. 3	. 3	17. 4	. 4	. 6	22	19	. 4	2	191	110	. 05	. 06	. 4	10
664	Candied	12. 0	339	. 5	. 2	86. 7	. 5	. 6	—	—	—	—	—	—	—	—	—	—
	Canned:																	
	Sour, red, solids and liquid:																	
665	Water pack	88. 0	43	. 8	. 2	10. 7	. 1	. 3	15	13	. 3	2	130	680	. 03	. 02	. 2	5
	Sirup pack:																	
666	Light	80. 0	74	. 8	. 2	18. 7	. 1	. 3	14	13	. 3	1	126	660	. 03	. 02	. 2	5
667	Heavy	76. 0	89	. 8	. 2	22. 7	. 1	. 3	14	12	. 3	1	124	650	. 03	. 02	. 2	5
668	Extra heavy	70. 1	112	. 8	. 2	28. 6	. 1	. 3	14	12	. 2	1	121	630	. 03	. 02	. 2	5
	Sweet, solids and liquid:																	
669	Water pack, with or without artificial sweetener	86. 6	48	. 9	. 2	11. 9	. 3	. 4	15	13	. 3	1	130	60	. 02	. 02	. 2	3
	Sirup pack:																	
670	Light	82. 0	65	. 9	. 2	16. 5	. 3	. 4	15	13	. 3	1	128	60	. 02	. 02	. 2	3
671	Heavy	78. 0	81	. 9	. 2	20. 5	. 3	. 4	15	13	. 3	1	126	60	. 02	. 02	. 2	3
672	Extra heavy	73. 0	100	. 8	. 2	25. 6	. 3	. 4	14	12	. 3	1	123	50	. 02	. 02	. 2	3
	Frozen, not thawed:																	
	Sour, red:																	
673	Unsweetened	84. 9	55	1. 0	. 4	13. 4	. 3	. 3	13	22	. 7	2	188	1, 000	. 04	. 07	. 3	5
674	Sweetened	70. 6	112	1. 0	. 4	27. 8	. 2	. 2	12	15	. 5	2	130	480	. 03	. 06	. 3	6
675	**Cherries, maraschino,** bottled, solids and liquid	70. 0	116	. 2	. 2	29. 4	. 3	. 2	—	—	—	—	—	—	—	—	—	—
676	**Chervil,** raw	80. 7	57	3. 4	. 9	11. 5	—	3. 5	—	—	—	—	—	—	—	—	—	9
	Chestnuts:																	
677	Fresh	52. 5	194	2. 9	1. 5	42. 1	1. 1	1. 0	27	88	1. 7	6	454	—	. 22	. 22	. 6	—
678	Dried	8. 4	377	6. 7	4. 1	78. 6	2. 5	2. 2	52	162	3. 3	12	875	—	. 32	. 38	1. 2	—
679	**Chestnut flour**	11. 4	362	6. 1	3. 7	76. 2	2. 0	2. 6	50	164	3. 2	11	847	—	. 23	. 37	1. 0	—
680	**Chewing gum**	3. 5	317	—	—	95. 2	—	1. 3	—	—	—	—	—	(0)	(0)	(0)	(0)	(0)

	Chicken:																	
	All classes:																	
	Light meat without skin:																	
681	Raw	73.7	117	23.4	1.9	0	0	1.0	11	218	1.1	50	320	60	.05	.09	10.7	—
682	Cooked, roasted	63.8	166	31.6	3.4	0	0	1.2	11	265	1.3	64	411	60	.04	.10	11.6	—
	Dark meat without skin:																	
683	Raw	73.7	130	20.6	4.7	0	0	1.0	13	188	1.5	67	250	150	.08	.20	5.2	—
684	Cooked, roasted	64.4	176	28.0	6.3	0	0	1.2	13	229	1.7	86	321	150	.07	.23	5.6	—
685	**Broilers**, flesh only, cooked, broiled	71.0	136	23.8	3.8	0	0	1.1	9	201	1.7	66	274	90	.05	.19	8.8	—
	Fryers (weight, ready to cook, with giblets, more than 1¾ lbs.):																	
	Flesh, skin, and giblets:																	
686	Raw	75.7	124	18.6	4.9	0	0	.8	12	201	1.9	—	—	730	.07	.38	5.6	—
687	Cooked, fried	53.3	249	30.7	11.8	2.9	—	1.3	13	254	2.3	—	—	820	.07	.57	9.1	—
	Flesh and skin:																	
688	Raw	75.4	126	18.8	5.1	0	0	.7	11	198	1.5	—	—	170	.05	.23	5.6	—
689	Cooked, fried	53.5	250	30.6	11.9	2.8	—	1.2	12	243	1.8	—	—	170	.06	.36	9.2	—
	Flesh only:																	
690	Raw	77.2	107	19.3	2.7	0	0	.8	12	203	1.3	58	285	90	.06	.25	6.4	—
691	Cooked, fried	58.6	209	31.2	7.8	1.2	—	1.2	13	257	1.6	78	381	90	.06	.35	9.7	—
	Skin only:																	
692	Raw	66.3	223	16.1	17.1	0	0	.5	9	174	2.4	—	—	550	.03	.13	2.0	—
693	Cooked, fried	32.5	419	28.3	28.9	9.1	—	1.2	8	186	2.4	—	—	490	.07	.41	7.0	—
	Giblets:																	
694	Raw	78.4	103	17.5	3.1	.1	0	.9	14	220	4.5	—	—	4,530	.16	1.36	4.9	—
695	Cooked, fried	51.7	252	30.8	11.2	4.7	—	1.6	18	335	6.5	—	—	5,760	.17	2.18	8.0	—
	Light meat with skin:																	
696	Raw	75.4	120	19.9	3.9	0	0	.8	11	211	1.3	—	—	130	.05	.16	6.7	—
697	Cooked, fried	55.0	234	31.5	9.9	2.4	—	1.2	11	260	1.5	—	—	130	.05	.27	11.9	—
	Dark meat with skin:																	
698	Raw	75.3	132	17.7	6.3	0	0	.7	12	185	1.7	—	—	200	.06	.30	4.7	—
699	Cooked, fried	52.1	263	29.9	13.6	3.1	—	1.3	12	228	2.0	—	—	210	.07	.45	6.7	—
	Light meat without skin:																	
700	Raw	77.2	101	20.5	1.5	0	0	.8	11	218	1.1	50	320	50	.05	.17	7.6	—
701	Cooked, fried	59.5	197	32.1	6.1	1.1	—	1.2	12	280	1.3	68	434	50	.05	.25	12.9	—
	Dark meat without skin:																	
702	Raw	77.3	112	18.1	3.8	0	0	.8	13	188	1.5	67	250	120	.06	.34	5.3	—
703	Cooked, fried	57.5	220	30.4	9.3	1.5	—	1.3	14	235	1.8	88	330	130	.07	.45	6.8	—
	Cut-up parts:																	
	Back:																	
704	Raw	73.3	157	16.5	9.6	0	0	.6	12	185	1.7	—	—	310	.05	.23	4.3	—
705	Cooked, fried	40.5	347	30.0	21.2	6.8	0	1.5	15	262	2.7	—	—	390	.07	.50	6.8	—
	Breast:																	
706	Raw	76.0	110	20.8	2.4	0	0	.8	11	214	1.2	—	—	80	.05	.16	7.9	—
707	Cooked, fried	58.4	203	32.5	6.4	1.5	—	1.2	12	276	1.7	—	—	90	.05	.22	14.7	—
	Drumstick:																	
708	Raw	76.5	115	18.8	3.9	0	0	.8	13	186	1.6	—	—	120	.06	.32	4.3	—
709	Cooked, fried	55.0	235	32.6	10.2	1.0	—	1.2	15	236	2.3	—	—	140	.07	.40	7.1	—
	Neck:																	
710	Raw	74.5	151	15.5	9.4	0	0	.6	11	182	1.9	—	—	310	.05	.25	3.0	—
711	Cooked, fried	50.2	289	26.7	17.4	4.5	—	1.2	12	234	2.7	—	—	350	.09	.41	5.7	—
	Rib:																	
712	Raw	76.2	124	17.7	5.4	0	0	.7	11	212	1.3	—	—	170	.04	.18	5.1	—
713	Cooked, fried	45.7	298	31.5	15.4	5.9	—	1.5	13	291	2.0	—	—	210	.05	.47	9.4	—
	Thigh:																	
714	Raw	75.5	128	18.1	5.6	0	0	.8	12	186	1.6	—	—	180	.06	.33	5.7	—
715	Cooked, fried	55.8	237	29.1	11.4	2.5	—	1.2	13	236	2.3	—	—	200	.06	.48	6.8	—
	Wing:																	
716	Raw	73.5	146	18.5	7.4	0	0	.6	10	203	1.5	—	—	240	.04	.14	4.1	—
717	Cooked, fried	52.6	268	29.0	14.8	2.7	—	.9	10	236	2.0	—	—	250	.05	.26	6.8	—
	Roasters:																	
	Total edible:																	
718	Raw	63.0	239	18.2	17.9	0	0	.9	10	176	1.6	—	—	920	.08	.19	6.7	—
719	Cooked, roasted	53.5	290	25.2	20.2	0	0	1.1	10	220	1.9	—	—	960	.07	.22	7.4	—
	Flesh, skin, and giblets:																	
720	Raw	67.5	191	19.6	11.9	0	0	1.0	12	194	1.7	—	—	760	.08	.21	7.3	—
721	Cooked, roasted	57.5	242	27.2	14.0	0	0	1.3	12	242	2.0	—	—	790	.08	.25	8.1	—
	Flesh and skin:																	
722	Raw	66.9	197	19.5	12.6	0	0	1.0	11	191	1.5	—	—	410	.08	.12	7.4	—
723	Cooked, roasted	57.0	248	27.1	14.7	0	0	1.3	11	239	1.8	—	—	420	.08	.14	8.2	—
	Flesh only:																	
724	Raw	73.3	131	21.1	4.5	0	0	1.1	12	203	1.3	58	285	150	.10	.12	7.7	—
725	Cooked, roasted	62.8	183	29.5	6.3	0	0	1.4	12	254	1.5	77	376	150	.10	.15	8.5	—

[46] Values for phosphorus and sodium are based on use of 1.5 percent anhydrous disodium phosphate as the emulsifying agent. If emulsifying agent does not contain either phosphorus or sodium, the content of these two nutrients in milligrams per 100 grams is as follows:

	P	*Na*
Item 653, American process cheese	444	650
Item 655, Swiss process cheese	540	681
Item 656, American cheese food	427	—
Item 657, American cheese spread	548	1,139

TABLE 1.—COMPOSITION OF FOODS, 100 GRAMS, EDIBLE PORTION—Continued

[Numbers in parentheses denote values imputed—usually from another form of the food or from a similar food. Zero in parentheses indicates that the amount of a constituent probably is none or is too small to measure. Dashes denote lack of reliable data for a constituent believed to be present in measurable amount. Calculated values, as those based on a recipe, are not in parentheses]

Item No.	Food and description	Water	Food energy	Protein	Fat	Carbohydrate		Ash	Calcium	Phosphorus	Iron	Sodium	Potassium	Vitamin A value	Thiamine	Riboflavin	Niacin	Ascorbic acid
						Total	Fiber											
(A)	(B)	(C)	(D)	(E)	(F)	(G)	(H)	(I)	(J)	(K)	(L)	(M)	(N)	(O)	(P)	(Q)	(R)	(S)
		Percent	Calories	Grams	Grams	Grams	Grams	Grams	Milligrams	Milligrams	Milligrams	Milligrams	Milligrams	International units	Milligrams	Milligrams	Milligrams	Milligrams
	Chicken—Continued																	
	Roasters—Continued																	
	Giblets:																	
726	Raw	72.4	135	19.8	4.8	1.7	0	1.3	15	218	4.4	—	—	4,290	0.09	1.07	6.7	6
	Light meat without skin:																	
727	Raw	72.3	128	23.3	3.2	0	0	1.2	11	218	1.1	50	320	100	.08	.08	10.6	—
728	Cooked, roasted	61.3	182	32.3	4.9	0	0	1.5	11	272	1.3	66	422	110	.08	.10	11.8	—
	Dark meat without skin:																	
729	Raw	73.2	132	21.0	4.7	0	0	1.1	13	188	1.5	67	250	150	.13	.16	4.7	—
730	Cooked, roasted	62.7	184	29.3	6.5	0	0	1.4	14	235	1.8	88	330	160	.12	.19	5.3	—
	Hens and cocks:																	
	Total edible:																	
731	Raw	56.9	298	17.4	24.8	0	0	.9	10	167	1.4	—	—	1,080	.06	.19	8.2	—
732	Cooked, stewed	45.9	369	24.0	29.5	0	0	.7	10	123	1.6	—	—	1,190	.04	.21	7.8	—
	Flesh, skin, and giblets:																	
733	Raw	61.7	246	19.0	18.3	0	0	1.0	11	185	1.5	—	—	900	.07	.20	9.1	—
734	Cooked, stewed	50.8	312	26.2	22.2	0	0	.8	11	136	1.8	—	—	990	.04	.23	8.6	—
	Flesh and skin:																	
735	Raw	61.3	251	19.0	18.8	0	0	.9	11	182	1.3	—	—	610	.06	.13	9.2	—
736	Cooked, stewed	50.4	317	26.1	22.8	0	0	.7	11	134	1.5	—	—	670	.04	.14	8.8	—
	Flesh only:																	
737	Raw	70.5	155	21.6	7.0	0	0	1.0	12	203	1.3	58	285	230	.08	.14	10.1	—
738	Cooked, stewed	60.4	208	30.0	8.9	0	0	.8	12	149	1.5	55	272	250	.04	.15	9.6	—
	Giblets:																	
739	Raw	66.8	191	18.6	11.6	1.8	0	1.2	15	214	4.4	—	—	4,300	.09	1.09	6.7	6
	Light meat without skin:																	
740	Raw	71.7	133	23.4	3.7	0	0	1.2	11	218	1.1	50	320	120	.05	.09	11.5	—
741	Cooked, stewed	62.1	180	32.2	4.7	0	0	.9	11	160	1.3	48	306	130	.03	.09	11.0	—
	Dark meat without skin:																	
742	Raw	71.2	154	20.2	7.5	0	0	1.1	13	188	1.5	67	250	240	.10	.18	8.7	—
743	Cooked, stewed	61.1	207	28.5	9.5	0	0	.9	13	138	1.8	64	239	270	.06	.20	8.3	—
	Capons:																	
	Total edible:																	
744	Raw	56.2	283	21.4	21.2	0	0	1.2	—	—	—	—	—	—	—	—	—	—
	Flesh and skin:																	
745	Raw	55.2	291	21.6	22.0	0	0	1.2	—	—	—	—	—	—	—	—	—	—
	Giblets:																	
746	Raw	63.3	220	20.4	14.6	.4	0	1.3	—	—	—	—	—	—	—	—	—	—
747	**Chicken, canned,** meat only, boned	65.2	198	21.7	11.7	0	0	1.4	21	247	1.5	—	138	230	.04	.12	4.4	4
	Chicken, potted. See Sausage, cold cuts, and luncheon meats: item 2008.																	
748	**Chicken a la king,** cooked, from home recipe	68.2	191	11.2	14.0	5.0	Trace	1.6	52	146	1.0	310	165	460	.04	.17	2.2	5
749	**Chicken fricassee,** cooked, from home recipe	71.3	161	15.3	9.3	3.2	Trace	.9	6	113	.9	154	140	70	.02	.07	2.4	0
	Chicken potpie:																	
750	Home-prepared, baked	56.6	235	10.1	13.5	18.3	.4	1.5	30	100	1.3	256	148	1,330	.11	.11	1.8	2
751	Commercial, frozen, unheated	57.8	219	6.7	11.5	22.2	.4	1.8	11	50	1.0	411	153	910	.10	.14	1.4	4
752	**Chicken and noodles,** cooked, from home recipe	71.1	153	9.3	7.7	10.7	Trace	1.2	11	103	.9	250	62	180	.02	.07	1.8	Trace
753	**Chickpeas** or garbanzos, mature seeds, dry, raw	10.7	360	20.5	4.8	61.0	5.0	3.0	150	331	6.9	26	797	50	.31	.15	2.0	—
754	**Chicory, Witloof** (also called French or Belgian endive), bleached head (forced), raw.[47]	95.1	15	1.0	.1	3.2	—	.6	18	21	.5	7	182	Trace	—	—	—	—
755	**Chicory greens,** raw	92.8	20	1.8	.3	3.8	.8	1.3	86	40	.9	—	420	4,000	.06	.10	.5	22
	Chili con carne, canned:																	
756	With beans	72.4	133	7.5	6.1	12.2	.6	1.8	32	126	1.7	531	233	60	.03	.07	1.3	—
757	Without beans [48]	66.9	200	10.3	14.8	5.8	.2	2.2	38	152	1.4	—	—	150	.02	.12	2.2	—
	Chili powder. See Peppers, item 1544.																	
	Chili sauce. See Peppers, items 1539, 1542; and Tomatoes, item 2287.																	
758	**Chives,** raw	91.3	28	1.8	.3	5.8	1.1	.8	69	44	1.7	—	250	5,800	.08	.13	.5	56
	Chocolate:																	
759	Bitter or baking [49]	2.3	505	10.7	53.0	28.9	2.5	3.1	78	384	6.7	4	830	60	.05	.24	1.5	0
	Bittersweet. See Candy, item 584.																	
	Chocolate sirup:																	
760	Thin type	31.6	245	2.3	2.0	62.7	.6	1.0	17	92	1.6	52	282	Trace	.02	.07	.4	0
761	Fudge type	25.4	330	5.1	13.7	54.0	.4	1.4	127	159	1.3	89	284	150	.04	.22	.4	Trace

	Chop suey, with meat:																	
762	Cooked, from home recipe	75.4	120	10.4	6.8	5.1	.5	2.3	24	99	1.9	421	170	240	.11	.15	2.0	13
763	Canned	85.5	62	4.4	3.2	4.2	.8	2.7	35	116	1.9	551	138	30	.05	.05	.7	2
	Chow mein, chicken (without noodles):																	
764	Cooked, from home recipe	78.0	102	12.4	4.0	4.0	.3	1.6	23	117	1.0	287	189	110	.03	.09	1.7	4
765	Canned	88.8	38	2.6	.1	7.1	.3	1.4	18	34	.5	290	167	60	.02	.04	.4	5
766	**Chub,** raw	74.9	145	15.3	8.8	0	0	1.0	—	—	—	—	—	—	—	—	—	—
	Cider. See Apple juice, item 27.																	
	Cisco. See Lake herring, item 1168.																	
767	**Citron,** candied	18.0	314	.2	.3	80.2	1.4	1.3	83	24	.8	290	120	—	—	—	—	—
	Clams, raw:																	
	Soft:																	
768	Meat and liquid	85.8	54	8.6	1.0	2.0	—	2.6	—	208	—	—	—	—	—	—	—	—
769	Meat only	80.8	82	14.0	1.9	1.3	—	2.0	—	183	3.4	36	235	—	—	—	—	—
	Hard or round:																	
770	Meat and liquid	86.2	49	6.5	.4	4.2	—	2.7	—	175	—	—	—	—	—	.13	—	—
771	Meat only	79.8	80	11.1	.9	5.9	—	2.3	69	151	7.5	205	311	—	—	—	—	—
	Hard, soft, and unspecified:																	
772	Meat and liquid	85.9	53	8.1	.9	2.5	—	2.6	—	197	—	—	—	—	—	—	—	—
773	Meat only	81.7	76	12.6	1.6	2.0	—	2.1	69	162	6.1	120	181	100	.10	.18	1.3	10
	Clams, canned, including hard, soft, razor, and unspecified:																	
774	Solids and liquid	86.3	52	7.9	.7	2.8	—	2.3	55	137	4.1	—	140	—	.01	.11	1.0	—
775	Drained solids	77.0	98	15.8	2.5	1.9	—	2.8	—	—	—	—	—	—	—	—	—	—
776	Liquor, bouillon, or nectar	93.6	19	2.3	.1	2.1	0	1.9	—	—	—	—	—	—	—	—	—	—
777	**Clam fritters** [50]	40.3	311	11.4	15.0	30.9	—	2.4	76	195	3.5	—	147	—	.03	.12	.9	—
	Cocoa and chocolate-flavored beverage powders:																	
778	Cocoa powder with nonfat dry milk	1.9	359	18.6	2.9	70.8	.5	5.4	589	545	1.8	525	800	20	.13	.73	.7	3
779	Cocoa powder without milk	1.3	347	4.0	2.0	89.4	1.0	2.5	30	171	2.1	268	500	—	.02	.09	.5	0
780	Mix for hot chocolate [51]	3.1	392	9.4	10.6	73.9	.8	2.6	275	290	1.4	382	605	10	.08	.41	.5	1
	Cocoa, dry powder																	
	High-fat or breakfast:																	
781	Plain	3.0	299	16.8	23.7	48.3	4.3	5.0	133	648	10.7	6	1,522	30	.11	.46	2.4	0
782	Processed with alkali	3.0	295	16.8	23.7	45.4	4.3	8.2	133	648	10.7	717	651	30	.11	.46	2.4	0
	Medium-fat:																	
	High-medium fat:																	
783	Plain	4.1	265	17.3	19.0	51.5	4.3	4.9	123	649	10.7	6	1,522	20	.11	.46	2.4	0
784	Processed with alkali	4.1	261	17.3	19.0	48.5	4.3	7.9	123	649	10.7	717	651	20	.11	.46	2.4	0
	Low-medium fat:																	
785	Plain	5.2	220	19.2	12.7	53.8	5.2	5.5	152	686	10.7	6	1,522	20	.11	.46	2.4	0
786	Processed with alkali	5.2	215	19.2	12.7	50.2	5.2	9.1	152	686	10.7	717	651	20	.11	.46	2.4	0
787	Low-fat	4.4	187	20.2	7.5	58.0	5.8	5.7	153	752	10.7	6	1,522	10	.11	.46	2.4	0
788	**Coconut cream** (liquid expressed from grated coconut meat).	54.1	334	4.4	32.2	8.3	—	1.0	15	126	1.8	4	324	0	.02	.01	.5	1
	Coconut meat:																	
789	Fresh	50.9	346	3.5	35.3	9.4	4.0	.9	13	95	1.7	23	256	0	.05	.02	.5	3
	Dried:																	
790	Unsweetened	3.5	662	7.2	64.9	23.0	3.9	1.4	26	187	3.3	—	588	0	.06	.04	.6	0
791	Sweetened, shredded	3.3	548	3.6	39.1	53.2	4.1	.8	16	112	2.0	—	353	0	.04	.03	.4	0
792	**Coconut milk** (liquid expressed from mixture of grated coconut meat and water).	65.7	252	3.2	24.9	5.2	—	1.0	16	100	1.6	—	—	0	.03	Trace	.8	2
793	**Coconut water** (liquid from coconuts)	94.2	22	.3	.2	4.7	Trace	.6	20	13	.3	25	147	0	Trace	Trace	.1	2
	Cod:																	
794	Raw	81.2	78	17.6	.3	0	0	1.2	10	194	.4	[52] 70	382	0	.06	.07	2.2	2
795	Cooked, broiled	64.6	170	28.5	5.3	0	0	—	31	274	1.0	110	407	180	.08	.11	3.0	—
796	Canned	78.6	85	19.2	.3	0	0	1.0	—	—	—	—	—	—	—	.08	—	—
797	Dehydrated, lightly salted	12.3	375	81.8	2.8	0	0	7.0	—	891	3.6	8,100	160	0	.08	.45	10.9	—
798	Dried, salted	52.4	130	29.0	.7	0	0	19.7	225	—	—	—	—	—	—	—	—	—
	Codfish cakes. See Fishcakes, items 1010–1011.																	
	Coffee, instant, water-soluble solids: [49] [53]																	
799	Dry powder	2.6	129	Trace	Trace	(35.)	Trace	9.7	179	383	5.6	72	3,256	0	0	.21	30.6	0
800	Beverage	98.1	1	Trace	Trace	Trace	Trace	.1	2	4	.1	1	36	0	0	Trace	.3	0
	Cola or coke. See Beverages, item 404.																	
	Coleslaw, [54] made with—																	
801	French dressing (homemade)	80.6	129	1.1	12.3	5.1	.7	.9	42	25	.4	131	197	110	.04	.04	.3	29
802	French dressing (commercial)	82.6	95	1.2	7.3	7.6	.7	1.3	42	26	.4	268	205	110	.04	.04	.3	29
803	Mayonnaise	79.0	144	1.3	14.0	4.8	.7	.9	44	29	.4	120	199	160	.05	.05	.3	29
804	Salad dressing (mayonnaise type)	82.9	99	1.2	7.9	7.1	.7	.9	43	28	.4	124	192	150	.05	.05	.3	29

[47] For further description of product, see Notes on Foods, p. 178.

[48] Contains not less than 60 percent meat, not more than 8 percent cereals, seasonings.

[50] Prepared with flour, baking powder, butter, egg.

[51] Values apply to products without added vitamins and minerals.

[52] Value is about 255 mg. per 100 grams if cod has been dipped or rinsed in brine.

[53] Contains 3,000 to 4,000 mg. caffeine per 100 grams of powder and 35 to 45 mg. per 100 grams of beverage made with 2.5 grams, or 1 rounded teaspoon of instant coffee per 8 fluid oz. of beverage.

[54] Values are for product immediately after preparation. Values for energy and fat are reduced if dressing drains from slaw and is not served.

TABLE 1.—COMPOSITION OF FOODS, 100 GRAMS, EDIBLE PORTION—Continued

[Numbers in parentheses denote values imputed—usually from another form of the food or from a similar food. Zero in parentheses indicates that the amount of a constituent probably is none or is too small to measure. Dashes denote lack of reliable data for a constituent believed to be present in measurable amount. Calculated values, as those based on a recipe, are not in parentheses]

Item No.	Food and description	Water	Food energy	Protein	Fat	Carbohydrate		Ash	Calcium	Phos-phorus	Iron	Sodium	Potas-sium	Vitamin A value	Thiamine	Ribo-flavin	Niacin	Ascorbic acid
						Total	Fiber											
(A)	(B)	(C)	(D)	(E)	(F)	(G)	(H)	(I)	(J)	(K)	(L)	(M)	(N)	(O)	(P)	(Q)	(R)	(S)
		Percent	Calories	Grams	Grams	Grams	Grams	Grams	Milligrams	Milligrams	Milligrams	Milligrams	Milligrams	International units	Milligrams	Milligrams	Milligrams	Milligrams
	Collards:																	
	Raw:																	
805	Leaves, without stems	85.3	45	4.8	0.8	7.5	1.2	1.6	250	82	1.5	—	450	9,300	0.16	0.31	1.7	152
806	Leaves, including stems	86.9	40	3.6	.7	7.2	.9	1.6	203	63	1.0	43	401	6,500	.20	(.31)	(1.7)	92
	Cooked, boiled, drained:																	
	Leaves without stems, cooked in—																	
807	Small amount of water	89.6	33	3.6	.7	5.1	1.0	1.0	188	52	.8	—	262	7,800	.11	.20	1.2	76
808	Large amount of water	90.2	31	3.4	.7	4.8	1.0	.9	177	48	.8	—	243	7,800	.07	.14	1.1	51
	Leaves, including stems, cooked in—																	
809	Small amount of water	90.8	29	2.7	.6	4.9	.8	1.0	152	39	.6	25	234	5,400	.14	.20	1.2	46
	Frozen:																	
810	Not thawed	89.7	32	3.1	.4	5.8	1.0	1.0	191	53	1.1	18	259	6,800	.07	.16	.7	68
811	Cooked, boiled, drained	90.2	30	2.9	.4	5.6	1.0	.9	176	51	1.0	16	236	6,800	.06	.14	.6	33
	Cookies: [55]																	
812	Assorted, packaged, commercial	2.6	480	5.1	20.2	71.0	.1	1.1	37	163	.7	365	67	80	.03	.05	.4	Trace
	Brownies with nuts:																	
813	Baked from home recipe, enriched flour	9.8	485	6.5	31.3	50.9	.7	1.5	41	148	1.9	251	190	200	.19	.12	.7	Trace
814	Frozen, with chocolate icing, commercial	12.5	419	4.9	20.6	60.7	.6	1.3	40	125	[56] 1.5	200	179	220	[56] .09	[56] .08	[56] .3	Trace
815	Butter, thin, rich	4.5	457	6.1	16.9	70.9	.1	1.6	126	94	.5	418	60	650	.03	.06	.4	0
816	Chocolate	4.0	445	7.1	15.7	71.5	.3	1.7	52	127	1.1	137	128	160	.04	.08	.5	Trace
	Chocolate chip:																	
817	Baked from home recipe, enriched flour	3.0	516	5.4	30.1	60.1	.4	1.4	34	99	2.1	348	117	110	.11	.11	.9	Trace
818	Commercial type	2.7	471	5.4	21.0	69.7	.4	1.2	39	114	1.8	401	134	120	.04	.07	.4	Trace
819	Coconut bars	3.8	494	6.2	24.5	63.9	.6	1.6	72	120	1.4	148	228	160	.04	.06	.4	0
820	Fig bars	13.6	358	3.9	5.6	75.4	1.7	1.5	78	60	1.0	252	198	110	.04	.07	.3	Trace
821	Gingersnaps	3.1	420	5.5	8.9	79.8	.1	2.7	73	47	2.3	571	462	70	.04	.06	.4	Trace
822	Ladyfingers	19.2	360	7.8	7.8	64.5	.1	.7	41	164	1.5	71	71	650	.06	.14	.2	0
823	Macaroons	4.4	475	5.3	23.2	66.1	2.1	1.0	27	83	.9	34	463	0	.04	.15	.6	0
824	Marshmallow	9.8	409	4.0	13.2	72.3	.3	.7	21	57	.5	209	91	260	.02	.06	.2	Trace
825	Molasses	4.0	422	6.4	10.6	76.0	.1	3.0	51	83	2.1	386	138	80	.04	.06	.7	0
826	Oatmeal with raisins	2.8	451	6.2	15.4	73.5	.4	2.1	21	102	2.9	162	370	50	.11	.08	.5	Trace
827	Peanut	2.3	473	10.0	19.1	67.0	.8	1.6	42	116	.9	173	175	200	.07	.08	2.8	Trace
828	Raisin	8.2	379	4.4	5.3	80.8	.9	1.3	71	157	2.1	52	272	210	.04	.08	.6	Trace
829	Sandwich type	2.2	495	4.8	22.5	69.3	.1	1.2	26	241	.7	483	38	0	.04	.04	.5	0
830	Shortbread	3.0	498	7.2	23.1	65.1	.2	1.6	70	156	.5	60	66	80	.04	.05	.5	0
831	Sugar, soft, thick, with enriched flour, home recipe	7.9	444	6.0	16.8	68.0	.1	1.3	78	103	1.4	318	76	110	.16	.16	1.3	Trace
832	Sugar wafers	1.4	485	4.9	19.4	73.4	.1	.9	36	80	.3	189	60	140	.01	.04	.5	0
833	Vanilla wafers	2.8	462	5.4	16.1	74.4	.1	1.3	41	63	.4	252	72	130	.02	.07	.3	0
	Cooky mixes and cookies baked from mixes:																	
	Brownie, with enriched flour:																	
	Complete mix:																	
834	Dry form	3.0	419	4.8	12.0	78.7	.5	1.5	21	105	1.2	299	163	90	.10	.11	.9	0
835	Brownies, made with water, nuts	15.3	403	4.9	18.7	59.8	.7	1.3	26	117	1.2	218	180	80	.16	.09	.7	Trace
	Incomplete mix:																	
836	Dry form	2.5	442	4.0	16.4	76.0	.5	1.1	42	118	1.8	194	149	Trace	.09	.09	.9	0
837	Brownies, made with egg, water, nuts	10.7	428	5.0	20.1	63.1	.6	1.1	45	137	1.9	166	168	100	.13	.10	.7	Trace
	Plain, with unenriched flour:																	
838	Mix, dry form	4.2	493	3.5	24.2	66.8	.1	1.3	86	147	.3	352	29	0	.02	.02	.3	0
839	Cookies, made with egg, water	4.5	493	4.8	24.3	65.0	.1	1.4	88	163	.5	347	42	120	.02	.05	.3	0
840	Cookies, made with milk	4.4	490	3.7	23.8	66.7	.1	1.4	95	151	.3	345	42	10	.02	.03	.3	Trace
	Cooky dough, plain, chilled in roll:																	
841	Unbaked	13.6	449	3.5	22.6	58.8	.1	1.5	33	66	.3	496	44	70	.02	.03	.2	0
842	Baked	4.5	496	3.9	25.0	64.9	.1	1.7	36	73	.3	548	48	70	.02	.03	.2	0
	Cooking oil. See Oils, item 1401.																	
843	**Corn, field,** whole-grain, raw	13.8	348	8.9	3.9	72.2	2.0	1.2	22	268	2.1	1	284	[57] 490	.37	.12	2.2	(0)
	Corn, sweet:																	
844	Raw, white and yellow	72.7	96	3.5	1.0	22.1	.7	.7	3	111	.7	Trace	280	[57] 400	.15	.12	1.7	12
	Cooked, boiled, drained, white and yellow:																	
845	Kernels, cut off cob before cooking	76.5	83	3.2	1.0	18.8	.7	.5	3	89	.6	Trace	165	[57] 400	.11	.10	1.3	7

846	Kernels, cooked on cob	74.1	91	3.3	1.0	21.0	.7	.6	3	89	.6	Trace	196	[57] 400	.12	.10	1.4	9
	Canned:																	
	Regular pack:																	
	Cream style, white and yellow:																	
847	Solids and liquid	76.3	82	2.1	.6	20.0	.5	1.0	3	56	.6	[9] 236	(97)	[57] 330	.03	.05	1.0	5
	Whole kernel:																	
	Vacuum pack, yellow:																	
848	Solids and liquid	75.5	83	2.5	.5	20.5	.8	1.0	3	73	.5	[9] 236	(97)	350	(.03)	(.06)	(1.1)	5
	Wet pack, white and yellow:																	
849	Solids and liquid	80.9	66	1.9	.6	15.7	.6	.9	4	48	.4	[9] 236	97	[57] 270	.03	.05	.9	5
850	Drained solids	75.9	84	2.6	.8	19.8	.8	.9	5	49	.5	[9] 236	97	[57] 350	.03	.05	.9	4
851	Drained liquid	91.7	26	.5	Trace	6.9	Trace	.9	3	45	.3	[9] 236	97	Trace	.03	.04	.9	7
	Special dietary pack (low-sodium):																	
	Cream style, white and yellow:																	
852	Solids and liquid	77.3	82	2.6	1.1	18.5	.3	.5	3	56	.6	2	(97)	[57] 270	.03	.05	1.0	5
	Whole kernel, wet pack, white and yellow:																	
853	Solids and liquid	83.6	57	1.9	.5	13.6	.5	.4	4	48	.4	2	97	[57] 270	.03	.05	.9	5
854	Drained solids	78.4	76	2.5	.7	18.0	.7	.4	5	49	.5	2	97	[57] 350	.03	.05	.9	4
855	Drained liquid	94.8	17	.5	Trace	4.3	Trace	.4	3	45	.3	2	97	Trace	.03	.04	.9	7
	Frozen:																	
	Kernels, cut off cob:																	
856	Not thawed	76.2	82	3.1	.5	19.7	.5	.5	3	78	.8	1	202	[57] (350)	.11	.07	1.6	8
857	Cooked, boiled, drained	77.2	79	3.0	.5	18.8	.5	.5	3	73	.8	1	184	[57] (350)	.09	.06	1.5	5
	Kernels, on cob:																	
858	Not thawed	72.1	98	3.6	1.0	22.6	.7	.7	3	102	.8	1	254	[57] (350)	.17	.09	1.9	10
859	Cooked, boiled, drained	73.2	94	3.5	1.0	21.6	.7	.7	3	96	.8	1	231	[57] (350)	.14	.08	1.7	7
860	**Corn flour**	12.	368	7.8	2.6	76.8	.7	.8	6	(164)	1.8	(1)	—	[57] 340	.20	.06	1.4	(0)
861	**Corn fritters**	29.1	377	7.8	21.5	39.7	.5	1.9	64	155	1.7	477	133	[58] 400	.16	.20	1.6	2
	Corn grits, degermed:																	
	Enriched:																	
862	Dry form	12.	362	8.7	.8	78.1	.4	.4	4	73	[59] 2.9	1	80	[57] 440	[59] .44	[59] .26	[59] 3.5	(0)
863	Cooked	87.1	51	1.2	.1	11.0	.1	.6	1	10	[59] .3	205	11	[57] 60	[59] .04	[59] .03	[59] .4	(0)
	Unenriched:																	
864	Dry form	12.	362	8.7	.8	78.1	.4	.4	4	73	1.0	1	80	[57] 440	.13	.04	1.2	(0)
865	Cooked	87.1	51	1.2	.1	11.0	.1	.6	1	10	.1	205	11	[57] 60	.02	.01	.2	(0)
	Corn muffins. See Muffins, corn: items 1347–1348.																	
	Corn oil. See Oils, item 1401.																	
	Corn products used mainly as ready-to-eat breakfast cereals:																	
	Corn flakes:																	
866	Added nutrients	3.8	386	7.9	.4	85.3	.7	2.6	17	45	1.4	1,005	120	(0)	.43	.08	2.1	(0)
867	Added nutrients, sugar-covered	2.2	386	4.4	.2	91.3	.4	1.9	12	24	1.0	775	—	(0)	.41	.04	1.9	(0)
	Corn, puffed:																	
868	Added nutrients	3.6	399	8.1	4.2	80.8	.4	3.3	20	90	5.8	1,060	—	(0)	.88	.18	2.7	(0)
	Presweetened:																	
869	Added nutrients	5.0	379	4.0	.2	89.8	.3	1.0	11	28	1.8	300	—	(0)	.42	.17	2.1	(0)
870	Cocoa-flavored, added nutrients	2.1	390	6.2	2.2	86.7	.5	2.8	20	90	6.0	850	—	(0)	.79	.18	2.5	(0)
871	Fruit-flavored, added nutrients	2.1	395	5.6	2.7	87.4	.3	2.2	30	70	5.0	600	—	(0)	.99	.17	2.5	106
872	Corn, shredded, added nutrients	3.0	389	7.0	.4	86.9	.6	2.7	5	39	2.4	988	—	(0)	.42	.18	2.1	(0)
873	Corn, rice, and wheat flakes, mixed, added nutrients	2.8	389	7.4	.7	86.1	1.2	3.0	39	120	1.8	950	—	(0)	.39	—	3.2	(0)
874	Corn, flaked, with protein concentrate (casein) and other added nutrients.	3.6	378	23.0	1.6	67.0	.2	4.8	310	330	17.9	1,100	—	(0)	1.65	1.96	14.2	35
875	**Corn pudding**	76.7	104	4.0	4.7	13.0	.5	1.6	66	84	.5	436	169	260	.03	.13	.4	2
	Corn sirup. See Sirup, table blends: item 2051.																	
	Cornbread, baked from home recipes:																	
	Cornbread, southern style, made with—																	
876	Whole-ground cornmeal	53.9	207	7.4	7.2	29.1	.5	2.4	120	211	1.1	628	157	[60] 150	.13	.19	.6	1
877	Degermed cornmeal, enriched	50.2	224	7.1	6.0	34.7	.2	2.0	109	156	[61] 1.4	591	157	[60] 150	[61] .17	[61] .24	[61] 1.1	1
878	Johnnycake (northern style cornbread), made with enriched, yellow degermed cornmeal.	37.9	267	8.7	5.2	45.5	.3	2.7	111	155	1.8	690	188	340	.20	.30	1.5	1
879	Corn pone, made with white, whole-ground cornmeal	51.8	204	4.5	5.3	36.2	.8	2.2	62	163	1.2	396	61	Trace	.15	.05	.9	0
880	Spoonbread, made with white whole-ground cornmeal.	63.0	195	6.7	11.4	16.9	.3	2.0	96	164	1.0	482	132	290	.09	.18	.4	Trace
	See also Muffins, corn: items 1347–1348.																	

[9] Estimated average based on addition of salt in the amount of 0.6 percent of the finished product.

[55] Products are commercial unless otherwise specified.

[56] Based on product made with unenriched flour. With enriched flour, approximate values per 100 grams are: Iron, 1.6 mg.; thiamine, 0.12 mg., riboflavin, 0.10 mg.; niacin, 0.5 mg.

[57] Based on yellow varieties; white varieties contain only a trace of cryptoxanthin and carotenes, the pigments in corn that have biological activity.

[58] Based on fritters made with yellow sweet corn; with white corn, value is 230 I.U. per 100 grams.

[59] Based on product with minimum level of enrichment.

[60] Based on cornbread made with white cornmeal; with yellow cornmeal, value is about 310 I.U. per 100 grams.

[61] For cornbread made with unenriched degermed cornmeal, values per 100 grams are: Iron, 0.7 mg.; thiamine, 0.07 mg.; riboflavin, 0.17 mg.; niacin, 0.4 mg.

TABLE 1.—COMPOSITION OF FOODS, 100 GRAMS, EDIBLE PORTION—Continued

[Numbers in parentheses denote values imputed—usually from another form of the food or from a similar food. Zero in parentheses indicates that the amount of a constituent probably is none or is too small to measure. Dashes denote lack of reliable data for a constituent believed to be present in measurable amount. Calculated values, as those based on a recipe, are not in parentheses]

Item No.	Food and description	Water	Food energy	Protein	Fat	Carbohydrate		Ash	Calcium	Phosphorus	Iron	Sodium	Potassium	Vitamin A value	Thiamine	Riboflavin	Niacin	Ascorbic acid
						Total	Fiber											
(A)	(B)	(C)	(D)	(E)	(F)	(G)	(H)	(I)	(J)	(K)	(L)	(M)	(N)	(O)	(P)	(Q)	(R)	(S)
		Percent	*Calories*	*Grams*	*Grams*	*Grams*	*Grams*	*Grams*	*Milligrams*	*Milligrams*	*Milligrams*	*Milligrams*	*Milligrams*	*International units*	*Milligrams*	*Milligrams*	*Milligrams*	*Milligrams*
	Cornbread mix and cornbread baked from mix:																	
881	Mix, dry form	5.7	432	7.5	12.8	71.0	0.3	3.0	28	474	[63] 2.5	1,156	81	[63] 320	[63] 0.33	[63] 0.21	[63] 2.6	0
882	Cornbread, made with egg, milk	50.8	233	6.1	8.4	32.9	.2	1.8	85	268	[63] 1.2	744	127	[63] 270	[63] .15	[63] .20	[63] 1.2	Trace
	Cornmeal, white or yellow:																	
883	Whole-ground, unbolted	12.	355	9.2	3.9	73.7	1.6	1.2	20	256	2.4	(1)	(284)	[57] 510	.38	.11	2.0	(0)
884	Bolted (nearly whole-grain)	12.	362	9.0	3.4	74.5	1.0	1.1	(17)	(223)	1.8	(1)	(248)	[57] 480	.30	.08	1.9	(0)
	Degermed, enriched:																	
885	Dry form	12.	364	7.9	1.2	78.4	.6	.5	6	99	[58] 2.9	1	120	[57] 440	[58] .44	[58] .26	[58] 3.5	(0)
886	Cooked	87.7	50	1.1	.2	10.7	.1	.3	1	14	[59] .4	110	16	[57] 60	[59] .06	[59] .04	[59] .5	(0)
	Degermed, unenriched:																	
887	Dry form	12.	364	7.9	1.2	78.4	.6	.5	6	99	1.1	1	120	[57] 440	.14	.05	1.0	(0)
888	Cooked	87.7	50	1.1	.2	10.7	.1	.3	1	14	.2	110	16	[57] 60	.02	.01	.1	(0)
	Self-rising:																	
	Whole-ground:																	
889	With soft wheat flour added	11.3	347	8.6	2.9	71.9	.9	5.3	[64] 301	624	[64] 1.6	1,380	[65] 212	[57] 380	[64] .25	[64] .07	[64] 1.7	(0)
890	Without wheat flour added	11.3	347	8.5	3.2	71.6	.9	5.4	[64] 300	641	[64] 1.7	1,380	[65] 234	[57] 450	[64] .28	[64] .08	[64] 1.8	(0)
	Degermed:																	
891	With soft wheat flour added	11.3	348	7.7	1.1	75.1	.5	4.8	[64] 292	524	[64] 1.0	1,380	[65] 109	[57] 350	[64] .12	[64] .05	[64] 1.0	(0)
892	Without wheat flour added	11.3	348	7.5	1.1	75.3	.6	4.8	[64] 290	524	[64] 1.0	1,380	[65] 113	[57] 420	[64] .13	[64] .05	[64] .9	(0)
893	**Cornsalad,** raw	92.8	21	2.0	.4	3.6	.8	1.2	—	—	—	—	—	—	—	—	—	—
894	**Cornstarch**	12.	362	.3	Trace	87.6	.1	.1	(0)	(0)	(0)	Trace	Trace	(0)	(0)	(0)	(0)	(0)
	Cottage pudding. See Cakes, items 528–530.																	
895	**Cottonseed flour**	6.1	356	48.1	6.6	33.0	2.0	6.2	283	1,112	12.6	—	—	60	1.21	.84	6.5	—
	Cottonseed oil. See Oils, item 1401.																	
	Cowpeas, including blackeye peas:																	
	Immature seeds:																	
896	Raw	66.8	127	9.0	.8	21.8	1.8	1.6	27	172	2.3	2	541	370	.43	.13	1.6	29
897	Cooked, boiled, drained	71.8	108	8.1	.8	18.1	1.8	1.2	24	146	2.1	1	379	350	.30	.11	1.4	17
898	Canned, solids and liquid	81.0	70	5.0	.3	12.4	.7	1.3	18	112	1.5	[9] 236	352	60	.09	.05	.5	3
	Frozen (blackeye peas only):																	
899	Not thawed	65.8	131	9.0	.4	23.6	1.5	1.2	28	179	3.1	[19] 50	387	170	.45	.12	1.4	13
900	Cooked, boiled, drained	66.1	130	8.9	.4	23.5	1.5	1.1	25	168	2.8	39	337	170	.40	.11	1.4	9
	Young pods, with seeds:																	
901	Raw	86.0	44	3.3	.3	9.5	1.7	.9	65	65	1.0	4	215	1,600	.15	.14	1.2	33
902	Cooked, boiled, drained	89.5	34	2.6	.3	7.0	1.7	.6	55	49	.7	3	196	1,400	.09	.09	.8	17
	Mature seeds, dry:																	
903	Raw	10.5	343	22.8	1.5	61.7	4.4	3.5	74	426	5.8	35	1,024	30	1.05	.21	2.2	—
904	Cooked	80.0	76	5.1	.3	13.8	1.0	.8	17	95	1.3	[4] 8	229	10	.16	.04	.4	—
	Crab, including blue, Dungeness, rock and king:																	
905	Cooked, steamed	78.5	93	17.3	1.9	.5	—	1.8	43	175	.8	—	—	2,170	.16	.08	2.8	2
906	**Crab,** canned	77.2	101	17.4	2.5	1.1	—	1.8	45	182	.8	1,000	110	—	.08	.08	1.9	—
907	**Crab, deviled** [66]	63.3	188	11.4	9.4	13.3	—	2.6	47	137	1.2	867	166	—	.08	.11	1.5	6
908	**Crab imperial** [67]	71.9	147	14.6	7.6	3.9	—	2.0	60	166	.9	728	131	—	.06	.12	1.1	5
909	**Crabapples,** raw	81.1	68	.4	.3	17.8	.6	.4	(6)	13	(.3)	(1)	(110)	(40)	(.03)	(.02)	(.1)	8
	Crackers:																	
910	Animal	3.0	429	6.6	9.4	79.9	.1	1.1	52	114	.5	303	95	130	.04	.10	.3	Trace
911	Butter	4.6	458	7.0	17.8	67.3	.3	3.3	148	260	.6	1,092	113	220	.01	.04	1.0	(0)
912	Cheese	3.9	479	11.2	21.3	60.4	.2	3.2	336	309	.9	1,039	109	360	.01	.10	.8	(0)
	Graham:																	
913	Chocolate-coated	1.9	475	5.1	23.5	67.9	.8	1.6	113	204	2.6	407	320	60	.07	.28	1.2	(0)
914	Plain	6.4	384	8.0	9.4	73.3	1.1	2.9	40	149	1.5	670	384	(0)	.04	.21	1.5	(0)
915	Sugar-honey coated	3.3	411	6.7	11.4	76.4	.8	2.2	88	329	1.6	504	270	—	.03	.02	1.0	(0)
916	Saltines	4.3	433	9.0	12.0	71.5	.4	3.2	21	90	1.2	(1,100)	(120)	(0)	.01	.04	1.0	(0)
917	Sandwich type, peanut-cheese	2.4	491	15.2	23.9	56.1	.5	2.4	56	179	.6	992	226	40	.03	.07	3.5	(0)
918	Soda	4.0	439	9.2	13.1	70.6	.2	3.1	22	89	1.5	1,100	120	(0)	.01	.05	1.0	(0)
919	Whole-wheat	6.9	403	8.4	13.8	68.2	2.4	2.7	23	190	.3	547	—	(0)	.06	.04	.9	(0)
	Cracker meal. See Crackers, soda: item 918.																	
	Cranberries:																	
920	Raw	87.9	46	.4	.7	10.8	1.4	.2	14	10	.5	2	82	40	.03	.02	.1	11
921	Dehydrated, uncooked	4.9	368	2.8	6.6	84.3	8.7	1.4	82	22	3.4	16	644	300	.17	.12	.8	32
922	**Cranberry juice cocktail,** bottled (approx. 33% cranberry juice).	83.2	65	.1	.1	16.5	Trace	.1	5	3	.3	1	10	Trace	.01	.01	Trace	([68])
	Cranberry sauce, sweetened:																	
923	Canned, strained	62.1	146	.1	.2	37.5	.2	.1	6	4	.2	1	30	20	.01	.01	Trace	2

924	Home-prepared, unstrained	53.9	178	.2	.3	45.5	.7	.1	7	5	.2	1	38	20	.01	.01	.1	2
925	**Cranberry-orange relish,** uncooked	53.6	178	.4	.4	45.4	—	.2	19	8	.4	1	72	70	.03	.02	.1	18
926	**Crappie, white,** raw	81.8	79	16.8	.8	0	0	1.0	—	—	—	—	—	—	Trace	.03	1.4	—
927	**Crayfish, freshwater; and spiny lobster;** raw	82.5	72	14.6	.5	1.2	—	1.2	77	201	1.5	—	—	—	.01	.04	1.9	—
	Cream, fluid:																	
928	Half-and-half (cream and milk)	79.7	134	3.2	11.7	4.6	0	.6	108	85	Trace	46	129	480	.03	.16	.1	1
929	Light, coffee, or table	71.5	211	3.0	20.6	4.3	0	.6	102	80	Trace	43	122	840	.03	.15	.1	1
930	Light whipping	62.1	300	2.5	31.3	3.6	0	.5	85	67	Trace	36	102	1,280	.02	.12	.1	1
931	Heavy whipping	56.6	352	2.2	37.6	3.1	0	.4	75	59	Trace	32	89	1,540	.02	.11	Trace	1
	Cream substitutes, dried, containing—																	
932	Cream, skim milk (calcium reduced) and lactose	1.4	508	8.5	26.7	61.3	0	2.1	82	—	.2	575	—	960	.05	1.17	.1	—
933	Cream, skim milk, lactose, and sodium hexametaphosphate.	.9	509	13.9	27.7	53.2	0	4.3	495	—	.3	—	—	520	.14	.71	.3	—
934	**Cream puffs** with custard filling	58.3	233	6.5	13.9	20.5	Trace	.8	81	114	.7	83	121	350	.04	.17	.1	Trace
	Cress, garden: [47]																	
935	Raw	89.4	32	2.6	.7	5.5	1.1	1.8	81	76	1.3	14	606	9,300	.08	.26	1.0	69
	Cooked, boiled, drained, cooked in—																	
936	Small amount of water, short time	92.5	23	1.9	.6	3.8	.9	1.2	61	48	.8	8	353	7,700	.06	.16	.8	34
937	Large amount of water, long time	92.9	22	1.8	.6	3.6	.9	1.1	58	44	.7	8	328	7,000	.04	.15	.7	23
	Croaker, Atlantic:																	
938	Raw	79.2	96	17.8	2.2	0	0	1.3	—	—	—	87	234	60	.12	.08	5.5	—
939	Cooked, baked	71.3	133	24.3	3.2	0	0	1.2	—	—	—	120	323	70	.13	.10	6.5	—
940	**Croaker, white,** raw	79.7	84	18.0	.8	0	0	1.3	—	—	—	—	—	—	—	—	—	—
941	**Croaker, yellowfin,** raw	79.0	89	19.2	.8	0	0	1.2	—	—	—	—	—	—	—	—	—	—
	Cucumbers, raw:																	
942	Not pared	95.1	15	.9	.1	3.4	.6	.5	25	27	1.1	6	160	250	.03	.04	.2	11
943	Pared	95.7	14	.6	.1	3.2	.3	.4	17	18	.3	6	160	Trace	.03	.04	.2	11
	Cucumber pickles. See Pickles, items 1558–1561.																	
	Currants, raw: [69]																	
944	Black, European	84.2	54	1.7	.1	13.1	2.4	.9	60	40	1.1	3	372	230	.05	.05	.3	200
945	Red and white	85.7	50	1.4	.2	12.1	3.4	.6	32	23	1.0	2	257	[70] 120	.04	(.05)	.1	41
	Cusk:																	
946	Raw	81.3	75	17.2	.2	0	0	.9	—	—	—	—	—	—	.03	.08	2.3	—
947	Cooked, steamed	74.3	106	23.4	.7	0	0	—	27	283	1.0	74	386	—	.03	.10	2.7	—
948	**Custard, baked**	77.2	115	5.4	5.5	11.1	0	.8	112	117	.4	79	146	350	.04	.19	.1	Trace
	Custard, frozen. See Ice cream, items 1139–1141.																	
	Custard dessert mix. See Pudding mixes, item 1829.																	
949	**Custardapple, bullocksheart,** raw	71.5	101	1.7	.6	25.2	3.4	1.0	27	20	.8	—	—	Trace	.08	.10	.5	22
	Daikon. See Radishes, oriental: item 1845.																	
	Dandelion greens:																	
950	Raw	85.6	45	2.7	.7	9.2	1.6	1.8	187	66	3.1	76	397	14,000	.19	.26	—	35
951	Cooked, boiled, drained	89.8	33	2.0	.6	6.4	1.3	1.2	140	42	1.8	44	232	11,700	.13	.16	—	18
	Danish pastry. See Rolls and buns, item 1899.																	
	Dasheens. See Taros, items 2271–2272.																	
952	**Dates,** domestic, natural and dry	22.5	274	2.2	.5	72.9	2.3	1.9	59	63	3.0	1	648	50	.09	.10	2.2	0
	Deviled ham. See Sausage, cold cuts, and luncheon meats: item 1993.																	
	Dewberries. See Blackberries, item 417.																	
	Dock (curly or narrowleaf dock, broadleaf dock, and sheep sorrel):																	
953	Raw	90.9	28	2.1	.3	5.6	.8	1.1	66	41	1.6	5	338	12,900	.09	.22	.5	119
954	Cooked, boiled, drained	93.6	19	1.6	.2	3.9	.7	.7	55	26	.9	3	198	10,800	.06	.13	.4	54
955	**Dogfish, spiny** (grayfish), raw	72.3	156	17.6	9.0	0	0	1.0	—	—	—	—	—	—	.05	—	—	—
956	**Dolly Varden,** raw	73.1	144	19.9	6.5	0	0	1.2	—	—	—	—	—	—	.06	.06	—	—
	Doughnuts:																	
957	Cake type	23.7	391	4.6	18.6	51.4	.1	1.7	40	190	[71] 1.4	501	90	80	[71] .16	[71] .16	[71] 1.2	Trace
958	Yeast-leavened	28.3	414	6.3	26.7	37.7	.2	1.0	38	76	[72] 1.5	234	80	60	[72] .16	[72] .17	[72] 1.3	0
959	**Drum, freshwater,** raw	77.0	121	17.3	5.2	0	0	1.0	—	—	—	70	286	—	—	—	—	—
960	**Drum, red** (redfish), raw	80.2	80	18.0	.4	0	0	1.3	—	—	—	55	273	—	.15	.05	3.5	—

[9] Estimated average based on addition of salt in the amount of 0.6 percent of the finished product.

[15] Average weighted in accordance with commercial practices in freezing vegetables.

[47] For further description of product, see Notes on Foods, p. 178.

[57] Based on yellow varieties; white varieties contain only a trace of cryptoxanthin and carotenes, the pigments in corn that have biological activity.

[59] Based on product with minimum level of enrichment.

[62] Based on mix made with enriched yellow degermed cornmeal. With unenriched cornmeal, approximate values per 100 grams are: Iron, 1.0 mg.; thiamine, 0.08 mg.; riboflavin, 0.06 mg.; niacin, 0.7 mg. If white cornmeal is used, vitamin A value is 160 I.U. per 100 grams.

[63] Based on mix made with enriched yellow degermed cornmeal. With unenriched cornmeal, approximate values per 100 grams are: Iron, 0.6 mg.; thiamine, 0.05 mg.; riboflavin, 0.14 mg.; niacin, 0.3 mg. If white cornmeal is used, vitamin A value is 210 I.U. per 100 grams.

[64] Value applies to unenriched product. Much of the self-rising cornmeal on the market is enriched. For enriched products, minimum values per 100 grams are: Iron, 2.9 mg.; thiamine, 0.44 mg.; riboflavin, 0.26 mg.; niacin, 3.5 mg.

[65] Amount of potassium contributed by cornmeal and flour. Small quantities of additional potassium may be provided by other ingredients.

[66] Prepared with bread cubes, butter, parsley, eggs, lemon juice, and catsup.

[67] Prepared with butter, flour, milk, onion, green pepper, eggs, and lemon juice.

[68] About 2 mg. per 100 grams is from cranberries. Ascorbic acid is usually added to approximately 40 mg. per 100 grams.

[69] Production of the European black currant in particular, and, to less extent, of other currants and of gooseberries, is restricted by Federal or State regulations that prohibit shipments of the plants to certain designated States and areas within some States. The regulations have been enacted to prevent further spread of the whitepine blister rust inasmuch as these plants are alternate hosts of this disease.

[70] Based on red currants only.

[71] Based on product made with enriched flour. With unenriched flour, approximate values per 100 grams are: Iron, 0.5 mg.; thiamine, 0.03 mg.; riboflavin, 0.06 mg.; niacin, 0.3 mg.

[72] Based on product made with enriched flour. With unenriched flour, approximate values per 100 grams are: Iron, 0.6 mg.; thiamine, 0.04 mg.; riboflavin, 0.08 mg.; niacin, 0.5 mg.

TABLE 1.—COMPOSITION OF FOODS, 100 GRAMS, EDIBLE PORTION—Continued

[Numbers in parentheses denote values imputed—usually from another form of the food or from a similar food. Zero in parentheses indicates that the amount of a constituent probably is none or is too small to measure. Dashes denote lack of reliable data for a constituent believed to be present in measurable amount. Calculated values, as those based on a recipe, are not in parentheses]

Item No.	Food and description	Water	Food energy	Protein	Fat	Carbohydrate		Ash	Calcium	Phosphorus	Iron	Sodium	Potassium	Vitamin A value	Thiamine	Riboflavin	Niacin	Ascorbic acid
						Total	Fiber											
(A)	(B)	(C)	(D)	(E)	(F)	(G)	(H)	(I)	(J)	(K)	(L)	(M)	(N)	(O)	(P)	(Q)	(R)	(S)
		Percent	Calories	Grams	Grams	Grams	Grams	Grams	Milligrams	Milligrams	Milligrams	Milligrams	Milligrams	International units	Milligrams	Milligrams	Milligrams	Milligrams
	Duck, domesticated, raw:																	
961	Total edible	54.3	326	16.0	28.6	0	0	1.0	(10)	(176)	(1.6)	—	—	—	(0.08)	(0.19)	(6.7)	—
962	Flesh only	68.8	165	21.4	8.2	0	0	1.2	(12)	(203)	(1.3)	74	285	—	(.10)	(.12)	(7.7)	—
	Duck, wild, raw:																	
963	Total edible	61.1	233	21.1	15.8	0	0	1.1	—	—	—	—	—	—	—	—	—	—
964	Flesh only	70.8	138	21.3	5.2	0	0	1.3	—	—	—	—	—	—	—	—	—	—
965	**Eclairs** with custard filling and chocolate icing	56.2	239	6.2	13.6	23.2	Trace	.8	80	112	.7	82	122	340	.04	.16	.1	Trace
966	**Eel,** American, raw	64.6	233	15.9	18.3	0	0	1.0	18	202	.7	—	—	1,610	.22	.36	1.4	—
967	**Eel, smoked**	50.2	330	18.6	27.8	0	0	2.4	—	—	—	—	—	—	—	—	—	—
	Eggs:																	
	Chicken:																	
	Raw:																	
968	Whole, fresh, and frozen	73.7	163	12.9	11.5	.9	0	1.0	54	205	2.3	122	129	1,180	.11	.30	.1	0
969	Whites, fresh, and frozen	87.6	51	10.9	Trace	.8	0	.7	9	15	.1	146	139	0	Trace	.27	.1	0
970	Yolks, fresh [73]	51.1	348	16.0	30.6	.6	0	1.7	141	569	5.5	52	98	3,400	.22	.44	.1	0
971	Yolks, frozen [73]	55.5	312	15.4	26.9	.6	0	1.6	125	502	4.9	63	100	2,990	.20	.42	.1	0
972	Yolks, frozen, sugared	50.7	315	14.3	24.0	9.9	0	1.1	113	455	4.4	57	91	2,710	.18	.38	.1	0
	Cooked:																	
973	Fried	67.7	216	13.8	17.2	.3	0	1.0	60	222	2.4	338	140	1,420	.10	.30	.1	0
974	Hard-cooked	73.7	163	12.9	11.5	.9	0	1.0	54	205	2.3	122	129	1,180	.09	.28	.1	0
975	Omelet	72.1	173	11.2	12.9	2.4	0	1.4	80	189	1.7	257	146	1,080	.08	.28	.1	0
976	Poached	73.3	163	12.7	11.6	.8	0	1.4	55	203	2.2	271	128	1,170	.08	.25	.1	0
977	Scrambled	72.1	173	11.2	12.9	2.4	0	1.4	80	189	1.7	257	146	1,080	.08	.28	.1	0
	Dried:																	
978	Whole	4.1	592	47.0	41.2	4.1	0	3.6	187	800	8.7	427	463	4,290	.33	1.20	.2	0
979	Whole, stabilized (glucose reduced)	2.0	609	48.9	42.9	2.5	0	3.7	194	832	9.0	444	482	4,460	.34	1.25	.2	0
980	White, flakes	14.6	349	75.1	.2	5.3	0	4.8	62	103	1.0	1,033	937	0	.04	1.87	.7	0
981	White, powder	8.8	37?	80.2	.2	5.7	0	5.1	66	110	1.0	1,103	1,000	0	.04	1.99	.7	0
982	Yolk	4.5	664	33.2	56.6	2.5	0	3.2	275	1,109	10.8	100	186	5,980	.41	.86	.1	0
983	Duck, whole, fresh, raw	70.4	191	13.3	14.5	.7	0	1.1	56	195	2.8	(122)	(129)	1,230	.18	(.30)	.1	0
984	Goose, whole, fresh, raw	70.4	185	13.9	13.3	1.3	0	1.1	—	—	—	—	—	—	—	—	—	—
985	Turkey, whole, fresh, raw	72.6	170	13.1	11.8	1.7	0	.8	—	—	—	—	—	—	—	—	Trace	—
	Eggplant:																	
986	Raw	92.4	25	1.2	.2	5.6	.9	.6	12	26	.7	2	214	10	.05	.05	.6	5
987	Cooked, boiled, drained	94.3	19	1.0	.2	4.1	.9	.4	11	21	.6	1	150	10	.05	.04	.5	3
988	**Elderberries,** raw	79.8	72	2.6	(.5)	16.4	7.0	.7	38	28	1.6	—	300	600	.07	.06	.5	36
989	**Endive** (curly endive and escarole), raw	93.1	20	1.7	.1	4.1	.9	1.0	81	54	1.7	14	294	3,300	.07	.14	.5	10
	Escarole, raw. See Endive, item 989.																	
990	**Eulachon** (smelt), raw	79.6	118	14.6	6.2	0	0	1.2	—	—	—	—	—	—	.04	.04	—	—
	Farina:																	
	Enriched:																	
	Regular:																	
991	Dry form	10.3	371	11.4	.9	77.0	.4	.4	25	107	[74] 2.9	2	83	(0)	[74] .44	[74] .26	[74] 3.5	(0)
992	Cooked	89.5	42	1.3	.1	8.7	Trace	.4	4	12	[74] .3	144	9	(0)	[74] .04	[74] .03	[74] .4	(0)
	Quick-cooking:																	
993	Dry form	10.3	362	11.4	.9	74.9	.4	2.5	500	561	([75])	250	83	(0)	[76] .44	[76] .26	[76] 3.5	(0)
994	Cooked	89.0	43	1.3	.1	8.9	Trace	.7	60	66	([75])	190	10	(0)	[76] .05	[76] .03	[76] .4	(0)
	Instant-cooking:																	
995	Dry form	10.3	362	11.4	.9	74.9	.4	2.5	500	396	([75])	7	83	(0)	[76] .44	[76] .26	[76] 3.5	(0)
996	Cooked	85.9	55	1.7	.1	11.4	.1	.9	77	60	([75])	188	13	(0)	[76] .07	[76] .04	[76] .5	(0)
	Unenriched, regular:																	
997	Dry form	10.3	371	11.4	.9	77.0	.4	.4	25	107	1.5	2	83	(0)	.06	.10	.7	(0)
998	Cooked	89.5	42	1.3	.1	8.7	Trace	.4	4	12	.2	144	9	(0)	.01	.01	.1	(0)
999	**Fats,** cooking (vegetable fat)	0	884	0	100.	0	0	0	0	0	0	0	0	—	0	0	0	0
1000	**Fennel,** common, leaves, raw	90.0	28	2.8	.4	5.1	.5	1.7	100	51	2.7	—	397	3,500	—	—	—	31
	Figs:																	
1001	Raw	77.5	80	1.2	.3	20.3	1.2	.7	35	22	.6	2	194	80	.06	.05	.4	2
1002	Candied	21.0	299	3.5	.2	73.7	—	1.6	—	—	—	—	—	—	—	—	—	—
	Canned, solids and liquid:																	
1003	Water pack, with or without artificial sweetener	86.6	48	.5	.2	12.4	.7	.3	14	14	.4	2	155	30	.03	.03	.2	1
	Sirup pack:																	
1004	Light	82.2	65	.5	.2	16.8	.7	.3	13	13	.4	2	152	30	.03	.03	.2	1
1005	Heavy	77.2	84	.5	.2	21.8	.7	.3	13	13	.4	2	149	30	.03	.03	.2	1
1006	Extra heavy	72.3	103	.5	.2	26.7	.6	.3	13	13	.4	2	146	30	.03	.03	.2	1
1007	Dried, uncooked	23.0	274	4.3	1.3	69.1	5.6	2.3	126	77	3.0	34	640	80	.10	.10	.7	(0)

1008	**Filberts** (hazelnuts)	5.8	634	12.6	62.4	16.7	3.0	2.5	209	337	3.4	2	704	—	.46	—	.9	Trace
1009	**Finnan haddie** (smoked haddock)	72.6	103	23.2	.4	0	0	3.1	—	—	—	—	—	—	.06	.05	2.1	—
	Fish. See individual kinds; Cod, etc. Also see table 13, page 183.																	
	Fish cakes, cooked:																	
1010	Fried [77]	66.0	172	14.7	8.0	9.3	—	2.0	—	—	—	—	—	—	—	—	—	—
1011	Frozen, fried, reheated	52.9	270	9.2	17.9	17.2	—	2.8	—	—	—	—	—	—	—	—	—	—
1012	**Fish flakes,** canned	72.1	111	24.7	.6	0	0	2.6	49	232	.8	—	—	—	—	—	—	—
	Fish flour:																	
1013	From whole fish	2.0	336	78.0	.3	0	—	19.7	4,610	3,100	41.0	170	430	—	.07	62	2.2	—
1014	From fillets	3.0	398	93.0	.1	0	0	3.9	920	610	8.0	40	80	—	—	—	—	—
1015	From fillet waste	3.0	305	71.0	.2	0	0	25.8	6,040	4,060	54.0	220	540	—	—	—	—	—
1016	**Fish loaf,** cooked [78]	72.2	124	14.1	3.7	7.3	—	2.7	—	—	—	—	—	—	—	—	—	—
1017	**Fish sticks,** frozen, cooked	65.8	176	16.6	8.9	6.5	—	2.2	11	167	.4	—	—	0	.04	.07	1.6	—
1018	**Flatfishes** (flounders, soles, and sanddabs), raw	81.3	79	16.7	.8	0	0	1.2	12	195	.8	78	342	—	.05	.05	1.7	—
1019	**Flounder,** cooked, baked	58.1	202	30.0	8.2	0	0	2.2	23	344	1.4	237	587	—	.07	.08	2.5	2
	Flour. See Corn, Rice, Rye, Soya, Wheat.																	
	Frankfurters. See Sausage, cold cuts, and luncheon meats: items 1994–2000.																	
1020	**Frog legs,** raw	81.9	73	16.4	.3	0	0	1.1	18	147	1.5	—	—	0	.14	.25	1.2	—
	Frostings. See Cake icings, items 570–579.																	
	Frozen custard. See Ice cream, items 1139–1141.																	
	Fruit cocktail, canned, solids and liquid:																	
1021	Water pack, with or without artificial sweetener	89.6	37	.4	.1	9.7	.4	.2	9	13	.4	5	168	150	.02	.01	.5	2
	Sirup pack:																	
1022	Light	83.6	60	.4	.1	15.7	.4	.2	9	12	.4	5	164	140	.02	.01	.5	2
1023	Heavy	79.6	76	.4	.1	19.7	.4	.2	9	12	.4	5	161	140	.02	.01	.4	2
1024	Extra heavy	75.6	92	.4	.1	23.7	.4	.2	9	12	.4	5	159	140	.01	.01	.4	2
	Fruit salad, canned, solids and liquid:																	
1025	Water pack, with or without artificial sweetener	90.1	35	.4	.1	9.1	.5	.3	8	11	.3	1	139	470	.01	.03	.6	3
	Sirup pack:																	
1026	Light	83.9	59	.3	.1	15.5	.4	.2	8	11	.3	1	136	460	.01	.03	.6	2
1027	Heavy	80.0	75	.3	.1	19.4	.4	.2	8	11	.3	1	134	450	.01	.03	.6	2
1028	Extra heavy	76.0	90	.3	.1	23.4	.4	.2	8	11	.3	1	131	450	.01	.03	.6	2
	Garbanzos. See Chickpeas, item 753.																	
1029	**Garlic,** cloves, raw	61.3	137	6.2	.2	30.8	1.5	1.5	29	202	1.5	19	529	Trace	.25	.08	.5	15
1030	**Gelatin,** dry	13.0	335	85.6	.1	0	0	1.3	—	—	—	—	—	—	—	—	—	—
	Gelatin dessert powder and desserts made from dessert powder:																	
1031	Dessert powder	1.6	371	9.4	0	88.0	0	1.0	—	—	—	318	—	—	—	—	—	—
	Desserts, made with water:																	
1032	Plain	84.2	59	1.5	0	14.1	0	.2	—	—	—	51	—	—	—	—	—	—
1033	With fruit added	81.8	67	1.3	.1	16.4	.2	.4	—	—	—	34	—	—	—	—	—	3
	Gin. See Beverages, items 395–399.																	
	Ginger ale. See Beverages, item 407.																	
	Gingerbread. See Cakes, item 533; Cake mixes, items 560–561.																	
1034	**Ginger root, crystallized** (candied)	12.0	340	.3	.2	87.1	.7	.4	—	—	—	—	—	—	—	—	—	—
1035	**Ginger root, fresh**	87.0	49	1.4	1.0	9.5	1.1	1.1	23	36	2.1	6	264	10	.02	.04	.7	4
	Gizzard:																	
	Chicken, all classes:																	
1036	Raw	75.0	113	20.1	2.7	.7	0	1.5	10	105	2.9	65	240	—	.03	.20	4.5	—
1037	Cooked, simmered	68.0	148	27.0	3.3	.7	0	1.0	9	71	3.1	57	211	—	.02	.21	5.1	—
1038	Goose, raw	73.0	139	21.4	5.3	0	0	1.0	—	—	—	—	—	—	—	—	—	—
	Turkey, all classes:																	
1039	Raw	70.3	157	20.3	7.3	1.1	0	1.0	—	—	—	58	170	—	.05	.13	5.0	—
1040	Cooked, simmered	62.7	196	26.8	8.6	1.1	0	.7	—	—	—	51	149	—	.03	.14	5.8	—
	Gizzard shad. See Shad, gizzard: item 2038.																	
	Gluten flour. See Wheat flours, item 2444.																	
	Goat milk. See Milk, goat: item 1335.																	
	Goose, domesticated:																	
	Total edible:																	
1041	Raw	51.1	354	16.4	31.5	0	0	.9	(10)	(176)	(1.6)	—	—	—	(.08)	(.19)	(6.7)	—
1042	Cooked, roasted	39.1	426	23.7	36.0	0	0	1.2	(11)	(240)	(2.1)	—	—	—	(.08)	(.24)	(8.1)	—
	Flesh and skin:																	
1043	Raw	49.7	371	15.9	33.6	0	0	.9	(11)	(191)	(1.5)	—	—	—	(.08)	(.12)	(7.4)	—
1044	Cooked, roasted	37.9	441	22.9	38.1	0	0	1.2	(13)	(260)	(1.9)	—	—	—	(.09)	(.16)	(8.9)	—
	Flesh only:																	
1045	Raw	68.3	159	22.3	7.1	0	0	1.1	(12)	(203)	(1.3)	86	420	—	(.10)	(.12)	(7.7)	—
1046	Cooked, roasted	54.8	233	33.9	9.8	0	0	1.5	(14)	(277)	(1.7)	124	605	—	(.11)	(.16)	(9.3)	—
1047	Giblets, raw	69.9	156	21.1	7.0	.6	0	1.4	—	—	—	—	—	—	—	—	—	—

[73] Fresh yolks include a small proportion of white; frozen yolks, a considerable amount.

[74] Based on products with minimum level of enrichment. In several brands, however, values for iron range from 2.8 to 7.1 mg. per 100 grams, corresponding to 0.3 to 0.8 mg. per 100 grams cooked form.

[75] Value of 42.4 mg. per 100 grams reported for one brand; corresponding values per 100 grams cooked form are 5.0 mg. for quick-cooking and 6.4 mg. for instant farina.

[76] Based on product with minimum level of enrichment. See Notes on Foods, p. 171.

[77] Prepared with canned flaked fish, potato, and egg.

[78] Prepared with canned flaked fish, bread cubes, eggs, tomatoes, onion, and fat.

TABLE 1.—COMPOSITION OF FOODS, 100 GRAMS, EDIBLE PORTION—Continued

[Numbers in parentheses denote values imputed—usually from another form of the food or from a similar food. Zero in parentheses indicates that the amount of a constituent probably is none or is too small to measure. Dashes denote lack of reliable data for a constituent believed to be present in measurable amount. Calculated values, as those based on a recipe, are not in parentheses]

Item No.	Food and description	Water	Food energy	Protein	Fat	Carbohydrate		Ash	Calcium	Phosphorus	Iron	Sodium	Potassium	Vitamin A value	Thiamine	Riboflavin	Niacin	Ascorbic acid
						Total	Fiber											
(A)	(B)	(C)	(D)	(E)	(F)	(G)	(H)	(I)	(J)	(K)	(L)	(M)	(N)	(O)	(P)	(Q)	(R)	(S)
		Percent	Calories	Grams	Grams	Grams	Grams	Grams	Milligrams	Milligrams	Milligrams	Milligrams	Milligrams	International units	Milligrams	Milligrams	Milligrams	Milligrams
	Gooseberries: [78]																	
1048	Raw	88.9	39	0.8	0.2	9.7	1.9	0.4	18	15	0.5	1	155	290	—	—	—	33
	Canned, solids and liquid:																	
1049	Water pack, with or without artificial sweetener	92.5	26	.5	.1	6.6	1.3	.3	12	10	.3	1	105	200	—	—	—	11
	Sirup pack:																	
1050	Heavy	76.1	90	.5	.1	23.0	1.2	.3	11	9	.3	1	98	190	—	—	—	10
1051	Extra heavy	69.2	117	.5	.1	30.0	1.2	.2	11	9	.3	1	95	180	—	—	—	10
	Gourd, dishcloth. See Towelgourd, item 2315.																	
1052	**Granadilla,** purple (passionfruit) pulp and seeds, raw.	75.1	90	2.2	.7	21.2	—	.8	13	64	1.6	28	348	700	Trace	0.13	1.5	30
	Grapefruit:																	
	Raw:																	
	Pulp:																	
	Pink, red, white:																	
1053	All varieties	88.4	41	.5	.1	10.6	.2	.4	16	16	.4	1	135	80	0.04	.02	.2	[79] 38
1054	California and Arizona (Marsh Seedless)	87.5	44	.5	.1	11.5	.2	.4	32	20	.4	1	135	10	.04	.02	.2	[79] 40
1055	Florida, all varieties	89.1	38	.5	.1	9.9	.2	.4	15	15	.4	1	135	80	.04	.02	.2	[79] 37
1056	Texas, all varieties	87.7	43	.5	.1	11.3	.2	.4	15	15	.4	1	135	([80])	.04	.02	.2	38
	Pink and red:																	
1057	Seeded (Foster Pink)	88.6	40	.5	.1	10.4	.2	.4	16	16	.4	1	135	440	.04	.02	.2	[79] 39
1058	Seedless (including Pink Marsh, Redblush)	88.6	40	.5	.1	10.4	.2	.4	16	16	.4	1	135	440	.04	.02	.2	[79] 36
	White:																	
1059	Seeded (Duncan, other varieties)	88.2	41	.5	.1	10.8	.2	.4	16	16	.4	1	135	10	.04	.02	.2	[79] 38
1060	Seedless (Marsh Seedless)	88.9	39	.5	.1	10.1	.2	.4	16	16	.4	1	135	10	.04	.02	.2	[79] 37
	Juice:																	
	Pink, red, and white:																	
1061	All varieties	90.0	39	.5	.1	9.2	Trace	.2	9	15	.2	1	162	80	.04	.02	.2	[79] 38
1062	California and Arizona (Marsh Seedless)	89.0	42	.4	.1	10.2	Trace	.3	9	15	.2	1	162	10	.04	.02	.2	[79] 40
1063	Florida, all varieties	90.4	37	.5	.1	8.8	Trace	.2	9	15	.2	1	162	80	.04	.02	.2	[79] 37
1064	Texas, all varieties	89.2	42	.5	.1	10.0	Trace	.2	9	15	.2	1	162	([80])	.04	.02	.2	38
	Pink and red:																	
1065	Seeded (Foster Pink)	90.0	38	.5	.1	9.1	Trace	.3	9	15	.2	1	162	440	.04	.02	.2	[79] 39
1066	Seedless (including Pink Marsh, Redblush)	90.0	39	.4	.1	9.3	Trace	.2	9	15	.2	1	162	440	.04	.02	.2	[79] 36
	White:																	
1067	Seeded (Duncan, other varieties)	89.6	40	.5	.1	9.5	Trace	.3	9	15	.2	1	162	10	.04	.02	.2	[79] 38
1068	Seedless (Marsh Seedless)	90.2	38	.5	.1	9.0	Trace	.2	9	15	.2	1	162	10	.04	.02	.2	[79] 37
	Canned:																	
	Segments, solids and liquid:																	
1069	Water pack, with or without artificial sweetener.	91.3	30	.6	.1	7.6	.2	.4	13	14	.3	4	144	10	.03	.02	.2	30
1070	Sirup pack	81.1	70	.6	.1	17.8	.2	.4	13	14	.3	1	135	10	.03	.02	.2	30
	Juice:																	
1071	Unsweetened	89.2	41	.5	.1	9.8	Trace	.4	8	14	.4	1	162	10	.03	.02	.2	34
1072	Sweetened	86.2	53	.5	.1	12.8	Trace	.4	8	14	.4	1	162	10	.03	.02	.2	31
	Frozen concentrated juice:																	
	Unsweetened:																	
1073	Undiluted	62.	145	1.9	.4	34.6	.1	1.1	34	60	.4	4	604	30	.14	.06	.7	138
1074	Diluted with 3 parts water, by volume	89.3	41	.5	.1	9.8	Trace	.3	10	17	.1	1	170	10	.04	.02	.2	39
	Sweetened:																	
1075	Undiluted	57.	165	1.6	.3	40.2	.1	.9	28	50	.3	3	508	20	.12	.05	.6	116
1076	Diluted with 3 parts water, by volume	87.8	47	.4	.1	11.4	Trace	.3	8	14	.1	1	144	10	.03	.01	.2	33
	Dehydrated juice (crystals):																	
1077	Dry form	1.0	378	4.8	1.0	90.3	.4	2.9	87	155	1.0	10	1,572	80	.36	.16	1.7	350
1078	Prepared with water (1 lb. yields approx. 1 gal.)	89.5	40	.5	.1	9.6	Trace	.3	9	16	.1	1	167	10	.04	.02	.2	37
	Grapefruit juice and orange juice blended:																	
	Canned:																	
1079	Unsweetened	88.7	43	.6	.2	10.1	.1	.4	10	15	.3	1	184	100	.05	.02	.2	34
1080	Sweetened	86.9	50	.5	.1	12.2	.1	.4	10	15	.3	1	184	100	.05	.02	.2	34
	Frozen concentrate, unsweetened:																	
1081	Undiluted	59.1	157	2.1	.5	37.1	.1	1.2	29	47	.4	2	623	380	.23	.03	1.1	144
1082	Diluted with 3 parts water, by volume	88.4	44	.6	.1	10.5	Trace	.4	8	13	.1	Trace	177	110	.06	.01	.3	41
1083	**Grapefruit peel, candied**	17.4	316	.4	.3	80.6	2.3	1.3	—	—	—	—	—	—	—	—	—	—
	Grapes:																	
	Raw:																	
1084	American type (slip skin) as Concord, Delaware, Niagara, Catawba, and Scuppernong.	81.6	69	1.3	1.0	15.7	.6	.4	16	12	.4	3	158	100	(.05)	(.03)	(.3)	4

No.	Food																	
1085	European type (adherent skin) as Malaga, Muscat, Thompson Seedless, Emperor, and Flame Tokay.	81.4	67	.6	.3	17.3	.5	.4	12	20	.4	3	173	(100)	.05	.03	.3	4
	Canned:																	
	Thompson Seedless, solids and liquid:																	
1086	Water pack, with or without artificial sweetener.	85.5	51	.5	.1	13.6	.2	.3	8	13	.3	4	110	70	.04	.01	.2	2
1087	Sirup pack, heavy	79.1	77	.5	.1	20.0	.2	.3	8	13	.3	4	105	70	.04	.01	.2	2
	Grapejuice:																	
1088	Canned or bottled	82.9	66	.2	Trace	16.6	Trace	.3	11	12	.3	2	116	—	.04	.02	.2	Trace
	Frozen concentrate, sweetened:																	
1089	Undiluted	52.8	183	.6	Trace	46.3	.1	.3	10	15	.4	3	118	20	.06	.10	.7	15
1090	Diluted with 3 parts water, by volume	86.4	53	.2	Trace	13.3	Trace	.1	3	4	.1	1	34	Trace	.02	.03	.2	4
1091	**Grapejuice drink,** canned (approx. 30% grapejuice) [81]	86.0	54	.1	Trace	13.8	Trace	.1	3	4	.1	1	35	—	.01	.01	.1	16
	Griddlecakes. See Pancakes, items 1453–1462.																	
	Grits. See Corn grits, items 862–865.																	
1092	**Groundcherries** (poha or cape-gooseberries), raw	85.4	53	1.9	.7	11.2	2.8	.8	9	40	1.0	—	—	720	.11	.04	2.8	11
1093	**Grouper,** including red, black, and speckled hind; raw	79.2	87	19.3	.5	0	0	1.2	—	—	—	—	—	—	.17	—	—	—
	Guavas, whole, raw:																	
1094	Common	83.0	62	.8	.6	15.0	5.6	.6	23	42	.9	4	289	280	.05	.05	1.2	[82] 242
1095	Strawberry	81.8	65	1.0	.6	15.8	6.4	.8	(23)	(42)	(.9)	(4)	(289)	90	.03	.03	.6	37
	Guinea hen, raw:																	
1096	Total edible	69.0	156	23.1	6.4	0	0	1.2	—	—	—	—	—	—	—	—	—	—
1097	Flesh and skin	68.9	158	23.4	6.4	0	0	1.2	—	—	—	—	—	—	—	—	—	—
1098	Giblets	69.8	157	20.8	7.0	1.2	0	1.2	—	—	—	—	—	—	—	—	—	—
	Haddock:																	
1099	Raw	80.5	79	18.3	.1	0	0	1.4	23	197	.7	61	304	—	.04	.07	3.0	—
1100	Cooked, fried [83]	66.3	165	19.6	6.4	5.8	—	1.9	40	247	1.2	177	348	—	.04	.07	3.2	2
1101	Smoked, canned or not canned	72.6	103	23.2	.4	0	0	3.1	—	—	—	—	—	—	.06	.05	4.2	—
1102	**Hake,** including Pacific hake, squirrel hake, and silver hake or whiting; raw.	81.8	74	16.5	.4	0	0	1.3	41	142	—	74	363	—	.10	.20	—	—
	Halibut, Atlantic and Pacific:																	
1103	Raw	76.5	100	20.9	1.2	0	0	1.4	13	211	.7	[84] 54	449	440	.07	.07	8.3	—
1104	Cooked, broiled	66.6	171	25.2	7.0	0	0	1.7	16	248	.8	134	525	680	.05	.07	8.3	—
1105	Smoked	49.4	224	20.8	15.0	0	0	15.0	—	—	—	—	—	—	—	—	—	—
1106	**Halibut, California,** raw	77.8	97	19.8	1.4	0	0	1.3	—	—	—	—	—	—	—	—	—	—
1107	**Halibut, Greenland,** raw	74.5	146	16.4	8.4	0	0	1.0	—	210	—	—	—	—	.01	—	—	—
	Ham. See Pork, items 1693–1707, 1765–1772, 1783.																	
1108	**Ham croquette**	54.0	251	16.3	15.1	11.7	.1	2.9	69	160	2.1	342	83	260	.28	.22	2.5	Trace
	Hamburger. See Beef, items 367-370.																	
1109	**Haws, scarlet,** flesh and skin, raw	75.8	87	2.0	.7	20.8	2.1	.8	—	—	—	—	—	—	—	—	—	—
	Hazelnuts. See Filberts, item 1008.																	
	Headcheese. See Sausage, cold cuts, and luncheon meats: item 2001.																	
	Heart:																	
	Beef, lean:																	
1110	Raw	77.5	108	17.1	3.6	.7	0	1.1	5	195	4.0	86	193	20	.53	.88	7.5	2
1111	Cooked, braised	61.3	188	31.3	5.7	.7	0	1.1	6	181	5.9	104	232	30	.25	1.22	7.6	1
	Beef, lean with visible fat:																	
1112	Raw	63.0	253	15.4	20.7	.1	0	.8	—	182	—	—	—	—	—	—	—	—
1113	Cooked, braised	44.4	372	25.8	29.0	.1	0	.8	—	169	—	—	—	—	—	—	—	—
	Calf:																	
1114	Raw	76.2	124	15.0	5.9	1.8	0	1.1	3	160	3.0	94	208	30	.63	1.05	8.1	1
1115	Cooked, braised	60.3	208	27.8	9.1	1.8	0	1.0	4	148	4.4	113	250	40	.29	1.44	8.1	Trace
	Chicken, all classes:																	
1116	Raw	74.3	134	18.6	6.0	.1	0	1.0	4	158	3.3	79	159	(30)	.06	.80	4.6	4
1117	Cooked, simmered	66.7	173	25.3	7.2	.1	0	.8	4	107	3.6	69	140	(30)	.06	.92	5.3	4
	Hog:																	
1118	Raw	77.4	113	16.8	4.4	.4	0	1.0	3	131	3.3	54	106	30	.43	1.24	6.6	3
1119	Cooked, braised	61.0	195	30.8	6.9	.3	0	1.0	4	121	4.9	65	128	40	.20	1.72	6.7	1
	Lamb:																	
1120	Raw	71.6	162	16.8	9.6	1.0	0	1.0	11	249	—	—	—	70	.45	.74	6.3	1
1121	Cooked, braised	54.1	260	29.5	14.4	1.0	0	.9	14	231	—	—	—	100	.21	1.03	6.4	Trace
	Turkey, all classes:																	
1122	Raw	71.3	171	16.2	11.2	.2	0	1.1	—	—	—	69	240	(30)	.23	.86	5.0	(4)
1123	Cooked, simmered	63.2	216	22.6	13.2	.2	0	.8	—	—	—	61	211	(30)	.25	.98	5.7	(4)

[78] Production of the European black currant in particular, and, to less extent, of other currants and of gooseberries, is restricted by Federal or State regulations that prohibit shipments of the plants to certain designated States and areas within some States. The regulations have been enacted to prevent further spread of the whitepine blister rust inasmuch as these plants are alternate hosts of this disease.

[79] Value weighted by monthly and total season shipments for marketing as fresh fruit.

[80] For white-fleshed varieties, value is about 10 I.U. per 100 grams; for red-fleshed, about 440 I.U.

[81] Fruit juice content ranges from 10 to 50 percent. Ascorbic acid may be added as a preservative or as a nutrient. Value listed is based on product with label stating 30 mg. per 6 fl. oz. serving. If label claim is 30 mg. per 8 fl. oz. serving, values would be 12 mg. per 100 grams. If thiamine and riboflavin have been added, the values expected would be 0.20 mg. and 0.24 mg. per 100 grams.

[82] Average for varieties grown in the United States; range is wide, from 23 to 1,160 mg. per 100 grams.

[83] Dipped in egg, milk, and breadcrumbs.

[84] Two frozen samples dipped in brine contained 360 mg. sodium per 100 grams.

TABLE 1.—COMPOSITION OF FOODS, 100 GRAMS, EDIBLE PORTION—Continued

[Numbers in parentheses denote values imputed—usually from another form of the food or from a similar food. Zero in parentheses indicates that the amount of a constituent probably is none or is too small to measure. Dashes denote lack of reliable data for a constituent believed to be present in measurable amount. Calculated values, as those based on a recipe, are not in parentheses]

Item No.	Food and description	Water	Food energy	Protein	Fat	Carbohydrate		Ash	Calcium	Phosphorus	Iron	Sodium	Potassium	Vitamin A value	Thiamine	Riboflavin	Niacin	Ascorbic acid
						Total	Fiber											
(A)	(B)	(C)	(D)	(E)	(F)	(G)	(H)	(I)	(J)	(K)	(L)	(M)	(N)	(O)	(P)	(Q)	(R)	(S)
		Percent	Calories	Grams	Grams	Grams	Grams	Grams	Milligrams	Milligrams	Milligrams	Milligrams	Milligrams	International units	Milligrams	Milligrams	Milligrams	Milligrams
	Herring. (See also Lake herring, item 1168.)																	
	Raw:																	
1124	Atlantic	69.0	176	17.3	11.3	0	0	2.1	—	256	1.1	—	—	110	0.02	0.15	3.6	—
1125	Pacific	79.4	98	17.5	2.6	0	0	1.2	—	225	1.3	74	420	100	.02	.16	3.5	3
	Canned, solids and liquid:																	
1126	Plain	62.9	208	19.9	13.6	0	0	3.7	147	297	1.8	—	—	—	—	.18	—	—
1127	In tomato sauce	66.7	176	15.8	10.5	3.7	—	3.3	—	243	—	—	—	—	—	.11	3.5	—
1128	Pickled, Bismarck type	59.4	223	20.4	15.1	0	0	4.0	—	—	—	—	—	—	—	—	—	—
1129	Salted or brined	53.8	218	19.0	15.2	0	0	12.0	—	—	—	—	—	—	—	.19	—	—
	Smoked:																	
1130	Bloaters	64.0	196	19.6	12.4	0	0	3.2	—	—	—	—	—	—	—	—	—	—
1131	Hard	34.6	300	36.9	15.8	0	0	13.2	—	—	—	6,231	157	—	—	—	—	—
1132	Kippered	61.0	211	22.2	12.9	0	0	4.0	66	254	1.4	—	—	30	—	.28	3.3	—
1133	**Hickorynuts**	3.3	673	13.2	68.7	12.8	1.9	2.0	Trace	360	2.4	—	—	—	—	—	—	—
	Hominy grits, dry. See Corn grits, items 862–865.																	
1134	**Honey,** strained or extracted	17.2	304	.3	0	82.3	—	.2	5	6	.5	5	51	0	Trace	.04	.3	1
	Honeydew melon. See Muskmelons, item 1360.																	
	Horseradish:																	
1135	Raw	74.6	87	3.2	.3	19.7	2.4	2.2	140	64	1.4	8	564	—	.07	—	—	81
1136	Prepared	87.1	38	1.3	.2	9.6	.9	1.8	61	32	.9	96	290	—	—	—	—	—
	Hyacinth-beans, raw:																	
1137	Young pods	88.8	35	2.8	.3	7.3	1.8	.8	57	53	1.0	2	285	580	.09	.11	.9	20
1138	Mature seeds, dry	11.8	338	22.2	1.5	61.0	6.9	3.5	73	418	5.1	—	—	—	.62	.18	2.1	—
	Ice cream and frozen custard: [85]																	
	Regular:																	
1139	Approximately 10% fat	63.2	193	4.5	10.6	20.8	0	.9	146	115	.1	[86] 63	181	440	.04	.21	.1	1
1140	Approximately 12% fat	62.1	207	4.0	12.5	20.6	0	.8	123	99	.1	[86] 40	112	520	.04	.19	.1	1
1141	Rich, approximately 16% fat	62.8	222	2.6	16.1	18.0	0	.5	78	61	Trace	[86] 33	95	660	.02	.11	.1	1
1142	**Ice cream cones**	8.9	377	10.0	2.4	77.9	.2	.8	156	198	.4	232	244	Trace	.05	.21	.5	Trace
1143	**Ice milk**	66.7	152	4.8	5.1	22.4	0	1.0	156	124	.1	[86] 68	195	210	.05	.22	.1	1
1144	**Ices,** water, lime	66.9	78	.4	Trace	32.6	Trace	Trace	Trace	Trace	Trace	Trace	3	0	Trace	Trace	Trace	1
	Icings and icing mixes. See Cake icings and Cake icing mixes, items 570–579.																	
1145	**Inconnu** (sheefish), raw	72.0	146	19.9	6.8	0	0	1.3	—	—	—	—	—	—	—	—	—	—
1146	**Jack mackerel,** raw	71.4	143	21.6	5.6	0	0	1.2	—	—	—	—	—	—	—	—	—	—
1147	**Jackfruit,** raw	72.0	98	1.3	.3	25.4	1.0	1.0	22	38	—	2	407	—	.03	—	.4	8
1148	**Jams and preserves**	29.	272	.6	.1	70.0	1.0	.3	20	9	1.0	12	88	10	.01	.03	.2	[87] 2
1149	**Jellies**	29.	273	.1	.1	70.6	0	.2	21	7	1.5	17	75	10	.01	.03	.2	[87] 4
1150	**Jerusalem-artichoke,** raw	79.8	([88])	2.3	.1	[8] 16.7	.8	1.1	14	78	3.4	—	—	20	.20	.06	1.3	4
	Jujube, common (Chinese date):																	
1151	Raw	70.2	105	1.2	.2	27.6	1.4	.8	29	37	.7	3	269	40	.02	.04	.9	69
1152	Dried	19.7	287	3.7	1.1	73.6	3.0	1.9	79	100	1.8	—	531	—	—	—	—	13
	Kale:																	
	Raw:																	
1153	Leaves, without stems, midribs	82.7	53	(6.0)	(.8)	9.0	—	(1.5)	249	93	2.7	(75)	(378)	10,000	.16	.26	2.1	186
1154	Leaves, including stems	87.5	38	4.2	.8	6.0	1.3	1.5	179	73	2.2	75	378	8,900	—	—	—	125
	Cooked, boiled, drained:																	
1155	Leaves, without stems, midribs	87.8	39	(4.5)	(.7)	6.1	—	(.9)	187	58	1.6	(43)	(221)	8,300	.10	.18	1.6	93
1156	Leaves, including stems	91.2	28	3.2	.7	4.0	1.1	.9	134	46	1.2	43	221	7,400	—	—	—	62
	Frozen:																	
1157	Not thawed	90.0	32	3.2	.5	5.5	.9	.8	134	50	1.1	26	241	8,200	.08	.18	.8	64
1158	Cooked, boiled, drained	90.5	31	3.0	.5	5.4	.9	.6	121	48	1.0	21	193	8,200	.06	.15	.7	38
	Kidneys:																	
	Beef:																	
1159	Raw	75.9	130	15.4	6.7	.9	0	1.1	11	219	7.4	176	225	690	.36	2.55	6.4	(15)
1160	Cooked, braised	53.0	252	33.0	12.0	.8	0	1.2	18	244	13.1	253	324	1,150	.51	4.82	10.7	—
1161	Calf, raw	77.4	113	16.6	4.6	.1	0	1.3	—	—	4.0	—	—	—	—	—	—	6
1162	Hog, raw	77.8	106	16.3	3.6	1.1	0	1.2	11	218	6.7	115	178	130	.58	1.73	9.8	12
1163	Lamb, raw	77.7	105	16.8	3.3	.9	0	1.3	13	218	7.6	200	230	690	.51	2.42	7.4	15
1164	**Kingfish;** southern, gulf, and northern (whiting); raw.	77.3	105	18.3	3.0	0	0	1.3	—	—	—	83	250	—	—	—	—	—
	Knockwurst. See Sausage, cold cuts, and luncheon meats: item 2002.																	
	Kohlrabi, thickened bulb-like stems:																	
1165	Raw	90.3	29	2.0	.1	6.6	1.0	1.0	41	51	.5	8	372	20	.06	.04	.3	66

1166	Cooked, boiled, drained	92.2	24	1.7	.1	5.3	1.0	.7	33	41	.3	6	260	20	.06	.03	.2	43
1167	**Kumquats**, raw	81.3	65	.9	.1	17.1	3.7	.6	63	23	.4	7	236	600	.08	.10	—	36
	Ladyfingers. See Cookies, item 822.																	
1168	**Lake herring** (cisco), raw	79.7	96	17.7	2.3	0	0	1.1	12	206	.5	47	319	—	.09	.10	3.3	—
1169	**Lake trout**, raw	70.6	168	18.3	10.0	0	0	1.1	—	238	.8	—	—	—	.09	.12	2.7	—
	Lake trout (siscowet), raw:																	
1170	Less than 6.5 lbs., round weight	64.9	241	14.3	19.9	0	0	.9	—	—	—	—	—	—	—	—	—	—
1171	6.5 lbs. and over, round weight	36.8	524	7.9	54.4	0	0	.6	—	—	—	—	—	—	—	—	—	—
	Lamb: [4]																	
	Carcass, raw:																	
	Total edible, including kidney and kidney fat:																	
1172	Prime grade (60% lean, 40% fat)	—	—	—	—	—	—	—	—	—	—	—	—	—	—	—	—	—
1173	Choice grade (67% lean, 33% fat)	—	—	—	—	—	—	—	—	—	—	—	—	—	—	—	—	—
1174	Good grade (70% lean, 30% fat)	—	—	—	—	—	—	—	—	—	—	—	—	—	—	—	—	—
	Composite of cuts (leg, loin, rib, and shoulder) trimmed to retail level:																	
1175	Prime grade (72% lean, 28% fat)	56.3	310	15.4	27.1	0	0	1.2	9	135	1.1			—	.14	.19	4.5	—
1176	Choice grade (77% lean, 23% fat)	61.0	263	16.5	21.3	0	0	1.2	10	147	1.2			—	.15	.20	4.8	—
1177	Good grade (79% lean, 21% fat)	62.5	247	16.8	19.4	0	0	1.3	10	151	1.3			—	.15	.21	4.9	—
	Separable fat:																	
	Raw. See individual cuts.																	
1178	Cooked	17.7	709	6.3	75.6	0	0	.4	—	—	—			—	—	—	—	—
	Retail cuts, trimmed to retail level:																	
	Leg:																	
	Prime grade:																	
	Total edible:																	
1179	Raw (79% lean, 21% fat)	60.8	262	16.9	21.0	0	0	1.3	10	152	1.3			—	.15	.21	4.9	—
1180	Cooked, roasted (79% lean, 21% fat)	50.4	319	23.9	24.0	0	0	1.7	10	195	1.6			—	.14	.25	5.2	—
	Separable lean:																	
1181	Raw	73.0	135	19.8	5.6	0	0	1.6	11	184	1.8			—	.18	.25	5.7	—
1182	Cooked, roasted	61.6	192	28.6	7.7	0	0	2.1	12	237	2.2			—	.16	.30	6.1	—
	Separable fat:																	
1183	Raw	15.8	730	5.9	78.1	0	0	.2	3	29	0			—	.05	.07	1.7	—
	Choice grade:																	
	Total edible:																	
1184	Raw (83% lean, 17% fat)	64.8	222	17.8	16.2	0	0	1.3	10	162	1.4			—	.16	.22	5.1	—
1185	Cooked, roasted (83% lean, 17% fat)	54.0	279	25.3	18.9	0	0	1.7	11	208	1.7			—	.15	.27	5.5	—
	Separable lean:																	
1186	Raw	73.6	130	19.9	5.0	0	0	1.5	12	185	1.8	(89)	(90)	—	.18	.25	5.8	—
1187	Cooked, roasted	62.2	186	28.7	7.0	0	0	2.0	13	238	2.2			—	.16	.30	6.2	—
1188	Separable fat:																	
	Raw	20.3	682	7.3	72.2	0	0	.2	4	44	0			—	.06	.09	2.1	—
	Good grade:																	
	Total edible:																	
1189	Raw (85% lean, 15% fat)	65.9	209	18.1	14.6	0	0	1.4	10	165	1.5			—	.16	.22	5.2	—
1190	Cooked, roasted (85% lean, 15% fat)	55.1	266	25.8	17.3	0	0	1.8	11	212	1.8			—	.15	.27	5.6	—
	Separable lean:																	
1191	Raw	73.8	127	19.9	4.7	0	0	1.6	12	185	1.8			—	.18	.25	5.8	—
1192	Cooked, roasted	62.4	183	28.7	6.7	0	0	2.1	12	238	2.2			—	.16	.30	6.2	—
1193	Separable fat:																	
	Raw	22.3	661	7.9	69.5	0	0	.3	5	51	0			—	.07	.10	2.3	—
	Loin:																	
	Prime grade:																	
	Total edible:																	
1194	Raw (67% lean, 33% fat)	52.0	351	14.7	32.0	0	0	1.1	9	127	1.0			—	.13	.18	4.3	—
1195	Cooked, broiled chops (61% lean, 39% fat)	41.7	420	19.5	37.3	0	0	1.4	8	150	1.1			—	.11	.21	4.5	—
	Separable lean:																	
1196	Raw	71.8	146	19.8	6.8	0	0	1.6	11	184	1.8			—	.18	.25	5.7	—
1197	Cooked, broiled	61.3	197	28.0	8.6	0	0	2.2	11	218	2.0			—	.15	.28	6.0	—
	Separable fat:																	
1198	Raw	12.2	770	4.6	83.2	0	0	0	3	14	0			—	.04	.06	1.3	—
	Choice grade:																	
	Total edible:																	
1199	Raw (72% lean, 28% fat)	57.7	293	16.3	24.8	0	0	1.3	9	145	1.2			—	.14	.20	4.7	—
1200	Cooked, broiled chops (66% lean, 34% fat)	47.0	359	22.0	29.4	0	0	1.7	9	172	1.3			—	.12	.23	5.0	—
	Separable lean:																	
1201	Raw	72.6	138	19.9	5.9	0	0	1.6	12	185	1.8			—	.18	.25	5.8	—
1202	Cooked, broiled	62.1	188	28.2	7.5	0	0	2.2	12	219	2.0			—	.15	.28	6.1	—
	Separable fat:																	
1203	Raw	18.4	699	7.0	74.2	0	0	.4	4	41	0			—	.06	.09	2.0	—

[8] A large proportion of the carbohydrate in the unstored product may be inulin, which is of doubtful availability. During storage, inulin is converted to sugars.

[85] Commercial products. Frozen custard must contain egg yolk which contributes somewhat more vitamin A value than is present in ice creams made with milk products only.

[86] Value for product without added salt.

[87] Higher values were found for the following jams or jellies: Gooseberry, 10 mg.; red cherry or strawberry, 15 mg.; guava, 40 mg.; black currant, 45 mg.; rose hip or acerola, 330 mg. per 100 grams.

[88] Values range from 7 Calories per 100 grams for freshly harvested Jerusalem-artichokes to 75 Calories for those stored for a long period.

[89] Average value per 100 grams of lamb of all cuts is 75 mg. for raw meat and 70 mg. for cooked meat.

[90] Average value per 100 grams of lamb of all cuts is 295 mg. for raw meat and 290 mg. for cooked meat.

TABLE 1.—COMPOSITION OF FOODS, 100 GRAMS, EDIBLE PORTION—Continued

[Numbers in parentheses denote values imputed—usually from another form of the food or from a similar food. Zero in parentheses indicates that the amount of a constituent probably is none or is too small to measure. Dashes denote lack of reliable data for a constituent believed to be present in measurable amount. Calculated values, as those based on a recipe, are not in parentheses]

Item No.	Food and description	Water	Food energy	Protein	Fat	Carbohydrate: Total	Carbohydrate: Fiber	Ash	Calcium	Phosphorus	Iron	Sodium	Potassium	Vitamin A value	Thiamine	Riboflavin	Niacin	Ascorbic acid
(A)	(B)	(C)	(D)	(E)	(F)	(G)	(H)	(I)	(J)	(K)	(L)	(M)	(N)	(O)	(P)	(Q)	(R)	(S)
		Percent	Calories	Grams	Grams	Grams	Grams	Grams	Milligrams	Milligrams	Milligrams	Milligrams	Milligrams	International units	Milligrams	Milligrams	Milligrams	Milligrams
	Lamb—Continued																	
	Retail cuts, trimmed to retail level—Continued																	
	Loin—Continued																	
	Good grade:																	
	Total edible:																	
1204	Raw (74% lean, 26% fat)	59.3	276	16.8	22.6	0	0	1.3	10	151	1.3			—	0.15	0.21	4.9	—
1205	Cooked, broiled chops (67% lean, 33% fat).	48.6	341	22.8	27.0	0	0	1.7	10	179	1.5			—	.13	.23	5.1	—
	Separable lean:																	
1206	Raw	72.9	135	19.9	5.6	0	0	1.6	12	185	1.8			—	.18	.25	5.8	—
1207	Cooked, broiled	62.5	184	28.2	7.1	0	0	2.2	11	219	2.0			—	.15	.28	6.1	—
	Separable fat:																	
1208	Raw	21.2	668	8.1	70.2	0	0	.5	5	53	0			—	.07	.10	2.3	—
	Rib:																	
	Prime grade:																	
	Total edible:																	
1209	Raw (58% lean, 42% fat)	45.3	424	13.0	40.8	0	0	.8	8	108	.7			—	.12	.16	3.8	—
1210	Cooked, broiled chops (53% lean, 47% fat)	35.5	492	16.9	46.5	0	0	1.0	7	128	.8			—	.10	.18	4.0	—
	Separable lean:																	
1211	Raw	69.7	169	19.2	9.7	0	0	1.4	11	178	1.7			—	.17	.24	5.5	—
1212	Cooked, broiled	59.1	224	26.9	12.1	0	0	1.9	11	211	1.9			—	.15	.27	5.8	—
	Separable fat:																	
1213	Raw	11.2	779	4.4	84.3	0	0	.1	3	12	0			—	.04	.05	1.3	—
	Choice grade:																	
	Total edible:																	
1214	Raw (68% lean, 32% fat)	53.4	339	15.1	30.4	0	0	1.1	9	132	1.0			—	.14	.19	4.4	—
1215	Cooked, broiled chops (62% lean, 38% fat).	42.9	407	20.1	35.6	0	0	1.4	9	156	1.1			—	.12	.21	4.6	—
	Separable lean:																	
1216	Raw	70.8	158	19.3	8.4	0	0	1.5	11	179	1.7			—	.17	.24	5.6	—
1217	Cooked, broiled	60.3	211	27.2	10.5	0	0	2.0	11	212	1.9			—	.15	.27	5.9	—
	Separable fat:																	
1218	Raw	16.5	722	6.2	77.1	0	0	.2	4	32	0	(**)	(**)	—	.06	.08	1.8	—
	Good grade:																	
	Total edible:																	
1219	Raw (71% lean, 29% fat)	56.1	312	15.8	27.1	0	0	1.2	9	139	1.1			—	.14	.20	4.6	—
1220	Cooked, broiled chops (64% lean, 36% fat)	45.4	378	21.2	31.9	0	0	1.6	9	165	1.2			—	.12	.22	4.8	—
	Separable lean:																	
1221	Raw	71.2	154	19.4	7.9	0	0	1.5	11	180	1.7			—	.17	.24	5.6	—
1222	Cooked, broiled	60.7	206	27.4	9.9	0	0	2.0	11	213	1.9			—	.15	.27	5.9	—
	Separable fat:																	
1223	Raw	18.8	697	7.0	74.0	0	0	.2	4	41	0			—	.06	.09	2.0	—
	Shoulder:																	
	Prime grade:																	
	Total edible:																	
1224	Raw (71% lean, 29% fat)	55.9	318	14.7	28.3	0	0	1.1	9	127	1.0			—	.13	.18	4.3	—
1225	Cooked, roasted (71% lean, 29% fat)	46.2	374	20.7	31.7	0	0	1.4	9	163	1.2			—	.12	.22	4.6	—
	Separable lean:																	
1226	Raw	71.4	158	18.4	8.8	0	0	1.4	11	169	1.5			—	.16	.23	5.3	—
1227	Cooked, roasted	60.4	215	26.6	11.2	0	0	1.9	11	217	1.8			—	.15	.28	5.7	—
	Separable fat:																	
1228	Raw	17.2	718	5.5	77.0	0	0	.3	3	24	0			—	.05	.07	1.6	—
	Choice grade:																	
	Total edible:																	
1229	Raw (74% lean, 26% fat)	59.6	281	15.3	23.9	0	0	1.1	9	134	1.0			—	.14	.19	4.4	—
1230	Cooked, roasted (74% lean, 26% fat)	49.6	338	21.7	27.2	0	0	1.4	10	172	1.2			—	.13	.23	4.7	—
	Separable lean:																	
1231	Raw	72.4	148	18.5	7.7	0	0	1.4	11	170	1.6			—	.16	.23	5.3	—
1232	Cooked, roasted	61.4	205	26.8	10.0	0	0	1.9	12	219	1.9			—	.15	.28	5.7	—
	Separable fat:																	
1233	Raw	23.1	659	6.3	70.1	0	0	.5	4	33	0			—	.06	.08	1.8	—

	Good grade:																	
	Total edible:																	
1234	Raw (75% lean, 25% fat)	61.2	265	15.5	22.0	0	0	1.2	9	136	1.1			—	.14	.19	4.5	—
1235	Cooked, roasted (75% lean, 25% fat)	51.1	322	22.1	25.2	0	0	1.6	10	175	1.3			—	.13	.23	4.9	—
	Separable lean:																	
1236	Raw	72.8	145	18.5	7.3	0	0	1.4	11	170	1.6	(89)	(90)	—	.16	.23	5.3	—
1237	Cooked, roasted	61.8	201	26.8	9.6	0	0	1.9	11	219	1.9			—	.15	.28	5.7	—
	Separable fat:																	
1238	Raw	25.8	633	6.7	67.0	0	0	.5	4	38	0			—	.06	.08	1.9	—
	Lambsquarters:																	
1239	Raw	84.3	43	4.2	.8	7.3	2.1	3.4	309	72	1.2	—	—	11,600	.16	.44	1.2	80
1240	Cooked, boiled, drained	88.9	32	3.2	.7	5.0	1.8	2.2	258	45	.7	—	—	9,700	.10	.26	.9	37
1241	**Lard**	0	902	0	100	0	0	0	0	0	0	0	0	0	0	0	0	0
1242	**Leeks,** bulb and lower leaf portion, raw	85.4	52	2.2	.3	11.2	1.3	.9	52	50	1.1	5	347	40	.11	.06	.5	17
	Lemons, raw:																	
1243	Peeled fruit	90.1	27	1.1	.3	8.2	.4	.3	26	16	.6	2	138	20	.04	.02	.1	[91] 53
1244	Fruit, including peel	87.4	[92] 20	1.2	.3	10.7	—	.4	61	15	.7	3	145	30	.05	.04	.2	77
	Lemon juice:																	
1245	Raw	91.0	25	.5	.2	8.0	Trace	.3	7	10	.2	1	141	20	.03	.01	.1	46
1246	Canned or bottled, unsweetened	91.6	23	.4	.1	7.6	Trace	.3	7	10	.2	1	141	20	.03	.01	.1	42
	Frozen, unsweetened:																	
1247	Single-strength juice	92.0	22	.4	.2	7.2	Trace	.2	7	9	.3	1	141	20	.03	.01	.1	44
1248	Concentrate	58.0	116	2.3	.9	37.4	Trace	1.4	33	47	.9	5	658	80	.14	.06	.3	230
	Lemon peel:																	
1249	Raw	81.6	(93)	1.5	.3	16.0	—	.6	134	12	.8	6	160	50	.06	.08	.4	129
1250	Candied	17.4	316	.4	.3	80.6	2.3	1.3	—	—	—	—	—	—	—	—	—	—
	Lemonade concentrate, frozen:																	
1251	Undiluted	48.5	195	.2	.1	51.1	.1	.1	4	6	.2	2	70	20	.02	.03	.3	30
1252	Diluted with 4⅓ parts water, by volume	88.5	44	.1	Trace	11.4	Trace	Trace	1	1	Trace	Trace	16	Trace	Trace	.01	.1	7
	Lentils, mature seeds, dry:																	
	Whole:																	
1253	Raw	11.1	340	24.7	1.1	60.1	3.9	3.0	79	377	6.8	30	790	60	.37	.22	2.0	—
1254	Cooked	72.0	106	7.8	Trace	19.3	1.2	.9	25	119	2.1	—	249	20	.07	.06	.6	0
1255	Split, without seed coat, raw	10.4	345	24.7	.9	61.8	1.7	2.2	46	260	6.8	—	—	60	.37	.22	2.0	—
	Lettuce, raw:																	
1256	Butterhead varieties such as Boston types and Bibb	95.1	14	1.2	.2	2.5	.5	1.0	35	26	2.0	9	264	970	.06	.06	.3	8
1257	Cos, or romaine, such as Dark Green and White Paris.	94.0	18	1.3	.3	3.5	.7	.9	68	25	1.4	9	264	1,900	.05	.08	.4	18
1258	Crisphead varieties such as Iceberg, New York, and Great Lakes strains.	95.5	13	.9	.1	2.9	.5	.6	20	22	.5	9	175	330	.06	.06	.3	6
1259	Looseleaf, or bunching varieties, such as Grand Rapids, Salad Bowl, Simpson.	94.0	18	1.3	.3	3.5	.7	.9	68	25	1.4	9	264	1,900	.05	.08	.4	18
	Lima beans. See Beans, lima: items 164–177.																	
1260	**Limes,** acid type, raw	89.3	28	.7	.2	9.5	.5	.3	33	18	.6	2	102	10	.03	.02	.2	37
	Lime juice:																	
1261	Raw	90.3	26	.3	.1	9.0	Trace	.3	9	11	.2	1	104	10	.02	.01	.1	32
1262	Canned or bottled, unsweetened	90.3	26	.3	.1	9.0	Trace	.3	9	11	.2	1	104	10	.02	.01	.1	21
	Limeade concentrate, frozen:																	
1263	Undiluted	50.0	187	.2	.1	49.5	Trace	.2	5	6	.1	Trace	59	Trace	.01	.01	.1	12
1264	Diluted with 4⅓ parts water, by volume	88.9	41	Trace	Trace	11.0	Trace	Trace	1	1	Trace	Trace	13	Trace	Trace	Trace	Trace	2
1265	**Lingcod,** raw	80.0	84	17.9	.8	0	0	1.2	—	—	—	59	433	0	.05	.04	—	—
	Liver:																	
	Beef:																	
1266	Raw	69.7	140	19.9	3.8	5.3	0	1.3	8	352	6.5	136	281	[94] 43,900	.25	3.26	13.6	31
1267	Cooked, fried	56.0	229	26.4	10.6	5.3	0	1.7	11	476	8.8	184	380	[94] 53,400	.26	4.19	16.5	27
	Calf:																	
1268	Raw	70.7	140	19.2	4.7	4.1	0	1.3	8	333	8.8	73	281	[94] 22,500	.20	2.72	11.4	36
1269	Cooked, fried	51.4	261	29.5	13.2	4.0	0	1.9	13	537	14.2	118	453	[94] 32,700	.24	4.17	16.5	37
	Chicken, all classes:																	
1270	Raw	72.2	129	19.7	3.7	2.9	0	1.5	12	236	7.9	70	172	[94] 12,100	.19	2.49	10.8	17
1271	Cooked, simmered	65.0	165	26.5	4.4	3.1	0	1.0	11	159	8.5	61	151	[94] 12,300	.17	2.69	11.7	16
1272	Goose, raw	66.9	182	16.5	10.0	5.4	0	1.2	—	—	—	140	230	—	—	—	—	—
	Hog:																	
1273	Raw	71.6	131	20.6	3.7	2.6	0	1.5	10	356	19.2	73	261	[94] 10,900	.30	3.03	16.4	23
1274	Cooked, fried	54.0	241	29.9	11.5	2.5	0	2.1	15	539	29.1	111	395	[94] 14,900	.34	4.36	22.3	22
	Lamb:																	
1275	Raw	70.8	136	21.0	3.9	2.9	0	1.4	10	349	10.9	52	202	[94] 50,500	.40	3.28	16.9	33
1276	Cooked, broiled	50.4	261	32.3	12.4	2.8	0	2.1	16	572	17.9	85	331	[94] 74,500	.49	5.11	24.9	36
	Turkey, all classes:																	
1277	Raw	70.4	138	21.2	4.0	2.9	0	1.5	—	—	—	63	160	[94] 17,700	.18	1.93	13.2	—
1278	Cooked, simmered	63.3	174	27.9	4.8	3.1	0	1.0	—	—	—	55	141	[94] 17,500	.16	2.09	14.3	—

[89] Average value per 100 grams of lamb of all cuts is 75 mg. for raw meat and 70 mg. for cooked meat.

[90] Average value per 100 grams of lamb of all cuts is 295 mg. for raw meat and 290 mg. for cooked meat.

[91] Applies to lemons marketed in summer.

[92] Based on the pulp. There is no basis for assessing the calorie value of the peel or the effect that inclusion of the peel may have on the digestibility of the product.

[93] Value cannot be calculated inasmuch as digestibility of peel is not known.

[94] Values vary widely in all kinds of liver, ranging from about 100 I.U. to more than 100,000 I.U. per 100 grams.

TABLE 1.—COMPOSITION OF FOODS, 100 GRAMS, EDIBLE PORTION—Continued

[Numbers in parentheses denote values imputed—usually from another form of the food or from a similar food. Zero in parentheses indicates that the amount of a constituent probably is none or is too small to measure. Dashes denote lack of reliable data for a constituent believed to be present in measurable amount. Calculated values, as those based on a recipe, are not in parentheses]

Item No.	Food and description	Water	Food energy	Protein	Fat	Carbohydrate		Ash	Calcium	Phos-phorus	Iron	Sodium	Potas-sium	Vitamin A value	Thiamine	Ribo-flavin	Niacin	Ascorbic acid
						Total	Fiber											
(A)	(B)	(C)	(D)	(E)	(F)	(G)	(H)	(I)	(J)	(K)	(L)	(M)	(N)	(O)	(P)	(Q)	(R)	(S)
		Percent	Calories	Grams	Grams	Grams	Grams	Grams	Milligrams	Milligrams	Milligrams	Milligrams	Milligrams	International units	Milligrams	Milligrams	Milligrams	Milligrams
	Liver paste. See Pâté de foie gras, item 1478.																	
	Liver sausage or liverwurst. See Sausage, cold cuts, and luncheon meats: items 2003–2004.																	
	Lobster, northern:																	
1279	Raw, whole	78. 5	91	16. 9	1. 9	0. 5	—	2. 2	29	183	0. 6	—	—	—	0. 40	0. 05	1. 5	—
1280	Canned or cooked	76. 8	95	18. 7	1. 5	. 3	—	2. 7	65	192	. 8	210	180	—	. 10	. 07	—	—
1281	**Lobster Newburg** [95]	64. 0	194	18. 5	10. 6	5. 1	—	1. 8	87	192	. 9	229	171	—	. 07	. 11	—	—
1282	**Lobster salad** [96]	80. 3	110	10. 1	6. 4	2. 3	—	. 9	36	95	. 9	124	264	—	. 09	. 08	—	18
	Lobster paste. See Shrimp or lobster paste, canned: item 2047.																	
	Lobster, spiny. See Crayfish, item 927.																	
	Loganberries:																	
1283	Raw	83. 0	62	1. 0	. 6	14. 9	3. 0	. 5	35	17	1. 2	(1)	170	(200)	(. 03)	(. 04)	(. 4)	24
	Canned, solids and liquid:																	
1284	Water pack, with or without artificial sweetener	89. 2	40	. 7	. 4	9. 4	2. 0	. 3	24	11	. 8	1	115	140	. 01	. 02	. 2	8
1285	Juice pack	85. 7	54	. 7	. 5	12. 7	2. 1	. 4	27	15	1. 2	1	170	150	. 02	. 03	. 3	12
	Sirup pack:																	
1286	Light	81. 4	70	. 7	. 4	17. 2	2. 0	. 3	23	11	. 8	1	111	130	. 01	. 02	. 2	8
1287	Heavy	76. 5	89	. 6	. 4	22. 2	1. 9	. 3	22	11	. 8	1	109	130	. 01	. 02	. 2	8
1288	Extra heavy	71. 5	108	. 6	. 4	27. 2	1. 9	. 3	22	11	. 8	1	107	130	. 01	. 02	. 2	7
	Longans:																	
1289	Raw	82. 4	61	1. 0	. 1	15. 8	. 4	. 7	10	42	1. 2	—	—	—	—	—	—	(6)
1290	Dried	17. 6	286	4. 9	. 4	74. 0	2. 0	3. 1	45	196	5. 4	—	—	—	. 04	—	—	28
1291	**Loquats,** raw	86. 5	48	. 4	. 2	12. 4	. 5	. 5	20	36	. 4	—	348	670	—	—	—	1
	Luncheon meat. See Sausage, cold cuts, and luncheon meats: items 2005–2006.																	
	Lungs, raw:																	
1292	Beef	78. 8	96	17. 6	2. 3	0	0	1. 0	—	216	—	—	—	—	—	—	6. 2	—
1293	Calf	77. 4	106	16. 8	3. 8	0	0	1. 2	—	—	—	—	—	—	—	—	—	—
1294	Lamb	76. 7	103	19. 3	2. 3	0	0	1. 2	—	180	—	—	—	—	—	—	—	—
	Lychees:																	
1295	Raw	81. 9	64	. 9	. 3	16. 4	. 3	. 5	8	42	. 4	3	170	—	—	. 05	—	42
1296	Dried	22. 3	277	3. 8	1. 2	70. 7	1. 4	2. 0	33	181	1. 7	3	1, 100	—	—	—	—	—
1297	**Macadamia nuts**	3. 0	691	7. 8	71. 6	15. 9	2. 5	1. 7	48	161	2. 0	—	264	0	. 34	. 11	1. 3	0
	Macaroni:																	
	Enriched:																	
1298	Dry form	10. 4	369	12. 5	1. 2	75. 2	. 3	. 7	27	162	[50] 2. 9	2	197	(0)	[50] . 88	[50] . 37	[50] 6. 0	(0)
1299	Cooked, firm stage (8–10 min.)	63. 6	148	5. 0	. 5	30. 1	. 1	1. 3	11	65	[50] 1. 1	1	79	(0)	[50] . 18	[50] . 10	[50] 1. 4	(0)
1300	Cooked, tender stage (14–20 min.)	72. 0	111	3. 4	. 4	23. 0	. 1	1. 2	8	50	. 9	1	61	(0)	. 14	. 08	1. 1	(0)
	Unenriched:																	
1301	Dry form	10. 4	369	12. 5	1. 2	75. 2	. 3	. 7	27	162	1. 3	2	197	(0)	. 09	. 06	1. 7	(0)
1302	Cooked, firm stage (8–10 min.)	63. 6	148	5. 0	. 5	30. 1	. 1	1. 3	11	65	. 5	1	79	(0)	. 02	. 02	. 4	(0)
1303	Cooked, tender stage (14–20 min.)	72. 0	111	3. 4	. 4	23. 0	. 1	1. 2	8	50	. 4	1	61	(0)	. 01	. 01	. 3	(0)
	Macaroni and cheese:																	
1304	Baked, made from home recipe [97]	58. 2	215	8. 4	11. 1	20. 1	. 1	2. 2	181	161	. 9	543	120	430	. 10	. 20	. 9	Trace
1305	Canned	80. 2	95	3. 9	4. 0	10. 7	. 1	1. 2	83	76	. 4	304	58	110	. 05	. 10	. 4	Trace
	Mackerel, Atlantic:																	
1306	Raw	67. 2	191	19. 0	12. 2	0	0	1. 6	5	239	1. 0	—	—	(450)	. 15	. 33	8. 2	—
1307	Canned, solids and liquid [98]	66. 0	183	19. 3	11. 1	0	0	3. 2	185	274	2. 1	—	—	430	. 06	. 21	5. 8	—
1308	Cooked, broiled with butter or margarine	61. 6	236	21. 8	15. 8	0	0	1. 6	6	280	1. 2	—	—	(530)	. 15	. 27	7. 6	—
	Mackerel, Pacific:																	
1309	Raw	69. 8	159	21. 9	7. 3	0	0	1. 4	8	274	2. 1	—	—	120	—	—	—	—
1310	Canned, solids and liquid [98]	66. 4	180	21. 1	10. 0	0	0	2. 5	260	288	2. 2	—	—	30	. 03	. 33	8. 8	—
	Mackerel:																	
1311	Salted	43. 0	305	18. 5	25. 1	0	0	13. 0	—	—	—	—	—	—	—	—	—	—
1312	Smoked	59. 4	219	23. 8	13. 0	0	0	2. 0	—	—	—	—	—	—	—	—	—	—
1313	**Malt,** dry	5. 2	368	13. 1	1. 9	77. 4	5. 7	2. 4	—	—	4. 0	—	—	—	. 49	. 31	9. 0	—
1314	**Malt extract,** dried	3. 2	367	6. 0	Trace	89. 2	Trace	1. 6	48	294	8. 7	80	230	—	. 36	. 45	9. 8	—
1315	**Mamey** (mammeeapple), raw	86. 2	51	. 5	. 5	12. 5	1. 0	. 3	11	11	. 7	15	47	230	. 02	. 04	. 4	14
	Mandarin oranges. See Tangerines, item 2262.																	
1316	**Mangos,** raw	81. 7	66	. 7	. 4	16. 8	. 9	. 4	10	13	. 4	7	189	4, 800	. 05	. 05	1. 1	35
1317	**Margarine** [99]	15. 5	720	. 6	81.	. 4	0	2. 5	20	16	0	987	23	3, 300	—	—	—	0
1318	**Marmalade, citrus**	29. 0	257	. 5	. 1	70. 1	. 4	. 3	35	9	. 6	14	33	—	. 02	. 02	. 1	6
	Marmalade plums. See Sapotes, item 1970.																	

No.	Food																	
	Matai. See Waterchestnut, Chinese, item 2422.																	
	Mayonnaise. See Salad dressings, item 1938.																	
	Meat loaf. See Sausage, cold cuts, and luncheon meats: item 2007.																	
	Meat. See Beef, Lamb, Pork, Veal.																	
	Mellorine. See Notes on Foods, page 182.																	
	Melons. See Muskmelons, items 1358–1361; and Watermelons, item 2424.																	
1319	**Menhaden,** Atlantic, canned, solids and liquid	67.9	172	18.7	10.2	0	0	3.8	—	—	1.3	—	—	—	—	—	—	—
	Milk, cow:																	
	Fluid (pasteurized and raw):																	
	Whole:																	
1320	3.5% fat [100]	87.4	65	3.5	3.5	4.9	0	.7	118	93	Trace	50	144	140	.03	.17	.1	1
1321	3.7% fat [100]	87.2	66	3.5	3.7	4.9	0	.7	117	92	Trace	50	140	150	.03	.17	.1	1
1322	Skim	90.5	36	3.6	.1	5.1	0	.7	121	95	Trace	52	145	Trace	.04	.18	.1	1
1323	Partially skimmed with 2% nonfat milk solids added.	87.0	59	4.2	2.0	6.0	0	.8	143	112	.1	61	175	80	.04	.21	.1	1
	Half-and-half (cream and milk). See Cream, item 928.																	
	Canned:																	
1324	Evaporated (unsweetened)	73.8	137	7.0	7.9	9.7	0	1.6	252	205	.1	118	303	320	.04	.34	.2	1
1325	Condensed (sweetened)	27.1	321	8.1	8.7	54.3	0	1.8	262	206	.1	112	314	360	.08	.38	.2	1
	Dry:																	
1326	Whole	2.0	502	26.4	27.5	38.2	0	5.9	909	708	.5	405	1,330	1,130	.29	1.46	.7	6
1327	Skim (nonfat solids), regular	3.0	363	35.9	.8	52.3	0	8.0	1,308	1,016	.6	532	1,745	30	.35	(1.80)	.9	7
1328	Skim (nonfat solids), instant	4.0	359	35.8	.7	51.6	0	7.9	1,293	1,005	.6	526	1,725	30	.35	1.78	.9	7
	Malted:																	
1329	Dry powder [101]	2.6	410	14.7	8.3	70.8	.3	3.6	288	380	2.1	440	720	1,020	.33	.54	.3	(0)
1330	Beverage [102]	78.2	104	4.7	4.4	11.7	Trace	1.0	135	122	.3	91	200	250	.06	.21	.1	1
	Chocolate drink, fluid, commercial:																	
1331	Made with skim milk	82.8	76	3.3	2.3	10.9	Trace	.7	108	91	.2	46	142	80	.04	.16	.1	1
1332	Made with whole (3.5% fat) milk	81.5	85	3.4	3.4	11.0	Trace	.7	111	94	.2	47	146	130	.03	.16	.1	1
	Chocolate beverages, homemade:																	
1333	Hot chocolate	80.5	95	3.3	5.0	10.4	.1	.7	104	94	.2	48	148	140	.03	.16	.1	1
1334	Hot cocoa	79.0	97	3.8	4.6	10.9	.1	.9	118	113	.4	51	145	160	.04	.18	.2	1
	Buttermilk. See Buttermilk, items 509–510.																	
1335	**Milk, goat,** fluid	87.5	67	3.2	4.0	4.6	0	.7	129	106	.1	34	180	(160)	.04	.11	.3	1
1336	**Milk, human,** U.S. samples	85.2	77	1.1	4.0	9.5	0	.2	33	14	.1	16	51	240	.01	.04	.2	5
1337	**Milk, reindeer**	64.1	234	10.8	19.6	4.1	0	1.4	254	198	.1	157	159	—	—	—	—	—
1338	**Millet,** proso (broomcorn, hogmillet), whole-grain	11.8	327	9.9	2.9	72.9	3.2	2.5	20	11	6.8	—	430	(0)	.73	.38	2.3	(0)
	Mixed vegetables, frozen. See Vegetables, mixed, frozen: items 2403–2404.																	
	Molasses, cane:																	
1339	First extraction or light	24.	252	—	—	[103] 65.	—	[104] 6.3	165	45	4.3	15	917	—	.07	.06	.2	—
1340	Second extraction or medium	24.	232	—	—	[103] 60.	—	[104] 8.5	290	69	6.0	37	1,063	—	—	.12	1.2	—
1341	Third extraction or blackstrap	24.	213	—	—	[103] 55.	—	[104] 10.5	684	84	16.1	96	2,927	—	.11	.19	2.0	—
1342	Barbados	24.	271	—	—	[103] 70.	—	[104] 1.6	245	50	—	—	—	—	.06	.20	—	—
	Mortadella. See Sausage, cold cuts, and luncheon meats: item 2010.																	
	Muffins, baked from home recipes:																	
	Plain, made with—																	
1343	Enriched flour	38.0	294	7.8	10.1	42.3	.1	1.8	104	151	1.6	441	125	100	.17	.23	1.4	Trace
1344	Unenriched flour	38.0	294	7.8	10.1	42.3	.1	1.8	104	151	.6	441	125	100	.04	.14	.4	Trace
	Other, made with enriched flour:																	
1345	Blueberry	39.0	281	7.3	9.3	41.9	.3	2.5	84	132	1.6	632	115	220	.16	.20	1.2	1
1346	Bran	35.1	261	7.7	9.8	43.1	1.8	4.3	142	405	3.7	448	431	230	.14	.24	4.0	Trace
	Corn, made with—																	
1347	Enriched degermed cornmeal	32.7	314	7.1	10.1	48.1	.2	2.0	105	169	1.7	481	135	300	.20	.23	1.6	Trace
1348	Whole-ground cornmeal	37.8	288	7.2	10.3	42.5	.5	2.2	112	216	1.4	495	132	310	.17	.17	1.0	Trace
	Muffin mixes, corn, and muffins baked from mixes: [105]																	
1349	Mix, dry form, with enriched flour	7.8	417	6.2	11.5	71.8	.5	2.7	300	473	1.8	660	76	150	.24	.16	2.1	0
1350	Muffins, made with egg, milk	30.4	324	6.9	10.6	50.0	.2	2.1	241	380	1.5	479	110	240	.18	.19	1.4	Trace
1351	Mix, dry form, with cake flour, nonfat dry milk	7.8	409	6.2	10.7	71.6	.2	3.7	222	328	.9	811	133	100	.13	.15	1.1	Trace
1352	Muffins, made with egg, water	33.1	297	4.5	7.8	51.9	.1	2.7	148	228	1.1	346	104	150	.12	.12	1.3	Trace

[94] Based on product with minimum level of enrichment.

[95] Prepared with butter, egg yolks, sherry, and cream.

[96] Prepared with onion, sweet pickle, celery, eggs, mayonnaise, and tomatoes.

[97] Prepared with enriched macaroni.

[98] Vitamin values based on drained solids.

[99] Values apply to salted margarine. Unsalted margarine contains less than 10 mg. per 100 grams of either sodium or potassium. Vitamin A value based on the minimum required to meet Federal specifications for margarine with vitamin A added; namely 15,000 I.U. of vitamin A per pound.

[100] Minimum standards for fat in different States vary considerably, and commercial milks may range somewhat above the required minimums. Selection of values to be used in dietary calculations may need to be based on information at the local level. The value, 3.7 percent, is considered valid as a national average for milk on the farm production basis.

[101] Values are based on unfortified products.

[102] Prepared with malted milk powder and whole milk.

[103] Value for total sugars.

[104] Value is for sulfated ash and overestimates ash by approximately 8 to 20 percent.

[105] Contain yellow degermed cornmeal.

TABLE 1.—COMPOSITION OF FOODS, 100 GRAMS, EDIBLE PORTION—Continued

[Numbers in parentheses denote values imputed—usually from another form of the food or from a similar food. Zero in parentheses indicates that the amount of a constituent probably is none or is too small to measure. Dashes denote lack of reliable data for a constituent believed to be present in measurable amount. Calculated values, as those based on a recipe, are not in parentheses]

Item No.	Food and description	Water	Food energy	Protein	Fat	Carbohydrate		Ash	Calcium	Phosphorus	Iron	Sodium	Potassium	Vitamin A value	Thiamine	Riboflavin	Niacin	Ascorbic acid
						Total	Fiber											
(A)	(B)	(C)	(D)	(E)	(F)	(G)	(H)	(I)	(J)	(K)	(L)	(M)	(N)	(O)	(P)	(Q)	(R)	(S)
		Percent	Calories	Grams	Grams	Grams	Grams	Grams	Milligrams	Milligrams	Milligrams	Milligrams	Milligrams	International units	Milligrams	Milligrams	Milligrams	Milligrams
1353	**Mullet,** striped, raw	72.6	146	19.6	6.9	0	0	1.3	26	220	1.8	81	292	—	0.07	0.08	5.2	—
	Mushrooms:																	
	Agaricus campestris, cultivated commercially:																	
1354	Raw	90.4	28	2.7	.3	4.4	.8	.9	6	116	.8	15	414	Trace	.10	.46	4.2	3
1355	Canned, solids and liquid	93.1	17	1.9	.1	2.4	.6	1.6	6	68	.5	400	197	Trace	.02	.25	2.0	2
1356	Other edible species, raw	89.1	35	1.9	.6	6.5	1.1	1.0	13	97	1.4	10	375	Trace	.10	.33	6.8	3
1357	**Muskellunge,** raw	76.3	109	20.2	2.5	0	0	1.6	—	227	.6	—	—	—	—	—	—	—
	Muskmelons:																	
	Raw:																	
1358	Cantaloups, other netted varieties	91.2	30	.7	.1	7.5	.3	.5	14	16	.4	12	251	[106]3,400	.04	.03	.6	33
1359	Casaba (Golden Beauty)	91.5	27	1.2	Trace	6.5	.5	.8	(14)	(16)	(.4)	(12)	(251)	30	(.04)	(.03)	(.6)	13
1360	Honeydew	90.6	33	.8	.3	7.7	.6	.6	14	16	.4	12	251	40	.04	.03	.6	23
	Frozen:																	
1361	Melon balls (cantaloup and Honeydew) in sirup, not thawed.	83.2	62	.6	.1	15.7	.3	.4	10	12	.3	9	188	1,540	.03	.02	.5	16
1362	**Muskrat,** cooked, roasted	67.3	153	27.2	4.1	0	0	1.4	—	—	—	—	—	—	.16	.21	—	—
	Mussels, Atlantic and Pacific, raw:																	
1363	Meat and liquid	83.8	66	9.6	1.4	3.1	—	2.1	—	—	—	—	—	—	—	—	—	—
1364	Meat only	78.6	95	14.4	2.2	3.3	—	1.5	88	236	3.4	289	315	—	.16	.21	—	—
1365	**Mussels, Pacific,** canned, drained solids	74.6	114	18.2	3.3	1.5	—	2.4	—	—	—	—	—	—	—	.13	—	—
	Mustard greens:																	
1366	Raw	89.5	31	3.0	.5	5.6	1.1	1.4	183	50	3.0	32	377	7,000	.11	.22	.8	97
1367	Cooked, boiled, drained	92.6	23	2.2	.4	4.0	.9	.8	138	32	1.8	18	220	5,800	.08	.14	.6	48
	Frozen:																	
1368	Not thawed	93.5	20	2.3	.4	3.2	1.0	.6	115	45	1.6	12	196	6,000	.04	.12	.4	34
1369	Cooked, boiled, drained	93.8	20	2.2	.4	3.1	1.0	.5	104	43	1.5	10	157	6,000	.03	.10	.4	20
	Mustard spinach (tendergreen):																	
1370	Raw	92.2	22	2.2	.3	3.9	1.0	1.4	210	28	1.5	—	—	9,900	—	—	—	130
1371	Cooked, boiled, drained	94.5	16	1.7	.2	2.8	.8	.8	158	18	.8	—	—	8,200	—	—	—	65
	Mustard, prepared:																	
1372	Brown	78.1	91	5.9	6.3	5.3	1.3	4.4	124	134	1.8	1,307	130	—	—	—	—	—
1373	Yellow	80.2	75	4.7	4.4	6.4	1.0	4.3	84	73	2.0	1,252	130	—	—	—	—	—
1374	**Nectarines,** raw	81.8	64	.6	Trace	17.1	.4	.5	4	24	.5	6	294	1,650	—	—	—	13
	New Zealand spinach:																	
1375	Raw	92.6	19	2.2	.3	3.1	.7	1.8	58	46	2.6	159	795	4,300	.04	.17	.6	30
1376	Cooked, boiled, drained	94.8	13	1.7	.2	2.1	.6	1.2	48	28	1.5	92	463	3,600	.03	.10	.5	14
	Noodles, egg noodles:																	
	Enriched:																	
1377	Dry form	9.8	388	12.8	4.6	72.0	.4	.8	31	183	[30]2.9	5	136	220	[30].88	[30].38	[30]6.0	(0)
1378	Cooked	70.4	125	4.1	1.5	23.3	.1	.7	10	59	[30].9	2	44	70	[30].14	[30].08	[30]1.2	(0)
	Unenriched:																	
1379	Dry form	9.8	388	12.8	4.6	72.0	.4	.8	31	183	1.9	5	136	220	.17	.09	2.1	(0)
1380	Cooked	70.4	125	4.1	1.5	23.3	.1	.7	10	59	.6	2	44	70	.03	.02	.4	(0)
1381	**Noodles, chow mein,** canned	1.1	489	13.2	23.5	58.0	—	4.2	—	—	—	—	—	—	—	—	—	—
	Nuts. See individual kinds.																	
	Oat products used mainly as hot breakfast cereals:																	
	Oat cereal with toasted wheat germ and soy grits:																	
1382	Dry form	8.7	382	20.5	9.0	58.6	3.5	3.2	70	590	7.1	8	—	(0)	1.06	.17	1.4	(0)
1383	Cooked	84.4	62	3.3	1.5	9.5	.6	1.3	13	96	1.1	292	Trace	(0)	.16	.03	.2	(0)
1384	Oat flakes, maple-flavored, instant-cooking:																	
	Dry form	7.4	384	14.6	4.2	72.3	.7	1.5	50	360	3.5	1	—	(0)	.35	—	—	(0)
1385	Cooked	83.0	69	2.6	.8	13.0	.1	.6	10	65	.6	107	—	(0)	.06	—	—	(0)
	Oat granules, maple-flavored, quick-cooking:																	
1386	Dry form	7.0	383	14.8	4.0	72.5	1.1	1.7	60	400	3.8	1	—	(0)	.40	—	—	(0)
1387	Cooked	85.2	60	2.3	.6	11.4	.2	.5	10	63	.6	72	—	(0)	.06	—	—	(0)
	Oat and wheat cereal:																	
1388	Dry form	10.0	364	14.7	5.0	68.3	1.5	2.0	53	423	3.9	2	—	(0)	.49	.18	2.6	(0)
1389	Cooked	83.6	65	2.6	.9	12.1	.3	.8	11	75	.7	168	—	(0)	.09	.03	.5	(0)
	Oatmeal or rolled oats:																	
1390	Dry form	8.3	390	14.2	7.4	68.2	1.2	1.9	53	405	4.5	2	352	(0)	.60	.14	1.0	(0)
1391	Cooked	86.5	55	2.0	1.0	9.7	.2	.8	9	57	.6	218	61	(0)	.08	.02	.1	(0)

	Oat products used mainly as ready-to-eat breakfast cereals:																	
1392	Oats, shredded, with protein and other added nutrients.	3.9	379	18.8	2.1	72.0	1.8	3.2	265	317	5.3	610	—	(0)	3.53	4.23	35.3	(0)
1393	Oats (with or without corn), puffed, added nutrients	3.4	397	11.9	5.5	75.2	1.1	4.0	177	408	4.7	1,267	—	(0)	.98	.18	1.9	(0)
1394	Oats (with or without corn, wheat), puffed, added nutrients, sugar-covered.	1.9	396	6.7	3.4	85.6	.7	2.4	72	202	4.4	588	—	(0)	1.03	.12	1.7	(0)
1395	Oats (with soy flour and rice), flaked, added nutrients	3.5	397	14.9	5.7	70.7	.9	5.2	150	350	8.5	1,200	—	(0)	.71	.33	8.5	(0)
	Ocean perch, Atlantic (redfish):																	
1396	Raw	79.7	88	18.0	1.2	0	0	1.1	20	207	1.0	79	269	—	.10	.08	1.9	—
1397	Cooked, fried [83]	59.0	227	19.0	13.3	6.8	0	1.9	33	226	1.3	153	284	—	.10	.11	1.8	—
1398	Frozen, breaded, fried, reheated	43.2	319	18.9	18.9	16.5	—	2.5	—	—	—	—	—	—	—	—	—	—
1399	**Ocean perch, Pacific,** raw	79.0	95	19.0	1.5	0	0	1.1	—	—	—	63	390	—	—	—	—	—
1400	**Octopus,** raw	82.2	73	15.3	.8	0	0	1.5	29	173	—	—	—	—	.02	.06	1.8	—
1401	**Oils,** salad or cooking	0	884	0	100.	0	0	0	0	0	0	0	0	—	0	0	0	0
	Okra:																	
1402	Raw	88.9	36	2.4	.3	7.6	1.0	.8	92	51	.6	3	249	520	(.17)	(.21)	(1.0)	31
1403	Cooked, boiled, drained	91.1	29	2.0	.3	6.0	1.0	.6	92	41	.5	2	174	490	(.13)	(.18)	(.9)	20
	Frozen, cuts and pods:																	
1404	Not thawed	87.9	39	2.3	.1	9.0	1.0	.7	94	51	.6	2	219	480	.17	.21	1.0	16
1405	Cooked, boiled, drained	88.3	38	2.2	.1	8.8	1.0	.6	94	43	.5	2	164	480	.14	.17	1.0	12
	Oleomargarine. See Margarine, item 1317.																	
	Olives, pickled; canned or bottled:																	
1406	Green	78.2	116	1.4	12.7	1.3	1.3	6.4	61	17	1.6	2,400	55	300	—	—	—	—
	Ripe:																	
1407	Ascolano (extra large, mammoth, giant, jumbo)	80.0	129	1.1	13.8	2.6	1.4	2.5	84	16	1.6	813	34	60	Trace	Trace	—	—
1408	Manzanilla (small, medium, large, extra large)	80.0	129	1.1	13.8	2.6	1.4	2.5	84	16	1.6	813	34	60	Trace	Trace	—	—
1409	Mission (small, medium, large, extra large)	73.0	184	1.2	20.1	3.2	1.5	2.5	106	17	1.7	750	27	70	Trace	Trace	—	—
1410	Sevillano (giant, jumbo, colossal, supercolossal)	84.4	93	1.1	9.5	2.7	1.2	2.3	74	20	1.6	828	44	60	Trace	Trace	—	—
1411	Ripe, salt-cured, oil-coated, Greek style	43.8	338	2.2	35.8	8.7	3.8	(9.5)	—	29	—	3,288	—	—	—	—	—	—
	Omelet. See Eggs, omelet: item 975.																	
	Onions, mature (dry):																	
1412	Raw	89.1	38	1.5	.1	8.7	.6	.6	27	36	.5	10	157	[107] 40	.03	.04	.2	10
1413	Cooked, boiled, drained	91.8	29	1.2	.1	6.5	.6	.4	24	29	.4	7	110	[107] 40	.03	.03	.2	7
1414	Dehydrated, flaked	4.	350	8.7	1.3	82.1	4.4	3.9	166	273	2.9	88	1,383	[107] 200	.25	.18	1.4	35
	Onions, young green (bunching varieties), raw:																	
1415	Bulb and entire top	89.4	36	1.5	.2	8.2	(1.2)	.7	51	39	1.0	5	231	(2,000)	.05	.05	.4	32
1416	Bulb and white portion of top	87.6	45	1.1	.2	10.5	1.0	.6	40	39	.6	5	231	Trace	.05	.04	.4	25
1417	Tops only (green portion)	91.8	27	1.6	.4	5.5	1.3	.7	56	39	2.2	5	231	4,000	.07	.10	.6	51
1418	**Onions, Welsh,** raw	90.5	34	1.9	.4	6.5	1.0	.7	18	49	—	—	—	—	.05	.09	.4	27
1419	**Opossum,** cooked, roasted	57.3	221	30.2	10.2	0	0	2.3	—	—	—	—	—	—	.12	.38	—	—
	Oranges, raw:																	
	Peeled fruit:																	
1420	All commercial varieties	86.0	49	1.0	.2	12.2	.5	.6	41	20	.4	1	200	200	.10	.04	.4	[79] (50)
	California:																	
1421	Navels (winter oranges)	85.4	51	1.3	.1	12.7	.5	.5	40	22	.4	1	194	(200)	.10	.04	.4	[79] (61)
1422	Valencias (summer oranges)	85.6	51	1.2	.3	12.4	(.5)	.5	40	22	.8	1	190	(200)	.10	.04	.4	[79] (49)
	Florida:																	
1423	All commercial varieties	86.4	47	.7	(.2)	12.0	(.5)	.7	43	17	.2	1	(206)	(200)	.10	.04	.4	[79] (45)
1424	Fruit, including peel (California Valencias)	82.3	[93] 40	1.3	.3	15.5	—	.6	70	22	.8	2	196	250	.10	.05	.5	71
	Orange juice:																	
	Raw:																	
1425	All commercial varieties	88.3	45	.7	.2	10.4	.1	.4	11	17	.2	1	200	200	.09	.03	.4	[79] 50
	California:																	
1426	Navels (winter oranges)	87.2	48	1.0	.1	11.3	(.1)	.4	11	18	.2	1	194	200	.09	.03	.4	[79] 61
1427	Valencias (summer oranges)	87.8	47	1.0	.3	10.5	(.1)	.4	11	19	.3	1	190	200	.09	.03	.4	[79] 49
	Florida:																	
1428	All commercial varieties	88.8	43	.6	.2	10.0	(.1)	.4	10	16	.2	1	206	200	.09	.03	.4	[79] 45
1429	Early and midseason oranges (Hamlin, Parson Brown, Pineapple).	89.6	40	.5	.2	9.3	(.1)	.4	10	15	.2	1	208	200	.09	.03	.4	[79] 51
1430	Late season (Valencias)	88.3	45	.6	.2	10.5	(.1)	.4	10	18	.2	1	203	200	.09	.03	.4	[79] 37
1431	Temple	88.0	54	(.5)	(.2)	12.9	(.1)	.4	(10)	17	.2	1	—	(200)	.09	.03	.4	[79] 50
	Canned:																	
1432	Unsweetened	87.4	48	.8	.2	11.2	.1	.4	10	18	.4	1	199	200	.07	.02	.3	40
1433	Sweetened	86.5	52	.7	.2	12.2	.1	.4	(10)	18	.4	1	(199)	200	.07	.02	.3	40
	Canned concentrate, unsweetened:																	
1434	Undiluted	42.0	223	4.1	1.3	50.7	.5	1.9	51	86	1.3	5	942	960	.39	.12	1.7	229
1435	Diluted with 5 parts water, by volume	88.2	46	.8	.3	10.3	.1	.4	10	18	.3	1	192	200	.08	.02	.3	47
	Frozen concentrate, unsweetened:																	
1436	Undiluted	58.2	158	2.3	.2	38.0	.2	1.3	33	55	.4	2	657	710	.30	.05	1.2	158
1437	Diluted with 3 parts water, by volume	88.1	45	.7	.1	10.7	Trace	.4	9	16	.1	1	186	200	.09	.01	.3	45

[80] Based on product with minimum level of enrichment.

[79] Value weighted by monthly and total season shipments for marketing as fresh fruit.

[83] Dipped in egg, milk, and breadcrumbs.

[93] Based on the pulp. There is no basis for assessing the calorie value of the peel or the effect that inclusion of the peel may have on the digestibility of the product.

[106] Value based on varieties with orange-colored flesh; for green-fleshed varieties, value is about 280 I.U. per 100 grams.

[107] Value based on yellow-fleshed varieties; white-fleshed varieties contain only a trace.

TABLE 1.—COMPOSITION OF FOODS, 100 GRAMS, EDIBLE PORTION—Continued

[Numbers in parentheses denote values imputed—usually from another form of the food or from a similar food. Zero in parentheses indicates that the amount of a constituent probably is none or is too small to measure. Dashes denote lack of reliable data for a constituent believed to be present in measurable amount. Calculated values, as those based on a recipe, are not in parentheses]

Item No.	Food and description	Water	Food energy	Protein	Fat	Carbohydrate		Ash	Calcium	Phosphorus	Iron	Sodium	Potassium	Vitamin A value	Thiamine	Riboflavin	Niacin	Ascorbic acid
						Total	Fiber											
(A)	(B)	(C)	(D)	(E)	(F)	(G)	(H)	(I)	(J)	(K)	(L)	(M)	(N)	(O)	(P)	(Q)	(R)	(S)
		Percent	*Calories*	*Grams*	*Grams*	*Grams*	*Grams*	*Grams*	*Milligrams*	*Milligrams*	*Milligrams*	*Milligrams*	*Milligrams*	*International units*	*Milligrams*	*Milligrams*	*Milligrams*	*Milligrams*
	Orange juice—Continued																	
	Dehydrated (crystals):																	
1438	Dry form	1.0	380	5.0	1.7	88.9	0.8	3.4	84	134	1.7	8	1,728	1,680	0.67	0.21	2.9	359
1439	Prepared with water (1 lb. yields approx. 1 gal.)	88.0	46	.6	.2	10.8	.1	.4	10	16	.2	1	209	200	.08	.03	.4	44
	Orange peel:																	
1440	Raw	72.5	([93])	1.5	.2	25.0	—	.8	161	21	.8	3	212	420	.12	.09	.9	136
1441	Candied	17.4	316	.4	.3	80.6	—	1.3	—	—	—	—	—	—	—	—	—	—
	Orange-cranberry relish. See Cranberry-orange relish, item 925.																	
1442	**Orange juice and apricot juice drink,** canned (approx. 40% fruit juices).	86.7	50	.3	.1	12.7	.2	.2	5	8	.1	Trace	94	580	.02	.01	.2	[108] 16
	Oysterplant. See Salsify, items 1961–1962.																	
	Oysters:																	
	Raw, meat only:																	
1443	Eastern	84.6	66	8.4	1.8	3.4	—	1.8	94	143	5.5	73	121	310	.14	.18	2.5	—
1444	Pacific and Western (Olympia)	79.1	91	10.6	2.2	6.4	—	1.7	85	153	7.2	—	—	—	.12	—	1.3	30
1445	Cooked, fried [83]	54.7	239	8.6	13.9	18.6	Trace	1.5	152	241	8.1	206	203	440	.17	.29	3.2	—
1446	Canned, solids and liquid	82.2	76	8.5	2.2	4.9	.1	2.2	28	124	5.6	—	70	—	.02	.20	.8	—
1447	Frozen, solids and liquid	87.4	—	6.1	—	—	—	.8	—	—	—	380	210	310	.14	.18	2.5	—
	Oyster stew:																	
	Commercial, frozen:																	
1448	Condensed	79.8	102	4.6	6.3	6.9	.1	2.4	131	116	1.1	680	205	190	.06	.16	.3	—
1449	Prepared with equal volume of water	89.9	51	2.3	3.2	3.4	Trace	1.2	66	58	.6	340	102	100	.03	.08	.2	—
1450	Prepared with equal volume of milk	83.4	84	4.2	4.9	5.9	Trace	1.6	127	106	.6	366	176	170	.05	.17	.2	Trace
	Home-prepared:																	
1451	1 part oysters to 2 parts milk by volume [109]	82.0	97	5.2	6.4	4.5	—	1.8	114	111	1.9	339	133	340	.06	.18	.9	—
1452	1 part oysters to 3 parts milk by volume [109]	83.7	86	4.9	5.3	4.7	—	1.4	117	109	1.4	203	138	280	.06	.18	.7	—
	Pancakes, baked from home recipe, made with—																	
1453	Enriched flour	50.1	231	7.1	7.0	34.1	.1	1.7	101	139	1.3	425	123	120	.17	.22	1.3	Trace
1454	Unenriched flour	50.1	231	7.1	7.0	34.1	.1	1.7	101	139	.6	425	123	120	.05	.14	.4	Trace
	Pancake and waffle mixes and pancakes baked from mixes:																	
	Plain and buttermilk:																	
1455	Mix (pancake and waffle), with enriched flour, dry form.	8.3	356	8.6	1.8	75.7	.4	5.6	450	590	3.1	1,433	162	0	.44	.34	2.9	0
	Pancakes:																	
1456	Made with milk	53.9	202	6.1	5.6	31.9	.1	2.5	221	242	.9	451	156	120	.14	.23	.8	Trace
1457	Made with egg, milk	50.6	225	7.2	7.3	32.4	.1	2.5	215	260	1.2	564	154	250	.15	.24	.8	Trace
1458	Mix (pancake and waffle), with unenriched flour, dry form.	8.3	356	8.6	1.8	75.7	.4	5.6	450	590	1.4	1,433	162	0	.12	.08	1.1	0
	Pancakes:																	
1459	Made with milk	53.9	202	6.1	5.6	31.9	.1	2.5	221	242	.4	451	156	120	.06	.15	.4	Trace
1460	Made with egg, milk	50.6	225	7.2	7.3	32.4	.1	2.5	215	260	.7	564	154	250	.06	.17	.4	Trace
	Buckwheat and other cereal flours:																	
1461	Mix, dry form	11.2	328	10.5	1.9	70.3	1.4	6.1	466	826	3.1	1,334	476	Trace	.36	.12	2.2	0
1462	Pancakes, made with egg, milk	57.9	200	6.8	9.1	23.8	.4	2.4	220	337	1.3	464	245	230	.12	.16	.7	Trace
	Pancreas, raw:																	
	Beef:																	
1463	Very fat	53.	357	11.8	34.	0	0	1.1	—	222	—	—	—	—	—	—	—	—
1464	Fat	57.	316	12.8	29.	0	0	1.1	—	267	—	—	—	—	—	—	—	—
1465	Medium-fat	60.	283	13.5	25.	0	0	1.2	—	270	—	—	—	—	—	—	—	—
1466	Thin	67.	217	14.9	17.	0	0	1.3	—	307	—	—	—	—	—	—	—	—
1467	Lean only, adhering fat removed	73.	141	17.6	7.3	0	0	1.8	8	330	2.8	67	276	—	—	.55	5.8	—
1468	Calf	69.7	161	19.2	8.8	0	0	1.4	—	326	—	—	—	—	—	—	—	—
1469	Hog (hog sweetbread)	63.4	242	14.7	19.9	0	0	1.1	11	282	1.0	44	217	—	—	—	—	—
1470	**Papaws,** common, North American type, raw	76.6	85	5.2	.9	16.8	—	.5	—	—	—	—	—	—	—	—	—	—
1471	**Papayas,** raw	88.7	39	.6	.1	10.0	.9	.6	20	16	.3	3	234	1,750	.04	.04	.3	56
1472	**Parsley,** common garden (plain) and curled-leaf varieties, raw.	85.1	44	3.6	.6	8.5	1.5	2.2	203	63	6.2	45	727	8,500	.12	.26	1.2	172
	Parsnips:																	
1473	Raw	79.1	76	1.7	.5	17.5	2.0	1.2	50	77	.7	12	541	30	.08	.09	.2	[110] 16
1474	Cooked, boiled, drained	82.2	66	1.5	.5	14.9	2.0	.9	45	62	.6	8	379	30	.07	.08	.1	10
	Passionfruit. See Granadilla, item 1052.																	
	Pastinas, enriched, dry form:																	
1475	Egg	10.4	383	12.9	4.1	71.8	.3	.8	35	194	[89] 2.9	5	—	220	[89] .88	[89] .38	[89] 6.0	(0)

	Vegetable:																	
1476	Carrot	10.0	371	11.9	1.6	75.7	.6	.8	38	160	[59]2.9	—	—	730	[59].88	[59].38	[59]6.0	(0)
1477	Spinach	10.1	368	12.4	1.6	74.8	.5	1.1	63	173	[59]2.9	—	—	640	[59].88	[59].38	[59]6.0	(0)
	Pastry shell, plain. See Piecrust, items 1598, 1600.																	
1478	**Pâté de foie gras,** canned	37.0	462	11.4	43.8	4.8	0	3.0	—	—	—	—	—	—	.09	.30	2.5	—
	Peaches:																	
1479	Raw	89.1	38	.6	.1	9.7	.6	.5	9	19	.5	1	202	[111]1,330	.02	.05	1.0	7
	Canned, solids and liquid:																	
1480	Water pack, with or without artificial sweetener	91.1	31	.4	.1	8.1	.4	.3	4	13	.3	2	137	450	.01	.03	.6	3
1481	Juice pack	87.2	45	.6	.1	11.6	.4	.5	6	19	.5	2	205	670	.01	.04	.9	4
	Sirup pack:																	
1482	Light	84.1	58	.4	.1	15.1	.4	.3	4	13	.3	2	133	440	.01	.03	.6	3
1483	Heavy	79.1	78	.4	.1	20.1	.4	.3	4	12	.3	2	130	430	.01	.02	.6	3
1484	Extra heavy	74.1	97	.4	.1	25.1	.4	.3	4	12	.3	2	128	420	.01	.02	.5	3
	Dehydrated, sulfured, nugget-type and pieces:																	
1485	Uncooked	3.0	340	4.8	(.9)	88.0	(4.0)	3.3	(62)	(151)	3.5	(21)	(1,229)	(5,000)	Trace	.10	7.8	14
1486	Cooked, fruit and liquid, with added sugar	66.6	121	1.1	(.2)	31.3	(.9)	.8	(15)	(36)	.8	(5)	(292)	(890)	Trace	.02	1.7	2
	Dried, sulfured:																	
1487	Uncooked	25.0	262	3.1	.7	68.3	3.1	2.9	48	117	6.0	16	950	3,900	.01	.19	5.3	18
	Cooked, fruit and liquid:																	
1488	Without added sugar	76.5	82	1.0	.2	21.4	1.0	.9	15	37	1.9	5	297	1,220	Trace	.06	1.5	2
1489	With added sugar	67.3	119	.9	.2	30.8	.9	.8	13	32	1.6	4	261	1,070	Trace	.05	1.4	2
1490	Frozen, sliced, sweetened, not thawed	76.5	88	.4	.1	22.6	.4	.4	4	13	.5	2	124	650	.01	.04	.7	[112]40
1491	**Peach nectar,** canned (approx. 40% fruit)	87.2	48	.2	Trace	12.4	.1	.2	4	11	.2	1	78	430	.01	.02	.4	Trace
	Peanuts:																	
1492	Raw, with skins	5.6	564	26.0	47.5	18.6	2.4	2.3	69	401	2.1	5	674	—	1.14	.13	17.2	0
1493	Raw, without skins	5.4	568	26.3	48.4	17.6	1.9	2.3	59	409	2.0	5	674	0	.99	.13	15.8	0
1494	Boiled	36.4	376	15.5	31.5	14.5	1.8	2.1	43	181	1.3	4	462	—	.48	.08	10.0	0
1495	Roasted, with skins	1.8	582	26.2	48.7	20.6	2.7	2.7	72	407	2.2	5	701	—	.32	.13	17.1	0
1496	Roasted and salted	1.6	585	26.0	49.8	18.8	2.4	3.8	74	401	2.1	418	674	—	.32	.13	17.2	0
	Peanut butters made with—																	
1497	Small amounts of added fat, salt	1.8	581	27.8	49.4	17.2	1.9	3.8	63	407	2.0	607	670	—	.13	.13	15.7	0
1498	Small amounts of added fat, sweetener, salt	1.7	582	25.5	49.5	19.5	1.9	3.8	61	395	2.0	606	652	—	.12	.12	15.3	0
1499	Moderate amounts of added fat, sweetener, salt	1.7	589	25.2	50.6	18.8	1.8	3.7	59	380	1.9	605	627	—	.12	.12	14.7	0
1500	**Peanut spread**	2.2	601	20.3	52.1	22.0	1.5	3.4	50	322	1.5	597	530	—	.10	.10	12.4	0
1501	**Peanut flour,** defatted	7.3	371	47.9	9.2	31.5	2.7	4.1	104	720	3.5	9	1,186	—	.75	.22	27.8	0
	Pears:																	
1502	Raw, including skin	83.2	61	.7	.4	15.3	1.4	.4	8	11	.3	2	130	20	.02	.04	.1	4
1503	Candied	21.0	303	1.3	.6	75.9	—	1.2	—	—	—	—	—	—	—	—	—	—
	Canned, solids and liquid:																	
1504	Water pack, with or without artificial sweetener	91.1	32	.2	.2	8.3	.7	.2	5	7	.2	1	88	Trace	.01	.02	.1	1
1505	Juice pack	87.3	46	.3	.3	11.8	.8	.3	8	11	.3	1	130	Trace	.02	.03	.1	2
	Sirup pack:																	
1506	Light	83.8	61	.2	.2	15.6	.7	.2	5	7	.2	1	85	Trace	.01	.02	.1	1
1507	Heavy	79.8	76	.2	.2	19.6	.6	.2	5	7	.2	1	84	Trace	.01	.02	.1	1
1508	Extra heavy	75.8	92	.2	.2	23.6	.6	.2	5	7	.2	1	83	Trace	.01	.02	.1	1
	Dried, sulfured:																	
1509	Uncooked	26.0	268	3.1	1.8	67.3	6.2	1.8	35	48	1.3	7	573	70	.01	.18	.6	7
	Cooked, fruit and liquid:																	
1510	Without added sugar	65.2	126	1.5	.8	31.7	2.9	.8	16	23	.6	3	269	30	Trace	.08	.3	2
1511	With added sugar	59.1	151	1.3	.8	38.0	2.6	.8	15	20	.6	3	244	30	Trace	.07	.2	2
1512	**Pear nectar,** canned (approx. 40% fruit) [4]	86.2	52	.3	.2	13.2	.3	.1	3	5	.1	1	39	Trace	Trace	.02	Trace	Trace
	Peas, edible-podded:																	
1513	Raw	83.3	53	3.4	.2	12.0	1.2	1.1	62	90	.7	—	170	(680)	.28	.12	—	21
1514	Cooked, boiled, drained	86.6	43	2.9	.2	9.5	1.2	.8	56	76	.5	—	119	(610)	.22	.11	—	14
	Peas, green, immature:																	
1515	Raw	78.0	84	6.3	.4	14.4	2.0	.9	26	116	1.9	2	316	640	.35	.14	2.9	27
1516	Cooked, boiled, drained	81.5	71	5.4	.4	12.1	2.0	.6	23	99	1.8	1	196	540	.28	.11	2.3	20
	Canned:																	
	Alaska (Early or June peas):																	
	Regular pack:																	
1517	Solids and liquid	82.6	66	3.5	.3	12.5	1.5	1.1	20	66	1.7	[9]236	96	450	.09	.05	.9	9
1518	Drained solids	77.0	88	4.7	.4	16.8	2.3	1.1	26	76	1.9	[9]236	96	690	.09	.06	.8	8
1519	Drained liquid	92.3	26	1.3	Trace	5.2	Trace	1.2	10	48	1.3	[9]236	96	Trace	.10	.04	1.0	10
	Special dietary pack (low-sodium):																	
1520	Solids and liquid	85.9	55	3.6	.3	9.8	1.3	.4	20	66	1.7	3	96	450	.09	.05	.9	9
1521	Drained solids	80.1	78	4.8	.4	14.3	2.0	.4	26	76	1.9	3	96	690	.09	.06	.8	8
1522	Drained liquid	94.1	22	1.4	Trace	4.1	Trace	.4	10	48	1.3	3	96	Trace	.10	.04	1.0	10

[9] Estimated average based on addition of salt in the amount of 0.6 percent of the finished product.

[59] Based on product with minimum level of enrichment.

[83] Dipped in egg, milk, and breadcrumbs.

[93] Value cannot be calculated inasmuch as digestibility of peel is not known.

[108] Ascorbic acid may be added as a preservative or as a nutrient. Value listed is based on product with label stating 30 mg. per 6 fl. oz. serving. If label claim is 30 mg. per 8 fl. oz. serving, value would be 12 mg. per 100 grams.

[109] Contains added salt and butter.

[110] Year-round average. Value for parsnips in the fall within 3 months of harvest is about 24 mg. per 100 grams, and drops to less than half this value if storage exceeds 6 months.

[111] Based on yellow-fleshed varieties; for white-fleshed varieties, value is about 50 I.U. per 100 grams.

[112] Average weighted in accordance with commercial freezing practices. For products without added ascorbic acid, average is about 11 mg. per 100 grams; for those with added ascorbic acid, around 41 mg.

TABLE 1.—COMPOSITION OF FOODS, 100 GRAMS, EDIBLE PORTION—Continued

[Numbers in parentheses denote values imputed—usually from another form of the food or from a similar food. Zero in parentheses indicates that the amount of a constituent probably is none or is too small to measure. Dashes denote lack of reliable data for a constituent believed to be present in measurable amount. Calculated values, as those based on a recipe, are not in parentheses]

Item No.	Food and description	Water	Food energy	Protein	Fat	Carbohydrate		Ash	Calcium	Phos-phorus	Iron	Sodium	Potas-sium	Vitamin A value	Thiamine	Ribo-flavin	Niacin	Ascorbic acid
						Total	Fiber											
(A)	(B)	(C)	(D)	(E)	(F)	(G)	(H)	(I)	(J)	(K)	(L)	(M)	(N)	(O)	(P)	(Q)	(R)	(S)
		Percent	Calories	Grams	Grams	Grams	Grams	Grams	Milligrams	Milligrams	Milligrams	Milligrams	Milligrams	International units	Milligrams	Milligrams	Milligrams	Milligrams
	Peas, green, immature—Continued																	
	Canned—Continued																	
	Sweet (sweet wrinkled peas, sugar peas):																	
	Regular pack:																	
1523	Solids and liquid	84.8	57	3.4	0.3	10.4	1.4	1.1	19	58	1.5	[9] 236	96	450	0.11	0.06	1.0	9
1524	Drained solids	79.0	80	4.6	.4	15.0	2.2	1.0	25	67	1.7	[9] 236	96	690	.11	.06	1.0	8
1525	Drained liquid	93.3	22	1.3	Trace	4.3	Trace	1.1	9	42	1.1	[9] 236	96	Trace	.12	.05	1.1	10
	Special dietary pack (low-sodium):																	
1526	Solids and liquid	87.8	47	3.3	.3	8.2	1.3	.4	19	58	1.5	3	96	450	.11	.06	1.0	9
1527	Drained solids	81.8	72	4.4	.4	13.0	2.0	.4	25	67	1.7	3	96	690	.11	.06	1.0	8
1528	Drained liquid	94.9	18	1.3	Trace	3.4	Trace	.4	9	42	1.1	3	96	Trace	.12	.05	1.1	10
	Frozen:																	
1529	Not thawed	80.7	73	5.4	.3	12.8	1.9	.8	20	90	2.0	[10] 129	150	680	.32	.10	2.0	19
1530	Cooked, boiled, drained	82.1	68	5.1	.3	11.8	1.9	.7	19	86	1.9	115	135	600	.27	.09	1.7	13
	Peas, mature seeds, dry:																	
	Whole:																	
1531	Raw	11.7	340	24.1	1.3	60.3	4.9	2.6	64	340	5.1	35	1,005	120	.74	.29	3.0	—
	Split, without seed coat:																	
1532	Raw	9.3	348	24.2	1.0	62.7	1.2	2.8	33	268	5.1	40	895	120	.74	.29	3.0	—
1533	Cooked	70.0	115	8.0	.3	20.8	.4	.9	11	89	1.7	[4] 13	296	40	.15	.09	.9	—
	Peas and carrots, frozen:																	
1534	Not thawed	85.4	55	3.3	.3	10.4	1.5	.6	26	59	1.2	[10] 92	171	9,300	.20	.07	1.3	10
1535	Cooked, boiled, drained	85.8	53	3.2	.3	10.1	1.5	.6	25	57	1.1	84	157	9,300	.19	.07	1.3	8
1536	**Pecans**	3.4	687	9.2	71.2	14.6	2.3	1.6	73	289	2.4	Trace	603	130	.86	.13	.9	2
	Peppers, hot, chili:																	
	Immature, green:																	
1537	Raw pods, excluding seeds	88.8	37	1.3	.2	9.1	1.8	.6	10	25	.7	—	—	770	.09	.06	1.7	235
	Canned:																	
1538	Pods, excluding seeds; solids and liquid	92.5	25	.9	.1	6.1	1.2	.4	7	17	.5	—	—	610	.02	.05	.8	68
1539	Chili sauce	93.9	20	.7	.1	5.0	1.0	.3	5	14	.4	—	—	610	.03	.03	.7	68
	Mature, red:																	
	Raw:																	
1540	Pods, including seeds	74.3	93	3.7	2.3	18.1	9.0	1.6	29	78	1.2	—	—	21,600	.22	.36	4.4	369
1541	Pods, excluding seeds	80.3	65	2.3	.4	15.8	2.3	1.2	16	49	1.4	25	564	21,600	.1	.2	2.9	369
1542	Canned, chili sauce	94.1	21	.9	.6	3.9	1.7	.5	9	16	.5	—	—	9,590	.01	.09	.6	30
	Dried:																	
1543	Pods	12.6	321	12.9	9.1	59.8	26.2	7.4	130	240	7.8	373	1,201	77,000	.23	1.33	10.5	[113] 12
1544	Chili powder with added seasoning	8.5	340	14.3	12.4	56.5	22.2	8.3	265	204	15.2	1,574	1,000	65,000	.19	1.13	8.9	10
	Peppers, sweet, garden varieties:																	
	Immature, green:																	
1545	Raw	93.4	22	1.2	.2	4.8	1.4	.4	9	22	.7	13	213	420	.08	.08	.5	128
	Cooked:																	
1546	Boiled, drained	94.7	18	1.0	.2	3.8	1.4	.3	9	16	.5	9	149	420	.06	.07	.5	96
1547	Stuffed with beef and crumbs	63.1	170	13.0	5.5	16.8	.7	1.6	42	121	2.1	314	258	280	.09	.17	2.5	40
1548	Mature, red, raw	90.7	31	1.4	.3	7.1	1.7	.5	13	30	.6	—	—	4,450	(.08)	(.08)	(.5)	204
1549	**Perch, white,** raw	75.7	118	19.3	4.0	0	0	1.2	—	192	—	—	—	—	—	—	—	—
1550	**Perch, yellow,** raw	79.2	91	19.5	.9	0	0	1.2	—	180	.6	68	230	—	.06	.17	1.7	—
	Persimmons, raw:																	
1551	Japanese or kaki	78.6	77	.7	.4	19.7	1.6	.6	6	26	.3	6	174	2,710	.03	.02	.1	11
1552	Native	64.4	127	.8	.4	33.5	1.5	.9	27	26	2.5	1	310	—	—	—	—	66
	Pheasant, raw:																	
1553	Total edible	69.2	151	24.3	5.2	0	0	1.2	—	—	—	—	—	—	—	—	—	—
1554	Flesh and skin	68.9	152	24.7	5.2	0	0	1.2	—	—	—	—	—	—	—	—	—	—
1555	Flesh only	67.9	162	23.6	6.8	0	0	1.3	—	—	—	—	—	—	—	—	—	—
1556	Giblets	71.4	139	20.8	4.9	1.6	0	1.3	—	—	—	—	—	—	—	—	—	—
1557	**Pickerel,** chain, raw	79.7	84	18.7	.5	0	0	1.2	—	—	.7	—	—	—	—	—	—	—
	Pickles:																	
	Cucumber:																	
1558	Dill	93.3	11	.7	.2	2.2	.5	3.6	26	21	1.0	1,428	200	100	Trace	.02	Trace	6
1559	Fresh (as bread-and-butter pickles)	78.7	73	.9	.2	17.9	.5	2.3	32	27	1.8	673	—	140	Trace	.03	Trace	9
1560	Sour	94.8	10	.5	.2	2.0	.5	2.5	17	15	3.2	1,353	—	100	Trace	.02	Trace	7

No.	Food																	
1561	Sweet	60.7	146	.7	.4	36.5	—	1.7	12	16	1.2	—	—	90	Trace	.02	Trace	6
	Chowchow (Cucumber with added cauliflower, onion, mustard):																	
1562	Sour	87.6	29	1.4	1.3	4.1	.6	5.6	32	53	2.6	1,338	—	—	—	—	—	—
1563	Sweet	68.9	116	1.5	.9	27.0	.9	1.7	23	22	1.5	527	—	—	—	—	—	—
	Relish, finely cut or chopped:																	
1564	Sour	(93.0)	19	(.7)	(.9)	(2.7)	(1.1)	(2.7)	(29)	(20)	(1.1)	—	—	—	—	—	—	—
1565	Sweet	63.0	138	.5	.6	34.0	.8	1.9	20	14	.8	712	—	—	—	—	—	—
	Pies:																	
	Baked, piecrust made with unenriched flour: [114]																	
1566	Apple	47.6	256	2.2	11.1	38.1	.4	1.0	8	22	.3	301	80	30	.02	.02	.4	1
1567	Banana custard	54.4	221	4.5	9.3	30.7	.2	1.1	66	82	.5	194	203	250	.04	.13	.3	1
1568	Blackberry	51.0	243	2.6	11.0	34.4	1.9	1.0	19	26	.5	268	100	90	.02	.02	.3	4
1569	Blueberry	51.0	242	2.4	10.8	34.9	.7	.9	11	23	.6	268	65	30	.02	.02	.3	3
	Boston cream. See Cakes, item 522.																	
1570	Butterscotch	45.1	267	4.4	11.0	38.3	Trace	1.2	75	81	.9	214	95	260	.03	.10	.2	Trace
1571	Cherry	46.6	261	2.6	11.3	38.4	.1	1.1	14	25	.3	304	105	440	.02	.02	.5	Trace
1572	Chocolate chiffon	33.0	328	6.8	15.3	43.7	.2	1.1	24	97	1.2	252	110	310	.03	.10	.2	0
1573	Chocolate meringue	48.4	252	4.8	12.0	33.5	.2	1.2	69	98	.7	256	139	190	.03	.12	.2	Trace
1574	Coconut custard	55.4	235	6.0	12.5	24.9	.2	1.2	94	116	.7	247	163	230	.06	.19	.3	0
1575	Custard	58.1	218	6.1	11.1	23.4	Trace	1.3	96	113	.6	287	137	230	.05	.16	.3	0
1576	Lemon chiffon	35.6	313	7.0	12.6	43.8	Trace	1.0	23	83	.9	261	81	170	.03	.08	.2	3
1577	Lemon meringue	47.4	255	3.7	10.2	37.7	Trace	1.0	14	49	.5	282	50	170	.03	.08	.2	3
1578	Mince	43.0	271	2.5	11.5	41.2	.4	1.8	28	38	1.0	448	178	Trace	.07	.04	.4	1
1579	Peach	47.5	255	2.5	10.7	38.2	.4	1.1	10	29	.5	268	149	730	.02	.04	.7	3
1580	Pecan	19.5	418	5.1	22.9	51.3	.5	1.2	47	103	2.8	221	123	160	.16	.07	.3	Trace
1581	Pineapple	48.0	253	2.2	10.7	38.1	.2	1.0	13	21	.5	271	72	20	.04	.02	.4	1
1582	Pineapple chiffon	41.1	288	6.6	12.1	39.1	.1	1.1	24	76	.9	256	98	350	.04	.09	.4	1
1583	Pineapple custard	54.3	220	4.0	8.7	32.1	.1	.9	50	65	.4	186	97	180	.04	.09	.4	1
1584	Pumpkin	59.2	211	4.0	11.2	24.5	.5	1.1	51	69	.5	214	160	2,470	.03	.10	.5	Trace
1585	Raisin	42.5	270	2.6	10.7	43.0	.3	1.2	18	40	.9	285	192	Trace	.03	.03	.3	1
1586	Rhubarb	47.4	253	2.5	10.7	38.2	.6	1.2	64	26	.7	270	159	50	.02	.04	.3	3
1587	Strawberry	58.4	198	1.9	7.9	30.9	.8	.9	16	25	.7	194	120	40	.02	.04	.4	25
1588	Sweetpotato	59.3	213	4.5	11.3	23.7	.2	1.2	69	84	.5	218	163	2,400	.05	.12	.3	4
	Frozen in unbaked form:																	
	Apple:																	
1589	Unbaked	56.3	210	1.6	8.3	33.2	.2	.6	7	17	.2	177	60	10	.02	.01	.2	1
1590	Baked	47.3	254	1.9	10.1	40.0	.3	.7	8	21	.3	213	72	10	.02	.02	.2	Trace
	Cherry:																	
1591	Unbaked	47.8	256	1.9	10.6	39.0	.1	.7	11	21	.2	202	72	280	.02	.02	.2	2
1592	Baked	40.6	291	2.2	12.0	44.4	.1	.8	12	23	.3	229	82	290	.02	.02	.2	2
	Coconut custard:																	
1593	Unbaked	58.0	205	5.2	8.5	27.1	.2	1.2	86	104	.6	238	157	190	.04	.15	.2	Trace
1594	Baked	51.2	249	6.0	12.0	29.5	.2	1.3	95	115	.6	252	172	160	.04	.16	.2	Trace
	Pie mix, coconut custard, and pie baked from mix:																	
1595	Mix, filling and piecrust, dry form	4.2	470	3.3	20.0	70.6	.7	1.9	13	46	.5	628	142	0	.02	.02	.4	0
1596	Pie prepared with egg yolk and milk, baked	57.6	203	4.3	7.9	29.1	.3	1.1	93	103	.4	235	154	210	.03	.14	.2	Trace
	Piecrust or plain pastry, made with—																	
	Enriched flour:																	
1597	Unbaked	20.9	464	5.7	31.0	40.7	.1	1.7	13	47	1.6	568	46	0	.24	.14	1.9	0
1598	Baked	14.9	500	6.1	33.4	43.8	.2	1.8	14	50	1.7	611	50	0	.20	.14	1.8	0
	Unenriched flour:																	
1599	Unbaked	20.9	464	5.7	31.0	40.7	.1	1.7	13	47	.4	568	46	0	.03	.03	.5	0
1600	Baked	14.9	500	6.1	33.4	43.8	.2	1.8	14	50	.5	611	50	0	.03	.03	.5	0
	Piecrust mix (including stick form) and piecrust baked from mix:																	
1601	Mix, dry form	8.6	522	7.2	32.7	49.5	.2	2.0	46	96	.5	693	63	0	.04	.04	.7	0
1602	Piecrust, prepared with water, baked	18.7	464	6.4	29.1	44.0	.2	1.8	41	85	.4	813	56	0	.03	.03	.5	0
	Pigeonpeas, raw:																	
1603	Immature seeds	69.5	117	7.2	.6	21.3	3.3	1.4	42	127	1.6	5	552	140	.40	.17	2.2	39
1604	Mature seeds, dry	10.8	342	20.4	1.4	63.7	7.0	3.7	107	316	8.0	26	981	80	.32	.16	3.0	—
1605	**Pigs' feet,** pickled	66.9	199	16.7	14.8	0	0	1.7	—	—	—	—	—	—	—	—	—	—
1606	**Pike, blue,** raw	78.8	90	19.1	.9	0	0	1.2	—	—	—	—	—	—	—	—	—	—
1607	**Pike, northern,** raw	80.0	88	18.3	1.1	0	0	1.1	—	—	—	—	—	—	—	—	—	—
1608	**Pike, walleye,** raw	78.3	93	19.3	1.2	0	0	1.2	—	214	.4	51	319	—	.25	.16	2.3	—
1609	**Pilinuts**	6.3	669	11.4	71.1	8.4	2.7	2.8	140	554	3.4	3	489	40	.88	.09	.5	Trace
1610	**Pimientos,** canned, solids and liquid	92.4	27	.9	.5	5.8	.6	.4	[115] 7	17	1.5	—	—	2,300	.02	.06	.4	95

[9] Estimated average based on addition of salt in the amount of 0.6 percent of the finished product.

[19] Average weighted in accordance with commercial practices in freezing vegetables.

[113] Based on 1 sample described as ground powder, stored; for freshly processed product, value is 154 mg. per 100 grams.

[114] If piecrust is made with enriched flour, increase values for nutrients in milligrams per 100 grams of pie by the following amounts:

	Iron	Thiamine	Riboflavin	Niacin
One-crust pie	0.3	0.03	0.03	0.3
Two-crust pie	.4	.06	.04	.5

[115] Federal standards provide for addition of certain calcium salts as firming agents; if used, these salts may add calcium not to exceed 26 mg. per 100 grams of finished product.

TABLE 1.—COMPOSITION OF FOODS, 100 GRAMS, EDIBLE PORTION—Continued

[Numbers in parentheses denote values imputed—usually from another form of the food or from a similar food. Zero in parentheses indicates that the amount of a constituent probably is none or is too small to measure. Dashes denote lack of reliable data for a constituent believed to be present in measurable amount. Calculated values, as those based on a recipe, are not in parentheses]

Item No.	Food and description	Water	Food energy	Protein	Fat	Carbohydrate		Ash	Calcium	Phos-phorus	Iron	Sodium	Potas-sium	Vitamin A value	Thiamine	Ribo-flavin	Niacin	Ascorbic acid
						Total	Fiber											
(A)	(B)	(C)	(D)	(E)	(F)	(G)	(H)	(I)	(J)	(K)	(L)	(M)	(N)	(O)	(P)	(Q)	(R)	(S)
		Percent	Calories	Grams	Grams	Grams	Grams	Grams	Milligrams	Milligrams	Milligrams	Milligrams	Milligrams	International units	Milligrams	Milligrams	Milligrams	Milligrams
	Pineapple:																	
1611	Raw	85.3	52	0.4	0.2	13.7	0.4	0.4	17	8	0.5	1	146	70	0.09	0.03	0.2	17
1612	Candied	18.0	316	.8	.4	80.0	.8	.8	—	—	—	—	—	—	—	—	—	—
	Canned, solids and liquid:																	
1613	Water pack, all styles except crushed, with or without artificial sweetener.	89.1	39	.3	.1	10.2	.3	.3	12	5	.3	1	99	50	.08	.02	.2	7
1614	Juice pack, all styles	84.0	58	.4	.1	15.1	.3	.4	16	8	.4	1	147	60	.10	.03	.3	10
	Sirup pack, all styles:																	
1615	Light	83.9	59	.3	.1	15.4	.3	.3	11	5	.3	1	97	50	.08	.02	.2	7
1616	Heavy	79.9	74	.3	.1	19.4	.3	.3	11	5	.3	1	96	50	.08	.02	.2	7
1617	Extra heavy	75.9	90	.3	.1	23.4	.3	.3	11	5	.3	1	94	40	.08	.02	.2	6
1618	Frozen chunks, sweetened, not thawed	77.1	85	.4	.1	22.2	.3	.2	9	4	.4	2	100	30	.10	.03	.3	8
	Pineapple juice:																	
1619	Canned, unsweetened	85.6	55	.4	.1	13.5	.1	.4	15	9	.3	1	149	50	.05	.02	.2	9
	Frozen concentrate, unsweetened:																	
1620	Undiluted	53.1	179	1.3	.1	44.3	.3	1.2	39	28	.9	3	472	50	.23	.06	.9	42
1621	Diluted with 3 parts water, by volume	86.5	52	.4	Trace	12.8	.1	.3	11	8	.3	1	136	10	.07	.02	.2	12
1622	**Pineapple juice and grapefruit juice drink,** canned (approx. 40% fruit juices).[118]	86.0	54	.2	Trace	13.6	Trace	.2	5	5	.2	Trace	62	10	.02	.01	.1	16
1623	**Pineapple juice and orange juice drink,** canned (approx. 40% fruit juices).[118]	86.0	54	.2	.1	13.5	Trace	.2	5	6	.2	Trace	70	50	.02	.01	.1	16
	Pinenuts:																	
1624	Pignolias	5.6	552	31.1	47.4	11.6	.9	4.3	—	—	—	—	—	—	.62	—	—	—
1625	Piñon	3.1	635	13.0	60.5	20.5	1.1	2.9	12	604	5.2	—	—	30	1.28	.23	4.5	Trace
1626	**Pistachionuts**	5.3	594	19.3	53.7	19.0	1.9	2.7	131	500	7.3	—	972	230	.67	—	1.4	0
1627	**Pitanga** (Surinam-cherry), raw	85.8	51	.8	.4	12.5	.6	.5	9	11	.2	—	—	1,500	.03	.04	.3	30
	Pizza, with cheese:																	
	From home recipe, baked:[117]																	
1628	With cheese topping	48.3	236	12.0	8.3	28.3	.3	3.1	221	195	1.0	702	130	630	.06	.20	1.0	8
1629	With sausage topping	50.6	234	7.8	9.3	29.6	.3	2.7	17	92	1.2	729	168	560	.09	.12	1.5	9
	Chilled:																	
1630	Partially baked	53.3	208	7.8	5.8	30.9	.3	2.2	121	126	.7	538	94	420	.06	.14	.9	6
1631	Baked	45.1	245	9.2	6.8	36.3	.3	2.6	143	148	.9	633	111	390	.06	.16	1.0	6
	Frozen:																	
1632	Partially baked	48.9	229	8.9	6.6	33.1	.3	2.5	146	146	.9	605	107	450	.06	.16	.9	5
1633	Baked	45.3	245	9.5	7.1	35.4	.3	2.7	156	156	.9	647	114	440	.06	.17	1.0	6
1634	**Plantain** (baking banana), raw	66.4	119	1.1	.4	31.2	.4	.9	7	30	.7	5	385	([118])	.06	.04	.6	14
	Plate dinners, frozen, commercial, unheated:																	
1635	Beef pot roast, whole oven-browned potatoes, peas, and corn.	76.3	106	13.1	3.2	6.1	.3	1.3	10	76	1.6	259	244	110	.06	.10	2.1	5
1636	Chicken, fried; mashed potatoes; mixed vegetables (carrots, peas, corn, beans).	66.1	173	12.8	8.5	11.3	.4	1.3	41	145	1.2	344	112	590	.07	.18	5.2	4
1637	Meat loaf with tomato sauce, mashed potatoes, and peas.	73.7	131	8.0	6.7	9.8	.3	1.8	19	117	1.3	393	115	430	.10	.14	1.7	4
1638	Turkey, sliced; mashed potatoes; peas	74.7	112	8.4	3.0	12.7	.3	1.2	26	87	1.1	400	176	130	.07	.09	2.3	4
	Plums:																	
	Raw:																	
1639	Damson	81.1	66	.5	Trace	17.8	.4	.6	18	17	.5	2	299	(300)	.08	.03	.5	—
1640	Japanese and hybrid	86.6	48	.5	.2	12.3	.6	.4	12	18	.5	1	170	250	.03	.03	.5	6
1641	Prune-type	78.7	75	.8	.2	19.7	.4	.6	12	18	.5	1	170	[119] 300	.03	.03	.5	4
	Canned, solids and liquid:																	
1642	Greengage, water pack, with or without artificial sweetener.	90.6	33	.4	.1	8.6	.2	.3	(9)	(13)	(.2)	1	82	(160)	(.01)	(.02)	(.3)	2
	Purple (Italian prunes):																	
1643	Water pack, with or without artificial sweetener.	86.8	46	.4	.2	11.9	.3	.7	9	10	1.0	2	148	1,250	.02	.02	.4	2
	Sirup pack:																	
1644	Light	82.4	63	.4	.1	16.6	.3	.5	9	10	.9	1	145	1,230	.02	.02	.4	2
1645	Heavy	77.4	83	.4	.1	21.6	.3	.5	9	10	.9	1	142	1,210	.02	.02	.4	2
1646	Extra heavy	72.4	102	.4	.1	26.7	.3	.4	8	9	.9	1	139	1,180	.02	.02	.4	2
	Poha. See Groundcherries, item 1092.																	
	Pokeberry (poke) shoots:																	
1647	Raw	91.6	23	2.6	.4	3.7	—	1.7	53	44	1.7	—	—	8,700	.08	.33	1.2	136
1648	Cooked, boiled, drained	92.9	20	2.3	.4	3.1	—	1.3	53	33	1.2	—	—	8,700	.07	.25	1.1	82

1649	**Pollock:** Raw	77.4	95	20.4	.9	0	0	1.3	—	—	—	48	350	—	.05	.10	1.6	—
1650	Cooked, creamed [120]	74.7	128	13.9	5.9	4.0	—	1.5	—	—	—	111	238	—	.03	.13	.7	Trace
1651	**Pomegranate pulp,** raw	82.3	63	.5	.3	16.4	.2	.5	3	8	.3	3	259	Trace	.03	.03	.3	4
1652	**Pompano,** raw	70.9	166	18.8	9.5	0	0	1.1	—	—	—	47	191	—	.41	.22	—	—
	Popcorn:																	
1653	Unpopped	9.8	362	11.9	4.7	72.1	2.1	1.5	(10)	(264)	(2.5)	(3)	—	—	(.39)	(.11)	(2.1)	(0)
	Popped:																	
1654	Plain	4.0	386	12.7	5.0	76.7	2.2	1.6	(11)	(281)	(2.7)	(3)	—	—	—	(.12)	(2.2)	(0)
1655	Oil and salt added	3.1	456	9.8	21.8	59.1	1.7	6.2	8	216	2.1	1,940	—	—	—	.09	1.7	0
1656	Sugar-coated	4.0	383	6.1	3.5	85.4	1.1	1.0	5	135	1.3	[96] 1	—	—	—	.06	1.1	0
1657	**Popovers,** baked (from home recipe with enriched flour).	54.9	224	8.8	9.2	25.8	.1	1.3	96	140	[121] 1.5	220	150	330	[121] .14	[121] .25	[121] 1.0	Trace
1658	**Porgy and scup,** raw	76.2	112	19.0	3.4	0	0	1.3	54	250	—	63	287	—	—	—	—	—
	Pork, fresh:																	
	Carcass, raw:																	
	Fat class:																	
1659	Total edible (41% lean, 59% fat)	33.4	553	9.1	57.0	0	0	.5	5	88	1.4			(0)	.44	.10	2.4	—
1660	Separable lean	68.0	185	17.3	12.3	0	0	2.4	10	197	2.6			(0)	.84	.20	4.5	—
1661	Separable fat	11.1	784	3.2	85.4	0	0	.3	2	10	.5			(0)	.16	.04	.8	—
	Medium-fat class:																	
1662	Total edible (47% lean, 53% fat)	37.3	513	10.2	52.0	0	0	.5	6	103	1.5			(0)	.50	.12	2.7	—
1663	Separable lean	69.3	171	17.8	10.5	0	0	2.4	10	204	2.7			(0)	.87	.21	4.6	—
1664	Separable fat	12.4	770	3.5	83.7	0	0	.4	2	14	.5			(0)	.17	.04	.9	—
	Thin class:																	
1665	Total edible (53% lean, 47% fat)	41.1	472	11.2	47.0	0	0	.6	6	116	1.7			(0)	.54	.13	2.9	—
1666	Separable lean	70.7	156	18.3	8.6	0	0	2.4	11	210	2.7			(0)	.89	.21	4.8	—
1667	Separable fat	13.8	755	3.7	81.9	0	0	.6	2	16	.6			(0)	.18	.04	1.0	—
	Wholesale cuts, raw:																	
	Bacon or belly:																	
1668	Fat class (25% lean, 75% fat)	26.4	631	7.1	66.6	0	0	.3	4	62	1.1			(0)	.35	.08	1.8	—
1669	Medium-fat class (33% lean, 67% fat)	30.3	588	8.2	61.3	0	0	.4	5	76	1.2			(0)	.40	.10	2.1	—
1670	Thin class (40% lean, 60% fat)	34.3	545	9.4	56.0	0	0	.5	5	92	1.4			(0)	.46	.11	2.4	—
	Backfat:																	
	Total edible:																	
1671	Fat class (100% fat)	6.4	841	1.7	92.4	0	0	.1	1	0	.3			(0)	.08	.02	.4	—
1672	Medium-fat class (100% fat)	7.5	827	2.1	90.7	0	0	.1	1	0	.3			(0)	.10	.02	.5	—
1673	Thin class (100% fat)	8.6	814	2.4	89.1	0	0	.1	1	0	.4			(0)	.12	.03	.6	—
	Shoulder:																	
	Total edible:																	
1674	Fat class (58% lean, 42% fat)	45.4	435	11.8	42.6	0	0	.6	7	124	1.8			(0)	.57	.14	3.1	—
1675	Medium-fat class (67% lean, 33% fat)	48.5	401	12.7	38.5	0	0	.6	7	136	1.9			(0)	.62	.15	3.3	—
1676	Thin class (75% lean, 25% fat)	51.7	368	13.6	34.4	0	0	.7	8	148	2.0	(122)	(123)	(0)	.66	.16	3.5	—
	Composite of trimmed lean cuts, ham, loin, shoulder, and spareribs:																	
	Fat class:																	
	Total edible:																	
1677	Raw (72% lean, 28% fat)	52.6	346	14.6	31.4	0	0	1.0	8	161	2.2			(0)	.71	.17	3.8	—
1678	Cooked, roasted (72% lean, 28% fat)	42.1	410	20.9	35.6	0	0	1.3	9	213	2.7			(0)	.47	.21	4.2	—
	Separable lean:																	
1679	Raw	68.0	182	18.8	11.3	0	0	1.4	11	217	2.8			(0)	.91	.22	4.9	—
1680	Cooked, roasted	56.4	245	27.6	14.1	0	0	1.9	12	287	3.5			(0)	.60	.28	5.4	—
	Separable fat:																	
1681	Raw	13.2	764	3.9	82.8	0	0	.1	2	19	.6			(0)	.19	.05	1.0	—
	Medium-fat class:																	
	Total edible:																	
1682	Raw (77% lean, 23% fat)	56.3	308	15.7	26.7	0	0	1.2	9	175	2.3			(0)	.76	.18	4.1	—
1683	Cooked, roasted (77% lean, 23% fat)	45.2	373	22.6	30.6	0	0	1.6	10	232	2.9			(0)	.50	.23	4.9	—
	Separable lean:																	
1684	Raw	69.0	174	19.1	10.2	0	0	1.4	11	221	2.9			(0)	.93	.22	5.0	—
1685	Cooked, roasted	57.2	236	28.0	12.9	0	0	1.9	12	292	3.6			(0)	.61	.28	5.5	—
	Separable fat:																	
1686	Raw	14.3	751	4.1	81.3	0	0	.4	2	22	.6			(0)	.20	.05	1.1	—
	Thin class:																	
	Total edible:																	
1687	Raw (81% lean, 19% fat)	59.5	276	16.7	22.7	0	0	1.2	10	188	2.5			(0)	.81	.19	4.3	—
1688	Cooked, roasted (81% lean, 19% fat)	48.0	341	24.0	26.4	0	0	1.6	11	249	3.1			(0)	.53	.24	4.8	—
	Separable lean:																	
1689	Raw	69.9	165	19.5	9.1	0	0	1.4	11	226	2.9			(0)	.95	.23	5.1	—
1690	Cooked, roasted	57.9	228	28.6	11.7	0	0	1.9	12	299	3.6			(0)	.63	.28	5.6	—

[96] Value for product without added salt.

[116] Fruit juice content ranges from 10 to 50 percent. Ascorbic acid may be added as a preservative or as a nutrient. Value listed is based on product with label stating 30 mg. per 6 fl. oz. serving. If label claim is 30 mg. per 8 fl. oz. serving, value would be 12 mg. per 100 grams.

[117] Values are based on products made with unenriched flour. With enriched flour, values per 100 grams are increased approximately as follows: Iron, 0.8 mg.; thiamine, 0.12 mg.; riboflavin, 0.08 mg.; niacin, 0.9 mg.

[118] Values per 100 grams range from 10 I.U. for white-fleshed varieties to as much as 1,200 I.U. for those with deep-yellow flesh.

[119] Value applies to all prune-type plums except Italian prunes and Imperial prunes, which average 1,340 I.U. per 100 grams.

[120] Prepared with flour, butter, and milk.

[121] With unenriched flour, values per 100 grams are: Iron, 0.9 mg.; thiamine, 0.05 mg.; riboflavin, 0.20 mg.; niacin, 0.3 mg.

[122] Average value per 100 grams of pork of all cuts is 70 mg. for raw meat and 65 mg. for cooked meat.

[123] Average value per 100 grams of pork of all cuts is 285 mg. for raw meat and 390 mg. for cooked meat.

TABLE 1.—COMPOSITION OF FOODS, 100 GRAMS, EDIBLE PORTION—Continued

[Numbers in parentheses denote values imputed—usually from another form of the food or from a similar food. Zero in parentheses indicates that the amount of a constituent probably is none or is too small to measure. Dashes denote lack of reliable data for a constituent believed to be present in measurable amount. Calculated values, as those based on a recipe, are not in parentheses]

Item No.	Food and description	Water	Food energy	Protein	Fat	Carbohydrate		Ash	Calcium	Phosphorus	Iron	Sodium	Potassium	Vitamin A value	Thiamine	Riboflavin	Niacin	Ascorbic acid
						Total	Fiber											
(A)	(B)	(C)	(D)	(E)	(F)	(G)	(H)	(I)	(J)	(K)	(L)	(M)	(N)	(O)	(P)	(Q)	(R)	(S)
	Pork, fresh [4]—Continued	Percent	Calories	Grams	Grams	Grams	Grams	Grams	Milligrams	Milligrams	Milligrams	Milligrams	Milligrams	International units	Milligrams	Milligrams	Milligrams	Milligrams
	Composite of trimmed lean cuts, ham, loin, shoulder, and spareribs—Continued																	
	Thin class—Continued																	
	Separable fat:																	
1691	Raw	15.4	737	4.5	79.6	0	0	0.5	3	27	0.7			(0)	0.22	0.05	1.2	—
	Separable fat, from lean cuts:																	
	Raw. See individual cuts.																	
1692	Cooked	11.1	773	4.8	83.4	0	0	.7	—	—	—			—	—	—	—	—
	Retail cuts, trimmed to retail level:																	
	Ham:																	
	Fat class:																	
	Total edible:																	
1693	Raw (72% lean, 28% fat)	54.3	327	15.2	29.1	0	0	.8	9	170	2.3			(0)	.74	.18	4.0	—
1694	Cooked, roasted (72% lean, 28% fat)	43.7	394	21.9	33.3	0	0	1.0	10	225	2.9			(0)	.49	.22	4.4	—
	Separable lean:																	
1695	Raw	70.2	160	19.7	8.4	0	0	1.1	11	229	3.0			(0)	.96	.23	5.1	—
1696	Cooked, roasted	58.2	225	29.3	11.1	0	0	1.5	13	303	3.7			(0)	.63	.29	5.6	—
	Separable fat:																	
1697	Raw	14.2	755	4.0	81.8	0	0	0	2	20	.6			(0)	.19	.05	1.0	—
	Medium-fat class:																	
	Total edible:																	
1698	Raw (74% lean, 26% fat)	56.5	308	15.9	26.6	0	0	.7	9	178	2.4			(0)	.77	.19	4.1	—
1699	Cooked, roasted (74% lean, 26% fat)	45.5	374	23.0	30.6	0	0	.9	10	236	3.0			(0)	.51	.23	4.6	—
	Separable lean:																	
1700	Raw	71.1	153	20.0	7.5	0	0	1.0	12	233	3.0			(0)	.97	.23	5.2	—
1701	Cooked, roasted	58.9	217	29.7	10.0	0	0	1.4	13	308	3.8			(0)	.64	.29	5.7	—
	Separable fat:																	
1702	Raw	15.0	746	4.3	80.7	0	0	0	2	24	.6			(0)	.21	.05	1.1	—
	Thin class:																	
	Total edible:																	
1703	Raw (77% lean, 23% fat)	59.2	281	16.7	23.2	0	0	.8	10	190	2.5			(0)	.82	.20	4.4	—
1704	Cooked, roasted (77% lean, 23% fat)	47.8	346	24.2	26.9	0	0	1.0	11	252	3.2	(138)	(138)	(0)	.54	.25	4.8	—
	Separable lean:																	
1705	Raw	72.0	147	20.4	6.6	0	0	1.1	12	238	3.1			(0)	.99	.24	5.3	—
1706	Cooked, roasted	59.3	210	30.2	9.0	0	0	1.5	13	315	3.8			(0)	.66	.30	5.8	—
	Separable fat:																	
1707	Raw	15.9	737	4.6	79.5	0	0	0	3	28	.7			(0)	.22	.05	1.2	—
	Loin:																	
	Fat class:																	
	Total edible:																	
1708	Raw (76% lean, 24% fat)	54.8	323	16.4	28.0	0	0	.8	9	185	2.5			(0)	.80	.19	4.2	—
1709	Cooked, roasted (76% lean, 24% fat)	43.7	387	23.5	31.8	0	0	1.0	10	245	3.1			(0)	.88	.25	5.3	—
1710	Cooked, broiled (68% lean, 32% fat)	40.2	418	23.5	35.2	0	0	1.1	10	256	3.2			(0)	.92	.27	5.6	—
	Separable lean:																	
1711	Raw	67.5	189	20.1	11.4	0	0	1.0	12	234	3.0			(0)	.98	.24	5.2	—
1712	Cooked, roasted	55.0	254	29.4	14.2	0	0	1.3	13	310	3.8			(0)	1.08	.31	6.5	—
1713	Cooked, broiled	52.6	270	30.6	15.4	0	0	1.5	13	324	3.9			(0)	1.13	.33	6.8	—
	Separable fat:																	
1714	Raw	15.5	739	4.8	79.7	0	0	0	3	31	.7			(0)	.23	.06	1.2	—
	Medium-fat class:																	
	Total edible:																	
1715	Raw (80% lean, 20% fat)	57.2	298	17.1	24.9	0	0	.9	10	193	2.6			(0)	.83	.20	4.4	—
1716	Cooked, roasted (80% lean, 20% fat)	45.8	362	24.5	28.5	0	0	1.2	11	256	3.2			(0)	.92	.26	5.6	—
1717	Cooked, broiled (72% lean, 28% fat)	42.3	391	24.7	31.7	0	0	1.3	12	268	3.4			(0)	.96	.28	5.8	—
	Separable lean:																	
1718	Raw	67.5	189	20.1	11.4	0	0	1.0	12	234	3.0			(0)	.98	.24	5.2	—
1719	Cooked, roasted	55.0	254	29.4	14.2	0	0	1.3	13	310	3.8			(0)	1.08	.31	6.5	—
1720	Cooked, broiled	52.6	270	30.6	15.4	0	0	1.5	13	324	3.9			(0)	1.13	.33	6.8	—
	Separable fat:																	
1721	Raw	16.7	723	5.2	77.7	0	0	4	3	36	.8			(0)	.25	.06	1.4	—
	Thin class:																	
	Total edible:																	
1722	Raw (85% lean, 15% fat)	60.0	268	17.9	21.2	0	0	.9	10	204	2.7			(0)	.87	.21	4.7	—
1723	Cooked, roasted (85% lean, 15% fat)	48.3	333	25.8	24.7	0	0	1.2	11	270	3.4			(0)	.96	.28	5.8	—

1724	Cooked, broiled (77% lean, 23% fat)	45.1	359	26.2	27.4	0	0	1.3	12	282	3.5			(0)	1.00	.29	6.1	—
	Separable lean:																	
1725	Raw	67.5	189	20.1	11.4	0	0	1.0	12	234	3.0			(0)	.98	.24	5.2	—
1726	Cooked, roasted	55.0	254	29.4	14.2	0	0	1.3	13	310	3.8			(0)	1.08	.31	6.5	—
1727	Cooked, broiled	52.6	270	30.6	15.4	0	0	1.5	13	324	3.9			(0)	1.13	.33	6.8	—
	Separable fat:																	
1728	Raw	18.2	706	5.6	75.6	0	0	.6	3	42	.8			(0)	.27	.07	1.5	—
	Boston butt:																	
	Fat class:																	
	Total edible:																	
1729	Raw (76% lean, 24% fat)	55.9	323	14.5	29.0	0	0	.7	8	160	2.2			(0)	.71	.17	3.8	—
1730	Cooked, roasted (76% lean, 24% fat)	45.0	389	20.9	33.2	0	0	.9	9	212	2.7			(0)	.47	.21	4.2	—
	Separable lean:																	
1731	Raw	68.1	196	17.7	13.3	0	0	.9	10	202	2.7			(0)	.86	.21	4.6	—
1732	Cooked, roasted	56.2	261	26.2	16.5	0	0	1.2	11	267	3.3			(0)	.57	.26	5.1	—
	Separable fat:																	
1733	Raw	17.6	721	4.7	77.7	0	0	.0	3	30	.7			(0)	.23	.05	1.2	—
	Medium-fat class:																	
	Total edible:																	
1734	Raw (79% lean, 21% fat)	59.3	287	15.5	24.5	0	0	.7	9	173	2.3			(0)	.75	.18	4.0	—
1735	Cooked, roasted (79% lean, 21% fat)	48.1	353	22.5	28.5	0	0	.9	10	229	2.9			(0)	.50	.23	4.4	—
	Separable lean:																	
1736	Raw	69.6	180	18.2	11.3	0	0	.9	11	209	2.7			(0)	.88	.21	4.7	—
1737	Cooked, roasted	57.5	244	27.0	14.3	0	0	1.2	12	277	3.4			(0)	.59	.27	5.2	—
	Separable fat:																	
1738	Raw	20.1	696	5.3	74.6	0	0	0	3	38	.8			(0)	.26	.06	1.4	—
	Thin class:																	
	Total edible:																	
1739	Raw (83% lean, 17% fat)	62.7	251	16.5	20.0	0	0	.7	10	187	2.5			(0)	.80	.19	4.3	—
1740	Cooked, roasted (83% lean, 17% fat)	51.2	317	24.2	23.7	0	0	.9	11	248	3.1			(0)	.53	.24	4.7	—
	Separable lean:																	
1741	Raw	70.9	166	18.7	9.5	0	0	.9	11	215	2.8			(0)	.91	.22	4.9	—
1742	Cooked, roasted	58.7	230	27.8	12.3	0	0	1.2	12	285	3.5			(0)	.60	.27	5.4	—
	Separable fat:																	
1743	Raw	22.5	671	6.0	71.5	0	0	0	3	47	.9			(0)	.29	.07	1.6	—
	Picnic:																	
	Fat class:																	
	Total edible:																	
1744	Raw (69% lean, 31% fat)	54.7	334	14.9	30.0	0	0	.5	9	165	2.2	([122])	([123])	(0)	.72	.17	3.9	—
1745	Cooked, simmered (69% lean, 31% fat)	41.5	420	21.8	36.2	0	0	.5	9	129	2.8			(0)	.51	.23	4.5	—
	Separable lean:																	
1746	Raw	71.0	165	19.1	9.2	0	0	.7	11	221	2.9			(0)	.93	.22	5.0	—
1747	Cooked, simmered	58.8	231	28.5	12.1	0	0	.7	12	173	3.6			(0)	.65	.30	5.8	—
	Separable fat:																	
1748	Raw	18.1	713	5.4	76.5	0	0	0	3	39	.8			(0)	.26	.06	1.4	—
	Medium-fat class:																	
	Total edible:																	
1749	Raw (74% lean, 26% fat)	58.9	290	15.8	24.7	0	0	.7	9	178	2.4			(0)	.77	.19	4.1	—
1750	Cooked, simmered (74% lean, 26% fat)	45.7	374	23.2	30.5	0	0	.6	10	139	3.0			(0)	.54	.25	4.8	—
	Separable lean:																	
1751	Raw	72.3	150	19.4	7.4	0	0	.9	11	225	2.9			(0)	.94	.23	5.0	—
1752	Cooked, simmered	60.3	212	29.0	9.8	0	0	.8	12	176	3.6			(0)	.66	.30	5.9	—
	Separable fat:																	
1753	Raw	20.9	685	5.8	73.2	0	0	.1	3	44	.9			(0)	.28	.07	1.5	—
	Thin class:																	
	Total edible:																	
1754	Raw (78% lean, 22% fat)	62.7	249	16.9	19.6	0	0	.8	10	191	2.5			(0)	.82	.20	4.4	—
1755	Cooked, simmered (78% lean, 22% fat)	49.7	329	24.9	24.7	0	0	.7	11	149	3.2			(0)	.58	.26	5.2	—
	Separable lean:																	
1756	Raw	73.7	135	19.8	5.6	0	0	.9	11	230	3.0			(0)	.96	.23	5.1	—
1757	Cooked, simmered	62.0	194	29.7	7.5	0	0	.8	13	180	3.7			(0)	.68	.31	6.0	—
	Separable fat:																	
1758	Raw	23.3	657	6.3	69.9	0	0	.5	4	51	.9			(0)	.31	.07	1.6	—
	Spareribs:																	
	Fat class:																	
	Total edible:																	
1759	Raw	49.2	390	13.7	36.8	0	0	.7	8	149	2.1			(0)	.67	.16	3.6	—
1760	Cooked, braised	37.2	467	19.7	42.5	0	0	.6	8	113	2.5			(0)	.40	.19	3.2	—
	Medium-fat class:																	
	Total edible:																	
1761	Raw	51.8	361	14.5	33.2	0	0	.7	8	160	2.2			(0)	.70	.17	3.8	—
1762	Cooked, braised	39.7	440	20.8	38.9	0	0	.6	9	121	2.6			(0)	.43	.21	3.4	—
	Thin class:																	
	Total edible:																	
1763	Raw	54.5	331	15.3	29.5	0	0	.8	9	170	2.3			(0)	.74	.18	4.0	—
1764	Cooked, braised	42.4	410	21.9	35.1	0	0	.7	9	129	2.8			(0)	.45	.22	3.6	—

[122] Average value per 100 grams of pork of all cuts is 70 mg. for raw meat and 65 mg. for cooked meat.

[123] Average value per 100 grams of pork of all cuts is 285 mg. for raw meat and 390 mg. for cooked meat.

TABLE 1.—COMPOSITION OF FOODS, 100 GRAMS, EDIBLE PORTION—Continued

[Numbers in parentheses denote values imputed—usually from another form of the food or from a similar food. Zero in parentheses indicates that the amount of a constituent probably is none or is too small to measure. Dashes denote lack of reliable data for a constituent believed to be present in measurable amount. Calculated values, as those based on a recipe, are not in parentheses]

Item No.	Food and description	Water	Food energy	Protein	Fat	Carbohydrate		Ash	Calcium	Phosphorus	Iron	Sodium	Potassium	Vitamin A value	Thiamine	Riboflavin	Niacin	Ascorbic acid
						Total	Fiber											
(A)	(B)	(C)	(D)	(E)	(F)	(G)	(H)	(I)	(J)	(K)	(L)	(M)	(N)	(O)	(P)	(Q)	(R)	(S)
		Percent	Calories	Grams	Grams	Grams	Grams	Grams	Milligrams	Milligrams	Milligrams	Milligrams	Milligrams	International units	Milligrams	Milligrams	Milligrams	Milligrams
	Pork, cured:																	
	Dry, long-cure, country-style:																	
	Ham:																	
1765	Fat	36.	460	14.6	44.	0.3	0	5.1	—	—	—	—	—	(0)	—	—	—	—
1766	Medium-fat	42.	389	16.9	35.	.3	0	5.4	—	—	—	—	—	(0)	—	—	—	—
1767	Lean	49.	310	19.5	25.	.3	0	5.8	—	—	—	—	—	(0)	—	—	—	—
	Light-cure, commercial:																	
	Ham, medium-fat class:																	
	Total edible:																	
1768	Raw (76% lean, 24% fat)	56.5	282	17.5	23.0	0	0	3.0	10	162	2.6	—	—	(0)	0.72	0.19	4.1	—
1769	Cooked, roasted (84% lean, 16% fat)	53.6	289	20.9	22.1	0	0	3.4	9	172	2.6	—	—	(0)	.47	.18	3.6	—
	Separable lean:																	
1770	Raw	66.4	168	21.5	8.5	0	0	3.6	12	188	3.2	1,100	340	(0)	.89	.24	5.0	—
1771	Cooked, roasted	61.9	187	25.3	8.8	0	0	4.0	11	200	3.2	930	326	(0)	.58	.23	4.5	—
	Separable fat:																	
1772	Raw	25.7	636	5.2	68.1	0	0	1.0	3	82	.8	—	—	(0)	.21	.06	1.2	—
	Boston butt, medium-fat class:																	
	Total edible:																	
1773	Raw (75% lean, 25% fat)	55.7	291	17.2	24.1	0	0	3.0	10	152	2.6	—	—	(0)	.71	.19	4.0	—
1774	Cooked, roasted (83% lean, 17% fat)	47.7	330	22.9	25.7	0	0	3.7	10	185	3.0	—	—	(0)	.53	.21	4.1	—
	Separable lean:																	
1775	Raw	63.2	200	20.9	12.3	0	0	3.6	12	179	3.1	(1,100)	(340)	(0)	.86	.23	4.9	—
1776	Cooked, roasted	53.9	243	27.8	13.8	0	0	4.5	12	218	3.6	(930)	(326)	(0)	.64	.25	5.0	—
	Separable fat:																	
1777	Raw	32.8	569	6.0	60.2	0	0	1.0	3	69	.9	—	—	(0)	.25	.07	1.4	—
	Picnic, medium-fat class:																	
	Total edible:																	
1778	Raw (70% lean, 30% fat)	56.7	285	16.8	23.6	0	0	2.9	10	150	2.5	—	—	(0)	.69	.19	3.9	—
1779	Cooked, roasted (82% lean, 18% fat)	48.8	323	22.4	25.2	0	0	3.6	10	182	2.9	—	—	(0)	.52	.20	4.0	—
	Separable lean:																	
1780	Raw	66.7	167	21.3	8.4	0	0	3.6	12	181	3.2	(1,100)	(340)	(0)	.88	.24	5.0	—
1781	Cooked, roasted	57.2	211	28.4	9.9	0	0	4.5	13	220	3.7	(930)	(326)	(0)	.65	.26	5.0	—
	Separable fat:																	
1782	Raw	33.9	553	6.4	58.3	0	0	1.4	4	79	1.0	—	—	(0)	.26	.07	1.5	—
	Pork, cured, canned:																	
1783	**Ham,** contents of can	65.0	193	18.3	12.3	.9	0	3.5	11	156	2.7	(1,100)	(340)	(0)	.53	.19	3.8	—
	Pork, cured. See also Bacon, items 125–129, and Salt pork, item 1964.																	
1784	**Pork and gravy,** canned (90% pork, 10% gravy)	56.9	256	16.4	17.8	6.3	0	2.6	13	183	2.4	—	—	(0)	.49	.17	3.5	—
	Potatoes:																	
1785	Raw	79.8	76	2.1	.1	17.1	.5	.9	7	53	.6	3	407	Trace	.10	.04	1.5	[124] 20
	Cooked:																	
1786	Baked in skin	75.1	93	2.6	.1	21.1	.6	1.1	9	65	.7	[125] 4	503	Trace	.10	.04	1.7	20
1787	Boiled in skin	79.8	76	2.1	.1	17.1	.5	.9	7	53	.6	[125] 3	407	Trace	.09	.04	1.5	16
1788	Boiled, pared before cooking	82.8	65	1.9	.1	14.5	.5	.7	6	42	.5	[125] 2	285	Trace	.09	.03	1.2	16
1789	French-fried	44.7	274	4.3	13.2	36.0	1.0	1.8	15	111	1.3	[125] 6	853	Trace	.13	.08	3.1	21
1790	Fried from raw	46.9	268	4.0	14.2	32.6	1.0	2.3	15	101	1.1	223	775	Trace	.12	.07	2.8	19
1791	Hash-browned after holding overnight	54.2	229	3.1	11.7	29.1	.8	1.9	12	79	.9	288	475	Trace	.08	.05	2.1	9
1792	Mashed, milk added	82.8	65	2.1	.7	13.0	.4	1.4	24	49	.4	301	261	20	.08	.05	1.0	10
1793	Mashed, milk and table fat added	79.8	94	2.1	4.3	12.3	.4	1.5	24	48	.4	331	250	170	.08	.05	1.0	9
	Scalloped and au gratin:																	
1794	With cheese	71.1	145	5.3	7.9	13.6	.3	2.1	127	122	.5	447	306	320	.06	.12	.9	10
1795	Without cheese	76.7	104	3.0	3.9	14.7	.3	1.7	54	74	.4	355	327	160	.06	.09	1.0	11
	Canned:																	
1796	Solids and liquid	88.5	44	1.1	.2	9.8	.2	.4	[126] (4)	(30)	(.3)	[126] 1	250	Trace	.04	.02	.6	13
	Dehydrated mashed:																	
	Flakes without milk:																	
1797	Dry form	5.2	364	7.2	.6	84.0	(1.6)	3.0	35	(173)	1.7	89	(1,600)	Trace	.23	.06	5.4	[127] 32
1798	Prepared, water, milk, table fat added	79.3	93	1.9	3.2	14.5	.3	1.1	31	47	.3	231	286	130	.04	.04	.9	[127] 5
	Granules without milk:																	
1799	Dry form	7.1	352	8.3	.6	80.4	1.4	3.6	44	203	2.4	84	(1,600)	Trace	.16	.11	4.9	[127] 19
1800	Prepared, water, milk, table fat added	78.6	96	2.0	3.6	14.4	.2	1.4	32	52	.5	256	290	110	.04	.05	.7	[127] 3
	Granules with milk:																	
1801	Dry form	6.3	358	10.9	1.1	77.7	1.5	4.0	142	237	3.5	82	1,848	60	.19	.30	4.2	[127] 16

1802	Prepared, water, table fat added	81.4	79	2.0	2.2	13.1	.3	1.3	31	44	.6	234	335	90	.03	.05	.8	[127] 3
	Frozen:																	
	Diced, for hash-browning:																	
1803	Not thawed	81.0	73	1.2	Trace	17.4	.4	.4	10	30	.7	8	170	Trace	.07	.01	.6	9
1804	Cooked, hash-browned	56.1	224	2.0	11.5	29.0	.7	1.4	18	50	1.2	299	283	Trace	.07	.02	1.0	8
	French-fried:																	
1805	Not thawed	63.5	170	2.8	6.5	26.1	.6	1.1	7	67	1.4	[125] 3	506	Trace	.14	.02	2.1	20
1806	Heated	52.9	220	3.6	8.4	33.7	.7	1.4	9	86	1.8	[125] 4	652	Trace	.14	.02	2.6	21
	Mashed:																	
1807	Not thawed	80.4	75	1.7	.1	17.1	.4	.7	16	39	.7	79	229	30	.07	.03	.8	6
1808	Heated	78.3	93	1.8	2.8	15.7	.4	1.4	25	42	.6	359	215	140	.06	.04	.7	4
1809	**Potato chips**	1.8	568	5.3	39.8	50.0	(1.6)	3.1	40	139	1.8	[128] —	1,130	Trace	.21	.07	4.8	16
1810	**Potato flour**	7.6	351	8.0	.8	79.9	1.6	3.7	33	178	17.2	34	1,588	Trace	.42	.14	3.4	(19)
	Potato salad, from home recipe, made with—																	
1811	Cooked salad dressing, seasonings	76.0	99	2.7	2.8	16.3	.4	2.2	32	64	.6	528	319	140	.08	.07	1.1	11
1812	Mayonnaise and French dressing, hard-cooked eggs, seasonings.	72.4	145	3.0	9.2	13.4	.4	2.0	19	63	.8	480	296	180	.07	.06	.9	11
1813	**Potato sticks**	1.5	544	6.4	36.4	50.8	1.5	4.9	44	139	1.8	[128] —	1,130	Trace	.21	.07	4.8	40
1814	**Pretzels**	4.5	390	9.8	4.5	75.9	.3	5.3	22	131	1.5	[129] 1,680	130	(0)	.02	.03	.7	(0)
1815	**Pricklypears,** raw	88.0	42	.5	.1	10.9	1.6	.5	20	28	.3	2	166	60	.01	.03	.4	22
	Prunes:																	
	Dehydrated, nugget-type and pieces:																	
1816	Uncooked	2.5	344	3.3	.5	91.3	(2.2)	2.4	90	107	4.4	11	940	2,170	.12	.22	2.1	4
1817	Cooked, fruit and liquid, with added sugar	50.7	180	1.2	.2	47.1	(.8)	.8	31	37	1.5	4	329	760	.03	.07	.7	1
	Dried, "softenized":																	
1818	Uncooked	28.0	255	2.1	.6	67.4	1.6	1.9	51	79	3.9	8	694	1,600	.09	.17	1.6	3
	Cooked (fruit and liquid):																	
1819	Without added sugar	66.4	119	1.0	.3	31.4	.8	.9	24	37	1.8	4	327	750	.03	.07	.7	1
1820	With added sugar	53.2	172	.8	.2	45.1	.6	.7	19	30	1.5	3	262	600	.03	.06	.6	1
1821	**Prune juice,** canned or bottled	80.	77	.4	.1	19.0	Trace	.5	14	20	4.1	2	235	—	.01	.01	.4	2
1822	**Prune whip**	57.3	156	4.4	.2	36.9	.6	1.2	22	33	1.3	164	290	460	.02	.14	.5	2
	Puddings with starch base, prepared from home recipe:																	
1823	Chocolate	65.8	148	3.1	4.7	25.7	.2	.7	96	98	.5	56	171	150	.02	.14	.1	Trace
1824	Vanilla (blanc mange)	76.0	111	3.5	3.9	15.9	Trace	.7	117	91	Trace	65	138	160	.03	.16	.1	1
	See also Bread; Rennin products; Rice; Tapioca; Baby foods.																	
	Pudding mixes and puddings made from mixes:																	
	With starch base:																	
1825	Mix, chocolate, regular, dry form	1.7	361	3.0	2.1	91.5	.6	1.7	20	94	1.6	447	95	Trace	.02	.07	.4	0
1826	Pudding made with milk, cooked	70.0	124	3.4	3.0	22.8	.1	.8	102	95	.3	129	136	130	.02	.15	.1	Trace
1827	Mix, chocolate, instant, dry form	.7	357	3.1	1.6	90.8	.6	3.8	245	88	2.0	404	85	Trace	.01	.06	.3	0
1828	Pudding made with milk, without cooking	68.7	125	3.0	2.5	24.4	.1	1.4	144	91	.5	124	129	130	.03	.15	.1	Trace
	With vegetable gum base:																	
1829	Mix, custard-dessert, dry form	.1	384	(0)	.1	98.9	Trace	.9	9	2	.1	297	25	0	0	0	0	0
1830	Pudding made with milk, cooked	70.0	131	3.1	3.5	22.6	Trace	.8	106	82	Trace	99	129	140	.02	.14	.1	Trace
	Pumpkin:																	
1831	Raw	91.6	26	1.0	.1	6.5	1.1	.8	21	44	.8	1	340	1,600	.05	.11	.6	9
1832	Canned [130]	90.2	33	1.0	.3	7.9	1.3	.6	25	26	.4	[125] 2	240	6,400	.03	.05	.6	5
1833	**Pumpkin and squash seed kernels,** dry	4.4	553	29.0	46.7	15.0	1.9	4.9	51	1,144	11.2	—	—	70	.24	.19	2.4	—
	Purslane leaves, including stems:																	
1834	Raw	92.5	21	1.7	.4	3.8	.9	1.6	103	39	3.5	—	—	2,500	.03	.10	.5	25
1835	Cooked, boiled, drained	94.7	15	1.2	.3	2.8	.8	1.0	86	24	1.2	—	—	2,100	.02	.06	.4	12
	Quail, raw:																	
1836	Total edible	65.9	168	25.0	6.8	0	0	1.6	—	—	—	—	—	—	—	—	—	—
1837	Flesh and skin	66.3	172	25.4	7.0	0	0	1.4	—	—	—	40	175	—	—	—	—	—
1838	Giblets	63.0	176	21.8	6.2	6.7	0	2.3	—	—	—	—	—	—	—	—	—	—
1839	**Quinces,** raw	83.8	57	.4	.1	15.3	1.7	.4	11	17	.7	4	197	40	.02	.03	.2	15
	Rabbit, domesticated:																	
	Flesh only:																	
1840	Raw	70.	162	21.	8.	0	0	1.	20	352	1.3	43	385	—	.08	.06	12.8	—
1841	Cooked, stewed	59.8	216	29.3	10.1	0	0	.8	21	259	1.5	41	368	—	.05	.07	11.3	—
	Rabbit, wild:																	
1842	Flesh only, raw	73.	135	21.	5.	0	0	1.	—	—	—	—	—	—	—	—	—	—
1843	**Raccoon,** cooked, roasted	54.8	255	29.2	14.5	0	0	1.5	—	—	—	—	—	—	.59	.52	—	—
	Radishes, raw:																	
1844	Common	94.5	17	1.0	.1	3.6	.7	.8	30	31	1.0	18	322	10	.03	.03	.3	26
1845	Oriental, including daikon (Japanese) and Chinese	94.1	19	.9	.1	4.2	.7	.7	35	26	.6	—	180	10	.03	.02	.4	32
	Raisins, natural (unbleached):																	
1846	Uncooked	18.0	289	2.5	.2	77.4	.9	1.9	62	101	3.5	27	763	20	.11	.08	.5	1
1847	Cooked, fruit and liquid, added sugar	41.4	213	1.2	.1	56.4	.4	.9	29	47	1.6	13	355	10	.04	.03	.2	Trace

[124] Year-round average. Recently dug potatoes contain about 26 mg. ascorbic acid per 100 grams. After 3 months' storage the value is only half as high; after 6 months', about one-third as high.

[125] Applies to product without added salt. If salt is added, an estimated average value for sodium is 236 mg. per 100 grams.

[126] Federal standards provide for addition of certain calcium salts as firming agents; if used, these salts may add calcium not to exceed 200 mg. per 100 grams of finished product.

[127] Value varies widely. It is dependent on content of ascorbic acid in raw potatoes, method of processing, and length of storage of dehydrated product. Present values for dehydrated forms range from 10 to 35 mg. per 100 grams.

[128] Sodium content is variable and may be as high as 1,000 mg. per 100 grams.

[129] Sodium content is variable. For example, very thin pretzel sticks contain about twice the average amount listed.

[130] May be a mixture of pumpkin and winter squash.

TABLE 1.—COMPOSITION OF FOODS, 100 GRAMS, EDIBLE PORTION—Continued

[Numbers in parentheses denote values imputed—usually from another form of the food or from a similar food. Zero in parentheses indicates that the amount of a constituent probably is none or is too small to measure. Dashes denote lack of reliable data for a constituent believed to be present in measurable amount. Calculated values, as those based on a recipe, are not in parentheses]

Item No.	Food and description	Water	Food energy	Protein	Fat	Carbohydrate		Ash	Calcium	Phosphorus	Iron	Sodium	Potassium	Vitamin A value	Thiamine	Riboflavin	Niacin	Ascorbic acid
						Total	Fiber											
(A)	(B)	(C)	(D)	(E)	(F)	(G)	(H)	(I)	(J)	(K)	(L)	(M)	(N)	(O)	(P)	(Q)	(R)	(S)
		Percent	Calories	Grams	Grams	Grams	Grams	Grams	Milligrams	Milligrams	Milligrams	Milligrams	Milligrams	International units	Milligrams	Milligrams	Milligrams	Milligrams
	Raja fish. See Skate, item 2053.																	
	Raspberries:																	
	Raw:																	
1848	Black	80.8	73	1.5	1.4	15.7	5.1	0.6	30	22	0.9	1	199	Trace	(0.03)	(0.09)	(0.9)	18
1849	Red	84.2	57	1.2	.5	13.6	3.0	.5	22	22	.9	1	168	130	.03	.09	.9	25
	Canned, solids and liquid, water pack, with or without artificial sweetener:																	
1850	Black	86.7	51	1.1	1.1	10.7	3.3	.4	20	15	.6	1	135	Trace	.01	.04	.5	6
1851	Red	90.1	35	.7	.1	8.8	2.6	.3	15	15	.6	1	114	90	.01	.04	.5	9
1852	Frozen, red, sweetened, not thawed	74.3	98	.7	.2	24.6	2.2	.2	13	17	.6	1	100	(70)	.02	.06	.6	21
1853	**Red and gray snapper,** raw	78.5	93	19.8	.9	0	0	1.3	16	214	.8	67	323	—	.17	.02	—	—
	Redfish. See Drum, red, item 960; and Ocean perch, Atlantic, items 1396–1398.																	
1854	**Redhorse,** silver, raw	78.6	98	18.0	2.3	0	0	1.2	—	—	—	—	—	—	—	—	—	—
	Reindeer, raw:																	
1855	Lean only	73.3	127	21.8	3.8	0	0	1.1	—	—	5.3	—	—	—	.33	.68	5.5	—
	Total edible:																	
1856	Side (84% lean, 16% fat)	63.3	217	20.5	14.4	0	0	1.0	—	—	—	—	—	—	—	—	—	—
1857	Forequarter (91% lean, 9% fat)	67.4	178	21.8	9.4	0	0	1.1	—	—	—	—	—	—	—	—	—	—
1858	Hindquarter (78% lean, 22% fat)	59.6	256	19.4	19.2	0	0	.9	—	—	—	—	—	—	—	—	—	—
	Rennin products:																	
1859	Tablet (salts, starch, rennin enzyme)	9.0	107	.1	1.0	24.3	0	65.6	3,510	200	—	22,300	—	0	0	0	0	0
1860	Dessert, home-prepared with tablet	81.1	89	3.1	3.5	11.6	0	.7	111	83	Trace	82	126	140	.03	.15	.1	1
	Dessert mixes and desserts prepared from mixes:																	
	Chocolate:																	
1861	Mix, dry form	1.0	387	2.8	3.3	91.5	.9	1.4	166	129	—	70	—	—	—	—	—	—
1862	Dessert made with milk	77.9	102	3.4	3.8	14.1	.1	.8	122	96	Trace	52	125	140	.03	.15	.1	1
	Other flavors (vanilla, caramel, fruit flavorings):																	
1863	Mix, dry form	.4	383	Trace	Trace	99.0	—	.6	[131] 117	[131] 91	—	6	—	—	—	—	—	—
1864	Dessert made with milk	79.7	95	3.2	3.6	12.8	0	.7	[131] 117	[131] 92	Trace	46	128	150	.03	.16	.1	1
	Rhubarb:																	
1865	Raw	94.8	16	.6	.1	3.7	.7	.8	96	18	.8	2	251	100	(.03)	(.07)	(.3)	9
1866	Cooked, added sugar	62.8	141	.5	.1	36.0	.6	.6	78	15	.6	2	203	80	(.02)	(.05)	(.3)	6
	Frozen, sweetened:																	
1867	Not thawed	80.1	75	.6	.2	18.5	.9	.6	93	14	.8	4	211	80	.02	.05	.2	8
1868	Cooked, added sugar	62.6	143	.5	.2	36.2	.8	.5	78	12	.7	3	176	70	.02	.04	.2	6
	Rice:																	
	Brown:																	
1869	Raw	12.0	360	7.5	1.9	77.4	.9	1.2	32	221	1.6	9	214	(0)	.34	.05	4.7	(0)
1870	Cooked	70.3	119	2.5	.6	25.5	.3	1.1	12	73	.5	282	70	(0)	.09	.02	1.4	(0)
	White (fully milled or polished):																	
	Enriched:																	
	Common commercial varieties, all types:																	
1871	Raw	12.0	363	6.7	.4	80.4	.3	.5	24	94	[132] 2.9	5	92	(0)	[132] .44	([132])	[132] 3.5	(0)
1872	Cooked	72.6	109	2.0	.1	24.2	.1	1.1	10	28	[132] .9	374	28	(0)	[132] .11	([132])	[132] 1.0	(0)
	Long-grain:																	
	Parboiled:																	
1873	Dry form	10.3	369	7.4	.3	81.3	.2	.7	60	200	[132] 2.9	9	150	(0)	[132] .44	([132])	[132] 3.5	(0)
1874	Cooked	73.4	106	2.1	.1	23.3	.1	1.1	19	57	[132] .8	358	43	(0)	[132] .11	([132])	[132] 1.2	(0)
	Precooked (instant):																	
1875	Dry form	9.6	374	7.5	.2	82.5	.4	.2	5	65	[132] 2.9	1	—	(0)	[132] .44	([132])	[132] 3.5	(0)
1876	Ready-to-serve	72.9	109	2.2	Trace	24.2	.1	.7	3	19	[132] .8	273	Trace	(0)	[132] .13	([132])	[132] 1.0	(0)
	Unenriched:																	
	Common commercial varieties, all types:																	
1877	Raw	12.0	363	6.7	.4	80.4	.3	.5	24	94	.8	5	92	(0)	.07	.03	1.6	(0)
1878	Cooked	72.6	109	2.0	.1	24.2	.1	1.1	10	28	.2	374	28	(0)	.02	.01	.4	(0)
1879	Glutinous (Mochi Gomi), raw	13.2	361	5.6	.9	79.8	.3	.5	36	100	2.0	10	130	(0)	.07	.04	2.0	(0)
1880	**Rice bran**	9.7	276	13.3	15.8	50.8	11.5	10.4	76	1,386	19.4	Trace	1,495	(0)	2.26	.25	29.8	(0)
1881	**Rice polish**	9.8	265	12.1	12.8	57.7	2.4	7.6	69	1,106	16.1	Trace	714	(0)	1.84	.18	28.2	(0)
	Rice products used mainly as hot breakfast cereals:																	
	Rice, granulated, added nutrients:																	
1882	Dry form	7.4	383	6.0	.3	85.9	.2	.4	9	96	5.4	—	—	(0)	.42	.11	5.8	(0)
1883	Cooked	87.5	50	.8	Trace	11.2	Trace	.5	2	13	.7	176	Trace	(0)	.06	.01	.8	(0)

	Rice products used mainly as ready-to-eat breakfast cereals:																	
1884	Rice flakes, added nutrients	3.2	390	5.9	.3	87.7	.6	2.9	29	132	1.6	987	180	(0)	.35	.05	5.4	(0)
1885	Rice, puffed; added nutrients, without salt	3.7	399	6.0	.4	89.5	.6	.4	20	92	1.8	2	100	(0)	.44	.04	4.4	(0)
	Rice, puffed or oven-popped, presweetened:																	
1886	Honey and added nutrients	1.8	388	4.2	.7	90.6	.2	2.7	46	74	.9	706	—	(0)	.33	—	4.6	(0)
1887	Honey or cocoa and added nutrients, including fat.	3.4	401	4.5	4.0	86.7	.4	1.4	51	82	3.3	358	61	(0)	.42	.06	6.3	(0)
1888	Rice, shredded; added nutrients	3.0	392	5.2	.3	88.8	.3	2.7	14	95	1.8	846	—	(0)	.39	—	7.0	(0)
	Rice, with protein concentrate, mainly—																	
1889	Casein, other added nutrients	3.0	382	40.0	.2	54.8	.5	2.0	159	318	17.6	600	—	(0)	1.70	2.10	17.6	53
1890	Wheat gluten, other added nutrients	2.5	386	20.0	.3	74.4	.5	2.8	53	187	12.4	800	—	(0)	1.40	1.70	17.0	35
1891	**Rice pudding** with raisins	65.8	146	3.6	3.1	26.7	.1	.8	98	94	.4	71	177	110	.03	.14	.2	Trace
	Rockfish, including black, canary, yellowtail, rasphead, and bocaccio:																	
1892	Raw	78.9	97	18.9	1.8	0	0	1.2	—	—	—	60	388	—	.06	.12	—	—
1893	Cooked, oven-steamed [133]	75.4	107	18.1	2.5	1.9	—	2.1	—	—	—	68	446	—	.05	.12	—	1
	Roe:																	
	Raw:																	
1894	Including carp, cod, haddock, herring, pike, and shad.	70.1	130	24.4	2.3	1.5	—	1.7	—	—	.6	—	—	—	.10	.76	1.4	14
1895	Including salmon, sturgeon, and turbot	61.3	207	25.2	10.4	1.4	—	1.7	—	—	—	—	—	—	.38	.72	2.3	18
1896	Cooked, baked or broiled, cod and shad [134]	71.3	126	22.0	2.8	1.9	—	2.0	13	402	2.3	73	132	—	—	—	—	—
1897	Canned, including cod, haddock, and herring, solids and liquid.	72.4	118	21.5	2.8	.3	—	2.0	15	346	1.2	—	—	—	—	—	—	2
	Rolls and buns:																	
1898	Baked from home recipe, with milk and enriched flour.	26.1	339	8.2	8.7	56.1	.2	.9	47	102	[135] 2.1	279	117	80	[135] .25	[135] .26	[135] 2.3	Trace
	Commercial:																	
	Ready-to-serve:																	
1899	Danish pastry	22.0	422	7.4	23.5	45.6	.1	1.5	50	109	.9	366	112	310	.07	.15	.8	Trace
	Hard rolls:																	
1900	Enriched	25.4	312	9.8	3.2	59.5	.2	2.1	47	92	2.3	625	97	Trace	.26	.23	2.7	Trace
1901	Unenriched	25.4	312	9.8	3.2	59.5	.2	2.1	47	92	.8	625	97	Trace	.05	.09	.8	Trace
	Plain (pan rolls):																	
1902	Enriched	31.4	298	8.2	5.6	53.0	.2	1.8	74	85	1.9	506	95	Trace	.28	.18	2.2	Trace
1903	Unenriched	31.4	298	8.2	5.6	53.0	.2	1.8	74	85	.7	506	95	Trace	.06	.09	.8	Trace
1904	Raisin rolls or buns	32.0	275	6.9	2.9	56.4	.9	1.8	75	91	1.4	384	245	Trace	.06	.10	.7	Trace
1905	Sweet rolls	31.5	316	8.5	9.1	49.3	.2	1.6	85	107	.8	389	124	70	.07	.15	.8	Trace
1906	Whole-wheat rolls	32.0	257	10.0	2.8	52.3	1.6	2.9	106	281	2.4	564	292	Trace	.34	.13	3.0	Trace
	Partially baked (brown-and-serve):																	
	Enriched:																	
1907	Unbrowned	33.0	299	7.9	6.8	50.6	.2	1.7	47	82	1.8	513	91	Trace	.24	.20	2.1	Trace
1908	Browned	26.9	328	8.7	7.8	54.8	.2	1.8	51	89	2.0	562	100	Trace	.26	.22	2.3	Trace
	Unenriched:																	
1909	Unbrowned	33.0	299	7.9	6.8	50.6	.2	1.7	47	82	.7	513	91	Trace	.06	.09	.8	Trace
1910	Browned	26.9	328	8.7	7.8	54.8	.2	1.8	51	89	.7	562	100	Trace	.06	.10	.8	Trace
	Roll dough and rolls baked from dough:																	
	Enriched:																	
1911	Dough, unraised, frozen	38.5	268	7.5	5.0	47.4	.2	1.6	33	76	1.7	482	82	Trace	.27	.20	2.2	Trace
1912	Rolls, baked	28.3	311	8.5	5.4	56.0	.3	1.8	39	88	2.0	560	96	Trace	.27	.22	2.3	Trace
	Unenriched:																	
1913	Dough, unraised, frozen	38.5	268	7.5	5.0	47.4	.2	1.6	33	76	.9	482	82	Trace	.08	.09	1.0	Trace
1914	Rolls, baked	28.3	311	8.5	5.4	56.0	.3	1.8	39	88	1.0	560	96	Trace	.08	.10	1.0	Trace
	Roll mix and rolls baked from mix:																	
1915	Mix, dry form	8.6	393	11.2	5.9	72.3	.2	2.0	74	128	[136] .8	412	162	Trace	[136] .08	[136] .16	[136] 1.1	Trace
1916	Rolls, made with water	30.6	299	9.0	4.5	54.5	.2	1.4	56	97	[136] .6	313	123	Trace	[136] .05	[136] .12	[136] .7	Trace
	Root beer. See Beverages, item 408.																	
1917	**Roseapples,** raw	84.5	56	.6	.3	14.2	1.1	.4	29	16	1.2	—	—	130	.02	.03	.8	22
	Rum. See Beverages, items 395–399.																	
1918	**Rusk**	4.8	419	13.8	8.7	71.0	.2	1.7	20	119	1.3	246	161	230	.08	.22	1.1	Trace
	Rutabagas:																	
1919	Raw	87.0	46	1.1	.1	11.0	1.1	.8	66	39	.4	5	239	580	.07	.07	1.1	43
1920	Cooked, boiled, drained	90.2	35	.9	.1	8.2	1.1	.6	59	31	.3	4	167	550	.06	.06	.8	26
	Rye:																	
1921	Whole-grain	11.	334	12.1	1.7	73.4	2.0	1.8	(38)	376	3.7	(1)	467	(0)	.43	.22	1.6	(0)
	Flours:																	
1922	Light	11.	357	9.4	1.0	77.9	.4	.7	22	185	1.1	(1)	156	(0)	.15	.07	.6	(0)
1923	Medium	11.	350	11.4	1.7	74.8	1.0	1.1	(27)	262	2.6	(1)	203	(0)	.30	.12	2.5	(0)
1924	Dark	11.	327	16.3	2.6	68.1	2.4	2.0	54	(536)	4.5	1	860	(0)	.61	.22	2.7	(0)

[131] Raspberry- and strawberry-flavored mixes contain about 170 mg. calcium and a trace of phosphorus per 100 grams. Values per 100 grams of prepared dessert are: Calcium, 121 mg.; phosphorus, 84 mg.

[132] Values for iron, thiamine, and niacin are based on the minimum levels of enrichment specified in standards of identity.

[133] Prepared with onion.

[134] Prepared with butter or margarine and lemon juice or vinegar.

[135] With unenriched flour, values per 100 grams are: Iron, 0.8 mg.; thiamine, 0.06 mg.; riboflavin, 0.14 mg.; niacin, 0.8 mg.

[136] Based on mix containing unenriched flour. If mix is made with enriched flour, approximate values in milligrams per 100 grams are as follows:

	Iron	Thiamine	Riboflavin	Niacin
Dry mix	2.6	0.40	0.34	3.3
Rolls	2.0	.25	.25	2.2

TABLE 1.—COMPOSITION OF FOODS, 100 GRAMS, EDIBLE PORTION—Continued

[Numbers in parentheses denote values imputed—usually from another form of the food or from a similar food. Zero in parentheses indicates that the amount of a constituent probably is none or is too small to measure. Dashes denote lack of reliable data for a constituent believed to be present in measurable amount. Calculated values, as those based on a recipe, are not in parentheses]

Item No.	Food and description	Water	Food energy	Protein	Fat	Carbohydrate		Ash	Calcium	Phosphorus	Iron	Sodium	Potassium	Vitamin A value	Thiamine	Riboflavin	Niacin	Ascorbic acid
						Total	Fiber											
(A)	(B)	(C)	(D)	(E)	(F)	(G)	(H)	(I)	(J)	(K)	(L)	(M)	(N)	(O)	(P)	(Q)	(R)	(S)
		Percent	Calories	Grams	Grams	Grams	Grams	Grams	Milligrams	Milligrams	Milligrams	Milligrams	Milligrams	International units	Milligrams	Milligrams	Milligrams	Milligrams
1925	**Rye wafers,** whole-grain	6.0	344	13.0	1.2	76.3	2.2	3.5	53	388	3.9	882	600	(0)	0.32	0.25	1.2	(0)
1926	**Sablefish,** raw	71.6	190	13.0	14.9	0	0	1.0	—	—	—	56	358	—	.11	.09	—	—
1927	**Safflower seed kernels,** dry	5.0	615	19.1	59.5	12.4	—	4.0	—	—	—	—	—	—	—	—	—	—
1928	**Safflower seed meal,** partially defatted	9.1	355	39.6	8.2	36.5	7.4	6.6	75	620	—	—	—	—	1.12	.40	2.2	0
	Salad dressings, commercial: [137]																	
	Blue and Roquefort cheese:																	
1929	Regular	32.3	504	4.8	52.3	7.4	.1	3.2	81	74	.2	1,094	37	210	.01	.10	.1	2
	Special dietary (low-calorie):																	
1930	Low-fat (approx. 5 Cal. per tsp.)	83.7	76	3.0	5.9	4.1	.1	3.3	64	47	.1	1,108	34	170	Trace	.07	.1	2
1931	Low-fat (approx. 1 Cal. per tsp.)	93.1	19	1.4	1.1	1.4	.1	3.0	35	24	.1	1,134	29	80	Trace	.04	Trace	2
	French:																	
1932	Regular	38.8	410	.6	38.9	17.5	.3	4.2	11	14	.4	1,370	79	—	—	—	—	—
	Special dietary (low-calorie):																	
1933	Low-fat (approx. 5 Cal. per tsp.)	77.3	96	.4	4.3	15.6	.3	2.4	11	14	.4	787	79	—	—	—	—	—
1934	Low-fat with artificial sweetener (approx. 1 Cal. per tsp.).	95.2	10	.4	.2	1.8	.3	2.4	11	14	.4	787	79	—	—	—	—	—
1935	Medium-fat with artificial sweetener (approx. 10 Cal. per tsp.).	78.8	156	.7	16.9	1.2	.3	2.4	11	14	.4	787	79	—	—	—	—	—
	Italian:																	
1936	Regular	27.5	552	.2	60.0	6.9	Trace	5.4	10	4	.2	092	15	Trace	Trace	Trace	Trace	—
1937	Special dietary (low-calorie, approx. 2 Cal. per tsp.).	90.1	50	.2	4.7	2.6	Trace	2.4	2	5	.2	787	15	Trace	Trace	Trace	Trace	—
1938	Mayonnaise	15.1	718	1.1	79.9	2.2	Trace	1.7	18	28	.5	597	34	280	.02	.04	Trace	—
1939	Russian	34.5	494	1.6	50.8	10.4	.3	2.7	19	37	.6	868	157	690	.05	.05	.6	6
	Salad dressing (mayonnaise type):																	
1940	Regular	40.6	435	1.0	42.3	14.4	—	1.7	14	26	.2	586	9	220	.01	.03	Trace	—
1941	Special dietary (low-calorie, approx. 8 Cal. per tsp.).	80.7	136	1.1	12.7	4.8	.5	.7	18	28	.2	118	9	220	.01	.03	Trace	—
	Thousand island:																	
1942	Regular	32.0	502	.8	50.2	15.4	.3	1.6	11	17	.6	700	113	320	.02	.03	.2	3
1943	Special dietary (low-calorie, approx. 10 Cal. per tsp.).	68.2	180	.9	13.7	15.6	.3	(1.6)	11	17	.6	700	113	320	.02	.03	.2	3
	Salad dressings, made from home recipe:																	
1944	French	24.2	632	.3	70.1	3.6	.1	1.8	6	3	.1	659	26	—	—	—	—	—
1945	Cooked	68.0	164	4.4	9.9	15.2	0	2.5	89	93	.6	728	116	490	.05	.16	.2	Trace
	Salad oil. See Oils, item 1401.																	
	Salami. See Sausage, cold cuts, and luncheon meats: items 2017–2018.																	
	Salmon:																	
	Atlantic:																	
1946	Raw	63.6	217	22.5	13.4	0	0	1.4	79	186	.9	—	—	—	—	.08	7.2	9
1947	Canned, solids and liquid	64.2	203	21.7	12.2	0	0	1.6	—	—	—	—	—	—	—	—	—	—
	Chinook (king):																	
1948	Raw	64.2	222	19.1	15.6	0	0	1.1	—	301	—	45	399	310	.10	.23	—	—
1949	Canned, solids and liquid	64.4	210	19.6	14.0	0	0	2.0	[138] 154	289	.9	[139] —	366	230	.03	.14	7.3	—
	Chum:																	
1950	Raw	—	—	—	—	—	—	—	—	—	—	53	429	—	.10	.06	—	—
1951	Canned, solids and liquid	70.8	139	21.5	5.2	0	0	2.6	[138] 249	352	.7	[139] —	336	60	.02	.16	7.1	—
	Coho (silver):																	
1952	Raw	—	—	—	—	—	—	—	175	231	—	[140] 48	421	—	.09	.11	—	1
1953	Canned, solids and liquid	69.3	153	20.8	7.1	0	0	2.4	[138] 244	288	.9	[139] 351	339	80	.03	.18	7.4	—
	Pink (humpback):																	
1954	Raw	76.0	119	20.0	3.7	0	0	1.2	—	—	—	[141] 64	[141] 306	—	.14	.05	—	—
1955	Canned, solids and liquid	70.8	141	20.5	5.9	0	0	2.3	[138] 196	286	.8	[139] 387	361	70	.03	.18	8.0	—
	Sockeye (red):																	
1956	Raw	—	—	—	—	—	—	—	—	—	—	48	391	150	.14	.07	—	—
1957	Canned, solids and liquid	67.2	171	20.3	9.3	0	0	2.7	[138] 259	344	1.2	[139] 522	344	230	.04	.16	7.3	—
1958	**Salmon, cooked,** broiled or baked	63.4	182	27.0	7.4	0	0	1.6	—	414	1.2	116	443	160	.16	.06	9.8	—
1959	**Salmon rice loaf**	74.4	122	12.0	4.5	7.3	—	1.8	—	—	—	—	—	—	—	—	—	—
1960	**Salmon, smoked**	58.9	176	21.6	9.3	0	0	9.4	14	245	—	—	—	—	—	—	—	—
	Salsify:																	
1961	Raw	77.6	([142])	2.9	.6	[8] 18.0	1.8	.9	47	66	1.5	—	380	10	.04	.04	.3	11
1962	Cooked, boiled, drained	81.0	([142])	2.6	.6	[8] 15.1	1.8	.7	42	53	1.3	—	266	10	.03	.04	.2	7

1963	**Salt, table**	.2	0	0	0	0	0	99.8	253	—	.1	38,758	4	0	0	0	0	0
1964	**Salt pork, raw**	8.	783	3.9	85.	0	0	3.5	Trace	Trace	.6	1,212	42	(0)	(.18)	(.04)	(.9)	—
	Salt sticks:																	
1965	Regular type	5.	384	12.0	2.9	75.3	.3	4.8	28	99	.9	1,674	92	Trace	.06	.07	1.0	Trace
1966	Vienna bread type	25.	304	9.5	3.1	58.0	.2	4.4	45	89	.8	1,565	94	Trace	.05	.08	.8	Trace
	Sanddab. See Flatfishes, item 1018.																	
	Sandwich spread (with chopped pickle):																	
1967	Regular	45.4	379	.7	36.2	15.9	.4	1.8	15	20	.7	626	92	280	.01	.03	Trace	6
1968	Special dietary (low-calorie, approx. 5 Cal. per tsp.)	80.2	112	1.0	9.0	8.0	.4	1.8	15	20	.7	626	92	280	.01	.03	Trace	6
1969	**Sapodilla**, raw	76.1	89	.5	1.1	21.8	1.4	.5	21	12	.8	12	193	60	Trace	.02	.2	14
1970	**Sapotes** (marmalade plums), raw	64.9	125	1.8	.6	31.6	1.9	1.1	39	28	1.0	—	—	410	.01	.02	1.8	20
	Sardines, Atlantic, canned in oil:																	
1971	Solids and liquid	50.6	311	20.6	24.4	.6	—	3.8	354	434	3.5	510	560	180	.02	.16	4.4	—
1972	Drained solids	61.8	203	24.0	11.1	—	—	3.1	[143] 437	[143] 499	2.9	823	590	220	.03	.20	5.4	—
	Sardines, Pacific:																	
1973	Raw	70.7	160	19.2	8.6	0	0	2.4	33	215	1.8	—	—	—	—	—	—	—
	Canned:																	
1974	In brine or mustard, solids and liquid	64.1	196	18.8	12.0	1.7	—	3.4	303	354	5.2	760	260	30	—	—	—	—
1975	In oil, drained solids	—	—	—	—	—	—	—	—	—	—	—	—	—	.01	.30	7.4	—
1976	In tomato sauce, solids and liquid	64.3	197	18.7	12.2	1.7	—	3.1	449	478	4.1	400	320	30	.01	.27	5.3	—
1977	**Sauerkraut,** canned, solids and liquid	92.8	18	1.0	.2	4.0	.7	2.0	36	18	.5	[144] 747	140	50	.03	.04	.2	14
1978	**Sauerkraut juice,** canned	94.6	10	.7	Trace	2.3	Trace	2.4	37	14	1.1	[144] 787	—	—	.03	.04	.2	18
1979	**Sauger,** raw	80.8	84	17.9	.8	0	0	1.1	—	—	—	—	—	—	—	—	—	—
	Sausage, cold cuts, and luncheon meats:																	
1980	Blood sausage or blood pudding	46.4	394	14.1	36.9	.3	0	2.3	—	—	—	—	—	—	—	—	—	—
1981	Bockwurst	61.9	264	11.3	23.7	.6	0	2.5	—	—	—	—	—	—	—	—	—	—
	Bologna:																	
1982	All samples	56.2	304	12.1	27.5	1.1	—	3.1	7	128	1.8	1,300	230	—	.16	.22	2.6	—
1983	All meat	57.4	277	13.3	22.8	3.7	0	2.8	—	—	—	—	—	—	—	—	—	—
1984	With nonfat dry milk	57.1	—	13.4	—	—	—	—	—	—	—	—	—	—	—	—	—	—
1985	With cereal	57.9	262	14.2	20.6	3.9	—	3.4	—	—	—	—	—	—	—	—	—	—
1986	Braunschweiger	52.6	319	14.8	27.4	2.3	—	2.9	10	245	5.9	—	—	6,530	.17	1.44	8.2	—
	Brown-and-serve sausage:																	
1987	Before browning	45.3	393	13.5	36.0	2.7	0	2.5	—	—	—	—	—	—	—	—	—	—
1988	Browned	39.9	422	16.5	37.8	2.8	0	3.0	—	—	—	—	—	—	—	—	—	—
1989	Capicola or Capacola	26.2	499	20.2	45.8	0	0	7.9	—	—	—	—	—	—	—	—	—	—
	Cervelat:																	
1990	Dry	29.4	451	24.6	37.6	1.7	0	6.7	14	294	2.7	—	—	(0)	.27	.23	5.5	—
1991	Soft	48.5	307	18.6	24.5	1.6	0	6.8	11	214	2.8	—	—	—	.11	.26	4.2	—
1992	Country-style sausage	49.9	345	15.1	31.1	0	0	3.9	9	168	2.3	—	—	—	.22	.19	3.1	—
1993	Deviled ham, canned	50.5	351	13.9	32.3	0	0	3.3	8	92	2.1	—	—	(0)	.14	.10	1.6	—
	Frankfurters:																	
	Raw:																	
1994	All samples	55.6	309	12.5	27.6	1.8	—	2.5	7	133	1.9	1,100	220	—	.16	.20	2.7	—
1995	All meat	56.5	296	13.1	25.5	2.5	0	2.4	—	—	—	—	—	—	—	—	—	—
1996	With nonfat dry milk	54.2	300	13.1	25.6	3.4	—	3.7	—	—	—	—	—	—	—	—	—	—
1997	With cereal	61.7	248	14.4	20.6	.2	—	3.1	—	—	—	—	—	—	—	—	—	—
1998	With nonfat dry milk and cereal	50.5	—	14.2	21.7	—	—	—	—	—	—	—	—	—	—	—	—	—
1999	Cooked	57.3	304	12.4	27.2	1.6	—	1.5	5	102	1.5	—	—	—	.15	.20	2.5	—
2000	Canned	66.0	221	13.4	18.1	.2	0	2.3	9	145	2.2	—	—	—	.03	.12	2.4	—
2001	Headcheese	58.8	268	15.5	22.0	1.0	0	2.7	9	173	2.3	—	—	(0)	.04	.10	.9	—
2002	Knockwurst	57.6	278	14.1	23.2	2.2	0	(2.9)	8	154	2.1	—	—	—	(.17)	(.21)	(2.6)	—
	Liverwurst:																	
2003	Fresh	53.9	307	16.2	25.6	1.8	0	2.5	9	238	5.4	—	—	6,350	.20	1.30	5.7	—
2004	Smoked	52.6	319	14.8	27.4	2.3	0	2.9	10	245	5.9	—	—	6,530	.17	1.44	8.2	—
	Luncheon meat:																	
2005	Boiled ham	59.1	234	19.0	17.0	0	0	4.9	11	166	2.8	—	—	(0)	.44	.15	2.6	—
2006	Pork, cured ham or shoulder, chopped, spiced or unspiced, canned.	54.9	294	15.0	24.9	1.3	0	3.9	9	108	2.2	1,234	222	(0)	.31	.21	3.0	—
2007	Meat loaf	64.1	200	15.9	13.2	3.3	0	3.5	9	178	1.8	—	—	—	.13	.22	2.5	—
2008	Meat, potted (includes potted beef, chicken, and turkey).	60.7	248	17.5	19.2	0	0	2.8	—	—	—	—	—	—	.03	.22	1.2	—
2009	Minced ham	61.7	228	13.7	16.9	4.4	0	3.3	8	89	2.1	—	—	(0)	.37	.22	3.4	—
2010	Mortadella	48.9	315	20.4	25.0	.6	0	5.1	12	238	3.1	—	—	—	—	—	—	—
2011	Polish-style sausage	53.7	304	15.7	25.8	1.2	0	3.6	9	176	2.4	—	—	(0)	.34	.19	3.1	—
2012	Pork and beef (chopped together)	53.5	336	15.6	29.9	0	0	1.0	9	174	2.3	—	—	—	—	—	—	—
	Pork sausage, links or bulk:																	
2013	Raw	38.1	498	9.4	50.8	Trace	0	1.7	5	92	1.4	740	140	(0)	.43	.17	2.3	—
2014	Cooked	34.8	476	18.1	44.2	Trace	0	2.9	7	162	2.4	958	269	(0)	.79	.34	3.7	—

[8] A large proportion of the carbohydrate in the unstored product may be inulin, which is of doubtful availability. During storage, inulin is converted to sugars.

[137] Values apply to products containing salt. For those without salt, sodium content is low, ranging from less than 10 mg. to 50 mg. per 100 grams; the amount usually is indicated on the label.

[138] Based on total contents of can. If bones are discarded, value will be greatly reduced.

[139] For product canned without added salt, value is approximately the same as for raw salmon.

[140] Sample dipped in brine contained 215 mg. sodium per 100 grams.

[141] Values for salmon dipped in brine averaged 473 mg. of sodium and 126 mg. of potassium per 100 grams.

[142] Values for raw salsify range from 13 Calories per 100 grams for the freshly harvested vegetable to 82 Calories for the product after storage; corresponding range for boiled salsify is from 12 to 70 Calories.

[143] Values for sardines without skin and bones canned in oil are: Calcium, 54 mg. per 100 grams; phosphorus, 319 mg.

[144] Values for sauerkraut and sauerkraut juice are based on salt contents of 1.9 and 2.0 percent respectively in the finished products. The amounts in some samples may vary significantly from this estimate.

TABLE 1.—COMPOSITION OF FOODS, 100 GRAMS, EDIBLE PORTION—Continued

[Numbers in parentheses denote values imputed—usually from another form of the food or from a similar food. Zero in parentheses indicates that the amount of a constituent probably is none or is too small to measure. Dashes denote lack of reliable data for a constituent believed to be present in measurable amount. Calculated values, as those based on a recipe, are not in parentheses]

Item No.	Food and description	Water	Food energy	Protein	Fat	Carbohydrate		Ash	Calcium	Phosphorus	Iron	Sodium	Potassium	Vitamin A value	Thiamine	Riboflavin	Niacin	Ascorbic acid
						Total	Fiber											
(A)	(B)	(C)	(D)	(E)	(F)	(G)	(H)	(I)	(J)	(K)	(L)	(M)	(N)	(O)	(P)	(Q)	(R)	(S)
	Sausage, cold cuts, and luncheon meats—Continued	Percent	Calories	Grams	Grams	Grams	Grams	Grams	Milligrams	Milligrams	Milligrams	Milligrams	Milligrams	International units	Milligrams	Milligrams	Milligrams	Milligrams
	Pork sausage, canned:																	
2015	Solids and liquid	42.1	415	13.8	38.4	2.4	0	3.3	8	150	2.1	—	—	(0)	0.19	0.19	3.3	—
2016	Drained solids	43.2	381	18.3	32.8	1.9	0	3.8	11	210	2.8	—	—	—	—	—	—	—
	Pork sausage, link, smoked. See Sausage, country-style: item 1992.																	
	Salami:																	
2017	Dry	29.8	450	23.8	38.1	1.2	0	7.1	14	283	3.6	—	—	—	.37	.25	5.3	—
2018	Cooked	51.0	311	17.5	25.6	1.4	0	4.5	10	200	2.6	—	—	—	.25	.24	4.1	—
2019	Scrapple	61.3	215	8.8	13.6	14.6	.1	1.7	5	64	1.2	—	—	—	.19	.09	1.8	—
2020	Souse	70.3	181	13.0	13.4	1.2	0	2.1	—	—	—	—	—	(0)	—	—	—	—
2021	Thuringer	48.5	307	18.6	24.5	1.6	0	6.8	11	214	2.8	—	—	—	.11	.26	4.2	—
2022	Vienna sausage, canned	63.0	240	14.0	19.8	.3	0	2.9	8	153	2.1	—	—	—	.08	.13	2.6	—
	Scallops, bay and sea:																	
2023	Raw	79.8	81	15.3	.2	3.3	—	1.4	26	208	1.8	[145] 255	[145] 396	—	—	.06	1.3	—
2024	Cooked, steamed	73.1	112	23.2	1.4	—	—	—	115	338	3.0	265	476	—	—	—	—	—
2025	Frozen, breaded, fried, reheated	60.2	194	18.0	8.4	10.5	—	2.9	—	—	—	—	—	—	—	—	—	—
	Scrapple. See Sausage, cold cuts, and luncheon meats: item 2019.																	
	Scup. See Porgy, item 1658.																	
2026	**Seabass**, white, raw	76.3	96	21.4	.5	0	0	1.4	—	—	—	—	—	—	—	—	—	—
	Seaweeds, raw:																	
2027	Agar	16.3	—	—	.3	—	.7	3.7	567	22	6.3	—	—	—	—	—	—	—
2028	Dulse	16.6	—	—	3.2	—	1.2	22.4	296	267	—	2,085	8,060	—	—	—	—	—
2029	Irishmoss	19.2	—	—	1.8	—	2.1	17.6	885	157	8.9	2,892	2,844	—	—	—	—	—
2030	Kelp	21.7	—	—	1.1	—	6.8	22.8	1,093	240	—	3,007	5,273	—	—	—	—	—
2031	Laver	17.0	—	—	.6	—	3.5	11.0	—	—	—	—	—	—	—	—	—	—
	Sesame seeds, dry:																	
2032	Whole	5.4	563	18.6	49.1	21.6	6.3	5.3	1,160	616	10.5	60	725	30	.98	.24	5.4	0
2033	Decorticated	5.5	582	18.2	53.4	17.6	2.4	5.3	110	592	2.4	—	—	—	.18	.13	5.4	0
	Shad or American shad:																	
2034	Raw	70.4	170	18.6	10.0	0	0	1.3	20	260	.5	54	330	—	.15	.24	8.4	—
	Cooked:																	
2035	Baked [146]	64.0	201	23.2	11.3	0	0	1.4	24	313	.6	79	377	30	.13	.26	8.6	—
2036	Creole [147]	73.3	152	15.0	8.7	1.6	—	1.4	19	190	.6	73	280	450	.09	.16	5.1	8
2037	Canned, solids and liquid	71.1	152	16.9	8.8	0	0	2.8	—	—	.7	—	—	—	—	.16	—	—
2038	**Shad, gizzard** (gizzard shad), raw	67.8	200	17.2	14.0	0	0	1.2	—	—	—	—	—	—	—	—	—	—
2039	**Shallot** bulbs, raw	79.8	72	2.5	.1	16.8	.7	.8	37	60	1.2	12	334	Trace	.06	.02	.2	8
	Sheefish. See Inconnu, item 1145.																	
2040	**Sheepshead, Atlantic,** raw	75.9	113	20.6	2.8	0	0	1.3	—	197	—	101	234	—	—	—	—	—
	Sheepshead, fresh water. See Drum, item 959.																	
2041	**Sherbet,** orange	67.0	134	.9	1.2	30.8	0	.1	16	13	Trace	10	22	60	.01	.03	Trace	2
	Shortbread. See Cookies, item 830.																	
	Shrimp:																	
2042	Raw	78.2	91	18.1	.8	1.5	—	1.4	63	166	1.6	140	220	—	.02	.03	3.2	—
2043	Cooked, french-fried [148]	56.9	225	20.3	10.8	10.0	—	2.0	72	191	2.0	186	229	—	.04	.08	2.7	—
	Canned:																	
2044	Wet pack, solids and liquid	78.2	80	16.2	.8	.8	—	4.0	59	152	1.8	—	—	50	.01	.03	1.5	—
2045	Dry pack or drained solids of wet pack	70.4	116	24.2	1.1	.7	—	3.6	115	263	3.1	—	122	60	.01	.03	1.8	—
2046	Frozen, breaded, raw; not more than 50% breading	65.0	139	12.3	.7	19.9	.1	2.1	38	111	1.0	—	—	—	.03	.03	2.0	—
2047	**Shrimp or lobster paste,** canned	61.3	180	20.8	9.4	1.5	—	7.0	—	—	—	—	—	—	—	.26	—	—
	Sirups:																	
2048	Cane	26.	263	0	0	68.	0	1.5	60	29	3.6	—	425	0	.13	.06	.1	0
2049	Maple	33.	252	—	—	65.	—	.7	104	8	1.2	10	176	—	—	—	—	0
2050	Sorghum	23.	257	—	—	68.	—	2.4	172	25	12.5	—	—	—	—	.10	.1	—
	Table blends:																	
2051	Chiefly corn, light and dark	24.	290	0	0	75.	0	.7	46	16	4.1	68	4	0	0	0	0	0
2052	Cane and maple	33.	252	0	0	65.	0	.1	16	1	Trace	2	26	0	0	0	0	0
	Siscowet. See Lake trout, items 1170–1171.																	
2053	**Skate** (raja fish), raw	77.8	98	21.5	.7	0	0	1.2	—	—	—	—	—	—	.02	—	—	—
	Smelt, Atlantic, jack, and bay:																	
2054	Raw	79.0	98	18.6	2.1	0	0	1.1	—	272	.4	—	—	—	.01	.12	1.4	—
2055	Canned, solids and liquid	62.7	200	18.4	13.5	0	—	5.4	358	370	1.7	—	—	—	—	—	—	—
	Smelt, eulachon. See Eulachon, item 990.																	

2056	**Snail, raw**	79.2	90	16.1	1.4	2.0	—	1.3	—	—	3.5	—	—	—	—	—	—	—
2057	**Snail, Giant African, raw**	82.2	73	9.9	1.4	4.4	—	2.1	—	—	—	—	—	—	—	—	—	—
	Snapper, red. See Red and gray snapper, item 1853.																	
	Soft drinks. See Beverages, items 402–409.																	
	Sole. See Flatfishes, item 1018.																	
2058	**Sorghum grain, all types**	11.	332	11.0	3.3	73.0	1.7	1.7	28	287	4.4	—	350	(0)	.38	.15	3.9	(0)
	Sorrel. See Dock, items 953–954.																	
	Soups, commercial:																	
	Canned:																	
	Asparagus, cream of:																	
2059	Condensed	85.8	54	2.0	1.4	8.4	.6	2.4	22	31	.6	820	100	250	.03	.07	.6	—
2060	Prepared with equal volume of water	92.9	27	1.0	.7	4.2	.3	1.2	11	16	.3	410	50	130	.02	.04	.3	—
2061	Prepared with equal volume of milk	86.4	60	2.8	2.4	6.8	.3	1.6	72	64	.3	436	123	200	.03	.12	.3	Trace
	Bean with pork:																	
2062	Condensed	68.9	134	6.4	4.6	17.3	1.3	2.8	50	101	1.8	806	316	520	.11	.06	.8	2
2063	Prepared with equal volume of water	84.4	67	3.2	2.3	8.7	.6	1.4	25	51	.9	403	158	260	.05	.03	.4	1
	Beef broth, bouillon, and consomme:																	
2064	Condensed	91.6	26	4.2	0	2.2	.1	2.0	Trace	26	.4	652	108	Trace	Trace	.02	1.0	—
2065	Prepared with equal volume of water	95.8	13	2.1	0	1.1	Trace	1.0	Trace	13	.2	326	54	Trace	Trace	.01	.5	—
	Beef noodle:																	
2066	Condensed	86.4	57	3.2	2.2	5.8	.1	2.4	6	40	.7	764	64	50	.04	.05	.9	1
2067	Prepared with equal volume of water	93.2	28	1.6	1.1	2.9	Trace	1.2	3	20	.4	382	32	20	.02	.03	.4	Trace
	Celery, cream of:																	
2068	Condensed	84.6	72	1.4	4.2	7.4	.4	2.4	40	30	.5	796	90	170	.01	.04	.4	1
2069	Prepared with equal volume of water	92.3	36	.7	2.1	3.7	.2	1.2	20	15	.2	398	45	80	.01	.02	Trace	Trace
2070	Prepared with equal volume of milk	85.8	69	2.6	3.8	6.2	.2	1.6	81	63	.3	424	118	160	.02	.11	.3	1
	Chicken consomme:																	
2071	Condensed	93.7	18	2.8	.1	1.5	Trace	1.9	10	59	1.0	602	—	—	—	—	—	—
2072	Prepared with equal volume of water	96.8	9	1.4	Trace	.8	Trace	1.0	5	30	.5	301	—	—	—	—	—	—
	Chicken, cream of:																	
2073	Condensed	83.8	79	2.4	4.8	6.7	.1	2.3	19	29	.4	809	66	350	.01	.04	.5	Trace
2074	Prepared with equal volume of water	91.9	39	1.2	2.4	3.3	.1	1.2	10	14	.2	404	33	170	.01	.02	.2	Trace
2075	Prepared with equal volume of milk	85.4	73	3.0	4.2	5.9	.1	1.5	70	62	.2	430	106	250	.02	.11	.3	1
	Chicken gumbo:																	
2076	Condensed	87.6	46	2.6	1.3	6.1	.2	2.4	16	21	.5	792	89	180	.02	.03	1.1	4
2077	Prepared with equal volume of water	93.8	23	1.3	.6	3.1	.1	1.2	8	10	.2	396	45	90	.01	.02	.5	2
	Chicken noodle:																	
2078	Condensed	86.6	53	2.8	1.6	6.6	.1	2.4	7	30	.4	816	46	30	.01	.02	.7	Trace
2079	Prepared with equal volume of water	93.3	26	1.4	.8	3.3	.1	1.2	4	15	.2	408	23	20	.01	.01	.3	Trace
	Chicken with rice:																	
2080	Condensed	89.6	39	2.6	1.0	4.7	.1	2.1	7	21	.3	764	82	130	Trace	.02	.6	—
2081	Prepared with equal volume of water	94.8	20	1.3	.5	2.4	Trace	1.0	3	10	.1	382	41	60	Trace	.01	.3	—
	Chicken vegetable:																	
2082	Condensed	84.5	62	3.4	2.0	7.7	.3	2.4	15	33	.5	845	80	1,800	.02	.03	.9	—
2083	Prepared with equal volume of water	92.2	31	1.7	1.0	3.9	.1	1.2	7	16	.2	422	40	880	.01	.02	.4	—
	Clam chowder, Manhattan type (with tomatoes, without milk):																	
2084	Condensed	83.7	66	1.8	2.1	10.0	.3	2.4	29	38	.9	766	150	710	.02	.02	.9	—
2085	Prepared with equal volume of water	91.9	33	.9	1.0	5.0	.2	1.2	14	19	.4	383	75	360	.01	.01	.4	—
	Minestrone:																	
2086	Condensed	79.0	87	4.0	2.8	11.6	.6	2.6	30	49	.7	813	255	1,900	.06	.05	.9	—
2087	Prepared with equal volume of water	89.5	43	2.0	1.4	5.8	.3	1.3	15	24	.4	406	128	960	.03	.02	.4	—
	Mushroom, cream of:																	
2088	Condensed	79.3	111	1.9	8.0	8.4	.2	2.4	34	43	.3	795	82	60	.01	.10	.6	Trace
2089	Prepared with equal volume of water	89.6	56	1.0	4.0	4.2	.1	1.2	17	21	.2	398	41	30	.01	.05	.3	Trace
2090	Prepared with equal volume of milk	83.2	88	2.8	5.8	6.6	.1	1.6	78	69	.2	424	114	100	.02	.14	.3	Trace
	Onion:																	
2091	Condensed	86.9	54	4.4	2.1	4.3	.4	2.3	23	23	.4	875	86	Trace	Trace	.02	Trace	—
2092	Prepared with equal volume of water	93.4	27	2.2	1.0	2.2	.2	1.2	12	11	.2	438	43	Trace	Trace	.01	Trace	—
	Pea, green:																	
2093	Condensed	72.8	106	4.6	1.8	18.4	.9	2.4	36	91	.7	734	160	280	.04	.05	.9	6
2094	Prepared with equal volume of water	86.4	53	2.3	.9	9.2	.4	1.2	18	46	.4	367	80	140	.02	.02	.4	3
2095	Prepared with equal volume of milk	79.9	85	4.2	2.6	11.7	.4	1.6	79	94	.4	393	153	210	.04	.11	.5	4
	Pea, split:																	
2096	Condensed	70.7	118	7.0	2.6	17.0	.4	2.7	25	122	1.1	767	220	360	.20	.12	1.1	1
2097	Prepared with equal volume of water	85.4	59	3.5	1.3	8.4	.2	1.4	12	61	.6	384	110	180	.10	.06	.6	Trace
	Tomato:																	
2098	Condensed	81.0	72	1.6	2.1	12.7	.4	2.6	11	27	.6	792	188	810	.05	.03	.9	10
2099	Prepared with equal volume of water	90.5	36	.8	1.0	6.4	.2	1.3	6	14	.3	396	94	410	.02	.02	.5	5
2100	Prepared with equal volume of milk	84.0	69	2.6	2.8	9.0	.2	1.6	67	62	.3	422	167	480	.04	.10	.5	6
	Turkey noodle:																	
2101	Condensed	84.6	65	3.6	2.4	7.0	.1	2.4	12	36	.5	832	64	160	.04	.04	1.0	Trace
2102	Prepared with equal volume of water	92.3	33	1.8	1.2	3.5	.1	1.2	6	18	.3	416	32	80	.02	.02	.5	Trace

[145] Based on frozen scallops, possibly brined.

[146] Prepared with butter or margarine and bacon slices.

[147] Prepared with tomatoes, onion, green pepper, butter, and flour.

[148] Dipped in egg, breadcrumbs, and flour or in batter.

TABLE 1.—COMPOSITION OF FOODS, 100 GRAMS, EDIBLE PORTION—Continued

[Numbers in parentheses denote values imputed—usually from another form of the food or from a similar food. Zero in parentheses indicates that the amount of a constituent probably is none or is too small to measure. Dashes denote lack of reliable data for a constituent believed to be present in measurable amount. Calculated values, as those based on a recipe, are not in parentheses]

Item No.	Food and description	Water	Food energy	Protein	Fat	Carbohydrate		Ash	Calcium	Phos-phorus	Iron	Sodium	Potas-sium	Vitamin A value	Thiamine	Ribo-flavin	Niacin	Ascorbic acid
						Total	Fiber											
(A)	(B)	(C)	(D)	(E)	(F)	(G)	(H)	(I)	(J)	(K)	(L)	(M)	(N)	(O)	(P)	(Q)	(R)	(S)
	Soups, commercial—Continued	Percent	Calories	Grams	Grams	Grams	Grams	Grams	Milligrams	Milligrams	Milligrams	Milligrams	Milligrams	International units	Milligrams	Milligrams	Milligrams	Milligrams
	Canned—Continued																	
	Vegetable beef:																	
2103	Condensed	83. 8	65	4. 2	1. 8	7. 9	0. 4	2. 3	10	39	0. 6	854	131	2, 200	0. 03	0. 04	0. 8	—
2104	Prepared with equal volume of water	91. 9	32	2. 1	. 9	3. 9	. 2	1. 2	5	20	. 3	427	66	1, 100	. 02	. 02	. 4	—
	Vegetable with beef broth:																	
2105	Condensed	83. 4	64	2. 2	1. 4	11. 0	. 5	2. 0	16	32	. 7	690	196	2, 500	. 03	. 02	1. 0	—
2106	Prepared with equal volume of water	91. 7	32	1. 1	. 7	5. 5	. 3	1. 0	8	16	. 3	345	98	1, 300	. 02	. 01	. 5	—
	Vegetarian vegetable:																	
2107	Condensed	83. 7	64	1. 8	1. 7	10. 6	. 4	2. 2	16	32	. 8	684	140	2, 300	. 03	. 03	. 7	—
2108	Prepared with equal volume of water	91. 8	32	. 9	. 8	5. 4	. 2	1. 1	8	16	. 4	342	70	1, 200	. 02	. 02	. 4	—
	Dehydrated:																	
	Beef noodle:																	
2109	Mix, dry form	6. 1	387	13. 6	7. 4	65. 3	. 6	7. 6	48	148	2. 0	2, 369	230	120	. 53	. 28	4. 1	4
2110	Prepared with 2 oz. mix in 3 cups water	93. 1	28	1. 0	. 5	4. 8	Trace	. 6	4	11	. 2	175	17	10	. 04	. 02	. 3	Trace
	Chicken noodle:																	
2111	Mix, dry form	5. 7	383	14. 5	10. 0	58. 1	. 4	11. 7	59	143	2. 4	4, 278	146	330	. 52	. 27	4. 2	5
2112	Prepared with 2 oz. mix in 4 cups water	94. 7	22	. 8	. 6	3. 2	Trace	. 7	3	8	. 1	241	8	20	. 03	. 02	. 2	Trace
	Chicken rice:																	
2113	Mix, dry form	9. 8	353	9. 0	6. 8	62. 8	. 2	11. 6	45	69	. 6	4, 362	71	Trace	. 04	. 02	1. 1	—
2114	Prepared with 1½ oz. mix in 3 cups water	94. 9	20	. 5	. 4	3. 5	Trace	. 7	3	4	Trace	259	4	Trace	Trace	Trace	. 1	—
	Onion:																	
2115	Mix, dry form	2. 8	349	13. 9	10. 6	53. 9	1. 8	18. 8	97	113	1. 4	6, 676	553	60	. 11	. 07	. 7	15
2116	Prepared with 1½ oz. mix in 4 cups water	95. 8	15	. 6	. 5	2. 3	. 1	. 8	4	5	. 1	287	24	Trace	Trace	Trace	Trace	1
	Pea, green:																	
2117	Mix, dry form	3. 1	362	22. 4	4. 1	61. 6	1. 2	8. 8	60	313	5. 4	2, 360	874	120	. 44	. 46	4. 1	1
2118	Prepared with 2 oz. mix in 3 cups water	86. 7	50	3. 1	. 6	8. 4	. 2	1. 2	8	43	. 8	325	120	20	. 06	. 06	. 6	Trace
	Tomato vegetable with noodles:																	
2119	Mix, dry form	3. 7	348	8. 7	8. 0	62. 7	1. 5	16. 9	46	112	2. 0	6, 137	173	2, 400	. 30	. 19	2. 6	26
2120	Prepared with 2½ oz. mix in 4 cups water	92. 5	27	. 6	. 6	5. 1	. 1	1. 2	3	8	. 1	427	12	200	. 02	. 01	. 2	2
	Frozen:																	
	Clam chowder, New England type (with milk, without tomatoes):																	
2121	Condensed	78. 5	107	3. 7	6. 4	8. 6	. 2	2. 8	75	68	. 8	870	185	50	. 03	. 07	. 4	—
2122	Prepared with equal volume of water	89. 2	54	1. 8	3. 2	4. 4	. 1	1. 4	38	34	. 4	435	92	20	. 02	. 04	. 2	—
2123	Prepared with equal volume of milk	82. 8	86	3. 7	5. 0	6. 7	. 1	1. 8	98	82	. 4	461	166	100	. 03	. 12	. 2	Trace
	Oyster stew. See items 1448–1450.																	
	Pea, green, with ham:																	
2124	Condensed	71. 8	113	7. 6	2. 3	16. 0	1. 4	2. 3	25	102	1. 6	750	201	180	. 15	. 06	1. 0	—
2125	Prepared with equal volume of water	85. 9	57	3. 8	1. 2	8. 0	. 7	1. 2	12	51	. 8	375	100	90	. 08	. 03	. 5	—
	Potato, cream of:																	
2126	Condensed	79. 8	87	2. 7	4. 3	10. 0	. 3	3. 2	48	51	. 7	980	185	340	. 04	. 05	. 4	—
2127	Prepared with equal volume of water	89. 9	44	1. 4	2. 2	4. 9	. 2	1. 6	24	26	. 4	490	92	170	. 02	. 02	. 2	—
2128	Prepared with equal volume of milk	83. 4	76	3. 2	3. 9	7. 5	. 2	2. 0	85	74	. 4	516	166	240	. 04	. 11	. 2	Trace
	Shrimp, cream of:																	
2129	Condensed	76. 6	133	4. 0	9. 9	7. 2	. 3	2. 3	32	40	. 4	860	48	90	. 03	. 05	. 3	—
2130	Prepared with equal volume of water	88. 3	66	2. 0	5. 0	3. 5	. 2	1. 2	16	20	. 2	430	24	50	. 02	. 02	. 2	—
2131	Prepared with equal volume of milk	81. 8	99	3. 8	6. 7	6. 2	. 2	1. 5	77	68	. 2	456	97	120	. 03	. 11	. 2	Trace
	Vegetable with beef:																	
2132	Condensed	82. 7	70	5. 4	2. 3	7. 0	. 5	2. 6	22	63	. 8	792	145	2, 200	. 04	. 07	1. 5	—
2133	Prepared with equal volume of water	91. 4	35	2. 7	1. 2	3. 4	. 2	1. 3	11	32	. 4	396	72	1, 100	. 02	. 04	. 8	—
2134	**Soursop,** raw	81. 7	65	1. 0	. 3	16. 3	1. 1	. 7	14	27	. 6	14	265	10	. 07	. 05	. 9	20
	Souse. See Sausage, cold cuts, and luncheon meats: item 2020.																	
	Soybeans:																	
	Immature seeds:																	
2135	Raw	69. 2	134	10. 9	5. 1	13. 2	1. 4	1. 6	67	225	2. 8	—	—	690	. 44	. 16	1. 4	29
2136	Cooked, boiled, drained	73. 8	118	9. 8	5. 1	10. 1	1. 4	1. 2	60	191	2. 5	—	—	660	. 31	. 13	1. 2	17
	Canned:																	
2137	Solids and liquid	81. 8	75	6. 5	3. 2	6. 3	. 7	2. 2	55	100	2. 9	[9]236	—	—	. 09	. 09	—	8
2138	Drained solids	76. 7	103	9. 0	5. 0	7. 4	1. 4	1. 9	67	114	2. 8	[9]236	—	340	. 06	—	—	2
	Mature seeds, dry:																	
2139	Raw	10. 0	403	34. 1	17. 7	33. 5	4. 9	4. 7	226	554	8. 4	5	1, 677	80	1. 10	. 31	2. 2	—
2140	Cooked	71. 0	130	11. 0	5. 7	10. 8	1. 6	1. 5	73	179	2. 7	[4]2	540	30	. 21	. 09	. 6	0

	Fermented products:																	
2141	Natto (soybeans)	62.7	167	16.9	7.4	11.5	3.2	1.5	103	182	3.7	—	249	0	.07	.50	1.1	0
2142	Miso (cereal and soybeans)	53.0	171	10.5	4.6	23.5	2.3	8.4	68	309	1.7	2,950	334	40	.06	.10	.3	0
	Sprouted seeds:																	
2143	Raw	86.3	46	6.2	1.4	5.3	.8	.8	48	67	1.0	—	—	80	.23	.20	.8	13
2144	Cooked, boiled, drained	89.0	38	5.3	1.4	3.7	.8	.6	43	50	.7	—	—	80	.16	.15	.7	4
2145	**Soybean curd** (tofu)	84.8	72	7.8	4.2	2.4	.1	.8	128	126	1.9	7	42	0	.06	.03	.1	0
	Soybean flours:																	
2146	Full-fat	8.0	421	36.7	20.3	30.4	2.4	4.6	199	558	8.4	1	1,660	110	.85	.31	2.1	0
2147	High-fat	8.0	380	41.2	12.1	33.3	2.2	5.4	240	650	9.0	1	1,775	—	.89	.36	2.3	0
2148	Low-fat	8.0	356	43.4	6.7	36.6	2.5	5.3	263	634	9.1	1	1,859	80	.83	.36	2.6	0
2149	Defatted	8.0	326	47.0	.9	38.1	2.3	6.0	265	655	11.1	1	1,820	40	1.09	.34	2.6	0
	Soybean milk:																	
2150	Fluid	92.4	33	3.4	1.5	2.2	0	.5	21	48	.8	—	—	40	.08	.03	.2	0
2151	Powder	4.2	429	41.8	20.3	28.0	.2	5.7	275	—	—	—	—	—	—	—	—	—
	Soybean milk products, sweetened: [51]																	
2152	Liquid concentrate	74.4	126	4.8	7.3	12.3	.2	1.2	30	59	.8	43	237	Trace	.06	.03	.2	0
2153	Powder	3.7	452	20.4	23.2	48.4	.5	4.3	115	285	5.0	1	915	20	.30	.24	1.4	0
2154	**Soybean protein**	8.2	322	74.9	.1	15.1	.4	1.7	120	674	—	210	180	—	—	—	—	0
2155	**Soybean proteinate**	5.5	312	80.6	.1	7.7	.6	6.1	—	—	—	1,200	—	—	—	—	—	0
2156	**Soy sauce**	62.8	68	5.6	1.3	9.5	0	20.8	82	104	4.8	7,325	366	0	.02	.25	.4	0
	Spaghetti:																	
	Enriched:																	
2157	Dry form	10.4	369	12.5	1.2	75.2	.3	.7	27	162	[59] 2.9	2	197	(0)	[59] .88	[59] .37	[59] 6.0	(0)
2158	Cooked, firm stage, "al dente" (8–10 min.)	63.6	148	5.0	.5	30.1	.1	1.3	11	65	[59] 1.1	1	79	(0)	[59] .18	[59] .10	[59] 1.4	(0)
2159	Cooked, tender stage (14–20 min.)	72.0	111	3.4	.4	23.0	.1	1.2	8	50	[59] .9	1	61	(0)	[59] .14	[59] .08	[59] 1.1	(0)
	Unenriched:																	
2160	Dry form	10.4	369	12.5	1.2	75.2	.3	.7	27	162	1.3	2	197	(0)	.09	.06	1.7	(0)
2161	Cooked, firm stage, "al dente" (8–10 min.)	63.6	148	5.0	.5	30.1	.1	1.3	11	65	.5	1	79	(0)	.02	.02	.4	(0)
2162	Cooked, tender stage (14–20 min.)	72.0	111	3.4	.4	23.0	.1	1.2	8	50	.4	1	61	(0)	.01	.01	.3	(0)
	Spaghetti in tomato sauce with cheese:																	
2163	Cooked, from home recipe	77.0	104	3.5	3.5	14.8	.2	1.2	32	54	.9	(382)	163	430	.10	.07	.9	5
2164	Canned	80.1	76	2.2	.6	15.4	.2	1.7	16	35	1.1	382	121	370	.14	.11	1.8	4
	Spaghetti with meat balls in tomato sauce:																	
2165	Cooked, from home recipe	70.0	134	7.5	4.7	15.6	.3	2.2	50	95	1.5	407	268	640	.10	.12	1.6	9
2166	Canned	78.0	103	4.9	4.1	11.4	.1	1.6	21	45	1.3	488	98	400	.06	.07	.9	2
2167	**Spanish mackerel,** raw	68.9	177	19.5	10.4	0	0	1.2	71	249	1.0	68	264	—	.13	.14	4.8	—
2168	**Spanish rice,** cooked from home recipe	78.5	87	1.8	1.7	16.6	.5	1.4	14	39	.6	316	231	660	.04	.03	.7	15
	Spinach:																	
2169	Raw	90.7	26	3.2	.3	4.3	.6	1.5	93	51	3.1	71	470	8,100	.10	.20	.6	51
2170	Cooked, boiled, drained	92.0	23	3.0	.3	3.6	.6	1.1	93	38	2.2	50	324	8,100	.07	.14	.5	28
	Canned:																	
	Regular pack:																	
2171	Solids and liquid	93.0	19	2.0	.4	3.0	.7	1.6	85	26	2.1	[9] 236	250	5,500	.02	.10	.3	14
2172	Drained solids	91.4	24	2.7	.6	3.6	.9	1.7	118	26	2.6	[9] 236	250	8,000	.02	.12	.3	14
2173	Drained liquid	96.8	6	.5	0	1.3	Trace	1.4	2	25	.9	[9] 236	250	Trace	.02	.07	.3	14
	Special dietary pack (low-sodium):																	
2174	Solids and liquid	92.8	21	2.5	.4	3.3	.7	1.0	85	26	2.1	34	250	5,500	.02	.10	.3	14
2175	Drained solids	91.3	26	3.2	.5	4.0	1.0	1.0	118	26	2.6	32	250	8,000	.02	.12	.3	14
2176	Drained liquid	96.7	8	.5	0	2.0	Trace	.8	2	25	.9	32	250	Trace	.02	.07	.3	14
	Frozen:																	
	Chopped:																	
2177	Not thawed	91.6	24	3.1	.3	3.8	.8	1.2	113	45	2.1	57	354	7,900	.09	.16	.5	29
2178	Cooked, boiled, drained	91.9	23	3.0	.3	3.7	.8	1.1	113	44	2.1	52	333	7,900	.07	.15	.4	19
	Leaf:																	
2179	Not thawed	91.3	25	3.0	.3	4.2	.8	1.2	105	45	2.5	53	385	8,100	.10	.16	.5	35
2180	Cooked, boiled, drained	91.8	24	2.9	.3	3.9	.8	1.1	105	44	2.5	49	362	8,100	.08	.14	.5	28
	Spinach, New Zealand. See New Zealand spinach, items 1375–1376.																	
	Spiny lobster. See Crayfish, item 927.																	
	Spleen, raw:																	
2181	Beef and calf	76.9	104	18.1	3.0	0	0	1.4	—	272	10.6	—	—	—	—	.37	8.2	—
2182	Hog	77.4	107	17.1	3.8	0	0	1.4	—	298	29.4	—	—	—	—	.40	—	—
2183	Lamb	74.4	115	18.8	3.9	0	0	1.6	—	—	—	—	—	—	—	—	—	—
	Spot:																	
2184	Raw [149]	65.3	219	17.6	15.9	0	0	1.2	—	—	—	61	—	—	.16	.22	—	—
2185	Cooked, baked	53.8	295	22.8	21.9	0	0	1.5	—	—	—	[150] 312	—	—	—	—	—	—
	Squab (pigeon), raw:																	
2186	Total edible	58.0	279	18.6	22.1	0	0	1.5	17	411	—	—	—	—	—	—	—	—
2187	Flesh and skin	56.6	294	18.5	23.8	0	0	1.4	—	—	—	—	—	—	—	—	6.6	—
2188	Flesh only	72.8	142	17.5	7.5	0	0	1.2	—	—	—	—	—	—	—	—	7.6	—
2189	Light meat without skin	74.0	125	20.4	4.2	0	0	1.2	—	—	—	—	—	—	—	—	—	—
2190	Giblets	69.8	154	19.8	7.2	1.2	0	2.0	—	—	—	—	—	—	—	—	—	—

[9] Estimated average based on addition of salt in the amount of 0.6 percent of the finished product.

[51] Values apply to products without added vitamins and minerals.

[59] Based on product with minimum level of enrichment.

[149] Values are based on samples caught in October. Content of fat may vary greatly from this average at other seasons of the year.

[150] Based on fish with salt added in cooking.

TABLE 1.—COMPOSITION OF FOODS, 100 GRAMS, EDIBLE PORTION—Continued

[Numbers in parentheses denote values imputed—usually from another form of the food or from a similar food. Zero in parentheses indicates that the amount of a constituent probably is none or is too small to measure. Dashes denote lack of reliable data for a constituent believed to be present in measurable amount. Calculated values, as those based on a recipe, are not in parentheses]

Item No.	Food and description	Water	Food energy	Protein	Fat	Carbohydrate		Ash	Calcium	Phosphorus	Iron	Sodium	Potassium	Vitamin A value	Thiamine	Riboflavin	Niacin	Ascorbic acid
						Total	Fiber											
(A)	(B)	(C)	(D)	(E)	(F)	(G)	(H)	(I)	(J)	(K)	(L)	(M)	(N)	(O)	(P)	(Q)	(R)	(S)
	Squash:	Percent	Calories	Grams	Grams	Grams	Grams	Grams	Milligrams	Milligrams	Milligrams	Milligrams	Milligrams	International units	Milligrams	Milligrams	Milligrams	Milligrams
	Summer:																	
	All varieties:																	
2191	Raw	94.0	19	1.1	0.1	4.2	0.6	0.6	28	29	0.4	1	202	410	0.05	0.09	1.0	22
2192	Cooked, boiled, drained	95.5	14	.9	.1	3.1	.6	.4	25	25	.4	1	141	390	.05	.08	.8	10
	Crookneck and Straightneck, Yellow:																	
2193	Raw	93.7	20	1.2	.2	4.3	.6	.6	28	29	.4	1	202	460	.05	.09	1.0	25
2194	Cooked, boiled, drained	95.3	15	1.0	.2	3.1	.6	.4	25	25	.4	1	141	440	.05	.08	.8	11
	Scallop varieties, white and pale green:																	
2195	Raw	93.3	21	.9	.1	5.1	.6	.6	28	29	.4	1	202	190	.05	.09	1.0	18
2196	Cooked, boiled, drained	95.0	16	.7	.1	3.8	.6	.4	25	25	.4	1	141	180	.05	.08	.8	8
	Zucchini and Cocozelle (Italian marrow type), green:																	
2197	Raw	94.6	17	1.2	.1	3.6	.6	.5	28	29	.4	1	202	[151] 320	.05	.09	1.0	19
2198	Cooked, boiled, drained	96.0	12	1.0	.1	2.5	.6	.4	25	25	.4	1	141	[151] 300	.05	.08	.8	9
	Winter:																	
	All varieties:																	
2199	Raw	85.1	50	1.4	.3	12.4	1.4	.8	22	38	.6	1	369	[152] 3,700	.05	.11	.6	13
	Cooked:																	
2200	Baked	81.4	63	1.8	.4	15.4	1.8	1.0	28	48	.8	1	461	[152] 4,200	.05	.13	.7	13
2201	Boiled, mashed	88.8	38	1.1	.3	9.2	1.4	.6	20	32	.5	1	258	[152] 3,500	.04	.10	.4	8
	Acorn:																	
2202	Raw	86.3	44	1.5	.1	11.2	1.4	.9	31	23	.9	1	384	[152] 1,200	.05	.11	.6	14
	Cooked:																	
2203	Baked	82.9	55	1.9	.1	14.0	1.8	1.1	39	29	1.1	1	480	[152] 1,400	.05	.13	.7	13
2204	Boiled, mashed	89.7	34	1.2	.1	8.4	1.4	.6	28	20	.8	1	269	[152] 1,100	.04	.10	.4	8
	Butternut:																	
2205	Raw	83.7	54	1.4	.1	14.0	1.4	.8	32	58	.8	1	487	[152] 5,700	.05	.11	.6	9
	Cooked:																	
2206	Baked	79.6	68	1.8	.1	17.5	1.8	1.0	40	72	1.0	1	609	[152] 6,400	.05	.13	.7	8
2207	Boiled, mashed	87.8	41	1.1	.1	10.4	1.4	.6	29	49	.7	1	341	[152] 5,400	.04	.10	.4	5
	Hubbard:																	
2208	Raw	88.1	39	1.4	.3	9.4	1.4	.8	19	31	.6	1	217	[152] 4,300	.05	.11	.6	11
	Cooked:																	
2209	Baked	85.1	50	1.8	.4	11.7	1.8	1.0	24	39	.8	1	271	[152] 4,800	.05	.13	.7	10
2210	Boiled, mashed	91.1	30	1.1	.3	6.9	1.4	.6	17	26	.5	1	152	[152] 4,100	.04	.10	.4	6
	Squash, frozen:																	
	Summer, Yellow Crookneck:																	
2211	Not thawed	93.4	21	1.4	.1	4.7	.6	.4	14	32	.7	3	167	150	.07	.04	.4	10
2212	Cooked, boiled, drained	93.4	21	1.4	.1	4.7	.6	.4	14	32	.7	3	167	140	.06	.04	.4	8
	Winter:																	
2213	Not thawed	88.8	38	1.2	.3	9.2	1.2	.5	25	32	1.0	1	207	3,900	.03	.07	.5	10
2214	Heated	88.8	38	1.2	.3	9.2	1.2	.5	25	32	1.0	1	207	3,900	.03	.07	.5	8
2215	**Squid,** raw	80.2	84	16.4	.9	1.5	—	1.0	12	119	.5	—	—	—	.02	.12	—	—
	Starch. See Cornstarch, item 894.																	
	St. Johnsbread. See Carob flour, item 617.																	
2216	**Stomach,** pork, scalded	74.0	152	16.5	9.0	0	0	.6	—	118	—	—	—	—	—	—	—	—
	Strawberries:																	
2217	Raw	89.9	37	.7	.5	8.4	1.3	.5	21	21	1.0	1	164	60	.03	.07	.6	59
	Canned, solids and liquid:																	
2218	Water pack, with or without artificial sweetener	93.7	22	.4	.1	5.6	.6	.2	14	14	.7	1	111	40	.01	.03	.4	20
	Frozen, sweetened, not thawed:																	
2219	Sliced	71.3	109	.5	.2	27.8	.8	.2	14	17	.7	1	112	30	.02	.06	.5	53
2220	Whole	75.7	92	.4	.2	23.5	.6	.2	13	16	.6	1	104	30	.02	.06	.5	55
	Sturgeon:																	
2221	Raw	78.7	94	18.1	1.9	0	0	1.4	—	—	—	—	—	—	—	—	—	—
2222	Cooked, steamed	67.5	160	25.4	5.7	0	0	—	40	263	2.0	108	235	—	—	—	—	—
2223	Smoked	63.7	149	31.2	1.8	0	0	1.9	—	—	—	—	—	—	—	—	—	—
	Succotash (corn and lima beans), frozen:																	
2224	Not thawed	73.0	97	4.3	.4	21.5	.9	.8	14	89	1.1	[19] 45	273	(300)	.11	.06	1.5	9
2225	Cooked, boiled, drained	74.1	93	4.2	.4	20.5	.9	.8	13	85	1.0	38	246	(300)	.09	.05	1.3	6
2226	**Suckers, including white and mullet suckers, raw**	76.4	104	20.6	1.8	0	0	1.2	—	220	—	56	336	—	Trace	—	1.2	—
2227	**Sucker, carp, raw**	76.2	111	19.2	3.2	0	0	1.2	—	—	—	—	—	—	—	—	—	—
2228	**Suet** (beef kidney fat), raw	4.	854	1.5	94.	0	0	.1	—	—	—	—	—	—	—	—	—	—

	Sugars:																	
	Beet or cane:																	
2229	Brown	2.1	373	0	0	96.4	0	1.5	85	19	3.4	30	344	0	.01	.03	.2	0
2230	Granulated	.5	385	0	0	99.5	0	Trace	0	0	.1	1	3	0	0	0	0	0
2231	Powdered	.5	385	0	0	99.5	0	Trace	0	0	.1	1	3	0	0	0	0	0
	Dextrose:																	
2232	Anhydrous	.5	366	0	0	99.5	0	—	—	—	—	—	—	0	0	0	0	0
2233	Crystallized	9.	335	0	0	91.	0	—	—	—	Trace	—	—	0	0	0	0	0
2234	Maple	8.	348	—	—	90.	—	.9	143	11	1.4	14	242	—	—	—	—	0
2235	**Sugarapples** (sweetsop), raw	73.3	94	1.8	.3	23.7	1.7	.9	22	41	.6	11	275	10	.10	.14	1.0	34
2236	**Sunflower seed kernels,** dry	4.8	560	24.0	47.3	19.9	3.8	4.0	120	837	7.1	30	920	50	1.96	.23	5.4	—
2237	**Sunflower seed flour,** partially defatted	7.3	339	45.2	3.4	37.7	4.6	6.4	348	898	13.2	56	1,080	—	3.6	.46	27.3	—
	Surinam-cherry. See Pitanga, item 1627.																	
	Swamp cabbage:																	
2238	Raw	89.7	29	3.0	.3	5.4	1.1	1.6	73	51	2.5	—	150	6,300	.07	.12	.7	32
2239	Cooked, boiled, drained	92.7	21	2.2	.2	3.9	.9	1.0	55	32	1.5	—	88	5,200	.05	.08	.5	16
	Sweetbreads (thymus):																	
	Beef (yearlings):																	
2240	Raw	67.8	207	14.6	16.0	0	0	1.6	—	393	—	96	360	—	—	—	—	—
2241	Cooked, braised	49.6	320	25.9	23.2	0	0	1.3	—	364	—	116	433	—	—	—	—	—
	Calf:																	
2242	Raw	78.4	94	17.8	2.0	0	0	1.8	—	—	—	—	—	—	.08	.17	2.6	—
2243	Cooked, braised	62.7	168	32.6	3.2	0	0	1.5	—	—	—	—	—	—	.06	.16	2.9	—
	Lamb:																	
2244	Raw	79.5	94	14.1	3.8	0	0	1.3	—	220	—	—	—	—	—	—	—	—
2245	Cooked, braised	64.6	175	28.1	6.1	0	0	1.2	—	204	—	—	—	—	—	—	—	—
	Sweetbread, hog. See Pancreas, hog: item 1469.																	
	Sweetpotatoes:																	
	Raw:																	
2246	All commercial varieties	70.6	114	1.7	.4	26.3	.7	1.0	32	47	.7	10	243	8,800	.10	.06	.6	21
2247	Firm-fleshed [153] (Jersey types)	74.0	102	1.8	.7	22.5	.9	1.0	32	47	.7	10	243	[154] 9,200	.10	.06	.6	23
2248	Soft-fleshed [153] (mainly Porto Rico variety)	69.7	117	1.7	.3	27.3	.7	1.0	32	47	.7	10	243	[155] 8,700	.10	.06	.6	20
	Cooked, all:																	
2249	Baked in skin	63.7	141	2.1	.5	32.5	.9	1.2	40	58	.9	12	300	8,100	.09	.07	.7	22
2250	Boiled in skin	70.6	114	1.7	.4	26.3	.7	1.0	32	47	.7	10	243	7,900	.09	.06	.6	17
2251	Candied	60.0	168	1.3	3.3	34.2	.6	1.2	37	43	.9	42	190	6,300	.06	.04	.4	10
	Canned:																	
	Liquid pack, solids and liquid:																	
2252	Regular pack in sirup	70.7	114	1.0	.2	27.5	.6	.6	13	29	.7	48	(120)	5,000	.03	.03	.6	8
2253	Special dietary pack, without added sugar and salt.	88.0	46	.7	.1	10.8	.3	.4	13	29	.7	12	120	5,000	.03	.03	.6	8
2254	Vacuum or solid pack	71.9	108	2.0	.2	24.9	1.0	1.0	25	41	.8	[156] 48	200	7,800	.05	.04	.6	14
	Dehydrated flakes:																	
2255	Dry form	2.8	379	4.2	.6	90.0	3.2	2.4	60	80	2.2	181	562	[157] 47,000	.06	.13	1.3	45
2256	Prepared with water	75.7	95	1.0	.1	22.6	.8	.6	15	20	.6	45	140	[157] 12,000	.02	.03	.3	11
	Sweetsop. See Sugarapples, item 2235.																	
	Swisschard. See Chard, Swiss: items 639–640.																	
	Swordfish:																	
2257	Raw	75.9	118	19.2	4.0	0	0	1.3	19	195	.9	—	—	1,580	.05	.05	8.0	—
2258	Cooked, broiled [158]	64.6	174	28.0	6.0	0	0	1.7	27	275	1.3	—	—	2,050	.04	.05	10.9	—
2259	Canned, solids and liquid	78.0	102	17.5	3.0	0	0	1.5	—	—	—	—	—	1,580	.01	.05	11.4	—
2260	**Tamarinds,** raw	31.4	239	2.8	.6	62.5	5.1	2.7	74	113	2.8	51	781	30	.34	.14	1.2	2
2261	**Tangelo juice,** raw	89.4	41	.5	(.1)	9.7	Trace	.3	—	—	—	—	—	—	—	—	—	27
2262	**Tangerines,** raw (Dancy variety)	87.	46	.8	.2	11.6	.5	.4	40	18	.4	2	126	420	.06	.02	.1	31
	Tangerine juice:																	
2263	Raw (Dancy variety)	88.9	43	.5	.2	10.1	(.1)	.3	18	14	.2	1	178	420	.06	.02	.1	31
	Canned:																	
2264	Unsweetened	88.8	43	.5	.2	10.2	(.1)	.3	18	14	.2	1	178	420	(.06)	(.02)	(.1)	22
2265	Sweetened	87.0	50	.5	.2	12.0	(.1)	.3	18	14	.2	1	178	420	(.06)	(.02)	(.1)	22
	Frozen concentrate, unsweetened:																	
2266	Undiluted	58.	162	1.7	(.7)	38.3	(.3)	1.3	62	48	.7	2	613	1,460	.20	.06	.4	96
2267	Diluted with 3 parts water, by volume	88.1	46	.5	(.2)	10.8	(.1)	.4	18	14	.2	1	174	410	.06	.02	.1	27
2268	**Tapioca,** dry	12.6	352	.6	.2	86.4	.1	.2	10	18	.4	3	18	(0)	(0)	(0)	(0)	(0)
	Tapioca desserts:																	
2269	Apple tapioca	70.1	117	.2	.1	29.4	.1	.2	3	4	.2	51	26	10	Trace	Trace	Trace	Trace
2270	Tapioca cream pudding	71.8	134	5.0	5.1	17.1	0	1.0	105	109	.4	156	135	290	.04	.18	.1	1
	Taros, raw:																	
2271	Corms and tubers	73.0	98	1.9	.2	23.7	.8	1.2	28	61	1.0	7	514	20	.13	.04	1.1	4
2272	Leaves and stems	87.2	40	3.0	.8	7.4	1.4	1.6	76	59	1.0	—	—	—	—	—	—	31

[150] Average weighted in accordance with commercial practices in freezing vegetables.

[151] Applies to squash including skin; flesh has no appreciable vitamin A value.

[152] Value based on freshly harvested squash. The carotenoid content increases during storage, the amount of increase varying according to variety and conditions of storage. More information is needed on the relative contents of the individual carotenoids and their rates of increase under usual storage conditions before a suitable vitamin A value can be derived for the stored product.

[153] Term refers to the flesh of the cooked product.

[154] Values for commercial varieties having deep-orange flesh average about 10,000 I.U. per 100 grams; light-yellow, about 600 I.U.

[155] Values for commercial varieties range from 8,000 to more than 20,000 I.U. per 100 grams. Porto Rico, the main variety, has a value around 8,000 I.U.

[156] Applies to regular pack. For special dietary pack (low-sodium), value is 12 mg. per 100 grams.

[157] Value varies widely; it is related to variety of sweetpotato. Range in dehydrated form is 21,000 to 72,000 I.U. per 100 grams, and 5,000 to 18,000 I.U. in product prepared for serving.

[158] Prepared with butter or margarine.

TABLE 1.—COMPOSITION OF FOODS, 100 GRAMS, EDIBLE PORTION—Continued

[Numbers in parentheses denote values imputed—usually from another form of the food or from a similar food. Zero in parentheses indicates that the amount of a constituent probably is none or is too small to measure. Dashes denote lack of reliable data for a constituent believed to be present in measurable amount. Calculated values, as those based on a recipe, are not in parentheses]

Item No.	Food and description	Water	Food energy	Protein	Fat	Carbohydrate		Ash	Calcium	Phosphorus	Iron	Sodium	Potassium	Vitamin A value	Thiamine	Riboflavin	Niacin	Ascorbic acid
						Total	Fiber											
(A)	(B)	(C)	(D)	(E)	(F)	(G)	(H)	(I)	(J)	(K)	(L)	(M)	(N)	(O)	(P)	(Q)	(R)	(S)
		Percent	Calories	Grams	Grams	Grams	Grams	Grams	Milligrams	Milligrams	Milligrams	Milligrams	Milligrams	International units	Milligrams	Milligrams	Milligrams	Milligrams
	Tartar sauce:																	
2273	Regular	34.4	531	1.4	57.8	4.2	0.3	2.2	18	32	0.9	707	78	220	0.01	0.03	Trace	1
2274	Special dietary (low-calorie, approx. 10 Cal. per tsp.)	68.1	224	.6	22.4	6.7	.3	2.2	18	32	.9	707	78	220	.01	.03	Trace	1
2275	**Tautog** (blackfish), raw	79.3	89	18.6	1.1	0	0	1.1	—	227	—	—	—	—	—	—	—	—
	Tea, instant (water-soluble solids) carbohydrate added:																	
2276	Dry powder	3.8	294	—	Trace	80.	.1	6.1	11	—	1.6	—	4,530	—	—	.95	8.9	—
2277	Beverage	99.4	2	—	Trace	.4	Trace	Trace	Trace	—	Trace	—	25	—	—	.01	Trace	—
	Tendergreen. See Mustard spinach, items 1370–1371.																	
2278	**Terrapin** (diamond back), raw	77.0	111	18.6	3.5	0	0	1.0	—	—	3.[illegible]	—	—	—	—	—	—	—
	Thuringer. See Sausage, cold cuts, and luncheon meats: item 2021.																	
	Tilefish:																	
2279	Raw	80.3	79	17.5	.5	0	0	1.4	—	—	—	—	—	—	—	—	—	—
2280	Cooked, baked	71.6	138	24.5	3.7	0	0	1.1	—	—	—	—	—	—	—	—	—	—
2281	**Tomatoes, green,** raw	93.0	24	1.2	.2	5.1	.5	.5	13	27	.5	3	244	270	.06	.04	.5	20
	Tomatoes, ripe:																	
2282	Raw	93.5	22	1.1	.2	4.7	.5	.5	13	27	.5	3	244	900	.06	.04	.7	[159] 23
2283	Cooked, boiled	92.4	26	1.3	.2	5.5	.6	.6	15	32	.6	4	287	1,000	.07	.05	.8	24
	Canned, solids and liquid:																	
2284	Regular pack	93.7	21	1.0	.2	4.3	.4	.8	[115] 6	19	.5	130	217	900	.05	.03	.7	17
2285	Special dietary pack (low-sodium)	94.1	20	1.0	.2	4.2	.4	.5	[115] 6	19	.5	3	217	900	.05	.03	.7	17
2286	**Tomato catsup,** bottled	68.6	106	2.0	.4	25.4	.5	3.6	22	50	.8	[160] 1,042	363	1,400	.09	.07	1.6	15
2287	**Tomato chili sauce,** bottled	68.0	104	2.5	.3	24.8	.7	4.4	20	52	(.8)	[160] 1,338	(370)	(1,400)	(.09)	(.07)	(1.6)	(16)
	Tomato juice:																	
	Canned or bottled:																	
2288	Regular pack	93.6	19	.9	.1	4.3	.2	1.1	7	18	.9	200	227	800	.05	.03	.8	16
2289	Special dietary pack (low-sodium)	94.2	19	.8	.1	4.3	.2	.6	7	18	.9	3	227	800	.05	.03	.7	16
	Canned concentrate:																	
2290	Undiluted	75.0	76	3.4	.4	17.1	.9	4.1	27	70	3.5	790	888	3,300	.20	.12	3.1	49
2291	Diluted with 3 parts water, by volume	93.4	20	.9	.1	4.5	.2	1.1	7	19	.9	209	235	900	.05	.03	.8	13
	Dehydrated (crystals):																	
2292	Dry form	1.0	303	11.6	2.2	68.2	3.1	17.0	85	279	7.8	(3,934)	3,518	13,100	.52	.40	13.5	239
2293	Prepared with water (1 lb. yields approx. 1¾ gals.).	93.5	20	.8	.1	4.5	.2	1.1	6	18	.5	(258)	231	860	.03	.03	.9	16
2294	**Tomato juice cocktail,** canned or bottled	93.0	21	.7	.1	5.0	.2	1.2	10	18	.9	200	221	800	.05	.02	.6	16
2295	**Tomato paste,** canned	75.0	82	3.4	.4	18.6	.9	2.6	27	70	3.5	[161] 38	888	3,300	.20	.12	3.1	49
	Tomato puree, canned:																	
2296	Regular pack	87.0	39	1.7	.2	8.9	.4	2.2	13	34	1.7	399	426	1,600	.09	.05	1.4	33
2297	Special dietary pack (low-sodium)	88.0	39	1.7	.2	8.9	.4	1.2	13	34	1.7	6	426	1,600	.09	.05	1.4	33
2298	**Tomcod, Atlantic,** raw	81.5	77	17.2	.4	0	0	1.0	—	—	—	—	—	—	—	.17	—	—
	Tongue:																	
	Beef:																	
2299	Very fat, raw	62.	271	14.4	23.	.4	0	.7	—	—	—	—	—	—	—	—	—	—
2300	Fat, raw	65.	231	15.7	18.	.4	0	.8	—	—	—	—	—	—	—	—	—	—
	Medium-fat:																	
2301	Raw	68.	207	16.4	15.	.4	0	.9	8	182	2.1	73	197	—	.12	.29	5.0	—
2302	Cooked, braised	60.8	244	21.5	16.7	.4	0	.6	7	117	2.2	61	164	—	.05	.29	3.5	—
2303	Thin (very thin), raw	70.	175	17.4	11.	.4	0	.9	—	—	—	—	—	—	—	—	—	—
2304	Smoked	48.9	—	17.2	28.8	—	0	—	—	—	—	—	—	—	.04	.21	3.0	—
	Calf:																	
2305	Raw	74.3	130	18.5	5.3	.9	0	1.0	—	—	—	—	—	—	—	—	—	—
2306	Cooked, braised	68.5	160	23.9	6.0	1.0	0	.7	—	—	—	—	—	—	—	—	—	—
	Hog:																	
2307	Raw	66.1	215	16.8	15.6	.5	0	1.0	29	186	1.4	—	—	—	.17	(.29)	(5.0)	—
2308	Cooked, braised	59.4	253	22.0	17.4	.5	0	.7	26	119	1.4	—	—	—	.07	(.29)	(3.5)	—
	Lamb:																	
2309	Raw	69.5	199	13.9	15.3	.5	0	.8	—	147	—	—	—	—	—	—	—	—
2310	Cooked, braised	60.2	254	20.5	18.2	.5	0	.7	—	102	—	—	—	—	—	—	—	—
	Sheep:																	
2311	Raw	61.0	265	13.7	21.8	2.4	0	1.1	—	—	—	—	—	—	—	—	—	—
2312	Cooked, braised	51.6	323	19.8	25.3	2.4	0	.8	—	—	3.4	—	—	—	—	—	—	—

	Tongue, canned or cured (beef, lamb, etc.):																
2313	Whole, canned or pickled	56.6	267	19.3	20.3	.3	0	3.5	—	—	—	—	—	—	—	—	—	—
2314	Potted or deviled	52.8	290	18.6	23.0	.7	0	4.9	—	—	—	—	—	—	.04	.11	1.3	—
2315	**Towelgourd**, raw	94.5	18	.8	.2	4.1	.5	.4	19	33	.9	—	—	380	.03	.04	.4	8
	Tripe, beef:																	
2316	Commercial	79.1	100	19.1	2.0	0	0	.4	127	86	1.6	72	9	—	—	.15	1.6	—
2317	Pickled	86.5	62	11.8	1.3	0	0	.3	—	—	—	46	19	—	—	—	—	—
	Trout. See Lake trout, items 1170–1171.																	
2318	**Trout, brook**, raw	77.7	101	19.2	2.1	0	0	1.2	—	266	—	—	—	—	—	.07	—	—
	Trout, rainbow or steelhead:																	
2319	Raw	66.3	195	21.5	11.4	0	0	1.3	—	—	—	—	—	—	.08	.20	8.4	—
2320	Canned	63.2	209	20.6	13.4	0	0	2.4	—	—	—	—	—	—	—	—	—	—
	Tuna:																	
	Raw:																	
2321	Bluefin	70.5	145	25.2	4.1	0	0	1.3	—	—	1.3	—	—	—	—	—	—	—
2322	Yellowfin	71.5	133	24.7	3.0	0	0	1.4	—	—	—	[163] 37	—	—	—	—	—	—
	Canned:																	
	In oil:																	
2323	Solids and liquid	52.6	288	24.2	20.5	0	0	2.4	6	294	1.1	800	301	90	.04	.09	10.1	—
2324	Drained solids	60.6	197	28.8	8.2	0	0	2.0	(8)	234	1.9	—	—	80	.05	.12	11.9	—
	In water:																	
2325	Solids and liquid	70.0	127	28.0	.8	0	0	1.2	16	190	1.6	[163] 41	[163] 279	—	—	.10	13.3	—
2326	**Tuna salad** [164]	69.8	170	14.6	10.5	3.5	—	1.6	20	142	1.3	—	—	290	.04	.11	5.0	1
	Turkey:																	
	All classes:																	
	Total edible:																	
2327	Raw	64.2	218	20.1	14.7	0	0	1.0	—	—	—	—	—	—	—	—	—	—
2328	Cooked, roasted	55.4	263	27.0	16.4	0	0	1.2	—	—	—	—	—	—	—	—	—	—
	Flesh and skin:																	
2329	Cooked, roasted	57.3	223	31.9	9.6	0	0	1.2	—	—	—	—	—	—	.07	.16	8.1	—
	Flesh only:																	
2330	Raw	68.3	162	24.0	6.6	0	0	1.1	8	212	1.5	66	315	—	.08	.14	8.0	—
2331	Cooked, roasted	61.2	190	31.5	6.1	0	0	1.2	8	251	1.8	130	367	—	.05	.18	7.7	—
	Skin only:																	
2332	Raw	48.2	405	12.1	39.2	0	0	.5	—	—	—	—	—	—	.03	.04	4.6	—
2333	Cooked, roasted	40.0	451	17.0	42.0	0	0	1.0	—	—	—	—	—	—	—	—	—	—
	Light meat:																	
2334	Raw	73.0	116	24.6	1.2	0	0	1.2	—	—	1.0	51	320	—	.06	.11	11.3	—
2335	Cooked, roasted	62.1	176	32.9	3.9	0	0	1.2	—	—	1.2	82	411	—	.05	.14	11.1	—
	Dark meat:																	
2336	Raw	73.6	128	20.9	4.3	0	0	1.1	—	—	2.0	81	310	—	.09	.18	4.7	—
2337	Cooked, roasted	60.5	203	30.0	8.3	0	0	1.2	—	—	2.3	99	398	—	.04	.23	4.2	—
	Giblets:																	
2338	Raw	71.0	150	20.1	6.6	1.2	0	1.1	—	—	—	—	—	—	—	—	—	—
2339	Cooked (some gizzard fat), simmered	61.0	233	20.6	15.4	1.6	0	1.4	—	—	—	—	—	—	—	2.72	—	—
	Young birds (24 weeks and under), raw:																	
2340	Total edible	71.5	145	21.4	6.0	0	0	1.1	—	—	—	—	—	—	—	—	—	—
2341	Flesh and skin	72.0	151	19.8	7.4	0	0	.8	—	—	—	—	—	—	—	—	—	—
2342	Light meat	73.8	108	24.5	.4	0	0	1.3	—	—	—	—	—	—	—	—	—	—
2343	Dark meat	75.7	111	20.6	2.6	0	0	1.1	—	—	—	—	—	—	—	—	—	—
	Medium-fat birds (26–32 weeks), raw:																	
2344	Total edible	63.3	227	19.9	15.8	0	0	1.0	—	—	—	—	—	—	—	—	—	—
2345	Flesh and skin	65.7	197	21.6	11.6	0	0	1.1	—	—	—	—	—	—	—	—	—	—
2346	Light meat	73.0	115	24.7	1.1	0	0	1.2	—	—	—	—	—	—	—	—	—	—
2347	Dark meat	73.9	127	20.8	4.2	0	0	1.1	—	—	—	—	—	—	—	—	—	—
	Fat mature birds (more than 32 weeks), raw:																	
2348	Total edible	51.3	343	18.4	29.3	0	0	.9	—	—	—	—	—	—	—	—	—	—
2349	**Turkey, canned**, meat only	64.9	202	20.9	12.5	0	0	1.7	10	—	1.4	—	—	130	.02	.14	4.7	—
	Turkey, potted. See Sausage, cold cuts, and luncheon meats: item 2008.																	
	Turkey potpie:																	
2350	Home-prepared, baked	56.2	237	10.4	13.5	18.5	.4	1.4	27	101	1.4	273	198	1,330	.11	.13	2.5	2
2351	Commercial, frozen, unheated	62.3	197	5.8	10.4	20.1	.3	1.4	12	56	.9	369	114	890	.09	.08	1.6	2
	Turnips:																	
2352	Raw	91.5	30	1.0	.2	6.6	.9	.7	39	30	.5	49	268	Trace	.04	.07	.6	36
2353	Cooked, boiled, drained	93.6	23	.8	.2	4.9	.9	.5	35	24	.4	34	188	Trace	.04	.05	.3	22
	Turnip greens, leaves, including stems:																	
2354	Raw	90.3	28	3.0	.3	5.0	.8	1.4	246	58	1.8	—	—	7,600	(.21)	(.39)	(.8)	139
	Cooked, boiled, drained, cooked in—																	
2355	Small amount of water, short time	93.2	20	2.2	.2	3.6	.7	.8	184	37	1.1	—	—	6,300	.15	.24	.6	69
2356	Large amount of water, long time	93.5	19	2.2	.2	3.3	.7	.8	174	34	1.0	—	—	5,700	.10	.23	.5	47

[115] Federal standards provide for addition of certain calcium salts as firming agents; if used, these salts may add calcium not to exceed 26 mg. per 100 grams of finished product.

[159] Year-round average. Samples marketed from November through May average around 10 mg. per 100 grams; from June through October, around 26 mg.

[160] Applies to regular pack. For special dietary pack (low-sodium), values range from 5 to 35 mg. per 100 grams.

[161] Applies to the more usual product with no salt added. If salt is added, the sodium content is about 790 mg. per 100 grams.

[162] Brined sample contained 439 mg. of sodium per 100 grams.

[163] One sample with salt added contained 875 mg. of sodium per 100 grams and 275 mg. of potassium.

[164] Prepared with tuna, celery, mayonnaise, pickle, onion, and egg.

TABLE 1.—COMPOSITION OF FOODS, 100 GRAMS, EDIBLE PORTION—Continued

[Numbers in parentheses denote values imputed—usually from another form of the food or from a similar food. Zero in parentheses indicates that the amount of a constituent probably is none or is too small to measure. Dashes denote lack of reliable data for a constituent believed to be present in measurable amount. Calculated values, as those based on a recipe, are not in parentheses]

Item No.	Food and description	Water	Food energy	Protein	Fat	Carbohydrate		Ash	Calcium	Phosphorus	Iron	Sodium	Potassium	Vitamin A value	Thiamine	Riboflavin	Niacin	Ascorbic acid
						Total	Fiber											
(A)	(B)	(C)	(D)	(E)	(F)	(G)	(H)	(I)	(J)	(K)	(L)	(M)	(N)	(O)	(P)	(Q)	(R)	(S)
	Turnip greens, leaves, including stems—Continued	*Percent*	*Calories*	*Grams*	*Grams*	*Grams*	*Grams*	*Grams*	*Milligrams*	*Milligrams*	*Milligrams*	*Milligrams*	*Milligrams*	*International units*	*Milligrams*	*Milligrams*	*Milligrams*	*Milligrams*
2357	Canned, solids and liquid	93.7	18	1.5	0.3	3.2	0.7	1.3	100	30	1.6	[8] 236	243	4,700	0.02	0.09	0.6	19
	Frozen:																	
2358	Not thawed	92.3	23	2.6	.3	4.0	1.0	.8	131	41	1.7	23	188	6,900	.06	.11	.5	34
2359	Cooked, boiled, drained	92.7	23	2.5	.3	3.9	1.0	.6	118	39	1.6	17	149	6,900	.05	.09	.4	19
	Turtle, green:																	
2360	Raw	78.5	89	19.8	.5	0	0	1.2	—	—	—	—	—	—	—	—	—	—
2361	Canned	75.0	106	23.4	.7	0	0	.9	—	—	—	—	—	—	—	—	—	—
	Veal:																	
	Carcass, raw:																	
	Including kidney and kidney fat:																	
2362	Fat class (76% lean, 24% fat)	62.	248	18.0	19.	0	0	.9	10	178	2.7			—	.13	.24	6.0	—
2363	Medium-fat class (81% lean, 19% fat)	66.	207	18.8	14.	0	0	1.0	11	190	2.8			—	.14	.25	6.3	—
2364	Thin class (86% lean, 14% fat)	70.	173	19.4	10.	0	0	1.0	11	199	2.9			—	.14	.26	6.5	—
	Excluding kidney and kidney fat:																	
2365	Fat class (79% lean, 21% fat)	65.	223	18.5	16.	0	0	.9	11	185	2.8			—	.14	.25	6.2	—
2366	Medium-fat class (84% lean, 16% fat)	68.	190	19.1	12.	0	0	1.0	11	193	2.9			—	.14	.25	6.4	—
2367	Thin class (88% lean, 12% fat)	71.	156	19.7	8.	0	0	1.0	11	201	3.0			—	.14	.26	6.6	—
	Retail cuts, untrimmed:																	
	Chuck:																	
	Fat class:																	
2368	Total edible, raw (83% lean, 17% fat)	67.	198	19.0	13.	0	0	1.0	11	191	2.8			—	.14	.25	6.4	—
	Medium-fat class:																	
	Total edible:																	
2369	Raw (86% lean, 14% fat)	70.	173	19.4	10.	0	0	1.0	11	199	2.9			—	.14	.26	6.5	—
2370	Cooked, braised (85% lean, 15% fat)	58.5	235	27.9	12.8	0	0	.8	12	151	3.5			—	.09	.29	6.4	—
	Thin class:																	
2371	Total edible, raw (90% lean, 10% fat)	73.	139	19.9	6.	0	0	1.1	12	206	3.0			—	.15	.26	6.7	—
	Flank:																	
	Fat class:																	
2372	Total edible, raw (49% lean, 51% fat)	49.	387	14.5	36.	0	0	.7	8	126	2.2			—	.11	.19	4.9	—
	Medium-fat class:																	
	Total edible:																	
2373	Raw (61% lean, 39% fat)	56.	314	16.5	27.	0	0	.8	10	155	2.5			—	.12	.22	5.5	—
2374	Cooked, stewed (60% lean, 40% fat)	43.8	390	23.2	32.3	0	0	.7	11	117	3.0			—	.05	.22	4.2	—
	Thin class:																	
2375	Total edible, raw (73% lean, 27% fat)	63.	240	18.1	18.	0	0	.9	10	179	2.7	(105)	(109)	—	.13	.24	6.1	—
	Foreshank:																	
	Fat class:																	
2376	Total edible, raw (84% lean, 16% fat)	70.	173	19.4	10.	0	0	1.0	11	199	2.9			—	.14	.26	6.5	—
	Medium-fat class:																	
	Total edible:																	
2377	Raw (87% lean, 13% fat)	71.	156	19.7	8.	0	0	1.0	11	203	3.0			—	.14	.26	6.6	—
2378	Cooked, stewed (86% lean, 14% fat)	60.1	216	28.7	10.4	0	0	.8	12	154	3.6			—	.05	.26	5.0	—
	Thin class:																	
2379	Total edible, raw (91% lean, 9% fat)	74.	131	20.1	5.	0	0	1.1	12	209	3.0			—	.15	.27	6.7	—
	Loin:																	
	Fat class:																	
2380	Total edible, raw (80% lean, 20% fat)	65.	215	18.6	15.	0	0	1.0	11	187	2.8			—	.14	.25	6.2	—
	Medium-fat class:																	
	Total edible:																	
2381	Raw (85% lean, 15% fat)	69.	181	19.2	11.	0	0	1.0	11	195	2.9			—	.14	.26	6.4	—
2382	Cooked, broiled (77% lean, 23% fat)	58.9	234	26.4	13.4	0	0	1.3	11	225	3.2			—	.07	.25	5.4	—
	Thin class:																	
2383	Total edible, raw (89% lean, 11% fat)	71.	156	19.7	8.	0	0	1.0	11	203	3.0			—	.14	.26	6.6	—
	Plate:																	
	Fat class:																	
2384	Total edible, raw (66% lean, 34% fat)	59.	281	17.3	23.	0	0	.9	10	168	2.6			—	.13	.23	5.8	—
	Medium-fat class:																	
	Total edible:																	
2385	Raw (74% lean, 26% fat)	64.	231	18.3	17.	0	0	.9	11	182	2.7			—	.13	.24	6.1	—
2386	Cooked, stewed (73% lean, 27% fat)	52.1	303	26.1	21.2	0	0	.7	12	138	3.3			—	.05	.24	4.6	—
	Thin class:																	
2387	Total edible, raw (82% lean, 18% fat)	68.	190	19.1	12.	0	0	1.0	11	193	2.9			—	.14	.25	6.4	—

	Rib:																	
	Fat class:																	
2388	Total edible, raw (76% lean, 24% fat)	62.	248	18.0	19.	0	0	.9	10	178	2.7			—	.13	.24	6.0	—
	Medium-fat class:																	
	Total edible:																	
2389	Raw (82% lean, 18% fat)	66.	207	18.8	14.	0	0	1.0	11	190	2.8			—	.14	.25	6.3	—
2390	Cooked, roasted (82% lean, 18% fat)	54.6	269	27.2	16.9	0	0	1.3	12	248	3.4			—	.13	.31	7.8	—
	Thin class:																	
2391	Total edible, raw (87% lean, 13% fat)	70.	164	19.5	9.	0	0	1.0	11	200	2.9	([165])	([166])	—	.14	.26	6.5	—
	Round with rump:																	
	Fat class:																	
2392	Total edible, raw (84% lean, 16% fat)	68.	190	19.1	12.	0	0	1.0	11	193	2.9			—	.14	.25	6.4	—
	Medium-fat class:																	
	Total edible:																	
2393	Raw (87% lean, 13% fat)	70.	164	19.5	9.	0	0	1.0	11	200	2.9			—	.14	.26	6.5	—
2394	Cooked, broiled (79% lean, 21% fat)	60.4	216	27.1	11.1	0	0	1.4	11	231	3.2			—	.07	.25	5.4	—
	Thin class:																	
2395	Total edible, raw (91% lean, 9% fat)	73.	139	19.9	6.	0	0	1.1	12	206	3.0			—	.15	.26	6.7	—
2396	**Vegetable juice cocktail,** canned	94.1	17	.9	.1	3.6	.3	1.3	12	22	.5	(200)	(221)	700	.05	.03	.8	9
	Vegetable main dishes, canned:																	
	Principal ingredients:																	
2397	Peanuts and soya	55.3	237	11.7	16.9	13.4	.9	2.7	—	—	—	—	—	—	—	—	—	—
2398	Wheat protein	72.9	109	16.3	.8	8.8	.1	1.2	—	—	—	—	—	—	—	—	—	—
2399	Wheat protein, nuts or peanuts	52.4	212	20.3	7.1	17.7	.4	2.5	—	—	—	—	—	—	—	—	—	—
2400	Wheat protein, vegetable oil	63.5	189	19.1	10.4	5.2	—	1.8	—	—	—	—	—	—	—	—	—	—
2401	Wheat and soy protein	73.4	104	16.1	1.2	7.6	.3	1.7	—	—	—	—	—	—	—	—	—	—
2402	Wheat and soy protein, soy or other vegetable oil	66.6	150	16.1	5.6	9.5	.6	2.2	—	—	—	—	—	—	—	—	—	—
	Vegetables, mixed (carrots, corn, peas, green snap beans, lima beans), frozen:																	
2403	Not thawed	82.1	65	3.3	.3	13.7	1.2	.6	26	66	1.4	[19] 59	208	5,000	.13	.07	1.2	9
2404	Cooked, boiled, drained	82.6	64	3.2	.3	13.4	1.2	.5	25	63	1.3	53	191	4,950	.12	.07	1.1	8
	Vegetable-oyster. See Salsify, items 1961–1962.																	
2405	**Venison,** lean meat only, raw	74.	126	21.	4.	0	0	1.	10	249	—	—	—	—	.23	.48	6.3	—
	Vienna sausage. See Sausage, cold cuts, and luncheon meats: item 2022.																	
	Vinegar:																	
2406	Cider	93.8	14	Trace	(0)	5.9	—	.3	(6)	(9)	(.6)	1	100	—	—	—	—	—
2407	Distilled	95.	12	—	—	5.	—	Trace	—	—	—	1	15	—	—	—	—	—
2408	**Vinespinach** (basella), raw	93.1	19	1.8	.3	3.4	.7	1.4	109	52	1.2	—	—	8,000	.05	—	.5	102
	Vodka. See Beverages, items 395–399.																	
	Waffles:																	
	Baked from home recipe, made with—																	
2409	Enriched flour	41.4	279	9.3	9.8	37.5	.1	2.0	113	173	1.7	475	145	330	.17	.25	1.3	Trace
2410	Unenriched flour	41.4	279	9.3	9.8	37.5	.1	2.0	113	173	.9	475	145	330	.05	.18	.4	Trace
2411	Frozen, made with enriched flour	42.1	253	7.1	6.2	42.0	.2	2.6	122	208	[167] 1.8	644	158	130	[167] .17	[167] .16	[167] 1.2	Trace
	Waffle mixes and waffles baked from mixes:																	
2412	Mix, with enriched flour, dry form	5.6	458	6.4	19.2	65.4	.2	3.4	118	196	1.6	1,027	85	120	.22	.18	1.7	Trace
2413	Waffles, made with water	38.6	305	4.8	14.0	40.2	.1	2.4	76	127	1.0	560	55	80	.12	.11	1.0	Trace
2414	Mix, with unenriched flour, dry form	5.6	458	6.4	19.2	65.4	.2	3.4	118	196	.6	1,027	85	120	.04	.08	.4	Trace
2415	Waffles, made with water	38.6	305	4.8	14.0	40.2	.1	2.4	76	127	.4	560	55	80	.02	.05	.3	Trace
2416	Mix (pancake and waffle), with enriched flour, dry form.	8.3	356	8.6	1.8	75.7	.4	5.6	450	590	3.1	1,433	162	0	.44	.34	2.9	0
2417	Waffles, made with egg, milk	41.7	275	8.8	10.6	36.2	.2	2.7	239	343	1.3	686	195	230	.14	.23	.9	Trace
2418	Mix (pancake and waffle), with unenriched flour, dry form.	8.3	356	8.6	1.8	75.7	.4	5.6	450	590	1.4	1,433	162	0	.12	.08	1.1	0
2419	Waffles, made with egg, milk	41.7	275	8.8	10.6	36.2	.2	2.7	239	343	.9	686	195	230	.08	.19	.4	Trace
	Walnuts:																	
2420	Black	3.1	628	20.5	59.3	14.8	1.7	2.3	Trace	570	6.0	3	460	300	.22	.11	.7	—
2421	Persian or English	3.5	651	14.8	64.0	15.8	2.1	1.9	99	380	3.1	2	450	30	.33	.13	.9	2
2422	**Waterchestnut,** Chinese (matai, waternut), raw	78.3	79	1.4	.2	19.0	.8	1.1	4	65	.6	20	500	0	.14	.20	1.0	4
2423	**Watercress** leaves including stems, raw	93.3	19	2.2	.3	3.0	.7	1.2	151	54	1.7	52	282	4,900	.08	.16	.9	79
	Water ice. See Ices, water: item 1144.																	
2424	**Watermelon,** raw	92.6	26	.5	.2	6.4	.3	.3	7	10	.5	1	100	590	.03	.03	.2	7
2425	**Waxgourd** (Chinese preserving melon), raw	96.1	13	.4	.2	3.0	.5	.3	19	19	.4	6	111	0	.04	.11	.4	13
	Weakfish:																	
2426	Raw	76.7	121	16.5	5.6	0	0	1.2	—	—	—	75	317	—	.09	.06	2.7	—
2427	Cooked, broiled	61.4	208	24.6	11.4	0	0	2.6	—	—	—	[168] 560	465	—	.10	.08	3.5	—
2428	**Welsh rarebit**	70.2	179	8.1	13.6	6.3	0	1.8	251	186	.3	332	138	530	.04	.23	.1	Trace
	West Indian Cherry. See Acerola, item 3.																	
2429	**Whale meat,** raw	70.9	156	20.6	7.5	0	0	1.0	12	144	—	78	22	1,860	.09	.08	—	6

[9] Estimated average based on addition of salt in the amount of 0.6 percent of the finished product.

[19] Average weighted in accordance with commercial practices in freezing vegetables.

[168] Based on fish with salt added in cooking.

[165] Average value per 100 grams of veal of all cuts is 90 mg. for raw meat and 80 mg. for cooked meat.

[166] Average value per 100 grams of veal of all cuts is 320 mg. for raw meat and 500 mg. for cooked meat.

[167] With unenriched flour, approximate values per 100 grams are: Iron, 1.1 mg.; thiamine, 0.06 mg.; riboflavin, 0.09 mg.; niacin, 0.4 mg.

TABLE 1.—COMPOSITION OF FOODS, 100 GRAMS, EDIBLE PORTION—Continued

[Numbers in parentheses denote values imputed—usually from another form of the food or from a similar food. Zero in parentheses indicates that the amount of a constituent probably is none or is too small to measure. Dashes denote lack of reliable data for a constituent believed to be present in measurable amount. Calculated values, as those based on a recipe, are not in parentheses]

Item No.	Food and description	Water	Food energy	Protein	Fat	Carbohydrate: Total	Carbohydrate: Fiber	Ash	Calcium	Phosphorus	Iron	Sodium	Potassium	Vitamin A value	Thiamine	Riboflavin	Niacin	Ascorbic acid
(A)	(B)	(C)	(D)	(E)	(F)	(G)	(H)	(I)	(J)	(K)	(L)	(M)	(N)	(O)	(P)	(Q)	(R)	(S)
		Percent	Calories	Grams	Grams	Grams	Grams	Grams	Milligrams	Milligrams	Milligrams	Milligrams	Milligrams	International units	Milligrams	Milligrams	Milligrams	Milligrams
	Wheat, whole-grain: [168]																	
2430	Hard red spring	13.0	330	14.0	2.2	69.1	2.3	1.7	36	383	3.1	(3)	370	(0)	0.57	0.12	4.3	(0)
2431	Hard red winter	12.5	330	12.3	1.8	71.7	2.3	1.7	46	354	3.4	(3)	370	(0)	.52	.12	4.3	(0)
2432	Soft red winter	14.0	326	10.2	2.0	72.1	2.3	1.7	42	400	3.5	(3)	376	(0)	.43	.11	(3.6)	(0)
2433	White	11.5	335	9.4	2.0	75.4	1.9	1.7	36	394	3.0	(3)	390	(0)	.53	.12	5.3	(0)
2434	Durum	13.0	332	12.7	2.5	70.1	1.8	1.7	37	386	4.3	(3)	435	(0)	.66	.12	(4.4)	(0)
	Wheat flours:																	
2435	Whole (from hard wheats)	12.	333	13.3	2.0	71.0	2.3	1.7	41	372	3.3	3	370	(0)	.55	.12	4.3	(0)
2436	80% extraction (from hard wheats)	12.	365	12.	1.3	74.1	.5	.65	24	191	1.3	2	95	(0)	.26	.07	2.0	(0)
2437	Straight, hard wheat	12.	365	11.8	1.2	74.5	.4	.46	20	97	1.4	2	95	(0)	.12	.07	1.4	(0)
2438	Straight, soft wheat	12.	364	9.7	1.0	76.9	.4	.42	20	97	1.1	2	95	(0)	.08	.05	1.2	(0)
	Patent:																	
	All-purpose or family flour:																	
2439	Enriched	12.	364	10.5	1.0	76.1	.3	.43	16	87	[30] 2.9	2	95	(0)	[30] .44	[30] .26	[30] 3.5	(0)
2440	Unenriched	12.	364	10.5	1.0	76.1	.3	.43	16	87	.8	2	95	(0)	.06	.05	.9	(0)
	Bread flour:																	
2441	Enriched	12.	365	11.8	1.1	74.7	.3	.44	16	95	[30] 2.9	2	95	(0)	[30] .44	[30] .26	[30] 3.5	(0)
2442	Unenriched	12.	365	11.8	1.1	74.7	.3	.44	16	95	.9	2	95	(0)	.08	.06	1.0	(0)
2443	Cake or pastry flour	12.	364	7.5	.8	79.4	.2	.31	17	73	.5	2	95	(0)	.03	.03	.7	(0)
2444	Gluten flour (45% gluten, 55% patent flour)	8.5	378	41.4	1.9	47.2	.4	1.0	40	140	—	2	60	(0)	—	—	—	(0)
2445	Self-rising flour, enriched (anhydrous monocalcium phosphate used as a baking acid). [169]	11.5	352	9.3	1.0	74.2	.4	4.0	265	466	[30] 2.9	1,079	[170] —	(0)	[30] .44	[30] .26	[30] 3.5	(0)
2446	**Wheat bran,** crude, commercially milled	11.5	213	16.0	4.6	61.9	9.1	6.0	119	1,276	14.9	9	1,121	(0)	.72	.35	21.0	(0)
2447	**Wheat germ,** crude, commercially milled	11.5	363	26.6	10.9	46.7	2.5	4.3	72	1,118	9.4	3	827	(0)	2.01	.68	4.2	(0)
	Wheat, parboiled. See Bulgur, items 497–501.																	
	Wheat products used mainly as hot breakfast cereals:																	
	Wheat, rolled:																	
2448	Dry form	10.1	340	9.9	2.0	76.2	2.2	1.8	36	342	3.2	2	380	(0)	.36	.12	4.1	(0)
2449	Cooked	79.7	75	2.2	.4	16.9	.5	.8	8	76	.7	295	84	(0)	.07	.03	.9	(0)
	Wheat, whole-meal:																	
2450	Dry form	10.4	338	13.5	2.0	72.3	2.2	1.8	45	398	3.7	2	370	(0)	.51	.13	4.7	(0)
2451	Cooked	87.7	45	1.8	.3	9.4	.3	.8	7	52	.5	212	48	(0)	.06	.02	.6	(0)
	Wheat and malted barley cereal, toasted:																	
	Quick-cooking:																	
2452	Dry form	6.4	383	12.0	1.6	78.5	1.5	1.5	50	350	2.6	1	—	(0)	.34	.06	—	(0)
2453	Cooked	84.1	65	2.0	.3	13.2	.2	.4	9	59	.4	72	Trace	(0)	.05	.01	—	(0)
	Instant-cooking:																	
2454	Dry form	6.6	382	14.0	1.6	76.2	1.6	1.6	40	390	4.1	1	—	(0)	.34	.09	—	(0)
2455	Cooked	80.0	80	3.0	.3	16.1	.3	.6	9	82	.9	102	Trace	(0)	.07	.02	—	(0)
	Also see Farina, items 991–998.																	
	Wheat products used mainly as ready-to-eat breakfast cereals:																	
	Wheat bran. See Bran, items 439–442.																	
2456	Wheat flakes, added nutrients	3.5	354	10.2	1.6	80.5	1.6	4.2	41	309	4.4	1,032	—	(0)	.64	.14	4.9	(0)
2457	Wheat-germ, toasted	4.2	391	30.0	11.5	49.5	1.7	4.8	47	1,084	8.9	2	947	110	1.65	.98	5.3	10
	Wheat, puffed:																	
2458	Added nutrients, without salt	3.4	363	15.0	1.5	78.5	2.0	1.6	28	322	4.2	4	340	(0)	.55	.23	7.8	(0)
2459	Added nutrients, [171] with sugar and honey	2.8	376	6.0	2.1	88.3	.9	.8	26	150	3.3	161	99	(0)	.48	.18	6.4	(0)
	Wheat, shredded:																	
2460	Without salt or other added ingredients	6.6	354	9.9	2.0	79.9	2.3	1.6	43	388	3.5	3	348	(0)	.22	.11	4.4	(0)
2461	With malt, salt, and sugar added	3.2	366	9.1	2.9	81.7	2.2	3.1	39	370	3.4	697	—	(0)	.09	.15	4.8	(0)
2462	Wheat and malted barley flakes, nutrients added	3.1	392	8.8	1.3	84.3	1.8	2.5	49	250	2.6	780	—	(0)	.46	.11	3.9	(0)
2463	Wheat and malted barley granules, nutrients added	2.9	391	10.0	.6	84.4	1.5	2.1	53	176	2.8	710	230	(0)	.46	.07	5.3	(0)
	Whey:																	
2464	Fluid	93.1	26	.9	.3	5.1	0	.6	51	53	.1	—	—	10	.03	.14	.1	—
2465	Dried	4.5	349	12.9	1.1	73.5	0	8.0	646	589	1.4	—	—	50	.50	2.51	.8	—
	Whisky. See Beverages, items 395–399.																	
	Whitefish, lake:																	
2466	Raw	71.7	155	18.9	8.2	0	0	1.2	—	270	.4	52	299	2,260	.14	.12	3.0	—
2467	Cooked, baked, stuffed [172]	63.2	215	15.2	14.0	5.8	—	1.8	—	246	.5	195	291	2,000	.11	.11	2.3	—
2468	Smoked	68.2	155	20.9	7.3	0	0	3.7	22	274	—	—	—	—	—	—	—	Trace

	White sauce:																	
2469	Thin	78.7	121	3.9	8.7	7.2	Trace	1.5	122	97	.1	351	146	320	.04	.17	.2	Trace
2470	Medium	73.3	162	3.9	12.5	8.8	Trace	1.5	115	93	.2	379	139	460	.04	.17	.2	Trace
2471	Thick	67.9	198	4.0	15.6	11.0	Trace	1.5	107	90	.3	399	133	570	.05	.16	.3	Trace
	Whiting. See Kingfish, item 1164.																	
2472	**Wildrice,** raw	8.5	353	14.1	.7	75.3	1.0	1.4	19	339	4.2	7	220	(0)	.45	.63	6.2	(0)
	Wine. See Beverages, items 400–401.																	
2473	**Wreckfish,** raw	76.5	114	18.4	3.9	0	0	1.2	47	171	3.2	—	282	—	—	—	—	—
2474	**Yam,** tuber, raw	73.5	101	2.1	.2	23.2	.9	1.0	20	69	.6	—	600	Trace	.10	.04	.5	9
2475	**Yambean,** tuber, raw	85.1	55	1.4	.2	12.8	.7	.5	15	18	.6	—	—	Trace	.04	.03	.3	20
	Yeast:																	
	Baker's:																	
2476	Compressed [173]	71.0	86	(12.1)	.4	11.0	—	2.4	13	394	4.9	16	610	Trace	.71	1.65	11.2	Trace
2477	Dry (active)	5.0	282	(36.9)	1.6	38.9	—	8.3	(44)	(1,291)	(16.1)	(52)	(1,998)	Trace	2.33	5.41	33.7	Trace
2478	Brewer's, debittered	5.0	283	(38.8)	1.0	38.4	1.7	7.1	[174] 210	1,753	17.3	121	1,894	Trace	15.61	4.28	37.9	Trace
2479	Torula	6.0	277	(38.6)	1.0	37.0	3.3	7.7	[175] 424	1,713	19.3	15	2,046	Trace	14.01	5.06	44.4	Trace
2480	**Yellowtail** (Pacific coast), raw	72.7	138	21.0	5.4	0	0	1.3	—	—	—	—	—	—	—	—	—	—
	Yoghurt:																	
2481	Made from partially skimmed milk	89.0	50	3.4	1.7	5.2	0	.7	120	94	Trace	51	143	70	.04	.18	.1	1
2482	Made from whole milk	88.0	62	3.0	3.4	4.9	0	.7	111	87	Trace	47	132	140	.03	.16	.1	1
	Youngberries. See Blackberries, item 417.																	
2483	**Zwieback**	5.0	423	10.7	8.8	74.3	.3	1.2	13	69	.6	250	150	40	.05	.07	.9	(0)

[59] Based on product with minimum level of enrichment.

[168] Values for moisture are based on product as it reaches the mill prior to tempering; data for other proximate constituents are adjusted to this basis.

[169] The acid ingredient most commonly used in self-rising flour. When sodium acid pyrophosphate in combination with either anhydrous monocalcium phosphate or calcium carbonate is used, the value for calcium is approximately 120 mg. per 100 grams; for phosphorus, 540 mg.; for sodium, 1,360 mg.

[170] 90 mg. of potassium per 100 grams contributed by flour. Small quantities of additional potassium may be provided by other ingredients.

[171] Values are based on the addition of iron, sodium (as salt), thiamine, riboflavin, and niacin; however, not all of these nutrients are added in every brand. If the label does not indicate the addition of a specified nutrient, values per 100 grams are: Iron, 2.2 mg.; sodium, 10 mg.; thiamine, 0.03 mg.; riboflavin, 0.04 mg.; niacin, 3.5 mg.

[172] Prepared with bacon, butter, onion, celery, and breadcrumbs.

[173] Product is sometimes fortified. For fortified compressed yeast, value for thiamine ranges from 2.6 to 25.1 mg. per 100 grams; for niacin, from 111 to 176 mg.

[174] Values range from 70 mg. to 760 mg. per 100 grams.

[175] Values range from 60 mg. to 1,000 mg. per 100 grams.

BIBLIOGRAPHY

Additives in Your Food, George Sullivan. Cornerstone Library, 1976.

Alexis Lichine's Encyclopedia of Wines & Spirits, Alexis Lichine *et al.* Knopf, 1967.

All About Apples, Alice A. Martin. Houghton Mifflin, 1976.

All About Meat, Leon and Stanley Lobel. Harcourt Brace Jovanovich, 1975.

The American Food Scandal, William Robbins. William Morrow, 1974.

American Metric Beef Cookbook, Beef Industry Council, 1976.

The American Woman's Cook Book, edited and revised by Ruth Berolzeimer. Doubleday, 1972.

America's Best Vegetable Recipes, selected and tested by the food editors of *Farm Journal*. Barnes & Noble Books, 1970.

Annemarie's Cookingschool Cookbook, Annemarie Huste. Houghton Mifflin, 1974.

Ann Seranne's Good Food Without Meat, Anne Seranne. William Morrow, 1973.

The Anytime, Anywhere Barbecue Book, Beth Merriman. Grosset & Dunlap, 1972.

The Art of Eating, M. F. K. Fisher. Macmillan, 1954.

The Art of Making Sausages, Pâtés, and Other Charcuterie, Jane Grigson. Knopf, 1976.

Barbecue with Beard, James Beard. Golden Press, 1975.

Bean Cuisine, Beverly White. Beacon Press, 1977.

Beard on Food, James Beard. Knopf, 1974.

Bellybook, James Trager. Grossman, 1972.

The Best of Beard, James Beard. Warner Books, 1974.

Better Homes and Gardens Barbecue Book, Bantam, 1972.

Billy Joe Tatum's Wild Foods Cookbook and Field Guide, Billy Joe Tatum. Workman Publishing, 1976.

The Blessings of Bread, Adrian Bailey. Paddington Press, 1975.

The Blue Sea Cookbook, Sarah D. Alberson. Hastings House, 1968.

The Book of Drinking, John Doxat. Triune Books, 1973.

The Book of Herb Cookery, Irene B. Hoffman. Award Books, 1957.

The Book of Spices, Frederick Rosengarten, Jr. Pyramid Books, 1973.

The Bread Book, Carlson Wade. Barnes & Noble, 1973.

The Bread Book, Carolyn Meyer. Harcourt Brace Jovanovich, 1976.

Breadcraft, Charles and Violet Schafer. Yerba Buena Press, 1974.

Breads of the World, Mariana Honig. Chelsea House, 1977.

The Captain's Cookbook, Walter Kaprielian. Holt, Rinehart and Winston, 1976.

A Celebration of Vegetables, Robert Ackart. Atheneum, 1977.

The Changing American Diet, Letitia Brewster and Michael F. Jacobson. Center for Science in the Public Interest, 1978.

Charcoal Cookbook, Ed Callahan. Nitty Gritty, 1970.

Cheers, Francesca White. Paddington Press, 1977.

Cheese and Wine, Carol Truax. Ballantine Books, 1975.
The Cheese Book, Vivienne Marquis and Patricia Haskell. Simon and Schuster, 1965.
The Cheese Handbook, T. A. Layton. Dover, 1973.
The Cheeses & Wines of England & France, John Ehle. Harper & Row, 1972.
Cheeses of the World, The U.S. Department of Agriculture. Dover, 1972.
The Chemicals We Eat, Dr. Melvin A. Benarde. McGraw-Hill, 1971.
Chocolate!, Nika Standen Hazelton. Simon and Schuster, 1967.
Coffee, Charles and Violet Schafer. Yerba Buena Press, 1976.
The Coffee Book, John Svicarovich *et al.* Prentice Hall, 1976.
Commercial Foods Exposed!, Gaye Deamer Horsey. Hawkes Publishing, 1975.
The Compleat Blueberry Cookbook, Elizabeth W. Barton. Phoenix Publishing, 1975.
The Complete Barbecue Cookbook, John and Marie Roberson. Roberson, 1967.
The Complete Book of Cheese, Bob Brown. Gramercy, 1955.
The Complete Book of Egg Cooking in Color, Paul Hamlyn, 1972.
The Complete Book of Fruits and Vegetables, F. Bianchini and F. Corbetta. Crown, 1975.
The Complete Book of Meat, Phyllis C. Reynolds. William Morrow, 1963.
The Complete Book of Outdoor Cookery, James Beard and Helen Evans Brown. Royal Books, 1971.
The Complete Book of Pasta, Enrica Jarratt and Vernon Jarratt. Dover Publications, 1977.
The Complete Book of Pasta, Jack Denton Scott. Bantam, 1970.
The Complete Book of Vegetable Cookery, Myra Waldo. Bantam, 1969.
The Complete Cookery Encyclopedia, Tudor, 1973.
The Complete Fish Cookbook, Dan and Inez Morris. Stoeger Publishing, 1972.
The Complete Food Catalogue, Jose Wilson and Arthur Leaman. Holt, Rinehart & Winston, 1977.
The Complete Food Handbook, Rodger P. Doyle and James L. Redding. Grove Press, 1976.
The Complete Kitchen Guide, Lillian Langseth-Christensen and Carol Sturm Smith. Grosset & Dunlap, 1968.
The Complete Rice Cookbook, Carlson Wade. Pyramid Books, 1973.
The Complete Seafood Cookbook, Arthur Hawkins. Bonanza Books, 1970.
The Confident Cook, Irena Chalmers. Praeger, 1975.
Cooking à la Cordon Bleu, Alma Lach. Harper & Row, 1970.
The Cooking Collectarium, Loyta Wooding. Nash Publishing, 1971.
Cooking for the Professional Chef, Kenneth C. Wolfe. Van Nostrand Reinhold, 1976.
Cooking with Michael Field, edited by Joan Scobey. Holt, Rinehart & Winston, 1978.
Cooking Without Recipes, Helen Worth. Gramercy, 1965.
Cooking with Spices and Herbs, the editors of Sunset Books and *Sunset Magazine*. Lane Books, 1974.
Cooking with Understanding, H. L. Nichols, Jr. North Castle Books, 1971.
Cooking with Vegetables, Alex D. Hawkes. Simon and Schuster, 1968.
Cook's and Diner's Dictionary, Funk & Wagnalls. Funk & Wagnalls, 1968.
The Cook's Companion, Doris McFerran Townsend. Rutledge, 1978.
The Cook's Companion, Frieda Arkin. Avon, 1970.
Cook's Quick Reference, Catherine Storr. Penguin, 1971.
Craig Claiborne's Favorites, from *The New York Times*, Volumes 1 to 4, Craig Claiborne. Times Books, 1975-1978.
Craig Claiborne's Kitchen Primer, Craig Claiborne. Knopf, 1969.
Culinary Arts Institute Encyclopedic Cookbook, edited by Ruth Berolzheimer. Culinary Arts Institute, 1972.
Cutting-Up in the Kitchen, Merle Ellis. Chronicle Books, 1975.
The Dairy Cookbook, Olga Nickles. Celestial Arts, 1976.

The Delicious World of Raw Foods, Mary Louise Lau. Rawson Associates, 1977.

A Dictionary of Cooking, compiled by Ralph and Dorothy De Sola. Meredith, 1969.

A Dictionary of Food Supplements, Lee Fryer and Annette Dickinson. Mason/ Charter, 1975.

Dictionary of Gastronomy, André L. Simon and Robin Howe. Overlook Press, 1978.

The Dictionary of Health Foods, Jeffrey Blish. Galahad Books, 1972.

Dictionary of International Food & Cooking Terms, Myra Waldo. Macmillan, 1967.

Diet for a Small Planet, Frances Moore Lappe. Ballantine Books, 1975.

The Diner's Guide to Wines, Howard Hillman. Hawthorn, 1978.

The Doubleday Cookbook, Jean Anderson and Elaine Hanna. Doubleday, 1975.

Dry and Save, Dora D. Flack. Woodbridge Press, 1977.

Ducks & Geese in Your Backyard, Rick and Gail Luttman. Rodale, 1978.

Easy Game Cooking, Joan Cone. EPM Publications, 1974.

Eating, Drinking & Thinking, Phylis Magida. Nelson-Hall, 1973.

The Edible Wild, Berndt Berglund and Clare E. Bolsby. Charles Scribner's Sons, 1971.

The Egg Book, Gayle and Robert Fletcher Allen. Celestial Arts, 1975.

The Encyclopedia of Fish Cookery, A. J. McClane. Holt, Rinehart and Winston, 1977.

The Encyclopedia of Food, Artemas Ward. Peter Smith, 1941.

The Encyclopedia of Organic Gardening, the staff of *Organic Gardening Magazine*. Rodale Press, 1978.

Encyclopedia of Practical Gastronomy, Ali-Bab and translated by Elizabeth Benson. McGraw-Hill, 1974.

Escoffier's Basic Elements of Fine Cookery, A. Escoffier. Crescent Books, 1966.

The Everything Cookbook, Betty Wason. Galahad, 1970.

Exotic Food, Rupert Croft-Cooke. Herder and Herder, 1971.

Fabulous Feasts, Madeleine Pelner Cosman. George Braziller, 1976.

Farm Journal's Choice Chocolate Recipes, Elise W. Manning. Doubleday, 1978.

Feasting Free on Wild Edibles, Bradford Angier. Stackpole Books, 1972.

Feasts of a Militant Gastronome, Robert Courtine. William Morrow, 1974.

The Fine Art of Food, Reay Tannahill. A. S. Barnes, 1968.

Fish and Seafood Cook Book, Better Homes and Gardens Books, 1971.

The Flavor-Principle Cookbook, Elisabeth Rozin. Hawthorn, 1973.

Flower Cookery, Mary MacNicol. Fleet Press, 1967.

The Food Book, Charles Patti. Fleet Press, 1973.

Foodbook, James Trager. Grossman, 1970.

Food for People Not for Profit, edited by Catherine Lerza and Michael Jacobson. Ballantine Books, 1975.

Food for Thought, Robert Farrar Capon. Harcourt Brace Jovanovich, 1978.

Food in History, Reay Tannahill. Stein and Day, 1973.

The Food of the Western World, Theodora Fitzgibbon. Quadrangle, 1976.

Foods, Margaret M. Justin *et al.* Houghton Mifflin, 1948.

Food: The Gift of Osiris, Volumes 1 and 2 by William J. Darby *et al.* Academic Press, 1977.

Food: Where Nutrition Politics & Culture Meet, Deborah Katz and Mary T. Goodwin. Center for Science in the Public Interest, 1976.

Four Seasons Cook Books, Audrey Ellis. Two Continents, 1975.

Frank Schoonmaker's Encyclopedia of Wine, Frank Schoonmaker. Hastings House, 1975.

Fresh Food, edited by Sylvia Rosenthal. Tree Communications, 1978.

Future Food, Barbara Ford. William Morrow, 1978.

Galley Guide to Fine Food, Richard Bock. Lorenz Press, 1977.

The Game Cookbook, Geraldine Steindler. Stoeger Publishing, 1977.

The Game Cookery Book, compiled by Julia Drysdale. Collins, 1975.

The Game of Wine, Forrest Wallace and Gilbert Cross. Doubleday, 1976.

The Garden-to-Table Cookbook, edited by Helen Witty and Burton Wolf. McGraw Hill, 1976.

Gastronomique, Ida Bailey Allen. Doubleday, 1958.

Gastronomy, Jay Jacobs. Newsweek Books, 1975.

The Gentle Art of Flavoring, Robert Landry and translated by Bruce H. Axler. Abelard-Schuman, 1970.

Getting Food from Water, Gene Logsdon. Rodale, 1978.

Gods, Men and Wines, William Younger. Wine and Food Society, 1966.

Going Wild in the Kitchen, Gertrude Parke. McKay, 1965.

The Gold Cook Book, Louis P. De Gouy. Galahad Books, 1948.

The Good Cook's Guide, Hilary Fawcett and Jeanne Strang. David & Charles, 1974.

Good Cooking, Nicholas Roosevelt. Collier Books, 1966.

The Good Egg, Loretta White. Paperback Library, 1967.

Good Food & How to Cook It, Ann Seranne. William Morrow, 1972.

The Gourmet Cooking School Cookbook, Dione Lucas with Darlene Geis. Bernard Geis Associates, 1964.

Gourmet International Barbecue, edited by Carol D. Brent. Doubleday, 1971.

Gourmet in the Galley, Katharine Robinson. Quadrangle, 1973.

A Gourmet's Book of Beasts, Faith Medlin. Paul S. Erikson, 1975.

The Gourmet's Guide to Meat and Poultry, William and Chesbrough Rayner. New American Library, 1971.

The Grammar of Cooking, Carol Braider. Holt, Rinehart and Winston, 1974.

Grand Diplôme Cooking Course, Volumes 1–20. Danbury Press, 1972.

The Great American Food Hoax, Sidney Margolius. Walker and Company, 1971.

The Great American Ice Cream Book, Paul Dickson. Atheneum, 1978.

The Great Book of Wine, Edita Lausanne. World, 1970.

Great Bread!, Bernice Hunt. Viking Press, 1977.

The Great Cooks Cookbook, James Beard, *et al.* Ferguson/Doubleday, 1974.

Great Recipes from the New York Times, Raymond A. Sokolov. Quadrangle, 1973.

The Great Wines of Italy, Philip Dallas. Doubleday, 1974.

The Greengrocer Cookbook, Joe Carcione. Celestial Arts, 1975.

The Green Thumb Cookbook, the editors of Organic Gardening and Farming. Rodale Press, 1977.

Grossman's Guide to Wines, Spirits and Beers, Harold J. Grossman and revised by Harriet Lembeck. Charles Scribner's Sons, 1977.

Guide to Organic Foods Shopping and Organic Living, edited by Jerome Goldstein and M. C. Goldman. Rodale Press, 1970.

Health Food Cookery, Marguerite Patten. Hamlyn, 1972.

Herbal, Joseph Wood Krutch. David R. Godine, 1976.

An Herb and Spice Cook Book, Craig Claiborne. Bantam Books, 1965.

Herb & Spice Cookery, Monica Mawson. Hamlyn, 1970.

Herbs for the Kitchen, Irma Goodrich Mazza. Little, Brown, 1975.

Herbs, Spices & Essential Oils, the editors of *Sphere Magazine*. Sphere Magazine, 1977.

Herbs, Spices and Flavorings, Tom Stobart. McGraw-Hill, 1970.

Hering's Dictionary of Classical and Modern Cookery, translated by Walter Bickel. Fachbuchverlag Dr. Pfanneberg, 1974.

A History of Brewing, H. S. Corran. David & Charles, 1975.

The Horizon Cookbook, William Harlan Hale and the editors of *Horizon Magazine*. Doubleday, 1968.

House & Garden's New Cook Book, the editors of *House & Garden*. Condé Nast, 1967.

How to Enjoy Eating without Committing Suicide, Charles D. Ewart. Cornerstone Library, 1971.

How To Shop for Food, Jean Rainey. Barnes & Noble, 1972.

How To Win the Grocery Game, Delight

Dixon Omohundro. Drake Publishers, 1973.

Impromptu Cooking, Glenn Andrews. Atheneum, 1973.

Innards and other Variety Meats, Jana Allen and Margaret Gin. 101 Productions, 1974.

The International Meat Cook Book, Bee Nilson. Drake, 1972.

The International Wine and Food Society's Guide to Cheese and Cheese Cookery, T. A. Layton. Bonanza Books, 1967.

The International Wine and Food Society's Guide to Meat, Ambrose Heath. Bonanza Books, 1968.

The James Beard Cookbook, James Beard. Dell, 1972.

James Beard's New Fish Cookery, James Beard. Little Brown, 1976.

James Beard's Theory & Practice of Good Cooking. Knopf, 1977.

Jeannette's Secrets of Everyday Good Cooking, Jeannette Seaver. Bantam, 1976.

Joy of Cooking, Irma S. Rombauer and Marion Rombauer Becker. Bobbs-Merrill, 1975.

The Joy of Eating, Katie Steward. Stemmer House, 1977.

Julie Dannenbaum's Creative Cooking School, Julie Dannenbaum. Popular Library, 1971.

The Kitchen Almanac, compiled by Stone Soup. Berkley, undated.

The Kitchen Garden Book, Stringfellow Barr and Stella Standard. Penguin Books, 1977.

Kitchen Tricks, Ben Charles Harris. Barre Publishing, 1975.

Larousse Dictionary of Wines of the World, Gérard Debuigne. Larousse, 1970.

Larousse Gastronomique, Prosper Montagné. Crown, 1961.

La Technique, Jacques Pépin. Times Books, 1976.

Le Répertoire de la Cuisine, Louis Saulnier. Barron's Educational Series, 1976.

Long Island Seafood Cook Book, J. George Frederick. Dover Publications, 1971.

The Los Angeles Times Natural Foods Cookbook, Jeanne Voltz. New American Library, 1973.

Madame Prunier's Fish Cookery Book, edited by Ambrose Heath. Dover Publications, 1971.

The Making of a Cook, Madeleine Kamman. Weathervane Books, 1975.

Managing Your Personal Food Supply, edited by Ray Wolf. Rodale Press, 1977.

The Maple Sugar Book, Helen and Scott Nearing. Schocken Books, 1971.

The Mariner's Cookbook, Nancy Hyden Woodward. Castle Books, 1969.

Mary Bought a Little Lamb, Rhoda Nation. Bailey Brothers and Swinfen, 1975.

Massee's Wine-Food Index, William E. Massee. Bramball House, 1962.

McCall's Cook Book, the food editors of *McCall's*. Random House, 1963.

Meat, The Lobel Brothers. Harcourt Brace Jovanovich, 1971.

The Meat and Poultry Cook Book, Beth Bailey McClean and Thora Hegstad Campbell. Pocket Books, 1960.

The Meat Board Meat Book, Barbara Bloch. McGraw-Hill, 1977.

The Meat Book, Travers Moncure Evans and David Greene. Charles Scribner's Sons, 1973.

The Meat Cookbook, John and Marie Roberson. Collier Books, 1966.

Meat Cookbook, Tess Mallos. Paul Hamlyn, 1970.

Methods and Manners of Cooking, Bruce H. Axler. Funk & Wagnalls, 1969.

Michael Field's Cooking School, Michael Field. M. Barrows, 1965.

Michele Evan's All Poultry Cookbook, Michele Evans. Dell, 1974.

The More-Beef-for-Your-Money Cookbook, Mary Dunham. Peter H. Wyden, 1974.

Mrs. Restino's Country Kitchen, Susan Restino. Quick Fox, 1976.

Ms. Pinchpenny's Book of Kitchen Management, Dorothy Parker. Penguin, 1977.

Mushrooms of North America, Orson K. Miller, Jr. E. P. Dutton, 1977.

The New Fruit Cookbook, Cynthia & Jerome Rubin. Henry Regnery, 1977.

The New York Times Book of Wine, Terry Robards. Quadrangle, 1976.

The New York Times Cook Book, Craig Claiborne. Harper & Row, 1961.

The New York Times International Cook Book, Craig Claiborne. Harper & Row, 1971.

Nobody Ever Tells You These Things, Helen McCully. Holt, Rinehart & Winston, 1967.

The Nutrition Cookbook, Stephen N. and Susan L. Kreitzman. Harcourt Brace Jovanovich, 1977.

The New Vegetarian, Gary Null with Steve Null. William Morrow, 1978.

Nutrition Scoreboard, Michael F. Jacobson. Avon, 1975.

The Oats, Peas, Beans & Barley Cookbook, Edith Young Cottrell. Woodbridge, 1976.

1001 Questions Answered about Cooking, Charlotte Adams. Dodd, Mead, 1963.

The Onion Cookbook, Jean Bothwell. Dover Publications, 1976.

The Original Boston Cooking-School Cook Book, Fannie Merritt Farmer. Plume, 1974.

The Other Half of the Egg, Helen McCully, *et al.* M. Barrows, 1967.

Out of the Garden into the Kitchen, Beryl M. Marton. David McKay, 1977.

The Passionate Palate, Jeanine Larmoth. William Morrow, 1975.

Pasta! Pasta! Pasta!, compiled and edited by Ursel Norman. William Morrow, undated.

Pâtés for Kings and Commoners, Maybélle Iribe and Barbara Wilder. Hawthorn, 1976.

The Pennysaver Cookbook, Inez & Dan Morris. Funk & Wagnalls, 1969.

The Pleasures of Seafood, Rima and Richard Collin. Holt, Rinehart & Winston, 1976.

Portrait of Pasta, Anna del Conte. Paddington Press Ltd., 1976.

The Potato Book, Myrna Davis. William Morrow, 1973.

The Potato Cookbook, Gwen Robyns. Stemmer House, 1976.

The Provincetown Seafood Cookbook, Howard Mitchum. Addison-Wesley, 1977.

Pure & Simple, Marian Burros. William Morrow, 1978.

The Quick & Easy Vegetarian Cookbook, Ruth Ann Manners & William Manners. M. Evans, 1978.

The Random House Book of Etiquette, Volume 1. Random House, 1967.

The Random House Treasury of Cooking, Volume 2. Random House, 1967.

Reader's Digest Creative Cooking, *Reader's Digest*. Reader's Digest Association, 1977.

The Rodale Cookbook, Nancy Albright. Rodale Press, 1973.

The Romance of Food, edited by Frederick Heider and Barbara Loots. Hallmark, 1976.

Roots & Other Edible Tubers!, Jeffrey Feinman. Zebra Books, 1978.

The Salad Book, Michele Evans. Henry Regnery, 1975.

Salad Days, compiled and edited by Ursel Norman. William Morrow, 1974.

The Sausage Book, Richard Gehman. Weathervane Books, 1969.

The Seafood Book, Shirley Ross. McGraw-Hill, 1978.

Seafood Cook Book, the editors of *Sunset Magazine* and Sunset Books. Lane Books, 1972.

The Seasonal Kitchen, Perla Meyers. Vintage, 1973.

Secrets of Better Cooking, *Reader's Digest*. The Reader's Digest Association, 1973.

7 Steps to Rock-Bottom Food Costs, Sally Sgerwin. William Morrow, 1976.

The Signet Book of American Wine, Peter Quimme. New American Library, 1975.

The Signet Book of Cheese, Peter Quimme. New American Library, 1976.

The Signet Book of Coffee and Tea, Peter Quimme. New American Library, 1976.

The Signet Book of Sausage, Richard Gehman. New American Library, 1969.

The Signet Book of Wine, Alexis

Bespaloff. New American Library, 1971.
The Something-Went-Wrong-What-Do-I-Do-Now Cookbook, John and Marina Bear. Award Book, 1970.
Spice Cookery, Helmut Ripperger. George W. Steward, 1942.
Spices of the World Cookbook, prepared and tested for McCormick by Mary Collins. Penguin, 1969.
Spices, Seasonings and Herbs, Sylvia Windle Humphrey. Collier Books, 1965.
Stalking the Wild Asparagus, Euell Gibbons. David McKay, 1973.
The Steak Book, Arthur Hawkins. Gramercy, 1966.
Sunset Barbecue Cook Book the editors of Sunset Books and *Sunset Magazine*. Lane Books, 1973.
Sunset Cook Book of Breads, the editors of Sunset Books and *Sunset Magazine*. Lane Publishing, 1977.
Sunset Ideas for Cooking Vegetables, the editors of Sunset Books and *Sunset Magazine*. Lane Books, 1974.
Sunset Salad Book, the editors of Sunset Books and *Sunset Magazine*. Lane Publishing, 1977.
Supermarket Counter Power, Adeline Garner Shell. Warner Paperback, 1973.
The Supermarket Handbook, Nikki and David Goldbeck. New American Library, 1976.
Supershopper, David and Marymae Klein. Praeger, 1973.
The Taste of America, John L. Hess and Karen Hess. Grossman, 1977.
A Taste of the Sea, Theodora Fitzgibbon. A. S. Barnes, 1977.
The Taste of Wine, Pamela Vandyke Price. Random House, 1975.
The Taster's Guide to Beer, Michael A. Weiner. Collier Books, 1977.
Tea, Milane Christiansen. Ventures International, 1972.
That We May Eat, U.S. Department of Agriculture, 1975.
Things You've Always Wanted to Know about Food & Drink, Helen McCully. Holt, Rinehart & Winston, 1972.
Tropical Fruit Recipes, compiled and edited by Dr. Mabel W. Richardson. The Rare Fruit Council International, 1976.
Understanding Food, Lendal H. Kotschevar and Margaret McWilliams. John Wiley, 1969.
Unusual Vegetables, the editors of Organic Gardening and Farming. Rodale Press, 1978.
Veal Cookery, Craig Claiborne/Pierre Franey. Harper & Row, 1978.
The Vegetarian Alternative, Vic S. Sussman. Rodale Press, 1978.
The Vegetables Cookbook, Southern Living Progressive Farmer. Favorite Recipes Press, 1972.
Vegetables Money Can't Buy But You Can Grow, Nancy Wilkes Bubel. David R. Godine, 1977.
Vermont Maple Syrup Cook Book, edited by Reginald L. Muir. Phoenix Publishing, 1974.
The Vintage Wine Book, William S. Leedom. Vintage, 1963.
The Weed Cookbook, Adrienne Crowhurst. Lancer Books, 1972.
What You Need To Know About Food & Cooking For Health, Lawrence E. Lamb, M.D. Viking Press, 1973.
Where the Great German Wines Grow, Hans Ambrosi. Hastings House, 1976.
The Wild Food Trailguide, Alan Hall. Holt, Rinehart & Winston, 1976.
The Wild Gourmet, Babette Brackett and Maryann Lash. David R. Godine, 1975.
Wine, Hugh Johnson. Simon & Schuster, 1966.
The Wine and Food Society's Guide to Eggs, Margaret Sherman. David & Charles, 1968.
Wines and Spirits, Alec Waugh. Time-Life Books, 1968.
Wines of France, Alexis Lichine and William E. Massee. Knopf, 1965.
The Wines of Germany, Heinrich Meinhard. Stein and Day, 1976.
The Wines of Italy, Cyril Ray. Octopus, 1966.
The Wines of Italy, Sheldon Wasserman. Stein and Day, 1976.
Wines of the World, edited by Andre L. Simon. McGraw-Hill, 1967.
A Wine Tour of France, Frederick S. Wildman Jr.. William Morrow, 1972.

Wings of Life, Julie Jordan. The Crossing Press, 1976.
The Wise Encyclopedia of Cookery, Grosset & Dunlap, 1971.
Woman's Day Encyclopedia of Cookery, Volumes 1–12. Fawcett, 1976.
The Wonder of Food, K. Cyrus Melikian and Lloyd K. Rudd. Appleton-Century-Crofts, 1961.
The World Atlas of Cheese, Nancy Eekhof-Stork. Paddington Press, 1976.
The World Atlas of Food, Simon & Schuster, 1974.
World Atlas of Wine, Hugh Johnson. Mitchell Beazley Publishers, 1971.
The World Book of Fish Dishes, Nina Froud. Pelham, 1965.
The World Encyclopedia of Cooking, edited by the staff of Culinary Arts Institute. World Publishing, 1972.
The World Guide to Cooking with Fruit & Vegetables, John Goode. E. P. Dutton, 1973.
The World of Cheese, Evan Jones. Alfred A. Knopf, 1976.
The World of Cooking, Mary Owens Wyckoff. Prentice-Hall, 1978.
World of Drinks and Drinking, John Doxat. Drake, 1971.
A World of Nut Recipes, Morton Gill Clark. Funk & Wagnalls, 1967.
World Wine Almanac and Wine Atlas, Grace Treber. International Wine Society, 1976.

INDEX

Emmentaler cheese, 98